Bribes

Bribes

—————John T. Noonan, Jr.—————

UNIVERSITY OF CALIFORNIA PRESS
Berkeley   Los Angeles

University of California Press
Berkeley and Los Angeles, California

Library of Congress Cataloging-in-Publication Data
Noonan, John Thomas, 1926–
     Bribes.
     Includes index.
     1. Bribery—History. 2. Bribery—Moral and
ethical aspects—History. I. Title.
K5261.N66 1988   364.1'323   87-13924
ISBN 0–520–06154–3 (alk. paper)

Printed in the United States of America
1   2   3   4   5   6   7   8   9

To John, Rebecca, and Susanna

munera Dei

Contents

Acknowledgments

I am greatly indebted to the following for reading all or portions of the manuscript and making suggestions for its improvement: W. D. Davies of Duke University (Scripture), Charles Duggan of London University (medieval history), Ze'ev Falk of Hebrew University (Jewish law), Koichiro Fujikura of Tokyo University (Japanese law), Elisabeth Gray of Harvard University (Celtic society), Kenneth Pennington of Syracuse University (Innocent III), Robert E. Rodes, Jr., of the University of Notre Dame (law, theology, style, and grammar), and my colleagues at the University of California, Teodolinda Barolini (Dante), William Bouwsma (Reformation history), Carlo Cipolla (prices), Edwin Epstein (campaign law), Erich Gruen (Roman history), Ann Kilmer (Assyriology), Leonard Lesko (Ancient Egypt), Robert Post (American law), Hugh Richmond (Shakespeare), Harry Scheiber (American history), Frank Zimring (American criminal law), and my father, John T. Noonan (law, style, and common sense). My wife, Mary Lee, has provided ideas, criticism, and encouragement. Sally Drach checked citations of American law and Dean Donovan other citations in English. Louise McCahan Cronenwett has patiently and ably put on the word processor the numerous drafts. I thank all these persons who have helped so generously.

Three institutions have funded my research: the University of California School of Law (Boalt Hall); the John Simon Guggenheim Memorial Foundation; and the Woodrow Wilson International Center for Scholars. With this work I gratefully reciprocate.

John T. Noonan, Jr.

Introduction

This book is about bribes and those who take them, give them, or condemn them in a variety of cultures from ancient Egypt to modern America. The concept of the bribe at work is the book's theme and matter. By "at work" I mean in use to affect action or thought, conduct or language—in criminal prosecutions, in the text of laws, in administrative rules, in political slogans and political campaigns, in confessions, homilies, editorials news stories, and diaries. Put to work, the concept has had physical, social, spiritual consequences. When, as has happened infrequently, a person has been sent to prison for bribetaking, all three kinds of consequence are observable. Socially, spiritually, the impact of the bribe is no less palpable when it figures in Chaucer's *The Canterbury Tales,* in Shakespeare's *The Merchant of Venice* and *Measure for Measure,* and in Dante's *Inferno* and *Purgatorio.*

The core of the concept of a bribe is an inducement improperly influencing the performance of a public function meant to be gratuitously exercised. The core turns out to be remarkably constant if its elements are taken with enough abstractness. The concrete constituent elements—what counts as "an inducement," what counts as "improperly influencing," what counts as "a public function," what functions are "meant to be gratuitously exercised"—change with the culture. The concept of a bribe contracts or expands with conventions, laws, practices. Relativized, it does not disappear. The idea is used in postexilic Jerusalem, late Republican Rome, imperial Ravenna, seventh-century Yorkshire, thirteenth-century Paris, seventeenth-century London, eighteenth-century Calcutta, nineteenth-century Washington, twentieth-century Tokyo. Cross-culturally compared in these very varied settings, the abstract central concept—with no forcing of the evidence—recurs.

Bribery is a legal concept, hence the law determines what counts as bribery in a particular society. This is easy to say but legal definitions turn out to be only superficially helpful. Is the law the edict issued by the prince and the statute written on the books or is the law that which is actually enforced? If one takes the proclaimed rule as the measure, one chooses a standard that is often demonstrably unreal. If one answers that the law is that which is actually enforced, then one is led to ask: How many trials must take place before a law is enforced? Is prosecution enough for enforcement or must conviction follow? Is conviction enough or must serious punishment be imposed? Is there enforcement if only small offenders but not large ones are seriously sanctioned? Actual enforcement is not a clear and simple measure.

Probing of the various meanings of any law on bribery leads to perception of a tension between it and the morals of any community. Typically, the morals in practice are less demanding than the law on the books and the morals in public expression are more exigent than the law enforced. Often a society has at least four definitions of a bribe—that of the more advanced moralists; that of the law as written; that of the law as in any degree enforced; that of common practice. If one is to say that an act of bribery has been committed, one should know which standard one is using. The great advantage of the concrete materials drawn on here— trials, confessions, letters, poems—is that one can see what bribery means in these contexts; one can conclude with some assurance as to which standard was in play and what a bribe meant for a particular prosecutor or poet, politician or publicist in a particular society.

This book, however, is not a history of bribery, that is, a history of all acts of bribetaking or all famous bribes. Such an encyclopedic undertaking would be as practically feasible as a history of all homicides and as intellectually profitable as a history of all famous murders. Interest here is in the idea, not in repeated or even in all notorious instances of the offense. Trials are employed illustratively for their rich documentation of the meaning and application of the concept. The cases range from Cicero's defense of attempted murder in Larinum to Thomas Puccio's prosecution of offenses committed in Washington, New York, and New Jersey.

No writer at several removes from the evidence can give unchallengeable verdicts about guilt or innocence. It is not the purpose of this book to give such verdicts. Yet we are so constituted by nature to be judgmental, or so formed to be so by the same cultural inheritance that frames our view of bribery, that the question, "Did he do it?," is irresistible. When I have dealt with trials or accusations I have not avoided giving my opinion as to clear guilt, clear innocence, or the probability of one or the other. Freshly discovered evidence or new analysis could challenge my conclusions. The challenge would not affect the value of the cases as illustrations of the concept in action.

What I have resisted is a temptation almost equally irresistible—to quantify. Modern moral argument, not to mention sociology and criminology, depends heavily on quotable numbers. When the subject is bribery, an economic transaction, it seems that numbers should be available. Tourists and journalists are very free in judging that a society is "corrupt" or "very corrupt." Historians and political scientists have not been far behind them. Surely, it may be supposed, the confident judgments that have often been made rest on a foundation of figures.

Quantification is conceivable. It has never been systematically attempted. There are no existing sets of figures by which one could conclude that the Roman Empire, for example, was more or less corrupt than the British Empire or the United States. In the absence of this kind of data it is wrong, I believe, to create an illusory certainty by using comparative terms.

Judgment about corruption in a society need not rest on a statistical basis. But with bribery several factors operate to make unquantified judgment difficult. First, the act is criminal and consensual; the victim where there is one is not made aware of the arrangement as it affects his case; consequently a number of acts of bribery remain secret and undiscovered. Second, accusations of bribery are often politically motivated or are made in order to satisfy certain social or psychic needs; one cannot judge from the accusations alone whether acts of bribery have actually occurred. Third, the amount of legal attention bribery receives is misleading. One society may be uncensorious of most reciprocities with its officeholders; there may be no legal response to them at all, and the appearance will be given of integrity everywhere. A different society may define bribes, legislate against bribetakers, and prosecute bribery in such a way as to suggest that the crime is ubiquitous. A common mistake is to use the number of laws enacted or convictions obtained as an index of corruption. Fourth, some critics have strong inclinations to exaggerate the corruption of their own day, and others have strong inclinations to denigrate past times or aliens or members of another race, religion, or class. Their criticisms will then be used as evidence that corruption is worse now or worse then, or worse with certain groups than others. Impassioned complaint will function as though it were hard evidence.

Fifth, there is the fallacy of the perfectly corrupt man—the belief that vices are linked and that unless a man is thoroughly corrupt in every aspect he can be no bribetaker or bribegiver. Moral judgment is held at bay by the kindly family man or illustrious genius who is also a taker or giver of bribes. Francis Bacon, Samuel Pepys, Warren Hastings are not merely respectable; they are heroes—respectively the founders, in the view of their admirers, of British science, the British navy, and British India. Bacon was a bribee by the law as actually enforced; Pepys a bribee by his own measure; Hastings a bribee by the law that was being made. Apologists by the score have hesitated to give their bribetaking its proper name. As for bribers, judgment has always been even more charitable, the underlying assumption being that they are the victims of extortion. When the persons involved have been preeminently just, judgment has often been entirely suspended. Who thinks of Thomas Becket or John Quincy Adams as giving bribes? The fallacy of the perfectly corrupt man prevents seeing bribery in transactions which, measured by at least one of the standards in use in their own time, were corrupt although executed by men of otherwise eminent virtue.

Finally, there is great difficulty in accepting a society's own standards when one approaches the society as a traveler or as a historian. Bribes are a species of reciprocity. Human life is full of reciprocities. The particular reciprocities that count as bribes in particular cultures are distinguished by intentionality, form, and context. What is a bribe depends on the cultural treatment of the constituent elements. The observer outside the culture, like the cynic or rigorist within it, is inclined to see the conventional differences as arbitrary and to reduce all reciprocities of a given kind to bribes—to treat, say, any gift to an officeholder as a bribe. Doing so, the outsider imposes his own standard and reaches a judgment that is unreasonable if the culture's own norms are used.

These major reasons for mistake—the rarity of proof of actual bribery; the abundance of accusations; the misleading impressions given by legal activity in its regard; prejudices of many kinds; the fallacy of the perfectly corrupt man; and the reductionism that eliminates conventions and looks only at function—mean that broad generalizations about the amount of bribery in a society must be made with caution and with caveats and without great confidence in their reliability. But evidence of bribery within the law enforcement standards of the day has at times been produced (Oakes Ames's admissions about payments to members of Congress). Givers of largess to public officials have on occasion furnished documentation of their activities enabling readers of the document to conclude that by some moral or legal standard of their day their donations were bribes (Carl Kotchian's *Lockheed Sales Mission*). More rarely, recipients have recorded their receipts in such a way as to show awareness that by their own standards they were taking bribes (the entries of Samuel Pepys in his famous diary).

Confession, autobiographical commemoration, admission against interest occur because the bribe is of significance to the person acknowledging its existence. Chronicles and newspaper stories stand at the other end of the spectrum of reality. Journalist or chronicler is typically retelling what he has heard from others, who are often not identified at all. The reporter is interested in making a sensation or in scoring a polemical point. He is personally remote from the situation reported. Anonymous hearsay, his report generally does not rise above the level of rumor. But the concept of a bribe is alive in such rumor. If the scandal were not significant to the society, it would be ignored. Often unreliable as a record of events, chronicles and newspapers are invaluable as witnesses to tastes, interests, and popular values.

Anthropology, it has been said, did not advance until it turned from the study of witchcraft to the study of accusations of witchcraft. My method has been to use not only admissions and accounts of bribery but also accusations—understanding by accusations the sermons of preachers and the censures of citizens as well as specific criminal charges. Where accusations abound—where sermons on the sin are copious, where prosecutions proliferate, where laws multiply—the idea of bribery is being put to work. It is being put to work not necessarily, as it were, for its own sake, but as an instrument of a religious reform or a political program. The reality of the concept in the society is indicated by its invocation, even though the extent to which the idea affects official conduct cannot be closely calculated. Accusations—sermons, moral treatises, moral censures, imperial edicts, didactic legislation—are intermediate between confessions and chronicles. When addressed to bribery, they characteristically evidence concern—the problem is serious enough to talk about in a high style. They also seek accountability: someone is being held responsible. Those who speak reflect a sense of the significance of bribery even if immediacy and involvement on their own part are seldom present. Preachers, theologians, emperors, legislators, concerned citizens grapple with the phenomenon using generalizations that cost them little yet reflect their estimate of the importance of bribery in their society and their view of the standard determining what counts as bribery in their milieu.

Exceptions to the detachment of the moralizers exist. As an authority on bribes, St. Augustine does not have the preeminence he enjoys in sexual morality, yet a judge in Hippo and a suitor in Ravenna, he contributed to the concept from a life full of litigation. Of all those who have written on bribes, his known deeds most match his words. Innocent III, ambiguous in his conduct, clear in his standards, was deeply involved in litigation before his curia. Edmund Burke was a politician who knew the patronage game well when he moralized on Warren Hastings. The most celebrated moralist of all on bribery, Cicero, formed his ideas as he worked his way up the slippery ladder of elected office to the consulship. For these men the concept of a bribe—moral rhetoric in their expositions—was also tied to what they had faced in professional practice. I draw as much as possible on these moralists seasoned by experience and burdened by responsibility for action.

Subject and sources I have accounted for. Need I say why bribery is of interest? For myself the interest began as a boy in Brookline, Massachusetts, where the merits of candidates for office were often discussed in terms of their corruption or corruptibility. Later, a student in Washington, D.C., I observed the drama in the Senate Caucus Room when Senator Homer Ferguson investigated bribery in Air Force procurement, calling witnesses who included Howard Hughes, then a sleek, still youthful-looking millionaire, whose company was the source of the payments; a corrupted Air Force general; and an inconspicuous accountant, cuckolded by the general, who now supplied the evidence that convicted the general of income tax evasion but Hughes of nothing. Back in Massachusetts, I saw the Chief Justice of the Supreme Judicial Court, Stanley Qua, a man of remarkable rectitude and energy, conduct an inquiry into the bribegiving of Judge John Derham; I still recall the moment when Derham, trapped by his own lies, was given a chance to name the high official of the Commonwealth to whom he had paid a bribe, and refused. Derham was disbarred; the high official exonerated because no witness remained against him. Later I watched an equally memorable judicial inquiry managed by Federal District Judge Charles E. Wyzanski with the collaboration of District Attorney Elliott Richardson into the bribegiving of Thomas Worcester, civil engineer, to William F. Callahan, the head of the Massachusetts Turnpike Authority. Later, an officeholder myself, chairman of the Brookline Redevelopment Authority, I saw the integrity of the board and the success of our principal project threatened by bribery—a threat ultimately defeated only with the help of a courageous colleague named

Trustman and the decision of a judge named Good: not only in literature are names appropriately allegorical, as, in this book, Hog, Bacon, and Khashoggi, not to mention Bagwell and Sharpeigh, Savage and Wild, also attest.

As a lawyer and a teacher of professional ethics to law students, I have become conscious of the heavy responsibility members of the American bar bear for facilitating, disguising, and even delivering bribes, as well as for prohibiting, detecting, and prosecuting them. As a father, I have been led to ponder whether my offerings to my children—the *munera* to whom this book is dedicated—are legitimate inducements, gifts, or bribes. As a believer in religion, I have asked how prayer and sacrifice to God are different from bribes.

For Americans generally, bribery has nearly always had a high interest. Treason and bribery are the two crimes mentioned by name in the Constitution. Charges of corruption have often decided elections. Within the last twenty years one president has been forced to resign after impeachment was voted for offenses whose criminal core could be reduced to bribery; another president has been biographically portrayed in convincing detail as a habitual bribetaker and bribegiver. One vice-president has been forced to resign after conviction of crimes based on the concealment of bribes; another vice-president was shown in the hearings on his nomination to practice what was arguably generic bribery by the standard of federal criminal law. Seven members of Congress have been convicted of bribetaking after the most elaborate investigation of legislative corruption ever conducted in any society. Confessions of large American corporations, solicited by the Securities and Exchange Commission, have produced the most abundant documentation of bribegiving known to history. One criminal statute, enacted in 1970, elevates to the level of federal felony any pattern of bribery in any police department, traffic court, mayoralty, state legislature, or gubernatorial office in the nation. Hundreds of officials, including four governors, have in the last decade been sent to prison under this or other federal laws against bribery. Another recent federal statute, unique in the history of the bribe, makes it a crime anywhere in the world for an American corporation to bribe an official of a foreign government. Enmeshed in politics at home, the bribe is now part of an American standard enforced throughout the globe.

At the very time when the concept of the bribe has carried all before it—never were there so many laws against bribery, never were the laws so often enforced by prosecutors, never were there so many convictions of high officials for bribetaking—at this moment the concept is challenged. There are those who would ignore the moral dimension of bribery, treat bribes as a neutral economic category, and rationalize bribery as giving the flexibility needed by many political systems. Typically this counter-concept to the moral notion of the bribe is most boldly applied to the underdeveloped countries. In the same way the argument most subversive of the old concept of usury was first advanced by European moralists in relation to the Chinese. Like usury, bribery could be demoted from a master moral category to a description of a type of economic exploitation.

To look at the bribe at this crisis in its life has the advantage of stimulating comparison with another area of the Western moral tradition in more obvious throes. Here not a single concept but a cluster—chastity, contraception, homosexuality, marriage—has been revamped or reweighed. The relation between bribery and the sexual ethic goes beyond simple comparison. Metaphors drawn from the vocabulary of sexual sin are used to describe the bribetaker. Since the time of the Roman Republic, "to corrupt" has meant both to seduce a woman and to pay off an officeholder. One "betrays" a lover or an office. One is "faithless" to a spouse or a public trust. The same religions, the same kind of commandments and examples, the same kind of sanctions have addressed acts of bribery and acts of unlawful intercourse. Taken at a certain level of generality, the same substantive goods are protected and promoted by both ethics. Each sets enormous store by fidelity. Each lays down the lines that separate a gift, understood as an identification of one person with another person, from the manipulative or exploitative use of one person by another person. As the sexual ethic disintegrates, or appears to disintegrate, before our eyes, we can ask whether the ethic governing bribes will follow suit.

The two areas can be seen as related although now destined to follow divergent paths. If the detailed rules for sexual purity are read not in terms of the substantive goods to which they are overtly directed but anthropologically in terms of their overall social function—if they are seen as ways of resolving ambiguities, safeguarding the vulnerable entrances and exits of social relations and imposing order on the chaotic flux of experience—it could be hypothesized that as these rules disappear there is a greater need for other rules that perform the same function, albeit in a different realm of conduct. The bribery rules, especially as they are embodied in the criminal law, do resolve ambiguities and do impose order. They set apart certain functions and specify explicitly how those performing those functions must be approached. They deal with entrances and exits to the system. They set up safeguards where the system is vulnerable. Their remarkable expansion in recent American history could be accounted for functionally as a social adjustment necessary as the other set of rules governing purity declined. In Henry James's *The Ambassadors* the bribery ethic, applied by analogy, is more important to the protagonist than the sexual ethic—an anticipation of what appears to be happening in American society.

In the time of the prophet Ezekiel, violation of the bribery ethic was regarded, like other offenses such as intercourse during menstruation, as the cause of national disaster inflicted by foreign armies: the impurity of the violations had led to divine punishment. The language in which bribery has been described since at least Roman times reinforces the hypothesis that bribery rules are rules promotive of purity, designed to deter social pollution. A bribe is "filth" in Roman law. Bribe money in both Latin and English is "dirty." A bribetaker "soils" his hands.

Bribegivers, aware of the linguistic odium attached to their actions, seek to make delivery in "as cleanly a manner as possible," as Sir George Hastings said of his way of bringing a bribe to Francis Bacon. Bags, briefcases, or envelopes regularly put a decent cover over the polluting cash.

To regard the rules on bribery, like the rules on sexual purity, as antipollutant is not to deny that the specific issues addressed by both sets of rules are important. It is to acknowledge that, as well as fostering fidelity and other specific values, they have an overall order-producing function. Another comparison may seem even more threatening to the objective basis for bribery rules, but is not. This is the analogy, already hinted at, between bribery and witchcraft, a major pollutant of premodern societies. Similarities are several. Both bribery and witchcraft are socially disapproved ways of influencing the accomplishment of a result the practitioner desires and believes he cannot accomplish openly by legal means or by force. Bribery, like witchcraft, is often believed to be widely practiced, but no one will voluntarily admit publicly to practicing it. Everyone knows of someone else who does it. Accusations of bribery, like accusations of witchcraft, serve a variety of social functions beyond identifying the guilty. Just as accusations of witchcraft sometimes worked to clarify and strengthen the social structure, so have accusations of bribery, as did Burke's indictment of Hastings. Just as accusations of witchcraft sometimes confused and weakened the structure, so have accusations of bribery—such was Bernardino of Siena's implicit judgment of the accusations of bribery so common against the papacy in fifteenth-century Italy. Where the system is most ambiguous or even at war with itself, antipollution rules multiply. Witchcraft accusations multiply in the fourth-century Roman empire and in Elizabethan England. Accusations of ecclesiastical bribery multiply when the Church assumes the highly ambiguous role of deprecating the accumulation of worldly goods and of amassing them for the service of God; so modern prosecutions begin to bear on legislators who are in the highly ambiguous role of rulers and representatives of constituents.

There are other likenesses. Both bribery and witchcraft work in the same way, in our modern understanding of them—that is, both achieve their effects psychologically. The victim of witchcraft feels tormented. The beneficiary of bribery feels obligated. Response in each case is not to physical pressure but to expectations affecting the mind. Witchcraft and bribery also have been subject to the same kind of sanctions. Until the twentieth century, although each crime was sometimes prosecuted, regular sanctions for either were social disapproval and supernatural displeasure. No one wanted to be known publicly as a witch; no one wanted to be known publicly as a bribetaker. The witch was accursed; and from the Book of Deuteronomy to the speeches of Edmund Burke the sanction most often invoked against a bribetaker was divine retribution.

The material harm done by either witchcraft or bribery has often been slight, at times incalculable. No one, for example, showed that the United

States as a whole was worse off because the backers of the Union Pacific Railroad bribed the Republican leadership in Congress. The crime was punished not because of material harm done, but because of the affront to intangible ideals of propriety. The major evidence that bribery or witchcraft has actually been practiced comes from confessions or admissions from those involved. Until modern times there were more confessions by those who had engaged in witchcraft than by those who had been a briber or bribee. If one puts accusations aside and goes simply by trials in which the defendant was found guilty, there is far more documentation, prior to modern times, of the existence of witchcraft than the existence of bribery. Today we doubt the voluntariness or the accuracy of the witchcraft confessions and regard the trials as aberrations; but there is little doubt that there were persons who engaged in witchcraft and who thought it worked, with circumstantial evidence corroborating their belief in its efficacy, however unlikely the causal connection now seems to us. As for bribery, the most comprehensive admissions I have found prior to the nineteenth century (by Bacon, Pepys, Hastings) all deny that what was called a bribe worked at all—that is, while admitting facts that were socially stamped as bribery, those involved claimed that other factors were decisive for them. If we still conclude that the bribes did work we make a causal connection that depends as much on our own experience, beliefs, and values as did earlier generations' conclusions about the efficacy of witchcraft. Today we assume that payment by an interested party to an officeholder is corrupting and we have even changed our statutes so that any such payment is generically bribery—no causal connection showing that the payment obliged the official and influenced his action has to be proved. But it is our desire to be rid of the pollution—not a demonstrated correlation between payment and action—that makes the statutes rationally acceptable.

To press these points of resemblance is not to say that the prosecution of bribetaking officials are witch hunts and that bribery is in general an imaginary crime. The chief difference is that our experience, as colored by our beliefs, makes us disbelieve that witches could set supernatural powers in action, while our experience, as colored by our beliefs, makes us confident that reciprocities can be created and that certain reciprocities conflict with a duty of fidelity we desire to promote. We cannot make an equation of witchcraft and bribery without denying our experience and changing our beliefs and values.

Analogies are always labile, dependent on what features are selected for emphasis. Analogies between bribery and witchcraft, between bribery and usury, between bribery and the sexual ethic and its antipollutant function depend on a selection of features that is speculative, that from a variety of interacting causes isolates and emphasizes certain factors without being able to demonstrate that these factors are in fact crucial. Speculation of this kind may be fed by what is provided in this book, but it remains speculation. Less speculatively, let me say what I have learned from making this account, what may be learned from reading it. To state summarily what may be best understood by following the story in detail, I take these points to be established:

First. Bribes—socially disapproved inducements of official action meant to be gratuitously exercised—are ancient, almost as ancient as the invention in Egypt of scales which symbolized and showed social acceptance of the idea of objective judgment.

Second. The bribe has a history, divisible into discernible epochs. From approximately 3000 B.C. to 1000 A.D. the idea of nonreciprocity struggles against the norms of reciprocation which cement societies whose rulers are both judges and the recipients of offerings. In the second period from, say, 1000 A.D. to 1550 A.D., the antibribery ideal is dominant in religious, legal, and literary expressions; its active enforcement is attempted in successive waves of reformation. The third period of the idea, as far as English-speaking people are concerned, begins in the sixteenth century with its domestication in English bibles and English plays and English law and ends in the eighteenth century with its proclamation as a norm for the English empire. The fourth stage is the American, when the heirs of the successive reformations and of English politics begin to apply it and then to expand its sway until it is asserted as an American norm around the earth; and the rest of the world—not merely as a result of American influence but because of the general expansion of the Western moral tradition—makes at least verbal acknowledgment of the norm.

Third. Bribes are today universal; that is, every culture, with insignificant exceptions, treats certain reciprocities with officials as disapproved.

Fourth. The bribe is a concept running counter to normal expectations in approaching a powerful stranger. Linguistic ambiguity in the term for bribe in Hebrew, Greek, and Latin marks the cultural resistance encountered by the concept. Historically, the limitation of the concept to one class of officials—judges—is a second sign of the resistance. Reluctance to apply the concept against the bribegiver is a third. Lack of specific sanctions against the bribetaker is a fourth indication of the precarious hold the concept, historically, has enjoyed.

Fifth. The bribe in its origins depends on religious teaching. Reciprocity is so regularly the norm of human relations that the conception of a transcendental figure, a Judge beyond the reach of ordinary reciprocities, was of enormous importance for the idea that certain reciprocities with earthly officials were intolerable. That conception of a transcendental Judge was shaped in the ancient Near East. Communication of this image to the West was largely dependent on religion. Accepted as divine revelation, Scripture by commandment and paradigm inculcated a teaching on impartial judgment. The concept of the bribe was cast in a biblical mold.

Sixth. Religion—Jewish, Christian, pagan—has been, however, profoundly ambivalent in its teaching on reciprocity. The Judge beyond influence has been placated by pagans, offered prayers and slaughtered animals by Jews, and seen by Christians as accepting a special redeeming sacrifice. Religion can be viewed as bribery on a grand scale, organized for the highest end, man's salvation, and practiced to persuade the Supreme Authority. Indulgences, systematized to support enterprises from basilicas to bridges, constitute an especially striking example of this kind of religion. Even in its most primitive form, Christianity rests on a transaction carried out between God and the Son of God which theology labeled the Buy Back, a term in Roman civilization often used to mean payoff to a judge to escape punishment. Job and Jesus himself to the contrary, religion can be read as reinforcement of the iron law, "I give that you may give," a law requiring reciprocity with every powerholder including God.

Seventh. The double message conveyed by the several religious traditions is paralleled in Western cultures by the elimination of certain reciprocities as bribes and tne retention of others as acceptable quid pro quos. Words alone seem to mark the distinction between certain acceptable and condemned offerings. In sixteenth-century Europe payment to obtain a spiritual favor was the sin of simony; a *contributio* to obtain an indulgence was legitimate. In twentieth-century America, payment to a candidate for his vote is a penal offense; a licensed contribution to a campaign committee is lawful. In some instances, there is only verbal camouflage; in some instances, the verbal distinction points to a real difference.

Eighth. Although the definition of a bribe depends on the conventions of the culture, so that ceremony and context, form and intention, determine whether an exchange counts as a crime or a virtuous act, ultimately the distinction between bribe and gift has become fundamental. Without this distinction the condemnation of bribes appears arbitrary, and intermediate offerings such as a tip or a campaign contribution are indiscriminately lumped into a single category which includes all reciprocities. With bribe and gift set at polar opposites, a spectrum with shades of discrimination exists. For our culture—Western culture, now the dominant world culture—the difference between bribe and gift has been most powerfully developed by reflection, theological and literary, on the Redemption.

Ninth. Bribes come openly or covertly, disguised as an interest in a business, as a lawyer's fee, or, very often, as a loan. Bribes come directly, paid into the waiting hands of the bribee or, more commonly, indirectly to the subordinate or friend performing the nearly indispensable office of bagman. Bribes come in all shapes as sex, commodities, appointments, and, most often, cash. In the shape of sex, bribes have been both male and female: a slave, a wife, a noble boy. As commodities, they have included bedspreads, cups, dogs, fruits, furniture, furs, golf balls, jewels, livestock, peacocks, pork, sturgeon, travel, wine—the gamut of enjoyable goods. As appointments, they have often been rationalized or justified by the merits of the appointee—a double effect, one good, one bad, being achieved by the bribe. As cash they have come as contingent payments and down payments, as payments for the life of the contract and payments for the life of the recipient and as cash on the spot. They have come at the rate of so much a car towed, so much a prostitute undisturbed, so much a plane purchased, so much a guinea spent, at such a percentage, and at a flat rate. They have been as little as 1 percent of a contract and as high as 20 percent or more. They have been as small as $2.50 for a Connecticut voter and as much as $12,000,000 for the prime minister of Japan and his associates. A representative list of prices appears in the Appendix.

Tenth. Bribers have included every variety of business, from very small to multinational; all the professions; every manner of criminal defendant; and the ordinary citizen in line for an inheritance or in need of a traffic ticket being fixed. Bribees have ranged from constables and sheriffs to the Speaker of the House (U.S., nineteenth century), the Speaker of the House of Commons (U.K., seventeenth century), the president of Honduras, the president of Italy, the prime minister of Japan, the prince-consort of the Netherlands, the Lord Chancellor of England (seventeenth century). Bribe-takers and bribegivers are not distinguished by any of the characteristics commonly associated with criminality. Sometimes they are oppressed and bribe to escape harassment. Sometimes they are oppressed and therefore accept bribes. Often they are possessed of high office and comfortable income, bribe to maintain or expand their power or wealth, and accept bribes given as tributes to their power or wealth. Their crimes have not been shown to depend on any oedipal fixation, sexual need or malfunction, or uncontrollable instinct. They are not vicious in all respects; they are often otherwise decent individuals. They are of all nationalities and sects and have been in the past more often men than women.

Eleventh. The bribe is ideologically neutral—that is, charges of bribery can be made by an established class attacking a new class (John Randolph pursuing the Yazoo speculators; George Templeton Strong scorning the Tweed Ring); by a new class attacking an old class (the Protestants assailing the papacy; Andrew Jackson censuring Adams and Clay); and in intraclass warfare (Coke against Bacon; the Carter administration against the Abscam defendants). The bribe is a concept which can be effectively evoked by "the center" or existing hierarchy, as fourth-century Roman emperors and popes like Gregory I, Gregory VII, and Innocent III illustrate. It is a concept which is useful to "the border" or sectarian groupings within a society, as is shown by the writings of John Wyclif and Jan Hus.

Twelfth. Enforcement of law against bribes has nearly always been a function of prosecutorial discretion. Prosecutions for bribery have often depended on motivations distinct from the desire to punish the bribe. The watershed for widespread federal prosecution of bribery occurred in the 1960s. Whatever social causes account for it, at this time the pursuit of bribery became a national enterprise in the United States. Watergate is the consequence not the cause of this phenomenon. In the Orwellian prophecy for the year 1984, sexual Puritanism is the rule, enforced by electronics. In the actual America of 1984, it is the purity of political reciprocities that is enforced by wire taps, tape recordings, and television cameras.

Thirteenth. The commonest sanctions against bribes are moral—the invocation of guilt before God and shame before society, guilt and shame being equally relied on. Political sanctions—repudiation at the polls, forced resignation from office, loss of promotion—are frequently invoked. Sanctions prescribed by law are more often indirect than direct—not the crime of bribery itself but a related offense is usually punished. Until very recent times application of direct criminal sanctions to highly placed bribetakers was rare.

Fourteenth. Prosecutors, politicians, and journalists are those most attentive to contemporary corruption. Academic lawyers, anthropologists, psychoanalysts, and theologians have had little to say. Political scientists and sociologists, intent on understanding the function of social practices, sometimes give little weight to the moral impact of corruption. Biographers and historians, despite a tendency at times to act as advocates or apologists, give a kind of secular last judgment on the corrupt. Those who have most powerfully articulated the antibribery ethic are the masters of Western literature—above, all, Chaucer, Dante, and Shakespeare

Fifteenth. The material injury bribers and bribees inflict is often undemonstrable. Their actions always subvert the trust that accompanies public office and distinguishes office from power. For Jews, for Christians, for those who share their moral heritage, the bribe is not a morally neutral concept.

Writing at this interesting time in the history of the bribe, I venture a prediction that is a projection of my values. That will come at the end. History itself is not prediction but the selection of significant actions, words, and characters to be remembered—drama more than process. "Remember! Remember! Remember!"—Burke's incantation after his prosecution of Warren Hastings had ended in defeat. If all that is collected here survives in memory, this account has been worth making.

John T. Noonan, Jr.
Berkeley, California
March 25, 1984

I

Kings, Judges, and Offerors

3000 B.C.—A.D. **1000**

1

Bending the Bond of Reciprocity

At the beginning there is no specific, unambiguous word for bribe, no common terms designating and denigrating the briber and the bribee, no noun summing up the action to be shunned and naming it bribery. There are only a range of reciprocities. Reciprocity is in any society a rule of life, and in some societies at least it is *the* rule of life. In a variety of archaic communities, as anthropologists have shown, relations with peaceful strangers are established by an exchange whose essential function is to oblige the offeree. The recipient is bound by receiving. If he does not accept what is offered he is hostile. If he does not respond after accepting he is hostile. The requirements of acceptance and reciprocation make exchange risky. Offerings are, however, a necessary way of creating relationships beyond kinfolk and tribe.[1]

That bribery is wrong, that a bribe must distort judgment—assumptions which may seem too obvious to need justification—are not self-evident. Bribery is an act distinguished from other reciprocities only if it is socially identified and socially condemned. The exchange of favors with a powerholder is otherwise like other reciprocal transactions in the society.

A bribe is not distinguished from other ways of eliciting a benevolent response.

Organized in terms of reciprocation, a society finds anomalous a relationship in which reciprocation is eliminated. To approach another not bound to one in the special reciprocity of family and to bring nothing is unusual. The gods themselves must be approached with offerings that they may be changed from potential enemies to allies. Powerful strangers are to be turned into friends by the creation of family connections or by the acceptance of a present. Officials are approached with offerings like everyone else. Fault lies not with the giver but with the nonreciprocator.

The Mayor Who Does Not Deliver. Gimil-Ninurta, a poor but free man, a citizen of Nippur in Mesopotamia, seeks to improve his lot. All he has is his goat. Leading the goat by his left hand, he brings it to the residence of the mayor and is made to wait. But when the mayor hears that he has something to offer he is indignant at his slaves. A citizen of Nippur, he says, should be admitted promptly. He sends for Gimil-Ninurta and asks, "What is your problem that you bring me an offering?" Gimil-Ninurta says nothing but greets him with his right hand, invokes blessings on him and gives him the goat. The mayor announces he will hold a feast. But when the feast is held, all that Gimil-Ninurta receives is a bone and a sinew of the goat and stale beer. He asks the meaning of such treatment. In reply he is beaten at the mayor's orders. He departs vowing vengeance.

Later, Gimil-Ninurta visits the king of the entire country and offers him one mina of gold in return for the use of the royal chariot for a day. The king asks no questions but agrees at once. In the chariot Gimil-Ninurta returns to Nippur where the mayor receives him as a high official of the realm. Installed in the mayor's residence, he secretly opens the chest he has brought and pretends the gold he says was in it has disappeared. He implies that the mayor is guilty of stealing it and gives the mayor three beatings for his crime. The mayor also placates him with "a gift" of two minas of gold.[2]

This story, celebrated among specialists in Akkadian literature under the title "The Poor Man of Nippur," dates from about 1500 B.C. It might be seen as a form of the folk tale in which men are visited unaware by gods. Gimil-Ninurta, in his triumphant return in the royal chariot, unrecognized by the mayor as the man he had mistreated, does appear to be a *deus ex machina*. As in the biblical story of Lot and the angels (Gn 19:1–26), there is even a hint of the divine in the fact that Gimil-Ninurta is poor and abused.

Nonetheless, the story stays on a secular level. No god is named or invoked. Moral structure is supplied by the rule of reciprocity. The king is said "to do justice." He responds royally when he is offered gold. He does not need to ask questions when tendered such an offer. He needs only to make the exchange requested. The mayor expects something—his expectation is not criticized. The mayor knows that something is expected of him—"What is your problem that you bring me an offering?" He becomes the villain only when he takes what is given and fails to reciprocate adequately. Gimil-Ninurta himself dominates the action, a hero as shrewd and enterprising as Figaro. His action is tricky: left-handed action carries this connotation. But his expectation is not condemned. He proceeds on clear principles of reciprocity, allowing for the demand of retributive justice that punishment be proportionate to malice: he returns threefold the unprovoked beating. His revenge is measured. Reciprocity is the norm.[3]

The same rule is reflected in complaints circa 1500 B.C. from another Mesopotamian city, Nuzi. An investigation into the conduct of Kushshiharbe, its mayor, and Peškilišu, the mayor's lieutenant, reports these charges:

> Thus Hinzurima the wife of Ziliya: I gave one sheep to Peškilišu as an offering (tātu), saying: 'Concerning my fields, attend to my lawsuit with Kariru.' But he did not attend to my lawsuit, and when I spoke concerning my sheep he struck me and kept my sheep.
> Thus Hatartema: When I arrived from Hanigalbat, on account of my lawsuit they handed me over to Peškilišu. Ahumiša gave a sheep, a mixing bowl of bronze, and two doors to Peškilišu as an offering, yet he did not attend to my lawsuit.
> Thus Huzirima: I gave Peškilišu six shekels of purified silver, saying: 'Give to Kushshiharbe in order that he should attend to my lawsuit.' . . . But they did not attend to my lawsuit.'

In each case Kushshiharbe failed to deliver. He did not reciprocate and therefore did wrong.[4]

In Nuzi, as in Nippur, no objection is made to influencing official conduct. In another set of documents of the same period, written in Middle Assyrian, conditional contracts are made with court officials: the promisor will perform his promise if the official will take care of his affair. In one case, for example, the promisor is a woman whose son is in trouble "because of a crime." She makes an agreement to deliver a slave girl as an offering (šulmānum) to Ashur-aha-iddina, a member of a prominent family, if the son's matter is arranged. Witnessed and sealed, contracts of this kind are a precaution against nonreciprocation by the official. Assurance of reciprocity is their aim.[5]

Nippur and Nuzi are in this respect like the very different Polynesian and North American Indian societies investigated by Mauss. In all of them, reciprocity is the norm. The way of offerings is the great avenue by which peaceful relations with strangers are established. Nonreciprocity is what needs to be explained, especially nonreciprocity with a powerful stranger. Two impulses, both rooted in religion, break the common pattern.

The Widow and the Scales.   About 2400 B.C., Urukagina, king of Lagash, makes a treaty with his god, Ningirsu. In return for Ningirsu's favor, he agrees, among other things, not to do injustice to "the widow and the orphan." Reciprocity of course exists between Urukagina and Ningirsu, but the widow and the orphan, who cannot be expected to reciprocate, are made the objects of the king's care. Provision is made for nonreciprocators.[6]

Three centuries later, another Mesopotamian king, Ur-Nammu, records how he has ruled Ur on behalf of the god Nanna: "The orphan was not delivered up to the rich man; the widow was not delivered up to the mighty man; the man of one shekel was not delivered up to the man of one mina. . . ." Ur-Nammu boasts, in effect, of how he has dealt with those who could not reciprocate. He presents his conduct as meritorious although reciprocation is the general order of society in this world and the next. When Ur-Nammu dies in battle, he goes to "the Great Dwelling" equipped with oxen, sheep, leather bags, and jewels to distribute to the seven gods, the scribe of the nether world, and important dead like Gilgamesh. Care by the ruler for the poor coexists with the belief that reciprocity is normally necessary.[7]

In an Egyptian story, circa 2000 B.C., a peasant, Khun-Anup, is robbed of his cattle. He seeks redress from Rensi, the chief steward of the pharaoh, and reminds him, "You are the father of the orphan, the husband of the widow, the brother of the divorcee, the apron of him that is motherless." But the pharaoh determines to test the peasant. At his order, Rensi has Khun-Anup beaten. The peasant persists: "Do justice for the sake of the Lord of Justice, the justice of whose justice exists." He is again thrashed. The ninth time, the pharaoh has Rensi judge in his favor. Perseverance is rewarded, the appeal to help the powerless is acknowledged. The modern title of the story, "The Protests of the Eloquent Peasant," catches Khun-Anup's dependence on the rhetoric which sets a nonreciprocal standard for the judge.[8]

The most famous lawgiver of antiquity, Hammurabi, makes it the recommendation of his decrees for Babylon that they are issued so that "the strong might not oppress the weak and that justice might be dealt the orphan and the widow." The theme by 1700 B.C. is familiar. The claim to protect the helpless goes with the staff of royal authority. The ruler's claim depends on divine inspiration. Hammurabi legislates "by the order of Shamash, the great Judge of heaven and earth."[9]

Several millennia later it is difficult to read of a powerful man professing his solicitude for the widow, the orphan, and the poor without a cynical response. How many thousand times have the interests of widows and orphans and the poor been invoked by kings, city-states, national states, corporations, candidates for office, bureaucrats, legislators, and Daumieresque lawyers in order to rationalize their demands or justify their own status and power! There is no way of telling now how sincere or how effective the Near Eastern rulers were in their promises or boasts: the story of the eloquent peasant contains a double message—rulers should respond to the rhetoric of justice, those who rely exclusively on rhetoric have a hard time. Sluggish, careless, or conventionally interested in gifts as the rulers may often have been in fact, the edicts do announce an awareness of a special responsibility to those whom the rulers cannot expect to reciprocate in person.

There is, however, a reciprocal relation. It is with the god. The poor are the god's stand-ins. He has, in effect, allotted them his own share. The relation is most succinctly stated, centuries later than Urukagina, in the words of the Wisdom literature of Israel:

> He who oppresses the poor insults his Maker;
> he who is generous to the needy honors him.
>
> (Prv 14:31)

The norm of reciprocity is not abandoned. There is a displacement. The ruler's reward is to be from on high, not from the particular poor man he aids.[10]

Every litigant is in a sense a poor man, subject to being outbid by an unscrupulous adversary. Special solicitude for the poor man flows into a second current of thought, the exaltation of objective justice.

Inscriptions in Egyptian tombs of the third millennium B.C. convey the belief that after death the merits of the deceased will affect his future, but do not indicate how these merits will be ascertained or how fair the process of ascertainment will be. Scales had been invented by 3000 B.C., a splendid symbol of objective judgment, once turned to this use. Near the end of the third millennium, between 2200 and 2050, tomb writings refer to "that balance of Re, in which he weighs *ma-at*." Re is the sun god. *Ma-at* is "Order," "Right," "Truth," "Justice." The scales in which Re weighs truth is now seen as the instrument of determining truth, the means of giving judgment. The symbol implies that the judgment is objective; nonetheless, it is also said that the deceased's "offerings [shall be] in front of him." The ambiguity is captured in a Coffin Text of the Middle Kingdom (post 2050), where a spell prays, "May your sin be erased by those who weigh in the balance on the day of reckoning characters." The weighers are invoked so they may cleanse the deceased before the weighing. Still, scales are expected to register the decisive verdict. Weighers open to influence co-exist with an objective measure.[11]

Khun-Anup, whose story is roughly contemporary with this spell, knows of Anubis, the god who does the weighing, and Thoth, the god who is the recorder of the balance. Khun-Anup merges his plea for mercy with a call for the kind of justice which Anubis and Thoth provide. "I shall go that I may appeal about thee to Anubis," he tells Rensi in his final and successful plea for justice. "You need the pen, the papyrus, and the palette of Thoth," he earlier asserts. "Is it the hand-scales?—It does not tilt. Is it the stand-balance? It does not incline to the sides." He addresses the chief steward: "Does the hand-scales err? Does the stand-balance incline to the side? Is even Thoth partial?" Another metaphor merges the scales with the Nile: "Good full justice neither falls short nor overflows."[12]

The ideal of objectivity is appealed to by Rekh-Mi-Re, a real vizier of the pharaoh in fifteenth-century Egypt, who records in his tomb how he was told to carry out his office: "An abomination of the god is partiality. This is the instruction, and thus shalt thou act: Thou shalt look upon him whom thou knowest like him thou knowest not, upon him who has access to thee like him who is far away."[13] Rekh-Mi-Re was in effect deputy pharaoh, supervising everything from the administration of the forts to the annual plowing; but he was preeminently responsible for justice: "the carrying out of justice [is] the produce of the vizier." That responsibility is linked to what he calls "the instruction." In an autobiographical eulogy, also in his tomb, Rehk-Mi-Re declares that Ma-at appointed him; and he has made Ma-at's beauty "circulate the width of the earth." Specifically, "When I judged the petitioner, I was not partial." Objectivity in justice is proclaimed as the great merit of a judge.[14]

By this time, circa 1500 B.C., vade mecums to go with the deceased in the next world are prepared to accompany named pharaohs or nobles after death. Standardized spells "for the rising of the day"—labeled as the Book of the Dead by Egyptologists—they contain an elaborate protestation of innocence of specified crimes for the dead man to recite. They also contain pictures showing how judgment is thought to take place. Objective measurement, judges open to influence—the mixture continues.

In one of the most celebrated of these works, prepared for Ani, treasurer of the temples of Thebes and Abydos in the Nineteenth Dynasty (post 1305 B.C.), three scenes depict the judgment. Scene One: The antechamber of the Judgment Hall. Ani carries a platter stacked with cake, fruit, and meat—supplies for himself or offerings for others, it is not immediately clear. Scene Two: The Judgment Hall itself. Anubis, the jackal god, weighs Ani's heart against a feather, a hieroglyph signifying "Ma-at." Thoth records the balance. Set apart from the weighers, although visible to twelve other gods and goddesses in the background, is the platter of food. The weighing, the actual act of judgment in which the heart can be neither lighter nor heavier than truth, is done without a gift on the scales. In this critical act, no reciprocity with the judge is shown; or rather, reciprocity is converted from a relation between Ani and his judges into a relation between the two pans of the scale. The connection of judge and judged undergoes a transformation. Reciprocity remains only in the balance of the two weights. Scene Three: A reception room beyond the Judgment Hall. Ani, whose heart has balanced the feather, offers the platter of food to Osiris, the great god of the underworld.[15]

From this series it may be learned that the judgment-seeker does not come empty-handed nor seek access to the court without gifts, nor does he fail in thankfulness. Reciprocity between judge and judged has not been totally transformed. The scales' peculiar conversion of reciprocity into an objective binary form nonetheless remains. In the Judgment Hall, at the most decisive moment in a man's life, he does not make an offering to those who weigh him.

The moment, it could be objected, was not so solemn. Recital of the magic formulary stating his innocence assured the deceased a safe passage. He often had a scarab with a spell to prevent his heart rising to bear witness against him. By the time of Ramses II (1290–1224 B.C.) it was even possible in certain sacred towns to anticipate the judgment by going through the weighing on earth. A supplicant's heart, made of lapis lazuli, would be weighed against an image of truth, and he would be instructed to make "full and complete offerings of oxen and birds, terebrinth, bread, beer, and vegetables." But all these practices—the formulary, the scarab, the pre-death ritual—testify to the Egyptians' extreme anxiety about the event and underline its momentousness. What human being would not want to make the outcome certain? All the more striking, then, that the books for the rising of the day teach that the weighing is carried out with no offering in the balance.[16]

The Subordinate's Offering Rejected.   Knup-Anup's story stands in contrast to Gimil-Ninurta's. The latter can deal with a powerholder only by giftgiving; the former's reliance on the rhetoric of justice is ultimately successful. Implicit in the rhetoric of the ruler as the champion of the widow and the orphan, implicit in the image of the scales is a teaching that the judge is not to be swayed by an offering from the litigant. The teaching is only implicit. Explicit condemnation lags.

Scarcely legislation in a modern sense, the royal apologiae issued as laws in Mesopotamia reflect what the king thought appropriate signs of his concern for justice. They state or imply the existence of judges who hear cases. But in these laws there is nothing on the judges receiving or not receiving gifts from those they judge. The laws of Ur-Nammu (circa 2100 B.C.) have nothing on this topic. The laws of Lipit-Ishtar (circa 1975 B.C.), nothing. The laws of Eshnunna (pre-1700 B.C.), nothing. The most completely preserved laws, Hammurabi's for Babylon (1711–1669 B.C.), nothing.[17]

Hammurabi does set out a penalty for a judge who changes his decision—he is to be fined, disgraced, and barred from future services. Hammurabi's English editors ask why a judge should change his mind and give one obvious answer: he has been bribed to reverse himself. Making the assumption that of all possible bribes only this kind of retroactive bribery has been singled out for punishment, they read Hammurabi as threatening permanent retirement to judges bribed to reverse themselves. They entitle this section of the laws of Babylon "The Corrupt Judge."[18]

Their interpretation is ethnocentrically Western. It overlooks the horror Hammurabi must have had of sheer inconstancy. In the ancient Near East, stability is the mark of a god's decision making. Inconstancy undermines the divinity surrounding judgment. The god Nunamnir, in a hymn of Ur-Nammu, speaks of his "life-giving commands and decisions" as "unalterable." It is the mark of his divinity. For the Egyptians a chief characteristic of *Ma-at* is immutability. In a Shamash hymn from the library of Ashurbanipal, the god giving a verdict is celebrated because "your manifest utterance may not be changed."[19] Among the Hebrews, Samuel tells the discarded Saul, "God who is the Splendor of Israel does not deceive or change his mind; he is not a man that he should change his mind" (1 Sm 15:29). Paradoxically, this truth is insisted on although a few verses earlier the Lord has had to "repent" in order to discard Saul (1 Sm 15:11). For a judge to change is for him to undo the sanctity surrounding judgment. His changeability is reason enough to sack him.

In the background of Hammurabi's legislation there may be judges like Kushshiharbe, the mayor of Nuzi who took *tātu* and did not reciprocate. A judge who delivers a decision and then changes his mind may be a judge who receives a present, gives the expected verdict, and then reneges. Legislation that punishes such a judge can only confirm a custom of giftgiving, not condemn it. Hammurabi's editors comment that there is no "known instance of the bribery of a Babylonian judge in legal documents, although there can be little doubt that it frequently occurred; but Assyrian religious texts imply that it was known when they assert that Šamaš punishes the judge who accepts a bribe." The question this comment raises is, by whose standards is bribery determined? If the laws neither define nor punish bribetaking, what act constituted the crime?[20]

A letter of Hammurabi does read:

> Summan-la-ilu has reported saying an offering (*tātu*) is present in Durgurguru and the man who took the offering and the witness who has knowledge of these matters is there.
> [Hammurabi sends an officer to conduct an examination and instructs him:] If an offering is present, set a seal on the money or whatever is offering [indecipherable] and cause it to be brought. And the men who took the offering and the witness who had knowledge shall you send to me.

Each time a form of *tātu* appears in this passage it could be translated "bribe." Doing so, a modern translator adds, "From this letter it seems that Hammurabi was anxious to remove corruption from his officials. Moreover, the successful recovery of any bribe which had been given tended to fill the royal coffers, as we may see from the fact that instructions are given for the bribe to be confiscated and dispatched under seal."[21]

The commentary goes beyond the text. What is being investigated is an offering. Was it given to influence official conduct? We do not know. Central to any allegation of bribery of a judge or royal officer would be an indication of the recipient's rank and function. Here the recipient is vaguely a "man" or "men." The recipients might well have been bribed as witnesses. Nothing shows that they were officials. Nor is it entirely clear that Hammurabi is confiscating the offering to his own advantage; he could be asking for the evidence. Only by reading in a set of Western assumptions about bribery and proper ways of combating it can it be concluded that a bribe to an official is meant. If this conclusion should be correct, Hammurabi's investigation is the first known inquiry into bribetaking; but the conclusion is uncertain.

To move from seventeenth-century Babylon to fifteenth-century Egypt, not only is impartiality exalted, but specifically the rejection by a judge of an offering from a petitioner is upheld as an ideal: the vizier Rekh-Mi-Re in the autobiographical eulogy of himself declares, "I did not turn my brow for the sake of reward (*feqa*)." In this context, there can be no doubt that an offering to a high official is regarded as undesirable; Rekh-Mi-Re boasts that he has not accepted one.[22]

The same idea appears more emphatically in the Edict of Horemheb (1342–1314 B.C.). The pharaoh, Horemheb, announces that he has chosen viziers for the North and the South and has taught them not to "receive the reward of another, not hearing [undeciphered]." He goes on to ask the judges how they can judge others "while there is one among you committing a crime against justice." He then remits an obligation of members of the official staff to pay the pharaoh a percentage of their income. After this apparently administrative detail affecting compensation, he continues: "Now, as for any official or any priest of whom it shall be heard, 'He sits among the official staff appointed for judgment to execute judgment, and he commits a crime against justice therein,' it shall be against him a capital crime." Taking reward from one litigant and not hearing his adversary is inferably the "crime against justice" which the pharaoh condemns with his rhetorical question. Arguably, it is also the "crime against justice" for which he provides capital punishment. If this interpretation is correct, Horemheb's Edict is the first law with a secular penalty for a form of bribe-taking.[23]

The ideal excluding offerings that influence judgment is clearly stated of the Sun-god who is hailed as He who "places the gods in their places," who is "eternal God, Judge." This judge protects the orphan and "does not put out his hand to the mighty." This "just Judge takes no reward." The god's rejection of reward is fused with his function of protecting the poor. Another eulogy of the god Amon-Re, circa 1230 B.C., declares that he, "the first to be King, the God of the primeval time, the Vizier of the poor, takes no reward from the guilty, and speaks not to him who brings testimony and looks not at him who promises." Amon-Re's impartiality is admirable. That he takes no reward "from the guilty" states a qualification probably understood in other Egyptian texts even when it is not stated: only the reward that perverts justice, only the gift that distorts the decision is deplored, no absolute ban on offerings is intended.[24]

The ideal is manifest, its realization in practice is not. Further isolated fragments of legislation or reports of investigations may no doubt exist or be discovered. But the wholly disputable example from Hammurabi's laws, the single ambiguous report on an inquiry by him, and the far from clear provisions of Horemheb are representative of the fragility, ambiguity, and meagerness of the evidence that any provision was made for punishing bribery in the ancient Near East; and we have no examples whatever of punishment actually applied. In the 100,000 cuneiform tablets of Mesopotamian civilization preserved in modern museums, no one has found the record of a specific punishment meted out to a gifttaker. In the inscriptions of four millennia of Egyptian civilization no one has produced evidence of a gifttaker actually suffering as a criminal. Somewhere in this vast storehouse of the past such an account may yet be found. But it can be said that the cases of punishment must have been so rare as to be virtually nonexistent. If the measure of a law is its enforcement, in no part of the ancient Near East was there a law against a judge receiving gifts. Indeed the chief distinction often made between legislation and literature—the presence of sanctions—should not be pressed. The codes are one way of expressing a moral ideal, no different in this respect from Rekh-Mi-Re's self-serving autobiographical tomb.[25]

Reliance is not on human enforcement but on divine assistance. That the judge speaks for the god is a recurrent assumption which sustains a litigant in danger of being outbid before a human tribunal—it is already apparent in Khun-Anup's appeal to the judgment of Anubis. Explicitly, in a papyrus of about 1230 B.C., the god Amon-Re is addressed as he presides in a human court. He is asked to "give ear" to one "alone in the law court, who is poor," from whom "the scribes of the mat" have already had "gold and silver" (so his poverty is relative). The petitioner prays, "May it be found that Amon assumes his form as the vizier in order to permit the poor man to get off. May it be found that the poor man is vindicated. May the poor man surpass the rich." The rich man in court may "seize like a crocodile," ran the proverbial wisdom of Ptahhotep. Assuming the form of the vizier, Amon must forestall the bite of wealth.[26]

Egyptian wisdom literature, six centuries later, contains the same message in the form of exhortation to the judge himself. "The Instruction of Amen-Em-Opet" (circa 650–550) reads:

> Give not your consideration only to him clothed in white,
> Nor give consideration to him that is unkempt.
> Do not accept the reward of a powerful man,
> Nor oppress for him the disabled.

The ideal of impartiality continues to be unmistakably linked to the injunction against receiving reward. No enforcement mechanism has been developed.[27]

That the god of justice will punish the one who gives reward is neither stated nor implicit. The focus of exhortation is on the judge not the litigant. It is no doubt implicit, but it is not said, that the god will punish the judge who *takes* reward to do injustice. Egyptian literature does not specify what the divine penalty will be. Babylonian wisdom literature—preserved in the seventh-century library of Ashurbanipal at Nineveh and reflective of an earlier era—offers a sanction of some specificity with this anonymous warning or curse:

> If a king does not heed justice his people will be thrown into chaos and his land will be devastated. . . . If citizens of Nippur are brought to him for judgment

but he accepts a present (*kat-ra*) and improperly convicts them, Enlil, lord of the lands, will bring a foreign army against him to slaughter his army, whose prince and chief officers will roam streets like fighting cocks. . . .

In the style of Babylonian omens, this "Advice to a Prince" sets out an event and what will follow that event as its necessary consequence. Taking an offering that produces an unjust criminal judgment is followed by disaster, divinely produced.[28]

Looking back at the fall of Babylon, a prophet of Eshaddon declares: "They were oppressing the poor and putting them in the power of the mighty. There was oppression and acceptance of offerings within the city. Daily, senselessly, they were robbing each other's property." Retroactively, the prophet sees that catastrophe followed a course of oppressive gift-taking.[29]

Supernatural sanction against the whole class of unjust judges is invoked in a hymn to the sun-god Shamash, also in the library of Ashur-banipal. Shamash is celebrated as he watches over all the people of the world, judging the good and the wicked, heaven and earth, and condemning, among others, these evil-doers:

> The unrighteous judge thou does make to see chains.
> The receiver of an offering (*tātu*) who perverts—thou
>   does make to bear punishment.
> The nonreceiver of an offering, the raiser-up of the
>   badge of the poor man, is well-pleasing to Shamash,
>   lengthens his life.
> The careful judge who pronounces a judgment of
>   righteousness shall prepare a palace—the abode of
>   princes his dwelling.

Not his country but the judge himself is threatened with supernatural punishment if he receives a gift that perverts his judgment. No more specific retribution exists in the judical literature of the age.[30]

To summarize: from the fifteenth century B.C. on, there has been a concept that could be rendered in English as "bribe," the concept of a gift that perverts judgment. It is the hieroglyph *fK3* (*feqa*) in Egypt. Its Mesopotamian counterparts are *kat-ra* and *tātu* as these words are used in the contexts quoted above. The problem in translating any of these terms as "bribe" is that the ambiguity of the original words is resolved into a clear unambiguous meaning. *Tātu*, for example, is used for the gifts made by those complaining about Kushshiharbe—the complainants are not saying they gave bribes to pervert his judgment. The parallel term for the present given to Ashur-aba-iddina is *šulmānum*, a word etymologically connected with *šulmum*, health. Originally a *šulmānum* meant a present brought by a guest to wish health to his host; it came to apply to any offering brought by one in a role subordinate to the receiver. Such offerings are often customary, acceptable, praiseworthy in the eyes of the society in which they are tendered. *Feqa* and *tātu* are analogous—they are, generically, the offerings of subordinates; a negative sense attaches only by context. To preserve the ambiguity of *feqa, kat-ra,* and *tātu* in translation, it is necessary to use terms like "reward" or "offering" which often have positive meanings but which can be used ironically to mean something improper. The purely negative terms, "bribe," "briber," "bribery," "corrupt," and "corruption" have no verbal counterparts in the ancient Near East. At the same time the concept of impartial judgment and the concept of a subordinate's offering which should be rejected by a judge have been formed. The ideal of impartiality and rhetoric supporting the ideal do exist in Egypt, Assyria, and Babylon.[31]

The Bribe in the Bible.   Neither the Book of the Dead nor a pharaoh's edict nor a vizier's tomb nor Sumerian stele nor Babylonian wisdom furnished the ideas that were to provide recurrent inspiration and direction in later history. The gropings, the tentative lunges forward, the high rhetoric of Near Eastern literature would have been so many broken shards if the main concepts had not been expressed in Hebrew Scripture.

The Hebrew term that functions in context like *feqa* and *tātu* to express a disapproved payment is *shohadh,* here translated ambiguously as "offering." The first specific criticism of *shohadh* in a judicial context appears directed at witnesses rather than judges. In the "Code of the Covenant," circa ninth century B.C., God speaks to Moses on Mount Sinai and after setting out the Ten Commandments gives further instructions for Israel. He ordains:

> You shall not spread a baseless rumor.
> You shall not make common cause with a wicked man by giving malicious evidence.
> You shall not be led into wrongdoing by the majority, nor, when you give evidence in a lawsuit, shall you side with the majority to pervert justice; nor shall you favor the poor man in his suit. . . .
> You shall not deprive the poor man of justice in his suit. Avoid all lies, and do not cause the death of the innocent and the guiltless; for I the Lord will never acquit the guilty. You shall not take shohadh, which makes the clear-eyed blind and the words of the just crooked.
>
> (Ex 23:1–3, 6–8)

While the text could be applied to judges, the commands focus on those who make accusation or offer evidence. The Lord is the judge—"I will never acquit the guilty." Witnesses before the judge, Israelites, are not to lie or take *shohadh* to slant their testimony.

A story independent of the events on Sinai but eventually incorporated into the narrative of Exodus shows Moses receiving the advice of his father-in-law, Jethro, in appointing judges. Jethro tells him to make leaders or judges those "who hate loot" (*béytza*) (Ex 18:21). The term employed is too imprecise to say whether Jethro excluded all reward or merely unusual and exorbitant profit. Exodus contains no distinct condemnation of judges who are willing offerees.

Offerings to the judges of Israel are attacked in the mid-eighth century B.C. when prophets speak out against offerings to God himself. Amos, self-identified as a shepherd from Tekoa, reports that the Lord addresses the rulers in these terms:

> *I know how many are your crimes*
> *and how countless your sins,*
> *you who persecute the guiltless, hold men to ransom,*
> *and thrust the destitute out of court.*

(Am 5:12)

The rulers have turned "justice itself into poison" (Am 6:12). The Lord rejects what they offer:

> *I hate, I spurn your pilgrim feasts;*
> *I will not delight in your sacred ceremonies.*
> *When you present your sacrifices and offerings*
> *I will not accept them,*
> *nor look on the buffaloes of your share-offerings.*
> *Spare me the sound of your songs.*
> *I cannot endure the music of your lutes.*
> *Let justice roll on like a river*
> *and righteousness like an ever-flowing stream.*

(Am 5:21–24)

Hosea, Amos's contemporary, has a similar message (Hos 6:6); and so, later in the eighth century, does Micah (Mi 6:6–8). Isaiah, Micah's contemporary, brings to a climax the denunciation of judges who take offerings. To them, through Isaiah, the Lord speaks:

> *Your princes are rebels, accomplices of thieves*
> *All are greedy for offerings* (shoḥadh) *and itch for presents* (mattana).
> *They do no justice to the orphan.*
> *They never hear the cause of the widow.*

(Is 1:23)

Denouncing these rulers, the Lord rejects their efforts to propitiate him. Through Isaiah, the Lord declares:

> *I have no desire for the blood of bulls,*
> *of sheep and of he-goats.*
> *Whenever you come into my presence—*
> *who asked you for this?*
> *No more shall you trample my courts.*
> *The offer of your gifts is useless.*

(Is 1:11–13)

Seventh-century law keeps pace with the prophets. The "Holiness Code" in Leviticus instructs the judges of Israel in these terms:

You shall not do evil in judging either by lifting up the faces of the poor or by lifting up the faces of the rich. You shall judge your countrymen in justice.

(Lv 19:15)

The passage builds upon Exodus 23:3 where witnesses are explicitly instructed not to favor the poor. Whereas Rekh-Mi-Re spoke of the judge's brow wrongly responding to partisan considerations, the gesture of favoritism here is toward the head of the litigant to recognize him as the person with whom the judge identifies. The idiom is analogous to an Akkadian expression, "to lift up the forehead," meaning to become a surety or guarantor for the one whose forehead is touched.[32] The action is condemned, be the litigant rich or poor. The judge is not to identify with the one before him. The final provision of the Holiness Code—"You shall not pervert justice in measurement of length, weight or quantity" (Lv 19: 35)—expresses the spirit that predominates in the Code's instruction on judging. The Egyptian symbol of objectivity is merged with other measuring instruments to inculcate impartiality. No more than the weigher at the scales is the judge to cheat in measuring what is just.

Pondering the stories and rules which eventually became Genesis, Exodus, Leviticus, and Numbers, the seventh-century authors of Deuteronomy, "the Fourth Gospel of the Pentateuch," reworked the tradition to fuse the prophets' polemic, the old religion, and the newer insights of Wisdom literature. The Lord on the mount tells Moses:

Circumcise the foreskin of your hearts, and be stiff-
necked no longer.
For the Lord your God is God of gods and Lord of lords,
the great, mighty, and terrible God,
Who does not lift up faces and does not take shoḥadh.
Who secures justice for widows and orphans
and loves the alien who lives among you,
giving him food and clothing.

(Dt 10:16–18)

God is just, impartial, and simultaneously the champion of the underdog. Specifically as a judge He does not discriminate (lift up faces like one creating suretyship); and He does not take an offering when He judges.

What is said of God as judge is expected of men as judges, for two reasons. Throughout the Near East the belief that the judge acts for the divinity is strong. The justice of Hammurabi was to prevail "by the order of Shamash, the great Judge of heaven and earth." Amon-Re was beseeched to assume "the form of the vizier." In Deuteronomy itself, Moses tells his appointees as judges, "Have no fear of men; for judgment is God's" (Dt 1:17). Acting as God or as God's deputy, the judge is also under an obligation, probably implicit in Egyptian theology, explicit in Hebrew, to imitate God. The divine model provides the motive for all the injunctions of the Holiness Code of Leviticus: "Be holy, for I the Lord your God am holy" (Lv 19:1). In Deuteronomy the divine paradigm of the Judge, set out by the Lord himself in self-description, becomes controlling for the human judges of Israel. God on the mount commands Israel:

> You shall appoint for yourselves judges and officers, tribe by tribe, in every settle-ment which the Lord your God is giving you, and they shall dispense true justice to the people. You shall not pervert the course of justice nor shall you lift up faces nor shall you take shoḥadh, for shoḥadh blinds the eyes of the wise and makes the just answer crookedly. Justice and justice alone shall you pursue, so that you may live and occupy the land which the Lord your God is giving you.
>
> (Dt 16:18–20)

Not only does the Lord provide himself as exemplar. In the tradition of Wisdom, He gives a reason and a reason of the strongest kind in a book devoted to Wisdom. In Exodus *shoḥadh* blinded "the clear-eyed"; the ef-fect was on a witness, and the effect was on his eyes (Ex 23:8). Here it is the judges who are affected, the wise themselves who are blinded by a gift. Finally the Lord himself pledges a reward to the just judges—the land itself will be their recompense.

After the prophets and Deuteronomy the denunciations of *shoḥadh* mul-tiply. The date and authorship of Psalm 26 are uncertain but it is remark-ably close in standards to the Assyrian hymn to Shamash; its singer speaks of human judging:

> I wash my hands in innocence
> to join in procession round your altar, O Lord
> singing of your marvellous acts,
> recounting them all with thankful voice.
> O Lord, I love the beauty of your house
> the place where your glory dwells.
> Do not sweep me away with sinners
> nor cast me out with men who thirst for blood,
> whose fingers are active in evil
> and whose right hands are full of shoḥadh.
>
> (Ps 26:6–10)

Whether the poet has in mind a witness or a judge, his criticism comprehends both. Although the last line by itself could be read to mean or to include givers as well as takers, it is probable on the basis of the other biblical texts that only takers are meant. The bloodthirsty are identified with those who take *shohadh* instead of doing justice. As the right hand in particular should be clean, its use to receive offerings is an additional reason for reproaching them.

Psalm 15 voices the same position, celebrating "the man of blameless life, who does what is right." This man does no wrong to his neighbor, he speaks the truth, he scorns the reprobate and honors the religious, he keeps his oath, he does not put out his money at usury, and, last, "he takes no *shohadh* concerning an innocent man." Such a man may dwell on the holy mountain of God. The encomium embraces the truthful witness and the just judge. Like the avoidance of usury, the avoidance of offering has become the requirement of righteousness. Psalm 15's encomium reappears, slightly varied, in an expansion of Isaiah praising:

The man who lives an upright life and speaks the truth,
who scorns to enrich himself with loot (béytza)
who snaps his fingers at offering (shohadh) . . .
that is the man who shall dwell on the heights.

(Is 33:15–16)

The usury of Psalm 15 is replaced by loot; and loot, the term used in Exodus 18:21 as something the leaders and judges are to avoid, now is made precise as a parallel to *shohadh*.

After the fall of Jerusalem in 587 B.C., the Lord speaks through Ezekiel to condemn the princes of Israel whose conduct brought on the disaster. These rulers, like those denounced by Isaiah, shed blood, oppressed the alien, and grieved the orphan and widow. They despised the Lord's sanctuaries. They caused the innocent to die, slandering them. They indulged in incest, had intercourse with the menstruous, and committed adultery. The Lord's culminating charge against Jerusalem is: "In you men have taken *shohadh* to spill blood, and they have practised feneration and exacted usury on their loans" (Ez 22:12).

Looked at anthropologically, *shohadh*-taking has risked danger and in fact brought about disaster by polluting the community. Like the violated sexual rules, the commandment against *shohadh*, if observed, would have protected the nation. Looked at from Ezekiel's standpoint, the consequences of *shohadh* in the condemnation of the innocent make its heinousness clear. Like usury from one's countrymen, *shohadh*-taking has violated a norm of Deuteronomy, established by command of God himself to Moses on Mount Sinai. Now it is the Lord himself who through his prophet points to *shohadh*-takers as the wicked rulers who caused the nation to be led captive.

After the return from exile in 538 B.C. the literature then taking its final shape repeatedly sets out the divine paradigm of Judge. "The heavens proclaim his justice," says Psalm 50:6, "for God himself is the Judge." God, declares Psalm 9:8, "will judge the world with justice"; He will pronounce "true judgment." As Judge, God is petitioned to judge a man on his merits: "Give me justice, O Lord for I have lived my life without reproach" (Ps 26:1). As Judge, He is exhorted, "Let your eyes be fixed on justice" (Ps 17:2). As Judge, He challenges "the gods themselves": "How long will you judge unjustly and show favor for the wicked. You ought to give judgment for the weak and the orphan" (Ps 82:2–3). As Judge, He is an exemplar; and as Judge He judges according to the truth with attention to the poor.

Even Proverbs, a mixed bag of secular and spiritual advice, incorporates maxims hostile to gifttaking:

> *A grasping man brings trouble on his family,*
> *but he who spurns* mattana
> *will enjoy long life.*

> (Prv 15:27)

Mattana in the first books of the Pentateuch means a gift given to the Lord (Ex 28:38; Lv 23:38; Nm 18:7), and in Deuteronomy a holy and permitted gift of this kind stands in direct contrast with forbidden *shohadh* (Dt 16:17–19). Here in Proverbs 15:27 the term comprehends any gift avariciously sought. Proverbs also teaches:

> *A wicked man accepts* shohadh *under his cloak*
> *To pervert the course of justice.*

> (Prv 17:23)

These texts join the Wisdom of Babylonia, of Amen-Em-Opet, of Deuteronomy in attacking certain kinds of gifttaking.

Offerings have now been repeatedly rejected by God as Judge and declared wrong for human judges to accept. The dominant message is repeated in the third century B.C. when the Chronicler, drawing on earlier accounts, gives his summary of the appointment of judges in Israel. King Jehosaphat tells the appointees:

> *You do not exercise the judgment of man, but of God.*
> *He is with you whenever you judge.*
> *May the fear of the Lord now be on you.*
> *Take care what you do,*
> *For the Lord our God*
> *Has no part in injustice*
> *Or in lifting up faces*
> *Or in taking* shohadh.

> (2 Chr 19:6–7)

The offering binding the judge to reciprocate by giving an unjust decision has been condemned.

Reciprocity Denied.   At the pinnacle of Wisdom literature, the Book of Job carries the teaching on reciprocity to a new level; but there are within the story itself two views of the matter. The self-righteous Eliphaz the Temanite declares,

> *For the godless, one and all, are barren, and their homes, enriched by* shohadh *are consumed by fire.*

> (Jb 15:34)

Shoḥadh-taking, godlessness, and divine punishment (sterility; destruction) are not accidentally connected. Elihu, another self-righteous counselor, tells Job that God "thinks no more of the rich than of the poor" (Jb 34:19). God "repudiates the high and mighty . . . but allows the just claims of the poor and suffering" (Jb 36:5–6). Job must reform himself when he acts as a judge:

> But you did not execute justice on the wicked.
> You cheated orphaned children of their rights.
> In future beware of being led astray by riches
> or corrupted by fat kopher.
> Prosecute the rich not merely the penniless;
> strong-armed men as well as those who are powerless.

(Jb 36:17–19)

Kopher is the life-price which Samuel, a just judge, is said to have spurned (1 Sm 12:3). Here it is broadly any judge-corrupting gift.

Job has been presented at the start of the story as a man "of blameless and upright life," who "feared God and set his face against wrong-doing" (Jb 1:1). Could such a man have taken *kopher*? The easy answer, supported by other textual arguments, is that Elihu's speech is an interpolation. But Elihu only makes explicit what Eliphaz implies: Job is being punished for his wickedness. God is reciprocating his evil. His misery is deserved. Both Elihu and Eliphaz, merely human counselors, speak on a level where reciprocation is the rule. Self-satisfied, they may be spiritually inferior to Job in the eyes of the author, but their sentiments are as usual in their society as Polonius' are in his. At the story's end, when Job has passed his tests, he also meets with reciprocity—God gives him 14,000 head of small cattle, 6,000 camels, 1,000 yoke of oxen, 1,000 she-asses, seven sons, and three remarkably good-looking daughters (Jb 42:11–15). All these blessings the final editor of the Book of Job thinks to be Job's due. The main thrust of the work is different. Reciprocity as seen by Elihu and Eliphaz is surpassed.

After Job has begun to be tested by Satan and has lost his oxen, asses, camels, and children and had his skin covered with boils, he does not curse God to his face but he asks,

> What is the lot prescribed by God above,
> the reward from the Almightly on high?
> Is not ruin prescribed for the miscreant
> and calamity for the wrongdoer? . . .
> Let God weigh me in the scales of justice,
> and he will know that I am innocent.

(Jb 31:2–3, 6)

> I would plead the whole record of my life
> and present that in court as my defense.

(Jb 31:37)

God is asked to be objective, to be fair, to reciprocate Job's goodness. He is even asked—it is the only passage in the Bible to indicate explicit that God uses scales to measure a man—to weigh Job.[33]

> God answers out of the whirlwind,
> *Where were you when I laid the earth's foundations? . . .*
> *In all your life have you ever called up the dawn*
> *or shown the morning its place?*

> (Jb 38:4, 12)

God challenges Job to silence:

> *Is it for a man who disputes with the Almighty to be stubborn?*
> *Should he that argues with God answer back?*

> (Jb 40:2)

To these words, Job says,

> *What reply can I give thee, I who carry no weight?*

> (Jb 40:4)

God's power establishes disequilibrium. Job's confession acknowledges its existence and his helplessness. He has nothing, not even his blameless life, to put in the scales. Job cannot bind God to reciprocate. With such a God the court etiquette of *The Book of the Dead* makes no sense. God is unreachable. The thrust of the narrative moves beyond the idea of God as judge; Job cannot plead his own merits. The scales will always tilt against him. Yet judgment is not discarded. God remains a judge, who asks, "Dare you deny that I am just?" (Jb 40:8).

In that great work of old age, *The Laws*, Plato says that the contention "that the gods when they receive gifts can be appeased by the entreaty of wrongdoers is one that no one should admit, and we must try to refute it by every means in our power." A little later, specifying the kinds of impiety to be punished by the state, he classifies as impious the belief that the gods are "appeased by entreaty." Probably the qualification "by wrongdoers" is again understood. The distance between divinity and men is not so ruthlessly and dramatically established as in Job.[34]

The breach in reciprocity goes too far, so we may think; perhaps so the author thought; and certainly so thought the final editor who assigned Job so much livestock and the comely daughters. But the breach is made. It leaves only a whirlwind or only a mystery through which God speaks. The breach functions to make it unthinkable that God can be bound by a gift. At the apex of judgment, at the center of the tradition, in response to the figure who becomes a prototype of Jesus, the Judge is incorruptible because He cannot be bound by anything He has created. Pointless to say that such a Judge does not take *shoḥadh*, pointless to qualify the teaching of Amos and Isaiah and say that the Lord rejects only the offerings of the unworthy. Even the just life of a good man is not enough to bind Him. The bond of reciprocity is rejected, if not forever, at least so seriously that no petty bribes can restore it. At the zenith of Wisdom, *Job* is an *a fortiori* statement that offerings intended to influence God are vain.

Mixed Message.   God himself is beyond *shohadh*, and God acts when a judge gives judgment. This biblical message is complicated by the lack of biblical sanctions for the common custom of making offerings, by the ambiguity of biblical language, and by information, biblically conveyed, about God's practices.

First, as to the lack of sanctions: In the Book of Samuel, a story set in the eleventh century B.C. and reworked in the seventh, the lots identify Jonathan as disobedient and his father Saul sentences him to death. As Jonathan is the hero of the battle, the people seek to save him. Ultimately they "ransom Jonathan," paying Saul to pardon him. Implicitly, the story contrasts the sinful Saul with Samuel, an unusually good judge, but Saul takes the ransom without incurring any penalty (1 Sm 14:45).

At the end of his outstanding career Samuel boasts,

> *Whose ox have I taken, whose ass have I taken?*
> *From whom have I taken life-price and a shoe?*
> *Testify against me, and I will make restitution.*[35]

(1 Sm 12:3)

The ordinary judge, Samuel suggests, not only takes life-price; he bargains for it—the transaction, like an arrangement for *šulmānum* in Assyria, is so standardized that it is solemnized with the ceremonial delivery of a shoe. The shoe-sealed judicial bargain is common enough in mid-eighth century to be treated as proverbial in the denunciation of it by Amos (Am 2:6). Samuel, here set forth as a model by a seventh-century editor, does not expect any criminal penalty if he should be proved to be boasting idly—his single penalty will be to restore what he has taken. His sons, Joel and Abiah, judges in Beersheba, are said to "take *shohadh* and pervert justice" (1 Sm 8:3). They do suffer one sanction, or rather, their failure to inherit their father's authority is interpreted by the author of Samuel as a sanction; the people's preference for another kind of ruler is connected with their conduct. They are not condemned by their honest father, nor are they prosecuted as criminals. In the same way Ezekiel interprets the fall of Jerusalem as a sanction: there is no specific criminal penalty he can retroactively cite against the faithless, *shohadh*-taking princes of Israel (Ez 22:12).

Certain stories which could be shaped to show a sanction for bribetaking do not in fact have this focus. The serpent's temptation of Eve with the apple is sometimes thought of today as a bribe. But the serpent does not offer the apple, he merely points out the beneficial consequences of eating; and Eve's sin is not bribetaking but disobedience (Gn 3:1–7). Delilah is offered 1,100 pieces of silver by each of the Philistine lords to discover the secret of Samson's strength and deliver him to the Philistines. The narrative focuses on her persuasion of Samson, as effective as the serpent's of Eve. The structure of the story underlines Delilah's betrayal of her husband and his credulity in trusting her. Nothing is said of Delilah's subsequent fate. No word approximating bribe is used to describe the Philistines' offer, which in itself appears to be a stratagem of war. Delilah herself, whom we might see as a kind of bribe, is not put in such a category (Jgs 16:4–22).

The enforcement of any law by actually applied human sanctions is not a prominent feature of biblical history. Vengeance is normally divine. There are also departures from law that are so taken for granted that they are neither avenged nor criticized nor explained: the murder of all the relatives of a dethroned monarch is accepted as normal palace politics (2 Kgs 10:11). But as to some laws there are stories that indicate a tradition of enforcement. According to Genesis, Shechem was killed for seducing Dinah (Gn 34:1–26); Tamar was condemned to burning as a prostitute (Gn 38: 24); Amman was killed for raping Absalom's sister (2 Sm 13:1–29). Such stories suggest that some sexual sins were punished. There is nothing similar about a judge taking a bribe.

The absence of applied sanctions coheres with the difficulty, which would have been experienced if sanctions had been pressed, of prosecuting bribetakers. Bribetakers are among the powerholders in society: that is why they are bribed. In a modern society corporate bribers may be more powerful than the officials they bribe. In an ancient society, power and office are more likely to coincide. To bring the guilty to justice requires strong political backing for their prosecutors.

Biblical organization of authority does not support sanctions. Insufficient separation of powers, too little professionalism prevent the imposition of human penalties. Attribution to God of specific and diverse functions such as creating, judging, pardoning can be read as an adumbration of the separation of powers which in modern times has been so important to democratic political theory. God's role as Judge, it can be argued, is kept distinct from His role as Pardoner. On the human level, the appointing of "judges" also produces some separation of functions—the local judges are distinct from the king. Nonetheless, all powers ultimately are vested in the Divine Ruler, and the king's ultimate authority is not limited by any line between the judicial and the executive. Judges under the king are not a separate bureaucratic class, compensated by the crown for the execution of their office. There is no set of men, high or low, making their living simply as judges—there are only ad hoc judges like Job and the man of blameless life celebrated in Psalm 15. No body of lawyers exists with an interest in the integrity of the courts. The prophets—professional critics if one likes—do not have the competence or corporate esprit necessary to give regular enforcement to a commandment overriding ordinary expectations.

Bribery is a crime that because of its secret nature is likely to go undetected unless there is incentive to complain about it and a procedure for its discovery. There is a procedure set out in Deuteronomy for the detection and judgment of a bride suspected of unchastity (Dt 22:13–21). Nothing is provided for the detection of an unlawful offering. There is no provision in the Bible that judgments obtained by offerings shall be null, so litigants are given no incentive to object to an offering made by an opponent. Nor is incentive provided for officials to investigate an offering taken by other officials. The authors of Deuteronomy will not permit the fee of a male or female prostitute to be given to the Lord (Dt 23:18). They make no similar restriction as to *shohadh* given to a judge. The Deuteronomic prohibition against judges taking *shohadh* has attached to it no penalty of any human kind (Dt 16:18–20).

The absence of specific sanction against bribery stands out even more strongly when bribery is compared with false witnessing. The prevailing assumption of the law in the ancient Near East is that there are only facts to be determined. If the witnesses but speak the truth the facts will be evident. The judges, agents of the divine, will declare what is manifest to them from the testimony. The fear is that the witnesses will not testify truthfully. In the Bible the command not to bear false witness against a neighbor is one of the Ten Commandments (Ex 20:16). Repeated in Dt 5:20, the law is fortified by specific prescriptions for the punishment of the false witness by the law of the talion (Dt 19:16–21). When culpable miscarriages of justice are reported in the Bible they are due to false witnesses—the "two scoundrels" sicced upon Naboth by Jezebel (1 Kgs 21:8–14) and the two lechers who accuse Susanna (Dan 13, 1–43). In the Bible no judgments are corrupted by an offering and no judges punished for receiving one.[36]

Say that the principal sanction for *shohadh*-taking was the guilt of violating the law—the contention has force after the acceptance of Deuteronomy as the law. There is a specific curse provided for him "who takes *shohadh* to kill a man with whom he has no feud" (Dt 27:25).[37] The sanction was one-sided, operating only against the judge or witness receiving an offering, not against the offeror. Bribery and prostitution are both acts which it takes two to consummate. As a norm teaching what should be done, the rule against *shohadh* was like a norm against prostitution condemning only the prostitute. If only one can be guilty, the force of the norm is more than halved. The rule was the more seriously undercut because it had to operate on the more powerful party in the transaction while the less powerful was left unstigmatized. The rulers of the community were asked to consider it wrong for them to receive what it was no sin in others to give.

A further dilution: the norm against offerings made full sense only if a judge was guarded against partiality from more obvious sources. In any tribal culture and in any hereditary monarchy the most likely source of influence upon a judge was a relative. In no part of the Near East was there an effort to shield a judge from corruption through nepotism. Very occasionally there are suggestions that nepotism is to be avoided. As long as influence more compelling than any bribe was not reproached, the operation of an offering on a judge's mind was hard to understand as seriously sinful.[38]

An additional weakness: the norm was not developed in relation to the legislator. The ancient writers made no sharp distinction between legislator and judge, but in Israel there were written laws as well as individual judgments. As they were presented to the people, the laws were pronounced by the Lord. As the Lord did not take *shohadh*, no gift could have influenced their formulation. The actual work of drafting legislation was ignored by theocratic theory. A degree of secularism was indeed introduced in Deuteronomy when it supposed that the judges, God's stand-ins, needed to be enjoined from taking *shohadh*. God's delegates were in this way distinguished from God. No such distinction was made between the divine legislator and his legislative agents. No rule against *shohadh* was enunciated for the human draftsmen whose function was overlooked in the presentation of the law as revelation.[39]

It is, however, a mistake to measure law only by the sanctions it imposes. Law is not solely addressed to the bad who must be coerced, but to the good who want to do right and to the puzzled or uninstructed who seek guidance. Without the teeth of sanctions, a rule, a norm, an ideal can both channel conduct and teach what the community expects. The Bible presented a rule against *shohadh*-taking, unjust judges, and the ideal of a God-Judge above *shohadh*. It presented the rule and the ideal not as an inert text or a school lesson but as the words of the living Lord. Still, the conduct which the condemnation of *shohadh* channeled cannot be quantified; and the strength of the teaching was diluted by the ambiguity of the terms it employed and the limitations of its scope.

Compare the normative language on sexual conduct. Not only were stories told in which sexual sins were punished, but the principal proscribed act was identified: to commit adultery (Ex 20:14). Not only was the central sin marked off by a name, but a variety of unlawful acts—intercourse with a near relative, intercourse of a man with a man, intercourse with a beast—were verbally identified (Lv 18:6; Lv 20:13; Ex 22:19). The strength of the sexual norm was confirmed by its metaphorical employment to indicate national apostasy: disobedient Israel was an adulteress or a whore (Is 1:21; Hos 3:1). *Shohadh*-taking did not carry the same metaphorical punch. As late as Ezekiel, when a prophet looked for a metaphor of communal disobedience to the divine ruler, it was not the corruption of judges but the well-established image of harlotry that he evoked (Ez 23:1–49).

The standard term for an offering to an official was *shohadh*, and the failure to establish a clearly derogatory meaning for *shohadh* is the best proof of the countervailing strength of the culture in support of giftgiving to the powerholders. *Shohadh* in its more general sense is like *feqa*, *šulmānum*, and *tātu*, a gift to a superior.[40] It can be neutral or good. Ahaz sends *shohadh* to the Assyrian monarch, Tiglath-pileser (2 Kgs 16:8): in context, the gift appears as one squeezed from the donor; *shohadh* here has an ironic sound—the "offering" is extorted. *Shoḥadh* also designates an appropriate and expected tribute. In this sense it is put in the mouth of the just King Asa to describe what he is sending the king of Aram: his ambassador is instructed to say, "I now send you this *shoḥadh* of silver and gold (1 Kgs 15: 19). Second Isaiah praises Cyrus, who will let the Israelites go without paying "a ransom or *shoḥadh*" (Is 45:13). A ruler might have legitimately asked ransom for the release of foreign slaves or prisoners; *shoḥadh* is parallel to ransom as something that would ordinarily be expected. If *shoḥadh* were despicable, there would be nothing extraordinary in Cyrus waiving it. When Job replies to his friends, he asks:

> Did I ever say, "Give me this or that;
> pay shoḥadh to save my life;
> rescue me from my enemy;
> ransom me out of the hands of
> ruthless men?"

(Jb 6:22–23)

Job is not boasting that he did no evil but that he has not even made the requests usual among friends. The function of *shoḥadh* is to make sure that a powerful donee will reciprocate.

The usefulness of *shoḥadh* is celebrated in the Wisdom literature of Israel:

> He who offers shoḥadh finds it works like a charm.
> He prospers in all he undertakes.

(Prv 17:8)

> A gift (mattana) opens the door to the giver
> and gains access to the great.

(Prv 18:16)

The observations are not made sarcastically. They are intended as advice for success. The art lies in the discreet presentation:

> A present in secret placates an angry man,
> Shoḥadh slipped under the cloak pacifies great wrath.

(Prv 21:14)

The thought is picked up in the second century B.C. by Jesus, son of Sirach:

> A wise man advances himself by his words,
> a shrewd man will please princes.
> He who tills the soil will have a full harvest,
> he who pleases princes will secure pardon for his offenses.
> Presents and shoḥadh blind wise men's eyes
> and stifle rebuke like a muzzle on the mouth.

(Ecclus 20:27–31)

Deuteronomy objects to the blindness produced by *shoḥadh*. The adviser of those anxious to succeed turns the law against itself. As *shoḥadh* blinds, a wise man will use it.

Shoḥadh never becomes a concept confined to a criminal bribe. To translate *shoḥadh* in all contexts as "bribe," as is sometimes done, introduces a moral criticism where sometimes none is intended. To translate *shoḥadh* as "gift" in these contexts and "bribe" in the negative contexts is to be faithful to the meanings but to conceal a problem: How is the *shoḥadh* which is finally condemned by the law to be distinguished from the *shoḥadh* that is useful and acceptable? The problem is inherent in a culture that has not firmly marked out the difference between bribe and gift.

The functioning of an order in which reciprocation plays its vital role is splendidly illustrated in the historical books of the Bible. The Ark of God, sacrilegiously seized in battle, brings plagues of tumors and of rats; its divine owner must be appeased, not only by its return, but with gifts—gold tumors and gold rats (1 Sm 6:1–9). Nabal, whose name according to Abigail his wife means "churl," fails to reciprocate the respect shown his sheep by David and his soldiers; he is asked for a gift and refuses. Abigail, described by the narrator as intelligent, does what he should have done; she is rewarded and Churl dies (1 Sm 25:1–44). A spectacular exchange occurs in Kings: the Queen of Sheba gives Solomon 120 talents of gold, spices in an abundance never to be repeated, and precious stones. He gives her "all she desired, whatever she asked, in addition to all that he gave her of his royal bounty" (1 Kgs 10:10–13). The Queen of Sheba knew what she was doing, and Solomon understood the duties of a donee.

When one comes to a prophet, one does not come empty-handed: so Saul hesitates to approach Samuel: "There is no food left in our packs and we have no present for the man of God, nothing at all." Saul's servant comes up with a quarter-shekel of silver to solve the difficulty (1 Sm 9:7–8). The apparent exception in the story of Naaman and Elisha is only apparent. Naaman, cured of leprosy, naturally offers "a token of gratitude." Surprisingly, Elisha refuses. But he is a prophet and is playing for larger stakes. Naaman is still obligated, and he responds by promising to offer holocausts and sacrifices only to the Lord; he will pay back Elisha's master who is the true source of Elisha's power. The point is driven home when Elisha's own servant, Gehazi, tries to euchre a gift out of Naaman. He gets the gift and with it Naaman's leprosy (2 Kgs 5:15–27). In this variation of the theme of the dangerous gift, reciprocity is maintained, and Gehazi is punished for claiming a return to which he was unentitled and which had already been given at a higher level.

From the beginning of the priesthood, offerings form a substantial part of the income of the priests. At the old sanctuary of Shiloh, the priests have a right to whatever a three-pronged fork picks out of the cauldron while the meat of the sacrifice is stewing (1 Sm 2:13). According to King Jehoash (835–796), "Money from guilt-offerings and sin-offerings was not brought into the house of the Lord: it belonged to the priests" (2Kgs 12: 16). According to the accusation of the Lord in mid-eighth century, the priests "feed on the sin of my people" (Hos 4:8). A reform proposal in Deuteronomy is careful to provide that the Levites "shall eat the food-of-ferings of the Lord, their patrimony" (Dt 18:2). The rights of the priests to gifts are safeguarded in the postexilic plan of Ezekiel: "The grain-offering, the sin-offering, and the guilt-offering shall be eaten by them, and everything in Israel devoted to God shall be theirs" (Ez 44:29). For this economy to work, reciprocity has to be the rule.

God himself is approached with gifts. The first giftgivers are identified in the Yahwist narrative almost at the beginning of the human race— Cain who brings produce of the soil as "a gift to the Lord" and Abel who brings the fat portions of the first-born of his flock (Gn 4:3–4). In the Yahwist account of the flood, Noah sacrifices whole-offerings and "when the Lord smelled the soothing odor, he said within himself, 'Never again will I curse the ground because of man, however evil his inclinations may be from his youth upwards' " (Gn 8:21). God's response to a gift is matched in the Priestly narrative by the covenant God makes with Noah (Gn 9:9). In the Elohist contribution to the story of Jacob, contract and conditional gift are blended. Jacob vows:

> If God will be with me, if he will protect me on my journey and give me food to eat, and clothes to wear, and I come back safely to my father's house, then the Lord shall be my God and this stone which I have set up as a sacred pillar shall be a house of God. And of all that thou givest me, I will without fail allot a tenth part to thee.
>
> (Gn 28: 20–22)

The theme of reciprocity, woven into the narratives of Genesis, is put in terms of law in Exodus. In the Elohist "Book of the Covenant," the Lord requires gifts as part of the bargain. He sets as a command for Israel: "No one shall come into my presence empty-handed" (Ex 23:15). When the people are to be registered, the Lord speaks to Moses and tells him that "each man shall give a ransom for his life to the Lord, to avert plague among them during the registration" (Ex 30:12). In the Yahwist restatement, the law is put: "You shall buy back all the first-born of your sons"; and it is again added, "No one shall come into my presence empty-handed" (Ex 34:20).

It would be a work of supererogation to show how the different layers of Hebrew tradition contain legislation specifying what the presents are to be—the "food-offering of odour soothing to the Lord" of Numbers (Nm 15:11) or the animals, birds, grains to be offered according to the priestly prescriptions of Leviticus (Lv 1:1–17, 2:1–16)) Deuteronomy, the reform-minded work most critical of certain offerings, also gives instructions for the killing of animals and the offer of their blood to the Lord (Dt 12:13–28); for tithes to be paid the Lord (Dt 14:22–27); for a heifer which will atone for the shedding of innocent blood by unknown hands (Dt

21:9). Deuteronomy decrees that thrice a year the community is to gather before the Lord in a festival to which no one is to come "empty-handed" (Dt 16:16). The religion of Israel is a religion of gifts. Reciprocation with the almighty Powerholder is the rule.

In both sexual conduct and judging, what the Lord does is set out as a paradigm, reflecting the human ideal and in turn influencing that ideal. But there is a difference. The sexual norms are so established that it is superfluous to declare that the Lord is not an adulterer or that the Lord does not practice incest, homosexuality, or bestiality. The only sexual conduct predicated of the Lord is marital (Hos 2:19). It is otherwise with gifttaking. It is necessary to say in explicit terms that the Lord does not take *shohadh* (Dt 10:18). *Shohadh*-taking is not unthinkable of the Lord. That it is not unthinkable is a sign that the teaching on *shohadh* has not been fully assimilated as a fundamental precept.

Taken at the letter in some of their words, the prophets put the ax to the root of reciprocity. But who could bear their relentless words or understand them as rejecting the entire giftgiving religion of Israel? Did they really mean to be taken literally? Ezekiel—the greatest descendant of the pre-exilic prophets—is witness that they did not. Unsparing in denunciation of *shohadh* received by sinners, unsparing of the offerings which roused God's anger (Ez 20:28–29), he is also the man by whom the Lord declares, "I will demand . . . the best of your offerings, with all your consecrated gifts. I will receive your offerings of soothing odour . . . (Ez 20: 40–41). Only offerings from sinners are rejected.

The distinction is as old as Genesis: In the Yahwist story of Cain and Abel, the Lord received Abel's gift but not Cain's, and when Cain was angry, the Lord told him:

If you do well, you are accepted.
If not, sin is a demon crouching at the door.

(Gn 4:7)

The Lord, it is evident, receives only the gift of a worthy donor. Wisdom does not speak differently:

The wicked man's sacrifice is abominable to the Lord,
the good man's prayer is his delight.

(Prv 15:8)

The view is like that implicit in the Book of the Dead: even before the weighing, the gods receive Ani's gifts because his heart will be found to balance truth in the scales. The solution is an easy one for a divinity who know the human heart and who knows what the judgment will be. He can always distinguish the worthy donor from the unscrupulous wretch trying to influence him with *shohadh*.

As long as God was the Supreme Judge and as long as God received offerings, an ambiguous message was transmitted to human judges by the divine paradigm. From Babylon to Thebes, it was known that "gods love gifts."[41] No Near Eastern society attempted to distinguish explicitly the divine aspects—to say that as Judge the deity did not take gifts, that as Lord he did. No Near Eastern society rejected reception of gifts by the gods. Deuteronomy, the biblical book with the clearest teaching that the Lord did not take *shohadh*, was also the clearest on the reciprocity that governed the relations of the Lord with Israel.[42]

God does not take *shohadh*. He does receive ransoms and sacrifices from the worthy. He who is the Judge of the world, who instructs the gods themselves, who pronounces true judgment with his eyes fixed on justice, receives offerings from the good men He judges. He who is the paradigm of justice is also the paradigm of the powerful donee. Despite the voices of the prophets, despite the Book of Job, when the teaching of the Old Testament as a whole is considered it is the paradox that dominates. Unreconciled and in tension, the passages celebrating the just Judge co-exist with the passages in which He is presented as a willing Offeree.

2

The Preference of the Professionals

To move from the high aspirations, the broad exhortations, and the vague denunciations of the Near East to the world of a practicing Roman orator is, at first blush, to cease to trace the history of an ideal in order to sink into a sewer. Only Cato, Cicero was to say, could imagine that the Roman state resembled Plato's Republic: those who knew it realistically recognized it as "Romulus' refuse." Reciprocity abounded. Appeals to justice seemed cynical. What election, what trial occurred without an exchange of favors? Reciprocity was nonetheless more consciously channeled and the reciprocities classified as bribes were more severely censured in Cicero's Rome than in any of the kingdoms of Egypt, Mesopotamia, or Palestine.

To put an antibribery ethic into practice in even a limited sphere—as opposed to announcing what it should be—required men professionally interested in the process of judging; it required a corps of men whose skill consisted in the presentation of facts and law and argument. By Cicero's day in Rome a small corps of politician-orators existed. Professionally their work depended on the presentation of cases. Professionally they were valued highly. Next to generalship, said Cicero, the art most useful to the state was oratory, a skill that could not only check mad tribunes and bend the excited mob but resist largess.[1] Whatever dodges orators might use, whatever reciprocities they might invoke, whatever corruption they might connive in, their reliance in the exercise of their profession could not be on cash, for then the courts would be a mere extension of the markets, open to any trader. As orators, the advocates needed a forum in which their words counted as much as, or maybe more than, money. Professionally, if they were not to be pimps for the judges or panders for their clients, they had to discountenance bribes.

Greek city-states preceded Rome in the use of a political forum in which a charge of bribetaking was relevant.[2] Professional legal skills were more developed in Rome. Thanks to Cicero's public speeches and private letters, the Roman cases are better documented; and the Roman examples and formulations were of far greater influence in the subsequent development in the West. Ciceronian standards join biblical texts in the later Roman Empire to constitute the tradition that becomes ours.

The Staining of Staienus.   In 74 B.C., Marcus Tullius Cicero—then thirty-two, a highly nervous young man with only a half dozen years of practice—was asked by country folk in the provincial town of Larinum to undertake the defense of one Fabricius, charged with complicity in attempted murder. The trial itself was to be in Rome, a contest between two powerful knights from the provinces who had come to hate each other. The initiator of the proceeding was Aulus Cluentius Habitus and the principal defendant was his stepfather, Statius Albius Oppianicus, to whom he related as Hamlet did to his mother's husband.[3]

The prosecution's case was this: Oppianicus stood to gain a large legacy from his wife if her son, Cluentius, died before she did. Moved by greed, Oppianicus planned to poison him. He contacted Fabricius, a kind of thug-for-hire. Fabricius put to work his freedman, Scamander, and Scamander in turn got in touch with a slave who worked for Cluentius' physician. Scamander offered the slave a sum of money to do the job, Scamander providing the poison. The slave, however, was honest and reported Scamander's offer to the doctor and Cluentius. They instructed him to pretend to go along. Scamander was captured as he delivered the poison and a sealed packet of money to the slave.[4]

Publius Cannutius, the prosecutor, was retained—in accordance with Roman usage—by Cluentius himself. Cicero, never a man to underestimate himself, rated Cannutius extraordinarily high—"my equal."[5] Cannutius proceeded cannily, trying the defendants one at a time and trying his strongest case first. Cicero, brought in to act for Fabricius, thus found himself first defending his client's freedman, Scamander, who had no good explanation of why he should have been found in a wood with poison and a sealed packet.

During the course of the trial, however, an incident occurred which Cicero did not mention at the time but which he later brought to light. Oppianicus, the principal target of the prosecution, bestowed *dona* and *munera* on one of the judges, Gaius Aelius Staienus, turning him into "a more zealous partisan than the fidelity of a judge demanded." *Donum* (plural, *dona*) and *munus* (plural, *munera*) both mean "gift." *Donum* usually carries no negative implication. In one primary meaning *munus* means office or duty; it also means burden and a work or book. But its range of meanings when used in connection with employment are only background, intensifying the ambiguity of the term when used to describe a type of present. *Munus* is the equivalent of *shoḥadh*. It designates offerings with a string attached.[6] It cannot be simply translated as "bribe." Context determines whether the word is used with a pejorative connotation. In this instance Cicero is contrasting these "presents and offerings" given in Scamander's trial with what he calls "the big money" Staienus later got in Oppianicus' own trial. The implication Cicero leaves is that while Staienus behaved improperly after receiving them, there was no absolute barrier to a judge taking small gifts. But in this case, to his discredit, Staienus was the sole judge to vote for Scamander's acquittal.[7]

After Scamander was convicted, Cicero prudently withdrew as counsel for Fabricius, who was found guilty too, and Oppianicus went on trial. There was still a gap in the prosecutor's case—direct evidence of Oppianicus' arrangements with Fabricius. To convict a freedman and a rural thug was not the same as convicting a knight with Roman connections. Oppianicus had been a power—indeed a hometown tyrant—in the day of the dead dictator Sulla. The wheel of politics had turned against him, but he was not without friends and resources. For his advocate he had obtained a tribune, Lucius Quinctius, a skilled and successful politician on his way to becoming praetor. Cluentius could not have been sure that his prime target would be sunk. Much, both sides must have reasoned, would depend on the thirty-two *iudices*.[8]

Iudices are sometimes, because of their large number, their limited term of service, and their lack of professional legal training, described in English as jurors. The term misleads. They were far from being random representatives of the defendant's neighbors. Drawn from the ruling elite of Rome, they were members of the sovereign lawmaking body of the state. Senators, free to act without supervision, they had power to determine the law as well as the facts. Resembling, most of all, members of a special investigating committee of the Congress of the United States, they were not merely committeemen bringing in a report. They held power of life and death over the man before them. They exercised that power surrounded by the prestige and mystique of judges, the spokesmen of the divine. It is as judges that their exposure to corruption must be understood.[9]

To have the judges on one's side at the start was obviously a desideratum. "I have the judges I want," Cicero reported in the 60's when he was preparing to defend his then client Catiline; and on another occasion, apropos a bill governing the selection of judges in a particular case, he observed, "Everything was in that." In his celebrated prosecution of Hog a good deal of prosecutorial and defense time was spent on the composition of the court—Cicero's selection of "good guys" (*boni*) being met by his opponents' maneuvering to drain his carefully chosen panel for service in another case. In the defense of Oppianicus, things went badly for the defense. The president of the court, Iunius, was a friend of the prosecutor.[10]

As it turned out, the senators were so closely split that every vote was crucial. Near the end of the trial a vacancy occurred on the panel. The replacement was selected by Iunius, acting in conjunction with the city praetor or law officer. That officer in 74 B.C. was Hog, the corrupt villain of Cicero's later indictment; and it was with his collusion, Cicero was to maintain, that the senator chosen, Gaius Fidiculanius Falcula, came ready to vote for conviction. Although he had not heard any of the evidence, Falcula so voted. Popular rumor credited him with having received almost 50,000 sesterces for his vote.[11]

At about the same time, Oppianicus made an approach to Staienus whom he had already tested and knew to be responsive to inducements. Now he selected Staienus to be bagman for all the judges he needed bought; Staienus was to be the *sequester* (fixer) for the others. A tie was the same as an acquittal; Oppianicus needed sixteen votes. He calculated the cash necessary "with the precision of an Archimedes" and offered Staienus 640,000 sesterces or 40,000 per judge.[12]

Staienus went to work to enlist his colleagues on the panel. He signed up M. Atilius Bulbus and Tiberius Gutta, promised Bulbus 40,000, and urged him to recruit others.[13] But well into his efforts, Staienus backed off. The inference is virtually irresistible that he did so when Cluentius secretly offered him more money to vote for conviction and to bring colleagues like Bulbus and Gutta with him. According to the charges later made, these men, Falcula, and five other judges were all bought by Cluentius, using Oppianicus' bagman as his own instrument.

When the time came for the vote to be taken, Staienus was actually absent on business in another court. Oppianicus, with the anxiety of a man who waits to see what he has paid for delivered, insisted on his recall. He returned and voted for conviction. The final tally was 17 for "guilty," 10 for "not proven," 5 for acquittal. By a margin of one, Oppianicus was convicted.[14]

It is Cicero, defense counsel at the beginning of the trials and eight years later Cluentius' counsel in a kind of replay of Oppianicus' trial, who provides the information on the money paid. As Cluentius' counsel, he did not acknowledge that Cluentius had paid more than Oppianicus; he claimed instead that Staienus' shift was motivated by his desire to keep all 640,000 sesterces for himself.[15] In 70 B.C., when he was counsel for neither side, he voiced the popular view of what had happened, a view it may be believed he shared. He evoked the image of a corrupt judge by first naming Bulbus—literally "Onion," a godsend to counsel mocking him—and then Staienus. The "judgment of Iunius," as the verdict by Iunius' panel was labeled, he characterized as "that foulest of crimes." In a devastating sentence in which Staienus was not named but was unmistakably described, Cicero declared that he was "a senator who, when he was a judge, in the same trial received money from the accused which he distributed to the judges and from the prosecutor to condemn the accused."[16]

Stained with money from both sides—a veritable mayor of Nippur or Nuzi if these anachronistic comparisons may be allowed—Staienus took money for judgment in a case where life was at stake, political issues muted, counsel active. In this ordinary criminal trial of a provincial knight, money spoke to senatorial judges more effectively than Cannutius or Quinctius.

The Cleansing of Cluentius. Oppianicus, convicted of attempted murder, was not executed or severely punished. Temporarily disgraced, he was even able to make something of a comeback. He trapped Staienus into promising to repay the money he had given him at the trial and successfully sued for its recovery. No law barred him as an unsuccessful briber from getting back his bribe; the ethics of Nippur and Nuzi prevailed.[17]

His counsel, Quinctius, meanwhile protested the verdict. As a tribune of the people, he had a platform from which to denounce the corruption of the court. He did not fail to do so. "This touches each of us," he declared. "The courts are nullities. No one who has a rich enemy can be safe." Marcus Caesonius, a judge who had voted against conviction, backed up his denunciations.[18]

Iunius was brought to trial not long after his term as panel president was over. The charges were both specific and easily substantiated: he had failed to take the oath of a judge; he had failed to report the appointment of Falcula as a substitute. He was convicted on these technicalities—then as now, technicalities being used to punish a man believed guilty of greater but less easily proved or defined criminality.[19]

Falcula was put on trial as an unlawfully impaneled judge and acquitted. He was then charged directly with receiving money from Cluentius. The case was complicated by being held before the *Quaestio de pecuniis repetundis*, the Inquiry as to Reclaimable Moneys. The judicial panels of the Senate were set up to deal with specific types of crimes. This panel was for the protection of "the allies," the vassal jurisdictions ruled by governors sent from Rome, to redress wrongs unredressable in the allied state because the governor himself was the wrongdoer. The jurisdiction of this Inquiry was stretched to take up a domestic case.[20]

It is customary in translation to refer to this Inquiry as the "Extortion Court," and indeed the property reclaimed had often been extorted by the violent use of official power. But the translation is too narrow. The court functioned as a forum in which all kinds of political outrages could be aired and given a political-judicial resolution. Extortion and bribery are always close. Clearly by the 60s the Reclaimables Court was not just the "Extortion Court" but the "Extortion, Political Outrages, and Senatorial Corruption Court." Before it, Falcula maintained his innocence, declared that he had voted "guilty" because the trials of Scamander and Fabricius had decided the issue, and was for the second time acquitted.[21]

Next, Staienus and Bulbus were each tried for the vaguer if greater offense of treason. The crime involved conduct affecting the army not the courts, but no bounds of relevancy cramped a Roman criminal proceeding. In each case evidence was introduced of their taking money in the Oppianicus trial—from which party is not clear in Cicero's report. For good measure, evidence was produced that Staienus had taken another 600,000 sesterces in another trial. Each defendant was convicted of treason.[22]

Gutta and another judge, Publius Popilius, were prosecuted under the election practices law. Again, what they had been paid in Oppianicus' trial became part of the prosecution's case, and they were convicted. Gutta and another judge, Aquilius, were noted by the censors as guilty "of corrupt judgment" in their votes for Oppianicus' conviction. The censors' verdict was not a judicial conclusion but reflected the popular belief; the censors added that Cluentius was the payor. Gaius Popilius was convicted of embezzlement; his money-taking as a judge of Oppianicus was also used against him. Publius Septimus Scaevola, another judge, was not accused of corruption in his own trial by the Reclaimables Inquiry, but in the assessment of penalty, a nonjudicial proceeding following on conviction, his vote against Oppianicus was taken into account and he was penalized as "one who had taken money for something he would judge." Gnaeus Egnatius actually disinherited his son, declaring publicly that he did so because his son as a judge at the trial "had taken money to condemn Oppianicus."[23]

Staienus, Iunius, Bulbus, Gutta, Publius Popilius, Gaius Popilius, Aquilius, Septimus Scaevola, Egnatius Jr.—all believed to have been corrupted by Cluentius—were not tried on this charge. Criminal lawyers seemed impotent to isolate the crime and prove the case. After the failure to convict Falcula, it was not attempted. Indirectly, within five years of Oppianicus' trial in 74, these judges had been punished for their corrupt part in his conviction. In 66, Oppianicus Jr. hit on a way of bringing Cluentius himself to book.

Before the Murder Inquiry in Rome, Oppianicus Jr. charged Cluentius with poisoning his father in 72. In addition, he charged him in the earlier trial with "the encompassing of an innocent man in judgment." The law this charge invoked went back to a statute of C. Sempronius Gracchus in 123 B.C., now incorporated in Sulla's more general murder statute, the *lex Cornelia de sicariis*. It did not refer specifically to seeking a capital conviction by bribery. The operative verb *circumvenire*, to encompass or to hem in or to surround, was vague. It could be interpreted to include any scheme intended to bring about the death of another. Specifically, at his trial, Cluentius was accused of encompassing Oppianicus "by false judgment." The gravemen of the case was that he had paid money to the judges to achieve the conviction.[24]

On the defensive and beset, Cluentius looked for counsel and found the present President of the Reclaimables Inquiry, the praetor-elect of Rome, the brilliant prosecutor of Hog. Already advanced on the electoral escalator, Cicero was three years away from being consul. In his prime as an advocate, actively associated with Pompey and his power, Cicero was doubly desirable as an orator and as a politician. For a client in grave difficulty he had the boldness and self-confidence to sweep all suspicions away. That he had once represented the side of Oppianicus Sr. in a very closely related trial, he treated not as an obstacle but as an advantage.

Cluentius had three lines of defense. He had not paid any money. Oppianicus was not innocent. The statute applied only to senators. Untroubled by what he had said earlier about the judgment of Iunius as the foulest of crimes, Cicero took all three positions.

"Teach us what money he gave, what he gave it from, how he gave it. Show us a single trace of money proffered by him." Cicero's challenge to the prosecutor was a classic defense. Cluentius' account books, scrupulously kept, were clean of suspicious payments. As long as he and his agents stayed silent, as long as no paid judge turned informer, the prosecutor had no direct evidence to offer.[25]

The crime charged was to encompass an innocent man. But, Cicero maintained, the deceased had not been innocent. He told three stories to demonstrate his character. In Rome itself Oppianicus had once been implicated in the murder of a rich young wastrel from Larinum. His confederate had been apprehended, brought before Q. Manlius, a *triumvir* or police commissioner, and scared into confessing. Oppianicus was picked up on the commissioner's orders. Commissioner and suspect quickly realized that they had mutual interests. Manlius "came to an understanding with Oppianicus and accepted money from him." The case was marked closed.[26]

Within his own family, Oppianicus had used money to induce betrayal of a trust. A legacy would fall to Oppianicus Jr. if a child in the womb of a widow were not born. The widow's husband, the testator, had thoughtfully provided that his wife would not get her own legacy unless she gave birth to the child. Oppianicus Sr. settled the matter by a cash payment to the widow. She "took this price and also many offerings (*munera*) which are disclosed in Oppianicus' account books." In short, she "sold the promise which, entrusted to her by her husband, she held in the womb." The child was aborted. Oppianicus Jr. got the legacy.[27]

A third story: Oppianicus Jr. would have a legacy of 400,000 sesterces if there were not in existence one Marcus Aurius, a young man who had fought in the Social War and had disappeared after the capture of Asculum in 88 B.C.. An informant let his mother know that he was held as a slave by a senator on the Adriatic coast. She died before she could obtain his ransom. Oppianicus contacted the informant, "corrupted him by money," found out where the son was, and arranged for his extermination.[28]

Triply guilty of corrupting others, Oppianicus had attempted to corrupt the panel that had tried him. "If it is established that this judgment is cor-

rupted," said Cicero, "It was corrupted either by Cluentius or by Oppianicus." The implication was that it was a logical dilemma, that both
could not have been guilty of corruption. Oppianicus had the character
and the motive which made him the probable villain. One or the other, no
doubt, had paid off Staienus. "The man who was in danger corrupted
him."[29]

Corrupere, "to corrupt," the verb employed by Cicero to describe Oppianicus' action, had been in use before Cicero adopted it. It was a term
exact enough to describe the evil act of paying a judge to decide unjustly
in one's favor. It drew strength from its parallel employment in a sexual
sense as in the phrase "to corrupt a virgin." The corresponding Greek
term, *dekasthō*, "to pay ten," focused only on the financial aspect of the
transaction with the judge. The Latin word fused disdain for the payment
with a significance derived from sexual mores; it implied that the judge
had been invaded like a seduced virgin.[30]

Cluentius had paid nothing to the judges. Oppianicus Sr. had not been
innocent. And a third argument: the law against encompassing by false
judgment did not apply to a person in Cluentius' position. The statute—at
least that portion of it which Cicero thought it worth his while to quote
—was a general conspiracy statute, with some focus on false testimony
or its subornation. It enumerated certain classes of persons—"whoever of
them conspires, has conspired, combines, or has combined, or has agreed
that, or speaks testimony so that anyone is condemned by a public
court."[31] Cicero emphasized the words "of them." Who could be referred
to by this phrase except the ennumerated groups—holders of certain civic
offices and all members of the Senate? Cluentius was neither an officeholder nor a senator. Whatever the evidence against him, he did not fall
within the statute's terms. The statute's strict limits must be observed.
After all, the law was "this bond of that status we possess in the state." It
was "this foundation of liberty." It was "this fount of justice." All citizens
were slaves to the law in order to be free. A city without law would be
"like a body without a mind, unable to use its sinews, blood and limbs."
The courts themselves were constituted by law, and without law they
would not exist. To convict Cluentius without a law applicable to his act
would be to destroy the basis of the courts, liberty, society.[32]

As he developed the case for interpreting the law literally, Cicero
launched an appeal to two groups possessed of great power and influence.
Since the trial of Oppianicus in 74, the courts had been reorganized. Senators could compose only one-third of a panel. The remainder was reserved
for *equites*, knights, and a subclass of knights known as *tribuni aerarii*.[33]
Cicero's argument, addressed to the nonsenatorial majority on the panel,
was that any extension by interpretation of the *lex Cornelia* was a threat to
them. Strictly interpreted, the statute spoke only of judges who were senators. No matter how much a knight conspired or combined he was beyond
the law. This was fair enough, Cicero contended. Senators were bound by
stricter laws because they had a higher status and received greater privi-

leges. The members of the other orders should not be held to the same standard.[34]

No argument could have emphasized more crudely the power politics that affected the Roman courts. Cicero said in so many words to the knights, "Who would dare to judge truly and bravely a man of even slightly greater wealth than himself if he saw that a case might be alleged against him because he conspired or agreed?" In other, non-Ciceronian words, in a system where money talked, who would dare to be a judge unless he were immune from being tried for his judgment? Only a senator, protected as he was by high political status, should be required to run the risk. Why should the knights endanger their power and influence by enlarging their liabilities?[35]

Cicero had spent much of his professional life counseling the tax farmers and bankers and provincial magnates who composed the nonsenatorial group. "I observe that order," he once confessed, "passionately."[36] He knew the kind of argument to which they would respond. He put the argument addressed to their self-interest at the climax of his long address. The judges acquitted Cluentius.

We cannot tell which line of defense was decisive. But in Cicero's rhetoric we catch the concept of the bribe at work. A partisan, he exaggerates, puts in a bad light, is not scrupulous. What he states as fact can be treated only as allegation. Nonetheless what he finds significant about the conduct of Oppianicus Sr. assumes the acceptance by his audience of an ethic deprecating the use of money to bring about betrayal. The *munera* given to the pregnant widow are viewed negatively; Oppianicus Sr. is seen as corrupting the informant who betrayed the enslaved heir; Oppianicus Sr. is a villain when he corrupts the court. The negative force of these incidents rests on shared beliefs.

As to the actual law on bribery we can be less certain. What Cicero declares to be the law must be understood to be his interpretation of the law. He is tendentious in his interpretation. When he takes his first line of defense and insists on Cluentius' simple innocence of making any payment, he plainly assumes that it is important to be able to clear him on the facts—*munera*-giving to judges is not something innocuous which he can concede his nonsenatorial client has committed. When he takes his third line and asserts that the statute does not apply at all, he is saying that there is no law against bribing two-thirds of the present judges. The social condemnation of bribery to effect betrayal has, if his interpretation is correct, not been very fully incorporated into law. Nonetheless, the sanctions imposed on the nine *munera*-takers of Oppianicus Sr.'s trial show that, circuitously, legal measures support the moral condemnation of the judge who receives *munera*.

Electoral Reform in the Late Republic.   Cicero became consul in 63 B.C., and in the year's course of his consulate he sponsored a new statute on *ambitus*, the crime of illegally soliciting votes. Related to our own "ambition" and "ambitious," *ambitus* could be committed by any ambitious politician. Under Cicero's comprehensive statute, *ambitus* became the payment of men to greet a candidate or to follow him; the reservation of places for voters at the public games; the giving by a candidate of banquets open to the public; and the sponsoring of gladiatorial contests by a candidate. Within a year of passage of the bill, L. Licinius Murena, consul-elect, was charged with *ambitus* by his defeated opponent and by the most uncompromising man in the Senate, Cato. Murena's counsel was ex-consul Cicero.[37]

It was not *ambitus*, Cicero argued, to invite friends to dinner or to give tickets to a game—the new law made it criminal only if the public was indiscriminately invited. The grandstands at all the games, filled with Murena's followers, had been provided by his friends not by the candidate. The crowds that met and followed him were not hired. Some of them were poor men, to be sure, but "humble folk have only one way of deserving favors from our order or repaying them—by this kind of work and attendance in our campaigns." If humble folk "shall have nothing except their vote, they shall have—even if they vote—no clout. As they themselves say, they cannot plead in court for us, they cannot be our sureties, they cannot invite us to their homes." Only campaign work gave them leverage.[38]

Gratia, here translated "clout," was what everyone sought in the system. It was the favor, influence, power earned by having an officeholder under obligation to you. Being someone's advocate, being someone's surety, being someone's host, as Cicero implied, were three upperclass ways of imposing an obligation and gaining *gratia*. *Gratia*, as much or more than cash, was what compensated the politician-orators who were the professional advocates. The acquisition of clout, his speech for Murena assumed, was the legitimate aspiration of everyone. Political loyalty in exchange for favors from the powerful—it was the essence of the republican system.

Murena had offered the electorate treats during the campaign. In the harsh image of his prosecutor, Cato, a man with these morals must have been seeking election as head pimp. His commission of *ambitus* was clear. Not at all, said Cicero. Cato's comparison was "uncouth." The Roman people were entitled to election games, gladiators, banquets. Cato was refuted by "experience, life, custom, and the republic itself." Besides, Cicero observed, if Murena were disqualified, an opening would be given to the evil adherents of Catiline. *Ambitus*, it was apparent, was a flexible crime whose discernment required astute political judgment.[39]

A third element of Murena's offense had been to pay the *divisores* or distributors of money at election times. The Romans voted by "tribes" of varying size, some indigenous, others artificial. When in ancient times a leader had stood for election he had looked for support from his tribe and the tribe had looked for his appreciation; his gifts had reciprocated tribal loyalty; the *divisores* distributed his largess. By Cicero's day the election agents, like managers of "boxes" in parts of the American South, took money from any candidate, within or outside the tribe. The term describing them is often mistranslated as "bribery agent." The Roman Republic did not make this legal judgment. Legislation of 67 B.C. which attempted to reach the *divisores* was so little enforced that its content is unknown. Cato's later legislation merely succeeded in banning the maintenance of a *divisor* in one's own home.

Cicero's reference, in another context, to "the training of a thief and a distributor," as though they were parallel professionals, may be understood as wit, not law or politics. In his defense of Murena, Cicero said he would come to the money paid the managers. He never did. He did not have to. After defending the right of the common people to gain *gratia* and to be given entertainment in reciprocation for their campaign efforts and votes and after invoking the dread shadow of the banished Catiline, Cicero had done all he needed for his client. Murena was acquitted. Achieved by the advocacy of the sponsor of the law, the acquittal accurately demonstrated the fragility, flexibility, porousness, of the statute governing exchanges between candidate and electorate. In these aspects the law was strikingly anticipatory of the Corrupt Practices Act later designed to govern federal elections in the United States.[40]

Ambitus is often rendered in English as "electoral bribery" or simply "bribery," translations that are triply defective. First, the Roman term was deliberately different from any word used in connection with judicial bribery. Second, it included practices involving no payoff to an individual voter. Third, to an even greater degree than judicial bribery, its meaning depended on shifting legal definitions and political discretion and was vague apart from particular cases. None of the shame risked by the corrupt judge attended the voter who was the recipient of a candidate's largess; the receptive voter was neither violator of law nor social outcast. The voter was not regarded as exercising a divine prerogative in voting; no divinity hedged in his vote. No paradigm of uninfluenced voting was appealed to. Without the support of shame, without a divine model to invoke, law alone was too weak an instrument to restrain the normal force of reciprocity.

Judicial Reform in the Late Republic.   Campaigns were beyond legal control. Did the revolving judiciary of senators and knights present a picture equally bleak? In 61 B.C., two years after Cicero's consulship, Clodius Pulcher ("Pretty Boy"), a younger senator whom Cicero detested, disguised himself as a woman and joined the Vestal Virgins in a sacrifice. To try him for his sacrilegious romp, a bill was introduced in the Senate permitting the praetor to choose the judges without opportunity for challenge by the defendant. As Cicero advised his friend Atticus, "everything depended on that." There were those who thought the case clear; Cicero was too aware of "the wants of the judges." When the bill failed, the judges, selected after vetoes by both prosecutor and defendant, were a sprinkling of "good guys" (*boni*) and a majority of "stained senators, naked knights, and tribunes who were not cash-carriers but cash-takers." Clodius' acquittal was secured in two days by a friend, the Bald One, employing a single slave, an ex-gladiator, to carry the appropriate offers. As Cicero observed to Atticus, the Bald One "made himself available to everyone; he promised; he gave security; he gave. Good gods, what abandoned proceedings! Even the nights of certain women were awarded to certain judges, and introductions to certain noble young men were offered, to cap the hire offered."[41]

Clodius' friends, according to Cicero, admitted that his crime had been "bought back from the judges." *Redemptam*, "bought back," from the verb *redimere*, characterizes the corrupt purchase of release from an obligation. Carrying a tincture of irony, *redimere* is not as precise a term as *corrupere*; in context, its negative connotation is clear. Significantly, in terms of social development, the pejorative verb has its nounal counterpart. The action of buying back a crime had become so common that the linguistic stage was reached where the substantive noun, *redemptio*, designated the corrupt purchase of release from punishment.[42]

Later in the year of Clodius' acquittal, Cato offered a bill in the Senate to condemn all who "took money for judgment." The glaring gap in the law's failure to include two-thirds of the judges was to be remedied and the bribery law was to be extended beyond capital cases. Clodius' case no doubt was the immediate inspiration, but as Cicero is witness, the problem was more general. Indeed, in a civil case Cicero had illustrated the sanctity of the written law by a polemical comparison between it and ordinary judicial proceedings. He had extolled the written law because "that excessive power which dominates civic life is silent only here. It cannot get to work, approach a judge, signal with a finger." To the written law, "neither the power nor the clout of anyone can make an approach; and further—to show how great and holy the written law is—a judge in a case of this kind cannot be corrupted even by a price." A *gratiosus*—a man with clout—may tell a court, "Judge that this was done or never done; believe this witness; admit these accounts"; he cannot dictate a different law.[43]

Cicero deplored the domination of the judges by the wagging finger of a rich man. He felt Clodius' acquittal to have been outrageous. Now when his best clients were threatened, he was on their side. The knights were angry that their immunity as judges should be removed. They actually preferred the rule of money in the courts to the risk of prosecution of themselves as judges for corruption. "What more just," Cicero wrote confidentially to Atticus, "than that he who takes money for judgment should come to judgment?" But the knights "made war" when this was put to them. The war was "on the Senate, not me, for I dissented." Cicero's dissent—his opposition to the bill removing the knights' immunity —prevailed.[44]

When Cicero had praised the written law as free from the motion of a finger or the payment of a price, the implication had been that the law was fashioned in some higher way than the judgments of courts. Now as a practicing politician Cicero pointed to a different reality as he wryly and candidly acknowledged to Atticus the compromised spirit in which he opposed the bill. At the surface of his consciousness, not articulated, are thoughts about the responsibilities of a legislator. Is a lawgiver corrupt when he responds to the pressures of his constituents? In Rome, as in Egypt and Israel, no law even attempted to regulate the reciprocities at play when law was made by the supreme legislative authority. Rome was not a theocracy with God as its legislator, but if law in Rome was not seen as tablets handed down on Sinai and therefore beyond criticism, still no senator suggested that as legislators he and his colleagues could be as corrupt as they sometimes were as judges.

Writing Atticus, and as it were shuffling his feet with embarrassment, Cicero was somehow aware of the ignobility of his role. "In an immodest cause," he wrote, "I was nonetheless grave and fluent." As for Cato, who tried to carry the bill, his consummate fidelity to the republic "sometimes injured the public welfare." It was observing him attempting to subject all the judges to an anti-bribery rule that Cicero concluded that Cato "pronounces judgment as though he lived in Plato's republic, not in Romulus' refuse."[45]

The Chutzpah of Cicero. A politico-judicial system in which "box money" is paid to election agents and other largess is given the voters, subject only to the lightest and most political scrutiny by a criminal court; in which bagmen and fixers are recognized by generic names and buying off criminal convictions is a practice subject only to a highly politicized judicial inquiry; in which clout is the due of every citizen and the reward of every lawyer; in which gifts with strings attached are so innocent that an advocate can admit that his client gave them to a judge—such is the system suggested by *ambitus, divisor, gratia, munera, redemptio, redimere,* and *sequester.* In such a system was it really possible to corrupt, *corrupere,* a court?

Could corruption be distinguished from customary reciprocity? The difficulty was not unique to Rome. It was to recur in every society where a concept of corruption became current. A man "puts aside the part (*persona*) of a friend when he puts on that of a judge," Cicero wrote primly in *Duties,* the moral homily dedicated to his son; but he regularly wrote letters to friends who were judges, remarking to them that particular litigants before them were his friends. Despite his usual request for "impartial" consideration of the case, the intended effect of such letters must have been to incline the judge toward the friend of his friend Cicero. These commendations have been noted by modern commentators as exercises of *humanitas* or civilized benevolence. No doubt they were conventional and too common to be criticized. But what did a powerful Roman politician expect to happen when he recommended a litigant to a judge?[46]

As for the special friendship represented by relationship, Roman politics were largely conducted on the basis of blood and marriage. The ties of kin were strong in the courts. When the consul-elect Metellus took steps to stop the prosecution of Hog, Cicero asked in exasperation, "What would

you do for an innocent kinsman, if you forsake duty and dignity for an utterly abandoned man, who is no kin?"[47] He implied what must have been
the norm—strenuous exertion at every level of office on behalf of an accused relative. The family connections were inseparable from political
connections. If the father of a family was condemned, his son would sometimes wait till he thought the moment politically propitious to avenge his
father by prosecuting his father's prosecutor—Oppianicus Jr. is an example of such a son who miscalculated.

Major trials necessarily had heavy political coloring. It was a political act
to prosecute a former governor or an incumbent senator or a country big
shot like Oppianicus. Although evidence was not actually irrelevant, politics had to play a part in the decision to convict or acquit. The senatorial
judges were making the foreign policy of Rome or scoring in domestic
contests for office.

"Most of the time," Cicero wrote, he spent in the law courts—no doubt
an exaggeration but true in the feeling it expressed that the law courts
were his territory and his home.[48] He had as deep an interest as possible in
their good name. Yet he also expected something from them—in two
words, cash and clout. In theory at one time gratuitous, advocacy was paid
for by money or by the gratitude of a client. "Ingratitude," Cicero wrote
feelingly as he contemplated an ungrateful freedman—"in that vice no
evil is missing!" Freedmen were expected to be grateful. Those for whom
an orator spoke were expected to be grateful. Oratory, Cicero exclaimed,
was indeed what won "the greatest gratitude." Cicero's fine Roman house
was due to the generosity of a shady client. The *boni*, the good guys, whose
approbation Cicero sought and whose standards he applauded, were
those already posessed of power, whom he hoped to join. Their goodness
went with their possession of power. How did they show their goodness
to him except by being grateful for his exertions?[49]

When expectations of reciprocity governed the relations of orators and
clients, how could the judges be exempt from tugs of gratitude? In a context that was almost always political, how could they immunize themselves from political demands? In family-motivated prosecutions, how
could they resist the claims of family? "This judge is my friend; that one is
the friend of my father," a candid litigant would mutter.[50] Cicero's
exclamation, "I have the judges I want," spoke to the kind of impartial justice sought.

It was horrible for Cicero when an enemy escaped just punishment by
the courts. "They took cash and wiped out all law and right," he wrote to
Atticus of the judges acquitting Clodius of sacrilege. What not only men
but even beasts knew had happened, "Talna, Flatfoot, Sponge and others
of this breed decreed never happened."[51] The cry was Swiftian: judges had
said "the thing which is not." The idea as ancient as Egypt that the judge
was to ascertain the truth was at the top of Cicero's consciousness. Still,
what had he persuaded the judges of Cluentius to say?

When Catiline went on trial the first time, Cicero wrote Atticus that the judges would convict him unless they could "judge that it does not shine at noon."[52] Nature, reality, truth appeared to be his criteria of judgment. Still, he was willing in this case to be Catiline's advocate and persuade the judges that it was dark at noon. All should know, he said in his final word to the judges of Cluentius, "that assemblies are the place for prejudice, trials for truth." At the same time he appealed to these judges' basest prejudice, their self-interest in immunity from prosecution for taking payoffs.[53]

In a system in which so many influences other than the evidence operated on the minds of the judges, one could even wonder what the difference was between paying cash and employing an advocate:

> Since nothing ought to be so incorrupt in the state as vote and judgment, I do not understand why he who corrupts them with money is worthy of punishment, but he who corrupts them with eloquence wins praise. Indeed it seems to me that he who corrupts a judge by oratory does more evil than corrupting a judge by money; for no one can corrupt a prudent man by money, but one can by speech.

The passage is attributed to Cicero—an excerpt, preserved while the surrounding context has vanished. No doubt if we knew the exigencies of the case we would understand why it was spoken.[54] No doubt he would have said that his own eloquence was always on the side of the truth. He knew better. No one, he remarked defending Cluentius and explaining his earlier negative references to Cluentius' purchase of Oppianicus' conviction, should think our speeches to be "our certified opinions. All of them are for the case and the occasion, not for the advocate himself, not for ourselves an men."[55] But if oratory corrupted, no standard for judging corruption in the courts remained. All was *gratia*, the clout of cash arranged by a fixer and delivered to a bagman, the clout of one's father or a close connection, the clout of a politician, the clout of a brilliant and unscrupulous orator.

And yet. And yet. Cicero's musings on the corrupt orator were a familiar rhetorical move—to start from what was accepted as evil and to expand the standard by analogy. His intention was not to jeopardize the prime analogate, the evilness of corruption by money, which could not corrupt a prudent man. In the end, the line between the use of words and the use of money was distinct. The public conviction persisted that the courts were not markets, that reciprocities could be distinguished, that a judge's role was different from a prostitute's. Pieties were offended by cash corruption. Limits to its sway were sought and, if often violated, never forgotten.

Cicero's own self-image did not permit a view of his profession equating him with a *sequester* or fixer. The letters to Atticus, in which a relative candor prevails, here confirm the stance adopted before a larger public. Publicly and privately he saw corruption ravaging the courts. Publicly and privately he did not abandon the conception of the courts in terms of which payments to judges were corrupting. It was his sober private judgment—the judgment of a man who knew courts, judges, and clients well—that Cato's proposed law against payments to all judges was utopian. Yet, standing in what he found to be the filth of the Roman Republic, Cicero had the effrontery to practice advocacy not as an exercise in purchasing votes but as a profession depending on persuasion. In the prosecution of Hog he was given the opportunity to fly his standard.

The Hubris of Hog.   When, in 74 B.C., Hog was praetor, or chief civil law officer in Rome, much came his way. His first opportunity for profit was in the shaping of his edict, the set of pronouncements on the law he would apply in the coming year. After his election he had contacted, or been contacted by, Lucius Annius, the reversionary heir of P. Annius Asellus, whose will had left his main estate to his daughter. Their conversation brought out that the praetor's edict could put the testator within a class forbidden to bequeath to daughters; Lucius Annius could take all. Having talked to the reversioner, Hog contacted the daughter's guardians—he would prefer, he said, to deal with them. But they did not see how they could account for a large payment to him; and he issued a rule that disqualified the daughter and transferred her legacy to Annius. In a second ruling, Hog's edict provided that in case of dispute over an intestate inheritance, the party in possession would be given preference. The absurdity of the rule—which made everything turn on who got there first —was as palpable as the rule was unprecedented. As law it could not be explained unless a payment had been taken by the praetor. In a third case, P. Trebonius left his property to several persons including his freedman, on condition that the heirs swear to give half of what they received to Trebonius' outlawed brother, who was ineligible to take directly. The freedman loyally swore, the others claimed the condition was invalid; they dealt with Hog and got the inheritance anyway, including the freedman's portion. In a fourth case, Hog personally told Ligus, a man of property, that he, Hog, "had many needs" and attendants to maintain. Ligus was unlikely to win the estate he sought unless he "also took Hog into account."

Hog had a mistress, Chelidon. During his rule as praetor her house was "full" of lawyers and litigants. Their business was strictly commercial: "Some were counting out cash, others were signing promissory notes." Procedural rulings, rulings on the law, judgments were all handled at Chelidon's for Hog's very fat account. As praetor Hog had administrative duties that included the oversight of certain temples. Among other actions he inspected the columns of the temple of Castor and Pollux and found that they "were not quite straight." Liability could be placed on those who had contracted to keep them in repair. The repair contract had been inherited by a young man still a ward. Hog arranged for the ward's guardian to pay him personally and he waived the ward's liability. He hired a contractor to do the straightening and took a second payoff from him. The year following his term as praetor Hog was sent to Sicily as the supreme embodiment of Roman law.[56]

In Sicily in 73 Hog's opportunities multiplied. He took money as before to award legacies. He took money to dismiss judges displeasing to the accuser of a defendant. He took money to let a pirate captain disappear without trial. He took money to let a master retrieve his slave from criminal prosecution. He took money to let a negligent sea captain escape punishment and money to release senators from duty. He took money in Messana to relax its treaty obligations, in Halaesus to appoint a provincial senator, in Cephaloedium to rig the election of the high priest. He took money to appoint favorable tax assessors. He took money from prisoners for their necessities and money from their relatives to visit the prisoners; he took money that a man be executed with minimal suffering; he took money that executed men receive burial. The high and the low, the prosperous and the bereaved, the living and the dead were those from whom he took.[57]

On occasion Hog in his greed went beyond reciprocity: Sopater of Halicyae, a wealthy Sicilian, was on trial before him for a capital offense. Hog's freedman, Timarchides, contacted Sopater and informed him that the prosecutors were offering the governor money for his conviction; he added that Hog would prefer to let him go. Sopater responded that he lacked ready cash, but he would think it over. With the help of friends he was able to raise 80,000 sesterces on the spot, which he tendered Timarchides. The money was received, but the case was continued. Timarchides returned the next day to tell Sopater that the prosecutors had increased their offer to top 80,000; if he knew what was good for him, he would see about doing something more. Sopater could or would go no higher. Timarchides did not return his money. The next day Hog found Sopater guilty as charged and imposed on him sentence of death.[58]

Hog also indulged in bisexual lust. As a boy he had paid his gambling debts "with the fruit of his youth." His interest in young men continued as governor of Sicily. He was even more passionately interested in women. At the very start of his career, he had caused a riot by his unrestrained craving for a respectable woman of Lampsacus. In Rome the role of his mistress, Chelidon, had enhanced the disreputableness of his reign as praetor. His governorship of Sicily was stained with promiscuous affairs. Corrupt in judgment, Hog was also lubricious.[59]

Cruelty accompanied his concupiscence for flesh and money. Cruel in avenging himself at Lampsacus on the father and brother of the respectable woman he insulted, cruel to the freedman of Trebonius in the matter of his legacy, cruel to Sopater of Sicily, Hog's culminating cruelty was to Gavius, a merchant and Roman citizen resident in Sicily. Imprisoned for an unspecified offense, Gavius had escaped and started for Italy to complain about his imprisonment. He was recaptured at Messana. Hog did not like complainers. Gavius was flogged. His complaints persisted: "I am a Roman citizen." Then, at Hog's order, he suffered the death that could be imposed on no Roman. Placed so that he could see across the straits to Italy, Gavius was crucified. Violent, shameful, painful, lawless death inflicted on a citizen—the act expressed the spirit of Hog.[60]

He was also sacrilegious. He did not scruple to steal the property and the images of the gods from their temples. He robbed the temple of Aesculapius at Agrigentum of its statue of Apollo. He took the trophies of Juno at Malta. As a crowning blasphemy, at Henna, the center of the ancient and universal cult of mother Ceres, the goddess of all Sicily and protectress of its fertility, he invaded the shrine, found the marble statue of the goddess too big to move, broke a statuette of Victory from her hand, and carried off a bronze replica of Ceres herself. His criminal violation of her sanctuary and her divinity led to a blight falling on the land.[61]

When Hog returned to Rome in 70 B.C. he was pursued by outraged Sicilians seeking vindication for their wrongs and those of their dead relatives. Under fire, he secured as his advocate Q. Hortensius, a leading member of the establishment and candidate for the supreme leadership as consul. When Hortensius was elected, an old consul told Hog, "By today's election, you're acquitted." Although he would not take office for several months, Hortensius wasted no time in exerting his influence. He suggested to the Sicilian witnesses that they come by his house for a conversation. The Sicilians knew that the suggestion was an attempt at intimidation. The other consul-elect, Metellus, was also Hog's friend; Hog had contributed to his election, too. Metellus reminded the Sicilians that the present governor of Sicily was his brother and remarked that already a good deal of trouble had been taken to keep Hog safe; the message to the witnesses was clear. Rumors to complete the complainants' rout were circulated. Their own advocate, it was said, was bought: he had received "big money" to throw the case. To cap everything, Hog put money down to buy the court. Again "big money" was involved. He had spent three years in Sicily. The saying went that the first year had gone to himself, the second to his lawyers, and the "very fat, wholly lucrative third year" to the judges.[62]

The Sicilians' advocate was Cicero, who had once served in Sicily and had been signed up by the Sicilians to prosecute their case in the Reclaimables Inquiry. He had not in fact taken Hog's money, but the other rumors about the deployment of cash he not only believed but insisted on. "Big money" had been used to put him personally on the defensive. As Hog's trial began, he was himself a candidate for public office, seeking to become an *aedile*. About ten "baskets of Sicilian gold" were paid a key knight to assure his defeat. A meeting of all the *divisores* or election agents was held at Hog's home. They were reminded of "how liberally" in his own election as praetor in 74 and in the recent consular elections, "he had treated them." The meeting agreed that 50,000 sesterces were enough to do the trick of defeating Cicero's candidacy. The figure was the price of two senators on Iunius' panel—not an overwhelming amount but not unflatteringly small.[63]

Cicero persevered. He was elected *aedile*. He continued the prosecution. The panel's president, Marcus Glabrio, was his friend. Under Glabrio's supervision, he challenged the members of the court he thought

Hog had reached, and on Cicero's motion, without the need of proving their corruption, they were replaced. The bought court vanished. Hog now spent his money to delay the case. It was August. If he could hold out until January 1, the two consuls who were his would actually be in office and the new president of the Reclaimables Court would also be his friend. Hog's efforts were in vain. The trial went on.[64]

The Humbling of Hog. Did Hog exist? Did there exist such a man whose hoggish swindles and extortions were so much beyond the ordinary that they could be described as not even "human"? Did there exist such a scoundrel who, "moved by madness and hubris openly made impious and always sacrilegious war" upon the gods?[65] Before Cicero's case against him was completed, Hog ran; so Hog's story we do not know. We have only the prosecutor's word for his character and conduct and the prosecutor's summary of the evidence actually offered against him. We may be confident that witnesses testified to many of the deeds attributed to him, and that Cicero relied on hearsay for the stories of his early career. We may also be confident that Cicero put every unfavorable construction possible on what was testified, did not distinguish hearsay and first-hand accounts, generalized single cases into patterns of conduct, and offered his own version of events such as those of Hog's boyhood of which no witness may have spoken. The darkest colors of Hog's character were, we may even speculate, projections of blacknesses within the prosecutor. But for our purposes the undeterminable guilt of Hog is not the issue. For our purposes it is enough that Hog, praetor and governor, did exist and was tried and at his trial became the incarnation of purchased justice and its accompanying vices of greed, lust, cruelty, and impiety. A master advocate, controlled to a degree by the facts but untrammeled in their organization and development, presented to the judges of Rome the image of a man they could fear and hate and desire to destroy.

The shamefulness of Hog's acts—for shame is what his image embodies—is conveyed by the sexual parallel, by signs, by direct denunciation, and by his name: *Verres*, meaning boar, swine, hog. The name is the shame. The only perfect parallel is the name of the bishop who condemned Joan of Arc: Pierre Cauchon, Peter Pig. Claudel makes appropriate use of this godsend in his text for Poulenc's oratorio where "Cauchon, Cauchon, Cauchon" mocks the murderous judge. The defendant's name is Hog. Cicero will never let his auditors forget that wonderful fact. His first name, Gaius, is mentioned. But for eternity he is Hog.[66]

Cicero seized upon the name when in a preliminary hearing he first established his right to conduct the prosecution. He told of one act of justice performed by the governor of Sicily and then, he said, "suddenly, instantly, as if by some Circean potion from being human he became Hog; he returned to his own self and his habits." The light allusion to the swine of Circe joined the gross insult to the future defendant. "This hog will not beget a hoglet unless he's paid," ran a line of a famous play by Plautus: the metonymy of swine for man was well-known. Other hunters of corruption, Cicero declared, had only the smell of faint footsteps of the prey. He had an easier task—to pursue "the Hog, who I discovered by marks on his whole body had rolled in the mud." Cicero was even to double the pun. The Roman people, he reported, found something thin in *ius verrinum*—pork gravy or Hog's law. The recurrent association of graft with pork, and the grafter with a pig has this classic precedent. The Roman people, according to Cicero, joked that this hog should have been sacrificed.[67]

Sexual corruption was associated with Hog as part of his swinish charactor. Like many themes of Roman politics, the precedent had been set in Greece. In the classic attack of Aeschines on Timarchus, for example, "the wages of his [homosexual] prostitution" were treated as parallel to "the fruits of his bribery" in office.[68] Association of sexual and judicial license played to popular prejudice and envy. A man like this, Cicero suggested, would do anything and could get away with everything. More fundamentally, the association rested on a psychological assumption: the man who had no care of his integrity in sexual matters would have none in rendering justice. Corrupt in one way, he was corrupt in the other.

The uncleanliness of Hog's activity was reflected in two kinds of indirection attributed to him. It was usual, Cicero said, for the paid judge to receive his money through an intermediary, an *interpres*, a go-between or fixer. If a court were to accept as a valid defense "I did not receive the money myself," no judge would ever be convicted. In Hog's case, Chelidon and Timarchides were his fixers. Cash paid them must necessarily be judged to be cash paid into his hands.[69] A similar indirection attended Hog's requests for payoffs. Cicero need not be assumed to have reported verbatim the conversations of Timarchides and Sopater and Hog himself with Ligus; he understood how such conversations would go. They did not consist in straightforward offers of a marketable commodity. Rather, Hog spoke of the importunities of the other litigant or the expenses of his staff. His bagmen expressed his demand in phrases such as "if you're wise."[70] Reluctance to specify the actual transaction, to name the deed, was a second badge of its shame.

Cicero's severest word for Hog's action was *turpe*—foul. From a Sanskrit root meaning "to be ashamed," *turpe* had first been applied by Romans to the disgraceful appearance of a man, later to disgraceful deeds. It suggested dirt. Clodius' acquittal was due to the *sordes iudicum*, "the filth of the judges." Bribed judges thrived in "Romulus' refuse." The judgment of Iunius was "the foulest" of crimes.[71] In the same way, Hog's deeds of selling justice were dirty, filthy, *turpe* or foul.

How central were Hog's giving and taking of money to the case against him? First, as to giving, "the big money" deployed against Cicero before the trial and in his election was emphasized to enhance Cicero's stature and to compliment the court. Against loaded odds Cicero had persisted, against them the court would prevail. Further, although no statute made it criminal to pay money in order to delay a case, to obtain an acquittal, or acquire voting support, each was an instance of an attempt to corrupt. The man who corrupted the integrity of the voters was like a man who corrupted the integrity of the judges. The man who strove to prevent the hearing of his case, to delay it, to have his friends on the court, to have paid-off judges acquit him, to prevent the ascertainment of the truth, was acting to corrupt. On behalf of Hog, Consul-elect Metellus had brought pressure on the witnesses. "What is it to corrupt judgment," Cicero asked, "if this is not?" Payments, intimidation, the use of clout—all the means which a powerful senator might use to escape conviction—Cicero put on a par as corrupting.[72]

Falcula's case showed that the expanded jurisdiction of the Reclaimables Inquiry could include corrupt taking in Rome as well as abroad. Hog's taking in Rome had been of the blackest kind. For two thousand years widows and orphans had been set up as the special object of the law's solicitude. Not accidentally, when Cicero sought to express the depth of Hog's iniquity, he visualized Hog exclaiming, "Boy orphans, girl orphans—they are the surest booty for praetors!" Hog could even be reproached with something worse: "May you tear away the wishes of a dead man?" "Why," he could be asked, "did you inflict this sorrow on his ashes and bones?"[73]

In Sicily where Hog took "money for judgment," the act was unquestionably criminal—money taken to give a false judgment to condemn the innocent in a criminal case. Cicero dwelt, however, not on the illegality but on the turpitude of the act. "To take money for a matter to be judged" was "wicked." Indeed, "it seems to me"—Cicero speaks for himself and for the listening judges—"of all the things in the world the most foul and the most wicked." The act of the corrupted criminal judge condemning the innocent was the paradigm of evil. But there was something beyond even that: "How much more wicked, vicious, shameful is it to take money from a man to acquit him and then condemn him!" Such was Hog's crime in selling out to Sopater and then selling Sopater. Here he had showed less honor than a bandit. To sell one's honor in judging in a province was a crime, yet "perhaps there has been someone now and then who has done something of the sort"—an understatement of course not without irony when made to a panel of senators! But to take another's money, transfer your conscience to him, then sell out to his enemy, and "not even return the money to the man you deceived"—not even stained Staienus had gone so far.[74]

In this negative hierarchy of corruption, violation of the ethic of reciprocity remained the greatest evil. After all, Hog might have said, "The man was guilty. I was wrong to take his money. At least I was not so wicked as to free him. I did the right thing in the end, with a reward for my restored virtue." Such a rejoinder was impossible; Cicero did not bother imagining it made. To the judges of Hog and to Cicero himself, worse than taking money, worse than freeing the guilty, was the betrayal of reciprocity. The crime of the mayor of Nippur was still the most basic treachery.

Next to that act more wicked than the most wicked, more foul than the foulest, was the act of selling criminal justice. Not all Hog's acts were mercenary. His crucifixion of Gavius was lawless vindictiveness without money being given or asked, and it was his gravest offense against a citizen of Rome. Not all Hog's acts were corrupt. His offense against Ceres was sacrilege, and it was his gravest offense against the Sicilians. But for Cicero, "of all the things in the world," his sale of criminal judgment was the foulest.

The paradigm of the judge remained as crucial for the law as it had been in Egypt and in Israel. The notion of corruption had been enlarged. Hog the paymaster of election agents was a corruptor. Hog, the purchasable praetor, the trafficking supervisor of probate, the building inspector running a shakedown and topping it with a scam, was a man corrupted. But rhetoric and imagery and religious tradition converged to make the corrupt judge central.

To a degree, no doubt, self-interest can explain Cicero's emphasis. If judges were for sale, who needed an orator? Why should a prosecutor like Cicero laboriously seek out witnesses and documents and accounts if evidence did not count? Why should oratory rank next to generalship if money could do the trick with senators? The court known to be corrupt became a market where the most prized abilities were those of the shrewd purchasing agent.

The judges, too, had a self-interest to protect. Their status was endangered if their votes were commodities. The judges Cicero addressed were senators whose status was expressly threatened by the legislation, then pending and later enacted, to reduce their share of judicial seats to one-third. To preserve their monopoly they had a powerful motive to be just, or to appear to be so, and Cicero appealed to their sense of self-preservation when he made them sharers in his view that the foulest of acts was taking money for something judged. "Hold fast, hold fast the man in your city," Cicero admonished them. "Spare him, preserve him, so it may be he who judges with you." The outrageous irony took it for granted that the last thing senatorial judges now would want was the corrupt Hog as a fellow judge.[75]

In a broader context of social expectations, the corrupted judge violated *fides*—that is, faith and honor and fidelity. Just as in Cicero's stories about Oppianicus the payment of money led to betrayals, so the paid judge betrayed a trust. Just as the mother paid by Oppianicus to abort her child violated her office as a mother, so a corrupted judge violated the cardinal function of his office. The counselors of a true judge were "law, religion, fairness and fidelity." The purchased judge abandoned these counselors. There was, it was true, a kind of reciprocity binding the judges—the reciprocity of *fides*. The fidelity of the judges was reciprocation for the fidelity of the prosecutor. "Let my fidelity in acting," Cicero told the judges of Hog, "be yours in judging."[76]

By oath the judges called the gods to witness their fidelity. The divine presence was more than merely supervisory. "You judges," Cicero told the judges of Cluentius, "are as if you were gods" in judging life or death. Divinity went beyond their lawful power over life. Divinity was in them as judges. It was palpable in each man's *conscientia mentis suae*, his inner self, his rational mind. *Conscientia*, Cicero declared, "we receive from the immortal gods; it cannot be torn from us." To be corrupt was to deny the divine that spoke within. As Cicero put it to the judges of Murena, "All the power of the immortal gods has been transferred to you or at least it is shared with you." The judges acted for the gods. For this ultimate reason a judge should "not think himself alone, not himself free to do whatever he wants."[77]

How sincerely was the identification of judgment with the gods believed by the judges, by Cicero, by anyone? How seriously were appeals to truth and fidelity taken? These questions cannot be confidently answered. Cicero's own view of the gods wavered between moderate skepticism and measured faith in the "divine guidance" he personally received.[78] But what Cicero personally believed was not at issue. Speeches at trials were for "the case and occasion"; they did not disclose "the man himself." What Cicero proclaimed was the public belief. His addresses to judges, whether delivered at the trial or, as often the case, largely written after the event, were rhetoric. They were effective rhetoric because they depended on the images and paradigms his audience accepted. Against his profoundest professional interest, Cicero's arguments testified to corruption in the courts. At the same time they testified to what the publicly accepted symbols were. What he invoked to win in the judicial forum he invoked because it was the public belief. What he appealed to as decisive, along with the self-interest and political instincts of the judges, was the public standard by which corruption was evil.

In the faith that was the foundation of the law and the cornerstone of the courts, the judge depended on divinity. That was why his oath was required. That was why his inner rational mind, his *conscientia*, could be addressed. That was why corruption was foul. As in Egypt and Israel, the judge in Rome was the bearer of divinity.

In the peroration of the case against Hog, Cicero broke into prayer. He addressed the gods and goddesses whom Hog had despoiled—Jupiter and Juno, Minerva, Latona, Apollo, Diana, Mercury, Hercules, the mother of Ida, Castor, Pollux, Libera, and Ceres—and all the other gods and goddesses against whom the insane Hog "had waged impious war." It was they who should grant his prayer that the senatorial judges now pronounce on Hog a judgment worthy of his unheard-of crimes, of which the foulest was the sale and resale of judgment.[79]

The Roman gods are gifttakers as well as judges. The Romans have no unambiguous word for bribe. The Roman notion of corruption is not comprehensive. The supreme legislative body, the Senate, is never treated as open to bribes in its legislation. The ultimate source of power, the electorate, is subject to no sanction for what it accepts from politicians, and the judgment as to what constitutes too much inducement on an ambitious politician's part is largely political. Even where judges are concerned, the law does not go very far. Substantial cash payments to a judge for a vote contrary to the evidence are criminal. Small gifts are tolerated. Payments for a correct judgment are not considered. Influence with the judge is not guarded against. There are no police actions to detect bribetakers. There is no statute aimed at bribery as such. The tension between the ethic of reciprocity and an ethic that insists in certain areas of government on nonreciprocity remains high. The newer ethic is still not fully grasped.

At the same time the concept of a bribe has more scope than in the ancient Near East. There are verbs, *corrupere* and *redimere*, designating the wrongful act of paying others to betray their trust. There are nouns, *corruptio* and *redemptio*, designating the evil practice. There are derogatory terms for the brokers of corruption. There is an incentive to prosecute corruption of judgment: a good advocate will win recognition, gratitude, clout. There is a forum in which corruption can be prosecuted: the judges themselves, interested in the subject by their rank and role, can be asked to vindicate integrity. There are methods by which corruption can be proved: account books can be examined. Albeit indirectly, bribegivers to judges, as well as bribetakers, are sometimes punished. Unlike Isaiah's and Ezekiel's denunciations of a class of bribetakers whose offenses are not particularized and whose doom is divinely produced catastrophe, Cicero's denunciations are of named individuals; the circumstances of their bribes are spelled out; concrete penalties are sought. The trial is the thing which in itself demonstrates dramatically the superiority of speech over money.

Cicero and the prophets are still very similar in their approach. Each depends on words for his effect. For each, shame on earth and divine vengeance are the most reliable sanctions. Each depends on the prevalence of a religious faith. The faith of Cicero was to die in the destruction of the Republic, the faith of Isaiah and Ezekiel to be gravely wounded by the destruction of Jerusalem. Could a new faith draw on the old and sustain the ideal of incorruptible judgment?

3

The Morals of the Christians

Bribery is a subject on which the stories and images and moral exhortation and theology of the New Testament bear only indirectly. The word is not used. The idea is at most implicit. The authors are very far from the advocate's concern with corruption in the courts. Their focus is on "Christ Jesus, and him crucified" (1 Cor 2:2). Exchanges nonetheless occur or are attempted which would furnish subsequent Christians food for reflection on bribery. Even in their original narration the episodes show a certain awareness of the concept.

Much more central to our theme are the New Testament views of judgment. The bribery ethic as developed in the ancient Near East and the Mediterranean world rested on the assumption that the judge must be impartial. The basis for opposing bribery disappeared if the judge could have favorites or be influenced by offerings to change his decree. What the New Testament said on impartiality, redemption, and favor was critical to the moral position of the Christians on bribery. The problems are more apparent in the fourth century, when the Christians come to power, than in the first century, but for our understanding of the later development it is necessary to look at the way matters stood in the beginning.

In the Beginning

Five cases occur in the telling of the stories of Jesus and the early Church where actions are performed which could be related to bribery. The actions and even more dramatically the actors provide possible prototypes for later Christian admiration or reprobation.

Persons as Possible Paradigms. "Hoping that money would be given him by Paul, he frequently met and spoke with him" (Acts 24:26). So runs the only reference in the New Testament to the expectation of a bribe. No word of condemnation is attached to the expectation, nor is it thought necessary to add that Paul does not pay. The "he" is Felix, the Roman governor of Judea. Paul is in protective custody, accused by Jewish enemies as a stirrer up of sedition and subject to possible trial before Felix. Of Felix we are also informed that he has ruled the province "for many years"; that his wife, Drusilla, is a Jew; that he knows about the Christian "way"; and that he and his wife are willing to listen to Paul preach about "the way."

Paul does preach to them on "faith in Christ Jesus" and on "justice and chastity and the future judgment." Two of the four topics bear on the responsibilities of a judge. In the subtle style of Luke, these subjects are set off against Felix's hope of making money off his prisoner. When Paul selects chastity as a theme, Luke does not report that Drusilla is a daughter of Herod and, according to Jewish law, an adulteress—a divorcee living with a man not her husband; nor does he enlarge upon the moral implications of Felix's position as a judge expecting money from his prisoner. The portrait of a weak and corrupt man is made in three sentences, so that it is no surprise that "wishing to offer a favor to the Jews, Felix left Paul bound" (Acts 24:27). The later Christian reader knew that this judicial favor to his enemies was the first step to Paul's death.

Moral indignation is explicitly conveyed in another incident: Simon, a practitioner of magic in Samaria, known popularly as "The Great Power of God," is converted by Philip and baptized. Peter and John are sent from Jerusalem to lay hands on the Samaritan converts so they will receive the Holy Spirit. When Simon sees this happening, he is moved to action:

> . . . he offered them money, saying, "Give me too this power, so that on whomsoever I lay hands he will receive the Holy Spirit." But Peter said to him, "Your cash and you go to perdition; for you have thought that the gift of God might be possessed through money. You are no participant nor sharer in this Word; for your heart is not right before God. Repent, therefore, of this wickedness of yours, and pray the Lord that you may be forgiven the thought of your heart. For I see you to be for bitter poison and the fetter of unrighteousness." But Simon said, "Pray for me to the Lord that nothing which you said will come upon me."

> (Acts 8:18–24)

Two distinct synonyms are used for money in this short episode: *chremata* (money or property), and *argurion*, (money or silver or cash). Attempted exchange of money for power over the Spirit is wickedness, offense against God, an occasion for Peter to curse the offeror and to pronounce this new Christian's separation from the community. The predicted fate of Simon—poison and fetter—identify him with his evil gift, which itself is bitter poison and an unrighteous chain. His mild reply shows him abashed but not really repentant or aware of the enormity of his attempt. Few actions in Luke's narrative are so strongly characterized as wicked as this unsuccessful effort. Describing Felix, Luke is merely observing the corruption of the old order. Reporting the sin of Simon, he is defending the essence of the new. The Spirit is central to the Church. The Spirit is its guide, its life, its source of morality. It is from the Spirit that "love, joy, peace" arise (Gal 5:22). The enormity of Simon's action lies in his attempt to use cash to reduce the Spirit to his power.[1]

There is a further aspect of the sin of Simon—of Simon Magician, as he comes to be called—which is memorable. Biblical condemnations of bribetaking had focused on the bribetaker. Here the act stigmatized as heinous is the offer. Scripture, when Acts became Scripture, now provided the paradigm of a bribegiver. Scripture now showed a person whose name could stand for every evil offeror of money in exchange for what could not be sold.

The scene with Simon Magician was associated, in later commentary, with one saying and one action of Jesus. In Matthew 10:8 when he sends out his disciples on their first mission, he instructs them, "You have taken freely. Give freely." The iron law of reciprocity is here set out and put on a higher plane. What is received as a gift must be given as a gift. The saying occurs only in Matthew.

The action is recorded in all four Gospels. It is the expulsion of the vendors from the Temple (Mk 11:15–16; Lk 19:45–46; Mt 21:12–13; Jn 2:14–16). The deed is accorded the greatest prominence in John where it is set near the beginning and is the first act performed by Jesus in Jerusalem. Its meaning is underlined by the words, "Do not make the house of my Father a house of selling" (Jn 2:16). In Mark, Matthew, and John the vendors driven out by Jesus include those "who sold doves." At Jesus' baptism "the Spirit as a dove descends onto him" (Mk 1:10; Mt 3:16; cf. Lk 3:22, Jn 1:32). The birds sold in the Temple were ordinary objects of sacrifice, but when the same kind of bird was presented by each Gospel as the symbol of the Spirit, a connection could be seen between the sales Jesus attacked and the sale of the Spirit. Patristic exegesis made explicit the latent reference.

Neither Simon's purchase nor Felix's sale is consummated. Two bargains are. One is that made by anonymous Roman soldiers. They are asked by the chief priests to report that the disciples of Jesus stole his body while the guard was asleep. The priests give "enough silver," and the soldiers do as bidden. Their false report is said to have been widely known and current in Jewish circles of the day (Mt 28:11–15). No characterization is made of the exchange, but it is fair to say that the transaction looks shabby. The chief priests have already been portrayed as agents of Jesus' death (Mt 27:1). Now they are presented as being willing to pay for a lie. The soldiers are the only officials in either Testament portrayed as accepting money for a breach of duty. If we were to apply anachronistically the modern American meaning of bribe, we would say they were bribetakers—the only actual bribetakers in the Bible. A contemporary Roman would have said that they had taken *munera*. The New Testament itself does not supply any concept to cover the transaction.

The second sale is that of Jesus himself. According to Mark, Judas Iscariot, one of the Twelve, goes to the high priests "to betray Jesus to them," and they promise they will "give him money" (Mk 14:11; cf. Lk 22:3). In Matthew, the desire to work out parallels between events affecting Jesus and events commemorated in the Old Testament leads to the amount being specified: "thirty pieces of silver" (Mt 26:15; cf. Zec 11:12–13). Judas later attempts to return the sum, the chief priests are unwilling to put the money in the Temple treasury, "for it is blood price," and they finally use it to buy a burial place for aliens (Mt 27:3–8). Judas recognizes his guilt: "I have sinned, betraying just blood" (Mt 27:4). In Mark, Matthew, and Luke, Jesus says of him, "Woe to that man by whom the Son of man is betrayed" (Mk 14:21; Mt 26:24; Lk 22:22). Matthew and Mark have Jesus add, "Good for that man if he had not been born." Two Gospels tie the betrayal to Satan: "Satan entered Judas" (Lk 22:3); "Satan entered into him" (Jn 13:27).

In the Gospel of John, Judas is described by Jesus as *diabolos* (Jn 6: 71–72), a term meaning "false accuser," "enemy," or "devil." In controversy with Jewish opponents Jesus characterizes the *diabolos* as "a liar and a liar's father" (Jn 8:44–45). There is a link between the two passages and Judas's act. His betrayal is a lie, a denial of the truth, expectable of one who is the devil. In Matthew, Judas hangs himself (Mt 27:5).

Judas's betrayal is not of loyalty in the abstract, but of the Lord. It leads directly to the arrest of Jesus and, as Matthew makes explicit, to his death. It is an action evil enough to be attributed specifically to Satan. Judas himself is without excuse and his end is miserable. That the betrayal is a sale is emphasized by Matthew's focus, in pursuit of his scriptural pedagogy, on the amount paid and its character of blood price. The Gospel of John reflects meditation on the earlier accounts. When Jesus speaks to Judas at the Last Supper, some of the disciples think that Jesus said to him, "Buy what we need for the feast" or what he might give the needy (Jn 13:29–30). The Johannine irony is that the disciples understand the exact opposite of what is happening: Judas is about to sell what is needed, to sell what is to be given for the needy: Jesus himself. At the brook of Cedars Judas is described as *ho paradidous*, "the deliverer," as if he delivered a hostage or a purchase (Jn 18:2)[2]

When the fault of the woman about to be stoned is described, she is said to have been taken "in adultery" (Jn 8:5). When Jesus warns against the lust of the eyes or against remarriage after divorce, "to commit adultery" is the verb he expands to include the condemned behavior (Mt 5:28). The basic sexual sin is well-established. No comparable category is available to characterize the acts of the chief priests, Felix, Simon, Judas, or even to identify unmistakably any one of the transactions. Felix asks, the priests and Simon proffer "money," not a "a bribe"; Judas gets a concrete sum, not "a payoff." Their actions, disapproved as they are, are not distinguished as specific sins.

By their place in the historical narrative, however, the chief priests, Felix, Simon, and Judas invite moral judgment. The chief priests and Felix are sketched unfavorably, Simon the Great Power of God is denounced, Judas is said to be in the power of Satan. That Simon the Great Power of God is a double, a negative image of Simon Rock, the leader of the Apostles, is part of the narrative from the beginning. In each story it is assumed that there are sales and purchases that cannot be made, that reciprocity in human relations is bounded by what may be made the object of reciprocity. Explicit abstractions of this sort are foreign to the New Testament. The characters of Felix, Simon, Judas are concrete; they have the potential of becoming symbols as Simon Rock became the symbol of the fallen and forgiven penitent. Would a Christian judge tempted by a bribe be moved by remembering that Felix looked for money from Paul and, to do the enemies of Christ a favor, set him on the course to his execution? Would the denunciation of Simon for trying to buy God's gift move a prospective briber? Would someone tempted to deny the truth recall the priests who did deny it with a payoff? Would a judge identify with Judas if he sold a condemnation for money or blinded his eyes to deny the truth? Much would depend on the sensibilities of the Christian reader, much on what was chosen by the Christian community for pedagogic emphasis. Later generations would select which if any of these villains would function as an exemplar. In the long run, in the development of an ethic affecting bribery, Simon was to provide the most powerful paradigm. Each of these negative images, however, is as nothing compared to the positive paradigm presented by Jesus.

Judge, Buyer, Ransomer, Donee, and Donor.   A parable, found only in Luke, presents a judge described as "an unrighteous judge" and one "who did not fear God and did not reverence man" (Lk 18:3, 6). He is importuned by a widow asking him to hear her case against her opponent. He refuses to act for a long time, but in the end to avoid a black eye—that is, disgrace—he consents to take up her case (Lk 18:4–5). In the background of the story is a view of bribery. The widow is the archetypical suitor who cannot pay. The unjust judge postpones action—what is he waiting for except an access payment? Unjust though he is, he is finally shamed by persistent entreaty; his conduct makes God's response to prayer an *a fortiori* probability. How differently the story would teach about God and man if the judge acted only when the widow scraped together enough money to make a payment.[3]

The story contains a double message. An adulterer, a homosexual, an incestuous man is never used as an analogue to God: the repugnance to sexual sin is too strong and the sensitivity to possible misinterpretation too great. The acceptability of an unjust man as an analogue implies a degree of tolerance or even respect for him. The judge gets a measure of sympathy. But his action has been bad—that is the second and dominant part of the message. The parable would lack its bite if it were about a good judge who did not expect a reward for hearing a case.

What is the model of judgment held in mind by Christians? Writing the community in Rome, Paul sets out an apocalyptic commonplace, that there will come a "day of anger and of revelation of the justice of God," when God "will pay each for what he has done" (Rom 2:5–6). He had already instructed the Corinthians about that day, "the day of our Lord Jesus" (2 Cor 1:14). On that day, when "each is to be repaid according to what he has done in the flesh, good or bad," the summons will be universal: "all of us must appear before the court of Christ" (2 Cor 5:10).

Paul makes explicit what is implicit in the parables of the Gospels that end in scenes of judgment—the usurer's talents (Mt 25:14–30; Lk 19: 11–26); the wheat and the tares that will be burnt (Mt 13:24–30; cf. Mt 3: 12); the guests ejected for lack of wedding garments (Mt 22:11–14), to give three examples. The "day of judgment" is also spoken of directly as in the teaching that on the day of judgment one will account even for his idle words (Mt 12:36). Apocalypse 20 provides a vision of thrones for the just "to whom judgment was committed" and of a great white throne occupied by One alone before whom stand the dead "great and small," who are judged "upon the record of their deeds," written in books which are then opened.

A single grand scenario of judgment, however, is dominant, that presented by Matthew as the climax of Jesus' prediction of the last days: Christ will come in glory with all his angels "and shall sit on his throne of glory, and before him shall be gathered all the nations, and he shall separate them from each other as the shepherd separates the sheep from the goats, and he will place the sheep on his right hand and the goats on the left." Then he, "the king," will welcome those on his right to his kingdom and dispatch to everlasting fire those on the left (Mt 25:31–46).

No lawyers, no offering of evidence, no weighing of merits in a balance—only the quick and sure decision of the shepherd. The only sort of acts on which judgment is passed are those of charity—feeding the hungry, giving drink to the thirsty, clothing the naked, housing the homeless, visiting the sick and the imprisoned. For two millennia rulers had been announcing that they were protectors of the poor: now a judgment seat is set up where their claims will be judged. It is a judgment scene which is an antijudgment scene. The shepherd is a conventional enough Near Eastern metaphor for a ruler, but none of the conventional crimes established by law are condemned. What is punished is failure to do justice to the poor.[4]

In this court where no advocates contend and no argument is heard, no room is left for bribery or influence with the judge. The very possibility of chicanery is excluded by Matthew's extraordinary combination of majesty with the metaphor of the pasture. The enthroned king surrounded by angels is unapproachable. The shepherd acts with an immediacy that permits no palaver. The judge has no scales like Anubis. He does not need them. He simply looks. Needless to say he is not blinded. Sheep and goats cannot change their category by gifts. Forever as part of the Christian message stands this scene of austere and irrevocable judgment by a Christ who sees only two kinds of human being and disposes of them instantly on the basis of what he sees.

Deuteronomy had taught that God does not "lift up faces" (Dt 10:17), and the Septuagint rendered the quoted phrase into Greek literally with the word *prosōpolemptes*, "face-lifting," more idiomatically in English paraphrase, "face-noticing." Making his own translation, Paul invokes Deuteronomy when he asserts his equality as an apostle with the leaders at Jerusalem: "God does not lift up a man's face" (Gal 2:6). In his later writing he adopts the Septuagint's adjective or makes variations on it. At the apocalyptic day of anger Jews and Greeks will receive equal justice, for "there is no face-noticing (*prosōpolempsia*) with God" (Rom 2:11).

The root term becomes standard. The Apostle Peter uses it when he hears of the vision God has granted the Gentile Cornelius: "Now I comprehend in truth that God is not face-noticing" (Acts 10:34). Luke puts into the mouths of Pharisees the acknowledgment that Jesus "does not take up a face" (Lk 20:21). Here Christ is recognized as an impartial teacher, diluting his doctrine for no one. But normally, as in Deuteronomy, the impartiality celebrated is that of a judge. Merging the images of judge and owner, Colossians instructs its readers "to slave for Christ as their Master." They should know that "the unjust man shall be repaid his injustice, and there is no face-noticing" (Col 3:25). The "Master in heaven" oversees them impartially.

As the judges of Israel were told to imitate God by taking no account of faces, so Paul's teaching about Christ comes to function as a norm for Christians. "Do not in face-noticing keep the faith of our glorious Lord Jesus Christ," the Letter of James advises (Jas 2:1). This means for James that the rich are not to be better treated at meetings than the poor. The "sovereign law" is, "Love your neighbor as yourself." The command outlaws discrimination: "If you notice faces, you commit a sin" (Jas 2:9). The injunction faithfully reflects the conception of the judicial Christ's freedom from partiality. But another set of metaphors strikes a different note.

Paul warns the Corinthians not to soil their bodies with sexual foulness and gives a reason: "You have been bought back at a price." (*egorasthete*) (1 Cor 6:20); and again, a few lines later Paul tells his reader that if he has been called as a free man he is now a slave, "Christ's slave—you have been bought back at a price" (1 Cor 7:23).

In Galatians 3:13, Paul declares explicitly that "Christ bought us back from the curse of the Law, becoming a curse for us." The verb used in these passages is *exagorazein*, a term whose root is the Greek word *agora* or marketplace. The idea of purchase is picked up in post-Pauline writings. In Apocalypse 5:9 the Lamb is saluted because "You were slain and your blood bought us back for God," and in Apocalypse 14:3 the new song of the Lamb is sung by the 144,000 "who have been bought back from the earth." In 2 Peter 2:1, the writer denounces teachers "who deny the Lord who bought them back."

The metaphor of Christ's repurchase of mankind is buttressed by a second set of metaphors clustered about the two related nouns *lutron* and *apolutrōsis* and the verb *lutrousthai*. In Mark 10:45, paralleled in Matthew 20:28, Jesus says he has come "to serve and to give his life a ransom (*lutron*) on behalf of many." In Paul, Christ Jesus is "our justification and holiness and redemption (*apolutrōsis*)" (1 Cor 1:30). In Ephesians 1:14, the Spirit is said to assure us that God will bring us "into the purchased redemption (*apolutrōsis*)." In Luke 24:21, the disciples on the road to Emmaus say they thought that Jesus was going "to ransom (*lutrousthai*)" Israel. Luke 21:28 points out that when Jerusalem is surrounded by armies and strange signs appear in the heavens and the Son of Man comes in a cloud with majesty and power, then "your redemption" (*apolutrōsis*) is at hand. In later writing the readers of 1 Pt 1:18 are reminded that they "were ransomed" (*elutrōthete*) not by silver or gold "but with precious blood." The readers of 1 Timothy 2:6 are told that there is "one God, one go-between between God and man, the man Christ-Jesus, who gave himself exchange-ransom (*antilutron*) on behalf of all." The addressees of Titus 2:13–14 are instructed that "our great God and Saviour Jesus Christ" "gave himself on our behalf to ransom (*lutrosetai*) us from all wickedness and to purify us, making for himself a people zealous to do good."

The metaphors of purchase, ransom, and redemption raise two questions. Do they imply a seller as well as a purchaser, a recipient of the price as well as a price? Are they inconsistent with the idea of Christ as judge? Neither of these questions are addressed by the New Testament itself. To raise the questions and to attempt to answer them necessarily involves a theology of the New Testament. If one sticks to the texts of the New Testament itself, the questions are merely implicit, present in the ambiguity of meanings of the metaphors in play.

On the one hand, secular Greek literature furnishes an example of *exagorazein* used to describe the repurchase of Plato by his friends after the tyrant Dionysius had sold the philosopher as a slave—here the idea of buying back is central. *Lutron* and the related verb *lutroun* are frequently found to describe the ransoming of slaves. There is even an instance in Josephus's *The Jewish War*, published 75–79 A.D., where Lucceius Albinus, the Roman procurator in Judea in 62–64 A.D., is described as Cicero had described Hog—a plunderer of the natives, a tyrannical tax collector, and one who "accepted ransoms (*apelutrou*) from their relatives on behalf of those who had been imprisoned for robbery by local councils or former procurators; the only ones left in prison as wicked were those who did not give." Ransom here is like *redemptio* in Cicero, an ironic term for payoff.[5]

On the other hand, *exagorazein* was not commonly used in Greek to describe slave redemptions, and *lutron* was frequently used by a first-century A.D. writer like Philo in a very broad sense, for example, "every wise man is the ransom (*lutron*) of a wicked man." Far more important, the Septuagint offered a number of examples of an expansive use in Greek of ransom or redeem. In Ex 6:5–7 the Lord announces that He will free Israel from the Egyptians and "will ransom (*lutrōsomai*) you by my outstretched hand." In Deuteronomy 7:6–8, it is recalled how the Lord "has redeemed (*elutrōsato*) you from the house of slavery, from the hand of Pharaoh, king of Egypt." In Ps 110:9 God is celebrated for sending "redemption" (*lutrosis*) to his people. In these and a variety of other Old Testament contexts, it is plain that purchase, purchase price, and seller are not suggested. The Lord by his mighty hand rescued Israel from bondage. He paid a ransom to no one. Yet by his rescue of the enslaved Israelites, God became their new owner. His possession was sealed by the covenant at Sinai (Ex 19:5). Hence the Old Testament frequently speaks of Israel as a people God "has acquired" (e.g., Ps 73:2). In this Old Testament usage, acquisition is without payment, and redemption is liberation gratuitously conferred by the Lord on those whom he chose to be his own. "You were sold for nothing, and you shall be redeemed without money," Isaiah 52:3 rejoices in the paradoxes of divine mercy. "Purchase" and "ransom" both describe God's way of uniting his choice to himself.[6]

It is reasonable to argue that the broad Old Testament meanings control the metaphors of purchase and ransom in the New. Nonetheless, the surface ambiguity is there, and argument is required to resolve it. "Did the hagiographers of the N. T. apply to the work of Christ the term 'redemption' because they envisaged it as a price paid to some person?" ask the authors of a modern study of the matter; and eventually they answer No, the New Testament authors wanted to evoke the Old Testament concept of a graciously liberating God acting gratuitously. But it requires forty pages of exegesis and argument to reach this conclusion as to ransom and to buy back. Other interpreters in the course of history were to reach—less persuasively no doubt—different conclusions.[7]

If Christ is the new owner, and the metaphors of acquisition are pursued, the ransom must have been paid an old and unrightful owner. Christ, Colossians says, has "carried us off" from "the power of the darkness" (Col 1:13). This power is not named as the seller; the inference could be drawn that it is. In a weaker form the same idea is present in the passage already quoted from Ti 2:14. Another possible answer, with another set of Jewish roots, is given in the Letter to the Hebrews. The ritual of

Israel was centered on the giving of gifts to God. The Gospel of Matthew assumes that the ritual will continue: "when you bring your gift (*dōron*) to the altar," you are to make peace with your brother and "only then come back and offer your gift" (Mt 5:23–24). The recognition of Jesus in Matthew begins with the gifts (*dōra*) brought by the magi (Mt 2:11). The developed theology of Hebrews declares there is now a new high priest whose relation to God is that of giftgiver and covenant-maker. The new high priest is "at the right hand of the throne of Majesty in the heaven" and has come with a gift because "every high priest is appointed to offer gifts (*dōra*) and sacrifices—this one too must have something to offer" (Heb 8:3). What he in fact has offered is "his own blood" (Heb 9:12) or "himself" (Heb 9:14). The offeror is Christ. The offering is the offering indicated by the rest of the New Testament. The offeree is explicitly God. The problem—implicit not raised—is how a gift taken by the Supreme Judge is reconcilable with the Judge's justice.

Dōron, the term for gift in ordinary Greek and in particular in Matthew and Hebrews, is also the term in Greek for bribe. In each of the places in the Old Testament where the Hebrew used *shohadh* to mean a corrupt gift, the Septuagint employed *dōron*. Thus, "You shall not take *dōron* which makes the clear-eyed blind" (Ex 23:8). God "does not lift up faces and does not take *dōron* (Dt 10:17), and the judges of Israel "shall not take *dōron*, for *dōron* blinds the eyes of the wise" (Dt 16:20). The Psalmist prays not to be cast out with men "whose fingers are active in evil, and whose right hands are full of *dōra* (Ps 26:10); the man who dwells on the holy mountain of God "takes no *dōra* against an innocent man" (Ps 14:5). The wicked man "accepts *dōron* under his cloak to pervert the course of justice" (Pv 17:23). For a Greek-reading Jew the range of meaning in *dōron* was always before his eyes in Scripture.

How, then, does a *dōron* to God to liberate us from sin differ from a payment to a judge to release a guilty prisoner? No New Testament author puts this question. But the question is present once the theology of Hebrews is juxtaposed with the presentation of God as judge. God the supreme judge is seen as influenced by the offering which Christ presents to him. Why is the offering not the kind of *shohadh* condemned by Deuteronomy?

As in the Old Testament, context controls meaning. *Shohadh* or *dōron*, taken by God, is always good. The goodness of a repurchase price, conceived as offering to God, is unquestioned. No effort is made by any New Testament author to bring together the images of God as gifttaker and God as judge. Yet God, judge and gifttaker, is the model for the mimesis of the Christian.

The metaphors centered on purchase and ransom convey a further teaching: Jesus has given us the gift of salvation and given it freely. We are the beneficiaries of his free, saving action. The text from Matthew 10:8, "You have taken freely, give freely," could be read to underscore the lesson. The example of this uncalculated, unreciprocable gift was eventually

to transform the meaning of gift itself, to found a sharp distinction between a true gift and a bribe. For the Christian, God is not only Judge and
Donee, but Donor.

Just as in the Jewish world from which the Gospel came the holiness of
man was founded on the imitation of God, so in the New Testament imitation is inculcated. Sometimes the imitation is specified as that of sons: "Be
imitators, therefore, of God as beloved children . . ." (Eph 5:1), "Love your
enemies . . . and you will be sons of the Almighty for he is kind to the
ungrateful and the wicked" (Lk 6:35–36). Sometimes the Father is to be
imitated as in the quoted texts, sometimes Christ. The quotation from
Ephesians continues, "and walk in love just as Christ loved you and gave
himself for you . . ." (Eph 5:2). "Be imitators of me as I am of Christ," Paul
writes elsewhere (1 Cor 11:1). The divine model is presented as mandatory by Jesus himself in Matthew: "Be perfect as your heavenly Father is
perfect" (Mt 5:48). When Jesus presents the "two great commandments"
of the law as love of God and love of neighbor (Mt 22:37–40) the term
"love" is given substantial content by the requirement of divine imitation.[8]

With God proposed as the being to imitate, consider the story told by
Jesus in Matthew of the landowner who wills to pay the laborers he hired
at the end of the day as much as those who have borne the whole day's
labor. These naturally conclude that they are being underpaid, and mur-
mur. The storyteller takes pains to deny that there has been injustice. He
has the landowner speak to a murmurer: "Friend, I do you no injury. Did
you not agree with me for a denarius?" The story insists that the landowner's generosity is not bounded by his justice (Mt 20:1–16).

The Gospel which presents the arbitrary and gracious landowner as an
image of God is also a Gospel that compares Christ to a usurious owner
(Mt 25:14–30; Lk 19:11–26); and the scene of the usurer demanding an accounting is the immediate prelude to Matthew's Last Judgment, the most
formidable judgment on the merits in all of Scripture. The parables of the
landowner and the usurer and the vision of judgment are all parts of a
complex whole. Together they maintain a paradox which is present in the
New Testament taken in its entirety: God is a just God, who gives favors
—above all the gift of himself. It is this God who is to be imitated.

Does not, however, one aspect predominate over the other when God is
set out as the being to imitate? "Be merciful, therefore, as your Father is
merciful," the followers of Jesus are told (Lk 6:36); and in the next verse,
"Judge not and you shall not be judged" (Lk 6:37; Mt 7:1). Is it not clear
that Christians are to imitate the Father of Christ in mercy but not in judgment, which is reserved to God alone? Nonetheless, it is impossible in the
style of fundamentalists to reduce the total message to a few clear texts.
Despite the forceful injunction against judging in Luke and Matthew, the
New Testament authors themselves are constantly judging individuals,
and, in addition to their moral censures, a recurrent image is forensic.
Whatever the letter, the Christian is invited to imitate a God who judges.

The Variety of Moral Instruction.   No one has ever understood all of the New Testament literally. It is impossible to do so for its images clash with each other if they are each accorded a literal reading. God is Creator, Father, Judge, Employer. Christ is Son, Purchaser, Redeemer, Judge, and Shepherd, as well as Bridegroom (Mk 2:19), Farmer (Lk 8:5), and Vine (Jn 15:1). To reconcile the images, to say one should be pressed in a literal sense, another be interpreted only figuratively is to write theology. When the New Testament is read as a historical document, the plentitude of imagery and instruction must be reported. No variety can be suppressed in the name of symmetry or sense.

"The preaching and teaching of Christ," objected Volusianus and other members of the Roman ruling elite of a later era, "are in no way suitable for the morals of the state: that is demonstrated by the commands to return no one evil for evil, to offer the other cheek to him who strikes one, and to give one's cloak to him who seeks to take one's tunic." The Roman rulers posed a rhetorical question: "Who would not wish by right of war to return evil to the ravager of a Roman province?"[9]

Volusianus' fifth-century complaint is echoed by the twentieth-century historian Paul Veyne. Was Christian charity, he asks, "to transform the political order, or was it only a spiritual refuge? Was it an ethic of commitment, of responsibility?" Jesus, he replies, "did not ask such questions," for "they can only be asked by the great, by those who hold the levers of power." Jesus and his followers had to accept the established order as "unbreakable like nature; humble folk can only endure it. What is left for them to do? To help each other, to treat each other as brothers in mercy, to beg those among them who are the modest agents of the powerful not to abuse their morsel of power." Jesus does not counsel such "modest agents" to abandon their occupation: "they are humble like him, and the humble are not heroes. He counsels them to earn their bread without being too zealous in their masters' service and without abusing their power." This is an "'irresponsible ethic,' if you please, for the good reason that it is made by a man and for a man who had no share in responsibility." This irresponsible ethic was, according to Veyne, the starting point for the Christians who after the conversion of Constantine shared responsibility for the Roman Empire.[10]

When they find the New Testament without bearing on the exercise of responsible power, Volusianus and Veyne read the New Testament literally. They also read it selectively as a literalist is inevitably forced to do. They select the maxims that prove their point. But these maxims cannot be isolated without distortion from the whole made up of exemplars and parables and postulates and exhortations and metaphors. There is not a single word in the entire canon of the New Testament on the morality of bribery, but there is a variety of material bearing on bribes, judges, and the responsible exercise of power.

The Gospels do not tell the tale of a poor boy who came to a sad end, but the story of the Son of God doing mighty deeds. Nothing could be more misleading than to characterize the ethic conveyed as the unheroic ethic of a man not in power. From the perspective of the storytellers, Jesus speaks with the authority of God. His followers are invited to imitate God.

The being these followers are asked to imitate is a judge, a judge ever vigilant, incorruptible, discriminating in no one's favor. They are specifically admonished to be like him in not discriminating. They are given for their guidance a figure who meets them in the final hour not in any family relationship, not as father, son, or brother, but in the form of a civil magistrate. It is in "Christ's court" that Paul expects each to stand. That the Judge is also Ransomer means, for moral mimesis, that love is joined to power. How the human imitator is to join love to power is left, with numerous hints, to be worked out.

In the New Testament the poor are explicitly stand-ins for the divine. In the judgment scene of Matthew he who has helped the poor discovers that he has helped Christ, and his conduct receives divine recompense. The ethic of divine reciprocity is expressed again in the teaching in Luke 14: 12–14: "When you give a lunch or a dinner, do not invite friends or brothers or relatives or rich neighbors, for they will invite you in return and what you did will be repaid. But when you give a feast, invite the poor, the crippled, the lame, and the blind, and you will be blessed that they will not be able to repay you; for you shall be repaid in the resurrection of the just." Reciprocity is not abolished; God pays for the poor. If this is said of giving a dinner, the implications for judgment are there. The just judge need not fear going unrecompensed if he forgoes a bribe from the poor litigant; God will repay.

The Christian is presented with pictures of men marked as bad—the chief priests, Felix, Simon, Judas, the unjust judge. None of these save Judas is presented as so bad that he does not have a kind of inner coherence of his own. They are presented as persons one might meet, that one would treat with a certain respect. But their conduct is condemned. They are far from being followers of Jesus. These negative images reject, with varying degress of vehemence, those who give and take payoffs for breaches of trust, for things that are unsalable, for denial of the truth, for injustice. That these negative images could operate to inculcate ways contrary to their authors' intention should not be overlooked. Contraception in Western culture was modeled, in part, on Onan. Christian traitors had Judas as a paradigm. The negative image provides a model fo the Christian who rejects the Christian message. The negative image gives coherence to conduct he might have viewed more casually. Normatively, however, the negative image rejects the behavior it incorporates.

Peter's classic defense of Gentile Christians begins with the declaration that God is not face-noticing and reaches its climax with the claim that God has designated Jesus as "judge" (Acts 10:34–43). In the catechesis traditionally ascribed to Peter the judicial paradigm set before Christians is recalled with its Old Testament roots and juxtaposed with the image of ransom:

> . . . like the holy being who has called you, you must be holy in all you do, for it is written "Be holy as I am holy." And if you call Father him who judges without noticing faces according to the work of each, you must live in fear of him all the time you live here, knowing that you have not been ransomed from the follies of your ancestral way with corruptibles, silver and gold, but with precious blood. . . .

(1 Pt 1:15–19)

Out of power or in power, the Christian has been gratuitously bought and freely paid for.[11] His purchase has not freed him from an arbitrary yet impartial Judge, whom out of power or in power he must imitate.

In Power

Flavius Marcellinus, imperial state secretary and tribune and conscientious Christian layman, stationed in Carthage, received Volusianus' challenge to the Christians' capability to be Roman rulers and passed it on to a friend who was the intellectual leader of the Church in Africa —Augustine, bishop of Hippo Regius. Augustine answered thoughtfully and promptly. The Gospel itself assumed that it was right for men to be soldiers (Lk 3:14). Maxims such as turning the other cheek were to be applied to one's interior disposition, not acted upon literally. Marcellinus, Augustine did not have to say, had no obligation to renounce his governmental role or his judicial responsibilities.[12]

Queries like Volusianus' were taken seriously; they could puzzle a scrupulous Christian; but they were not of the kind to cause an institutional crisis. By the beginning of the fifth century most Christians saw no incongruity between their beliefs and the exercise of power. If individual Christians—Augustine himself was an example—left the life of the court, they did not condemn or reject their brothers who sought office; indeed Augustine rejoiced to have a "very dear and deeply loved son" like Marcellinus in high place. If a precedent were sought, had not Paul himself in the seedtime of the faith made a point—perhaps a boast—of the faithful who were in "the household of Caesar" (Phim 4:22)? "God does not reject the powerful, for He is powerful"—so ran Job 36:5 in the version by Jerome which became the Latin Vulgate. The thought does not appear in the Hebrew, the Greek, or the old Latin of Job 36:5, but Jerome faithfully catches what was to be a working assumption of Latin Christendom.[13]

Institutional crises in the Western Church when power came were of a different sort. First, in fourth-century Africa, a Roman Africa celebrated for its contentious lawyers, the Donatists contended that the Church could extend no mercy to those who had denied their faith under persecution. Then, as that controversy abated after about a hundred years of acrimony, Pelagius and his followers reduced or qualified the mercy granted those on earth by God himself. These doctrinal squabbles were in fact intimately tied to secular conceptions of justice and judgment—not that the doctrinal issues were faced with the conviction that they bore directly on secular society but that secular conceptions of justice and judgment shared by both sides to the debates made the treatment of mercy, favor, and impartiality crucial.

Where else but in human experience did Donatus or Pelagius and his ally Julian and his opponent Augustine derive their ideas of what justice and judgment should be? Acting on that experience they seized on certain images and expressions of Scripture as significant for their faith. The controversy between Augustine and the Pelagians, in particular, demonstrated how deeply entrenched in Roman and Christian consciousness the conception of impartial judgment was. In contrast to, or even in conflict with, this conception were central Christian concepts of grace, of offering, and of redemption. Just judgment, on the one hand, grace, offering and redemption, on the other—the combination recapitulated tensions of the Old Testament, exacerbated in the Roman empire by the double meanings of *gratia*, *munus*, and *redemptio*.

The Impartiality of Justice.   Holding the words of Scripture in common, what did both Pelagius and Augustine agree was significant? That God is not an *acceptor personarum* and that when God gives judgment there is no *acceptio personarum*. With these phrases the Latin Bible rendered the teaching of the Septuagint that God does not lift up faces and the teaching of the New Testament that on Judgment Day God will not lift up faces. The Latin imitated the Greek in using a verb, *accipere*, that implied an action by the judge: the verb in English may be translated "to take up." In Latin as in English, the sense of a physical gesture, the judge raising the litigant's face, was lost. Greek had used a single word, incorporating within it *prosōpon*, a triply ambiguous word meaning "face," "mask" or "person." Latin eliminated any literal reference to "face" and used *persona*, a term meaning either "mask" or "person." In the phrase *accipere personam*, the sense of "mask" was not emphasized.

Augustine's definition of the nounal phrase ran, "*Acceptio personarum* is rightly used where he who judges, leaving the merit of the case about which he judges, patronizes one against the other because he finds something in his person worthy of honor or mercy." Literally, *acceptio personarum* is translated as "the taking up of persons." Idiomatically, the phrase should be simply translated as "discrimination." *Acceptio personarum* paradigmatically occurs in judgment by a judge who does not decide on the merits, who becomes the sponsor of one side, swayed by the consideration of something in the person of the litigant.[14]

God is not a taker-up of persons, taught the Latin Old Testament. The Father is not a taker-up, taught the Latin Peter, Christ is not a taker-up, taught the Latin Paul and Luke. Christians should not be takers-up, taught the Latin James. The phrase was scriptural, the teaching on impartial judgment was canonized in Scripture, the importance of the teaching was born of experience.

If the bishop is not of good conscience, said the Syrian *Didascalia Apostolorum*, and takes up a person for a certain foul profit on the offerings which he receives, and spares one who impiously sins and suffers him to remain in the Church, the bishop has polluted his congregation with God and with men. The teaching uses sexual imagery to convey the rebuke: the bishop "pollutes" as one does by an unlawful genital act. His "lewdness" provides a terrible example for youths and maidens. Such was the experience of third-century Christians in Syria. The Latin version of the *Didascalia* adopted the same vocabulary: the bad bishop takes *turpe lucrum*, "filthy profit." *Inquinavit*, "he has stained," his church. He has been guilty of *intemperantia*, "incontinence."[15]

"'Woe to those who say sweet is bitter and bitter is sweet', They say this who in judging do not consider the case but the person. The fruit of Christ, who is justice, who is most sweet, they turn to bitterness. Whosoever in judging is led by kinship, or by friendship, or contrariwise by hostile hatred or by enmity, therefore perverts the judgment of Christ, who is justice, and turns his fruit to bitterness." Such was the comprehensive condemnation of partiality in judging offered by the fourth-century's leading authority on Scripture, Jerome, here quoting one Old Testament prophet, Isaiah, to interpret another, Amos, and integrating both with Christ, identified as incarnate justice. Jerome's rejection of those who "do not consider the case but the person" is common ground for orthodox and unorthodox Christians.[16]

In a passionate passage the Pelagian leader, Julian of Eclanum, declared the deity was inconceivable without impartial justice: "Beyond doubt, then, there is justice, without which there is no divinity; which if it were not, God would not be. There is, however, God. Therefore, without cavil, there is justice. But *it* is nothing other than the virtue containing all and giving to each his own, without fraud, without favor." The anti-Pelagian bishop of Carthage, Quodvultdeus, was no less emphatic: "For we wait the Day of Judgment. Then will come that most equal judge who takes up the person of no powerful man, whose palace no one corrupts with gold and silver." Augustine himself, expounding Psalm 45:6, "God in his center shall not be moved," declared: "God is said to be in the center. That means he is equal toward all and does not take up persons. For what is in the center is equidistant to every boundary. Thus God is said to be central as he takes care for everyone equally."[17]

Pelagians and opponents alike held the conviction that Christians must be like God in their justice, difficult though it was for human judges to be equidistant from everyone. God, Pelagius observed, "without taking up persons has spared neither his friends nor the sinning angels. But human judgment is corrupted in many ways. By love, hate, fear, and greed the integrity of judgment is violated; and sometimes mercy inclines against the rule of justice." Love, hate, fear, and greed—Pelagius named the stock corruptors. As Christians, both Pelagius and Augustine were especially sensitive to the need to preserve justice from corruption by mercy. "Some-times," Augustine wrote, expounding Psalm 32,

> You hear a case between two men. One of the two is rich and the other is poor; and it happens that the poor man has a bad case but the rich man a good one. Now if you are not learned in the kingdom of God, thinking to do well for your-self, you will as it were be merciful to the poor man and hide and conceal his injustice. . . . But your God says to you, "Take not up the person of the poor in judgment." We are easily advised not to take up the person of the rich. This every man sees, would that every man did![18]

The Latin Bible supplied no adjective for "face-lifting" corresponding to the Greek *prosōpolemptes* (Acts 10:34), but the Latin text known to Augustine did provide a related adverb. In John 7:24 Jesus rebukes the crowd for censuring his cure of a man on the Sabbath and says, "Do not judge according to height *(kata hupsin)*, but judge according to just judgment." The Latin Vulgate translated *kata hupsin* "secundum faciem"—"according to the face." Augustine's Latin text translated it *"personaliter"*—"by the person." He expounded the text as follows: "Do not judge by the person. . . . To escape this vice, brothers, which the Lord marked in this place, is a matter of great labor in the world. . . . Who is he who does not judge by the person?" If he had been speaking, Augustine would have paused at this point. He continued with an answer that made his question not rhetorical. The answer was hard: "He who loves equally. Equal love makes for a non-taking up of persons." Such equal love was observed by a judge, he added, when he judged for the cause that was good. Equal love of this kind was commanded by Christ.[19]

That a judge should not sell his judgments followed as a deduction from the teaching on impartial justice. Augustine had occasion to elaborate on the matter in a letter, subsequently celebrated, to Macedonius, Roman governor of Africa in A.D. 414. The apparent reason for the letter was Macedonius' criticism of Augustine's conduct in intervening in criminal cases to ask clemency from the governor. Answering that criticism, Augustine went on to put his correspondent on the defensive. He agreed that every criminal had an obligation to make restitution of any property he had wrongfully taken; otherwise his sins would not be forgiven. He progressed to consider what payments were subject to restitution. They did not, he said, include all unwilling payments—often one does not want to pay a physician or a worker, yet they receive an honorarium or salary without injustice. What of a judge or witness selling his just judgment? Augustine paused to explore the question of the differences between a judge and an advocate. An advocate sells his advocacy. A counselor sells his counsel on the law. They need not restore what they receive. But advocate and counselor are known to be partial to the party for whom they act. Judge and witness must act fairly toward each side. Their necessary impartiality excludes their selling their services to either party.[20]

By his seemingly remote inquiry about the venal judge, Augustine, it appears probable, meant to touch Macedonius. A venal judge's obligation to make restitution if *his* sins were to be forgiven was implied but never stated. Why was Augustine so insistent on what justice required in a judge and so reticent on what a sinful judge must do unless he meant to hint to Macedonius that he too had sins? Explicitly he invoked the analogy of the Lord with the accusers of the woman taken in adultery. The Lord too had charged no accuser directly; a reminder had sufficed. Intermixed with the veiled rebuke to the governor was Augustine's condemnation of any payment to a judge.

But did not the central Christian transaction with the divine Judge subvert the model of uncorrupted secular judgment? The Latin translation of the New Testament emphasized the notion of purchase already present by adopting forms of *emere*, to buy, to translate both *exagorazein* and *lutron* and its variants, therby effectively fusing "buy back" and "ransom." Where Paul spoke of us as "bought back" (1 Cor 5:20 and 7:23), the Vulgate used *empti*, the past perfect of *emere*, to buy. Where the Apocalypse speaks of the Lamb who bought us back, the Vulgate used the verb whose root was *re-emere*, to repurchase (Rv 5:9). When *lutron*, ransom, or *antilutron*, exchange–ransom appeared, the Vulgate also relied on *emere*. Christ gave his life for our *redemptio* (Mk 10:45; Mt 20:28). He has given himself as *redemptio* for all (1 Tim 2:6). When he is seen coming with power and majesty, we are to know our *redemptio* is at hand (Lk 21:28). *Redemptio* in respectable Latin meant "ransom." In equally respectable Latin since the time of Cicero, in connection with a judge it meant "payoff."

In fourth- and fifth-century legislation, good and bad senses are both found. Christian slaves "are to be ransomed" (*redimantur*) from Jewish owners; prisoners will be ransomed (*redempti*) from the barbarians; and general legislation deals with ransom (*redemptio*) from slavery. Yet guardians may be suspect of being paid off (*redempti*); chaperons may be paid off (*redempti*) to act as go-betweens; creditors may transfer their rights of action to more powerful claimants and thereby buy up (*redimant*) enforcers for their debts. Most spectacularly, in Constantine's basic legislation of A.D. 331 against access payments to provincial governors or to members of their staffs, it is provided, "Let the chamber curtain of the judge not be for sale, nor access bought up (*redempti*)." Purchase of this kind, the emperor suggests, is foreign to fundamental equality: "Let the ears of him who judges be open equally to the poorest and the rich." *Redimere* in such legal usage is tied to payment for breach of trust, especially to payment made to a judge, especially to unequal justice. A Christian theologian, lamenting corruption in the courts, can say, "What can be bought off (*redemi*) is not feared—so Cyprian writing in third-century Africa. "He who is poor and prudent when he sees judgment bought up (*redemptum*) will be silent in that time, because it is a bad time"—so Jerome writing in Bethlehem about A.D. 400 and speaking against those who "take *munera*." To apply *redemptio* boldly to describe the Christian's liberation from the judgment of God was to attempt a reversal of meaning, a transvaluation of values, to celebrate a paradox where purchase of freedom was rightly bought.[21]

The negative implications of *redemptio* do not appear to have distressed Pelagius or Julian, and the term was fully accepted by Augustine. In the course of the Pelagian controversy itself he wrote, "When *redemptio* is uttered, price is understood." He compared the purchaser—Christ—to a bishop ransoming slaves who have fled for protection to his church. He named the price—"The merchant himself speaks: 'Here,' he says, 'is my blood . . .'" Like Paul, he did not name the seller. Elsewhere he did. Preaching on Christ as foretold by the Psalms, he asked, "From whom does he ransom us?" and he answered, "From the devil." In the anti-Pelagian treatise, *Marriage and Concupiscence*, he said again that we are ransomed "from the power of the devil." Giving this answer he affirmed his understanding that *redemptio* was a reciprocal transaction but avoided the implication that it was a purchase of Christians from their Judge. Writing on the Trinity, he affirmed, "In this buy back the blood of Christ is given as price on our behalf; and the devil, accepting it, is not enriched but obliged"—that is, the devil was forced to give us up and was somehow deprived of the benefit of his bargain.[22]

In this understanding of the reciprocal character of the Redemption, Augustine was not innovating. His own instructor in the faith, Ambrose, bishop of Milan, had explained that there was no need for blood sacrifice, and therefore no need for circumcision, after the blood sacrifice of the Lord Jesus "which, necessarily, was to be paid to him to whom by our sins we had been sold." The same view was held by Augustine's and Ambrose's contemporary, Jerome in Judea, who wrote of "the bloody sometime victor accepting the price given for us." Nor were the Latin Fathers different from the Greek. Their contemporary, John Chrysostom, described God as being like a master who had sold an obviously incompetent slave but then saw him being mistreated by a new and wicked master and so "gives a price and buys him back." In our case the devil had bought us by our sins, and we stood in need of God's deliverance. This kind of exegesis went back at least as far as the third century when Origen asked, "But to whom did he give his soul as ransom for many? Because it was not to God. Was it not therefore to the Evil One? For he had us in his power until on our behalf the soul of Jesus was given to him, deceived as if he could possess it." Like Augustine, Origen thought the devil was tricked, as well as bought off. That the payee did not keep the price somehow softened the similarity with payment to obtain *redemptio* from an unjust judge.[23]

This line of speculation worked out the implications of buy back and ransom. The Letter to the Hebrews, however, had spoken of a gift to God. What of *munus* to God the judge? Where the Septuagint had translated *shoḥadh* by *dōron*, the Latin translators of the Old Testament used *munus*, offering, or its plural *munera*, offerings. Where the Greek New Testament said *dōron*, the Latin said *munus* or *munera*. Latin readers were told that God did not take *munera*, that his judges did not take *munera*, and that the man who lived on the holy mountain of God did not take *munera*. The Latin construction indeed emphasized the parallel between "taking up" persons and "taking" offerings: in each case the verb was *accipere*, to take. In each case taking was forbidden.

Here the tendency of Augustine was precisely parallel to that of rabbinic commentators on the Old Testament—to enlarge, with sensitivity, the ways a judge might be corrupted. *Munera* in the bad sense were "money" and "gold and silver." They included *xenia* or "guest presents," the euphemism employed to describe small offerings to officials. And Augustine went further, exactly like Cicero, whose work he knew, and the rabbis, whose work he probably did not know. *Munera*, he taught, included the stroking of the judge. Blandishment or praise was a gift that could corrupt like gold. Like cash it was to be shunned by the judge. In the Latin Vulgate, Psalm 25 spoke disdainfully of those "in whose hands are iniquities, their right hands are filled with *munera*." The judge who stretched out his hand to accept such gifts, Augustine said, "has lost the judgment of his own conscience." Whether by a sale or by the reception of offerings, the judge, called to impartiality, was not to be in reciprocal relation with a litigant.[24]

Yet in the infancy story Jesus was given *munera* at Bethlehem. Worshippers in Matthew brought *munera* to the altar. The new high priest of Hebrews offered himself as *munus*. And how did the Church itself live except by *munera*? How had Jesus himself lived? As Augustine observed in the very passage in which he rejected *munera* for the judge, "Peter took, the Lord took. He had coins—those which were sent and Judas carried off." It was impossible, *tout court*, to condemn offerings. The tradition, even if it did not furnish a vocabulary, contained the resources for a distinction. Psalm 49 in the Vulgate, for example, presented God uncompromisingly rejecting all conventional gifts—why should He want them when everything was His (Ps 49:7–15)? Commenting, Augustine made a traditional move. God was rejecting not all gifts, only those of the wicked man. Apostrophising this designing creature, Augustine exclaimed, "You want to have God as a participant and, as if He were a corrupt judge, a partner in your plunder." Like Cain, the unworthy could not give; the bad man's offering would be unaccepted. Otherwise, so the implication ran, *munera* were not unwelcome to God.[25]

Entrenched in Scripture and in practice, *munera* had to be considered good from the good, bad from the bad. *Munera* had to be recognized as carrying two meanings, like *gratia*. The calm acceptance by everyone of giftgiving to God is refutation of the hypothesis that somehow the Pelagians' objections to *gratia* were tied to their concern with what was done in human courts.[26] If Pelagius had actually feared that the paradigm provided by the divine would corrupt the courts, what could have given a worse example than the *munera* offered the Supreme Judge and accepted by Him? The problem did not trouble him at all. The Pelagians' theological assault was not launched against what man brought to God but against the arbitrariness of God's will. But as arbitrary favor is so easily seen as the consequence of bribery, the meaning of favor must be further examined.

Favor and Favoritism.   That God has chosen a people is one message of the New Testament as it is one message of the Old. To choose among several means to favor some. In Greek, what God gives is *charis;* in Latin, *gratia;* in English, "favor." The celebration of God's choosing of a people and of individual persons runs through the New Testament. "Hail, highly favored," the angel greets Mary at the beginning of the Gospel of Luke (Lk 1:28). The Word, "full of favor," came among us, the Gospel of John begins. "Of his fullness we have all received favor after favor" (Jn 1:14 and 16). *Charis,* in Greek, *gratia,* in Latin, favor cannot be eliminated from the New Testament without disemboweling surgery.

The teaching boldly risks misunderstanding. *Charis* can designate a generous act or unjustified partiality. Used in connection with a judge, it at least signifies a departure from judicial regularity. Thus in the New Testament itself, what Felix does for Paul's enemies at Caesarea, leaving him imprisoned, he does as *charis,* favor, to Paul's opponents. The Jewish leaders in Jerusalem than ask his successor Festus as a "favor" to them to move Paul's trial to Jerusalem (Acts 25:3). Festus rebuffs the request, and the trial opens in Caesarea; but Festus, wishing to give a "favor" to the Jews, asks Paul if he will agree to go to Jerusalem (Acts 25:9). In these instances favor amounts to favoritism. Yet Luke, the author who so pointedly disparages favor here, celebrates God's favor given to Mary. The negative sense of the term is no embarrassment to its positive employment.

In the secular law of the fourth century, *gratia* continued to function homonymously. Cicero had employed *gratia* in the sense of "influence" or "clout"—the exercise of pressure by the powerful on the courts. *Gratia* continued to be used in this sense in such legislation as Constantine's of 319, directed to Corsica: any official who has been corrupted by a payment (*pretium*) or by influence (*gratia*) and has judged unjustly is subject to suit by the party injured. Similarly, a decree of 373 to the Senate denounced "the most disgraceful baseness of sycophantic influence" (*gratia*). *Gratia* designated not only the influence that unfairly affected judgment. It was also understood as the unjustified act of favoritism itself. A decree of 385 provided for the fine of a judge whose "negligence or favoritism" (*gratia*) had delayed the hearing of a case. A decree of 398 permitted a bishop to intervene in any judicial case where human life would be taken "through the mistake or the favoritism" (*gratia*) of the trier. Whether it was exercised on the judge or by the judge, *gratia* was objectionable. In these senses, *gratia* was anathema to churchmen as well as lawyers. "Let us not take up a person in judgment. Let favoritism (*gratia*) be banished. Let them decree the merits of the case," taught Ambrose, bishop of Milan, an ex-judge himself. When the General Council of Africa met in Hippo in 393 (Augustine, not yet a bishop, a leading spirit in this assembly), the Council referred with scorn to ecclesiastical judges "depraved by cupidity or by clout" (*gratia*). It is these usages of *gratia* that a modern historian has in mind when he writes, "*Gratia* in common parlance stood for official corruption in the courts, for official hanky-panky of all kinds in public life. . . ." *Gratia* also stood for lawful favors granted by the emperor or his delegate.[27]

The Roman legal system was honeycombed like the American with a vast array of privileges and exemptions—what tax system is tolerable without them? Do our universities, churches, unions, and governmental authorities regard their favored tax status as corrupt? Yet we are at least as egalitarian in our ideology as the emperors who in 372 proclaimed: "A favor (*beneficium*) for some is to the injury of the people." Certainly the artisans (including architects, carpenters, stonecutters, silversmiths, blacksmiths, fullers, potters, plumbers, and furriers), the bishops, the teachers of painting, the imperial officials, the physicians, the professors, and the secret service who were among the beneficiaries of Roman privilege or exemption did not think they were recipients of wrongful bounty. The emperors could declare, "A general regulation must be preferred to a special favor (*beneficium*)"; but special favors could be lawfully sought and were often lawfully granted.[28]

In 383, for example, an imperial decree abolished tax exemption for the imperial household and proclaimed, "Now the favor (*gratia*) of particular exemptions has been abolished"; the decree did not deny the legitimacy of the favor as it had existed. The emperors in fact went on granting special tax exemptions. Sixteen years later another decree declared, "Let favor (*gratia*) relieve no one." Uniformity of tax assessment was again announced as the rule; but the power and right of the emperor to relieve by favor went unconfined. In the same way the emperor had an unrestricted power of pardon. As a decree of 381 put it, a pardon did not "take away the infamy of the crime," but it did "make a favor of the penalty" (*poenae gratiam facit*), that is, it remitted punishment. The forgiveness granted was a legitimate favor. In a system of criminal justice whose hair-raising sanctions were not unlike the terrors of the Christian hell it would have been a cruel man who said that such favor had no place.[29]

Ambrose, an authority on the imperial court, praised the dead emperor Valentinian as "full of incorrupt favor" (*integrae plena gratiae*). He used the angel's words about Mary with the addition of *integer*—incorrupt—to offset any bad connotation of *gratia* and to stress that the favors the emperor had granted were wholesome and good. In his funeral oration on Theodosius I, Ambrose exclaimed, "How great, then, it is to set aside the terror of power and to prefer the sweetness of favor." When Theodosius had used the terror of power he had been a tyrant—Ambrose did not dwell on those episodes; Theodosius had repented. "And I," Ambrose declared, pausing and emphasizing the personal pronoun, "I loved the man of mercy." Ambrose would have banished *gratia* from the judge's chamber but when it took the form of executive clemency, *gratia* became "great." Its lovable dispenser could be formally compared to Christ: for, as Ambrose said, so Christ "preferred to come into this world as repurchaser, not judge." The emperor blessed like Mary, the emperor of sweet mercy, the Christ-like emperor, was the emperor dispensing favor.[30]

Openly the legal system acknowledged that the asking of favor from the emperor or his delegate was one task of a bishop. The imperial decree of 398, already cited, recognized the limited right of a cleric to intervene and appeal where a judge's "negligence or favoritism" threatened the safety of a defendant. Augustine understood this concession broadly. In his view it was as publicly accepted that a bishop should intercede for any convicted criminal as that a prosecutor should prosecute or a defender defend. In the letter which had provoked Augustine's discussion of payments to judges, Macedonius had not challenged Augustine's view of the law, but had written him, "I strongly doubt that this [duty] arises from religion." The Church itself permitted public penance only once. Why should a bishop approve crime by asking that it go unpunished? Augustine had replied with a massive defense of mercy. We should love evil men not for their evil but "because they are men." As a bishop he intervened not to approve their deeds but to spare their lives. In this he imitated God, who kept much for the Last Judgment. If the Church did not grant sinners a second chance publicly, God did. "Let us be imitators, as the Lord Christ exhorts us." We prayed to the Father to forgive us as we forgave others. Should we not forgive criminals and show them mercy? Jesus himself was an intercessor for the woman taken in adultery. She was guilty, but he successfully intervened on her behalf by reminding her judges of their own sins. Could not a Catholic bishop follow him by reminding a Roman governor of his sins?[31]

When in the Pelagian controversy Augustine's devotion to "Christ's favor," as he was to call it, and his opposition to "the enemies of favor" (hostes gratiae), as he was to call them, appear extraordinarily theoretical, his personal dedication to obtaining favor for convicted criminals cannot be neglected. For him as for Pelagius, gratia could be corrupt. Favor could be bought, the consequence and the sign of a bribe. But in his own experience there was also the gratia that saved men's heads from the ax.[32]

The Sale of Gratia. Favoritism was closely connected with, if not always the same as, favor that was bought. The character of purchased favor was raised in an ecclesial context where the gratia which was the object of barter was specifically God's—the gratia which it was believed he bestowed at ordination on one ordained a priest or bishop. As the underground and persecuted Church became in the early fourth century the tolerated Church and then, in time, the official religion of the empire, the use of money to obtain a bishopric became an observable problem. Implicit in the practice—not at first articulated—was the question whether money was being used to buy God's gratia.[33]

By the latter part of the fourth century there was already in parts of the

East an established custom of bishops' taking money from those they ordained, together with criticism of the custom, and a developing defense of its legitimacy. Basil's *Moralia*, a collection of New Testament teachings, delivered the critique. Rule 58 declared, "It must not be thought that the favor (*charis*) of God can be bought by money or by any art." Basil buttressed the flat declaration by citations of Peter's rebuke of Simon Magician and Christ's words, "The favor (*charis*) you have received freely, give freely." On becoming bishop of Caesarea in 370, Basil wrote his suffragans that he had heard that "some of you receive money from those who are ordained and cover it in the name of piety." Bishops of this kind had forgotten the words addressed to other purchasers of a share in the Holy Spirit, "You and your money go to perdition." The sellers were worse than the purchasers. They introduced their petty commerce into the Church which held a different kind of deposit—the body and blood of Christ. Contrary to Christ's words, they sold for a price what they had received gratis. They put forward a distinction that was no defense. There was no sin, they said, because unlike Simon Magician the donors did not offer money in return for God's favor; they gave only after ordination. "But," Basil insisted, "taking is always taking." Accordingly the recipients would be deprived of God's favor (*charis*) as if they had sold themselves to Satan. In Basil's implication their case was that of Judas. Contemporaneously, the *Apostolic Canons*, a pseudonymous collection, expressed the same doctrine in the name of the Apostle Peter: Purchaser and seller of God's favor were to be cut off from communion "as Simon Magician was cut off by me, Peter."[34]

The rule was clearer than its enforcement. John Chrysostom, writing at Antioch in the 380s, observed, "There are many who snatch the priesthood with money; and they have no one who rebukes them, nor do they hear what Simon Magician once heard from Peter." John supposed that they would be punished by God.[35] Later, in 400, now bishop of Constantinople, he was himself called to act against the practice. The account of what he did comes from one of his partisans, purportedly an eyewitness; it is intended to refute the bishop of Alexandria's charge that John acted arbitrarily and illegally; and it must be discounted for bias. But it is good testimony to contemporary problems and standards.

At a gathering of twenty-two bishops in Constantinople, Eusebius of Valentinopolis suddenly charged his metropolitan, Antoninus of Ephesus, with seven offenses, including the custom of selling episcopal ordinations "on the basis of the revenue." John tried to discourage Eusebius from pressing the case. Eusebius persisted, pointing out that Antoninus and five bishops who had paid him were present. All the accused denied the charges. Reluctantly, John consented to an investigation by three bishops. Antoninus bought off Eusebius, witnesses could not be found, the investigation stalled. Antoninus then died, and in 401 the clergy of Ephesus invited John to come and see for himself the state of their Church, despoiled by Arian heretics and by Catholics lusting for money and power. John came and presided over a synod called to choose the new bishop. The accusations against the dead Antoninus were renewed. Witnesses now appeared—priests, laymen, women—who testified to the pledges they had made (presumably on behalf of candidates for the episcopacy). Six bishops who were implicated defended themselves: "We thought," they said, "that it was customary." If their practice was right, they asked to be kept in the ministry. If it was wrong, they wanted their money back. John persuaded the synod to order the heirs of Antoninus to pay back what he had taken. The bishops were deposed.[36]

The story catches nicely the state of doctrine and enforcement in the East at the end of the fourth century—an entrenched local custom of taking money by a metropolitan from bishops; high doctrinal objections; hesitation as to how hard the sellers should be pursued; doubt as to how much the buyers should be made to suffer. The reciprocity actually enforced was that of Nippur and Nuzi. Nothing having been conveyed by the money taken, the money has to be returned.

The scriptural passages evoked in the East to condemn purchased favor were evoked again in the West and added to. Ambrose, commenting on the Gospel, brought to mind Gehazi who sought to make money out of Naaman. The leprosy he contracted was the sign of the stain spread on the soul by money evilly acquired. The sale of holy orders not only resembled the attempt of Simon Magician and not only violated the precept of the Lord, "You have taken freely. Give freely" (Mt 10:8): the sellers were like those who sold doves in the Temple and were ejected by Christ. They, too, had "marketed the favor (*gratia*) of the Holy Spirit." Jerome extended the comparison. The money-changers selling doves were like those who now sat as bishops, priests and teachers "selling the gifts of the Holy Spirit." What was taken gratis must be given gratis, except for an interesting qualification which the Lord had appended: "The laborer is worthy of his food" (Mt 10:10). You could take what was necessary for food and clothing. Only the sale of the Spirit was condemned. Augustine added, "The Lord expelled from the Temple those who sold doves. But the dove signifies the Holy Spirit. Simon, therefore, wanted to buy the Dove and to sell the Dove." The scriptural circle was complete. The express teaching of Christ, Peter's condemnation of the would-be purchaser, Christ's expulsion of the dove-sellers stood arrayed to reject traffic in the favor given freely by God.[37]

The Creator's Impartial Choice. God's favor could not be bought—common ground of the Catholics and the Pelagians. But why could it not be bought? The fundamental answer to this question, as it emerged in conflict with Pelagius, was that no human action could compel God's response. The manipulation of God which Simon Magician and his imitators failed to achieve was only a special case of a general truth. Nothing man could do required God to reciprocate.

Most of the New Testament did not confront head-on the relation of God's merciful choosing to his impartial justice. Paul, pondering God's choice of the Jews and God's offer to the Gentiles, took up the issue in a letter to the Christian (largely Jewish Christian) community at Rome, a letter which was to be the source of so many inspirations, controversies, and agonies for later believers. In it Paul softened the tension between justice and mercy by sketching what was, in effect, a three-stage scenario of action: judgment, mercy, judgment. Man first was justly condemned for Adam's sin. Second, the "gift in favor (*dorea en chariti*) in the one man Jesus Christ" canceled Adam's sin and won man's "acquittal" from the first judgment (Rom 5:15–16). Finally, the Day will come when man will stand for judgment again in "God's court" (Rom 14:10). Stretching out the divine action over these stages permitted a rhythm like that of justice on earth in the empire where amnesty could follow conviction, and a new conviction could follow upon pardon.

Having reduced the conflict by postulating a three-part time frame, Paul intensified it to the breaking point by introducing a divine perspective on time which included divine omniscience as to the fate of his creatures. God "knew his own before they ever were." These "He chose, and called, and justified" (Rom 8:30). But if He knew in advance who would be justified, how was He just to those whom He did not choose? Paul provided no answer to that question except to ask another question, the most basic of all questions about reciprocity between God and man: "Who first gave to Him to be repaid?" (Rom 11:35).

The question shows meditation on the Book of Job and God's answer to Job out of the whirlwind in Job 41; the Latin Vulgate was to read Paul's answer back into Job 41:2. But Paul is more precise than Job, more focused on the fundamental basis for an exchange. Creatures have nothing of their own by which to compel their Creator. With the possibility of real reciprocity denied, Paul has to exclaim, "How unsearchable his judgments, how untraceable his ways!" (Rom 11:33).

In that impenetrable mystery, the union of justice and mercy in an omniscient, omnipotent being might have been left to rest. It was no more and no less a contradiction, paradox, or problem than a Repurchaser-Judge, and it no more or less risked practical misapplication in human affairs than a Judge who took offerings. But as the controversy over original sin and infant baptism took shape and developed between Pelagius and Augustine, Pelagius insisted on the irreconcilability of divine justice and divine favor. Julian of Eclanum quoted Job 41:2 without finding in it the decisive message Paul had discovered. For Pelagius, Job was not the man humbled by the voice from the whirlwind, but a man of strenuous personal virtue, "that most famous athlete of God."[38]

God, the Pelagians said, cannot be the God of Augustine's African theology. God would be "a taker-up of persons" if "He has mercy on whom he wills, without any preceding merits." "It is unjust," they said, "in one and the same bad case to free this man and punish that one." God, they reiterated, is a "taker-up of persons when in one and the same case his mercy falls on some."

The strength and popularity of the Pelagians' argument rested on legal analogy. The force of their argument depended on how deeply and how comprehensively the Creator's relation to his creatures was taken to be that of Judge and defendants. In the view of Pelagius, God is the Judge; all mankind is on trial; for everyone it is "one and the same case;" it is a bad case for all; and a just judge will not prefer one doomed defendant to another.[39]

Answering, Augustine was bound by the same conception of impartial justice. He could not admit that God was guilty of discrimination as a judge. All of us were condemned. The act that freed some was gratuitous, yet it was not a discrimination based on the personal characteristics of those freed. There was "no taking up of persons where one and the same mass of condemnation and offense is involved, so that he who is freed learns from the non-freed that punishment would be appropriate for him too, unless favor had aided; but if it is favor surely it is not given in return for any merits but granted by gratuitous goodness."[40] Favor itself created the discrimination. God's *gratia* was not a response or a reciprocation. It was a free choice by the Creator. It was—Augustine himself did not adopt the analogy—like the act of the emperor giving pardon. Like any lawful favor it was the exercise of a prerogative that co-existed with, and exceeded, justice.

The perspective Paul, and Augustine following Paul, adopted was that of the Creator, owing nothing to anyone, acting as He chose. Whenever the perspective shifted to that of human beings contending for salvation, the Pauline pose appeared intolerable. Had not the Psalmist cried out, "The Lord shall repay me according to my justice, and according to the purity of my hands he shall repay me" (Ps 17:21)? When Julian insisted that there is no God if there is no justice, and that if there is justice and a God, He "restores to each his own without fraud, without favor," he stood with the Psalmist and with every human being who thinks that what he has done must count with a just Creator.[41]

In his commentary on Romans, Augustine acknowledged that *gratia* could be understood in a bad sense: "Not every favor is from God. Evil judges proffer favor when, enticed by some kind of covetousness or frightened by fear, they take up persons."[42] But God was not evil. Just as no gift could corrupt him, compelling his reciprocation, so no gift from him could be a discrimination influenced by the donee. "You," Augustine replied to Julian, "are he who denies that, where there is no taking up of persons, there is favor."[43] For Augustine, as for Paul, there was impartiality and favor, justice and *gratia*. The mystery that combined mercy and justice in God could not be abandoned. The Creator was a Father who made gratuitous choices and yet was fair.

The parable of the generous landowner was Augustine's apposite answer to Julian's impassioned plea: "Tell me, I ask you, how did he give so much to them who were one hour at work without favor? Did he perhaps abandon justice? Then restrain yourself. Assuredly divine justice defrauds no one. But to those not deserving it, it grants much favor."[44]

In power, the major theologians had set out an ethic explicitly excluding the sale of judgment; the Church had adopted an institutional posture against the purchase of ecclesiastical preferment. Incorporating the ideals of Hebrew prophets and Roman senators, the new ethic perpetuated the old tensions and added to them the two cosmic dramas of Redemption and Judgment. Standing at the confluence of Roman law and Jewish theology, of Greek political thinking and Christian eschatology, Augustine articulated the elements that were to form the Western paradigm of the Judge transcending any reciprocal tie to the litigants—the Judge uninfluenced by *munera*. The concept of the judge is central because of human anxiety about what happens after death. It is as Judge that, according to Christian belief, God is then to be encountered. It is this Judge, so firmly centered in Christian consciousness, who is seen as incorruptible.

Only a consciousness committed to the mystery of Christian particularism—that God chose this people, this virgin, these apostles, these converts, this Church—could have insisted so fiercely that God acts gratuitously. Only a consciousness committed to the requirements of an impartial judge could have felt so keenly the force of the cry that God is a just Judge. Only the mystery that the Judge is also the Repurchaser, the Redeemer, the Giver of himself could have made beliefs in impartiality and in favor bearable. Meditation on that mystery would suggest the great division between a gift and a bribe. Development of that distinction, however, was to be postponed in the next succeeding centuries by more elementary struggles.

4

"Lest Money Should Prevail at the Department..."

It happens that you are made a judge. You are not corrupted because you do not seek what is not your own. No one gives you a reward (*praemium*) and says, "Judge against my adversary.".... See what evil you will do for what is your property. Perhaps he who wants you to judge wrongly and issue a judgment for him against his adversary is a powerful man, and he is able to slander you so that you will lose what is your own. You note his power. You think of it. You think of your property which you have and love, which you have not possessed wrongly but have clung to wrongly.... You will judge wrongly, not when you seek what is another's, but when you keep your own.

Pressure, not profit, is what will influence an otherwise honest judge, according to Augustine preaching here on avarice.[1]

Two men bring a case before "God's slave" (a bishop). Each thinks his case is just—otherwise "he would not seek a judge." Each says, before the judge decides, "I embrace your judgment. Whatever you judge, heaven forbid that I should scorn it. What do you pronounce? Judge what you will, but judge." The judge is tempted. By what? By praise. He is loved by both. He wants to please both. But if he accepts the gift of praise, he loses the gift of office. Where must he look? To God. Looking at God, he will decide between the two. When he does, he will forfeit the love of the loser. The disappointed litigant will "turn blind eyes against the judge." He will "slander him as much as he can." What does the loser say? "'He wanted to please that man,' he says, 'he favors the rich man.' Or he says, 'He feared to offend him.'" In a word, "he accuses him as if he has taken a *munus*." God's slave has kept his eyes on the Lord. The unseeing eyes which Scripture ascribes to the corrupt judge have become the eyes of the disgruntled litigant crying out against the effect of favor and offerings.[2]

The vignette is painted by Augustine expounding Psalm 25 in the Latin Vulgate (Ps 26 in the New English Bible) at the line, "Their hands are full of *munera*." God's slave as bishop of Hippo Regius had had experience of the temptation and of the criticism; and he must have known also the temptation of the honest judge under pressure from the powerful and unscrupulous litigant. His experience of judging was neither slight nor casual. By public law a major function of a Catholic bishop was to judge, and Augustine was a bishop from 395 until his death in 430. The jurisdiction he exercised was not narrow and not wholly dependent on the parties. Legislation originating with Constantine had determined that a case brought before "episcopal judgment" could not be removed to an imperial court. Almost a century later, Honorius' decree of 408 specified that a bishop's judgment was "valid for all persons who consent to be heard by priests." By the terms of this decree, a bishop's decision was not like a mere arbiter's, enforceable only after application for an order of enforcement from the public courts; it was entitled to execution directly "through a public department staff." Submission to episcopal jurisdiction was also not entirely voluntary. By Honorius' decree of 399 for Africa, "an action involving matters of religion" must be conducted by bishops; and by his decree of 411, directed to Rome, clerics "must not be accused except before bishops." When Augustine spoke of the influences brought to bear upon a judge and the charges a judge must endure he spoke as a public official who had borne these burdens.[3] He was also to bear the burden of being a successful litigant.

Horses and Heirlooms.   "You talk wildly with women and with all the barrackroom boys and officers. Eighty or more horses, bred in almost every part of Africa, have recently been presented to them by your Alypius."[4] And, again: "Why have you rented crowds to stir up upheavals in Rome? Why from the proceeds of the poor have you, by Alypius, sent to the tribunes and centurions herds of horses bred in almost every part of Africa? Why with the offerings made you of the heirlooms of matrons have you corrupted the powers of the world so that the straw of public favor burned against us?"[5] The accuser is the young Pelagian leader Julian, bishop of Eclanum. The accused is Augustine, here charged along with the other African bishops from whose lands the horses have come. The price is eighty horses, plus heirlooms. The alleged go-between is Alypius, Augustine's old friend from the days before his conversion, now bishop of

Thagaste in Africa and the lawyer par excellence of the African hierarchy. The payees, at least broadly described, are members of the imperial military staff.

Relying on these allegations, one modern historian has suggested that a gift "was probably necessary to gain official attention for the plea." A second has concluded, "It is possible that the Africans had strengthened their intervention in a wider circle of the court by bribery." A third has gone further: "On one mission, Alypius had carried with him the promise of eighty Numidian stallions, fattened on the estates of the church, as *douceurs* for the cavalry-officers, whose views on grace had proved decisive." And again: "Alypius, distributing eighty stallions to the Imperial Court, was doing his best, as far as the means of the church of Africa allowed, to live down to the diplomatic methods used by Theophilus of Alexandria against John [Chrysostom]."[6]

Access payment, possible bribery, *douceurs* according to the modern writers, the horses and the heirlooms appear to have played a substantial part in the resolution of a great theological controversy. The premier moralist of the West is involved in their presentation, if the accusations are proved. The context of the accusations needs to be summarized. In 411, questions relating to Pelagius' position on divine favor had come to the attention of Marcellinus in Carthage. As an interested believer rather than as an imperial official he had consulted Augustine and had drawn from him the treatise *The Merits and Forgiveness of Sinners*, and, on pursuing his questions further, a second anti-Pelagian work, *Spirit and Letter*.[7] From this point on, Augustine took the lead in bringing the African bishops as a body to reject Pelagius and his followers. In 416 the rejection became formal in the African Church Councils of Carthage and Milevis. The African decisions were sent to Rome, to "the Apostolic See," recognized by the African Church as its fount, possessed of "greater favor," and recognized by imperial law as the norm of Catholic Christianity. Innocent I, bishop of Rome, in January 417 confirmed the African doctrine on God's favor and condemned Pelagius. But on Innocent's death two months later, his Greek successor, Zosimus, reopened the case and concluded from his own examination of Pelagius that he was no heretic. The Africans refused to be conciliated, and relations between the Apostolic See and Africa came to an impasse.[8]

The stalemate was broken by action with the emperor at Ravenna, and the probability is that the Pelagians initiated the action. What they wanted, according to Julian himself, were "judges"—that is, imperial judges—to "correct a record deformed by deliberate dishonesties."[9] No doubt they were following up their success with Zosimus, who, they could reasonably suppose, could not have been elected bishop of Rome without tacit approval from high authorities in Ravenna and must still stand high with his patrons at the imperial court.

Suddenly the Pelagians met a snag. Their request for imperial intervention backfired. A rescript from Ravenna on April 30, 418, denounced

Pelagius as a heretic, exiled him from Rome, and barred advocacy in his defense. Zosimus himself, with some delay, followed suit and condemned Pelagius again in the summer of 418. In less than a year the Pelagians had moved from triumph to defeat.[10]

What is not clear are the channels which the Africans used to win their stunning victory. There has been much guesswork by modern historians. The most powerful man at court, Constantius, had been a friend of the now dead Marcellinus. Was he appealed to? Constantius' wife, Galla Placidia, was a strong Catholic, with enough interest in ecclesial politics to take a hand the following year in a disputed election to the bishopric of Rome. At that time she wrote a letter addressed in common to Augustine, Alypius, and four other African bishops and a separate letter to the bishop of Carthage. The letters show her regarding the Africans as her natural clients; it is reasonable to infer that the relation antedated 419. Was she in mind when Julian accused Augustine of "talking wildly to women?" It is a plausible guess.[11]

What is known for certain as to contacts between Augustine and Ravenna is this: He had addressed several letters to a known Christian at court, Count Valerius, without getting an answer. Later in 418 or early 419 a bishop, Vindemialis, and a priest, Firmus, came to Hippo with word from Valerius.[12] Firmus spoke highly of Valerius' Catholic faith, conjugal chastity, and humble bearing in high office; he also reported that Valerius was a reader of Augustine. Responding to this report, Augustine acknowledged Valerius' part in combating the Pelagian heresy at Ravenna. "I am resisting these profane novelties by argument," Augustine wrote him. "You have efficaciously resisted them by governing and pursuing with power."[13] It is a reasonable inference that Firmus, who in late 417 had carried correspondence between Augustine and the Roman clergy concerning Pelagius, proceeded to Ravenna in 418 with at least one appeal by Augustine to Valerius. Nothing of this evidence shows any payment or gift, even to get attention.[14] Since the days of Donatus, the Africans had been dealing with Ravenna, and the reputation of high officials like Valerius with a taste for theology was well known to them. Julian, the accuser himself, doubted that Valerius helped Augustine, professed to think well of him, and honorably commemorated his name in his own book.[15] There is no suggestion by Julian that Valerius was among the tribunes and centurions he charged were paid off. Yet Valerius is the only official with whom Augustine is known to have been in contact before the imperial rescript of April 30, 418, against Pelagius.

Julian's accusations appear to bear on a later stage of events—"appear," because no date is given yet they apply to Alypius, who is known to have been in Ravenna in the spring of 419 on a mission from Augustine. The mission involved the delivery of Augustine's latest anti-Pelagian tract, dedicated to Valerius in recognition of his exemplary marriage and his earlier service against the Pelagians.[16] Delivering the tract, Alypius is for Julian "the slave boy of sinners." But Julian does not say Alypius gave either horses or heirlooms to Valerius; the recipients are nameless others buttered up at the same time. Whatever he did, Alypius' visit was followed by a second stunning African triumph. The imperial proscription of Pelagius and Pelagians was extended from Rome to the entire empire.[17] Julian left Italy to go into exile in Greece. He advanced his charges against Augustine at a distance of time and space from the events in Ravenna.

Augustine was for Julian "the African," a description that, employed by a native of Italy, could only have been intended to convey contempt. Augustine was also known to Julian as "the asses' advocate"—no need to underline the bitterness of this description.[18] A loser and a bitter loser—what is the worth of his charges unsupported by any scrap of documentation? The charges, if true, affected not only Augustine but also Alypius, his former student, his lifelong friend, an official of "amazing" integrity, commemorated as "the brother of my heart."[19]

Julian's allegations are repeated by Augustine and in the same breath answered. They are denied. When he restates them the first time in the passage on the barrackroom boys and horses, Augustine adds, "Either you slander with a lie or you do not know what you are talking about. Either, therefore, you are a liar or what you say you say rashly. What is worse than you if you yourself invented these things? What is stupider than you if you believed those who invented them?"[20]

The second time Augustine reports Julian's charge—two books later in the same tract—he writes, "The crimes which you object against us are as false as the teachings you imagine for yourselves. But say as much evil as you lyingly can against us defending against you the Christian and Catholic faith. How difficult is it to return such maledictions to you rather than to believe the Gospel and rejoice, because by these most false maledictions of yours our reward shall be increased in heaven."[21]

Augustine's denials could not be clearer, nor more compelling. He takes the accusation of making a payoff hard. He brands the charge a malicious invention of Julian or his sources. He is willing to have his lot in heaven improved by suffering such malice to be spoken of him, as Matthew 5: 11–12 had foretold would be spoken of the followers of Christ. Augustine would have to be a man of brazen immorality to be guilty of the charge, repeat it in order to deny it, and claim merit with God as one meekly suffering slander. Impossible to believe in his general honesty and not feel the force of his denials.

Even without these denials, Julian's allegations would be in the category of rumor and loose talk by a loser. Do they show the "probable" necessity of an access gift? That is not their thrust. Do they show that bribery was "possible" by the Africans? No more than if they had not been made—bribery is always "possible." Here the possibility of bribery is met by Augustine's denial. If veracity in a man known to prize the truth is to be respected although the man is dead, no bribe was given. No evidence whatsoever supports the charge.

The Context of Suspicion.   That bribery should be common enough to be suspected and that the charge of bribery is serious enough to be damaging—these are the twin inferences to be drawn from Augustine's sermon-stories and Julian's accusations against him, and again from Augustine's involvement in an event at Cirta. In 409, Faventius, a tenant on a large estate, became involved in a legal quarrel with the estate owner. He sought refuge with Augustine in Hippo. His powerful opponent simply had him picked up by officers, held incommunicado, and then whisked off to Cirta to be tried before a tribunal there. The law was flouted in the hustling of Faventius out of town. Augustine wrote Fortunatus, bishop of Cirta, to intercede with Generosus, the imperial representative, to delay the case as permitted by law and let Augustine have time to work out a friendly settlement. "The fear is," Augustine remarks, "that perhaps he will suffer some evil when he is produced before the consular department—since he has a case with a very wealthy man—even though the integrity of the judge is spoken of as famous. Lest, however, money should prevail at the department . . . ," and Augustine goes on to instruct Fortunatus to give Generosus the letter he has sent him directly. A short note is enclosed to "The Excellent Lord, Deservedly and Honorably Famous, His Dearest Brother Generosus," who, Augustine tells him, "will surely do what befits not only a true and upright but Christian judge."[22]

Clearly, corruption is a fear when your opponent is rich and unscrupulous enough to shanghai you. Clearly, Augustine is fighting threatened corruption with a counterforce, his circumspect intimation to Generosus that his staff ("the department") is under observation. Augustine's intervention is at once testimony to the likelihood of bribery in the proconsular court in such circumstances and testimony to the belief or hope that public opinion or a bishop's nudge will keep the judge upright. It is also evidence of the etiquette to be observed. Judges are not to be accused to their face. If corruption exists, it is to be blamed on the office staff.

In ancient Israel and Rome the judge had appeared as a stand-in for the divine, and corruption was a blinding of the representative of the divine. While this belief also animates the Christian view of the judge, by the fourth century it is commonly realized that in the imperial bureaucracy the judge is in fact highly dependent on his *officium*—his "office staff" or more simply "department," in the sense that a government administrator refers to his associates and secretaries as his department. Partly as a matter of etiquette, partly as a matter of realistic strategy, efforts against corruption focus on "the department."

The starting point of law against corruption was the ancient law of the Inquiry as to Reclaimables (*Repetundae*), the law intended to protect the provincials. This had been expanded by Julius Caesar in the *lex Iuliana* of 49 B.C., and the *lex Iuliana* had been interpreted by the jurists of the third century A.D. to include taking money to put a man in chains or to take off chains; to give a judgment or not give a judgment; to engage a public contractor or to remit a tax; in a word, "to do more or do less than is required in the exercise of office."

Magistrates might legally accept gifts up to 100 goldpieces in one year. Anything beyond was "filth" (*sordes*). The corrupt judge "made the case his own." In Papinian's summary, the crime of *repetundae* was committed "whenever money is taken and a publicly-conferred duty is violated." These later jurists said what Cicero had assumed to be the law in 70 B.C. when he had prosecuted Hog for similar deeds.

Punishment for violating the *repetundae* law was "exile or something harsher." If an official took money to put a man to death, the penalty was capital. Alternatively the perpetrator could be deported to an island, "as many have been punished," according to the jurist Macer. Petty judges found "corrupted by money" were to be either suspended or exiled. There was also, according to Ulpian, a distinct crime of *concussio*—"shakedown" or "extortion"—committed by an official pretending to have an order against a subject and using it to obtain money from him. The crime, Macer added, could be prosecuted under the Cornelian law on homicide if the shakedown was based on a capital accusation against an innocent man.

These surviving fragments of the jurists suggest a world in which rude abuse of the law was familiar, where corruption was a hazard, and where sanctions at least sometimes were invoked. It was also a world in which the jurists themselves were not immune from raw violence. Papinian (d. 203), and Ulpian (d. 223), each the praetorian prefect, the highest legal officer of the empire, died by murder. The sway of law was precarious yet precious and defended by the formal prohibition of accepting payment for the exercise of office.[23]

Imperial response to the problems of corruption may be profitably compared to American legal responses between 1940 and 1975 to air pollution caused by automobiles. Pollution control is control of a physically measurable phenomenon, the emission of toxic substances into the atmosphere, but what counts as "pollution" has a strong symbolic component, and what risks of pollution are acceptable depend on changeable political evaluations. Bribery control is control of a physically observable phenomenon, the payment of money to officials, but what payments are to count as bribes depends on the symbolic function of the official, and what risks of bribery are acceptable depends on political assessments. American air pollution measures have been described as "limited, local measures addressed to specific, readily identifiable problems," consisting in "band-aid solutions," avoiding any radical attack on the roots. The scope and vigor of these incremental measures constantly "escalated" but were always "too little and too late." The reasons for this pattern have been hypothesized to be two: (1) "great uncertainty about the origins and harmfulness of pollution," and (2) the collective nature of environmental quality which makes individuals see the cost of pollution control as greater than the benefit they receive. *Mutatis mutandis*, the pattern recalls the imperial edicts addressed to particular abuses or particular provinces with escalating scope and vigor. For particular individuals the cost of curbing corruption appeared greater than the benefit they would get from a decrease in corruption. As to uncertainty, although neither the emperors nor the moralists were uncertain that corruption was harmful, there was great uncertainty as to what forms of reciprocation with officials should be treated as corrupt—for example, the sale of the lesser public offices was common and a gray zone existed as to the offices that could be sold. Incremental increases in control, with legal draftsmen responding to crises and learning by blunder—these features of the American experience were anticipated by the Roman.[24]

Heirs of Cicero, Caesar, and the jurists, the fourth-century emperors legislated at least a dozen times between A.D. 316 and 398 against judicial corruption. The most important decree is Constantine's of 331, addressed from Constantinople to "the Provincials." Governors are told to conduct trials in public. They shall not "hide themselves in their private council chambers." They shall not judge civil cases "only at a price." Bailiffs, court clerks, centurions on court duty, the chief of the department and his assistants—all these bureaucratic categories are enumerated; and payments to any of them to obtain a hearing are made criminal. Other decrees are directed against government accountants, both military and civilian, who cover up fraud. Targeting the accountants, the court personnel, and the office staff, the legislator seeks to put his hand on the key professionals. Not in Egypt, not in Mesopotamia, not in Israel, not in the Roman Republic is there any law like Constantine's specifically condemning the oldest threat to judicial integrity, the taking of an access payment.[25]

The outright sale of judgment is heavily condemned. Capital punishment is threatened the judge who even in private litigation is paid by one side. Financial liability that descends to his heirs is imposed. Provincials are invited to inform the emperor of abuses. Clerics are given official standing to complain. Investigation is promised. Opportunities for corruption—appeals, secret meetings, and, above all, access payments—are identified and condemned.[26]

The fourth-century chronicler most interested in criminal trials, Ammianus Marcellus, notes the presence of corrupted judges on seven principal occasions in the fourteen years between 354 and 369. Sometimes an observer of the scene, sometimes the reteller of well-authenticated gossip, Ammianus is always shrewd and usually biased, and he is fond of stories of cruelty and scandal. Like a daily newspaper, he gives evidence of what was popularly believed. In only two instances—that of Constantine's nephew Gallus Caesar and that of state secretary Paulus—does he report retribution overtaking the principal offenders and then not precisely for corruption. Their corrupt reputation, however, is a factor in the fate of execution which they ultimately suffer. The picture Ammianus conveys is remarkably like that of Rome in Cicero's day. Judicial corruption is a crime. Sanction for it, if applied at all, is applied indirectly through punishment for some other offense.[27]

A judge who made "the case his own" could be sued for restitution by the aggrieved litigant; but there are no reported instances in law or literature of such a suit.[28] There is even significant negative evidence that suits were at all usual. Analyzing the obligation to restore ill-gotten money in the letter to Macedonius, Augustine observes, "He who purchases a just judgment usually seeks to recover the money as if it had been wrongly taken from him, for judgment should not be for sale; but he who gives for an unjust judgment would like to recover it except he is afraid or ashamed that he bought."[29] Speaking of what is usual (*solere*), Augustine does not even mention suit by the litigant victimized by a bribe. It may be inferred that restitution to the victim was rare. What seems capable of recovery is a payment for a "just judgment," that is, a payment extorted by the judge for doing justice. Augustine does not appear to regard such extortion and such efforts at redress as unusual. He may even, as suggested in Chapter 3, think Macedonius not beyond the obligation to make restitution himself.

Augustine speaks out of an African context; he had also known Milan. His distinction between types of payment to a judge should be supplemented by his observations on payments to court officers. Constantine in his decree of 331 had treated court access payments comprehensively as extortion. Draconian legislation addressed to Illyricum about 370 banned under pain of capital punishment even voluntary "guest gifts or little offerings" to the chief of the department staff and to those serving the governor; that the presents were customary was to be no defense.[30] But Augustine, writing Macedonius in 413, makes reference to no legislation and remarks that lower court officials commonly receive payments from both sides. What they extort immoderately, he observes, can be recaptured in an action for restitution. What they take "by tolerable custom" is not normally sought back. Indeed, "we"—he means himself and other dispassionate citizens—"disapprove more of those who seek its recovery than of those who took it by custom." Reason is given for this tolerance: many officials, "necessary to human affairs, are held, even against their will, by such advantages." The recipients, in other words, are doing work essential to the functioning of the government; they are held, that is, bound by the prevailing custom. If they seek to live a more perfect life, they should give what they have gotten to the poor. They are, however, under no obligation to return it as though it had been extorted from the payors.[31]

This highly nuanced judgment, introduced into a discussion of criminal justice, shows some distaste for what amounts to tipping the staff and hints at the need which the staff may have for the tips. To call such baksheesh corrupt would be to confuse a tip and a bribe: clearly such customs do not prevail without the tacit acquiescence of superiors willing to have subordinates supplement their salary. Legislation might lump all payments together. Custom was more discriminating.

The lack of evidence for the enforcement of sanctions, Ammianus' stories of major payoffs, the imperial decrees, Faventius, and Augustine's fear of corruption in the consular court at Cirta, the popularity of the cry of corruption among losing litigants whether they were Pelagians at Ravenna or suitors in an episcopal court, the custom of tips to court employees—all may converge to a conclusion: this was a judicial system in which bribery ruled; judgment was merely a public ware. Such a conclusion would chime with a conclusion Roman writers had been reaching since the first century A.D.

Martial observes, "The judge asks and the advocate asks"; a litigant might as well pay his opponent and forget about litigating. In Petronius' *Satyricon* the question is put, "What do the laws do where only money rules?" Nowadays, the poem maintains, "judgment is nothing except public merchandise." Apuleius recalls the story of Paris corrupted by the golden apple and says, since the original judgment between gods and men was sold by the judge for his own profit, it is no surprise that "now so many judges market their own decisions for a price."[32] The negative assessments made by poets and satirists and storytellers show that, from the beginning of the empire, popular and sophisticated belief held that judges were corrupt. The fourth-century evidence appears merely to confirm the long-standing belief.

Modern historians of the late Empire concur. "Everyone steals. . . . Functionaries traffic in judicial hearings," writes a French authority. "The whole of the Roman Empire lived in the blind lust for gold. . . . Nothing could be done without baksheesh," declares a Hungarian historian. "The age was one of venal and corrupt judges and judges' staffs," exclaims an American expert; the "corruption and injustice of the times" were "ubiquitous." The most recent English analyst of Roman administration joins in: "[J]udicial corruption was normal and systematic in the provincial courts." Provincial governors were "almost invariably venal." Despite the "excellence" of Roman law, the judges who applied it "were as a rule venal." Judicial corruption was "an endemic evil."[33]

The Working of Justice.   Ancient critics, popular suspicion, and modern assessment agree. We are back in seventh-century B.C. Jerusalem—all the princes take *shoḥadh*. We are back in the late Republic, Romulus' refuse. Where, however, is hard evidence for the poets' belief that corruption was universal or the historians' belief that it was systematic? The lack of evidence of enforcement of sanctions has been mentioned. We have found a similar lack of evidence of enforcement in Egypt and Israel and Republican Rome. We can infer in each case that the antibribery ethic was weak but we are not given quantitative information on the extent of corruption.

Next, there are stories like Ammianus' of payoffs. All, or nearly all, are hearsay; Ammianus did not participate in the payments; he retells what was believed. Such chroniclers' accounts merge with the popular cry of corruption by losers and the prudent fear of a knowledgeable man like Augustine—they convey suspicion. Is suspicion evidence?

"The hands of bailiffs shall instantly stop their rapacity. They shall stop. If after due warning they do not stop, they shall be cut off by the sword."[34] These are the opening words of Constantine's comprehensive decree of 331 to the Provincials against access payments. Horrendous activity, it is implied, is going on everywhere. It is prohibited, but not merely prohibited; it is categorized morally in a strongly derogatory way. The tone of command is peremptory; it conveys desperate urgency. The sanction is savage and, to modern minds, disproportionate. The agency of punishment is vague; "the sword" is supposed to fall as though the governor and his staff, the subjects of the legislation, did not wield it. Desperate, disproportionate, and vague, legislation in this style has been a principal reason why generations of historians have held that the courts of the later Roman Empire were normally corrupt.[35]

But of course legislation of this kind is no more than an accusation. Bailiffs, Constantine's decree says, have been taking money from litigants. Who, how much, where? We are not told. As a charge of corruption the decree is far less precise than Cicero's charges against Hog, and it is undocumented. Imperial legislation does not indicate the information on which it was based.

Even if the emperors had entirely trustworthy informants and were legislating for conditions they knew to exist in large portions of their domain, what was asserted as a justificatory fact in legislation would have to be examined with a cautious sense of probable political motivations at work. The central authorities had reason to make themselves look good and to put blame, if blame there was to be, on their subordinates. The Edwardian historian Dill derived from his reading of the Theodosian Code the impression "that fraud and greed are everywhere triumphant," but he cannot help feeling that the central authority was keenly alive to its duties: "Almost every part of the Code bears witness to the indignant energy with which the Emperor and his Council strove to check the anarchy of the provincial administration."[36] What more could a self-serving bureaucracy want than the picture of rampant evil being combated by a stern and compassionate emperor?

The sources feeding the emperor's mind must often have been uninformed or colored by personal or political prejudice. The emperors' decrees were normally addressed not at large but to particular officials concerned with particular problems and areas. The difficulty of using the decrees to draw sure inferences about actual and universal corruption is clear. The difficulty is exacerbated by the style of the draftsmen. Hectoring, blustering, bullying, they are also determinedly didactic, and their didacticism often operates by denunciation. The style does not favor cool assessment of actual realities. Its modern counterpart is a Maoist communiqué on the corruptions of the running dogs of imperialism—we are not well informed on how many running dogs there are or in what their corruption consists.

A final obstacle to firm inference from the legislation is the punishment prescribed. When torture which can cripple and penalties which include death are laid down, the modern reader is inclined to suppose that a mighty evil is being assailed. The emperors, however, relied on cruel punishments for a multitude of offenses. Their methods and sanctions reflect insensitivity to individual suffering more than they establish the enormity of the crimes denounced.

Peter Brown, describing the abundance of accusations of sorcery in the fourth-century Empire, doubts that there was "any absolute increase in fear of sorcery or in sorcery practices." Rather, accusations abound because of ambiguity, tension, and conflict in the social structure. There is a clash between articulate power, authority vested in precise persons, success gained by recognized channels on the one hand, and on the other, inarticulate power, "the disturbing intangibles of social life, the imponderable advantages of certain groups, personal skills that succeed in a way that is unacceptable or difficult to understand." On the one hand, there is a highly hierarchical, caste-oriented society, its richest class a landowning aristocracy; on the other, a bureaucracy conducive to social mobility, infiltrated by a Christianity which "had seeped triumphantly upwards, just at this time, from the lower-middle classes into a court aristocracy of *parvenues*." Where articulate and inarticulate power clash it is easy for the upholder of recognized authority to blame the sorcerer, the man who has "brought in the unseen to redress the balance of the seen." His accusers are those committed to an image of society "in which everything that happens, happens through *articulate* channels only." Rhetoricians—men successful through a personal skill—are particularly subject to charges of sorcery, as the career of Libanus of Antioch illustrates. Pagans associated with the old aristocracy are particularly prone to give currency to sorcery charges. Ammianus is a great supplier of them. And there are real sorcerers, that is, actual practitioners of the art. However doubtful we may be of the efficacy of the means they used, there did exist persons who regularly resorted to black acts to affect results.[37]

Ambiguity, tension, conflict can, no doubt, be found in every society if one probes far. These broad social factors should be seen as contributing to the climate in which the witchcraft accusations flourished without being the sole causes of their popularity and without determining that the suspicions of the day take shape in charges of witchcraft.

In the fourth-century Empire fear of bribery was as rational as fear of sorcery, and in the eyes of those concerned with government, bribery was as good an explanation for success as reference to the occult. The same ambiguity, tension, and conflict that account for the climate in which accusations of witchcraft abound also provide the climate in which accusations of bribery occur. In these accusations, too, articulate power affirms the single image of society. The briber is the one who has brought in the unseen to redress the balance of the seen. The briber is the one whose personal skills have succeeded in ways that are unacceptable or difficult to understand. And beyond argument, there are real practitioners of bribery.

That all the accusations and suspicions could flourish without some experience of corruption in practice is hard to believe. That a society would have continued to rely so heavily on machinery that was totally corrupt is almost equally incredible. That the profession of advocacy did not wither offers a measure of evidence counter to popular suspicion and the popular conclusions. Ammianus, an old army officer, thought advocacy an art "hateful to a good man," and his caricature of lawyers is classic. In his long and amusing catalogue of their failings he notes that these miserable parasites sometimes have to deal with judges who bought their offices with "heavy cash" and who accordingly "shake out booty from other men's bosoms." Yet even Ammianus says these judges are met with only "sometimes." He does not see lawyers as merely bagmen for the judges. If they lose, almost all litigants blame not their judges but their lawyers—a quaint custom if in fact winning depends on paying the judge.[38]

Augustine, much more sympathetic to the legal profession than Ammianus, discusses lawyers in the letter to Macedonius. Championing his own role as intervenor for mercy, he had, earlier in his letter, reminded Macedonius of the need for professional roles in a trial: Macedonius himself, he observed, had once been a defense lawyer whose work was "to mitigate or cover up crimes." As Augustine considers the matter further, he wonders if role is sufficient excuse for injustice. Suppose an advocate who has "acted against the truth, assisted injustice, deceived the judge, oppressed a just cause, won by falsity. . . . A multitude of very respectable and very learned men are seen to carry on only with impunity but with renown." Their life is unjust and, if they are to repent, they must return what they received for their injustice. In this catalogue of unjust acts, bribegiving is not mentioned. In this sharp indictment of a crowd of criminal lawyers, forensic battles are seen as decided by evidence, sometimes by false evidence. Augustine does not suggest that trials are usually decided by money paid the judge.[39]

Giving a sermon on adultery, Augustine recalls a case that had happened seventy years ago in Antioch under Acindinus, praetorian prefect in 338–340: A certain man owed one gold pound to the treasury and had not paid. Acindinus, exercising arbitrary authority, announced the debtor would die if by a fixed date the gold was not forthcoming. The man had a particularly good-looking wife. A rich admirer of hers told her he would pay the fine if she would sleep with him. She consulted her husband, who told her to go ahead. She went to the rich man's house and carried out her part, but he substituted earth for gold in the package he gave her. When she discovered she was cheated, she denounced the cheat to Acindinus. The prefect extracted the gold for the treasury from the rich delinquent and awarded the woman the portion of his land from which the earth had been taken. Augustine's focus is on marital chastity, not bribery; the story itself shows the prefect as arbitrary but honest. There is not the slightest suggestion that the victim has to pay to get her case heard or her complaint answered. The story is valuable in the assumption it conveys, that a Roman judge will be interested in the truth and will not have to be moved by money.[40]

The same assumption underlies Augustine's sermon on the judge under pressure from a rich man, his sermon against favoritism to the poor (see

Chapter 3 above), and his exposition of the Psalm on those "whose right hands are filled with offerings." That the well-meaning judge is more open to pressure than to money is the theme of the sermon on the judge's temptations. The offerings which distort judgment are not cash but praise and threats of slander. That the ordinary Christian judge will be more inclined to favor the poor than to help the rich is the point of the homily on evenhandedness. Corruption does not seem "systematic" or "endemic" in the views which Augustine, writing as a moralist, provides. Only once, at Cirta, is he concerned "lest money prevail at the department."

What bureaucrats receive by "tolerable custom"—to use Augustine's words—does not fall within the class of gifts condemned as bribes. Poorly paid, dependent on fees and gifts to support themselves—at least to support themselves in a fashion society thought appropriate—they could not have thought of what they were given as morally evil. They had bought their offices—often borrowing to buy them—or inherited them. They were sometimes pluralists, holding a variety of offices. Often enough they carried out their duties by delegates. A bureaucracy whose only requirement for entry was literacy could not place a large premium on special skills, even though the rhetoric of the day praised the industrious and faithful officeholder. A high degree of elitism, a sense of governmental purpose and of the honor of a technocratic corps that would have rejected offerings from those it dealt with, did not exist.[41]

Judges were a different matter. They were not a professional class, learned in the law, educated in the edicts, promoted on merit to higher and higher judicial place. They were not even exclusively judges. Like other "judges" of the Ancient World they were not specialists but rulers and administrators with much else to do and to decide. Yet as guardians of justice they were judged by a higher standard.

Ammianus actually lists a substantial number of judges he characterizes as just. His praise is not more certainly deserved than his blame; but it shows how mixed the reality is for him. Just judges in his opinion include Leontius, prefect of Rome in 355; Apronianus, prefect in 364; Symmachus, also prefect in 364; Viventius, prefect in 366; Praetextatus, prefect in 367; and Olybrius, prefect in 368; also Liberius, bishop of Rome, spirited off by the emperor in 355 because he would not condemn Athanasius without a hearing; also Mavortius and Ursulus, respectively praetorian prefect and count of the largesses, "of one heart in their love of the right and the just," who condemned certain false informers to death in 356; also Constantius' head eunuch, the Armenian Eutherius, an exception to his class in "never having burned to increase his wealth"; also Julian when he served as ruler of Gaul in 359 and later when he became emperor in 362. Valentinian is presented as a cruel and arbitrary emperor, but not corrupt. Ursicinus, the general on whose staff Ammianus served for years, is shown as surrounded by corrupt judges in the Antioch treason trials of 354 and cooperating with them under pressure, but as a man of integrity when he conducted the treason trials in Cologne in 356. Particularly striking is the story of Romanus, a negligent commander in Africa, who corrupts the state secretary sent to investigate him with the result that it is his accusers who are savagely punished; but ultimately, the accusers who survive are vindicated by the proconsul Hesperius and his deputy Flavianus, "whose justice was most even."[42] Ammianus' own liberal exposure to palace intrigue, tyrannical princes, and corrupt judges was not enough to extinguish a sense that justice on occasion prevailed. When Gallus Caesar meets his end, Ammianus sees it as "the work of Adrastia or Nemesis, who, the old theologians say, is the daughter of Justice." The fraud of Romanus is revealed because "the vigilant eternal Eye of Justice" does not close.[43] It is, in this case, honest provincial rulers who are its agents. The daughter of Justice works "sometimes—would it were always."[44]

Corruption, if ubiquitously feared, was not universal. Lawyers, bureaucrats, and emperors struggled to make justice work. The draftsmen of imperial edicts attempted to safeguard free access to the judge; focused on the accountants who were privy to financial transactions; subjected the bureaucracy to antibribery rules; and repeatedly set out sanctions to deter bribetaking judges. Laws do not testify to social fact; they do testify to social consciousness. The laws of the Empire testify to the persistent belief, the unquenchable hope, that just judges exist. Their existence is the predicate of all the laws. Who else will enforce them? And just judges do exist. For that we have the opinion of Ammianus, the indirect evidence of Augustine, and the life, now to be examined, of Marcellinus. The apprehension that money would prevail at the department stained the system. The system worked, justice was sometimes done, because part of the time money did not prevail.

The Partial Judge.   "Your bishops say: the trial judge was corrupted by a reward." The time is the summer of 411, the place North Africa, the context the final phase of the century-old conflict of Catholics and Donatists. "Your bishops" are Donatists; it is they who circulate the accusation. The accused is the imperial state secretary, Flavius Marcellinus. The reporters of the accusation are the Catholics (Augustine among them), who report it to refute it. Known only through the Catholic report, denied, and uncorroborated, the charge itself cannot count as evidence. Its interest lies in its use and prominence. At the end of a great ecclesiastical battle, as the final rallying point for Christians who began by refusing to readmit to the Church those who had buckled under persecution, the cry is against a judge "corrupted by a reward." The term used for "reward," *praemium*, is like *munus* multivalent and like *munus* it must be translated by a word that can have at times a positive or neutral meaning and at times, in context, an ironic or unfavorable meaning. *Praemium* has its root in *emere*, to buy, and the word can have the negative value we, in similar contexts, associate with "a payoff." The accusation has popular resonance and immediate persuasiveness.[45]

There had, in fact, been no trial. There had, rather, been a public confrontation over which Marcellinus presided, rendering at the end a verdict to which he had been committed from the start. The popular Donatist objection, however, is not the bias of the judge, but his corruption by material means. The claim is so serious that in a letter from Catholic bishops intended to persuade the Donatist rank and file that their cause is hopeless, it must be set out by the Catholics at the beginning. If Donatist waverers are to be persuaded, the charge must be met head-on. The importance given the allegation is remarkable testimony to the plausibility of a charge of corruption against an imperial agent. At the same time it is remarkable testimony to the store set on judicial probity even in forums that were far from the properly judicial. If the claim shows that people easily believed the worst of an official from Ravenna, it is also proof of what the worst was thought to be.

The extraordinary good fortune that has preserved the verbatim record of the proceeding, made by imperial scribes, permits a closer evaluation of the kind of contest in which corruption could be a telling charge.[46] What had taken place was a species of debate between Catholics and Donatists in the Garglian baths, Carthage, on June 1, 3, and 8, 411. There were 286 Catholic bishops, 284 Donatist bishops, but the numbers were not decisive. What determined the course of the proceeding was the legislation of the past century and the orders of the Emperor Honorius who had arranged for the meeting to be held.

Almost a hundred years earlier, in 317, Constantine had decided against the Donatists and begun to enact imperial laws against them.[47] They had survived, sometimes enjoying peaceful co-existence, sometimes securing legal toleration, but always separated from the other Catholic episcopates in the empire, and usually bearing the odium of official disfavor.[48] In the six years preceding the conference the disfavor of Honorius for them had been marked.

An imperial decree of February 12, 405, to the Praetorian Prefect had treated the Donatists as heretics and prescribed for their correction the confiscation of their property and the manumission of any of their slaves whom they subjected to rebaptism. An edict of the same date proclaimed them guilty of "madness," announced that they would be caught "in the toils of innumerable constitutions," and declared that only "one Catholic worship" should exist. Two further decrees, of March and December 405, addressed to the authorities in Africa, pressed the execution of the edict. When the fall of Stilicho, the minister in power in 405, raised hopes among the Donatists of a change in policy, they were swiftly rebuffed: a decree sent to the proconsul of Africa denounced their "new and unaccustomed audacity" and urged containment of "the pestilence." Finally, to cap this settled course of repression, the instructions given Marcellinus of October 14, 410, by the emperor were to "abolish the new superstition" and to keep the Catholic faith "incorrupt and inviolate." Nothing that Honorius had done indicated or implied that he was open to having an impartial reexamination of the issues.[49]

Nor was a trial in the mind of the Catholic bishops who asked the emperor to convoke a conference. It would have been strange for them to have forfeited their privileged position in the law and to have asked the imperial authorities to decide over again who was right. What they wanted was a chance to convince the Donatist bishops and the Donatist waverers by measures somewhat more irenic than confiscation of their property. As Augustine put it to Marcellinus, "You were sent for the good of the Church." As Marcellinus put it at the meeting itself, "Not a trial judge, but a colloquy was asked for." To him the emperor had delegated his judgment.[50]

Marcellinus made no secret of the orders he obeyed or his view of his role. He had the instructions read aloud on the first day of the conference. The emperor had said that out of his desire for peace and favor (*gratia*) he was granting the Catholic bishops' request to gather the Donatist bishops in order that debate be held and "manifest reason confute superstition." The Donatists, the emperor had remarked, "discolor Africa with their empty error."[51] It was in the context of these instructions that Honorius had designated Marcellinus "trial judge in the place of the prince"—a prince anxious "to strengthen the Catholic faith."[52] Marcellinus was surely not to be a judge in the sense of judging between heresy and orthodoxy. He was not to reverse his prince's law. He was to be a judge who was to proclaim its force, "the new superstition abolished." A Catholic layman, he had been selected from the imperial chancery for his interest in theology and his reputation as "an eminent Christian."[53] In his summons of the Donatists to the conference, dated January 19, 411, Marcellinus published the substance of his instructions announcing publicly that the emperor saw Africa "discolored" by difference of religion and wanted a disputation so that "manifest reason will conquer superstition."[54] Read against the background of the past six years of imperial legislation, his summons left no doubt as to what the emperor thought was "manifest reason" and who he thought "discolored" his realm.

If the conference could in no sense be considered a trial, why was Marcellinus named as judge? The answer must be "by analogy, in tribute to the prestige of the judicial process." It was evident to the imperial chancery, if not to the Catholic bishops who asked for the conference, that there had to be someone to run the meeting and there had to be some way of ending the meeting if the Donatist bishops failed to be convinced by "manifest reason." An emperor-like authority ("in place of the prince"), with the title "trial judge," was the form chosen. Marcellinus himself then went very far to give equality in the deliberations: he offered twice—once in his summons, once on the first day—to accept a co-judge, named by the Donatists, to sit with him.[55] The offer went beyond what the emperor had specified, but was, Marcellinus observed, within his discretion to make. If it had been accepted, it would have put the Donatists on a par with the Catholics procedurally if not substantively, and it even offered the likelihood of a deadlock as to a concluding verdict. In the defeatist spirit that the Donatists often relished, the offer was refused. Marcellinus, in fact, made procedural rulings with admirable impartiality, but it was already determined what his "judgment" would be when the discussion was over.

Why didn't the Donatists cry that Marcellinus was "a taker up of persons," corrupted by love or hate? Perhaps they did, and the evidence is lost. But if we assume that their most significant charges are preserved in order to be answered in the Catholic bishops' letter, their silence on this point needs explanation. This hypothesis may be offered: A "taker up of persons" was one who favored a particular person, not one who championed a cause. Then, as now, commitment to a point of view on some large issue of the day was not the same as bias for an individual. To say that a judge was prejudiced in favor of imperial law would not have been a persuasive objection.

Marcellinus' role may be compared to that of a Redevelopment Authority in federal urban renewal programs of the 1950s. Under the federal legislation, the Authority was expected to designate land for clearance and renewal, obtain local support, and convince a federal bureaucracy that its plan was sound. It was *then* required by federal legislation to hold a public hearing on the desirability of the plan which it had originated, voted for, and nurtured. At the public hearing the plan's supporters and opponents were heard by the Authority. There was not the slightest doubt how the Authority would vote when the hearing was over.[56]

In the case of the Donatists and in the case of the redevelopment plan, a forum for public dissent was provided. In a restrained degree, the dissenters were given a chance to be formally recognized and to air their grievances. In return for this opportunity those in control—the imperial or the federal officials—profited from the prestige of a quasi-judicial hearing preceding the final approval of their program. In each case to refer to "judges" or a "hearing" was a sham when no proper adjudication was intended. But it was not the parody of judicial form, so palpable upon reflection, that was the object of the Donatists' complaint. The simulacrum of a court was accepted. "Payoff" was the telling charge.

Corruption had in fact once been the cry of the Catholics against the Donatists. At the very beginning of the schism in 312 a court of seventy Numidian bishops had deposed the consecrated bishop of Carthage, making way for the election of Donatus. They were said to have been paid for their votes by Lucilla, who was wealthy, a Spaniard, and a woman. Evidence taken eight years afterwards in the imperial court in Numidia identified Silvanus, bishop of Cirta, as receiving the lion's share. No evidence showed that all were tainted.[57] But Augustine, presenting the Catholic cause generations later, cited a judicial summary that made the corruption encompass the entire body: "the bishops in Carthage were corrupted by the money of Lucilla." The deposed Catholic bishop had refused to appear before those who were "no true judges but enemies and corrupted."[58] As a charge, corruption told against the Donatists' origins; so a charge of corruption now told against the Catholics' conclusion of the quarrel. The

Donatists struck at the most vital nerve when they did not yell "bias" but "payoff"; and the Catholics took up their most important defense when they denied the accusation and offered the record itself in proof of their prejudiced presiding officer's financial probity.

The Memory of Marcellinus. One sequel of the Conference of Carthage did lead to proceedings which were purely judicial. The left wing of the Donatists, known as Circumcellians or "Hide-Abouts," had engaged in sporadic violence against the orthodox. Some of them were now to be tried as ordinary criminals. Marcellinus presided at their trials in Carthage. A group from Hippo were convicted of stoning a priest to death and of gouging out the eye and cutting off the finger of another. They were liable to the death penalty. Its imposition was in the power of Marcellinus and his older brother Apringius, proconsul of Africa. For these convicted enemies from his own diocese Augustine asked favor.[59]

Marcellinus, by letter, was apostrophised as "a Christian judge" who must "perform the duty of a merciful father," who must cure, not wreak vengeance. If he would not listen to "a friend petitioning," let him "hear a bishop counseling." As a Christian it was even fitting for him—"excellent and justly distinguished lord and most beloved son"—to hear Augustine as "a bishop commanding." As sons of the Church, both he and his brother should be merciful.[60] To Apringius, a less devout man and no special friend, Augustine wrote with more restraint but no less pointedly. In giving judgment he was "to think of the divine judgment at which judges too will stand to give an account of their judgment." The Church would benefit more from mercy than severity. "On account of Christ," he, "a Christian judge" acting in "a case of the Church," should be obediently merciful.[61] In a follow-up to the first two letters Augustine assured Marcellinus that if his brother would not yield, Augustine himself would ask clemency of the emperor.[62]

That the grace was given is not stated in the surviving correspondence. But the continuing closeness of the ties between Augustine and Marcellinus is virtual proof that the bishop was not let down.[63] To this remarkable man who had already moved him to take up the battle on grace with Pelagius, Augustine was to dedicate the first books of his greatest work, *The City of God*, owed he said to Marcellinus "as a debt"; and he was to let the dedication stand after Marcellinus himself had been executed.[64] In his eulogy of Marcellinus after his death Augustine was to exclaim of him, "What splendor of favor (*gratia*)!"—a wonderful phrase fusing the *gratia* God had shown him and the *gratia* Augustine had seen him show others.[65]

Mercy and justice, as Augustine saw it, had met in Marcellinus. Soon Marcellinus was in need of both himself. An unsuccessful revolt against Honorius by the military ruler of Africa, Heraclian, was suppressed in June 413. Honorius' successful general, Marinus, followed Heraclian back to Carthage and, on the emperor's orders, had the rebel executed. Other high officials in the African province naturally were under suspicion. Sometime during the summer Marcellinus and his brother were arrested.

They were kept in prison, and Augustine was able to visit them. The African bishops were assured that their case would not even be examined until a bishop could go to Ravenna and obtain an order for their release from Honorius. Marinus himself was a Catholic. His close adviser was a former praetorian prefect, Caecilian. Apringius had once done Caecilian a serious injury, but Caecilian was a Catholic catechumen and supposed to be a friend of Augustine. Everyone knew how central Marcellinus' role had been in the recent Catholic triumph in Carthage.[66]

On September 12, 413, Caecilian saw Augustine and expressed the hope that no harm would come to the brothers, adding that as a farewell present to him Marinus would grant their release. The following day was the eve of the feast of the great martyr of the African Church, St. Cyprian. Augustine was startled by a messenger informing him that the brothers had been moved from prison and were now on trial. He thought that Marinus meant to celebrate the feast with their release. The next messenger brought the news that they had been beheaded.[67]

African custom prescribed that the saints be honored by bringing to their shrines a basket of cakes and bread and wine—the gifts were not unlike those brought by Ani the Egyptian to his gods. Augustine's mother Monica had followed this custom even at Milan until it was forbidden by Ambrose as an occasion of tippling and too much like pagan superstition. After Ambrose's prohibition she brought to the shrines her prayers and presents for the needy. From a giver to the dead, she became a petitioner to God and a giver to the poor. By prayers and gifts to the living she honored the memory of the saints.[68] His mother's son, Augustine honored Marcellinus not by cakes and bread and wine but by a letter on his life and death.

The basis of Marcellinus' conviction, Augustine writes, was the false testimony of one witness: "It was not a big deal to procure someone who when his safety was promised would say what he [Marinus] ordered to be said." At that time "everything was 'influenced.'" The verb is the passive form of *suffragare*, "to obtain by patronage or payoff." The bribe goes to the witness.[69] Orosius, the church historian and Augustine's friend, was to speculate that Marinus had either been moved by zeal "or corrupted by gold"—the popular suspicion that judges are bought will not down.[70] But Augustine, who had no reason to conceal such a suspicion, is clear. Perjury, not bribery of the court, procured the conviction; and the perjury was the result of the power of the senior military commander to give a quid pro quo to a witness. The death of Marcellinus was "impious cruelty," "wicked cruelty," "blind cruelty," "gratuitous cruelty." What it was not in the view of Augustine, throbbing with anguish at the loss of his friend and the deceit of the perpetrators, was venal cruelty. The author of the execution, Marinus, is now in disgrace; this deed, among others, did not please the emperor.[71] For Augustine his sin is so dark that he will not mention his name. The entire letter in which he is a principal villain is written without naming him—his fate is worse than Hog's. Marinus is simply "he." Memory of him is to be blotted out. Yet Augustine does not accuse this cruel man of being himself corrupted by money.

In the course of the letter Augustine introduces a panegyric, based on personal knowledge, of Marcellinus: "He lived religiously and was much a Christian in heart and life." His character was upright, his judgment measured, he was merciful in giving aid and benevolent in forgiving. His decency was remarkable, his favor (gratia) known.[72] No need to say that this judge's favor was not corrupt. No need here to deny that he had ever taken munera for judgment. When he ponders the meaning of Marcellinus' modest hope, expressed in prison, that "my sins may be punished here and not reserved for my future judgment," Augustine thinks of only one kind of secret sin—sexual incontinence. The age abounds with accusations of corrupt judges. Here was an imperial commissioner who had been publicly accused of being corrupted as well as a judge who had sat on capital cases and shown mercy. Yet speaking of this judge of known reputation it is unnecessary even to anticipate an accusation of bribetaking by denying it or to refute the Donatists' stale charge. It does not enter Augustine's head to suppose that Marcellinus' secret sin was graft.

Marcellinus was married to Anapsychia, a Christian as intellectual as he himself.[73] Augustine reports his relief when in prison Marcellinus told him he had had no intercourse before or after marriage except with his wife. As in the New Testament itself, a higher significance is placed on chastity—it is more suspect, more jealously guarded, more prized—than on the integrity of a judge which even in a corrupt time is taken for granted. In Augustine's indictment of his killers the judicial dedicatee of The City of God is celebrated for his sexual self-control.[74]

Another New Testament value was to predominate as legend gathered about Marcellinus. Jerome, writing in Bethlehem, asserted that he was "an innocent man slain by the heretics." Presumably he meant that the Donatists had contrived his death.[75] As a martyr who had given his life for the faith, St. Marcellinus entered the Roman Martyrology with the feast day of April 6.[76] Augustine, on the scene in Carthage with far more reason to dislike the Donatists than Jerome, said his death pleased "the impious," but made no such charge. For Augustine the chief slayer was a Catholic, the chief accomplice a catechumen. In the usual way, Jerome's accusation has been picked up by a modern historian. "The truth is," he writes, "that he [Marinus] acted under pressure from the Donatists."[77] The truth is that Jerome's report is one more accusation without evidence.

There is instruction to be derived from Jerome and the Martyrology. To be a hero of the faith a blameless life as a chaste husband and just judge was not enough. The highest honors were only for him who had imitated the Redeemer by the giving of his blood. For Augustine, however, Marcellinus' life was enough.

The recipient of Augustine's epistolary memorial to Marcellinus was Marinus' adviser, Caecilian, the catechumen in power at the time of the killings. In the letter to him the execution is described as a deed of perfidy, but Augustine does not say in so many words that Caecilian engineered it while lulling the Catholic bishops with false promises. He makes no formal accusation. He asks Caecilian to tell him, "What were you doing on the day it happened? How did you learn it? What did you do then? Did you see him [Marinus]? What did you say to him? What did you hear from him?"[78] The questions form an implicit indictment.

At the end of the letter, after his praise of Marcellinus, Augustine turns again to Caecilian. Why has he, a man of such maturity and such probity (how deep the irony is), remained a catechumen? Why has he not been baptized and joined the faithful? It is "as if the faithful, the more faithful and the better they are, would not be able to administer the state the better and more faithfully."[79] Augustine does not observe that Christ the judge-to-be gave his life for those he ruled. He sets before Caecilian the image of an imperial judge who was "much a Christian in heart and life." Marcellinus' suspected murderer thinks that he himself has been a better servant of the state by not accepting Christ. Augustine leaves him to consider who has been the more faithful Christian, the better judge.

In this way Augustine returns, glancingly, to the challenge of Volusianus which Marcellinus had once sent him: could a Christian be a ruler? He calls to mind—the mind of the accomplice of the tyrant executioner—that the best Christian ruler they both knew was one whom the tyrant, after a hasty parody of a trial, had put to death.

In Augustine's letter to Caecilian his assumptions about Roman justice in the late empire are clear: Fair judges are central to the system. False witnesses are a danger to innocent life. Bribes are not the necessary explanation of a wrong judgment. There are judges, of whom Marcellinus is an example, who give favor without being corrupt, whose integrity is such that, after their death, it is unnecessary even to say that they gave judgment without bribes.

Byzantium

"Four large wool rugs, two smaller wool rugs, four pillows . . . two ostriches; and that he may help us in the case about which we have written him, fifty pounds of gold." These words open a schedule of presents to be delivered to Paul, an official of the imperial court at Constantinople. The schedule continues with a list of other recipients and what they are to receive in furniture, rugs, cloths, and money. Over 1,000 gold pounds are to be distributed. The donees include Marcella and Droseria, ladies of the emperor's maiden sister Pulcheria, if they will work on the empress; Helleniana, wife of the prefect of the praetorium if she persuades the prefect; Florentius, the prefect's assessor; the master of offices; and a variety of other officials and assistants at the court of Theodosius II. The largest amount (200 pounds of gold) is destined for an opponent, Chrysoretes, the grand chamberlain or highest functionary in the household, to persuade him to desist from opposition. Scholasticus, a lesser chamberlain

and an opponent, is down for 100 pounds, with 50 pounds for his aide
Theodosius if he helps persuade his boss. The *mediator* or go-between for
these transactions is identified, the priest Claudianus. The schedule is attached to a letter from Epiphanius, archdeacon of Alexandria, to Maximianus, bishop of Constantinople. Epiphanius is acting for Cyril, bishop
of Alexandria, who is in trouble. If the letter and schedule are genuine,
they constitute a master plan for bribing the court. With figures given,
donor, donees, *mediator* named, with the expected quid pro quo indicated,
no better documentation of bribery exists.[80]

   The Cyril File.   Letter and schedule form a part of a dossier compiled on
one of the great theological controversies of the fifth century. Nestorius,
newly elected bishop of Constantinople in 428, objected to calling Mary
"the mother of God." He was attacked by Cyril, bishop of Alexandria, an
older see long jealous of the rise of Constantinople. Nestorius asked for a
council, and the Eastern Emperor, Theodosius II, called one in 431 at
Ephesus. Cyril arrived, accompanied by forty Egyptian bishops, and
without waiting for the Syrians, believed to side with Nestorius, opened
the Council. In Nestorius' view, Cyril not only rushed the opening, he
violated fundamental justice by moving from accuser to judge, in fact
dominating the other judges. The Council promptly anathematized Nestorius and sent him its decision, addressing him as "the new Judas." Five
days later the Syrians arrived, held their own council, and excommunicated Cyril. Eventually an imperial commissioner put both Nestorius and
Cyril under house arrest. Nestorius lost his see, was replaced by Maximianus, and was relegated to a monastery in Syria. Cyril escaped and
made his way back to Alexandria. There he was under imperial pressure to
be reconciled with the Syrian bishops and to drop the dogmatic exposition
he had championed against Nestorius. In these circumstances Cyril had
need of friends at the court, and it is inferable that the letter and schedule
of Epiphanius were sent at this time. Peace was made with the Syrians
without Cyril abandoning his formulas. If the documents are authentic,
the presents presumably neutralized the opposition, enlisted Pulcheria
and the praetorian prefect, and carried the day.[81]

   Are the documents genuine? They survive in two Latin copies, one of
the thirteenth century, one somewhat earlier. The Latin collection from
which they come was made about 565 by Rusticus, a Roman deacon, who
had stayed at a monastery in Constantinople where apparently he found
and translated the Greek originals. These originals were part of the
Tragoedia, a work composed by Bishop Irenaeus over a century earlier,
about 450, or within a generation of Cyril's difficulties. It is apparent that
the documents we possess are in a language different from the originals
and separated from them by at least two compilers, Rusticus and
Irenaeus.[82] More important, we have no information on how Irenaeus obtained the letter and schedule of Epiphanius. There is no evidence proving
their authorship apart from the claim made by the letter itself that it comes
from Epiphanius. The only basis for believing the letter is his is the likeli-

hood that no one else would have composed it and palmed it off on him. Technically the assertion that it is Epiphanius' is hearsay.

The style of the letter is a striking mixture of sycophancy, beginning with the address to "My Most Holy Lord and Dearest Friend of God," Maximianus, and abruptness: Cyril is "sad that you are not putting out your soul. . . . Let your holiness hustle. . . ." It is a tone appropriate for addressing the patriarch of Constantinople by men to whom he owes his office. The letter shows a detailed knowledge of connections at the court and of Cyril's finances. Maximianus is instructed to borrow from Count Ammanius, to whom the letter says Cyril already owes 1,050 pounds. There is a realistic two-pronged strategy set out as to the principal opponent, Chrysoretes: he is to be given double, but meanwhile Pulcheria is to be pressed to have him removed from office. There is nothing in the documents that betrays a forger's hand. Two references—to the "avarice which you know" and to "whatever of avarice is lacking to them in the palace"—are less than tactful, but understandable in a letter meant to be confidential. The presents to be given are designated by standard euphemisms—*eulogiae* or *benedictiones*—terms literally meaning "praises" or "blessings" and actually used to mean gifts to an official. The *mediator* is described tactfully in the body of the letter as "your messenger" or "your angel." On their face, the letter and schedule are the work of a shrewd and knowledgeable manipulator laying out a battle plan for the corruption of the powerholders.

If the documents were forgeries, this is precisely the impression they would be intended to make. The purpose of a forger would be to persuade his readers that Cyril was an experienced operator in a bribable court, working particularly through women and the eunuch chamberlains. If a forger wanted to blacken Cyril, these documents would do it convincingly. Have we reason to believe they are forgeries?

Rusticus, although in a later epoch an anti-Cyrillan, may be presumed to have merely copied Irenaeus. Irenaeus' motives and knowledge are different. In 428 he was a count of the empire and a friend of Nestorius, who regarded him as "a man who lived in God and served him with his possessions and with his soul and with his body." He accompanied Nestorius to Ephesus. He was sent by the Syrian bishops to Constantinople to report their action of deposing Cyril. He wrote a detailed account of the perils he encountered at the court which "the Egyptians" had reached first and filled with their "calumnies." He persevered in upholding Nestorius' position. In 436 he suffered exile for his involvement with him. In 443 he was rehabilitated, ordained, and made bishop of Tyre, but after fresh intrigues he was deposed in 448; the following year a council formally condemned him. At this point after twenty years of fighting, having suffered greatly for his beliefs, he composed the work to which he gave the name *Tragoedia*, the same title Nestorius had given to his own account of his defeat. Irenaeus' *Tragoedia* was intended to vindicate Nestorius and to prove that he himself was right in sticking with his teaching. The battle was still going on. Nestorius, still alive in exile, was to be vindicated. Cyril, dead in 444, was the archenemy to be destroyed. In these circumstances, where revenge is a clear motive, and where Irenaeus would have possessed a detailed knowledge of the court as it existed in the 430s, he had both reason and ability to concoct letters portraying Cyril as a corruptor.[83]

Batiffol, who accepted the documents as genuine, went to some pains to show that the offer of gifts at court was "d'étiquette."[84] If that were true, there would have been no reason for Irenaeus to have inserted the documents in what is a highly polemical account of doctrinal controversy. Their preservation by Irenaeus must reflect his judgment that the documents were disgraceful, a blot on the memory of Cyril.

To win points by depicting the chief opponent as a villain had been a tactic of the Cyrillans from the beginning. The description of Nestorius as "the new Judas" was followed in due course by a sermon in which Cyril preached against him as a corrupt man, as one who did not examine the Scripture, but "examined gold and silver."[85] When on August 3, 435, Theodosius II issued a decree formally condemning the Nestorians, the emperor declared that from this time forward this "nefarious sect" was everywhere to be called "Simonians." In this way, the decree said, they might "appear to have rightly received the name of him whose crime they, deserting God, imitated."[86] The Nestorians were to be forever stigmatized as imitators of the paradigmatic purchaser of the Spirit. Surely the imperial tactics and Cyril's own sneer could foster the Nestorians' desire to picture Cyril as the briber par excellence.

The counteraccusation had already been raised against Cyril. The source was a venerable bishop—believed to be over a century old—Acacius of Boroea, writing his friend Alexander, bishop of Hieropolis. According to this accusation, Theodosius II had found on the death of the eunuch Scholasticus that the eunuch had left "infinite gold." Further investigation had led to a chest containing "many pounds of gold he had received from Cyril." According to Acacius' information it had been delivered by Paul, a nephew of Cyril, who was then "count of the consistories." In addition, "there were other *munera* which in various forms were offered to various persons."[87] Here *munera* presumably translates *dōra* and, in context, means offerings operating as bribes. Acacius' gossip could be taken to be confirmation of Cyril's strategy outlined in Epiphanius' letter for payments which Paul was to manage (the detail, of course, differs, with Scholasticus being a prime recipient), or it could be read as typical of the suspicions which could have inspired Irenaeus to compose documentation proving Cyril's guilt.

Nestorius himself, meanwhile, at roughly the time Irenaeus was at work, was composing his own new account of the controversy—a book like Irenaeus' *Tragoedia* which blended dogmatic argumentation, autobiography, and accusations against Cyril. In particular, Nestorius accused Cyril of giving money to the imperial commissioner who had had both of them arrested at Ephesus; in Cyril's view, the commissioner's zeal had slackened after the payment. Nestorius also accounted for Cyril's escape from Ephesus as the work of money. According to Nestorius, Cyril then came back to Ephesus having "filled ships with all things and presents as though for the Emperor and for the imperial family and for the chief persons as much as was sufficient for their rank and according to their honour." The tactic worked so well that Cyril "sat with the emperor upon the first throne—and I mean the emperor's—while the emperor sat on the second." But when the presents were exhausted, the emperor commanded "that the gold should be exacted, the two thousand pounds to which he was pledged by written documents."[88]

Nestorius' story was clearly composed without the benefit of Irenaeus' book and without consultation between them. There is little agreement between Nestorius and Irenaeus or between them and Acacius. Pulcheria, a key figure to be won by money in the letter of Epiphanius, is not mentioned in connection with money by Nestorius. Rather, he acknowledges her as a young maiden, a virgin, who had already become his enemy while he was bishop because of his uncompromising stand in relation to another woman, presumably her protégé: she "fought against me because I was not willing to be persuaded by her demand that I should compare a woman corrupted by men to the bride of Christ."[89] Nestorius' accusations are not even entirely coherent with each other. He has Cyril pledged "by written documents" to pay 2,000 pounds, but, unable to do so, leaving after giving "pledges"—one would suppose that a defaulting bribegiver would very quickly have fallen from favor. Vague and unpersuasive as his charges are, far less persuasive than the detailed letter of Epiphanius, Nestorius' autobiography does show that Nestorius himself clung to the belief, as late as 450, that money had been the reason for Cyril's victory. He, Nestorius, the incumbent bishop of Constantinople, the friend of the emperor and the chief men of the empire, had been ousted from his own see by an Egyptian. He was still flabbergasted by the event. How had it been brought about? Money beat us, was the explanation cherished by him and his friends.

On balance, tempting as it is to pounce on Epiphanius' letter and schedule of gifts as hard evidence of corruption, the temptation must be resisted. In the annals of bribery such documentation is unique. Irenaeus does not show how he obtained it. We do have little reason to accept Nestorius' assessment of his high character: their association was too close for Nestorius to have been dispassionate. Irenaeus had personal religious motives to destroy Cyril. He had the knowledge to do so skillfully. He put together his *Tragoedia* after he had been condemned by the orthodox, deposed from his see, left with nothing. It is not fair on the basis of his hearsay to conclude that Cyril had authorized the bribes so lovingly detailed in the correspondence Irenaeus claimed to reproduce.[90]

What the correspondence does prove, what Acacius' gossip proves, what Cyril's sermon against Nestorius and Nestorius' attack on Cyril prove, are that it was a common belief that money and other gifts were efficacious in influencing the court and that it was considered disgraceful to employ such means. We do not know if the Nestorian charges were true. We do know that after twenty years of the great dogmatic battle over the nature of Christ the most telling personal argument against the Cyrillans was the charge that Cyril had paid for his victory. Challengeable and doubtful as proof of Cyril's corrupt conduct, the letter and schedule of Epiphanius are precious evidence that at a moral level the briber was regarded with contempt. It was because Irenaeus hated Cyril that he preserved forever the correspondence, true or false, that would cover the Father of Ephesus with shame.

The Canon of Chalcedon.   A decree of Theodosius II in 439 provided that men chosen to rule a province should obtain office "neither by too much effort (*ambitio*) nor by price (*pretium*)." Those chosen were to swear that they had given nothing on their own behalf, or "by means of any person interposed in fraud," or "by title of gift, sale, or the veil of any other contract whatsoever." The emperor granted to everyone the faculty of accusing both the recipients and the givers "as of a public crime," and the penalty was to be four times the amount paid for the office. This strenuous attempt to prevent purchases of secular office and to anticipate stratagems for cloaking purchases went further than any earlier surviving legislation. It is not known to have been conspicuously effective. It offered a model for the Church.[91]

Twenty years after Ephesus, in 451, the Council of Chalcedon capped the Christological debates that had erupted in the conflict with Nestorius, correcting or at least compromising and nuancing the stark line of Cyril. The disciplinary canons adopted were subordinate to the dogmatic concerns; but significance may be found in the council's first measure. After reaffirming "the canons of the Fathers," the council provided against the sale of ecclesial office. The canon showed the commitment of the victorious orthodox to high standards of church government; it implicitly contrasted them once again with "the Simonians" who were the heretics. It provided explicitly that if anyone "ordains for money and puts a price on unsalable favor," he is to lose his own rank, and "the one ordained" is to obtain nothing from "the ordination or promotion."[92]

The phrasing left open whether the purchased ordinations were automatically void or not. If the Spirit's favor could not be sold, what did the buyer have? Yet the decree went beyond those receiving holy orders to include stewards of church property and the *defensores* or church advocates, functionnaries who did not seem to require the favor of the Spirit to exercise their roles. These men appeared to hold positions that would continue to be theirs unless tainted acquisition of them was shown. Would not the same rule then apply to priest or bishop, the office would be his until the defect was proved? Not addressing problems of proof or presumptions of innocence, the council did not deal with the major defenses known a century earlier to Basil—custom, and the more or less voluntary character of offerings made *after* ordination. It struck only at the most flagrant kind of case—a negotiated purchase; and it included not only the seller and purchaser but also their agents, the bagman who would receive and the broker who would give money. The term chosen to designate the intermediary who took or gave was *mesites*, the term used by the New Testament (1 Tm 2:5) to designate Christ as our go-between with the Father. Undoubtedly the choice was deliberate, to contrast ironically the mediator in sales of divine favor with the Mediator who had freely redeemed us.

A canon of this kind was by no means self-executing. It provided a basis for action and development. Within the decade, Gennadius, patriarch of Constantinople, followed it up with an "encyclical letter" addressed to all metropolitans and to "the Pope of Rome." Gennadius signaled neglect of the canon in Galatia: that must stop. More broadly, he denounced all attempts to conceal the offense by sophistry. It was clear from Chalcedon, he said, that money could not be given before or after. The canon embraced all *dōrodokia*—all bribery. Unclean hands should not be at work. You could not serve God and mammon; and "favor (*charis*) must always be favor (*charis*)." As Christ taught, "You have received freely, give freely."[93]

In 469, a generation after Chalcedon, the Emperor Leo embodied its teaching in imperial legislation: "Let no one market the priesthood by a sale of a price." In the argumentative style of much Roman law: "What place can be safe, what cause blameless, if the venerable temples of God are assaulted by cash? . . . What in short can be safe and secure if incorrupt holiness is corrupted?" In the epigrammatic style favored at times by the imperial chancellory: "Not by price but by prayers let a bishop be ordained." In the exhortatory fashion of the emperors: a candidate for episcopal office "should be so distant from ambition that he does not seek the office but is compelled to it." The penalty for giving or taking something to ordain was set at degradation from the priesthood and perpetual infamy. The crime was to be treated like *lèse majesté*.[94]

Novel 8.   The Leonine law entered the Code of Justinian in 534 in the chapter on "Bishops and Clerics." The great codifier also declared that there were "four holy Councils": Nicaea, Constantinople, Ephesus, and Chalcedon.[95] Although Justinian gave Chalcedon this position apropos Christological dogma, all the canons of the Council were given a special position by the cross-reference. Confirming the Church's view of Chalcedon, the emperor implicitly elevated its canon against the sale of ecclesial office to the status of imperial law.

In the Digest that was to become the encyclopedic resource of Europe, Justinian incorporated Papinian and the other third-century jurists on the comprehensive scope of the Julian law on Reclaimables; he thought it desirable to add Ulpian in a special section entitled *Concussio* or "Shakedown."[96] The excited edicts of fourth-century emperors flailing corruption appeared in his new Codex. All trial judges were once more told to "keep their hands off moneys and patrimonies." Anyone "shaken down" by a judge was once more invited to inform the emperor and win glory.[97] But these restatements were to yield pride of place to his own legislative efforts.

"Every night and every day we spend in laborious study and thought wanting to offer something useful and pleasing to God. . . ." So begins the most elaborate composition of Roman legislation on the sale of secular office, Novel 8, issued by Justinian in May 535. It would be better, says the emperor, if the governors of provinces "abstained from taking from anyone" and lived on the salaries paid from the Treasury. But this desirable course is impeded by the practice of purchasing appointment. (Apparently Theodosius II's edict of 439 was a dead letter.) Is it not evident to everyone, asks the emperor, that he who gives gold and so buys his office pays not only the price fixed for the office but something extra to those who award the office or promise it to him? "He who makes the gift must solicit among many hands." To meet his needs he must borrow, and borrow at interest. His expenses are heavy. To recoup, he takes from his subjects triple or even ten times what he gave. The Treasury suffers from his exactions. In civil cases he sells justice. In criminal cases, even capital cases, he "sells the guilty their crimes" and condemns the innocent to get money from them. No one is afraid to commit robbery, murder, rape when "whatever someone does illegally he çan buy back (redemit) by giving money." Priests, officials, proprietors flee to Constantinople groaning at the thievery and injustices of the provincial administrators. The start of all these evils is the taking of payment (suffragium) from judges.[98]

This preamble to Novel 8 reads like a cento of Roman rhetoric on the rapacity of provincial judges. It could as well have applied to Hog in Sicily in the first century B.C. as to the Byzantine governors of the sixth century A.D. It strikes the same themes as the satirists of Roman justice in the classical era. It evokes the same images as the emperors of the fourth and fifth centuries: the administrators appointed by the emperor are corrupt, they exploit the people, the emperor will protect the people from his appointees. Almost 600 years after Cicero nothing appears to have changed in candid denunciation of provincial maladministration and rhetorical devotion at the center to the purest ideals of justice.

"Having thought about all these things"—that is, the obvious consequences of the sale of provincial office—and "having consulted her who is the gift of God" (that is, Theodora; so Justinian puns on his wife's name), the emperor decreed that there should be minimal standard fees paid for the badges and documents of office. He attached a specific schedule of fees. A total of 136 gold solidi were, for example, to be paid various court officers by the proconsul of Asia. The charges allowed were far from the prices that great office could command. They were no more than the clerical costs of a bureaucratic process. The governing principle was that the sale of office was abolished. Appointment was to be gratis.[99]

To enforce the principle, a variety of sanctions were set out. As former law required, governors were to stay fifty days in their provinces after their term of office ended; any governor leaving earlier would be treated as a runaway slave. Appointees were to give an oath that they had given or promised no one anything for patronage and had not agreed to send anyone anything from a province and that they would live only on the revenues allotted by the emperor, "keeping their governorship with pure hands and rendering account of it to God and to us." In particular they were to swear to be impartial in judging cases. The oath was to be given before the emperor or his delegate or in the provinces before the bishop, officeholders, and inhabitants of the city at the judgment seat of the province. If any magistrate violated the edict by giving or taking for office he should undergo confiscation of his property, beatings, torture, and exile. Bishops in the provinces were exhorted to report derelictions to the emperor. Patriarchs and archbishops were instructed to place the text of the law itself, as a thing "dedicated to God," with the sacred vessels of the church; they would do better if they also had it "engraved in stone on the porticos of their cathedrals." Finally the judgment of God was also invoked. Those who committed perjury in swearing consented in their oath to be punished "here and in the future world at the terrible judgment of the Great Lord God and Our Saviour Jesus Christ," and "to have a share with Judas, with the leper Gehazi and with the fearful Cain."[100]

Novel 8 blended exhortation, sanctions, preventative oaths, and biblical archetypes. Whether it was more successful than the efforts of the past 600 years cannot be determined. It would be unduly cynical to say it accomplished nothing, and naive to suppose that it reformed daily practice. That Justinian could with a straight face not only describe it as the result of laborious cogitation but actually prescribe that its issuance should be celebrated by hymns of thanksgiving shows that the tradition of "running against oneself," of denouncing the corruptions of one's own government, still had a powerful attraction for those at the center of society. Whatever its practical impact, Novel 8, a little summa of scriptural and legal learning on bribery, was the last major statement of the East to become part of the Western tradition on corruption.

Accusations abound. Hard evidence of corruption is hard to come by. Ammianus, avid for gossip, tells us of no judge actually convicted of bribetaking. The poets engage in generalities. The modern historians of the Empire appear to rely chiefly on the accusations made by the emperors themselves in imperial laws designed to deter corruption. Where specific charges can be examined—that of the Donatists against Marcellinus, of Julian against Augustine, of Cyril against Nestorius, of the Nestorians against Cyril—persuasive documentation cannot be found; indeed only in the case against Cyril is there any documentation at all and its authenticity is not established. A moralist as acute as Augustine appears to treat a false cry of corruption by a losing litigant as a more serious probability than a true case of a judge being corrupted by money. Yet he is aware that the possibility does exist that "money will prevail at the department." The perception of the power of money and the fear that it will prevail in a judicial or judicial-like proceeding are a perception and a fear of his society. To guard against the danger the most stringent anti-access legislation ever attempted has been enacted by Constantine, and a variety of threats and exhortations have been enacted into law by emperors from Constantine to Justinian. The accusatorial mode adopted by emperors and losing litigants is eloquent testimony to the function of bribery accusations in the society—for the loser it accounts for his opponent's undeserved success; for the imperial draftsman the accusation reaffirms the single image of the society in which the channels of power are firmly marked and regulated. In their popularity the accusations draw on Jewish and Roman ideals, nicely blended in the precepts of patristic moralists. The point is firmly fixed in the public mind that to take money for giving a corrupt judgment is evil. One kind of accusation reflects a development. The accusation against Augustine by Julian, against Nestorius by Cyril, against Cyril by Irenaeus is an accusation that assumes that bribe*giving* is sinful and shameful. No such accusations occur in the Old Testament and they are no more than a subordinate theme in Cicero's critique of Oppianicus. Now this kind of accusation is prominent in politico-religious battle. Its prominence can be accounted for by the attention given the sin of Simon. In terms of an ideal held up as a standard by which to exhort and accuse, the ethic rejecting reciprocities with him who judges had never been more vigorously embraced or more vitally employed.

5

The Saints and the System

Western Europe, beset by new peoples by the time of Justinian, offered not a bureaucracy to discipline but tribes and nations to initiate into the paradigms breaking the rule of reciprocity. Offerings to the powerful were the norm. Jewish and Roman images of impartiality, Christian emphasis on the gift freely given clashed with native customs. Who had the authority, the desire, the education, the energy to champion the morality of nonreciprocation? If there were those who did, where was a professional class like the Roman advocates with the competence and interest in assuring that in deciding cases offerings did not count more than rhetoric?

Saints—that is, men subsequently recognized in Catholic hagiography as holy—were the spokesmen and actors. Mostly monks or bishops, or monks become bishops, they announced in this area of tradition as in other areas the remembered morals of the Christianized Empire. Alternatively, without apparent difficulty or objection, they acquiesced in the exchanges customary among the tribes and nations new to Roman ways. A mixed record: between the sixth and eleventh centuries the ideal of nonreciprocity was, not without struggle, preserved. In select and remarkable instances it was exemplified. Seldom was it enforced.

The British Missionary to Ireland. Nowhere is the clash of custom with ideal more sharply caught than in the autobiography of Patrick, the most famous missionary to Ireland. Writing near the end of his life in mid-fifth century in a land beyond Roman rule but not beyond Roman thought, he declares to his flock, "I spent for you that they might receive me." In these words with a distinct Pauline echo, Patrick presents the image of a bringer of the gospel giving from his own resources to make himself available to his flock. The sentence is a claim on the flock's devotion, a boast of what the missionary had been willing to do; in no sense is it the confession of a sin. At the same time, it affords a glimpse of the practice prevailing in the country of the Airgialla and other pagan Celts. The spending for his sheep is by way of exchange with the secular authorities: "In addition to the wages paid their sons who travel with me, I have been giving rewards to the kings."[1]

Patrick's words are delicately chosen. The sons receive *merces* (wages). The kings receive rewards (*praemia*). The term could connote "payoff" as in the accusation of the Donatists against the Catholics at Carthage; it could also mean merely "recompense." *Praemium* here has just enough flavor of the unusual to suggest a kind of bonus. Bonuses and wages function as protection money, offered to get the local rulers to wink at the activities of an alien, a Roman Briton, arrived in Ireland as an emissary from outside the island. Recipients are specifically "those who judged in all the districts I have visited," that is, the chiefs or, more probably, the brehons or legal advisers of the chiefs. The amounts given are no secret: "You know how much I have paid." The amounts are even a matter for emphasis: "So that you might enjoy me and that I might always enjoy you in the Lord, I judge that I have distributed to them not less than the price of fifteen men."[2]

Gifttaking by Patrick himself was different. Penitents, he relates, tendered him many offerings (*munera*). Pious women offered many small presents (*munuscula*). Female converts gave of their own ornaments and put them on the altar. Patrick refused the offerings, the small presents, the altar donations. Baptizing thousands, ordaining clergy everywhere, he took nothing—not "half a screpull" from any. Keeping scruples over a screpull, a small coin of little value, Patrick is refusing to sell the sacraments. He is applying Chalcedon, he is following Peter rebuking Simon. Neither the Council nor the New Testament are what he cites. His standard is that of that exemplary Old Testament judge, Samuel, and like the Old Testament itself Patrick repudiates receiving, not giving *munera*. When the Lord ordained clerics through me, he writes, echoing Samuel, "If I asked from any of them the price of my shoe, speak against me and I will return it to you."[3]

Local mores were against him. The devout were scandalized when he rejected what they tendered. His seniors—his superiors at his home base outside Ireland—told him he was wrong. "Guided by God," as he saw it, and shaped by Scripture (the Psalms his favorite Old Testament book), he was obstinate. Nonreciprocity was to be the rule for him even as he paid life-price to the chiefs or their counselors. Helpless to alter others' mores, he gave the example of a Christian chief who was a giver but not a taker of offerings.[4]

The Archbishop of Arles.   "Those who lead a wicked life and observe neither charity nor justice and, as they hear cases, receive rewards against the innocent—they will have to endure eternal punishments for as many persons as those to whom they give the example of an evil life."[5] This homilectic threat against judges was uttered by Caesarius, a contemporary of Justinian, a monk of Lérins, and from 503 to 542 archbishop of Arles. Predicting no particular temporal sanction against the corrupt, Caesarius projected a divine punishment which paralleled, with a difference, the divine trial he had envisaged for a woman who committed abortion. The latter "should not doubt that before the tribunal of Christ she will have to plead as many cases as the number of those she killed when they were already born or still in the womb."[6] The delinquent judge was not to be tried or punished per corrupt judgment but per person scandalized by his conduct—a loss of specificity in the measure used, an increase in the amount of punishment predicted.

"Live so your children will imitate you" was Caesarius' theme in "A Sermon Necessary in Parishes." Those who hear cases "should decide them justly and not 'take offerings against the innocent,' for 'offerings blind the heart of the wise and change the words of the just.' While they are gaining money, they may lose their souls." The preacher conveyed the scriptural message on *munera*; his emphasis again was on a supratemporal sanction.[7]

How frequent was the offense? In "An Admonition to Those Who Frequently Give Alms But Still Commit Robbery and Adultery Every Day" Caesarius observed that the devil taught them that "although they commit sins every day they believe they buy them back by daily almsgiving. They suppose that God, after the custom of corrupt judges, takes money and forgives their sins."[8] In "On Almsgiving and on the Heavenly Mercy to Which We Attain by Mercy on Earth" he preached,

> Every man who knows he is going to plead his case before an earthly judge, dearly beloved, seeks useful patrons for himself and tries to obtain skilled advocates. Thus a man prepares himself when he is going to plead his case before a judge whom he can circumvent, surprise, or deceive, turn from justice by eloquent arguments, perchance corrupt by offerings, or pervert by false praise and false argumentation.

On earth, Caesarius assumed that there would be such intercessors; the taking up of persons was a sin he left unmentioned. In heaven, he continued, mercy should be our patron "ever interceding on our behalf." On earth, Caesarius thought, corruption was only a shade less usual than the use of patrons or the tricks of forensic advocacy.[9]

How seriously did Caesarius struggle against *munera*-taking? In the longest and most deliberate of his surviving writings, a circular letter to the bishops of his province setting out major moral rules, he dealt with the subject just after condemning the use of magic and just before condemning the use of abortifacients. "Let no one," he wrote, "try to oppress a good case by taking offerings."[10] The command was clear, sharp, and stated with a brevity and in a context that gave it attention but not emphasis. It was confined to receivers not extended to givers. Caesarius continued the Old Testament tradition without notably enlarging it or leaving any record of its application to the particular Visigoths, Ostrogoths, or Franks who in his forty years as archbishop populated his see.

The Legislator of Braga.   On the Iberian peninsula, on June 1, 572, a council called by King Miro met at Braga under the presidency of Braga's vigorous archbishop, Martin, another former monk in high office. The council recalled the words of Christ on gratuitous giving and "the ancient definition of the Fathers," that is, Chalcedon, about ecclesial ordinations. It noted that "some" who were "stained by many crimes" had obtained the ministry by a "profusion of offerings." It recalled that both giver and receiver were anathema. It taught that it was necessary to ordain clerics "not by the favor of offerings (*gratia munerum*) but by careful discussion followed by the testimony of many." The headnote of this canon ran, "Let a bishop in the ordination of clerics take no stipend." Stipend (*commodum*) broadly covered all temporal rewards.[11] In the same vein, the council declared that a bishop should take nothing for the holy chrism, lest he seem to sell, "as Simon Magician seemed to buy, the gift of God with money." Bishops were not to demand money for consecrating a church, nor priests for baptizing. Many poor people, the council warned, withheld their children from baptism because of clerics who demanded money or a pledge from the needy. Loopholes were left: both bishops and priests might take what was voluntarily offered at the consecration of a church or at a baptism. No church was to be consecrated without "a dowry" for its maintenance. The measures to be taken to raise the dowry were left to episcopal imagination.[12]

In the kingdom of the Suevians, Martin's legislation incorporated scriptural injunction and imagery, restated the Fathers, continued Roman terminology. Most strikingly, it retained from the Acts of the Apostles and Chalcedon the denunciation of payor as well as payee. Purely ecclesial in scope, it left secular affairs untouched. Summation of current abuses, prescription to eliminate them, Braga was churchly housekeeping, the assertion of the nonreciprocal ideal in the dispensation of God's favor.

The Ruler of Rome.   Three kinds of *munera* or offerings exist: from the heart, from the mouth, from the hand. From the heart comes the service offered by one who is unduly subject or servile—it is commonly called influence (*gratia*). From the mouth comes flattery; its respectable name is glory. From the hand comes money; it is presented as a reward (*praemium*). In this Augustinian way the monk Gregory analyzed the offerings condemned by the Lord speaking through Isaiah. All were to be rejected by the just man.[13]

Gregory spoke as a monk, but as a monk who had once been a ruler—prefect of Rome—and who perhaps suspected he would be a ruler again. At the time he spoke he was the pope's emissary to the court at Constantinople where no doubt all three kinds of *munera* were known, and he was addressing the monks who had come with him from Rome. For their benefit and his own he was reflecting on what he saw before his eyes. The central figure of these contemplative moral meditations on the active life was Job, a man of sorrows.

"God does not reject the powerful because He is powerful," Jerome's imaginative translation of Job 36:5, was before Gregory as he spoke to his monks on morals, and commenting on the text, he spoke on the perils of power. A ruler, he declared, could easily become "like the angel of apostasy," that is, like the devil himself. Why? Because a ruler might aspire to be like God and, although a man, disdain to be like men. It was a frightening insight—presumably it was related to Gregory's own earlier experience as the senior secular authority in Rome. In 590, not long after Gregory had formulated this fearful truth, he accepted election as bishop of Rome and, with the approval of the emperor in Constantinople, was consecrated.[14]

Election to the most powerful position in the Western world did not remove the fear and self-doubt that the meditations on Job had made explicit. A few months after he had been in office Gregory wrote a distant friend, Theoctista, the emperor's sister, revealing his idealism, perplexity, and anguish. He had been trying, he wrote, to go daily "beyond the world," to "become beyond the flesh." His new pastoral office had called him back to worldly affairs. He knew that in what he was now doing he was not abandoned by God. "God does not reject the powerful," he quoted, "because He is powerful." The reminder was not enough. The business of office was for him "difficult." It was, in fact, "very burdensome." He concluded with a startling burst of self-deprecation, in which the recollection of his great predecessor, Leo I, played a part. The emperor, he wrote, has ordered an ape to become a lion (*leo*). After that, "the ape can be called a lion. But he cannot be a lion." The reference was unmistakably to himself, and the sense of hopelessness was absolute: "he cannot be a lion." It was with this acceptance of power as godlike, this inner craving to "become beyond the flesh," this conviction that he was only another monkey that Gregory considered the effect of offerings on judgment.[15]

In the first year of his pontificate he sent to John, archbishop of Ravenna, the *Pastoral Rule,* a work doubtless matured earlier, but issued now as a kind of moral manifesto at the start of the pontificate. Self-doubt was erased in an emphasis on purity. A ruler, he wrote, must be "clean in thought, so that no uncleanness pollutes him." He must have clean hands, which he took care to wash of dirt (*sordes*). He must be careful lest "what he touched with his hands stained anything he touched, lest he pursue what was mud and be held by what was dirt." Isaiah had said, "Be clean, you who bear the vessels of the Lord" (Is 52:11). Purity of this kind was freedom from corruption. It paralleled a purity Gregory insisted on in sexual matters. Even the married, he taught, "befouled" copulation by mixing pleasures with it. After lawful conjugal intercourse—so Gregory was to instruct Augustine, the missionary bishop he had sent to Canterbury—the spouses should seek "purification" by water and by abstaining from entering a church. "Cleanness" was required to receive the body of the Lord. The best cleanness was "the cleanness of those who are continent." For Gregory, the antipollution ethic in sexual morals as in government morals reflected a strong impulse "to become beyond flesh." Cleanness meant being free from the desire of earthly things. Judging the causes of his subjects "when set in the divine place," the ruler must not let his mind be darkened by "the importunity of dusty desire for terrestrial things."[16]

In the same year Gregory gave a series of homilies on the Gospels —again they no doubt reflect prior work, now taking on special significance as the words of the new pope; John Paul II's homilies at St Peter's today are a good parallel. "Weeping," he spoke to priests, some of whom he knew "sell spiritual favor for rewards" (*praemia*). Did they not recall the words of the Lord, "What you have received freely, give freely" Did they not know that the Repurchaser had overturned the tables of those who sold the doves? And did not the dovesellers today take a price for selling the Spirit?[17]

These declarations can be compared to the proclamations of the rulers of Ur-Nammu and Babylon or the reform edicts of fourth-century Roman emperors: clearly high ideals are being enunciated. But Gregory also put these ideals forward as internal guides for himself. "Sacred Scripture in operation is a bow in hand. . . . The bow is well held in hand when whatever is known by the study of the sacred tongue is accomplished by living. . . . The Word of the Lord is wonderful not only to know but to do." His public scorn for the hypocrisy of those who were hearers of the Word only was intense. He was keenly aware that the ruler was in a position where "outside" evil "corrupts" what is "within." He wanted to be better than an ape with a lion's name.[18]

Scandal in Sardinia led him to address the Empress Constantina in June 595. Pagans on the island had given "the judge" (the governor) a reward (*praemium*) to permit them to continue to sacrifice to idols. Some pagans had now become converts. The judge wanted the new Christians to continue paying. Upbraided by Gregory's representative, he replied that he "had promised such a large payment for office" that without such income his promise could not be met. Gregory asked the empress to command that "nothing be collected with sin." Payment for office, *suffragium*, had supposedly been outlawed by Justinian's Novel 8. Gregory did not himself characterize the *suffragium* as either unlawful or sinful. It is not clear whether he regarded it as normal custom or mentioned it to get the governor in trouble with the empress. His focus was on the payments extorted from the Christians, and he sought to put a crimp in the governor's operations.[19]

Small gifts, *xenia*, were by implication in a different category; or it may be that Gregory thought of the offeror as being in a position different from that of the recipient. Subdeacon Peter, a trusted agent sent by him to Sicily, received specific instructions in July 592 to pay "some small offering" (*exenium*) to military recruiters "to make them agreeable," and "some ancient customary amount" was to be deposited at the praetor's office "so you may win their favor." Gregory showed no moral diffidence in this kind of accommodation. In the same letter he noted he had examined the monk Cyriacus, another agent, recently returned from Sicily, about receiving money in the case of a certain woman. He was satisfied by Cyriacus' answer, which Subdeacon Peter had approved. The payment was described as *praemium*—here a reward was found to be acceptable.[20]

In July 592 Gregory wrote Honoratus, his representative at the court in Constantinople, ordering him to support the petition of Venantius, "nephew of the patrician Opilio," to obtain the title of ex-consul, and observed that Venantius was ready to spend thirty gold pounds for the title. "He is such a man," Gregory lamely added, "to whom honor is due even without a payment." Willingness to make an illegal payment had not lost him Gregory's backing; or Gregory may again have judged givers more lightly than takers.[21]

Dealing with rulers, Gregory was also not an inconspicuous donor of nonmonetary *munera*. In 597, Queen Brunichildis, ruler of Austrasia and Burgundy, asked for the pallium for her favorite, Syagrius, bishop of Autun. This small band of wool conveying a special mark of papal favor was unprecedented for Autun and was to be denied to Autun's metropolitan at Lyons, but Gregory was ready to oblige. He rationalized his concession as justified by Syagrius' help to Augustine and the mission Gregory had sent to England. By his own stricter standards, Gregory was tendering the queen a service that constituted a *munus* of the heart. Brunichildis herself, a Visigothic tigress in popular repute, living in incest with her nephew, was the object of generous offerings from the pope's mouth—for example, "The government of your kingdom and the education of your son testify to a goodness of Your Excellency which pleases God and must be proclaimed." A modern biographer of Gregory is reminded of Disraeli addressing Queen Victoria.[22]

Coping with the world, the pope clearly did not abandon conventional ways of winning reciprocity from the powerful. Within the Church his attitude was stiffened by a conclusion he had probably reached as a monk and did not give up as pope. For a churchman to accept any offering —with offering understood broadly as any of the three kinds of *munera* of the hand, of the mouth, of the heart—in exchange for an ecclesiastical benefit was "what the sacred canons condemn as the simonian heresy."[23] As pope, Gregory found the simonian heresy ubiquitous.

"The sacred canons"—presumably Gregory meant Chalcedon—had condemned the act of buying God's favor but had no noun to describe the action. Patriarch Gennadius had called it "bribery" (dōrodokias). Gregory knew no Latin equivalent but coined or adopted the cumbersome phrase "simonian heresy" as a substitute for the nonexistent action noun. The phrasing did more than identify a practice. It escalated the level of denunciation. Before Gregory the view that Simon Magician was a heretic was common; and Theodosius II's decree against the Nestorians showed how the tag "simonian" could be applied to disgrace new heretics. But Gregory pioneered in calling the practice of purchasing God's grace a heresy in itself and labeling a common sin as a form of doctrinal perversity.

The one place Gregory did not press hard with the harsh word "heresy" was Rome itself. In 595 he presided over a Roman synod of some twenty-three bishops and legislated: "Following the ancient rule of the Fathers, I decree that nothing is ever to be taken for ordinations or for the giving of the pallium or from the handing over of the documents. Nothing is to be taken from the new fraud which self-seeking (ambitio) has invented which is called 'pasturage.'" The lector was not to charge for his reading at the service nor the notary for his pen; and pasturage (pastellum) for the clergy was to be no excuse. One exception, inviting evasion, was left. Gregory declared himself unwilling to condemn what was offered voluntarily "out of thanks" (gratia) after the ceremony." The "simonian heresy" was not associated with the bad Roman customs.[24]

In the rest of the world, Gregory read custom differently. "No one in the regions of Gaul and Germany," Gregory wrote on August 12, 595, "attains to holy orders, as I have learned from information provided me by certain persons, without giving a stipend" (commodum). This ominous observation was addressed to a successor of Caesarius (himself silent on the topic), one Virgil, bishop of Arles. Gregory went on to instruct him on the evil: "Our Repurchaser" drove the sellers of doves from the temple, because "to sell the dove is to receive a temporal stipend for the Holy Spirit. . . . " Vice fed on vice: "Already spoiled in the very root of his advancement, the one who was promoted for a price is the more ready to sell to others what he bought." What becomes of the teaching of Christ, "You have received freely, give freely"? The simonian heresy was the first to spring up in the Church. It should now be extirpated everywhere. Letters to the same effect went out to all the bishops of the Franks and to their king, Childebert.[25]

In the same month the East was similarly addressed. God, John of Corinth was told, wanted to end "the wicked plague of pollution" that had infected his church. John was better than the previous regime, but Gregory had heard that no one in his territory attained to orders without a stipend. This selling of the dove was denounced. Gregory went on to blame equally each of the three kinds of offering: "You must not consent to anyone coming to holy orders, or permit it, by means of a stipend or by means of favor or through the request of others." In less detail he sent the same exhortation to all the bishops of Greece.[26]

Images and argument were representative of Gregory's use of familiar scriptural symbols, amplified on occasion by reasoning on the pernicious effects of the practice. Earlier he had taken up simoniacal sales in a disciplinary case from Byzacena in Africa; instructed John, the new bishop of Prima Justiniana in Illyricum, about them; and admonished Januarius, the chronically delinquent bishop of Caligari in Sardinia. In September 596 he drew the simonian heresy to the attention of Theodoritus, Demetrius, Philip, Zeno, and Àlcison, bishops of Epirus, and also took up the particular case of Maxim of Salona. In September 597 he brought the matter up with Brunichildis of Austrasia and Burgundy. In April 599 he looked East and upbraided Anastasius of Antioch. In July of the same year he attempted to stir up Virgil again, along with Syagrius of Autun, Etherius of Lyons, and Desiderius of Vienne. Another missive quickly followed to Aregius, bishop of Gap. He wrote Kings Theudebert of Austrasia and Theodoric of Burgundy jointly in the same month. Isacius of Jerusalem, another eastern patriarch, received a reminder of the problem in 601. A spate of letters went to Gaul in June of that year—to King Theodoric, to King Theudebert, to Queen Brunichildis, to King Clothar II, to Bishop Aregius. African bishops Columbus and Victor each received a letter on the topic in 602. A friend in Alexandria, Patriarch Eulogius, was told in 603 to clean up his practices. The counterargument occasionally anticipated in the letters, that the money raised went to the poor or to monasteries and hospitals, Gregory dismissed. What was offered to God "from a crime" did not "placate his anger but aroused it."[27]

Recipients of these missives were not appointees of Gregory and for the most part they were beyond his control. The eastern patriarchs in Alexandria, Antioch, and Jerusalem would not have taken his direct orders, and it could not have been welcome to them to be told that Gregory had "heard" that "no one in the Churches of the East attains to holy orders except for a stipend." In the one case (Alexandria) where Gregory mentioned a source it was an anonymous person, who had studied medicine there and had known a youth "of extreme depravity" who had been suddenly ordained after giving "rewards (*praemia*) and gifts (*donationes*)." There is no indication that the patriarchs even acknowledged these rebukes; Gregory's complaints were based on rumor and were not notably sensitive to local customs and nuances.[28]

In the West, in Frankish kingdoms, Gregory's sources of information were no better identified, and the action he obtained was no more responsive. His royal correspondents, Brunichildis and her grandchildren Theudebert and Theodoric, were unlikely candidates as reformers. Gregory tried to bargain with Syagrius over the pallium Brunichildis asked for him—he would get it if he first presided over a council correcting what must be corrected, including simoniacal abuses. No council was called. Syagrius was a prominent politician, and if not the kind of bishop likely to be ironic about Gregory's bargaining to prevent bargaining, also not the kind of bishop likely to wage war on a system in which his career had been made. For several years Gregory pressed Gallic rulers and bishops to convoke a reform synod. When synods were finally held in 601 and 603, they left no decrees on the sale of orders. When Clothar II, having unified the Franks and murdered Brunichildis, held a synod at Paris in 614, the matter was not touched by the synodal canons or by the accompanying edict of the king.[29]

Even the Roman synod imposed no sanction of a human kind on those whom old custom or new pretense led to pasture on the ordinands. God's judgment, the synod observed, would overtake those who disobeyed. Only occasionally did Gregory have the opportunity to try to enforce the rules anywhere with specific penalties. Requesting Clement of Byzacena to restore a petitioner to his priestly appointment, he instructed him that the priest who had supplanted the petitioner was to be "deprived of the order of the priesthood" if he had obtained the post by means of "the simonian heresy." Actual application of the sanction was left to Byzacena.[30]

Factional fighting in Dalmatia produced a more complex affair. In the face of Gregory's advance disapproval, Maxim was chosen bishop of Salona. Gregory summoned him to Rome to meet the charge that he owed his election to "the simonian heresy." Maxim did not come. After four years of ecclesiastical fulminations and political skirmishing, Gregory let him off in return for his doing a few hours of public penance in Ravenna for his disobedience. The charge of the simonian heresy was satisfied by his taking an oath that he was innocent. God was made the judge in place of Gregory.[31]

Gregory's teaching on the sale of the Spirit could be understood narrowly to apply to the sale of ordination or, as at Chalcedon, to include the sale of any ecclesial office or, very broadly, to include the sale of justice. Patriarch Gennadius in his encyclical had taught that the canon of Chalcedon embraced all dōrodokias, all bribery; but it was plain from his context that in fact he meant only bribery to win office in the Church. No extension of the canon was made to the sale of justice by judges, even if they were ecclesiastical judges. Linguistically there was a difficulty. Chalcedon barred the sale of favor (charis). What judges gave was by definition not favor but justice. No comprehensive theory existed covering both the sale of favor and the sale of justice. Novel 8 had linked the sale of secular office to injustice in the execution of the office. Analogously, Gregory linked the sale of ecclesial office to further abuse of office. He paralleled Justinian rather than incorporated him. Embattled representative of Christian tradition in a collapsing West, he did not pursue both ecclesial and secular sale of office, both ecclesial and secular taking of bribes. Nor did he extend the campaign against "the simonian heresy" to the practices of monasteries receiving gifts from candidates.

After fourteen years of the pontificate of the most determined foe of the sale of holy orders to sit in the seat of Simon Rock it is hard to find a single case where an accusation of the simonian heresy had been made, proved, and the offender punished by the pope. "God's consul," as his epitaph proclaimed him, legislated but did not prosecute.[32] What Gregory did accomplish was a restatement of the standard on giving money for the Spirit in regions where the standard was forgotten or unknown. Ineffective in immediate results, his letters on the simonian heresy were to furnish the arsenal of reformers following, centuries later, in his footsteps.

Gregory's epistles had not only the prestige of a pope who had raised the Roman see to a new eminence, but his letters came from a man who was to appear to the Christian West of the next several centuries as its preeminent moral teacher or at least to share that position with St. Augustine. Gregory's lectures on Job to his monks he sent as a present to Leandro, archbishop of Seville. They were eventually copied all over Europe, in the course of time receiving the ultimate compliment of translation into the vernacular—into German in the tenth century, into Spanish in the eleventh, into French in the twelfth. His *Pastoral Rule* was equally diffused—for example, in the late 890s King Alfred had it translated into Anglo-Saxon. The three kinds of *munera* denounced in the meditations on Job and the purity from pollution insisted on by the *Pastoral Rule* were to be known to all medieval students of the morality of political life. In retrospect, Gregory did not appear to be an ape but a lion greater than Leo. His strong injunctions were to be the basis of reform in the West.[33]

The Encyclopedist of Seville.   On the separate track of secular bribery a summation of the ancient standards was offered in Spain. Ysidro (Isidorus)—one of four children all later regarded as saints—succeeded his older brother Leandro as archbishop of Seville in 600 and held office until 636; the combined rule of the two brothers in the most important see in the Iberian kingdom of the Visigoths lasted over fifty years. Bent on instructing the now settled invader in the Roman heritage, Ysidro set out didactically the duties of a prince and the duties of a good prince's good judges. Such men give judgment "without taking up persons," their justice unweakened by "the flame of avarice." They do not "take offerings" and give judgment. They look only to their eternal salvation. Wicked judges out of greed "delay or pervert judgments, and do not complete the business begun by the parties until they have exhausted the purses of the litigants." These "judges" are "like wolves in the evening"; and "in the manner of wolves they snatch at everything and leave scarcely anything for the poor," wounding "their own people" more savagely than the cruelest enemies. Even the many good judges often had grasping assistants. Scylla, who had a human shape and doglike heads, symbolized them: "not otherwise does it happen to certain powers that their own humanity is disturbed by the inhumanity of their unjust associates."[34]

Pursuing his indictment, Ysidro provided a separate section devoted to "The Taking Up of Persons." "It is written," he wrote, "'Do not take up a person in judgment.'" The judge who perverts judgment "by favor of kinship or friendship or hatred of enemies" sins "against Christ, who is truth and justice." "The Taking Up of Persons" was followed by a chapter called "Offerings" (*munera*) dealing explicitly with the judge "who judges rightly and from that looks for a compensatory reward" (*praemium remunerations*). Such a judge "perpetrates a fraud against God because justice, which he should impart gratis, he sells by taking money." The taking of offerings was "the undoing of the truth." The rich man "quickly corrupts the judge with offerings." Of Gregory's three kinds of offerings, cash "most easily" perverts the soul. In summary, "human judgment is corrupted in four ways—by fear, greed, hate, and love." On account of these motives justice is "often" violated, innocence "often" harmed.[35]

Interested in language, Ysidro accepted without comment the range of *redimere*: Christ bought back man gloriously and man bought back his crimes wickedly. *Redimere* means, he wrote, "to buy what was properly one's own." No crimes, he taught, "can be bought back by alms if one remains in one's sins." The guilty wrongly think "to buy back their fault with cash."[36] He showed awareness of the nuances of two of the Latin terms for present. His *Differences of Words* taught that "*munus* is offered to men, *donum* to God." Amplifying a little later, he said that *munus* is "owed to a patron," *donum* is a free gift (*honorarium*). His *Etymology* explained that *munera* are "services which poor men pay to rich men" and so "*munus* is given to man, *donum* to God." Ysidro was unable to maintain this distinction consistently. When he spoke of bad judges, he said that they "look not at the case but at the *dona*."[37]

Classical satire blended with Scripture in Ysidro to set the standard for the judge. His comments on corruption form a small proportion of the total corpus of his work, but he clearly regarded the risk of corruption as real. His anger, his sense that the poor were the victims, was palpable; and the offense to the poor man merged for him with offense to God. Sellers of justice committed frauds on God by selling what should be gratis—so Ysidro adapted to the courts the standard objection to the sale of divine favor; but he himself did not acknowledge the connection, mentioning "the Simonians" only to identify their name as derived from Simon, the man who "wanted to buy the favor of the Holy Spirit for money."[38] His focus was on the sale of justice.

For centuries after his death, in monasteries far north and east of Seville, Ysidro's encyclopedias were to be an easy source of knowledge. Along with all the other information they contained, they provided teaching on the judge's sin of taking up persons and the judge's sin of taking money. His words repeated, reinforced, and propagated the basic biblical commands.[39]

The Hagiographers of Iona and Ripon and the Historian of Wearmouth.   Colum-Cille (Columba d. 597) was venerated in his own life as a holy man. Visiting the diocese of Coleraine, he found that the bishop in preparation for his coming had taken care to collect "almost innumerable

gifts" from the people for him. The gifts were laid out in the monastery courtyard and duly inspected and blessed by Colum-Cille. One he praised in particular as the gift of a generous man. Another, he said, he could not "taste"; the giver must be "wise and avaricious." The embarrassed donor came forward, acknowledged his sin, and promised to be liberal in the future. A similar incident occurred when Colum-Cille visited the church of Death-rib. Each time Colum-Cille's problem with giftgiving was the inad- \
equate size of the gift, not its acceptance.[40]

So at least the stories were told a century later, about 690, by Adomnán, abbot of Iona, writing one of the earliest of Irish biographies. Colum-Cille's interest in gifts did not in the least detract from his saintliness in Adomnán's eyes. The biographer left no doubt that Colum-Cille, of the royal clan of the O'Neills, had a royal sense of giftmanship. He had begun life as Cremthann, the Fox. In monastic life he became Columba, the Dove, and he was called Colum-Cille, or Church Dove, to distinguish him from a namesake. Adomnán, himself a monk later to be acclaimed a saint, enlarged on the significance of the Dove as a "simple and innocent" bird and the form taken by the Holy Spirit.[41] His theme did not lead him to speak of buyers of the Dove. His chosen word for the gifts Colum-Cille received was *xenia*, the Roman term for small gifts to an official or patron. Adomnán saw no more difficulty in gifttaking than the royal Colum-Cille himself. That gifts, in any community accustomed to giftgiving, normally carry an expectation of reciprocation was not perceived as a problem.

Offerings have greater moral ambiguity and far greater social importance in a work written between 710 and 720 at the monastery of Ripon. Aedde, its author, was a priest from Kent, called to Northumbria about 669 to be a singing master for Wilfrid, archbishop of York.[42] Forthright, unpretentious, partisan, Aedde gives an account, often based on personal observation, of the ups and downs of his patron and hero. Offerings play a substantial part.

Aedde arrived in the time of the archbishop's prosperity. Wilfrid was performing miracles, building monasteries and churches, instructing the sons of the nobility. Above all, he was "always giving gifts and offerings (*dona et munera*) to spiritual men and to secular men, so lavishly that no one was found to be his equal."[43] Aedde said nothing of what Wilfrid got in return. As in any tribal situation the munificent *munera*-giver was a big man. The chapter setting out Wilfrid's liberality was entitled "The Goodness of Our Bishop."

Wilfrid's stature stirred the jealousy of Queen Iurminburg, who worked on her husband King Ecgfrith. Together they approached Archbishop Theodorus of Canterbury and persuaded him to intervene in York. Theodorus marked off a portion of Wilfrid's territory, divided it into three new dioceses, and appointed three new bishops. What brought about this interference by Rome's Greek appointee to Canterbury? According to Aedde, Ecgfrith and Iurminburg had tendered him *munera* "which blind the eyes of the wise."[44] As Aedde saw it, offerings were motivation enough to bring Rome's man into action.

Wilfrid decided to appeal this highhanded intrusion to the pope. He had visited Rome as a young man and studied for three years at Lyons, so he was not wholly ignorant of Roman law or Roman ways. Northumbrian enemies, determined to hamper his appeal without taking open responsibility, sent *munera* to the rulers of Neustria so that they might rob him en route. Aedde here again uses *munera* to designate the necessary and evil quid pro quo for a service.[45] Aedde's assumption about the purpose of this stratagem is also instructive. He takes it for granted that Ecgfrith and Iurminburg would be content if Wilfrid got to Rome without money.

Escaping the trap by taking another route, Wilfrid stopped in Austrasia, whose king, Dagobert II, he had once befriended in exile. Dagobert, "mindful of his gifts," pressed him to become bishop of Strasbourg in his country. When Wilfrid refused, Dagobert sent him on his way with an escort and "great offerings and gifts" (*munera et dona*).[46] *Munera* are here used to describe the appropriate response of a host who has once been a needy guest. They are meant to ensure that Wilfrid will reach Rome in style.

In Rome Theodorus' report had come first. Nonetheless, Wilfrid's case was examined by the bishops of Ostia and Porto and then heard by Pope Agatho and a synod. The result was a compromise. The diocese remained divided, but Wilfrid was to be allowed to pick the bishops. Aedde has nothing to say of giftgiving by Wilfrid in Rome but he does report that Wilfrid went shopping. From "select men" he obtained a great many relics for the churches of Britain. The *munera* he brought from Austrasia did not, we may infer, remain unspent. Pope Agatho, we know from Roman sources, was a Sicilian and interested in financial affairs; breaking custom, he had appointed himself the Treasurer of the Roman Church and personally signed receipts. Like Wilfrid, he has been regarded as a saint.[47]

On his return, Wilfrid presented to the king, the chief men, and the religious leaders "the written judgment of the Apostolic See." Displeased, some asserted that "the writings had been bought back (*redempta*) for a price." "Redeeming" is here used in its old meaning of paying off a judge; the first move of those confronted with an unpleasant verdict from the pope is to assail the integrity of the Roman administration. For the next 800 years of English history this reaction was to recur. Aedde underlines the enormity of the accusation, leaving indefinite its victim, although it is apparently Wilfrid. They "defamed," he writes, "to the peril of their souls."[48]

Suspect, Wilfrid was cast into prison. There Ecgfrith brought pressure on him, in the end offering a compromise: part of his diocese "and other gifts not at all small" if he would deny that the decisions from Rome were "true." Wilfrid said he would rather have his head removed. Eventually Ecgfrith was led to release him. Wilfrid had refused the king's *munera* and refused to accuse the pope of *munera*-taking, and the malicious accusation of *munera*-obtained decrees had not been fatal to him. In the long run Archbishop Theodorus himself acknowledged him as the man in England "most learned in the judgments of the Romans." Theodorus could be suspected of irony, but not Aedde: in his report, Theodorus is being made to acknowledge the authority of the papal decision, untainted by defamatory suspicions.[49]

About 708, Wilfrid suffered an illness that led him to prepare for death. He ordered his treasurer at Ripon to bring out his hoard of gold, silver, and precious stones and to divide them in four parts before eight witnesses. Wilfrid told the witnesses that he had once thought that he would "again invoke the see of St. Peter the Apostle" and doing so would take one quarter of the treasure to bring gifts to the church of St. Mary and to offer *munera* to the church of St. Paul. As approaching death now prevented execution of this plan, Wilfrid directed that the offerings be carried in his name to the two Roman churches; that a second quarter of the treasure be given to the poor "for the buy back of my soul"; a third quarter should go to those who had shared his exile; and the fourth quarter should be divided by the abbots of Ripon and Hexham, Wilfrid's major foundations, "so that with offerings they will be able to obtain the friendships of kings and bishops."[50]

In this last testament, redemption of one's soul is obtained by offerings, old friends are rewarded by offerings, churches are endowed with offerings, and the means for abbots to gain the support of secular rulers and of bishops are explicitly stated to be offerings. One quarter of Wilfrid's total treasure had been saved for an appeal to Rome. At death he offers it without a case in view. The implication left is that his original provision had been prudent, a precaution necessary if he were to succeed in litigation. *Munera* in multiple modes are acknowledged by Wilfrid's last directions as puissant and legitimate in his society.

Writing his *Ecclesiastical History* at Wearmouth less than a decade after Aedde, Bede took a different view. Telling of the apostleship of Aedhán (latinized as Aidan) to England, he writes, "He was never accustomed to give any money to the powerful of the world, only food when he received them as guests; rather, those gifts of money which were distributed to him by the rich he spent, as we have said, for the use of the poor or dispensed for the buy back of those who had been unjustly sold." Of the bought-back he made disciples and priests.[51] Like Colum-Cille, Aedhán appears as a gifttaker; unlike Wilfrid he is not a giftgiver to the powerful. Buy back, *redemptio*, is restricted to the recovery of actual slaves.

Contrast between Bede and Aedde increases when Bede draws on Aedde for his own account of Archbishop Wilfrid. All references to the charges against Theodorus of taking *munera* or against Wilfrid for buying his judgment in Rome disappear. For Bede, Theodorus is a man "of venerable age" (sixty-six!) and "upright morals," and Bede is not one to repeat derogatory rumor about Rome. Offerings play no role in his history of Wilfrid. His last directions are not restated.[52]

Bede does bring out a view of Adomnán invisible in Adomnán's life of Colum-Cille. Engaged in conflict with the Irish over their peculiar tonsure, Bede took the position that the author of this style was Simon Magician. Arguing with Adomnán, Bede challenged him directly: why did he wear a tonsure that had such an author? Adomnán replied, according to Bede, "Although I wear the tonsure from the custom of my country, I detest with my whole soul the simonian treachery and spit upon it."[53] Reported first-hand by a reliable historian, Adomnán must be believed to have spoken in this fashion. His answer and Bede's question are evidence that English and Irish ecclesiastics were conscious of the sin of Simon, evidence that the sin itself was a more active concept than the penitentials or the hagiographers suggest. It is not a heresy as in Gregory. It is not yet described by the action noun *simonia*. It is seen as a betrayal, for money, of God.

The Poet of Orléans

Why shall I delay? Pressingly the mob promises offerings
Whatever it wants, it thinks done, if it will give.

The lines are from a poem, written circa 800, entitled *Versus Contra Iudices—Against the Judges*. Their author, Teodulfo (Theodulfus), was himself a judge, and he was writing autobiography.[54]

Visigoth in origin, Teodulfo had left his Spanish homeland to enter Charlemagne's service as a cleric. By royal favor he had become bishop of Orléans. In 798 he was sent on a tour as a "judge"—in effect a royal deputy or *missus* with plenipotentiary power—to do justice, restore order, and promote prosperity. He was accompanied by another ecclesiastic, Lei-dradus, Alcuin's favorite pupil. Vienne, Valence, Rochemore, Orange, Avignon, Nîmes, Maguelonne, Soutancion, Agde, Béziers, Carcassonne, Arles, Aix, and Cavaillon were inspected by the two, and they held a particularly important judicial session in Narbonne, the principal city of the Midi. *Against the Judges* was based on these visitations.[55]

Nine years earlier, Charlemagne had given other royal deputies directions for judging. "Judge justly, sons of men," he declared and para-phrased the familiar words of Deuteronomy on the blinding effect of offerings and warned against corruption by adulation, love, fear, or reward (*praemium*). He quoted Chalcedon against ordaining for money and referred to "the heresy in Simon Magician." *Munus* to God, offered by a man of peace, was good. Upright bishops might expect a *praemium* with those enjoying eternal happiness. On earth, "having deliberated with priests and counsellors," Charlemagne condemned those who looked for gifts and offerings.[56] From Teodulfo's verse it must be inferred that these instructions had been hard to follow.

Everywhere in 798 Teodulfo and Leidradus were met by crowds, male
and female, old and young, rich and poor, all carrying offerings, all believing offerings were essential to win the deputies' favor. Payoffs to witnesses were occasionally attempted; principally the litigants concentrated
on the two judges. Offerings were their flying missiles, offerings were
their battering rams.[57] Great and small, litigants offered in accordance
with their means. Linen work, wool, headcoverings, boots, gloves, boxes
for manuscripts, wax for writing were tendered by the less prosperous.
Cordova leather in red or white, colored clothing of Arabic workmanship,
ingeniously embroidered, were presented by the rich. Calves, cows, bulls,
even vineyards were promised.[58]

Turbulently, the scene recreates itself: This one promises a crystal drinking vessel and jewelry "if I make him the owner of a farm." That one
brings Arabic money "if he may get a house." An ancient vase on which
Hercules is depicted in struggle with Nessus is Teodulfo's "if you favor
my hopes." Imports from Spain, treasures of the past, local farm products
are physically set before the judges. Fruits, eggs, bread, wine, goat cheese,
chickens and other edible birds—all these are put more or less literally in
their laps. Openly, unself-consciously, persistently the litigants take it for
granted that reciprocity with the judge is proper. In a word, "all rely on an
offering."[59]

Dependent on court attendants, servants, and local assessors who sit
with them, the royal judges are handicapped from the start. "Every
doorkeeper loves gold," thought Teodulfo. Not "one in a thousand of
them" is honest. The judges' servants are obvious targets. Constant vigilance is necessary to assure their integrity. One or another is ready to say
how a case can be decided in a suitor's favor without the judge shouldering
"the weight of sin." The servant's words are persuasive, his hands
"loaded with money." Assessors, drawn from the native nobility, have
pleas or gifts ready to press upon the court. They take their cue from
friends in the crowd, winked at by one man, hand-signaled by another.[60]

Teodulfo's poetic record of bribes offered a judge who refused them is
unique. No doubt he heightened the coloring and looked for picturesque
detail. His favorite poets were Virgil and Ovid, and he put to work Ovid's
technique of overstatement joined to sharp concrete examples.[61] He drew,
for example, a portrait of a married judge besieged by a wife seeking to influence his decision. Kissing his cheek, hands, neck, and knees, she offers
soft words to bend his mind. If he stands firm, a child or nurse reproves
him, "Why do you despise our mistress' words?"[62] Domestic intercessors
of this kind were presumably not known to Leidradus or himself; he was
indulging in conventional satire. Exaggerated as it may be, his picture of a
populace that expects offerings to operate in obtaining justice is convincing.

Teodulfo reported with gusto the gifts offered and took a stern, scriptural
view of their propriety. Samuel, Hezekiah, Josiah were examples that
showed they must not be taken. "Taking an offering usually turns weak

minds from the truth." The judge who accepts "sells what it is fitting that he should give gratis." A good judge should be looking out for the widow and the orphan, the aged and the sick. He should be helping those "whose voices and whose feet tremble." But "with an offering the rich man quickly disturbs the mind of the judge." Indeed the man who can say " 'Receive,' when he pleases, carries everything off; he dares anything if he is able to give more." As for the judge who "seeks barbarous rewards (*praemia*) for just judgment, he does your wicked work, O Enemy Fraud." The sanction was divine. "The High-Throned" observes what he does. "The last day must always be kept in sight." When Christ returns to judge "it will be with the voice of the Thunderer that he comes."[63]

As for himself, Teodulfo noted that often, when he upbraided others for taking, they said behind his back that he was one of them. Despite the assaults of the siege engines and battering rams of offerings, "I stood firm like a strong city after a battle and could not be taken by their arts." What he did take were "the little things," fruit, eggs, wine, bread, chickens. These were offered "not by a barbarous but a kindly hand." In this controlled and attenuated form Teodulfo permitted the rule of reciprocity to survive.[64]

Scriptural standard, popular expectations—the gap was enormous. Charlemagne's court proclaimed the standard in poetry and legislation. Enforcement was not apparently attempted.[65] Even education of the giftgivers appeared to be beyond what was possible. Charlemagne's *General Instruction* of 789 listed sins against which preaching was appropriate. Bribery and the simonian heresy were not among them. As bishop of Orléans, Teodulfo enacted two sets of "statutes" or regulations for the spiritual discipline of his diocese. He provided explicitly against a priest giving offerings to obtain another priest's parish. He said nothing about a litigant giving offerings to obtain a judgment.[66] When it came to specifics he mentioned robbery, usury, and false testimony. Bribetaking and bribegiving were not mentioned for inquiry.[67] Conscious of the tide of *munera* washing upon judges, convinced of the sinfulness of taking *munera* in judgment, Teodulfo gave no more attention to the problem for penitents that did his Irish, Anglo-Saxon, or Frankish predecessors.

The Masters of Penance. For killing a layman, seven years of penance; for the practice of coitus interruptus, two years; for anal intercourse, four years: in this way, for those disposed to receive their discipline, the monks between the sixth and tenth centuries set out tariffs for sin, at once informing confessor and penitent of what acts were sinful and giving an indication of the sin's relative gravity.[68] On the simonian heresy and bribetaking, a sharp contrast is found between the teaching of Saints Patrick, Caesarius, Martin, Gregory, and Ysidro and the message of these manuals.

Sins of covetousness fell within the penitentials' purview. From Patrick's first encounter with the pagan Celts it was evident that a standard rejecting gifts was new and puzzling to the pious. The custom of secular chiefs expecting payments was obviously engrained. Baptism could scarcely have erased the habit. Was there not a need to legislate about offerings to judges and bishops? Was there not a necessity to teach about offerings in the discipline enforced on the laity by the monks? The penitentials, by their silence, answered these questions negatively.

Abbot Finnian, author of the earliest Irish penitential (mid-sixth century) had a general provision against clerical covetousness, which he called idolatry, and a specific provision against clerical swindlers who raised money "under the false pretence of the buy back of prisoners." Nothing specific was said on bribery or the simonian heresy. Cummaine Fota (d. 662), bishop of Clonfert, modeled his penitential—the most comprehensive and the one much admired and circulated on the Continent—on the eight capital sins catalogued by Abbot Cassinian. Avarice was one of these principal sins. Theft, hoarding, and deceit were dealt with under this heading, so it was not for inability to specify particulars that bribery and Simon's sin were ignored. The closest Cummaine came to these topics was false witnessing; it was not very close. In the same way a penitential among the oldest of preserved works of prose in Old Irish, circa 850, treated generally of "Avarice" and, specifying the sins of false witnessing and false judging, did not link them explicitly to bribery; no doubt there was an implicit association between falsity in judging and a judge's desire for money. Books remarkably specific on sexual sins were vague on bribery and silent on the simonian sin.[69]

Simonians, Pope Gregory had believed, were everywhere. No contemporary professed greater devotion to Gregorian ideals than Columbanus (circa 543–615), the Irish educator of the Continent. He had read Gregory's *Pastoral Care* and found it "sweeter than honey." He was in touch with Candidus, Gregory's envoy to Brunichildis and Childebert. He wrote Gregory to ask if he should communicate with "the Simonians"; there were, he observed, "many in the province." Yet the penitential of Columbanus, which was to be exemplary for the Franks, was devoid of references to Simonians or the simonian heresy.[70]

Anglo-Saxon penitentials did not show a stronger interest in corrupt reciprocities. Gregory himself had launched the Roman mission to England with the sending of Augustine and his companions to Canterbury. Works from this English foundation such as *The Canons of Gregory* did not treat the topic. Later, in 668, Rome had reinforced its earlier connection by choosing the Greek Theodorus of Tarsus as archbishop of Canterbury—the man who according to Aedde was seduced by the offerings of King Ecgfrith and Queen Iurminburg. The penitential issued in St. Theodorus' name said nothing on this sensitive topic. Bede, ecclesiastical historian, writing in a Northumbrian monastery circa 725–730, did have a sharp comment on the betrayal of Jesus for cash:

Many today are shocked at the crime of Judas as inhuman and wicked: he sold his own lord and master and God for money. Yet they do not avoid it. For when they speak false testimony against anyone for offerings, they assuredly—for they deny the truth for money—sell God. For he himself said, "I am the truth."

By implication only, the passage was a rebuke to judging falsely for a bribe; as to the simonian heresy it drew no lessons. Bede's own penitential had nothing on either subject. The penitential of Egbert, archbishop of York, 731–767, was equally blank. So were two other penitentials circulated under the names of Bede and of Egbert.[71]

An exception exists. A penitential in Old Irish composed at the monastery of Tallaght, probably before 800, and based on earlier, lost Latin texts, prescribes a penance of three and a half years for anyone who "takes a reward to kill a man or to bear false witness or to bring a false suit or to give false judgment." The crimes here associated together recall the Roman law on conspiracy to condemn someone in court. An additional section provides a penance of one year for perjury committed out of friendship, and seven years penance if done for payment. The provisions show that the possibility of influencing testimony or judgment was understood while it remained unemphasized.[72]

Augustine, Caesarius, and Ysidro were familiar to many of the monasteries where the penitentials were composed or revised. The Bible itself was known to all of the composers. Old Testament commandments, New Testament images, patristic elaborations were all bypassed by the handbooks in the predominant silence on Simonians and bribetakers. Unquestionably a devout penitent instructed by a monk following a penitential would have known that avarice was evil. He would not have been instructed as to measure or mode in receiving gifts offered by way of reciprocity.

Social patterns, meanwhile, not only checked the teaching on gift-free actions; they provided a model influencing penitential discipline itself. Three stages of development can be discerned. The first is reflected in the oldest Irish penitential, that of Abbot Finnian. The sin of magic, Finnian stated, "can be bought back (redimi) by penance." Negligence leading to the death of a child without baptism "can be bought back by penance." A false oath "can scarcely or not at all be bought back." In this usage penance was exchangable for guilt. The transaction was not entirely voluntary. Once committed, the sin was unexpiated until paid for by the penance. Payments were physical and severe—for example, one year on bread and water, while not sleeping in the same bed, for the negligent parents of the child; one to three years on bread and water for various kinds of magic.[73]

Finnian used redimere or redemptio in another context when he spoke of persons pretending to collect money "to buy back captives" or "for the buy back of captives." Buying back guilt was an analogous transaction, modelled on the reciprocity required in many ancient societies when a neighbor had been killed or injured. Irish canons of an early if undetermined date set out a list of the payments to be made for various kinds of killings, woundings, or kidnappings. A rule ascribed to Patrick said that a thief from a king, bishop, or scribe "shall pay the price of seven female slaves or do penance for seven years with the bishop or scribe."[74] In the case of sins less definite than bodily assault or theft, no identified person was to be paid except God who had been offended by the act. In Latin terminology the sin was "bought back" by the penance. In Finnian the buy backs were made through personal suffering, not with money.

A second stage was reached by the seventh century in the coinage of a term for buy backs and the elaboration of equivalents for standard penances. The term came from the Irish *ar-ren*, "pays for, pays instead of."[75] The noun indicating the action of paying for or instead of was *arre*, latinized as *arreum* and translatable as "commutation," "redemption," or "buy back." A seventh-century Irish list of such commutations provided, for example, that the *arreum* of one year of penance was "a month of great pain from which one does not die."[76] A more elaborate late eighth-century list in Old Irish, probably from the monastery of Tallaght, commuted "a black fast" to a hundred blows with a scourge. Some sins—for example, kin-slaying, druidism, adultery—were beyond remission of the penance. Buy backs were provided for "rescuing a soul out of hell"; they consisted in prayers, fasts, and scourging. Cash buy backs were not usual. By analogy, these redemptions of penances were like the redemptions of guilt. Basic to each was the exchange.[77]

In the third stage, cash was frequently used. Illustrative are penitentials prepared on the Continent in the eighth and ninth centuries such as Pseudo-Cummean's [Cummaine], post 750, and Pseudo-Bede and Egbert's (post 850). Pseudo-Cummean had a chapter entitled, "The Rich or Powerful Man: How He Buys Himself Back on Account of His Criminal Sins." The cases dealt with under this rubric were restricted. Where the victim could not be found, the sinner could substitute charity to the poor and the Church or "buy back captives." A poor man unable to make restitution was assigned a graduated scale of fasts and almsgiving over a three-year period.[78] Pseudo-Bede-Egbert contained one section entitled, "The Price of a Buy Back." A rich man who could not fast and who had means "whereby he could buy back" was to give twenty *solidi* in exchange for seven weeks of fasting. Not so rich, he was to give ten. "Very poor," he was to give three. Money was acceptable in place of physical suffering, even if acceptance was limited to donors unable to fast. It was to go for "the buy back of prisoners" or for the altar or to the Christian poor.[79]

In exchanges of personal suffering for sin, exchanges of more intense suffering for protracted suffering, and exchanges of money for suffering, reciprocity governed. When money was substituted in hard cases, the commutation had a form difficult to distinguish from an offering by which a spiritual benefit was purchased. The difficulty did not appear to have been generally experienced. Reciprocity, the great principle, was being observed. The "system"—that is, the mutual expectations of rulers and ruled in secular society and in the Christian Church—was satisfied even by money equivalences. Scriptural standards, saintly examples were not effective to stop such popular and comprehensible arrangements.

Preserving the word of God in Scripture, and the texts of Fathers, councils, and popes, the monks handed down the tradition. Judgment was to be given without offerings. The Spirit's gifts were free. Martin, Gregory, and Charlemagne elaborated the teaching by legislation, Caesarius by preaching, Ysidro by learned compilation. Bede reported that Simon's sin was spat upon. Teodulfo satirized in verse the gift-bearing litigant. Patrick presented his own self-denial as example. The tradition was neither unknown nor unfruitful nor unlived. It was overshadowed by the system—by customs, practices of the people, expectations of the powerful. Freely accepting gifts Colum-Cille did not follow Patrick; Adomnán still saw Colum-Cille as a saint. Wilfrid knew that offerings were required both in Northumbria and Rome; he is Aedde's hero. The penitentials were silent on the sins involving offerings. Penitential discipline was itself adapted to the practice of exchange. The protests against gifttaking were almost as sporadic as those in Israel of the seventh-century B.C. The mechanisms to carry out the legislative aspirations of Pope Gregory were not in place. The competent professional class was missing. As the millennium was reached in 1000, the system was the obvious reality. Was it possible that in European society a desire, an energy, an authority could be found that would shake the system?

II

Recurrent Reformation

1000–1530

6

Sins of the Stomach

Reform, a term with a scriptural pedigree, was a theme popular with the Fathers. Renewal, restoration, reassertion of spiritual values were its senses. Multiple in the modes it took, broad in its significance, reform was an idea not narrowly confined to the correction of corruption. The large patristic concept was necessarily present in the literature that a later and less privileged age drew on to form its own aspirations and purposes. "You," the Mass, addressing God, prayed at the offertory, "have formed the nobility of human nature and you have still more wonderfully reformed it." The idea of reform as restoration could not have been more succinctly or more centrally expressed.[1]

Now, however, after one thousand years of Christianity, reform was to become more specific, more connected to concrete corruptions. Invaders, unacquainted with the tradition regulating reciprocity, had continued to despoil Western Europe in the ninth and tenth centuries. Links to Greco-Roman and Mediterranean culture declined. Impoverished, the churches were exploited for personal profit. By 950 the papacy had reached its nadir. A century later, a band of clerics, strategically placed in Rome, raised the

banner of reform in the immediate and practical sense of eliminating corruption in the appointments and administration of the Church. Reform
was to become the cry of the day.

The standard that was to be *the* criterion of ecclesiastical administration
for the next 500 years was set out between 1050 and 1170 in statutes and
satire, theoretical analyses and anecdotal chronicles, personal letters and
official judgments. It centered on that special subdivision of bribery
which involved the purchase of the Spirit. The charge of selling the Spirit
was to become the most potent of political accusations. Parties and programs formed around it. Popes came to office pledged to extirpate the
practice and were judged, often harshly, by their own success or failure in
living up to the reformers' measure of purity. In the spiritual sphere, no
doubt was to remain that reciprocation for spiritual office was an evil.

Reform was always partial, always hampered by the arrangements of
administrative organization and the assumptions of the age about gifts.
The central organization was chronically in need of money. Curial offices
were not supported from a common treasury but depended on the fees
paid for exercise of the function. Clear lines had not been drawn between
funds held in trust for particular public purposes and funds at the personal
disposition of an officeholder. Organizational needs for money, the association between exercise of office and a fee, the confusion between public
and personal property converged to make it hard for churchmen in office
to be as pure as the reformers wished. At the same time the old assumptions about giving had not been eliminated. Europeans tendered offerings
to those in power. Offerings could not be banned. Yet offerings—
munera—were exactly what were condemned when given to influence
judgment. No unambiguous word for bribe existed. In the canon of the
Mass itself, the bread and wine about to be consecrated were described as
dona and *munera*—gifts and offerings. In the most sacred context, *munera*
were still acceptable. As the reform intensified, distinctions were to be
driven between *munera* that were murderous—that indeed led to murder—and the only *munera* that a Christian could rightly offer.

Bribery as Heresy. "More detestable than ambitious Catiline," the
bishops and priests of the Church have connived in the spread of a monstrous evil. "Led by blind ambition," they have failed to combat a stupen-
dous assault upon the Church. Silently, they have seen enemies—the very
robbers and thieves denounced by the Supreme Shepherd in John
10:1—enter not by the true gate but by the window. Once within, once enjoying office, these robbers have let churches and monasteries fall into
ruin. Alienating ecclesiastical revenues and possessions, they have
employed "diabolical contracts" to convey away what was rightfully
God's. Wasting the Church in Italy, they have done more harm to it than
the Vandals, the Goths, the Huns, the Lombards, or even the Hungarians![2]

Determined, unscrupulous, ubiquitous, who are these internal enemies,
now to be fought tooth and nail, hammer and tongs? Their name—not the
name they chose but the name that must be pinned upon them—is

"Simonians." Descendants of Simon Magician who are now everywhere, they must be identified, execrated, and extirpated from the sheepfold.

Such in mid-eleventh century, in 1057, were the words of Humbert of Silva Candida, cardinal of the Roman Church in the pontificate of Leo IX. Such was the burning spirit of the reformers at the ancient center, the center to be restored, of the ecclesial organization. Cardinals Humbert and Hugues and Frédéric (the future Stephen IX)—Lorrainers all—were now at the top of an administration that had disintegrated for two centuries. They had recruited to their enterprise Pietro Damiani of Tuscany and Ildebrando of Rome (the future Gregory VII). Thanks to the patronage of the emperor, Henry III, his cousin Bruno had become pope as Leo IX. The others were Bruno's protégés. Half a dozen men, they represented a resurgence in Rome of standards occasionally recalled, sometimes forgotten, often ignored, and generally unenforced.[3]

Three practices were identified by them as evil and allied—concubinage or marriage by the clergy; investiture of laymen with churches; purchase and sale of holy orders. Ten years after the inauguration of Leo IX's reign a council in Rome summed up their program: No one was to hear the mass of a priest who kept a concubine. No priest was to obtain a church, either at a price or gratis, from a layman. No one was to be ordained or promoted "to any ecclesiastical office whatever" by means of "the simonian heresy."[4] Lay investiture was linked with unworthy, that is, simoniacal appointments; clerical celibacy was considered a mark of self-control contrary to the looseness and self-indulgence manifested by the venal. Purity—purity both sexual and administrative—was what the reformers sought. If in the United States a band of reformers decided that politicians living unchastely should be barred from office, that corporations should not favor candidates, and that no one should be elected to any office who received a campaign contribution from a corporation, the task before them would be comparable. Political battles, physical warfare lay ahead for the reformers. Our focus will be on the rhetorical and legal combat against bribery itself, a combat centered on "the simonian heresy."

Against it were marshaled words and images—words and images turned into invective and shaped, at times, as sanction. Scripture was fundamental. The universal paradigm of the faithless cleric was Simon Magician. The ubiquitous sin was his effort to buy the Spirit—a species of bribery that, remarkably, tainted the giver as much as, or more than, the donee. The condign punishment was Peter's curse, "Your cash and you go to perdition." Dove-sellers condemned by Christ, Gehazis turned to lepers by their greed, Judases "betraying God himself"—these were the sellers of the Spirit, scripturally regarded.

Scripture was reinforced. The "Canons of the Apostles" were cited. Chalcedon was invoked. Ambrose and Augustine were set out at length. Above all, Gregory the Great—his correspondence collected by his biographer Giovanni the Deacon—was used. His decree in the Roman Synod of 595, his letters to Brunichildis, John of Corinth, Theoderic, Theudebert,

Victor, and Virgil were extensively quoted. Missiles made 400 years earlier became weapons in the hands of the new reformers.[5]

As for sanctions, the most explosive was this: orders acquired simoniacally were invalid. All of the ancient authorities, as Cardinal Humbert read them, led to this conclusion. Ordaining, the Simonian conferred nothing. Ordained, the Simonian took nothing. Orders, purchased, were utterly void. No synod was needed to determine their voidness and to depose "the pseudo-bishops" simoniacally ordained. Automatically, from the nature of the transaction, they were without grace, power, or office.[6]

Simonians objected that Gregory I, even in denouncing the act, spoke of "the Spirit being sold and conferred." That showed, they said, that the pope believed that the grace purchased was conveyed. They failed to understand, wrote Cardinal Humbert, that Gregory merely meant that there was an attempt to confer the Spirit. "In this manner of speaking, it is said almost daily that one sells God when he sells justice." It is evident that neither God nor grace nor justice can be sold although "each can be trampled on for a price."[7]

Two formidable consequences flowed from Humbert's logical exposition of automatic invalidity—chains of null ordinations and utter uncertainty among the faithful. If A, a bishop, received no grace on his simonian consecration, then B, C, and D, candidates for ordination, received no grace when ordained by A; and if B became a bishop, he began his own chain of null ordinations. If a priest had been invalidly ordained, how was a layman receiving the sacraments from him to know? As Humbert acknowledged, a large effort had been made to separate the efficacy of the sacraments from the personal holiness of the priest: the orthodox position was that a priest in a state of sin could still validly celebrate mass. Humbert's doctrine on Simonians, in an age where Simonians were ubiquitous, offered reason to doubt the validity of the sacrament one received—reason remarkably analogous to the doubt caused by the view that sacramental grace depended on its dispensers being in a state of grace. Bonizo, an ardent Milanese reformer, gave it as his opinion in 1059 that "scarcely five out of one thousand [priests] could be found who were not stained by the simonian heresy"[8]; and even the pure five might have been ordained by simoniacally ordained bishops and so themselves be without orders. Was anyone sure of receiving a valid sacrament from a valid priest? Six years after Humbert had articulated his unanswerable syllogisms, a synod in Rome under Alexander II acknowledged that there existed "scarcely any church which is not corrupted in this way in some part" and decreed, "Therefore, not so much from the prompting of justice as from the instinct of mercy, we permit those who up to this time have been ordained gratis by Simonians to remain in the orders they have received."[9] The synodal decree cut the inexorable chain of invalidity for the innocent. It did not explain how the synod could supply the grace which was missing. Nullity was too powerful a weapon to wield effectively.

Almost equally difficult to manage in the long run was the sanction that classified Simonians among the heretics. Humbert derived this view from the repeated assertions of Gregory the Great and embroidered it. Like other heretics, the Simonians put on the character of Antichrist and did the work of Antichrist. Not only was the simonian heresy the first, it was the worst. Arians said the Son was a creature but did not try to merchandise Him. Novatians divided God's Church but did not try to dispose of Him for a price. Montanists located the Spirit in creatures but did not believe they could sell the Spirit daily. The essential false belief of the Simonians was that the Spirit *could be* sold. The heretical character of their faith was manifest.[10]

The evil act of buying or selling orders became so well known, so delineated as a type of conduct that a substantive action noun was needed to designate the disgraceful behavior. *Simonia*, that is, "simony," emerged. The new word was a sign both of the awkwardness of treating Simonians as heretics and the frequency of accusations against them. Cumbersomely, "simonian heresy" lingered in official documents. The new coinage measured the success of the reformers, the popularization of their critique. The Greeks had had *dōrodokias* to designate bribery generically; the Latins had lacked a word. Now, for the first time, an apt and specific term described the use of bribes to acquire the Spirit.[11]

As long as heresy was not investigated and pursued by elaborate mechanisms, characterization of simony as heresy was effectively abusive without entailing other consequences. When, later, heresy trials became more common, leading Simonians were not prosecuted as manifest heretics. What the reformers did do in the way of actually removing Simonians was selective and sporadic. In 1049, the first year of his pontificate, Leo IX presided over a council at Reims. The bishops of Nevers and Langres were accused of having purchased their orders. Nevers confessed that his relatives had given money without his knowledge of their action. He wept and was forgiven. Langres, accused of adultery, murder, and sodomy as well, was still defying his accusers when his lawyer "was divinely deprived of the motion of his tongue, so he could offer no defense." So state the records of the council, adding that the pope proceeded to excommunicate the bishop.[12]

In 1056, Ildebrando, as archdeacon, represented Pope Victor II at another council in France. A "very eloquent" archbishop was accused of the simonian heresy. As Bonizo reports what happened, "By night he makes all the accusers his friends by money. In the morning he taunts the judge, saying 'Where are they who accuse?'" Ildebrando asked him to recite the Gloria. He got as far as "Spiritus" and was unable to go on. He tried again, and again, and could not do it. He fell at Ildebrando's feet and admitted that he was a Simonian. He and a number of other guilty bishops then resigned.[13] The truth of the story is vouched for by Ildebrando's older colleague, Pietro Damiani. According to William of Malmesbury, a monastic chronicler, Pietro heard the tale from Hugues, abbot of Cluny, who used to lead the penitent bishop about with him and call on him to confirm that it had happened.[14]

Bribes and legal arguments were barriers to effective enforcement of the anti-simonian campaign. Miracles were needed to overcome them. Nonetheless the reform went on. This much is indicated by the anecdotes. Cardinal Hugues, a leading reformer, was himself accused of "simony" by the monks of Cluny. Other stories suggest the slow pace at which reform proceeded. In 1073 Ildebrando was elected pope and became Gregory VII. For a quarter of a century the reformers had been at work in Rome. On taking office he found that a crowd of laymen—some married, some, as the expression went, "concubined"—had custody of Saint Peter's. Pretending to be priests, they made a living from gulling Lombard rustics. Gregory VII ended their sway by locking them out. Swindlers, they were routed only by physical papal action.[15]

In the same first year that he overcame these petty crooks in Rome, Gregory VII made the move which was to start the conflict that came to dominate his reign. He sought the removal of Goffreddo, who reigned as archbishop of Milan due to his investiture by Emperor Henry IV. The pope called on other secular rulers, in particular Beatrice of Tuscany and her daughter Matilda, to help against this man "guilty of the simonian heresy."[16] The great struggle, which was to put pope against emperor, to lead the emperor to do barefoot penance at Canossa, and the pope to die in exile at Salerno, was begun, and among its causes was the desire for canonical justice on a Simonian.

Imperfect Image

> How precious are the martyrs Rufinus and Albinus! How they should be preached! How they should be praised! He who has their relics is justified immediately instead of being a sinner; he is made heavenly instead of earthly; he is turned from impious to innocent. We have seen simoniac, sacrilegious bishops, wasters of their churches, come to the Pope and because of the relics of the aforesaid martyrs be purged by the apostolic benediction, be disentangled from guilt, and, having no more of the old, become new. As if born again, they return to their own country. . . . Come, come, simoniac archbishops, bishops, archdeacons, abbots, deans, and priors too. Offer the two martyrs to the Roman Pontiff. By them the door is open into the Roman Church. Behold, he stands at the entrance with open hands. He calls you all. He exhorts you all. He solicits you all. He rejects no one—he who professes Albinus and Rufinus. Seek, therefore, by Albinus and you shall receive. Seek by Rufinus and you shall find. Knock by either martyr and it shall be opened.

Such was the judgment of Cardinal Gregory of Pavia pronounced before a gathering of cardinals and the reigning pope, Urban II. Pope and cardinals confirmed the judgment, prayed to Saints Albinus and Rufinus, and began to eat and drink freely until they fell asleep. Albinus is silver. Rufinus is gold. Every sin, this judgment indicates, can be absolved for money at the Roman Curia.[17]

Pseudonymous political cartooning of the year 1099, complete with a

pinguissimus papa or plumpest pope winebibbing with his gluttonous colleagues, this satire known as *Garsia's Tract* provides a picture of the
papacy very different from the image of Ildebrando sweeping out the
swindlers at Saint Peter's and bringing the Simonians to a stammering
stop. Monastic reformers, however, were still at the helm of the Church
when the satire was written. Eudes de Châtillon had been a monk and
prior of Cluny when, at a comparatively young age, he had caught the eye
of Gregory VII and had been made cardinal-bishop of Ostia. Two years
after Gregory's death he succeeded him as pope, taking for his name the
saint's on whose feast day Gregory had died. Jeeringly described by a rival
as Gregory's "footfollower," Urban II was by commitment and experience
Ildebrando's worthy successor. Joyfully he wrote his old abbot, Hugues, a
bulwark of the reform, to announce his election; eagerly he summoned his
old master Bruno, founder of the Carthusians, to counsel him in Rome. Er-
udite in Scripture and ecclesiastical tradition, trained in churchly politics,
commonly regarded as intelligent and courageous, he had been an ideal
choice for carrying out the reformers' program. The gap between Garsia's
caricature and the man chosen appears unbridgeable.[18]

How could unkind observers draw the satirist's conclusion about the
power of Albinus and Rufinus in the pontificate of Urban II? Three criminal matters were handled in this way: Gervin, bishop of Amiens, charged
by members of his clergy with acquiring his see and the abbey of St.
Riquier through "the simonian wickedness," took himself to Rome in
1091. His accusers did not follow. Urban II permitted him to purge himself
by swearing that he had not given or promised money for either the episcopacy or the abbey, nor to his knowledge, had anyone else on his behalf.
The pope confirmed his election and quashed an attempt to revive the
charge before the bishops of the province.[19] Foulque, bishop of Beauvais,
was accused by members of his clergy in 1094 of having been the patron of
murderers and of having acquired his bishopric by his father's purchase
of it. At Urban's order the bishop came to Rome where he offered to resign. His father and a canon of Beauvais swore before the pope that he was
free from any suspicion of simonian guilt. Urban judged him cleared and
restored him to office. An attempt by the archbishop of Reims to reopen
the case was rebuked.[20] Humbaldus, the bishop of Limoges, answered in
Rome to a charge of uncanonical election. "Under hope of mercy," he
resigned and made a pilgrimage to Jerusalem. On his return he again
implored mercy, and the pope committed his case to the archbishop of
Lyons. His accusers failed to prove him a Simonian, and he was permitted
to swear that he neither gave nor promised money, nor that to his knowledge anyone else had on his behalf. In October 1094, the Pope restored
him to office.[21]

Each of these cases, as set out in letters of Urban himself, was marked by
a striking lack of evidence supporting the accusations made and by a
procedure that permitted the accused to clear himself by his own oath. In
each case, a dispassionate observer might have remarked, the essential el-

ement appeared to be the accused's obeisance to the see of Peter. Nothing in Urban's letters indicates that the absolved bishops made gifts to pope and curia, but if they did it would have been easy for a hostile observer to conclude that the gifts were as important as the formal obeisance. Perfunctory judicial investigation followed by acquittals would have fed this cynical analysis.

Two marriage cases, also described by Urban himself, afforded a stronger basis for inferences uncomplimentary to the system of papal justice. Within the first year of Urban's pontificate, Jourdain I, prince of Capua, asked him to annul the marriage of his daughter to Renaud Ridel, duke of Gaeta. Jourdain had been an important supporter of the papacy: beginning with Gregory VII, the popes had relied on the Normans in southern Italy. Urban issued a rescript ordering the marriage to be held null if it were true, as Jourdain's envoys represented, that the daughter and her parents and relatives had been coerced into consenting to the marriage. Annulment on the grounds of coercion was, at the time, scarcely precedented. Proof of the pressure allegedly exerted by Renaud was made as easy as the proof of innocence for bishops. For evidence the rescript provided that the pope's legate need only take Jourdain's oath. The focus was so much on the father that the name of his daughter was not even mentioned in the rescript. It would not have been unreasonable for an observer to conclude that the case was decisively affected by Jourdain's standing as an ally.[22]

A second case: Sancho Ramirez, king of Aragon, wrote Urban II to acknowledge that Aragon was a feudatory of St. Peter and to pledge that the king and his sons should pay the pope 50 marks apiece annually as long as they lived. Replying in July 1089 to this letter from "our dearest friend" (friend, not son), Urban II took up a case the king had presented: Sancho Ramirez had promised his niece in marriage to a certain knight. He now asserted that he had acted under pressure and the girl herself was unwilling to marry the man. Urban II assured him that his niece was not to be married against her will. Her right to marry freely outweighed a promise that the king regretted having made. The decision represented unexceptionable theory; it was given in a letter specifically referring to the annual tribute which the petitioner had just promised the judge.[23]

Jourdain's daughter's case, Sancho Ramirez's niece's case show Urban II insensitive to the procedural requirements of impartial justice. No doubt he might have defended himself—I took Jourdain at his word; any sin was on his head; I was a ruler as well as a judge. Was I to give up judging my subjects because they paid me tribute? On behalf of an institution intended to be the center of reform these excuses would not have been highly persuasive. Whatever the pope's belief in his own sincerity and good faith, the linkage of money, power, and judicial results was palpable. At the very climax of the reform the curia acquired a reputation of susceptibility to influence and money. For centuries the reputation could not be shaken.

Collectors' Rules.   Ideologically, for purposes of the reform, individual papal acts did not loom as large as standards extractable from the Fathers, the Councils, and the decrees of past popes. The force and focus of the reform can be measured in the changing content of the collections of canons available to the reformers as weapons. The most famous of contemporary collections, often drawn on by the first generation of reformers, was that made by Burchard of Worms circa 1010 and available in Italy in 1050.[24] In a detailed set of instructions on sins as to which confessors should inquire, Burchard provided nothing specific on secular bribery or simony: here he was in the tradition of the silent penitentials.[25] He did, however, provide under "The Primacy of the Church" one decree from the Council of Meaux against the simonian heresy and a decree of Pope Gelasius I speaking of the sin of Simon Magician.[26] Under "Accusers and Witnesses" he put a rule of the Council of Châlon-sur-Saône, "Never in judgments let them take up either offerings or persons"; and he supplemented this canon with two of St. Ysidro's vigorous teachings on the taking up of persons and the taking of money.[27] If, however, Giovanni the Deacon's *Life* of Gregory I had not also been available, the reformers would have starved for Gregorian texts on the subject.

Near the end of the century, Yves, bishop of Chartres—a man well acquainted with the curia of Urban II—made a collection to be of much importance in the first part of the twelfth century.[28] The reform had been in progress forty years or more. Yves provided only a single canon, taken from a law of Charlemagne, against judges judging unjustly "or on account of offerings (*munera*)" and against judges "selling just judgment." But he set out twenty-five canons against the simonian heresy. Gregory I's homilies and his letters to Syagrius and the other Gallic bishops, to Brunichildis, and to Maxim formed a substantial part of this array.[29]

By 1130 the reform was history, its institutional objectives of an unmarried clergy and clerical control of investiture substantially advanced. About this time the greatest collection of all, *Concordantia discordantium canonum (A Harmony of Unharmonious Canons)* was begun at Bologna. Ascribed to an otherwise unidentified "Graziano" (Gratian), it reached its present form about 1150 in the papacy of Eugene III and as standard legal equipment for church courts and lawyers became known as the *Decretum*.[30] Simony by now was a major theme of the law.

Part II, the problem-focused core of the *Harmony*, began with Case One, a carefully constructed hypothetical intended to raise a variety of questions: "A certain man had a son and offered him to a very rich monastery. The abbot and brethren demanded ten pounds from him, which he paid, in order that his son might be received; the latter, by virtue of his age, was unaware of this." In the course of time the boy's merits win him election as a bishop; his father simultaneously makes a payment to a counselor of the archbishop, the son again being in ignorance of the payment. Once made bishop he gives his priestly blessing gratis to the ordinands but takes the money of some to ordain them. Ultimately he is accused of simony and convicted before his metropolitan. The first question which this plausible hypothetical raises is this, "Is it a sin to buy spiritual things?"[31]

The opening situation centered on an old custom that had recently been drawn into serious question. From at least the time of the rule of St. Benedict, monasteries had been accustomed to accept gifts from those they were about to admit: The novice from the day of entrance was to know that henceforth he would never have even "power over his own body." He gave his possessions with himself. The case was not so simple when, as the Rule of St. Benedict itself envisaged, a noble family offered a minor son to a monastery giving with him a voluntary offering "for their own reward (*merces*)." In the course of time such offerings were sometimes freely given, sometimes mandated by custom, often negotiated, occasionally waived. They were an important source of monastic endowments. When they consisted of land, as they frequently did, they helped a monastery to round out its boundary lines and to settle or avoid property litigations with its neighbors. Avaricious seeking of such gifts had been condemned by the twelfth-century reformers, but they had not applied the harsh term "simoniacal" to practice common and, so it seemed, necessary for most monasteries. As the concept of simony had become established and extended, however, an unsettling possibility was contemplated: the gift at entry to religious life could be analyzed as a quid pro quo, as something paid for the spiritual good of being admitted, as in fact simony. A German layman had raised a rumpus in Cologne around 1130 by making this charge against the monks of Saint Pantaleon. Gerhoch of Reichersberg, an outspoken clerical reformer, stated in 1135 that the entry offering (*oblatio*) was sought with "simoniacal avarice." Among all the little foxes who destroyed vineyards—the reference was to the Song of Songs 2:15—simony was "the most astute." This fox constantly disguised himself. Here in the monastery he was scarcely recognized when he appeared in the skin of a domesticated sheep. Reading Gerhoch, monks could suppose that a prize sheep was about to be denied them as a fox. Gratian, working within a decade of Gerhoch's blast, stepped into the middle of the controversy.[32]

Addressing it, a problem specifically covered by no authority, Gratian's *Concordantia* cites forty-nine texts from popes, councils, and fathers of the Church, the accumulation of centuries of opposition to the sale of the Spirit. Cardinal Humbert's teaching that "favor (*gratia*) is not favor if not given or received gratis" is chapter one (the author of the thought being mistakenly identified as "Pope Leo"). Chalcedon forms chapter eight, important but not given pride of place. Gregory I's homilies and letters are liberally quoted: no single authority is more often invoked. The plenitude of later authorities does not completely obscure biblical bases for objection. At least the biblical images stand out—the leprosy of Gehazi as the sign of the soul's stain when it sells God's gift; Peter's rebuke to Simon Magician; the Lord's ouster of sellers of the Dove from the temple; Judas's sale of Jesus as the paradigm of all who make money out of the Spirit.[33]

There was indeed no discord, no conflict of canons on the question of the sinfulness of selling the Spirit; and while Gratian has to describe the object sold broadly as "spiritual things" (entrance to a monastery was, after all, not a sacramental grace), the same answer holds for the monks' demand of the ten pounds as for the bishop's sale of ordinations: for the monks, and for him who gave to them, it was the crime of simony.

The hard question, not put by Gratian but answered by him, was whether orders acquired from Simonians were void. After much consideration of analogies pro and con, he concluded that they were void if knowingly received, but if received in ignorance that the ordainer was a Simonian they were valid. As the sale of Christ by Judas conferred the gifts of grace not on the seller or on the buyer but on beneficiaries unaware of the transaction, so the sale of the Spirit conferred grace on those in ignorance of the defect. The answer was strong in Scripture, tolerant in cutting the chain of invalidity.[34]

Tagged on at the end of the 125 chapters exploring the effect of purchasing the Spirit were five citations from Roman law on corruption. Like other additions of Roman law in the *Concordantia*, these were an afterthought inserted by a reviser; they were awkwardly attached to the long discussion of simony. All were from Justinian's *Codex*: the decree of the Emperors Gratian, Valentinian, and Theodosius of 386, also found in the Theodosian Code, encouraging anyone to report if "shaken down"(*concussus*) by a judge; a penalty set by law of four times the money paid a witness in cases of calumny; an extension of the Cornelian law to those falsely accusing or testifying for money; and two comments on the Julian law against any one entering a judgment or decree for money. Similarly tacked on in Case Two, at the end of a discussion of dilatory appeals, was a provision of Novel 47 that purchased judgments were null. These additions to the *Concordantia* called the attention of its reader to the Roman standards; they were not integrated into the analysis.[35]

Elsewhere within the work a diligent reader could find a scriptural comment on shakedowns. Answering in Case Twenty-Three the question, "Is it a sin to fight?," Gratian cited John the Baptist's reply to the soldiers who asked him, "What shall we do?" In the translation of the Vulgate, John answered, "Shake down no one, calumniate no one, be content with your wages" (Luke 3:14). An anonymous commentator (identified by Gratian as "Augustine") observed, "Whosoever is paid publicly-set wages and seeks more is condemned as a calumniator and shake-down man (*concussor*) by the judgment of John."[36] Here was a text applicable to all salaried officials, but its teaching on extortion was unrelated to the thrust of Case Twenty-Three and undeveloped by Gratian.

More firmly located in the *Concordantia*'s presentation, if still an excursus, were several patristic texts on unjust judgment. These were set in Case Eleven, whose main question was whether one was bound to obey the unjust sentence of a bishop. The *Concordantia* adduced Ysidro on the four forces (fear, hate, greed, love) that pervert human judgment; to this it added Jerome on "perverting the judgment of Christ, who is justice." It continued with Bede on false witnesses like Judas and those who followed Judas to "sell God." Bede's words were made general enough to arguably include judges by being introduced with the sentence, "He who denies the truth for money or speaks false testimony against anyone is proved to deny or sell God."[37] In the context of the same discussion stood the strong text of Ysidro on the judge who seeks a reward for a just judgment, described as one "perpetrating a fraud on God." With it went Ysidro's lapidary phrase, "The taking of money is the undoing of truth."[38] Interspersed with other texts on judgments wrongly motivated by wrath, Ysidro was quoted, "Justice is quickly violated by gold"; and Augustine's letter to Macedonius was recalled, slightly paraphrased, "Although it may be lawful for an advocate to sell his just advocacy and for a jurisconsult to sell right counsel, it is not lawful for a judge to sell a just judgment."[39]

The letter to Macedonius was drawn on again, three cases later, to answer the question, "Can alms be given out of usury?" The argument ran that what was unjustly acquired must be restored to its true owner. To the contrary, Gratian cited the words to Macedonius teaching that lower officials who by "tolerable custom" took payments from those doing business with them should give the money to the poor if they changed their lives for the better. This concession to human weakness was surrounded in Gratian's text by the whole paragraph of Augustine declaring that payments to judges were always wicked and giving the rationale that the judge must not be bound to one side.[40]

The double quotation of Augustine to Macedonius, the single quotation of Jerome, the multiple citations from Ysidro, the analogy with Judas from Bede offered as staunch a rejection of judicial corruption as can be found in any earlier moral teaching. Innocent misattributions undoubtedly enhanced their authority. Just as Cardinal Humbert's teaching on favor was credited to Leo I and the anonymous dictum on shakedowns to Augustine, so two of the three citations of Ysidro were credited to Gregory the Great, and Jerome on justice appeared as Augustine. The most influential moralist and the most important pope were presented as quotable authorities against payments to a judge. To them were added the reviser's citations of Roman law.

In terms of the *Concordantia*'s own problematic, the antibribery texts bore only obliquely on the questions being pursued. But, as often in this work, the questions were a peg on which to hang texts which the compiler wished to preserve. Later commentators generally ignored the questions and used the collection as a treasure trove from which to dig apposite teaching. In effect, the patristic authorities arrayed by Gratian formed a compelling case against the taking of offerings by judges. Far less emphasized and far less focused than the major texts on simony assembled in Case One, the fathers' and emperors' warnings against corruption of the courts were there for all to read. Generations of European lawyers were to read them.

After seven centuries in which emperors had issued edicts and popes decrees, in which saints had exhorted and homilists denounced, the *Concordantia* left no doubt in legal theory and legal teaching that neither the Spirit nor justice could be sold. Still, the preference of academic lawyers has always been to ignore the subjection of rules to the forces of money and influence. Bribery was a matter to which less than 1 percent of the *Concordantia* was devoted. If one went by counting texts the practice was inferably rare and the subject insignificant. Yet if money spoke more powerfully than texts, the 99 percent dedicated to exposition of the rules was less important than the 1 percent directed to preserving the integrity of the judges. If the courts were not incorruptible, no rule of law was beyond bending. At the end of the evolution of which Gratian's work was the crown, can we make some assessment of the extent to which theory and practice coincided in the twelfth century? The letters of the most energetic reformer of the day, the memoirs of the greatest literary genius of contemporary England, and the experience of a martyr afford a means.

Cistercian and Curia.   In 1145, as the *Concordantia* was nearing its final form, Bernardo of Pisa was elected pope and took the name Eugene III. Monk of the famous reform abbey of Clairvaux where his teacher and sponsor, the more famous Bernard, presided, he came from outside the curia. At the time of his elevation he was abbot of Sant' Anastasio, a Cistercian monastery near Rome, so that he joined the experience of an administrator to the austerity of a son of Clairvaux, for whom Clairvaux in retrospect was "Paradise." Pious and energetic, he was the kind of man whose election in the darkest days of the tenth-century papacy would have seemed miraculous. His choice now after a century of monastic reformers could seem the climax of the great fight for a better Church begun by Leo IX and Gregory VII.[41]

The other Bernard, his old mentor, wrote him at once a letter mixing congratulations and warnings. Eugene had come to a sublime and terrible place. His only hope for salvation lay in imitation of the first prince of the Apostles. He was to make his model the first pope, Peter, a man "who had shaken from his hands every offering."[42] Like Peter he must be able to say, "Silver and gold I have none" (Acts 3:6). To a prize pupil placed in such awful temptations, Bernard did not hesitate to be emphatic: he recalled what Peter had said to Simon, "Your cash and you go to perdition" (Acts 8:20); and he added as commentary: "Voice of thunder! Voice of nobility! Voice of virtue."[43] These thunderous words must reverberate in Eugene's heart if his pontificate was to fulfill its promise.

In late March of 1148 Raoul, count of Vermandois and Valois, seneschal and ex-viceroy of France, came with a request and a handicap to Eugene III. The scene was a palace in Reims where the pope, accompanied by a few cardinals, had come to celebrate a reform council of French and English prelates. Raoul, a married man living with Petronilla, a noble lady not his wife, asked the annulment of his existing marriage. He was under a handicap because his case had already been investigated by Innocent II in

1142 and found wanting. Innocent had excommunicated him for flouting his marital obligations, and the excommunication had been confirmed by Innocent's successors, Celestine II and Lucius II. Would Eugene lift their ban and pronounce Raoul's marriage void?[44]

The proceedings were observed and reported by a subordinate on the pope's staff, a man of sharp eye and sharper pen, John of Salisbury. Norman English, John had pursued philosophical studies at Paris for about a dozen years and then, a brilliant young cleric, had been recruited by a curia of international composition, receptive to talent backed by a patron. Out of the doings at the papal court he made a fragmentary history, too candid to be published in his lifetime and remarkably fresh in its details. For John the trial of Raoul's marriage was one of the more memorable events he witnessed. Without obvious bias or self-interest and on the basis of first-hand sources and his own eyesight he set down what happened.

Eleanor of Aquitaine, wife of Louis VII of France, was Petronilla's sister. Through this connection Raoul had the king's support. Before departing on crusade the king had asked the pope to absolve Petronilla's friend and end the first marriage. Now, before the pope in Reims, Raoul relied on "the aid and counsel" of two of Eugene's cardinals, Giovanni Paparo and Gregorio di Sant' Angelo. There was, John said, naming the two, "the suspicion that money passed."[45] Inferably, he means it passed to them.

As the pope opened the proceedings at Reims, John thought he seemed embarrassed. He made a point of cultivating "the woman" (the wife whom John does not name) and "her party." Eugene was about to reverse a judgment which "was believed to be perfectly just" and so, John inferred, was "ashamed to do in the sight of the Church what he was doing." He offered the woman, up till now not given an audience, an opportunity to be heard. She turned out to be "not anxious to return to the court" and modestly declined the pope's offer. Then Barthélemy, bishop of Laon, stepped up to swear to the existence of kinship between her and her husband which made their marriage invalid. He started to touch the Gospels, but the pope said it was enough if the bishop, having looked at the sacred books, spoke his testimony. Like us, John of Salisbury apparently wondered if Eugene thought an oath on the Gospels in this case too sacrilegious. The bishop gave his testimony, and the pope pronounced the annulment. When Raoul was then ordered to return the dowry and said that he had already done so, "everyone presumed that the parties had colluded." No one ventured to suggest that the testimony be reassessed or the annulment undone. Only Bernard of Clairvaux cried out that no good fruit would come from the bed of Raoul and Petronilla.[46]

Bernard, John wrote, was "a very holy man" and "a very violent lover in the observation of religion and the bestowal of benefits on Christ's poor." John's account of Raoul's case ends with Bernard's malediction. The conclusions which he intended his readers to reach appear from his selection of details—Louis VII's words to the pope, the rumored payoff to the cardinals, the pope's embarrassment and his sensitivity about the oath, the plain evidence of prearrangement in the return of the dowry, the belief that the earlier excommunications by three popes had been just, the reaction of Bernard. Eugene does not go away with gold and silver; he does leave this scene with a shrunken sanctity, seen as the instrument that power and money have used to achieve a judgment against the truth.

If we combine John's account with more general first-hand comments a somewhat different impression emerges. Bernard rated Giovanni Paparo as one of the few good cardinals: he could not have thought that he was in the habit of taking money.[47] Gregorio di Sant'Angelo, however, was said by another contemporary to have been "a very easy speaker and a deeply clever man, with a truly Roman soul"[48]—the words were not necessarily complimentary; moreover, he owed his cardinalate to having been Innocent II's nephew. He remains an object for suspicion as far as the passing of money is concerned. As for the pope himself, in *De consideratione,* a remarkable set of letters to Eugene on his opportunities and failings, Bernard of Clairvaux specifically freed him from any taint of avarice. In great want Eugene has turned down great gifts: in his regime "a new thing! When up to now has gold been refused by Rome?"[49] "You," Bernard wrote, "are said to account money straw. No, no, not on that account is anything to be feared in judgments which are yours."[50] But there are two faults of which Eugene is implicitly guilty: one is "an easy credulity"; the other is "the taking up of persons." It is "no small sin," Bernard informed Eugene, "if in this way you lift up the faces of sinners and do not judge cases on their merits."[51] In these words, probably written within three or so months after Raoul's annulment at Reims, Bernard restored the force of the old Hebrew metaphor: a judge guilty of partiality looked at the litigant rather than the law. Although Eugene had presided so far "without much complaint about any of these things," Bernard put it to him directly without mention of specific cases. To the pope he had seen yield to the French king and the counsel of his cardinals and the testimony of the bishop of Laon, Bernard wrote, "Look to it yourself, whether you be without fault."

The Eugene who appears in two later marriage cases, recorded with the same fidelity and candor by John of Salisbury in his history, was a different man. When Eleanor of Aquitaine herself came to the curia out of sorts with Louis and seeking an annulment for consanguinity, the pope prepared a bedchamber in royal style and "made them sleep in one bed." Afterward, he sent them on their way united, with his blessing, and instead of taking offerings he gave them gifts.[52] (It was to be the unsavory task of a council of French bishops two years later, when Eleanor and Louis had given up on each other, to pronounce their marriage void. The pope had no part in this outrageous "taking up of persons."[53]

The other marriage case is set off by John with an artist's eye against Raoul's release at Reims. Hugues, count of Molise, a Norman from Apulia, sought an annulment on the ground of consanguinity. He arrived before the pope at Ferentino supported by the deputies of the king of Sicily and other nobles of Apulia and Calabria and by the bishops of his country "who knew it would please the king." He produced his witnesses, his advocates presented the case, and "he had corrupted the curia, so that in considering the judgment, there were not two who objected to the annulment." Eugene listened to the cardinals and then interrogated the witnesses himself. How did they know of the asserted blood tie between the spouses? They replied they had lived a long time in Apulia and had been witnesses in two other annulments. The pope was shocked and said so. "We will rarely hear any witness in more than one annulment, and for a third time we are hearing you men who are strangers, unknown and suspect!" With a fine disregard for the judicial record before him and a keen scent for a bad case, Eugene announced that the truth was known to him from other sources. He pronounced the marriage good. Weeping, he then rose from his seat and running, threw himself at the count's feet, his mitre falling in the dust before the feet of the "stupefied" count of Molise. The cardinals raised him, but he continued to beg the count to love his wife. If he would, Eugene informed him, he the pope would answer at the Day of Judgment for all the sins he had committed to date. The assembled prelates began to weep too, the count was overcome, the pope ordered husband and wife together to approach him, and he put on the count's finger his own ring as a sign of the count's agreement to take back his wife with affection.[54]

In this scene the integrity of judgment is preserved by the pope. The Last Judgment stands in the background, a reference point which the pope invokes decisively when he identifies himself with Hugues. Eugene emerges as the Christian judge par excellence, a judge ready to answer for the one he judges, whose goal is not formal accuracy but active love. The Dostoevskian dénouement is recounted by John with the emotion of a participant, his confidence in the pope restored. But as for the cardinals and John's colleagues in office! As for John himself! Hugues "had corrupted the curia." No honest man spoke up until the pope cut through the circle of bribes and lies.[55]

Honest pope, corrupt curia—the same refrain appears in Bernard's later expostulations to Eugene, four years after those written in 1148. The pope himself has acted well in the cases known to Bernard: Two Germans, "both rich, both guilty," came to Rome for a papal favor. "Grace was given gratis to one; the other, unworthy I believe of grace, heard from you, 'Depart, wearing the cloak with which you came.'" Eugene had spoken like Peter.[56] Again, across the sea, almost from the ends of the earth, a man came to Rome to buy a bishopric, and to pay for it with his own and other men's money. He knew what was expected. He "had bought before." He fell "into other hands more mighty in taking than giving." He had to pay "to avoid the envy of those who love offerings." He had no wish "to be marked down as ungenerous." But the pope surprised him. Eugene himself secretly supplied the money to be given the curia. An unlikely, even absurd, situation—Eugene observing curial practice by putting up the money his curia was getting from the suppliant. The taking of offerings was so ingrained that even the pope must appear to conform.[57]

Good cardinals, according to Bernard, once existed. He invoked the memory of Martino Cibo, eight years dead—a legate "who returned from the land of gold without gold, who rejected a horse from the bishop of Florence as soon as he learned that the bishop had a case in the curia. "What do you say, my Eugene?" Bernard asked, "Is it not something from another world?[58] Another legate, Géoffrey, bishop of Chartres, on legation in Aquitaine was offered a sturgeon by a priest; he insisted on paying five *solidi* to the embarrassed offeror. Tendered two or three pretty wooden dishes by a lady, he declined them; he could ask like Samuel, "From whose hand have I taken an offering?" (1 Kgs 12:23).[59] These stories were like the accounts of exceptionally just rabbis preserved in the Talmud; they were used to illustrate what was wanting today. Bernard imagined Eugene sighing and saying to himself, "Do you think what is said could ever be?—Would that in my lifetime I might see the Church of God resting on such pillars."[60]

How long would Eugene sleep? He must pick men for the curia who were already good, "for the curia does not easily make men good." He must choose those who like Paul "look not for the gift but the fruit" (Phil 4:17), who "do not calculate the profit of commissions," who "go not after gold but after Christ," who "do not stroke but frighten the rich," who "do not exhaust purses but relieve hearts," who "do not hurry to enrich themselves and their families with the widow's dowry and the Crucified's patrimony but who give gratis what they took gratis, rendering judgment gratis."[61]

In Bernard the great texts against simony merged with admonitions against corrupt judging. Whether it was an act of ecclesiastical administration or an act of ecclesiastical judgment, the pope's act was to be done freely without offerings. A curia operating without offerings was still a goal to be achieved. A Cistercian at the center, a reformer at the top, had not yet been able to purge the central administration from the power of *munera* tendered to those in power.

Munera and Murder

John of Salisbury did not end his reporting on the curia with the *Papal History* quoted above. Much later he helped compose a letter written by "the clerks of Thomas Becket" to the archbishop of Sens after Thomas's murder. To the extent that the letter is John's, it comes from a man familiar with the principal characters and probably in a position to assess the truth of its allegations, which concern Roger of Pont-l'Evêque, archbishop of York, at the time of the story a senior clerk of Archbishop Theobald of Canterbury. According to the writers, Roger had a lover, a boy named Walter. As Walter aged and talked of the affair, he became an embarrassment. Roger "corrupted the judges who conducted secular affairs" and had Walter hanged for some unspecified crime. Roger was still not out of trouble; he turned to his fellow-clerk, Thomas Becket, for help. Thomas with the aid of two bishops persuaded Archbishop Theobald to let Roger purge himself—that is, appear with friends swearing to his innocence—before a closed chapter of the monks of Canterbury. The crime of which he was "purged" is not specified but appears to have been the homosexual acts Walter had accused him of; nothing was made of the corruption of the judges. The purgation itself was uncanonical, because secret and monastic and not in open court. Someone at Eugene's curia heard of it and objected. Roger came to Rome "to that very famous man of affairs Gregorio Cardinal of Sant'Angelo." Through him, "with a multitude of offerings sprinkled in the curia," Roger succeeded in returning home 'justified.'"[62]

Principal English historians of this period such as Reginald Poole and David Knowles have noticed Roger's alleged crime as homosexuality, burying in silence the letter's more awful charge that the royal judges corruptly put his lover to death and the scarcely small crime of his acquiring absolution for a price. The hostility of the letter-writers to Roger is evident, so the charges must be discounted for bias. The writers assert, nonetheless, that they are not revealing anything new: the main elements of the story have been frequently retold, to the shame of the Church. The story is not proved by its retelling. It is evidence of the common view of the corruptibility of courts, royal and papal.[63]

Engraved on John's mind was one more episode confirming his overriding impression of the curia. It occurred at Ferentino where Eugene and his staff spent the winter of 1155–1156. Prominent among the curialists was Cardinal Guido—variously known as the Tooth and the Girl—a Genoese, a jurist, and a fighting priest who had commanded a papal army that retook Rome from its rebellious citizenry.[64] John made some observations to the pope and cardinals that called forth Guido's scorn at John's naiveté. The Tooth roundly declared that love of money was rooted in the Roman Church. He "blazed out," John recalled, "at my innocence." John does not say that either the pope or the other cardinals contradicted the Tooth. The avarice of the curia was, as it were, an acknowledged weakness. John published this story and its damning generalization in his lifetime when, three years later, back in England, he wrote his magnificent essay on politics and government, the *Policraticus*.[65]

This book in its strictures on the ways of courts represented largely, though not wholly, John's mature reflections on his eight years under Eugene. Since then he had worked as a curialist for Archbishop Theobald of Canterbury, and he was familiar with secular courts such as Henry II's. By his own account a close friend of Cardinal Nicholas Breakspear, he had stayed with him on an extended visit to Italy after Nicholas had become pope in 1154 as Adrian IV.[66] These experiences, and no doubt his reading, were integrated into his pictures of an imaginary court of an unwise prince. Still, his primary impressions of practice at a court must have been formed as Eugene's clerk.

Satirically evoking what he had experienced "a thousand times in his dealing with the aides of princes," he began by observing, "Do not suppose justice, truth or godliness is at home with those who are putting all things up for sale." Christ himself is "shut out." If He knocked, the door would be closed. These men flee grace (*gratia*) and do nothing *gratis*. "With them the more corrupt a man is in character and the more he corrupts with offerings, the more blessed is he." If "petitions are to be furthered, if a case is to be examined, if execution is to be issued on a judgment, if security is to be furnished, money does everything. . . ."[67]

In the bureaucratic warren an official on the take lurks in every cubbyhole. Here is Cossus, ready to prepare your papers if you will pay for his pen and ink, throwing in your belt or your hat if he likes the look of them. Here is Vegento whom you must supplicate to get his attention. After you have deployed words and offerings to achieve this much, he will find fault with your documents unless your advance stroking has softened him: "there is always a knot which needs money to conquer." Delay is the officials' stock in trade. Charon, who never spares anyone, is more merciful. He charges the dead a coin. These officials demand "whole pounds, multiplied."[68]

John's wit had been sharpened by the masters of Latin satire. Cossus and Vegento come from Juvenal, and John had Juvenal's delight in exaggeration. Ovid on the art of love was quoted to illustrate the litigant's need to pay *munera*:

Although you come accompanied by the Muses, Homer,
Out you go, Homer, if you have brought nothing.[69]

Classical embellishment was meshed with Bernard ("Saint Clairvaux") on the corruption of Eugene's court: the three great subverters of the judgment of prudent men were "the love of offerings, the taking up of persons, and credulousness."[70] Juvenal, Ovid, Bernard confirmed what John had experienced: neither eloquence nor sincerity will avail in litigation "unless a price intervenes."[71]

Defenders of the bureaucrats would say that someone has to pay for pen and ink and the daily sustenance of the officeholders, why not the user? John has a double answer. First, these men are not taking routine fees, they are getting "whole pounds." Second, in a well-run government, they would have fixed fees and not be expected to make booty of the cases that come their way.[72] They could, John concedes, receive true gifts, *munera* in a good sense, spontaneously offered. Depending on the circumstances of their offering, *munera* "shine or sully." These sullied. It is axiomatic that "to take a benefit is to sell one's liberty." What more shameful for those who are supposed to rule than by taking gifts to become "slaves?" Officials of this sort have indeed sold themselves twice—once in asking, again in delivering.[73]

John's censures fell chiefly on access payments or on the costs of getting administrative action, not on decision giving itself. Yet John was categorical: in this milieu, neither justice nor truth were "at home." He found Isaiah 5:23 apposite and paraphrased it, "The Lord declares it is wicked to judge for the unrighteous in return for *munera.*"[74] Offerings in his account contaminated all the actors in the process. "He who touches pitch," he quoted Ecclesiasticus 13:1, "is stained by it."[75] Those who learned to live at the court, however innocent their past, were defiled and deformed by their associates.

The sting of satire was not turned wholly outward. Just as in his companion observations on repentance after satisfying lust ("the beginnings of desire are sweet above honey and the honeycomb, but its dregs are more bitter than any wormwood"),[76] an autobiographical edge could be felt in John's remarks. Still he did not adopt the form of outright confession. His book bore a subtitle revealing the split in his personality: "The Games of Courtiers and the Tracks of Philosophers." He had played the games and he had left the tracks. The philosopher at the curia, he wrote, becomes an hermaphrodite. Corrupted, he loses his virility, that is, his virtue, and becomes another gamesman. A curialist-philosopher, he concludes, is "a monstrous thing."[77] Who was this monster but the student from Paris who had plunged into the service of the Cistercian reformer Eugene III?

The Emerald Offering.   In 1155 Nicholas Breakspear ruled as Adrian IV. Henry II was king of England. Thomas Becket, late of Archbishop Theobald's staff at Canterbury, sat as the king's all-powerful chancellor, the king's "heart and wisdom," without whose will nothing happened.[78] Thomas chose John of Salisbury, still in Theobald's service, to go to the curia on an important mission for the king.

The mission was nothing less than to obtain papal permission to invade Ireland. Under a vague expansion of the fictitious donations of Constantine it was believed that the pope had a superior sovereignty over the islands of the world, Ireland included.[79] The plan was to have the pope in exercise of this power authorize an invasion. John was the ideal emissary, a churchman knowing in the ways of the curia and a friend of Adrian from the days when both Englishmen had served Eugene.

John journeyed to the papal court in Benevento and settled into residence for almost three months. The pope, he was to boast later, "with a certain special favor (*gratia*) marked by charity loved me beyond our other countrymen."[80] He certainly gave John some latitude in frank speech. At the end of the visit John came off with what he had come for. He describes it—with just a little puffery—as a grant of Ireland to Henry II and his heirs in perpetuity.[81] The actual bull, *Laudabiliter,* wobbled. Authorizing Henry to enter Ireland "to expand the boundaries of the Church, to restrain the course of the vices, to correct morals and implant virtues, and to increase the Christian religion"—all objectives that could be accomplished without permanent dominion—it continued: "let the people of that land receive you honorably and venerate you as if lord". Here was a concession of quasi-dominion with no conditions attached except that the churches were to be unharmed and the right of the Roman Church to an annual payment of one penny per house was to be preserved. Henry's wish to pay this tax was also set out among the considerations moving the pope's action.[82] No doubt it was a sweetener of special interest to Adrian who, as a cardinal, had regulated the Holy See's affairs in Norway. The document suggested a connection between the payment offered the pope and his disposition of a land whose sees were in no more need of reform than, say, the bishoprics of Winchester or York. Moral backing for Henry's contemplated use of armed force in Ireland was sealed by Adrian's bestowing on the king a ring of sinister significance—a gold ring, set with a magnificent emerald, given in token of Henry's authority "to rule Ireland."[83] Beyond argument the emerald was a *munus* from the Pope. Did it not reciprocate *munera* from Henry? John says nothing here that would imply such an exchange. He avoids the term *munus* when he speaks of the emerald. He says nothing of his bringing gifts on Henry's behalf. Yet he writes (without reference to *Laudabiliter*) that at Benevento he said to the pope, "If you therefore are a father, why do you look for *munera* and *retributiones* (offerings and reciprocities) from your children?"[84] The words would scarcely have been appropriate if John himself had received a big favor gratis. They fit a mission where offerings had played a necessary part.

John's question to the pope was recorded by him in the *Policraticus* where he no doubt consolidated conversations held over three months into a single exchange, shaping the dialogue to his present purpose but presumably preserving the substance. In this account Adrian begins by asking him what men thought of him and the Roman Church. John replies that many say, "She shows herself to others more a stepmother than a mother. . . . Scribes and Pharisees render justice not so much for truth as for price. For everything has a price today. And tomorrow you will obtain nothing without a price."[85] "And you yourself," the pope asks, "what do you say?"

John says he felt trapped. Was he to lie or flatter? Was he to be evasive or presumptuous? He began by recalling the Tooth's blast at his own innocence at Ferentino. He observed that he had "never seen more honest clerks than in the Roman Church"—for example, Cardinal Bernard of Redon, a Cistercian at Eugene's court, was the kind of person of whom one could say, "The man has not been born from whom he would take an offering." Cardinal Guarino of Bologna, bishop of Palestrina, even abstained from sharing in the curia's communal property. There were "many others" who were austere and modest. The curia was not, or had not been, all bad. But John continued, "Since you urge and press and command me," he would be blunt: "The faults of a few bring stains to the pure, and infamy to the whole Church." Bolder still, he asked the key question: "If you therefore are a father, why do you look for offerings and reciprocities from your children?" John then passed (or at least in recollection passes) from answering Adrian to lecturing him: "What you took gratis, give gratis.

Justice is the queen of the virtues. She blushes to be bartered for any price."[86]

At this frank and earnest exhortation, John says the pope broke into laughter. He told John the fable of the stomach: The other members of the body once complained that they did all the work, seeing, hearing, walking. The stomach did nothing but ate what they produced. The arms and legs and all agreed to abstain from work and to starve the idle greedy stomach. In three days they were faint. Then they knew that the stomach had to be supplied if anything was to be distributed to them. Brother, he said, the Roman Church is like the stomach.[87]

John adds no comment. The fable was a very fine defense for the financing of a central organism by levies on its lesser members. It came from Livy, who, writing under Augustus, said that Menenius Agrippa in 494 B.C. told the story to the alienated plebians to induce them to accept the rule of the patricians. It is, in its original telling, as in its use by Adrian, "a masterpiece from the point of view of the haves, threatened by an opting out of the have-nots."[88] Beyond demonstration it failed to answer John's complaint that justice was sold at the curia.

The pagan fable had a Christian counterpart. "For just as the body is one," Paul had written the Corinthians,

> and has many members, but all the members of the body, many as they are, are one body, so Christ. For in one Spirit we all have been baptized into one body— whether Jews or Greeks, slaves or free men—and we all have been saturated in one Spirit. For the body is not one member but many. If the foot says, "I am not hand, I am not of the body," not on that account is it out of the body; and if the ear says, "I am not eye, I am not of the body," not on that account is it out of the body. If the whole body were eye, where would be hearing? If all hearing, where smelling? Now God has arranged the members, each of them, in the body as He willed. If all were one member, where would be the body? Now there are many members, one body. Eye is not able to say to hand, "I need you not"; or again, head to feet, "I need you not." But even the more fragile members of the body are indispensable and what we think the dishonorable in the body we surround with greater honor, and our disgraceful members get a greater decency which our decent members need not. But God has so ordered the body and given greater honor to what it lacked so that there is no conflict in the body, but one member in turn cares for another. And if one member suffers, all members suffer. If a member is glorified, all members together rejoice. You are Christ's body, members in turn.
>
> (1 Cor 12:12–27)

In Paul's metaphor "the more disgraceful members," which are better clothed than the others, are the pudenda; the genitals are meant by the term as in the Septuagint's translation of Leviticus 18:7. Elsewhere in the letter to the Corinthians, the stomach is used by Paul as a stand-in for the genitals as he discusses immorality (1 Cor 6:12–13). It is not clear from Corinthians what Paul thought were the equivalent of the stomach or the pudenda in the Church. But if the metaphor is pressed, the stomach or genitals should be that part of the organism better clothed than the rest.

Pope Adrian did not make this comparison, nor did John of Salisbury advert to it. It could scarcely have been absent from the mind of such a scholar as John that the passage in Paul was both a rebuke to a greedy stomach and a wry comment on the nature of the organ that was given the most honor.

In the episodes of Count Raoul, of Count Hugues, of the rich Germans, of the poor bishop helped by the pope, of Roger of York and Gregorio di Sant'Angelo, in Bernard of Clairvaux's warnings and remonstrances, in John's eyewitness accounts and in his satirical generalizations, in the Tooth's cynical rebuke, in Adrian's own words, justice at the curia appears expensive, precarious, and chancy. Good cardinals struggle against corruption. Law in practice is very different from Gratian's noble song. How different was to be experienced in person by John when he became the confidant and counselor of an archbishop of Canterbury who turned to the law and the curia for vindication.

Game Plan. By 1163 relations between Henry II and his old chancellor Thomas, now archbishop of Canterbury, had deteriorated badly. In 1164 Thomas gave in to the king, agreeing to observe the Constitutions of Clarendon, but then repented of his agreement as a surrender of rights of the Church.[89] From this point until death ended the battle, Thomas and Henry were locked in a conflict that often took a legal shape; and the legal shape most frequently taken was that of appeals to Alexander III by Thomas or by bishops loyal to the king attacking Thomas. It was never State against Church, as modern ideology tends to see the conflict, but king and bishops (sometimes a majority of bishops, although some were coerced) against archbishop; and the pope was often cast in the role not of defender of the Church but of judge or at least arbitrator between quarreling members of the English hierarchy. In the course of this six-year struggle, in which the pope acted as judge, arbitrator, conciliator, and diplomat as well as head of the Church, *munera* at the curia played a part.

Alexander III was not entirely adverse to his cardinals receiving gifts. In 1162 or 1163 he had occasion to write on the topic to Lucás Bánffius, the scrupulous archbishop of Esztergom. The archbishop's brother had given Cardinal Peter de Mizo a single horse when the cardinal came to Hungary to deliver the pallium to Lucás. Lucás was unaware of the gift at the time, but it was delivered before he received the pallium. Had he been guilty of benefiting from simony? Alexander III reassured him. In general, three things were to be considered: the quantity of the offering, the time of its donation, and "the quality" of the donor and donee. "Blessed is he who shakes every offering from his hands" was written of gifts likely to "allure or pervert the soul." In Rome it was customary to offer some good wine of small value—it was not condemned. Here, considering the affluence of Lucás's brother, the need of the cardinal (he had arrived with few horses), and the quality of both persons, the gift was "not to be considered of such price that it should much move the soul of the recipient." There was no sin. Alexander's answer, the decretal *Etsi quaestiones*, left room for the exercise of discretion. If its careful limitations were followed, it was not a charter for the curia to traffic in litigation. It accepted the principle that gifts to gain clout were iniquitous. Cynics could read the answer as opening the door for the unscrupulous, just as some today see legalized political action committees as a cover for corruption. On its face, the answer drew common sense lines. It was not law for the whole Church—Alexander's answers were not yet part of a universal law book. It was an indication that gifts were neither unknown nor unwelcome in Rome.[90] Their role in the business of Thomas Becket can be gathered from his correspondence.

The first relevant letter is to Thomas from John of Salisbury. John, Archbishop Theobald's trusted assistant and legal adviser, had become Thomas's on his accession to the archbishopric in 1162; and in 1164, even before the final breach between king and archbishop, John had gone to France to promote Thomas's cause. From there he wrote to advise his master that he had visited Louis VII and "expounded to him your case in orderly fashion." Louis had promised "to do what he can" with the pope. Next, John had made arrangements to present the situation to Louis VII's brother, Henri, the archbishop of Reims. He urged Thomas to send this high prelate a letter "along with some small gift" (munuscula) to make friends with him: whatever his personal qualities, he was a big man in France; also he could "do much in the Roman church" both on account of his brother and on account of the eminence of his see. For Thomas the French connection was, in fact, to be essential.[91]

John reported that he had also written two cardinals, Enrico of Pisa and Guglielmo of Pavia, setting out what a calamity it would be for the Roman church if the measures against Thomas were permitted to proceed—the letters were to forestall representations by prelates coming to see the pope on Henry's behalf. John went on to analyze Thomas's prospects in the curia:

> But what we can do there, I do not clearly see. Many things make against you, few for you. Big men will come, lavish in spending money—which Rome has never spurned. They will lean not only on their own authority but on the lord king's—whom the curia will dare to offend in nothing. . . . Can we—humble, poor, defenseless—trick the Romans? Those men have learned from the comic playwright "not to pay a price for a hope." But you write that, if no other way is open, we may promise two hundred marks. Assuredly the adverse party, before it is disappointed, will give three hundred or four hundred. "If you fight with munera, Iollas will not give up." And I promise that the Romans out of love for the king and reverence for his messengers would rather receive more than hope for less.[92]

The letter spells out a program: with the help of high French officials including the French king, with the aid of friends at the curia, and with the judicious employment of money—a small gift at Reims; up to 200 marks with the cardinals—Thomas's cause against the king will be promoted. The letter reveals no scruple at all about using influence—that is taken to be the nature of the game; big men regularly throw their weight. The letter shows, on John's part, a nice sense of a distinction between a *munus* and a *munuscula*. Although a "little gift" from one archbishop to another archbishop might have looked large to a poor man, its purpose is to win benevolence not corrupt judgment. The letter suggests, on Thomas's part, reluctance ("if no other way is open"), but not repugnance, to enter on a less innocent course of paying at the curia. Two hundred marks was a substantial sum but not enormous if, as seems likely, it was to be divided among several persons. Divided and distributed, ten marks here, forty marks there, it would have functioned to buy access and attention. Instructively, it is not expected that the other side will pay large bribes, only enough to beat Thomas's offering. John takes a realist's not a moralist's view of Thomas's tactics, tastefully expressing his judgment in classical quotations. Terence has taught the cardinals not to trade what they deliver "for a hope." Virgil's *Eclogues* has instructed John that Iollas does not lose a fight dependent on offerings. John's conclusion is that the other side has more influence and more money and so will win. Thomas would do well if he could, the epistle ends, to regain Henry's favor. "God can mend, but the Roman church will not bring aid."[93]

In this letter John is not indulging in the freedom of a satirist, nor is he, as he did later, speculating suspiciously about what the other side has done. He is giving his own best estimate and quoting Thomas. When it is recalled that both of them had had years of dealing with the curia, the letter is precious evidence as to curial customs and prices. The notion of a judicial process beyond diplomatic influence does not exist. It is taken for granted that one will enlist one's friends. In addition, there is a price tag. What is expected is not big money. Marks, not pounds, are being calculated. Yet money is necessary. Justice is not free.

There was one occasion on which Thomas was accused of paying a lot—"many thousands of marks," a figure at least ten times the amount later slated for the curia. According to his bitterest enemy, Gilbert Foliot, bishop of London, the money was paid to obtain appointment as Henry's chancellor. The accusation occurs in a letter addressed to Thomas himself reviewing his shortcomings. Foliot sets out the payment as something "our whole world knows" and links it to Thomas's subsequent promotion to archbishop.[94] The implication, not developed, is that Thomas was guilty of simony, paying for a royal office which customarily led to advancement to a bishopric. Borne on this "tide of gold" Thomas reached "the port of Canterbury." Foliot's charge was neither admitted nor denied by Thomas— mere accusation, it must be considered unproved.[95] What it is evidence of is a belief that to obtain high office with the king one had to pay. John of Salisbury observed that in the days of his chancellorship Thomas was "a great gamesman."[96] As John's letter on the 200 marks implies, Thomas was still a gamesman when the battle with the king began.

In the judgment of his most astute biographer, David Knowles, Thomas's personality changed in the course of the conflict. The decisive break with the ways of the world, Knowles says, occurred at Northampton in October 1164 when Thomas's confessor advised him, "The affair is no longer in your hands but God's, and He will be with you. Stand fast in your just cause." Henceforth, Knowles writes, Thomas "carried his cross with a realization of its power and of its message."[97]

Like every Christian in power and dealing with power, Thomas still had to decide what carrying his cross meant. Evidence indicates that a decisive break with the ways of the world came not in 1164 but in 1170, only after six years of purgation in France, six years of frustration by the force of *munera*. Two years after the events of 1164 at Northampton, the inexorable Foliot was to tell him, "The Lord set a child as example to the Apostles. . . . He Himself is a remarkable exemplar of virtue—He who absolved those crucifying Him. . . . What can that humility not do with our lord the king?"[98] These words in Foliot's mouth have the reek of odious self-righteousness, but they are essentially accurate in contrasting Thomas's conduct with Christ's. During the six years of exile, Thomas was not a lamb led to the slaughter, but a petitioner in the curia, litigating his case.

The barons of England, acting at Northampton in 1164 at the king's behest, had judged Thomas and found him guilty of not accounting for funds he had received as the king's chancellor. Thomas asked the pope to quash the verdict of this secular court unlawfully judging a bishop. Yielding to the king's pressure, the other bishops of England petitioned the pope to condemn the archbishop or at least let the case against him be tried in England.[99] Facing these irreconcilable judicial and political pleas, and uneasily in residence in France with larger political problems of his own on his mind, Alexander procrastinated. Doing nothing about the bishops' request, he effectively killed it.[100] The verdict against Thomas was intolerable as a matter of church policy; the pope eventually quashed it with a formal decree. But he put off acting for a good while. In the meantime he ordered Thomas not to assert his rights in England.[101]

A year and a half passed. The wait was hard to bear, not only for Thomas personally but for his relatives. Henry II, with an inhumanity shocking to his contemporaries, expelled from England all of Thomas's kin, even "girls and babes in cradles," and told them to show themselves to Thomas as the one responsible for their misfortune.[102] The existence of this group of entirely innocent victims must be borne in mind as one measures the role of delay in the lawsuits. As with all protracted litigations, one looks back and wonders where all the time did go. Was it all wasted? Here the time was mainly spent in sporadic efforts by the pope to find ways of reconciling the king and the archbishop. Meanwhile, Thomas and his relatives suffered.

When, in April 1166, the pope unleashed the archbishop, Thomas promptly excommunicated a number of his enemies. Against the excommunications, appeal was taken by the English bishops.[103] At this juncture John of Salisbury wrote Thomas again as to what he could expect:

> I do not have much confidence in the Roman church, whose character and needs are well known to us. Surely the Pope is a holy and just man, and Cardinal Alberto, many say, models himself on him; but his needs are so many and so great, and the greed and wickedness of the Romans so great, that the Pope sometimes uses the license of power and obtains by way of dispensation what is said to be expedient for the common good although it is not expedient for religion. I fear that we must wait for the day set for the appeal and when it has come that those who love *munera* will seek reciprocities.[104]

"Those who love offerings will follow after offerings." John had already invoked Isaiah 1:23 in the *Policraticus* when he analyzed the ways of courts. Now he modified the line and applied its analysis to Thomas's situation. Reciprocities (*retributiones*) was what the men of the curia would want. He alluded to what both he and Thomas knew of "the needs" of the stomach as well as what they knew of the character of Alexander III. The conclusion was bleak: offerings would affect the handling of the appeal.

To a sympathetic English bishop, Bartholomew of Exeter, John confided his cynicism: "Perhaps the Apostolic See thinks ecclesiastical laws are like civil laws which, as Anacarsis the Scythian said, are like spiders' webs, catching flies and letting greater flying things through."[105] Already John expected vindication only hereafter: "Christ, I summon You. I bring an action against You who are truth unfailing. If reason permits, I will on the last day of Judgment prove Your lie, unless one is judged by the judgment by which he judged and unless he receives due measure for measure."[106] Reciprocity was to rule in heaven as Jesus had promised (Mt 7:2). That reciprocity was to be very different from the give and take of the curia.

Prepare himself as he might for disappointment, John suffered "the hurt of a wounded mind" when Alexander did act on January 1, 1167, appointing to decide the bishops' appeal two legates, one supposed to favor Thomas and the other the king.[107] John did not conceal "the hurt" from the pope, writing to him directly to upbraid "the vicar of the Crucified" for abandoning those exiled for Christ.[108] As the year 1167 wore on, and the legates, instead of deciding, listened to both sides and worked at reconciliation, John wrote again to Alexander looking for vindication before the Last Judgment: "Some of us dying in the defense of justice look to God and the Church for the revenge of innocent blood."[109] At the time the reference to dying was rhetorical. He criticized the appointment of a legate whom Henry had requested by name, a man who, John said, was "looking for profit" from his appointment.[110] To a friend, John was even franker. Rumor had it that both legates had decided "to make void the justice of our case for money"—money which it would not be "lawful to put in the treasury, for it is the price of blood."[111] John did not hesitate to invoke the line which Matthew 27:6 applied to Judas's sale of Christ.

The line had, perhaps, been put in his mind by its use by Gilbert Foliot. In his searing indictment of Thomas, directed to the archbishop in person, Foliot had noted that Thomas, in France, was demanding the revenues of his see. But it was the bishops of England who would have to risk the king's anger—"When the lion roars, who does not tremble?"—if they paid anything to Thomas: "Why do your annual returns mean so much to you, my father, that you want to get them for yourself by the blood of your brothers? Even the Jews, when Judas brought back the money, spurned it because they recognized what was blood-price."[112]

Thomas should follow the Lord forgiving his executioners, Thomas was a Judas selling out his colleagues for money. Both images occurred in Foliot's cruel and masterly letter. The images of Jesus and Judas were the images which shaped the symbolism, and to some extent, the minds of the parties to the controversy. There is the danger that negative images will actually function to fashion the behavior of those who know they are negative. Foliot himself, for example, holding up Judas with scorn while addressing Thomas as "my father," insensibly cast himself in the Judas-like role of betraying his father the archbishop and his lord Jesus.

John of Salisbury was acutely aware of this perverse phenomenon. In indirect commentary on Foliot's letter, John wrote Thomas that Judas had "left an example of treason and of parricide to our own scribes and pharisees."[113] Later, in 1168, he recounted in his own words a remarkable exchange between Thomas and certain Carthusian and Grandimontine monks speaking for the king. Refuting the king's appeal to custom, Thomas told them, "Moses is not to be imitated in lack of trust, David in treachery or adultery, Peter in perjury, Paul in foolish zeal." Even those figures of Scripture who were, on the whole, good could function as negative guides. Of the exemplars provided by Scripture, Thomas said, only one was to be imitated: "the model of Christ."[114] That model, as Thomas apparently still believed in the fourth year of litigation, authorized him to seek God's justice from the pope.

Guglielmo of Pavia had been one of John's chosen correspondents at the curia in 1164. There was reason to believe that he took an interest in English affairs. Since then, he had been suggested by the king as a legate, and, now named legate by the pope, he was suspect of partiality. John wrote him: "I trust in the Lord that with you the taking up of persons and offerings will not be so great that you will do something to harm the Church, generate scandal in the world, darken the clear light of your good name. These are the works of those who know not the law or do not fear the Lord of the law. You are not such."[115] John had previously warned Thomas against tactlessly attacking the suspect legate.[116] If this was tact—to say to his face that it was hoped he would not be over-partial and over-avaricious—one has a measure of the thickness of skin of a hardened curialist.

When the two legates reported to Alexander, criticizing Thomas's intransigence,[117] John was convinced that they had sold out: "They take the *munera* of the Moabites," he wrote an English friend, the bishop of Poitiers. "They have not been afraid to lie against the archbishop of Canterbury in the letter which they sent the Pope."[118] John began a small campaign at the curia to offset their influence. He wrote Cardinal Alberto, a canonist who later became Gregory VIII, to assert directly what he had diplomatically denied in the letter to legate Guglielmo—the latter was indeed a man who preferred "the king's power and favor (*gratia*) to the truth." He urged Alberto as one "with whom there is no taking up of persons" to stiffen the courage of his colleagues and the pope. John's own associates reckoned it unsafe, he wrote, to try Thomas's case before a legate influenced by offerings, fear, and favor.[119]

Continuing the counterattack, John wrote Cardinal Gualtero, an appointee of Adrian, boldly invoking the friendship the dead pope had had in a special way for John. How could Gualtero's honor, or the curia's, stand "if you [a plural you] are takers up of persons and of offerings?" To pardon Christ's enemies because "they are opulent, we poor," was this "the way of the Lord?" Considering this possibility, John piled up his questions: "Where is the law? Where the prophets? Where the Gospel of Christ? Where the decrees and the saints' examples?" Like Cicero he affirmed that the law itself was unbreakable, although in the same breath he gave a Christian, not Ciceronian, reason for this belief: "by what judgment you judge, you shall be judged." Vindication was hereafter. "But maybe little men seem unworthy that on their account such great princes must be troubled; and the rigor of justice should be exercised only in favor of equally powerful men." To accept such a distinction, he observed, was to return to the exploded position of Thrasymachus that justice was whatever could do most for the powerful. True justice "frees the poor man from the powerful and decrees its rewards by merits not by persons."[120] Such a sermon on justice John thought necessary for a wavering cardinal in the curia. About the same time he advised John of Poitiers that Thomas had told the legates that "his poverty" was not equal to the expenses of litigation.[121]

No resolution of the case, or cases, took place. John continued to point to the power of money, writing his friend at Poitiers in May 1168 that the king had told Roger, bishop of Worcester, to fear nothing "because now he has the lord pope and all the cardinals in his pocketbook." John also had the names of three more cardinals said to be actively enlisted on the king's side. He hoped that the pope would provide for his conscience, and the cardinals would bring to mind "the judgment of God."[122] Slightly more buoyantly, John wrote Thomas himself about this time: The Romans, as Juvenal had observed, could not be trusted. "Generally they twist the purpose of the laws and the canons, so he who is powerful in offerings is more powerful in law." But the pope was not wholly "broken" and was actually showing signs of "inchoate virtue." His acts, which were not proven to be perverse, should be interpreted for the best. Maybe he would cheat the king![123]

Not much later, July 1168, John was in despair. The king was boasting of a letter from the pope which "gave him immunity in sinning" (it had, in fact, prohibited Thomas from issuing any more excommunications in the king's territories). In John's view, expressed to Lombardo of Piacenza, a friendly canonist at the curia, "the cause of God and the favor of Christ were sold for a wretched price." A few cardinals had made the deal. "Would that those golden ounces had never existed which drove those to fall who should have been pillars of the Church!" Henry, so John heard, was savoring the names of those who took the gold and not concealing which cardinals had distributed it, "more to some, less to others," in proportion to their contribution to his case.[124] Hostile and embittered hearsay, these comments are good evidence of what John thought the curia capable.

Alexander, while reining Thomas, was actually putting new pressure on the king to be reconciled, and with the help of the king of France almost brought it off at Montmirail on January 6, 1169.[125] When this parley of the parties ended in bitter disagreement, the pope appointed two new legates, Viviano, an experienced advocate at the curia, and Graziano, a papal notary not, it seems, the famous canonist.[126] Being less than cardinals, these men did not have much status independent of the pope, and they were explicitly instructed that, unless peace was made (an exception meant to motivate them) they were "to abstain" from the king's *munera* and not even to accept their expenses from him.[127]

Graziano's appointment was a godsend to Thomas. A nephew of Eugene III, known to Thomas from his student days at Bologna, he was joyfully greeted by John as a virtuous friend—also a courageous man—now in a position to do the right thing in England. John learned from him in July 1169 that now "the Pope and the Roman Church much favor Canterbury."[128] Graziano was thereafter saluted by Thomas himself as the one emissary from the Roman church "who did not hurt the Church."[129] He was hailed by Thomas's associates as one immune from "the corruptible gold and silver and various worldly vanities of a pander by which he [the king] is accustomed to corrupt those dealing with him" and as one glad to work gratis for the Church while her enemies "corrupted others" with "the spoils taken from us."[130] He was recognized by Thomas after further experience of his qualities as a man immovable "by prayer or price, blandishment or threat."[131] These outspoken praises of sheer honesty can be read as measuring Thomas's disillusionment with Graziano's colleagues. They can also be seen as the *munera* of flattery offered a friend in power.

In the fall of 1169 Henry increased the pressure on the pope by promulgating a law forbidding anyone to bring a papal interdict into the country. Alexander in January 1170 responded with the appointment of new legates (a step back from Thomas' perspective) and the threat of an interdict (a step forward). The move forward was undone a little later by the king's agent at the curia obtaining the Easter Day absolution of Bishop Foliot; Foliot was now freed from Thomas's excommunication. For Thomas this was the last straw. He wrote Cardinal Alberto, "I know not by what arrangement the Lord's party is always slain in the curia, so that Barabbas escapes and Christ is killed." Against the Gospel the pope had forgiven the impenitent. Why? "Are not the spoils our own, or rather the Church's, which the king's envoys grant and promise to the cardinals and curialists?" Prepared as he now said to die for the liberty of the Church, Thomas called on God to rise and judge. To Graziano he poured out the same cries: The persecutors of the Church were giving the cardinals and curialists "our spoils," and "so Barabbas is dismissed, Christ crucified." The Lord, "that terrible Majesty," would have to judge.[132]

To Cardinal Alberto, he wrote, "I have no intention of troubling the curia further." To Graziano, "We shall not intentionally trouble the curia. We yield it to those whose wickedness is accepted there, who preach its venality." These letters mark a critical moment in the long struggle. In them Thomas gave up what he calls "the Roman way." *Munera* had effected Foliot's absolution. Thomas would no longer trust the pope but God. Now in 1170, not in 1164, he broke with the ways of the world. Now he chose a way that could not trouble the Roman curia.[133]

The famous meeting between Thomas and the king at Fréteval in July 1170 was the sequel of this decision. The king had consistently refused to give Thomas the kiss of peace, saying he had sworn never to do so and ignoring the pope's power to dispense from such an unreasonable oath. Thomas knew that the refusal was "sinister in the extreme." Now he accepted the king's offer of reconciliation without the kiss, and took at full value the protestations of Henry that the status of the Constitutions of Clarendon and the restoration of Thomas's confiscated property could be worked out later. With open eyes, knowing he was dealing with a double-dealer, abandoning the conditions for peace he had always said were essential, Thomas went through the form of a reconciliation with the king.[134]

Beaten by *munera*, he returned to England at the beginning of December 1170. He found his property unrestored, the Constitutions of Clarendon enforced, and he himself not much better than a prisoner. On the afternoon of December 29, 1170, he was visited by four knights of Henry II's entourage. When they threatened him, he declared, "I commit myself and my cause to the Judge of all men." A little later in the day the knights killed him in his cathedral.[135]

Christian Munera. Offerings had another relationship to Thomas's murder. Foliot had been absolved in 1169. But when in 1170, he, Jocelin of Salisbury, and Roger of York participated in the coronation of Henry II's son, they were excommunicated again by Alexander III at Thomas's instigation. On December 3, 1170, their messengers asked Thomas to lift the excommunication. The immediate cause of his death was the anger of the king, hotly expressed in the presence of his knights, at Thomas's claim that it was beyond his competence to grant the request. Gilbert and Jocelin were for submitting. But Roger, it is alleged by Thomas's biographers, dissuaded them, saying he "sometimes had the Pope and the king in his coffers." If this account is to be believed, it was the bishops' confidence in the might of *munera* that moved them to challenge the excommunications and as a consequence to rouse the king to anger at the excommunications having been issued.[136]

Whether in fact Roger talked this way we cannot be certain. The story coheres with his "business," years before, with Cardinal Gregorio di Sant'Angelo, and with another impression of his ways, recorded in a report by Thomas's man at the curia in 1164. Hearing that Roger's representative was approaching the curia with three horses, he concluded that Roger's envoy was coming "loaded."[137] And there is a final report of the same character. Horrified by Thomas's murder, Alexander III refused to see any Englishmen for a week. He then prepared to excommunicate the king and the three bishops who had stirred the king up—"your trinity," as he satirically called them.[138] But when Holy Thursday came, when papal excommunications were traditionally announced, no names were mentioned and only the actual murderers and unnamed conspirators with them were condemned. According to one of Henry's emissaries at the curia, this result had been preceded by "the intervention of certain cardinals and big money."[139] Roger of York in the end escaped with the requirement that he purge himself by oath of any complicity in the killing; and he gleefully gave the oath.[140]

Most of these impressions of Roger's potent *munera* must be discounted as the tales of hostile observers; but the final report of money spread around the curia comes from the king's side. Consistent though they are, we cannot be certain that all the stories are true. Nor can we be certain that John of Salisbury and Thomas himself were right in concluding that "Christ was sold" at the various times that their cause was undercut at the curia. The effect of protracted litigation on the minds of those who are its victims is often such as to make them seek a reason for their frustrations in the bad faith of their judges. Neither Thomas nor John was a firsthand observer of any bribery by their opponents. Their reliance was on scuttlebutt, supplemented by the inferences they made when a cause, obviously just to them, was sidetracked. They made little allowance for the diplomatic needs of a pope harassed by an antipope and a hostile emperor. They made even less allowance for any papal realization that total victory over the king of England in England was unlikely or for any papal desire to heal and reconcile rather than judge. What they wanted was absolute justice. The maxim frequently cited by both came from Augustine's letter to Macedonius, "Unless stolen property is returned, the sin is not remitted." They knew the maxim from the *Concordantia* where it was surrounded by Augustine's strictures against bought judgments.[141] Restoration of all their rights by the king or by judicial order of the pope was what they sought. Compromise until Fréteval was compromise with sin.

That the taking of *munera* was sinful was the predicate of Thomas's and John's complaints about the curia. Strikingly, their reliance was on the moral objection to, the scriptural condemnation of, the practice. At no point did these two men, both experienced in the work of chanceries, attempt to give a legal cast to their criticism, to contend that a papal decision was invalid because it had been paid for. At no point did they invoke the Roman laws which, as appended to Gratian's *Concordantia* or as they stood in Justinian, would have been available to give their position a legal shape.[142] Citing the *Concordantia* frequently for the words of Augustine on restitution, they ignored the teaching contained in the same text on payoffs to a judge. The gap between academic law and actual practice could not be more clearly demonstrated. The great problem of litigants in the curia was the play of offerings. The *Concordantia* was useless in helping litigants counteract the power of money at the top of the system.

If the standards set by the *Concordantia* applied to the litigation between Thomas and his adversaries and the rumors heard by John of Salisbury were true, simony was being committed by cardinals and those paying them; and, as Alexander III's own decretal *Insinuatam* set out the general rule, a notorious Simonian was to be deposed, and a person not notorious but defamed as a Simonian was bound to undergo judicial purgation.[143] Even by the norm provided the archbishop of Esztergom in 1162, the gifts being given were simonian for they were intended to "allure and pervert" minds. No one, however, as far as can be seen, invoked the sanctions of canon law against simony to stop the giftgiving. Where offerings were in play, the law was a dead letter.

The focus of Thomas and his supporters on justice made them more or less wilfully blind to the true nature of the proceeding in which they were engaged. They themselves had not scrupled to enlist the king of France and his brother, the archbishop of Reims, on their side as men powerful in influence at the curia. They saw nothing wrong in having an old friend like Graziano appointed as legate, partial though he was to them from the start. Influential friends on their side were seen simply as the friends of Christ and the truth. When the king obtained influential friends at the curia, it was corruption, and when friends of his like Guglielmo of Pavia were made legate, it was manifestly unfair and wrong. Thomas and company chose then to think of the legates as true judges, not as they actually functioned, as arbitrators and conciliators.

The failure of pope, curia, and canon law to sort out such different functions made a monumental contribution to the suspicions Thomas's side voiced about the role of *munera* in curial action. We cannot be sure that all the suspicions were true. We can be sure that Thomas believed them to be true. Once a great gamesman, he was willing in 1164 to play the game himself. In 1164 the problem was that his resources put a limit on what he could pay to play. When later he said he was too poor to litigate, and again in 1170 when he exclaimed to Graziano that "his creditors were worn out," were these not allusions to the cost of *munera* to sustain his case?[144] Only in the spring of 1170, after the final disillusionment of Alexander's absolution of Foliot, did he abandon the curial game and remit his cause wholly to God.

In his last days at Canterbury in December before his death Thomas was once more a bishop judging cases in his own court. In his time as chancellor he had served the king as a secular circuit justice, holding the king's court in at least ten counties.[145] Now back in Canterbury his court was not much used by the rich and powerful; in fear of the king they stayed away. Humbler folk sought a judge who had been absent nearly seven years. To all of them who came—John of Salisbury reported with edification to Pierre, abbot of Saint-Rémi—"he in person gives the law with a bishop's serious care, assuredly without taking up persons and offerings."[146]

Acting in person, not discriminating among persons, not taking *munera*, Thomas had been in his last days a true judge. When John wrote his only letter on the circumstances of Thomas's death, this image of his justice came back: he was "a judge most incorruptible and surely the taker up of neither persons nor gifts." It was this judge who, as John now put it, "used to offer Christ's body and blood on the altar, and now prostrate before the altar, offered his own...."[147] The follower of the way of Christ at the end so redeemed his case with the only *munera* a Christian could afford.

Reformers, chiefly monks, had worked for over a century to shape the see of Peter so that it could be the center from which justice radiated to the spokes. To a seasoned administrator like Adrian IV, it was still the stomach. Would administrators formed by education in the canons collected by Gratian and instructed by the example of Thomas and imbued in the new theological learning beginning to be dispensed at Paris be different from their predecessors? In the offertory part of the Mass the gift of sharing the divine nature was asked from God who had "wonderfully reformed man's nature." The generic reform had been accomplished by Christ. It remained for each one in particular to be reformed as to the taking of offerings. A pope, the most brilliant of the thirteenth century, was to show how difficult of accomplishment this was at the seat of power.

7

The Quarter and the Road

Pierre le Chantre, Stephen Langton, Robert Courson, Robert of Flamborough, Thomas of Chobham, Gerald of Wales, Thomas of Marlborough, Alain de Lille, Jacques de Vitry, Lotario dei Conti di Segni—men whose teaching, writing, judging, lawmaking or deeds gave meaning to the doctrine on *munera*. Coming from different parts of Western Christendom, they had a common bond forged in the life of the Latin Quarter and the schools of the Cathedral of Notre Dame. On the royal Ile-de-la-Cité they had been able to study the seven sisters of the Liberal Arts, or, as a student at the university puts it, to hear the canon and civil law "read with the thundering trumpet of the noblest eloquence"; they were able to "irrigate the spirit" by drawing from the "three most linked rivers" of historical, allegorical, and moral interpretation of Scripture.[1] Here, in the students' quarter of Paris, in the last part of the twelfth century, theology was given a practical turn. The demands of Christian life and the proper dispensing of the sacrament of penance became serious subjects. Among a multitude of moral topics the purchase of justice, ecclesiastical office, or spiritual advantage was not the smallest. Enough of these earnest teachers and students were to leave the protecting shadow of Notre Dame and voyage in the greater world for what they learned to be put to the test of action.

The Master. Most influential of all the moralists of Paris was Pierre le Chantre, whose surname—"Cantor," or "Chanter"—reflected his administrative post in the great cathedral. He spoke about judges from observation and experience. His *Abbreviated Word*—a series, composed 1191–1192, of scripturally inspired moral reflections—had a chapter entitled "Against The Takers of Offerings for Justice Done or To Be Done, Accelerated or Omitted." The first kind of offerings (*munera*) were those given for no unjust reason. They were always dangerous, for the receiver of them "sold" his freedom. The third kind of *munera* came from extortion and taking beyond a prescribed stipend. They were always sinful. The second kind was given for justice done—"which was Gehazite"; or justice to be done—"which was simoniacal"; or not to do justice or to accelerate justice—"which was unjust"; or to do injustice—"which was diabolical." "Against the second kind," le Chantre collected a battery of texts, mostly from the Old Testament, many of them ingeniously interpreted to bear on unjust judging. These were fortified by such Fathers as Augustine, Gregory, and Jerome and by such Romans as Sallust and Cicero. Le Chantre's position was uncompromising. He endorsed the view that even little offerings (*munuscula*) were corrupting, as Jerome had said. A wife who accepted a small offering from outside her home gave "a sign of her own corruption"; in the same way, "from a judge who takes even a small offering, no judgment will issue except a corrupt one." Let the judge "in giving judgment have not a friend but only God in mind." These severe standards were joined to severe language on the pastors and prelates of the Church who as judges took offerings for justice done or to be done, accelerated or omitted. They were not shepherds, but shearers. They were skinners, hair-pullers, nose-wipers of money—the piling up of invective reflected le Chantre's disdain of the whole corrupt crowd.[2]

Suppose, le Chantre asked in 1192, that someone has business in the prince's court. He "cannot obtain justice without money." He borrows from a usurer, having to pay usury and the charge of a guarantor of the loan plus the charge of the man who arranged the loan. "I say," le Chantre taught, "without any doubt the judge is bound to make restitution," a restitution including all the costs occasioned by the loan. The hypothetical was instructive. Le Chantre assumed that if you could not obtain justice without money at the secular court, a payoff must go to the judge. He applied general principles of restitution to determine the amount the judge was bound, under pain of sin, to pay back, and he added, "If you are a judge, look to it that you have something to live on. For, to sell judgment, when judgment is attached to the office of a judge and to justice, is—even though you are in need—simonian." With this bold equation, le Chantre classed corrupt judges generally, not merely corrupt ecclesiastical judges, with Simonians, and trained on judicial corruption of all kinds the batteries assembled against simony. "Along with Judas," he wrote elsewhere, the Simonian "sells God and Justice."[3]

A comparable boldness was shown by le Chantre in his treatment of *acceptio personarum*. Suppose a bishop bestowed a benefice on a relative because he was a relative. Le Chantre held the appointment to be "the taking up of flesh and blood," the equivalent of the sinful act of taking up a person. Bias in administration was equated with bias in judging. The appointee was also guilty of simony. Spiritual goods should be bestowed gratis; here they were conferred for a consideration.[4]

Identifying both corrupt judgment and *acceptio personarum* with simony, le Chantre set severe standards for the courts. *Nemo presbyterorum*, composed by Hincmar of Reims and in le Chantre's time sometimes treated as a decretal of Alexander III, could be read to support this result. But le Chantre's teaching was qualified: he advanced his view "rather by way of objection and opinion than by way of assertion." Directly contrary was Uguccione of Ferrara, the leading canonist of his day, who wrote, "a judgment is neither spiritual nor attached to the spiritual," so that in itself it could not be an object of simoniacal sale unless the case itself involved the spiritual. Uguccione did not care to apply to every case the whole arsenal of texts developed against simony; and he did not even consider putting *acceptio personarum* in this drastic category. In contrast to the canonist's restraint, le Chantre's position appeared to be the academic speculation of a master in the schools of Paris.[5]

But le Chantre, a teacher with a passionate interest in moral questions, was no mere theorist. Experienced as an ecclesiastical judge and often active as a papal judge-delegate, he attacked the ecclesiastical bureaucrats of his day with the fury of a reformer and the sharpness of a satirist. An *officialis* (an "official," the bishop's delegate in holding an ecclesiastical court) and a collector (an authorized alms-gatherer or *quaestor*) were, in his view, the indispensable agents of prelates of the Church who were not fishers of souls but "fishers of cash." They were "less officials than they were robbers." By fear, fraud, and violence they acquired cash. "If you want to offend God beyond all other sinners," le Chantre quoted an observer, "become the official or the collector of the palace of a bishop." Men like these stood under the judgment of John the Baptist's words to the soldiers, "Shake down no one" (Lk 3:14).[6]

An excommunicate today, le Chantre reported, was not absolved until he satisfied a prelate's judgment that he had been contumacious. "Satisfaction" was provided by paying money for the prelate's private use. In such a case the prelate was guilty of both a shakedown and simony; he had sold absolution. An archdeacon would not agree to let the parties to a case before him reach a compromise with each other unless "his hand was preoiled,"—unless his palm was greased we would say. The great area of canonical shuffling—the area of impediments to marriage based on remote degrees of blood relationship and in-law relationship, impediments scarcely comprehensible by experts and incomprehensible to most people—was manipulated by ecclesiastical "gladiators" seeking to capture money with "nets and tridents." For a price they would whisk away an impediment, for a price they would find one in existence and end a marriage. "At our pleasure," they boasted, "we join whom we will and, when we will, we separate them." These practices, never identified with a particular diocese, were, by implication, what le Chantre knew to go on in Paris and perhaps in his home diocese of Reims. These were not the distant abuses of Rome but incidents observed or heard of in France.[7]

Was there any excuse for such abuses? Le Chantre contemplated none when he spoke of shakedowns. In the Roman curia he had heard auditors (*examinatores*) say that they were "renting their labor or selling their writing." He had even heard them say that they could charge for accelerating their work. It appeared to him, he told his students mildly, that these practices gave "birth to simony." Similarly, "it seemed to him" that a judge-delegate who took money to travel to hear a case was guilty of simony though ostensibly the money was compensation for his trouble in making the trip. On no account should there be a charge for the use of a seal, which was the very sign of office. As for two and one-half shillings taken before trial from each litigant—known as "the penny of justice"—he hesitated to condemn the practice or accept it. Was it not "usury" to take such a sum from an innocent man? Le Chantre would permit a charge for parchment, ink, and the labor of writing a document. Nonetheless he knew one exemplary bishop who "prohibited his chancellor to receive anything for attestation, seal, pen, parchment, ink or even the knife." The heroic example he evoked was that of an old Paris boy, much revered now as a martyr, "St. Thomas of Canterbury," as he administered his archdiocese in the few months of his life after he returned from exile.[8]

As to the responsibility of the giver of *munera*, le Chantre had not much to say. If a prelate has granted me a letter gratis, ran one of his hypotheticals, and the notary refuses to give it to me without a price, may I buy back (*redimam*) my right? The question was not answered. The usual ambivalence as to the giver of a gift prevailed. The question itself was weighted in its phrasing: the giver was not bribing, but redeeming. Le Chantre did call attention to what a really good man would do. Archbishop Lukás of Esztergom (an old Paris boy of an earlier generation) sent his archdeacon to Rome for a privilege highly necessary for his church. When the archdeacon returned, Lukás asked if he had paid anything for it. He replied that they had asked nothing when they heard that the archbishop spent everything he had on the poor; he added, "Still I gave a certain notary three solidi to make me a better than usual letter." Lukás hurled the privilege into the fire. In le Chantre's presentation, the action of Lukás like those of Thomas rose above the ambiguities of analysis. The exemplary archbishops showed what should be done.[9]

The Confessor's Friends. Stemming from the same Parisian milieu came new models of an old genre, handbooks designed to guide confessors in hearing sins and imposing penance. Alain de Lille, le Chantre's contemporary, writing about 1200, and le Chantre's English pupils writing a little later, all adopted the crucial position that simony was a sin in whose absolution restitution must be imposed by the confessor—that is, "restitution" must be practiced in the sense of giving up what one had received and paying it to the Church or the poor. Beyond this principle Alain had relatively little to say on corruption. He declared, very generally, that an ecclesiastical judge should be free from sin when he judged—otherwise he condemned himself. He prescribed restitution if "by false patronage" or "by false judgment" one had "extorted things." He prescribed "offerings (*oblationes*) and charities" as the medicine for avarice: "These remedies redeem." He said that a priest might not remit a penance "for money." In his much more detailed analysis of sexual sin, he held a man's sin was less if the girl was pretty, because then the man "was more compelled"; but he did not adapt the principle to a judge tempted by cash. One may guess that some of his students did. *Munera* as such were not analyzed.[10]

A Derbyshireman, Robert Courson, writing between 1204 and 1208, showed the same realism as his master, le Chantre.[11] Teaching while Notre Dame de Paris was still unfinished, he asked: what is to be said of "the hucksters" (*quaestuarii mercenarii*) sent out by bishops to raise money for church building? The hucksters came equipped with schedules showing how much remission of penance would be obtained per offering, a tariff of reductions purchasable in exchange for donations. They preached that "in whatever manner you come" and "whoever you are," you could participate in the "remissions." They proclaimed that if the soul of anyone was in hell it could be repurchased by such offerings. They promised—what living person would not be moved by such a promise?—that, at the very least, part of a soul's punishment in hell would be mitigated by an offering for the building. These teachings, Courson observed, "smack of heresy." Proclaimers of them were false preachers, and the bishop who commissioned them was guilty of their sin. The "simple parish priest" who saw them coming should denounce them even if the bishop would excommunicate him and turn him out of his parish—Courson seemed to believe a bishop would go this far to protect his building drive. Courson himself was not utterly uncompromising before such pressures. The money-raisers, if they did no more than read aloud the bishop's announced tariff of reduced penances for living penitents, could be "tolerated."[12]

At the level of the parish clergy, especially the rural clergy, and religious houses, Courson found it a common abuse for penances to be imposed as a way of enriching the priest or house, rather than to correct the soul of the penitent. A confessor of this sort was himself "Simon Magician." Particularly objectionable was the practice of commuting penance where restitution to an injured party should have been required—a kind of discount where, it is implied, the discounter took a percentage. Commutation was never lawful unless the penitent restored "as much as he could. What he could give was to go to make up the injury, not enrich his confessor." As for a bishop who had promoted an unworthy person—"a case by which the Church is afflicted every day"—he was bound to make restitution for the losses his appointee had caused. An unworthy appointment was "lefthanded work." Instead of following the Gospel maxim, "Let not your left hand know what your right hand is doing," (Mt 6:3), the bishop's left hand had "absorbed his right." If he had made the appointment because the man was a relation or if for any other reason he had put God second, he—although not his appointee—was guilty of simony.[13]

Courson had words too for the man at the top, then Innocent III. Supercilious flatterers existed who said that since the Lord Pope "has the plenitude of charity" he could by his nod "dispose of everything" without incurring "the sin of simony." These men, and those like them who egged on secular princes to think that at will they could dispose of all secular property, were incendiaries. The pope was "not to be heard" if he acted against faith or morals; and if he did something against the liberty and ancient statutes of a church—did it for money or other unworthy motive was the implication—the pope was guilty of simony.[14]

Robert of Flamborough, a Yorkshireman, another English pupil of le Chantre, became the penitentiary or principal confessor of St. Victoire in Paris.[15] In his *Liber poenitentialis*, written between 1208 and 1213, he catalogued judicial corruption under "Simony" and had his model confessor ask directly, "Have you ever sold justice, or have you withheld what should have been done, or have you accelerated or delayed for money? If you have done so, it is simony." Like le Chantre, he saw that the grant of a procedural advantage could be as corrupt as the sale of a judgment. Speeding up a case was sin when done for money.[16]

Under "Avarice," Robert's inquiring confessor asked, "Have you ever been corrupted as a judge, witness, advocate, assessor, or arbiter?" If the answer was affirmative, the priest was to proceed, "You are bound to satisfy the one you injured as to his loss, his expenses, and his harassment." Offerings were analyzed in the ancient terms of Gregory the Great— *munera* of the hand, *munera* of the tongue, and *munera* of service. Any offerings given for a spiritual good constituted simony.[17]

Thomas of Chobham, a third English pupil of le Chantre, returned from Paris to be the *officialis* of Salisbury and to write for the English clergy a *Summa Confessorum*.[18] He was as detailed in his diagnosis as Flamborough and milder in his prescriptions. A judge who sold justice was selling neither a sacrament nor a virtue but his judgment; by implication, he was not guilty of simony. He was, however, guilty of sin and was bound to give what he received either to the poor or to the person injured by his judgment. "Judges have large incomes so that in their office they can maintain justice, and therefore they should receive nothing." The passage from Augustine in Gratian holding that lesser officeholders did not have to make restitution did not apply to judges, but, according to many, applied to "apparitors" or court bailiffs. As to them,

Luke 3:14 spoke, "Shake down no one." A shakedown, Thomas added, was "to harass a man unjustly until he gives something." It was possible, however, without sin "to buy back one's own right from a judge when one cannot otherwise have it." Redeeming his right, a litigant received "nothing from the judge except what is his own or what is owned to him." In this way, le Chantre's hypothetical about the recalcitrant notary was answered and broadly extended by his pupil.[19]

The Preacher.   Nero in hell was boiling in molten gold when he was surprised to see a group coming. Who should they be but lawyers! The moral for this "venal race of men" was evident—"Lawyers, beware, lest you sell your souls to the devil." The homilist did not specify that lawyers would pay *munera* to win. Their avarice was globally satirized.[20]

A second, more current case: It was believed that the ecclesiastical judges of Lorraine were particularly partisan. They would cite a party to appear before them at a certain place and time and then pretend that the citation had been misunderstood, the defendant should have come earlier somewhere else; he must now be excommunicated for contempt. Such judges should be deprived of every office and compelled to pay the expenses and damages of those they afflicted. By implication, they acted for money. The moral: "Judges must exercise their office gratis."[21]

A third story: a "poor little woman" was not able to get her right from a notoriously venal judge. She was told, "Unless his hands are oiled, you will never obtain justice." She obtained grease from a pig and began to oil the judge's hand in the courtroom. "Woman, what are you doing?," he exclaimed. "Lord, it was said to me that unless I oiled your hands, I could not get justice from you." The judge blushed and was covered with confusion that his ways should be so well-known. The moral: "You, dearest brothers, judging or pleading, conduct yourselves so that you can render a secure account of the talent committed to you before the Supreme Judge, our Lord."[22] The parable of the talents and the Last Judgment were here combined. Going further than the insistent litigant before the unjust judge in the Gospel, the poor woman made a gesture that actually punctured the suave decorum of the court. The key verb, "to oil," probably came from le Chantre's use. The association of bribetaking with an animal reputed to be filthy and voracious was as old as Cicero and Hog, but no echo of Cicero need be supposed. The preacher appealed to an image immediately graspable by countrymen.

The preacher—the most famous of his age—was Jacques de Vitry, a native of Reims, later a participant in the Fifth Crusade, bishop of Acre, and a cardinal, another student of le Chantre, another ecclesiastical leader whose moral ideals were formed in Paris.[23]

The Pope.   Of all the students of the schools of Notre Dame the one who was to be best known was an Italian, Lotario dei Conti di Segni. He came as a young man and drank deeply of the aspirations of the Quarter. Reforms advocated by le Chantre—marriage for prostitutes, interest on dowries, abolition of the ordeal, reduction of the canonical gobbledygook on consanguinity and affinity—were to become his reforms. The Parisian schools themselves were to receive papal recognition from him as a university. His own teacher, Pierre Corbeil—another "rock from the quarry" of the Quarter—he made an archbishop. At the height of power, pressed by a thousand problems of politics and all the needs of his own assertive family, Lotario promoted to the cardinalate two Parisian masters, both English, both uncompromising to the point of being difficult: le Chantre's pupil, Courson, and le Chantre's colleague, Stephen Langton. His call of the Parisians to power suggests what the Quarter must have meant to him. Other students such as Gerald of Wales and Thomas of Marlborough were to cross his path as he himself sat in the seat of justice.[24]

Lotario left Paris for Bologna where, for an undetermined but inferably substantial time, he studied law.[25] He then returned to Rome where his connections were excellent, and his rise in the curia meteoric. Clement III (1187–1189) made him a cardinal, assigning him the pope's former titular church—a very special promotion, a dazzling start at court for someone no older than twenty-nine.[26] Clement died a few months later; the new pope, Celestine III, eighty-five years of age, used Lotario as an auditor in legal cases, but the young cardinal had enough leisure for moral reflection to write a small treatise, *The Misery of the Human Condition*.[27]

Lothario's book was composed in the first months of 1195 as he observed the old pope and his colleagues in the curia; he dedicated it to another cardinal, Pietro Galloccia, whom it was important for him to impress. Not apt to move a reader very much today, the moral tract was a remarkable production for a curialist. Lotario coined, or at least made current, the great phrase "the human condition." His book was praised by Petrarch and used by Bernardino of Siena. Chaucer thought well enough of it to translate the first part under the title "The Wrecched Engendryng of mankynde" (the translation is lost) and to draw on it in *The Canterbury Tales*. To generations of Europeans it conveyed a vivid didactic message on the connection between bribes and injustice.[28]

With simplicity and skill *The Misery of the Human Condition* was divided into three parts—entrance, progress, exit. Entrance into life and exit from it were filled with dangers. Its course was marked with moral temptations. Chapter titles such as "The Taking Up of Persons," "The Sale of Justice," and "The Insatiable Desire of the Greedy" suggested reflections stirred by Lotario's life in Rome. Three "very big things," the young cardinal wrote, "are accustomed to affect men very greatly: riches, pleasures, honors." Each of the first fourteen chapters of Book Two was a cento, drawn from Scripture, against avarice. "Woe to you," Lotario preached. "You do not attend to the merits of the cases but to the merits of the persons. You attend not to the laws but the *munera*, not to justice but to money." "You"—an indefinite you—"with delay neglect the poor man's case, with urgency you press the rich man's." "You"—still indefinite—"do not give favor (*gratia*) gratis or justice justly." As an adage ran, "Profit in the coffer, loss in the conscience." The measure of the greedy was distorted, their vision was directed at what they could get: "Insatiable is the eye of the avaricious."[29]

Against these unidentified sellers of justice, Cardinal Lotario invoked not the canon law but the law of Deuteronomy, the rebukes of Isaiah and Ezekiel, and the words of St. Matthew and St. James. He put before the Simonians and the corruptors the shameful examples of Gehazi and Judas, the good examples of Abraham and David. It was not a sin to have wealth—was that to be a chink in the young cardinal's armor? He was a rich young man, whose resources for the restoration of his titular Roman church caused wonder—but one must be as one having nothing and possessing all, finding in God the satisfaction of limitless desire. The doctrine was entirely orthodox and not original. Lotario sought to expound not novel insights but traditional truths. Yet his homiletic phrases were not in the air. When he wrote, as he did, that the expenses of litigation often exceeded the fruit won, he spoke at close range to the cases, a brilliant, ambitious, underemployed young theologian looking from the inside at the center of Christendom, its temptations, and those who had succumbed to them. Realism about the needs of the Stomach was not apparent. His rhetoric was sententious and severe.[30]

The climax of *The Misery of the Human Condition*—its final lines—was a description of the damned on "the Day of Wrath, that Day":

There will be weeping and gnashing of teeth, groans and moans, cries and sighs and agony, shrieking and screeching, shaking and shuddering, suffering and travailing, fire and stink, darkness and dread, bitterness and boisterousness, ruin and waste, distress and dejection, oblivion and disorder, torturings and piercings, torments and terrors, hunger and thirst, frigidity and boiling heat, brimstone and fire burning for ever and ever.

The Old Testament Prophet Zephaniah and the Gospel of Matthew were amplified in this way to conclude a judgment clearly contrasted with judgments familiar to the author:

> Wealth will then not avail.
> Honors will not be a defense.
> Friends will not provide patronage.

Over this "strict judgment" there is to preside "the justest Judge," from whom no one can appeal. As the Apocalypse puts it, "He shuts, no one opens. He opens, no one shuts." Him "no one can corrupt." He "does not swerve from the path of righteousness for prayer or price, love or hate. Always treading the royal road, He will pass over no evil unpunished. He will leave no good unrewarded."[31]

Already in Eugene III's day "the royal road" designated the path of the just judge. The phrase echoed the Epistle of James 2:8 where *acceptio personarum* was banned by the sovereign or royal law of love. Lotario cherished the curial, biblical image.

"The Miserable Entrance into the Human Condition," the first part of Lotario's work, had two striking discussions of food not without psychological bearing on Lotario's view of gifttaking. Chapter 4, "The kind of food by which the embryo is nourished in the womb," asserted that the embryo fed on the unclean menstrual blood of his mother. The biology was common to the time, the emphasis on the uncleanliness of the meal unusual; and the chapter was peculiarly set off against the climax of Book I, "A certain horrible crime." The tale came from Josephus' history of the fall of Jerusalem. Among the inhabitants reduced to starvation was a mother who devoured her son. Lotario elaborated the circumstances and dialogue including the eater's command, "Be food for mother." One thinks of a modern author's observation on the physical origin of male insecurity: "The archetypal image of the devouring mother has a biological base: what mother eats is, or at one point was, good for you—if only she doesn't make a mistake and eat you too."[32] In exegesis of Lotario: The primal gift, food, was necessary but unclean. The giver could become dangerous, devouring, fatal—an exegesis and a prophecy when Innocent became responsible for the Stomach.

A little earlier Lotario had discussed "the terror of dreams" and remarked, "Dreams terrify. Visions disturb. And although what dreamers dream are not in truth sad or terrible or laborious, yet in truth the dreamers are saddened, terrified, and fatigued." Lotario in fact had a dream not revealed in this book, but later. It was a dream or vision that visited him recurrently: he was marrying his mother.

The authority for this information is a biography written in his lifetime by an anonymous intimate so close to him, so apt to use his favorite phrases, and so familiar with his mind, that the work is kin to autobiography. Lotario did not interpret his dream with the help of vulgar Freudianism, nor did his intimate biographer feel the need to explain the symbolic significance of the dream, obvious to any ecclesiastic. Claricia, Lotario's mother in the flesh, was—strikingly enough—commemorated in the first paragraph of the biography. But the mother of the dream was of course the Church, whose spouse was Christ. The repeated dream could only mean that Lotario would become his Mother's Head by marriage.[33]

On January 8, 1198, the day Celestine died, Lotario, still not a priest, was put forward to succeed the deceased nonagenerian. His age—thirty-seven—was objected to, but the objection was brushed aside. He became Pope Innocent III. The next day he wrote the French episcopate to describe how he had been chosen: the electors had perhaps thought to find a Benjamin who was "a great silver vase."[34] His energy, his youth, his stature, and his eloquence—besides being youthfully dynamic, he was a short man with a good voice—were physical factors that may be inferred to have affected his conduct of the papacy. His sense of his aristocratic family was also important: at the beginning of his biography the point was emphasized that he was of "the counts of Segni," and his brother Riccardo actually became count of Sora as a consequence of his pontificate.[35] His immersion in the law helped to form his aspirations and his sense of his capabilities. But at a conscious level it was his theology that dominated his actions when he acted as a judge.[36]

In Lotario's theology, any pope had very special status, as his dream had suggested. On the day of his consecration as bishop of Rome he, preaching, described the pope "as Vicar of Jesus Christ, successor of Peter, the Anointed of the Lord, God of the Pharaoh"—God over the forces of evil, as God had set Moses over Pharaoh. He declared the pope to be "set in the middle between God and man, less than God, but bigger than man." The pope, he added trenchantly, "judges everyone, and is judged by no man." "To me," he quoted Jeremiah, "it is said in the Prophet, 'I have set you over peoples and kings to root out and destroy, to waste and dissipate, and to build up and plant.'" Self-conscious of his authority, self-assured in proclaiming and exercising it, he acknowledged no difficulty in being larger than any other human being.[37]

The image of himself as judge was a high one, explicitly insisted on in his early decretals, and his own standards were deliberately put forward for other judges. To Philip II of France he wrote in the spring of the year of his election, chastising the king for failing to return to his wife. As a cardinal with knowledge of the French court, he had followed Philip's case with interest and impatience. As he understood the situation, Philip, a widower, had decided to marry a Danish princess, Ingeborg. When he got a good look at her at the coronation ceremonies, he turned white with shock. He was advised to get to know her in bed, but this did not work at all, according to the king; at least it did not change his mind. His uncle, the archbishop of Reims, pronounced a divorce on the usual ground of affinity. Ingeborg, ignorant of French, stammered "Roma"; Celestine III took cognizance of her appeal and quashed the Reims proceeding, but the old pope had then procrastinated in forcing Philip to obey. Meanwhile the king had married Agnes, "a right pretty girl," as Lotario had heard. On taking office, Innocent was determined to show the king that with him in charge there would be no favoritism.[38]

Indebted as he recalled he was to his studies at Paris and to Philip's kindness while he was there, he would not tolerate the scandal of Philip's disobedience. Philip should expect no concession from him:

> With the Lord giving inspiration, We have an immoveable mind and an unbreakable intention. Not by prayer, not by price, not by love, not by hate shall we swerve from the path of righteousness. We shall walk the royal road. We shall not swerve to the right. We shall not deviate to the left. We shall make judgments without taking up persons. For there is no taking up of persons with God.[39]

No judge more deliberately took his own embodiment of divine power as the basis for excluding all partiality.

In *The Misery of the Human Condition* the young author had presented the paradigm of man's last Judge, treading the royal road of incorruptibility, the road that had been James's law of love. Now often invoked as an image of the pope the royal road was not especially connected with love. Innocent used the phrase on occasion to indicate "the right path" in a purely political context. Messina, for example, was said "never to have swerved from the royal road" in a battle over control of Sicily.[40] In particular it was a favorite expression of Innocent for the work of a good judge, especially his own work. The transmutation of the scriptural term, its elaboration and integration into a standard for judges were his doing.

In the end Innocent moved no faster than Celestine with Philip. Fourteen years went by before the French king was brought into a species of common life with Ingeborg. But when Agnes died in childbirth after the pope's first intervention he inferred that he was on the right track. The Lord, he wrote, had ."judged her case."[41]

In his first papal year Innocent also had the opportunity to instruct the king of England on the topic of judicial integrity. The monks of Christ Church, Canterbury, had been engaged in controversy for a dozen years with the archbishop of Canterbury over the archbishop's attempt to set up a college of secular canons with a church which would draw on Canterbury's income and supplant the monks. Lotario, there is reason to believe, had been approached on the matter much earlier. He had visited Canterbury in person, probably in early 1187. He had, apparently, been seen even then as an influential person whom the monks wanted to have on their side. He had a great veneration for St. Thomas, the martyr whose cause the monks identified with their own. He was reported to have worked for them as an advocate. Certainly King Richard the Lionheart, an ally of the archbishop, showed a good deal of nervousness about how impartially the new pope would decide the case and undertook to educate him on his duties. The royal admonition stimulated Innocent to observe that he already knew that he owed his position to "the divine gift (*munus*)" and that he already knew that it was "incumbent on us to safeguard the rights of every one whomsoever, and therefore we do not will, either in this or any other business, to swerve from the path of justice on account of favor for anyone whomsoever." His protests of impartiality, repeated at the end of the letter, were fulsome. At the same time he observed critically that the archbishop of Canterbury would be better advised to reside in the place which "Martyr Thomas had consecrated with his blood."[42]

The monks, so the pope thought, had not a friend in the world except God and himself. According to the monks who came to Rome, "Our opponents offered an infinite sum of money to turn the soul of the Lord Pope or at least to impede the business lest due effect follow; but in vain because that man is founded on the Rock and is a taker up of neither persons nor offerings." The monks were right in their confidence in their champion.[43] The pope's decision was wholly in their favor. Like Jeremiah, Innocent exercised his mission to "root up." The archbishop was instructed to remove physically the church he had constructed to the monks' prejudice. Writing King Richard to ask him not to interfere, Innocent described the decision as "divinely revealed." He added—no doubt he meant a bite to be felt—that he had acted after being "invited by the salutary exhortations of your royal prudence and being willing to tread the royal road prudently and to swerve not to the right or to the left." In a follow-up to the king he declared, "We have God alone before our eyes. We sought to decide according to the divine pleasure. If in this matter we wanted to take up persons or perchance to take up *munera*, beyond doubt we should have preferred the party of the archbishop of Canterbury to the party of the monks." As Innocent saw it, royal pressure and royal offerings had been useless. Better than le Chantre's "have not a friend but only God in mind," Innocent's image for impartiality was physical and his phrase entirely positive. To the ocular image of the avaricious man in *The Miserable Condition* he opposed the image of the impartial judge whose gaze was Godward.[44]

The same standard was embraced in the whirlwind activity of the first year in a quarrel with Filippo di Lampugnana, archbishop of Milan, over the appointment of the chancellor of Milan. The pope backed a candidate different from the archbishop's and formed the view that the archbishop's choice had been secret and simonian. Innocent took a high line. "That our judgment may proceed from the face of God and that our eyes may see justice," the decretal *Ut nostrum* began, "we must walk the royal road and swerve neither to the left nor to the right, judging the great like the small, for with God there is no taking up of persons." Here the eyes fixed upward were combined with the metaphor of the road—the mixture seemed to the pope utterly appropriate. What he conveyed was the sense of a vision that rose above material inducements and a progress or process that was like God's because it was free from corruption.[45]

Still in the first year of his pontificate the pope stated his standards in a rule for his delegates. Addressing the prelates and the priests of Lombardy in the decretal *Cum ab omni* he again put himself in the place of Jeremiah. His mission was "to root out and to destroy, to build up and to plant"—an unwelcome mission to a settled clerical establishment. Judges-delegate got their living expenses from the litigants: that was customary and acceptable. They were also accustomed to receive compensation (*salarium*) in amounts that varied regionally and which sometimes came to one-tenth the value in litigation. Judges-delegate took pledges from the parties that the *salarium* be paid. The pope found this practice of compensation from the litigants lamentable and worse. Judges should not be "reaching out their hands to filthy profits or bending their eyes to unjust offerings." "Filthy profits" (*turpia lucra*, our English "filthy lucre") was already the term used to describe a variety of shameful gains, among them the fee of a prostitute. "Filthy profits" were what Innocent called the litigant-derived compensation of the judges. The term was one of art: it implied wrongdoing, disgraceful conduct, not necessarily injustice. The pope was not saying that every such payment was a bribe; and there was a great deal of litigation where no material object by which compensation could be measured was in contention. But wrongful offerings (*munera*), the pope asserted, could be involved. Judges-delegate were ecclesiastics, assigned benefices by the Church, Innocent said, so "they could live decently." They must impart justice gratis.[46]

The pope invoked the gratuitous standard set for spiritual acts without applying the canons against simony. His anger and his sanctions were specific and controlled. He was aware of the way the judges sometimes covered themselves, by asking that their assessors be paid. The assessors, Innocent implied, split with the judge. The practice of payments to the assessors, he concluded, could not be tolerated.

The same informed and practical spirit of reform was manifested in Rome itself. "Near the kitchen well" of the Lateran Palace, at the time of his accession, moneylenders and moneychangers had an office for the convenience of the litigants in the curia. Their wares included silver cups suitable for presentation. Innocent—no doubt with the Gospel story of the moneychangers in his mind—had them expelled from the precincts of justice. He himself, as his letter to the French hierarchy had intimated, was a great silver cup. He was not to be bought by lesser ones.

Another reform: the papal notaries were guarded by doorkeepers from the importunities of litigants in need of documents. To gain admittance one paid. A payment to a doorkeeper was, so it seemed, different from payment to an officeholder: the old rationalization of access payments had taken this transparent form. Innocent had the doorkeepers dismissed. Most practically, he published a schedule of fees to be paid both the writers who prepared documents and the sealers who sealed them. Not for Innocent the costless and impractical justice that le Chantre had celebrated in St. Thomas of Canterbury. A public schedule would set modest limits. Other acts in the legal process at the curia were, the pope added, to be free.[47]

Above all, it was his boast that he heard cases in public frequently and in person. In "a major case," he took an active part in stating each side. He threw himself into the role of raising the most difficult objections to the advocate of each party in turn, so that each side hearing him would be sure he was on their side. Then, after mature deliberation, he decided. The Lord Chancellor's famous line in *Trial by Jury*, "And I, my Lords, embody the law," could have been uttered by him with "justice" substituted for "the law."[48]

Cash and Cups.   Reforms did not purify the expectations of litigants. In 1199, the year after his rebuff in the matter of the monks, Archbishop Hubert of Canterbury, backed by King John of England, engaged in litigation over the election to the see of St. David's in Wales. He was opposed by Gerald de Barri, a Welshman rightfully elected, as he believed; and Gerald, a former scholar of Paris, came to Rome to pursue his case.

According to Gerald's postlitigation account, Hubert and the king paid "a large sum of money" to get Innocent to defer decision; but Gerald obtained from the pope the judges-delegate he asked for. When the case resumed in Rome in January 1203, Gerald, arguing before Innocent in person, alleged that his adversaries were relying on "gold and silver." The pope told him bluntly to pay no attention to boastful lies. The case in fact seemed to go well for Gerald. "Be strong and act confidently," he was advised. "Justice is with you, and the Lord Pope, too." His opponents then gave 200 pounds to the pope's chamberlain, "as if by this to salute the Pope," plus individual gifts to the cardinals and bigwigs in the curia, coupled with promises of more if their man won. The case continued into April. As Palm Sunday and decision time neared, his opponent's offers to "the chamberlains and counsellors, the Pope and the cardinals" intensified. He strove "to corrupt them with an immensity of treasure." The cardinals divided, the "more healthy part" for Gerald, "the corrupted" others for his opponent.

Gerald had relied on witnesses for the other side being subject to various disqualifications, including excommunication. He was asked not to press his points—asked, he says, "by almost all the confidential clerks and secretaries of the Pope" and finally by Cardinal Ugolino, the pope's cousin, now "wholly corrupted." This view of what was happening, however, came late to Gerald. At the time he was "still ignorant of such great corruption," and credulously withdrew some of his objections to the witnesses. The pope, now a party to the corruption in Gerald's later view, pushed him to withdraw even the objection of excommunication. Easter came, and on April 16, 1203, the pope pronounced sentence, quashing Gerald's election and his opponent's—a tie that led to a new election which the pope arranged to be conducted by English bishops hostile to the independent Welshman.

Gerald's complaint against Innocent was the fruit of bitter memory; it was retroactively constructed out of "what must have happened" for Gerald to lose. The pope's active participation in bringing the case to a head was construed as connivance in corruption. To a losing litigant Innocent was far from being above suspicion. A modern commentator says that Gerald's details of corruption "carry conviction." But Gerald is not very specific, and details are always meant to "carry conviction." His story shows what was often believed of the curia and the pope, and what Gerald was willing to say publicly in a book intended to influence Stephen Langton, the Innocent-backed appointee to Canterbury.[49]

In the year 1200, Innocent's integrity was put to a more subtle test. Konrad of Querfurt, bishop of Hildesheim, had arranged to be transferred to the much richer see of Würzburg. In Innocent's view, moving about like this could be done only with papal permission, which had not been granted. Konrad was an old friend from younger days. That weighed little with the pope. One thinks of Henry Adams's adage: "A friend in power is a friend lost." Konrad was excommunicated. The usual combination of offerings and political pressure was then employed on his behalf. Konrad was the chancellor of Philip of Swabia. The envoys he sent to negotiate were viewed by Innocent as "honorable." But the pope stood fast. Then Konrad came to Rome. He removed the pallium and his shoes, put bonds of slavery about his neck, lay before Innocent on the ground, stretched out his hands as on a cross, and with tears begged for mercy. The pope was moved, so the biographer close to Innocent tells us, but he ordered his old friend to resign both Hildesheim and Würzburg. Konrad complied.[50]

At the same time, our knowledgeable biographer reports, Konrad sent offerings to the pope. The *munera* were "silver cups, beautiful to see." The silversmiths still did business in Rome if no longer in the Lateran. The pope—again our informant is close to Innocent's mind—was puzzled. He did not want Konrad "to think that by the giving of offerings he could be corrupted." Yet to refuse the gifts would have seemed unforgiving. He did not want Konrad "to despair utterly of his favor." He kept the cups and sent Konrad a single cup of gold more valuable than the set of silver ones he had received. There was no corruption, for judgment had not been bought; no churlishness, because courtesy was received and reciprocated. Within the year Innocent approved the re-tender to Konrad of Würzburg.[51]

Cups continued to be purchasable and usable in Rome. In November 1204 Thomas of Marlborough arrived there on a mission from his monastery of Evesham. Thomas was yet another alumnus of the Paris schools, a pupil of Stephen Langton, and a late vocation to monastic life. He had drawn on his knowledge of the law to persuade the monks of Evesham to defy Bishop Mauger of Worcester's claim to have jurisdiction over them, and the first round of litigation had ended in an interlocutory decree in England upholding the bishop's rights. Thomas was in Rome to get the pope to suspend the decree of his delegates. At the first audience Innocent indicated he would. "Delighted," Thomas spent six marks and presented him with a silver cup.[52]

There is little reason to doubt Thomas's own account of this episode, told almost twenty years later when, as the prior of Evesham, he wrote the abbey's history. He seems to have had no motive in telling this tale unless it was true, although it did give him the occasion to show a certain sophistication about Rome. As his own sequel revealed, the gift was actually unavailing. The pope on further thought declined to suspend the judgment. Thomas, seeing the case to be hopeless for the time being, decided in April 1205 to leave. Before going, however, he "visited on the Lord Pope 100 pounds sterling" and on the cardinals 400 marks. Several cardinals no doubt divided the 400. If one makes the reasonable assumption that no more than half a dozen would have been in line, they got over 60 marks apiece, while the pope received a considerably larger amount personally. All the donees refused to accept these sums "until it was established that we had no case in the curia." They then took the money willingly.[53]

Within the year, as quickly as October, Thomas was back in Rome to press the merits, not now of an interlocutory order, but of the main case. He hired four advocates, paying them per day of employment, respectively, 50, 40, 40, and 20 solidi. Among them were Pietro da Benevento, a chaplain of the pope, and Guglielmo, a clerk of the papal chancellor.

Thomas paid them, he says, so "that I might learn certain secrets of the curia; and so I did." These small payments, one may notice, were for information not influence. Pietro, a well-known canonist whom Innocent had brought from Bologna to the curia, subsequently became a cardinal.[54]

By April 1206, after public argument in which Innocent participated with relish, Thomas had the judgment he wanted and was ready to go home. The official documents he needed were in pawn to Roman merchants who had advanced him forty marks. The merchants departed for England, taking with them the documents, to be released only when Evesham paid up. Thomas, still in Rome, believed that it was "fitting for the victor" to "visit" the pope and cardinals—"visit" in the sense of visiting gifts upon them. At the time of his calling on them he thought he would have received a few extra documents that would have been nice to have—a renewal "of all our privileges" and "a letter about the bishop refunding our expenses." But Thomas did not have any more money for "visiting" purposes; so he left town secretly. He had paid nothing for the judgment he had won. He left in his chronicle the indelible impression that gifts at appropriate times were expected by Innocent and his cardinals.[55]

The Gilded Cup. In *The Misery of the Human Condition* the young cardinal had described "the ambitious man," who calls on Simon Magician and comes close to Gehazi—that is, a climber who uses the methods of simony to climb. Such a one "imprudently snatches a dignity by the patronage of friends and the kindness of kin." The scenario was part of a rake's fall entitled, "The Blameworthy Progress of the Human Condition." When he wrote in 1194 Lotario was acutely conscious of the kindness of kin. In the course of his pontificate his kindness to his own kin was to severely compromise his high standard of justice.

In 1204 Innocent entered judgment in a case where the defendants, Abaiamonte de Montorio and his son, were in contempt of court, having been cited several times to appear before Innocent and having been excommunicated for continued contumacy. A panel of six named judges and five advocates was assembled before Cardinal Ugolino, the pope's relative, and gave the pope "counsel" to proceed with the judgment, which he accordingly issued, investing the plaintiff, Giovanni Oddone, with possession of Montorio, the land of the Abaiamonti. Nothing would be exceptional about the decision if it were not that Giovanni Oddone was Innocent's cousin. The Abaiamonti's unwillingness to come to court, even though they had been guaranteed "the fullest security in going, returning and litigating," appears entirely comprehensible. They had been offered no security as to the impartiality of their judge. Were they expected to defend their position before their opponent's blood relation?[56]

A case that turned out to cause Innocent far more trouble began in 1202 and was ended by judgment in the summer of 1204. The Poli family held a fee from the Roman Church, granted under Adrian IV and irrevocable unless they committed an act against the pope. They were sued by an abbey claiming prescriptive rights in the land and brought the case before their overlord, the pope, who referred it to auditors. "Meanwhile"—a significant "meanwhile" by which Innocent's biographer links this litigation to what follows—Odo de Poli began to negotiate a marriage between his son and the pope's niece, the daughter of his brother Riccardo. Contracts between the two families were signed; the pope's cousin, Cardinal Ottaviano, married the couple. Niece and nephew-in-law, unnamed, now disappear from the story as seen from Innocent's perspective. As a result of the marriage alliance and accompanying arrangements, Riccardo bailed out the heavily mortgaged Poli estates and received some kind of conveyance of their property. At the end of the transactions he claimed to own what until then the Poli had thought was theirs.

Riccardo offered to have their claims examined before the pope or before "other prudent men" and the pope offered to pay the necessary legal expenses of the impoverished Poli. But the Poli, like the Abaiamonti, were not keen on appearing before Innocent or men beholden to him. To shame Riccardo and his mighty brother they resorted to an ancient Roman device. They paraded through the streets naked, clutching crucifixes and crying out that the pope's family had despoiled them of their heritage. Their demonstrations excited popular hostility against the pope. Their next move was to convey the disputed lands to the commune of Rome. Innocent at this point entered the conflict in person, took the position that the Poli had no lands to convey, and ordered his brother Riccardo to defend the property as the Church's. Innocent's difficulties were enhanced by his mother's family, the Scotti, engaging in a murderous feud with the Bobone, the family of the old Pope Celestine. With disorder raging in the streets of Rome, the Poli, aided by the Roman commune, occupied and wasted Riccardo's tower. Innocent himself was forced to withdraw from Rome.[57]

By the summer of 1204 the pope had the upper hand over the Poli and his other Roman opponents. He had put his brother-in-law Pietro Annibaldi in charge of destroying the towers of the opposition, and brother Riccardo had helped to finance the building of wooden siege turrets and the fortification of baths and churches. The Poli on the run, Innocent gave interlocutory possession of their lands to Riccardo. The case, he observed punctiliously, was "not yet judged in our court"; so his award was not in final form. But Riccardo was given the property until the Poli compensated him for the losses they had inflicted and the expenses they had put him to. For the time being—and inferably until the Poli came into "our court"—Riccardo was recognized as the tenant, and Innocent promised to defend him as a good overlord should defend his vassal. The interlocutory decree was good for over 600 years. The family kept the property until the line ran out in 1808. Even Riccardo's ruined tower was ultimately made up to him. The pope built him a bigger one, tremendous in size, which as long as it lasted, was one of the wonders of Rome.[58]

A third case involved Riccardo's second oldest boy, Stefano. In 1205,

Magister Robert came to Rome to defend his claim to have been elected bishop of Bayeux. While in Rome he arranged for the canons of Bayeux to assign a rich benefice, paying 120 livres annually, to Stefano. In April Innocent chose the bishop of Dol and two abbots as judges-delegate, and they swiftly decided Robert's case in his favor. By February 1206 he was consecrated as bishop. Stefano, however, was left with a lawsuit over his benefice. It turned out that, much earlier, Robert had assigned the same prebend in perpetuity to Jean, a priest of Bayeux, in return for a fixed income of 34 pounds. The assignment had been modified and confirmed by Innocent III's predecessor and great patron, Clement III. Jean was not afraid to assert his prior and superior right in the pope's court itself.

Innocent heard the case with keen interest and set out in detail the pros and cons of the argument he heard. The answer of Stefano's side to the documents establishing the earlier assignment and its papal confirmation was essentially simple. Master Robert had farmed his prebend "in perpetuity," true, but the "perpetuity" lasted only as long as he held the prebend. On his becoming bishop, the farm "finished"—he had nothing to assign. Stefano's title, it now appeared, came from the chapter of Bayeux, hence Jean's tenancy lapsed when Robert was promoted. So Innocent judged, condemning Jean to make restitution of the three churches to Stefano and to desist from further litigation. Stefano went on to become a cardinal in 1216 and in the closing days of the pontificate to be noticed "as the cardinal nephew."[59]

The date of Innocent's judgment for his nephew, July 11, 1208, was shortly after the climax of a political affair which underlined—if underlining were necessary—how close Riccardo stood to the pope. From the beginning of his regime Innocent III had worked to expand the Patrimony of Peter over which as he put it, the pope had unmediated authority, having received this great power in temporal matters "from the Lord Himself."[60] Part of his plan was to expel the German rulers of the imperial fiefdom of Sora on his southern flank. His major opponent here was Markward, count of Molise, who lay siege to the monastery of Monte Cassino. Innocent first sent his cousin Landone de Montelongo and then two cardinals (one of them cousin Ottaviano) to the monastery's relief, and they succeeded—Innocent's biographer reports with satisfaction—in "corrupting some of Markward's army with money." The siege was raised. Markward tried to negotiate, promising "offerings" of gold and an annual tribute, but Markward proved unreliable, and Innocent was frustrated.[61]

Late in 1207 new opportunities presented themselves. The local nobility was reduced by its alien masters, Innocent heard, to public begging. The cardinal abbot of Monte Cassino and the lords of Aquino helped launch a local revolution in Sora against the Germans. The pope dispatched troops led by his chamberlain and by brother Riccardo. The abbot and the lords of Aquino of course thought that they would reap the harvest of their activities. But the end result was the installation of Riccardo in place of the defeated Germans. The abbot and the lords of Aquino were left to nurse their grievances. Innocent rounded out the territory acquired by exchanging the abbot's prisoners plus 1,000 gold ounces and twenty horses for Rocca d'Arce and Pescosolido, adjacent unconquered land.[62]

Facing the fait accompli, the emperor ceded Sora to, as Innocent's biographer puts it, "Riccardo, brother of the Lord Pope, and his heirs in perpetuity." The actual legal document appears to have been a conveyance to the pope, who then enfeoffed Riccardo. By the spring of 1208 Innocent had notably enlarged the papal domain, and Riccardo was count of Sora.[63]

A further enterprise, financial rather than military, increased Riccardo's holdings, this time in the Campagna. The land of Valmontone was owned by the canons of the Lateran and heavily mortgaged. Innocent paid off the debt and acquired the lease, which was then assigned to Riccardo. In a letter from the pope to his brother reciting the details of the transaction, Innocent explained that he had acted in his own name lest "those envious of you impede it." The "large and mighty price," he acknowledged vaguely, had been paid "partly from your goods and partly from ours." Riccardo and his heirs were to have the lease and the option to renew the lease on the same terms. If the prior and canons of the Lateran should defy this "apostolic statute" and refuse to renew, Riccardo should "nonetheless" hold the land directly "by apostolic commission." In perpetuity, so far as Innocent could assure it, control of Valmontone passed from the Lateran to his own family. Riccardo built a palace there and when, much later, he divided his property, his oldest son Paolo inherited the tenancy.[64]

In October 1208 at Ferentino, before an audience of cardinals and local lords, Riccardo did homage to his brother as overlord of Valmontone and the lands once belonging to the Poli. "And the Lord Pope," the notary records, "invested the count by means of a silver cup, gilded in gold." Innocent had seen himself, at the start of his pontificate, as a great silver goblet. To his brother he gave silver mixed with gold.[65]

To another count who was proving stubborn in resisting his plans for southern Italy, Innocent in 1206 wrote a letter of expostulation that ended with an instructive comparison. Innocent would not give way on this point where the Church was concerned, "for anyone born of woman, not even for our own brother if he were in your straits."[66] Innocent put the extreme case. What would he not have done for Riccardo? For him he had commingled papal and family funds, disadvantaged the Lateran "in perpetuity," waged war on imperial vassals, outwitted the abbot of Monte Cassino and the lords of Aquino, and acquired Sora. For his brother's son he had let his delegates decide the episcopal election in Bayeux in favor of his nephew's benefactor and he had then ensured his nephew's prize by himself entering judgment in his favor. Such a judge had felt no difficulty in his interlocutory grant of the lands of the Poli to his brother. Blood relationship disqualified a judge delegate, *Postremo* X2, 28, 36. Could Innocent not see the application of the principle to himself? Kindness to his kin had submerged all his preachments about the royal road.

The Road Resumed.   Very occasionally Innocent became aware of what knowledgeable men actually thought of his court. In the spring of 1204 he addressed a sharp and distinctly personal rebuke to the bishop of Fiesole. The pope was opposing a Florentine plan to move the bishop and he was incensed at the bishop's resistance to papal directions. Informing him that he would be suspended and summoned to Rome if he disobeyed, Innocent added, "You will be set before Us, and you will know for sure whether your money can—as it is said you boast—redeem your fault with Us." The bishop must have used *redimere* in the old sense of buying off an unjust demand. The implication of Innocent's answer was that the bishop would learn for sure that the pope was incorruptible.[67]

Addressing three judges-delegate in northern Italy in 1206 in what was to become one of his most famous decretals, *Qualiter et quando,* Innocent set out procedures to be followed by a judge inquiring into the conduct of a bishop. He opened with the words of the Master to the Unjust Steward, "What are these things I hear of you? Render an account of your stewardship" (Lk 16:2). God himself in Genesis had descended to investigate the outcry against Sodom and Gomorrah (Gen 18:20)—a suggestively ominous analogy. Proceeding, therefore, on the basis of reports, judges were to inquire into abuses and to remove the steward who could not account. The ecclesial judge was to keep in mind that he would be judged by a strict judge, "where with what measure you have measured it shall be measured to you" (Mt 7:1). The judge was to observe the prescribed procedure; "set aside favor (*gratia*) and fear; have God alone before [his] eyes; and walk the royal road without taking up of persons." The words were a reworking of those of 1198. The judge's attention was to be not on the litigants nor on their offerings, but above: God *alone* was to be before him.[68]

In 1208 or 1209 the intimate biography was written to commemorate the deeds of the first decade of the pontificate. Describing Innocent's standards, the biographer repeatedly used the pope's own words. When people wondered at the young cardinal's restoration of his titular church, they were surprised at his resources because "he had shaken his hands free from every dirty *munus,* taking no gift or promise from anyone before a man's affair was judged, demanding nothing from anyone, always walking the royal road, swerving neither to the right nor to the left." At the beginning of his regime Innocent was described as meditating reform: "Among all plagues, he held venality the most hateful, and he took thought how he could root it out from the Roman Church."[69]

When his alter ego, having set out at length Innocent's operations benefiting Riccardo in Sora and the South, turned from "temporal" to "spiritual acts," the first topic he addressed was Innocent's judicial activity. His pontificate had begun with cases between the archbishops of Compostela and Braga and seven Iberian bishops, which the pope decided with "a supereminent intelligence commended by all." There followed "from the whole world" an innumerable succession of cases, in whose handling all wondered at the pope's "subtlety and prudence," and highly educated men and lawyers declared "they learned more in his consistories than they had learned at school." In all the cases Innocent "walked the royal road, never swerved to right or left, did not take up persons and did not take offerings." Only once did the biographer quote a line that could have contained a hint of reflective doubt. Innocent found his immersion in "what was to be reformed in the Patrimony" odious and often used to say, "Who touches pitch is stained by it." The relation of this line from Ecclesiasticus 13:1 to bribes was to be pondered by both Dante and Bacon, as it had been by John of Salisbury. But Innocent did not believe his hands touched anything sticky. The Innocentian self-image of absolute integrity was unshaken.[70]

In 1211 Innocent wrote two judges-delegate at the center of legal studies, Bologna. Instructing them, he again took the opportunity to assert his integrity. The "vice of venality" was enormous. "By the favor (*gratia*) of the divine office (*munus*) We struggle to keep the Roman Church free from slipping into it." The sentence punned masterfully. By *gratia* the Pope gave gratis. By God's *munus*, he avoided man's *munus*. The declaration was germane to the business before his delegates. In the case they were hearing, the bishop of Alessandria in Lombardy was being sued by his creditors, certain Roman merchants, for repayment of money borrowed in the course of litigation before the curia. It had turned out, so the bishop himself had testified, that the borrowing had been on a sliding scale—the bishop had authorized a loan of one hundred pounds for expenses; the loan was to go to one hundred and fifty pounds if the bishop could get possession of as many as eight disputed churches; it was to go to three hundred if the bishop was given possession of S. Martino de Foris. The scale implied that the bishop would be buying the results, paying more as he got more. "From this," wrote Innocent, "it is evident what the said bishop thought of Us." Punishment for such an approach to the pope was severe. The delegates were told to announce publicly the bishop's suspension from office. Innocent would not tolerate such an open challenge to his self-image.[71]

Overlord and Vassal. In 1215 a document usually of greater interest to common law lawyers than to canonists came before the pope: the charter of liberties known to all English-speaking people as *Magna Carta*. Bishops and barons of England, led by Stephen Langton, Innocent's cardinal and choice as archbishop of Canterbury, had negotiated with King John at Runnymede and, to settle a barons' revolt, had obtained his consent to a statement promising a rich variety of reforms in royal administration. Feudal homage, widows' dower, the practices of sheriffs and bailiffs, the loans of the Jews, and the rights of the Welsh were all covered. Among sixty-one remarkably heterogeneous chapters mixing the trivial and the serious, the local and the national, ran a pledge by the king, "To no one shall we sell, to no one shall we deny or delay, right or justice."[72] This single sentence, in lapidary form, affirmed for the land of St. Thomas of

Canterbury the Innocentian ideal. It had been won by Innocent's archbishop. But the document came to Rome not as the legal embodiment of an
Innocentian standard. It was presented to the pope as a piece of extortion.[73]

To understand the context in which Innocent then acted requires a summary of his relations with King John since the see of Canterbury had
become vacant in 1205. The suffragan bishops, backed by the king, had
contended with the monks of Christ Church for the right to choose the
new archbishop, and the case was appealed to Rome. St. Thomas had
"laid down his life for the Church's liberty" and still "his blood" had
borne no fruit. The English king continued to dominate the church. The
pope now saw his opportunity. Over 11,000 marks, he understood, were
ready to be spent, but Innocent "detested *munera*." He "trod the royal road
prudently," as he had with Richard in 1198.[74] He rebuffed the existing
claimants to the see, quashing the elections that had already been held and
called to Rome fifteen representatives of Christ Church. Voting in his
presence the monks chose "a man surely outstanding in life, knowledge,
and reputation, and of English origin, whom the Lord Pope in the same
year had raised from the magisterial chair he ruled in Paris to be cardinal
priest"—none other than Stephen Langton.[75]

Innocent must have regarded Langton as the embodiment of the moral
ideals of the Quarter; his move to Rome could only have reflected the
pope's personal admiration for him. For the mess existing in England the
Lincoln-born Stephen must have struck the pope as a heaven-sent envoy.
Perhaps, too, a few months of Langton in person at the curia had led Innocent to think that this sterling moralist could be better employed at a
distance. For King John, Langton's election was more than a slap in the
face. It struck him as intolerable that a man so unknown to him and so
close to Innocent should hold the premier see of his realm. He asked the
pope to reconsider.[76]

Langton was not yet consecrated as archbishop, and John did what
seemed appropriate to him to influence reconsideration. Early in 1207 the
royal accounts show payments of 30 marks to Paolo, "son of Riccardo the
brother of the Lord Pope"; 60 marks to Pietro Annibaldi; and 20 marks to
"the nephew of the Lord Pope." The king was not sure of the nephew's
name. He gave instructions that it was to be ascertained. Presumably
young Stefano, prebendary of Bayeux, was the nephew he was searching
for. A wish to benefit Innocent's family, whoever they turned out to be,
could not have been more clearly expressed.[77]

The royal strategy took into account almost a decade of experience with
Innocent and his court. Sending cash to Riccardo's first-born, Paolo, and to
Paolo's unnamed brother, and to the pope's soldierly brother-in-law Pietro Annibaldi, John was not acting out of the goodness of his heart.
Nonetheless his investment gained him no immediate advantages. The
pope, "strong and steady," as his alter ego puts it, consecrated Langton
with his own hands four months after the royal bounty to his relatives.[78]

John dug in. He expelled from their monastery the hapless community whose representatives had elected Langton. He let it be known that the new archbishop could not land in England. In Lincoln, Langton's father fled for his life, the crown confiscated his estate. Innocent responded to the king's violent intransigence with threat of a general interdict of England, and after five months of fruitless negotiations, in March 1208 the interdict took effect.[79]

For five years, Innocent and John warred with each other. John confiscated the clergy's property; Innocent stood firm on his sanctions. By 1213 France was threatening an invasion, and the king was cornered. On May 13, 1213, he submitted to the papal representatives and offered restitution. On May 15, 1213, by an arrangement not without benefit to him, he conveyed the kingdoms of England and Ireland to the pope and his successors. "We have offended God and Our Mother Holy Church in many things," John declared. In satisfaction of such debts, "we will to humble ourselves." By the same conveyance he put himself in the position of vassal to Innocent, holding the kingdoms from his papal overlord in consideration of doing homage as a liegeman of the pope, vowing to defend "the Patrimony of Blessed Peter and in particular the kingdom of England and the kingdom of Ireland," and paying an annual tribute in cash. The tribute was set at 700 marks sterling for England, 300 marks sterling for Ireland, the whole 1,000 to be paid in semi-annual installments of 500 marks on St. Michael's Day and Easter.[80]

The amount was a great deal less in the short run than the 11,000 marks Innocent could have had in 1206. It was, however, a great deal more than his net yield from Peter's Pence. From that ancient annual collection, after withholding by English bishops, he got no more than 300 marks. In the long run, by 1327, the income from the English royal vassal—who did not always pay on time or in full, but like other reluctant debtors could be pushed to pay on account—amounted to over 78,000 marks. The road "prudently" taken by Innocent had led him to be John's lord with an income to accompany his lordship.[81]

From the point of view of the monastic chroniclers of St. Albans, who loathed both pope and king and wrote the history of this transaction a generation later, John knew Innocent to be "an insatiable thirster for money and quick and ready for any crime, in exchange for payoffs given or promised."[82] So Innocent who had moralized on the insatiably avaricious was himself moralized over. From Innocent's viewpoint it was no payoff he received but reparation owed for the outrage offered to God and God's Vicar for five years. He celebrated the new "priestly kingdom" he had in the British Isles with a letter to the king. Not only God but God's vicar was King of kings.[83]

The role of vassal suited John as wonderfully as the role of overlord suited Innocent. From this point on, Innocent thought it a prime duty to preserve peace and royal authority in England. In 1214, as bargaining went on in England and Rome over the amount of restitution due the English

Church by John, Count Riccardo and brother-in-law Pietro Annibaldi again appeared on John's payroll along with Riccardo's son Stefano and Cardinal Ugolino, the pope's cousin.[84] But the harmony of pope and vassal was complicated by the archbishop of Canterbury and the barons. With John's defeat Stephen Langton arrived in England, and within the year a draft document had been prepared containing reforms the king must effect: "King John grants that he will not take men without judgment nor accept anything for doing justice, nor perform injustice." The promise paralleled a reform Langton promulgated as a canon for Canterbury reflecting the teaching of le Chantre at Paris: "We forbid that anything be taken for doing, delaying or accelerating justice, or that for anything spiritual anything be contractually promised, given or taken. If this shall be done, let the one who gives as well as the one who takes know they shall be bound by judgment of excommunication." Clause forty of *Magna Carta* existed in embryo, except Langton went further, reaching the payor as well as the payee.[85]

By early 1215 mutinous barons were in motion against the king, while a larger number of barons waited to see what happened. The pope from a distance took the position that the barons must not use force. The pope was planning a crusade and the king had taken the cross. The barons could not be allowed to disrupt the crusade. The pope was planning a General Council to be held in the fall, and he did not want his new realm in civil war. By March 1215 he was instructing the barons to petition the king for redress peacefully. At the same time he addressed to Langton a stinging rebuke suggesting that he was responsible for stirring them up. From this date to the issuance of *Magna Carta* in July 1215, Innocent looked on the king's critics as troublemakers.[86]

What was actually presented to Innocent as *Magna Carta* is not known; the St. Albans chronicle suggests that only certain offensive clauses were read to him.[87] Of these the most offensive would have been a provision that wrestled with the oldest of problems: who would guard the guardians? The document provided a baronial council of twenty-five to oversee the king's observance of *Magna Carta*, an innovation that Stephen Langton may have fathered, but one which cramped royal prerogatives and entirely overlooked the pope's overlordship. On August 24, 1215, three weeks or so after the document reached Rome, Innocent pronounced *Magna Carta* void.[88]

There was in Innocent's letter, *Etsi karissimus*, language indicating his sense that he was performing a judicial act. In canon law fear which would coerce "a steady man" would annul a marriage. John, the pope declared, had been subjected to fear which would coerce "the steadiest man." The pope's main reliance was not on his role of Judge or his role of Overlord, but on his position as God's Vicar. It was to the pope that God had spoken through the prophet Jeremiah, making it his part "to root out and destroy, to build and to plant"—the phrases of his coronation year were once more invoked. On the basis of his comprehensive divine commission Innocent determined that *Magna Carta* would dishonor the Apostolic See, injure the king's right, shame the English, and jeopardize the crusade. Nullifying it in toto, he excommunicated all who would support it.[89]

An old decretal of Alexander III to England, *causam quae*, held that an overlord was a suspect judge in the case of his vassal. It is difficult to believe that Innocent would have paid any attention if the decretal had been raised as an objection. In the terrible Last Judgment of *The Misery of the Human Condition*, the young cardinal had spoken of that trial where "the same one will be accuser and advocate and judge."[90] The necessary confusion of roles had not been a reason for him to abandon the recognition of God as Judge. Innocent showed a similar indifference to his own mixture of roles.

In November 1215 Innocent presided over his great reform council, Lateran IV. The council was called for two principal purposes: "the reformation of the whole Church" and the liberation of the Holy Land. The plague of venality was central to the first topic. In a moving opening address to the Council Fathers, beginning with the Pauline quotation, "Because, for me to live is Christ and to die gain . . .", Innocent declared, "Every corruption among the people principally proceeds from the clergy." By "their example" the laity fell. The Fathers were exhorted that "no taking up of persons occur in you."[91]

Incorporating the pope's concern, the canon *Irrefragabili* provided "by an unbreakable constitution" that prelates should correct the abuses of their subjects, especially clerics. In so doing they should take care not to turn correction "into a quest for money." When a bishop acted he must "have God before his eyes." Issued a year before Innocent's death, *Irrefragabili* echoed the letter to Philip II of his coronation year when the pope had declared his intention "unbreakable." It set out once more the teaching of his letter to the Lionheart that the eyes of a judge should be turned to God. Once more, for all of Catholic Christendom, the Innocentian standard was held high. The voice of le Chantre, the accent of the Quarter, was heard in the legislation of the Universal Church. Along with that voice went the acts of Innocent, judging for his cousin Giovanni Oddone, judging for his nephew Stefano, judging for his brother Riccardo, and overthrowing *Magna Carta* on behalf of his vassal John.[92]

Satire and Style.   At the crude level of clerical satire Innocent III's justice was mocked as his patron Clement III's had been, as Urban II's had been, as the curia's had been since time immemorial. A contemporary, an anonymous Anglo-Norman, wrote "A Dialogue about the Bad Customs of the Curia Between a Traveller to the Curia and a Man Coming from Rome." The latter tells how he "has suffered torments." The cardinals "call you son if you give to them," they have a sharp bite if you don't. The Pope, "father of the family," calls the churches his daughters and has commerce with them: as in English, *commercium* carries the double meaning of "business" and "intercourse." The pope in short is incestuously involved with his daughters. Even the doorkeepers are as bad as ever, Cerberuses who bark if you don't pay up.[93]

At a more refined level, certain correspondence was put forward in the pontificate of Innocent III as taking place over the election of the archbishop of Magdeburg. The chapter of Magdeburg to their candidate:

> The majority has elected you, but there is objection and opposition. Get to Rome ahead of your opponent, "and with prayers and offerings obtain judges delegate who must offer patronage to your party."

THE CANDIDATE: It's too much to get into.

THE CHAPTER: The Emperor is your blood relation and supports you. The archbishop of Treves, recently back from Rome, says it is yours if you spend 5000 marks.

THE CANDIDATE: I agree. I will spend twice as much.

THE CANDIDATE TO "A CERTAIN CARDINAL":   I am sending you 5000 marks "to be divided and spent usefully. . . . Secretly offer the Lord Pope 1000 marks and his brother 500," the rest divide as you see fit "among the cardinals, notaries, chaplains and other officials of the Curia." Keep something good for yourself.

THE CARDINAL TO THE CANDIDATE: The 5000 have been received and spread around. The Pope's chamberlain is "a bit angry that he did not have more *munera* from you." If you could placate him, all would go well.

THE CANDIDATE'S AGENT TO THE CANDIDATE: Don't believe the cardinal. The other side offered 10,000 marks, "of which the chamberlain is said to have had one-third. Therefore a venal curia has yielded to the one offering more."

THE OTHER SIDE'S AGENT TO THE OTHER CANDIDATE: "By the grace of God and the merits of the blessed martyrs Albinus and Rufinus," the Lord Pope "in full consistory quashed the election of your opponent and solemnly and magnificently confirmed yours."[94]

This little drama was a part of the *Ars Rhetorica* of Buoncompagno, a Florentine rhetorician working in Bologna. The work was a form book meant to instruct students in epistolary styles appropriate to many legal and ecclesiastical occasions. Was Buoncompagno being satirical or being serious and cynical in providing forms exalting the power of money to pay off the pope? A handbook, it might be argued, is meant for serious use. Modern scholars such as Barraclough and Cheney have understood these forms as meant to be copied by ecclesiastics congratulating bishops who have won contested elections.[95] On the other hand, there are other letter sequences in Buoncompagno so outrageous that they are seen, even today, as elephantine humor. Letters on the episcopal confirmation of the election of an abbess immediately follow the forms touching the curia. Where a woman's fate is at stake the misogynistic twists of Buoncompagno's mind so distort the forms that Barraclough has no difficulty in labeling them as "obviously ironical."[96] The Magdeburg correspondence is not different. In Buoncompagno's own day, "the blessed martyrs" Albinus and Rufinus were shopworn equivalents for cash discreditably given, the "stock-in-trade of all the satirists of the age," as Barraclough acknowledges. It would have been a bold agent who thought he could congratulate his boss by telling him in effect that he had won "by graft and corruption." The other agent denouncing the curia as "venal," after he himself has tried to buy it for 5000 marks, is not a wholly credible model either.

According to his admiring biographer, Innocent expounded cases "so subtly and prudently that all wondered at his subtlety and prudence, and many very learned men and lawyers frequented the Roman Church to hear him, and learned more in his consistories than they had learned in school, especially when they heard him give judgments." Dispatching the decretals of the first twelve years of his pontificate to Bologna as a mark of his esteem for the law school, Innocent had included *Cum ab omni* on judges delegate and filthy profits. But Buoncompagno's work was crowned with laurel at Bologna in 1215 in the presence of the law faculty. The applause at Bologna for Buoncompagno suggested how stories of the new Solomon and his brother Riccardo must have circulated in the law faculty. Wryly, even morbidly, Buoncompagno's jest at the expense of the Segni brothers would have been relished at Bologna. Cynical or more probably satirical, his imaginary letters were a tragic measure of how far below the stated papal ideal the justice of Innocent III was reputed to be. That the story could be savored at Bologna and nothing effectual proposed to remedy the system demonstrated the gap between academic lawyers and practice that has always been the badge and shame of the former.[97]

Evidence about Innocent's curia comes not only from litigants and rhetoricians: it is furnished by the curia itself. Tommaso di Capua, briefly archbishop of Naples, apparently came to Innocent's notice during the great council of 1215. He stayed on in Rome as a papal notary. A busy, practical man with a good literary style, he was promoted in Innocent's last creation of cardinals in March 1216 and became the head of Innocent's chancery. In the pontificate of the next two popes he was a major figure in the curia, functioning as grand penitentiary and exercising his literary ability by writing two hymns in honor of St. Francis of Assisi.[98] His letters from 1215 to 1239, edited as a *Summa dictaminis* in 1268, did for curial officials what Buoncompagno's and other handbooks did earlier for the provinces: they provided a set of examples appropriate to the situation. As the letters were first composed for official use, the edited version can scarcely be suspected of satire.[99]

A substantial number of Tommaso's forms deal with presents—presents which are acknowledged, presents which are sent back, presents which are sought. Among the gifts enumerated there are a horse, a mule, food, a double bedspread, cloth, vases, Greek wine, marten skins, and a hundred gold ounces—in a word, everything but sex. The presents are named *xenia* once, *beneficium* once, *munuscula* or little gifts several times, and often *dona* or *munera*. There is no sense of impropriety in calling the presents *munera* and still receiving them. The senders are usually unidentified in the formbook. Those who are identified by the body of the letter include a monastery, a Hungarian prelate, someone on the business of the archdeacon of Norwich—enough to suggest the European range of the cascade of gifts showered on the curia. The thankful donee is always Tommaso.[100]

Some gifts are sent back for various reasons. We have just become friends, don't rush it, one letter says in substance. Another is firmer: I refuse to be held under obligation, "I desire to serve you in full liberty, from pure liberality." In another the donee's "right hand" has been attracted, but "the prohibition of a superior" (presumably the pope) is an obstacle. In another it is "the rigor of a certain intention of my own" that stands as an objection. In another a petitioner is told that his proctor promised money in another case which has not been paid. The pope "is making himself difficult" in the new matter. It is better to drop it than "by mention of your business to stir him up to seek the hoped-for money."[101]

Other letters do not reject gifts but give thanks for what has been received and set a prohibition against giving more. "As a *munus*, no more *munera*," one letter puns. "Content at heart, we do not seek a hand." The last word is another pun, *manus*, hand, standing also for *munus*, gift. In the same spirit another letter says that "as a *donum*, I seek no *dona*"; "I do not look for a *munus* in the *manus* of a friend." In another, to the man on the Norwich business, the writer declares, "Obligation does not bind you to thanks. Praise is not owed us if justice pays you what it should." Another letter accepts a gift, refuses further gifts, and implicitly encourages them: "Although what was sent was welcome, still we refuse now to thank the sender lest we seem tacitly to revoke the edict of prohibition which we remember we made against sending. Yet lest we be judged wholly ungrateful when your sending stops, we shall rise to thanks."[102]

Several letters say "More, please." "We are prepared to stretch out ready hands for your gifts," reads one formula. Be prepared to come back later, reads another, "with fatter recompense (*retributio*). Therefore let your ready hand not grow lukewarm in the future nor put obstacle to later payments so that with repeated benefits you make your friend more devoted." A very short form reads, "Our hands have been educated to receive your welcome *munera* with welcome and are ready to receive more when you send them." In a similar formula the donee's "educated hands" are "producing a hope to receive more." When Tommaso wants something, his expressions are unmistakable.[103]

To what extent do these letters establish corruption in Innocent's curia? In Innocent's defense it can be said that few of the letters used as examples in the *Summa dictaminis* can be definitely dated to his day. Even when they can be shown to go back to the time that Tommaso was Innocent's notary, as does the letter advising against "stirring up the Pope," there is no proof positive of Innocent's personal involvement. This letter refers to Tommaso's learning of the pope's attitude from another notary: maybe, it can be argued, the other notary or Tommaso himself was using a dodge to squeeze more money out of the petitioner; the pope might have known nothing. Further, Tommaso sometimes acted as an advocate in matters where he was not the judge and sometimes acted to further petitions of grace where justice was not at issue.[104] Remuneration as an advocate or reward as the broker of a favor would not be the same as taking bribes in the course of a case. Finally, it may be noted, Tommaso did draw lines, turn gifts back, note on occasion the pope's prohibition.

What the letters establish is not an air-tight case of corruption against Innocent personally or even against the curia corporately. What they convey is an atmosphere—an atmosphere which must have prevailed in 1215 when Tommaso entered the chancery, for nothing there changed overnight. The atmosphere is one where *munera* are important, where high officials give great attention to them, where the acquisition of gifts is an art. Many of the letters refusing reward have the flavor of "No, but" or an air of "If you insist" or "See me later." An anxious or a sophisticated litigant could have read them as refusals which were close to being invitations. If the heroic task of breaking the rule of reciprocity was to be accomplished along the lines formally proclaimed by Innocent's decretals, if the royal road of impartiality was actually to be walked, a ruder and sterner style than that of these unctuous missives was required. Too easily they were read in the fashion of the cynical bishop of Alessandria or of the Anglo-Norman satirist or of the saturnine Buoncompagno.

Road's End.   One of the most beautiful of all hymns to the Spirit, *Veni, Sancte Spiritus,* prayed,

> Veni, pater pauperum
> Veni, dator munerum.[105]

"Come, Father of the poor. Come Giver of gifts." The hymn's author, the upright Stephen Langton himself, saw no difficulty, where the rhyme required it, in describing the seven gifts of the Spirit as *munera. Munera* remained essentially ambiguous, their good or evil character dependent on context. When they came from the Spirit, they were, as everyone knew, good and gratuitous. In the same prayer Langton asked the Spirit to wash away the *sordidum,* the foul, usually associated with corrupt gifts.[106] The Spirit, as celebrated by Langton and worshipped by all, gave without having a Stomach that sought support. The task of the pope was to act for the Spirit and not to neglect the Stomach.

Innocent III was more thoroughly educated in law and theology, more energetic, and more intelligent than most medieval popes. If he emerges in this book on bribes more as "Guilty III," there are three reasons. One, he expressed his ideals explicitly: so he provided his own measure. Two, he preserved his judgments: so his decisions in favor of his brother and his nephew stand forever as monuments to kindness for kin overpowering his ideals.[107] Three, he maintained the curial institution he inherited without recognizing that the reciprocities built into its rhythms jeopardized his ideal of reform.

The third reason may be further elaborated. Innocent detested *munera*. Innocent took *munera*. In his mind he took *munera* in a way that did not buy his judgment. The standard he employed is clear in the biography where, speaking of his freedom from corruption as a cardinal, he is said to have taken no gift or promise "before a man's affair was judged." The standard was publicly articulated in the same way by Innocent in his protest at the plans of the bishop of Alessandria when the pope declared he permitted "no price or agreement or promise": he added that "sometimes," after "an affair is judged," he received what "appears to be not extorted by necessity but conferred by devotion." What was given after judgment and given freely did not fall within his strictures. He provided the same rule in setting the fee schedule for the writers and sealers: gratuitous gifts were not outlawed.[108]

The standard used as to when a matter was judged (when a *negotium* was *terminatum* in Innocent's phraseology) turned out to be flexible. To generalize from Thomas of Marlborough's account, the silver cup given after a preliminary ruling was not out of bounds, and the "visiting" of pounds on the pope and marks on the cardinals occurred on the basis that the monks of Evesham had "no case" in the curia, when in fact all that was over was the interlocutory appeal and it took little imagination to foresee that the main case eventually would be appealed to the curia. The presents from King John were a larger instance of the same general problem: the pope and curia did not easily end a relationship with a litigant. The king's relationship was ongoing. There was no point at which his overlord could say that his vassal's affairs were judged.

Voluntariness of gifts, Innocent's other criterion, was far more ambiguous than he acknowledged. Gifts that were expected, gifts for whose nondelivery the pope would make himself difficult, were not wholly voluntary. Thomas of Marlborough as a litigant, Tommaso di Capua as a curialist show that for litigants expectation translated itself as demand.

As to the effect of gifts upon the curia, Innocent in his own reflections on the cups of Konrad of Querfurt saw the problem clearly. A gift always implied a response. Gifts to judges were not given gratis. A willing hand expected to be met by a ready hand. The judge who took gifts could be no freer than the litigant who gave them by customary compulsion. At the Lateran Council a scheme was proposed to finance the curia from revenues assigned to it by the dioceses and monasteries. Its details are unknown because Innocent backed off in the face of opposition. His successor, Honorius III, a cardinal at the time of the council, brought the idea forward again in 1225. In return for the churches accepting this kind of taxation he proposed that all curial business be free: there would be no requests, express or tacit, direct or indirect; the curia would even refuse what was "voluntarily offered"; and sanctions would be applied to "any Gehazi" who accepted anything. Honorius fared no better than Innocent with this practical plan for providing a central fund and eliminating occasions of corruption. What he agreed to give up—the tacit, indirect requests and the voluntary offerings—had become routine.[109]

As reflected in his biography, Innocent's priorities included the push of the Patrimony to the South, the welfare of his family, the Fourth Crusade, and the conduct of litigation in the curia. He was also a man, self-seen, as *munificus*, open-handed. He gave substantial gifts to churches, hospitals, and the poor. He found bishoprics for his old teachers and benefices for his staff. He gave away a great deal. To be generous, to finance family and crusade, to push South meant that he could always put money to use.[110]

Mediator between God and man as he saw himself at the start, Innocent was Head of the Church and Supreme Judge, ruler of the papal patrimony and peacemaker of Europe, chief shepherd of the flock and secular overlord of secular kings, preacher and politician, moralist and protector of his family. The multiple roles clashed. Trusting in his own ability and in divine help, Innocent never acknowledged, except by the fierceness of his denials, the pecuniary pressures upon him. Mediator between God and man, he walked a path strewn with presents. His eyes, he told himself, were fixed only on God.

Once the pope had a dream of the basilica of the Lateran tottering, upheld on the back of a little religious of miserable appearance. It was a dream quite far from the dream which had presaged his passage to the Headship of the Church. The Pope said he knew the meaning of the dream when Francis of Assisi came to see him and told him this parable: In the desert there was a poor but beautiful woman who was loved by a king. He married her, and from him she had handsome sons. "Do not be ashamed that you are poor," the mother told them. "You are all sons of that great king. Go rejoicing to his curia and ask from him what is necessary for you." And the king received them joyfully at his table. In this parable Francis was the mother, the desert was the sterile world, the sons who scorned riches were the followers of Francis, the king was the Son of God.[111]

This conversation, if it occurred, would have happened in 1210 when Francis came to Rome for papal approval of the rule of his new community.[112] The conversation reportedly ended with Innocent acknowledging Francis as "he who will sustain the Church." Francis was a very different kind of sustainer of the Church than brother Riccardo and brother-in-law Pietro. His support of the Lateran was very different from that which the pope had given the Lateran by picking up its obligations in order to turn its fief into family turf. The miserable religious who turned out to be a mother was a very different mother from the one Lotario had married in his youthful dreams. Reciprocity in this parable was not banished but transformed. Those who embraced poverty were rewarded by feasting in a curia which was God's.

The source for the later dream and the exchange between Innocent and Francis is far less reliable than the source for Innocent's dream of his mother. The account comes not from Innocent's biographer but from Francis'. It was not like those early dreams of Lotario which "saddened, terrified, and fatigued." Whether it was the pope's own dream or a legend of the new order, the dream and Francis' parable projected an institutional vision that Lotario might have glimpsed once in the Quarter and had lost from sight, often completely, as he traveled the road.

8

Buy Backs

Put aside the corrosive effect of nepotistic example. The legacy of the Innocentian years was a stronger set of standards, sanctions, and institutions hostile to bribetaking. Innocentian images and rhetoric firmly upheld the ideal of nonreciprocity with judges and with dispensers of the Spirit.

As to standards: Innocent's initiative in sending a collection of decretals to Bologna was followed on a grand scale by his cousin Ugolino, now Gregory IX. For the use of "the courts and the schools," so that "appetite" be "confined under the rule of law," he dispatched to Bologna in 1234 a comprehensive, logically organized, and definitive edition of papal decrees.[1] Mostly taken from the past eighty years and particularly from the legal corpus of Alexander III and Innocent III, these decisions and rulings, joined to Gratian and occasionally supplemented by later legislation, were to stand for almost 700 years as "the canon law." Gregory's editor, the Spanish Dominican, Raimundo da Peñafort, was good at pruning. Stripped of most of their context, the decretals stated principles whose deformation or ineffectiveness in practice was obscured when they were presented as lapidary insights. The principles appeared as indisputable truths, and in this ideal way were communicated to generations of European lawyers.

Innocentian imagery was especially preserved by his *Qualiter et quando*, entered under the title "Accusations, Inquiries, and Denunciations" (X 5, 1, 17). The royal road was set before everyone. The taking up of persons was formally condemned by law. *Irrefragibili*, with its solemn call to reformation by the higher clergy, "God before their eyes," formed part of the teaching on "The Office of the Ordinary Judge" (X 1, 31, 13). *Cum ab omni*, now a canon in "The Life and Honesty of Clerics" (X 3, 1, 10), continued to proclaim that judging must be gratis.

These vintage pieces of Innocent's regime chimed with Alexander III's *Causam quae*, the rejection of an overlord as a judge in the case of his tenant, a decretal now inserted in "The Office and Power of the Judge Delegate" (X 1, 29, 17). Under "Simony," Alexander III's *Etsi quaestiones* (X 5, 3, 18), *Matthaeus* (X 5, 3, 23), and *Cum essent* (X 5, 3, 12) set strict rules. *Ad aures* (X 5, 3, 24) continued to forbid absolution from excommunication being "bought back" (*redimatur*); and *Nemo presbyterorum* (X 5, 3, 14), ascribed to Alexander, treated "respect for person or kinship" as simonian an act as a sale of the Spirit for money.

The diffusion of these ideals was enhanced by another measure adopted under Innocent in his great general council: the requirement that every Christian confess his sins once a year. The handbooks of the Paris theologians had preceded the requirement. Now the legislation made the handbooks a practical necessity, and any confessor who consulted writers like Robert of Flamborough or Thomas of Chobham could find instruction on our subject. Raimundo da Peñafort himself issued a summa for confessors where the traditional demand that restitution precede absolution reinforced the canonical insistence that judging not be for money. The judge who took something, "to judge evilly or to judge well or merely to judge," was bound, Raimundo taught, to surrender what he had received. Where the giver gave to corrupt the judge, the money was not to be returned to him but "to the one in injury of whom the judge receives." Where the giver gave with "a good intention, to wit, to preserve his right and peace," he was the one entitled to restitution. If the judge had in fact issued an unjust decision due to the corruption, he was bound to make up the entire loss he had inflicted on the litigant.[2]

Institutionally, Innocent III had recognized Bologna as the repository of the law and confirmed the statutes of Paris. Under Gregory IX the Decretals bolstered Bologna in its central place in legal education, while Paris received its own "Magna Carta." Detached from the pressures of any secular or ecclesial curia, the universities could be expected to provide a dispassionate critique of corruption. Enhancement of their role and prerogatives could be understood as the creation of a giant counterweight to bribery and nepotism. Especially was this true of Paris with its new breed of university professors drawn from the two new mendicant orders, the

Dominicans and the Franciscans, communities approved under Innocent III and vowed to poverty. Here were teachers who had renounced personal wealth and who lived in academic centers where the acquisition of property was far from the dominant activity. Here were men who had the independence, if they had the knowledge and interest, to set out the sins of those who were corrupt in office.

High and specific standards provided by laws widely communicated, an at least annual necessity of restitution as a sacramental sine qua non, bodies of learned men disciplined to disvalue money—these were forces to break the "natural" hold of reciprocity. For the next several hundred years these forces were at work. The result was a tension, at times unbearable, between the accepted ideal of nonreciprocity in office, now well-known and diffused, and its implementation.

The tension was reflected, indirectly, in theology and in law. The task of the theologians of the thirteenth century—that greatest of theological ages—was to expound, systematize, surpass the teaching on justice and judgment, redemption and gift-giving, simony and unfair discrimination and divine favor. Nothing was to be discarded. Yet as the disparate themes and images were more deeply explored the balance became precarious. To maintain that God was our strict Judge, also our Redeemer, also the One placated by the Redemption, while discriminatory judgment was wrong and the purchase of spiritual reconciliation was sinful—to set out the theological drama and the moral agenda—was not easy. The danger was always that a debased view of the great Buy Back be taken over into the spiritual and legal affairs of men. For this was the century of the Buy Back—the mystery of it holding the key to a fundamental distinction between generous giving and sordid bribing; the metaphor always exposed to the risk of being understood too literally and put to use too venally; the objectivity and integrity of judgment always exposed to the pressing pleas of intercessors seeking mercy and to legal structures in which pardon became purchasable.

The Moderation of the Friars.   The embrace of the Lady Poverty by Francis and his followers, the announced mendicancy of Dominic and his, offered lifestyles in distinct contrast to that of beneficed clergy; and as members of the great new religious orders became leaders at Paris it might have been supposed that academic moralism, reinforced by evangelical zeal, would have redoubled the university assault upon corruption. In particular, a man who in middle life, holding several benefices as an absentee, gave them all up to follow Christ as a Franciscan, and a young man of noble family who for two years resisted the physical compulsion of his relatives and persevered in his Dominican vocation, might have been thought inclined to a puritanical view of ordinary ecclesiastical business. In 1236 Alexander of Hales—Shropshireman, university teacher at Paris since 1210, absentee canon of St. Paul's, London, with a prebend in Holborn, then absentee canon of Lichfield and archdeacon of Coventry—astounded the comfortable clerical world when, over fifty and accounted rich, he became a simple Franciscan; and in 1244, Thomas Aquinas, a cadet of the feudal Aquino family linked to the imperial cause in southern Italy, defied the family plan that he at least become the abbot of Monte Cassino, and became instead a poor Dominican.[3]

"Can you buy the kingdom of heaven?" Alexander had asked before he entered the order; and he had answered, "He who gives for the kingdom buys from him who can sell it." The seeker must give what the seller wants. Reciprocities were maintained, but transmuted. Glory was bought by humility, abundance by hunger, life by death, and the kingdom by poverty.[4] Alexander and Thomas made the bargain. Yet neither Alexander nor Thomas adopted the moral stance that a rigorously severe view of reciprocities would have dictated. A Pascal, if he had existed in the thirteenth century, would indeed have found much in Alexander and Thomas on which to exercise the mordant wit and self-righteousness of the *Lettres provinciales*. To a striking degree the mendicant moralists left loopholes through which the worldly churchmen of their day might pass. It was simony, for example, for a preacher to preach to make money; it was no simony, Alexander said, for him to sermonize to stir his congregation to "help others," provided that this was his "secondary intention." Alexander did not specify that the "others" whom the congregation helped need exclude the preacher, and this loophole was visibly available for the wordly homilist. It was simony to confer a benefice in exchange for service, and the appointee agreeing to give service offered one of the three types of condemned *munera*. It was, however, neither simony nor acceptance of a *munus*, Alexander taught, to receive service from another provided the service was honest and not bargained for, even though it was given in reciprocation for appointment to a spiritual benefice. As long as a contract was avoided, it appeared that a prelate could get benefits from the offices he conferred.[5]

It was simony according to *Nemo presbyterorum* to discriminate in appointments to benefices on the basis of kinship. Appointing relatives to spiritual benefices was customary practice, Thomas observed. It was sinful discrimination, Alexander and Thomas held, to choose a relative over a worthier candidate. But neither treated the sin as simony. For Thomas simony had to involve the payment of money or "a price which can be measured in money." Affection based on blood did not fall within this category. Hence Thomas did not mention *Nemo presbyterorum*, and Alexander explicitly for this reason rejected the contrary opinion of le Chantre. It was not a sin at all, according to Alexander and Thomas, to prefer a relative if two candidates were equal, unless the preference gave scandal to the populace: the relative could be considered superior because the appointing prelate would have greater confidence in him. For Alexander it was not a sin to prefer the good to the better man in appointments below that of bishop: it was enough that a good man was chosen. As to secular appointments Alexander was even more liberal. To confer a temporal benefice on a relative, if he was a good man, and to do so *ex intentione consanguinitatis*—"intentionally because of the relationship" was legitimate.[6]

It was simony to sell absolution to an excommunicate. It was not a sin, Alexander maintained before he was a friar, to take money when one absolved an excommunicate if the money were taken not in exchange for the absolution but as the exaction of a penalty imposed on the excommunicate's contemptuous behavior—the distinction had escaped le Chantre. It was not simony, Alexander taught as a Franciscan, "to buy back harassment" (*redimere vexationem*), where a spiritual right was being withheld from one "unjustly," and there was no superior from whom one could obtain redress. This was not the purchase of a spiritual good, for what was bought was relief from the harassment, and harassment was "a temporal thing." Nothing was specified as to who made the crucial decision that the withholding of the right was "unjust." By implication the decision was made by the man doing the "redeeming."[7]

Casuistry reduced remarkably the sin of *acceptio personarum*. Was it a taking up of persons to honor a prelate? No, answered Alexander, for he had received power from God. Is it this sin to honor a prelate, a prince, or a parent? asked Thomas. No, for they are properly honored as representatives of God. What of honor to the rich? It was all right to give them honor, said Alexander, lest the rich "be scandalized" at the poor being preferred. It was a sin only if a man was seen as the richer, the better. It was all right, said Thomas, to acknowledge the rich man's "greater place in the community."[8]

In none of these instances did Alexander or Thomas lack a reason for his conclusion. In some cases, as in that of "buying back harassment," a papal decretal could be invoked in support of their conclusions.[9] At the same time, they took off the sharp edge of criticism of customs bordering on the corrupt or leading to corruption. They accommodated more than they challenged.

Persons and Masks.   Elastically treated where honor was at issue, *acceptio personarum* was a dispositive category in a more fundamental area, that of justice. After all, it had been very recently a main theme in Innocentian rhetoric on the duty of a judge. For different reasons, each perhaps theological, Alexander and Thomas offered new definitions of the sin, each distinctive. Writing of "The Sins of the Heart," Alexander defined *acceptio personarum* as "the injustice by which, for an undue cause, one person is preferred to another person," a conventional phrasing of the matter. But Alexander was aware of a problem: "Person" refers to what is divine in man, that is, to what should be cherished; therefore persons should be taken up. To this undeveloped objection he replied: "Taking up a person is spoken of when a person is attended to not on account of that which is divine in the person, but on account of what is extrinsic to the person. *Persona* is then understood by way of similarity to the *persona* in the theatre which is called a mask."[10]

To paraphrase, for Alexander *acceptio personarum* is "the taking up of masks." It is not consideration of the human person as possessed of a divine element. It is judging on the basis of a mask. The central paradox is that we should revere *personae*, persons, but we should disregard *personae*, masks. Implicit in the pun is the belief that the sin of *acceptio personarum* consists in judging on the basis of disguises like wealth or poverty. So understood, the sin was committed in every bribed judgment. Alexander's insight went deep. His re-definition was comprehensive. Neither he nor his successors developed the implications or spelled out the applications.

Within fifteen years of Alexander's teaching, Thomas Aquinas at Paris fashioned a new approach out of Aristotle. In what was to be the best known of all his works, the *Summa theologica*, he treated "The Vices Opposed to Justice" and dealt, first of all, with "The Taking Up of Persons." What is the essence of this vice? At its center is the violation of distributive justice. In Aristotelian terms, distributive justice is the virtue by which one distributes "different things to different persons in proportion to the worthiness of the persons." In a just distribution all do not necessarily share equally. Proportion is what is required. The proportion is rightly determined by consideration of only two factors: the thing being distributed and the worthiness of the person to receive that thing. If other factors are considered, the sin of taking up persons occurs.[11]

Thomas furnished two examples, one of conformity with distributive justice, the other contrary to it. In the first, a man is made a Master because of his learning. Here "due cause, not the person" is attended to. The good distributed (the title of Master) and the recipient (because of his learning) are in just proportion. In the second example, something is conferred on a man "only because he is this man, say Peter or Martin." No attention is given to "some reason which makes him worthy." There is no proportionality between the good given and the recipient's entitlement. The distribution sinfully violates justice: it is a disproportionate discrimination.

The structure set up by this analysis was simple in outline and capable of accommodating infinite particular judgments. The factors appropriate to consider in distribution depended on the distributees and on what was distributed. Blood relationship, for example, entitled one to be an heir, but not to be appointed to a prelacy: "The same status of a person taken into account in one matter creates the taking up of persons, but does not in another." Proportion, in effect, was determined by the purpose of the distribution and the relevance of the distributees' status or qualities to the purpose pursued.

Thomas's theory was broad enough to cover all discriminatory acts of officials, a remarkable transposition into an Aristotelian key of the old Hebrew sin of lifting up a face—but there was a specifically Aristotelian difficulty with it. In Aristotle, equality of exchange is governed by commutative justice.[12] When a litigant comes to court seeking what is his due, he seeks restoration of what is his due exactly. He asks for commutative justice. How then is the judge who decides his case governed by distributive justice?

Distributive justice, Thomas taught, is the justice governing the relation of the whole to the parts, the relation, that is, of a community to its members. A judge acts for the whole. Consequently, the "form" of every act of judgment is distributive. But the same act performs a second function. It restores a good which is owed according to commutative justice. Accordingly, the judge's act is an act of both distributive and commutative justice. Both, it is implied, are violated if the judge takes into account something other than the merits of the case. In court the proper proportion, it is implied, is that between the justice of the cause and the good distributed by the judge's judgment. The "form of judgment" is for a judge to "take from one and give to another, and this belongs to distributive justice." The unjust judge's act, like other takings up of persons, is a violation of what distributive justice requires; he gives in disproportion to the merits of the case.[13]

Analysis of this sort appears to be a kind of natural law argument, that is, it appeals to no specifically theological tradition and rests on an analysis of justice which should be valid for everyone. The argument does require the supposition that a community exists, but similar suppositions are necessary for any natural law argument about justice in a community. Strikingly, however, Thomas, devoted as he is in other contexts to the natural law, makes no reference to it here. He does not explicitly contend that the violation of distributive justice is contrary to natural law. He says nothing about acceptance of a bribe being contrary to the rational nature of man. In the case of usury Thomas vigorously develops the argument that it is against the nature of consumptibles to be made the means of profit.[14] In the case of bribetaking there is no emphasis on the unnaturalness of using the judicial function as a means of profit. The rhetoric of natural law is not used as a bulwark for the condemnation of bribes. In this silence as to bribery, Thomas is representative of the medieval theologians working in the natural law tradition.

Looked at from one perspective, Thomas's analysis clashed radically with Alexander's. According to Thomas, the essential sin of *acceptio personarum* was committed when a good was conferred "simply on the person." According to Alexander, the person was to be taken into account; what was sinfully considered was what was extrinsic to the person. Alexander used *persona* to mean "mask"; Thomas used it to mean "this particular individual." From another perspective, the difference in theory came to nothing, for Alexander did not work out what it would mean for a judge to respond to "the divine in a person." In application, he, like Thomas, held it wrong for a judge to take into account a factor other than the merits of a case. "Not by reason of this *persona* or that *persona*," Alexander wrote, "let there be swerving from the truth."[15]

Neither Alexander nor Thomas related *acceptio personarum* explicitly to offerings. In a separate question, "The Office of the Judge," Alexander identified *munera* with money and held that the judge was governed by the rule, "What you took gratis, give gratis." The ecclesiastical judge, although not the secular judge, who sold justice was a Simonian. The obligation of both kinds of judge to make restitution was affirmed.[16]

Thomas devoted a whole question, containing four articles, to "The Injustice of a Judge in Judging" and did not speak of *munera* at all.[17] His silence may be thought unsurprising—all extrinsic considerations in judging had already been condemned by his analysis of *acceptio personarum*. Yet *munera* constituted a specific moral topic, not easily passed over. Thomas's own Dominican teacher, Albert the Great, commenting on Psalm 25, had spoken of "*munus* from the hand" and defined it as "a purse full of money or a gold cup, which fills the hands of evil judges."[18] For Thomas not to mention *munera* meant no discussion of the judge's duty of restitution, no discussion of the sale of justice as simony, and no spelling out of the link between the taking up of persons and the taking of offerings. When one reflects on the skimpy examples of unjust judging given by Thomas and the cumbersomeness of his relating of distributive justice to judges, it is surprising that he paid no attention to what would seem to be an obvious disturbance affecting the distributor of justice. Thomas had known the customs of his noble family, he had known Naples, he had known the papal court: he could not have been unaware of the ambiguities of *munera*. Thomas was not indifferent to the morality of economic transactions (his analysis of usury became classic) and not indifferent to the problems of princes (his short treatise on kingship was a model). Yet he who was to be the most influential moral teacher of the age has no analysis of bribetaking, bribegiving, or the difference between a bribe and a gift. His silence contrasts with what he had to say on reciprocation and on gift when he treated the Redemption.

The Great Reciprocation. Since Augustine, since Paul, since the images used by Jesus, Christians had lived with a God against Whom sin was an offense and Who Himself judged the offense, with a God Who was Judge of sin and Buyer-Back from sin, with a God who according to some theologians accepted the death of His Son in satisfaction for sin. The difficulty of these notions depended on how literally they were taken, how seriously the requirements of just judging were understood, and how prominently the Judgment figured in Christian thought.

In the thirteenth century the Judgment loomed large. *Dies irae*, the most popular of Latin hymns, anonymously composed in the late twelfth or early thirteenth century and translated into many Western vernaculars, paralleled the spectacular ending of Lotario's popular book on the misery of the human condition:

> Day of wrath, that day:
> Into dust dissolves the world,
> As David and Sybil testify.

What great trembling there will be
When the Judge shall come
To examine everything with strictness.

A trumpet spreading wondrous sound
Through the tombs of earth
Compels all before the throne.

Death and nature are struck dumb
When the creature again rises
To respond to Him who judges.

The written book is proffered
In which all is contained
By which the world is judged.

When then the Judge shall sit
Whatever hides shall appear.
Nothing will remain unavenged.[19]

Summons, written documentation, sitting judge—all these elements dramatically informed the Christian of the importance of the occasion. The human being who rose from the dust at "the trumpet spreading wondrous sound" was

Judicandus homo reus

"Man, the defendant, about to be judged," a human being reduced to a judicial category with a future expressed totally in terms of the judgment about to be pronounced upon him.

This great poem apart, theological opinion even identified where the judgment would take place. Honorius (circa 1080–1156), a monk of the community of Irish Benedictines at Regensburg, in a catechetical question and answer form affirmed definitively that the judgment would be given in the valley of Josaphat. Peter Lombard the leading theologian of Paris in 1150, cited Joel 3:12 in support of the site but understood that Christ would not descend, remaining, rather, in the air.[20] Thomas Aquinas agreed that the place would be near Josaphat and Mount Olivet, as suggested by Acts 1:12. Would there be space enough to accommodate the throng? Thomas thought there would be since Christ, in the air, would be visible at a great distance.[21] Thomas had more reservations about the time it would take to read the record, "in which is written the entire life of everyone." Following Augustine, he thought the judgment would not be read, but communicated mentally, in an instant.[22] This conclusion was characteristic of theological thought on the Judgment: not everything about it was understood literally, but a blend of the symbolic and the literal left a permanent impression of a definite place and time where a specific Judge would pronounce judgment.

At the Judgment, as Lotario reported the common belief, "the same will be accuser and advocate and judge."[23] That fusion of roles did not trouble Lotario, but it ran against fundamental ideas of human justice. Could one maintain a view of divine justice that was deficient by human standards? Were the great theologians not driven by their own explicit teaching on simony and on the taking up of persons to explain how divine judgment did not suffer defects, to say how a Redeemer could be a Judge?

Usage of *redimere* in the special sense of buying off or paying up to avoid harassment was not remarkably far from the euphemistic or ironic usage of *redimere* in Cicero to indicate a payoff to a judge. Decretal law admitted that if a layman unjustly held tithes, a church could "redeem" them; and Alexander of Hales had generalized the decretal's principle to defend any buying off of harassment. But expounding Peter Lombard, he had made an exception. If a cleric was unjustly suspended from office, he could not "buy back" (*redimere*) the right to act. Unlike buying off harassment in other cases, he would here be purchasing something immaterial. "Reconciliation is something spiritual. One cannot buy it back."[24] One cannot buy it back because to buy a spiritual good is the sin of simony. But if reconciliation cannot be bought, what of the redemption of mankind by Christ?

Nothing followed for the theology of the Redemption if Redemption were taken as a vague metaphor not connected with the root of the word; and if "Redeemer" were predicated of Christ poetically and imprecisely, he could be understood as simply "freeing" us from our sins when he accomplished our Redemption. But for Thomas, to be "Redeemer" is "proper to Christ as man," that is, the term "Redeemer" is properly not metaphorically predicated of Christ.[25] Thomas, moreover, returned *Redemptio*—already becoming a theological cliché detached from its literal meaning—to its roots. *Redemptio*, he wrote, comes from *emere*, to buy. An *emptio* is a purchase. A *re-(d)emptio* is a repurchase.[26] There is a buyer, a price, a good. The buyer was Jesus Christ. He was in fact an agent acting by "the mandate of the Father as the primordial author." The price the agent paid was his death, usually expressed as his blood.[27] The good repurchased was "us,"—all of humankind. Only as to a seller did Thomas noticeably hesitate. The prior sale, now being reversed, was "that sale by which we sold ourselves to the devil by consent to sin."[28] One would suppose that the devil was then the seller. But Thomas did not describe Christ as paying off the devil. Instead, he declared that Christ bought us back from the devil as "by the labor of battle a king buys back a kingdom occupied by an enemy." The commercial metaphor became a military one. The blood was offered not to the devil but to God.[29]

No payoff to the devil, no reciprocation between Christ and the devil—these principles may be inferred to underlie Thomas's abrupt switch of metaphors. But the conclusion reached here in his youthful commentary on Peter Lombard's *Sentences* is forced and fails to cohere with the preceding analysis of a sale. In maturity, in the *Summa theologica*, with the same underlying but unarticulated principles at work, he provided a different theory of the buy back of man, eluding even more elaborately any payoff to the devil. By man's own fault, he taught, man became the devil's slave; but the punishment of slavery was inflicted by the devil merely as God's agent. God was the one to whom payment was due if man were to be released. It was "in respect to God, not in respect to the devil that justice demanded that man be bought back." Accordingly, "the price of our redemption" was offered "not to the devil but to God."[30]

A firm grasp of the place in human experience of reciprocity was central to such theology. In his commentary on Peter Lombard's *Sentences* Thomas expressed its essence: "In the passion of Christ there was a certain exchange: he accepted death and he bestowed life." There was "a kind of purchase."[31] The wages of sin were death, so, Thomas later wrote, Christ sought to pay the death we owed. The reciprocity was such that the tree of the Cross canceled out the tree of Eden. Or, as he put it in a Parisian quodlibet, Christ died so that "the price of the human buy back" would be "of the same genus" as the penalty: "by death he would buy us back from death." Any part of the suffering of Christ—*passio* comprehended any suffering—could have redeemed us. As St. Bernard of Clairvaux had said, a drop of his blood was enough.[32] But there was a rightness in death being the price. Death was the most difficult of all difficulties, the ultimate human penalty, the end to which all terrors were directed, the maximum. In exchange for our death Christ gave his.[33]

But reciprocity gave way, in Thomas's lyrical celebration of Redemption, to generosity. "How singular and admirable the liberality where the giver comes as gift, and the gift is completely the same as the giver!" exclaimed the bull *Transiturus* in 1264 establishing the feast of Corpus Christi to celebrate the institution of the Eucharist.[34] The emphasis on the Redeemer as giver and gift was paralleled in the contemporaneous poem Thomas composed for the feast:

> Record, tongue
> The mystery of the glorious body
> And the blood of great price.
> Fruit of noble womb,
> The king of peoples poured it
> For the price of the world.

The gift of himself in the Redemption was reenacted when Christ "with his own hands" gave "himself" at supper.[35] The food offered in *The Book of the Dead* to the gods was now food offered by God to man.

In the reading for the office of Corpus Christi, Thomas declared that God's Son "poured out his own blood for a price and simultaneous laver, so that, bought back from miserable slavery, we might be cleansed of all sins." The exchange was taken to an even higher level: "He put on our nature, willing that we be participants of his own divinity." Thomas turned into an affirmation the most audacious of human prayers, already a part of the Mass, "Give to us that we may be co-sharers of his divinity who saw fit to become participant of our humanity." God, Thomas taught, took our nature that we might share in his. He still did not state explicitly the difference between God's free and saving action and a transaction whereby God's pardon was purchased.[36]

In these insights, a gift becomes something totally different from a bribe—it is an identification of the donor with the donee to the point of giving the donee the donor's nature. Propitiation of a powerful being by an offering is not in question. The powerful being gives himself. The manipulative use of *munera* has nothing in common with this free and saving transaction. But Thomas did not find any occasion to develop this contrast explicitly, to set down in so many words the distinction between bribe and gift. Could the reason for his nondevelopment of the distinction have been the difficulty, at least obscurely apprehended, of reconciling this view of Christ's action with the literal sense Thomas had elsewhere attributed to *Redemptio*? And was it possible to keep this literal view and the standard moral analysis of simony? Was not the price paid for human ransom, the blood of Christ, a corporeal thing? Was not the price paid in exchange for a spiritual good? Was it not simony to buy forgiveness or reconciliation? Thomas did not ask.

Difficulties doubled with Thomas's teaching about the judge of our sins at the Last Judgment. The judge, he affirmed in orthodox fashion, will be Christ, and it will be Christ as he is man. Just as the primordial Author of Redemption is God, so God is the primordial Author of Judgment.[37] But just as the actual Redemption was carried out by Christ in the flesh, so will be the Last Judgment. The basis of the assertion is scriptural: "He has given him power to give judgment, because he is the Son of Man" (Jn 5:27); and "God has established him Judge of the living and the dead" (Acts 10:42).[38] Thomas connected these verses to the mystical union of the members of the Church: it is fitting that Christ in his humanity, as the head of the Church, be the Judge. And a reason of convenience is urged: such a judgment will be "sweeter to man."[39] In a special way the judicial power to be exercised at the Last Judgment, Thomas held, is to be attributed to Christ in his humanity.[40]

Reconciliation of mercy and justice can be treated as a paradox, resolved in the mysterious depths of divine being. Insistence on the humanity of the Redeemer-Judge scarcely permitted such a putting off of the paradox even though his Redeemer-Judge was God as well as man. The unasked question pressed, how does Christ in his humanity judge for their sins those whom in his humanity he has redeemed from their sins? The answer that the Redemption was of human nature in general but not of individuals was anticipated and formally excluded by Thomas. When "he paid the price for us," Christ freed us "from the sins proper to individuals."[41] Must not then Christ, the Supreme Human Judge, recognize Christ, the Head of humanity mystically united to every man? How could Christ the Judge not be biased in favor of those he had bought back?

> Recall, dear Jesus,
> I am the reason for your way.[42]

In these words, the *Dies Irae* itself boldly reminded the Judge of his other role. How were the roles reconcilable if Christ was human and the roles were real? Thomas did not ask or answer.

Redemption and Judgment were understood by Thomas literally enough to cause incoherence when the images were pressed against each other. He kept them apart; and he brought neither into close conjunction with his view of God's gift to man which was the paradigm of perfect gifts, the gift of the divine nature. From the disparate strands in his thought there could be derived different implications for teaching as to bribery. At one level the difference between a perfect gift and a corrupt bribe was decisively established. At another level the integrity of the Judge was not perfectly maintained. At another, the literal aspects of Redemption, transferred to transactions on earth, provided the model for a degenerate form of spiritual traffic.

The Purchase of Pardon.   "The Vow and the Buy Back of the Vow" ran the title of Book 3, Section 34, of the Decretals of Gregory IX; it dealt with the commutation of vows for cash. Opening with the bishop of Exeter asking if a vow to make a pilgrimage could be "bought back by charitable offerings," Section 34 provided Alexander III's answer: the bishop should weigh the circumstances as to whether "the recompense would be better and more acceptable to God." In the following canon Alexander III instructed the bishop of Norwich that by charitable offerings a crusader could redeem his vow to go to Jerusalem—in particular he could redeem his vow by agreeing to support one poor man for life. In chapter 8 of Section 34, Innocent III instructed the archbishop of Canterbury that if crusaders were permanently prevented from carrying out their vows "a buy back is to be imposed" and they were to pay in aid of the Holy Land the equivalent of their expenses and labor in going in person. Innocent III also thought it appropriate for nonfighting men "to buy back the vow"; and women not rich enough to bring troops at their own expense should definitely "buy back the vow."

In themselves these substitutions of money for labor and hardship were in the line of earlier penitential practice substituting money and alms for corporal penance. Critics existed who saw the practice as an exercise in greed: Peter Abelard, in his *Ethics or Know Yourself,* a short treatise on sin and its forgiveness written about 1137, commented in these terms on the action of a number of bishops at dedications of churches, consecrations of altars, blessings of cemeteries, or wherever a large crowd led them to expect substantial offerings of money. The bishops on these propitious occasions proffered pardons of punishments, good, as they said, on earth and in heaven. If the bishops were pardoning (*indulgentes*) part of the punishment for sin out of charity, why didn't they open heaven for everyone, beginning with themselves?[43] The practice, however, had been accepted by canon law. Under the heading "Penances and Pardons" it was regulated at a diocesan level by another decretal of Alexander III to the archbishop of Canterbury (X 5, 38, 4). The Pope spoke of "pardons (*remissiones*) made at the dedications of churches or for those contributing to the building of bridges." He left the implication that it was customary and proper to grant a pardon even for such a secular but communal purpose as raising money for a bridge.

At the papal level, pardons were most prominently associated with the popes' encouragement of the crusades. At Clermont in 1095 a council under Urban II had legislated as to those going on the First Crusade that the journey to Jerusalem would "be counted for all penance."[44] Reporters of Urban II's actual speech at the time understood him to say that the crusaders would obtain "pardon of sins," and he himself used the expression "pardon of all sins" (*remissio omnium peccatorum*) in writing the Flemish. Those who had been mercenaries for a few pennies, the Pope was reported to have preached, "now acquired eternal rewards (*praemia*)." The popular understanding of what the pope promised was that a dead crusader went straight to heaven, needing to suffer no more on earth or in purgatory.[45]

That this kind of exchange of temporal labor for spiritual bliss was itself simoniac was not entertained, or rather, was countered by applying the rhetoric of spiritual trading. Deliberately, at the time of the Third Crusade, Bernard of Clairvaux used the language of business. Summoning French and Bavarians and English to the crusade in 1146, he told the young that God

> wills to be held a debtor so that He may return to those fighting for Him their wages—pardon of sins, eternal glory. . . .
>
> If you are a prudent merchant, if you are a searcher in this world, I show you remarkable bargains. See that they are not lost. Take up the sign of the cross, and of all that you confess with a contrite heart you shall obtain pardon. The material itself, if bought, is of little value. Worn on a devout shoulder it is worth without doubt the kingdom of God.[46]

Bernard's term for pardon, *indulgentia*, meant amnesty in Roman law. He saw only heroism in purchasing it. The journey to Jerusalem was a spiritual enterprise like the purchase of the pearl of great price (Mt 13:46) where profit was to be expected. In the course of the twelfth century, however, papal pardons were extended to those who merely contributed to the expenses of the crusades, and a concrete connection between a cash payment and the pardon obtained was evident.[47]

At Lateran IV in 1215 the reformers concentrated on the abuse of pardons by "the collectors of charitable offerings." It was apparent that they had in mind the practices already attacked by Pierre le Chantre and Cardinal Courson. The collectors, the Council decreed, were to be modest and discreet, they should not run up large expenses, and they should not stay in taverns. In particular, they must possess a valid papal or episcopal letter of authorization and not go beyond it in what they promised their audiences. The decree entered the Decretals in the title "Penances and Pardons" as *Quum ex eo* (X 5, 38, 14). A form letter for collecting money for a hospital was even approved by the Council as a model and preserved in the canons. It began with a reminder that "we shall all stand before the tribunal of Christ" and so should sow on earth to collect in heaven. For "the pardon of sins" the bearer was exhorted to provide aid to the hospital so that "by these good things and others which you do with God's inspiration you can come to eternal joys." Not wholly free from ambiguity—especially in its use of the phrase "pardon of sins"—the form letter did not categorically promise eternal bliss in exchange for what was given.

Lateran IV even went beyond attempting to control the collectors to criticize local bishops. By their indiscriminate granting of pardons the latter had brought into disrepute the keys of the Church and actually weakened the practice of penance. Bishops were instructed that they could give no more than a year's pardon (*indulgentia*, now the word generally in vogue) when a church was dedicated. They were called to follow the moderation of the Roman pontiff. The Council said nothing at all in criticism of the pope; and, as Innocent III had a crusade very much in mind, he extended the full pardon of sins obtainable by a crusader to all those paying, according to their means, to support a crusader.[48]

The more common it became to equate the journey to Jerusalem with payment for the expenses of the journey, the easier it became to buy back the vow to go. In effect the vow followed by a buy back became simply another means of raising cash for a crusade. By mid-thirteenth century it was taken for granted that a buy back would usually be made. The decision whether to go or pay became that of the vowed crusader. Form receipts were in use by papal collectors acknowledging that A had paid so much "for the buying back of the cross." The amount varied considerably. Five shillings was the norm in England. Some bought back the cross for as little as three. The repurchasers retained the benefit they had acquired by vowing—entrance into paradise without penance or purgatory.[49]

Institutionally, vow and buy back functioned together, while money from them became an international source of papal revenue—of revenue sometimes used for general papal purposes as no segregation of the funds appears to have been made if they were forwarded to Rome.[50] At mid-century when the great theologians of Paris were writing their moral treatises, the institution was established. Confronted by customs of this kind, what would the mendicant theologians say?

Thomas Aquinas approached the practices involved with a high degree of abstractness. He addressed the question of the commutation of a vow in general and found it easy to conclude that the pope, having care for the whole Church, could commute a vow of pilgrimage to something better for the common utility of the Church; he avoided analysis of the practice of vowing and buying back in a single transaction. He did not link the vow and buy backs with the pardon given in exchange for the vow.[51]

Thomas did approach with more circumspection the meaning of "pardon." What was a "pardon of sins" by the pope? A pardon (*remissio*) could be of fault or of punishment. Analysis of the ambiguity seemed essential. To be forgiven a fault, one must be contrite and confessed: the pope could not do these things for someone else. Consequently, the pardon must be understood to be of punishment—an amnesty for one sorry for his sins.[52] Thomas had earlier established that A could make satisfaction for B, as Christ had done for our sins. The pardon extended by an indulgence was only a particular application of this proposition: God's justice was not cheated because the sufferings of Christ substituted for the debt owed by the sinner. In Thomas's words, one "is not absolved, strictly speaking from the debt of punishment, but there is given to him that from which he pays the debt."[53]

The heart of the doctrine, then, was the great buy back already effected by the great Repurchaser. Thomas dressed up the doctrine with a phrase taken from Hugues de Saint Cher, a senior colleague, the first Dominican to be made a cardinal. What was being drawn on when indulgence was given was "the treasure" of the Church, that is, the sufferings of Christ and of all the saints. The metaphor was doubly attractive: it gave a kind of concrete value to suffering, and the idea of treasure led naturally to the idea of administration. Who administered the treasure of the Church? The living head of the Church on earth, the pope. The pope could dispense the treasure "as the benefit or need of the Church requires." He distributed the treasure to individuals "as much as seems opportune to him up to the total pardon of punishments."[54]

Five characteristics of indulgences completed the economy they created: (1) They were valid to remit punishment not only in life but also after death, for the Lord had given Peter keys which bound or loosed in heaven. (2) Like other *suffragia* or intercessions by the living for the dead, they were effective for the dead who were not damned. (3) They could not change the state of a soul from misery to felicity but they could be multiplied to the extent that they eliminated the punishment of those in Purgatory—a contrite crusader, dying, could escape Purgatory altogether by force of the papal indulgence. (4) They could be obtained for others by those not personally in the state of grace, as, for example, a sinful priest offering mass for the dead. (5) They were "worth as much as they were preached," that is, the value of an indulgence was what it was proclaimed to be, and a complete pardon of all punishment by a plenary indulgence was effective before God. The Church, accordingly, had a treasure, principally administered by the pope, which (being infinite) was inexhaustible; which could be used to free the dead; whose efficacy was vouched for by the Church; and the use of which to benefit others did not require the user's freedom from sin. The possibility that the economy of indulgences might displace the economy of ordinary Christian morals was glanced at by Thomas—indulgences could be given "inordinately"—but not seriously pursued.[55]

Suppose, he did ask, that an indulgence was given consisting in the pardon of the punishment of one-third of one's sins to anyone giving assistance to the erection of some building. If an indulgence "is worth as much as it is preached," one could give a penny and get the one-third remitted and then another penny for another third and a final penny to be free of all punishment, "which seems absurd." Thomas's answer focused on the meaning of "giving assistance." A king giving a half-penny to someone did not give him assistance; similarly someone able to give all three pennies was not "giving assistance" when he doled them out one by one.[56] But Thomas, glimpsing how indulgences could be made a matter of barter, did not deal with the case soon to be common where a definite amount was fixed as the price of the indulgence. Then anyone with the cash was in a position to buy smaller or larger remissions of punishment. If an indulgence, say, remitted punishment equivalent to 1,000 days of penance for 1 florin, a rich man could buy the equivalent of 10,000 days for 10 florins; a poor man could not spend as much. Those with money had an advantage over those who did not, even though the prices were often low and the very poor were permitted to obtain the indulgence by prayer.[57]

Thomas did ask the question he had not asked apropos the great Buy Back: why was simony not involved? The pardon of punishment for sins was "something spiritual," the exercise of a spiritual power by the Church. To give spiritual things in return for temporal things was simony. The objection was simply and strongly stated, and the answer as clearly given: "To the contrary is the common custom of the Church, which makes indulgences for pilgrimages and charitable offerings." Custom, not attacked as evil custom, was to be decisive.

For temporal things alone, Thomas argued, an indulgence "cannot be made," but it could be given "for temporal things ordered to spiritual things, such as the repression of the enemies of the Church who disturb the peace of the Church; or such as the construction of churches and bridges and the collection of other charitable offerings." From this it followed that "simony does not occur there, because the spiritual is not given for the temporal but for the spiritual."[58]

In this analysis a crusade was a temporal thing ordered to a spiritual good; a bridge (an example doubtless taken from Alexander's letter in the Decretals) was ordered to a spiritual good; and any charitable collection was ordered to a spiritual good. By the extraordinarily simple move of categorizing as spiritual every temporal act ordered to the spiritual, the sin of simony no longer endangered the exchanges by which crusades were organized, churches built, and civic improvements financed. An economy was validated in which one of the most spiritual of objects, the fate of the soul after death, could be affected by cash laid out on earth, and the exchange would not count as an exchange of the earthly for the heavenly.

Was such a transaction really not simoniacal? Thomas did not pursue the question further. No doubt it was clear from the terms of his presentation that the pope had to act for the benefit of the Church; he could not give indulgences to benefit himself. In the Thomistic presentation, the administrator of the treasure spent a spiritual good in return for receipt of an earthly good directed to a spiritual good. There was no corruption in the Church's presiding officer using the treasure to pay a member's debt to God.

Among the Franciscans, Alexander of Hales's great pupil, Bonaventura, in general not differing from Thomas on this topic, perceptibly hesitated over the objection of simony. Commenting in 1252 on Peter Lombard's *Sentences*, he asked, "Should indulgences be made for a spiritual or for a corporeal benefit?" He noted that the relaxation of punishment was a spiritual thing and that the standard definition of simony precluded giving the temporal for the spiritual. But "the common practice of the Church" was otherwise. He concluded that the treasure of the Church could be expended for the glory of God, so indulgences could be given for the construction of churches, for visiting churches, or for preaching; and the treasure could be spent for the common benefit, so that indulgences could be given for the defense of the Holy Land or the faith. Bridge-building was conspicuously absent from this analysis. To the objection that a temporal good was being given for a spiritual, Bonaventura replied that what was obtained was a reduction of punishment with the remainder due being paid by the Church "from favor." Seeing, perhaps, that this answer was not responsive to his own objection, Bonaventura added as an alternative that the pardon was not given for an exterior action alone but in consideration of the good will from which the act proceeded.[59]

Bonaventura did not consider the obvious implication that all simony would then depend exclusively on the intention with which money was offered. Lack of rigor at the point where the traditional law on simony pressed hardest on practice suggested how difficult it was for the speculative theologians of the mendicants to come to grips with what was going on. At a time when vows, buy backs, and complete pardon of punishment had become an ecclesial institution, the great masters rationalized the foundations of these practices and adopted the economic metaphor of a celestial treasure to explain what was happening. Indulgences were accepted, blessed, defended by the intellectual leaders of the Dominicans and the Franciscans. The ease with which indulgences were now acquired was itself a manifestation of the tension between justice and mercy in the account of the Judgment and the Buy Back—a manifestation, the theologians thought, in the direction of the mercy already shown by the Judge who had died for our sins.

The Crucified Judge. The tension, paradox, contradiction between the role of the human Judge and the human Ransomer were eventually captured in nonverbal images more concrete than Thomas's theology. The earliest representation of the Last Judgment that has survived, an early fourth-century sarcophagus, showed no sign of the conflict. The biblical text it invoked was Christ's separation of the sheep from the goats. Paulinus of Nola followed the same text in decorating the apse of his early fifth-century church. In such a scene Christ discerned the good from the bad objectively.[60] A more formal Last Judgment—the nucleus of later Byzantine representations of the event—in the sixth-century church of St. Apollinare in Classe showed Christ, flanked by two angels, judging, without a sign of a countercurrent.[61]

Conflict came with the introduction of evidence of the Passion into the scene of Judgment. A poem describing a Last Judgment at the monastery of St. Gall in the eighth century relates that "in the heavens the Cross shines."[62] No more may have been intended than to represent the harbinger of the Judgment in Matthew 24:30, "The sign of the Son of Man shall appear in the sky"; but the conjunction of Cross and Judgment brought more than complexity. In the twelfth century, as the Last Judgment took sculptured form in the West, the abbey of St. Pierre, at Beaulieu in the Midi, showed Christ judging with his wounded hands extended as if still on the cross. The pattern was followed in 1135 at St. Denis de Paris and inspired Notre Dame de Corbeil. With variations, the showing of the Judge's wounds became standard. At Chartres, circa 1200, for example, in the central bay of the north portal, Christ the Judge bared his wounded side and held up his pierced hands.[63] To reinforce the recollection of the Passion, the instruments of his suffering—the nails, the lance, the crown of thorns, and, above all, the cross—were regularly represented in the background.[64]

The difference between verbal and pictorial reminiscence of the Passion was striking. Honorius in his vivid dialogue on the Judgment asked, "In what form will the Lord appear there?" and answered, "To the elect in that form in which he appeared on the Mount; but to the damned in that form in which he hung on the cross."[65] Sculpture could not present a scene that would vary with the spiritual state of the beholder, but it would be foolish to suppose that by choosing the crucified Christ the sculptors implied that they and their contemporaries were damned. Thomas Aquinas taught that the Cross would appear at the Judgment in order that "the condemnation of those who have neglected such great mercy may, by it, appear more just"; and the wounds on Christ the Judge's body would be marks of the virtue by which Christ triumphed. It would be rash to deny that the sculptors' views might have been like Thomas's, but the effect, at least for many beholders, was very different. When the Judge raised wounded hands, how could he be about to condemn? Visually, compassion prevailed.[66]

Typically, in these twelfth-century Judgments, at a level below the seated Christ, the weighing of souls went on. Nothing in the Gospels provided this image. It came from the Egyptian *Book of the Dead* to Coptic Christianity, to Byzantine Christianity, to Western Europe.[67] The task was now performed not by the jackal-god Anubis but by the Archangel

Michael, who had been scripturally represented in the Apocalypse 12:7 as battling the great dragon, and in the Epistle of Jude, verse 9, "as disputing with the devil over the body of Moses."

The offertory of the Mass for the dead, already in use in the eleventh century, prayed:

> Lord Jesus Christ, King of glory, free the souls of all the faithful dead from the pains of hell and the deep lake. Free them from the lion's mouth lest the Underworld suck them up, lest they fall into darkness. But let Standard-bearer Saint Michael bring them back into the holy light which you once promised Abraham and his seed. To you, Lord, we offer offerings and prayers of praise. Receive them on behalf of those souls we commemorate today. Make them pass, Lord, from death to the life which you once promised Abraham and his seed.[68]

In this remarkable plea the vision was not that of the after-life passage visualized by Augustine, in which souls with venial imperfections passed through purifying fire. Here it was supposed that all the souls of the dead, the recently deceased and the long deceased, were in transition. As in the *Book of the Dead*, offerings to God could affect their destiny—only here the offerings were made not by the deceased themselves but by the living. Trials and dangers, it was even implied, still threatened. A watery hell stood ready to lap over them. The head of the heavenly army, its *signifer* or standard-carrier, would have to lead them through.

Nothing in the offertory mentioned weighing, but when, against the background of this prayer and his scriptural role, Michael was chosen by sculptors to be the master of the scales, it was an ally of humankind who was chosen. In some representations, for drama or humor, his battle with the devil was continued. At the abbey church of Sainte Foy in Conques, a demon pressed his thumb on the scales. In the cathedral of St. Lazare at Autun a devil threw a toad in the pan.[69] St. Michael, who had wrestled with the great dragon, was not likely to be fooled by these tricks of a rascally grocer; and, after all, he was not completely impartial himself.

Two judgments, two judges—the theologians had not suggested this double operation now visually presented in a variety of churches. Michael, like the *officialis* of a bishop, was shown doing the actual work of judging but appeared subject to reversal by his superior, the God-man, Christ. If the theologians had been followed, there would have been a double operation of another sort. Following a thought of Augustine, Peter Lombard taught that after death and before the general resurrection of the dead, the souls of the dead would exist in "different receptacles" according to their merits. As developed by Thomas Aquinas, the soul which was separated from the body "either is submerged in hell or flies to heaven unless it is impeded by some guilt for which it is necessary to delay the flight until the soul is purged." In this vision no scales were necessary—the state of the soul by itself achieved its fall, its place of purgation, or its flight; and the Last Judgment confirmed what was already determined by the soul's state. If such theology had been embodied in art, there would have been no role for Michael, and the Last Judgment itself would have appeared as an anticlimax.[70]

Artists opted for a Last Judgment which was a focus of excitement, and they kept the weighing as well. Introduced at Conques in the Midi, post 1125, the scales were repeated in cathedral art, in part, no doubt, for their dramatic interest; in part, perhaps, as an image of objectivity. Integration of the two judgments was sometimes attempted as at Bourges by setting the chalice of Christ's blood in the scale on the soul's side. In a spectacular scene at thirteenth-century Amiens, the weight of a devil's head in one scale was outweighed by the Lamb of God set in the other. Here the Redeemer replaced the soul under examination; the Judgment appeared as the affirmation of a Redemption already accomplished. The impartial scales registered the buy back previously made.[71]

How many judgments of man were there if one went by Scripture, the theologians, and the artists? At least four: the First, by which Adam, and all humanity in Adam, were condemned; the Last, where Christ, the Son of Man, judged all; the anticipatory, rendered to each soul as it left the body; and the weighing. The last two were apparently not the same, because in the artists' rendition of the weighing there was a line of souls; the scales were not individually present at a deathbed; and the theologians, not discussing the weighing, talked of "receptacles" for the souls separated from their bodies.

How many of these judgments were affected by Christ's Passion? The First, because man was given another chance. The Last, because Christ was a merciful Judge. By extension, as has been seen, the weighing was affected, and by implication, no doubt, the judgment at death. Without counting the times man was set before God as Judge, learned theologians and popular writers rested their hopes on the sufficiency of Christ's Buy Back, with some additional trust in the effectiveness of saintly and angelic patrons. Multiplication of the judgments of man invited multiplication of the means of influencing the heavenly Judge.

The Judge's Mother.   The main stream of Parisian theology from Peter Lombard to Thomas Aquinas followed what were read as the indications of Scripture that the saints had a part to play at the Last Judgment. "They shall judge nations," declared Wisdom 3:8. "Amen, I say to you," Jesus promised in Matthew 19:28, "that you who have followed me shall, when the Son of Man at the Resurrection sits on the seat of his majesty, sit on twelve seats judging the twelve tribes of Israel." To him "who has overcome," the Lord said in Apocalypse 3:21, "I shall give to sit with me on my throne just as I have overcome and sit with my Father on his throne."

Read more or less literally, these predictions or promises appeared to say that the saints would sit as judges much as the gods of Egypt sat to oversee the weighing of souls in *The Book of the Dead.* The saints would include more than the Apostles—Paul could not be left out; indeed all the perfect would be there; and being among the judges, they would not now be subject to judgment themselves. They would judge, Peter Lombard said, "with authority and power."[72] Thomas saw the saints juridical role as announcing to those being judged the sentence already passed on them by Christ. Nothing in these accounts allowed for the saints being active as intercessors.[73] In Honorius' detailed dialogue, it was asked, "Will the just have defenders or the evil accusers?" The answer was, "They will have their consciences." Mary and John the Evangelist were described by him as leading the just as they rise; they had no other role.[74] Lotario was entirely orthodox when he wrote of the Last Judgment, "No friends will offer patronage," and acknowledged as our advocate only the Judge Himself.[75]

Marian piety took a different track, giving the mother of the Judge a prominent role at the time of judgment. Formulated most influentially by Bernard of Clairvaux, the role drew on the language of law but did not distinguish clearly between the activity of one pleading a case, an *advocatus*, and a go-between or intercessor pleading with the judge. Bernard thought in terms in which many bribegivers have thought: it must be right to reach the judge, to get his ear, to have access. Mary provided access. She was described as "the discoverer of favor" (*inventrix gratiae*). She was "our advocate." She was our go-between (*mediator; mediatrix*). "By you," Bernard declared in so many words, "we have access to the Son." Mary was "the royal road itself." Daring paradox: it was the go-between's *integritas*, both physical and moral, which excused "our corruption."[76]

Many of Bernard's invocations of Mary might be read as prayers for her help during life, before the Judgment. But the rise of the juridical metaphors suggested a role at the Judgment, and at times Bernard appeared to locate in Mary, at the Judgment, the mercy usually recognized as God's: Christ

learned compassion by the things that He suffered, so that he became merciful. Nonetheless, He keeps His power of judgment. Our God is, in truth, a consuming fire. Shall not the sinner fear to approach the presence of God lest, as wax flows before fire, he himself perish before God? Now see how she, the woman who is blessed among women, will not appear indifferent. She will find a place for herself in this reconciliation. For a go-between is needed with the go-between himself.

From "her fullness," all receive. She brings to the prisoner his "buy back."[77] In another sermon, celebrating Mary as "the aqueduct" as well as "the advocate," Bernard told his congregation that the Father gave Jesus as the go-between. But if they still wanted an advocate to Jesus, "Have recourse to Mary."[78] The closest secular parallel to Bernard's vision of Mary's pressure on the Judge was Teodulfo's portrait of the judge's wife tugging at his knees before he rendered judgment.

Another Bernard, a native of Morlas in the Pyrenees and a monk of Cluny, in a long poem, the *Mariale*, asked,

> To whom shall I stretch out
> To escape the awful judgment?
> Whom shall I seek
> By whom shall I flee the Judge's wrath?

His answer was Mary, "the go-between":

> If you fear Christ,
> The Judge of the living and the dead
> You should know that
> She does not want
> Her petitioner to perish.

Mary, he prayed,

> Give gifts of favors
> To the soul beseeching you.

and,

> Good mother, give us
> Your patronage.

and,

> Give them and me
> The prayers of your intercessions.

and,

> Star of the sea, force
> The ears of the Supreme Judge
> So that the heavenly King unites us
> To angelic feasts.

and,

> Make the formidable Judge
> Mild by your pleas
> Lest angered at our guilt
> He hand us over to savage fires.

and,

> Just Judge, we beg you
> Give pardon to all
> Who love the memory
> Of Mary, your mother.[79]

Mary's part in softening the Judge was decisive. She was the go-between (*mediatrix*), providing patronage (*patrocinium*), intercessions (*suffragia*), and offerings of favors (*munera gratiarum*). She was to assault her Son's ears until He heeded.

Popular piety extended Mary's influence to the procuring of a pardon after judgment. In the legends of her miracles collected between 1218 and 1227 by Gautier de Coinci, prior of Saint Médard, Mary is petitioned by St. Peter on behalf of a monk of Cologne who has already been judged and dragged off to hell. The monk has apparently nothing to recommend him, and God has already refused St. Peter's direct request. Peter turns to Mary:

> Beg Him as your Father.
> Command Him as your Son.

Mary at once agrees. When the Lord sees Mary He seats her and asks her wish, which, as soon as He hears, He grants.[80] Orthodox theology said, as Lotario phrased it in *The Misery of the Human Condition,* that "there is no buy back in hell." Mary's pull set orthodoxy aside.

Architecture and art also favored a role for Mary. The Last Judgments created in churches on the periphery of the Byzantine Empire preceded the Last Judgments of the West. In the Byzantine church at Torcello, an island near Venice, rebuilt at the beginning of the eleventh century, Mary was shown pleading before a seated Christ.[81] The Western recognition of Mary's role was gradual. In the mid-twelfth-century cathedral of Autun, Mary was shown seated not far from Christ.[82] She was now more than an advocate—else why should she sit? She was half assessor, half intercessor. At Chartres, about 1200, in the South Portal, Mary was still sitting in the Judgment scene, but she extended her hands in an unmistakable gesture of prayer.[83] In thirteenth-century Amiens and Notre Dame de Paris, she was on her knees.[84] Advocacy and intercession had become vigorous.

In the Judgments, Mary is represented on one side of the Judge. The usual scene required for aesthetic balance a complementary figure on the other side. Mary needed a partner in her brokerage of mercy. Who could it be? The Twelve Apostles were normally depicted as assessors, judging the twelve tribes. John the Baptist had no role assigned by Scripture at the Judgment, and so he was available to intercede with Mary. In some representations he is the other intercessor. But a different symbolism, as old as Byzantine Torcello, came to prevail. John the Evangelist had stood with Mary by the cross in John 19:26. Even if he were supposed to be busy judging, was it not fitting for him to be reminding the Judge of His passion? At

Amiens and Notre Dame de Paris, it was John the Evangelist who knelt with Mary to influence the Judgment.[85]

The treatment of Mary in direct relation to Christ judging was amplified and modified by other treatments which the variety and vastness of a cathedral made possible. In an almost frivolous vein Mary was sometimes shown putting her rosary on the scales where the souls were weighed.[86] Here she showed no more respect for the process than the demons loading the scales in *their* favor. In a profound way Mary's cathedrals proclaimed that she had unlimited influence with her Son. There was no need for her to extend her hands or kneel.

No doubt different temperaments have read different meanings where the language was complex, varied, and not that of words, but Henry Adams's famous interpretation of the Virgin above the high altar at Chartres, the infant Jesus on her knees, captures the message many must have read: Suppliants "look up to the light, clear blues and reds of this great space. . . . There is Heaven! and Mary looks down from it. . . . She is there as Queen, not merely as intercessor."[87] In the Last Judgment on the western rose window Christ is on the clouds, but for many, as for Adams, Mary's majesty and grace must have been uppermost: "To the Virgin and to her suppliants . . . the Last Judgment was not a symbol of God's justice or man's corruption, but of her own infinite mercy. The Trinity judged, through Christ—Christ loved and pardoned through her."[88]

These words are close to St. Bernard's, and it is not unwarranted to find the meaning the architecture had for many in the teaching of Mary's panegyrist. When, in thirteenth-century Notre Dame de Paris, the western rose window—traditional locus of the Last Judgment—was given over wholly to Mary as Queen, was not the teaching similar or likely to be interpreted similarly? Whether Mary was enthroned, or tipped the scales, or formally intervened, the mother of the Judge had a part in the judicial process which substantially limited the moralists' formal rejection of *acceptio personarum*. No person was more important in the judgment of man than the mother of God.

The basic exchange constituting the great Buy Back, the roles of Jesus as Judge and Redeemer, Son of an offended God and son of a merciful mother, the development of Mary as advocate and as intercessor, even the assignment of supervision of the scales to man's champion Michael, conveyed an image of a judicial process in which reciprocities had a part. The heavenly court, however, was not brought into a relationship with the criteria used to measure human justice. The gap was most evident in the indifference of cathedral art to treating bribery on a human level. Among the myriad scenes from the Gospels recorded by medieval artists, none that I have seen or heard of shows the one incident of completed corruption narrated in Scripture, the bribery of the soldiers guarding Jesus' tomb. No doubt the story had nothing to contribute to the glory of the Resurrection.[89]

Judas's betrayal, which could be analogized to an act of bribetaking, was frequently memorialized; but the part of his deed closest to bribery, his actual receiving of the money, was rarely evoked. At thirteenth-century Naumberg, in Saxony, a splendid stone choir does show the scene with psychological realism: The high priest sits, stretching out a hand as he pours silver into Judas's cloak. A man whispers in the high priest's ear, and another man whispers to another at Judas's right. The face of Judas himself is distorted with disgust. The whispering suggests secret corruption. But the high priest, paying, looks far more like a judge than the miserable Judas. The scene, in short, satirizes Judas, not the general act of corrupting an official.[90] Christian iconography, as it was embodied in the cathedrals, did not express an interest in *munera*-taking human judges. Avoiding the subject while contemplating the Judge-Redeemer, it was not unlike the teaching of Thomas.

The Last Judgment and the Judges.   In the most comprehensive treatise of national law known to the Middle Ages, one of the two or three most important books ever written on English law, the Last Judgment occupied as critical a place as it did in any cathedral's tympanum. *The Laws and Customs of England* was the work of a priest-judge or, more probably, two priest-judges: Henry de Bratton, the traditionally identified author, whose name is traditionally misspelled as Bracton; and Bratton's mentor, William de Ralegh, principal judge of Henry III in the 1230s and subsequently bishop of Winchester.[91]

Their book, a marvelous fusion of English cases, classical Roman law, medieval Roman law, canon law, custom and reason, was written, they said, for the instruction of "the lesser judges."[92] They gave up on the self-sufficient big judges with plenty of political weight. But even the teachable ones had to be told not to be corrupt. It was here that the Last Judgment played its part.

Discussing the elements of a civil action, Ralegh-Bratton taught that a judicial proceeding required "at least two persons between whom the dispute arises and at least a third who acts as judge." Without "the triune acts of three persons" there was no judicial proceeding.[93] In these simple lines the essential paradigm of a court was presented, and the essential requirement of judicial impartiality was stated. A judge was told to employ "the truth of judgment"; and the truth of judgment was said to consist in "the impartial and equal reception of the parties." Deuteronomy 1:16–17 and Deuteronomy 16:18–20 were quoted. The judge was not to take up persons nor take up *munera*. The divine paradigm was dominant. As 2 Chronicles 19:6–7 put it, "With the Lord our God there is neither iniquity nor taking up of persons nor desire of *munera* which blind the eyes of the wise and pervert the words of the just." The reason the divine paradigm was dominant was that "Judgments are not of man but of God; so, therefore, the heart of a king who rules well is said to be in the hand of God."[94]

The offerings which the judge must shun were the three kinds set out by

Gregory the Great—of the hand, that is, anything corporeal; of the tongue, "a public eulogy, a symphony of vainglory" (a pungent Ralegh-Bratton definition); and of service, "for which the probity of judgment is bent." To these were added *munus a sanguine*, "offering from blood relationship"; for, Ralegh-Bratton said, in one of those plays on words in which they took delight, "the line of straight judgment is curved for the line of blood." "All of these offerings," our authors declared, were "justly called filthy," and the judge who received them was "filthy in fact." Such a judge, "corrupted by filth," was rightly punished by the human law. As the Code of Justinian prescribed, he must restore fourfold what he received whether it had been under the pretext of a gift or a purchase. Upon him our authors pronounce a kind of curse: "Woe to that filthy man by whom the truth becomes filthy in the swamps of the courtyards."[95]

Matched against their rhetoric, the remedy Ralegh-Bratton provided was small. The fourfold penalty was based on Justinian; the practical legal questions were: To whom was the penalty to be restored? Who was to sue for it? In a book whose core consisted of cases and writs, there was no case holding a corrupt judge accountable and no writ providing an action to recover the penalty. Compared to their immense and intricate analysis which Ralegh-Bratton made available of ways for asserting possession of land, their treatment of corrupt judges was puny.

Impartiality was insisted upon, but Ralegh-Bratton did not comment on all the cases where it was clearly in jeopardy. Intrepidly they taught that where a crime of lèse majesté was charged the king could not judge "because he would be in his own complaint the actor and the judge in a trial of life, members, and disinheritance"; nor could the king's justices judge "since in trials they represent the person of the lord king of whom they are vicars." Judgment must, then, be by "the court and peers."[96] But the analysis was not extended. Great monasteries, wealthy religious bodies (e.g., the Knights Hospitaler of St. John), peers of the realm kept royal judges on retainers. The practice was not universal, but common enough to be known.[97] Ralegh-Bratton passed over it in silence. Royal judges also acted as advocates where the king's property was involved in a case.[98] Ralegh-Bratton said nothing about the judges who then should judge such cases.

Payments to King John's judges had sometimes been made to secure procedural advantages. Apparently these payments continued despite the promise in *Magna Carta*. In a case decided by Henry III and his council in 1233, a report of the case noted that the winner "voluntarily" paid the king five marks "for hastening his judgment."[99] Ralegh-Bratton, who were probably familiar with the report—Ralegh was a royal judge at the time—cite the case for its substantive holding on wardship without commenting on the payment by one party and the sense in which it was "voluntarily" offered.[100]

Most remarkable of all, at least from the perspective of later myth, Ralegh-Bratton did not invoke *Magna Carta* against corrupt judges. Ralegh and Bratton were both appointees of Henry III, whose guardians had reinstated *Magna Carta* after Innocent III's invalidation of it. Both were devoted to the concept of limited royal authority, so that in terms of their political theory *Magna Carta*'s restrictions were good law. But the great promise, "To no one shall we sell, to no one shall we deny or delay right or justice," they left unmentioned. As to bribes, *Magna Carta*, noted by them occasionally in other contexts, had neither teeth nor magic.[101]

What Ralegh-Bratton did rely on to curb corruption was set out in their introduction: Let not an unwise and unlearned man ascend the judgment seat which is, "as it were, the throne of God"; and let a judge not fall from on high, from "as it were, the throne of God." Let each judge take care not to judge against the laws "for prayer or price" and "for the advantage of a small temporal gain" acquire eternal sorrow.

And let him not on the Day of Fury of the Lord feel Him, avenging—Him who said, "Vengeance is mine, I shall repay"; on the Day when kings and princes of the earth when they see the Son of Man will weep and wail for fear of His torments, when gold and silver will not avail to free them. Who may not fear that trial in which the Lord will be the accuser, the advocate, and the judge? Yet from his judgment there can be no appeal, for the Father has given all judgment to the Son. He shuts, no one opens. He opens, no one shuts. How strict the judgment in which men shall give an account not only of acts but of every idle word whatsoever they have spoken!

And Ralegh-Bratton continue with the final passage from Lotario's *The Misery of the Human Condition* where the moans and groans, sighs and cries, and torments of sinners are set out with such energy and gusto. They conclude:

Let each one beware of that judgment where there is a Judge terribly strict, intolerably severe, offended beyond measure, His judgment incommutable, His prison inescapable, His punishments without end or interval. . . .[102]

In this extended passage there is an oblique reference to the Redeemer: the Judge is also the Advocate, contrary to the tripartite requirement of human justice. The dominant image is that of the Son as Judge—a Judge who has been offended beyond measure, a Judge who looms as a ferocious Vindicator. This Judge steps from the Last Judgment of Lotario to be the ultimate sanction Ralegh-Bratton know against the *munera*-taking judge. Mightier than *Magna Carta* and Justinian, He sits in the central arch of English justice.

The Other Passion.   "At that time a certain noble king went away into a distant country to take up tribute, and he called his servants and handed over to them his possessions and gave them power to give judgment and to do justice." With this parody of the parable in Matthew 25 and Luke 19, *The Passion of the Justices* begins, a clerical-legal satire on real judges in England two generations after Ralegh's day.[103]

The departure of Edward I for Gascony in 1286 and his return in 1289 is compared to the master's journey in the parable. While the king is gone, the sins of his servants left "to do justice" are several. They are described in a paraphrase of Psalm 25: "They sat secretly with the rich to kill the innocent, and their right hands are full of offerings." Three years later, the king returns. The servants try to buy him off with offerings; but the king declares, "Vengeance is mine. I shall repay." And he does.[104]

In this updating of the parable, *munera*-taking is a major part of the bad behavior of the royal ministers, and *munera*-giving is their major defense when discovered. The king steps out of the tympanum to administer retribution on earth. The title of the work emphasizes the inversion of the entire Gospel: these justices suffer a passion and redeem no one.

Actual events of 1289–1290 are described not too dissimilarly in roughly contemporaneous monastic chronicles: "Meanwhile the cry of the poor came to him [the king] because the justices and other ministers whom he had set over his kingdom had been corrupted by *munera* and subverted judgment." On the king making inquiry, the delinquent judges were "scarcely saved by a very heavy buy back" (*redemptio*); and Chief Justice Hengham, imprisoned in the Tower, "bought peace for himself—his buy back, as one says, and a right heavy one." Or another account: "Afterwards, passing through England, he [the king] punished in proportion to their trespasses his own justices and ministers. In his absence, blinded by offerings, they had perverted judgment and erred in other ways." Or, according to a third account, the king announced that those with complaints about injuries "against justice" should come to Parliament and they would receive "the complement of justice." Then the accused sheriffs, bailiffs, and judges were "struck with a pecuniary buy back (*redemptio*) in proportion to the quality or the quantity of their crimes; from which the lord king's fisc took not a little." The central role of *munera* and the condign royal retribution, both set out with the flavor of biblical reminiscence—such is the story the clerical historians tell, and it chimes with *The Passion of the Justices*.[105]

The surviving judicial records of the time give a picture that is both confirmatory and strikingly different. Edward I, returning to England in 1289, set up a royal commission of seven trusted priests and laymen to hear complaints against any royal official for acts done in his three-year absence. Complaints poured in against bailiffs, sheriffs, court clerks, and judges. The records do agree with the satirists and chroniclers that the judicial establishment was not trusted.

Royal administration under Edward I had already taken a strong public stand against bribetaking. Inquiry had been made at the beginning of his reign, in 1274–1275, into a variety of offenses by officials in the justice system. Royal commissioners had systematically put local citizens on oath to answer as juries if, among other things, they knew of sheriffs or their bailiffs, or coroners or their bailiffs, "taking *munera* to consent to conceal felonies"; if they knew of any sheriff or bailiff taking *munera* to remove recognitors from assizes or juries; if they knew of anyone who had received gifts (*dona*) or profits (*lucra*) from exercising or not exercising their office; if they knew of any sheriff, seneschal or bailiff who took a buy back (*redempcio*) from men for a verdict given before the justices.[106] Asked the length and breadth of England to the small local units known as hundreds, the inquest produced a large number of charges of corruption. For example, the hundred of Flitte, County of Bedford, reported that the coroner took one-half mark to exercise his office and his bailiff two pence. Dustebery Hundred in Buckingham County said the coroner "took whatever he can for exercising office." Geldecross Hundred, Norfolk, reported that a named bailiff had taken one pound from a named chaplain to conceal his felony, and it made three other accusations of money taken by officers to conceal robberies. Haywardeshow Hundred, Lincoln, accused a sheriff and bailiff of taking "buy-backs from jurors," that is, of making jurors ransom themselves because of their verdicts. The town of Lincoln reported that three foreigners licensed by the king to export wool had to pay two marks to the sheriff to get him to honor the license.[107]

These instances, selected at random, are representative of the multitude of complaints that came, not from every hamlet but with sufficient frequency to indicate pervasive problems. To be sure, the charges were alleged, not proved; and although names were named and amounts often given, dates tended to be imprecise. Actual prosecution came years later, sporadically.[108] The king had a motive in the questionnaire—to appear to be interested in doing justice, and the questionnaire suggested that something be said by the jurors.[109] Nonetheless, the product of the inquest, the Hundred Rolls, was not self-serving like imperial edicts; they testified to a widespread belief that local officers were corrupt; and the testimony was sometimes given at the risk of reprisals.[110] The First Statute of Westminster (1275) and the Second Statute (1285) were designed to remedy the evils complained of.[111]

Neither the inquiries nor the statutes spoke to the situation of royal justices. They had presided over the inquest and drafted the remedial statutes and ignored their own conduct. Now in 1289 the question was raised whether the big fish were not as guilty as the small. As in 1274 the king had been abroad and now returned to demand an accounting. Thomas de Weyland, Chief Justice of Common Pleas since 1278; Ralph de Hengham, Chief Justice of the King's Bench since 1274; William de Saham, justice of the King's Bench since 1271; Nicholas de Stapleton on the King's Bench from 1278 to 1287 and an itinerant judge since 1274; William de Brompton, a justice of Common Pleas since 1274; and Solomon de Rochester, an itinerant royal judge since 1274, were among the accused.[112]

Chief Justice Weyland's crime and punishment were the most dramatic. He was accused of sheltering the murderers of a named individual. No *munera* were mentioned, nor was there need to show any. The suspects he had helped were from his own household. The Chief Justice, if the charge was true, was an accessory to murder. He fled; sought sanctuary with the

Franciscans; got a statement from the archbishop of Canterbury that he was really an ordained cleric instead of what he appeared to be, a married layman; was nonetheless starved out of sanctuary by the king; imprisoned; and, without trial, exiled. He departed for the Continent a barefoot penitent and was never heard of again. No evidence exists of his taking or trying to give *munera*.[113]

Hengham, Chief Justice of the King's Bench, was a defendant in nine complaints, accused *inter alia* of favoritism, false judgment, and refusal to hear a case. In one, where he was said to have favored the abbot of St. Edmund's the abbot was reported to have induced him and his colleagues *per munera* to keep or eliminate certain witnesses as the abbot chose; and Chief Justice Weyland and Justices John de Lovetot and Richard de Boyland were alleged to have aided the abbot with advice.[114] But no judgment is recorded in this and two other of the cases involving Hengham. In five others he was formally acquitted and in one he was convicted of misdating a writ by four days. He nevertheless paid the king a very large amount, 4,303 pounds, for a pardon. Ten years later he was again a judge, and in 1301 he became Chief Justice of Common Pleas.[115]

Brompton, a Common Pleas justice, was accused of misconduct in twenty-eight complaints. Ten of the complainants never appeared; in four cases he was acquitted; in ten there was no recorded judgment including one case where he was charged with refusing, for *munera*, to give judgment; in two he was ordered to produce money found to be wrongfully withheld; and in two the plaintiffs were restored to the state they had before his judgment. In the last four cases the reason for Brompton's erroneous actions may have been favoritism or bribery, but the evidence has not survived. He paid the king 3,666 pounds in exchange for a pardon.[116] Saham, the King's Bench judge, charged by seven complainants, was acquitted in two cases; four did not come to judgment; and he was convicted of the same misdating as Hengham. Solomon, the itinerant judge, was acquitted thrice, while one complaint did not come to judgment. Saham, nonetheless, paid 1,666 pounds and Solomon 2,100 pounds for their pardons. Brompton and Saham did not serve as justices again; Solomon was on eyre in 1292.[117]

The royal records show that the sums I characterize neutrally as payments were actually received by the fisc. They were large amounts, particularly if compared to the judges' salaries. Hengham's 4,303 pounds, for example, was over one hundred times his income as a judge.[118] What significance is to be given them? Are they evidence of ill-gotten booty? Are they tacit admissions of guilt?

In Hengham's case we know that he was not only a cleric but a cleric who was a pluralist—among other benefices, he held, like Bratton, the chancellorship of Exeter cathedral.[119] It might be argued that his ability to pay a monumental fine came from these "livings," frugally husbanded and invested in land, rather than from takings on the bench. As to the other judges we have less information as to other sources of income;

typically, when they were laymen, they were landlords.[120] As for being admissions of guilt, the sums paid were officially registered as "fines" not in the sense of judicially imposed penalties but in the sense of moneys paid to obtain quittance of the king ("fine" being related to *finis*, the end). They bear no evident relation to the recorded results of the judges' trials. They could be argued to measure the king's anger and his financial needs rather than the judges' fault. After all, it could be observed, Edward I had in 1287 squeezed the Jews of England.[121] Now he was squeezing his own ministers. Functionally, the payments resembled bribes—they were offered by accused men to settle a case and obtain freedom. Yet they differed from bribes in being publicly registered with the fisc. The king took a righteous public posture in collecting them. Edward may have been squeezing them, but these victims were not selected arbitrarily. Is it not a fair inference that the judges' conduct had made them vulnerable? The fees, in short, do not make guilt of corruption certain beyond a reasonable doubt, but they do make it inferable.

Only Nicholas de Stapleton, a judge of King's Bench from 1278 to 1288, was seriously pursued of taking bribes, and here the recorded accusation avoided the biblical term *munera*, employing instead the less damaging *dona*, gifts.[122] The case was this: Richard le Fraunceys and others had been accused of murdering one Nicholas, the brother of Amice of Goldington, in the county of Westmoreland. Amice and her husband charged that Stapleton had been assigned the case and then had taken "large gifts" from a relative of the defendant; that thereupon he had made inquiry about the murder in Northumbria, a county far distant from Westmoreland; and that he had called as witnesses only Richard's relatives. Stapleton's reply was that he had been taken ill and so held the inquiry where he could, not being able to travel further. Amice retorted that Stapleton had been in good health, and that the reason for the judge's conduct was ten marks he received from the defendant's father-in-law. Stapleton denied taking the money.[123]

A trial was set to determine if Stapleton had "received some gifts." The sheriff failed to summon the jurors, but when, after a delay of a whole court term, a jury was finally assembled, the accused produced a pardon from the king. According to this document, Stapleton had promised to pay the king 300 marks in three installments, and because of this the king pardoned him and remitted "any action" he had or could have against him. Amice's case was dismissed.[124] No bribe had been proved. Still, a pardon purchased in the course of a trial—and purchased at a price more than seven times the defendant's salary—suggests that Stapleton did not believe he would prevail before the jury. The king's overt public act of justice was to mulct him severely, in effect imposing a condign punishment on a bribetaker.

Royal justice, at the levels of politics, propaganda, and journalism, emerged vindicated. The bad guys were put to rout, to shame, to large financial expense. In the eyes of the populace, for whom the chroniclers speak like modern newspapermen, *munera*-taking was appropriately sanctioned. In the eyes of the legal community, for whom *The Passion of the Justices* was designed, the judges rightly suffered on earth some of the torments Ralegh-Bratton had held out for corrupt judges at the Last Judgment. But the judicial machinery of Edward I—sometimes thoughtlessly called "the English Justinian"[125]—had not functioned to prove corruption by the king's justices. The king's vengeance had taken a form that was strangely like *munera*-taking by the Crown. Or to put it more exactly, the crimes of corruption had been "redeemed." Buy backs on a grand scale had released the justices from their passion and their guilt.

Redemption in this bastardized secular form consisted of payments to purchase pardons by defendants who thought they might be found guilty. Redemption in its bastardized ecclesiastical form consisted of payments to purchase pardons by penitents who knew that they had committed sins. Redemption in its literal theological presentation consisted in the purchase of pardon for guilty humankind. In each of these forms redemption was a form of reciprocity. The difference between these permitted reciprocities and the reciprocities rebuked as simony and *munera*-taking could become invisible. The invisibility could threaten belief in justice in earth or in heaven.

Bribetakers were supposed to fear the Last Judgment. Wealth, honor, patrons would not avail them there. Sporadic, indirect, ineffective human measures against corruption would be supplanted by divine punishment. Paradigm of justice, promise of just retribution for the corruption of the earth, the Last Judgment affirmed human belief in the baseness of bribes. God did not take *munera*. But the image of impartial justice was intolerable. The heavenly Judge responded to a woman's influence. Patronage affected the process. As in ancient Egypt, purchases in this life offered immunity: buy backs—the small ones and the great-acquired pardon. The Judge himself had set the example in the Redemption. In a Church still committed to reformation, what voices would be raised to insist that certain reciprocities were intolerable?

9

The Pouches and the Pitch

Canto 21

From bridge to bridge in this fashion
We spoke of things my Comedy cares not to sing.
We reached the crest and held it when we stopped to see
The other ditch—of Bad Pouches and other futile cries.
And I saw it, wonderfully dark.

As in winter in the armory of the Venetians
The sticky pitch boils
For caulking unsound ships,
And at that time, for they cannot navigate,
One makes a new ship and one stops up the ribs of her who has made
    many voyages,
One hammers at the prow, one at the poop,
Another makes oars and another sews sails and one twines rope, another
    patches reef and mainsail,

In the same way, not by means of fire but by means of divine design,
A thick tar boiled below.
It smeared the bank in every part.

I saw it, but I did not see in it
Except the bubbles the boiling raised.
The whole heaved and, compressed, sank.
While I looked fixedly downwards,
My leader said to me,
"Watch, watch."
And he drew me to him from the place where I was standing.

Then I turned, like a man who has delayed to see
What he should flee and whom sudden fear disarms
So that to see he does not put off going.
And I saw beyond us a black devil running
To come up on the rock.

Wings open, feet light—how ferocious his looks, how harsh his action
    seemed to me.
Sharp and high, his shoulder
Carried both thighs of a sinner,
And he held him by the sinews of the feet.

From our bridge he spoke:
"Here, Badclaws, an Alderman of Saint Zita. Put him under.
I return to that land which is well-furnished with him;
Every man there is a grafter, but Bonturo.
'No' there for money becomes 'Yes.'"

He threw him below, and turned back over the hard rock.
Never was an unleashed dog in such a hurry
To follow a thief.
The other sank and turned up head down.
The demons who had cover from the bridge
Shouted: "Here the Holy Face has no place;
Here you swim differently than in the Serchio.
If you do not want our hooks, surface not
Above the tar."

Pricking him with more than a hundred
Prongs, then they said,
"Dance, covered. It is fit.
Snatch in secret, if you can."

Not differently do cooks make their slaveys
Sink the meat with tongs into the middle of the pot,
So that it does not float.

The good teacher to me: "In order that it not appear

That you are here,
Squat below
Behind a splinter which will give you some defense.
Do not fear on account of any offense done me;
I have taken count and another time was in such dispute."

He passed beyond the head of the bridge.
As he touched the sixth bank, he needed a steady face.
With the fury and storm of dogs
Who rush upon a poor man who suddenly stops and begs,
Those under the little bridge came out.

They turned all their pincers against him; but he shouted,
"None of you be foul.
Before your tongs bend me, let one step forward to hear me,
Hook me then if it is advised."

"Badtail go," all shouted.
One therefore moved, and the others, holding firm,
Came to him, saying, "How does it help him?"
"Do you believe, Badtail," my teacher said,
"That you see me come here safe
From all your defenses
Except by divine will and favorable fate?
Allow me to go.
In heaven it is willed that I show another
This wild road."

His pride, then, so fell that he let the hook
Fall at his feet,
And to the others, "Well, no striking now."
And my leader to me: "You who sit
Asquat the splinters of the bridge
Now join me safely."

I therefore moved and came to him quickly;
And all the devils advanced,
So that I feared whether they would keep the compact.
In the same way I once saw infantry fear
Who came out of Caprona by compact
And saw themselves among so many enemies.

I put myself next to my leader
With my whole body,
Not turning my eyes from those whose looks were not
Benevolent.

And they bent the prongs, and one said to another,
"Shall I touch him on his arse?"

And he replied, "Yes. Nick him."
But the demon who had conversed with my leader
Turned instantly and said,
"Hold, hold, Rumpler."

Then he said to us, "You cannot go further
On this rock;
The sixth arch lies, completely shattered, at the bottom.
And if it still pleases you to go further,
Go above by this bank.
Another rock is near which makes a path.

"Five hours later than this hour of eight, yesterday,
One thousand two hundred and sixty-six years ago,
This way was broken.
I will send these to see if any there display themselves.
Go with them. They will not be harmful."

"Step forward, Bentwing, Trampleage and Curnose," he began,
"And Curlbeard lead the ten.
Walleye and Dragonnose, come,
Tusked Hoggie and Clawdog,
Little Devil and mad Blusher.

"Look around the boiling glue,
These are to be safe to the rock bridge
That goes unbroken above the dens."

"Teacher, what is that I see?" I said. "Please,
Let us walk alone without escort,
If you know how to go.
For myself I do not seek it.
If you are as wise as usual, do you not see
They grind their teeth, and troubles threaten in their brows?"

And he to me, "I do not want you frightened.
Let them grind if they like.
They do it for those boiled in pain."
By the left dike they turned.
But first, each had as a signal
Bitten his tongue toward
The leader;
And he had made a trumpet of his rump.

Canto 22

I have sometimes seen cavalry move camp,
Begin attack and draw up lines,
And at times I have seen their backs departing.

I, Artines, have seen scouts in your land, the swoop of raiders,
The clash of tournaments, the rush of jousts,
With trumpets with bells with drums with castle noises, our own and for-
    eigners';
But I never saw cavalry or footsoldiers
Or a ship at sign of land or star
Move to such a distinct
Bagpipe.

We walked with the ten demons.
Fierce company; but in a church with saints and in a tavern with
Gluttons.
The pitch was my attention, to see the content of the pockets
And the people who were burning within them.

Like dolphins when they make signs by the arching of their backs
To mariners to work to save their ship,
In the same way, to lighten the pain,
Sinners showed their backs and hid like lightning.
And as at the edge of water in a ditch
Frogs stand with snouts outside
So that they hide feet and remaining bulk,
Sinners squatted everywhere.
When Curlbeard approached, they withdrew below
The boiling.

I saw, and my heart still shudders at it,
One wait, as it happens that a frog remains
When the rest jump;
And Clawdog, who was closer to him,
Hooked his head's tarred hair
And hauled
So that he seemed to me
An otter.

I already knew the names of all of them,
Noted when they were elected.
When they called to one another, I listened.
"Sink your claws in him, Blusher.
Flay him,"
Shouted all together these hateful beings.
And I: "My teacher, if you can, find out who is the unlucky man
Fallen into the hands
Of his adversaries."

My leader approached his side and asked from where he was,
And he answered: "I was born in the kingdom
of Navarre.

My mother put me in the service of a lord.
For she had borne me of a loser,
Destroyer of himself and of his property.
I was in the household of good king Thibaut; there I began
To graft.
For this in this heat I account."

Hoggie, on each side of whose mouth a tusk
Protruded like a hog's,
Made him feel how one of them would tear him.
The mouse had come among bad cats.

But Curlbeard closed his arms about him, and said, "Stand back,
I'll fork him."
And he turned his face to my teacher.
"Ask," he said, "if you want to know more before another mangles him."

My leader: "Tell. Do you know if there are any
Italians among the guilty
Under the pitch?"
And he: "A little while ago I left one who was
A neighbor of such. Would I were still with him, covered;
I would not fear a claw or hook."

And Walleye: "We have stood too much."
He hooked his arm and ripped and carried off
A sinew. Dragonnose, too, wanted to seize a leg.

Hence their dean with sour looks
Went round and round them.
When they were a little pacified,
And he was still examining his wound,
My leader without delay said to him:
"You say that by an unlucky move you left another to come
To shore. Who was he?"

And he answered,
"Friar Gomita of Gallura,
Vessel of every fraud.
He had his lord's enemies in his hands and did for them
In a way all praise.
He took money and, as he says, quietly released them.
In other duties too he was no small but sovereign
Grafter.
Lord Michele Zanche of Logodoro mixes with him.
Their tongues do not tire of Sardinia.

"Look at the gnashing of that other;
I would say more but I fear
He prepares to scrape my mange."

The great Provost turned to Little Devil who widened
His eyes to strike. "Off, noxious bird," he said.

He who had been scared began again:
"If you want to see or hear Tuscans or Lombards,
I'll make them come.
Let the Badclaws hold back a little,
So that they do not fear their vengeance.
Sitting where I am, for one of me I'll make seven come
When I whistle
As our custom is if one of us gets out."

At these words, Curnose raised his snout
And shook his head
And said, "Hear his cunning; so he thinks
To throw himself below."
At this he, who had tricks in rich abundance, answered,
"I am too cunning when greater grief I get
For my own."

Bentwing did not restrain himself and
Unlike the others said to him,
"Drop. I'll not be after you at a gallop, but
Beat the pitch with my wings.
Leave the height. Let the bank be shield.
See if alone you can do more than
All of us."

You who read, hear new sport.
Each turned his eyes toward
The other slope,
He first who to do it had been most unready.

The man from Navarre chose his time, put
His feet on the earth, and
Bounded. From the Provost he was free—
Blunder afflicting all, and most
Him who was its cause.
He stirred and shouted, "You
Are caught."

It was of small effect. His wings
Could not advance to reach
The suspect, who went
Under; the other, diving, came up
Breast up.
Ducks do not otherwise submerge
When falcons near, and they turn away
Angered and beaten.

Enraged by the joke, Trampleage flew,
Following him,
Charmed because he was escaping
To have a row;
And when the grafter had gone,
He turned his claws on his associate,
Clutching with him above the ditch.

The other was a hawk,
Ravenous to claw him;
And both fell within the boiling pond.
They were unclutched instantly by the heat,
But not to rise; they had glued their wings.

Curlbeard, sorrowing with his men, made four
Fly to the other slope
With all the hooks. Soon from here and there, they came
Into position and stretched
The hooks toward those ensnared.
But already they were within the crust and
Cooked.

And we left them there entangled in this fashion.

Canto 23

Silent, sole, without company,
We walked,
One in front and the other behind,
As Friars Minor go on the road.

The brawl turned my thought
To the fable of Aesop
Where he spoke of the frog and the mouse.
"Now" and "at once" are not more alike
Than one is with the other,
If beginning and end of each are compared
With mind fixed.

As one thought explodes out of another, there was
Born from that one another, which doubled
My first fear.
I thought in this way:
"They have been mocked, hoaxed, damaged;
Their irritation must be huge.
If anger adds to malice, they will come
After us more cruelly than
Dogs on hares they hunt."

I was already aware of all my hair
Rising with fear;

And I stood intent on what was behind.
I spoke:
"Teacher, unless you quickly
Hide me and yourself, I fear the Badclaws.
Already they are behind us;
I imagine I already hear them."

And he: "If I were a glass set in a leaden mirror,
I would not more quickly draw to myself
Your outer image than
I obtain what is within you.
Even now your thoughts come
Among mine with similar face and appearance;
I form a single plan from the mix.
If on the right the bank so lies
That we can descend into the next pocket,
We shall flee the hunt
Which you imagine."

He had not completed giving this plan when
I saw them coming,
Wings stretched,
Not very far away,
Wanting to take hold of us.

My leader suddenly snatched me up,
Like a mother roused by the roar
Who sees next to herself a fire
And snatches up her son and flies and does not stop,
Caring more for him than for herself,
Clothed only in a shirt.

Down the neck of the hard bank, on his back,
He slid
To the hanging rock
Plugging one side of the next pocket.

Water never ran so fast through sluices
To turn the wheel of a riparian
Mill when it comes closest
To the blades,
As my teacher ran on that edge,
Carrying me on his chest
Like a son not like a companion.

Scarcely had his feet met the bed
Of the bottom below
Than they were on the hill
Above us;
But he did not doubt

That high Providence, whose will
Made them servants of the fifth ditch,
Took from them all power to depart from there.[1]

Dante Alighieri and Virgil in their descent into hell have reached the Eighth Circle, one away from the bottom of the pit. At the very beginning of his journey in Canto 1 Dante had encountered a wolf "that in her leanness seemed burdened with craving." The wolf turns out to be the deadliest of enemies; the *Purgatorio* exclaims,

> Cursed be you, old wolf.
> More than all the other beasts you have
> Prey; for your hunger desires
> Without end.

The hunger without end is for wealth, and the wolf's prey are the deeds to which the hunger leads. To speak without symbols, as Dante does in *De monarchia*, the desire for wealth is "the worst enemy of justice." In the journey just described one batch of sinners who have been dominated by it are being punished by demons who are themselves remarkably vicious.

Dante does make a distinction between those who surrender to the desire for wealth and those who pursue wealth by unjust deeds. Earlier the travelers had encountered those who had given in to their passions, among them avarice. Beginning with the Seventh Circle they meet those whose sins include malice—that is, sins of which "injustice is their end." The mark of injustice is this: its accomplishment always "afflicts someone else." Those who have harmed others by violence are in the Seventh Circle. In the Ninth are traitors, who have not only failed to keep a natural love for their fellow men, but have broken faith with those to whom they owed personal loyalty. Between the Seventh and the Ninth are "the pouches" where fraud is punished.[2]

Fraud—*la frode*—is a comprehensive term for the injustice brought about by the wolf's hunger and man's use of his intellect. As Dante teaches in the *Convivio*, justice is "the most human" of virtues. Conversely, fraud—the opposite of justice—is "man's proper vice."[3] For this reason it is worse than violence—God's penology is unlike that of human courts, generally tender of white-collar crime and punishing most severely those who have used force. As Virgil explains the plan of hell,

> . . . because fraud is the proper evil
> Of man, it more displeases
> God.
> And therefore the fraudulent
> Stand below; and greater pain
> Assails them.[4]

Fraud is also counter to love, to Dante an essential element of justice. In

De monarchia he writes of "charity or upright love which sharpens and gives light to justice." Over the gate of hell is the inscription,

> "Divine Power, Supreme Wisdom, Primal Love
> Made me."

Difficult as it is to comprehend, unless the punishments are seen as symbols of the soul's own choices, the torments of the damned are the works of love. Yet the love that fraud violates is not the kind of personal loyalty whose breach excites Dante most. Hence the merely fraudulent are not in the Circle of the traitors. Their fraud

> . . . appears to sever
> Only the love which
> Nature makes.

This vice is —surprisingly perhaps—universal:

> Fraud, by which every conscience
> Is bitten.[5]

Sinners—a subclass of the fraudulent—who are punished in the fifth pouch of the Eighth Circle are first characterized in the lines from Canto 21:

> Every man there is *barattier*, but Bonturo.
> "No" there for money becomes "Yes."

In the following Canto the man from Navarre declares,

> "there I began
> To do *baratteria*";

and he describes Gomita as sovereign *barattier*.[6] How should the italicized words be translated?

"Grafter" is an appropriate term for any kind of official who trades his assent for money—the *barattier*; and "to do *baratteria*" may be rendered, slightly more succinctly than in the Italian, as "to graft." Translators such as John Ciardi (1954) and Mark Musa (1971) have chosen these terms. Their translation would need little comment except for an extraordinary tradition in English. The first complete English version of *The Divine Comedy*, by Henry Boyd in 1802, offered these verses for Canto 21's description of Bonturo and his compatriots:

> Prone to State-Simony, a sordid tribe,
> Bonturo singly scorns the golden bribe
> Nor sells the honours of his parent state.

"State-Simony" was the awkward circumlocution of a translator—the chaplain of Lord Charleville—more familiar with clerical precedents than with politics. It did convey the idea that official power was being sold, and the key idea was captured by "golden bribe." In Canto 22, Gomita was made to confess that his sin had been to "sell" gifts. These translations acknowledged that what was punished in this pouch was the sale of the exercise of secular authority. But in an introductory summary of the canto, Boyd added, "The Poets see below the Department of Baratry [sic], where the State Simonists, or they who were guilty of selling Offices, or making traffic of Justice, are confined."

Boyd thereby introduced as well as misspelled a fatal concept: "barratry." Obviously for him "barratry" designated official corruption, a meaning that could not have been found in the great contemporary authority, Samuel Johnson's Dictionary. It seems unlikely that Boyd could have encountered the term in common usage in the sense he gave it. Presumably, antiquarian research had led him to some ancient book where the word seemed to be used with the meaning he adopted. Neither "graft" nor "grafter" were then in English use; why he did not use "bribe" and its compounds is not evident.

The next translator, Henry Francis Cary, another clergyman, writing in 1805–1806, had Friar Gomita describe himself as "peculating," a verb then virtually unknown in English; and he characterized Bonturo's compatriots as "barrators." The verb "to peculate" had a Latin root which suggested that its meaning was "to embezzle"; it was too specialized a term to embrace Gomita's crime and was not favored in later translations. Meanwhile, "barrator" as well as "barratry" were now fairly launched among translators of Dante. Charles Eliot Norton provides a late nineteenth-century example: Bonturo's countrymen are barrators, Gomita confesses to having committed barratry.

The tradition did not end with the nineteenth century. It has been perpetuated by Dorothy Sayers (1949), Geoffrey Bickersteth (1965), and Charles Singleton (1970). In English, however, a barrator is one who stirs up litigation, and barratry is the illegal or unethical encouragement of litigation. The words do not convey any sense of official corruption. They were in some use when legal ethics frowned on the promotion of lawsuits. In an age in which litigation thrives, they are virtually obsolete. In any event they do not describe a sin Dante finds punished in the lower depths of hell. Cary, Norton, Sayers, Bickersteth, and Singleton have translated the sound and not the sense.[7]

Singleton, to whom otherwise such a debt is owed for his elucidation of Dante's journey, compounds the matter here by declaring that barratry is "the buying and selling of public office."[8] There is warrant for this definition in the New English Dictionary; but the examples it provides are from the early seventeenth century, from eighteenth-century Scottish law, and from nineteenth-century translators of Dante. In fact the definition had become defunct at least by the nineteenth century outside of the tiny circle of Dante's translators. Modern Baltimore has been filled with charges like those against the sinners of this pouch. If Singleton should step outside the precincts of Johns Hopkins University to denounce the city's barrators, how many Baltimoreans would understand him? Would there be one? And even if barratry could indicate to a modern student of Dante the corrupt sale of public office, the sin condemned in the poem is far broader. The sin is that of an official making "No" "Yes" for money. Dante's definition is exact and comprehensive. He has, as will be seen, turned into an Italian verb, *barattare*, the Latin *committere baratterias* describing a crime with which he himself was charged. In his own case, the specific crimes charged included not only the sale of office but also the sale of orders and licenses. In the poem, Gomita is a *barattier* for releasing prisoners for money—no sale of office there. As observed by Pietro Alighieri, Dante's son, the fraud of those judged here is in "judging or administering."[9] "Grafter" and "to graft" are the best English equivalents of the noun and the compound verb describing their corruption.

Two grafters are identified by name, two by country: Friar Gomita and Michele Zanche; the Navarrese, and the man from near the River Serchio, that is, a citizen of Lucca. One fourteenth-century commentator supplied the name Ciampolo for the Navarrese, and tradition has so linked the gloss to the text that Ciampolo is often referred to as a well-known character; but all the information about him comes from his own words in hell, and no name is included. Gomita worked for Dante's Pisan friend, Nino Visconti, who put him to death for the treachery commemorated here. Nino himself appears in the Purgatorio as "noble Judge Nino," in the process of being cleansed of his negligence as a ruler; he was a "judge" in the sense of being the head of a district.[10] Zanche, of whom little is known, was killed by a Branca (Claw). Perhaps no more than the coincidence of the name of his slayer and the collective name of the demons makes him occur to Dante here. The poet makes little of the circumstances in which the grafters have acted. Sardinia, however, was a Pisan colony, and the two in Canto 22 who never tire of talking of Sardinia were corrupt colonial exploiters. Navarre was a small independent kingdom. Why Lucca should be singled out as generally corrupt is not known. Bonturo, the sole official excepted from the charge, was identified in fourteenth-century commentary as Bonturo Dati, a man associated with "the party of the people," that is, an anti-aristocrat, pro-middle class party boss; according to one oft-told tale he boasted of being "half of Lucca" in his day. It has plausibly been suggested, though not demonstrated from anything outside the text, that the reference to him is ironic.[11]

Not every kind of graft is comprehended by these examples. Strikingly, there is no reference to the paradigmatic case of a judge bribed to give a false judgment. Less striking, but notable, there are no instances of payors being punished, only payees. It is sometimes thought that Dante's hell is encyclopedic in its list of sins or at least comprehensively Thomistic. It is in fact selective. To take the analogous area of sexual sin, contraception, simple fornication, and masturbation—all sins dealt with by Thomas Aquinas—are not punished in the Inferno; so here only certain species of bribery are dealt with. The proportion of the Inferno addressed to the subject is still very substantial. If Canto 19 on simony is added, three and one-third, out of thirty cantos on the inhabitants of hell, are devoted to bribe-takers and their fate.

Activity, obscurity, viscosity, and filth—these are the chief characteristics of the grafter's life encountered in the Eighth Circle. It is not as though Dante found symbols corresponding mechanically to each aspect of that life. Rather, psychological and moral tones of the grafter's existence are conveyed by converging images and action. Beginning with the memorable metaphor of the Venetian armory, the poet meets movement, agitation, bustle. The grafters are busy and quick-moving. Lively animals—dolphins, frogs, otters—represent their swift shifts of position. Their industry stands in contrast with the static state of the Simonians met in another pocket, who are encased in baptismal fonts. Paradoxically their speedy motions are not slowed up by the viscous medium in which they move. Pitch or tar—the terms are used interchangeably—covers them. "Those who touch pitch are stained by it," teaches Ecclesiasticus 13:1. No doubt the line, already used by John of Salisbury and Innocent III to rebuke grafters, suggested to Dante what their element should be. His son, Pietro, says he "believes" Ecclesiasticus was the source.[12] The pitch has a double function. First, it hides the grafters. They operate in the dark, mostly invisible. A snout shows, a back flashes. It is hard to see a whole man or speak face to face. Second, it stains them. They are smeared and blackened. They are sordid creatures, dirtied by the stream they infest.

The supervisors of the stream are themselves violent. They hook and tear and dismember the grafters dodging grafters, each in turn feared greatly. They rush upon Virgil like dogs. They pursue Virgil and Dante in violation of the safe-conduct their leader granted, and their pursuit is crueler than hunting dogs'. They are vulgar as well as vicious. Like malicious urchins they salute their leader with their tongues, and he responds with a fart to which the poet gives monumental dimensions. The implicit suggestion is that these are the kind of politicians who punish grafters.

Dante's own sense of jeopardy is unique in his entire account of hell. He begins by being aware only of the heaving and the bubbles; he has no idea of what is going on beneath the surface. His leader first warns him to watch, then draws him from the place where he was standing. Almost too late, already weak with fright, he is aware of his danger from a devil running toward him. His leader tells him to hide. He must squat, an undignified action, behind a splinter, an inadequate defense. His leader is challenged in ferocious fashion. He himself cowers in the cracks. He continues to fear, as he had once seen Ghibellines surrendering at Caprona in 1289 fear treachery. He huddles close to his leader while two of the supervisors discuss nicking his rump. He distrusts the menacing escort which is offered and pleads to go alone. He escapes when the supervisors begin chasing the escaped grafter, turn to fighting each other, and end by getting stuck in the pitch—that is, they begin to graft themselves. Escaped, Dante is taciturn and without company, and he fears the pursuit, which is in fact launched. The pursuers come very close. Virgil's desperate action—a mother saving a child from fire—saves him.

The emphasis laid on the analogy with the Aesopian fable is also germane to Dante's personal involvement. The beginning and the end of the fable are to be compared, he says, with the beginning and the end of his adventure here: Virgil and Dante were offered a safe passage across a dangerous obstacle by the devils, as the frog offered assistance to the mouse in crossing a stream. The devils were ready to betray them, as, in the middle part of the fable, the frog actually began to eat the mouse. The devils were themselves caught, just as a hawk at the end of the fable made off with the frog. A comparison of beginnings and ends suggests that treacherous apparent friends were trapped as they tried to trap the poet. The frog (ranocchia) struck Dante, perhaps, as a particularly apt analogue for his demonic pursuers because the author of the Florentine decree confirming his banishment in 1315 was named Ranieri.[13]

Another sign of the poet's personal involvement is the outburst of preteen vulgarity—a source of embarrassment to the graver commentators. Pietro, his son, goes on at length apologizing for it, making matters worse with the implausible claim that by the extended comparisons with the military at the beginning of Canto 22, "the author intends to excuse himself for his shameful account."[14] The jeer and prolonged jest do appear, rather, to reflect the author's desire to strike at the supervisory demons any way he can, above all by making them ridiculous as well as hateful.

Pietro Alighieri says the demons "symbolize the passions and affections assaulting them [the grafters] and infecting them in such deeds and secret machinations."[15] In this view, grafters lead a divided and turbulent inner life. Pietro's focus is too exclusive. It does not give weight to the indications that the devils are also objective and entirely independent of the sinners they torment. A modern commentator believes the devils are themselves grafters operating a ring; hence their organization and the role of Boss Curlbeard.[16] They are so successful that they undergo no tortures themselves except by accident. A third way of viewing the demons is to see them based on Dante's own experience in Florentine politics.

From June 15 to August 14, 1300, Dante was one of six priors in the rotating council governing Florence. The times were turbulent. The independence of the city was under threat from Pope Boniface VIII. Earlier in the year Florence had tried in absentia three papal bankers connected with the Florentine firm of Simone de Spini and condemned them to fines of 1,000 florins apiece or to having their tongues cut out. The pope, bearing the commune of Florence, as he said, "in the bowels of charity," wrote from Anagni to the bishop of Florence ordering him to annul the trial, instigated by hatred and held, the pope observed, in the defendants' absence. Boniface forbade further proceedings without his special permission. In a follow-up to the bishop and the inquisitor of the city on May 15, 1300, he characterized as "not so much heretical as insane" the suggestion of certain Florentines that he lacked power to intervene in a Florentine trial. The Roman Pontiff was the vicar "of Him who has been established by God as judge of the living and the dead." The Roman pontiff "rules kings and kingdoms." The Roman Pontiff "holds first place over all mortals." To him "every soul must submit," and "all the faithful of whatever eminence or state must bow their necks." Men cannot live without law and a superior. The Roman Pontiff supplied that need. The Florentine detractors of this power had broken out "in canine barkings." The pope had decided "to constrain the jawbones of such barkers with a bit and a muzzle." The refractory citizens and the officials of the commune were to be cited to appear before the pope in eight days; otherwise the pope would order the seizure of the property of all the citizens of Florence "in the different parts of the world" and would order all the debtors to Florentines not to pay their debts and would proceed against those who dared "to bite our authority" as against fosterers of heresy.

Unperturbed by this barrage, Dante in the first days of his priorate joined in ratifying the judgment against Boniface's friends. The quarrel escalated. The city, basically Guelf or pro-pope, was divided between Whites or moderate Guelfs like Dante and Blacks or ultras in their pro-papal position. In November 1301 Boniface's ally, Charles of Valois, took control of the city, abetted by the Blacks arrayed on Boniface's side. In December 1301 a legate arrived to represent Boniface's interests. By January the Whites were being tried and proscribed. On January 27, 1302, the Podestà entered a judgment directed at Dante and three other named persons.[17]

The Florentine Four were found to have received money, property, or a written promise of money, in exchange for the election of new priors and standard-bearers; to have "received something improperly, unlawfully or unjustly" for electing or appointing other officers, for enacting or not enacting ordinances, and for issuing orders and licenses to officials of the Commune; to have drawn from the Treasury beyond the amounts authorized; to have given or spent sums "against the Supreme Pontiff and Lord Charles" and against the agreement between the Guelf Party and the Commune; to have received money or property from "some particular college" by reason of "some threats of extortion"; and to have separated Pistoia from Florence, creating divisions in it, and expelling from it "the Blacks, the devoted faithful of the Holy Roman Church." The introductory clauses characterized the crimes involving money as "graft (barattaria), unlawful profits, and unjust extortions," and the crimes involving Pistoia as "fraud, falsity, trick or malice, graft or illicit extortion."[18]

Notably imprecise, these findings may be compared with a judgment issued on the same day against another ex-prior, Gerardo. In his case—also one of graft—the accuser, the amount, and the payor were all named.[19] In the case of the Four none of these things were mentioned. The findings read more like a comprehensive indictment than substantiated conclusions—the Four "or some one of them" did the acts of graft; they acted "through themselves or through others"; the acts were performed as priors or not as priors or after they ceased to be priors. The findings as to harming the Blacks of Pistoia suggest the political nature of the proceeding. In form a judgment, the decree is a set of vague allegations, composed by partisans. The podestá's charges are no more evidence against Dante than Julian's charges were against Augustine. Was Dante in fact guilty? "Every conscience is bitten by fraud."[20] His sense of vulnerability to the demons of the pitch is extreme. But the Inferno is no confession, and he indignantly denied the truth of the podestá's charges. His own claim of innocence "manifest to everyone" must be accepted.[21]

None of the Four had dared to appear in person and make a defense. Found guilty in absentia, they were sentenced, so the judgment read, that "they might partake of the harvest's fruit according to the quality of what was sown." They were condemned to make restitution, to pay fines of 5,000 florins apiece and to undergo exile for two years. Boilerplate at the end said that their names were to be inscribed forever in the statute book and that, "as counterfeiters and grafters," they were to be barred in perpetuity from public office and public benefits. If they did not pay within three days, their property was to be "wasted and destroyed." As they remained absent and in contempt, a new judgment was issued by the podestà on March 10, 1302. If any one of them at any time should enter Florentine territory, he was "to be burned by fire in such a way that he dies."[22]

The ironies of Dante's hell are apt to strike a reader as cruel, but they are not crueler than this Florentine decree on the fruits of the harvest and its penalties as to property and life. By never returning to Florence Dante avoided death by fire; nothing, except what his wife could claim as her dowry, prevented the laying waste of all he had. "Every thing loved most dearly, you shall leave."[23] Aged thirty-seven, he was a fugitive from justice and an exile for good. Found guilty of at least five crimes—graft, unlawful profits, extortion, fraud, and trick—Dante chose to commemorate graft in Cantos 21 and 22 along with the cruel prosecutors of it. The devils who made him cower are those who drove him from Florence. Their collective name, Bad Claws, *Malebranche*, is the plural form of the family name of a nephew of Nicholas III, Cardinal Latino Frangipani or Malebranca, who intervened in Florentine politics in 1280.[24] The cardinal, a Dominican, could have been viewed as a peacemaker; but as the bearer of Orsini influence into Florence, he could also be seen as the source of later woes and a symbol of papal intervention. The harsh treatment of Nicholas III and family in Canto 19 shows that Dante held the Orsini in particular disfavor. The other names, it is reasonable to suppose, are derisive distortions of family names, physical characteristics, or moral qualities of the poet's persecutors. He had noted these guardians when they were "elected."[25] In mangled form he has preserved their memory.

The greatest pictorial commentator on Dante has been William Blake,

because he has not mechanically followed the letter of the poem but has by
intuition attained to Dante's spirit. His powerful prints and watercolors
for Cantos 21 and 22 focus on the demons. They are sleek, prosperous,
even cheerful, bristling with energy and self-confidence—the very model
of triumphant politicians. Hoggie, his tusks curled like an elegant mous-
tache, is especially self-satisfied. Dante and Virgil are timid creatures
beside them, and the Navarrese, his arm being skewered, a hapless victim.
Blake has captured the central place Dante has assigned the supervisors of
the pitch, the bosses who condemned him.[26]

Accusations of bribery are often political. Accusation is not proof. Accusers may themselves tumble into the pitch. No one has conveyed these
recurrent features of the concept of the bribe more vividly than Dante.
Squatting behind his splinter, then in mortal fear of pursuit, he has had
experience to provoke ambivalence or the awareness that charges of bribery can be baseless and employed exploitatively. The same ambivalence or
awareness is not apparent when he addresses simony. The man behind
the unjust judgment that exiled him, Dante was certain, was Benedetto
Caetani, Boniface VIII, and even in Paradise the memory of this pope is
recalled with loathing. Beatrice, speaking as of 1300, predicts Dante's fate
to him as though already at this time the pope had his personal exile in
mind. Boniface is seen at the center of the simonian sale of grace:

> So from Florence you must depart.
> This is wanted. This is already planned.
> And soon it will be done by him
> Who ponders it there
> Where every day Christ is sold.[27]

Earlier in the Inferno Boniface VIII has been commemorated in Canto 19
on the Simonians. Hated as these ecclesiastics are by Dante, he puts them
slightly higher in hell than the civic grafters; and there is no sense of near
personal involvement in their sin. The Canto follows:

Canto 19

> Simon Magician and Simon's vile followers:
> The things of God which ought to be
> Brides of goodness,
> You rapaciously make adulteresses
> For gold and silver.
> It is now fit that the trumpet
> Sound for you,
> For you stand in the third
> Pouch.
>
> We were already at the next tomb
> Having mounted the rock at that point
> Which drops over the middle of the ditch.

Great is the art, Supreme Wisdom,
You show in the heavens, on earth, and in the evil
World, and very justly Your Power
Dispenses!

I saw on the slopes and on the bottom
Ashen stone
Full of holes of a single size.
Each one was round.
They did not appear to me less ample or greater
Than those which are in my beautiful St. John's,
Made as stations for those baptizing there,
One of which—it is still not many years ago—
I broke
So that one within would not drown.
Let this be the seal so that every man may be undeceived.

Out of the mouth of each protruded
Feet and legs of a sinner up to
The calves. The rest remained within.

On fire were both soles,
On account of which their joints
Quivered so intensely
That they would have shattered
Ropes and chains.

Flame moves above the outer surface
Of oiled objects—so it did there
From heels to tips of toes.

"Who is he, teacher, so tormented,
Quivering more than his associates,
Sucked by a redder flame?"
I asked, and he to me: "If you wish
That I carry you below
By that lower bank,
You shall know of him from himself
And of the wrongs he did."

And I, "I like
What pleases you.
You are lord and know that I
Do not depart from your will;
You know that which is not said."

We came then onto the fourth embankment,
Turning left to descend below
Into the tight and pitted bottom.

My good teacher still did not displace

Me from his hip until
He brought me to the opening
Of him who wept with his shanks.

"Whatever you are who are held upside down,
Sad soul, set like a stake,"
I started to say. "Speak if you can."

I was standing like a friar
Who hears the confession of a treacherous assassin,
Who, after he is fastened, calls him back
To delay death.
And he shouted, "Do you stand there already?
Do you stand there already, Boniface?
The writing lied to me by several years.
Are you so quick with that you seized,
Which to possess you did not fear
To rob by trick the Beautiful Lady, and afterwards
Outrage her?"

I did like those who stand as if mocked,
Not understanding what is replied to them,
Not knowing how to answer.
Then Virgil said, "Say to him quickly,
'I am not he, I am not he you think.'
And I replied as ordered.

At that the spirit twisted hard both feet,
Then sighed and crying said to me,
"Then what do you ask of me?
If to know who I am has brought you down
So much that on that account you have run the bank,
Know that I was clothed with the great mantle.
And I was truly the Bear's son,
So greedy to advance the cubs
That above I put wealth, here I put myself
Into a pocket.

"Flattened in the fissures of the stone
Under my head are drawn those
Who proceeded me in practising
Simony.
I shall fall lower also
When he comes who I thought you were
When I put my sudden question.

"But I have already cooked
My feet and stood headfirst
More time than he will stand
With red feet.

For after him will come from the West
A shepherd without law, of uglier works,
Fit to cover him and me.
A new Jason he will be, of whom one reads
In Maccabees.
As his king was soft toward him,
So to the other will be he who rules
France."

I do not know if I was too much a fool
Answering him in this metre:
"Come tell me: how much treasure did Our Lord
Want from St. Peter
To place the keys in his power?
Surely he sought nought except 'Follow me.'
Neither Peter nor the others took gold or silver
From Matthias,
When he was chosen for the place lost by the guilty soul:
Stay here. You are well punished.
And watch well the ill-gotten money
Which made you hot against Charles.

"And if reverence for the supreme keys,
Which in glad life you held,
Did not still forbid me,
I would use yet graver words.
Your avarice afflicts the world,
Trampling on the good and comforting
The wicked.

"The Evangelist saw you shepherds
When he saw her who sits on the water
Whoring with kings.
I mean she who was born with seven heads
And had the ten horns as sign
As long as her virtue pleased her spouse.

"You have made gold and silver God.
Are you different from an idolator
Except he prays to one and you
To one hundred?
Constantine, of what evils was the mother
Not your conversion, but that dowry which
The first rich Father got
From you."

And while I sang to him these notes,
Anger or conscience bit him;
With both feet he kicked out hard.

I well believe my leader was pleased.
With a contented look he listened all the time
To the true words I pronounced.
He therefore took me up with both arms
And when he had all of me upon his breast
Remounted by the way he had descended.

Nor did he tire of holding me tight
Until he had carried me
Above the crown of the arch
Which joins the fourth and fifth embankments.
Here he sweetly rested his burden,
Sweetly for the rock was marred and steep,
And would be hard passage for goats.

From it another valley was disclosed to me.[28]

There is, it would appear, no doubt that the sin punished here is simony. Simon Magician is addressed at the start. The pope being punished—Giovanni Gaetano Orsini, Nicholas III—declares that those below him preceded him *simoneggiando*, "simonizing." Jason, the purchaser of the high priesthood in 2 Maccabees 4:7–8, is another Simonian invoked as comparison. Yet simony is taken in a broad sense. In his commentary Pietro quotes the canonical definition of simony and that of Thomas Aquinas, but neither applies to the specific conduct mentioned. Pietro also refers to the sale of Christ by Judas; but this kind of treachery is reserved by Dante for the Ninth Circle. The chief charge against the pope is that he was greedy to advance the bear cubs (*orsatti*), a charge documented by Dante's commentators with examples of Orsini nepotism. Only a severe, and by now ancient, moralist like Pierre le Chantre held such conduct to be simonian. If Dante had been following Thomas, here would have been an opportunity explicitly to punish *acceptio personarum*; but the sin is completely submerged in simony in the Inferno. Le Chantre's analysis is accepted.[29]

A second charge implied against Nicholas III is that he had taken "ill-gotten" money to work against Charles—meaning Charles of Anjou, king of Naples and Sicily.[30] The charge is essentially political. As for the two popes for whom places are reserved, Dante condemns their operations globally. Boniface VIII, we learn from the *Paradisio*, lives where "every day Christ is sold."[31] It is no doubt the height of irony that the poet should be mistaken for this unforgiven enemy. The shepherd from the West, Bertrand de Got, Clement V, is characterized as "lawless" and by implication owes his throne to Philip the Fair; the king's good will is not said to be owed to money but to the king being "soft," *molle*, toward him, an adjective suggesting a sexual attraction.

Dante's commentators have responded enthusiastically to this Canto by reporting that all three popes were notorious for their simony.[32] But nothing really distinguishes what is known about Nicholas III and Clement V as Simonians from many of their predecessors of the past five centuries. The reputation of Boniface VIII is different. His French enemies, seeking to have him tried posthumously by a Council, claimed that he had "heretically dogmatized that simony did not touch the Pope," his position being expressed in his question, "Is not the Roman Pontiff the Lord of all things and in particular of the goods of the Church?" Having instigated the notorious attack on Boniface at Anagni, the French had an interest in showing that he was a heretic. Clearly the old teaching that any Simonian was a heretic was not good enough for their purposes. Not merely his practice of simony, but his *ex professo* defense of its lawfulness for the Pope was necessary if his heresy was to be established. The French did specify certain simonian practices they attributed to Boniface: election cases were not tried "in the course of justice by those having God before their eyes," and were, instead, settled by a go-between (*mediator*) who would come to agreements with both parties or with one of them; large, noncustomary sums were asked for papal provisions to benefices; the pope had agents—*exploratores* or investigators—to determine how much money a prelate had; and his exactions were so great "that no accountant could count them." His Florentine banker, Simone de Spini, was singled out as the chief go-between in these sinful financial transactions. None of the charges was proved, and Boniface VIII's memory never came to judgment. The French claims do show that, to others besides Dante, Boniface appeared as unusually corrupt; but he was also hated with unusual vehemence, and the hatred fed the charges.

Strikingly, the charge of being "a manifest Simonian" pales in the French list beside other charges brought against Boniface: he was, the French said, a manifest usurer, an incorrigible sodomite, and a heretic believing in neither the resurrection of the dead nor the reality of Christ in the Eucharist. Of all these terrible allegations, given public notoriety before Clement V in 1310–1311, and all worthy of hell in his book, Dante chose simony as the sin by which his enemy was to have earthly immortality.[33]

Unlike some other satirists and rumormongers Dante is uncompromising as to where the blame lies. The popes are not to be excused by shifting responsibility to the curia. The supreme pontiffs are personally liable. The contrast is particularly striking with the civic grafters where three out of four are lower officials and even the fourth, the alderman from Lucca, is one who shared power. The condemned Simonians are at the apex of the governmental pyramid.

The Simonians are upside down. That is the capital physical fact conveying their total inversion of what should be done. It is the moral fact about their lives equivalent to the grafters' entanglement in pitch. Two corollaries: they cannot see what they are doing; and they are immobilized. In the Purgatorio where Pope Adrian V is purged of avarice, he lies facing the ground and says:

> No punishment the mountain has
> Is more bitter.
> Just as our eyes did not adhere
> To that on high,
> So justice here has turned them
> To the earth.
> As avarice wasted our love for every good
> And so destroyed our work,
> So justice here binds us tight,
> Hands and feet captured and bound.
> And as long as it pleases the just Lord,
> So long shall we be immobile
> And stretched out.[34]

In the Inferno, the sinners' feet are not only bound but on fire—another inversion. Their souls should have been on fire with the flames of the Holy Spirit. In fact it is their lower extremities which burn with a material flame. They are enclosed by what look like sources of sacramental salvation but are in fact deadly traps. The fonts of St. John the Baptist hold refreshing water. These simulacra burn. They burn those who are like "oiled objects" (cose unte). These priests were at ordination touched with holy oil. Now they are oiled in a different sense: the popular metaphor for payoff finds a place in this description of their punishment.

Pouches are what all sectors of the Eighth Circle are called but the name is particularly apt for the habitations of the grafters and the Simonians. The latter, it is at least implied, have their money with them: Nicholas III is told to guard what he has got. The presence of coin fulfills Simon Rock's curse of Simon Magician: "Your cash go with you to hell" (Acts 8:20). The pope even puns on his punishment: he pocketed money, now he pockets himself.[35]

In great contrast to the grafters the Simonians suffer only from the conditions proper to their state; they are not tormented by active demons. If the demons primarily represented passions they would be needed here, too. Their absence suggests, perhaps, that Dante did not see the Simonians—at least those at the top—as bothered by anyone. Even more, their absence confirms the part which Dante's own experience played in making the devils such a major factor in the world of the civic grafters.

Sexual metaphors for corruption—absent from the grafters' pouch—are recurrent in Canto 19. Simon Magician and his followers avolterare their brides. There is no corresponding verb in English, and one has to translate "make adulteresses of their brides," not merely "prostitute," as translators often put it. The theme is picked up in specific relation to Boniface VIII who has taken the Beautiful Lady, the Church, and then farne strazio

—"outraged her." He has made his own bride a harlot—rented her out for money. A fourteenth-century commentator observes, "No greater outrage can a man do to the wife whom he has married than to make her submit for money to him who gives the most."[36] The climax of these metaphors is the denunciation derived from Apocalypse 17:1, "Come I will show you the condemnation of the great whore who sits on many waters with whom the kings of the earth have fornicated." In the original probably the Roman Empire is meant. Dante means not geographical Rome, for the papacy when he wrote was already in Avignon, but Rome as the pope. As Pietro Alighieri puts it, "Whore—that is, the administration of the Church."[37]

Not rejecting the institution of the papacy, Dante sees its major crime as simony. "Your avarice" he says to Nicholas III, employing a plural "your" to include many popes, "Your avarice afflicts the world." No reformer, before or since, has made a simpler or more passionate indictment.[38]

Dante expects no help from the corrupt papacy. He finds civic corruption punished by cruel politicians who themselves get into the pitch. Cynical despair would be the easy outgrowth of such realism. Yet on the sixth star in *Paradisio* he sees written by angels in "human language,"

"LOVE JUSTICE YOU WHO JUDGE THE EARTH"

The star seems "silver patterned with gold."[39] The monetary agents of corruption have become transformed and transcended. Dante prays,

> Sweet star, how great and how many jewels
> Showed me
> That our justice is done
> By the heaven of which you are the gem.
> Therefore I pray to the Mind, in Whom begin
> Your motion and your power,
> That He look intently there
> Where the smoke rises which mars your ray
> So that another time He will at last
> Present himself to those
> Selling and buying in the temple,
> Walled with signs and martyrs.[40]

The bribery of churchmen and civil leaders is corrected only by God's grace. The terrible indictments of corruption, which could be a call to revolution, end in this prayer.

10

The Monkeys and the Bears

Dante's journey through a hell and purgatory marked by bribery and simony ended in personal salvation and prayer for reform of the Church. Reform had been the cry since Gregory I had tried it from the top. Would the cry ever end?

Sparks. In the growing literature designed to instruct on sins to be confessed in confession, neither simony nor secular bribetaking was overlooked. For the upper class layman there were, for example, translations of the *Somme Le Roi,* a treatise by a Dominican, Lorens of Orléans, written in the thirteenth century for a royal penitent, Philip the Bold. Translated in the fourteenth century into Midland dialect as the *Book of Vices and Virtues,* and into Kentish dialect as the *Ayenbite of Inwit* (the title made famous by James Joyce), it took up the seven deadly sins and under the third branch of covetousness spoke of great prelates who were wolves eating the sheep. It moved on to decry bailiffs, beadles, constables, and reeves who, the Midland version said, "raunsomen men and wommen," especially poor men, poor women, and children who cannot help themselves: the sin of these minor officials was, in effect, extortion under color of authority. The "lady of couetise," Lorens taught, also had many scholars, clerical and unlettered, who learned to practice avarice in lawsuits. They included judges who leaned to one side more than the other in response to gifts, orders, or requests; judges who for the same reasons delayed cases; and judges who sold just judgment. All were bound to make restitution equivalent to the harm that they had done.[1]

Simony, named for a "iogelour" who lived by the devil's craft, was, according to this text, one of the greatest sins of all. "Symoners," those buying or selling "gostly" things, included buyers or sellers of the sacraments; those preaching principally for silver; and those bestowing benefices in response to gifts, orders, requests, armed force, or charms. Many other sins belonging to simony but pertaining principally to clerics were intentionally omitted from this book addressed to laymen. Laymen, Lorens said, needed to know what simony was in three cases: when helping kin or friends to come into a church dignity, when endowing a church, and when giving a child to religious life.[2]

Apparitors, beadles, and the catchpoles of secular judges who forced innocent men "to buy back their harassment" were also arraigned in Memoriale presbiterorum, a representative manual for confessors written in 1344. The author, an anonymous English canonist at Avignon, also called the confessor's attention to the sins of "the archdeacons of our times" and the sins of their servants. "Hounds of hell," the servants oppressed those subject to them, inventing farfetched or feigned grounds for their oppressions and being particularly prone to extort offerings (munera).[3] Simony was personified in Manuale sacerdotis, written about 1400 to instruct a relative by John Mirk, a Shropshire prior. Dramatizing the contrast with the good vicar he wanted his kinsman to be, Mirk showed an unworthy, worldly priest who was aided by Master Symon, "potent in word and work with the bishop and all his servants." Employing Gregory the Great's triple classification of offerings, Mirk found scarcely anyone promoted in the Church except for money, flattery, or service. The sin of simony once committed by such means had unpleasantly long sequelae: "he who enters his benefice with sin must of necessity live henceforth in sins." The sinner most offensive to God—Mirk followed Pierre le Chantre—was a collector for a bishop.[4]

Simpler works gave less attention to the sins involving gifts. Mirk's own Instructions for Parish Priests, a Latin manual, had under Avarice merely the question, "Have you practised simony, spiritual things to sell or buy?"[5] The Instructio of Cardinal John Thoresby—a kind of Latin catechism prepared in 1357 by an ex-chancellor of England and present archbishop of York, translated into English verse by a monk—briefly listed the sins of avarice, generically defined as "immoderate love of temporal goods," and mentioned simony among its species.[6]

Manuals of this sort do not show what was in fact confessed. A remarkable public confession was made in 1354 in the Livre des Seyntz Medicines, where conventional sins were appropriated by the repentant author and acknowledged to be his own. Aged forty-four and commonly reputed to be a good man, Henry, duke of Lancaster, admitted that out of sinful lust he had seduced women and that, as a consequence of his sinful anger, men had been beaten, maimed, and killed.[7] Nothing so specific as these self-accusations came into his mind as to simony or bribetaking. When he confessed to covetousness, he admitted that his feet were fast to seek sinfully "un beau present," but he did not charge himself with distorting judgment or buying ecclesiastical office for friends or relatives.[8] Like the laymen visualized by the simpler books on confession, he seemed to himself clean of corrupt acts and thoughts. Near the apex of the social order he was not troubled by guilt as a simoniacal ecclesiastical patron, a bribegiving litigant, or a bribetaking judge.

At the same time Duke Henry had no hesitation in appealing to influence in the heavenly court where he, "a false traitor" to his God, would be judged. On judgment day Jesus the Judge would show his wounds and the instruments of his passion. The mercy of the Judge would need reinforcement. Before St. Michael who would weigh his sins, the duke would need "all aid and favors." The Queen of Heaven was requested to "sweetly supplicate from her heart her blessed very dear Son, that he pardon me." The duke prayed: "Against my great sins, Lord, let there be in the balance the sufferings which your very sweet mother suffered for love of you in this life and also those of the men and women who are saints." Verbally the equivalent of the judgment scenes done in stone on the tympana of cathedrals, the duke's prayers were like the offerings of the mouth denounced by Gregory the Great when operating in an earthly context. Unself-consciously they reflected a judicial process in which powerful intercessors, especially queens, made a difference.[9]

Penitential literature reminded confessors and, indirectly, those who came to confession that simony and bribe-seeking were sins. Individual penitents could be complacent. Against complacency were the preachers or at least some preachers. Available about 1350 for those with access to a manuscript of it was John Bromyard's *Summa praedicantium*, a compendium for homilists, chiefly on moral topics.[10] Under a variety of headings—Adultery, the Clerical Order, Correction, Honor, Judges, Justice, Offering, Simony, the World—Bromyard struck again and again at corruption. Native of Hereford, student of Oxford, orthodox Dominican, he found corruption everywhere. Mixing didacticism and satire, argument and illustrations, despair and exhortation, Bromyard provided an arsenal of ammunition for anyone ready to give a sermon against corruption in Church or society.

Under "Offering" (*Munus*), Bromyard begins with the verse become familiar to nearly every priest from the use of Psalm 26 in the mass, "Those whose right hands are full of offerings." The sin of *munera*, he says, is sometimes only that of the receivers, sometimes of both receivers and givers. It is not a sin to give offerings openly to a lord who is harming one, or secretly to servants and bailiffs in order to lessen delays: here one buys back one's harassment (*redemit vexationem*); here the praise of Proverbs 21:14 for a hidden offering has a place. Why in other cases is it wrong to give offerings? Clearly it is sinful when it leads to an unjust decision. In other cases, it does spiritual harm to the givers when they acquire victory unworthily. It is a "daily abuse" that some give offerings willingly—for example, it has recently been reported that a man regularly gave a great prelate twenty pounds to keep his concubine, stopping his payments when he decided to dismiss her. Others pay the judge's assistants (*assessores*) to do justice, "which, as to the truth of the matter, is injustice." Skillfully accommodating the biblical texts favorable to giftgiving, admitting the standard justification of buying off harassment, Bromyard nonetheless insists that *munera*-givers will often be sinners. The influenced recipients—whether of offerings of the hand or of the mouth—are unsparingly condemned. The most serious of feudal faults is charged against them. *Munera*-taking judges are guilty of "treason" to God. They are bound to make restitution to those injured by them. The judgment on them is the judgment of Job 15:34: "Fire shall devour the tabernacles of those who freely take offerings."[11]

Against the *munera*-takers Bromyard employs a bestiary. They are like pigs—"Call to one to give him something and all run and clamor seeking something for themselves." Dogs, they are angriest when anything is taken away or discontinued. Wolves, they frighten into silence those who seek justice from them. Wolves, they want something for their children—a benefice for a son at school, a pension for a son practicing law. Worse than the wolves who brought up Romulus and Remus, they despoil orphans, widows, and other simple wards. Beavers, they hold men in their teeth. Crueler than lynxes, who can be satiated, they have eye and hand open for offerings whether their belly is full or not. They are like Gehazi, the leper, and Judas, the traitor, and worse than either: those men sought offerings for their lawful wives and children; the modern *munera*-takers seek offerings for their concubines and bastards. *Munera* go to prelates' nephews to be spent by them on whores, so a whore's hire—the harsh word from Micah 1:7 is read as a prophecy—circles round to a whore. Receiving offerings, they take justice away from those deserving it, blind their own eyes, deny God and themselves, and act as though it were God who were "deaf and blind."[12]

Sinful *munera*-takers specifically include prelates and their servants who receive offerings "for buy back of sins" especially from those in religion, who sin doubly by using the property of the Church to redeem themselves. Bailiffs, constables, and summoners (process-servers) are another class of *munera*-takers—they cite those who fail to give "until something is given and harassment is bought off by throwing something in the dog's mouth." Jurors—"the twelve Apostles of falsity and Antichrist"—who go to London to declare the truth of a matter and will take one day from one party and the next from the other and be aggrieved if one juror gets more than another are among these sinners. Judges who will take twelve pence from the false side but say that for only six pence they will decide for the just side are *munera*-takers. Judges who take plead custom for what they accept. They act unreasonably and contrary to the charity they should have for themselves, for those they judge, and for God. Damaging "the whole community" are judges who, either before or after imposing a death sentence on robbers, let them "buy back their lives at a bargain"; so that a thief today can steal one hundred pounds and redeem his life for twenty.[13]

Judges are meant to be pillars of the Church. Judges today are rotten or weak or slanted pillars, of bad marble, not straight under great pressures, so slanted toward cupidity that "the whole superstructure falls," crushing beneath it the judges' subjects. Judgments are often marked by discrimination (*acceptio personarum*). When is it seen in an ecclesiastical or a secular court that a judge condemns a friend? The service and livery of a worldly lord or great prelate is a shield, a letter of protection, a safe conduct from all correction.[14] Corrupt judges are particularly visible in marriage cases—cases that would be decided in the court of the bishop. The marriages of Christians have become like those of the debauched: "so now when a wife displeases or another is lusted after on account of her beauty or this sort of thing, an annulment is procured." Under *Advocatus* Bromyard ridicules advocates for always believing their clients because their fees came from them. Almost alone among medieval moralists he also explicitly charges lawyers with giving offerings to judges, court officials, and jurors. Under Adultery he accuses both advocates and judges of receiving *munera* and acquiescing—often, though not invariably—in false testimony.[15]

Judges exist, Bromyard observes, who accept offerings and do nothing in return for them. They are not free from fault. Ingrates, they should restore the gifts to the givers. He knows in fact of a magistrate whose chamberlain received a splendid gold cup from a litigant seeking a manor, and when it came to his attention he ordered it returned. The story is told with approval. Bromyard was not ready to treat every offering as illicit and forfeit and so to be given to the poor. Implicit in his story is the ineffectiveness of secular law and the absence of any clear secular rules governing the reception and restitution of gifts by judges.[16]

Munera are also hard to distinguish from officially imposed commutations of corporal penances for cash. Bromyard wonders if there is a difference. Ecclesiastical judges making these commutations, he says, "punish a purse" and reduce sins "to a farm under an annual rent." As the income from fines goes to the officeholder imposing the fine, the distinction between a commutation and the taking of *munera* is hard to see. In a single sentence Bromyard merges payoffs and commutations: "Adulterers and fornicators can always stay together by means of a little money given to the summoners or to the ecclesiastical judges." Making these commutations, the judges have been seduced by cupidity and have become "proctors of the devil and promoters of the vices." At other points, Bromyard separates commutations from *munera* and ponders the penology involved. Why are commutations, as distinct from *munera*, wrong? He answers that the authorities are supposed to be applying medicine. Commutations are medicine applied not to the sinner's wound but to his cash. Authorities say that they are afflicting the sinner. They do not do so in a divine way: he who sins in the body should be afflicted in the body. They say the money paid as commutation goes to charity for the poor. The answer is that of Judas (cf. John 12:4–5). They say that sinners fear the pecuniary penalty. Why then do kings and lords of the earth come to the judges asking commutation of corporal penances to money offerings? The cupidity of the judges is not to be wondered at; it is natural and regrettable. The majority accept office not with zeal to do justice but with the intention of collecting money. They have a partnership with devils: as devils take joy that many sin, so these "take joy in this, that many sin so that they may acquire profit from their crimes."[17]

Among the clergy, simony is rampant. Scarcely one in a hundred priests would seek priesthood or promotion if not for the stipend or benefice attached. "I have come to have life more abundantly than I otherwise would have" is their cynical variation on Jesus' promise in John 10:10. Their sin lies in their intention, like the seven husbands who preceded Tobias and were struck dead for their lustful intentions toward Sarah (Tobias 6 and 7). Some, it is true, avoid paying *munus* in cash or property. "Scarcely anyone" avoids the simony of offerings of flattery or service: so those who write in support of any unworthy candidate or who order or who request his appointment, and those who respond to the order or request, are simoniac. Some who do not dare offer cash as a gift do offer cash as a loan, with the simoniacal intent of being promoted. Simonians include laymen who buy or sell the patronage of churches, and those who give *munera* to be made advocates or defenders. Simonians include prelates who license pardoners to go about their dioceses and "receive big money and a share of what they make from all their lies." Bishops would issue licenses to pardoners gratis if the pardoner's work were just.[18]

Unworthy men are simoniacally elected or chosen by patrons for benefices. Such electors or patrons "stain the Church because they put pigs in it, that is, those leading a piggish life." When a prelate attempts to correct "a damned pig," the pig takes the rebuke as an affront; all his accomplices and supporters run to his aid. Rectors of churches hire vicars at a small part of the parish income. "Middlemen and mercenaries," the hirelings cannot perform the tasks of a good parish priest. What account will the rector give to God "when he takes more and yet does not put in personal labor?" With God it is not to be believed that there be "such injustice or such discrimination (*acceptio personarum*)" as to acquit the rectors. From him who takes more from the sheep, more will be demanded at the final accounting. Rectors should recall Deuteronomy 23:1: a eunuch —"that is, one impotent to generate spiritual sons"—"shall not enter the Church of God."[19]

Under *Honor,* Bromyard addresses corruption in the Roman curia, tactfully sparing the pope: "Coming to aid my father's nakedness I intend to veil the pudenda." He speaks instead of the lifestyle of the cardinals who live on "offerings and exactions." Need is pleaded by the curia. The excuse fails. The cardinals themselves have fallen into need by superfluous expenses spent on servants and horses and incurred by inordinate affection for relatives. Income of a diocese for the first year from those consecrated at the curia, or income of a vacant diocese, could be taken by the cardinals without great sin yet still not without great scandal. Those who have to pay these large sums must borrow at usury, pledge the revenues of the churches to their creditors, and exercise tyranny over their subjects to pay off the loans. Scandalizing "the weak flock who believe in Christ and who were bought back by his blood," the cardinals should recollect themselves and restrain their demands. Let them henceforth live on assigned portions, not on *munera* and exactions. If one turns to *Munus,* one sees that Bromyard has treated the cardinals like those servants whose guilty master has made them live on offerings and filthy lucre (*turpe lucrum*). The master is responsible for the servants' sins.[20]

Job and Isaiah, Psalms and Proverbs, negative images like Gehazi and Judas and positive images like Samuel—again and again Bromyard grounded his discourse in the Bible. Canons and Roman law, Augustine's letter to Macedonius, Pietro Damiani's story of Ildebrando and the tongue-tied simonian bishop, John of Salisbury on the Cerberuses of the curia, St. Bernard's rebukes to Eugene III in *De consideratione,* Lotario's *The Misery of the Human Condition,* Jacques de Vitry's tale of the woman who oiled the judge's hands, not to mention pagan authorities such as Cicero and Seneca and pagan exemplars like Cambyses, rounded out the homiletic matter. References to local bailiffs and London jurors had the ring of experience; Bromyard's view of the curia seemed largely shaped by John of Salisbury, St. Bernard, and Innocent III. To use him was to plunge into a grand cornucopia on corruption. Under the covers of one book he gathered the themes and texts of the antibribery tradition.[21]

Against the stern background of the tradition, his judgment of the power of *munus* was classically severe:

> With the clergy as with the religious orders, *munus* or *nummus* (cash) is the lord of the sciences and of the churches. Everywhere it opens the palaces of the earth and the doors of chambers. And in all the earth it kills and brings to life; it leads to hell and brings back. It opens and closes prisons. It kills souls which do not die and brings to life souls which do not die . . . . It closes and no one opens. It opens and no one closes. And briefly, if fortitude is sought, it is very strong; if melody or jollity, it is very jolly. Cash conquers, cash reigns, cash commands the world.[22]

Bromyard has inverted Innocent III's invocation of the Christ of the Apocalypse. Now it is money that opens and shuts irrevocably. Without offerings, "nothing happens."

Infidels, scandalized, now hold the Christian faith in contempt. Christian princes and lords, whose ancestors built the walls of the Church, now hold cheap the ecclesiastical state and now tear down the walls. Because of the crimes of individuals the Church should not be despoiled, but the behavior of lords today is not a remarkable response to the Church's "most open ruin and infamy." "The state of the modern Church and of Christianity" is "most filthy and quasi-destroyed." Enemies are within. Bad clergy abound. "It is probably to be feared that in this the wound of the Church has been made incurable."[23]

Taken at face value, Bromyard's account was of a system seriously if not mortally impaired. He still did not reject the system. Respectful of the pope, cautious toward the cardinals, he was harsh on prelates, patrons, and priests, and even these Simonians he did not denounce as heretics. If he labored so hard in a literary way, if he marshaled satire and exhortation so strenuously, it had to be—at least in terms of conscious purpose—that he harbored hope of reformation and believed that corruption could be corrected by knowledge and repentance. Preachers in the same path, drawing on his repertoire, followed.

The church in England, preached Thomas Brunton, Benedictine, bishop of Rochester, and Edward III's confessor, is in greater servitude than under Pharaoh. Bishops who desire great office or want to be moved to richer sees predominate. Dumb dogs, they are silent as to evils and fawn upon the powerful. Simon Magician, he had heard, tried to resurrect the dead: such is the omnipotence of money today that it is necessary to point out that Simon Magician was not successful.[24] "Redempcioun, that is forbiggynge," said an anonymous vernacular sermon, "is what officials and deans call the silver they take, but it is open extorcioun or robbynge." Officials and deans, preached John Waldeby, Austin friar, cite and despoil the poor and the simple, not strong enough to resist, but license fornicators for money. The judges of the Church, Thomas Wimbledon, secular chaplain, stated in a sermon, have only a single medicine, which they call the "pecuniary penalty." If it is medicine, it should be called "a laxative medicine for purses," not "a medicine for souls." Most priests are worse than most laymen, preached Nicholas Philip, Franciscan. They are priests of Baal and of Dagon in their lust for "benefices, offices, pensions," collecting money for "their own nephews, their sons, and prostitutes." Like Solomon (1 Kgs 10:22), the Church has brought apes from Tarshish when it has promoted these priests to prelates.[25]

Multiple functions were performed by these sermons against corruption. Castigating others, they implicitly presented the preacher as a champion untainted by the faults he perceived. Like the fourth-century edicts of the emperors they shifted blame from the speaker. A form of permitted discontent—although at times, according to Brunton, actually forbidden by royal officials—they performed the valuable function of verbal criticism without physical consequences.[26] Titillating their audiences with the scandals which they reproved, they acted like a modern newspaper, simultaneously exposing wrong and bringing profit to the exposer. Calling for personal and corporate reform, they sometimes subverted all effort by setting standards too high or describing conditions as beyond earthly repair. On occasion, their satire, their idealism, their clear call to conscience must have stirred the embers of charity. The preachers proclaimed a conflict between perceived practices and established categories of sin. To the homilists and to parts of their audience the categories were measures with spiritual significance. Austins, Benedictines, Carmelites, Cistercians, Dominicans, Franciscans, secular clergy, and bishops—if only a distinct minority of any of these groups—thought that the categories must be communicated and applied if changes in the contemporary Church were to occur.[27]

Here is one of the most famous preachers of this age of preachers, Richard FitzRalph, archbishop, preaching to his colleagues: Greater and lesser prelates exist who are adulterers with several whores. Others are drunkards. There are also prelates who are stealers of church property, who give not only movable goods but immovables to nephews and nieces (he will not speak of sons and daughters). "Prelates there are who are ravishers, robbers and thieves and so are they who take the fruits of churches and hold ministerial service in total contempt, who always exert themselves crying 'Shear, shear. Take, take,' and never fulfill the command, 'Feed, feed.' They feed themselves, they destroy their subjects." Others are "merchants, selling to laymen for definite sums of money not only tithes but the advantages flowing from their spiritual jurisdiction." The common and greatest peril of ecclesiastical office is simony, the sin of Simon Magician and Gehazi and Balaam. The sin is especially committed in seeking office. "Perhaps scarcely any among those promoted" is free of simony. The sin does not consist merely in giving money—Simon Magician did not complete his gift: "the crime of simony was his bad will by which he wanted to possess God's gift for money." He could have committed the sin by offering clothes, horses, sheep, cows, or the prayers of others. "And how many these days are not promoted by petitions procured by them which—not to lie—are clearly their own *munera*; for they commonly buy the petitions dearly enough from the petitioners. Very few would be heard unless offerings effactually interceded." What are the consequences? "As long as one detains a benefice simoniacally acquired, so long does he hold what is not his own and is a thief and a robber." Whether the sin of simony committed is mortal or venial, a benefice acquired by simony is "infected in its title." Any title is invalid if won by simoniacal means. "And who is he, my brothers, if he truthfully examines his own conscience, who does not report in his obtaining of office the brokerage of sin? I think that such a man is found most rarely."[28]

FitzRalph, primate of Ireland, addressed these words to an unknown number of bishops and other dignitaries of the Church gathered in a provincial synod at Drogheda, February 7, 1352. Stopping just short of calling simony a heresy—he did associate the Balaam of Numbers 22 who received *munera* to curse Israel with the heretical Balaamites denounced in the letter of Jude—FitzRalph unmistakably implied that most of his audience held their offices sinfully. Anticlimactically, he added that he had heard that "some prelates" scarcely ever conferred a benefice except for cash paid or assured advantage post factum. "As Joseph instructed his brothers," FitzRalph meant to instruct his fellow bishops. "Before the tribunal of the High King, Christ," when called to render their accounts, they would, he prayed, be found shepherds, not merchants. In this Latin address which cannot have taken more than forty minutes to deliver, FitzRalph, Joseph-like, fulfilled his mission.[29]

FitzRalph's own career in the Church was a moderate success despite his outspokenness and keen sense of sin. Born in Dundalk, of Norman descent, he had been a student at Oxford and in 1332–1334, still in his thirties, its chancellor. Thanks to the friendship of Jean Grandisson, a Burgundian who was bishop of Exeter and a friend of the reigning pope, Benedict XII, he had become dean of Lichfield in 1335. Conducting litigation for Lichfield at Avignon, he became known to the pope himself. When in 1346 he was asked for as their archbishop by the canons of Armagh, the pope agreed—a recognition, he could think, of his abilities as a theologian and administrator. An English-speaking native of Ireland, familiar with the curia, he was an obviously sound political choice for a see under English domination. Perhaps FitzRalph himself was one of those unusual men who never asked another to get him office; still, at Avignon he himself had obtained Irish benefices for three of his own nephews. Armagh itself was an honor, but to judge from the time he spent away from it—about half of his incumbency—it was not the most attractive of sees. In Ireland, after his death, he was reputed a saint, and the cult of "St. Richard of Dundalk" lasted into the seventeenth century. At Avignon, where he died in 1360 after three years of prolonged controversy with the friars, he remained uncanonized.[30]

When FitzRalph was in Avignon it was the custom of the curia to invite him to preach before it on one of the two feast days of St. Thomas of Canterbury. On July 7, 1340, or December 29, 1340, he exhorted the prelates on business at the curia to take St. Thomas as a model and to judge whether they were mercenaries or pastors. On July 7, 1341 or December 29, 1341, in the *audientia causarum* or courtroom, he attacked simony, discrimination in favor of relatives, the simoniacal chase for prebends, and corrupt judges. Asked to address the Dominicans in their own church, he punned fearlessly, describing the Dominicans (*Domini canes*) as *canes muti non valentes* or dumb ineffectual dogs.[31]

Back in Avignon in 1349 he again exhorted his curial hearers to imitate St. Thomas and spoke boldly against *munera*-takers. He added, "I do not say these things because I suspect some such are here, because I do not think that ever in the Church of God can such just judgments be found as in the apostolic palace." In his own experience, in the seven-year long case of the canons of Lichfield against the archbishop of Canterbury, "a much more powerful adversary," every judgment had been in the canons' favor: "God will give a good turn to those judges for their just judgments to my person; and in that whole time I did not find in them the vice treated here." A "good turn" was another pun, a kindly wish for the judges whose panels were turns upon the wheel of the Rota. That equally just judgments were not to be found elsewhere had to be rhetorical exaggeration. Yet it is hard to believe that this intrepid preacher in his flattery stooped to falsehood. His sermon must stand as one testimony to integrity at the curia.[32]

Bromyard observed that general friends are received in the hall, particular friends in the bedchamber—he wanted sermons to be particular so that they could be intimately received.[33] He and the classic preachers of the fourteenth century abounded in illustrations. Yet even as forthright a man as FitzRalph used examples, when he spoke critically, which lacked names, dates, places. We get no information about identified sinners. We are far from a case in court. We are sure only of the preacher's sense that the problem is pressing and general. Declamatory and denunciatory, sometimes satirical, the sermons cannot be read literally as exact sociological description. Quantification on the basis of their sweeping statements would be hazardous.

The more outspoken sermons have been described as "a primary literature of secular revolt" which "has not been exceeded, probably, by the most outspoken champions of social revolution in any age"; and the sermons have been seen not only as bringing social discontent to a boil but as affecting the foundations of the Church, as "the prelude to a revolt."[34] The truth of these claims has not been demonstrated. The evidence on which they are based includes Bromyard's summa and FitzRalph's sermons, and these were in fact addressed to special audiences unlikely to be moved to revolution by a depiction of ecclesiastical evils. Not a single bishop resigned his see after FitzRalph at Drogheda had spelled out the consequences of simoniacal acquisition.[35] Were all his hearers the rare innocent men? Only by accumulation and slow wear on the conscience do sermons usually work. Yet preaching itself, as FitzRalph's own diary indicates, was generally limited to Advent, Lent, and the Easter season and then normally tied to the Epistle or Gospel of the day.[36] A sermon on corruption would not have been a regular Sunday's fare. Isolation of the material on corruption produces a misleading picture of a massive assault made by men alienated from the hierarchy. Instead, most of the critics—Bromyard, Brunton, FitzRalph are illustrative—throve within the establishment. Far from being revolutionaries themselves, they did not seek to overturn the system. What they did perpetuate was a cluster of themes as old as John of Salisbury, St. Bernard, and Innocent III and what they did provide was a set of stereotypes of corrupt officials. In more powerful literary hands these themes and types would become enduring criticism; in bolder hands they could be used to stir revolt. The words of preachers, John Bromyard said in the Prologue to his summa, are called sparks and like sparks they ought to fly to different places. Like sparks, too, they could fall on bare ground and die or they could ignite a conflagration.[37]

The Mastery of Mede.   In a vision William the poet sees a woman in scarlet dress banded with gold and trimmed with the finest fur, a crown on her head, amethysts, beryls, diamonds, sapphires, rubies on her fingers. He asks his guide, Holy Church, her identity. Holy Church, a lady herself, has told him that of all treasures truth is the best, and she now introduces the other woman: "That is Mede the mayde," and procedes to delineate her character.[38]

Mede, Holy Church declares, has often been where she is:

> In the popis paleys • she is as pryve as my-self.
>
> (*Piers Plowman*, 2, 22)

That is, Mede is as familiar as the Church with the pope. But she is to be avoided at all costs. As Psalm 14 teaches, he who takes *munera* does not dwell with the Lord (2, 38). Mede is in fact a bastard, the daughter of Fals, and she is about to be married to Fals Fikel-tonge. The ceremony is being attended by a vast assembly of knights, clerics, jurors, summoners, sheriffs, beadles, bailiffs, brokers, victuallers, and lawyers. Those who are most familiar of any of the men with her are Symonye, Cyuile, and the jurors (2, 62). A wedding deed is produced announcing that Mede is being married only for her property. The wedding, however, is interrupted by Theologye who denounces it as contrary to truth. Mede, she protests, is "a mayden of gode." She is kissing kin of the king and intended by God for honest work (2, 131–132).

By personification the poet has captured the ambiguity of the basic Latin word for bribe. *Munus* can be the honest return given a laborer or it can be the chief mischief-maker in the pope's palace and the corrupt friend of simony, secular law (Cyuile), and jurors. Truth taught by the Church will expose the character in which it acts. In the poem *Munus* is Mede.[39]

The lawfulness of Mede's marriage to Fals Fikel-tonge is tried in the king's court at Westminster. Mede is well-received by all, the clerks declare that they are hers, and some judges, with the clergy's leave, take pains to comfort her, assuring her that she can marry as she wills (3, 9–19). She responds with gifts of

> Coupes of clene gold • and coppis of siluer,
> Rynges with rubies • and ricchesses manye.
>
> (3, 22–23)

—gold and silver cups, many valuables, and goldpieces for the least retainers. The clergy come to comfort her as the judges have done. She assures them she'll make them lords and that she is known where learning would not help them (3, 32). Her confession is then heard by a friar who offers her absolution for a load of wheat. Growing bolder, he suggests she pay for a stained-glass window that will bear her name. She offers to roof his church, build his cloister, whitewash his walls, and glaze his windows if he will be similarly easy on all lords and ladies who are lechers (3, 51–64). The king escorts Mede into his private chambers and offers to arrange a marriage for her with his knight, Conscience. Conscience, however, refuses. Mede has ruined those who love her gifts. She has poisoned popes and corrupted Holy Church and destroyed the king's father. She is "tikil of hire taile," that is, sexually excitable and promiscuous (3, 130). She is, it is true, respected by jurors, summoners, jailors, and sheriffs. She and Symonye seal the pope's own bulls (3, 147). She makes illiterates into bishops and provides livings for priests with concubines and children. At the royal court she does more in one month than the king's privy seal can do in six. In law courts, "She ledeth the lawe as hire list," that is, she decides the law; and a case will not end unless she provides presents or pence (3, 157, 160–161). Poor men have no power to get redress (3, 167). Mede brings disaster to all honest men.

Mede's reply is that she would have won France for the king's father (Edward III) if Conscience had not given him a coward's advice to make peace. Moreover, she points out, it becomes a king to give mede himself:

> Mede maketh hym biloued • and for a man holden.
>
> (3, 211)

Giving gifts, he becomes beloved and a real man in reputation. Emperors and earls and every kind of lord use gifts to keep young men about them. The pope and all prelates partake of presents and themselves "medeth men," that is, give them *munera*. Beggars seek mede, and minstrels for making mirth seek mede. Those that teach children want mede. Priests who preach ask mede; merchants and mede must go together. No one on earth "with-oute mede may libbe" (3, 224). The king is left in admiration:

> bi Criste! as me thynketh,
> Mede is well worthi • the maistrye to have!
>
> (3, 227–228)

Conscience will not concede Mede's mastery. There are "two manere of medes." The one is what God gives by his grace. The other is what is condemned by Psalm 26, "Their right hands are full of *munera*" (3, 247). What laborers receive is not mede at all, but hire, and what merchants get is an exchange, one pennyworth for another. Conscience's voice swells to prophesy of a time when Mede shall no more prevail and reason shall rule and law will be an honest workman (3, 283, 297). Mede retorts by quoting Wisdom: "He who gives *munera* acquires honor" (3:333). Conscience responds with another quotation "It [*munus*] takes away the soul of those taking it" (3:346). In short,

The soule that the sonde taketh • bi so moche is bounde.

(3, 349)

The soul that takes a gift is bound by it.

The king continues to seek to bring Conscience and Mede together and for advice turns to Resoun, that is, Reason, a figure identified at points with the Logos or Christ. A case comes before the king where the defendant Wrong is charged with abduction, rape, robbery, forestalling, and incitement to murder. Wrong goes to Wisdom and Wit who turn to Mede to get a pardon for him (4, 63–77). The king stands firm and orders him fettered. Wisdom and Wit press the king to let Wrong be bailed. Mede offers the complainant a present of pure gold to agree to this settlement. Resoun advises the king to stay firm. Meanwhile Mede is winking at the lawyers. Chuckling, they desert Resoun to join her. Yet most people in the hall and many of the great men think Mede a slut, and the greater part of the court call her a whore. The king's verdict is in accord with Resoun's; Wrong is sentenced; bail is refused. In the future the king will have honesty in law. Conscience remarks that without the help of the community, this will be "ful hard" (4, 183). By Christ on the cross Resoun swears to rule if the king will give him power. By Mary the king swears not to leave Resoun (4, 185–188).

Three books out of twenty of William Langland's *The Vision of William concerning Piers Plowman* are devoted to these adventures and the final discomfiture of *Munus*, alias Mede. At one point the poet deserts the central allegory for an animal fable: When Mede goes to Westminster, Cyuile and Symonye ride on the summoners as horses. Deans, subdeans, archdeacons, *officiales*, and registrars are also to be pressed into service:

Lat sadel hem with siluer • owre synne to suffre.

(2, 174)

So saddled, they are to carry bishops on their visitations. At another point the poet altogether abandons imagery to exhort in his own voice. He attacks offerings given to the Church out of pride, denounces officers and mayors who take money, plate, and rings to let fraudulent retailers stay in business undisturbed, and quotes the doom predicted by Job 15:34 on those "who freely take *munera*." He translates:

this latyn is to mene,
That fyre shal falle, and brenne • al to blo askes
The houses and the homes • of hem that desireth
Giftes or yeresgyues • bi-cause of here offices.

(3, 96–99)

—fire from heaven, houses in livid ashes for those taking gifts by reason of office either in the course of the year or, as must have already been the custom, at New Year's. The biblical judgment, first set out in Latin, is stern and absolute.[40]

Reciprocity also rules in heaven. When a poor man comes to Judgment, Pacience declares, he can plead and prove by pure reason that God should treat him well:

> Ioye that neuere ioye hadd • of rightful Jugge he axeth.
>
> (14, 110)

Never having had joy, he who was created for joy, dares ask joy from his just Judge. A rich man, on the contrary, has been paid by God in advance. He can get another reward after death only if he "rewarde wel the pore" (14, 46).

In the final book of *Piers*, after the seven deadly sins have been reviewed, the necessity of restitution inculcated, lords urged to take over the Church's corrupting possessions, kindness to the poor insisted upon, the life of Christ-like love extolled, and the passion, death, and resurrection of Jesus recounted, William dreams of the coming of Antecryste. He comes in the form of a man, he roots up truth, and he is much followed by the friars; Symonye appoints prelates who take his side. At the king's court, covetousness takes the form of a bold baron who with gold bears down most of "the witte and wisdom of Westmynster halle" (20, 132). A few words in a justice's ear "overtilte al his treuthe" (20, 134). Earlier the poet has suggested that justice nowadays depends upon a present, a prayer, or a prince's letter (19, 304). At the ecclesiastical Court of Arches, the baron turns civil law into simony, beginning with payments to the *officialis*:

> For a mantel of menyuere • he made lele matrimonye
> Departen al deth cam • and deuors shupte.
>
> (20, 137–138)

—that is, for a mantle of miniver or ermine the baron made true marriage depart before death and set up annulments. Conscience wishes the baron were a Chrsitian, he is such a keen fighter "while his bagge lasteth" (20, 141). Life laughs at this naïve hope and goes off with his concubine, Fortune.

Unlike the triumph of Conscience and Resoun over Mede in the earlier part, no victory is provided in the time of Antecryste. The poem ends somberly. The friars are crawling everywhere, Sloth and Pride are attacking Conscience, and Piers Plowman, a figure variously identified with Saint Peter or Christ, is absent. Conscience leaves on a pilgrimage to find him, crying aloud for grace (20, 384).

On the margin of society, William Langland voiced complaints that are marked by the anger, alienation, and vagueness of an outsider looking at a system whose motions he does not entirely understand. He draws on a century of sermons in the tradition of Bromyard's sermon topics and on a variety of vernacular verse—for example, *The Simonie*, whose anonymous author had also found Truth afraid to enter the pope's palace and arch-deacons taking mede of this one and that one.[41] He had fed on the scholastic tradition—for example, the identification of ecclesiastical bribetaking with simony going back to Pierre le Chantre and his English pupil Thomas Chobhan—and on conventional satire of the curia, satire here handled with great restraint. Scripture had nourished him most. Out of these public themes, the poet made a personal work—the life project of a man uncelebrated by his contemporaries, a professional acolyte paid for his prayers, with a wife Kitte and a girl Kalote (18, 426), now old, bald, and impotent if the autobiographical parts can be trusted (20, 183, 195), who entered upon his project carrying on his back the mark of Job.[42]

In *Piers*, a man wrestles with evil, and a large part of that evil as he observes it takes place in acts of bribery in the king's court and the bishop's. No more brilliant analysis has ever been made of the ambiguity of *munera* and the omnipresence of reciprocity in human affairs than the allegory of Mede the maid. The allegory is enriched by full exploitation of the sexual metaphors for the bribetaker, boldly applied to Mede herself as a bribegiver. The concluding world under Antichrist, so far from the kingdom ruled by the Logos, is amazingly bleak—mundane, one might say. Its evils are social. Escape from it is personal and by God's gift. In the time of Antichrist—that is, now 1378—Resoun and Conscience do not hold sway at the Arches, Westminster, or the pope's palace.[43]

The Quasi-Indelible Stain.   The pope commits simony when he seeks the office for worldly motives; when he multiplies laws for his own gain; and when he appoints pastors for temporal advantage. And in fact today "the Avignonian nest" is the very fount of simony. The "worst merchants" buy from the pope. Annates paid the pope—the regular tax on the first year's revenues of a newly appointed bishop—are simoniacally taken. The pope appoints to benefices not from the love of souls but out of "Luciferian domination" and for "the profit of his own temporalities." Apologists who say that all the goods of the Church belong to the pope so he cannot commit simony, or who say that what the pope does cannot be sinful as if he were impeccable, set him up as Antichrist. Today there reigns a pseudo-pope, an antipope, an Antichrist.[44]

Bishops commit simony when they enter office for temporal profits; when they spend the poor's money on themselves, maintaining large households and grooms for their horses; when they collect money for their services as they do, for example, by charging five marks for the consecration of a holy place; when they wink at charges by their servants (there is even a small charge made by the clerk registering the names of the newly ordained); or when they sell staff appointments like the office of summoner. To say that what they get is given voluntarily is a sophism: if one did not pay one would get nothing from them. They say they charge only for their labor—they are like vendors who claim to give away some things but actually charge more for the total. Today in England few or no prelates are not simonian heretics.[45]

Today in England few or no clergy are promoted without simony. Priests are Simonians when they pay for promotions or when they go to Rome with a simonian will, seeking benefices and in fact doing business with the cardinals and their servants. Monks are Simonians preferring kinfolk and the rich to the devout in admitting candidates. Monks are Simonians appropriating the revenues of parishes. Monks are Simonians aspiring to be prelates. Simony flourishes as well in collegiate churches and in universities. Simony is practiced by the laity who sell the patronage of ecclesiastical appointments "like cattle" and by the laity who appoint to livings those priests they prefer by reason of the tie of blood or marriage. Simony is practiced by all the lords who defend and foster simony. It is practiced also by judges and advocates who unlawfully sell justice. It is practiced by ecclesiastical judges who judge cases involving benefices and act for money or at the request of secular lords. It is also committed by all those who cooperate in its commission—those who act to arrange it; those who defend it in scholastic disputes; those who counsel it; and those who are silent about it out of servile fear or for temporal gain, as are the majority of the mendicant friars in England, who in public preaching or private exhortation, in counseling or in confession, keep mute about the sin.[46]

Corruption of the Church in England in 1379 is described in these terms by John Wyclif in his Latin tract, *De simonia* (*Simony*). His strictures must be understood in the framework of his more general view of the Church. Earlier in the 1370s he had focused on a concept used more moderately by Richard FitzRalph—*dominium*, that is, dominion, lordship, mastership, or absolute ownership. In the age of grace, Wyclif had written, dominion rightly belonged only to a person in a state of grace. The person not in grace lost his title, and the property was forfeit to the Crown. Specifically the doctrine applied to the endowments of the Church in England. Possessed by sinful men, they should be taken over by the king. A battery of English legal concepts was mounted to support the central thesis: eminent domain could be exercised by the civil government in such necessity as now existed; the Statute of Mortmain of 1279 had been repeatedly violated by ecclesiastical bodies; the endowments were forfeit for the treason of their evil possessors.[47]

Legal arguments of this kind gave a technical force to Wyclif's breathtakingly simple theory. Enjoying John of Gaunt's support, he was protected against ecclesiastical reaction in England. At the curia, where his work became linked with antipapalist names like Marsilius of Padua, English critics took care to secure a condemnation from Gregory XI. Papal bulls against him arrived in England. In response to these threats from Rome, Wyclif turned to the ancient doctrine on simony. As in *Civil Dominion* he had crafted legal arguments to support confiscation, so in *Simony* he employed a canonical-theological arsenal to the same effect. The outbreak of the Great Schism and the ambiguities created by the existence of two popes had given Wyclif a little breathing space. After 1378 the English government adhered firmly to Urban VI, and Wyclif needed an ecclesiastical case to meet the censures of the Church, backed by the king.[48]

Simony offered two advantages over "dominion" as a weapon. In terms of it he could speak of the existing ecclesiastical establishment almost as sweepingly as he had done in *Civil Dominion* while using a category of sin with a pedigree of a thousand years. Pursued by his enemies for heresy, he could turn the tables, for if there was any heresy at all simony was heresy. Indeed heresy was of three kinds, apostasy, blasphemy, and simony, and "the first and the pre-eminent" heretic had been Simon Magician. The old term "simonian heresy"—for a century or more understood less than literally—he revived. Few or none of the bishops of England were in his view not heretics, because few or none were not Simonians.[49]

Wyclif said simony consisted in "the inordinate will of exchanging spiritual things for temporal."[50] The novelty of the definition has sometimes been exaggerated. Its emphasis on the subjective did permit him to find simony where there was illicit desire alone, as in the popes, bishops, and monks who aspired to office for worldly motives, and to treat a bishop's lavish expenditure as itself an instance of preferring temporal things to spiritual. Yet Wyclif emphasized intention no more than Bromyard or FitzRalph. Usury—in the whole entirely orthodox tradition of canon law—was analogously treated as determined by the lender's illicit hope of profit.[51] Most of the actual transactions Wyclif assailed could, with a little analysis, have been brought within the canonical definition of simony. It was Augustine and Gregory who taught that there were three kinds of corrupting *munus*—of money, of service, and of flattery—and it was their teaching that Wyclif invoked. Old-fashioned views—Pierre le Chantre's that nepotism was simoniacal and that bribed judges were Simonians —were what he adopted.

The terms in which he emphasized the evil were entirely conventional and often drawn from the texts assembled in Gratian. Simonians were the dove-sellers expelled by Christ. They were lepers covered with leprosy like Gehazi. They were, he said—here following a favorite author of his, the thirteenth-century Dominican summist Guillaume Pérault—spiritual sodomites, "for just as, contrary to nature, the seed from which an individual of the human race is formed is lost in bodily sodomy, so in this sodomy the seed of the Word of God by which spiritual generation is created in Christ Jesus is thrown away." Simonians—here again Wyclif followed Pérault—were worse than Judas for they sold the Son and the Spirit.[52]

Applying the ancient lore, Wyclif showed the boldness and simplicity of a brilliant intellect, mixed with the crankiness sometimes associated with scholarly superiority. No mere scholar—he had served Edward III in negotiating with papal envoys at Bruges and had been for a time John of Gaunt's protégé at court—Wyclif, a former fellow and master of Balliol, can be imagined sitting comfortably in a modern Common Room. Some modern academics have resisted the analogy; it is basically sound. Wyclif possessed an academic's capability of detached criticism of institutions while enjoying their benefits: he himself held several benefices, the most notable, Lutterworth, having been awarded by the king for entirely temporal work. Simonian by his own standard, unless his intent in serving the king had been remarkably pure, he owed restitution of all the income he had received if his own uncompromising analysis was applied to his own holdings. To the end of his life he continued to enjoy his livings while he enjoined reform upon the despised establishment.[53]

How could reform come? It could come from Pope Urban VI. But that would be "an immense and unexpected miracle." It could come from secular lords. But they were afflicted by hypocritical blindness to the evil. It was useless to look to the courts or the bishops. The hierarchy had cleverly insulated itself from criticism by determining that no one was to be called a Simonian unless he was convicted of simony. The Simonians who were the judges would favor rather than punish a Simonian. As a colorblind man could not tell colors, so these judges could not tell simony when they saw it.[54]

The evil was left to be redressed by another judge. Who could wipe out such a stain which was "quasi-indelible"? Who could heal a wound which "had seared so widely"? Where earlier writers would have said "Christ," Wyclif put his trust in the people. The people should reject "the old men" when they are "drunk with avarice"—a remarkably revolutionary note associating age with corruption and making the metaphor of intoxication stand for absorption in wealth. The people should withhold from the ecclesiastics their offerings, their tithes, their gifts, or their bequests creating endowments. *Simony* called for rebellion by the faithful, the peaceful rebellion of noncooperation with the economic system of the Church.[55]

As a by-product of his main endeavors, Wyclif addressed the most vulnerable aspect of the ecclesial economy, indulgences. Clement VI in the bull *Unigenitus*, issued January 27, 1343, had formally adopted Thomas Aquinas's theory of the treasure administered by the pope.[56] With the freedom of one academic correcting another, Wyclif attacked Thomas not Clement. Written before he tried to cast all abuses within the net of simony, his analysis was added as a kind of appendix to his general treatise, *De ecclesia* (*The Church*), and the pope whose administration of indulgences he had principally in mind was the Avignonese Gregory XI.[57] Theological foundation for the traffic in pardons was, Wycliff asserted, wanting: no one "can be entirely released from his debt to God." As he put it in other terms, there is an essential connection between sin and punishment, and from it God himself cannot dispense; or as he less rigidly expressed it, satisfaction for sin is part of the *regalia* or royal prerogatives of God, release from which He cannot permit to be performed vicariously. Moreover, the merits of the saints go to their own account and are not available for distribution. God determines who will profit by the saints' merits. Merits of past deeds cannot be appropriated to help future persons. The whole idea of a treasure of merits gained by suffering and administered by the pope was an invention arising out of "fantastic imagination."[58]

Near the close of his life, in the summer of 1383, Wyclif's attack on indulgences took a more specific shape. The election of rival popes had led not only to schism but to Urban VI declaring a crusade upon his rival and issuing a *Cruciata* or Crusade Bull promising the crusader's pardon to all who enlisted in, or gave to, the campaign. Henry Spencer, bishop of Norwich, was raising troops and money in England with the *Cruciata* as an instrument for recruiting and fund-raising. Wyclif was at first willing to think that "our Urban does not authorize this crime," but when he saw that it was the pope who was behind it, he noted that Paul had rebuked Peter, Bernard had rebuked Eugene III, and he would not refrain from saying that any pope fighting for mastership was violating the law of Christ and was himself an Antichrist. Urban VI's frivolous claim that he had suffered injury was no excuse to kill Christians. In "this cause of the devil," it was a "manifest lie and the abomination of desolation" that it should be said that Christ was granting pardons to participants in the crusade. By "one lie about its future treasure," Satan had "devastated the whole Western Church."[59]

Wyclif had other teachings—on transubstantiation, on confession, on the nature of the Church—which were far from accepted views; and his theory that lawful dominion depended on being in a state of grace was revolutionary if applied to secular property and government. The Peasants' Revolt of 1381—a rising squashed in a month—was seen by his enemies among the friars as the consequence of his doctrine. As always, it is difficult to calculate the force of an idea on social conditions. Economic distress underlay the peasants' move. Other factors at work were popularized versions of Wyclif's ideology and perfectly orthodox preaching against corruption. Sparks spread.[60]

What did not happen was what Wyclif most clearly called for—stripping the Church of endowments, extirpation of simony, the end of indulgences. No rebellion against the ecclesiastical establishment occurred. In 1382 at Oxford, those in control of the English Church, led by William Courtenay, archbishop of Canterbury, condemned Wyclif's teaching on the Eucharist, confession, the papacy, dominion, and endowments (his views on indulgences and simony were not touched). Parliament in May 1382 passed a statute making unauthorized preaching a crime. In June 1382, Richard II accelerated enforcement of the law by authorizing Archbishop Courtenay to imprison unlicensed preachers without resort to the secular courts. Acting in concert, Church and king moved to wipe out Wyclifism.[61]

As a campaigner against corruption, Wyclif had done four things Bromyard and FitzRalph had not: he had treated Simonians as heretics; he had attacked indulgences at their root; he had attacked popes by name; and he had called for a kind of layman's boycott of the corrupt establishment. The legacy of Wyclif to those he taught or among whom his works were popularized was a violent sense of abuses in the Church without practical remedies—withholding contributions was about as practical as a tax revolt in the United States today. The abusive term "Lollard" came into fashion to designate not only those who held radical Wyclifite propositions but to denigrate anyone too interested in reform. Like "Manichee" in the fourth century or "Puritan" in the twentieth, it was a term to put down the zealous. Obscure in origin, "Lollard" had an etymological link with *lollen*, to mumble. Calling all reformers Lollards or mumblers was ironically to invert the real charge against those who too trenchantly repeated the sharp charges articulated by the Oxford scholar.[62]

Chaucer's Choice. "By thyn owene experience," you will be able to speak of hell better than Virgil or Dante: so a summoner is informed by a demon in *The Canterbury Tales*. The addressee of this remark has already confidentially told the demon that without "extorcioun" he could not live. A summoner or process-server—canonically an "apparitor"—was provided with blank citations in which to fill in the names of sinners for summoning before the ecclesiastical court. An unscrupulous summoner could operate on his own, filling in names for his own purposes. This summoner employs girls to trap male customers whom he then shakes down, or he simply fills out summonses which he tells illiterate folk will not be served if they will fill his purse:

> Certeyn he knew of briberyes mo
> Than possible is to tell in yeres two.
>
> (*Canterbury Tales*, F 1367–1368)

"Briberyes" in this context are essentially frauds and extortions. As the story begins, the summoner is

> Feynyenge a cause, for he wolde brybe.
>
> (F 1378)

"Brybe," the verb, designates the action of the official; it is the equivalent of "extort under color of office." The summoner goes on to threaten a poor widow with a bogus excommunication unless she pays him twelve pennies. By her curse he is hauled off to hell. A partner of devils, found already in the pages of Bromyard, he is the sinister, story-within-a-story counterpart of the Somonour who is one of the principal pilgrims riding with Frere Hubert, the teller of this tale.[63]

The Somonour plays the same game himself, less cruelly:

> A bettre felawe sholde men noght fynde.
> He wolde suffre for a quart of wyn
> A good felawe to have his concubyn
> A twelf month, and excuse hym atte fulle.
>
> (P 648–651)

The Somonour is thoroughly irritated at Frere Hubert's lampoon. We have been told of Frere Hubert himself that he is "an esy man to yeve penaunce" to any penitent likely to pay and that he takes a gift to a poor religious order to be a sign of repentance. The Somonour is not now to be put down by his sanctimonious smoothness. He retorts to the friar's story with an anecdote in which 20,000 friars are discovered to live in the devil's arse and with a longer account of a friar, John, whom he introduces preaching "trentals" or thirty masses for the dead. Pay now, free a soul from purgatory at once, is Frere John's message:

> "Delivereth out," quod he, anon the soules!
> Ful hard it is with flesshhook or with oules
> To been yclawed, or to brenne or bake.
> Now spede yow hastily, for Cristes sake!
>
> (ST 1729–1732)

Hooks or awls, frying or baking—these are the tortures from which a small donation to the preacher will release the dead.[64]

Skilled in begging, Friar John is unctuous with women and adroit with men. Attempting to get a big gift from Thomas, a sick layman who has already spent a lot on the friars, he is told he will receive something if he will divide it with his brothers. Groping down Thomas's back for the offering, he receives an immense fart, whose dimensions are dwelt on like the devil's fart in Dante.[65] From his own experience, as it were, the Somonour tells Frere Hubert that this is what friars seeking money should receive.

A third low-level figure from the ecclesiastical world rides on the famous pilgrimage to the shrine of Thomas Becket. He is, in the language of Lateran IV, a collector or, in other terms, an indulgence man, simply identified as the Pardoner. He has come straight from "the court of Rome," and his bag is stuffed with pardons "comen from Rome al hoot."[66] Along with the pardons he carries pseudo-relics—a pillowcase he presents as part of Mary's veil, and a piece of the sail of Peter's fishing boat. His preaching is smooth "to wynne silver" and in one day he can get more out of a poor parson ("person") and his parish than the parson gets in a year:

> And thus, with feyned flaterye and japes
> He made the person and the peple his apes.
>
> (P 705–706)

Simple folk are the Pardoner's apes or monkeys, but when he tries his line on the pilgrims—for cash every mile they can get pardons "newe and fressh"—he is rudely cut off by Harry Baillie, the Host:

> I wolde I hadde thy coillons in myn hond
> In stide of relikes or of seintuarie,
> Lut kutte hem of, I wol thee helpe him carie;
> They shul be shryned in an hogges toord!
>
> (PT 952–955)

The Pardoner—already described as "a geldyng or a mare"; like Brom-yard's spiritual eunuch he cannot enter the kingdom—is told that the Host would prefer his genitals pickled in hogshit.

Frere Hubert and Frere John, the two summoners, the Pardoner, these are the figures in *The Canterbury Tales* most connected with churchly justice on earth or in heaven. The process-servers and the Pardoner are depicted as conscious frauds; by implication the two friars are no better. No disrespectful word is said of the papal bulls as such; but the bulls come out of the same bag as the pillowcase and Peter's sail. Without the pardons hot from Rome, how does the Pardoner turn pastor and people into his monkeys? No disrespectful word is said of the theology of indulgences or the treasure of the Church administered by the pope; but an indelible impression is made of the operation of these doctrines in practice. Chaucer, a translator of part of Lotario's *The Misery of the Human Condition*, is unlikely to have forgotten its account of avarice at the curia. The effect is similar to the Canon's Yeoman's Tale where one man teaches another to transmute quicksilver and copper into silver and gets 40 pounds for his instruction. Read at one level, the story is about alchemy and godless science. However, the instructor is a canon, and his dupe—for the instruction is entirely fraudulent—is a priest. A dealer in illusions sells to someone credulous enough to buy an illusion. In the words of the teller of this tale—they echo the comment on the Pardoner and the parson—"the preest he made his ape."[67]

The effect is not dissimilar in "The Clerk's Tale," an account of a Roman annulment given in a story taken from Petrarch by the Oxford cleric who tells it. Walter, a rich, knowledgeable noble, wants to test the patience of his poor and uneducated wife, Griselda. An ultimate test is to get an annulment in order to marry another:

> He to the court of Rome, in subtil wyse
> Enformed of his wyl, sente his message,
> Comaundynge hem swiche bulles to devyse
> As to his crueel purpos may suffyse,
> How that the Pope, as for his peples reste,
> Bad hym to wedde another, if hym leste.
>
> I seye, he bad they sholde countrefete
> The popes bulles, makynge mencion
> That he hath leve his first wyf to lete,
> As by the popes dispensacion,
> To stynte rancour and dissencioun
> Betwixe his peple and hym; thus seyde the bulle
> The which they han publiced atte fulle.

(CT 737–749)

The bull, like the Somonour, excuses "atte fulle" or fully. Nothing is said about the ease with which the curia connives in a fiction. Indeed the pope is personally freed from responsibility for the counterfeit. In Petrarch, a "simulated" apostolic letter is also obtained, but no point is made of the curia being informed of Walter's will.[68] In Chaucer the implication left is that illusions of this kind are readily obtainable from Rome.

Chaucer, it has been argued, does not tip his spiritual hand, does not reveal his reactions to religion. Alternatively, it has been contended that there "are chinks in Chaucer's narration through which can be glimpsed a black pessimism."[69] True, the author can be inferred to have had many moods. That he doubts can scarcely be doubted; that he believes can still less be denied, and his belief bears on his view of bribes. Consider in this connection what is intrinsic to the stories—the grades of punishment: money-sniffing Frere John is made ridiculous by his final sniff; the shake-down specialist goes to hell; the Pardoner suffers a public jibe at his most private parts. The Frere's Tale asks the reader to rejoice in the fate of the rascally summoner; the Somonour's Tale invites the reader to join the laugh on the unctuous friar; and the Pardoner's Tale supposes that the reader will not be offended by the Host's rude wish. In each of these stories, stock figures of English sermons are given life and treated as harshly as in any homily on simony. There is a community of values shared by author and reader. At the moment of greatest emotion in the Pardoner's Tale, the Pardoner himself breaks out:

> And Jhesu Christ, that is oure soules leche,
> So graunte yow his pardoun to receyve,
> For that is best; I wol yow nat deceyve.
>
> (PT 916–918)

The lines have the ring of truth for the character who so surprisingly utters them; it is not rash to see the author agreeing. The pardon freely given by Jesus is very different from the pardons purchased of the Pardoner. At the end of the whole work, where "taketh the makere of this book his leve," Chaucer prays to the "preest over alle preestes, that boghte us with the precious blood of his herte." The author's prayer is far from *pro forma*. All the other priests of his book are measured by the Priest to whom he prays, all other bargains by the Redemption.

Two personages of the pilgrimage are presented in terms congruent with this distinction between the Redemption won by Jesus and the sale of forgiveness: the Clerk and the Persoun. The Clerk, an ecclesiastic, has neither benefice nor secular office. By these negations we are informed that he is free of simony. He spends what he has on books and prays for the souls of those who gave him money to study. He is not wordy, but what he does say conveys Truth:

> Sownynge in moral vertu was his speche,
> And gladly wolde he lerne and gladly teche.
>
> (P 308-309)

Not accidentally, it would appear, the Clerk comes from Oxford, the university where cries for reform have been heard. Not accidentally, he is praised as an articulate moralist. His "sownynge" recalls the sower of good seed in Luke. The reciprocity he practices recalls the command of Christ to give freely what one has received freely. The Clerk is not connected particularly with the Persoun, but they are from the same cloth.

The tale told by the Persoun comes last and is by far the longest, almost one-sixth of the whole, to the discomfiture of those who think poetry should not end in a tract of moral theology. It may be right to argue that it should not be read as a gloss on the earlier stories—they stand on their own[70]—but it is a remarkably comprehensive vision of the vices the stories describe. Neither its length nor its explicit function—"To knytte up al this feeste"—can be accounted for except by the interest of the author in what the Persoun has to say, "to shewe yow the wey." The relation of his tale to the earthly pilgrimage is put plainly:

> I wol yow telle a myrie tale in prose
> To knytte up al this feeste, and make an ende.
> And Jhesu, for his grace, wit me sende
> To shewe yow the wey, in this viage,
> Of thilke parfit glorious pilgrymage
> That highte Jerusalem celestial.
>
> (Pers 46–51)

Piers Plowman ended with the start of a pilgrimage. *The Canterbury Tales* ends with a moral map for the wayfarer to heaven. Specifically, as to corruption, the Persoun does not pick up Langland's use of mede, except at one point. "Meede," he says, is taken by false accusers and false witnesses (Pers 795). Otherwise, secular justice is generally neglected; there is nothing like Langland's portrayal of Westminster. Simony is treated more personally and more passionately. It consists, according to the Persoun, in "espirituel marchandise," that is, he says, "ententif desir to byen thing espirituel" (Pers 780). The definition is objective like the canon law's, while the Persoun's gloss stresses volition like Bromyard and Wyclif. Simony can be committed in buying spiritual things by money, by entreaty, or by the petition of kinfolk or other friends. To appoint a man "oonly for wikked flesshly affecioun that they han into the persone" is "foul symonye"—the old view, and Wyclif's too, that *acceptio personarum* is simony. Indeed this kind of simony, resulting in the devil's own sons being put in charge of churches, is "the grettest synne that may be, after the synne of Lucifer and Antecrist." The heinousness of the sin is brought out by its harm to souls that God "boghte with his precious blood. . . . They sellen the soules that lambes sholde kepen to the wolf that strangleth hem" (Pers 785–791). The reference to the Redemption chimes with Chaucer's own prayer.

The Persoun is reserved but clear as to the pope who "calleth hymself servant of the servantz of God": lords that are like wolves devouring the property of poor folk shall receive "by the same mesure that they han mesured to povre folk" (Pers 772, 774–775). These words—menacing, but applied to no specific pope—are put under the analysis of avarice. The Persoun also hints, in a reserved and allusive way, at his view of indulgences, already harshly handled in the presentation of the Pardoner and his wares. The Persoun points out that time for repentance is better "than al the tresor of this world" and that a man "may acquiten hymself biforn God by penitence in this world, and nat by tresor" (Pers 176–177). Clearly the treasure of this world is being contrasted with true penance, but "tresor" is not accidentally chosen. It not only refers to money used to buy indulgences but it also recalls that other "tresor" which is the theologians' basis for indulgences. Penance now, not treasure of either kind is the Persoun's doctrine. His meaning becomes unmistakable when, treating of the third part of penance, satisfaction for one's sin, he sees a sinner's necessary atonement accomplished by bodily pain, alms to the needy, and prayer—acts performed by the penitent himself. The Persoun has no place for satisfaction accomplished by purchasing a pardon.

Host Harry Baillie smells a Lollard in the Persoun's readiness to preach—the Host's is the vague, rude reaction of a man restive before too much piety (MLT 1177–1178). But unlike Wyclif, the Persoun is insistent on confession, and even as to moral matters he does not denounce simony as heresy or pursue its ramifications throughout the hierarchy in a Wyclifite mode; there is no talk of Church endowments being forfeit. He probably knew Wyclif's writings, as Chaucer—the brother-in-law of Wyclif's patron John of Gaunt—probably knew Wyclif in person. He could not be convicted of Lollardry.

In the Prologue the Persoun is described as learned, poor, virtuous, and holy (P 478–480, 490). The description is without irony, the author's tribute. Even his name contains a pun suggesting his special place. "Persoun" is "parson," but it is also "person." The parson is *persona ecclesiae*—"the person of the Church." The pun, good in the Latin *persona* or in Middle English, is preserved in the objection to preference for "persons" on a fleshly basis: the worst sin, according to the Persoun, is this kind of bias for persouns.

Thomas Aquinas had already written that the only perfect *persona* is God.[71] The Persoun comes close to being Christ on earth. As the Prologue puts it, "A bettre preest I trove that nowher noon ys" (P 524). In Chaucer's words, he gives a "noble ensample to his sheep":

> Ne maked him a spiced conscience,
> But Cristes loore and his apostles twelve
> He taughte, but first he folwed it hymselve.
>
> (P 526–528)

Men of integrity among manipulators who are making money out of religion, the Clerk and the Persoun follow the Redeemer of Chaucer's world.

Frere Hubert, the Somonour, the Pardoner, the Clerk, the Persoun, are not central to *The Canterbury Tales*. Who is, except the Host? But if they were removed, their stories would be poorer or lost. Present as storytellers, they are a substantial part of the pilgrimage. Their characters depend on the difference the author sees between the free gift of salvation and sales of salvation as if it were a commodity. For the Persoun the old categories identifying corruption are valid. For Chaucer himself they govern not only the Persoun's analysis but also the tales told of or by the friars, the summoners, and the Pardoner. A layman (customs controller of London, clerk of the king's works at Westminster and Windsor, royal forester in Somerset), Chaucer reveals extraordinary sensitivity to the state of the Church. For him the Apocalypse is not about to happen, his personal salvation is not assured, the Antichrist is not at hand. Accepting the free pardon available from Jesus, a Christian goes about his business, laughing at illusions, unmasking manipulators when he can, satirizing savagely the modern Simonians, insisting on the reciprocity of God's judgment that will give appropriate measure to those who have been wolves on earth.

The Sincere Sienese. "If a wound in need is not burnt with fire or cut with steel but only ointment is put on it, it not so much lacks health as festers completely and many times receives death. Woe! Woe! Sweetest daddy, this is the cause that your subjects are all corrupt, full of impurity and iniquity." The year was 1376. The writer was Caterina Benincasa, aged thirty-one, laywoman of Siena. The addressee was Pierre Roger de Beaufort, aged forty-five, for the past five years Gregory XI. "My Daddy, sweet Christ on earth, follow that sweet Gregory"—Follow your great namesake Gregory I, the Avignonese pope was told.[72]

A cat may look at a king, but the king will not necessarily look back. Gregory XI looked and listened to Caterina, an Italian stranger writing him personally for the first time. Already she had told a representative of his that prelates were "re-sellers of divine grace." Already she had told her confessor that Jesus himself had informed her of his intention to drive out once again those "filthy, greedy, grasping merchants" selling and buying "the graces and gifts of the Holy Spirit."[73] Messages from Caterina to the pope continued. Wounded, the Church bought by Christ's blood was near death: "so much blood has been sucked out of her by wicked gluttons that she has gone pale all over." What did God want of the pope? Arrived in Avignon in June 1376, Caterina told him: "His will is this, father, and so He requires of you: He requires of you that you make justice of the abundance of great iniquity committed by those who nourish themselves and graze in the garden of Holy Church. He says that animals ought not to nourish themselves on the food of men." The animals must be brought to justice. "You must use your power and might. Not willing to use it, better to resign. . . . Watch, as you hold life dear, that you commit no negligence. . . . I, if I were you, would fear lest the divine judgment come upon me."[74]

Papal Avignon was, as Petrarch had put it earlier, Babylon, the whore of Apocalypse 17:1–6 clothed in purple and scarlet and wearing horns: in Petrarch's words, "impious Babylon, from which all shame has fled"; "nest of treachery," enriched by impoverishing others; "avaricious Babylon which has filled the bag of God's anger"; Babylon who against her founders Peter and Paul has raised the horns of a "disgraced whore."[75] This view of the central administration of the Church, essentially Dante's, gave a special emphasis to its location in exile; and one of Caterina's objectives was to persuade the pope to go back to Rome. Her letters to Gregory, however, focused more on his associates than on geography. As she wrote him while she was in Avignon itself, vices and sins specially abounded in "prelates and shepherds." Now "wolves" nourish themselves on "the mystical body of Holy Church." Gregory himself seemed to stand "like a lamb in the midst of wolves." If he had good advisers, their advice would attend not to self-love but "to the salvation of souls and the reformation of Holy Church."[76]

Caterina, at most, reinforced a resolution the pope had already taken to return to Rome. She did not get the kind of reformation which her strong, if vague, words sought. Her language to Gregory, like her letters to others and her one book, reflected a view of the Church and the corruption of its central administration that can be called "standard international," from Petrarch to Wyclif. Her images and themes came from her circle, from friends such as William Fleet, English Austin, and Raimundo da Capua, Italian Dominican. Her sources were the usual ones. Ideas of which Bromyard's summa had been one great repository were, by the 1370s, the common property of critics of the Church's government. Animals were at large attacking the flock. Simony was rampant. Wounded, the Church was not far from death. Reformation must come from the top. Personal in her urgency, Caterina pressed on the pope the same view of corruption that a congregation would have received from a well-read preacher. What was most remarkable about her was that a woman of the age should speak out publicly on church administration and that a woman should be heard. Half daughter, half mother, she cajoled Gregory XI with childlike affection and threatened with the standard international themes. For her audience her authority came from her close communication with the Lord. Nothing she said was unorthodox or unconventional enough to prevent her, eighty-one years after her death, from being canonized in 1461.

Constance. Caterina, Langland, and Wyclif were writing contemporaneously; Chaucer composed *The Canterbury Tales* a few years later. Alive at the same time but a man of a younger generation was Jan Hus of Husinec—John Goose of Goosetown, a Catholic priest and scholastic theologian at the brandnew University of Prague. Hus's mind had been set on fire by Wyclif's writings, brought to him from Oxford in 1401 by his close friend Jerome of Prague. Aware that Wyclif had been pursued for heresy, Hus believed he could extract the solid core and avoid the errors. In this spirit, in 1407–1409, he lectured on the *Sentences* of Peter Lombard at Prague, incorporating Wyclif's attack upon the simonian heretics. In this spirit in 1411 he attacked a Crusade Bull of Baldassare Cossa, Pope John XXIII, issued against supporters of John's rival for the papal throne, as Wyclif had attacked the Crusade Bull of Urban VI. In this spirit in 1413 he published in the vernacular *O svatokupectví (Simony)* following Wyclif's *De simonia*.[77]

Little in Hus is new to a reader of Wyclif. Occasionally he is more concrete, often he is more discreet. Priests pay for their benefices. Priests demand payment for baptisms, marriages, funerals; they ask for legacies before they confess the dying. Vicars pay a *groschen* to get episcopal permission to hear confessions and then charge their penitents a *groschen* or more per confession. Priests sell masses at a *groschen* a mass. Priests rent out their parishes to vicars who "diligently shear and milk the sheep." Very few priests are free of the simonian sin. The priests urge custom in defense of their fees, but when has evil custom ever been a defense against express laws? The monks are equally culpable. They sin especially by offering the pope, priests, or nobles money to obtain parishes attached to their monasteries. Bishops are Simonians, charging two *kopy* (= 120 *groschen* = 120 days' pay for an unskilled laborer) for each consecration of an altar and more than two *kopy* for consecration of a church. The bishops say they are selling their labor, not their blessing. They are like innkeepers who serve food free and charge more for beer than the cost of the food and drink combined. And the bishops enter into office simoniacally paying the pope. Many thousand *gulden* are paid to obtain the archbishopric of Prague. The annates regularly and openly demanded by the pope from episcopal appointees are simoniac. The pope does not even use "a Gehazi": he himself has set the rate. Old Nick (Lucifer) may say that the pope grants a benefice without any demands being made and that he takes the appointee's money later, so there is no trafficking. "But Hodek the baker or Húda the vegetable woman would answer Old Nick that when he has bread for sale and someone comes in and in silence lays the money on the counter, either before or after taking the bread, Hodek or Húda concludes that the customer has bought the bread."[78]

The laity are similarly "besmirched" with many kinds of simoniacal practice. At the coarsest level they dispose of ecclesiastical appointments in exchange for money or services; or they make ecclesiastical appointments to a relative or a man who is a good hunting companion. A layman presenting a cleric for a benefice "because of money, gifts, material service, worldly favor, blood or marriage relationship, flattery or to oblige another" is among the Simonians. The sin includes in its sweep those families who send their children to school "that they may become rich, receive honor in the world, and become able to help their relatives." The fathers and mothers send their sons "with evil intent" and their children pursue their studies with "evil intent." Finally, there are the Simonians who cooperate in the commission of simony as its abettors, counselors, and defenders.[79]

When Hus attacked John XXIII's Crusade Bull and its attached indulgences, he did not include Wyclif's reference to the Church's treasure as invention based on imagination. He began with safe canonical doctrine. Commonly, he observed, the papal indulgences were bought and sold, and he invoked the canonical rule that the sale of the spiritual conveyed nothing. He pointed to the discretion vested in the papal commissioners executing the bull to set the amount of money or property necessary to pay for the pardon. "Look, a blind man can here feel whether a pardon of sins is being given according to a rate of temporal property." Did not priests in turn buy from the commissioners a license to grant the indulgence? "Where, I ask, can simony be more manifest?" "With what face," that is, with what chutzpah, did John XXIII grant plenary pardon and the reward of the just? Here Hus pushed close to Wyclif's fundamental challenge to the papal power. "With what face does the Pope presume to condone God's injury unless God expressly commanded him to do this?" How can any man escape judgment at the tribunal of Christ? The reality of that judgment was invoked against the easy escape from all punishment offered by pardoners who "extend their palms and say, 'Whoever puts money here, his sins will be forgiven,' and 'Now you can buy back your ancestors by these pardons.'"[80]

Suspicion of his sympathy for Wyclif—a suspicion whetted by his criticism of simoniac clerics—led Zajic Zybnek, archbishop of Prague, to proceed against him. Unbelievably for a man who had taken Wyclif to heart, Hus' response was to appeal from his archbishop to the curia of John XXIII. It was while his case was in the curia that he chose to attack John XXIII's Crusade Bull. After two years, in 1412, the case terminated with Hus being excommunicated for failing to obey a citation to appear in person.[81] By this time he had adopted the viewpoint of many disappointed litigants in Rome: the cardinals hearing the case

> accepted from my foes beautiful horses, silver goblets and precious rings and refused to pass judgment. The Pope then turned the case over to others, but the same thing happened. . . . After that, the Pope once again assumed charge of the trial, saying that he himself wished to be its judge and that 'Everyone else has already profited by that trial except me.' . . . He was looking for the golden knights, but the Goose did not have them nor wish to send them to him.[82]

Hus's suspicions are not evidence, and it is not clear how he knew what John XXIII said. It is clear that old denunciations of curial iniquity rang in his mind as fresh truths. Denouncing papal simony, Hus quoted St. Bernard's trenchant advice to Eugene III, not quite 300 years old.[83] When later his old friend and present enemy, Stefan Palec, taunted his side with, "Why do they not go to the Roman Curia?," Hus replied, "The Roman Curia does not take a sheep without its wool." The line was a tag from a Latin satire 200 years old.[84] In the spirit of Thomas Becket, Hus went beyond the canons to appeal his case to God "the supreme and most just Judge, who is not terrified by fear or deflected by love or suborned by an offering or deceived by false witnesses."[85] The Goose was finished with the curia.

He was not finished with the Church. In 1414 a Council opened in Constance. In the view of leading churchmen of the day—Jean Gerson, chancellor of the University of Paris; Cardinal Pierre d'Ailly; Cardinal Francesco Zabarella—a Council was the only way to end the Great Schism, which had now produced three rival popes; it was, moreover, a heaven-sent opportunity to reform the Church. Uncompromising preaching from Bromyard to Hus was one kind of response to corruption, the Council was another. When it gathered—cardinals, bishops, abbots, generals of religious orders, university theologians, curial officials, John XXIII, and the Emperor Sigismund—it looked bigger and better than any visible claimant to the See of Peter. Hus, who once had thought he would be vindicated in Rome, now believed he would address the Council and be vindicated by it.[86]

The Goose, Hus wrote, was not afraid of being cooked. He put not only his case but his person within the power of John XXIII. Almost immediately the pope had him arrested and imprisoned. The Roman case against him was reopened—a criminal trial for heresy. The Council, its scholars in particular, entered on the work (apparently not uncongenial for them) of identifying his doctrine with Wyclif's and finding it equally heretical, although today, half a millennium later, it is hard to find the heresy he actually held. Not for his orthodox attack on simony was he condemned, not for his questioning of indulgences. Nor was he condemned because his judges were bribed. Certain that he held heretical views on civil authority and on the nature of the Church, despite his denials that he held them, the Council condemned him to be degraded from the priesthood and turned over to the secular arm. He was burnt on July 6, 1415.[87]

The Council, meanwhile, had set about trying John XXIII himself. He was ordered to appear on May 14, 1415. On his nonappearance he was suspended from office. On May 16 two prosecutors appointed by the Council offered seventy-four charges against him including the poisoning of his predecessor, incest with his brother's wife, and simony. Cardinals whom the pope asked to act as his proctors declined to do so. He remained absent. Nine days later, May 25, 1415, the prosecutors informed the Council that fifty-four charges had been sufficiently established for the Council to act. Assassination and incest disappeared. Nearly all the remaining charges of a serious and fairly specific character involved simony. The Council was not told the name of any witness to the charges but it was given the rank of each witness and informed whether he testified "to the truth" or to common report.[88]

At this critical juncture the Council did not indulge in the evasion of later apologists that Baldassare Cossa reigning as John XXIII was an antipope, elected in a line of succession that had been in schism since 1379.

Nor did the Council take either of two courses which the old canons suggested—to treat Cossa's orders as null because simoniacally acquired or to try Cossa himself as a notorious heretic because he was a notorious Simonian. The Council had been called into being by Cossa. At this moment it did not seek to subvert its legitimacy. The Council proceeded by way of deposition.[89]

The first charge the prosecutors reported to the Council as established was that

> from the time of his youth or while he was still called Baldassare Cossa, he was a man of evil character, shameless, immodest, mendacious, rebellious and disobedient to his parents, and given to many vices, and commonly spoken of, held, believed and reputed by all having information about him as such and for such; and he still is spoken of, held, believed and reputed as such and for such; and was and is manifestly and openly, publicly and notoriously so known.

A Hog from the beginning. The charge was reported to have been "proved" by two cardinals, one protonotary, two auditors, one clerk of the Chamber, one licensed canonist, one archbishop, one writer, one proctor of a great order, one canon of a great metropolitan church, one bishop, and many other notable men.[90]

The second charge was that John XXIII had acquired a copious treasure by simony and other illicit means. Two cardinals and others testified to public report of this, two cardinals to its truth. The third article charged that he paid a great sum of money for his promotion to the cardinalate. One cardinal and one archbishop testified to the truth of this, other witnesses to hearsay about it. The seventh article charged him with giving benefices for money. Two cardinals and others swore to its truth. The twelfth article charged him with requiring payment for copies of apostolic letters so that many litigants, lacking the funds to get them, failed in their proofs. This was proved by two auditors, a writer of apostolic letters, and two proctors. The twentieth article declared that he had "sold for cash" pardons and absolutions from punishment and guilt. A cardinal, an archbishop, two bishops, two auditors, a canonist, and a proctor all testified that such was the common report.[91]

In a memo penned a few months after the event, Jean Gerson, the theological genius of the Council, summed up his views on the sin at issue. The "simonian slip" (*simoniaca labes*), as Gerson rather mildly called it, was not in itself heresy, for it could result "from only a distortion of the affection through avarice, while the judgment of right understanding remains that to act in this way is to sin." By "presumption of law," nonetheless, "every Simonian can be held suspect in faith." It was a sin which the pope could escape by suspending the positive law defining certain acts as simony, but the pope could not suspend the divine law by which any contract of the character "I give if you give" or "I give that you may give" governing the transfer of spiritual goods for goods measurable in money was condemned. Where there was no contract, simony could be avoided by a "rectification of intention," that is, by seeking money not for the spiritual good being given but as decent sustenance befitting one's status. Even where there was a contract, simony could "perhaps" be excused in one compelled to pay, as cooperation in usury was excused in one compelled to borrow: "buy back of harassment" could be invoked as a defense. Neither intention nor compulsion justified the great amount of simony commonly committed, and "the worst argument" was that "the crowd do this, therefore it's lawful."[92] Assuming that the Council majority would have agreed with the principal points of Gerson, John XXIII had at least one arguable defense—good intention. He could also have taken the position that he was avaricious in affection, but no heretic. As it turned out, no defense was offered. Fugitive from the Council and recaptured, the pope told the Council's emissaries on May 27 that he would not defend himself.[93]

On May 29 the Council proceeded to judge the pope. It found the fifty-four articles proved, it declared that the pope had freely submitted to judgment, and it judged specifically that John XXIII was a notorious Simonian, a notorious pillager of the property of many churches, and an evil administrator, scandalizing the Church by his detestable life and morals before and after his election to the papacy. The Council deposed him from office.[94]

An assembly of the most learned prelates in Europe had actually removed the head of the Church on earth for buying and selling the Spirit. From the perspective of satisfied participants, Constance was a success: the schism was substantially ended; the accountability of pope to Church was established; a decent pope was elected; the unorthodox boldness of subordinating pope to Council was compensated for by the condemnation of Wyclif's writings and Hus's person.[95]

Viewing the proceedings from a Franciscan prison a month before he himself was judged, John Hus had written,

> These men have condemned and anathematized the seller, while they themselves remained buyers and middlemen and continue to sell at home. . . . O that the Lord Jesus would have said to the Council, "He that is among you without sin of simony, let him condemn Pope John!" It seems to me that they would have run out one after another! . . . Are they not guilty who have themselves committed simony along with him?[96]

A jury of thieves convicting a thief? Since the days of Cicero, scarcely unusual where bribery was the crime. If the exemplary effect of the Council's action was weakened by selectivity in the culprits punished, it was even more undermined by the secrecy and haste with which John XXIII was condemned and by the absence of counsel and witnesses for him. The grand example of punishing a pope for simony was also muffled by what was finally done to the deposed pope. Temporarily imprisoned but not treated like Hus as a heretic, Baldassare Cossa survived to be bishop of Frascati.[97] The proceedings against him at best looked like a grand jury presentment, not a trial, and could be seen as political theater: his submission was not a confession. Everyone could see the political motive at work: when the Council disposed of one of the two principal popes it had reduced the schism to manageable size. Finally, in the eyes of Bohemia the Council had made a martyr of the country's most powerful critic of corruption. Constance—the great general council intended to remedy corruption—was compromised, a failure, even before the conciliar flops of the later fifteenth century ended hope in the ability of a council to achieve reform.[98]

The Not Entirely Silent Sienese.   The most remarkable preacher of the fifteenth century, Bernardino of Siena, took a course very different from Hus or Wyclif, FitzRalph or Bromyard. Simony, the simonian heresy, the sin of *acceptio personarum* in ecclesiastical appointments, restitution of simoniacal profits, the simoniacal sale of indulgences—these topics he left alone in his preaching and in the treatises prepared from his sermons. "All the family are made bishops today," he remarked once, tersely and disapprovingly,[99] but he provided no dissection of the sin which Chaucer's Persoun had found almost the greatest. Where ecclesiastics were concerned, scandal, dissension, schism were to be avoided, and for him the corollary apparently followed that public homilies against ecclesiastical abuses were not to be given. Entering the Franciscan order in 1402 at the relatively mature age of twenty-two, he was drawn to the stricter followers of Francis, the Observants, and he was the Observants' provincial in Tuscany from 1414 to 1417, their vicar general for Italy from 1438 to 1442. Example, change from within the friars, devotion to the development of observance of the rule—these were Bernardino's methods of reform. The most effective speaker of his day, he seems to step from the pages of *Piers Plowman*, a silent watchman on walls crumbling under attack. To an experienced Venetian diplomat, he was a man "engaged in correcting the morals and customs of peoples, powerful in example as in word . . . seeking no human compensation." He was not burned at the stake like Hus or disinterred like Wyclif, but canonized in 1450 only six years after his death.[100]

The deliberateness with which Bernardino chose tactful taciturnity emerges even more sharply when his own statements on the moral obligations of a preacher are examined. Preachers, he declared, often fail to preach the truth out of *negligentia* or tepidity of spirit, out of false humility, or out of craven fear. These motives he scorned. His declared opinion was: "Justice is to be preached to the unjust, truth to the blindly ignorant, salvation to the despairing impious."[101] He did take the position that punishment might be suspended if there was danger of "worse sins" if it were imposed, but he was adamant that judgment itself was not to be falsified for fear of scandal.[102] What he taught as to judgment held equally of preaching. Failure to preach the truth endangered the people "who were immersed in worldly things." The people depended on the exponent of the Gospel to enlighten them.[103] When Bernardino chose to be silent about simony, he renounced his voice, his most powerful professional in-strument, to use means more modest and less disruptive. It was a decision that went beyond tact. For him policy dictated that public indictments of clerical corruption be muted.

As to secular bribery, he had much and little to say:

There are those who go to steal secretly and with fear, as do thieves who secretly enter homes and steal what they can. Robbers who infest ways and woods and despoil the passers-by are like them, and such are called forest thieves. And there are many others who with open faces under the pretext and insignia of jus-tice, flag flying in the name of common utility, come to office to skin the people. How many extortions, disembowelings, frame-ups, wickednesses, frauds, false promises, undue favors, impious terrors and other evil machinations they engage in to draw in money, the unhappy peoples who have experienced such things in certain countries know. These are domestic thieves, and they are so much the more pernicious than the forest thieves as among other things they are so much the more secure; for they are not punished and hung as robbers and thieves but defended, praised and honored by those who are like them, and each becomes an example and a safeguard for the other.[104]

Heartfelt denunciation of crooked politicians set out in a series of Len-ten sermons, "The Eternal Gospel," this paragraph would appear to be only a prelude to one of Bernardino's masterly dissections of the tricks of a class of crafty wrongdoers. It is a prelude to a definition of *concussio* or shakedown, which, Bernardino says, includes three kinds of acts by of-ficials—extorting money by fear; refusing to carry out a legal duty unless given money; extracting in anyway something beyond salary. The defini-tion encompassed what Chaucer meant by "briberey" and what is often meant by bribery today.

Shakedown and its spiritual counterpart, simony, Bernardino says, con-stitute one of the four sins arising from avarice for which God beats cities and countries with His anger. Along with the other three sins—robbery, oppression of the poor, and ingratitude for divine benefits—it draws from God the collective punishment of the community. Knowing the unsparing character of Bernardino's denunciation of other sins, one would expect him to give details, to bring the guilt home to those responsible. But the passage says only that these domestic thieves have been experienced by people "in certain countries." No specific suggestion is made as to where such creatures may be found.

"Truth in the world," Bernardino preaches on another occasion, "is not defended" because of fear, lechery, or avarice. "Because of avarice," he ob-serves, "many do not defend the truth as they are bound by obligation to do." He illustrates not by a judge taking a bribe, not by any instance from Siena or any Italian city, but from the court of Herod when Salome asked for John the Baptist's head. There were "the princes and tribunes and first men of Galilee"—these words are from the Gospel of Mark 6:21—and Ber-nardino adds, "They preferred to serve desire rather than stand for the truth." So, "in these times," he continues, there are those "who do not favor the truth, as they are bound to do, lest they give up gain. They have many accomplices in their crime." In a few words, with a slight expansion of the Gospel text, Bernardino has evoked the picture of complaisant courtiers too selfish to risk their positions to speak out for an innocent man. But the scene is far from home; there is no indication of where such courtiers exist in Italy.[105]

In a third sermon, in the Lenten series, "The Christian Religion," Bernardino puts a case with stronger tones of local color. There are those accused of crime and incarcerated either by the *podestà* or others. Before judgment is passed on them they pay intercessors to plead for them, and the *podestà* frees them. If they were guilty, Bernardino says, they gave the money unjustly and the intercessors took it shamefully. If they were innocent, "perhaps they could not otherwise be helped since they had powerful adversaries and had stayed a long time in prison and had spent much and suffered many other harassments." It was morally lawful, he concludes, for them "to buy back their harassment." It was also lawful for the intercessors, if they were not salaried officials of the commune or the lord, to "take a benefit for their work." In short, Bernardino speaking in Siena as one might have spoken in Hog's Sicily, supposes that the only way an innocent man may get out of jail is to make a payoff to someone with influence with the ruler, be he *podestà* or tyrant. Not only does Bernardino visualize such conditions existing; he defends both those making and those arranging the payoffs. He does not pause to criticize those who make them necessary.[106]

In the Lenten series of 1425, preaching in Santa Croce in Florence, he proclaims, "There are twelve evils which undo your city and all others." The first is "the false judge in the consistory;" the eleventh is "the avaricious man in office who for money commits every evil and every act of graft (*baratteria*)."[107] In another Florentine sermon of 1425, he declares, "Many of your officials and rulers and other officials have become little tyrants and disgrace your country and your land"; and he sweepingly announces, "Better to live without bread than without justice."[108] Again, at Florence he preaches that the Venetians do not do as the Florentines do, and so the Venetians have a reputation for justice and the Florentines do not. The Venetians remove from office and bar from future appointment any ruler who receives "a single present."[109]

More generally he strikes at bribery in his indictments of avarice and selfishness. In a splendid sermon he apostrophizes "Self or Private Love," as follows:

> O most cruel beast . . . you corrupt all virtues. . . . You love no one unless it is reciprocal. . . . You are distraught if you do not receive. . . . O worst of beasts, in judgments you pervert the just.[110]

Identifying the requirement of reciprocation as the demand of self-love, Bernardino identifies the central psychological mechanism by which corruption works. He puts his finger on the essential of every corrupt transaction—the demand of a quid pro quo by an official bound to act gratuitously and without reciprocity from the one for whom he acts.

Still, he says nothing, or next to nothing, about the political mechanisms by which corruption worked. The problems of restitution arising from the receipt of bribes and the resultant injury to litigants were presumably enormous. Bernardino picks up the problems perfunctorily, invoking Augustine as quoted in Gratian. As to bribes given to judges, Bernardino accepts the view of Alessandro Lombardo, the Franciscan master general in 1313, that if a litigant paid to assure his right then the judge was bound to return the money to the litigant. If the bribe was given "to corrupt the mind of the judge," then the repentant judge was bound to give it to the poor. Bernardino's general principles, stated elsewhere, required restitution by anyone unjustly causing harm. He makes no specific mention of the obligation of the bribed judge to make up the loss caused by his corrupt decision. He frees from any obligation of restitution the intercessors paid for their work in obtaining the release of an innocent man. He says the intercessors find merit with God and pays no attention to the shabby network in which they must be a part.[111]

Bernardino sweepingly attacks the whole system by which usury infests Siena. He gives the closest attention to the ruses and disguises of the usurers. Not merely manifest usurers like pawnbrokers, but foreign-exchange dealers, merchants of wool, sellers on credit are indicted from his pulpit. He insists that the duty of restitution of property usuriously acquired passes to wives, to children, to donees and the beneficiaries under wills, so that scarcely a propertied person is unaffected by the spreading obligation. It is not Bernardino's style to denounce sinners by name, but with usury he leaves no doubt of the extent to which nearly everyone in the bourgeoisie is entangled. His analysis of usury stands in strong contrast to his treatment of civic corruption. The latter is condemned but it is not pursued into its varieties, its refinements, its restitution. In his published Latin sermons and in the vernacular sermons, there is no analysis of civic corruption resembling his extended treatment of usury. Where Bernardino does speak, he is as strong against civic corruption as Dante or Langland. The eleventh of his evils that undo cities—the avaricious man in office—is indeed an echo of Dante on Lucca, and he uses Dante's word, *baratteria*. Why then does he not say more and speak more specifically?[112]

Can a clue to his relative reticence in developing the theme be found in his imagery? A recurrent phenomenon in the vernacular sermons is Bernardino's recourse to animal analogies to describe the corrupt officeholder. A man who leaves his own trade to "despoil the city" is like the cat who sits before a mousehole waiting to seize the mouse who comes out—the mouse is the countryman or poor man.[113] The avaricious man in office who is prepared to "pluck this one and to plunder that one and to butcher this one" is like a wolf who stuffs himself on a pig. The ruler who does not give justice is like the lion who acquitted the predatory animals and found the lamb worthy of death.[114] Bad rulers, he tells the Florentines, are the locusts of the Apocalypse. They are insatiable insects with swollen bodies. "They eat and they bite, these bad rulers, with teeth of iron. . . . They eat their subjects."[115]

Pouncing cat, gluttonous wolf, hypocrite lion, iron-toothed locust—the bestial images accumulate. The great beast, Self-Love, takes the form of many different animals, and, in general, Bernardino is not reluctant to point out how sin bestializes man. Historically, tales and images of animals have always been a way for the oppressed to express popular complaint against a ruling class. The animal images figure prominently in Bromyard's repertoire. When Bernardino employs these similes he is speaking for the oppressed without attacking individual officeholders. In one of his most striking stories, told in the Campo in Siena in 1426, he tells of the bear and the monkeys at the French court: The bear, being stronger, ate a baby monkey. The mother monkey ran from one person to another looking into their faces "as if asking for justice." No one responded. "As no one does justice for the fault of that bear, I will do it myself," declared the mother monkey. She went to the hay-loft where the bear slept, took hay, piled it round the bear, and set it on fire, burning the bear alive. "And she did justice herself."[116]

If the cats, wolves, lions, locusts, and bears who corruptly denied justice evoked such an allegory, it may be that they were rarely found as penitent or receptive members of Bernardino's audience. Speaking to poor monkeys, he could denounce the sins of the unidentified bigwigs unsparingly; he voiced a view that the monkeys shared. Bears were not even awake to benefit from an extended analysis of their sins. Or perhaps the same sense of discretion that kept him silent about ecclesiastical abuses kept Bernardino from carrying further a dissection of sins whose only earthly remedy would be the fire of revolution. A final, functional reason: Preaching against bribery was necessarily accusatorial; a preacher could not provide a trial. Accusations of bribery functioned to express social dissatisfaction and social criticism. This function was fulfilled by Bernardino's sustained attack on the multitude of usurious practices. No need for him to duplicate the function that the great sermons against voracious usury already performed.

The story of the monkey and the bear was itself a parable with as much force for the Church as for any secular community. If justice was not upheld in the Church by those appointed to uphold it, Christians would do it themselves. For almost 400 years, reform had been sought by popes and councils, by the passage of statutes and by personal conversions, in the founding of orders and the multiplication of universities. Reform, if Hus and Wyclif, Chaucer and Langland, preachers and professors and poets could be believed, was still far from realized. Bernardino worked for it from within, without public denunciations of the evils. Others were gathering hay—much of it from Bernard, Innocent III, and the canons to be found in Gratian and Gregory IX—for a large conflagration. Sparks from preaching were falling here and there. The bears within the Church were still asleep or at large.

Fire

> In all things, look to the end,
> and how you will be judged before a strict Judge,
> from whom nothing is hidden;
> who is not placated by offerings
> and does not accept excuses,
> but will judge what is just.

These are lines from the great spiritual classic of the fifteenth century, *The Imitation of Christ*. The austere figure of the Judge at the Last Judgment is drawn in implicit contrast to human judges who do not judge what is just, who accept excuses, who take *munera*. This kind of piety is not revolutionary but reflects a sense that justice without offerings is an ideal to be realized by divine judgment. Other spiritual authorities looked to reform now.[117]

Bromyard had seen the Church as gravely wounded by corrupt clergy. Wyclif had seen the curia as corrupt. Caterina had seen the necessity of reformation if catastrophe were to be avoided. In the years immediately preceding the move of Martin Luther, the old and familiar themes, warnings, and proposals were all heard again. In 1512, Julian II convoked the Fifth Lateran Council. Addressing its opening session, Egidio da Viterbo, master-general of the Augustinian hermits, declared: "We have seen Christ sleeping in the boat. . . . We have seen evil greed and thirst to get gold and silver. We have seen, I say, violence, rapine, adulteries, acts of incest—in short the universal plague of crimes has so confused all things sacred and profane and so beaten against the holy boat that its side has nearly given way to the waves of crimes and it has almost foundered and sunk." The bark of Peter close to destruction. Gold and silver rampant. Christ himself asleep. Could a harsher judgment be pronounced?[118]

Succeeding Julian in 1513, Leo X continued the Council. It had been called, he observed, because of "the frequent complaints about the officials of the Roman Curia." It was his intention, he told the Council Fathers, "to carry out a universal reformation"; and he did in fact in 1514 issue a "Bull of Reformation of the Curia," which adopted, without real sanctions, Bromyard's ideal of cardinals who lived modestly, were not "discriminators" (*acceptores personarum*), and did the business of the Curia "freely and graciously." Reformation was the cry of officialdom at the highest level. It had been, from time to time, since Gregory VII, since Gregory I.[119]

When reformation then came in shapes very different from what high officialdom expected, the old rhetoric and the old analysis of shameful traffic in the spiritual played a part—if only a part—in what happened. By

itself the kind of criticism found in, say, Bromyard was not enough to ignite a revolution. Even when combined with unorthodox views of the sacraments and the Church, as in Wyclif, the critique of corruption had not
been sufficient—absent other conditions—to bring about major changes.
The break-up of the papal supervision of the churches of half of Western
Europe was a complex concatenation, with multiple causes—among them
national and international politics, dynastic calculations, ethnic loyalty,
personal greed, spiritual hunger, commercial growth, capital accumulation, new learning, new methods of communication, new concentrations
of energy. "The Reformation" was a vast series of events whose religious
impact was often liberating for those affected. In the words of a memorable essay by Lucien Febvre, it would be "ridiculous and profoundly
puerile" to believe that the spiritual manifestations of the Reformation era
were caused by impersonal abuses or "by the fairly habitual lack of shame
of the merchants of the temple, those eternal parasites of the divine."[120]

Rejection of what once was a stereotype of the Reformation goes too far,
however, if it overlooks the part played by the tradition on bribery
(including simony), corruption, and reform. In three ways the tradition affected what took place. First, it had a supportive, if not generative, role in
the theology of Redemption which was critical for Luther's thought. Second, it affected the ability of the Roman authorities to reassert themselves.
Third, it occupied a prominent place in Rome's perception of the problems
posed and channeled much of the Roman response.

First, as to theology: The old, quasi-hagiographic account of Luther was
of a devout German first scandalized by a visit to Rome in 1510, then
shocked into remedial remonstrance by the crude commercialism with
which Roman pardons were peddled in Germany in 1517. Dispassionate
examination has shown that his new religious views came from his interi-
or struggles, his own sense of utter unworthiness to cross the abyss
separating man from God, his search for certainty of his own salvation;
and the struggles, and the views they issued in, antedate 1517. One theological counterpart to the resolution of his personal crisis was the overriding significance of the great Buy Back effected for the Christian by Christ.
Christ, as Luther was to preach in 1518, has "absorbed" our sins and given
us instead his righteousness. Christ, he came to write in 1520, has made
with the soul a happy exchange, marrying her, "a poor, outlawed, evil
whore," taking from her all evils and endowing her with all goods. Christ,
as he taught in the *Small Catechism* of 1529, has "redeemed, acquired and
gained me, a lost and condemned man, from all sins, from death, and from
the power of the devil, not with gold and silver, but with his holy,
precious blood and with his innocent suffering and death in order that I
may be his own. . . . " The extraordinary act of reciprocity, by which Christ
identified with man and served him, did not need to be repeated by a
series of small buy backs.[121]

This theology, it should be observed, does not stand in a social vacuum.
It offers not only assurance of salvation, it offers a way out of some of the

worst of medieval abuses. Luther had seen with his own eyes the Church which Egidio, the master general of his own order, described in such harsh terms to the pope and the Fathers of Lateran V. It is difficult to believe that Luther constructed his theology unaware of its bearing on the abuses. In any event, this theology was affronted, this theology was given opportunity for exposition by the crude commercial operation of agents of Leo X and the Fugger banking house acting through Archbishop Albrecht. It has often been observed that Luther, although he attacked indulgences, gained the support of the secular ruler of Wittenberg, Frederick the Wise, himself a great collector of indulgences for his city's cathedral. The observation underlines how Luther's complaints were crafted to connect what he criticized with the pope. If it is naïve to suppose that a specific sale of pardons in Germany provoked Luther to action, it is equally naïve to suppose that the expression of pure theology would have captured the attention of the world or won the local support essential to Luther's security. Luther got that support because he drew on traditional themes which chimed with his broader theology. In *Against Hans Sausage*—a late work (1541) and a highly angry one, it is true—he describes his reaction to Tetzel's preaching of pardons and how he opposed them although "the song might be too high for my voice." He continues: "This is the first real fundamental beginning of 'the Lutheran ruckus' which not Duke Frederick but the bishop of Mainz began through his fleece-pocket or pickpocket, Tetzel—or rather through his shameful preaching (as heard) which aimed to steal and to rob the people of their cash to pay for his pallium and pomp."[122] It is a rash historian who knows Luther's career better than he himself did.

Albrecht of Brandenberg owed the pope 24,000 ducats (14,000 of *servitia* and taxes, 10,000 as the fee for a dispensation), a debt incurred so that he could be bishop of three sees, Mainz, Magdeburg, and Halberstadt. To pay the pope he borrowed from bankers, the Fuggers. To repay the Fuggers he arranged to have the pardon which was attached to contributions to the building of Saint Peter's in Rome preached for eight years in his dioceses, the pope to get half the proceeds, the Fuggers to be paid from the rest, the Fugger agents to accompany the pardoners so that they could check the receipt of cash as it came in. This businesslike way of financing the taxes imposed by the Roman curia—taxes of the kind deplored by Bromyard and a variation on the license to preach pardons equally deplored by him—was regarded at the Roman curia as a routine legal transaction.[123]

Archbishop Albrecht himself issued a "Summary Instruction" for the subcommissioners designated to execute "the business of the most plenary pardons." Rates were set. Kings, queens, archbishops, and bishops were to pay twenty-five gold Rhenish florins. Poorer citizens needed only contribute one florin. Those without money could contribute prayers and fasts. Religious prevented by their superiors from contributing could solicit alms from others to be given on their behalf. Wives could contribute from their dowries, though their husbands objected. If one was contributing for a soul in purgatory, the rate was determined by one's own rank, not the soul's. There was no need for "contributors to be contrite in heart" if they were contributing to obtain the favor (*gratia*) of release of another from Purgatory, "since such favor rests on the charity in which the deceased died and on the contribution of the living." The pardons for the dead were described as working "most surely" by way of papal intercession. The living could also "buy back" for themselves confessional letters, promising participation "now and forever" in the prayers of the Church plus the privilege of confessing to the confessor of their choice sins ordinarily reserved for absolution to the pope or bishop. Subcommissioners were also authorized to make compositions with Simonians who sought forgiveness. Nothing was to be required as remuneration for hearing confessions "because it would be simoniac." The purpose of the fund-raising was said to be to keep the resting place of Peter and Paul from remaining "unfinished and rainy." Nothing was said of the Fuggers' share.[124]

Acting under these instructions, Johann Tetzel, Dominican of Leipzig, came to preach the Saint Peter pardon near Wittenberg, announcing, "You shall have plenary pardon of all penalties" and singing the same song as Chaucer's Frere John. Speaking in the voice of a departed relative, he declared, "We are in the harshest punishments and torments, from which with a small alms you can buy us back, and you refuse." The striking linguistic development from Chaucer's day was the elegant standard term in the Summary Instruction for the purchasers of the pardon. They were neither buyers nor donors but *contribuentes*, "those contributing," and what they gave was not a purchase price, not a mere gift, not a naked bribe but a *contributio*.[125]

In the face of this operation, Luther's attack—the attack which had such revolutionary reverberations—maintained:

27. They preach man who say that as soon as cash clinks in the chest, the soul flies up.

28. It is certain that when cash clinks in the chest, profit and avarice may be increased; but the intercession of the Church is in the discretion of God alone.

50. Christians are to be taught that, if the Pope knew the exactions of venal preachers, he would prefer that the basilica of St. Peter turn to ashes rather than that it be built with the skin, flesh and bones of his own sheep.

66. The treasures of pardons are nets with which they now fish for the wealth of men.

81–82. This licentious preaching of pardons so operates that even learned men cannot buy back the reverence of the Pope from calumnies or definitely shield it from the acute questions of laymen, such as, "Why does not the Pope empty purgatory for the sake of most holy love and the supreme need of souls—the most just of all reasons—if, as if for the slightest reason, he buys back an infinite number of souls in exchange for the most deadly money with which to build his basilica?[126]

Proposition 27 repudiated a sloganeering way of preaching indulgences, satirized in Chaucer and formally condemned by the Sorbonne in 1482.[127] Proposition 50 was complimentary to the pope, if uncomplimentary to his agents. Proposition 66 was about as critical of "nets" for money as Pierre le Chantre had been. Propositions 81–82 were another form of a question asked as early as Bonaventura and answered by him in terms of the pope's discretion to decide what most benefited the Church. It may have been impertinent but it was surely unheretical to raise the question again in this nuanced way. These specific charges corroborated, as it were, Luther's general rejection of pardons and gave his more radical underlying view credibility and persuasive power with conventional minds.

When Rome replied, and Leo X and Luther were engaged in debate before the eyes of Europe, Luther was able to take the stance of the many reformers who had preceded him. "If St. Bernard lamented his Pope Eugene at a time when the Roman See, although already poisoned, ruled with better hopes, how much more—Luther wrote Leo—shall we lament you, we who have had these three hundred years such an overwhelming excess of evil!" Traditionally, too, he offered the pope the chance of defending himself by separating his person from the Roman Curia: "in that Babylon, Satan himself reigns more truly than you." The power of this rhetoric was that it appealed to a tradition accepted in Rome as much as Germany. Essentially, on corruption Luther said no more than Egidio of Viterbo had said to the Fifth Lateran Council.[128]

Criticism of this kind had not in the past destroyed Roman authority. Now, joined to a bold new theology, it helped complete the destruction. The popular impact may be measured in a play performed in Bern in the Lent of 1523, Nicholas Manuel's *Die Totenfresser*. The "eaters of the dead" invoked by the play's title are the pope, a cardinal, a bishop, etc. The dead are seen as the prelates' source of wealth—"they are our food and prey." The sale of the spiritual is satirized repeatedly. The bishop, for example, rejoices that priests, unable to marry or to be chaste, pay him fees to allow them concubines. If they could marry lawfully, "we would lose the fat in our sausage." The criticism is Chaucerian. Now, in a city that is moving away from Rome, it effectively blocks a hearing for the Roman claim. The eaters of the dead who so abuse the people are to be laughed out of town. The old charges and old images work, if not to produce the new order, to insulate it from the claims of the old.[129]

Luther in 1541 could still invoke the rule of law that a partial judge was no judge: the pope could not judge his own case against him. He could also appeal to the Dantean tradition and speak specifically of paintings of the Last Judgment in which pope, cardinals, bishops, priests, monks were depicted in hell. He could bring into play the whore of Hosea and the scarlet whore of the Apocalypse. He could denounce the Roman church as "an archdevil's whore," "anti-Christlike and anti-God," "the last and most shameless bride of the devil." Sexual imagery merged with the scatalogical to convey what happened in his exit from it: "we once found ourselves seriously stuck in the behind of the hellish whore. . . . But God be praised and thanked who redeemed us from the scarlet shameful whore." No doubt there is a distance between the reform preaching of a

John Bromyard and the polemics of Luther: "anti-God" is a strong term. Still, the basic images are traditional. It is no accident that the Bible translated into German by Luther and published in 1540 carries an illustration of the Book of the Apocalypse in which the great whore of Babylon is the pope. Dante's and Petrarch's image is now a talisman for the reformers.[130]

Rome itself saw the problems which Luther and his allies posed in the traditional terms where a cry of corruption should be met by measures of reform. The first Roman response, of course, was to defend the general lawfulness of indulgences.[131] After that, as the crisis worsened, a new pope, Adrian Florensz, Adrian VI, was elected. An imperial Diet met in Nuremberg holding out the possibility of a settlement in Germany. Writing to his nuncio Francesco Chieragato to convey his views to the Diet in November 1522, the pope declared, "In this Holy See now for some years there have been many abominations. . . . As corruption has emanated from it into all lower parts, so also from it will come the cure and reformation of all." The "inveterate disease" has become "various and multiple," so the means to heal it must be many and cannot all be adopted at once. "We"—Adrian VI—"desire reformation." At the same time he asked Chieragato to send him the names of "good and learned" Germans, who were poor, and who could be given benefices.[132]

"One Hundred Complaints," drafted by the lay estates at the Diet, meanwhile reinforced Adrian's confession of corruption. First on the list was "Dispensations Bought Back by Cash." Innumerable obstacles to marriage, the laymen said, had been invented. Money was then able to obtain the favor of dispensing from them. "Money thus makes lawful for the rich what is freely prohibited to the poor." Complaint number three was "The Burdens of Papal Pardons," by which the popes were said to have "sucked everything from the simple and too credulous Germans." Indulgences destroyed piety. Every purchaser of them "promises himself impunity in sinning." The fourth complaint was that the money so raised was spent "on the luxury of relatives," and the fifth was that the pope reserved cases of absolution to Rome as a way of raising money.[133]

A detailed, inside-outsider's view of the curia was provided in 1523 by Johannes Eck, the champion of Catholic orthodoxy in debates with Luther and his adherents and "Doctor Sow" to Luther. Professor of theology at Ingolstadt, Eck had been called to Rome to advise Adrian. He prepared a set of candid, confidential memos to the curia. In them the importance of the indulgence issue and corruption generally were given a reading from the Catholic side: "The heresy of Luther first arose because of the abuses of the Roman Curia, and it grew and spread because of the corrupt morals of the clergy." To meet these evils, SDN (Sanctissimus Dominus Noster = Our Most Holy Lord) should publish "a bull of reformation," and he should call a general council. Specifically, SDN should not appoint non-Germans to German benefices, should not take annates at more than the ancient rate, should not take annates more than once a year even though the benefice becomes vacant twice, should not permit laymen to be dragged before ecclesiastical tribunals in lay cases, and should excommunicate only in grave cases. Bishops should not permit "notorious concubines" to be tolerated, and should in particular avoid "the wicked name and fact of toleration where they take money and leave the delinquent unpunished." Bishops should choose vicars who do not rob the churches, and they should control the preachers. Pardons "are to be moderated." Scandals have arisen from their collectors, who have used indulgences to pay for hospitality and "what is most foul of all, as a nocturnal wage for wicked women." Germans as well as Romans now bargain over indulgences. The emperor will not allow indulgences "unless he has a part of the Lord's tunic." Indulgences now are so common that they are sold cheaply. If there were not so many, the pope could raise a bigger subsidy from the Germans to fight the Turks. The pope would do well never to grant plenary pardons to be dispensed by particular churches in the provinces. They are not productive: "for three years pardons were collected for the building of San Pietro and yet a horse can scarcely stand there."[134]

Benefices are a worse problem. Those in Rome traffick in them, getting ten, twenty, thirty benefices—"the patrimony of Christ is set before dogs, pimps, and whores. O gods!" In litigation over benefices, fraud is frequent, "and wolf agrees beautifully with wolf." So litigants collude with notaries and others who are promised half of what they win: "when one man is the notary and constant companion of the judge before whom the litigation is conducted, he does everything. . . ." His co-conspirator is the victorious litigant. Another abuse is the buy back (*redemptio*) of pensions: buy backs of them are the trade of "hucksters" (*cauponatores*). Again, a benefice-holder, properly appointed, will be threatened by a fraudulent claim. He buys off his harassment by agreeing that his opponent can succeed him on his death; "then by regression the Roman beast is first in the nest." The threat of litigation over a benefice never ceases, as Eck knows from experience with the university parish he holds in Ingolstadt. He has been sued three times, and "if I oiled the hands [of the last], I would still not be safe from some fourth beast who would be raised up."[135]

Settlements, savoring of simony, are frequently used to settle benefice cases. Settlements for cash are also the rule with the Sacred Penitentiary, the tribunal handling sins reserved to Rome: "All other kinds of satisfaction are now excluded. Commutation alone remains. Silver and gold only." If a couple has married within the prohibited degrees of relationship and need a dispensation, they are always told "You must pay. Only pay, and you shall have. I cannot do it for less." Not surprisingly the office of penitentiary is a salable office, so that its incumbents make money to get a return on their investment and know less of Scripture and the Fathers "than an ass about a lyre." Confessors of the penitentiary hurry penitents saying, "This is nothing. This is nothing. Say something serious." They are not interested in souls but in getting two or three julians per penitent. To make money the penitentiaries release monks from their vows and tighten the canonical way of computing the degrees of kinship and teach proctors of the parties to say what is necessary, "not caring if it be true or false."[136]

Not out of Salisbury or Bromyard but out of observation Eck drew this picture of the Rome which Martin Luther was rejecting; and not for the purpose of polemic or preaching but to distinguish between the pope and the Roman curia: as friendly advice for the pope's ear Eck composed this account. Indulgences—never questioned by him in theory—are treated like a potentially valuable product, spoiled by flooding the market and being entrusted to irresponsible salesmen. Their reform is important—in a later memo he said "by the abuse of pardons, the rashness of the commissioners and certain other things, we have come into this great labyrinth"[137]—but their misuse is only one part of the picture of the traffic in the spiritual. Money commutations, benefice-hunting, and corruption in litigation loom larger. His personal interest in the handling of benefices stands out. A subsequent Eck memo speaks cynically of their centrality: "Finally, I know what the nature and quality is of the Lutherans' claim by which that matter is agitated, and I believe that if twenty of the most learned Germans were provided with some benefices, so the learned would not appear to be disdained, the middle part would be pacified—for it is sometimes necessary to placate Cerberus with offal."[138] Cerberus is now not the papal doorkeeper but the German academic. Reciprocity still rules, Eck thought, as he followed the lead of Adrian VI is searching for practical measures for which "*munera*-giving" would have been a true if tactless label.

Adrian VI, the Diet, Eck were reformers. Their criticisms of the system of which they formed a part were unambiguous. Unless corruption were corrected they thought that Martin Luther's movement could not be contained. Their admissions, complaints, and prescriptions reflected their awareness of the fire now ready to devour their tabernacles. But they were not only prisoners of the system, unable to purge it of salable pardons, marketable benefices, payoffs to placate critics; they were also prisoners of the tradition that identified reformation with the correction of corruption.

From Gregory I to Leo X, reform of corruption had been attempted in many ways, direct and indirect, through sanctions and channeling and teaching, by increased centralization of government and active papal intervention in local affairs; by the founding of religious orders intended to be poor or live on alms; by the cultivation of moral theology and canon law in universities removed from some of the pressures of office-seeking; by preaching, by instruction in the confessional, by personal exhortation; by literature which, reaching its height in Dante and Chaucer, excoriated the bribetaker, the seller of the spiritual, the corrupt Church. Purity had been insisted on. Accusations had multiplied. No charm had worked. Corruption remained.

The tradition also remained. The tradition so relentlessly established and asserted—theological in its roots and in its ultimate sanction of the Last Judgment; literary in its most effective expositions; political in its implications for judges and rulers on earth—was the embodiment, the ultimate "work" of all the preaching and legislating and moralizing and exhorting against bribetakers and Simonians. This tradition, so formidable in its contributors, its scope, and its bulk, had sustained the recurrent reformation which had gone on since the eleventh century, and that reformation had in turn shaped the tradition, making possible—not causing singlehandedly—the Protestant Reformation and the Catholic Counter Reformation. The tradition needed only to be put into the vernacular to provide a basis for other reformations in the secular governments which were now to occupy center stage.

III

The Englishing of the Tradition

1530–1800

11

To Ransom and Redeem, But Not Corrupt

Inheritor of a tradition shared for 900 years with continental Europe and conveyed principally in Latin, England possessed a biblical teaching on bribery that theology, preaching and poetry already made part of English culture. The tradition was now to be Englished in the sense of being put into modern English and in the sense of being expanded, in succeeding centuries, to a range of English institutions.

Energies released by the Reformation, national consciousness high, the educated elite of the sixteenth century wanted in their own tongue not only God's Word but this portion of the Word in particular. They were to do more than translate the tradition. No word existed, in Egypt, Greece, Israel, or Rome, meaning only "a corrupt gift." The word was found in English. Beyond linguistics, as English drama reached its climax in the early seventeenth century, its greatest playwright was to explore, with a subtlety, force, and focus unequaled by earlier theologians, the relations of a corrupt gift to Christian Redemption.

The Word Found. Good judges today are rare: "These bribing judges have been suffered of a long time: and then it was *quasi non fuisset rex in*

Anglia. To suffer this is as much as to say, There is no king in England." These judges who take bribes touch pitch for "bribes may be assembled to pitch."

> Why, you will say we touch none. No, marry, but my mistress your wife hath a fine finger, she toucheth it for you: or else you will have a servant *a muneribus*; he will say, "If you will come to my master and offer him a yoke of oxen, you shall speed never the worse; but I think my master will take none." When he hath offered them to the master, then comes another servant and says, "If you will bring them to the clerk in the kitchen, you shall be remembered the better." This is a friarly fashion, that will receive no money in their hands, but will have it upon their sleeves.[1]

Joshua, a true judge, was "no gift-taker, he was no winker, he was no by-walker." The judge condemned by Cambyses was "a briber, a gift-taker, a gratifier of rich men, he followed gifts as fast as he that followed the pudding, a hand-maker in his office. . . ." Today, "Omnes diligunt munera: 'they all love bribes.' Bribery is a princely kind of thieving. They [sic] will be waged by the rich, either to give sentence against the poor, or to put off the poor man's causes. This is the noble theft of princes and magistrates. They are bribe-takers."[2]

Bribes occur in the administration as well as in the courts, for "Lady Covetousness is a fruitful woman." Offices are bought, and "if they buy, they must needs sell." "This buying of offices is a making of bribery; it is an inducing and enforcing and compelling of men to bribery. . . . This cometh from the devil's consistory, to pay five hundred pound for one office. If they pay so much, it must needs follow that they take bribes, that they be bribe-takers."[3]

Bribes occur in the award of benefices. Thirty apples were given one patron, sent to him through his servant. The patron said he had as good apples in his own orchard. Urged to try the presents, he cut one open. It had ten goldpieces within, and so did all the rest. The donor got his benefice. "Get you a graft of this tree," said the patron, "and I warrant you it will stand you in better stead than all the learning of St. Paul."[4]

Bribes occur in secret, yet there are bribes the preacher knows of: "He that took the silver basin and a ewer for a bribe, thinketh that it will never come out: but he may know now that I know it; I know it not alone, there be more beside me that know it. Oh briber and bribery!" There is the case he knows where one man killed another and was cleared by a jury who received a crown apiece. There is the case he knows where a woman delivered triplets out of wedlock, killed them at birth, and was found not guilty "through bearing of friends, and bribing of the judge." There are the bribes paid by the king's disbursing officers. Say I have spent 20,000 pounds for the king, "Well when I have laid it out, and do bring in mine account, I must give 300 marks to have my bills warranted." Why? "What needeth any bribes-giving except the bills be false?"[5]

What is the remedy for all this bribery? Like Cambyses' judge, the judges must be skinned. "Surely it was a goodly sign and a goodly monument, the sign of the judge's skin. I pray God that we may once see the sign of the skin in England.'"[6] On capital punishment of a more conventional kind for bribed judges:

> But I am sure this is *scala inferni*, the right way to hell, to be covetous, to take bribes and pervert justice. If a judge should ask me the way to hell, I would show him this way: First, let him be a covetous man, let his heart be poisoned with covetousness. Then let him go a little further and take bribes, and last, pervert judgment. Lo, here is the mother and the daughter and the daughter's daughter. Avarice is the mother, she brings forth bribe-taking; and bribe-taking, perverting of judgment. There lacks a fourth thing to make up the mess, which, so God help me if I were judge, should be *hangum tuum*, a Tyburn tippet to take with him, and if it were the judge of the king's bench, my lord chief judge of England; yea, and it were my lord chancellor himself, to Tyburn with him.[7]

In these words, Hugh Latimer preached on avarice before Edward VI and his court in 1549 and 1550. Born about 1490, son of a yeoman, graduate of Cambridge, ordained Catholic priest, Latimer had become bishop of Worcester in the new Anglican establishment under Henry VIII. He had been forced to resign and was then imprisoned by the same king. Released under Edward and now an elder statesman of the Reformation, he spoke with the freedom of one not in office and the sharpness of an ex-prisoner. "Unpreaching prelates," he declared, were why the king was blind. Class-conscious, he insisted that it was yeomen's sons who became preachers. A bishop too blunt to keep his bishopric and too independent to want it back, destined to perish as a martyr under Mary, Latimer put to Edward in plain English the teaching of Christendom on bribery.[8]

Bromyard and Brunton, Scripture and medieval theology lived in Latimer. The *Book of Vices and Virtues*'s "lady of couetise" was reinforced by Cambyses as painted by Herodotus. The pitch of Proverbs and the sin of Gehazi were joined to a jibe at the friars and coupled to a modern Latin construction, "servant *a muneribus*," roughly translatable as "bribe minister," to constitute a rousing assault on bribetakers, above all on "bribing" (that is, bribetaking) judges, with a climax, prophetic in fact, of a bribetaking lord chancellor. What was different about the old writers living in Latimer was that now they spoke in an English made precise and cogent by "bribe," "briber," "bribery," and "bribing."

"Simony" did not disappear from use, but as Latimer's sermon on bribery in benefice-giving showed, the old ecclesiastical term had become less vital than the modern English word which scooped it up and made it (at least in its principal form of purchase of office) a subcategory of "bribery." "Bribe" and its derivatives had been employed in English since Chaucer, although shaded more to extortion than to voluntary offering. "Mede" in the fourteenth century had been a rival. It was a better word for capturing the soft ambiguity of *munus*, if preservation of the ambiguity was wanted.

An immense difference existed psychologically between saying, "You give him an offering," where offering could be either a corrupt inducement or gift acceptable to God, and saying, "You give him a bribe." Ambivalence was eliminated. The offering was stigmatized. The new usage no longer tolerated the double-meaning words of the classical languages.

Scriptural translation slowly moved in the same direction. Fourteen years earlier, in 1535, Miles Coverdale, Cambridge graduate and ex-Augustinian, translating the Bible into English from the Vulgate with the help of more modern versions, used "gifts" at two key texts in Deuteronomy. God, he translated, "regardeth no persons and taketh no gifts" (Dt 10:7). Israelites were commanded to "know no person, also not take giftes" (Dt 16:19). He similarly translated *munera* as "giftes" in 1 Samuel 8:3, 1 Samuel 12:3, Psalm 26:10 and Ecclesiasticus 35:12. Nonetheless, he introduced "brybes" at Ecclesiasticus 40:12. Where the Vulgate read, "Omne munus et iniquitas delebitur"—a broad, contextless reference to *munus*—he translated, "All brybes and unrighteousness shalbe put awaye." Two years later, the Matthew Bible, based on William Tyndale's unpublished translation, introduced "brybe" into 1 Samuel 12:3: "Whose ox have I taken—of whose hand have I receaved any brybe to blynde mine eyes?"[9] Coverdale in 1539, redoing his own work for the Great Bible, followed this emendation. The passage was singled out by Latimer in his preaching before King Edward: "I can commend the English translation," he declared, "that doth interpret *munera*, bribes, not gifts."[10]

Neither Martin Luther, who used *Geschencke* in the key texts, nor Calvin, who used *dons*, *presens*, or *rancon*, found a single word in German or French to express *munera* in an unambiguously negative sense. When in 1560 the Bible was translated from the Hebrew and the Greek by learned English exiles in Geneva—Calvin's brother-in-law William Whittington prominent among them—the precedents set by Calvin might have been followed. The Geneva Bible did still prefer "gift" or "reward" in a majority of cases. Twice, however, it employed "bribe," once (following the Matthew Bible) at 1 Samuel 12:3 and once at Psalm 26:10, referring in the singular to one whose "right hand is ful of bribes." An editor's headnote to Samuel announced that here Samuel was declaring "his integretie." In the London 1578 publication of the Geneva Bible the Psalms were printed in parallel columns "according to the Hebrew" and "as used in common prayer." The first column translated "whose right hands are full of gifts." The translation for liturgical use had "bribes." The King James translation, published in 1611, continued to use "gift" or "reward" more often than "bribe," but it did follow the Geneva Bible at 1 Samuel 12:3, and it made 1 Samuel 8:3 consistent ("took bribes"). It also adopted "bribes" in Psalm 26:10.[11]

Seventy-five years of translation, therefore, had by 1611 established "bribe" as an acceptable although not necessary rendition of *shoḥadh*, *dōron*, or *munus*. "Lady Munera" and "meede," as well as "brybe" were used by Edmund Spenser in *The Faerie Queene* (1594). But the popularity of the Psalms gave "bribe" a currency beyond other terms. "Now-a-days," Latimer had preached in 1550, "they call them gentle rewards. Let them leave their colouring, and call them by their Christian names, bribes."[12] With the Geneva and King James translations, their Christian names were fixed.

Plays on Bribes.   Comedy in 1578—*Promos and Cassandra* by George Whetstone—begins with Promos being made judge in the city of Julio. He announces he will judge all on their merits:

> Ne yet shall Coyne corrupt or foster wrong.

He condemns to death Cassandra's brother for intercourse with the brother's own fiancée. Cassandra pleads for mercy for the condemned man and awakens Promos's desire. He offers her her brother's release and the possibility of marriage if she will sleep with him. Cassandra prefers death to this "raunsome." Urged by her brother, she agrees to it:

> "Cassandra is wonne, thy raunsome great to paye."

Dressed as a boy page, "apparelled thus monstrous to my kinde," she goes to Promos; but once he has had her he orders her brother to be "released" by death. A kindly jailer lets the brother secretly escape. Cassandra denounces Promos to the king of Hungary and Bohemia and tells the story of her brother, "raunsomed with the spoyle of my good name." The king observes:

> If love or hate from Justice leads the Judge,
> Then money sure may overrule the case.

He pronounces her "forced fault" to be "free from evil intent" and finds Promos guilty of worse than rape with Cassandra and of breaking his oath to release her brother. He is sentenced to marry Cassandra and then to be executed. He begs for mercy, but the king says it will be done to him "as he did to others." Before the execution takes place, the brother's escape is discovered. Cassandra thereupon asks the king to spare her husband. He does so, telling Promos to "measure Grace with Justice evermore."[13]

A subplot parallels the main. Promos's legal deputy is Phallax, who says,

> . . . by wit or wyle I have an office got,
> By force whereof every lycence, warrant, pattent, pasport,
> Lease, fyne, fee *et cetera*, pass and repass through Phallax hands.
> Disordered persons brybe me wel to escape from Justice bands.

He is brought a bawd, Lamia, for judgment. Without hesitation or bargaining he releases her. He then asks her for "som grace." She points out he risks the death penalty. He says,

> I have been, my Girle, a Lawier too too long
> If at a pinche I cannot wrest the Law from right to wrong.

Soon he is so close with her that "halfe his brybes unto her share will goe."[14]

Two "promoters" arrest John, a smooching yokel, on the suspicion of lewd behavior. "A share of their venture belongs to me," says Phallax. He advises the protesting young man to pay his captors:

> Phallax: Grease them well in their handes, and speak them fayre.
> John. O Leard God, our tallowe potte is not here.
> Phallax. Tush, clawe them with money.
>
> (II, 3, 2)

John hands over ten shillings and thirteen pence and is told the arrest was all a joke. He asks for his money back and is told "thee tooke thy money in earnest." Later the king issues a proclamation that subjects are to certify and prove to him their grievances. If any officer, "by the corruption of brybes, affecting or not favoring of the person," has wronged them, the king will act. Phallax is denounced before the king as "a common Barriter"; he is discharged from office, and his goods are confiscated to repay his victims.[15]

Derived from a tale by Gianbattista Giraldi Cinthio, a noble of Ferrara, the play's forerunner was published in Italian in 1565. Juriste [= Lawman], the wicked judge in Cinthio's story, actually defends his breaking of his promise to release the brother: "since without offence to Justice he could not be allowed to live." The emperor instructs him that he is wrong: "it would have been more fitting to keep faith with his sister."[16] The norm of reciprocal obligation overrides the public, nonreciprocal duty of the judge. Most audiences will instinctively agree. Whetstone's comedy assumes the point without even going into it.

Cinthio's story differs in a more fundamental way from his imitator's. The brother is not rescued; he is put to death. The difference means that the later pleading of his sister, Epitia [= Pity], to spare Juriste's life is a true act of mercy and forgiveness. But it is an incredible act whose success condemns her to remain the wife of her beloved brother's executioner.

St. Augustine's account of the wife who raised the money for her husband's fine by sleeping with her rich admirer is sometimes cited as a parallel or ancestor of these tales; but the stories are at most distant cousins.[17] No bribery occurs in Augustine for no official is paid off, and the whole question is whether, arguably, a husband might allow this use of his wife's body. In Cinthio and Whetstone, there is no possibility of the brother's consent constituting authorization for his sister. Focus is on the bribe and its requital. In Whetstone more than in Cinthio the subplot and the langauge emphasize the bribery which is at the center of the plot.

"Bribe" is used for what Phallax takes. "Reward" designates what goes to Promos. Just as in the Geneva Bible, no significant difference exists between the two words. The king's proclamation is described as "against Usurie, brybrie, and barrating."[18] "Barrating" is bribery's synonym, and the bribetaker is a "barriter," a term so close to barrister—a term already in vogue—that no lawyer could have relished the closeness. The key verb for paying off a low-level official is "grease," a vigorous Englishing of the old Latin term *ungere*, to oil. The earliest documented use of the term is 1526.[19]

"Raunsom," that is, "redemption," is used to describe Cassandra's sacrifice to rescue her brother. This redemption, by monstrous means, fails. No redemptions are in fact accomplished, even later. Promos and Phallax both confess; but Phallax leaves town unrepentant, and Promos's confession does not save him—he escapes punishment only by the accident of the brother's reappearance. Cassandra is more realistic and less magnanimous than her model, Epitia. The king is a conventionally just monarch who responds to what meets his eye; he is not above the other players. *Promos and Cassandra* shows the nature of bribery well understood. Its relation to redemption is not explored very far.

Corrupt Judge, Corrupt Generals.   For Shakespeare, the verb "to corrupt," and the adjective "corrupt" are recurrent terms. To be corrupt is to be rotted, made evil in a generic way. Joan of Arc upbraids York in Part One of *Henry VI:*

> . . . you that are polluted with your lusts,
> Stain'd with the guiltless blood of innocents,
> Corrupted and tainted with a thousand vices.
>
> (5, 4, 45)

Pollution and stain are natural accompaniments of this impure condition. "To corrupt" is to reduce to an evil state as in Sonnet 144:

> . . . my female evil
> Tempteth my better angel from my side,
> And would corrupt my saint to be a devil.

"To corrupt" means specifically to seduce a woman from virtue. Bertram, the married French count in *All's Well That Ends Well*, wooing a Florentine girl, is said "to broke," that is, to be a broker or go-between, "to pimp." Bertram

> . . . brokes with all that can in such a suit
> Corrupt the tender honor of a maid
>
> (3, 5, 67–68)

"To corrupt" also means specifically to seduce an official from duty. Cardinal Wolsey in *Henry VIII* begins to speak to Queen Katherine of his *integritas.* She says, "O good my lord, no latin." He continues to boast of his "integrity" while he and his Italian colleague advise her to submit to the king's demands. She says:

> Is this your Christian counsel? Out upon ye!
> Heaven is above all yet: there sits a Judge
> That no king can corrupt.
>
> (3, 1, 99–101)

By implication the cardinals' integrity is wanting; they have been corrupted by the king.[20]

Sexual meaning and civic meaning are brought together in *Coriolanus*. A citizen comments after Coriolanus' banishment from Rome:

> I have heard it said the fittest time
> to corrupt a man's wife is when she's fallen
> out with her husband.
>
> (4, 3, 32)

Analogously, Coriolanus is ripe to be seduced. "To corrupt" politically is paralleled to "to corrupt" sexually.

Corruption is also specifically invoked in connection with the sale of indulgences by the pope. In *King John*, Cardinal Pandulph has told John he must admit Archbishop Stephen Langton to England; the king of France supports Pandulph; John rebukes him and all the kings who are

> . . . led so grossly by this meddling priest,
> Dreading the curse that money may buy out,
> And by the merit of vile gold, dross, dust
> Purchase corrupted pardon of a man
> Who in that sale sells pardon from himself.
>
> *KJ* 3, 1, 163–166

King John in Shakespeare is not a villain but a figure of mixed merits. Neither Wyclif nor Chaucer's Host more succinctly denounced pardoners than John's hyperbaton attributing "corrupted" to "pardon."

Corrupting is explicitly linked to bribery in *Part III of Henry VI*; but before this happens a scene is presented of a would-be bribetaker in action. The new king, Edward IV, is approached by Lady Grey, whose husband has been slain in the Yorkist cause and whose lands have then been confiscated. York triumphant, she petitions for their restoration. Edward puts her off, hinting and then finally saying plainly that she will not have the lands until she lies with him. She says she will not "purchase" the lands with loss of her honesty. Immediately after this incident, without any change of scene, the king's brother, humpbacked Gloucester, who has witnessed it, soliloquizes on his "lustful" brother and his own chance at the crown. By an association of ideas with what he has just seen, this image for the cause of his own defect comes to mind:

> She [Love] did corrupt frail nature with some bribe
> To shrink mine arm up like a wither'd shrub,
> To make an envious mountain of my back,
> Where sits Deformity to mock my body.
>
> (3, 2, 155–158)

A metaphorical bribe has produced a corrupt effect and the effect is monstrous.

That a charge of bribery can do serious political damage, especially to an officeholder who is in jeopardy, is plain in *Part Two of Henry VI:*

> Thy sale of offices and towns in France—
> If they were known, as the suspect is great—
> Would make thee quickly hop without thy head.
>
> (2 H. 1, 3, 138–140)

So Queen Margaret speaks to the lord protector, maliciously mixing the sale of towns (treason) and the sale of offices (a more ambiguous offense). The protector makes no reply here. Later he is accused directly, just before he is arrested, by the duke of York:

> 'Tis thought, my lord, that you took bribes of France.
>
> (3, 1, 104)

He answers,

> Nor ever had one penny bribe from France.
>
> (3, 1, 109)

The accusation is not seriously explored, for the conspirators murder him before his trial. What is striking is that Shakespeare's historical sources do not mention the charge. He adds it as dramatically appropriate against a falling minister. Similarly, in the same play, Lord Say, surrounded by an angry, antilawyer mob, defends himself:

> Justice with favor have I always done;
> Prayers and tears have moved me, gifts could never.
>
> (4, 7, 72–73)

Say is politic enough not to introduce the inflammatory word "bribes" even in denying he took them.

Say's speech makes a contrast between what can and cannot legitimately move a judge. In *King John*, Queen Constance says to Queen Elinor apropos the tears of the disinherited Arthur:

> Ay, with these crystal beads heaven shall be brib'd
> To do him justice and revenge on you.
>
> (*KJ* 2, 1, 171–172)

The paradox that tears can be a lawful bribe is played with. Constance also says his tears are "in nature of a fee."

Like Latin *corrupere* and Latin *corruptus*, "to corrupt" and "corrupt" gain force by invoking a range of images of evil. No progression occurs in Shakespeare in his use of the terms. Whenever they are used they designate what destroys wholesomeness. Development does take place in Shakespeare's presentation of the corruption of justice by bribery. Three plays, *The Merchant of Venice, Julius Caesar,* and *Measure for Measure,* mark the progress.

Portia, when Bassanio wins her, pledges her love with a ring, and Bassanio promises to keep the ring as long as he lives. Bassanio then goes to the ducal court where Shylock is claiming against the bond of Antonio, Bassanio's surety for 3,000 ducats. The ducats have not been paid and Antonio is liable on the bond, which calls for a pound of his flesh. Portia enters disguised as a doctor of laws. The duke delegates decision to her in her capacity of learned jurisconsult. She decides that the bond does not permit the creditor to take less or more than a pound. She tells him

> . . . nay if the scale do turn
> But in the estimation of a hair—
> Thou diest, and all thy goods are confiscate.
>
> (*The Merchant of Venice* 4, 1, 330–331)

The principal of the debt she declares forgiven by Shylock's refusal of it in open court. She further holds that, as he indirectly plotted against the life of a citizen, both his life and goods are already forfeit. This draconian sentence is modified by the duke, so that Shylock is at least allowed life and a portion of his property on condition of changing his religion.

After these remarkable judgments have been given, Bassanio acknowledges that he and Antonio have both been acquitted "of grievous penalties." He asks the doctor of laws to accept "in lieu" of these penalties the 3,000 ducats: "We freely cope your courteous pains withal" (4, 1, 412). The winners want to "cope," that is requite, the doctor's decision in their favor. Portia refuses the offering, saying, "He is well paid that is well satisfied." Bassanio presses: "Take some remembrance of us as a tribute / Not as a fee" (4, 1, 421). Portia yields and takes his glove and the ring she herself had given him. Bassanio protests that the ring is "a trifle"; he is ashamed to give it. Portia says she wants it. Bassanio now says more depends on the ring than its value, and he will give the dearest ring in

Venice if he can keep this. Portia pretends disappointment. He yields and sends the ring after her. Portia's lady-in-waiting, Nerissa, disguised as her law clerk, then gets her own husband's ring by begging for it "as a fee" (5, 1, 164). Both women, restored to their own dress, tease their husbands for so easily parting with their rings. The disclosure of their ruse and the teasing provide a cheerful close to the comedy.

Implicit in the incident of the rings is the assumption that a gift, even a gift as large as 3,000 ducats, to a judge who has already decided in one's favor is not corrupt. The cash is "freely" tendered by Bassanio. It lies within Portia's lawful power to accept or refuse. Nothing illicit or improper is suggested when Portia qua judge actually designates the present she prefers. That the ring is extraordinarily dear to the affected litigant does not make it criminal or even impolite to accept it. Portia's innocence in taking the ring conceals her deeper corruption.

Partial Portia!—the paradox of a partial judge being the instrument of justice was present in Ser Giovanni's *Il Pecorone*, the fourteenth-century source which Shakespeare followed.[21] Unnamed, the disguised wife in *Il Pecorone* gives the judgment that exonerates the surety of her husband. Copying the plot, Shakespeare skates over the difficulty: Portia is a judge acting in a case where she has an interest affecting her integrity. She is hearing the case of her husband's surety. She is deciding that her husband's debt has been canceled by his creditor's actions. She is condemning her husband's enemy to further forfeitures. She is as highly a prejudiced judge as could be found. In form she is an impartial stranger, in fact a deeply interested party to the case. If Bassanio were seen paying her 3,000 ducats in advance of her judgment, everyone would be disgusted at her prejudice. We are actually given equivalent information. We know that releasing her husband's surety and declaring his debt canceled will enrich Bassanio and herself by 3,000 ducats. Her relationship to Bassanio would disqualify her if it were known. In actual Venice, famous for its justice, such prejudice would have been intolerable. Even in Shakespeare's imaginary Venice, a spouse could not have sat openly in judgment of her husband's debt and her husband's surety. Only the slight of hand which presents Portia as a doctor of laws from Padua conceals her bias from the court and from the audience. Only the apparent magnanimity of her refusal of the 3,000 ducats conceals the fact that she, the released debtor's wife, has already enriched herself by this amount by her own judgment. Psalm 71:6 teaches that is is justice which falls like rain from heaven; for Portia it is mercy (4, 1, 85). She makes her famous speech urging such heavenly mercy on Shylock while she herself is seriously deficient in elementary justice.

Portia does have other defects—often overlooked in the era before women's liberation when she was treated as a paragon of her sex; in Boston, Massachusetts a law school was even named for her. She cheats in arranging the music to point out the right casket to Bassanio when he is her favored suitor. She gains the upper hand over him when he is her husband by her trick of getting his ring, and she exploits her advantage. It is she who issues the completely merciless sentence on Shylock. She does not have a very tender conscience. She may even be made to speak with unconscious irony when, refusing Bassanio's money, she declares she is already "well paid" (4, 2, 417): indeed, she is. Yet the tone of the play is not designed to focus on Portia's deficiencies. She is the principal heroine, she is the prize sought by the suitors, she is the resourceful wife who procures the delivery of her husband's friend, she is the "Daniel come to judgment," as with Johannine irony Shylock is made to predict (4, 1, 223). No bystander suggests that a partial judge is no judge at all or that bias by hate or love is as great a bias as that caused by gold or that Portia in fact has a financial interest in the case. Shylock, having been cast as the villain, must be brought to book. The monstrousness of the bond he is enforcing dwarfs all other considerations. Portia is presented as a *dea ex machina* in effecting the result.

Portia saves Antonio. She saves him without risk to herself, by a putting on of another's identity. She saves him as a learned man helps others, by putting his wit at their service. Portia's self remains self-possessed, rejoicing even in the superiority exhibited. She delivers a homily on the need of all for mercy, but she effects her delivery of Antonio by legal quibbling. Bassanio, at the moment where Antonio's life seems about to be taken, says he would give both himself and his wife "to deliver" his friend. Portia's comment at the suggestion of self-sacrifice is tart:

> Your wife would give you little thanks for that
> If she were by to hear you make the offer.
>
> (4, 1, 288–289)

Portia has a safer, surer way than offering herself. The law is used to confound the law. She even puts the ancient image of the impartial scales to an innovative use in service of her judgment. Like the devil himself in some theologians' view of the Redemption, Shylock is tempted to his own destruction by desire for blood—the blood of a man who is guiltless. Focus on the fall of Shylock obscures Portia's less than honest part. That for her judgment Bassanio will give a reward that is a breach of his own fidelity, that in her judgment she is a biased judge using the scales as an instrument of partiality are ironies below the surface, which Shakespeare does not care to probe, even if the unevenness of Portia's character invites their exploration. At no point, at any rate, does anyone in the play call Antonio's delivery a redemption or Portia a redeemer.

The Merchant of Venice was written between 1596 and 1598. By 1599 Shakespeare had finished *Julius Caesar.* Ironies involving bribery are pressed harder here; a whole scene depicting character depends on their treatment.

Brutus and Cassius have been the leaders in the assassination of Caesar. They are now encamped with an army arrayed against Caesar's heirs.

They have begun to quarrel and go to Brutus' tent to do so privately. Cassius begins:

> That you have wrong'd me doth appear in this:
> You have condemn'd and noted Lucius Pella
> For taking bribes here of the Sardians;
> Wherein my letters, praying on his side,
> Because I knew the man, were slighted off.

BRUTUS: You wrong'd yourself to write in such a case.

CASSIUS: In such a time as this it is not meet
> That every nice offense should bear his comment.

BRUTUS: Let me tell you, Cassius, you yourself
> Are much condemn'd to have an itching palm
> To sell and mart your offices for gold
> To undeservers.

CASSIUS: I an itching palm!
> You know that you are Brutus that speaks this,
> Or, by the gods, this speech were else your last.

BRUTUS: The name of Cassius honors this corruption,
> And chastisement doth therefore hide his head.

CASSIUS: Chastisement!

BRUTUS: Remember March; the ides of March remember.
> Did not great Julius bleed for justice sake!
> What villain touch'd his body that did stab
> And not for justice? What, shall one of us,
> That struck the foremost man of all this world
> But for supporting robbers—shall we now
> Contaminate our fingers with base bribes
> And sell the mighty space of our large honours
> For so much trash as may be grasped thus?
> I had rather be a dog and bay the moon
> Than such a Roman.

CASSIUS: Brutus, bait not me!
> I'll not endure it. You forget yourself
> To hedge me in. I am a soldier, I,
> Older in practice, abler than yourself
> To make conditions.

$$(4, 3, 1–32)$$

"Fee" and "tribute" had been used in *The Merchant of Venice*, "bribe" not at all. Here the precise term crackles in Cassius' reproach and Brutus' indictment. Caesar himself, according to Brutus, has been killed for complicity in evil. The bribes over which the generals quarrel are of two kinds: local Sardians' payoffs to Pella, and Cassius' sale of offices. What is objectionable to Brutus is selling to "undeservers." To do this is "corruption," calling for punishment. It is the mark of a greed that is analogized with lust. Cassius' palm is said to itch the way Kate in Trinculo's song in *The Tempest* (2, 2, 55) is said to itch for a tailor.

Purchase and sale of office was a common practice in Elizabethan England. Take one example involving two men of generally good reputation acting in regard to a matter where the seller had duties to the Queen and to the orphan involved: William Cecil, Lord Burghley, in his capacity as Master of the Court of Wards, sold the guardianship of Walter Aston, a rich orphan, to Attorney General Edward Coke for 1,000 pounds. Coke found it an immensely profitable transaction, eventually making Aston pay him 4,000 pounds when Aston married. Neither Cecil nor Coke had committed a crime. Such sales were a substantial source of income to Cecil. A profit like this enabled Coke to become a famously uncorrupt judge. Nonetheless, Cecil's private compilation of his profits from the wardship sales was marked "to be burned"—a notation that would not have been used if the income was beyond reproach. Ambivalence attended the sale of office. Shakespeare gives to Brutus the high-minded sentiments of the most sensitive members of the community. Cassius does what officeholders in Elizabeth's court ordinarily do.[22]

Brutus speaks not in terms of criminal law but in terms of honor. Bribes are dirty, "base," and "trash." It is dishonorable to be a taker. Brutus would rather metamorphose himself into an animal. Cassius sees himself as a practical fellow. Pella's bribery is an offense too special to be followed up in wartime. Cassius himself has more experience than Brutus in making "conditions," that is, in managing affairs. Yet for Cassius the charge of corruption is unsupportable. That is the first irony. The practical man cannot hear his practice called by its right name.[23]

The scene continues:

BRUTUS: There is no terror, Cassius, in your threats
          For I am arm'd so strong in honesty
          That they pass me by as the idle wind,
          Which I respect not. I did send to you
          For certain sums of gold, which you deni'd me;
          For I can raise no money by vile means.
          By heaven, I had rather coin my heart
          And drop my blood for drachmas than to wring
          From the hard hands of peasants their vile trash
          By any indirection. I did send
          To you for gold to pay my legions
          Which you deni'd me. Was that done like Cassius?
                                              (4, 3, 66–77)

With the repetition of a single phrase, "which you deni'd me," the irony of Brutus' position, and of all honorable politicians like Brutus, is made clear. He will not soil his hands with bribes, but he will use the money a bribetaker has gathered; in fact, he has to. He is dependent on the vile means of Cassius to pay his troops. Unconscious of the irony, he avows his repudiation of "indirection," that is, crookedness. Cassius can be the crook. Cassius can deserve chastisement. With his cooperation Brutus will keep his honor clean. At the end of the encounter Brutus appears to be baying at the moon with an idealism impossible to make a reality on earth.

Redemption Foul and Fair.   From the first, and by title, *Measure for Measure* takes up the nature of reciprocity. Exploring it profoundly, the play illuminates the difference between bribery and redemption. It is the only work of Shakespeare that takes its title from words of Jesus:

For with what measure ye mete shall it be measured to you.

> *(Mt 7, 2)*

Reciprocity in the ultimate sense of the Gospel of Matthew is the theme of the play.

Angelo has been left by the duke to rule Vienna in his place. He is a person of great apparent virtue, marked by icy self-control. Sexual probity —his blood is "very snow-broth" (1, 4, 58)—is the symbol of his general integrity. His name announces his extraordinary virtue. He thinks of himself as Christ-like before temptation: he scarcely admits "that his appetite / Is more to bread than stone" (1, 3, 51–53). He enforces the law against fornication by condemning to death Claudio who has got his fiancée pregnant. Claudio's sister, Isabella, intercedes for him:

ANGELO: Your brother is a forfeit of the law,
And you but waste your words.

ISABELLA: Alas, alas!
Why, all the souls that were were forfeit once,
And he that might the vantage best have took
Found out the remedy. How would you be
If he which is the top of judgment should
But judge you as you are? O, think on that!
And mercy then will breathe within your lips
Like man new made.

> (2, 2, 71–78)

Angelo, a seeming Christian, is urged to judge like Christ, to judge as one made new in Christ. He insists that he most shows pity when he shows justice, "For then I pity those I do not know." As Isabella is dismissed, having failed, she says

Hark how I'll bribe you! Good my lord, turn back.

ANGELO: How? Bribe me?

(2, 2, 145–146)

"Bribe" rings an alarm with the ruler. Flat offer is a challenge and an insult. Isabella answers,

> Ay, with such gifts that heaven shall share with
> you. . . .
> Not with fond sicles of the tested gold
> Or stones whose rates are either rich or poor
> As fancy values them; but with true prayers. . . .

(2, 2, 147–151)

Prayer appears to be acceptable. Angelo tells her to come tomorrow.

The "crystal beads" which were a lawful way of bribing in *King John* have reappeared. The sexual bribe demanded by a ruler to do his office, sketched in *Part III of Henry VI*, is now to be used as the basis of a more profound investigation. When Isabella has gone, Angelo meditates on what he may be given. Like carrion in the sun, he thinks he is becoming "corrupt with virtuous season" (2, 2, 165–167). When Isabella returns he asks her,

> Which had you rather—that the most just law
> Now took your brother's life or, to redeem him
> Give up your body to such sweet uncleanness
> As she that he hath stain'd?

(2, 4, 52–55)

Isabella at length replies,

> Better it were a brother died at once
> Than a sister, by redeeming him,
> Should die for ever.

ANGELO: Were not you then as cruel as the sentence
> That you have slandered so?

ISABELLA: Ignomy in ransom and free pardon
> Are of two houses. Lawful mercy
> Is nothing kin to foul redemption.

(2, 4, 106–113)

Angelo pursues:

> . . . Redeem thy brother
> By yielding up thy body to my will. . . .

(2, 4, 163)

Redemption by Christ has been put by Isabella as the model for Angelo, but he has responded by asking her to redeem her brother with herself, and redemption has come to seem, like *redemptio* in much Roman usage, filthy. Paid-for forgiveness stands in contrast to lawful mercy. Differences between a prayer as a bribe and a body as a bribe, and between a body offered as living sacrifice and a body offered for lust, are not stated, but assumed.

The duke reappears as a friar to advise Isabella how to "redeem your brother from the angry law" (3, 1, 207). She is to promise Angelo "satisfaction," but her place will be taken at the tryst by Mariana, Angelo's jilted fiancée. Unlike the heroine of Cinthio's tale and Whetstone's comedy, Isabella will not have to pay the price in person. This trick is carried out. Angelo has intercourse with Mariana thinking she is Isabella. But instead of releasing Claudio, he orders him executed. Without Isabella knowing, this command is frustrated by the duke. In the final act, the duke returns in his own person. Isabella asks him for "justice, justice, justice, justice" (5, 1, 24). He tells her to ask it of Angelo. She says, "You bid me seek redemption of the devil!" (5, 1, 29), and denounces Angelo as a murderer, oath-breaker, adulterer, and virgin-violator. The duke tells her Angelo's "integrity / Stands without blemish." He advises Angelo,

> In this I'll be impartial; be you judge
> Of your own cause.
>
> (5, 1, 166–167)

The duke prolongs the charade but finally reveals his knowledge of Angelo's guilt and calls him to account. Angelo abandons all defense, saying "[L]et my trial be my confession" (5, 1, 377). The duke renders justice. The first step is to make Angelo formalize his marriage with Mariana. He then comes before the duke for sentencing,

> Being criminal in double violation
> Of sacred chastity, and of promise-breach
> Thereon dependent for your brother's life.
>
> (5, 1, 409–411)

The duke, pretending still that Claudio has been killed, adds that the "very mercy of the law cries out,"

> 'An Angelo for Claudio! death for death!'
> Haste still pays haste, and leisure answers leisure;
> Like doth quit like, and Measure still for Measure.
>
> (5, 1, 414–416)

Mariana pleads for his life. The duke refuses. Isabella, who thinks Angelo her brother's executioner, is then appealed to by Mariana: "Sweet Isabel, do yet but kneel with me." Isabella kneels in intercession. The duke reveals Claudio is alive and pardons Angelo, who is restored to Mariana; the duke proposes to Isabella. The play ends with justice vindicated, reconciliation effected, love regnant; modern readings which have Isabella turning silently away from the duke's proposal fail to acknowledge the harmonies established.

All's Well That Ends Well is a title that could well apply to this ending; and indeed the two plays are close in time and spirit. *All's Well* is earlier and comparatively simple—the story of Bertram who seeks to "corrupt" a Florentine girl and finds that he has bedded his own wife in disguise. Her chaste devotion is what saves him from paying the penalty of a corruptor of virgins. Through his wife's trick he is restored to wholeness. *Measure for Measure* is deeper, richer, more complex; it intertwines the sexual motifs with the great issue of good and evil reciprocities.

Interest in Shylock's usury in *The Merchant of Venice* overshadows Portia's corruption. *Measure for Measure* faces openly what *The Merchant of Venice* conceals. When Isabella calls for "justice, justice, justice, justice," she receives justice at the level where appearances dominate. As Shylock's demand for justice led to his downfall so apparently does hers. Strict justice requires strict proof. She cannot provide it. She and Mariana are treated as slanderers, Angelo as their wronged victim who will be permitted to vindicate his wrong by condemning his accusers. Only, as the audience is cognizant of his villainy, this kind of strict justice by a prejudiced judge is being criticized. When, without Portia's disguise, Angelo is put in Portia's place to judge his own case, the duke's comment underlines the criticism. "I'll be impartial," he declares, making Angelo his own judge. Justice on this purely human level not only boomerangs against the one seeking it; it is gravely flawed in its embodiment.

Near the climax of *King Lear*—in the scene of Lear mad on the moor, which is a climax in itself—the contradictions in human justice provide Lear with matter for his outpourings:

> Thou rascal beadle, hold thy bloody hand!
> Why dost thou lash that whore? Strip thy own back.
> Thou hotly lusts to use her in that kind
> For which thou whip'st her. The usurer hangs the cozener.
> Through tatter'd clothes small vices do appear;
> Robes and furr'd gowns hide all. Plate sin with gold,
> And the strong lance of justice hurtless breaks;
> Arm it in rags, a pigmy's straw doth pierce it.
> None does offend, none—I say none! . . .
>
> (KL 4, 6, 159–168)

Because wealth shields sin (not only bribery but discrimination based on wealth is meant), because men are punishing their own sins in others, there is no place for human justice—"none does offend, none." Yet is this not madness, "matter with impertinency mixed," as Edgar says of Lear's speech? If offenses are to be wiped out, more than comradeship in sin is needed.

Angelo is the rascal beadle, engaged in the very act he presumes to punish in another. Yet, like Brutus, he is in his own eyes an honorable man. Like Brutus, he pursues an abstract ethical ideal. Like Brutus, he is self-sufficient yet deficient in love. Like Brutus, he is corruptible. But while Brutus hid from himself his dependence on Cassius' corrupt means, Angelo sins openly and falls self-consciously.[24]

Measure for Measure in one respect does not try to move beyond the human level established in its English and Italian forerunners. Without argument the play assumes that Angelo should have kept the promise to free Isabella's brother. Failing to do so, he is, in Isabella's words, "a murderer," and in the duke's judgment, guilty of "promise-breach." From Cicero to Cinthio to Shakespeare it is apparent that the obligation of reciprocity is felt as stronger than the judge's duty to enforce the law.

Measure for Measure goes beyond its predecessors in Isabella's redemptive act. As long as the heroine paid the price for her brother's life by her own sexual submission, she was herself redeemer, corruptor, and corrupted. When Shakespeare borrowed from *All's Well That Ends Well* and let Mariana be the substitute, he left Isabella without a role in her brother's salvation; she became as peripheral as the nearly forgotten Florentine in the other play. Isabella is nonetheless the heroine. She remains so not by saving her brother but by saving Angelo; and here her work is not bribery but true redemption.

Isabella's action may be overshadowed by the duke, who plays a role far greater than Whetstone or Cinthio's ruler. On one level the duke is an ideal human monarch, whose inspirations owe something to *Basilikon Dōron*, the treatise on royal government written by England's new king, James I. In these instructions for his son Henry, James had insisted on the importance of integrity in judges. He advised, "And therefore delite to haunt your Session, and spie carefully their proceedings; take good heed, if any briberie may be tried among them, which cannot over severely be punished."[25] The duke is taking James's advice literally. He is haunting his court of justice and taking special care that bribery not be practiced by his judges. *Measure for Measure* was put on at King James's court on St. Stephen's Day, December 29, 1604. The allusions to the book in the duke's remarks on government are deliberate compliment; the carrying out of James's advice, a felicitous correspondence of the plot to the king's view of royal oversight.[26]

Measure for Measure was also a Christmas play; and the duke—"more than Prospero"[27]—stands not only for royalty but also for divinity. His actions are like those of the divine stand-ins in the parables. Such modern readings as a recent Ashland, Oregon production in which the duke was a moody sadist take no account of the biblical clues to his role. At the beginning he is like the master in Matthew 25 who leaves his servants with the talents they must employ profitably. At the end he is like the master of

Matthew 18 who judges the unmerciful servant by his own standard.[28] Throughout, he knows everything, anticipates everything, arranges everything. As he prepares the dénouement he announces:

> Look th' unfolding star calls up the shepherd.
>
> (4, 2, 215)

He becomes the Shepherd who separates sheep from goats. As he pronounces judgment on Angelo, he follows the prophecy of Chaucer's Persoun: wolflike lords shall receive mercy in the same measure they have measured to poor folk.[29] As in *The Merchant of Venice*, like is given for like—only now by a fair and godlike arbiter. Impartially judging, unlike Portia or his own corrupt counterpart Angelo, he is Christ the Judge. Impartial judgment, however, is not the climax of the play.

The structure of the play hangs on redemption, fair and foul. Isabella seeks to redeem Claudio with a plea. She is asked to give her body. Her stratagem for his release then fails. Only the knowledge and power of the ubiquitous disguised duke saves Claudio. The redemption Isabella does achieve is of Angelo. She brings him from death to life. She does it by forgiveness. Like Portia she had only used words when she had entreated Angelo for mercy. When she kneels to the duke on Angelo's behalf, she practices mercy herself.[30]

Isabella's act is internal and so simple that there is a risk that it seem perfunctory. Shakespeare gives it a physical dimension, emphasized by Mariana thrice asking Isabella to "lend a knee." That the act is psychologically difficult is suggested by what has already been seen of Isabella. She prays Angelo for mercy for her brother only as spurred on by Lucio. She ranks Claudio's life with her own and thinks Angelo his murderer. She puts her chastity above her life and knows Angelo has tried to violate it. She now forgives an enemy who has injured her intimately. Behind the apparent simplicity of her action lie the words of the Shepherd in the judgment scene in Matthew, "When I was hungry you gave me food . . . when in prison you visited me" (Mt 25:33–37)—that is, an act done in charity for any human being is an act done to Christ. In act not word Isabella obeys Christ's teaching, "For if you forgive others the wrongs they have done, your heavenly Father will also forgive you" (Mt 6:14). The reciprocity of redemption is forgiveness matched by forgiveness. When the duke is still testing Isabella, he calls for "an Angelo for Claudio" and states the iron law by which a death matches a death. Isabella's act of mercy breaks the bind and introduces a new measure where mercy reciprocates mercy.

Cinthio's story had presented salvation won by forgiveness; Whetstone's play had suggested the ambiguity of "raunsom" describing Cassandra's tender of sex to Promus. Shakespeare's most immediate inspiration was James I's punning title, *Basilikon Dōron, Royal Gift, Royal Bribe*. *Measure for Measure* distinguishes gift from bribe, resolves the ambiguity of "raunsom," shows salvation won by forgiveness.

Images and ideas of the redemption of mankind by Christ are explicit and played with. Isabella's offer of a prayer is "to bribe"; the proposed purchase of her brother with her body is "to redeem." When Isabella exclaims, "You bid me to seek redemption of the devil," her statement punningly evokes the line of Christian theologians who taught that redemption was *from* the devil. When Angelo asks her to "lay down the treasures of your body" (2, 4, 96), the redemptive treasury of Christ's sufferings is recalled. The climax of her great speech for mercy is, "Why, all the souls that were were forfeit once."

Concentrating on the lofty parallel, Shakespeare drops the low-level bribery of Phallax. He does not use the pungent but low-level word "grease." More boldly than any major Christian theologian, Shakespeare focuses attention on the similarity in structure of a bribe to God and the redemption won by Christ. Using the "Christian names" of *munera* he asks what is the difference.

Angelo thinks there is no difference. Isabella answers him by intuition: "Lawful mercy / Is nothing kin to foul redemption." The reason is not given. By itself her statement is unpersuasive. The theologians' paradox of a Supreme Judge satisfied by His Son's death is not solved in words. Imitating Christ in an act of forgiveness, Isabella shows how redemption is lawfully won. Virginal intercessor, she is more than an advocate. Salvation comes from her simple action. By it the iron law of reciprocity is transmuted to a higher sphere. Mercy for another is obtained by the merciful. Redemption occurs when wrong is forgiven by a victim. Such redemption is no bribe offered to corrupt the judge.

Words existed to designate in English the sin of bribery. Was it also a crime? Were denunciations of bribery to be confined to the pulpit and the theater, or could *Measure for Measure* be enacted not on an English stage but at the center of the English system of justice?

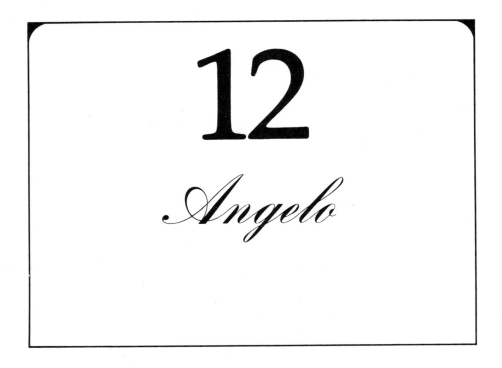

12

Angelo

Haile, happie Genius of this antient pile!
How comes it all things so about thee smile?
The fire, the wine, the men! and in the midst,
Thou stand'st as if some Mysterie thou didst! . . .
Fame, and foundation of the English Weale . . .
Englands *high Chancellor: the destin'd heire*
In his soft Cradle to his fathers Chaire,
Whose even Thred the Fates spinne round, and full,
Out of their Choysest, and their whitest wooll.[1]

So Ben Jonson celebrated Francis Bacon's sixtieth birthday in January 1621. In the same month James I invested him as a viscount, and as Lord St. Albans he wrote the king: "So this is the eighth rise or reach, a diapason in music, even a good number and accord for a close. . . . Then I must say, *quid retribuam?* I have nothing of mine own." He had only an undivided heart to give, "hoping that your Majesty will do, as your superior doth; that is, that finding my heart upright, you will bear with my other imperfections."[2]

Very few imperfections, however, seemed to exist to be borne, except that James I would sometimes be heard to mutter, reading St. Albans's latest book, the *Novum Organum*, "It is like the peace of God—it passeth all understanding."[3] Against his legal work for the Crown, the king had no complaints. The king's solicitor-general from 1607 to 1613, attorney general from 1613 to 1617, lord keeper in 1617, and lord chancellor since 1618, Bacon had served the king longer than any other man in high legal office, and none had been more approved by James. If the king wanted a learned, devout, and devoted counterpart, who could fill the role more perfectly? Indeed when the king left for Scotland in 1617 he invested Bacon with royal authority as his regent in England; and as Chancellor, St. Albans had a conscience meant to be the measure of the King's.

Another poet, John Donne, preaching to the lawyers at Lincoln's Inn in 1620, had a vision more prophetic than Ben Jonson's birthday verse: "No attribute of God is so often iterated in Scripture, no state of God so often inculcated," Donne preached, "as this of Judge, and Judgment, no word concerning God so often repeated . . . and he will judge the world, and the Judges of the world; other Judges, die like men, weakly; and they fall, that's worse, ignominiously; and they fall like Princes, that's worst. . . ."[4]

Wrenham's Complaint.   Two years after Bacon had become the holder of the great seal of Chancery and the official keeper of the king's conscience, a complaint was made to the king against him. The complainant, John Wrenham, had begun a suit in Chancery in 1606 against Sir Edward Fisher for breach of a long-term lease. In 1608 the then lord chancellor decreed that Wrenham should have the leased land, but Fisher had encumbered the lease with conveyances and claimed that these antedated Wrenham's suit. Wrenham had to bring a new bill in Chancery to show that Fisher's conveyances were fraudulent. He seemed near success when he imprudently yielded to a suggestion of the old chancellor that he let Fisher buy him out. Agreeing to this compromise, he let the master of the rolls set the value of the land. In 1610 the master of the rolls set it at 200 pounds per year. Wrenham objected and asked for new hearings on the value. These resulted in the old lord chancellor setting the value at 340 pounds. Fisher then moved to back out of the compromise and give up the lease, paying Wrenham the profits he had had in the meantime from the land; and it was so decreed by the old chancellor, subject to Wrenham returning to Fisher a down payment Fisher had made on the compromise. Wrenham, however, failed to return the money. The case was in this posture when Bacon inherited it in 1617. Bacon then decreed that Fisher and Wrenham should return to the compromise, but using the master of the rolls' valuation of the land of 200 pounds per year.

To reach this result, highly unsatisfactory to Wrenham, it had taken Wrenham eleven years of litigation in Chancery. The issues of the original lease, of alleged offsetting debts of Wrenham to Fisher, of the fraudulent conveyances, and of the value of the land had been heard by various masters in Chancery, by the master of the rolls, by Bacon's predecessor, and by

Bacon. In the piecemeal style of Chancery—the cat-and-mouse style as it looked to outsiders from Wrenham to Dickens—there had been some twelve reports by officers of the Chancery, forty-six orders issued by Chancery judges, and over eighty hearings. Wrenham had in the last stages of the case been represented by the king's own attorney general, Henry Yelverton, and Fisher had been represented by almost equally eminent counsel, Sergeant Crewe. Wrenham had spent close to 3,000 pounds, and by Bacon's last decree was losing, he calculated, over 40 percent of the value of his property. The harm was accomplished, as Wrenham saw it, by Bacon's "raising out of Hell" the master of the rolls' report which had died seven years earlier.[5]

Wrenham had then recalled the words of the king on justice. In a speech to the Star Chamber in 1616 James had declared that all judges must account to him and that he was especially bound in conscience to keep Chancery "free from corruption." Turning to his subjects, the king had advised them to acquiesce in any judgment against them. "Do not complain and importune me against Judgments. . . . Be satisfied and content when Judgment is passed against you. [T]rouble me not. . . . But," he added, "if you find bribery or corruption, then come boldly; but when I say boldly, beware of coming to complain except you be very sure to prove the justice of your cause. . . . Your accusing of an upright judge deserves double punishment. . . . And be not tild [tilted] on your own Lawyers' tales, that say the cause is just for their own gain; but believe the judges that have no hire but of me."[6] Wrenham was familiar with this speech, printed in 1616; but he ignored the king's caveats and the king's stress on bribery or corruption. He had been subjected to injustice. He would let the king know. He petitioned the king for relief, setting out the conflicting valuations of Bacon and his predecessor. The king procrastinated. Wrenham filed two more petitions. The king remarked that if he reheard every case of a dissatisfied litigant, "No other business would be done by us." He pressed Wrenham, "Will you charge my Lord Chancellor with injustice or bribery?" Again Wrenham failed to catch the accent on bribery. Convinced that he had been unjustly treated, he said the chancellor had been unjust. At that James said he would ask the chancellor, and Bacon produced the master of the rolls' report, adding he was sorry that it should have hurt Wrenham. Fearing the king would not go beyond this one-sided evidence and seeing Bacon's apology as evidence of "a guilty conscience," Wrenham then prepared an elaborate statement of the case. He introduced it with the charge that Bacon covered oppression "with cunning and rhetoric" and had "racked all out of joint." He had the manuscript wrapped in black velvet and presented it to the king on Good Friday. Shortly thereafter, Wrenham was brought before the Star Chamber for slander of the chancellor.[7]

Wrenham's prosecutors were familiar with the original case. One was his old counsel, Attorney General Yelverton; the other, Fisher's counsel, Sergeant Crewe. No one commented on these switches of role, except that

Yelverton made something out of his own moderation in pursuing Wrenham's cause "as far as equity would suffer," in contrast to Wrenham's own wild charge. Both Yelverton and Crewe emphasized that Wrenham had not alleged any bribery. "The razor of his tongue," Yelverton declared, "cannot charge him [Bacon] that any thing came between God and his own conscience, but the merits of the cause." Bacon had judged like the virtuous son of a virtuous father, himself once lord keeper. The lord chancellor, said Crewe, "hath always despised riches and set honor and justice before his eyes." He had judged "out of his noble conscience and integrity of his heart." The "sign of a corrupted estate," a "bribed magistrate," was not to be found here. Yelverton neatly combined reprobation of bribery with an appeal for reciprocity: "As justice is not to be recompensed in price, so ought not the scandal hereof to go unpunished." Wrenham's black velvet book had been black and foul. Such slander operated "to discourage judges and vilify justice." Yelverton asked that his old client be punished as, in the second year of James I, one Foorth (Ford) had been punished.[8]

Wrenham undertook his own defense, a man "so perplexed with so many miseries," that he "knew not how to behave." How could he defend himself without repeating the slander? How could he show he had been given an unjust decree without showing the chancellor to be unjust? Eleven years of suit, eighty hearings, forty-six orders, twelve reports, all overturned by the last decree. He was ruined by the suit; he who had once given bread to others must now beg his own; his wife and four children (the eldest only five) must beg. His miseries had "enforced" him to petition the king; "for misery made patient Job break out and swell against God himself."[9]

Wrenham went on to try to explain the ins and outs of his complex case, but he was cut off by Yelverton: "Mr. Wrenham, for you to shift it off, doth but aggravate your offense." Thereupon Wrenham knelt and threw himself on the mercy of the court.[10] Sir Edward Coke then spoke as one of the judges. Wrenham had attacked the dead master of the rolls. "I never heard him taxed of corruption," Coke said. Wrenham had attacked the king, saying "Let the King rise," as if the king were asleep. There had indeed been corrupt chancellors—de la Pole and Wolsey; and "if a judge's conscience be oiled and moistened with corruption, then all is naught." But all Wrenham had shown was a difference of opinion among chancellors. Coke was walking what he himself enigmatically called "a very slender bridge." He was not in favor of slander of judges. As attorney general he had procured Foorth's punishment. But the present chancellor was his ancient enemy, responsible for his own loss of the chief justiceship of Common Pleas. If he was circumspect in saying nothing against his honesty, he said nothing for it, but simply called for Wrenham to be punished like Foorth.[11]

Sir Laurence Tanfield, lord chief baron of the Exchequer, noted that Wrenham had accused "the principal officer and magistrate of justice in the kingdom," the man who nominated all justices of the peace and all sheriffs, who not only was "sole judge in chancery," but chief judge of the Star Chamber itself. "And shall we think that this man is bought and sold to corruption . . . ?" He concurred with Coke.[12]

"Can you, Mr. Wrenham, charge your judge with corruption?" asked Sir Edward Mountague, lord chief justice. The question was rhetorical and called for a negative. The slander of a chief justice in the days of Henry VII, he recalled, had cost a knight both his ears and a time in the public pillory. Wrenham deserved Foorth's judgment.[13]

Those bishops who were also judges of Star Chamber then spoke. Launcelot Andrewes, the great Anglican divine, who was the king's favorite preacher, royal almoner or official dispenser of charity, and bishop of Ely, had once delivered lectures at Cambridge on the Ten Commandments. Bribery he had said was against the Ninth Commandment. The lawyer who paid "a gift or a bribe"—Andrewes did not say to whom—or who "by any wrong means" sought "to bolster out any matter" fell under the prohibition against false witnessing. As for a judge, without mentioning bribery, Andrewes had said he too could transgress the Ninth Commandment: "it is most perilous on his side, for Deuteronomy 1, 17, the judgment is God's; and therefore what judge soever giveth a wrong sentence, *facit Deum mendacem*, he 'maketh God to speak a lie.'"[14] Now sitting in a case where a judge had been accused of having made God lie, he peremptorily upheld sentencing the accuser. Such a complaint "in so foul a manner, against so great a person, in so high a place, deserves sharp punishment." John King, bishop of London, spoke as Andrewes had written earlier: Judges "sit in God's seat and execute his, not their own judgments." Yet though they gave God's judgments, they were, Bishop King observed, men, and in fact differed with each other. It was, then, wrong, indeed unnatural, to complain of differing judgments.[15] George Abbot, archbishop of Canterbury, followed up the bishop of London's first thought and declared that Wrenham "hath blasphemed," speaking "not against God yet against those that are the image of so great a God." He recalled the boast of a good judge in the words of Samuel, "Whose ox or ass have I taken? From whom have I received a reward?"[16]

The sixteen judges of Star Chamber present being in agreement on his crime and punishment, John Wrenham was then sentenced to Foorth's punishment. It was that he be fined 1,000 pounds, put on a horse with his face to the tail with his fault "written on his head," be paraded in this fashion from Fleet Prison to the law courts at Westminster where he should acknowledge his fault in all the courts, that he should then stand in the pillory "a reasonable time," that one ear should then be cut off, that he should be returned to the Fleet and then paraded to Cheapside where his other ear would be removed, and after that he should be "perpetually imprisoned."[17] It was indeed, as Launcelot Andrewes put it, "sharp punishment" for having taken James I too literally when he said to bring complaints about his judges to him. Viscount Wallingford, another Star

Chamber judge, remarked that, though he was sorry for Wrenham, he was "very glad in this bold and quick-sighted age that other men, by his example, may take heed not to exceed the bounds of modesty."[18] The exemplary danger of complaining about a lord chancellor was established.

The Shaken Icicle. On the day that Parliament opened in 1621, Bacon sat on the king's right hand, and Launcelot Andrewes preached. "God standeth in the congregation of Princes," ran his text from Psalm 82. "In the midst will he judge the gods." God judges, he said, "that is, calls to account, every god of them." By gods, he said, were meant all persons in authority. The term was a title of "God's own giving," used by Christ in John 10:34. The gods judged by God were those to whom Andrewes now spoke.[19]

"When they have done judging, they shall come to be judged themselves. *Dii caduci, dii iudicandi,* 'Gods that shall fall, gods that must come to judgment.'" For what would they be judged? God would judge them for "how they used themselves in their deity." He would judge them for what they did "when they sat in His place and went under His name." And the judgment which was future was also now. God was "in the midst of the gods." Where was He? "There in the midst, in their heart, their conscience accusing them, and a worm there gnawing. . . ."[20]

Parliament opened on January 30, the first Parliament in seven years. It had been called because James needed money to make a show of strength against Spain, and in the king's view the voting of money was to be its main business. Bacon had advised on the agenda and on the selection of members to represent the crown effectively.[21] A veteran of four terms in the Commons, Bacon as lord chancellor now represented the king to the Commons—"I am his mouth to you"—and presided over the Lords.[22] It was this Parliament that was to accuse, judge, and condemn the chancellor.

On February 3, Bacon responded to the Commons' presentation of their speaker to the king. James had graciously agreed that the Commons besides supplying money might draw complaints to his attention. The speaker had complimented the king on his judging—"no judges being freer from corruption."[23] Bacon now declared that if the king had "opened himself up," there were two limitations. The Commons were not to "hunt after grievances" or "heap up grievances." The Commons could forward the citizen's legitimate complaint. But members were not to suppose they were in "Plato's commonwealth." Like Cicero confronted by Cato, the chancellor found Platonic perfectionism irritating and illusory. A striking simile completed his exhortation to moderation: "It is certain that the best governments, yea and the best men, are like the best precious stones, wherein every flaw or icicle or grain are seen and noted more than in those that are generally foul or corrupted." If any icicles were visible on the gems of the Crown, the Commons were not to shake them.[24]

One matter was general enough in its consequences to trouble the Commons and move their indignation. This was the granting of royal monopolies to royal favorites and in particular to Sir Giles Mompesson, holder of a remarkable royal patent permitting him to license the inns and taverns of England. There was little disposition on the part of James I to defend Mompesson, who himself confessed that he had abused the license.[25] If anyone else was to be blamed, Mompesson's patron, the duke of Buckingham, was the logical target. But the Commons took note that the king had referred all royal licenses to his legal advisers for an opinion on their legality. In the House Sir Lionel Cranfield asked why the referees had approved Mompesson's license to begin with.[26] The question touched Bacon who had in fact been one of four judges certifying the king's power to grant a lawful monopoly. But Cranfield's question named no names and was the merest indication that the Commons would not be afraid to trouble the highest counsellors of the king.

Other grievances touching Chancery itself concerned Bacon more closely but still peripherally. Chancery was a busy court, but not an entirely popular one. Its practice of preventing the collection of a debt by a "bill of conformity" was bound to annoy merchants and was one grievance that interested the Parliament. Another was a particular *cause célèbre* where Bacon's court and the Court of Wards headed by Sir Lionel Cranfield each had claimed jurisdiction, and the party who won in one court was imprisoned for contempt by the other court, and vice versa. A third was a report that to increase their fees, which depended on the number of orders and injunctions issued, registrars of Chancery would make up fictitious orders and attribute a request for them to lawyers in pending cases. These complaints lapped at Bacon's feet. They did not touch the lord chancellor in any essential way. On February 17, Bacon told the Commons' Committee on the Courts, chaired by his apparent friend Sir Edward Sackville, "Any man might speak freely anything concerning his Court."[27]

The next week, the Commons' Committee on the Courts began examining a deputy registrar, John Churchill, and quickly found that he had engaged in the practice of making up fictitious orders. Churchill confessed his fault and at the same time, or a little later, after Bacon had removed his seal, indicated that he had more to confess about others.[28] At approximately the same date, the last week of February, perhaps emboldened by accounts of what Churchill could say, perhaps acting independently, a defendant harassed by suits in Chancery, Christopher Aubrey, sent a message to the chancellor.

Aubrey had since 1608 been a patentee or holder of a license to collect the fines of defaulting jurors, a source of revenue rented out by the king for 1,000 pounds per year. He had been sued in chancery by his co-licensee, Sir William Bronker, for an accounting. The suit was dismissed. Bronker sued again in Exchequer, and Aubrey again won. Bronker reopened the Chancery suit, and this time, under Bacon's chancellorship, the case went Bronker's way. Three reports, thirty orders, and eight years after the case started, Aubrey was 2,000 pounds poorer and had lost the case. With boldness he sued Bronker in the Star Chamber, alleging that he had coerced witnesses and falsified a report in the Chancery case.[29] He also let Bacon know that if the case were not opened again in Chancery, he would have to let the Commons know that he had already paid Bacon 100 pounds to have the matter settled.

Aubrey's counsel was Sir George Hastings, an MP from Leicester and old hand in Chancery. According to Hastings, Bacon's response to this blackmail was to send for Hastings, who found the lord chancellor in his bed. Bacon told Hastings to come close and everyone else to leave and then said, "George, I am sure you love me and I know that you are not willing that anything done by you shall reflect any dishonor upon me. I hear that Aubrey intends a petition against me. He is a man that you have some interest in, you may take him off if you please."[30]

Hastings did his best, and got Aubrey to see Bacon. But Bacon gave no assurance that he would end the suit. Hastings, who had been involved in the passing of the original 100 pounds, now backed Aubrey up. He told Bacon that he "must lay it on him." Bacon replied, "If you lay it upon me, George, I must upon my honor deny it."[31]

By the end of February, then, Bacon was aware of a problem, but no doubt it did not appear to be a major one. He had brushed off Aubrey's attempt at blackmail. Aubrey had made no public accusations. Wrenham's example was freshly before all suitors in Chancery. Aubrey could be expected to value his ears and his liberty. Bacon's own position, reputation, and integrity were unassailable. His views on judicial corruption had been public for many years. Writing "Of Great Place" before he had achieved it, he had observed,

> The vices of authority are chiefly four—delays, corruption, roughness, and facility. . . . For corruption; do not only bind thine own hands or thy servants' hands from taking, but bind the hands of suitors also from offering. For integrity used [i.e., practised], doth the one; but integrity professed, and with a manifest detestation of bribery, doth the other. And avoid not only the fault, but the suspicion.

He had gone on to observe that changeability in judgment would cause suspicion; that a servant or favorite cherished for no apparent reason was "commonly thought but a by-way to close corruption"; and that "facility," that is, too quick a readiness to please, was worse than bribery, for it was a constant temptation while "bribes come but now and then."[32] Reflecting in Latin on "The Dignity of the Sciences and Their Augmentation," he had repeated the thought—*munera* were "not brought by everyone"—and interpreted Proverbs 28:21 to be an injunction against the evil of "recognizing a face in judgment" and so "deserting the truth." This "wisdom of Solomon" was to be preferred to "the bad arts" of Machiavelli. A corrupted judge, as Solomon's more general language in Proverbs 25:26 suggested, was a befouled fountain.[33]

These maxims were those of a man who had seen and admired his father as the head of Chancery, who had practiced much in the courts, and who professed reverence for biblical wisdom. When he had taken office as lord keeper in May 1617 his opening address had been marked by its strong moral tone. "Justice is a sacred thing," he had said. Continuing the metaphor of the judge as fountain of justice, he had announced that he would water law "at the root."[34] In July 1617, with the king in Scotland, he had charged the judges going on circuit, "Do good to the people, love them and give them justice." He had paralleled the famous line of Luke 6:35, *Nihil inde sperantes*, "hoping nothing thereby," so long used as the basis for an absolute prohibition on usury, with another line: "Let it be, as the Psalm saith, *nihil inde expectantes*, looking for nothing, neither praise nor profit."[35] With such proclaimed maxims as his guide, with such dexterity and diligence in dealing with a thousand decrees or orders per year, with such jealous defense of his reputation by Star Chamber, Bacon could not have supposed at the end of February 1621 that anyone would actually call him to public account, unless he had believed Launcelot Andrewes when he said that God stood in the midst of the gods.

White Crow. The Commons proposed a conference with the Lords on the punishing of Mompesson. Before it took place Mompesson fled the country. The conference was held anyway on March 7. Bacon wrote Buckingham in anticipation of it that Cranfield "who had formerly been the trumpet" was backing off from attacking the referees, and he feared only Coke; "but I think a word from the King mates him." Bacon dated the letter, "March 7, the day I received the seal."[36]

James responded to this suggestion on Saturday morning, March 10, with an appearance before the Lords so sudden that they were not robed to meet him. The question of the licenses he told them "cannot but reflect on me," putting them on notice that they trod on dangerous ground. Bacon then gave the Lords the history of the licenses. James spoke again, acknowledging that the Lords could act as a court and that for any irregularity in the issue of the licenses the lord chancellor and the lord treasurer must "answer for themselves," for "if they cannot justify themselves, they are not worthy to hold and enjoy those places they have under me." These words were by way of concession. The Lords were free, he added, even to judge Buckingham, adorned as he was with honors by the king. They were to judge him not as the king had made him but "as he was when he came to me as poor George Villiers," and "if he prove not himself a white crow he shall be called a black crow." On his knees Buckingham said that if he could not clear himself, "I am contented to abide your Majesty's censure and be called the Black Crow."[37] Buckingham, in short, believed himself safe even if he proved himself to be what he was. But a black crow with pretensions to a different color might have reflected on the king's announced preference for honest color.

The main thrust of the king's remarks was not directed at Buckingham. In the conference Coke had cited precedents for the Lords' punishing offenders. No doubt Bacon had been sure that the king had understood where those precedents came from. They came from the kings who had been "usurpers or tyrants." James resented Coke's implication. "For though Sir Edward Coke be very busy and be called the father of the Law, and the Commons' House have divers young lawyers in it, yet all is not law that they say, and I could wish, nay I have told Sir Edward Coke, that he would bring precedents of good kings' times. . . ." James did more than resent Coke's disobedience. His directions to the Lords were clear. In "vouching" such precedents Coke had made himself subject to punishment. "I hope," the king said flatly, "you will punish him."[38]

James was not accustomed to expressing empty hopes. To be sure the Lords did not misunderstand, he cited the precedent of the Star Chamber, "an inferior court to this." The Star Chamber, he declared "will punish *pro falso clamore.*" Such an offense of false accusation, he did not need to add, had been punished in John Wrenham's case; nor did he need to say that Wrenham's slur on a great officer of the realm, serious though it had been, was less than Coke's slur on the king. He did say, however, how great Coke's offense had been: "I think him an enemy to monarchy and a traitor to me that mentions my actions with such kings as I have told you."[39]

There seemed no doubt now how Bacon would be saved—by the king condemning his enemy. If there was any doubt, it was resolved by one of those homely metaphors in which the king delighted. Common law lawyers like Coke, he rose again to add, were "wind instruments their tongue being their pipe," and like bagpipes they made greater noise and less music than a viol. In contrast his judges were "men of great understanding and gravity." There was a time for testing all things. The day of judgment itself had come.[40]

James had set the stage for Bacon, Buckingham, and the treasurer to clear themselves. They all spoke. Buckingham said he must become a Papist and believe in Purgatory for now he must be purged by the king. The treasurer said the licenses he had approved were legal in themselves, however the patentees had abused them. Bacon took the same position and then turned with an explicit challenge to his old enemy, about to be brought down: "for all my Lord Coke has said, I hope in future ages my acts and honesty shall well appear before his and my honesty over balance and [out]weigh his and be found heavier in that scale." The longstanding rivalry of Coke and Bacon had reached its climax with Bacon asking to be weighed against Coke in the scales of justice. The king closed by saying he would willingly join in punishing Mompesson.[41]

The king's expressed wish that Coke be punished was a high moment for Bacon in a rivalry that stretched back almost thirty years between him and the one other lawyer in England with an intelligence, a learning, and a boldness that fairly matched his own. In 1593, Bacon, then only thirty-three, had sought the attorney-generalship, with the backing of a royal favorite, the earl of Essex; Coke, nine years his senior and far more experienced in courtroom work, had received the appointment. In 1598, Bacon had sought to marry a rich, pretty, and youthful widow, already related to him by marriage; Coke married her. In 1601 Coke triumphantly prosecuted

Essex for treason; Bacon clearing himself, had to join the prosecution of his former patron. After a verbal quarrel in Exchequer Court, Bacon wrote Coke, "You take a liberty to disgrace and disable my law, my experience, my discretion. . . ." Coke was knighted, then in 1606 made chief justice of Common Pleas; Bacon's career had not yet taken off. In 1610, asserting a principle fundamental to the concept of a judge, Coke went a little too far. He had to decide whether the censors of the Royal College of Physicians could exercise their statutory monopoly and fine a Cambridge University graduate, Thomas Bonham, who did not have a license from the Royal College. Noting that the College got half the fine, Coke held that the censors could not be both judges and parties, since "no one ought to be judge in his own case"; he felt constrained to go further and say that an Act of Parliament "against common right and reason" could be judged void. In the same year, Coke advised James he could not create crimes by royal proclamation; the advice did not sit well. Bacon's star began to rise. In 1613, on Bacon's recommendation, James moved Coke to a position where he could cause less trouble, the chief justiceship of the King's Bench—a kick upstairs which Coke resented and knew Bacon had arranged. In 1616 Coke refused to delay a case at the king's request, transmitted by Bacon, now attorney general. Coke held the delay contrary to law. James spoke in Star Chamber on his special supervision over the courts; he asserted that the king was the Judge, from whom, under God, all other judgment was derived. Coke was suspended from office and told to review and correct his book of law reports. In October 1616 he had to report to a committee of four, including Bacon, the errors he found. After this humiliation, Bacon advised James that Coke could be dismissed for "deceit, contempt, and slander of the government" and even judged by Star Chamber to "his utter overthrow." In November 1616, on Bacon's continued nudging, Coke was removed and, at sixty-five, left public service in disgrace. From this nadir he began a comeback by marrying off his fourteen-year-old daughter to Buckingham's thirty-year-old brother; Bacon, getting in the way, suffered a royal rebuke. Now in 1621, Coke, just turned sixty-nine, seemed ripe to be knocked down for good.[42]

If the Lords had done what they were expected to do, James's speech would have decided everything. They needed no more in order to decide that the Black Crow was Coke, punishable for slander far worse than Wrenham's. But Bacon did not move for immediate judgment on his enemy; and Coke with his ears, his liberty, and perhaps his life at stake, took the only course open to save himself. He threw into motion a full-scale attack on the chancellor. When one asks how the charges of bribery that were to bring Bacon down became suddenly public and how a swarm of witnesses appeared from nowhere and were organized to testify against him—witnesses risking Wrenham's punishment for slander, witnesses defaming themselves by their accusations—one has to find behind the scenes a powerful mind and persuasive advocate with a compelling reason to act. The person with ability to act with rapidity and energy in the mobilization of a case, and the person with urgent motivation to do so, was Coke. Bacon had asked that they be weighed against one another. Coke stood behind the scenes, but at crucial moments—twice when it was a key issue of admissible evidence, once when there was a procedural ploy of the king—he intervened decisively. Cranfield no doubt stood his second. And when it came time for punishment to be assessed, Coke was there with precedents for punishment. With all that each held dear as the penalty for losing, Coke checkmated Bacon.

On Wednesday, March 14, four days after James's intervention, Cranfield presented to the Committee on the Courts a petition to stop Chancery enjoining the collection of debts. The petition was one "to pare the nails of the Chancery," a mild way of saying "to cut the claws of the chancellor."[43] The petition served to remind the Commons of the hated Chancery practice. On the same day Christopher Aubrey went public with his charge against the chancellor. The Committee on the Courts received his petition stating he had paid 100 pounds to Bacon for help in his suit. The petition was buttressed with copies of three letters, dated November 22, 1619, June 21, 1620, and July 19, 1620, respectively, from Aubrey to the chancellor, each letter pressing Bacon to do something in return for the money. Sir George Hastings, Aubrey's counsel, then rose in the Commons and confirmed the story, adding by way of exculpation of himself and his client, "I think that never any man suffered more injustice. He was willing to deliver himself out of purgatory." Hastings said he had taken the money in the form of gold in a box and presented it to Bacon "in as cleanly a manner as I could." Bacon had remarked, "It is too much," but returned none of it. John Finch, a Bacon choice as MP and soon to be a legatee in his will, rose in his place to suggest that Hastings kept the money himself.[44]

The Committee received a second petition from Sir Edward Egerton, who as a litigant in Chancery had also dealt with Bacon. He had given first a silver basin or ewer worth 51 pounds. He had then been told by Robert Sharpeigh, Bacon's steward, that for 1,000 pounds to Bacon and 100 pounds to Sharpeigh himself, he would get his decree. Thereupon he had recourse to a lender for 500 pounds, changed the money he got into gold, had 400 pounds delivered to the chancellor and the 100 pounds asked by Sharpeigh to him. Sir Richard Young, Egerton's counsel, affirmed that he and Hastings had carried the 400 pounds to the chancellor.[45]

Hastings and Young were challenged on the floor of the House by Bacon's "chief secretary," Thomas Meautys, himself a member of Parliament. These gentlemen, he observed, had "but chalked out the way for others to follow." He prayed that their aspersions which "blowed" on the chancellor would not "blast" him. He also opined that "others might come perhaps to pass through this purgatory after him."[46] The veiled menace of this remark was evident. It is not unlikely that the substance of the threat and even its phrasing had had the chancellor's approval.

On the same day Bacon wrote the royal favorite Buckingham,

> Your Lordship spake of purgatory. I am now in it. . . . I know I have clean hands and a clean heart; and I hope a clean house for friends or servants. But Job himself, or whosoever was the justest judge, by such hunting for matters against him as hath been used against me, may for a time seem foul, especially in a time when greatness is the mark and accusation is the game. And if this be to be a Chancellor, I think if the great seal lay upon Hounslow Heath nobody would take it up.

This remarkable letter must have been written after the two petitions had been brought to the Commons' notice. Bacon recognized at once how it looked for him. Like John Wrenham, he thought of himself as Job. He also thought of a remedy: "the King and your Lordship will, I hope, put an end to these miseries one way or other." If these cares continued, he wrote, he foresaw he would be sick.[47]

The next day in the Commons, Hastings "did now more plainly discover the matter." He disclosed that he and Aubrey had had conversations with the chancellor, and that the chancellor had made efforts to dissuade them from making these conversations public. He revealed that only yesterday Bacon had talked to him and told him he would deny his story if he spoke.[48] Bacon's ally Finch then intervened, saying that no one "should fall by the testimony of one who had most reason to excuse himself for so foul a fact as the delivery of a bribe." It was the first time the opprobrious word had been used to describe what Bacon had received. On March 17, Robert Phelips reported for the Committee on the Courts. He said, "The principal thing wherein I desired to be satisfied was whether at the time of giving those gifts to the Lord Chancellor there were any suit depending before him." Hastings's testimony had satisfied him. Giving the gold, Hastings had said, "That it was to help Aubrey in his cause." Egerton had mortgaged his estate to raise the 400 pounds, and Young and Hastings had given it to Bacon "as a gratuity from the gentleman, for that my Lord when he was Attorney had stood by him." Bacon had again observed, "It was too much," but took it, saying not only did this "enrich him but laid a tie on him to assist him in all just and lawful business." Phelips indicated that the just and lawful business for which Egerton had mortgaged his land to raise the money for Bacon was a Chancery suit then pending.[49] After losing it, Egerton had entered on a further scheme with the bishop of Landulph to get the decree reversed for 10,000 pounds; but this had not come off.[50]

Sackville, Bacon's friend, attacked the witnesses as not competent. First, "because they spoke to discharge themselves." Second, "because, if he be guilty, they were they that tempted him to it."[51] Finch, Bacon's man, challenged the implications of the report. One Egerton proposal had been rejected. The other was put to St. Albans as a gift for "former kindness." How could he be expected to remember that Egerton had a suit before him? As for the Aubrey matter, there was only one witness, Hastings, not entirely consistent in his story and guilty himself if it were true.[52] As all who knew Scripture knew, two witnesses must prove a crime. At this point Coke entered the debate. "You will make bribery to be unpunished if he that carrieth a bribe shall not be a witness." *Particeps criminis*, a participant in the crime, was "often taken for two good witnesses. And therefore we have a rule that if an offense be committed in a brothel-house, the testimony of brothels shall be admitted." Unflattering as it may have been to George Hastings to be compared to a brothel, that is, a prostitute, Coke's point was clear and his analogy apt. Like prostitution, bribery was to be proved from the mouths of those who had transacted the business.[53]

The Committee's report called forth general, uncomplimentary descriptions of Chancery—"an inextricable labyrinth, wherein resideth such a Minotaur, as gormandizeth the liberty of all subjects whatsoever." It moved members to quote Scripture, "Corruption in justice destroyeth the land," and from Thomas Crewe, a friend of Bacon, "Bribes blind the eyes of the just." It led to speculation as to what the precise offense was in a judge taking a bribe. The crime, it was said, was a kind of perjury, for it was contrary to the oath of a judge; the crime was "against the King," "by falsely distributing the King's conscience," that is, violating distributive justice.[54] No statute condemned bribery. Like many other crimes, including murder, the offense, if it existed, had to be found in "common law," the precedents to be found in judicial practice. No particular precedents were reported on this occasion, although Coke, already the acknowledged "father of the common law," affirmed that the criminality of bribery was clear. As Coke pressed the case, the Commons agreed to refer the charges to the Lords for judgment.[55]

A conference with the Lords was set up for March 19, two days later. The psychosomatic illness Bacon feared broke out. His "heart" and his "back" were sick. He could not come.[56] He had to surrender his symbolic place presiding over the Lords. He had to abandon the field of battle to Coke. He was not present to hear his acts characterized as stained by "great Bribery and Corruption."[57] The field being abandoned was nearly lost.

The king, however judicial, was still on his side and put forward a plan that might have tempered the full force of the storm. He proposed that a commission be set up of twelve members of the Commons and six of the Lords to examine the charges. He "hoped the Chancellor was free, yet if he should be found guilty, he doubted not but you would do him justice." Coke sensed a trap. He warned the Commons "to take heed the commission did not hinder the manner of our parliamentary proceedings." The king was politely rebuffed.[58]

The following day, March 20, was a busy one in both Commons and Lords, a day on which the energetic work of Coke and company manifested itself. Another petition had been brought against Bacon by Montagu Wood and his wife for what had happened in their case against Lady Dorothy Wharton. Bacon, they said, had taken money from her and given her a decree; not only that, but on hearing that the Woods were going to complain to Parliament, Bacon reversed himself. This led Lady Dorothy to prepare her own petition to Parliament, "which my Lord stops by renewing the order"; and so the Woods went ahead with their charges.[59]

Details of the case were supplied the Committee on Courts by Churchill, the Chancery registrar, and by Richard Keeling, Lady Dorothy's solicitor. Churchill related that her suit had been dismissed by consent of counsel on both sides, but she objected and, taking Churchill with her in her coach, carried him to the lord chancellor where she "so wrought that he was willed not to enter the last order."[60]

Keeling, the solicitor, had had qualms about testifying and on the same day, being examined as to a bribe paid by Sir John Trevor, asked "to be spared to answer because he was entrusted with his secrets, being employed in the cause." The chairman, Phelips, was about to let him off, finding this reticence "commendable modesty." Coke intervened. Secrets "which only concern the Cause" a counselor might keep, but "matters which are offenses against the common wealth you are bounden upon lawful demand to reveal, for you owe more faith to the common wealth."[61] Keeling's scruples were overcome. There had been, in all, five injunctions in Lady Dorothy's case and five times the injunctions were dissolved. She had finally made him set down "the words and style" he should use in delivering 100 pounds to Bacon; but then she had decided to go to Bacon's London residence, York House, and deliver it herself in a purse. "My Lord asked her what she had in her hand. She said a purse of her own making and presented it to him, who took it and said, 'What Lord could refuse a purse of so fair a lady's working.'" After this Bacon wrote out an order for her, but it was not entered.[62]

At this point, according to Keeling, another lawyer, Robert Shute, had played a prominent role. In the Parliament of 1621 Shute had been selected by Bacon to be one of the representatives of his titulary domain, St. Albans; so it is reasonable to believe that the chancellor thought him discreet and trustworthy.[63] Shute suggested to Lady Dorothy that 200 more pounds would bring the order to "life." She did not have the ready money. Shute said she could convey a remainder interest in her estate to the chancellor instead. Keeling thought this was too much. Shute replied she could get it back when the 200 pounds was paid; in short, he did not seek to obtain Lady Dorothy's land for the chancellor but merely security that she make the payoff. In the end, she found the money, and "her decree had life."[64] Bacon's secretary, Sir Thomas Meautys, an MP himself, replied to this report that Churchill was guilty by his own confession and that Keeling was "a common solicitor"—two observations that failed to damage the circumstantial strength of the Committee's narrative.[65]

Churchill had further told the Committee that Sir Richard Young had delivered 100 pounds to the chancellor in the case of Sir John Trevor; that in *Hoddy v. Hodie*, Hoddy and his counsel Sir Thomas Pereint had given a jewel thought to be worth 500 pounds, though Hoddy had called it a "trifle"; and that in *Peacock v. Reynell* much had been given on both sides. Barker, the plaintiff in *Barker v. Hill*, claimed that he was 800 pounds out in gifts since his case began. In *Smithwick v. Wyck*, Smithwick gave 300 pounds but lost the case and got back his money in installments. "In this and other causes," according to Churchill, "my Lord would decree part and then when he wanted more money he would send for more money and decree another part." It was customary, he added, for Bacon's servants to take one side or the other, so "it was usual for counsellors when their clients come to them to ask what friends they had at York House."[66]

Meanwhile, the Lords sent a message to Bacon advising him to defend himself; called seven witnesses, including the opponents of Aubrey and Egerton, "to be examined whether they gave any Bribe on their Part"; and heard the bishop of Landulph defend himself against the charge of being a broker in Egerton's attempt to reverse the result in his case by bribery.[67] The success of the bishop in exculpating himself in person emphasized the implication of Bacon's absence. Apropos the witnesses, the Lords discussed the liability of a bribegiver. The prevailing opinion appeared to be that at least a bribegiver who testified to his bribe would not be punished; and on a subsequent day it was further agreed that no judgment should be affected by testimony before the Lords that a bribe had been paid in the case.[68]

Next day, March 21, the Lords set up three committees complete with legal counsel to hear testimony. Fifteen witnesses were sworn, including Bacon's secretary, Meautys, and Hunt, another aide; they both asked that their examination be delayed, a sign, it must have been observed, of uncertainty in the chancellor's camp. Questions were set out which the Committees were to use: Whether they "by themselves or any other person have given Money or other Gratuity" to the chancellor or his servants, friends, or followers; whether they had so advised or directed anyone else to do; whether they knew of any who had so done; whether they had any cause or suit pending before the chancellor or intended to have any; whether they had "contracted for any gratuity so to be given, though not performed." These interrogatories comprehensively covered transactions that might have occurred between litigants or their lawyers and the chancellor and his staff. They used the neutral term "gratuity," leaving the Lords to decide whether a gratuity in a given case was a bribe. They recognized that the relation of the gratuity to pending or intended litigation was important.[69]

Sir George Reynell was examined in "open court" and set down in writing under oath his "knowledge of bribes given by him to the Lord Chancellor." He had had a suit in Chancery for "a fair house" and valuable lands. He gave 200 pounds to John Hunt, who told him he had delivered them to the chancellor. He also sent the chancellor a diamond worth between 500 and 600 pounds. He had, however, lost his suit. He supposed that his opponent, William Peacock, "went deeper than he."[70]

Next day, March 22, Peacock and Lady Dorothy and thirteen others were sworn as witnesses of the Lords, and Churchill's statement on "Bribes and Abuses in Chancery" was received from the Commons. Peacock admitted he had given 1,000 pounds to the chancellor in connection with the suit by Reynell, but he described it as a loan. He was asked to set out in writing what security he had taken, the time for repayment, and the purpose for which the money was borrowed. There was, in fact, nothing he could set down. Hunt and another follower of Bacon were questioned. In another case touching "bribes" to Bacon, Robert Barker was deposed. Two more cases were forwarded by the Commons. In *Hull v. Hollman*, Hollman had been committed to the Fleet prison; he had been released at a cost "one way or the other" of 1,000 pounds. In *Smithwick v. Wyck*, John Borough, a lawyer "close to the Chancellor," asked Smithwick for 200 pounds, which he had paid either to Borough or to John Hunt "to the use of the Lord Chancellor." But he received only part of the decree he wanted. He was asked for another 100 pounds and paid it. The final decree, however, went against him. He asked for his money back and "had it all, save Twenty Pounds, kept back by Hunt for a Year."[71]

Between March 19 and March 21 the Lords had heard of nine cases in which bribetaking by Bacon was alleged—Aubrey's, Egerton's, Wharton's, Reynell's, Trevor's, Hoddy's, Barker's, Hollman's, and Smithwick's. They had the depositions of Reynell and Smithwick swearing to sums paid in the course of Chancery suits. Three lawyers—Sir George Hastings, Sir Richard Young, and Richard Keeling—had informed the Commons of further sums paid. An ex-Chancery registrar had told the Commons of "Bribes and Abuses." Bacon had made no reply. His agents had sniped at the credibility of the hostile witnesses and put off their own testimony. A prima facie case—the case a grand jury would need for an indictment—existed against the chancellor.

Popular opinion held Bacon "utterly lost and ruinated for ever," although one who had observed him before thought, "I know when he shall come to word it, he is excellent at that."[72] The Keeper of the King's Conscience stood accused. The man the king had once left to rule the kingdom in his stead was in grave peril. Bacon, whose blood had seemed snowbroth, whose own celebration of the public virtues was matched by the public celebration of his own virtues, was suspect of corruption; and no one denied that the bribery if proved was base; the corruption alleged, criminal; the charges, if true, fatal.

The King's Virgin. In *Basilikon Dōron (Royal Gift, Royal Bribe)* James I had embraced the ancient insight that when he judged, a king acted in God's stead. He had told his son, "When ye are there, remember the throne is God's and not yours, that you sit in, and let no favor nor whatsoever respect move you from the right." Before Star Chamber James had repeated, "The seat of Judgment is properly God's." This belief was intimately tied to James's view of judicial bribery. As the king acted for God, so did lesser judges act for the king. In this delegated capacity they must judge "without delay, partiality, favor, or bribery," "with clean and incorrupt hands." Those "found in fault" were to "expect punishment at God's hand and mine." Bacon was familiar with the public posture of the king. In his flattering phrase, *Basilikon Dōron* had "filled the whole realm as with a good perfume or incense." He had been present in person when James had lectured the judges of Star Chamber on their duty. Since Coke's rebuff of March 19, James had watched the storm. If he was now ready to have judgment pronounced on his erring double, by what means could Bacon save himself?[73]

On March 25 Bacon sent Buckingham a letter to be delivered to the king. Why, he wondered, had this "tempest" come upon him? He had been "no avaricious oppressor of the people." The Commons had always liked him, and the Lords knew him to be "without crooks or angles." As for "the briberies and gifts with which I am charged, when the book of hearts shall be opened I hope I shall not be found to have the troubled fountain of a corrupt heart in a depraved habit of taking rewards to pervert justice; howsoever I may be frail, and partake of the abuse of the times." Hence, when he answered in the Lords he would not "trick up" his innocence, but he would "excuse, extenuate, or confess" as his heart indicated. Meanwhile by his "matchless friend," Buckingham, he asked what James would do for him: "I have ever been your man, and counted myself but an usufructuary of myself, the property being yours." He signed himself as "clay in your Majesty's gracious hands."[74]

James had not wholly made up his mind. The Easter vacation was at hand. He would address Parliament before it recessed. The tone and temper he adopted on the whole gave no comfort to Bacon. They were at one with his earlier formal pronouncements on justice: "God hath made Me the great Judge of this land under him, and that I must answer for the same." He would respect "no private Person whatsoever, were he never so dear with me." Under the king, the Lords were "the Supreme Court of Justice." His instructions to them were to "proceed judicially and spare none."[75] Yet James introduced an idea that could have seemed mere chaff and banter but was so pointed that Bacon meditated upon its meaning. James alluded to his son Charles's role in the Lords: "Because the World at this time talks so much of Bribes, I have just cause to fear the whole body of this House hath bribed him to be a good Instrument for you on all Occasions." "What Father," he added, "could refuse a Son when God himself could not refuse his Son?"[76] Bacon pondered the analogy over Good Friday and Easter. Charles, his later notes ran, was "ever my chief patron. The work of the Father is creation, the Son redemption."[77] Meanwhile, he was not yet convinced that he needed redemption; he might still prevail with the king on his merits.

He did have Meautys make notes on past judges who had committed great offenses and had been eventually pardoned by the king.[78] More aggressively, he prepared a memo for an interview with James. He could have received gifts while a case was pending which he had neglected to note was "fully at an end or no." But he had never had a "bribe or reward in my eye or thought when I pronounced any sentence or order." He might also, he noted, have received gifts after a case was ended, but these he would have received "without fraud." Such was his defense to the king: everything was either received after the case was over or when he was unaware that it was not over. Nothing had been paid corruptly for judgment. This was the case to be put, as he wrote, "without fig-leaves or subterfuges."[79]

The opportunity came on April 16. For the first time since his troubles began, Bacon was given audience by James. Presumably he presented the ideas contained in his memorandum. But a new distinction had occurred to him as crucial. Whatever he had taken in private litigation, he had taken nothing in anything affecting the king. "I am," Bacon told James in person, "still a virgin for matters that concern your person or crown."[80]

Shakespeare had used the ancient analogy between sexual corruption and bribery in *Measure for Measure*. Coke had referred to the analogy awkwardly when he spoke of "the brothel's" testimony and compared the *bribegiver* to a prostitute. Bacon reverted to the classic form in which the corrupted official was the whore. Preparing for the king, he had decided to go "without fig-leaves"—he would show how his genitalia worked. Speaking to the king he had carried out his plan—he had shown his innocence in the king's affairs, and, by implication, his guilt in others.

Bacon's posture as the king's virgin no doubt tickled James. But as an argument or plea it failed doubly: it claimed merit, so that redemption was not needed; it conceded sin, so that punishment was justified. James told Bacon he must look only to the Lords.[81]

The following day, April 17, Parliament resumed, and the Lords swore in seventeen more witnesses in the case against him. On April 19, a report on several examinations was made, with particular attention being given to Aubrey's letters to Bacon referring to his payment and to letters by Bacon in a case involving the London Vintners in 1618–1619. The earl of Southampton also reported that his committee had heard that the chancellor, "having ordered Matters in open Court, did afterwards alter and reverse the same orders upon Petitions." Instances of such reversals had been found and more were being investigated.[82]

Bacon then, on April 20, wrote James, comparing him to Christ: "I see your Majesty imitateth him that would not break the broken reed nor quench the smoking flax." When he received the charges he would "without fig-leaves" excuse, extenuate, or confess as he could.[83] This was a very brief letter, whose brevity was explained the next day as due to an "extremity of head-ache upon the hinder part of my head." The pain had now become "tolerable," and so Bacon wrote James at greater length. The king was now addressed as God with language taken from Christ's prayer to the Father: "If not *per omnipotentiam* (as the divines speak) but *per potestatem suaviter disponentem*, your Majesty will graciously save me from a sentence with the good liking of the House and that cup pass from me, it is the utmost of my desires." If not by omnipotence at least by power sweetly ordaining let James judge. Losing the seal, Bacon continued, would be punishment enough. If the king would let the Lords Counselors know, and if Prince Charles would so move, and if Buckingham exerted his influence, and if Bacon himself humbly sued the Lords to this effect, it would be brought off. After "eight steps of honor," Bacon prayed that he be "not precipitated altogether." He repeated that he was a virgin as to the king's business. He concluded with the kind of wit that James appreciated: "Because he that hath taken bribes is apt to give bribes, I will go further and present your Majesty with a bribe." The bribe would be "a good history of England and a better digest of your laws."[84] The bribe was as spiritual as Isabella's offer to Angelo, and unexpected from Angelo.

On April 24 James addressed the Lords. He thanked them for the subsidies voted and went on to note the "many complaints" being made about the courts. The king said he would add to the complaints and their redressing. He proposed, "that no orders be made, but in Public Court, and not in Chambers; that excessive Fees be taken away; that no Bribery nor Money be given for the Hearing of any Cause."[85] On the same day the Commons asked for a conference on the bribery committed by Sir John Bennett, a judge of the Canterbury Prerogative Court. And on the same day Bacon sent the Lords his "humble submission and supplication."[86]

Hereafter, Bacon wrote, "the greatness of a judge or magistrate shall be no sanctuary or protection of guiltiness; which, in a few words is the beginning of a golden world." After this, "judges will fly from any thing that is in the likeness of corruption." For these reasons he rejoiced in being fortune's anvil. For himself he would imitate Job, who said, "I have not hid my sin as did Adam." He, Bacon, would "without fig-leaves" confess that he understood, though not formally, "the charge" against him and was moved "to desert the defense." He could not "remove all the needles." He would not try to "extenuate the offense, in respect of the time or manner of the gift," though the Lords might if they pleased. He asked only that the king take the seal, "which is a great downfall and may serve I hope in itself for an expiation of my faults." The Lords might remember there were "vices of the day," distinct from "vices of the man," and note that this reformation could spread and hurt others besides himself. It was a subtle letter, blending admissions and argument for mercy, a hint of a threat, and a frank plea that he lose no more than his office.[87]

The letter was read twice aloud, first by the clerk, then by the lord chief justice sitting in the chancellor's place, and "Noe Lord spoke to it, after it was read, for a long time." Suffolk observed that the confession was not sufficient "for he desires to be a judge, to lose his Seal, and that to be the sentence; wherefore it is far short of that we expect." The attorney general read aloud the Committees' "proofs of the corruption," the specific charges, and, for the third time, Bacon's submission. It was agreed that it was "not full enough." It was debated whether to make Bacon appear and answer. "Shall the Great Seal come to the bar?," asked the Lord Chamberlain. It was voted to send the charges and await his response.[88]

The conference with the Commons on the charges against Bennett followed. Coke took the occasion to show "how grievous to the commonwealth a bribing Judge is." According to him, three judges had been hanged for bribery.[89] These precedents would not have been lost on the Lords weighing Bacon, nor were they meant to be.

On April 25, Baron Denham who had seen Bacon reported that he would make "no manner of defense." He was given till 10:00 A.M., Monday, April 30, to make his confession.[90] On Monday the Lords received "The Confession and humble Submission of me, the Lord Chancellor." It began, "I do plainly and ingenuously confess that I am guilty of corruption." He then confessed to each of twenty-eight specific charges, adding at points details that might soften judgment but saying at the end that he did not seek extenuation and that there was here "a great deal of corruption and neglect." For this he was "heartily and penitently sorry." He said most or all matters were almost two years old, so he had not been getting worse. His estate was poor. He begged for mercy.[91]

The twenty-eight charges were based on twenty-one cases. Three related to a dispute where Bacon had acted as an arbiter between a society of grocers allied with apothecaries on the one side and a new society of grocers on the other. The Lords had heard witnesses in April who deposed that Bacon had 200 pounds from the grocers, a taster of gold worth 400 to 500 pounds from the apothecaries, and another 100 pounds from the new company of grocers.[92] Bacon commented this was "no judicial business" but a composition between the parties, and he had thought "all had received good," so he took from all. "If I had taken it in the nature of a corrupt bribe, I knew it could not be concealed," because of the accounting the companies would make.[93] These distinctions—that he had not sat as a judge, that each party had received something, that the payments could not have been hidden—were offered to distinguish these charges from the others.

In another commercial matter, Sir Thomas Smith had approached Bacon on behalf of a company of French wine merchants who complained of price-fixing by the London wine dealers. Smith offered Bacon 1,000 pounds to help the French company. Bacon proceeded to negotiate on their behalf. But when negotiations faltered, the company filed a formal petition with the king, who then referred the matter to Bacon for action.[94] Bacon admitted all this, and further that after the king's committing it to him, "I dealt more earnestly and peremptorily in it; and, I think, restrained in the messengers' hands for a day or two some that were the most forward." The wine dealers, he insisted, still had "a very competent gain"; but they had settled with the chancellor's client after he had used his power to deprive their leaders of liberty. In this matter Bacon had been promised his money in advance of any official act, although he took pains to point out he received the 1,000 pounds from the French company only when it was over.[95]

In some other cases Bacon claimed the payment was after the final decree, implying but not actually saying that there had been no antecedent promise or agreement. In Sir Thomas Monk's case he had received 100 pounds, as Sir Thomas's lawyer, Sir Henry Helms, had deposed. In the cause of Mr. Dunch he had received 200 pounds, delivered to his seal-bearer William Hatcher. The go-between had been Bevis Thelwall, a relative of Eubule Thelwall, a master in Chancery. In the case of Sir Henry Ruswell, Bacon's own servant John Hunt had deposed that he had received "a purse." Bacon specified that it contained 300 or 400 pounds, adding that he had framed the decree with the help of two other judges. In Robert Barker's case, both Barker and Edward Shereburne, one of seven gentlemen of Bacon's "chamber" and "much used in his most confidential business," had deposed that he had received 700 pounds. Bacon confirmed their depositions. In *Wroth v. Mainwaring,* an inheritance case, the parties had agreed, and after his decree Hunt brought Bacon 100 pounds from Wroth. In Hoddy's case, the original story of John Churchill of a jewel had been amended by Hoddy's lawyer, Sir Thomas Pereint, the son of the old chief justice of Common Pleas. Pereint had delivered, he said, not a jewel but a dozen buttons of gold, worth fifty pounds. Bacon confirmed this account. In Wrenham's case against Fisher, Mr. Shute had advised Fisher, as he deposed, to give Bacon hangings worth over 160 pounds. Bacon received them, Bacon now said, when he was about to move to York House and was furnishing it with the help of presents from others who "were no way suitors." Fisher had testified to the gift. John Wrenham, if he were still alive, was not called.[96]

In only one case was there an explicit difference between a deposition and Bacon's memory. From Richard Scott, "after his cause was decreed," he had received 200 pounds from the hands of Mr. Shute. But Shute had deposed that the money was paid on a precedent promise, of which Bacon professed to know nothing. Sir John Lentall had also paid him 100 pounds through Shereburne, Lentall being a third party benefited by the decree for Scott.[97] Putting this case aside, there were eleven judicial cases where Bacon confessed to receiving money before the case was at an end. He had received 500 pounds from Sir Rowland Egerton after he had made his award, although before Sir Rowland sued "to have the award confirmed." When he first came to the seal, he also had received a "purse" of 400 pounds which was delivered on behalf of Edward Egerton, though "it was expressed by them that brought it to be for favours past, and not in respect of favours to come." He had received 200 pounds "and an hundred pieces" from Lady Dorothy. He had received 100 pounds from Aubrey. These three cases which had stirred the Commons to action were all confirmed by his confession.[98]

In addition, he had received 100 pounds from Sir John Trevor, the plaintiff in *Trevor v. Ascue.* Keeling, the solicitor, had so deposed. Bacon noted that the money came as a New Year's gift, so "I neglected to inquire whether the cause was ended or depending." In Lord Mountague's case, Bevis Thelwall had brought 600 to 700 pounds and promised more, and St. Albans specifically recalled Thelwall saying that Mountague would be "further thankful if he could once get his quiet." The decree in the case had been entered but in fact its enforcement had required many later orders. From Sir George Reynell he had received 200 pounds for house furniture before any suit began. Later he received the diamond "and though it were at new year's tide, yet it was too great a value for a new year's gift; though as I take it nothing near the value mentioned," that is, 500 or 600 pounds. From Peacock, Reynell's opponent, Bacon admitted having 100 pounds as a present on taking office, before any suit began. He later borrowed 1,000 pounds from Peacock without interest, note, or security, with the understanding that "I should take my own time for payment of it." In Sir Ralph Hansby's inheritance case, as Sir Ralph had deposed, Bacon had had 500 pounds, given after his decree awarding the land but before his decree on the chattels. The intermediary had been Bacon's friend Toby Mathew.[99]

In a number of cases Bacon had taken money and then entered decrees injurious to the payor. Aubrey's and Sir Rowland Egerton's indignation at this treatment had led to their being easily induced to testify. In Compton's case, after Bacon took a loan from him, Compton was pressed for 400 pounds by a creditor of his own, Huxley. Bacon asked Huxley to forbear. Compton understood that Bacon was assuming his debt to Huxley in satisfaction of his debt to Compton. But Bacon did not have the money, and when Huxley then sued Compton, Bacon gave judgment for Huxley, leaving Compton with the sense that he had been done in by the judge who should have been liable for the debt.[100]

Again, in the case of Young, Bacon admitted to having had 100 pounds from Young himself or through Toby Mathew. He understood now that Young's opponent Hollman had also paid his seal-bearer, William Hatcher, although Bacon professed not to have known of that.[101] In *Kenneday v. Vanlore*, Bacon was charged in James Kenneday's deposition with receiving from him a rich cabinet valued at 800 pounds. Bacon admitted having received it, though not wanting it and finding it "nothing near half the value" stated. In this case he also borrowed 2,000 pounds of the defendant, Peter Vanlore, an amount described by Bacon as "a true debt."[102] In *Smithwick v. Wyck*, Hunt had indeed received 200 pounds from Smithwick and it had been repaid.[103] Bacon did not note that he had received a letter on November 18, 1618, from Buckingham "desiring your lordship to show what favor you lawfully may unto Mr. Wche [sic] according as the justness of the cause shall require." Letters in this style, frequently written by the favorite to the chancellor, were little short of commands. In Hansby's inheritance case, for example, Buckingham had referred to the evidence and suggested that Hansby was in "no way liable." There, there was a happy coincidence between Buckingham's suggestion and the 500 pounds Hansby paid the chancellor. In Wyck's case, where Buckingham and bribe diverged, it was understandable that Bacon felt he could not keep Smithwick's money.[104]

Angelo, finally caught, had cried, "Let my trial be my confession." Bacon was not so simple. For almost every one of the rewards received he had an excuse. Reynell's ring and Trevor's money had come as New Year's gifts, Peacock's as a present on taking office. Reynell's money had come before the lawsuit started; Edward Egerton's and Aubrey's for past favors; Barker's, Dunch's, Fisher's, Lentall's, Ruswell's, Scott's, Wroth's, and Young's after the case was over; Rowland Egerton's, Hansby's, Mountague's after all the legal issues were decided. Kenneday's cabinet had been a nuisance which he wanted to return and Smithwick's money he had returned. The French company had paid him as a negotiator. The apothecaries and grocers had paid him as an arbiter. Compton, Peacock, and Vanlore had merely loaned him money. Only one transaction was in fact left without its figleaf—the 300 pounds taken from Lady Dorothy. Here Bacon merely grumbled that there was "some shuffling between Mr. Shute and the Register in entering some orders, which afterwards I did distaste."[105] With this conspicuous exception, everything was explained.

Occasionally the specific excuse was advanced that Bacon had been uninfluenced by a gift: to Thelwall's hint of Mountague's future thankfulness "I gave little regard." More often this suggestion was implicit, especially in the practice—five cases are a practice—of taking from both sides. A running general excuse was that it was his servants' doing. In his confession Bacon acknowledged that it was "a great fault of neglect in me that I looked no better to my servants."[106] Even when admitting the unexcused taking from Lady Dorothy, he made an effort to shift the focus to Shute and Churchill.

The suddenness of Bacon's fall—no more sudden, of course, then Angelo's—could lead to speculation that there had been an inner collapse or that, alternatively, his confession had been extorted from him like the confesion of a defendant in a show trial of a totalitarian state. Neither speculation is supported by the evidence. To a remarkable degree Bacon's unsuccessful older brother Anthony was subject to physical breakdowns in moments of crisis; Bacon behaved similarly when he fell sick at the time of trial and the time of judgment. But there is no indication of mental paralysis. The confession was crafted with a lawyer's skill. It admitted only what could not be effectively denied. It argued that in each instance Bacon was excusable or innocent.

The total impression overwhelmed the close and careful argument. As he presented his court and himself, the Chancery was a money-making machine, and the chancellor the chief money-maker. The New Year's gift of 100 pounds and the ring too valuable to be a New Year's gift, why did he suppose they were made? His old client's remembrance of his past services were "too much," as Hastings and Young recalled him remarking. The loans accepted from litigants he could scarcely have supposed were made as business propositions. They were to be uncollectable, as Compton's experience showed. They were without interest or security and in Peacock's case without a note. Even in an age when interest was still morally marginal, loans without interest were favors. If Peacock and Vanlore tried to prove their claims later against Bacon's estate, it was only after his public confession had categorized them as his debts.

The excuse that payment was made after the decree was hurt by the indication that intermediaries like Shute fixed the amount before the decree, and it was undermined completely by the piecemeal Chancery practice in which a decree by itself was not self-executing and to have final force needed to be backed by contempt proceedings. By itself a decree was a piece of paper to negotiate with and the chancellor's continuing favor was a must if one was to pin down a squirming opponent, as Sir Rowland Egerton, Lord Mountague, and John Wrenham all discovered. In Chancery there was hardly any point at which one could say the case could not be reopened.

In both commercial matters his excuse was that he was not paid as chancellor. In the grocers and apothecaries' matter the excuse had limited force. But that the division he approved was not satisfactory to all was plain from the complaint against him deposed to before the Lords. One side remunerated him nine times as much as the other—enough of a disproportion to make his impartiality unlikely. In the other matter, he had entered on judicial duties affecting the wine dealers and had used official force after he was on retainer to their opponents.

Putting it on his servants did not wash when he confessed to receiving substantial sums from Hatcher, Hunt, and Shereburne. These and such friends and agents as Bevis Thelwall, Robert Shute, and Toby Mathew appeared in the confession as bagmen, busily negotiating for payments from litigants and doing Bacon the double service of screening him from contact and of letting him accomplish more business than he could have handled by himself. Bacon presided over a ring whose modus operandi was familiar to members of the bar such as George Hastings, Richard Keeling, and Richard Young. With the connivance of such counsel, the collaboration of Chancery personnel like Churchill, and the judicious employment of bagmen, Bacon had made Chancery produce cash.

The earlier excuse that the vice was "of the times" not "of the man" had color and even force when it is observed that noble families like the Comptons, ladies like Lady Dorothy, lawyers like Hastings, Young, Keeling, and Pereint engaged in the practice and abetted Bacon in his game. The elite of the land, or at least a portion of the elite, were Bacon's collaborators, while the king's chief minister Buckingham openly indicated what litigants he favored. Yet that what was customary could also be vicious was clear when Bacon himself had remarked on several payments that they were "too much"; when the king had made it public that he expected his judges to have "hire" only of him; when both the English Bible and the London stage treated bribes as corrupt; and when Bacon had personally diagnosed the evil of a judge receiving *munera*. From the beginning of the inquiry by the Commons he acknowledged that bribery was "base." He was not able in law or custom to distinguish much of what he received from bribes.[107]

What drove him to it? The son of Nicholas, a yeoman's son who had risen to Lord Keeper, did he want to maintain a figure as great or greater than his father's? Did his mother, Ann, a learned puritanical nag, so chide within him that his compulsions included the compulsion to succeed whatever the cost? Did he, the younger brother of neurasthenic, restless, unfortunate Anthony, in his self-conscious steadiness and shrewdness conceal a patch of his older brother's wildness and will to fail? What part in his later attitudes was played by events in his earlier life? Did the memory of poverty and debts in his beginning years as a lawyer make him want to abound in wealth? Did his own "great betrayal," prosecuting his patron Essex for treason and sending him to have his head cut off, haunt him so the memory could be obliterated only in magnificence and opulence? Was he—so self-controlled in his demeanor, so rational in his speculations—simply unable to control his expenses, so that he was always living beyond his means as chancellor, always pressed for ready cash? Did accumulating debt drive him to desperate expedients? What part had his view of law, whose chief deficiency he imagined to be its lack of certainty? Did he divorce too radically the law he announced from his own responsibility for shaping it? Was pride his basic vice, so that he whose assertions were "rather like oracles than discourses" thought himself above the law? Was he like Angelo so imprisoned in his confidence in his own competence and self-sufficiency that he was the ready victim of great temptations? Was he an intellectual who mistakenly sought power instead of the life of the spirit, so that, as he put it in a prayer, his soul had "been a stranger in the course of my pilgrimage"? Available evidence permits these psychological speculations without proving them. He was at all events no Hog, no orator's creation without redeeming characteristics; but a man who fell.[108]

It has often been said that the charges against Bacon were political. It was not an excuse he offered but no doubt they were. The Commons and the Lords were political bodies. To mobilize 400 or so members of the Commons and 100 or so lords required political energies to be at work. The motives of the leaders, Coke and Cranfield, were both personal and political. But from Hog to Bacon bribery in high places had been a crime that needed political motivation for its detection and denunciation. The objective character of the offense was not altered by the motivations of the prosecutors.[109]

Salary, plus fees and perquisites regarded as legitimate, made the office of Lord Keeper in Bacon's father's day worth about 2,500 pounds per annum. In Bacon's own day a similar estimate of lawful income put it at about 3,000 pounds. It was one of the largest incomes in the kingdom in an age when a laborer might receive no more than 30 pounds a year.[110]

To supplement his lawful income and to triple his total, Bacon, in two years of chancellorship (the cases not going beyond 1619) had received from Fisher, Hoddy, Kenneday, and Reynell goods worth either 1,610 pounds (his estimate) or 2,610 pounds (theirs). From Compton, Peacock, and Vanlore he had loans of 3,500 pounds. From Aubrey, Dunch, the two Egertons, Hansby, Lentall, Mountague, Reynell, Scott, Smithwick, Trevor, Wharton, Wroth, Young, and the French company and the two companies of grocers he had received 6,100 pounds. Reducing this by Smithwick's refund of 200 left a grand total of 11,010 or 12,010 pounds, depending on the property's valuation.

After Bacon's fall Buckingham told Meautys that he had heard that Bacon must have had 100,000 pounds in gifts since he became Lord Keeper, that is, 25,000 pounds per year. Bacon denounced the report as an "abominable falsehood." He listed for Buckingham the areas in which he had taken nothing extra: "I never took penny for any benefice or ecclesiastical living, I never took penny for releasing any thing I stopped at the seal, I never took penny for any commission or things of that nature, I never shared with any servant for any second or inferior profit."[111] In short, as chancellor he had sold neither Church appointments nor royal commissions; he had not extorted money for pardons and the like which required his seal; and he had not made his servants share their own booty with him. That left a wide swatch of judicial and administrative business in Chancery where by implication he had "taken penny." He offered no estimate of his own. Later he wrote Buckingham, "I have lost six thousand pounds by year, besides caps and courtesies," that is, besides salutations of respect and honor. Six thousand pounds per annum was double his legitimate income but only two-thirds of what his lawful income plus the confessed bribes amounted to annually. It is unlikely that the twenty-one cases brought to light in a few weeks comprised his total bribery income. He issued a thousand orders or decrees a year. Even if bribes came only "now and then," his retinue was organized for profit in more cases than in a mere ten per year. If Buckingham's 25,000 pounds is too high a guess, 6,000 and even 9,000 are too low.[112]

A statement of Bacon's "Receipts and Disbursements" for three months in the summer of 1618 shows him spending 3,711 pounds—more than a whole year's lawful income—and receiving 4,160 pounds. Among the items are 400 pounds from Toby Mathew, 100 pounds from "Mr. [George?] Hastings," and 1,200 pounds from a master in Chancery not named as a bribe-bearer in the later trial.[113] It is a fair inference that bribe income makes up part of the total sum which is so much larger than his legitimate twelve-month income, and on an annual basis amounts to 16,640 pounds—a not improbable estimate of the chancellor's takings from all sources. Whatever the correct estimate, the amount was substantial and higher than the incomes of most persons in the kingdom.

No Jesuit Nor No Leper. Bacon's detailed confession was read aloud to the Lords on Monday morning, April 30. A deputation was sent to him to confirm that it was indeed his act. The delegates returned and reported him as saying, "My Lords, it is my act, my hand, my heart. I beseech your Lordships, be merciful to a broken reed." The Lords moved to ask the king to remove the seal and adjourned to meditate their judgment.[114]

Bacon had reason to ask mercy. From the beginning of the session when the Lords had committed to the Fleet a deputy clerk whose sole offense had been dropping three customary words from the summons to Parliament, the Lords had shown a ferocious severity in punishing affronts and crimes.[115] Mompesson in absentia had been convicted, deprived of all his property, stripped of all titles, declared an outlaw, to be imprisoned for life if captured, and made "infamous forever."[116] Edward Lloyd, judged later in May to be guilty of malicious speech against Princess Elizabeth, was given a sentence only slightly less savage than that imposed on John Wrenham by the Star Chamber.[117] It might have been reasoned that selling the king's justice was an offense greater than Mompesson's or Lloyd's or Wrenham's. On May 3 the House of Lords formally voted, without dissent, that Bacon was guilty of every crime with which he was charged. The extenuations, qualifications, and argument of his confession were ignored. Debate about his punishment followed.[118]

The Lords agreed at once that they would not take his life or banish him forever like Mompesson. They debated if he should be degraded, that is, deprived of his titles, and decided against it by a majority vote. For sparing him these fates Bacon credited Prince Charles.[119] ("Ever my chief patron. The work of the Father is creation; of the Son redemption"). Charles did not, however, object to other penalties, and only Buckingham dissented when the Lords agreed that he be fined 40,000 pounds; that he be imprisoned in the Tower as long as the king pleased; that he should be incapable of "any office, place or employment in the State"; that he should never sit in Parliament; and that he should not come within "the verge" (twelve miles) of the Court. With the sentence agreed on, the Lords robed and met formally with the Commons, whose Speaker recalled the "many exorbitant offenses of bribery and corruption" of which the Commons had complained and now formally asked judgment. The Lord Chief Justice then pronounced the judgment of the Lords on the chancellor for "crimes and corruptions of like nature."[120]

Such was the formal verdict, in Bacon's own estimate a "sentence just, and for reformation sake fit," but yet intolerable for one who in his own view had been "the justest Chancellor" in the five changes since his father held the seal.[121] It was in that frame of mind that he had received assurances from Buckingham that the proceedings in Parliament were an empty charade. The king would pardon "the whole sentence."[122]

The king would do more, Buckingham said. He would provide financial help. Bacon would be given assistance in paying or postponing his debts. He would have a pension of at least 2,000, perhaps 3,000 pounds per annum.[123] If Buckingham could be relied on, Bacon would have lost nothing but the seal and the burdens and the takings of the chancellor.

The promises were delivered on. He was allowed to wait until the end of May, when his health was better, to enter the Tower. On May 31 he wrote Buckingham, "Procure the warrant for my discharge this day," and he was out by June 4, writing thank you notes to his royal master and the royal favorite.[124] The fine was disposed of with even greater success. Bacon prepared an assignment of the fine by the king to persons Bacon himself should nominate.[125] In other words, the fine would consist in paying 40,000 pounds to assignees who would be in effect trustees not for the king but for Bacon. Bishop Williams, Bacon's successor as chancellor, sealed this document while gasping at its adroitness: by it, he observed, Bacon "had deceived his creditors."[126] He had taken the money from where it could be reached for his debts and put it where it could only be used for his benefit. The fine became a boon.

The next step was the pardon. Again the drafting was Bacon's and it was done with care. In one version both the alteration of records and the "receiving of moneys and rewards" were pardoned; in a second version, which reached Bishop Williams at the seal, the "receiving" pardoned was for "false judgments or decrees." In neither case was the term "bribes" used. Excepted from the pardon were not the crimes condemned by the Lords but "all fines, imprisonments, penalties and forfeitures" adjudged by Parliament. This exception was artfully done.[127]

Signed by James, the pardon went to Bishop Williams to be sealed. Williams observed that Bacon was "too cunning for me." He had drafted the pardon to except the fine as though that were still in force; but the fine was already remitted. Williams wondered if Parliament would not find itself "mocked and derided with such an exception."[128] He could have observed the same as to the illusory exception of imprisonment from which Bacon was already released. While appearing to leave in force Parliament's punishments, the pardon as drafted restored to Bacon everything except capacity to hold office; and no doubt Buckingham had said it was too soon for that.

Williams's objection would not have had any impact if Bacon had not forgotten that in his new position he could not expect to deal with Buckingham as a colleague. Tangible quid pro quos were necesary if Buckingham's promises were to be kept. Buckingham in fact had a concrete suggestion. It was that he take over Bacon's London residence.

York House had been the chancellor's father's residence and his own boyhood home. He held it on a long-term lease. He balked at the thought of losing it. Buckingham, of course, offered to pay, though it would have been understood that he set the price. But loss of his home, more than financial harm, troubled Bacon. "At least no money nor value shall make me part with it," he was to tell another would-be purchaser.[129] In any event he put off Buckingham, who wrote him, "I would rather provide myself otherwise than any way incommodate you."[130] At the same time Buckingham saw to it that Bacon would recall a lesson that over thirty years at court had not sufficiently impressed on him: one did not get favors without reciprocating. Bacon's pardon stayed stopped at the seal. In the father's theology the son might be the redeemer; but the favorite was the way of access.

In the next several months Bacon tried other avenues. He consulted the learned John Selden as to whether the Parliament that had condemned him had been a "true Parliament." Selden replied that it had been a true Parliament but set out a new distinction for Bacon to grasp. There had been no recording of the judgments, so "it may be justly thought that they are of no force."[131] The quibble, if it had any weight, was one which a patron would have to put before the king. Again, Bacon addressed the House of Lords to lift the ban on his entering the vicinity of the court, so that "out of the carcase of dead and rotten greatness (as out of Samson's lion) there may be honey gathered for the use of future times." Again, Bacon drew on an old friendship—with Diego de Gondomar, the Spanish ambassador, hoping that this alien could procure from the king what he could no longer get for himself.[132]

Bacon now wrote of himself that he was "no Jesuit nor no leper." His treatment reminded him of the status of these outcasts.[133] To get what he wanted he had to go back to Buckingham. As he put it in upbeat terms, "I had rather sojourn in a college in Cambridge than recover a good fortune by any other but yourself."[134] He came with an outright present—the offer of one of his country residences, Gorhambury, a place whose sentimental value was possibly greater than York House, for it was the house his father had built. Gorhambury was, Bacon informed Toby Mathew, his bagman turned go-between, "the best means I have now left to demonstrate my affection to his Lordship." The purpose of the gift was made clear in a draft memorandum. Conveyance was to be made to Buckingham "if my Lord should prevail for me in my suit." He added, "If my Lord like better to proceed by way of bargain . . . I will deserve his favor and express my love in a friendly pennyworth."[135]

Buckingham had harsher terms, designed to remind Bacon of the folly of one in his position refusing an offer from one in Buckingham's position. Bacon must still give up York House, must still surrender his sentimental desire to die where he had been born. Only now he must work out the terms not with Buckingham but with one of the two principal instruments of his downfall, Lionel Cranfield. Bacon, if he was to get his "liberty" and something for his "poor estate," must please Cranfield, to whom these matters had not been referred by the king.[136] Bacon knew that this was to reduce him to "servile dependence" on an enemy. He would rather "beg and starve than be fed at that door."[137] But he knew now about irrefusable offers. He wrote to Cranfield and congratulated him on his "great and noble heart." He asked him to have his man set what price he chose on York House.[138]

The forced dealing with Cranfield was only a prelude to the main transaction. Toby Mathew was instructed by Bacon to tell Buckingham that as to York House "whether in a straight line or a compass line, I meant it his

Lordship, in the way I thought might please him best."[139] In June of 1622 he conveyed his interest to Buckingham for 1,300 pounds; the transaction was protected against his creditors by a decree of Chancery.[140]

For the house, he got his liberty of movement restored.[141] He still had need to get his old pension paid or a new pension granted. Here Cranfield again toyed with him. Bacon's secretary, Meautys, reminded him that Cranfield and his crowd had "such a savage word amongst them as fleecing." Bacon himself declared that he was put off by messages and postponed appointments. He realized that Cranfield "doth but mean to coax me (it is his own word of old) and to saw me asunder." He appealed to Buckingham: "And for my house at Gorhambury, I do infinitely desire your Lordship should have it."[142] With what was left to him he begged and bargained.

No restitution was made by Bacon of what he had taken, even when he had taken from both sides. One exception was that his will, executed April 16, 1621, during the period of his purgatory, provides: "the great diamond I would have restored to Sir George Reynell."[143] This could only have been the diamond received in *Reynell v. Peacock,* whose value Reynell had put at 500 to 600 pounds and Bacon at "nothing near the value." The will was superseded by one of December 19, 1625, and the actual fate of the diamond is unknown.[144] Peacock, the other litigant, had to sue Bacon's estate on his "loan," as did Vanlore and Hollman; his executors defended on the ground that Bacon was "sentenced for them in Parliament as bribes."[145]

In the long run Bacon kept what he had taken, and he got from the king almost everything he sought. Imprisonment was momentary, the fine became his own asset, he was given freedom to enter the verge. The king continued his pension and gave him advances on it, helped with his debts, even consulted him on the reform of the law.[146] In his speeches and writings James had said that he would punish bribetaking judges, and that lawbreakers who were members of a monarch's court should be punished more severely than other criminals. Abstract theory had not stood up to the play of power and favor. When presented by Buckingham, Bacon's merits or past services outweighed his guilt; and Buckingham's presentations, as the king could reasonably have known, were not gratuitous but induced at least in part by what Buckingham was offered. What Bacon had lost by taking bribes as a judge he won back by favor purchased by his home and his humility.

There was one thing James would not do, and that was give Bacon a full pardon. Three years after his conviction Bacon drafted the appropriate document, which explicitly referred to the sentence of the Lords and removed "that blot of ignominy which yet remaineth upon him [Bacon], in incapacity and disablement."[147] He sent it to the king, who was once more addressed as a being analogous to the deity. Bacon asked "that I die not a condemned man, but may be to your Majesty, as I am to God, *nova creatura.*"[148] John Bennett, a judge in the Canterbury prerogative court, had been charged with bribery by the same Commons that indicted Bacon, had been allowed to escape by the Lords, but had been convicted by Star Chamber. [149] The king had pardoned him in full. Yet Bennett's offenses in ecclesiastical matters had presented a "black" case, in comparison to which Bacon's was "ash-colored." He who forgave Bennett could forgive him. God himself loved those he loved "to the end." James, he hoped, would do the same.[150] But James declined to give this final mercy; and Charles did no more when in 1625 he succeeded his father.

The punishment kept in being was symbolic. It was enough to satisfy the exigencies of a Dantean hell. The man who prized honor was left in a place of permanent inferiority, not capable of being elected an alderman. The reminder of his fault was as public as if he had suffered physical disfigurement in the pillory. With it went that "servile dependence" on others he had once regarded as colleagues or inferiors, whom now he had to pay to obtain their benevolence. He was, he had said, "no Jesuit," "no leper," but his position was not far different. Out of power and sick in 1624 he translated certain Psalms and captured in his version of the lot of the unjust man his own. It is among his own rare efforts at poetry. The unjust man is

> All as the chaff, which to and fro
> Is forced at mercy of the wind.
> And when he shall in judgment plead,
> A casting sentence bide he must:
> So shall he not lift up his head
> In the assembly of the just.[151]

The original spoke of the unjust in the plural; Bacon made it singular, and he added specifically "the casting sentence." He had been treated by Cranfield as a substance with no more weight than chaff. He was dependent on the wind of Buckingham's favor. He had heard the casting sentence of the Lords. He was not permitted to lift up his head with his peers. As a consequence he had to beg. Measure met measure. He who once had taken bribes was left to offer them.[152]

13

The Conscientious Clerk

1/27/63   Up and to the office, where sat till 2 a-clock; and then home to dinner, whither by and by comes in Creede and he and I talked of our Tanger business and do find that there is nothing in the world done with true integrity but there is design along with it; as in my Lord Rutherford, who designs to have the profit of victualling of the garrison himself, and others to have the benefit of making the molle. So that I am almost discouraged from coming any more to the Committee, were it not that it will possibly hereafter bring me to some acquaintance of the great men. Then to the office again, where very busy till past 10 at night; and so home to supper and bed.

2/10/63   This evening Sir W. Warren came himself to the door and left a letter and a box for me—and went his way. His letter mentions his giving me and my wife a pair of gloves. But opening the box, we find a pair of plain white gloves for my hand and a fair State-dish of Silver and cup with my armes ready-cut upon them, worth I believe about 18 £—which is a very noble present and the best I ever had yet.

3/5/63   This evening came captain Grove about hiring ships for Tanger. I did hint to him my desire that I could make some lawfull profit thereof—which he promises, that he will tell me of all that he gets and that I shall have a share—which I did not demand, but did silently consent to it—and money, I perceive something will be got thereby.

4/3/63   Thence going out of White-hall, I met Captain Grove, who did give me a letter directed to myself from himself; I discerned money to be in it and took it, knowing, as I found it to be, the proceed of the place I have got him, to have the taking up of vessells for Tanger. But I did not open it till I came home to my office; and there I broke it open, not looking into it till all the money was out, that I might say I saw no money in the paper if ever I should be Questioned about it. There was a piece of gold and 4 £ in silver.

5/1/63   This day Captain Grove sent me a side of porke, which was the oddest present, sure, that was ever made to any man; and the next, I remember I told my wife, I believe would be a pound of candles or a shoulder of mutton. But the fellow doth it in kindness and is one I am beholding to.

6/13/63   . . . and I to the office and there had a difference with Sir W. Batten about Mr. Bowyers tarr; which I am resolved to cross, though he sent me last night, as a bribe, a barrell of Sturgeon; which it may be I shall send back, for I will not have the King abused so abominably in the price of what we buy by Sir W. Batten's corruption and underhand dealing.

6/27/63   27. Up by 4 a-clock and a little to my office. Then comes by agreement Sir Wm. Warren; and he and I from ship to ship to see Deales of all sorts, whereby I have encreased my knowledge and with great pleasure. Then to his yard and house, where I stayed two hours or more, discoursing of the expense of the navy and the corruption of Sir W. Batten and his man Wood, that he brings or would bring to sell all that is to be sold to the Navy.

9/10/63   10. Up betimes and to my office. And then sat all the morning, making a great contract with Sir W. Warren for 3000 £ worth of Masts; but good God, to see what a man might do were I a knave—the whole business, from beginning to the end, being done by me out of the office, and signed to by them upon but once reading of it to them, without the least care or consultation either of quality, price, number, or need of them, only in general that it was good to have a store. But I hope my pains was such as the King hath the best bargain of Masts hath been bought these 27 years in this office.

12/12/63   At noon went home; and there I find that one Abrahall, who strikes in for the serving of the King with Ship-chandlery ware, hath sent my wife a Japan gowne; which pleases her very well and me also, it coming very opportune—but I know not how to carry myself to him, I being already obliged so far to Mrs. Russell—so that I am in both their pays.

To the Exchange, where I had sent Luellin word I would come to him; and thence brought him home to dinner with me. . . .

Then he begin to tell me that Mr. Deering had been with him to desire him to speak to me that if I would get him off with those goods upon his hands, he would give me 50 peeces. And further, that if I would stand his friend, to help him to the benefit of his patent as the King's merchant, he could spare me 200 £ per annum out of his profits. I was glad to hear both of these; but answered him no further then that as I would not by anything be bribed to be unjust in my dealings, so I was not so squeemish as not to take people's acknowledgment where I have the good fortune by my pains to do them good and just offices. And so I would not come to be at an agreement with him, but I would labour to do him this service, and to expect his consideration thereof afterward, as he thought fit. So I expect to hear more of it.

1/1/64   Among others, one came with the best New Year's gift that ever I had; namely from Mr. Deering, with a bill of exchange drawn upon himself for the payment of 50 £ to Mr. Luellin—it being for my use, with a letter of compliment. I am not resolved what or how to do in this business, but I conclude it is an extraordinary good New Year's gift, though I do not take the whole; or if I do, then give some of it to Luellin.

1/5/64   He being gone, then Luellin did give me the 50 pound from Mr. Deering which he doth give me for my pains in his business and which I may hereafter take for him—though there is not the least word or deed I have yet been guilty of in his behalf but what I am sure hath been to the King's advantage and profit of the service, nor ever will I. And for this money I never did condition with him or expected a farthing at the time when I did do him the service. Nor have given any receipt for, it being brought me by Luellin. Nor do I propose to give him any thanks for it—but will, wherein I can, faithfully endeavour to see him have the privilege of his Patent as the King's merchant.

1/20/64   But am resolved to better my care in my business, to make me stand upon my own legs the better and to lay up as well as to get money; and among other ways, I will have a good fleece out of Creeds coat ere it be long, or I will have a fall.

1/25/64   . . . and to the office upon a perticular meeting of the East India Company, where I think I did the King good service against the Company in the business of sending our ships home empty from the Indys, contrary to their contract. And yet, God forgive me, I find that I could be willing to receive a bribe if it were offered me to conceal my arguments that I find against them, in consideration that none of my fellow-officers, whose duty it is more than mine, had ever studied the case or at this hour do understand it, and myself alone must do it.

2/2/64   Thence to the Change again, and thence off to the Sun taverne with Sir W. Warren and with him discoursed long and had good advice and hints from him; and among [other] things, he did give me a pair of gloves for my wife, wrapped up in paper; which I would not open, feeling it hard, but did tell him my wife should thank him, and so went on in discourse. When I came home, Lord, in what pain I was to get my wife out of the room without bidding her go, that I might see what these gloves were; and by and by, she being gone, it proves a pair of white gloves for her and 40 pieces in good gold: which did so cheer my heart that I could eat no victuals almost for dinner for joy to think how God doth bless us every day more and more—and more yet I hope he will upon the encrease of my duty and endeavours. I was at great loss what to do, whether tell my wife of it or no; which I could hardly forbear, but yet I did and will think of it first before I do, for fear of making her think me to be in a better condition or in a better way of getting money then yet I am.

2/11/64   This noon Mr. Falconer came and visited my wife and brought her a present, a silver state-cup and cover, value about 3 or 4 £—for the courtesy I did him the other day. He did not stay dinner with me. I am almost sorry for this present, because I would have reserved him for a place to go in summer a-visiting at Woolwich with my wife.

2/12/64   ... and with him [John Creed] back to the Coffee-house, where with great seriousness and strangeness on both sides he said his part and I mine—he sometimes owning my favour and assistance, yet endeavouring to lessen it; as, that the success of his business was not wholly or very much to be imputed to that assistance. I to allege the contrary and plainly to tell him that from the beginning I never had it in my mind to do him all that kindness for nothing; but he gaining 5 or 600 £, I did expect a share of it; at least, a real and not a complimentary acknowledgment of him. In Fine, I said nothing all the while that I need fear he can do me more hurt with then before I spoke them. The most I told him was after we were come to a peace, when he asked me whether he should answer the Boards letter or no—I told him he might forbear it awhile and no more. Then he asked how the letter could be signed by them without their much enquiry: I told him it was as I ordered it and nothing at all else of any moment. ...

2/16/64   Up and to the office, where very busy all the morning; and most with Mr. Wood, I vexing him about his masts.

2/17/64   ... and by and by home and dined—where I found an excellent Mastiffe, his name Towzer, sent me by a surgeon.

2/27/64   Up, but weary, and to the office, where we sat all the morning. Before I went to the office there came Bagwell's wife to me to speak for her husband. I liked the woman very well and stroked her under the chin, but could not find in my heart to offer anything uncivil to her, she being I believe a very modest woman.

2/29/64   Thence I to the Change and thence to a Coffe-house with Sir W. Warren—and did talk much about his and Woods business. ...

3/2/64   This afternoon we had a good present of tongues and Bacon from Mr. Shales of Portsmouth.

3/16/64   This day I have a great barrel of Oysters given me by Mr. Barrow, as big as 16 of others and I took it in the coach with me to Mrs. Turner's and gave them to her.

3/31/64   ... and after supper to the making up my monthly accounts and to my great content find myself worth above 900 £, the greatest sum I ever yet had.

4/2/64   Up and to my office, and afterwards sat—where great contest with Sir W. Batten and Mr. Wood ... and so home to dinner, and thence to Sir W. Warren's and with him passed the whole afternoon ... And thence to Woolwich; and after seeing Mr. Falconer, who is very ill, I to the yard and there heard Mr. Pett tell me several things of Sir. W. Batten's ill managements; and so with Sir W. Warren walked to Greenwich, having good discourse; and thence by water, it being now moonshine and 9 or 10 a-clock at night, and landed at Wapping and by him and his man safely brought to my door; and so he home—having spent the day with him very well.

4/16/64   Up and to the office, where all the morning upon the dispute of Mr. Wood's masts.

4/27/64   ... and late to my office, concluding in the business of Woods masts; which I have now done and I believe taken more pains in it then ever any Principall Officer in this world ever did in anything to no profit to this day.

5/3/64   . . . I went to the Change, and there meeting with Mr. Hempson, whom Sir W. Batten hath lately turned out of his place, merely because of his coming to me when he came to town before he went to him. And there he told me many rogueries of Sir W. Batten. How he knows and is able to prove that Captain Cox of Chatham did give him 10 £ in gold to get him to certify for him at the King's coming in. And that Tom Newborne did make poor men give him 3 £ to get Sir W. Batten to cause them to be entered in the yard; and that Sir W. Batten hath oftentimes said—"By God, Tom, you shall get something and I will have some on't." His present Clerke that is come in Norman's room hath given him something for his place. That they live high and (as Sir Frances Clerkes Lady told his wife) do lack money as well as other people, and have bribes of a piece of Sattin and cabinetts and other things from people that deal with him; and that hardly anybody goes to sea or hath anything done by Sir W. Batten but it comes with a bribe; and that this is publicly true—that his wife was a whore and that he had Libells flung within his doors for a cuckold as soon as he was married.

5/18/64   And here I met a pretty Cabinet sent me by Mr. Shales, which I gave my wife—the first of that sort of goods I ever had yet—and very conveniently it comes for her closet.

5/27/64   But to comfort my heart, Captain Taylor this day brought me 20 £ he promised me for my assistance to him about his masts.

5/31/64   Dined at home; and so to the office, where a great while alone in my office, nobody near, with Bagwell's wife of Deptford; but the woman seems so modest that I durst not offer any courtship to her, though I had it in my mind when I brought her in to me. But am resolved to do her husband a courtesy, for I think he is a man that deserves very well.

6/3/64   This morning before I came out, I made a bargain with Captain Taylor for a ship for the Commissioners for Tanger, wherein I hope to get 40 or 50 £.

6/10/64   . . . and in the evening with Captain Taylor by water to our Tanger ship; and so home well pleased having received 26 £ profit today of my bargain for this ship—which comforts me mightily.

6/13/64   I rated at Captain Taylor, whom contrary to my expectation I found a lying and a very stupid blundering fellow, good for nothing; . . . I confess I am at a vile trouble for fear the rogue should not do his work and I come to shame for loss of the money I did hope justly to have got by it.

6/17/64   I perceive the corruptions of the Navy are of so many kinds that it is endless to look after them—especially while such as one as Sir W. Batten discourages every man that is honest.

6/24/64   . . . and at night, weary, home, where Mr. Creed waited for me. And he and I walked in the garden, where he told me that he is now in a hurry fitting himself for sea. And that it remains that he deals as an ingenuous man with me in the business I wot of, which he will do before he goes. But I preceive he will have me do many good turns for him first.

6/30/64   Then to the making-up my month's accounts; and find myself still a gainer and rose to 951 £, for which God be blessed.

7/2/64   After dinner sat close to discourse about our business of the victualling of the garrison of Tanger—taking their [Alsop and Lanyon's]
prices of all provisions; and I do hope to order it so that they, and I
also, may get something by it—which doth much please me, for I
hope I may get nobly and honestly, with profit to the King. They
being gone, came Sir W. Warren and he and I discoursed long about
the business of masts. . . .

7/14/64   At noon to the Change, and from the Change over with Alsopp and
the others to the Popes-head tavern and there stayed a quarter of an
hour; and concluded upon this, that in case I get them no more than 3
s 1¹/₂ d per week a man, I should have of them but 150 £ per annum,
but to have it without any adventure or charge. But if I got them 3 s 2
d, then they would give me 300 £ in the like manner. So I directed
them to draw up their tender in a line or two against the afternoon,
and to meet me at White-hall. . . . So with my heart light, I to White-
hall, and there, after understanding by a statagem and yet appearing
wholly desirous not to understand Mr. Gaudens price when he
desired to show it me—I went down and ordered matters in our
tender so well, that at the meeting by and by I was ready, with Mr.
Gaudens and his, both directed in a letter to me, to give the board
their two tenders; but there being none but the Generall Monke and
Mr. Coventry and Povy and I, I did not think fit to expose them to
view now, but put it off till Saturday—and so with good content rose.

7/15/64   . . . my head at this Juncture very full of business how to get
something—among others, what this rogue Creed will do before he
goes to sea—for I would fain be rid of him and see what he means to
do—for I will then declare myself his firm friend or enemy.

7/16/64   Up in the morning, my head mightily confounded with the great
deal of business I have upon me today. But to the office and there dispatched Mr. Creed's business pretty well, about his bill. . . . Thence to
White-hall to the Tanger Committee; and there above my expectation
got the business of our contract for the Victualling carried for my
people—viz., Alsop, Lanyon and Yeabsly.
    And by their promise I do thereby get 300 £ per annum to
myself—which doth overjoy me; and the matter is left to me to draw
up. Mr. Lewes was in the gallery, and is mightily amused at it; and I
believe Mr. Gauden will make some stir about it, for he wrote to Mr.
Coventry today about it, to argue why he should for the King's convenience have it; but Mr. Coventry most justly did argue freely for
them that served cheapest.

7/18/64   Povy, to my great surprize and wonder, did here [at his home] at-
tacque me in his own and Mr. Bland's behalf, that I should do for
them both with the new contractors for the victualling of the garrison—which I am ashamed that he should ask of me; nor did I
believe that he was a man that did seek benefit in such poor
things. . . . Thence home, and Creed with me; and there he took occasion to own his obligations to me, and did lay down twenty pieces
in gold upon my shelf in my closet; which I did not refuse, but wish
and expected should have been more; but however, this is better than
nothing, and now I am out of expectation and shall from henceforward known how to deal with him.

7/19/64   And then at home with Lanyon and Yeabsly till 12 and past, about their contract for Tanger; wherein they and I differed, for I would have it drawn to the King's advantage as much as might be—which they did not like, but parted good friends; however, when they were gone, I wished that I had forborne any disagreement till I had had their promise to me in writing.

7/21/64   Up, and to the office, where we sat all the morning; among other things, making a contract with Sir W. Warren for almost 1000 Gottenburg masts, the biggest that ever was made in the Navy and wholly of my composing, and a good one I hope it is for the King. . . . This morning to the office comes Nich. Osborne, Mr. Gauden's clerk, to desire of me what piece of plate I would choose to have, a 100 £ or thereabouts, bestowed upon me in—he having order to lay out so much, and out of his freedom with me doth of himself come to make this question: I a great while urged my unwillingness to take any, not knowing how I could serve Mr. Gauden; but left it wholly to himself. So at noon I find brought home in fine leather cases a pair of the noblest Flaggons that ever I saw all days of my life. Whether I shall keep them or no, I cannot tell; for it is to oblige me to him in that business of the Tanger victualling, wherein I doubt I shall not; but glad I am to see that I shall be sure to get something on one side or other, have it which will. So with a merry heart, I looked upon them and locked them up.

7/22/64   . . . comes Mr. Lanyon, who tells me Mr. Alsop is now become dangerously ill and fears his recovery, which shakes my expectation of 300 £ per annum by that business. And therefore bless God for what Mr. Gauden hath sent me; which from some discourse today with Mr. Osborne, swearing that he knows not anything of this business of the victualling but the contrary, that it is not that that moves Mr. Gauden to send it me, for he hath had order for it any time these two months. Whether this be true or no, I know not; but I shall hence with the more confidence keep it.

7/25/64   I met Mr. Lanyon, who tells me Mr. Alsop is past hopes—which will mightily disappoint me in my hopes there, and yet it may be not. I shall think whether it will be safe for me to venture myself or no—and come in as an adventurer.

7/27/64   Mr. Lanyon to me and brought my neighbour Mr. Andrews to me, whom he proposes for his partener in the room of Mr. Alsop; and I like well enough of it.

7/31/64   I to my accounts; and to my great joy and with great thanks to Almighty God, I do find myself most clearly worth 1014 £—the first time that ever I was worth 1000 £ before—which is the heighth of all that ever I have for a long time pretended to. But by the blessing of God upon my care, I hope to lay up something more in a little time, if this business of the victualing of Tangier goes on as I hope it will.

8/2/64   . . . to the Change and there walked two hours or more with Sir W. Warren—who after much discourse in general of Sir W. Batten's dealings, he fell to talk how everybody must live by their places; and that he was willing, if I desired it, that I should go shares with him in anything that he deals in. He told me again and again too, that he confesses himself my debtor 100 £, for my service and friendship to him in his present great contract of masts, and that between this and Christmas he shall be in stock and will pay it me. This I like well, but do not desire to become a merchant and there[fore] will put it off, but desired time to think of it.

8/5/64   ... so mounted upon a very pretty Mare, sent me by Sir W. Warren according to his promise yesterday—and so through the City, not a little proud, God knows, to be seen upon so pretty a beast....

8/7/64   ... and I showed my wife, to her great admiration and joy, Mr. Gaudens present of plate, and two Flaggons; which endeed are so noble that I hardly can think that they are yet mine. So blessing God for it, we down to dinner, mighty pleasant....

8/11/64   ... and by and by comes Mr. Creed, lately come from the Downes, and dined with me. I show him a good countenance, but love him not for his base ingratitude to me.

8/12/64   Up, and all the morning busy at the office with Sir W. Warren about a great contract for New England Masts; wherein I was very hard with him, even to the making him angry. But I thought it fit to do it, as well as just for me on the King's behalf.

8/27/64   At noon to the Change and there almost made my bargain about a ship for Tanger, which will bring me in a little profit with Captain Taylor.

9/1/64   And we cut up the great cake Morecocke lately sent us—which is very good.

9/9/64   They eyed mightily my great Cupboard of plate, I this day putting my two Flaggons upon my table; and endeed, it is a fine sight and better then ever I did hope to see of my own.

9/10/64   ... this night I received by Will 105 £—the first fruits of my endeavours in the late Contract for victualling of Tanger—for which God be praised. For I can with a safe conscience say that I have therein saved the King 5000 £ per annum, and yet got myself a hope of 300 £ per annum without the least wrong to the King.

9/14/64   ... at noon to the Change and there went off with Sir W. Warren and took occasion to desire him to lend me 100 £—which he said he would let me have with all his heart presently, as he had promised me a little while ago to give me, for my pains in his two great contracts of masts, 100 £; and that this should be it—to which end I did move it to him; and by this means I hope to be possessed of the 100 £ presently, within two or three days.

9/16/64   And among other things, Mr. Gauden coming to me, I had a good opportunity to speak to him about his present, which hitherto hath been a burden to me, that I could not do it, because I was doubtful that he meant it as a temptation to me to stand by him in the business of Tangier victualling. But he clears me it was not, and that he values me and my proceedings therein very highly—being but what became me; and that what he did was for my old kindnesses to him in despatching of his business—which I was glad to hear; and with my heart in good rest and great joy, parted and to my business again. At noon to the Change, where by appointment I met Sir W. Warren; and afterward to the Sun tavern, where he brought to me, being all alone, a 100 £ in a bag; which I offered him to give him my receipt for, but he told me no, it was my owne, which he had a little while since promised me and was glad that (as I had told him two days since) it would now do me courtesy. And so most kindly he did give it me, and

I as joyfully, even out of myself, carried it home in a coach—he himself expressly taking care that nobody might see this business done, though I was willing enough to have carried a servant with me to have received it; but he advised me to do it myself.

9/21/64   But it is a strange thing to observe, and fit for me to remember, that I am at no time so unwilling to part with money as when I am concerned in the getting of it most (as, I thank God, of late I have got more in this month, *viz.* near 250 £) then ever I did in half a year before in my life, I think.

9/26/64   ... so I have looked a little too much after Tanger and the Fishery—and that in the sight of Mr. Coventry. But I have good reason to love myself for serving Tanger, for it is one of the best flowers in my garden.

10/3/64   But meeting Bagwell's wife at the office before I went home, I took her into the office and there kissed her only.

10/17/64   And thence with Sir W. Warren to a cook's shop and dined, discoursing and advising him about his great contract he is to make tomorrow. And do every day receive great satisfaction in his company, and a prospect of just advantage by his friendship.

10/19/64   Coming home, weighed my two silver Flaggons at Stevens's; they weigh 212 oz. 27 dwt.—which is about 50 £—at 5 s. per oz.; and then they judge the fashion to be worth above 5 s. per ounce more.

10/20/64   Then I to my office, where I took in with me Bagwells wife; and there I caressed her, and find her every day more and more coming, with good words and promise of getting her husband a place, which I will do.

11/3/64   At noon to the Change; and thence by appointment was met with Bagwells wife, and she followed me into Moore-fields and there into a drinking-house—and all alone eat and drank together. I did there caress her; but though I did make some offer, did not receive any compliance from her in what was bad, but very modestly she denied me; which I was glad to see and shall value her the better for it—and I hope never tempt her to any evil more.

11/8/64   I to my office, where Bagwell's wife stayed for me; and together with her a good while, to meet again shortly.... This day Mr. Lever sent my wife a pair of silver candlesticks, very pretty ones—the first man that ever presented me to whom I have not only done little service, but apparently did him the greatest disservice in his business of accounts, as Purser generall, of any man at the board.

11/15/64   I to the Change; and thence Bagwell's wife with much ado followed me through Moor-fields to a blind alehouse, and there I did caress her and eat and drank, and many hard looks and sithes the poor wretch did give me, and I think verily was troubled at what I did; but at last, after many protestings, by degrees I did arrive at what I would, with great pleasure.

11/30/64   ... home again and long together, [with Sir William Warren] talking how to order things in a new contract for Norway goods, as well to the King's as to his advantage.

12/5/64   ... and then after I had discoursed an hour with Sir W. Warren, plainly declaring my resolution to desart him if he goes on to Joyne with Castle, who, and his family, I for great provocations I love not—which he takes with some trouble, but will concur in everything with me he says. Now I am loath, I confess, to lose him, he having been the best friend I have had ever in this office.

12/20/64   Up and walked to Deptford, where after doing something at the yard, I walked, without being observed, with Bagwell home to his house and there was very kindly used, and the poor people did get a dinner for me in their fashion—of which I also eat very well. After dinner I found occasion of sending him abroad; and then alone avec elle je tentoy à faire ce que je voudrais, et contre sa force je le faisoy, bien que pas à mon contentement.

12/31/64   ... and then to my accounts, not of the month but of the whole year also, and was at it till past 12 at night—it being bitter cold; but yet I was well satisfied with my work and, above all, to find myself, by the great blessing of God, worth 1349 £—by which, as I have spent very largely, so I have laid up above 500 £ this year above what I was worth this day twelvemonth. The Lord make me for ever thankful to his holy name for it.[1]

Such are diary entries over two years by Samuel Pepys, clerk of the acts to the Naval Board and member of the Tangier Committee. He had received from those interested in his official actions animals, clothing, food, furniture, silverware, cash, and sex—the mastiff from a ship's surgeon, the mare from Warren; the Japan gown from Abrahall; the cake from Morecocke, the oysters from Barrow, the pork from Grove, the tongue and bacon from Shales; the cabinet from Shales, too; silverware from Falconer, Gauden, and Warren; the cash from Creed, Deering, Grove, Taylor, Warren and the Tangier victuallers; and the sex from Bagwell.

He had been paid by suppliers to the Navy of tallow for candles (Abrahall and Russell); by a supplier of elm (Morecocke); by a supplier of food (Gauden); by a supplier of masts (Warren); and by a supplier of miscellaneous goods (Deering). He had been paid by a Navy creditor for getting his bill accepted (Taylor) and a naval officer for getting his accounts passed (Creed). He had been paid by the master of a ropeyard (Falconer), by a Navy storekeeper to whom he had assigned extra personnel (Barrow), and by a Navy victualling agent (Shales). He had been paid by a ship's doctor who had gotten a post (the owner of Towzer) and by the wife of a ship's carpenter who wanted a better post (Mrs. Bagwell). He had been paid by suppliers to Tangier of the garrison's victuals (Alsop, Andrews, Lanyon, and Yeabsly) and by suppliers to Tangier of ships (Grove and Taylor).

The nature of the services he rendered is in most cases evident from the diary entries, but elaboration may illuminate certain details. Pepys was only one of seven members of the Naval Board and only one of sixteen members of the Tangier Committee. As clerk he was among the principal officers of the Navy, but not the senior man in rank or experience. Most of the members of the Tangier Committee outranked him politically and socially. A master of bureaucratic detail, he dominated both Board and Committee by his command of data. He made sure that he was the first to understand new business like the Tangier victualling. The "whole business" of many supply contracts eventually came to be left to him.

The developing relationship with Sir William Warren and the consequent defeat of William Wood is most fully documented. When it began, William Wood was the supplier of the Navy's masts, his partner being the son-in-law of Batten, a senior member of the Navy Board. Warren and Pepys had both served the overthrown Cromwellian government, and on April 19, 1661, Pepys had dealt with Warren on behalf of the private business of Pepys's patron, Lord Sandwich. By June 23, 1662, Warren had begun to educate Pepys on the types of timber and to offer him hospitality. On July 4, 1662, they spent four hours alone together, passing from talk of timber "to discourse of Sir W. Batten's corruption and the people that he imploys"—a theme that Warren returned to the next year, specifically bringing up Batten's "man Wood." Before returning to this instructive topic Warren had made his first present to Pepys of the State-dish of silver and cup with his arms cut on them—a nonreturnable gift. Later in the year the first big contract for masts with Warren was signed, the occasion when Pepys realized "what a man might do were I a knave." Over four months later, on February 2, 1664, came Warren's larger present of forty gold-pieces, the joy of which deprived Pepys of appetite. Two weeks later Pepys was very busy vexing Wood about his masts. On Wood's deficiencies he continued to take Warren's advice, the April moonlit stroll from Greenwich being one of several occasions. Wood had been put down by the end of April, Pepys recording how he had worked for his defeat without profit to himself. By August 2 Warren was offering to make Pepys a partner in all his ventures, and as Pepys shied off, acknowledged that he owed him 100 pounds for the mast contract. In mid-September after a little hinting and pushing by Pepys the 100 pounds were secretly delivered. In October he was advising Warren about the "great contract" the Navy would give him the next day. At the end of November he was figuring out how a new contract could benefit both the king and Warren. On December 5 he exercised muscle to shake Warren from joining Wood's old partner Castle, Batten's son-in-law, while he candidly admitted to the Diary that Warren had been "the best friend I have ever had in this office."[2]

The Tangier victualling contract was a long-term agreement, managed by Pepys with skill. To begin with, Sir Dennis Gauden, the Navy's regular supplier, thought he had the business, as Pepys noted on January 26, 1663; but Pepys preferred to deal with the Plymouth merchants Alsop, Lanyon, and Yeabsly and on July 14, 1664, after getting their oral agreement to his share, set up the tenders for the Tangier Committee so that their price beat Gauden's. Gauden complained but at once recognized where the power lay by giving Pepys the two great flagons. On September 9, Pepys got a down payment of 105 pounds from the Plymouth crowd, and a week later was assured by Gauden that he could keep the flagons too. Gauden may have been more than a little ironic when he told Pepys on this occasion that Pepys's handling of the affair became him; but Pepys was more interested in the assurance than the irony, and Gauden was playing for the long run. Ultimately, he was cut into the Tangier business, and Pepys wound up, as he noted February 4, 1667, with 500 pounds from him "for the service I do him in my victualling business," that is, for Pepys not interfering in Gauden's old role as a Navy supplier, "and 100 £ for my particular share of the profits of my Tangier imployment."

In his appreciation of the benefits he had received Pepys's consciousness appears to have been undivided. When on February 2, 1664, he got the gloves with the gold inside he saw God's blessing in his increase. When at the end of June he found himself still a gainer, it was God he thanked. When on July 22 he realized the Plymouth syndicate might fail, he blessed God for the Gauden bounty. When his worth passed 1,000 pounds at the end of July he gave great thanks to God, now described as Almighty God. When the first fruits of Tangier came in on September 9, it was God he praised. When on September 21 he realized it would be his best half year ever, God was again thanked. And when on New Year's Eve he did his accounts past midnight, he could end the diary for the year with a prayer that the Lord keep him thankful for the great rise in his capital.

The religious emotion which attended the receipt of his emoluments seems more than perfunctory. The self-satisfaction and ease of conscience that manifest themselves in his joyous ejaculations stand in sharp contrast to the misgivings he occasionally expressed on his adventures in adultery. There a consciousness of evil, at times, obtruded on his satisfaction in obtaining his objective. The record of the pursuit of Mrs. Bagwell is illustrative. Most of the time the diary registers no sense of sin in the chase. But twice there are breaks in Pepys's composure—on November 3, 1664, when he was relieved by her modesty, and on December 20, when he resorted to French to describe his quasi-rape of her. At no time did he invoke the blessing of God or thank God for his luck with her. In this respect, the sexual payoff for official favor was dominated for him by its sexual character; it did not enter neatly into the account books or even rank with other consumables like cake and oysters.

Trying to ascertain more certainly Pepys' view of the payments he received, one is struck by the most basic fact of all—that he bothered to record them. Why? As he indicated on May 31, 1666, he had account books where his receipts were presumably recorded. He had other sources of income—his salary of 350 pounds a year plus fees and poundage for exercising official duties. He did not ordinarily record in his diary the payment of these lawful sums; only occasionally, as on June 15, 1660, unusually prompt payment of a bill of the Navy led to his recording the payment. Payoffs tickled his interest. Some, of course, were mouthwatering or flashy enough to be noteworthy in themselves; but even the payment of cash struck him as interesting enough to record. In the interest these payments had for the diary-keeper, they were very like his sexual successes. As to both payments and sex, Pepys was keeping score. The events were recorded because the scoring pleased him. From the scorer's point of view, morality did not enter in; but in some fashion the events scored were exciting and significant—principally, one might conclude, because they showed him how much he could make from his office.

What is most striking, if the entries of 1663–1664 are compared with those of 1660, the first year the journal was kept, is the increase in Pepys's sensitivity. On March 6, 1660, his patron Edward Montagu, Lord Sandwich to be, offered him the big opportunity that made him—to go to sea as his secretary in the fleet that was to restore Charles II to England. On the same day an anonymous seaman was introduced to him who was willing to pay ten pounds for a purser's place "which I think to endeavor to do." On March 14, 1660, he records: "Here I got half a piece of a person [= parson] of Mr. Wrights recommending to my Lord to be preacher in the *Speaker* frigate." Thereafter there are over a dozen entries recording the receipt of similar payments along with other entries gloating over his rapidly rising net worth. None of the payments seems secretive or furtive. Pepys appears to be operating on Sandwich's axiom that the greatest virtue in the world is gratitude and being sure that proper gratitude was shown him for any appointments he secured. The ugly word bribe does not enter his head in connection with his unofficial income.[3]

Three years later his consciousness is more mixed. The silver dish and cup from Warren on February 10, 1663 is a "present," the best he's had. The far less expensive sturgeon from Bowyers on June 13, 1663, is "a bribe." He is thinking of sending the sturgeon back—he can afford to give it a contemptuous name. By May 20, 1666, he can record that Yeabsly the Tangiers supplier, "hath presented my Lord Ashley with 100 £ to bespeak his friendship to him in his accounts now before us; and my Lord hath received, and so I believe is as to bribes, as what the world says of him." Pepys followed up this disapproving entry on September 23, 1667, when he went to Ashley's to dine and go over

> the business of Yeabsly, who God knows doth bribe him very well for it; and it is pretty to see how this great man doth condescend to these things and doth all he can in his examining of his business to favour him, and yet with great cunning, not to be discovered but by me that am privy to it. . . . I find how prettily this cunning Lord can be partial and dissemble it in this case, being privy to the bribe he is to receive.

The comment in form complimentary is tinged with contempt, and "bribe" used as a noun and repeated as a verb contains a negative judgment.

Mr. Cooling, the Lord Chamberlain's secretary, made a disagreeable impression on him on July 30, 1667, when he told Pepys and Creed in casual conversation that "his horse was a Bribe, and his boots a bribe, and told us he was made up of bribes, as a Oxford scholar is set out with other men's goods when he goes out of town, and that he makes every sort of tradesman to bribe him; and invited me home to his house to taste of his bribe-wine." Mr. Cooling had just been talking of sexual affairs "very lewdly," in Pepys's judgment, when he passed on to bribes. Back on July 5, 1660, Cooling had treated Pepys to dinner and told him "how he hath a project for all us secretaries to join together and get money by bringing all business into our hands." Then, Pepys had recorded his talk at face value. Now he notes, "I never heard so much vanity from a man in my life." Cooling's cynical prattle in 1666 was slightly disconcerting.

When Pepys discovers his own patron, Lord Sandwich, takes cash, his reaction is sour—partly no doubt because he's been left out, partly, perhaps, because he is disappointed by Sandwich's stooping. The occasion was December 27, 1667, when Sir Hugh Cholmly was talking to him

> about the method he will leave his accounts in if he should suddenly die, he says there is nothing but what is easily understood, but only a sum of 500 £ which he hath entered 'Given to E.E.S.', which in great confidence he did discover to me to be my Lord Sandwich [Earl Edward Sandwich] at the beginning of their contract for the Molle; and I suppose the others did the like, which was 1500 £—which would appear to be a very odd thing, for my Lord to be a profiter by the getting of that contract made for them.

The term "profiter" is studiously neutral, but "a very odd thing" betrays surprise, jealousy, criticism, all muted. That the comment is made at all contrasts with Pepys's silence three months later, on March 10, 1668, when his wife tells him that Sandwich, through an agent, and Sandwich's son had each solicited her sexually—outrages that Pepys could neither respond to nor treat verbally. The diary entry four years earlier of January 27, 1663, it may be recalled, had shown a sense of disillusionment when he had heard of Lord Rutherford, the governor of Tangiers, wanting "the profit of victualling of the garrison itself, and others to have the benefit of making the molle." Pepys had observed that he found that "there is nothing in the world done with true integrity but there is design along with it." Now he knew who "the others" were who had had "the benefit of making the molle," and who lacked "true integrity."

As the pattern of entries in 1663–1664 is more closely considered, it becomes evident that there was more than a trace of anxiety mixed with the spontaneous delight he took in a payoff. When the treasurer for Tangiers, Povey, on July 18, 1664, tried to muscle in on his deal, Pepys was "ashamed" for him and thought such "poor things" beneath a rich and elegant man. Pepys knew what the common word was for what he took. He heard it applied on May 3, 1664, to Batten when he heard talk about how hardly anybody went to sea without a bribe to Batten. Batten's bribes came in the form of satin, furniture, and cash, just as his own did. Batten took, or was said to take, a standard rakeoff on Navy yard jobs; Pepys had a varying schedule, with sex sometimes acceptable as well as less personal presents. The difference between Batten "living by his place" and Pepys himself was not very perceptible. If on July 17, 1664, the corruptions of the Navy appeared endless, he knew the way his own transactions could be characterized.

A need for secrecy is evident more than once in his own behavior and ir. those with whom he dealt. The first payment from Warren on February 10, 1663, came with the letter containing the fake message about gloves, in case anybody asked what his package had contained. The first payment from Deering came as a "New Year's Gift." The first payment from Grove on April 3, 1663, led Pepys to perform a charade he could refer to if "ever I should be Questioned about it." When on February 2, 1664, he chivvied Creed for his share in the Navy's settlement of Creed's account, he took pains to say nothing that could be used to "hurt" him later. The 100 pounds delivered in a bag by Warren in September 1664 was set up by Pepys as a loan, partly out of caution. Warren brushed this flimsy device aside but was clear that the bag should be handed over without even a servant to observe it. All of these concealments, artifices, dodges suggest that taking money for official actions was not accounted right and respectable in public.

Public rightness and respectability became Pepys's principal concern in 1668 when a hostile Parliament set up commissioners of accounts to examine the Navy Board. His first care was to talk to the witnesses who might damage him. On March 2, 1668, he recorded "and among others, I did prepare Mr. Warren, and by and by Sir D. Gawden, about what presents I had from them, that they may not publish them; or if they do, that in truth I received none on the account of the Navy but Tanger. And this is true to the former, and, in both, that I never asked anything of them. I must do the like with the rest." The damaging witnesses were to be coached to silence, or—since the Inquiry was focused on the Navy—to connect their gifts to Tangier, or at the very least to make their payments appear as voluntary offerings. The great mast contract with Warren of 1664 was to be buried. What was in the diary could not have stood the light of day.

On his own behalf, Pepys filed with the commissioners "a particular defence" of what he characterized as his "uprightness." Alluding to the diary without revealing its existence, he declared that he could give "an account of the particular manner of [his] employing" every day he had served the Board. He challenged "the whole world" to allege a single instance reflecting on his "integrity to my master and fair dealing towards those whom his service hath led me to have to do with." He roundly affirmed that he "did never . . . directly or indirectly . . . demand or express any expectation of fee, gratuity, or reward from any person for any service therein by me done or to be done him." A more comprehensive or inaccurate denial could not have been entered. But he shrewdly suspected that the commissioners would still be interested in how much money he had made in office. He ended his defense by saying he had not increased his estate "by 1000 pounds" (underestimating his profits as of this date by about 6,000 pounds). Confronted with unhelpful witnesses among the suppliers and Pepys's vigorous assertion of his purity, the commissioners found it hard to make their case.[4]

Still, a great deal turned on the king. There were two differences between Pepys's situation and Bacon's besides the commissioners' lack of forthcoming witnesses. First, Pepys's friends were in a stronger political position; the king was on their side. Second, Pepys was a bureaucrat not a judge; the basic paradigm of justice was not at issue. Charles II took up his defense. The commissioners were told that they must present the case to the king and his Council. Before the case opened, on January 4, 1670, the king conferred with his most intimate advisers with Pepys present. They reached the conclusion that "the matter should be managed" by Pepys. With his nominal judge actively on his side, Pepys easily put his parliamentary critics to rout.[5]

The public exoneration of Pepys, first achieved by political measures, has continued to this day. To Percival Hunt, with access to the diary, which would have destroyed Pepys before Parliament, he "stood up well . . . under attempts to bribe him." He was "at bottom a moralist;" he had rules and he wanted to act by conscience." His "large purpose to do justice to all men" he kept "inviolate."[6] For Arthur Bryant, he is "the Saviour of the Navy" and "the Father of the Civil Service."[7] Noting Pepys's own lies to the commissioners of accounts but not his tampering with the commissioners' witnesses, Bryant celebrates Pepys pouring "scorn on the poor shabby proofs which were all they could bring to support the accusations of nearly two years."[8] William Matthews, the editor of the splendid new edition of the diary, declares, "Pepys is rightly regarded as a great civil servant, a remarkable administrator and reformer."[9] Since Matthews thinks the story of Pepys's attempted seduction of Deb Willett, his wife's teenage helper, is the story of "the degradation that slowly came upon Deb"[10]—Deb's degradation, not Pepys's!—he may be suspected of some partiality. His co-editor, Robert Latham, is more circumstantial in his defense. Pepys "condemned" gifts "which obviously operated against the public interest," but not those made "merely to expedite business or to establish good personal relations." In fact, "surrounded as he was by the calculated generosity of merchants, he preserved his independence." He had "mastered the useful art of receiving gifts without becoming corrupt."[11] These judgments made by men highly familiar with the diary take Pepys at face value in his evaluation of his deals.

More than once Pepys said or hoped his profits were "noble," "honest," "just." His apologists believe they must have been. The distinction implicit in Pepys's use of the derogatory term "bribes" for Batten's takings would be that "bribes" for Pepys meant payments that brought about substantively wrongful official actions. What he himself got led to nothing wrongful. They were like—he does not use the word—tips, that is, rewards for special service given him with the tacit acquiescence of his superiors. But his insistence in the privacy of his journal on the integrity of his actions is scarcely comprehensible unless he was arguing with a contrary inner voice. One can hear that inner voice when he recorded on September 10, 1664, that he would make his profit on the Tangiers deal "without the least wrong to the King" and so "with a safe conscience."

The entry told his conscience that the transaction was not injurious to the Crown. Before his inner judge he customarily claimed to observe two rules: No one was hurt by what he took. What he got was voluntarily given. He had convinced himself on January 27, 1663, that "there is nothing in the world done with true integrity," but in these inner dialogues he did not make the defense that bribetaking was customary, the vice of the age, or what everyone else did. Here he announced his own, higher standard.

The two rules, which were interdependent, were both put in the little public lecture he gave Luellin on December 12, 1663, and thought worthy of reporting: He would be "bribed" by no one to be "unjust." He was not "squeamish" about subsequent "acknowledgments" from persons he had served. The diary went on to show both rules empty with an emptiness so evident that the holes must have been close to Pepys's consciousness.

He would not be unjust, but when he got a payment the money had to come from someone. His theory was that if he had saved money for the king, he was entitled to a percentage. The theory was expressed in the "safe conscience" entry of September 10, 1664. The king had saved 5,000 pounds. Pepys was taking only 300 pounds. That this 300 pounds was either subtracted from what was spent on the men's victuals, or reduced what the Navy might have saved, was not considered. Pepys's self-contented implication was that the Plymouth syndicate simply cut him into a share of its lawful profit. That the profit had depended, according to his agreement with the syndicate of July 14, 1664, on getting an extra halfpenny per week per man, Pepys did not mention. In this classic illustration where, by his oral contract with the Plymouth suppliers, his own compensation depended on the victuallers getting the higher price from the Navy, Pepys did not acknowledge that he had made at least 150 pounds by setting up the Navy Board so it would approve the higher price. The emphasis of the diary—"without the least wrong"—is telltale.

His concern for the Navy was equally tempered when he set down on November 30, 1664, that he was "long together" with his best friend Warren planning the new Norway mast contract to Warren's advantage and the king's. In this entry there was open admission that the Navy was being represented by an agent looking out for both sides. Equally candid was the entry the same day of his speech on bribes to Luellin, when he considered his relation to Abrahall and Russell: "I am in both their pays."

The claim Pepys pressed against Creed on February 12, 1664, arose from help he had given Creed in passing his accounts as master-muster and deputy treasurer of the fleet, 1660–1662.[12] As his "favor and assistance" and "kindness" had been extended to get Creed paid, he must have either taken money from the king that did not belong to Creed, or he must have stood ready to mulct Creed for getting paid something honestly due him. He must have hurt one or the other. He found Captain Taylor "good for nothing" on June 13, 1664, and not only kept him on the job for which Pepys was to be paid 40 or 50 pounds but retained him for the same kind of work on August 27. It is hard to see the use of the services of "a very stupid blundering fellow" as without harm to those he was supposed to serve.

If the harm is palpable in several of the situations, the bargained-for nature of the reward to Pepys is even more often evident. Obligations imposed by reciprocity were his theme. He was amazed at the candlesticks on November 8, 1664, from Lever for whom he had apparently done nothing. In general, Pepys made no difference between presents that preceded the award of Navy business and those that followed. Either way, the degree of favor measured the appropriate material response. He understood on June 24, 1664, that Creed "will have me do many good turns for him" before paying up. A month later he wrote Creed off for his failure to reciprocate properly: "I am out of expectation and shall henceforward know how to deal with him." When Warren gave the gloves with the gold on February 2, 1664, Pepys knew he could expect more if he increased his "duty and endeavours." After the great mast contract, he approached Warren for the "loan" that would compensate for his work. On the really big Tangiers deal Pepys negotiated his commission in advance. Even after making the speech to Luellin on bribes, he knew he had put matters clearly enough to convey what he really wanted, adding to the diary, "So I expect to hear more of it"; and less than three weeks later he received the New Year's Day note endorsed to Luellin, to be cashed for Pepys's benefit. Unlike the gods of the *Book of the Dead* who did not take Ani's cakes till after they had approved the judgment, he ate Morecocke's cake the day Morecocke's tender of elm was pending. The victuallers had to give their assent to his share before he acted for them. Reciprocity, not generosity, was the principle he understood to rule.

Only occasionally did he do worse than make an implicit contract and keep it, and each time the circumstances were extraordinary. Once was the use of force on Bagwell to subdue her to his use in her own home after her husband had given him dinner shortly before Christmas of 1664. But there sex provided an element beyond his usual objectives, and he later did write, albeit ineffectually, two letters seeking to promote her husband.[13] Another exception was when he received unexpectedly the dress for his wife from a tallow-maker, while already bound to buy tallow from Mrs. Russell. No entry appears as to the return of the dress, no doubt an awkward present as it had caught his wife's eye and came "very opportune." It must be assumed that he somehow made it up to Abrahall. A third exceptional case occurred when Gauden presented the splendid flagons. Pepys well understood how they were meant—"a temptation to me to stand by him" in the Tangiers victual contract. He accepted them on July 21, 1664, after he had made his deal with the Plymouth syndicate and had even used Gauden's Tangiers offer on July 14 as a foil to the better offer of the syndicate. He kept them and put them on display for his wife on August 8 and for his guests on September 9, all the while under the impression they were for the Tangiers trade. Gauden took him off the hook on September 16. If Pepys accepted Gauden's smooth explanation that they were for other past services, he also understood they were for services to come; and after the two months in which he could not reciprocate the gift the way he thought it was intended to be reciprocated, his heart was "in good rest and great joy." The exceptions to the rule of reciprocity confirm its reign.

At times Pepys did make a show of independence from his paymasters. He angered Warren on August 12, 1664, by riding him hard on one order of masts. He dressed down Captain Taylor for his incompetence. He pressed Lanyon and Yeabsly past midnight on July 19, 1664, to get better terms for the king on the Tangiers contract. In short, he did not sell out the king entirely. But his independence was necessarily qualified. He gave up none who rewarded him, not even the very stupid blundering Taylor. He did not push Warren so far that Warren stopped being his best friend. He worried that he might have lost Lanyon and Yeabsly by being sticky, but in fact he did well enough by them to get his first installment of money less than eight weeks later. Who, indeed, is likely to get higher rakeoffs—the official who is in a supplier's pocket or the one who occasionally shows mettle? Gauden's tribute to Pepys, ironic as it may be, also acknowledged his superiority at the art of extracting money—Pepys's proceedings with the Plymouth syndicate "being what became me."

If the king had abandoned him, would he have fared any better than Bacon? His most basic defense was similar, that he never took money to make a bad decision, or, as Bacon had put it, "to pervert justice." The defense was similarly implausible in that, in such subjective matters as the better of a legal argument or the better of goods offered, absolute right or wrong is hard to tell, and what is wanted is a judgment uninfluenced by extrinsic considerations affecting discretion. A soccer referee who is bribed but says he made all the right decisions anyway is incredible; so is a judge or a contracting officer.

When the recorded reciprocities are laid by the side of Pepys's self-justification, his excuses to his conscience seem so feeble that he himself must have been aware of their fragility. But Pepys also manifests a very considerable capacity to delude himself. The higher rate on Tangiers supplies did not "the least wrong" to the king. It was "true" that the presents he got from Gauden were only in connection with Tangiers, not the Navy. It was "true" that he "never asked anything" of either Warren or Gauden. There was no reason to record these misstatements in his diary unless at the time he did so he had convinced himself that a number of events which earlier he had said had happened had not happened. When he recorded that he would be able to tell as the truth, if questioned, that he had never seen money in the envelope he got from Grove, he had convinced himself that pouring the money out first made his answer true. With this ability at rationalization and self-delusion, he was capable of simultaneously believing that his graft injured no one, that it was voluntarily paid, and that those he favored owed it to him.

At the back of Pepys's consciousness must have been the size of the amounts involved, relative to the king and relative to himself. On the Tangiers deal, where almost 40,000 pounds was needed for a year's food supply, he took only 350 pounds, not quite 1 percent.[14] Apart from Tangiers, the Navy was spending about 350,000 pounds per year.[15] One percent of the amount was 3,500 pounds. If Pepys helped himself to 350 pounds, he took one tenth of 1 percent of such expenditure. Although this amount was insignificant to the king, relative to his own salary and estate it was enormous. He had a salary of 350 pounds as clerk plus the fees and poundage he collected by virtue of his offices. At a time when the mean annual income for a household was under 8 pounds and when not more than 5,000 persons earned over 240 pounds, this income by itself put Pepys in the upper class.[16] In 1664, if the diary entries are added, close to 300 pounds came to him from contractors, while his net worth rose over 500 pounds. Payoffs made 1664 his first bumper year, the first of his years of great prosperity. The man who began his career as clerk in 1660 with 25 pounds liquid capital, "discoursing of the changes that we have seen and the happiness of them that have estates of their own," became a man possessing over 7,000 pounds by the end of 1667. As his lawful income had not increased significantly, it must be inferred that his extra-legal arrangements were now paying out handsomely. In his editor's words, at the end of his career he had "grown rich in the service of the state and by investments."[17] When Pepys had first taken the job on August 6, 1660, he had received an offer to buy it from him for 1,000 pounds, "which made my mouth water," but he had been advised on August 16, 1660, by his patron Lord Sandwich "that it was not the salary of any place that did make a man rich, but the opportunities of getting money while he is in the place." Increasing his worth by almost 30,000 percent in six and a half years, he had realized those opportunities. Engaged in getting an estate of his own, he could no more listen to the voice of conscience than heed the fear of public exposure. The voice became "squeamish," the qualms were suppressed.

The parallel between Pepys's consciousness in regard to bribery and in regard to adultery is stronger than at first appears. A psychoanalyst who has ventured to analyze what moved Pepys to describe his sexual adventures with foreign words has observed that he could not "have seriously considered that this would have been a shield to prying eyes. . . . It would seem more probably that he was in this way attempting to separate those thoughts from himself, to make them less immediately part of his own consciousness and yet at the same time more titillating. Perhaps the remnant of the Puritan in him had to be deceived."[18] Similarly, he could not acknowledge as his own act the taking of a bribe.

Pepys's practice is not to apply the ugly categorical descriptions of either adultery or bribery to his own conduct, but to moralize about the adultery of his patron Sandwich (for example, on November 15, 1663) as he did about William Batten's bribetaking. The reservations he expresses on November 3, 1664, about Mrs. Bagwell doing "evil" are indeed stronger than anything he says explicitly about a cash bribegiver. But, in the course of time, his sensibilities to the evil of adultery were blunted. He began the seduction of Deb Willett with the same care that he set up his relations with the victuallers. If he did not praise God for his goodness in making her available, he did record his opening moves on August 6 and 31, 1668, with great matter-of-factness; no sign of a divided consciousness appears. Only when on October 25 his wife discovered him with Deb with "my main in her cunny," did he begin to want to stop; and only after enduring unrestrained wifely rage for a month did he resolve on November 20 "that it is much the best for my soul and body to live pleasing to God and my poor wife." Before he was seared by his spouse's anger, he concentrated on the satisfaction of his desires, and his conscience did not stir. If the king had left him to the mercy of the commissioners, it would have been like being surprised with his hand in Deb, and he would have undergone the suffering inflicted by a wrathful nation or a wrathful Parliament. We can even imagine that his response in this extremity, like his domestic response, would have been to turn to prayer. Bacon, whose view that every man was "the architect of his own fortune" he greatly admired, could have provided a model. But he never was tested by such a public crisis.[19]

In practice, to the degree that any morality operated under the heavy tar of greed, Pepys's morality as he made his way in the world was that of the Poor Man of Nippur. He expected a return for his goat. He tried not to be as bad as the mayor of Nippur, failing himself to reciprocate, even if Gauden easily convinced him he could keep the wonderful silver cups. What he took was in the tradition of the gifttakers of Mesopotamia, where one of the earliest recorded gifts to an official was a female slave and the other gifts were money. His worst words were reserved for the official who would not stay bought. On March 24, 1667, Hugh Cholmly spoke to him of "Lord Bellasses, who (he did tell me perticularly how) is as very a false villain as ever was born, having received money of him here upon promise and confidence of his return, forcing him to pay it by advance here and promising to ask no more there, when at the same time he was treating with my Lord Allington to sell his command to him. . . . I am glad I am informed hereof, and shall know him for a l[iar] etc." The phrase "as very false a villain as ever was born" speaks eloquently of Pepys's high sense of the obligation created by a payoff.

If Pepys had been prosecuted like Hog by a Cicero, a Cicero with access to honest witnesses and to the diary, he would not have come off well. The doubledealing with Gauden, the unconscionable taking from him while binding the others, would have been underscored. The mean advantage taken of a humble employee's wife, the gross exploitation of her husband's hospitality and home, the fact that the promised payoff by Pepys was ineffectual so she got nothing for her pains—these themes would have been enlarged on. No doubt a Cicero would have added that the money the victuallers spent on him must have come out of the food rations of poor sailors. Even a modern biographer, Richard Ollard, observes that "the lucrative deals by which money to feed them went to his own pocket [were] intellectualized and made abstract."[20] A Ciceronian prosecutor would have portrayed him more simply, as greedy for money as he was for sex and taking as much of both as he could get. Such a prosecutor would not have been enamored of Pepys's wonderful prose style nor enthralled by his catholic capacity to enjoy life. Such a prosecutor would have made an abstract man, the grafter, and failed to acknowledge that Pepys, though he committed adultery, loved his wife, and that, though he was in the pay of the Navy's suppliers and the king's contractors, loved the Navy and served the king.

Our focus is not on the man, but on what bribery meant for him morally and socially. The complexity of his consciousness is central. His payoffs were disguised and taken secretly, would not bear public examination, led him to suborn perjury in those who could have testified about them, and made it necessary for him when he wrote the commissioners to assert the contrary of what he had done. His payoffs were, in short, something of which he was ashamed. They were taken joyfully, industriously, with thin rationalizations and a suppressed conscience. They did come by bargain not true gift. They did work to fetter his discretion and blur his judgment. They were not excusable as the pickings of a poor man making up an inadequate salary. Added to a high lawful income they were the way of making him rich. They were, in his own language for others, corruption and bribes. He did not pay a public penalty for them because he was on the politically stronger side, he concealed them, and he was not a judge. The diary, rich as it is in many other aspects, also is the confession of a grafter.

Pepys's consciousness of the gifts he took as somehow significant may be profitably compared with two other kinds of contemporaneous judgment publicly offered: that of professional expositors of a morality more severe than his own and that of Parliament as to its own members.

The Moralists' Answers.   Representative of the handbooks of Puritan inspiration that answered moral questions in Pepys's youth is William Ames's *Conscience with the Power and Cases Thereof*, published in English in 1639. If—to entertain an improbable hypothesis—Pepys had consulted it on bribes, he would have found them treated under the question, "What sins ought a Judge especially to beware off?" By means of bribes he would have read, "[J]udgment is either corrupted, that it may bee unjust, or just judgment is sold, either of which is abominable." The sin was condemned by Deuteronomy 16:19 "and every where in Scripture." The description of the just man in Isaiah 33:15 did "especially belong to Judges and other administers of judgment." To be pricked by these admonitions, Pepys would have had to regard himself as an "administer" of judgment.[21]

Ames's exposition of the sin of simony, to buy or sell "a holy and Spirituall, for a Temporall" was unlikely to have struck Pepys as applicable to himself; still less would he have been tempted to apply Ames's conventional reproduction of Gregory the Great's three types of "simoniacal gift" or Ames's medieval insistence on the sin of mental simony.[22] Ames, however, went on to discuss "the sale of public offices." This "hath a dishonest corruptness, which thwarts the nature of them. . . . There are also so many evils which spring from this kind of traffick, that it is had in detestation with all ingenuous men."[23] By this comment Pepys's conduct with Captain Taylor and with Bagwell could have been caught. A penitent Pepys could have regarded his dealing with them with the eye of Ames's ingenuous men.

Arguably apropos was the question "What is Acception of Persons?" and Ames's answer: "the Personall qualities are onely respected, which are altogether impertinent to the end, which is intended in the cause in hand"—Thomas Aquinas's definition, without acknowledgment.[24] Ames then identified "Acception of Person" with "respect of persons." To the next question, whether respect of persons "bee a sin?," Ames answered that in its "owne generall nature" it was, citing Deuteronomy and the Epistle of James, and declaring it contrary to both justice and charity in "all kind of Judgment, Election, or Sentence." Indeed it governed "all cases about Election or Promotion of men to offices." If any make "choyce of an unworthy man," he committed the sin.[25] The offense could occur even in procedural matters "left to the discretion of the Judge, which kind are the prorogation or restraint of time." By analogy, a mind as perspicacious as Pepys's could have seen that the same principle applied in the administration of procurement. Nonetheless, he might have answered mentally, I only pick the fit; and he could stoutly have maintained that he was "no Judge."

Richard Baxter's *A Christian Directory, or A Summa of Practical Theologie, and Cases of Conscience*, another Puritan handbook, published in 1673, stated clearly that an "unrighteous judgment" was "a damnable sin," which "condemneth Christ himself in his members." To avoid it, Baxter advised, "Keep a tender conscience, which will not make light of sin. It is those that have seared their consciences by infidelity or by a course of sinning who dare venture with *Judas* or *Gehezi* for the prey and dare oppress the poor and innocent." The scriptural exemplars associated unrighteous action with bribetakers; the "infidelity" spoken of could have been in belief or in marriage: Pepys might have pondered the ambiguity if the book had come to his attention during his marriage. Nonetheless a judge, not he, was addressed when Baxter recalled St. Paul's corrupt judge, "Faelix," and exhorted, "Remember the day when all these causes must be heard again, and the righteous God will set all strait, and vindicate the cause of the oppressed."[26]

Under "Christian Politicks," Baxter asked, "May I give money to a Judge or Justice or Court officer, to hire him to do me justice, or to keep him from doing me wrong, or to avoide persecution?" He gave the old answer that it was permissible if "you cannot have your right by other means." But he added three qualifications not found in, say, Bernardino of Siena. Such payments were not to be made if forbidden by the law of the land; if they would accidentally do more hurt to others than benefit to you; and "when it will harden men in the sin of bribery, and *cause them* to expect the like from others." Even if permissible for the donor, such payments remained wrong for the donee to take.[27] Addressing "Simoniacal Contracts" for holy orders or benefices, Baxter observed sharply that "promised Gratitude is but a kind of contracting."[28] To the question, "May I buy an Office for money in a Court of Justice?," Baxter answered that it depended on the law and one's motive. The law could permit it. A proper motive was the common good, not "your own commodity or honor."[29] Neither of these questions addressed nonjudicial contexts, but what could have been morally done to get office in a court would have been acceptable to Baxter in less exalted places.

Pepys, in short, if he saw Baxter's principles confined to the sacred realms of justice and the spiritual, had nothing to learn; if he felt bound by analogies, he had much to teach himself. Two passages had a generality that could have given him pause. Under "Directions Against Scandal," Baxter paraphrased Scripture and said, "Gifts also have blinded the eyes of some who seem wise. . . . What scandals have preferments proved to the world, and how many have they ruined?" Under "Directions against Covetousness, or Love of Riches, and against Worldly Cares," Baxter numbered the signs of covetousness, among them, "When we make too *much ado* in the world for riches, taking too much upon us, or striving for preferment, and flattering great ones, and envying any that are preferred before us, or get that which we expected." Reflectively, Pepys might have noted that this and other signs fitted him, that he even deserved Baxter's conclusion that such a one was "a *worldly covetous* wretch."[30] Yet nothing in Ames or Baxter, strictly construed, condemned the gifts he took for procurement contracts. On August 25, 1661—early in his rise—Pepys heard "a very good and pungent sermon of Mr. Miles concerning the nature of Restitution." He records no further details, and there is no evidence that he ever felt under any moral necessity to restore any of his gains.

The Purity of Parliament. Just as the popular handbooks on Christian duty did not address the moral problems of procurement officers, so they left untouched the morals of legislators. Parliament, however, had been at least ready to investigate Pepys. What of Parliament's own standards? John Ashburnham's case is contemporaneous with Pepys's tenure at the Naval Board.

Ashburnham was from youth a courtier. Born into a family related to James I's favorite, the duke of Buckingham, he was made a groom of the royal bedchamber at the age of twenty-five. He stood by Charles I against the rebels, and in 1643, aged forty, became the treasurer of the king's army. He shared the king's flight after his defeat and was ultimately imprisoned by Parliament in 1648. At the Restoration he, too, was restored to his post at the bedchamber and became a member of Parliament from Sussex. Pepys observed him, two months before his fall, angrily dressing down the clerk of the great wardrobe for failing to keep up the supply of personal linen for the king: "still this old man (endeed, like an old loving servant) did cry out for the King's person to be neglected." On November 22, 1667, aged sixty-four, he became the first member of Parliament to be expelled for accepting a bribe.[31]

Ashburnham was an incidental casualty of a political storm. The earl of Clarendon, Charles II's chief minister, had just been jettisoned by the king as the result of general discontent over disasters in the naval war with the Dutch and domestic ills. Parliament was in the process of impeaching Clarendon, and he was about to flee the country for France. Among the evils complained of was a monopoly, licensed by the king, of the importation of Canary wine. Allegedly 4,000 pounds had been paid illicitly to Clarendon for the license, but the evidence establishing the bribe was not specific. The topic suggested inquiry into another royal license, that granted certain merchants for importing French wine; and Clarendon being pro-French, this license seemed particularly vulnerable. The licensees and their go-between were summoned before Parliament, and they talked.[32]

According to the merchants, Ashburnham had told them, "Since the King hath done so much for you, it is fit you present His Majesty with a New Year's gift of 1000 pounds." They gave him 500. The persistence of the New Year's gift cover for bribes, half a century after Bacon, is credible and striking. Whether Ashburnham passed any money on to Charles is not clear because he—loyal above all—said nothing.[33]

Defenders pointed out that if Ashburnham had done any wrong it was not "as a member of the House of Commons but as a Courtier." The House, however, was not to be swayed. Pursuing Clarendon and pushing Charles, with no effective ministry to restrain them, the Commons looked at Ashburnham's as an open and shut case; and perhaps Charles felt no inclination to help his father's old, fortune-beaten favorite. The House resolved that Ashburnham in receiving the money had "committed an Offense, to the Dishonour of this House, and contrary to his Duty, as a member thereof." He was expelled, ordered to receive his sentence on his knees at the Bar, and thereafter to be confined in the Tower. He pleaded gout and was excused from coming to the Bar and going to the Tower. His expulsion remained—a remarkable manifestation against bribery in a session where, it is believed, both the French and Spanish governments spent money to buy votes, and inexplicable except as an expression of parliamentary pique against a royal monopoly.[34]

Nonenforcement of the criminal penalty, the emphasis on "Dishonour of this House," and the political nature of the proceeding all showed that the application of the antibribery rule to a legislator was a novel and difficult business. Pepys, who recorded with such interest Ashburnham's solicitude for the royal linen, did not trouble himself to record the wardrobe keeper's flaw or fall. Ashburnham's disgrace was not a major event like Bacon's. The fall of a courtier in a political context had no larger teaching for Pepys on other servants of the Crown. By Parliament's political standards, Pepys had nothing to worry about as long as he stood in with patrons in power.[35]

The contrast with payments to a judge was sharp. Lord Ashley, according to what Yeabsly told Pepys on May 20, 1666, received 100 pounds to pass Yeabsly's accounts; Pepys on September 23, 1667 had marvelled at Ashby's "great cunning" in favoring Yeabsly. Ashley went on to become the earl of Shaftesbury and to be Lord Chancellor in 1678-1679. John Dryden saw him in 1681 as "Achitophel," the treacherous counsellor of a conspiracy against the king. Attacking him as strongly as he can, Dryden says of his year on the woolsack:

> Yet, fame deserv'd, no Enemy can grudge;
> The Statesman we abhor, but praise the Judge.
> In Israels Courts ne'er sat an *Abbethdin*
> With more discerning Eyes, or Hands more clean:
> Unbrib'd, unsought, the Wretched to redress;
> Swift of Dispatch, and easie of Access.[36]

Pepys was swift of dispatch and easy of access; but his hands could not have been described by the ancient metaphor of cleanliness, and "unbribed" would have been an inappropriate adjective for him. Achitophel—"to all succeeding Ages Curst"—stands as a judge in sharp contrast to the ingenious, busy, conscientious clerk who made such a good thing out of his place and provided the information and the measure by which he himself in the delicate realm of conscience was vulnerable to judgment.

14

Hog Two

He "did not only give and receive bribes accidentally." He "formed plans and systems of government for the very purpose of accumulating bribes and presents to himself." He descended into "the muck and filth of peculation and corruption." He was "not only a public robber himself, but the head of a system of robbery, the captain-general of the gang."[1]

In such and similar language did the most philosophical member of Parliament, Edmund Burke, describe the man who had for thirteen years, from 1772 to 1785, been the British governor of Bengal. The occasions of his descriptions were public and formal—sessions in the House of Lords in which Burke as the chairman of the managers of an impeachment committee of the House of Commons sought the conviction of the defendant. Of the object of these attacks, Warren Hastings, Burke observed, "Do you want a criminal, my Lords? When was there ever so much iniquity ever laid to the charge of any one?"[2]

Hastings, as portrayed by Burke, had been as cruel as he had been corrupt. Bent on taking all he could, he had instigated, approved, or collaborated with the use of torture to produce the revenues he needed; and he had not stopped at arranging a judicial murder to stifle an accuser. "Do you want a cause, my Lords? You have the cause of oppressed princes, of undone women of the first rank, of desolated provinces, of wasted kingdoms."[3]

Hastings had no doubt as to the model he was being made to fit. He did not wish to sustain "the vile and abhorred character of a Verres." Charles Fox, one of Burke's co-managers, explicitly evoked Cicero and paraphrased his appeal to the judges of Hog. Burke himself was wonderfully plain:

> We have all, in our early education, read the Verrine Orations. We read them, not merely to instruct us, as they will do, in the principles of eloquence and the laws of the ancient Romans, of which they are an abundant repository; but we may read them from a much higher motive. We may read them from a motive which the great author had doubtless in his view when by publishing he left to the world and to the latest posterity a monument by which it might be seen what course a great public accuser in a great public cause ought to pursue, and, as connected with it, what course judges ought to pursue upon such a cause. In those orations you will find almost every instance of rapacity and peculation which we charge upon Mr. Hastings.

A "great public accuser" in a "great public cause," Burke spoke as Cicero, and Hastings became Hog.[4]

The outcome, however, was different from the classic model. In 1795, after a trial of seven years—a very intermittent trial, for the Lords met thirty-five days the first year, five days the fourth year, etc.—Hastings was formally acquitted. Of some 250 Lords, only twenty-nine thought themselves sufficiently familiar with the case to vote, and no more than six of these found Hastings guilty on any count.[5] The East India Company reimbursed his legal expenses of 71,000 pounds and voted him an annuity of 4,000 pounds a year and a loan of 50,000 pounds without interest. In 1803 repayment of the loan was waived. In 1808 a company ship was named the *Warren Hastings*. In 1813 he was awarded an honorary doctorate of laws by Oxford. In the same year a parliamentary committee seeking his advice on Indian affairs uncovered their heads, as before royalty, in his presence. In 1814 he was made a privy councillor. He died in 1818, aged eighty-five, having lived the last twenty years in comfortable retirement in the house of his dreams, the old Hastings family estate at Daylesford.[6]

Not only did his material well-being and public reputation survive his long trial; Hastings's subsequent treatment by posterity has often been benevolent. In 1932, for example, the Royal Empire Society celebrated the bicentenary of Hastings's birth as if he were a hero. Thomas Macaulay, his most famous critic, passed over the charges of bribery as based on "a few transactions which would now be called indelicate and irregular, but which even now would hardly be designated as corrupt."[7] Biographers, by profession inclined to indulgence, have emphasized his greatness as an administrator and rationalized his faults. The furthest the author of a recent admiring life will go is to say that "the true charge must not be corruption but an insensibility, a legacy of the India in which he had been bred."[8] A modern historian of the impeachment, attempting evenhandedness between Burke and his target, holds that two of the dealings to be examined below were "very questionable" but refrains from calling them corrupt. He quotes critics of Hastings who thought the trial itself was an ordeal which he "did not deserve." He concludes, "It was Burke's tragedy that he could not see Hastings in perspective."[9] In this modern view Hog Two is a cruel caricature.

Hastings and the Company.   From the perspective of this book, Hastings is to be seen in terms of the accusation of taking bribes, the evidence supporting and refuting the charge, and the sanctions imposed and not imposed for what he had done; but for any understanding at all, a summary of his official position and the circumstances of his impeachment is essential.

After his mother died in childbirth and his father, a minister, abandoned him, Warren Hastings was brought up by a grandfather in genteel rural poverty. At ten he was sponsored by an uncle at the Westminster School in London, and after seven years of classical education there, sent out at eighteen to India as a clerk of the East India Company. His state of mind could not have been much different from that of other young men he later described who went out in the Company's service, "every one aspiring to the rapid acquisitions of lacs," a lakh being 100,000 current rupees or 10,000 British pounds, and from 25,000 to 100,000 pounds being regarded as a respectable fortune for an Englishman to acquire in India.[10]

One of a small band of British civilian employees—about 300 in Bengal—Hastings rose through the Company's ranks until in 1772, aged forty, he was made governor of Bengal. A director of the Company, informing Burke of the new appointment, wrote, "His name is Hastings, lately sent down from the Coast (Madras) and chosen for his good sense and integrity." Hastings was to remain in this position until his resignation and return to England in 1785.[11]

For thirteen years he was the most important holder of political power in Bengal. He had to deal with a variety of Indian rulers already in varying degrees of dependence on the British and to face their insubordination or revolts. He had to deal with hostile neighbors, both native and European, who became or were seen as threats to British interests. A Supreme Council made up of Englishmen appointed by the Company hampered him for a period when the majority were his critics. A Supreme Court of English judges was for another period intractable. But armed with inflexible determination and great resourcefulness, Hastings usually dominated the government. The population of millions ("Blacks" to the British), divided between a Hindu majority of many castes and a Moslem minority, submitted generally to what the ruler ordained for them, and there is little indication that Hastings consciously took their needs or interests into account; there was no institutional mechanism to compel him to do so. Hastings's accountability was at home, in England. As the Company's employee or servant, to use the misleading eighteenth-century term, he was responsible to the Company's directors in London. Orders on a variety of matters came from them, but given the distance from which they wrote and the time it took for their commands to arrive (four to five months at the best), Hastings had a latitude of discretion that in practice had few limits.[12]

The Company's supervision was further diluted by its structure. The East India Company—"the United Company," "the E.I. Co.," "John Company," or simply "the Company"—was a joint stock company in which every holder of over 500 pounds of stock possessed one vote, so that domination by a few big stockholders did not occur. Instead, the directors, occasional fallings-out aside, tended to perpetuate themselves. The directors' interest in patronage was often as keen as their interest in protecting the stockholders. Their official posture was the obvious one of requiring integrity in the Company's employees; but there were splendid opportunities for the employees to develop reciprocal relationships with the directors. One example will serve. In 1770 Stephen Sulivan, the son of Laurence Sulivan, a leading director, arrived in Bengal. Hastings appointed him judge-advocate general, loaned him 10,000 pounds charged to his father's account, and assigned him for four years the most lucrative of the Company's monopolies, the trade in opium. Laurence Sulivan was a strong backer of Hastings in the Company's headquarters at Leadenhall Street.[13]

Political pressure from England was also responded to in India by Company jobs for sons or dependents. But political pressure increased to the point where it could not be confined by the awarding of patronage. In part, greater involvement of the home government was inevitable when the Company became the de facto sovereign of a large and important nation, required British military support, and engaged in actual warfare. The Company's rapacious administration of Bengal in the 1760s had led to a terrible famine in 1770, and Bengal's misery had actually affected the Company's own fortune adversely. In 1773 Lord North's Regulating Act had intervened by statute in the Company's affairs: a governor-general's post was created by law with Hastings designated by name in the statute. A Supreme Court, to be chartered by the king, was authorized for Calcutta. By the same statute the governor-general was required to obey the orders of the directors, and the directors were required to furnish information on Company affairs in India to the government at home.[14]

Further government involvement accompanied the Company's increasing financial dependence on the state. By the 1780s the Company was not in flourishing condition. In Bengal its debt was immense, and its paper sold at a 25-30 percent discount. At home it was seriously in arrears on routine debts. In the summer of 1783 it was unable to pay cash to tradesmen. In March 1784 its offices were attached for 100,000 pounds owing the Customs. In the spring of 1785, it was offering to pay half of an outstanding arrearage on duties of 1,000,000 pounds. The Company's problems could be solved only by government aid, usually disguised and always indirect. The simplest expedient was to get the Treasury not to press for payment of the customs' duties. A slightly more complicated move was for the Company to issue annuities at $3^1/_2$ percent, guaranteed by the king. By 1783 the Company had borrowed almost 3,000,000 pounds on the strength of the royal guarantee. The credit and therefore the existence of the Company depended on the government, and knowledgeable persons in each institution were entirely aware that the Company had to be responsive to the administration in power.[15]

Hastings's Finances.   The Governor's salary was 25,000 pounds a year, plus perquisites of which the chief was the use of the Company's principal house in Calcutta as his residence—in all about 5,000 pounds of perks, for a total lawful annual compensation of 30,000 pounds. The significance of such a sum may be measured by comparing it with two other contemporary figures. When Burke was seeking to raise funds for refugees from revolutionary France, the committee decided that a priest—a single man of respectability—could live decently in England on less than 25 pounds a year. At the upper end of the scale, when Burke became paymaster general in the Coalition government of 1782, he was assured of "4,000 certain," plus a residence, while his son Richard became his deputy at 500. Burke described the paymaster general's job with the emoluments attached as "giving a person who had some pretensions his Baton de Marechal de France en argent comptant"—in short, as first-rate employment. Hastings, in other words, received over 1,000 times the income of a man in genteel poverty and at least seven times as much as a major official in the administration at home.[16]

With this salary and emoluments, Hastings—during two years for which records have been found, 1780–1781 and 1781–1782—spent more cash than he received by over 10,000 pounds. It may be assumed, given his style of life as governor-general and his generosity to his dependents, that in other years he saved little or nothing from his salary. Nonetheless, when he returned to England, rumors circulated about his great fortune. The Prince of Wales, a friend, applied for a loan of 200,000 pounds. His own representatives would not admit his wealth to be greater than 50,000 pounds, and a modern effort to estimate it puts it no higher in 1795 than 75,000 pounds. This figure is no pittance, but a matter of far greater interest for our purposes is not the ascertainable remainder of his property but how much he sent out of India. Here one has to leave aside guesses as to what he may have sent through the Dutch East India Company; its records reveal him in person buying one 15,000 pound bill of exchange, and his friends, Richard Barwell and George Vansittart, were its frequent customers and at times could have been his straws. But relying only on what is established by the records of John Company itself as to bills of exchange and diamonds sent home by Hastings, plus miscellaneous other records referring to him, it has been shown that Hastings, in his thirteen years of office from 1772 to 1785, remitted to England at least 218,527 pounds. This sum was nearly ten times his annual salary, nearly ten thousand times the an-

nual income of a poor gentleman. It is characterized by its modern calcula-
tor, a student of fortunes made in India, as "extremely large."[17]

Prosecution.   As early as 1780, when Lord North was in power, Edmund Burke, then an opposition member of Parliament, had voiced concern about great abuses by the Company in India. In 1781, he began to
focus in particular on Hastings. He was now supplied with data by a
former member of the Supreme Council in Bengal, Sir Philip Francis, an
avowed and unrelenting enemy of the governor. A Select Committee dominated by Burke began to issue reports on the administration of Bengal,
nearly all of them highly critical of Hastings. "I have undertaken a vast
Task," Burke wrote Francis, "but with your assistance I may get through
it."[18] In March of 1782 Burke's patron Rockingham came to power, and
Hastings was warned that Burke now sought his removal. Burke was supported by Charles Fox in the Rockingham administration and by Henry
Dundas, the opposition's leading authority on India; but the Company
resisted governmental pressure. Rockingham died and was succeeded by
Shelburne, and Burke was out of the administration. Returned to influence
in April 1783 as a member of the Coalition, Burke told Parliament "that he
would bring to justice, as far as in him lay, the greatest delinquent that
India ever saw."[19]

Reform bills for India, drawn by Burke and Fox, were sponsored by the
Coalition, presented to the Commons in November 1783, and defeated in
the Lords, with the consequent fall of the Coalition. The government of
William Pitt, which then took office, owed something to the Company interests that had opposed reform and had triumphed in the Lords, but Pitt's
main adviser on India was Dundas, and Pitt's alliance with Hastings
turned out to be "accidental and temporary." When Hastings returned in
1785, expecting a peerage, Burke, again in opposition, worked for his impeachment—impeachment in the British sense being a charge by the
Commons of violations of "the already known and existing law," tried
before the Lords as "the most high and supreme court of criminal jurisdiction." As one who had held a statutory appointment, Hastings was open
to impeachment.[20]

Burke observed to Francis that Hastings had been governor-general
under North, Rockingham, Shelburne, the Coalition, and Pitt, and that the
parties had been "so perfectly jumbled" in their relations with him that it
was "morally impossible to find any combination of them who can march
with the whole body in orderly array upon the expedition before us." Yet
before "a bribed tribunal," Burke insisted on pressing on. "Speaking for
myself," he wrote, "my business is not to consider what will convict Mr.
Hastings (a thing we all know to be impracticable) but what will acquit
and justify myself to those few persons and to those distant times which
may take a concern in these affairs and the Actors in them."[21]

In April 1786 charges of high crimes and misdemeanors, drafted by
Burke, were presented to the House. On May 1 Hastings spoke in response
to them. The rest of the month the House, meeting as a Committee of the

Whole, heard prosecution witnesses. The opposition was united in supporting impeachment; the Pitt administration's attitude was crucial to the outcome. Dundas was clearly hostile to Hastings. Pitt himself could well have calculated that he lost nothing by letting the impeachment proceed and that he risked criticism by blocking it. Those closest to him thought that he was persuaded on the merits that impeachment was justified. The matter of Hastings's "presents" was mentioned in particular to Hastings as something moving the First Minister against him. On a decisive vote on June 13 Pitt voted to support one charge. He did not make it an administration issue, but once he had decided personally against Hastings, he was followed by many ordinary members expressing their own "idealism and prejudices." Although Burke and Francis worked the chief oars, the impeachment would not have occurred without his approval. After an adjournment and the hearing in early 1787 of further witnesses, pro and con, actual impeachment was voted in May 1787.[22]

The Crime of Corruption.   The Preamble of the Articles of Impeachment announced that Hastings had held statutory office, "on the due and incorrupt Execution of which the Welfare of the said United Company, the Happiness of the native Inhabitants of India, the Honor of the Crown of these Kingdoms, and the Character of the British Nation did most materially depend." Hastings, it was asserted, was bound by the duties of this office. Sixteen articles followed, many of them setting out abuses of authority outside the scope of this book, all of them constituting "high crimes and misdemeanors," and each one of them being a ground for impeachment. The sixth article charged Hastings with having received "presents" and with having thereby "grossly violated the duties of his Station"—an invocation of the standard set by the Preamble. Breaching this standard, he was, the sixth article alleged, guilty of "Corruption, Peculation, and Extortion."[23]

For none of these "high crimes" was there a citation of the controlling law. Extortion would have required a showing of coercion which the managers of the impeachment did not attempt. "Peculation" was so unfamiliar to English law that it appeared in Blackstone only in its Latin form *peculatus*, defined as the embezzlement of public funds. The Company's money was not public, and even if it had been, the technicalities of the law of embezzlement kept immune from this crime an agent who received money in trust and simply failed to deliver it to his principal—Hastings's position if the charges were true. "Corruption" was the one crime involving the presents where conviction might have seemed possible. But what was "corruption," as defined by English law and applied to acts performed in India?[24]

The leading case was that of Thomas Earl of Macclesfield, a Lord Chancellor impeached in 1725. The gravamen of his offense was the sale by him of masterships and clerkships in Chancery. Although on other grounds the impeachment was sustained, the judges, when asked by the Lords, had specifically stated that the sale of an office which related "to the administration of justice" was not an offense at common law; and over a sharp dissent, this view had been followed by the majority of the Lords in assessing Macclesfield's punishment. *Macclesfield's Case* was reflected in a diluted way in Blackstone's definition of bribery in 1765 in his famous *Commentaries on the Laws of England*. Bribery was for him, as it had been for Coke, a crime committed by "a judge or other person concerned in the administration of justice." The implication, at least, was that the act had to involve a judicial decree or its execution. So limited, it might not reach the political or administrative actions of Hastings. True, Lord Mansfield in 1769 had held that the tender of money to the First Minister to "procure" a clerkship in Jamaica was a bribe at common law. Whether this advance in the law would stand was an open question. Mansfield, moreover, had limited the common law of bribery to England itself, finding that it applied in this case only from the circumstance that the clerkship was awarded under the Great Seal. None of Hastings's acts involved the use of such high English authority. Even if Mansfield were followed on the elements of the crime, none of Hastings's acts in India could constitute the crime of bribery or any other common law offense. The same conclusion was reached by reading Blackstone: the laws of England applied to the British isles. In "conquered or ceded countries"—the American plantations were instanced—common law did not apply, nor did statutes unless explicitly extended. Hastings by the standard rules of English jurisprudence was beyond the force of any law save one expressly made for India.[25]

By covenant with the Company in 1767, before he was governor, Hastings had sworn to accept from any Indian prince no more than 400 pounds as reward or gift; anything above the limit was to be held in trust for the Company. As governor he had sworn to do his duties faithfully. These two oaths appeared at least principally to be for the Company's benefit. If violation of them was a breach of law, it was difficult to see how breach of them was criminal, much less a "high crime." A statute was also germane—North's Regulating Act of 1773. It explicitly prohibited the governor-general from receiving from anyone "any Present, Gift, Donation, Gratuity or Reward, pecuniary or otherwise . . . any Usage or Custom to the Contrary thereof in any wise notwithstanding." This law seemed to fit the case exactly, sweeping aside all excuses based on Indian practices of giftgiving. The difficulty was in characterizing the violation of it as a crime. No criminal sanction was attached to it. Examined closely, it regulated the governor-general's conduct but did not make him a criminal if he disobeyed.[26]

Macclesfield's Case, however, was here of help to the prosecution. No statute had been shown to make the receipt of substantial presents by the chancellor a crime. He himself had argued that it was an old custom in disposing of the offices in Chancery. Nonetheless, he had been unanimously found guilty by the Lords. Innocent of bribery by vote of the majority, he was—at least by implication, for there were lesser charges of misconduct and no judgment separating them from the main charge—impeachable merely for taking presents in return for jobs in the justice system. If *Macclesfield's Case* was a good analogy, Hastings could be impeached for receiving presents in exchange for jobs. As the statute addressed the governor-general specifically, he did not have the defense that the statute did not apply in India.[27]

In eighteenth-century diction "presents" was a polite description of offerings from a suppliant to a superior; "bribes" were a critical description of the same offerings as in Alexander Pope's translation of the Iliad. Apollo's priest, Chryses, seeks to get his captive daughter, Chryseis, back from Agamemnon and prays,

> If Mercy fail, yet let my Presents move . . .

Agamemnon scornfully replies

> Mine is thy Daughter, Priest, and shall remain,
> And Pray'rs, and Tears, and Bribes shall plead in vain;
> And Age dismiss her from my cold Embrace,
> In daily Labours of the Loom employ'd
> Or doom'd to deck the Bed she once enjoy'd.

To the proud Trojan the Greek's presents are bribes; and so the chain of consequences was begun that led to Agamemnon's quarrel with Achilles.[28]

So here with little case law, and with Mansfield's decision going beyond *Macclesfield's Case*, it was not hard to identify the receipt of presents with bribery. Blackstone himself had already done this, saying in the passage where he spoke of bribery,

> In the east it is the custom never to petition any superior for justice, not excepting their kings, without a present. This is calculated for the genius of despotic countries; where the true principles of government are never understood, and it is imagined that there is no obligation from the superior to the inferior, no relative duty owing from the governor to the governed. . . . And some notable examples have been made in parliament of persons in the highest stations, and otherwise very eminent and able, but contaminated with this sordid vice.

Blackstone made no analysis of the state of mind of the recipient of a bribe, and he provided no cases. But written long before Hastings's trial, this passage must have struck the impeachment managers as a happy contrast of corrupt Eastern customs with English practice. When, frequently, in the course of arguments, the managers went beyond the articles to speak of Hastings's "bribes," they followed the conflation of bribery and present-taking suggested by Blackstone and by Mansfield; even in Article Six, they made one reference to a "Bribe or Consideration"; and they took no notice of the doctrine that bribery did not exist as a crime in the colonies.

The defendant and his counsel did not follow the course which the analysis just made might suggest. They did not contend that the law of bribes had no application in India. One must infer they thought this path too risky in a political proceeding. Instead, they strenuously maintained that, before the 1773 Act, customary presents were legal and that after the Act there was no prohibition against the governor-general receiving presents not for himself but for the Company. Hastings, it would seem, had reached this conclusion on advice he received before leaving India. As he told the Lords in his own defense, "No person ever suggested to me that the Act of Parliament deprived the Company of the right of receiving the customary presents." Corruption in this view consisted in the governor taking for himself. Everything Hastings had taken, he maintained, was for the Company. Lord North's Act had no application to this kind of situation. That was clear from the fact that under Pitt, in 1784, the Act had been amended to bar gifts to the Company. As all the charges against Hastings antedated the amendment, he was home free, he believed, if he could show he personally took nothing.[29]

Three examples—one dating from before North's Act of 1773, two after it—will show how the case was fought.

Entertainment by Munni Begam.   Munni Begam, the woman Hastings had appointed head of the household of the young nawab of Bengal had acknowledged to Company agents that she had paid Hastings 15,000 pounds. He admitted receiving the money. The reason both he and she gave was that an allowance to the governor-general was customary when he visited the nawab. Hastings had made such a visit in 1772 for over two months and accordingly had been allotted an "entertainment" allowance of 2,000 rupees, or 200 pounds, a day, amounting to 15,000 pounds in all.[30]

Munni Begam was reputed to be an ex-slave, and an ex-dancing girl, who had been taken in polygamous marriage by the old nawab. In the view of the managers she was unfit to be the guardian of the nominal ruler of the country, her stepson, especially in disregard of the boy's own mother. This unnatural and unfit choice, as the managers saw it, was made by Hastings to facilitate his bribetaking—the ex-dancing girl being his compliant agent—and to reciprocate the bribe she actually paid for the appointment. Hastings defended his choice and contended that what he had received had no connection with his selection.[31]

There was no possibility of Hastings denying that the money he had taken fell literally within the comprehensive terms of his covenant to take no "allowance" or "donation" or "compensation" from an Indian prince. (As the payment had been made in 1772 it was not covered by North's Regulating Act). But was Hastings's breach of his oath a crime? The question, as put to the Lords by Hastings's counsel Robert Dallas, was whether "established usage" did not grant "persons of distinguished rank" an "allowance for table expenses" when "resident at the court of eastern princes." The practice of earlier governors was cited as precedent; the allowance to the nawab himself when visiting the governor in Calcutta was invoked as parallel. Custom, Dallas argued, must be decisive as to whether the act was criminal. Even in England itself, there were "a great number of different practices with respect to the receipt of emoluments by persons in public situations" which would not bear legal scrutiny, but which, sanctioned by custom, could not be the basis of a criminal charge.[32]

To prove corruption the managers tried to rely on a record made before the Supreme Council in Bengal. The Lords ruled the record inadmissible.[33] Alone, the record would not have been convincing; but one circumstance strengthened its weight—the death of the accuser. Confined by less strict rules than the managers, we can look at what had happened in Bengal. In 1775 when Hastings was governor-general but was outnumbered on his own Council by opponents fresh from England, he had been accused before the Council of taking 35,000 pounds in bribes from Munni. His accuser, egged on by his English opponents, was a highly experienced Bengalese politician. Maharaja Nanda Kumar (Nundcomar to the English) was a Brahmin, at one time Hastings's foe, at another his friend, and the most influential Indian in Calcutta. He no doubt believed he was striking a defeated and vulnerable man.

Nanda Kumar made his charge on March 11, 1775, providing amounts, payors, and dates. The Supreme Council began to investigate. Meanwhile, George Vansittart, Hastings's friend, got in touch with Indians who were claiming that Nanda Kumar in 1769 had tried to defraud an estate by a forged acknowledgment of debt. Nanda Kumar was arrested, imprisoned by May 6, 1775, and put on trial by June 9. The English Chief Justice, Elijah Impey, an ally of Hastings, presided with three other English judges. There was a great deal of contradictory testimony from Indians, and the jury of Englishmen had to decide whom to believe. As a matter of law it was doubtful that the document Nanda Kumar was said to have forged fell within the terms of the English forgery statute; very probable—if Blackstone's treatise was to be believed—that the statute itself did not apply in Bengal; and almost certain that the Supreme Court did not have jurisdiction to try an Indian for a crime against another Indian. After six days, Nanda Kumar was found guilty and sentenced to death. Appeal, permission for which depended on the court, was denied. In a last petition to the Council, which had no control over the court, he asserted, "They put me to Death out of Enmity and Partiality to the Gentlemen who have betrayed their Trust." He was hanged in August. Opinions have differed as to whether the verdict was justified. Impey's rulings during the trial and his charge to the jury appear to have been fair. No one has disputed that the death sentence struck the Indians as "an act of savagery." No one has doubted the stunning effect the execution of the most powerful Brahmin in Calcutta had upon would-be accusers of Hastings. "The change which this execution has worked is easily perceived," wrote a backer of Hastings. "The Blacks know not which way to look." As Macaulay has observed, everybody, "idiots and biographers excepted," thought that "Hastings was the real mover in the business."[34]

Murder will out. When Impey returned to England and ran for a seat in the Commons against Richard Brinsley Sheridan, an impeachment manager, Sheridan's supporters followed Impey with the figure of a black man with a noose around his neck. It was enough to defeat Impey. But murder will not always out at the right time and place. An attempt to impeach Impey foundered on the Pitt administration's unwillingness to support the charges. No evidence was ever produced that Hastings dictated the result or interfered in any manner in the judges' conduct of the trial, so that "murder" seemed to many too strong a characterization of the proceeding. But it was and is a reasonable inference that Nanda Kumar would not have been prosecuted except for a nod given by Hastings, and if, as seems clear, the court had no jurisdiction, "murder" appears accurate. The murder of a witness by a defendant is not necessarily proof of the truth of the witness's testimony; but courts have admitted evidence of such murder as a circumstance the jury may consider in evaluating the murdered man's veracity. So here Nanda Kumar's accusations and the manner of his death may be weighed together. The inference can be drawn that Nanda Kumar had made charges that were too sensitive for Hastings to permit him to testify about them before a Supreme Council whose majority was unfriendly to the governor. The arrangements for the elimination of Nanda Kumar are evidence suggesting that Hastings perceived that the 35,000 pounds from Munni would have been regarded by the hostile Supreme Council as bribes.[35]

Anonymous Money from Dinajpur. In 1782 Hastings wrote the Secret Committee of the directors, accounting for certain sums which "have occasionally been converted to the Company's Property through my Means." He enclosed a paper headed, "An Account of sums received on the Account of the Honourable Company by the Governor General, or paid to their Treasury by his Order, and applied to their Service." Under this heading appeared the serial numbers, dates (October and November 1780), and amounts of three Company bonds, totaling 406,000 rupees (about 40,000 pounds) and the notation that these bonds were in the governor's possession but endorsed with the statement that he had no claim on them against the Company. Nothing further appeared in the Account as to why the bonds had been issued. A second sum was noted in the Account as a deposit, then more bonds were listed. In the body of the letter transmitting the Account, Hastings wrote,

> Why these Sums were taken by me; why they were except the Second, quietly transferred to the Company's use; why Bonds were taken for the First, and not for the Rest, might, were this Matter to be exposed to the view of the Publick, furnish a Variety of Conjectures to which it would be of little Use to reply. Were your Honourable Court [of directors] to question me upon these Points, I would answer that the Sums were taken for the Company's Benefit, at Times in which the Company very much needed them; that I either chose to conceal the First Receipts from publick Curiosity, by receiving Bonds for the Amount, or acted without any studied Design which my Memory could at this Distance of Time verify; and that I did not think it worth my Care to observe the same Means

with the Rest. I trust, Honourable Sirs, to your Breasts for a candid Interpretation of my Actions....[36]

The ambiguity, hesitations, mysteriousness of the passage are palpable. It furnished no clear information about the 40,000 £ worth of bonds which Hastings once had held and now was crediting to the Company.

The letter itself was dated May 22, 1782, but was not sent until December 16, 1782, when it was accompanied by a second letter from Hastings to the Secret Committee, saying that the sailing of the ship intended to carry it had been "protracted by various Causes" with "no other Conveyance since occuring" (an assertion later shown to have taken liberties with the facts). What was in fact the true date of the first letter had a bearing on its credibility. Hastings protested that it had been written when the "late Parliamentary Inquiries" [those of April 1782 during the Rockingham administration] had been unknown to him. He continued,

[The] Honourable court [of directors] ought to know whether I possess the Integrity and Honour which are the first Requisites of such a Station. If I wanted these, they have afforded me but too powerful Incentives to suppress the Information which I now convey to them through you. . . . Upon the Whole of these Transactions which to you who are accustomed to view Business in an official and regular Light may appear unprecedented, if not improper, I have but a few short Remarks to suggest to your Consideration. . . . The Sources from which these Reliefs to the publick Service have come, would never have yielded them to the Company publickly, and the Exigencies of your Service (Exigencies created by the Exposition of your Affairs, and Factions in your Council) required those Supplies.

I could have concealed them, had I had a wrong Motive, from yours and the publick Eye for ever.[37]

The directors, who received both letters in the spring of 1783, replied in March 1784, observing that with "so many Points so unintelligible" they would like more information. In particular they wanted to know when the sums were received and Hastings's "Motives" for withholding earlier knowledge of them.[38] The directors were as puzzled as the modern reader must be by the deliberate vagueness of their representative's report. They were not, however, so impolite as to remind Hastings that he had taken an oath to keep a daily account of all "Transactions and Occurences relating to his Trust."[39]

Hastings acknowledged the directors' inquiries over a year later, on July 11, 1785. The acknowledgment came after his return to England and after he had been "kindly apprized that the Information required as above is yet expected from me." He referred now to "the Presents" and said the dates they were received were about those "prefixed to them in the Account," that is, the dates on the bonds of October and November 1780. As to his motives, he quoted his letter of May 1782 and remarked, "It will not be expected that I should be able to give a more correct Explanation of my

Intentions, after a Lapse of Three Years." He continued, nonetheless, with suggestive amplifications:

> I should have deemed it particularly dishonorable to receive, to my own Use, Money tendered by Men of a certain Class, from whom I had interdicted the Receipt of Presents to my Inferiors and bound them by an Oath not to receive. I was therefore more than ordinarily cautious to avoid the Suspicion of it, which would scarcely have failed to light upon me, had I suffered the Money to be brought directly to my own House, or to that of any Person known to be in Trust for me; for these reasons I caused it to be transferred immediately to the Treasury. . . . Although I am firmly persuaded that these were my Sentiments on the Occasion, yet I will not affirm that they were. . . . Of this I am certain, that it was my Design originally to have concealed the Receipt of all the Sums, except the Second [the deposit] from the Knowledge of the Court of Directors. They had answered my Purpose of publick Utility; and I had almost totally dismissed them from my Remembrance. But when Fortune threw a Sum in my Way of a Magnitude which could not be concealed, and the peculiar Delicacy of my Situation at the Time in which I received it, made me circumspect of Appearances, I chose to apprise my Employers of it. . . . This, Sir, is the plain History of the Transaction.[40]

These three extraordinary letters said a great deal. Hastings would not expose to public conjecture "why these Sums were taken by me"; nor would he explain why he had taken bonds in his own name for money belonging to the Company. He could have concealed the receipt of the money forever and had first intended to do so. The money had come from persons who would not have paid the Company publicly and from whom it was prohibited to receive presents; but the sums were presents. At a time when his situation had become delicate, he had chosen to reveal them and make a species of accounting. He did his best not to connect this time with any inquiry in Parliament. For further answers his July 11 letter referred the directors to William Larkins who "possessed, I believe, the original Paper which contained the only Account that I ever kept of it."

Larkins was the Company's accountant-general in Bengal. An affidavit by him had been enclosed in Hastings's letter of December 16, 1782, stating that the earlier May letter and the enclosed account "were written by me, at the Request of the Honourable Warren Hastings, Esquire, on the 22d May 1782, from rough Drafts written by himself in my Presence." The purpose of this affidavit had been to confirm Hastings's claim that his disclosure was not prompted by the parliamentary inquires of April 1782. It had also appeared to put the Company's chief accounting officer in Bengal in the position of asserting that the enclosed account of "sums received on the Account of the Honourable Company" was known by him to be true.

Now, on August 5, 1786, writing from Calcutta on Hastings's directions and signing himself as Hastings's "attorney," Larkins sent the directors "Copies of the Papers which I kept as Memorandums of the Particulars of the Dates on which the Sums contained in Mr. Hastings's Account of 22d May 1782 were received." The first of these memos ("Paper No. 1") had under Dinajpur a list of moneys totaling 200,000 rupees set opposite dates beginning in August 1779 and ending in July 1780. It listed a "balance" owing from one "G.G.S." of almost 100,000 rupees. The Dinajpur account was then summarized as follows:

Cabooliats	Received	Balance
400,000	300,000	100,000

Dinagepore Peishcush.[41]

A "cabooliat" or *kabulyat* meant an agreement; "peishcush" or *peshkash* was money payable like a feudal fine on the installation of a new zamindar or feudatory revenue collector. The account, therefore, indicated that, by agreement at Dinajpur, 400,000 rupees were payable on the zamindar's investiture, of which 100,000 had not been paid. If the summary were read in conjunction with the preceding list of moneys, only 200,000 had been received, and 100,000 was still due from G.G.S. When these amounts were turned into pounds, the account stated that Hastings had collected 20,000 pounds of *peshkash* from someone at Dinajpur and was owed 20,000 pounds more, half from an unknown, half from G.G.S.

If this paper were compared with the "account" enclosed in Hastings's May 22, 1782, letter, which was supposedly based on it, two discrepancies were noticeable. The amounts received had been between August 1779 and July 1780, and the bulk of them, received in 1779, had not been received at all near the October–November 1780 dates on the bonds; and the amount of the bonds differed from the collection. Neither discrepancy was enormous. Both were surprising when one account was said to be based on the other. A different and more basic discrepancy was noticeable when records outside these accounts were consulted. The old zamindar had been in office until July 1780 when he died, and the small, regular *peshkash* paid by his successor was duly recorded in the Company's books on August 1, 1780.[42] Payments beginning in August 1779 could not have been *peshkash*.

Further discrepancies appeared as to the time when Hastings noted on the bonds that he had no claim on them against the Company. In his letter to the Company of July 11, 1785, Hastings said he had made this endorsement "in order to guard against their becoming a Claim on the Company as part of my Estate," and that he had made it in the middle of 1781. His letter of May 22, 1782, said the endorsement then existed. The bonds when they were produced for inspection carried a date of May 29, 1782, as the date of Hastings's notation. They were not in fact delivered for cancellation to the Company until January 1785.[43] By Hastings's own admission, then, he had held the bonds for a substantial period in his own name; he had publicly stated two dates for the endorsement which proved to be inaccurate; and he did not finally let the Company have the bonds until shortly before he left India. Larkins before the Lords was confronted with the Interest Book for 1781–1782, on which he had accrued the bonds' interest of 8 percent in Hastings's favor. The converging facts suggested that Hastings had only very belatedly decided to treat the bonds as not his own.[44]

A mystery, rather than a discrepancy, was the balance shown owed by G.G.S. He was identified in Larkins's letter of August 5, 1786: "Although Mr. Hastings was extremely dissatisfied with the Excuses which Gunga Govind Sing assigned for not paying Mr. Croftes [the Company subtreasurer] the Sums stated by Paper No. 1 to be in his Charge, he never could obtain from him any further payments on this Account."[45] Gangha Gobinda Sinha (Gunga Govinda Sing to the English) was the executive agent of the Committee of Revenue, appointed to this post by Hastings in 1781. It was not clear why Hastings should have permitted him to retain Company money. Cross-examination of Larkins by the managers before the Lords in 1794 revealed that G.G.S. had never been made to account for the 10,000 pounds. Larkins testified that Hastings had once told him that G.G.S. said he had spent the money on jewels or diamonds for the wife of Wheeler, a member of the Council. Larkins also testified that he believed part of the amount owing was paid by Nandalal, a revenue farmer with no clear connection with Dinajpur.[46] The only inference that could be drawn from these stories—inconsistent with each other and with Larkins's first tale of Hastings's dissatisfaction—was that Larkins did not know what had happened to the money.

Larkins's letter and testimony led to further discoveries about Hastings's accounting to the Company. "The Particulars of the Paper No. 1," Larkins wrote in the August 5, 1786, letter, "were read over to me, from a Bengal Paper, by his Banyan, Cauntoo Baboo." The reference was to Hastings's Indian *banyan* or business agent, Krishna Kanta Nandi. On examination, it turned out that Larkins did not read the Bengal language, but thought he would understand what was read to him. What he prepared in English was a translation of what he got from Kanta. What Kanta read to him "was a detached piece of paper put into Cauntoo Baboo's hands by Mr. Hastings." Larkins rejected the characterization of this document as "his account." It was "a mere Translate of an Account kept by another Person." Who that other person was he did not know.[47]

Perhaps the most damaging question asked Larkins was, "When you was making up this Account, whether you considered it as making an Account of the Company's Money?" He replied, "I considered myself as employed in drawing out an Account of Money which might eventually be the Property of the Company but which was not so until they had determined that it should be so." He also testified, "I was not upon this Occasion employed as Accountant General."[48] He had written down totals supplied by Kanta from a paper handed him by Hastings, and he had listed them as "sums received on the Account of the Honourable Company." But Larkins was not sure whose money he had given an account of.

Hastings had called on Larkins as the person who possessed the only record Hastings had ever kept of these mysterious transactions. On examination Larkins had proved incoherent.

Burke had a theory as to why the Dinajpur money had been paid and why Hastings took such trouble to conceal its origin. On the death of the old zamindar in July 1780, the succession had been disputed between his son, who suffered the double disadvantage of being a minor and adopted, and his half-brother. Hastings did not regard zamindaries as inheritable private property but as government property to which a zamindar was appointed as a government collector of revenue. But even he acknowledged that in practice the claims of the heir deserved recognition, and he never chose to defend the Dinajpur money as payment for his exercise of arbitrary power in the appointee's favor. On the view of zamindaries alternative to Hastings's, their succession was governed by law, and Hastings and his Council acted as judges in determining the true heir. The case in fact had gone to Hastings's Council for decision and been promptly decided in the son's favor. Burke claimed that the money was "corruptly taken" by Hastings "as a judge in litigation." It was irrelevant that, as a matter of law, the decision was correct. It was a payment for a judgment.[49]

This theory of course implied that Kanta's or Hastings's "Paper No. 1," showing payments from August 1779 to July 1780, was cooked. The intention would have been to show that nothing was received after the date of the dispute over the inheritance. The payments would have been recorded with whimsical irregularity in amounts and times. Since they could not have been *peshkash*, and since no agreement to pay them was ever produced, it could be fairly inferred that they were made up arbitrarily.

The receipt of the money by Hastings was admitted by him. The accounts furnished by him and on his behalf were, to say the least, unconvincing. Must one infer that he had received the money as a bribe? When a high official of a government acknowledges receiving a large sum of money from an anonymous source and provides no explanation of its purpose except a demonstrably inaccurate one, it is a reasonable conclusion that he received the money for a corrupt purpose. That there has been a corrupt payment is established by its size, its anonymity, and the payee's attempts to disguise its purpose. Such circumstances existed here. To them must be added Hastings's own acknowledgment to the directors that the amounts in Paper No. 1 were presents, received from persons from whom receiving presents was generally forbidden.

Hastings's defense had tried to merge the question of bribery with the question of what he did with the money. As Burke put it, "Mr. Hastings confesses it was a sum of money corruptly received, but honestly applied."[50] The first part of the sentence is inexact—Hastings did not confess to corruption but to facts from which Burke had inferred corruption—but the second part of the sentence correctly emphasizes Hastings's main contention: that he could not have been taking money corruptly when he was accounting for it and turning it over to the Company.

Charles Fox compared this defense to that of a British ambassador taking a bribe from a European prince and saying he used it for the king's secret service, or a member of Parliament taking a bribe for his vote and saying he had given it to the Sinking Fund.[51] To say that as a judge one had sold judgment to raise money for the Company could not have been said with a straight face; but as Hastings did not identify the source of the money, his claim that it was all for the Company's benefit had a certain plausibility.

Had there, in fact, ever been any intent on Hastings's part to benefit the Company? As Fox observed, the Dinajpur money was first applied to the Company's use in October 1780, much of it over a year after it had been received, according to Paper No. 1. If that memo were disregarded as fictitious, the capital facts remained that whenever the money was paid into the Company's treasury it was recorded as a loan made by Hastings personally; he took bonds from the Company for it; and interest accrued to him on what he advanced.

Why, then, had Hastings disclosed at all what by his own boast he could have concealed from "the publick Eye for ever?" For the very purpose for which the letters and account were used, and have been used with some success even to this day, to argue that such candor was incompatible with corruption. When the façade was probed the candor disappeared. The skillful operator of a shell game puts himself in the position that no matter what shell his victim picks the winning pea is under another; yet the shell game operator, to gull customers, must make a great show of candor, picking up and turning over each shell and demonstrating that all is open to the eye of the beholder. The shell game operator may stand as a pale analogue of Hastings. What he told the Company seemed to be a changeable amount, as flexible as his circumstances. Hastings had told the Secret Committee of the directors that he trusted them for "a candid Interpretation" of his actions, meaning a benevolent interpretation conceding him everything and asking no questions. His own candor was correlative to such benevolence; he revealed only what he thought his own side would swallow.

It was the heart of his defense that he had applied to the benefit of the Company the money he had taken as presents. With great sincerity he had told the Lords, "No person ever suggested to me that the Act of Parliament deprived the Company of the right of receiving the customary presents." He thought he had set up a plausible shelter for what he had taken when he provided a colorable story that it was for the Company. When he failed to make a coherent accounting of what he had given the Company, he stood the confessed recipient of illegal presents, guilty and impeachable.

A Loan from Nabakrishna. In 1783, Hastings observed, "the Company was in my debt, and it was not very convenient for them to pay it; but it was extremely convenient to me that my debt should be paid." He met the problem by "sending" to Nabakrishna and telling him "I wanted to borrow of him three lacs of rupees." Maharaja Nabakrishna had had in fact great experience with the British, had served both Governors Clive and

Verelst, spoke English "to a degree," and been particularly active in his friend Nanda Kumar's case, providing information on his friend of great value to the prosecution. Hastings knew Nabakrishna "to be rich because I had employed him in the service of the revenue." Nabakrishna not only agreed to Hastings's request but "intreated" Hastings to take the money without executing a bond—that is, he asked Hastings to take it as a gift. "I neither accepted the offer nor refused it," Hastings testified. The following year, 1784, he decided "to accept the money for the Company's use." He did so by paying himself what he said the Company owed him, an amount which exactly used up the three lakhs.[52]

Hastings wrote the Company about this setoff on February 21, 1784. Stating that he was crediting the Company with "a sum privately received," he said nothing as to its source. He declared that he was charging against it "many Sums" which "I have hitherto omitted to enter in my public Accounts." He appended a list of expenditures which he said he had made for the Company's benefit. These came out to equal the amount he now credited. The major items were of four kinds: academic, for the composition of a Code of Hindu law, a translation of Moslem law, and the foundation of a Moslem Academy; rent, for his aides-de-camp; secretarial and office; and transportation, for boats and budgerows or Ganges barges. In the appended list these charges were set out with much detail by Larkins, "Acting Attorney" for Hastings.[53]

On examination, Larkins maintained that he did not know when the money was borrowed from Nabakrishna and acknowledged that the "minute Expenditures" he had listed were furnished by "Cantoo Baboo's People." Asked why they had not been furnished before, Larkins indicated that Hastings was careless about his own finances. It was then put to him that Kanta was the person keeping Hastings's accounts through the whole period, and he was asked if he thought Kanta negligent. "I do not know that he was negligent," he replied. Kanta's ability to produce an itemized list of payments which carelessly had never been charged to the Company before remained unexplained.[54]

When Hastings informed the Company of the setoff he urged its appropriateness lest he furnish the precedent of a life "spent in the Accumulation of Crores for your Benefit and doomed in its Close to suffer the Extremity of private Want, and to sink in Obscurity." One crore equalled ten million rupees, so Hastings suggested that his services had been very beneficial. The charge he described as "the Aggregate of a contingent Account of Twelve Years." His remarkable story excited the skepticism and contempt of the managers. He meant, they said, "the rakings" of twelve years. By "some strange, unaccountable mistake," Manager John Anstruther remarked, Mr. Hastings "had forgot to charge" these claims before. As Burke put it, Hastings feigned and invented a service, "that he had, without any authority of the Company, squandered away in stationary and budgerows and other idle service, a sum amounting to this."[55]

According to Hastings's testimony, he had reimbursed himself "in a mode most suitable to the Company's affairs." Manager Anstruther commented, "And the mode most suitable to the Company's affairs is that of robbing one of the inhabitants of Calcutta of 30,000 pounds!" What Charles Fox observed of another gift received by Hastings and then of all his presents applied with particular force here: "even though he applies it to the Company's use, he does a fraudulent act, because that was not the intention of the giver." The intention of the donor, the managers contended, must have been to influence Hastings. It was not the practice of the merchant caste to which Nabakrishna belonged to make large gifts for nothing.[56]

What was the quid pro quo? Burke observed that Nabakrishna "immediately afterwards enters upon the stewardship or management of one of the most considerable districts in Bengal." In fact, on July 21, 1780, Nabakrishna had been appointed administrator of the zamindari of Burdwan. But Hastings had declared he got the loan in 1783. How could Burke be right? Anstruther accordingly speculated that at the time of the loan Nabakrishna was in arrears as collector and needed Hastings's indulgence. As it turned out, however, the true date of the transaction between Nabakrishna and Hastings was July 26, 1780, five days after Nabakrishna's appointment. Burke was right after all.[57]

The true date came out in a suit brought in Chancery by Nabakrishna himself in 1792. In Chancery, Nabakrishna denied that he had ever intended a gift and sought the recovery of his loan with interest. In Chancery, Hastings did not try to maintain that a gift had originally been made. Ultimately, he produced the bond, dated July 26, 1780, which he had executed for the money, and showed that at a later time it had been returned to him canceled.[58] Given this information, it was beyond argument that Hastings had misrepresented the transaction to the Company, the Commons, and the Lords. That the loan was in exchange for Nabakrishna's 1780 appointment was a reasonable inference from the coincidence of dates and the concealment. That the cancellation of the loan was for a fresh favor of the kind Anstruther had suggested was probable but not proved. But the managers' case was clear as to the original transaction. The Lords in May 1794 refused to admit the Chancery bill and answer in evidence.[59]

In summary, the managers in the instances examined here had shown that Hastings had violated his oath to the Company as to the taking of presents and the keeping of current, accurate accounts, and that he had violated the statute of 1773 as to the taking of presents. The managers were not able to provide as much data as we have today on the prosecution of Nanda Kumar, and the Lords' ruling on evidence handicapped their case as to Nabakrishna. As to Dinajpur they had shown a large sum paid to Hastings under circumstances from which his corruption could reasonably be inferred, and the existence of an equally large sum for which he had failed to account. As to both Dinajpur and Nabakrishna they had shown that what Burke called "Bengal bookkeeping" was not the product of carelessness but was characteristic of Hastings's operations.[60] The managers had taken full advantage of his admissions and demonstrated the incoherence of his explanations. They had shown Hastings's candor to be fraud. They had caught the shell game operator with his hand transferring the pea. Why did the prosecution fail to win a conviction?

The Failures of the Prosecution.   At the most obvious level, the prosecution failed because it had the wrong jury. The Lords were not a body likely to convict Hastings. Burke and Dundas were aware of this from the beginning when they maneuvered the Lords into moving the trial from their own limited quarters to the more spacious setting of Westminster Hall with the deliberate intent that the trial be before a wider audience than those who were the nominal judges.[61] The trial itself was presided over by the lord chancellor, Edward Thurlow, whose wishes in an appointment Hastings had met in India and whose legal rulings, supported by the other judges, almost always favored Hastings. In 1792 Pitt removed him as chancellor. Remaining as a member of the Lords, Thurlow then acted more as Hastings's advocate than his judge.

Thurlow once told Dundas that the bribes were "a very Nasty Business." "The Closetstool of Bribery," Burke thought, "is too potent to enable him to carry it off under his Robes," that is, the privy containing the filth could not be smuggled off by the chancellor. But this optimism was unfounded. Thurlow's view of the possibilities of India was scarcely concealed. It was, he told the Lords, "the weak part" of Hastings's character that had led him to need to borrow from Nabakrishna. He should have left Bengal "fairly and honorably possessed of 400,000 pounds from the known allowed emoluments of his office and the accumulating interest upon his fortune." That Hastings should have been tried at all was an outrage to Thurlow. As he was reported to have remarked, no one could consider the trial "but with horror."[62]

In Burke's analysis of the Lords, Thurlow was "at the bottom of the whole." But the corps of bishops in the Lords was also unsympathetic to the prosecution. "The humility of the Bishops will leave the honour of vindicating the Christian religion to others," Burke mordantly observed as early as 1787.[63] The most vocal was his own former friend, William Markham, archbishop of York, whose son had been Hastings's secretary. He interrupted Burke's examination of a witness to compare it to the work of a Marat or Robespierre—a comparison, which, given Burke's view of the French revolutionaries, could not have been more personal or unkind.[64] By 1793, Burke knew exactly how the score stood for Hastings in the Lords: "Of the thirty-six who attend, thirty are dead votes for him, who will not be shocked at his cruelties nor his corruptions. They will swallow the whole, Bribes, forgeries, every thing."[65]

The prosecution failed not only because of the character of the jury but because of the character of its case with its many separate issues, complex concatenations of facts, prolixity, argumentativeness, and, despite the great detail, abstractness. The attempt to prove Hastings guilty of multiple crimes was a conscious decision. "Even in a temper less favorable to Indian delinquency than what is now generally prevalent," Burke advised Francis, "the people at large would not consider one or two acts however striking, perhaps not three or four, as sufficient to call forth the reserved justice of the State." Before a *"publick political* tribunal," it was essential to show "a *corrupt, habitual,* evil intention."[66] In particular Burke was not confident that the showing of individual acts of bribetaking would be enough. People talked excusingly of "his taking but a bribe here and a bribe there." Hastings, he told the Lords, formed "systems" for "the very purpose of accumulating bribes." "Governors, we know very well, cannot with their own hands be receiving bribes—for then they must have as many hands as one of the idols in an Indian temple." Hastings had to be aided by a tribe of agents, "some white and some black," among them Larkins, Kanta, and G.G.S., "that most atrocious and wicked instrument of the most atrocious and wicked tyranny." Even Hastings's "system of peculation," in Burke's judgment, was not enough to awaken or sustain popular indignation; he must show its "consequences." When he came across a report of atrocities in revenue collection at Dinajpur, he wrote Francis, "I am clear that I must dilate upon it; for it has stuff in it that will, if any thing, work upon the popular Sense"; and he tried to link these alleged misdeeds to the money anonymously received at Dinajpur. If Hastings could have been tried like a common criminal at Old Bailey for the single offense of taking a bribe, Burke might have secured his conviction. But he catered to the popular temptation to think a bad man must be thoroughly bad: "There is, my Lords, always a close connection between vices of every description." Facing a political tribunal and making his own judgment of how seriously bribery would be rated by it, Burke took the Ciceronian route.[67]

That course had a momentum whose escalation can be measured by an incident in which Burke was publicly rebuked for exceeding his mandate. Opening the impeachment in February 1789, Burke spoke of Hastings's claim that no one in India complained of him and observed, "It is generally true. The voice of all India is stopped. All complaint was strangled with the same cord that strangled Nundcomar. This murdered not only that accuser, but all future accusers." Here, only a cord was specifically charged with murder. Two months later, expanding on the Article on the presents, Burke went further and became more specific: "There is an action which is more odious than the crimes he attempts to cover,—*for he has murdered this man by the hands of Sir Elijah Impey.*" The Commons had not charged Hastings with murder, and it promptly voted that Burke's words "ought not to have been spoken." Burke was reduced to explaining that he had used "murder" in "the moral and popular sense." A critic might have added that, applied to a country where no English bribery law was applicable, "bribe" too was used by Burke only in the moral and popular sense, and yet he used it ad infinitum.[68]

Cicero had touched on Hog's sexual misconduct. Burke said nothing of the relations between Hastings, his second wife, and his second wife's ex-husband, although they were the subject of London satirists. He did appear to consider the possibility that Hastings "might really be in love" with Munni Begam, but dismissed the fancy. He did use such a familiar sexual metaphor for corruption as "pollute"—with "purity" set in contrast—to characterize Hastings's conduct; and to describe Hastings's financial relations with Munni he quoted a stinging couplet from Swift's "The Progress of Love":

> They keep at Stains the Old Blue Boar,
> Are Cat and Dog, and Rogue and Whore.

His figures of speech were more often nonsexual. "Bribery, filthy hands, a chief governor of a great empire receiving bribes from poor, miserable, indigent people, this is what makes government itself base, contemptible, and odious in the eyes of mankind": so Burke had said in 1788, employing one of the most basic metaphors for a corrupt official, "filthy hands." When he neared the end in 1794 he told the Lords, "I have had a great encyclopedeia of crimes to deal with." Between those dates Hastings had been compared physically to a pig: "for years he lay down in that sty of disgrace, fattening in it, feeding upon that offal of disgrace and excrement. . . ." To another manager Hastings seemed to be the unjust steward, making money for himself by dealing with the Company's debtors. When Burke thought of New Testament comparisons, he recalled Satan surveying the kingdoms of the world and said of Hastings that "he looked out over the waste of Oude with a diabolical malice which one could hardly suppose existed in the prototype himself." Each of the metaphors or images dehumanized Hastings.

Minutely examined and marshaled in the final nine days of oratory, Hastings's faults made him evil personified. The degree of abstraction Burke reached is measured by his ultimate assault on the advice that one should "hate the sin and love the sinner," paraphrased by him as "hate the crime and love the criminal." Burke became incredulous that he should be asked to love a Nero or Domitian. "No," he affirmed, "we hate the crime, and we hate the criminal ten times more." The maxim of charity he represented as "the language of false morality." That as a convinced Christian he was required to love his enemies, he put to one side. He could not love the abstract symbol of corruption which Hastings had become. The inevitable correlative of this view of the defendant was an implied sanctity on the part of the prosecutor. Burke once said of an oration of the elder Pitt attacking "any sort of personal connections" that it was "a Speech too virtuous to be honest." Was not the whole prosecution of Hastings too virtuous to be honest?[69]

Cicero's Hog had run away. The real man had never stood for judgment by the court. But Burke's Hog was visible to everyone, a man devoted to his wife, generous to his relatives, kind to his dependents, admired by many of the English in India, trusted by many stockholders of the Company, on good terms with a variety of Indians, a friend of peers, above all a ruler who had some political successes to his credit. A political tribunal may be expected to reach its conclusions politically and pragmatically, balancing successes against derelictions, not exclusively vindicating justice. There was no such person as Hog Two, corrupt and cruel and dishonest in his every move. When asked to judge the abstract Hog, the embodiment of evil, the Lords judged the politician and the man.

Finally, the prosecution failed because it failed to touch Hastings. He could not at first take it seriously. When his agent John Scott told him that Thurlow was ashamed at the attention given "the ravings of a madman," he echoed Hastings's own sense of Burke as a fool. A later and more considered conclusion was that Burke was motivated by misanthropy. Hastings concluded that Burke's "hatred of others infinitely exceeds his love of himself"—a sharp judgment by a man himself so noticeably not deficient in self-love. Holding his chief prosecutor to be unnatural in his tendencies, Hastings preserved an attitude of icy disdain when on trial before the Lords. As Burke noted disparagingly, Hastings's demeanor lacked decorum and suggested audacity. Wearing such armor, he was not to be convinced that he had erred in any way. The armor reflected the inner man. Years before, in 1773, Hastings had written the Company that three-year appointments in India were too short, that they operated as a stimulus to rapacity. "The Care of Self-preservation," he wrote, "will naturally suggest the Necessity of seizing the Opportunity of present Power." The words put his own philosophy succinctly. Self-preservation was a duty. It implied the use of opportunities. Naturally its suggestions should be followed. It was not only natural but necessary that power while it was enjoyed should be used for oneself. A man who naturally had done what was necessary could not feel fright, remorse, or guilt when a hater of his fellow man denounced him as a criminal. Hastings's aplomb was unshaken.[70]

The Accomplishments of the Prosecution.   Untouched inwardly, outwardly complacent, Hastings nevertheless felt the strain of being tried. It began with the public humiliation of kneeling before the Lords at the opening of the trial, "punishment not only before conviction, but before the accusations" as he described it, with a Hastingsism which conveniently ignored the votes taken in the Commons. The strain continued with the publicity that attended the case and made him notorious in the public eye. His legal expenses, eventually recouped, were large—over 70,000 pounds. Expenses for propaganda and the promotion of selected candidates for seats in the Commons, never reimbursed, ran to at least another 26,000 pounds. Confident of his acquittal, untroubled in conscience, Hastings was acutely aware that he was involved in a process that could destroy him. For "nine, long years," as he put it, calculating from the Commons' first vote, he was "bound to the stake."[71]

By conventional standards trial is not punishment, and a trial that ends in acquittal is no sanction at all. But a trial of seven years on a large public stage was a punishment. To this sanction was added a second: for the period of the trial, and for well over a decade after the acquittal, Hastings existed in a political limbo. He experienced "total insignificance in public life." The most knowledgeable man in England on Indian affairs, he was given no voice in their management. At fifty-two he was retired, and when he was finally formally consulted in 1813 he was an old man speaking from another time. The third sanction was of a similar kind. He never received the peerage his position as governor-general led him to expect. Pitt put off his friends' importunities in 1784; the trial assured that he would never be elevated. The Lords were ready to acquit him. No administration was willing to make him a lord himself. In these ways, social not legal, pragmatic not theoretical, indirect and tempered, not direct and absolute, Hastings was sanctioned for the presents he had taken.[72]

The governor who replaced Hastings, John Macpherson, tried "to preserve what he could of the system which had enabled the group about Hastings to make their profits." But the next governor, Charles Cornwallis—the same Cornwallis known to Americans by his surrender at Yorktown—brought about reforms. Concentrating on the future, he himself took no interest in punishing Hastings. Personally Cornwallis found him "aimable" and regretted the prosecution. Publicly he testified before the Lords in support of his reputation: no one in India had complained to him about him; he was, in general, respected. But in the forums he thought appropriate Cornwallis left no doubt of his convictions: Writing the chairman of the directors in 1787, he said the directors knew "the shocking evils" of Hastings's era and had quarreled over whether their friends or Hastings's "should enjoy the plunder." Writing the directors in 1788, he enlarged on the need of breaking from "the temptations, dangers, and discredit of the former system of conceal'd emolument." Writing Dundas, head of the government's Board of Control for India, he mocked "the good old principles of Leadenhall-street economy" of "small salaries and immense perquisites," whose victims were not the directors but the British nation. Denouncing Governor Macpherson to Dundas, he found his conduct as impeachable "as Mr. Hastings'."[73]

Chosen by Dundas as one who had "no broken fortune to be mended," Cornwallis arrived in Bengal in the fall of 1786 as the impeachment proceedings were going on in the Commons. The "senior members of the Company's civil and military service were quickly made aware that the Bengal government would henceforth not be conducted for their private advantage." Governors still would come to India to seek their fortune, but Cornwallis's achievement was to be a substantial reduction of corruption among the Company's civil employees. A clash of cultures attended this accomplishment. Cornwallis declared, "Every native of Hindustan, I verily believe, is corrupt," and excluded Indians from all higher government posts.[74] The English who were employed were much better compensated than under former regimes. But better compensation is not the whole explanation of the Cornwallis reform. After all, Hastings had been munif-

icently compensated. Cornwallis's accomplishment can scarcely be understood apart from the sanctions visited on Hastings at home. If Hastings
had not been impeached, if he had not been tried, if he had not been
reduced to political impotence, if he had not been denied his peerage, the
efforts of Cornwallis would have been, if not derisory, at least very much
less effective. When, as any member of the Company could appreciate,
Hastings was paying a substantial social price in England for his conduct in
India, there were tangible sanctions supporting Cornwallis's requirements.

Domestically what the prosecution accomplished was less tangible.
Throughout the eighteenth century there had been caustic critics of the
way the government of England was conducted. In 1726 Swift's Gulliver
contrasts "English yeomen of the old Stamp" whose "pure native Virtues
were prostituted for a Piece of Money by their Grandchildren" at elections. To his Houyhnhnm master, Gulliver explains that Chief Ministers,
"having all Employments at their Disposal, preserve themselves in Power
by bribing the majority of a Senate or great Council." "The Palace of a
Chief Minister is a Seminary to breed up others in their own Trade. The
Pages, Lacquies, and Porter, by imitating their Master, become *Ministers of
State* in their several Districts, and learn to excell in the three principal
Ingredients, of *Insolence, Lying,* and *Bribery*."[75]

The same note was struck later in the century by James Burgh, author of
a contemporary tract on "Public Errors, Defects, and Abuses." The love of
power and the love of money were two weaknesses in human nature that
produced "bribery, corruption, and many other arts." In our day, love of
money predominated. Ministers took office "chiefly with a design of filling their *pockets*, and advancing their families and friends." They
proceeded by "bribing and buying parliament." For that purpose they
had places to offer in the collection of the customs, excise, and salt-duty; in
the army and navy; in the church; and as postmasters, surveyors of houses
and windows, receivers of land-tax, managers of lotteries, and commissioners of hackney coaches—in a word, in all appointments in the gift of
the government. Ministers could also give preferences in loans, subscrip-
tions, and remittances of public money. They could, as they did in 1769,
distribute 20,000 lottery tickets to members of Parliament, giving freely
what sold for two pounds apiece. They could award contracts to those
"with the greatest parliamentary interest." They could use the civil service
list and the secret service ("a huge cloak thrown over an immense sewer of
corruption") to reward their supporters. These were the normal practices
of the rulers of England—"the modern plan of government." To buy
"every necessary vote" was how a government stayed in power. Charles II
had ruled Parliament corruptly, but "the art of governing by regularly and
systematically bribing the House of Commons came in at the Revolution,"
that is, with William III. "Bribery" and "corruption," as Burgh uses the
terms, are not crimes—at least not crimes in terms of statutes which are

enforced. They are moral and political offenses condemned by a standard higher than that of most contemporaries. That higher standard was Burke's for Bengal, not Britain.[76]

No structural change, no legal change occurred as Burke orated against Hastings. If a censurious critic could have spoken like Burgh when the case against Hastings began, he could have done so equally vigorously when it was over. By adept use of patronage Dundas himself built a political machine in Scotland. His power as chairman of the Board of Control in India profited his relatives and his Scottish allies. The "Scottization" of India was his monument. Meanwhile his conduct at home led to his own impeachment by the Commons, and acquittal by the Lords, in 1805.[77]

Burke's own career conformed not to his standard for Hastings, but to the rules of English politics. At the age of thirty, an aspiring Irish writer from Dublin, a law studies drop-out without definite employment or income in London and with a wife and two children, Burke had entered the political realm by becoming the secretary of a minor English politician, William G. Hamilton. In 1761 Hamilton became chief secretary to the lord lieutenant of Ireland. After two years' service to Hamilton in this capacity, Burke was awarded a pension of 300 pounds per year chargeable to the Irish budget. Like many other government pensions of the era this was terminable at the government's pleasure. It was not retirement pay but an act of patronage intended to maintain loyalty to the patron. Samuel Johnson—though he was, with embarrassment, to take a pension himself—in his dictionary defined a pension as "an allowance made to any one without an equivalent. In England it is generally understood to mean pay given to a state hireling for treason to his country"; and he defined a pensioner as "A slave of state hired by a stipend to obey his master." Burke's candid view of his pension was that "if it had come from Hamilton's pocket instead of being derived from the Irish Treasury, I had earned it by a Long and Laborious attendance." The pension continued after both Hamilton and Burke had left Ireland, and they quarreled over whether Burke's taking it meant that he was bound to keep on working for Hamilton. Burke thought this a kind of servitude—he was perhaps not far from Johnson's view—but neither master nor man admitted any illegality in making the Irish compensate Burke for his past service to Hamilton. In the end, Burke gave up both the pension and his employer.[78]

In retrospect, Burke was glad to be free from Hamilton: "the wear and tear of mind, which is saved by keeping aloof from crooked politicks, is a consideration absolutely inestimable." When Burke wrote these lines he was private secretary to a major Whig politician, Lord Rockingham. He could not have meant that all politics were crooked; he was reflecting on the work of Hamilton—"extremely disgustful to me"—in a central position in the English government of Ireland. Hamilton acquired a "ministerial fortune" by his endeavors and gave Burke an insider's view of colonial government that Burke did not forget when he spoke of Hastings.[79]

Serving Rockingham, Burke became a member of Parliament and losing his constituency at Bristol was glad in the 1780s and 1790s to be the member from Malton, the Rockingham family's pocket borough. Here he owed his parliamentary existence not to the public will but to the good graces of his patron. Rockingham's heir could congratulate him on "the credit and reputation you have confer'd upon me by receiving the seat at my hands"; Burke nonetheless sat indebted to a single landlord's nod. When Rockingham came in in 1782, Burke had his share of the spoils— himself paymaster general of the Forces; his younger brother secretary to the Treasury; Champion, a debt-ridden backer, deputy paymaster; his own son Richard, another deputy. They were all out with Shelburne and back again with the Coalition.[80]

For Richard, the center of his care, "the best and dearest part of me" ("You need stipulate nothing, except for my poor Lad," he had told Rockingham) he struggled to secure a life sinecure, finally doing so under the Coalition. Richard was appointed receiver of land revenues, holding the position jointly with a straw who, even after Richard's unexpected death, held the office in trust for "Mr. Burke and his family," paying 7,000 pounds to their account. Richard's father saw the money as coming from a useful fund meant to provide "a reward for publick service," whether his own past service or his twenty-five-year-old son's future service is not clear. Even during the impeachment trial, Burke looked out for his relations: his brother became one of the paid counsel to the managers, son Richard served as one of their clerks.[81]

For a widowed sister in Ireland who had no public service to her credit he bestirred himself, unsuccessfully, to obtain a pension of 200 pounds a year for life. On behalf of his close friend, financial manager, and courtesy cousin, William Burke, he was more successful. William had made money by an investment in the East India Company in the 1760s, enabling their joint purchase of an estate at Beaconsfield, and then had lost heavily in Company stock. Broke, he set out for India itself, accompanied by a letter from Edmund to Sir Philip Francis, then on the Supreme Council in Bengal. Edmund wrote of Williams's departure as the loss of "a friend, whom I have tenderly loved," and added, "Indemnify me, my dear Sir, as well as you can for such a loss, by contributing to the fortune of my friend. Bring him home with you an obliged person and at his ease, under the protection of your opulence. . . . Remember that he asks those favours which nothing but his sense of honour prevented his having it in his power to bestow." A letter from a mutual friend to Francis informed him that to help William would "oblige E.B. by serving his nearest and dearest friend." When Rockingham took office, Edmund assured William that he would be taken care of "in the new Indian arrangements," and he finally made him deputy paymaster general in India, a lucrative position and a "most unnecessary job and a material hindrance to the public business," according to Cornwallis when he had seen William at work in India.

William traded on Edmund's name, securing in 1786 a "scandalous" rate of exchange on money for the troops from Governor Macpherson, who found this a way "to pay his court to Edmund Burke."[82]

One man's "reward for publick service" is another man's bribe, it might be observed. A family that feeds at the public trough cannot be reformed by the prosecution of someone who has succeeded more spectacularly; the prosecution may even be considered an outlet for their jealousy. Of course the prosecution had small impact at home when it was undertaken by those so thoroughly enmeshed in the system.

In informal conversation with Samuel Johnson and James Boswell in April 1778, Burke said of the House of Commons, "It is a mass by no means pure, but neither is it wholly corrupt, though there is a large proportion of corruption in it. There are many members who generally go with the Ministry, who will not go all lengths." Johnson replied, "We are all more or less governed by interest. But interest will not make us do every thing." He went on to accept the fact that in doubtful matters, interest—that is, personal interest—would govern a member. Corruption appears to be narrowed to voting against what one is sure is right. A year later Johnson was harsher. In Henry VIII's day, he indicated, the king went his way by coercion, "but the House of Commons is now no longer in the power of the crown, and therefore must be bribed." Johnson added, "I have no delight in talking of public affairs."[83]

Johnson's judgment of the House was that of a literary man and moralist, disenchanted with the political process. Burke's only slightly milder view was that of a member of Parliament who knew the House intimately. Both Burke and Johnson measured the government by a moral standard higher than the criminal law or contemporary practice. The same is true of the measure used by Burgh. It is a contemporary standard but higher than that commonly adopted. Where was the line drawn? At hard cash. By 1769 offering money for an office was a crime, as Lord Mansfield had held, adding, "If these Transactions are believed to be frequent, it is Time to put a stop to them." A quid pro quo in patronage, preferment, and even pensions was distinguished by eighteenth-century politicians from the payment of ready cash. Johnson, as has been seen, was more censurious. Fox's casual example of an MP taking money for a vote showed that everyone would have understood that act as indefensible. It was in an altogether different category from a parliamentary follower being remunerated by a plum. When Boswell sought Burke's help in getting office in the wake of Rockingham's victory, Burke wrote him "My friends in power have come in with equally long claims upon them with a divided Patronage, and a reduced Establishment. If I could serve you I tell you in sincerity that the bringing you to a residence here would be no mean Bribe to me." Burke to Boswell was as innocent as Isabella in *Measure for Measure* calling her prayer a bribe.[84]

With no sense of hypocrisy or irony—only with a nice and limited sense of the meaning of bribery—Burke told the Lords, "If there is any one thing which distinguishes this nation eminently above another, it is that in its offices at home, both judicial and in the state, there is less suspicion of pecuniary corruption attaching to them than to any similar offices in any part of the globe, or that have existed at any time." The emphasis here was on "at home" and on "pecuniary corruption." When Burke further told the Lords that bribes in England were indeed so "little known" that we "can hardly get clear and specific terms to distinguish them," he unconsciously confessed how little thought had been given to the variety of reciprocal exchanges in English political existence. But taking the English system as it was, he knew that a bribe was money paid for the specific use of official power. The assault of the prosecution on cash bribery could only reinforce the rules at home against it and do nothing to disturb the accepted forms of patronage—except that persons of another generation, less implicated in the system, might be led to reflect, reading Burke, that by his own principles there was much need of reform in England.[85]

The final accomplishment of the prosecution was that education of the future. Defeated, ill, despondent, Burke in 1797 wrote the impeachment managers' old counsel, French Laurence, laying on him the "solemn charge and trust" to write a history of Hastings's trial. "If ever Europe recovers its civilization, that work will be useful. Remember! Remember! Remember!" Laurence did not carry out the charge, but historians of all kinds have kept alive the memory. Not all have remembered it as Burke would have had it done, but his own words and deeds are available to anyone who cares to read.[86]

Burke complained on occasion that it was the policy of Hastings's party to treat the prosecution "as nothing more than the private Business of one Mr. Burke" and to make it out to be "no more than a scuffle between Mr. Burke and Mr. Hastings." Biographers of each have found it easy to fall into this trap, and every account of the trial inclines to this focus on the two chief combatants. A prosecution voted by Parliament with the consent of the government was clearly no vendetta in the sense Hastings's friends suggested, and Burke alone would have been powerless. Among the managers of the prosecution were John Anstruther, future chief justice of Bengal; Charles Fox, past first minister; John Grey, future prime minister; Richard Brinsley Sheridan, the leading playwright of the day; and they were aided by such counsel as the learned Laurence, later Regius Professor of Civil Law at Oxford. But Burke was the principal force in bringing the impeachment about, and in terms of the record made for posterity it is he who has had the greatest impact.[87]

For him, concrete responsibilities arose with particular employments. "Humana *qua parte* locatus es in re?" he quoted and italicized Persius's *Satires*. In what human place are you situated in the affair? This Burke pronounced "the best rule both in morals and in prudence." Of all situations public employment was the most demanding. "All political power which is set over men," he declared, arguing for the Coalition's East India Bill in 1783, "ought to be some way or other exercised ultimately for their benefit." All political power was therefore a trust; and "it is of the very essence of every trust to be rendered accountable." So Hastings must account. On this basis the Articles of Impeachment were framed in terms of the office Hastings held, and Burke could tell the Lords that "every office of trust, in its very nature, forbids the receipt of bribes."[88]

In one of the noblest of his speeches, on conciliation with America, spoken prophetically a month before the events at Concord and Lexington, Burke told Parliament that what gave it an army and a navy and a revenue was nothing but "the love of the people." His words, he said he knew, would appear "wild and chimerical" to "vulgar and mechanical politicians." To Parliament, near the close of his peroration, he addressed words taken from the Latin mass—"the old warning of the Church," as he described it—"*Sursum corda!*" Only by the members lifting up their hearts beyond "the gross and material" to the level where love reciprocated fidelity could revolution be avoided and government endure.[89]

Sealing these responsibilities of man was the "one law for all, namely that law which governs all law, the law of our Creator, the law of humanity, justice, equity, the Law of Nature and of Nations." For Burke this single law was not a legal or philosophical abstraction but was linked in a lively way to his religious faith. In an extraordinary letter to a young woman, Joshua Reynolds's niece, whose "friend" in India spoke ill of him, Burke wrote, "I have no party in this Business, my dear Miss Palmer, but among a set of people, who have none of your Lilies and Roses in their faces, but who are images of the great Pattern as well as you and I. I know what I am doing; whether the white people like it or not." The Indians without English complexions were his clients because they were made in the image of God. Service to them was based on the imitation of Christ. As he told the Lords in a rare direct evocation of his religion, "When the God whom we adore appeared in human form, He did not appear in a form of greatness and majesty but in sympathy with the lowest of the people and thereby made it a firm and ruling principle that their welfare was the object of all government, since the Person who was the master of Nature chose to appear Himself in a subordinate situation." That by the example of Christ the welfare of the people was "the object of all government" was the foundation of Burke's view of the trust that went with office.[90]

The view co-existed with Burke's immersion in the politics of patronage, the only political system he knew. It co-existed with a willingness to provide office for his relatives and friends. It co-existed with the belief that there were honest ways for Englishmen to enrich themselves while governing India. "My dearest Miss Palmer, God bless you; and send your friend home to you Rich and innocent," Burke's letter to Reynolds's niece concluded.[91] In the same way he had wanted William Burke's rectitude rewarded in Bengal. That becoming rich and remaining innocent in India were inconsistent goals, that serving oneself and the ones one governed were incompatible objectives, were propositions he would not have entertained.

In 1792 Burke, isolated from his old associates like Fox by his horror of the French Revolution, was harassed by a motion in the Commons by Hastings's agent, Scott. The motion asked that detailed accounts of the cost of the prosecution be rendered. Writing Dundas to get the administration's support against the bill, Burke observed that Hastings hoped to load "the whole of the public disgrace" upon a person who had "become obnoxious to his old party, without having secured protection from a new." Yet he, Edmund Burke, would pay all the costs, except that of the short-hand writer, if Hastings would not escape. "Twelve years have been spent in this one Indian pursuit," Burke wrote looking back to his committee service in 1780. "What but some irresistible Sense of Duty could induce me to continue so unthankful, unfruitful and unpleasant an occupation. . . . He who, in long publick service, obtains no rank, no emollument, no power, and no commendation from any publick party, expiates a good many smaller Offenses."[92] Plenty of other reasons could have been given—pride, stubbornness, lack of other occupation—as to why Burke went on with the case; and the reason he had no rank, power, or income was that he had chosen once, far back, not to join Pitt and had made the wrong choice in terms of political opportunities. Self-pitying as the letter to Dundas was, it was also true that he stuck to his task long after he knew of the stack of "dead votes" for Hastings. "God knows what I feel in my Mouth returning to my Indian Vomit," he wrote at the beginning of the last year of the case. Yet he went on, making the long closing speeches and urging the Lords to be "the perpetual residence of an inviolable justice."[93]

"Even my imputed thoughts," Hastings remarked before the Commons, "as at the final day of judgment, are wrested into accusation against me."[94] It was no accident that he should have had this sense of being arraigned before such an ultimate bar. When Burke set out on his "vast Task" to vindicate the principles of just government against Hastings, he had acknowledged that conviction of Hastings was impracticable. Realism of this kind vacillated with hope of victory as he proceeded, but his soberer belief was in vindication by a judgment of posterity that was an eighteenth-century stand-in for the Last Judgment; and at times Burke counted only on divine vindication.

In his peroration before the Lords, Burke spoke of Justice as "emanating from the Divinity." It "will stand," he declared, "after this globe is burned to ashes, our advocate or our accuser before the great Judge, when He comes to call upon us for the tenor of a well-spent life." Now knowing but not believing that the Lords would not convict, Burke put himself and his listeners before the tribunal at the end of time and made Justice herself a party to a final litigation. He did so to evoke for himself and the human judges the sense that the judgment now to be rendered would be reviewed by God.[95]

On April 23, 1795, the Lords judged formally that Hastings was not guilty. A month later the E.I. Co. proposed to indemnify his legal costs. Burke wrote to urge Dundas to prevent it, else "the House of Commons must go to the Dogs."[96] His protest was in vain, and the following year the Company awarded Hastings a pension. In Burke's view he was being "publicly remunerated" by the E.I. Co. by a reward for "crimes" that had been "*proved* against him."[97] Pitt and Dundas failed to prevent the Company paying. In 1797 Burke concluded that it was publicly established that he had "with such incredible pains both of himself and others, persevered in the persecution of innocence and merit."[98] To pragmatic minds his concern with principle, with past deeds, with vindictive justice had seemed ridiculous, misanthropic, mad. For starting such a quixotic crusade he could be characterized by even a modern historian as possessed of a "disordered mind."[99] Irony alone was left him, and his "Remember! Remember! Remember!"

What the Commons sought, he had told the Lords in May 1794, was to "see corrupt Pride prostrate under the feet of Justice."[100] What he furnished in his own person was a different image—a politician, an MP, an orator, suffering in heart and mind and spirit for his failure to achieve the chastisement of corruption. That his posture was more Christian if less comfortable than Cicero's might have occurred to him.[101]

IV

American Approaches

1776–1984

15

Thorough and Most Adroit Politicians

Appealing to "the Supreme Judge of the World" to judge that their intentions were possessed of "rectitude," the representatives of "the United States of America," meeting in Philadelphia in 1776, asserted the independence of the country. No higher or more appropriate image of God occurred to them than that of an omniscient court of last resort; and the famous Declaration itself was framed as an indictment of George III before civilized opinion and God. The rhetoric of the revolutionaries echoed the judgmental themes of Christian thought.

Among other "injuries and usurpations" charged against the king were "the obstruction of the administration of justice by refusing his assent to laws for establishing judiciary powers" and making "judges dependent on his will alone, for the tenure of their offices, and the amount and payment of their salaries." He was not, however, accused of corruption or of acquiescence in corrupted judges. Conscious of the divine paradigm of impartial justice, by whom they themselves asked to be judged, the revolutionaries did not enumerate bribed judges among the evils of which they complained. In the formation of the republic which followed, the founding fathers were to show an awareness, restricted in range and limited in results, of the harm to impartial justice that bribery could do.[1]

The Foresight of the Founders. When Virginia became a commonwealth and in 1777 established a court of Chancery, the oath for the chancellor was drafted by the chancellor-elect, America's first professor of law, George Wythe. "You,"—that is, the chancellor—were to swear to

> do equal right to all manner of people, great and small, high and low, rich and poor, according to equity and good conscience and the laws and usages of Virginia, without respect of persons. You shall not take by yourself, or by any other, any gift, fee, or reward, of gold, silver, or any other thing, directly or indirectly of any person, great or small, for any matter done or to be done by virtue of your office, except such fee or salary as shall be by law appointed.... You shall ... do equal and impartial justice without fraud, favour, affection or partiality. So help you God.

The old royal judges' oath had been almost the same. Wythe introduced the biblical "without respect of persons." His change invoked Jewish and Christian tradition and an exemplar, the mighty and impartial God of Deuteronomy.[2]

For the seal of the Virginia chancellor, Benjamin West proposed the story of Sisamnes. Wythe agreed and recorded his approval in a footnote to a judicial opinion in which he himself showed the finest impartiality by deciding a case against the interest of many fellow Virginians and to the benefit of a British subject and the benefit of his personal enemy. "The punishments of Sisamnes," he wrote, were deserved by a prejudiced judge; he did not bother to say that a bribed judge was contemptible.[3] All Wythe's judgments, an admirer claimed, were "as between A and B, for he knew nobody but went into Court as Astrea was supposed to come down from Heaven, exempt from all human bias."[4] This austere and learned man in his person as by his oath set a standard conformable to the noblest religious tradition of judicial integrity.

"A Declaration of the Rights of the Inhabitants of the Commonwealth of Massachusetts," enacted in 1780 by the legislature of Massachusetts, asserted it to be "essential to the preservation of the rights of every individual, his life, liberty, property and character, that there be an impartial interpretation of the laws, and administration of justice. It is the right of every citizen to be tried by judges as free, impartial and independent as the lot of humanity will admit." The Declaration went on to specify the means of securing this result: judges of the Supreme Judicial Court "should hold their offices as long as they behave themselves well; and they should have honorable salaries ascertained and established by standing laws." An act, passed the same year, set the justices' salaries at 300 pounds per year. The underlying thought was close to the idea implicit in the indictment of the king's treatment of judges in the Declaration of Independence—if a judiciary was set up with tenure and a proper salary, it was freed from subordination to the executive and could therefore be impartial. The most affecting note was struck by the sobriety or realism of the qualification, "as the lot of humanity will admit." For once, it was recognized that justice here below would imitate the divine paradigm imperfectly.[5]

The Maryland "Declaration of Rights" had a similar statement on the essential "independency and uprightness of judges" and acknowledged that "salaries liberal, but not profuse" should be paid the chancellor and judges. More specific than Massachusetts, it went on, "No chancellor or judge ought to hold any other office, civil or military, or receive fees or perquisites of any kind." Gifttaking was dealt with comprehensively as to the recipients, narrowly as to the donors: "nor ought any person in public trust to receive any present from any foreign prince or state or from the United States, or any of them, without the approbation of this state." The ancient ambiguity of a present that might be a bribe was recognized in this special treatment, surprisingly made part of fundamental Maryland law, of gifts from other sovereign entities.[6]

Virginia, of the three, most openly acknowledged the danger of bribery and attempted to anticipate the danger by oath and instruct against it by the seal. None of the three states enacted criminal statutes against bribing the judges. Here, as in most matters of criminal conduct, reliance was put on the common law. Only special situations—for example, the bribing of naval officers or of customs officers—were covered by particular statutes.[7] One branch of government conspicuously free of common law criminal precedents on bribery was also left conspicuously free of exhortations to, or enunciations of, impartiality. Gripped by the paradigm of unbiased divine justice, the draftsmen applied it to the judiciary and left the legislature to be the playground of interests.

When the convention to make a constitution for the United States met in Philadelphia in 1787, John Randolph of Virginia early offered a resolution to have a "national judiciary" to hold office "during good behaviour."[8] This positive phrase excluded corruption. How much else it excluded was left undefined. It stuck through various redraftings from May to September 1787, was not elaborated, and emerged in Article III, section 1, of the final document conferring tenure on the judges "during good behaviour." No special stress was put upon impartial judges. Their impeachment was provided for only indirectly, by a clause aimed mainly at the president.

Corrupt judges had not been on the revolutionists' mind; corruption by the Executive had. For much of the eighteenth century, English critics of English administration such as James Burgh had focused on the way the ministry ruled by corrupting Parliament with jobs and appointments. These partisan outpourings had been devoured in America and formed part of the ideology of those who made the Revolution. As firmly as educated European opinion in the later Middle Ages held the papacy to be corrupt, so it was accepted that corruption characterized British parliamentary rule. What Dr. Johnson took as true in coffee house conversation was also believed by educated colonials. "Soon after Sir Robert Walpole was made premier he reduced corruption into a regular system," wrote Charles Carroll in 1768; while his son Charles Carroll noted that "the sweets" of liberty were enjoyed in colonial America "in spite of a corrupt Parliament," and added that "the degenerate sons of some future age" could come "to prefer their own mean lucre, the bribes, and the smiles of corruption." In revolutionary ideology, corruption of the legislature by the executive was the way in which the people were deprived of liberty: "a corrupt and prostituted ministry" was what had sought to "enslave" Americans. Care to prevent such corruption could scarcely not have been a care of the constitution-makers.[9]

Impeachment, provided for by Article 2, section 4, was, for most of the Convention's sessions, a remedy exclusively for this evil. It was a remedy for corruption by or in the chief magistrate. "No point is of more importance," said George Mason of Virginia, "than that the right of impeachment should be continued. Shall any man be above Justice? Above all shall that man be above it who can commit the most extensive injustice? . . . Shall that man who has practised corruption and by that means procured his appointment in the first instance, be suffered to escape punishment, by repeating his guilt?" Gouverneur Morris of Pennsylvania admitted "corruption and some few other offenses to be such as ought to be impeachable, but thought these ought to be enumerated and defined." He added that the chief magistrate "may be bribed by a greater interest to secure his trust. . . . One would think the King of England well secured against bribery. He has as it were a fee simple in the whole Kingdom. Yet Charles II was bribed by Louis XIV. The Executive ought therefore to be impeachable for treachery." He added, "Corrupting his electors, and incapacity were other causes of impeachment." James Madison of Virginia stated a commonplace of English politics and Opposition criticism, that the Executive "might pervert his administration into a scheme of peculation or oppression" and that "loss of capacity or corruption" was "within the compass of the probable events, and either of them might be fatal to the Republic."[10]

On July 20, 1787, the Convention agreed that the Executive should be impeachable. The Committee on Detail, reflecting the concerns of Mason, Morris, and Madison, specified the grounds as "Treason, Bribery, or Corruption." In September the Committee of Eleven eliminated "Corruption." The change presumably reflected the sense that "Corruption" was superfluous. If it was, it was because "Bribery" was read both actively and passively, including the chief magistrate bribing someone and being bribed. Mason asked, "Why is the provision restrained to Treason and bribery only? . . . Hastings is not guilty of Treason." Making plain why Warren Hastings came to mind, he moved to add "maladministration." Madison replied, "So vague a term will be equivalent to a tenure during pleasure of the Senate." Mason then substituted "other high crimes and misdemeanours," which passed.[11]

To this point only removal of the president had been at issue. The Com-

mittee of Style added the vice-president and "all civil Officers of the United States," so putting in final form Article II, section 4. Clearly the clause
did not apply to the legislative branch, dealt with in Article I and probably
it was not intended to apply to the judiciary, the subject of Article III. But
bribery stood with treason as one of two crimes identified by name in the
Constitution.[12]

The line of thought reflected in the Maryland Declaration of Rights, that
presents might be distinct from bribes, was also alive. On motion of
Charles Pinckney of South Carolina, the need of "preserving foreign Ministers and other officers of the United States independent of external influence" was recognized by a provision that in its final form declared, "No
Person holding any Office of Profit or Trust under [the United States]
shall, without the Consent of the Congress, accept of any present,
Emolument, Office or Title, of any kind whatever, from any King, Prince
or foreign State." The proposal passed unanimously and became Article I,
section 9, clause 8.[13] Explaining it to the Virginia ratifying convention,
John Randolph reported, "This restriction is provided to prevent corruption. . . . An accident which actually happened, operated in producing the
restriction. A box was presented to our ambassador by the king of our
allies. It was thought proper, in order to exclude corruption and foreign influence, to prohibit any one in office from receiving or holding any
emoluments from foreign states." The "box" was apparently a snuff box
bearing Louis XVI's portrait, and the ambassador to whom it was given
was Benjamin Franklin.[14] As Article II, section 4, gave a sanction against
bribery, this second provision was an outer fence against bribery by
foreign governments. Unlike Article II, it could be construed to reach not
only the Executive Branch but Congress as well.

Article I, section 6, clause 1, provided that "for any Speech or Debate in
either House, they [the legislators] shall not be questioned in any other
Place." Easily accepted, this provision conferred immunity for speech;
how far it could be extended to cover other congressional conduct
remained to be determined. A companion of congressional immunity
was Article I, section 5, clause 2, giving each House power to "punish its
Members for disorderly Behaviour and, with the Concurrence of two
thirds, expel a Member." The two-thirds requirement was inserted after
Madison had observed "that the right of expulsion was too important to
be exercised by a bare majority of a quorum: and in emergencies of fac-
tion might be dangerously abused." It was assumed that the right to
"punish" would be exercised only after an offense, but what offenses
would be punishable was left to the discretion of future Houses.[15]

Congress itself, Madison thought, was less corruptible than the Executive. His reason was the old one of Aristotle—it was harder to corrupt a
multitude: "Besides the restraints of their personal integrity and honor,
the difficulty of acting in concert for purposes of corruption was a security
to the public. And if one or a few members only should be seduced, the
soundness of the remaining members would maintain the integrity and fidelity of the body." In the light of the revolutionists' own ideology,

Madison's reasoning was remarkable. What had been the object of corruption by British ministries other than the multitude in Parliament? Aristotle's view flew in the face of experience as English experience had been understood by the colonists.[16]

In the event, only a single clause was distinctly related to the maintenance of the integrity and fidelity of Congress. From the first, John Randolph had proposed that legislators be ineligible for appointment to public office during their term as legislators.[17] The proposal occasioned lively debate especially when Madison moved to limit the ineligibility to offices which the legislator in question had voted to create. The narrower restriction was vigorously opposed. Pierce Butler of South Carolina noted that George II had ruled Parliament by pensions, offices, and promotions to the House of Lords. George Mason referred to Virginia practice where all officers were appointed by the legislature, remarking: "Need I add, that many of their appointments are most shameful?" Madison's check "will soon cease to be any check at all. . . . [I]f we do not provide against corruption, our government will soon be at an end; nor would I wish to put a man of virtue in the way of temptation." (Not quite 200 years later the temptation to which the government might subject members of Congress was to be the great question of Abscam.) Elbridge Gerry of Massachusetts observed that during the Revolution a Roman virtue had prevailed. Now in politics "we have more land- and stock-jobbers than any place on earth." Gerry—whose own name was soon to be incorporated into the word gerrymander to express legislative shenanigans—was not contradicted.[18]

Supporting Madison, Rufus King of Massachusetts derided "the idea of preventing intrigue and solicitation of offices" as "chimerical." A legislator could still bargain on behalf of "his son, his brother, or any other object of his partiality." Or, he might have added, even under the broad proposal a legislator need only wait for appointment until his term was over. John Mercer of Maryland believed, "All Government must be by force or influence." The American government was not to rule by janissaries. Hence it must be allowed to have means of influencing the legislators (a view of administration unkindly described by Gerry, who did not give an alternative, as a "Government of plunder"). Madison himself declared,

My wish is that the national legislature be as uncorrupt as possible. I believe all public bodies are inclined, from various motives, to support [their] members, but it is not always done from the base motives of venality. Friendship, and a knowledge of the abilities of those with whom they associate, may produce it. If you bar the door against such attachments, you deprive the government of its greatest strength and support. . . . The legislative body must be the road to public honor.[19]

Madison's motion to create limited ineligiblity lost in June, but a substantially similar motion prevailed in September.[20] The result was Article

I, section 6, clause 2: "No Senator or Representative shall, during the Time for which he was elected, be appointed to any civil Office under the Authority of the United States, which shall have been created, or the Emoluments whereof shall have been encreased during such time; and no Person holding any Office under the United States shall be a Member of either House during his Continuance in Office." The convention refused to extend the disqualification for any period beyond actual membership in Congress.[21]

A distinctly modest barrier to corruption of Congress was thus set up by the Constitution—a barrier designed only to deter the legislature from collaborating with the executive to create or enhance office for the benefit of current legislators. No penalty was set for its violation. It was to be eventually flouted with impunity by Senator Hugo Black and President Franklin Roosevelt, who appointed Black to the Supreme Court after the Justices' emoluments had been increased while Black was a legislator.[22] What was treated as "corruption" by most participants in the debate was an administration's use of appointments to buy votes—the same concept of corruption which had prompted the provision permitting impeachment for bribery. Only Mercer appeared to defend "influence" as legitimate and as indeed indispensable. But by action, although not in words, the constitutional convention accepted Mercer's view. A dichotomy was accepted. The chief magistrate could be removed for bribing Congress or anyone else. The Congress was subject to no sanction if it was bribed.

The most famous commentary upon the Constitution, *The Federalist*, took the position in an essay by Alexander Hamilton that those with enough knowledge of the laws to be judges were few, "and making the proper deductions for the ordinary depravity of human nature, the number must be still smaller of those who unite the requisite integrity with the requisite knowledge." These considerations, Hamilton argued, supported tenure rather than a fixed term of office. Good judges being few, they must be kept. Great Britain, he observed, showed "the excellence" of judicial appointments lasting as long as good behavior.[23] Hamilton further supported the jury as "a security against corruption." A standing body of magistrates was always easier "to tamper with" than a jury summoned for a special occasion. Juries could be corruptly chosen by sheriffs or clerks of court, and those "promiscuously taken from the public mass" could be more corruptible than the government's chosen appointees. Nonetheless a jury "must still be a valuable check upon corruption. It greatly multiplies the impediments to its success." If a jury went wrong, the court could grant a new trial. Successful corruption would have to work on both. "By increasing the obstacles to success, it discourages attempts to seduce the integrity of either. The temptations to prostitution which the judges might have to surmount, must certainly be much fewer...." Easily and naturally Hamilton fell back upon the ancient sexual metaphors to explicate the dangers besetting a judge.[24]

Sexual imagery was also used by Hamilton when he gave an Aristotelian reason why the Constitution left the election of the president to the people: they were not a small body of men "who might be tampered with beforehand to prostitute their votes." As for the electoral college, none might be a member who "might be suspected of too great devotion to the President in office," and this temporary body, composed of men dispersed over the thirteen states, would not afford time for "the business of corruption" to do its work.[25]

Despite this lively sense of "the depravity" of man and "the temptations" in the path of jurors, judges, and electors, *The Federalist* showed no concern about the corruption of the legislature. Madison in the justly celebrated essay Number 10 wrote

> No man is allowed to be a judge in his own cause, because his interest would certainly bias his judgment, and, not improbably, corrupt his integrity. With equal, nay with greater reason, a body of men are unfit to be both judges and parties at the same time; yet what are many of the most important acts of legislation, but so many judicial determinations, not indeed concerning the rights of single persons, but concerning the rights of large bodies of citizens? And what are the different classes of legislators but advocates and parties to the causes which they determine?[26]

The conclusion was not that legislators could not vote. Like Dr. Johnson, Madison accepted the view that "interest" was inevitable. He did not suppose that the Constitution mitigated its impact even by the elementary rules intended to preserve the impartiality of judges. Interested and biased as they must be, legislators were not provided by the Constitution with any special protection against the temptations of corruption.

Was the virtue of congressmen safeguarded by statute? The first federal law on bribery, enacted in 1789, was part of a general statute directed to protection of the government's most important source of revenue, the customs. Specifically it made it a crime to receive or give "any bribe, reward, or recompense" for making a false entry as to a ship or merchandise. A fine of $200 to $2,000 was set as penalty, together with forfeiture of office. The next year, as one provision in a bill enumerating crimes against the United States, it became criminal to offer or accept money "or any other bribe, present, or reward, or any promise, contract, obligation or security" for the payment of money to procure "the opinion, judgment, or decree" of any federal judge. Draftsmen still hesitated to believe that "bribe" alone would cover all contingencies. Thoughtfully, the act extended to promises. Remarkably, no punishment was fixed except for disqualification from federal office. Fine or imprisonment was explicitly left to the discretion of the court. In statutory form the sanction prescribed was that inflicted on Bacon—forfeiture of office and the prospect of office, everything else open to remission.[27]

Only judges—not federal juries, federal district attorneys, federal marshals—were protected in this way from corruption. No statute was enacted against bribery of the Executive Branch or by the Executive

Branch. Arguably, the common law of bribery covered certain kinds of corruption, for example, buying an appointment, if Lord Mansfield were followed. Arguably, there was a federal common law of crime, at least until 1812 when the courts declared its nonexistence. But even at common law there was no clear criminal precedent on purchase of a vote for cash, still less was there authority covering purchase of a vote by an appointment or contract, the kind of corruption that Walpole had made into a system. Given the ideology of the Revolution and the revolutionaries' deep suspicion of such corruption, given the accumulated experience of English and American politics of the Fathers of the Constitution, given the unillusioned view of human nature of Hamilton and Madison, it must be inferred that the absence of constitutional or statutory protection of legislative integrity was deliberate. Lawmakers were not to be inhibited from bribery by law. The only sanction for legislative bribetakers was to be political.[28]

Yazoo.   In the first decade of the nation under the new Constitution the state of Georgia was to afford a spectacular example of what could be done in influencing a legislature. The original transaction was instructive as to the reciprocities which heroes of the Revolution, high federal officials, Fathers of the Constitution thought legitimate. The original transaction's sequel in Congress, the Executive Branch, and the Supreme Court was to be even more instructive as to the reciprocities that federal authority would tolerate, protect, and reward.

Georgia in 1795 had claim to 35 million acres of land from the present western boundary of the state to the Mississippi River and from the border of Tennessee to a Spanish strip on the Gulf, in effect to the territory comprising the two later states of Alabama and Mississippi. In the controversy that erupted, the Yazoo River gave its name to the whole area. Wild country, partially occupied and arguably owned by Chickasaws, Cherokees, Choctaws, and Creeks, the land was irresistibly attractive to speculators. At the beginning of 1795 they were sufficiently organized and capitalized to come to the village of Augusta where the Georgia legislature met and undertake to persuade the state to enact legislation conveying title to the 35 million acres to them.[29]

Four companies—not corporations but associations whose shares were convertible into acres of land—collaborated in the campaign. Investors in them included leaders in the law of Georgia: for example, Mathew McAllister, the federal district attorney for Georgia; William Stith, judge of the Superior Court, the state's highest tribunal; and Nathaniel Pendleton, the only federal judge in Georgia, who also signed the certificates of ownership the companies issued. Investors also reflected the national dimension of the enterprise: Southerners like Robert Goodloe Harper and Wade Hampton of South Carolina; Westerners like William Blount and John Sevier of Tennessee; and Northerners like Robert Morris and James Wilson of Philadelphia. The outside investors often had governmental connections, too. Harper and Hampton were congressmen; Blount was superintendent of Indian Affairs; Sevier was soon to be governor of Tennessee; Morris, financier of the Revolution, was a senator; and Wilson, like Morris a Father of the Constitution, was a justice of the Supreme Court of the United States. Wilson was on hand in person in Augusta as the campaign began. At its head was a brigadier-general of the Revolution, James Gunn, now United States Senator from Georgia.[30]

Gunn's method was simple—to pay a legislator what he had to to get his vote. Gunn instructed his agent Robert Flournoy that no member of the legislature "should or could have a share if he did not vote for the bill." As the next Georgia legislature was to hear, this method produced a variety of prices. Representative Thomas Raburn, for example, was reproached for selling his vote for $600 while others got $1,000. Raburn replied it showed he was easily satisfied and not greedy. Clement Lanier, a House member, who did not vote in favor of the act, was offered 75,000 acres (1 share) by William Longstreet, a state senator in favor of passage. Senator Thomas Wylly said he would get 8 to 10 "likely negroes" for his part in passing the bill. Later he felt "he had engaged too soon, that he was not so lucky as some of them who had held off until the last." Representative John Shephard, intending to vote No, was offered 42 pounds, a comparatively small sum, to leave town; he declined and remained in opposition. Flournoy, at Gunn's request, checked on Senator Robert Thomas, who assured him "he meant to be uniform"; Thomas later sold the shares he received for 3,000 to 5,000 dollars. Flournoy offered 75,000 acres to Senator Mitchell, which he refused. In the end the bill—discreetly entitled "An act supplementary to an act for appropriating a part of the unlocated territory of the State for the payment of the late State troops, and for other purposes therein mentioned"—passed the House 19–9 and the Senate 10–8. It disposed of the 35 million acres to the companies for $500,000, a price of under $1^1/_2$ cents per acre. According to the companies' own records, every member of the legislature—with a single exception—who voted for the bill was a shareholder in the purchases.[31]

Public indignation—surely fanned by disappointed rival speculators—became intense when the main features of the deal were known. County grand juries presented the legislature's conduct as a grievance. A statewide convention on May 10, 1795, pointed out that the majority who voted for the bill "were engaged in the purchase" and denounced "the atrocious peculation, corruption, and collusion by which the usurped acts and grants were obtained." There had been an inadequate price paid, fraud, an unauthorized and unconstitutional conveyance of state land, and, exclusive of all these acts, "corruption," which would suffice in equity, reason, and law to invalidate the contracts. Individual legislators who had voted for the bill were in physical jeopardy. The people of Hancock, for example, "had an idea that Thomas was bribed," so he was thought to "stand a good chance of chugging a sapling," that is, being ridden on a rail. Fortunately for public sentiment, a new legislature could be elected for 1796. Only two "Yazoo men" were returned. The new legislature took depositions on the corruption of the old and on February 13, 1796, annulled the act of the previous year. Not only was it voided, but the engrossed bill was ordered to be "publicly burnt in order that no trace of this unconstitutional, vile, and fraudulent transaction, other than the infamy attached to it by this law, shall remain in the public offices."[32]

Massive outrage, corruption proved and proclaimed, but no one went to jail or was even prosecuted. Georgia congressmen, testifying later before a federal commission, gave it as their opinion that Georgia had no law against bribery. The erring legislators had been punished at the polls. The purchasers who had put up the $500,000 got their money back, if they chose, from the state: over $300,000 was refunded. Corruption, exposed, did not seem to pay; it did escape all criminal censure. Those getting the refunds were pessimists. The optimists took another course.[33]

The Yazoo optimists conveyed their titles to others. As of February 13, 1796, the day of the enactment of the law annulling the sale, the Georgia Mississippi Company, for example, recorded the conveyance of its entire title to William Wetmore, Leonard Jarvis, and Henry Newman. A year later these three conveyed the land to a dozen other Massachusetts men, including Oliver Phelps, Seth Wetmore, and John Peck. These in turn put their land in a trust called the New England Mississippi Land Company. This trust became a major vehicle for representing the Yazoo claimants, and the Yazoo claimants took the position that the Georgia recission of the grant violated the federal constitution and was void and that they had title good against Georgia. Alexander Hamilton on March 25, 1796, gave a legal opinion to this effect. It did not put any money into the hands of the Yazoo owners. The prospect of enforcing Yazoo land titles in Georgia seemed remote.[34]

Thought was given to where compensation could be found: only one treasury was big enough. In 1798 a bill went through the Federalist-dominated Congress for an "amicable settlement" of land disputes between the United States and Georgia by providing for the United States to acquire from Georgia the entire Yazoo area. Massachusetts names had been prominent among those holding Yazoo titles in 1795 and 1796—among them Charles Bulfinch, the Boston architect, and William Scollay, a developer of Beacon Hill in Boston. After the rescinding act, speculation in the titles continued in Massachusetts: $2,000,000 was estimated to have been invested by Bostonians. But by 1798 Yazoo shares had been peddled widely. There were, for example, said to be 1,200 claimants in Maryland alone. The suspicion was voiced that certain respectable persons had been given shares free so their names would act as decoys to the multitude who were induced to buy. Georgia and Virginia congressmen suggested that the bill was intended to bring as much as $1,000,000 to the Yazoo claimants, and Harper, speaking for the bill, candidly admitted that the claimants had "no hope while Georgia possesses this territory." With cosmetic changes the bill passed; only two years later, in the first Jefferson administration, did it lead to action. The United States then bought the area from Georgia for $1,250,000. The commissioners to consider the Yazoo claims were James Madison, the secretary of State; Albert Gallatin, the secretary of the Treasury; and Levi Lincoln, the attorney general—three-fifths of the cabinet. They reported to Congress on February 16, 1803, setting out the facts relating to the first Georgia legislature's interest in the sale, the text of the depositions as to its corruption, and the annulling act. Their opinion was that "the title of the claimants cannot be supported." Nonetheless, they thought that it would be in the interest of the United States to offer a compromise—to price 5,000,000 acres at two dollars per acre and to offer this land or its equivalent in bonds to the claimants. The Jefferson administration, in a word, was willing to pay the claimants of a portion of the property more than the United States had paid for the whole. Having at one time nothing but a legal opinion, the Yazoo claimants now had the possibility of ten million dollars.[35]

To make sure that possibility became a reality, the Massachusetts trustees hired the postmaster general, Gideon Granger. Granger was a lawyer who had been rewarded (for nurturing a Republican minority in Connecticut) with presidential appointment to a position not yet of cabinet rank but with more patronage than any other department. He was himself a Yazoo titleholder; his work for his fellow Yazoo claimants was to be their lobbyist, and he even went on to the floor of Congress in their behalf. Half a century or so later such employment on the part of a government officer would be classified as a crime, a century later it might have been prosecuted as one. In 1803 it was acceptable enough that the attorney general, although declining to issue an opinion, told Granger that he saw nothing wrong with his double role.[36]

Opposition to Yazoo was led by John Randolph, not the Father of the Constitution but a thirty-year-old Virginian, chairman of the Ways and Means Committee, the most brilliant man in the House, so independent as to appear eccentric and so used to speaking his own mind as to be undisciplined. Randolph had read a good deal of Burke, and he held Burke's Ciceronian view of corruption; he had also been in Augusta when Georgia had annulled the Yazoo grants and burnt the offending statute, so that his sense of the offensiveness of Yazoo was strong. Against his own party and his own political interests, against his fellow-Virginian Madison, against the Jefferson Administration, Randolph declared that the Yazoo claimants should be paid nothing.[37]

Commenting on the extraordinarily quiet way the Yazoo claims had been handled in Washington, Randolph observed that Yazoo was "one of those subjects which pollution has sanctified." In the view of the backers of the bill—unnamed by him, the Jeffersonians in office were meant—"the hallowed mysteries of corruption [were] not to be profaned by the eye of public curiosity." Randolph would not be so reticent. The original grants were "obtained by bribery and fraud" and were therefore void ab initio. The "swindlers of 1795" had no title, nothing to pass on. As for those who claimed to have bought from them in ignorance and good faith, the Yazoo fraud was as notorious as the Stamp Act had been in its time. Everyone knew of it. Those claiming ignorance were "guilty of gross and wilful prevarication." The arguments on their behalf were "sophisticated trash."[38]

To this trash the Committee on Claims had been remarkably tender. Known for its niggardliness to veterans of the Revolution, this committee was generous to those whose title, according to Madison, Gallatin, and Lincoln would not stand up. It reminded Randolph of the Magdalen Charity in London, approached by a girl who said she was poor and innocent. The director told her, "This is a place of reception for prostitutes; you must go and qualify yourself before you can partake of our relief." Only claims "tainted with corruption" were relieved by the Committee on Claims.[39]

Lacking a good cause, the Yazoo men had hired as their agent a man who had "offices in his gift amongst the most lucrative and at the same time the least laborious or responsible under the Government." He came armed with "snug appointments and fat contracts," with $300,000 in funds he could employ, with a patronage limited only by the extent of the country. "Timeo Danaos et dona ferentes," Randolph quoted Virgil, and in the American vernacular he said, "Millions of acres are easily digested by such stomachs. . . . They buy and sell corruption in the gross, and a few millions, more or less, are hardly felt in the account."[40]

Most specifically, Randolph said he would breach a confidence and tell what another congressman had told him—that "a jackal" of the postmaster general had offered him a postal contract; that the congressman had accepted, adding, "I shall vote against the Yazoo claim notwithstanding." Next day the "obscene animal" who had approached him told him "that there had been some misunderstanding of the business" and the contract was withdrawn. This honest congressman had not been bought, but "the Yazoo squad"—a monstrous alliance of New England Federalists and Republicans—was at its silent work. "In the coarse language of the proverb, 'tis the still sow that sucks the draff'"—in other words, the pigs were quietly lining up at the trough.[41]

Granger wrote the House formally denying the story, asking for an investigation, and stating "I trust I have virtue enough not to attempt improperly to influence any man." Congressman Matthew Lyon of Kentucky, famous for a physical fight on the floor of the House and holder of several postal contracts, asserted he made no money on them, and that Randolph's charges came from "the disordered imagination of a young man" who had "got his head as full of British contracts and British modes of corruption as ever Don Quixote's was supposed to have been of chivalry." Lyon showed the sensitivity of one who might have considered himself to be the jackal and obscene animal of Randolph's story. He concluded his speech with an unmistakable reference to Randolph's physiognomy —he thanked God that He had not given him, Lyon, the face of an ape or a monkey. William Findley, a senior congressman from Pennsylvania, also defended Yazoo with an appeal to custom—the Pennsylvania legislature, he said, had been similarly interested in land grants it had made.[42]

Thanks to Randolph's oratory and the rank and file of southern Republicans, payment of the Yazoo claimants stalled in Congress. Meanwhile the claimants resorted to a device to bring new pressure. George Blake, a Yazoo titleholder as of 1797, had already obtained a judgment from the Supreme Judicial Court of Massachusetts treating the Georgia act of recission as void. Unfortunately, the writ of the Supreme Judicial Court did not run beyond Massachusetts. In May 1803, in Massachusetts, John Peck sold Robert Fletcher, a citizen of New Hampshire, 15,000 acres of Yazoo land with the warranty that Georgia had legally made the original grant and that no subsequent act of the Georgia legislature had impaired the title. Fletcher then claimed that these warranties had been violated; he sued Peck. As citizens of different states were involved, the federal courts were open, and in the circuit court on demurrer, Caleb Cushing, the Massachusetts man on the Supreme Court, obligingly upheld Peck's defense that the title was good. But what was needed was the imprimatur of the Supreme Court itself. Fletcher accordingly appealed, and John Quincy Adams, lately a senator from Massachusetts, was employed to defend the Yazoo title for Peck.[43]

At this point—by now it was 1809—the strategy of using the Supreme Court encountered a check. Chief Justice John Marshall intimated to counsel that the Court did not want to decide the case because it was "manifestly made up." In open court Marshall told counsel that it was clear from the pleadings themselves that Fletcher knew of the defects in title when he took the deed.[44]

One would have supposed that the case was over. However, the parties were given leave to amend the pleadings. In 1810 Joseph Story replaced Adams. Story's father-in-law, William Wetmore, a judge of the Court of Common Pleas in Boston, had been a heavy speculator in Yazoo, and Story was a prominent enough Republican in Massachusetts to be appointed in 1811 to the Supreme Court himself. Teamed with Robert Harper—the same Harper who had moved the federal purchase in 1798—Story argued for the validity of the title. His nominal opponent, Luther Martin, got drunk and was unable to complete his argument before the Court. Chief Justice Marshall delivered an opinion overlooking entirely the fictitious character of the case, and the real harmony of interests in the litigants. Marshall held that the Georgia act annulling the original grants was a violation of the federal Constitution's prohibition against a state "impairing the obligation of contracts"—at least it was such a violation when the title of a purchaser in good faith was affected; that consequently the Georgia voiding act was itself void; and that therefore Peck had conveyed a good title.

Marshall left open whether Georgia itself in a suit by the state could show the grant was acquired by corruption, although rhetorically casting doubt even on this possibility by speculating about the degree of corruption that would have to be shown and the difficulty of drawing a line. With true chutzpah the Chief Justice wrote, "It would be indecent, in the extreme, upon a private contract, between two individuals, to enter into an inquiry respecting the corruption of the sovereign power of a state." Corruption denounced by Georgia was at the core of Georgia's recission. By refusing to inquire about the corruption and by accepting at face value the pleadings' claim that Peck and Fletcher had no notice of the corruption—there was no trial of the facts since it was all worked by demurrers— Marshall let Peck as well as Fletcher appear as innocent purchasers. It was "indecent in the extreme" to ask about corruption. It was apparently entirely legitimate for the Court to give the Yazoo claimants a new stick to beat on Congress.[45]

Although no factual issue was determined, and although Georgia had never been heard, *Fletcher v. Peck* furnished the Yazoo holders with the argument that the Supreme Court had upheld their basic position. In the words of Henry Adams—here a true descendant of his grandfather—"the question whether the claimants had rights which the government would do well to compromise was for the law to decide and was ultimately settled by Chief Justice Marshall in their favor."[46] Of course nothing had been decided in their favor as to their rights against the United States; they had no rights at all which they could enforce. But the illusion of having rights which Congress should honor was effectively created. It must be a matter of speculation as to whether the broad implication of *Fletcher v. Peck* that a legislative grant, however corruptly secured, was safe from challenge was more of an incentive to later legislative corruption than the opposite view holding such a grant void *ab initio* (and so subject to corruption counteracting corruption). It is no speculation to say that in *Fletcher v. Peck*, a fictitious case managed by those seeking to manipulate Congress, the Marshall Court gave a substantial boost to the Yazoo titleholders. The indignation of Georgians was understandable. On the floor of Congress, Representative George M. Troup gave his view of Marshall's decision. The case taught, he said, that "the Representatives of the people may corruptly betray the people." "The archfiend" would have "issued a decree like that of the judges."[47]

Randolph still staved off capitulation by Congress. But in 1814 he was defeated for reelection, and Madison, the major mover of the compromise of 1803, was president. Five million dollars was appropriated as reimbursement for the Yazoo titleholders. How many of these were the same as those who had been in on the game in 1795 or in privity with them, how many were widows and orphans induced by the original swindlers to buy their titles, does not appear. In the nineteen years between the first bribes and the federal payoffs, there had been much swapping of, and speculation in, Yazoo titles. One can only observe that what cost the speculators a net $200,000 paid to Georgia in 1795 (plus bribes) was redeemed by the United States for a sum equal to one-third of the amount paid to Napoleon for the entire Louisiana Territory.[48]

Far less effective than Burke in creating a national drama out of Yazoo, Randolph himself never let go of the issue. Jefferson became for him "St Thomas of Cantingbury." His administration's bias toward the Yazoo interest was his government's "original sin." As late as the regime of Andrew Jackson, Randolph could and did discomfort an opponent with the accusation, "You are a Yazoo man." For him, "The Yazoo business is the beginning and the end, the Alpha and the Omega of our alphabet." Beyond doubt the affair showed at the start of the new Republic that bribery in legislative affairs ran only the risk of political sanction, and that that sanction could be effectively blunted.[49]

Silver in the Silver Age.   The high officers of government, reported one observer of Washington in 1824, "are not, in reality, quite so good as other men." The naïve observation could have been made by Ammianus in fourth-century, or Lotario di Segni in twelfth-century, Rome. Meanwhile, looking out on the provinces from Washington, the sharpest and most censorious eye of the day, that of John Quincy Adams, found them no better. Baltimore, for example, in the person of its federal officials was "as rotten as corruption can make it." Savannah, for another case, was distinguished by "deep and deadly villainy" in its piratical collector of customs. These were the thoughts of a man living in what became conventionally known as the Era of Good Feelings or the Silver Age of the American republic. Recording such and similar reactions and the conduct to which they responded, a recent historian has concluded that the age should be denominated "the nation's first Era of Corruption."[50]

The evidence on which such unflattering judgment is based invites examination by the standards of the day. No federal bribery statute applicable to the president, to the cabinet, or to Congress existed. The standards of the day as to corruption were moral and political. How did certain transactions conform to these criteria?

Sometime during the War of 1812, when he was Secretary of State, James Monroe borrowed $5,000 from John Jacob Astor, the head of the American Fur Company. The amount was the equivalent of Monroe's salary for one year. Astor normally loaned on mortgages, but this loan appears to have been made without security. The interest was 14 percent, but for at least three years, 1818—1821, Astor let the interest run without collecting or compounding it. The loan was presumably for a term; by 1821 it was indisputably overdue. Why Monroe, a Virginian in high office, should have borrowed from Astor, a successful German immigrant in New York, is not known, Monroe merely observing that Astor "offered" the loan "on hearing that I was pressed for money." How this interesting intelligence was communicated to Astor, Monroe did not say.[51]

Once the loan was made, Astor wrote to Monroe "with the utmost fullness whenever any menace hostile to the fur trade or to his own position therein appeared to be in view among the acts of government." The letters began in 1813 with a request for a federal license for a company ship. Engaged in attempting to monopolize the fur trade in all American territory and constantly involved in encounters with the Indians or with white foreigners, Astor needed a variety of favors from the federal government. From the highest issues of foreign policy—for example, the right of Canadians to engage in the trade in United States territory—to questions of detail, the federal authorities could be of critical assistance. For American Fur the years 1817 to 1825, the years of Monroe's presidency, were decisive in the company's phenomenal success.[52]

Astor did not hesitate to remind Monroe of the leash he was on. In January 1821, writing Monroe from Rome, Astor noted that the loan was in arrears and then stated his "under standing that Landed proper[ty] in the U.S. is at present not verry Saleable I presume you have not Sold any of your estates." Letting him off the payment of principal, he did not hesitate to comment on Monroe's mention of the fur trade in his message to Congress. He, Astor, he said, had $400,000 in the venture: "If any Change is contemplated I hope it will not be to oprate against Citzons who are at present engagd in that trade under the System which government adopted Some years ago." Astor's spelling was erratic, his tone was forthright and confident. The threat that he could make Monroe sell his property at this inconvenient time was delivered without unnecessary growling. The letter may profitably be compared to the alleged letter of Epiphanius to the bishop of Constantinople, whom he owned.[53]

Monroe's credit was good as long as he was president. When he left office, Astor congratulated him on his "honorable retirement," reminded him of the debt, and stated, "I would be glad if you would put it in a train of Sittlement." Three years later, in 1828, Monroe settled by selling slaves from his estate at Albemarle, Virginia, to Joseph White in Florida. It was commonly accounted inhumane to sell Virginia slaves for shipment to undeveloped, swampy areas like Florida, and Monroe felt the need to explain the sale to his friend James Madison. Hence a letter in which he mentioned that the slaves would go "in families" and referred to getting released from the Astor loan. Clearly he felt that the sale of his slaves "down the river" was, unexplained, more damaging to his reputation than the loan.[54]

Confessing, in a limited way, to his old patron, Monroe implicitly treated the debt as honorable. The obligation to repay obscured that Astor had conferred a benefit on him in giving him credit. Astor indeed had used a wonderfully effective way of securing influence, especially if the debt was in effect on demand, so that at any time the debtor could be pulled up short. The American Winston Churchill's nineteenth-century novel *Coniston* illustrates the creditor's power, as Jethro Bass, a shrewd villager, builds his political base in New Hampshire by mortgages taken from other farmers. What Bass got fictionally, Astor got in fact.

Having successfully invested in a man who became president, Astor made another investment in 1819 in Henry Clay, speaker of the House. He loaned him $20,000 for three years at 7 percent, secured by a mortgage on Clay's Kentucky home, "Ashland." The quid pro quo when one had the speaker as one's debtor became evident in 1822 when the loan was extended and legislation was enacted cutting out of the Army appropriation the money to run a "factory system" of trading with the Indians which competed with the American Fur Company. In 1823 Astor was still betting on Clay as a presidential hopeful: "I am glad to See that your prospect is So good." And as late as 1833, when presumably the first loan had been paid, Astor lent Clay another $20,000.[55]

The Bank of the United States, an entity existing by federal legislation and dependent on government deposits, also practiced the loan game. An undated, handwritten list of congressmen, federal officials, and newspaper editors, liable to the Bank as borrowers or guarantors, was kept by the Bank's president, Nicholas Biddle. It included James Monroe, down for $10,596; Henry Clay in the amount of $7,500; and Senator Daniel Webster of Massachusetts, liable for $17,782.86.[56]

Biddle's list did not become public in his lifetime. But in the 1830s two congressmen, George Poindexter of Mississippi and Josiah Johnson of Louisiana, were publicly reported to have borrowed $10,000 and $35,000 respectively from the Bank. They were accused in the press of being bribed.[57] The accusation came in the midst of a hot fight over the renewal of the Bank's federal charter; Johnson was in fact down on Biddle's list for $28,405. It is fair inference that if there had been an analogous battle over American Fur's special favors from the government, Monroe would have been regarded as bribed. The public standard, in short, was there. It was not applied to the Astor-Monroe loan because the loan never became the object of public scrutiny.

A second way of acquiring influence—less open to political polemic if it became known—was to hire a member of Congress as one's lawyer. Astor himself used Thomas Hart Benton, senator from Missouri, to attack the factory system in the Senate, and in the same year Benton became an attorney for American Fur. Henry Clay had among his clients James De Wolfe, renowned as a Rhode Island slave trader.[58] As long as the congressman did some actual legal work, it was hard for anyone to say that he was hired for his clout. The Bank of the United States found it useful to employ both Clay and Webster. In 1833, when the Bank was engaged in the mortal combat to keep its federal charter, Senator Webster coolly wrote Biddle, "Since I have arrived here, I have had an application to be concerned, professionally, against the Bank, which I have declined, of course, although I believe my retainer has not been renewed, or *refreshed* as usual. If it be wished that my relation to the Bank should be continued, it may be well to send me the usual retainers." In these phrases there was the suggestion that only Webster's professional allegiance was at stake. Delivered at a time of peril for the Bank in Congress the letter scarcely failed to convey the importance of keeping the senator satisfied.[59]

Not only could the legal services of members of Congress be legally bought; so could those of the attorney general himself. William Wirt, attorney general under Monroe and John Quincy Adams, conducted an extensive private practice. Among his clients was the Bank of the United States, from which he obtained a retainer of $250 in 1822 and the hope of trial fees of $1,500 to $2,000. These, he wrote his wife, "are the fees that *tell*." With a salary of $3,500, it is inferable how much private business might tell a man like Wirt who, in Adams's acidulous description, "appeared to think more about his salary, or what he called bread and meat for his children, than any other subject."[60]

A Judge Influenced, a Senator Suborned. The case of *The Antelope*, which began in 1820, is illustrative of how work as a lawyer and an officer of government could be lucratively combined while escaping public criticism because the payoff was camouflaged as a fee. Two hundred and eighty-one Africans were rescued from a slave ship bringing them into Georgia. Under federal law the Africans were free, and President Monroe was supposed to return them to Africa. They were claimed as property by the Spanish and Portuguese consuls purporting to represent honest Spanish and Portuguese slavers from whom they had been taken by a pirate, whose effort to import them illegally into the United States should not, the consuls said, work a forfeiture on the rightful owners. In fact the Portuguese certainly, and probably the Spanish, were fronts for American slaveowners (including Senator James De Wolfe of Rhode Island) unable themselves to appear in court without admitting criminal guilt. A secret agreement bound "the Spanish" and "the Portuguese" to divide their recovery. Without direction from the Monroe Administration, the district attorney in Savannah opposed the claims against the Africans and contended for their freedom. He was opposed before Federal District Judge William Davies by John Macpherson Berrien, a state court judge, locally celebrated as "the American Cicero." Judge Davies decided almost all issues in favor of the Spanish and Portuguese. One week after his final order he resigned from the bench and joined Judge Berrien in the practice of law. Berrien's clients stood to gain at least $30,000 by Davies's decree.[61]

Four years later, after political delays by the Monroe Administration, the United States argued the appeal for the Africans before the Supreme Court. Berrien, now a United States senator-elect, continued to appear for the Spanish. He was joined by Charles Ingersoll, United States district attorney for Philadelphia, representing the fictitious Portuguese. John Marshall decided almost all of the issues differently from Judge Davies, but although most of those Africans who had not died in the meanwhile were freed, thirty-seven were left who were treated as property, subject to a bond of $14,800, to be removed from the country. These thirty-seven represented a kind of pot, from which counsel hoped to be paid. Richard Wilde, a congressman from Georgia, wrote Senator Berrien expressing willingness to buy them and at the same time proposing that the bond be canceled. His proposal was accepted. He put up just enough cash to cover counsel fees and other expenses, acquiring the Africans at a substantial discount because of the bond. Simultaneously with his delivery of the cash in Savannah, Berrien introduced in the United States Senate a bill to cancel the bond. Referred to the Judiciary Committee of which Berrien was a member, the bill was quickly reported out favorably and passed the Senate. In the House it ran into some questioning by northern congressmen but Wilde's friends persevered and the bill carried; President Adams signed it into law.

Senator Berrien received $850 of the fees awarded in Savannah and funded by Wilde. He also received from the United States a bounty of $25 per head due under law for each freed African, no matter that many of them had died before freedom was finally established. How was Berrien entitled to the bounty? He had also represented John Jackson, the captain of the Treasury cutter that had rescued the Africans. Jackson received $400 of the bounty himself. The lion's share appears to have been assigned as contingent compensation to Berrien, who, representing conflicting claims, stood to win whoever prevailed. The United States paid him a total bounty of $5,100 with no questions asked by the Adams Administration about his inclusion of the dead Africans in calculating the total. The enslaved Africans were ultimately sold by Wilde to the same Joseph White who in the same year bought Monroe's slaves from Albemarle.[62]

"Conflict of interest" was a term not yet invented. In America in 1984 its use ranges from being a euphemism for the result of outright bribery to describing a situation in which one subject to a duty takes a position inconsistent with that duty. Ingersoll and Berrien arguably had conflicts of interest in the latter sense, that is, they had duties as officials inconsistent with representing plaintiffs in a case against the United States. But this conflict was known and not objected to by the government; hence the government may have waived it, as presumably John Jackson and "the Spanish" waived objection to Berrien representing their inconsistent interests. That Berrien had an understanding with Wilde about the bill to cancel Wilde's bond was not publicly known. The legislation to cancel Wilde's bond would not have sped through the Committee on the Judiciary and the Senate without Berrien's use of his position as a senator. It can be said politely that Berrien had an unwaived conflict of interest, or bluntly that he was bribed. Similarly, Judge Davies can be inferred to have made his arrangements with Berrien before his decision: euphemistically, he was involved in a conflict of interest; realistically he was paid off.

Since Berrien's arrangements with Wilde were secret, no public criticism of them was made. The ease with which a congressman bribed a senator to introduce a private bill is suggestive of the relaxed standards of the legislature. That no criticism was made of Davies has a different basis, the difficulty of converting a reasonable inference into proof, added to the fact that those harmed by his decision were the helpless Africans. Inferably, Davies had violated the statute against bribery of a federal judge. If that inference was not made, the appearance of evil remained.

Sensitivity to judicial impropriety was known to the age. In 1819 Chief Justice John Marshall wrote the opinion in the famous case of *McCulloch v. Maryland*, upholding the constitutionality of the federal charter of the Bank of the United States. In the midst of the later bank war, it was claimed that Marshall had been a stockholder in the Bank—in modern terms, a conflict of interest rather than a bribe, for his holdings had preceded the litigation. The claims found credence "so general is the belief of the universal corruption of the nation." Marshall and the Bank were assailed. Nicholas Biddle was delighted to be able to appeal to the stock transfer book of the Bank to show that the story was untrue: Marshall had disposed of his shares a month before the case was argued. To be sure, he had transferred a portion of them to his son Thomas, a rather close connection. Still, he was not judging in his own case.[63] Clearly, by his own standard, as well by the popular standard of what constituted corruption, a judge could not be personally interested in the subject of litigation. Davies escaped censure only by presenting his association with Berrien as a professional arrangement and implicitly defying anyone to show the contrary.

Toqueville, describing America at the end of the 1830s, remarked that it was a nation governed by lawyers.[64] That money paid to lawyers could be explained, or rationalized, or laundered as money paid for actual legal services was a substantial difficulty in isolating bribes paid to lawyers occupying official posts. With lawyer-congressmen the difficulty was doubled by the absence of statutes against the bribing of legislators and by the absence of a strong paradigm of the legislator as impartial. No national police, no Federal Bureau of Investigation, no Department of Justice existed to inquire into wrongdoing at the federal level. Abusive journalism was common, but true muckraking unusual. With the facts unknown or unproved, with legislators understood as partisan and influenced in a variety of ways, with many lawyers ready to take any paying client, the chicanery, fraud, and bribery attendant on *The Antelope* passed unremarked. Nonetheless, when before the eyes of everyone a favor appeared to be exchanged for an important vote, the cry of corruption rang through the land.

Bargain and Sale in 1825. The presidential election of 1824 failed to give a majority of electoral votes to any candidate, and, following Article Twelve of the Constitution, the House of Representatives had to choose between the three highest candidates. These were Andrew Jackson, who had a plurality in both the popular and electoral votes; John Quincy Adams, the incumbent secretary of State; and William Crawford, the incumbent secretary of the Treasury. Crawford, ailing with a stroke and trailing in the national voting, was not in a strong position. Jackson faced Adams, with the eliminated fourth candidate, Henry Clay, in a position to play a large role in determining the winner in the House. In that election each state counted for one vote, so that small states were as important as big ones, and, in a divided congressional delegation, the vote of a single congressman could swing one of the thirteen states necessary for a majority. The electors, in fine, were a small predetermined body precisely of the kind that Hamilton had feared "might be tampered with beforehand to prostitute their votes."

Adams kept a diary which, laconic and incomplete, conveys a sense of the pressures he was under when a finite number of persons were in a position to determine if he would be president. Among those he talked to in December 1824 and January 1825—the election in the House was set for February 9—were Jonathan Jennings, member from Indiana, a difficult delegation for Adams to win; John Scott, sole member from Missouri whose single vote would be the state's; and Isaac McKim from the divided Maryland delegation. To Jennings, Adams explained to his satisfaction how he, Adams, would choose the printers of federal laws in Indiana. Scott was also interested in federal printing in his state, but he had a bigger problem: his brother, a judge in the Arkansas Territory, had engaged in a duel, and territorial law made duelists ineligible for office. The duel was notorious—it had ended in the killing of a colleague on the bench, and months ago Monroe had been asked to remove the killer. Adams told Scott that Monroe, not having acted, would not act now. Unspoken was the implication that what Monroe did would be precedent for Adams. McKim had a constituent with a claim against Spain that needed government backing; he was also a person with an interest in having *The Antelope*, now delayed four years, argued before the Supreme Court, and it may be inferred that he induced Adams to agree to this, for the argument promptly followed the election.[65]

These visitors with varied problems were only a small fraction of those that Adams saw. "Long lists of persons calling daily, with their respective wishes, still remain, but they scarcely retain interest enough to merit the space they would occupy in these pages," writes Adams's son Charles Francis, the editor of the diary.[66] The daily callers with their respective wishes were not given negotiable instruments, written pledges, or express words; but it is a fair inference that the stream would have dried up, and Adams would not have been elected, if he had not on occasion used words that indicated, to those who came to him to declare their desires, his readiness to oblige them.

Of all the callers, the most critical was Henry Clay, who came on January 9, 1825. The way had been prepared by several conversations with Robert Letcher, Clay's messmate. "Incendo super ignes," Adams confided to the diary after the longest of these exploratory exchanges—"I walk upon fires." Clay himself asked for "some confidential conversation upon public affairs" on January 1, 1825. When he came on January 9 he disclaimed any intention to discuss "any personal considerations for himself." He and Adams were to discuss privately "some principles of great public importance." The result was what Adams described as "a long conversation explanatory of the past and prospective of the future." Adams left blank space in the diary to record the details of this conversation and never filled in the blank. The upshot of the evening was that Clay declared "he had no hesitation in saying that his preference would be for me."[67]

Anyone reading Adams's account would have to conclude that at no point was a gross promise made by Adams to appoint Clay to a particular office. Yet even historians sympathetic to Adams have inferred from this report, put in the context of subsequent events, that there was a meeting of minds as to what Clay would do for Adams and what Adams would do for Clay. In the words of Samuel Flagg Bemis, an admirer of Adams, there was "an implicit bargain—a gentlemen's agreement."[68]

After this discussion, Clay would write a supporter that he, Clay, could have any cabinet post he wanted in an Adams administration. Clay and Clay's friends worked hard to shift the Kentucky and Ohio delegations in particular to Adams. Clay supporters in Kentucky were assured by January 20 that if Adams would be elected president, Clay would be secretary of State, the post generally thought of as the highest in the cabinet and the usual stepping stone to the presidency. Two days after his election, Adams told Monroe of his intention to make Clay secretary of State, "considering it due to his talents and services, to the Western section of the Union whence he comes, and to the confidence in me manifested by their delegations." The last clause was the closest Adams came to acknowledging to anyone that the appointment was, even in part, in reciprocation for votes cast in the election in the House.[69]

A devout man, who invoked the blessing of God on his election, Adams did not even in the privacy of his diary admit fault or accuse himself of any mental sin in working for the presidency. All the diary reveals is awareness of the strain. On January 30, 1825, it underlines "the intenseness of interest in the issue." On January 31, it records "the excitement already great and every day inflaming." On February 3, "the excitement of electioneering is kindling into fury." The sense of fire which Adams had invoked in his Latin phrase in December was now acute. He made his observations on the warmth of the excitement as he read and heard the reactions of the Jackson camp to his alliance with Clay.[70]

Jackson, a lawyer far more famous as a soldier, was an outsider on the Washington scene, consciously guarding his purity. For three years spent largely in Tennessee he had ruminated on the national government, "corrupt," as he put it, "to the core." The attempt to select a presidential candidate by congressional caucus earlier in 1824 (Secretary Crawford was the choice) had failed. Jackson wrote, *"The great whore of babylon being prostrated, by the fall of the caucus,* the liberty of our country is safe. . . ." Biblical language of this kind came easily to him. Although not a regular churchgoer like his devout wife Rachel, he had Presbyterian roots and sentiments and was increasingly inclined to see events in a Christian perspective of good and evil, sin and retribution. When word of Clay's movement to Adams reached him he wrote, "Intrigue, corruption, and sale of public office is the rumor of the day. How humiliating to the American character that its high functionaries should conduct themselves as to become liable to the interpretation of bargain and sale of the constitutional rights of the people."[71]

The Jackson forces prompted a Pennsylvania congressman on January 28, 1825, to accuse Clay of trading votes in the House in exchange for appointment as secretary of State, but when a congressional investigation was at once launched, the accuser declined to appear and the investigation fizzled. The understanding between Adams and Clay was not to be proved by testimony but by what happened: the Clay camp worked for Adams, Adams made the appointment. "The acts of the villain," remarked Louis McClane, an unfriendly observer of Clay, "return the poisonous chalice to his own lips." The gift of office was seen as poison. "All the waters of the sweet Heavens cannot remove the iota of corruption."[72]

When he first heard of the deal, Jackson himself wrote, "The rumor of Barter of office, intrigue, and corruption still afloat, which I hope for the honor of our country there is no truth in." When Clay's appointment became known, Jackson declared, "So you see the *Judas* of the West has closed the contract and will receive the thirty pieces of silver. his end will be the same." And again, "Mr. Clay like *Judas of old* (it is said) *sold himself and his influence to Mr. Adams. . . .*" Andrew Jackson Donelson, the general's ward, wrote of "the nefarious drama" that would reach its climax on March 4 "when Mr. Adams is to seal with his oath all his corrupt bargains." Not only the understanding with Clay but all Adams's arrangements with congressmen were "rewards for the iniquity" of selling the Constitution, that is, for denying election to the people's choice. Ten days after the election, Jackson declared, "I weep for the liberty of my country. The rights of the people have been bartered for promises of office." He and his supporters could not get over the fact that Kentucky and Ohio and Missouri, where Adams had almost no popular support, had been voted by their representatives in the House for the New Englander. As Jackson put it, "the voice of the people of the west has been disregarded, and demagogues barter them as sheep in the shambles, for their own views, and personal agrandisement." The echo remained scriptural. The people, like Christ, were sheep led to the slaughter. The comparison was even more explicit—for it was the people not himself whom Jackson saw as betrayed—when he saw Clay as "the *Judas* of the West."[73]

Jackson's complaints reflected George Mason's words at the constitutional Convention. "Shall that man who has practised corruption and by that means procured his appointment in the first instance, be suffered to escape punishment . . .?" But the response to Mason at the Convention had been to make bribery an impeachable offense. It was unlikely that a Congress that had just elected a president would turn around and impeach him. No criminal statute spoke to Adams's conduct. When Jackson charged "corruption" he appealed to a moral ideal that could only be vindicated at the polls.

"Was there ever witnessed such a bare faced corruption in any country before!," Jackson exclaimed with a fine disregard for the enormities of the past. Once convinced of the deal, he could not put it out of his mind or not speak of it. On the way home to Tennessee he made his charges ring: "there was *cheating*, and *corruption*, and *bribery*, too." The presidential campaign of 1828 was already started. Its battle cry was to be "Jackson and Reform." Principled and priggish, Adams was to be defeated in part at least because outside of New England the charge of corruption against him was accepted.[74]

When in the 1830s the Jackson Administration entered its greatest fight, against the Bank of the United States, its strategy was the same: "Let the cry be heard across the land. Down with bribery—down with corruption —down with the Bank." And Jackson still cherished the Christ-like role ot the voters: "I cannot refrain from shedding a tear over the immorality of our congress, and the corruption of the times, still there are a redeeming spirit in the virtue of the people in which I trust." Redemption in this Anglo-American usage was the opposite of corruption. The Christian sense of the term had triumphed.[75]

Jackson transferred the religious sense of redemption to the action of the people or at least saw an analogy between their work and Christ's. If anyone in the Jackson camp had a more orthodox view of redemption, it was his wife. In one of her rare letters Rachel wrote her brother in 1821 that Jesus was "the hope of glory," adding, "may you say as pious job I know that my redeemer liveth."[76] Against her in 1828 was unleashed the fury of the friends of Adams's principal ally, Henry Clay. The strength of this attack, as much as Jackson's victory at the polls, measured the force of the Jacksonian indictment of Clay for "the corrupt bargain." Measure was meant to meet measure.

"This is Mr. Clay's fight," wrote Isaac Hill of *The New Hampshire Patriot*. "The country has him on trial for bribery, and, having no defense, he accuses the prosecution." Invoking its original technical invalidity thirty-eight years earlier, the Clay men assailed Rachel's marriage to Jackson as bigamous and adulterous. An adulterer, Jackson was guilty of a moral corruption outweighing Clay's. The vicious campaign did not persuade the voters; it did wound Rachel. Her health was already precarious. She collapsed under the charges and died; so that her life, as much as her belief, came close to that of pious Job, and her redemption was not by the people. Jackson's claim of political corruption—a moral claim not based on any statute—had been only too effective. It had set in motion the counterattack of sexual corruption that took the life of the person Jackson loved best.[77]

A Statutory Standard for Congress. Jacksonian reformers did not enact any criminal statute against the bribing of congressmen. That was to come almost a generation later, and then as an afterthought, in 1853. The occasion was the scandal generated by the handling of claims arising after the war with Mexico and in particular the engagement of a senator to prosecute for a contingent fee of 5 percent the claim of G. A. Gardiner before the Mexican Claims Commission.[78] The senator whose conduct was in question, Thomas Corwin, had become secretary of the Treasury in the administration of Millard Fillmore, a Whig lawyer who had become president at his predecessor's death. Fillmore, a blameless Unitarian, was embarrassed by the furor over Corwin. A lame duck himself, denied nomination by his party, Fillmore in his last annual message to Congress diverted attention from Corwin to "subordinate officers and clerks" who were "appointed to guard the approaches to the public Treasury." These persons, he declared, "occupy positions that expose them to all the temptations and seductions which the cupidity of peculators and fraudulent claimants can prompt them." It would be "a wise precaution to protect the Government against that source of mischief and corruption." The president recommended the passage of a law punishing anyone giving "bribes" to these officers or clerks.[79]

A committee of the House, appointed to look into the Corwin-Gardiner transaction, responded obliquely to Fillmore's request by reporting a bill making it a misdemeanor for any officer of the government, whether in the executive or in the legislative branch, to become interested in a claim against the government. An amendment to the bill was then successfully offered by Solomon G. Haven, Fillmore's former law partner and a past district attorney and mayor of Buffalo. He was no doubt familiar with the New York statute on bribery passed in 1846, providing a ten-year imprisonment for offering money or property to the governor, lieutenant governor, or any member of the legislature "with intent to influence his vote, opinion or judgment on any question." Haven's amendment made it criminal to offer "money, goods, right in action, bribe, present, or reward . . . or any other valuable thing whatever" to any officer of the United States or any member of Congress "to influence his vote, opinion, decision, or judgment or with the intent to bias his mind." The amendment made it equally criminal to accept such an offer. The penalty the amendment proposed was three years' imprisonment, a fine of three times the amount offered, and disqualification from office.[80]

Debate in the House focused on the practice of a "great number of members of Congress who have for many years and still are engaged in prosecuting claims against the government before the Executive Departments and in the courts of the United States." Vice President George Dallas, Senator Thomas Hart Benton, Senator Pierre Soulé of Louisiana, Senator Jesse Bright of Indiana were cited as persons well-known to have prosecuted claims against the United States. The dubious claim of George Galplin had been handled by John Forsyth, secretary of State, 1834–1841. The present bill, in the view of Thaddeus Stevens, member from Pennsylvania, was "an impeachment upon the whole House." Nonetheless the committee's chairman, Preston King of New York, stuck to his guns: "Some cases . . . by the large amount of the fee paid by the claimant have excited—perhaps I should say justly excited—suspicion that official and personal influence of the officer, as well as the legal skill of counsel, was sought by the claimant. This certainly no person would justify." The actual bribery provisions were not analyzed. The House—in a lame duck session where reform was easier for the departing members—passed the bill by a vote of 134 to 23.[81]

In the Senate, the bill was managed by George Badger of North Carolina, a former judge and secretary of the Navy, who was unsuccessfully nominated by Fillmore for the Supreme Court. He was interested in a bribery bill rather than a claims bill, but the House insisted on both in combination. Two modifications suggested by Badger were acceptable to the House. Conviction of bribetaking would not automatically deprive a member of his seat in Congress—Congress's constitutional power to expel its members itself was retained. The words "to bias his mind"—described as "near akin to a legal absurdity"—were removed along with the words "opinion" and "judgment," so that the crime was limited to influencing a "vote or decision."[82]

In the Senate as in the House, speakers centered on the traffic in claims. The most outspoken was John P. Hale of New Hampshire, the first antislavery candidate to be elected to the Senate, unsuccessful Free Soil candidate for president in 1852, and now apparently at the end of his office as a senator. Hale put the blame for this commerce on professional intermediaries rather than on congressmen: "Our influence, our countenance, our affection, everything is bartered away and sold by these agents, who block up the Capitol and block up the avenues to the Departments," making Washington "a great fountain of filth." A sailor, he said, could not get his pay unless he paid an agent ten dollars for his services. Senator Hale did not say how he thought the bill, directed at officers of the government, would affect the business of the agents. His implication as to how the agents were able to operate successfully was clear. If, in the ancient metaphor of dirt, the capital was filthy, the agents could not be effective without the connivance of the congressmen. The bill passed the Senate without a record vote. Under the misleading title of "An Act to prevent Frauds upon the Treasury of the United States," it was signed by Fillmore and became law on February 26, 1853.[83]

Between the date of its enactment and the outbreak of the Civil War, no prosecutions are known to have occurred. In the midst of war and in response to many efforts to get rich by the war, Senator Lazarus Powell, a Union Democrat from Kentucky, sought on June 18, 1862, to introduce stronger legislation. His bill was followed by a report by the new secretary of War, Edward M. Stanton, that James Fowler Simmons, senator from Rhode Island, had "exercised his official influence" to procure a gun-manufacturing contract from the Army and Navy for C. D. Schubarth, Schubarth agreeing to pay him $50,000 as "compensation" for an order for 50,000 breechloading rifles. The Judiciary Committee on June 27 reported out Powell's bill, enlarged to include payments to procure office as well as contracts. Committee chairman Lyman Trumbull of Illinois declared that the report needed no discussion. It was a wish devoutly shared by his colleagues. Who was so rude as to desire to discuss the connection between congressmen and contracts? John Hale of New Hampshire, who had spoken so bluntly of claims agents in 1853 and who had been reelected in 1855, broke the silence to say that he had heard of "improper practices" by congressmen and although he could not prove them he did not doubt them, but that there was not "the slightest doubt on earth" that "members of the Cabinet have prostituted their places to the grossest favoritism for the purpose of benefitting their friends in the bestowal of contracts." This was true, he said, despite this being "the purest Administration that has existed since the days of Washington." Senator Hale was "indisposed to let Congress be made the scape goat to carry off all the sins of this Administration or any other." He mentioned no names although everyone must have thought of the War Department under Stanton's immediate predecessor, Secretary Simon Cameron. Senator Morton Wilkinson of Minnesota replied that he had not noticed the administration favoring "good straight-out Republicans." Senator Powell declared that he had heard of persons receiving "large sums of money" but they were not cabinet officers. No other senator had the appetite to compare the relative guilt of the cabinet and Congress. Senator Hale's traditional imagery and his references to sin and Old Testament scapegoating showed how self-destructive opposition to the bill would have been. Who was going to be against purity and for prostitution? The bill passed without more than a half hour of discussion and without a record vote. In the background, figuratively, were the guns of war as the bloody battle of the Seven Days went on.[84]

The House Judiciary Committee had minor amendments, and the House like the Senate avoided debate. Charles Wickliffe, a Union Whig from Kentucky, aged seventy-four, asked if the bill covered "presents," giving this case as one that should be covered: "An oily contractor comes here and he goes to an equally oily member to help him procure a contract. After he gets the contract, the contractor becomes generous and makes the member a present of a carriage and horses." The oil of the proverbial briber had now spilled over the corrupted official as well. John Bingham of Ohio, chairman of the Judiciary Committee, assured Wickliffe that the case fell within the bill. Again without opposition or a record vote, the House on July 11 passed the bill. Lincoln signed it into law on July 16, 1862.[85]

In its final form, the statute applied to "any member of Congress" and "any officer of the government of the United States" who took money, property, or other valuable consideration to procure "any contract, office, or place" in the government; to those who gave for such purpose; and to any member of Congress who took money, property, or other valuable consideration for "his attention, service, action, vote, or decision." A misdemeanor, the crime was punishable by a fine of $10,000, two years in the penitentiary, and, at the option of the president, the voiding of the contract. Meanwhile, on July 14, the Judiciary Committee had reported out a resolution for the expulsion of Senator Simmons. The session was almost over. No action was taken, and Simmons was allowed to resign on August 15 and return with his loot to his yarn manufacturing business in Rhode Island.[86]

Like its predecessor of 1853, the new statute was drawn broadly enough to encompass any offer to a congressman. Practical limitations on these laws, when it came to patronage dispensed by the Executive Branch, were evident from the moment of their enactment. The limitations were to be illustrated most vividly by the process that ended in the emancipation of the slaves.

The Thirteenth Amendment.   In March 1861 the Thirteenth Amendment to the American Constitution was adopted by the requisite votes of two-thirds of each House and sent to the states for ratification. The amendment provided that slavery, as a form of property, should be beyond any interference by the federal government. The amendment had been accepted by the Republican leadership, including the president-elect, Abraham Lincoln. It was a final attempt to persuade the South that its peculiar domestic institution would not be threatened by Republican rule. It was the offer of a gigantic sop in return for southern loyalty to the Union. It died when southern guns fired at Fort Sumter.[87]

The origin of a very different Thirteenth Amendment lay in a very different reciprocation, one cast in the mold of Israel's response to Yahweh. In July 1862 Abraham Lincoln broached the idea of emancipation to his closest associates in the Cabinet. In September a Confederate army led by Lee entered Maryland, threatening Pennsylvania and the capital; it drew back after the battle of Antietam. Five days later, on September 22, 1862, Lincoln informed the Cabinet that he had "made a vow, a covenant, that if God gave us the victory in the approaching battle (which had just been fought), he would consider it his duty to move forward in the cause of emancipation." The result of this bargain with God and the convergence of such mundane factors as the cultivation of European public opinion and the political pressure of Republican radicals was the Emancipation Proclamation, liberating the slaves in the states still in rebellion, and a commitment by Lincoln to their continuing freedom so great that nothing could make him the instrument of their reenslavement. To assure against any such drastic postwar move, and to free the slaves in the loyal border states, a constitutional amendment was necessary.[88]

In the spring of 1864 a new Thirteenth Amendment passed the Senate. It provided that slavery should "not exist within the United States" and empowered Congress to enforce this proposition. On June 15, 1864, the amendment was defeated in a House of Representatives that had 94 Republicans, 64 Democrats, and 25 Unionists from border slave states. The vote was 93 in favor, 65 against. The required two-thirds of those voting was 105; the proponents were 12 votes short; 25 congressmen did not vote at all; and of the Democrats in the House only 4 voted in favor of the amendment.[89]

The November 1864 elections reduced the Democrats in the House from 64 to 35, but the new Republican members would not take office until March 1865. The old Congress met in the traditional lame duck session that ran from December until March. Lincoln in his presidential message asked the House to pass the amendment, speaking of the will manifested in the past election to maintain the Union and placing passage of the amendment among the means to that end.[90] This speech was addressed especially to border state Unionists and northern Democrats, some of whom had to be won over if he was to succeed. Meanwhile he went to work to get the necessary votes.

According to the recollections, twenty-three years later, of John B. Alley, then aged 71, at the time of the Amendment a Republican congressman from Lynn, Massachusetts:

> Mr. Lincoln was a thorough and most adroit politician as well as statesman, and in politics always adopted the means to the end, fully believing that in vital issues, "success was a duty." In further illustration of this feeling and sentiment, I need only refer to his action and conduct in procuring the passage of the constitutional amendment abolishing slavery. It required a two-thirds vote of Congress to enable the amendments to the Constitution to be sent to the legislatures for ratification, and there were two votes lacking to make two-thirds, which, Mr. Lincoln said, "must be procured." Two members of the House were sent for and Mr. Lincoln said that those two must be procured. When asked, "How," he remarked: "I am President of the United States, clothed with immense power. The abolition of slavery by constitutional provision settles the fate, for all coming time, not only of the millions now in bondage, but unborn millions to come—a measure of such importance that *those two votes must be procured.* I leave it to you to determine how it shall be done; but remember that I am President of the United States clothed with great power, and I expect you to procure those votes." These gentlemen understood the significance of the remark. The votes were procured, the constitutional amendment was passed, and slavery was abolished forever. Some, I know, would criticize Mr. Lincoln's methods. But he was a thorough politician, and believed most fully in this case the consequences resulting from his action justified him in resorting to almost any means to procure for that down-trodden race such a boon.

Alley does not say he was one of two sent for by Lincoln to procure the two needed votes. He writes as an admirer of Lincoln, asserting him to have been "among the greatest, wisest, and best who have ever lived in any country." He leaves the impression that he has heard the story from one privy to the presidential conversation.[91]

According to the recollections, twenty-seven years after the event, of Albert Gallatin Riddle, a Republican congressman from Ohio, the task of securing the needed two-thirds was entrusted to Congressman James M. Ashley of Ohio. The Republicans were told in confidence that Ashley could report "the acquisition" of the needed Democrats. One Democrat wanted "a place" for his brother in New York; another was told that an election contest in the next Congress "would depend entirely on his vote on the impending thirteenth amendment"; a third was a lawyer representing a railroad in Pennsylvania threatened by legislation pending in the Senate before a committee headed by Charles Sumner. Riddle implies that these three were satisfied. From the point of view of the proponents, every hostile member who stayed away at voting time provided help: their absence reduced the number required to constitute two-thirds of those voting. On January 31, 1865, the lawyer and 7 other Democrats stayed away; 175 members voted and the amendment carried 119–56—a margin of two votes.[92]

John Nicolay and John Hay, the secretaries and later quasi-official biographers of Lincoln, identify the railroad in question as the Camden and Amboy and state that the railroad "interest" definitely offered to trade the votes or absence of "the New Jersey Democrats" if Sumner would postpone the bill. They also state, however, that Lincoln said, "I can do nothing with Mr. Sumner in these matters." Nicolay and Hay, adding no more about this apparently abortive effort, say generally that "it is not unlikely" that influences of "selfish interest, operating both for and against the amendment, were not entirely wanting."[93]

James Rhodes, the American historian, prepared his work with the assistance of Congressman Ashley's son. He writes, "Money could probably have been raised for an attempt to buy up the wavering members but it is doubtful whether any was used for this purpose." The Democrats, he continues, were "won over through the process of logrolling." The term implies trading, votes on one issue being exchanged for votes on another. Congressman George W. Julian, Republican of Indiana, is more mysterious, writing that success "depended upon certain negotiations the results of which were not fully assured, and the particulars of which never reached the public." An account attributed to Thaddeus Stevens, a Republican leader in the war Congress, is bluntest: "The greatest measure of the nineteenth century was passed by corruption, aided and abetted by the purest man in America."[94]

Did Lincoln corrupt Democratic congressmen to pass the amendment? Alley and Stevens, whose own integrity was not spotless, could be suspected of trying to pull Lincoln down to their own level. Julian, Rhodes, and Riddle have no obvious motive for denigrating the president. None of these five, it must be observed, have the authority of eyewitnesses. Each speaks from a position in which he could have heard reliable hearsay. The quotation from Stevens, although it sounds like him, is undocumented as to time and place. The others wrote long after the events. Allowing for bias, error in memory, and error in transmission, it is probable, but not certain, that the president did bargain to get the swing votes. These circumstances support this conclusion: The Camden and Amboy Railroad bill was not reported out by Senator Sumner. Nicolay and Hay, knowledgeable insiders with no motive to hurt Lincoln, concede that selfish influences were at work without specifying the president's full view of their use. Patronage was the regular instrument by which Lincoln encouraged his Republican followers in Congress.[95] The difference between patronage and a specific act of reciprocity for a specific vote may have seemed insubstantial.

Would a presidential promise to appoint a congressman to a government job have violated the bribery statute of 1853? The act covered any "bribe, present or reward" or "any other valuable thing whatever" given in exchange for a vote. Would staying away from a vote constitute "services" or "action" or "decision" so that a congressman bargaining for his absence violated the 1862 statute? Certainly in terms of the corruption feared by the founding fathers, the use of "the immense power" of the president was the chief danger foreseen and ineffectually provided against by Article I, section 6 of the Constitution. In terms of law as actually enforced, Lincoln's use of presidential patronage was not bribery. As in the case of Adams's arrangements with Clay, if his conduct was to be categorized as corrupt, it would have to be in terms of a moral standard whose practical enforcement would have been political.

If Lincoln had lived, if the Democratic-controlled House in 1874 had investigated the circumstances of the passage of the Thirteenth Amendment, it is possible that a price would have been exacted—in political terms and to the detriment of Lincoln's reputation—for what was done in January 1865. The investigation did not occur, Lincoln did not live, and his death, overshadowing everything, became a redemptive act sealing the Emancipation in a way his use of patronage could never have achieved.

First, there was in March 1865 the Second Inaugural Address, that masterpiece of scripturally based theology, in which Lincoln understood the war in terms of sin and reciprocation:

Fondly do we hope—fervently do we pray—that this mighty scourge of war may speedily pass away. Yet, if God wills that it continue, until all the wealth piled by the bond-man's two hundred and fifty years of unrequited toil shall be sunk, and until every drop of blood drawn by the lash shall be paid with another from the sword, as was said three thousand years ago, so still it must be said, "the judgments of the Lord are true and righteous altogether."

Declining to judge those with whom the country was at war, "lest we be judged," declaring his charity to all, Lincoln identified his own duty and that of his countrymen with that of the good ruler and the God of Israel: "to care for him who shall have borne the battle, and for his widow, and his orphan."[96]

Assassinated less than six weeks later, Lincoln died on Good Friday. The coincidence was irresistible to many, even extending to the treatment of the assassin, unknown to Lincoln, as a "Judas." In Carl Sandburg's summation, "Over and over again were the parallels drawn of Lincoln and Christ in blood of atonement dying for mankind."[97] By his death Lincoln legitimated the emancipation and redeemed the slaves already freed by the bargains of congressional politics.

Four-score and nine years after the inception of the Republic, the United States had in place statutes making reciprocation with lawmakers a criminal offense. The country had also had substantial experience of legislators made serviceable to specific interests on specific votes by means of loans, legal fees, or presidential patronage. No one had ever been punished for these practices. Was there any combination of circumstances which could lead Congress to apply its announced standard to itself?

16

Credit Mobilier

Washington, Jan. 25, 1868

H.S. McComb, Esq.:

DEAR SIR: Yours of the 23d is at hand, in which you say Senators Bayard & Fowler have written you in relation to their stock. I have spoken to Fowler, but not to Bayard. I have never been introduced to Bayard, but will see him soon. You say I must not put too much in one locality. I have assigned as far as I have gone to 4 from Mass., 1 from N.H., 1 Delaware, 1 Tenn., 1 Ohio, 2 Penn., 1 Ind., 1 Maine, & I have 3 to place, which I shall put where they will do most good to us. I am here on the spot, and can better judge where they should go. I think after this dividend is paid we should make our capital to 4,000,000, and distribute the new stock where it will protect us, let them have the stock at par, and profits made in the future; the 50 per cent. increase on the old stock I want for distribution here, and soon . . . a part of the purchasers here are poor, and want their bonds to sell to enable them to meet their payment on the stock in the C.M. I have told them what they would get as dividend, and they expect, I think, when the bonds the parties receive as the 80 per cent. dividend, we better give them the bonds—it will not am't to anything with us.

. . . Yours, truly,

OAKES AMES.

Washington, Jan. 30, 1868.

H.S. McComb:

DEAR SIR: Yours of the 28th is at hand, inclosing copy of letter from, or rather to, Mr. King. I don't fear any investigation here. What some of Durant's friends may do in N.Y. courts can't be counted upon with any certainty. You do not understand by your letter what I have done, & am to do with my sales of stock. You say none to N.Y. I have placed some with N.Y., or have agreed to. You must remember that it was nearly all placed as you saw on the list in N.Y., & there was but 6 or 8 m. for me to place. I could not give all the world all they might want out of that. You would not want me to offer less than 1,000 m. to any one. We allow Durant to place 58,000 to some 3 or 4 of his friends, or keep it himself.

I have used this where it will produce most good to us, I think. In view of King's letter and Washburne's move here, I go in for making our bond dividend in full. We can do it with perfect safety. I understand the opposition to it comes from Alley; he is on the finance com'ee, and can raise money easy if we come short, which I don't believe we shall, & if we do we can loan our bonds to the company, or loan them the money we get from the bonds. The contract calls for the division, & I say have it. When shall I see you in Washington?

Yours, truly,

OAKES AMES.

Washington, Feb. 22, 1868

H.S. McComb, Esq.:

DEAR SIR: Yours of the 21st is at hand; am glad to hear that you are getting along so well with Mr. West; hope you will bring it out all satisfactory, so that it will be so rich that we cannot help going into it. I return you the paper by mail that you ask for. You ask me if I will sell some of my U.P.R.R. stock. I will sell some of it at par C.M. of A. I don't care to sell. I hear that Mr. Bates offered his at $300, but I don't want Bates to sell out. I think Grimes may sell a part of his at $350. I want that $14,000 increase of the Credit Mobilier to sell here. We want more friends in this Congress, & if a man will look into the law, (& it is difficult to get them to do it unless they have an interest to do so,) he cannot help being convinced that we should not be interfered with. Hope to see you here or at N.Y. the 11th.
    Yours, truly,

OAKES AMES.[1]

The author of these letters, Oakes Ames, was a sixty-five-year-old New Englander, a native of North Easton in the southeastern part of Massachusetts, senior partner of the great shovel-making business of Oliver Ames and Sons, and for the past seven years a Republican member of Congress. The letters accurately convey his energy, his decisiveness, his sense of purpose, his focus on the concrete, his practicality. The recipient, H. S. McComb, was his associate in the construction of the Union Pacific Railroad. Ames's letters deal with his disposition of stock in the company doing the construction, the stock's value, and a method of paying for it. The references to states in his first letter are references to members of the Senate or the House from the states named.[2]

Compared to the plan of bribery set out in alleged letter of Epiphanius of Alexandria to the bishop of Constantinople, Oakes Ames's letters are sketchy; but the outline of a strategy is evident. Stock of the C. M.—the initials stand for the Credit Mobilier—is being "put" or "placed" with members of Congress. The stock is regarded as a scarce commodity, opportunity to obtain it as a privilege. The purpose of distributing it in Congress is to "do most good to us." Congress, as will be seen, had already passed the basic statutes by means by which the C. M. could be a profitable venture; this basic legislation was not being paid for by these distributions. But a danger for the C. M. management was that new statutes could be passed—a threat even if the constitutionality of disturbing an existing contract could be challenged. An even more significant danger was that the way the existing arrangements were actually working could be investigated by Congress. When a good thing depended on the good will of the government, it was important to cultivate congressmen. Described in the kindest terms, the strategy outlined by Ames was a strategy for this cultivation of friends in legislative office. The stock, in Ames's words, was to go "where it will protect us."

The Union Pacific Railroad, like the East India Company, was a hybrid of private investment and public credit. The idea of a transcontinental railroad had gathered momentum as a patriotic enterprise during the Civil War. The first congressional legislation creating the corporation and giving it federal assistance had been passed in 1862. In 1864 additional legislation had materially increased the government subsidy. It consisted principally in the loan by the United States of thirty-year government bonds to the corporation at the rate of so many thousand dollars in bonds per twenty completed miles, and the grant to the corporation of alternating sections of land on each side of the track in the amount of 12 million acres. The corporation could sell the bonds for cash and, although after thirty years it would have to repay the government, it was permitted to subordinate the United States to the holders of an equal amount of first mortgage bonds of the corporation. It could also use the land, prior to sale, as a way of selling bonds, the land being the security. Five directors, nominated by the president to a board of twenty, were expected to look out for the government.[3]

Despite these inducements, there was little interest by private investors in buying the stock of the Union Pacific. By the spring of 1865, only a little more than $300,000 had actually been paid in, and over $250,000 had been spent in lobbying to get the favorable legislation of 1864. To build the first twenty miles of track and so be eligible to receive the government bonus and to issue its own bonds, the corporation needed $440,000, and it needed additional capital for engineering surveys, legal expenses, interest, and administration. After building twenty miles, however, it was entitled to receive $20 \times \$16,500$ in government bonds or $330,000 and to issue an equal amount of its own mortgage bonds; if the governments sold at close to par and the company's own at not too far below par, the cash would be on hand to finance the next twenty miles, and so on. Moreover, the government subsidy was to increase as the road entered the mountains, reaching $48,000 of bonds per mile. If the way through the Rocky Mountains turned out to be easier than was believed in 1864, the spread between the cost of construction and the cash the corporation was realizing through the bonds would be very large. What was needed to tempt capital was knowledge that there was an easier way through the Rockies and a means of getting at the cash that could be generated.[4]

Sophisticated capitalists shrank from risking money in an unbuilt railroad. A method used by several roads had been for the stockholders to form a construction company which was expected to build the road at a substantial profit. The method involved no unfairness to the stockholders if they all consented to deal with themselves in this fashion and held the same proportion of stock in the construction company as they did in the railroad. The method did subject the bondholders and other creditors to new risks, because the stockholders were given an incentive to drain the railroad of cash. Contracts between the construction company and the railroad could tilt heavily in favor of the construction company. The management of both companies being substantially the same and the stockholders identical, only the creditors of the railroad could complain. Applied to the Union Pacific, the method meant that the United States, committed by the legislation of 1864 to being a subordinated, long-term creditor of the road, was to run the risk of the railroad being bankrupt when the time came to pay the government. The method was adopted, made sweeter for the capitalists by the discovery of the Evans Pass in late 1866, affording easy access for the track through the Rockies.[5]

The vehicle for the transformation of the cash of the Union Pacific into realized profits for the promoters was a company inauspiciously named "The Pennsylvania Fiscal Agency." With a flair bordering on the flamboyant the promoters decided in 1864 to change the name to "The Credit Mobilier of America." The name, if the French words meant anything, suggested a lending association based on movables, that is, on non-real estate; it conveyed nothing of the company's purpose.[6] The company bought all the outstanding stock of the Union Pacific. The stock was canceled, and new shares of the Union Pacific were distributed as a dividend to the stockholders of the Credit Mobilier, so that the stockholders of both corporations were the same in the same proportions. The Credit Mobilier was eventually capitalized for $3,750,000 and began the construction of the railroad. By November 1866, 246 miles had been built. A disagreement then developed between two factions of stockholders—those who had been among the first to invest, largely a New York group, headed by Thomas Durant, and those who had come in in 1865, largely Massachusetts and Rhode Island men, headed by Oakes Ames and his brother Oliver. The standoff between these factions led to a new arrangement, consisting of a trust with seven trustees, three per faction, one neutral. The trustees had as their beneficiaries the stockholders of the Credit Mobilier. Their task was to construct the railroad. They also held in a voting trust a majority of the shares of the Union Pacific and elected its directors. Controlling the railroad, they set the terms on which they themselves would finish the road, and having made the appropriate contracts, they completed the bulk of the building.[7]

The spirit in which the cost of construction was determined was instructive. The U.P.'s chief engineer was Peter Dey, former mayor of Iowa City, and an old hand at the game of politics and railroading which had been played for a decade in Iowa, a person whose experience made him unlikely to be shocked. But when the first 247 miles of road were contracted for at $50,000 a mile, he remonstrated that $20,000 was the right figure and resigned in protest. "No man," he wrote Grenville Dodge, "can call $50,000 per mile for a road up the Platte Valley anything else but a big swindle—and thus it must stand for-ever."[8]

As first set up, the construction work done at the $50,000 per mile was to be by Hub Hoxie, the chairman of the Republican party in Iowa. By prearrangement, no doubt, Hoxie was given 100 shares of U.P. stock and $5,000 in return for which he assigned the contract to the C.M.[9]

The Credit Mobilier and later the trustees were paid by the Union Pacific in cash and in its first mortgage bonds and stock. In general these were distributed to the C.M. stockholders or beneficiaries, who could choose to keep the securities or to sell them at the market price if they did not depress the market by selling too many immediately. Those who chose to keep them, of course, made a decision to invest in the railroad, taking a risk separate from the risk run as builders. If the securities were valued at their market price when received—87 for the bonds and 10 to 30 for the stock—the beneficiaries by the time the road was completed in August 1869 had made a handsome profit.[10]

The exact profit was never disclosed. A congressional committee put it at $23,366,319, an exaggeration. The promoters preferred to state it as a percentage of cost. Thus, for example, on "the Oakes Ames contract," one of several construction contracts, Oakes Ames said the cost was $47,000,000 and the profit 15 percent or $7,000,000. The same method of calculation yields a profit of about $9,000,000 on a total construction cost estimated by Ames to be about $60,000,000. This method, however, has one glaring deficiency. The usual way of calculating a rate of return on an investment is to determine the rate on the money one has at risk. The promoters never had anything like $47,000,000 or $60,000,000 at risk; they were using mostly the bondholders' money.

The method is defective, and the percentage chosen, 15 percent, is misleading. Oakes Ames himself put the profit at 300 percent on the total capital of the Credit Mobilier. That capital was $3,750,000, and 300 percent would have been a profit of $11,250,000. This method is fairer in reflecting the return on the promoters' money. It is still, however, on the low side. Ames was, after all, not disposed to boast of the profits before Congress. The bookkeeping of the Union Pacific was—one thinks of Hastings and Krishna Kanta Nandi—"disgraceful." An unbiased modern investigator has calculated the profit at between $13,000,000 and $16,500,000. It has also been estimated that the average amount invested in the Credit Mobilier over five years was $2,700,000. The percentage of return therefore was a maximum of 600 percent, or 120 percent per annum. The significance of these magnitudes is best grasped by comparison. Government securities in the same period paid 6.02 percent. For some individual stockholders, like the favored congressmen who were allowed to pay for their stock out of dividends, there was no risk at all.[11]

The profits of the promoters do not include what was made on subcontracts. The promoters who arranged to contract with themselves when they spoke for the railroad had the same willingness to contract with themselves when they spoke as the Credit Mobilier; and in making sub-contracts, the stockholders of the C.M. and the sub were not always identical. Here fraud against the C.M. could be committed. The contract to provide coal for the railroad was with a company owned in part by Oakes Ames and his brother Oliver; the contract was approved by the Ames-dominated executive committee and signed by Oliver as president; it was later held fraudulent by a unanimous Supreme Court.[12]

The profits made by the promoters might have excited envy or admiration but not a congressional investigation were it not for the failure to convince one promoter, McComb, that he had been fairly treated in the allotment of Credit Mobilier stock. He sued Oakes Ames. The conversation that ensued is reported differently by the litigants: According to McComb, he was asked by Ames's counsel to return Ames's letters (those with which this chapter began). Instead, McComb suggested they reach an agreement. "Mr. Ames replied, exhibiting some petulance of feeling, 'You can publish any letters you have from me; everybody knows that members of Congress are bribed, and everybody does it.'" According to Ames, "the price of secrecy offered was the compromising with McComb." He did not do so because "I knew I had done or said nothing that meant anything wrong to a fair mind. The remark he puts in my mouth, viz. that all members of Congress are bribed, etc. is entirely untrue. I said nothing of the kind to him."[13]

The failure to agree led McComb to making the letters available to Charles Dana of the New York *Sun*, a Democratic organ. It published them on September 4, 1872, with the headline,

THE KING OF FRAUDS:
How the Crédit Mobilier Bought
Its Way into Congress

The time was the middle of a presidential campaign, Grant against Greeley, and the honesty of the Republican administration was a major issue. The *Sun*'s French accent mark on Credit was the foreign spice the paper added to an already spicy story, "the most damaging exhibition of official and private villainy and corruption," the *Sun* said, "ever laid bare to the gaze of the world." The names of prominent Republicans—the vice-president, Schuyler Colfax; the candidate for vice-president, Henry Wilson; the speaker of the House, James G. Blaine; the chairman of the House Appropriations Committee, James A. Garfield—ornamented the account. "All of them," the opening paragraph ran, "are proven, by irrefutable evidence, to have been bribed."[14]

SECRET CONFERENCE BARED. POWERFUL
REPUBLICANS BACKED INVESTIGATION

This headline, like subsequent headings in this chapter, is imaginary, written to convey with the boldness and inexactitude of headlines the main points in the unfolding story. It is, as will appear, derivable from the published diary of Garfield, who wrote on September 9, "I find my own name dragged into some story which I do not understand but see only referred to in the newspapers." Ten days later he observed, "The disruption of party organizations leaves the mere politician to fall back on personal scandal. The Credit Mobilier story started by the N.Y. *Sun* is one of the vilest and boldest pieces of rascality in the way of wicked journalism I have ever seen. I think this independent of the fact that my own name is unjustly involved in the lie." At this point, Garfield, running for reelection himself in Ohio, took counsel with an old friend and lawyer, his co-religionist in the Disciples of Christ, Jeremiah Sullivan Black.[15]

Black wrote him on September 29, 1872, advising him not to attempt to defend Ames: "You have, I believe, no idea of what it is like. It will turn out to be the most enormous fraud that has ever been perpetrated." Black went on to reconstruct what he said Garfield had told him of the matter in 1870 although the reconstruction has more the ring of what Black thought would clear Garfield than of an effort to recall an actual conversation:

> You regarded O.A. as a perfectly upright man—an example of solid integrity—had no suspicion that he had private interests to take care of as a member of Congress, much less that he was a ring-leader in any fraud. . . . During all this time you were not informed & did not suspect that the Cred. Mob. was connected with the U.P.R.R. Co. or that either of those companies was committing any wrong against the U.S. or any body else. . . . It relieves you entirely from every imputation w'h A's statement unexplained might cast upon you. It shows that you were not the instrument of his corruption, but the victim of his deception. O.A. did undoubtedly intend to corrupt the M.C.s to whom he gave the stock.[16]

The advice of Judge Black, as Garfield customarily called him, came from a man of exceptional experience and exceptional knowledge about the Credit Mobilier. A very prominent Democrat, once chief justice of the Supreme Court of Pennsylvania, Buchanan's attorney-general and secretary of State in the last months of his administration, Black had been among the counsel setting up the Credit Mobilier. "I believe we did it under the advice of Jerry Black," Oakes Ames was to tell him later to his face. When Ames had wanted to secure the appointment of his friend ex-Governor John Andrew as a government director, he had thought of Black as "the best channel" to the Johnson administration. But then Black became McComb's lawyer in the suit against Ames; and Black participated in the negotiations—blackmail in Ames's view—over the return of the letters and the settlement of the suit. Accepting his counsel, Garfield, a Republican leader, took the advice of a veteran Democrat and an agent of McComb.[17]

The basic McComb charge that Ames had distributed C.M. stock for the purpose of corrupting Congress had been contained in McComb's complaint in his suit begun in 1868. The exploitative relation of the Credit

Mobilier to the Union Pacific had been set out in a complaint in another suit, that of the speculator Jim Fisk against the U.P. in 1869. In the spring of 1869 the Credit Mobilier had been denounced in the Senate by Senators Stewart and Nye, both from Nevada and both friends of the U.P.'s Western rival, the Central Pacific. Stewart said he had heard that "leading members of Congress" had been "the recipients of enormous dividends" from the U.P. or C.M. and "for that very reason the thing would never be investigated."[18] His speech "excited a little curiosity," and Congress passed a joint resolution directing the attorney-general to investigate the legality of the Union Pacific's dividends. Ebenezer Hoar, Grant's upright attorney-general, did not go below the surface; nothing resulted from Congress's request.[19] The involvement of Black and Garfield in the business was critical in moving the Credit Mobilier affair from the realm of rumor and oratory to the arena of active congressional inquisition.

Grant won the election of 1872, and the Republicans retained control of Congress. The lame duck congressional session, December 2, 1872 to March 3, 1873, opened, the members being those elected to the Forty-Second Congress in 1870. Right after the election Black and Garfield discussed the desirability of an investigation by the House of Representatives, and Black wrote Speaker James G. Blaine about it. On December 1, 1872, Garfield's diary records, "Called on Speaker Blaine and urged the importance of requiring an investigation into the Credit Mobilier scandal and agreed to call a democrat to the Chair and ourselves introduce the resolution. Judge Black called in the evening and staid three hours."[20] The next day, immediately after the House had formally opened the session, "the Speaker introduced the Credit Mobilier resolution." It provided for a committee of five headed by Luke Poland, a former judge from Vermont, "to investigate whether any member of this House was bribed by Oakes Ames, or any other person or corporation, in any matter touching his legislative duty."[21] Judge Poland's committee was to have power to summon witnesses and documents and to employ a stenographer. The resolution passed easily on a voice vote. Black, Garfield, and Blaine had set in motion a legislative antidote or complement to the scandal generated by the *Sun*. In retrospect it was a mistake for Garfield and for Blaine.

SPEAKER EXONERATED.
BLAINE CLEARS SELF

The Speaker appeared before the committee on December 12, its first witness. He testified that Ames had offered to sell him Credit Mobilier stock in the spring of 1868, and he had not been interested in taking it. "I beg, however, to say in justice to Mr. Ames, but more especially in justice to myself, that it never once occurred to me that he was attempting to bribe me, or in any way influence my vote or action as a Representative." Blaine further swore, "Nor did I ever receive, either directly or indirectly, a single cent derived in any manner or shape from the Credit Mobilier or from the Union Pacific Railroad Company."[22]

So testified James Gillespie Blaine, Pennsylvania-born emigré to

Augusta, Maine; newspaper man; speaker of the Maine House; Republican congressman since 1863 and since 1869 speaker of the House of Representatives; a man to be the leading candidate for the Republican nomination for president in 1876, to be secretary of state in 1881 and 1887–1892, and to be the Republican presidential candidate in 1884; a man whose dealings with the Union Pacific Railroad were to affect the rest of his political life.

VICE-PRESIDENT CLEARED.

ONLY WIFE HELD STOCK

Henry Wilson, vice-president-elect, a senator from Massachusetts in 1867, appeared before the committee. He had boarded at the same house as Ames and often ate at the same table. He had bought 7 percent bonds of two other railroads from him. In 1865 a surprise party had been given him and his wife on their twenty-fifth wedding anniversary. "Before the company separated, a package was presented to my wife, I think by Governor Claflin, which was found to contain $3,800, with a letter and list of subscribers, containing a request that she would accept it as a gift to herself. . . . Mr. Ames was down for $200." Wilson consulted Ames about investing the $3,800 in more railroad bonds. Ames said there was

> stock that he believed would be of more value, which he said was the stock of the Credit Mobilier. . . . I told Mr. Ames that I believed much of the money put into the Pacific Railroad would be lost. . . . Mr. Ames said that he would guarantee the stock and that it should pay ten percent on condition that he should have one half of the excess if any. . . . Before accepting Mr. Ames's offer, I asked him if any more legislation for the Pacific Railroad would be required, and he assured me that there would not be . . . My position was a peculiar one. Having learned in early life that a poor man cannot do what a rich man can, and that a lawyer can do what an unprofessional man cannot do, I made up my mind, when I came here, that I would purchase no property that could be affected by legislation . . . . I came into the Senate from a mechanic's shop. I had a home that cost me about $4,000. I was doing a small business, and soon found that I must leave the Senate or abandon it. I closed my business, paid my debts, gave my wife a deed of my house, and had less than $1,000 left, with no profession, no capital, no business, no partnership. . . . [In 1867] I was not worth a thousand dollars.[23]

Wilson invested $2,000 of his wife's gift with Ames to buy the stock Ames had recommended. No stock was actually delivered. When Wilson heard of disputes among the managers of the Credit Mobilier and of the Union Pacific he asked "whether legislation would not grow out of these controversies." He then told Ames that he "should regard the transaction as incomplete." He made a settlement, in which Ames returned the $2,000 and Wilson "allowed to" Ames the dividends to that date, amounting to $814. He then made up to his wife from his own pocket the $814. "I am therefore $814 poorer and shall be till I die." As to his own view of the matter, "I did not know or suspect that there was anything wrong in the transaction. . . . In the transaction with Mr. Ames, I have done nothing which I did not feel that, as a member of Congress and a man, I had a perfect right to do; nothing to be palliated or excused; nothing I am called upon to apologize for to my fellow-men or my country; nothing I must take into my closet and ask God's forgiveness for."[24]

So testified Henry Wilson whose story until then had been a model of the Horatio Alger kind. He had begun life in New Hampshire as an indentured farm laborer—from the age of ten to the age of twenty-one he labored without receiving any wages in cash. At twenty-one he had changed his name from Jeremiah Colbath to Henry Wilson and began anew in Massachusetts as a shoemaker. By 1848 he was editor of the Boston *Republican*. He entered the Massachusetts legislature and by 1851 was president of its Senate. In 1855 he became a United States senator from Massachusetts. During the Civil War he was chairman of the Military Affairs Committee of the Senate. Grant's running-mate in 1872, now vice-president-elect of the United States, he appeared to be a living example of the "poor but honest" boy who by his own industry had risen from poverty to high office.[25]

From the memorandum book of Oakes Ames offered in evidence to the committee:

	Henry Wilson	
Rec'd of him	$1,000	
two bonds 1,600		
Less 3 pr cent	1,552	
Cash	70	
	2,622	
p'd Cash and Int'st		1,548
		1,074
2,000 Credit		
2,000 U.P. stock		

According to this statement, Ames had invested not $2,000 but $2,622 for Wilson; the money had come not from his wife's cash gift but in part from bonds; the investment was held not in the name of Mrs. Wilson but in Wilson's; the return was not $814 but $1548; and Ames had held and still held stock of $2,000 par value of the Credit Mobilier and stock of $2,000 par value of the Union Pacific in trust for Wilson.[26]

There was no suggestion by anyone that Ames falsified his book. The discrepancies between it and Wilson's story were blatant. The committee did not ask for an explanation. Wilson was technically a member of the Senate until his inauguration on March 4; the Senate took his tale at face value; and no one challenged the propriety of his taking office as vice-president.

DARTMOUTH PROFESSOR TO BE EXPELLED FROM SENATE: PATTERSON LIED, REPORT SAYS

James W. Patterson, senator from New Hampshire, testified that he "had no transactions with the Union Pacific Railroad, or with Mr. Ames, which, in my judgment call for investigation, or which any respectable business man would think of criticising." Between the summer of 1869 and 1871 he had bought for cash 300 shares of Union Pacific stock and some bonds from Ames at the market price and sold them through a friend in New York at a fair profit. He had never bought "one penney's worth of stock of the Credit Mobilier."[27]

From the memorandum book of Ames:

1868

Friday, February, 14

Paid J. W. Patterson for 2400 $ bonds of Union Pacific R.R. Co. as

dividend, less 3 pr ct.	2,328
Less interest paid	105
P'd cash	2,223
Per receipt.	
Rec'd of J. W. Patterson	
Cash and Interest	3,105.00
Rec'd for 3 Bonds	2,328
	5,433.00
Feb'y 14 to Cash	2,328
	3,105.00

3,000 U.P. stock
3,000 C.M.A.

According to this statement, contrary to Patterson's testimony, Ames had held $3,000 worth of Union Pacific and $3,000 of Credit Mobilier of America stock for him and Ames was the purchaser of his Union Pacific bonds. The account had a double X drawn through it which, according to Ames, showed the account had been settled by his paying Patterson. Ames said he had paid by drawing checks on the House sergeant-at-arms, who offered banking service as a convenience to members. One such check for $1,800 drawn in June 1868 was produced in evidence. It had been endorsed to bearer. Ames identified the payment as a cash dividend on Credit Mobilier stock. He also furnished the committee with a receipt dated February 14, 1868, signed by Patterson. It read, "Received of Oakes Ames $2,328, for three bonds of Union Pacific Railroad Company sold for me, being a dividend of 80 per cent in bonds on the stock of the Credit Mobilier of America, held by him as trustee on my account."[28]

The House committee referred Patterson's case to the Senate. On Patterson's own motion a special committee headed by Justin Morrill of Vermont looked into his case and that of several other members of the Senate. Patterson declared that he had a right to buy the stock and that errors in his testimony before the House had been unintentional. The character of congressmen, he said, must be "exceptionally exalted and pure" when ownership of a few shares of Credit Mobilier stock "so horrifies their colleagues." If Congress really wanted to "cut up by the roots all corruption," it would ban lobbying save by a body of parliamentary solicitors, subject to congressional discipline. As it was, "What a wild rage of self-destruction and of self-dishonor has during those months occupied the halls of Congress . . . all over $16,000 worth of Credit Mobilier stock."[29]

So complained James Patterson, like Henry Wilson a self-made native of New Hampshire. A farm worker and mill laborer, he had gone to Dartmouth and then studied theology at Yale. At the age of thirty-one he had become professor of mathematics at Dartmouth, later enlarging his academic field to include astronomy and meteorology. He had been elected as a Republican to the House in 1863, to the Senate in 1866. He had already been defeated for reelection when Morrill's committee filed its report at the end of the short session in March 1873. His complaints came as he contemplated the committee's conclusions. It found, first, that Patterson knew the "object of Ames in thus dealing with him"; and second, that Patterson had engaged in "a suppression of material facts" and a denial of others "which must have been known to him." It recommended his expulsion from the Senate.[30]

As a lame duck, without strong party connections, Patterson was very vulnerable. But his weakness had one advantage for him. He was not returning to the Senate and the session was over. No action of any kind was taken. Nonetheless, Patterson's public career was temporarily blighted. He was not reappointed at Dartmouth. He did become a state legislator. Eventually in 1881, he became superintendent of public instruction for the state of New Hampshire. In 1893, aged seventy, he was again appointed to the Dartmouth faculty, as professor of rhetoric and oratory, "a measure of vindication which he did not live to enjoy fully."[31]

VICE PRESIDENT GIFTED BY U.S. PRINTER:
CRACKLING BILLS AT THE BREAKFAST TABLE

Schuyler Colfax, vice-president of the United States in Grant's first term, testified that Ames "never paid me a dollar, or the value of a dollar, on any account whatever. . . . I state explicitly that no one ever gave, or offered to give me, any shares of stock in the Credit Mobilier, or the Union Pacific Railroad. I have never received, nor had tendered to me, any dividends in cash, stock, or bonds, accruing upon any stock in either of said organizations."[32]

From the memorandum book of Oakes Ames for 1868:

Colfax:

20 shares Credit M. cost	2,000.00
7 mos. 10 days' int'st	86.72
	2,086.72
Less 80 pr. ct. bds at 97	1,552.00
Paid March 5	534.72
2,000 U.P. stock	
2,000 C.M. stock	

According to this statement, Ames held for Colfax $2,000 par value of both the Union Pacific and Credit Mobilier, and had received $1,552 in dividends which were applied to Colfax's C.M. purchase, and Colfax had paid Ames on March 5, 1868, the balance of $534.72. A further entry showed a payment to Colfax on June 19, 1868, of $1,200. Ames testified that this was by a check drawn on the sergeant at arms. The sergeant-at-arms recalled a check made out to "S.C. or bearer" for $1,200. Records of the First National Bank of Washington showed that Colfax deposited $1,200 on June 22, 1868.[33]

Colfax, testifying to rebut Ames, concentrated on the $1,200. "Difficult as it is to recall all the transactions of five years of a public man's life, I will state to the committee where all the money came from deposited on June 22, 1868, and will add that it was the month immediately succeeding my nomination for the office I now hold." The total deposit was $1,968.63. Three innocent checks amounted to $768.63, leaving the $1,200 which had been deposited in cash. "Of the deposit of bills, two hundred dollars, I am positive, were paid me by my step-father, Mr. Matthews, on account of a debt which he owed me." Matthews had wanted to buy a Steinway piano for his daughter, and Colfax had advanced $566; the $200 was a partial repayment.[34]

That left $1,000 to be accounted for. Colfax's account continued: "About the time of this payment, and near as I can fix the date, about the middle of the month of June, and very soon after the payment by Mr. Matthews, I was opening my letter-mail at the breakfast-table, in accordance with my usual custom, and found an envelope within another envelope postmarked New York. . . . Enclosed in this letter was a greenback or national bank bill of $1,000." The letter was from one George F. Nesbitt congratulating Colfax on his nomination as vice-president and enclosing the money to aid in his election. Nesbitt said the contribution was to be kept secret, but Colfax could not refrain from passing the bill around the table. Those present at this scene were his mother, now deceased; his half-sister who now lived "in a distant Territory beyond the Rocky Mountains," but who came to Washington from Utah to testify that she could not positively say she saw the bill ("I knew of it, and I think I must have seen it"); and his stepfather, Matthews, a clerk in the House, who fully supported his story. As Matthews recalled the occasion, Colfax's mother had said, "Read the letter, Schuyler." Matthews and his wife spoke of the $1,000 bill "a great many times . . . We talked about it frequently."[35]

Nesbitt himself was dead, and his letter had not survived. He was described by Colfax as "a gentleman in New York in the stationery business, originally a printer." On further probing by the committee, Colfax produced other letters from Nesbitt. These contained a check of $1,000 for "personal expenses" in April 1868, a check of $1,000 for campaign expenses in July 1868, and the promise of another $1,000 "for your use" in November. According to Colfax he had received $4,000 in all from Nesbitt.[36]

Oakes Ames was then permitted to cross-examine Colfax:

Q.:   Was not this Mr. Nesbitt a contractor with the Post-Office Department for furnishing envelopes?

A.:   So I understand.

Q.:   For four or five years, while you were chairman of the Post-Office Committee?

A.:   I have no recollection of it; I had no connection with it. It was a contract given to the lowest bidder. . . .

Q.:   It seems that this man always got the contract every year, whether he was the highest or lowest bidder

A.:   That I know nothing about.

Q.:   So I am informed.

Oakes Ames pressed Colfax as to why Nesbitt had sent the money in cash in June when he had sent the contributions in April and July by check. He also asked, "Can you account for so much being said about that thousand dollars when the other three thousand dollars excited no attention at all?"

A.:   When I opened my mail at the breakfast-table and saw this one thousand dollar bill I was very much surprised. It was a bill which had evidently been somewhat worn, because I remember it had none of the crispness of a new bill; the rattle was all out of it. I held it up, and we talked of it.

Q.:   It made a rattling sensation at the breakfast-table which the checks did not make.

A.:   It lacked the rattling sensation.

Oakes Ames suggested that Nesbitt's gifts "may have been something as bad as Credit Mobilier stock." Colfax answered, "The only favor he ever asked me was to get tickets for his family to see the inauguration." Ames: "He must have been a singular man." Colfax: "He was a very large-hearted man." Ames: "No doubt of it."[37]

The committee had stumbled on to a matter not within its jurisdiction, and Colfax himself, for that matter, as vice-president was beyond its jurisdiction. At thirteen his family had moved to St. Joseph County, Indiana, from New York and at eighteen his stepfather (the later House clerk and corroborating witness) had appointed him deputy county auditor. At twenty-two he had bought the South Bend newspaper. In 1855 he went to Congress as one of the new Republican members. From 1863 to 1869 he was the speaker of the House. His election at forty-five as vice-president turned out to be the climax of a career that turned downward with his defeat by Henry Wilson for the vice-presidential nomination in 1872 and was "ruined" by the Credit Mobilier, the gifts of Mr. Nesbitt, and the story he told the committee. He became "Smiler" Colfax to the press, the incarnation of insincerity. *Frank Leslie's Illustrated Magazine* ran an editorial entitled "The Pious Vice Presidents—The Twin Pecksniffs," paralleling Colfax and Wilson as hypocrites; it finished Colfax off with a page-length cartoon showing him declaring, "I am an honest man. If Nesbitt were here, he'd say so. I never took anything that wasn't given to me."[38] W. Colfax St. and E. Colfax St. in South Bend still perpetuate his name.

GENERAL MADE BUCKS TOO.
"A LITTLE MEMORANDUM" BY J.A.G.

Of all the congressmen brushed by the Credit Mobilier affair, James Abram Garfield affords the best evidence of what the accusation and the involvement meant. Public testimony has to be used where Blaine, Wilson, Patterson, and Colfax are concerned. Garfield's diary—far as it is from being Pepysian—offers a more interior view. The day he testified he recorded, "I am too proud to confess to any but my most intimate friends how deeply this whole matter has grieved me. While I did nothing in regard to it that can be construed into any act even of impropriety much less than corruption, I have still said from the start that the shadow of the cursed thing would cling to my name for many years. I believe my statement was regarded as clear and conclusive." The shadow of the Credit Mobilier was with him almost to his death.[39]

Accompanied by Judge Black, who was permitted to feed him leading questions, Garfield testified that Ames had offered him $1,000 worth of stock at par in the Credit Mobilier in 1868 and that he declined because of the controversy he heard was going on with the Union Pacific; that he did not know the purpose of the Credit Mobilier was to build the railroad; and that Ames never attempted to influence his legislative action. He admitted borrowing $300 from Ames during the congressional session of 1868.[40]

From the memorandum book of Oakes Ames:

	J.A.G.	DR.
1868	To 10 shares stock Credit Mobilier of A	$1,000.00
	Interest	47.00
June 19	To cash	329.00
		1,376.00
1868	By dividend bonds, Union Pacific Railroad	
	$1,000 at 80 per cent. less 3 per cent	776.00
June 17	By dividend collected for your account	600.00
		1,376.00

In other words, the book had Garfield down for ten shares of C.M. stock, which had resulted in dividends to his account of $1,376. Subtracting $1,000 as the cost of the stock and $47 as interest, Ames owed him $329.

Ames testified that he had never delivered the stock to Garfield, that it had been paid for, as the account indicated, by the bond and cash dividends, and that he had paid the balance of $329 to Garfield by a check drawn on the sergeant-at-arms and made out to bearer. His records, whose sober matter-of-factness challenged all denial, conclusively refuted Garfield's story.[41]

Garfield to his diary: "He is evidently determined to drag down as many men with him as possible. How far he will be successful it remains to be seen. But in the present condition of the public mind, he will probably succeed in throwing a cloud over the good name of many people. He seems to me as bad as a man can well be."[42] A week later Ames testified that Garfield had "never asked me to lend him any money. . . . I did not know that he was short. . . . I never loaned him any." In three or four recent conversations Garfield had asked him to treat their transaction as a loan which Garfield had repaid. Ames had refused: "I told him that he knew very well it was a dividend. In one conversation he admitted it, and said, as near I can remember, that there was $2,400 due him in stock and bonds. He made a little memorandum of $1,000 and $1,400, and as I recollect, said there was $1,000 of Union Pacific Railroad stock, $1,000 of Credit Mobilier stock, and $400 of stock or bonds, I do not recollect which." Ames produced Garfield's memo which had these figures but no names. He said, "It was made in my room; I cannot remember the date. It was since this investigation commenced. . . . He felt very bad, was in great distress, and hardly knew what he did say."

Q.:   Did he make any request to you to make no statement in reference to it?

A.:   I am not positive about that.

Q.:   What is your best recollection in reference to it?

A.:   My impression is that he wanted to say as little about it as he could, and to get off as easily as he could.[43]

A friend, a physician, found Garfield "thoroughly demoralized," his condition "pitiful." He did not want to go back before the committee and explain why his testimony differed so from Ames's. A powerful congressman—the indications are it was Henry Dawes of Pittsfield, Massachusetts, chairman of the Ways and Means Committee—"induced Judge Poland not to recall him to the stand."[44]

Garfield was reassured by Judge Black that nothing in the case would "ultimately injure" him, but he remained apprehensive. For his benefit Black wrote the speaker of the House a letter asserting that Garfield's integrity "depended on whether he acted with his eyes open" and asserting that he had not known the purpose of the Credit Mobilier. It was the defense Black had outlined to Garfield when the scandal first broke in 1872. It bore no relation to Garfield's story to the committee that he had never bought any Credit Mobilier.[45]

In the presidential election campaign of 1880, when Garfield was the candidate of the Republicans, Black broke with him and, in support of General Hancock, the Democratic candidate, disclosed to the New York *Sun* why Garfield had not told the story Black had prepared: "the party would not let him take it. The accusation struck at the highest heads in the House and Senate. They had but one answer, and that was a positive denial that any stock had ever been taken by them. General Garfield, for the benefit of others, united in making this defense." Black's disclosure was treachery to a friend. It moved John Hay to advise Garfield bluntly to break with "the infamous old blackguard," and he did. Black's disclosure also had the ring of truth. When Garfield had helped get the investigation started he had never expected to be in the dock. When he saw himself there, or almost there, he apparently decided to tell the story he did. The party—at least the leaders of the party in the House—then stuck together.[46]

When the committee reported, it accepted Ames's account of his dealings with Garfield. Garfield had agreed to take Credit Mobilier stock and Garfield had received a cash dividend of $329. Nonetheless the committee offered no censure of Garfield for his testimony, and it adopted Judge Black's view that Garfield and a number of other congressmen were innocent because they had been unaware of the purposes and connections of the Credit Mobilier. Subsequent debate in the House focused on Ames. But an effort was made to censure Garfield and the others, and Garfield was nervous enough about the possibilities to abandon a case in the Supreme Court rather than leave the House. Yet the attempt against him was an anticlimactic fizzle. Garfield—a powerful speaker who liked to speak—kept his head low, contributed nothing to the debate, and was safe. When further inquiry was suggested, he rose only to say that such an "inquisition" could not "do more than to throw a shadow over men who now stand acquitted." The shadow was, however, already there.[47]

General Garfield, as he was known both publicly and privately, was, at the age of forty-two, a veteran of poverty, war, and politics. Like Wilson, Patterson, and Colfax he was an all-American success story. Poor boy from Ohio, graduate of Williams College, class of '56, self-taught lawyer, Ohio state senator in 1859, raiser of a regiment in 1861 and its colonel, eventually chief of staff at Chickamauga and finally a major-general, a congressman since 1863, chairman of the Military Affairs Committee when he got the stock, chairman of the Appropriations Committee since 1871, Garfield was a power in the House.[48] Yet he had by no means been single-minded in the pursuit of the power he held. His formation had been highly religious as one of the Campbellite brethren or Disciples of Christ. His skill in speaking had been developed as a preacher. He had once labored to translate for himself *The Imitation of Christ*, that *"aureum libellum,"* and wished that his soul was "golden too." The intense religious preoccupations of his twenties had faded, but he was still devout, a loving husband and father, a thoroughly respectable man. Vulnerable to temptations both of a financial and a sexual kind and unwilling to acknowledge their force,

Garfield never admitted to his diary that he had sinned or erred in the business of the Credit Mobilier. Even in the diary he referred to the attempt to censure him in the House as "the attempt to censure Kelley and Hooper."[49]

"I confess," began the journal entry on the day of his dishonest testimony, but the confession was ambiguous, Garfield spoke of how deeply he had been grieved: he viewed himself as victim. The Credit Mobilier was a "woe" visited on him from without. The same, for him strangely passive, note was struck when he reviewed the year at its end. It had been "the stormiest year of my life. . . . I have climbed to the heighth where the wind blows furiously and cold. I now look back to the peace and quiet of other years with a sadness that hardly becomes a man of forty-two years. I can do but little to direct my life. The very pressure of my surroundings determines my pathway." His surroundings, no doubt, had led him to accept the Credit Mobilier stock in the first place.[50]

His outward stance was unyielding. Black continued to counsel him to assert his rectitude. Worried about his reputation, he worked on an exculpatory pamphlet. Inevitably its villain was Ames. The only public sign of a divided conscience that he gave was that, when the House voted on Ames's guilt, Garfield abstained.[51]

The congressional elections of 1874 were a true political revolution. For the first time since 1861 the Republicans lost control of the House. Where they had held a two-thirds majority in 1872, they fell to just over one-third. Nine years after the War, the House could be referred to, at least by Republicans, as a "Confederate Congress." Difficult as it always is to sort out the converging issues that determine an election, it was generally believed that the Credit Mobilier affair was one cause for the Republican decline.[52] Garfield, running in a safe Ohio district, found it to be one of three issues used against him.[53] In his own constituency, about 2,800 Republicans, Garfield guessed, bolted. He still carried the district by over 3,000 votes. The district, the Western Reserve, was "celebrated all over the country for its intelligent and high-minded people; it was made up of inquisitive and reflecting voters. To these he argued his case and," one historian concludes, "received a vindication."[54]

American elections, however, are not normally a vote on the merits of a man or his case—they are necessarily comparative. A very able man with seniority and known flaws may be intelligently preferred to a novice whose ability and virtue have been untested. The only conclusion to be drawn from the action of the voters of the Western Reserve is that nothing believed about Garfield was so black as to destroy his comparative advantages over his competitor. The Credit Mobilier matter, however, was far from put to rest. In the long run, it haunted him more than any other charge. The Democrats made it a major issue in the presidential campaign of 1880 when Garfield was the Republican nominee. 329 was scrawled on all available surfaces—on fences, billboards, pavements. An epidemic or mania seemed to have seized the country in late September as the magic figure appeared everywhere. Its meaning of course was explicable only in the context of the testimony of Oakes Ames. To anyone who asked, "Why 329?," the answer had to be, "That's what Garfield got from the Credit Mobilier." It was not much compared to the millions of the promoters, but a cartoon in *Puck* made the point: A wedding being celebrated between a stern Uncle Sam and a demure Garfield was shown being interrupted by the chairman of the Democratic National Committee carrying a baby whose gown was embroidered with the legend Credit Mobilier; the abashed bride was saying, "But it was such a little one!"[55]

When Garfield was elected and shot, when he suffered for almost three months—*stangulatus pro respublica,* as he himself expressed it, that is, tortured for the republic[56]—when he died and civil service reform was sanctified by his death and a civil service bill passed Congress, memory of the little one receded. Only the work of historians has continued the connection between Oakes Ames, the Credit Mobilier, and Garfield.

IN THE BAG TOO? MANY
CONGRESSMEN BOUGHT FROM AMES

Frank Leslie's Illustrated Weekly offered two cartoon comments on the Credit Mobilier affair as Ames's testimony went on. In one Oakes Ames as a rogue elephant was dashing about the congressional barnyard trampling on chickens with the faces of distinguished congressmen. In the other Uncle Sam was looking at his Credit Mobilier cake, which had been partially eaten. Various urchins, with the faces of Colfax, Garfield, Wilson, and others were escaping. The First Boy said, "I didn't touch it, sir; I only smelt it." The Second Boy said, "I just took a little piece, sir, but I put it back again, whole." The Third Boy said, "I just had a very small piece, sir, but I found it had a bad smell about it, and I didn't keep it." Uncle Sam said, "Look you rascals, there are crumbs on all your fingers." The cartoons were cruel. Were they unfair?[57]

John A. Bingham, Republican of Ohio, chairman of the Judiciary Committee, one of the oldest members of the House, admitted that he bought 20 shares of C.M. stock from Ames in February 1868 at par, when the market value was substantially above par. A little later Congressman James A. Wilson of Iowa took ten shares from Ames at par, the market being much higher. Congressman William D. Kelley, a former judge of Common Pleas in Philadelphia, bought 10 shares from Ames at par in December 1867, when the value was above par. Congressman Glenni W. Scofield, a former Pennsylvania district judge, bought 10 shares at par from Ames, also in December; so did Congressman William B. Allison, Republican of Iowa, who was elected to the Senate in 1872. Henry L. Dawes, Republican from the Berkshire hills of Massachusetts, the chairman of the Ways and Means Committee, "The Father of the House," bought 10 shares in the same month at par. John A. Logan, Republican of Illinois, later senator from Illinois and Republican vice-presidential nominee, made an identical purchase from Ames in December. John B.

Alley from Lynn, Massachusetts, Samuel Hooper from Boston, and Benjamin Boyer from Philadelphia were among the earlier congressional investors in the Credit Mobilier, before the stock rose; so too was James Grimes, Republican senator from Iowa. The stock sold to the early congressional investors at market price was inferably made available to them to influence their official attitude. Unquestionably the stock later sold to congressmen at par but below market represented a benefit to them; and stock sold on credit, to be paid from dividends, was also a benefit. No reason has been found why Oakes Ames should have wished to confer benefits on Congressmen except the reasons given in his letters to Mc-Comb—to "do most good to us," to "protect us." In all, sixteen Republican members of Congress—Alley, Allison, Ames, Bingham, Boyer, Colfax, Dawes, Garfield, Hooper, Kelley, Logan, Scofield, J. Wilson, and Senators Grimes, Patterson, and H. Wilson—were stockholders of the Credit Mobilier during the time it was, in the view of the investigating congressmen, engaged in fraud on the government.[58]

In addition, General Benjamin Butler, Republican congressman from Lowell, Massachusetts, had been Ames's counsel in drawing up one of the construction contracts with the U.P.; he was intimately familiar with the relationship of the U.P. to the C.M. and received $6,000 for his services. James Harlan, Republican senator from Iowa, had received $10,000 from U.P. President Durant while Harlan was secretary of the Interior in the Johnson administration; the money, he testified vaguely, had been spent for the expenses of his campaign for senator, including the cost of putting up friends who came to Iowa City to lobby for him with the legislature that elected the senators. Edwin D. Morgan, Republican senator from, and former governor of, New York, was co-trustee with Oakes Ames for the bondholders of the Union Pacific; the job was a sinecure, unless one took seriously the trustees' responsibility to look out for the bondholders; there is no evidence of Morgan's activity on their behalf.[59] Thaddeus Stevens, Republican congressman from Pennsylvania and the chairman of the Pacific Railroad Committee, held $29,000 par value U.P. stock in 1868. Grenville Dodge, who became the U.P.'s chief engineer after his predecessor had objected to a cost of $50,000 per mile, ran for Congress from Iowa and was elected in 1866. He continued to serve the railroad. "The fact that I am Chief Engineer of the Union Pacific gives me good standing," he wrote about his role in Congress to his wife Anne, in whose name stood 100 shares of C.M. stock. In the same letter he told of "the Lobby," consisting of "unscrupulous thieves" and "pretty women"; these had been pointed out to him as "breakers to steer clear of." That he was part of "the Lobby" apparently did not occur to him.[60] In all, twenty-one Republicans, among them over half the Massachusetts congressional delegation, were stockholders or beneficiaries of the business of the Credit Mobilier.

What a young Pennsylvania congressman asked about one of these men might have been asked as to each. Could they really not have known or at least suspected "what kind of a hen was laying these golden eggs?" How could any experienced lawyer among them "plead ignorance or the baby act?" Yet if the committee recommended punishment for all of them what chance did it have of its report being adopted? It was even suggested on the House floor that the criticism in the press of the committee for not going further was secretly promoted by the guilty "in the hope of breaking down the report of the committee and raising a fog of dust and confusion under which all may escape." Moderation was the committee's key to success. "I am not disposed to blame the committee," said Job Stevenson of Ohio, "when they found all these leviathans of the great deep in their net that they were not quite able to haul them all into their little tub." Only one of the sixteen was selected for condemnation of the committee, Oakes Ames himself. But there was also one Democrat to be dealt with.[61]

DEMOCRAT SHARED IN BOUNTY.
SON-IN-LAW FRONT FOR BROOKS

James Brooks, a congressman from New York City, had been an active promoter of the Union Pacific and worked with Durant to induce investors to buy Credit Mobilier. He never denied that he had full knowledge of its connection with the Union Pacific. He contended, however, that he never owned any U.P. or C.M. stock. As a reward for his promotional work he said he had been given an option to buy 200 shares of C.M. at par. By the time he wanted to exercise the option, U.P. President Durant thought the stock worth double this amount and persuaded him to settle for 100 shares of C.M., then worth $10,000, and U.P. bonds and stock, worth $9,000. At this point, according to Brooks, scruples prevented him from going ahead and exercising the option. He had been named a government director of the Union Pacific, and a statute prohibited government directors from holding stock in the railroad. Technically, the C.M. was distinct, but Brooks feared he would be "misunderstood and misrepresented" if he acquired C.M. stock. In this dilemma he gave up his option to someone else—Charles Neilson, an insurance broker. Neilson, not he, became the owner of the C.M. stock and U.P. bonds.

The committee pressed him as to the reality of this transaction. Neilson was his son-in-law. The money to pay for the purchase, according to Brooks's own admission, went directly from Brooks to Durant. How were the securities Neilson's if Brooks had put up the money? It was a loan, Brooks testified. Neilson had borrowed from him to exercise the option. It was a loan although Neilson gave him no note, and he himself made no memorandum of the debt. How had he expected to collect if Neilson defaulted? Neilson, Brooks observed, "was my son-in-law; if he behaved badly, I had him in my power, in the benefit he might or might not receive from my will." What was the collateral and where was it kept? It consisted in the U.P. bonds which came with the C.M. stock, and they were kept in a safe in Brooks's house, where Neilson also lived; there was nothing in the safe to distinguish Brooks's property from Neilson's. The committee disbelieved that any loan was made. Neilson, if he had been involved at all, had been Brooks's straw.[62]

In January or February 1868, as the C.M. stock increased to about four times par, Brooks had called on Sidney Dillon, president of the Credit Mobilier, and insisted that he was entitled to 50 more shares at par, to be transferred to Neilson. Dillon obtained the consent of the majority of C.M. stockholders to this extraordinary demand and he himself, he said, loaned Neilson, a casual acquaintance, $5,000 to buy the stock. Dillon could not remember if the loan had ever been paid. The stock was recorded on the company's books as issued to a person whose name was erased when Neilson's was substituted. The committee concluded that the shares had originally stood in Brooks's name, and that as to these 50, as to the earlier 100, Neilson's ownership was "merely nominal and colorable," Brooks's "real and substantial."[63]

These findings led to the committee's judgment that Brooks had violated his duty as a government director. "Appointed to guard the public interests in the road, he joined himself with the promoters of a scheme whereby the Government was to be defrauded." The committee also invoked the bribery statute of 1853 making it a crime for a congressman to receive "any money, goods, right in action, bribe, present, or reward . . . [offered] with intent to influence his vote or decision . . . ," and declared that Brooks had violated the statute. His expulsion from the House was recommended. Brooks was a Democrat. Since the committee was recommending a similar fate for Oakes Ames there was "an exact balance between political parties" which a committee spokesman went out of his way to declare to be unintentional.[64]

In the debate which followed in the House, Brooks's defenders stressed chiefly the lack of power in Congress to punish offenses committed by members prior to their election. What Brooks had done occurred in 1867 and 1868 while he was a member of the Forty-First Congress. His faults, so far as the current Congress was concerned, were absolved by his reelection to the Forty-Second Congress in 1870. Any retroactive jurisdiction was attacked as dangerously discretionary and not conferred by the simple phrase in the Constitution which empowered Congress "to expel" members. Brooks could not have been bribed, his defenders also argued, when no intent to bribe him had been established on the part of Durant as to the 100 shares, or on the part of Dillon as to the 50 shares. His principal spokesman, Daniel Vorhees, a Democrat of Indiana, went on to emphasize that no acts of Brooks in exchange for a bribe had been shown. If he had been paid for his vote or decision in Congress, what had he done for the money? As to the claim that Neilson was a dummy, if Brooks had intended to commit a fraud "he would not have selected a member of his own family." What proof was there that both Brooks and Neilson had perjured themselves about the loan? Vorhees asked that Brooks not be sacrificed to public clamor.[65]

Expulsion looked to many members of Congress like a harsh penalty —an excommunication, a casting into outer darkness of one of their col-leagues. Even if Brooks had taken the stock and even if Brooks had tried to cover his tracks with an improbable yarn, was there not genuine legal doubt about this Congress's jurisdiction over offenses against another Congress? The Republican leadership did not want to be vindictive. A substitute resolution embodying a penalty milder than expulsion was proposed and put in place of the committee's recommendation by a vote of 115 to 110, 15 not voting. By its terms, the House absolutely condemned the conduct of James Brooks in procuring for "himself or family" the stock of the Credit Mobilier. The resolution passed 174 to 32, not voting 34.[66]

With passage of this censure Brooks's public career ended and, it seemed to some, his life. A journalist originally from Maine; a graduate of Waterbury (later Colby) College; a school teacher; a writer for the Portland *Advertiser;* the editor of the New York *Express,* a Whig organ; a Cop-perhead during the War; a congressman from 1848 to 1850 and from 1864 to 1873, Jem Brooks was basically a newspaperman. The world he inhabited was that of "public opinion." His health had not been good. The issue in the House meant more to "this sick and feeble man," his de-fender Vorhees had said, "than life or death." Aged sixty-three, he died two months after the vote. His honor, Vorhees had said, was "dearer to him than life." A tarter comment came from the great New York diarist George Templeton Strong: "Died . . . (of Napoleon's disease) the 'Hon.' James Brooks, the meanest of political mankind, except his brother, Erastus, or 'Rat.'"[67]

A CHRISTMAS TREE FOR POLS;
OTHER BENEFACTIONS OF THE U.P.

While one committee probed the distribution of Credit Mobilier stock, a second under Jeremiah Wilson of Indiana investigated where the gov-ernment's subsidy to the Union Pacific had gone. The scope of its inquiry included suspicious disbursements of cash by the U.P. Among other things, it turned up the following:

One. Thomas Durant (originally a physician in Pittsfield, Mas-sachusetts), the big man in the U.P. in 1864, spent $435,000 for which he had sought reimbursement from the company. The official story, retailed by Oliver Ames, Oakes's brother and the U.P.'s president from 1867 to 1871, was that the money had been spent settling the claims of various other railroads. Curiously, no compromise agreements, no releases, no receipts, and no canceled checks showing these settlements were in the U.P.'s possession—everything had been paid for in cash, and large and presumably serious claims had been bought off with no single piece of paper showing what had been agreed to. The official story was not designed to deceive the sophisticated. The Ames crowd, in fact, had first believed that Durant had embezzled the money for himself but was ul-timately convinced that he had spent it for the company when he produced "a tin box containing . . . vouchers." These vouchers had been retained by Durant as his personal property and were never shown to the investigating committee. The committee did discover that they had nothing to do with the settlement of the claims of other railroads. According to the U.P.'s own records, they had been approved by a special committee of U.P. directors "appointed to approve vouchers on congressional expenses." The time of the expenditures correlated with the vital 1864 amendments increasing the government's subsidy and subordinating the government's loan to the company's first mortgage bonds.[68]

One signer of the vouchers turned out to be Joseph Stewart, a lawyer-lobbyist with twenty-seven years of experience in presenting claims to Congress. He was called as a witness and took credit for drafting the most important section of the 1864 bill. He had been paid $30,000 for his services, and he admitted to having been given $100,000 or $150,000 of U.P. bonds. He denied having given any to anyone in Congress and absolutely refused, on the ground of the lawyer-client privilege, to disclose what he had done with them. The Wilson committee told him that he was wrong about the privilege but did not pursue him for contempt of Congress.[69]

The most specific information about Durant's transactions obtained by the committee was that $80,000 had gone to Thaddeus Stevens, now deceased, then chairman of the House Committee on the Pacific Railroad as well as a major power in the war Congress. Oliver Ames testified to this expenditure. Although his story was hearsay about an expense incurred before he was president, and although Durant denied it, Ames was in a position to have found out and had no clear reason to lie unless it be supposed that he was trying to satisfy the committee's interest in names with that of a dead man.[70] In fact Stevens held 2,900 shares of U.P. stock by 1868. That some congressmen had been bought off, and that they were connected with the Committee on the Pacific Railroad, was circumstantially proved by Stewart's silence and the U.P.s own description of the vouchers being for "congressional expenses." No other plausible accounting of the money was given.

Two. In December 1868 a government commissioner, Cornelius Wendell, refused to approve forty miles of track ending at Bryan, Wyoming, unless he was paid $25,000. The general superintendent at Omaha, Webster Snyder, testified that Wendell "wanted it as blood." Given "the exigencies" of the road, Snyder paid him after two weeks of hesitation. The amount was charged either to "Contingencies" or "Construction." Oliver Ames, then the U.P. president, who heard about it later, did nothing to try to get the money back. As he understood what had happened: "Mr. Johnson sent Wendell out there to make a raid to raise some money" and the money went for some of "Johnson's paper"; that is, Wendell was acting for President Andrew Johnson who needed it to pay off his personal obligations; it would have been a waste of energy to have complained. Wendell, the only commissioner the U.P. admitted paying, was now dead.[71]

Three. In February 1869 the Union Pacific was sued by Jim Fisk, the famous Wall Street speculator, who contended that the Credit Mobilier was a fraud on U.P. stockholders. The case was in a Manhattan trial court before a judge of the state Supreme Court, George Barnard. Barnard was notoriously corrupt and was later impeached and removed by the New York legislature for corruption. The company's New York lawyers, Charles F. Tracy and William Fullerton, proposed to Oliver Ames that they could settle the case if they had $50,000. The money was at once made available to them and spent. The lawyers said it had gone to Fisk. The U.P. received no receipt, acknowledgment, or agreement from any one in return. The implication was very strong that at least in part the money must have gone to the judge.[72]

Fisk, in fact, did not drop the suit and in March obtained from Judge Barnard an injunction against the U.P. holding its annual meeting. The Ameses saw the injunction as obviously purchased. Their worst suspicions were confirmed on March 17, 1869, when Barnard appointed a receiver for the Credit Mobilier and the receiver was William M. Tweed, Jr., the son of the legendary Tammany Hall boss. The Ameses countered with another family connection. On March 25 they succeeded in having the case moved to the federal court before Samuel Blatchford, the son of a stockholder in the Union Pacific. Nonetheless they were not wholly happy in New York. Oliver wrote, "When we can get our books away from New York and cleared out from that sink of corruption, we shall feel safe and not till then." In April Congress obligingly passed legislation changing the U.P.'s headquarters to Boston.[73]

SEVEN SHARES FOR SEVEN WHOS?
"SIMPLY A LITTLE ERROR"

Among the items that intrigued the Wilson committee was a resolution of the U.P. directors of March 9, 1871, approving $126,000 for "special legal expenses." Six days earlier, on March 3, 1871, another piece of legislation vital to the U.P. had become federal law. In December 1870 Secretary of the Treasury George Boutwell, acting on an opinion from Attorney General Amos Akerman, had decided to withhold from the U.P. all of what the government owed for the use of the road, with the view of offsetting these amounts against what the company owed in interest on the government bonds lent to it as subsidy.[74] The effect was catastrophic for the U.P.'s cash flow and the price of its securities. In the words of Cornelius Bushnell, a major U.P. stockholder and director, "It was a very extreme case and required a very extreme and extraordinary effort."[75] A team of U.P. officers and directors went to Washington. Working feverishly in February they lobbied Congress for corrective legislation. Among them were General Dodge, now an ex-congressman, and Bushnell, who had acquired much

experience of government as a navy contractor during the war. In Bushnell's words, "In less than ten or fifteen days we had the bill through
Congress just exactly as we wanted it, and just exactly right."[76]

Ideally, legislation of this benevolent kind should have three features. It
should avoid debate. It should avoid a recorded vote. It should be veto-
proof. The bill benefiting the Union Pacific had all these qualities. The
Forty-First Congress expired at midnight March 3, 1871. On February 17
the Army Appropriations Act passed the House. On February 24 the
Senate Judiciary Committee reported that Secretary Boutwell was wrong
and that the proper construction of the 1864 law did not permit the United
States to offset all transportation charges against the interest on the bonds.
On March 1 an amendment expressing this position was added in the
Senate, without debate, to the Army Appropriations Act; by its terms the
secretary of the Treasury was directed to resume the old practice. On
March 2 a conference committee of three members of the House and three
members of the Senate met to consider this and other disagreements on
the bill between the House and the Senate. Pointing to the Judiciary Committee's report, the Senate conferees insisted on the Senate amendment,
and the House conferees receded. On March 3, the last day of the session,
with dozens of bills being pushed through, the Army Appropriations Act
was must legislation. In the five minutes allotted for explanation, a House
conferee reported on the Senate's insistence on the amendment. There was
no time for debate. The amended bill passed both House and Senate
without any recorded vote. A veto was out of the question. Veto the Army
Appropriations Act! President Grant signed it into law the same day. In
the whole smooth process it was difficult to identify who had brought it
about. The senator who introduced the amendment was not identified.
Matthew Carpenter, Republican of Wisconsin, gave the report of the Judiciary Committee, a crucial step. The cooperation of the House conferees,
the appointees of Speaker Blaine, was essential.[77]

The $126,000, voted by the directors six days after the bill became law,
was divided into $82,500 for Bushnell to buy bonds of the U.P.; $24,500 to
Grenville Dodge, the company's chief engineer, who had gone to Washington as part of the lobbying campaign; and $19,000 to Thomas Scott,
president of the Pennsylvania Railroad and a director of the U.P. Bushnell
testified that the money was not merely for "special legal expenses." The
directors' resolution so describing it was "simply a little error." It should
have read "special and legal expenses." The $82,500 he himself had
received was a bonus for earlier agreeing to set up a syndicate to buy two
million dollars' worth of the U.P.'s land bonds; the $19,000 was a payment
on account to Scott, who had helped finance this deal; only the $24,500 to
Dodge had any relation to Washington, and it was compensation to the
chief engineer for his trouble in coming to Washington for a few weeks.
The payments had been approved by an ad hoc directors' committee
whose members were Dodge, Scott, and Bushnell. Bushnell could give no

explanation why the U.P. should have given him a bonus, Scott a down payment, or Dodge, a company employee, such large special compensation; or why those receiving the compensation should have composed the committee that approved it.[78]

Dodge was an old hand at lobbying. In Iowa in 1859–1860 he had been the chief lobbyist with the state legislature for the Mississippi and Missouri Railroad, and his practice, his biographer observes, had been "to reward every politician who worked with him." He became a general during the Civil War, was an Iowa congressman for a term in 1866–1868, and for forty years functioned as a leader of "the Des Moines Regency," the rulers of the Republican party in Iowa. Dodge was subpoenaed by the investigating committee, but dodged the process servers. When he was finally interrogated by another congressional committee three years later, he told a completely different tale from Bushnell's. The $24,000 he received from Bushnell, he then said, was money owed him on a stock transaction.[79]

Benjamin Spence, assistant treasurer of the U.P. at the time of the transaction, had retained a rough memo given him when he issued the checks. On its back he had made notations including these:

	25	
126	7	7000 L
	175	17500
Dodge, 24,500		G.M.D.

The "L"—for lobbyist?—was not identified. The inference was that Dodge's $24,500 was made up of seven shares of $2,500 apiece plus $7,000 for L. Spence testified that he understood from the conversation of the U.P. treasurer and Bushnell that the $126,000 was used "for the purpose of securing a reversal of Secretary Boutwell's action." He testified further that Bushnell at once gave a check for $2,500 to E. H. Rollins, the company's secretary. He understood, and Rollins later testified, that this was to reimburse Rollins for $2,500 borrowed by him for Bushnell in Washington; the lender had been Ordway, the sergeant-at-arms of the House. Finally, a memo offered by Spence showed that the $19,000 check—said by Bushnell to have gone to Scott—had gone to ex-Congressman Jeremiah Wilson, no kin of the committee chairman and at the time a government director of the U.P.[80]

Oliver Ames was questioned about the $126,000. President of the U.P. during the period of the lobbying effort, he had gone out of office at the same March meeting of directors that approved the payment. He was asked what special legal services had been performed for the money. He answered, "That I cannot tell you. I do not know anything about it. I suppose it was for the purpose of securing favorable legislation." He was asked why he did not inquire. He answered, "Our board of directors—that is, myself and the majority of us—had always looked to Mr. Oakes Ames to look after our matters at Washington, and believed he would do whatever might be necessary for the interest of the road."[81]

In summary, Bushnell's story as to $107,000 of the $126,000 was implausible to the point of impudence. It was supported by no document and contradicted by the official records of the directors and by Ames and Spence. The official story of "special legal expenses" also did not stand up. There had been eminent counsel retained to give opinions supporting the U.P.'s legal position—ex-Attorney-General Ebenezer Hoar, ex-Supreme Court Justice Benjamin R. Curtis—but these specially hired lawyers had been publicly identified and separately paid. They were not the nameless persons put under the $126,000 item. If neither the minutes nor Bushnell could be trusted, there was the clear belief of Ames and Spence that the entire $126,000 had been spent in Washington. The reasonable inference could be drawn that the committee had uncovered cash spent in a few weeks to bribe members of Congress, that seven members received $2,500 apiece, and that Bushnell had borrowed another $2,500 from the sergeant-at-arms to make another payment of the same sort. It was also a reasonable inference that the knowledgeable head of the lobbying team was the man "looked to" to "look after our matters at Washington," Oakes Ames. The Wilson Committee, focusing on the big question of the U.P.'s relationship with the Credit Mobilier, made no findings on this matter; and it was left to the Poland committee to pursue Ames on the surer evidence of his own letters.

AMES GUILTY AS CHARGED.

MASS. MILLIONAIRE BRIBED CONGRESS

From the beginning Ames was the center of attention. His difficulties with McComb had started the scandal. He was the representative of the Union Pacific who had been the principal liaison with Congress in distributing the stock of the Credit Mobilier. Added to these facts was his own great wealth—his "millions," as they were sometimes called—which excited both respectful admiration and envy. To his supporters he was the man who had taken on "his own broad shoulders" the building of the Union Pacific when Durant and the first adventurers had faltered. To him was owed the enlistment of the necessary capital; and he was portrayed as risking his own fortune in agreeing to "the Oakes Ames contract," the largest of the contracts by which the road was constructed. In the portrait painted by his chief congressional champion, General Benjamin Butler of Massachusetts, "old Oakes Ames," was a man who spoke with the simplicity of "a blacksmith." He was "a mechanic of Massachusetts, a shovel-maker of Massachusetts, a man who by his own right arm carved out a fortune. . . ." If everyone sought his advice on investments, it was because "in him there was no guile." He had been patriotic in promoting the Union Pacific; honest and so trusted by many men with their property; truthful in his testimony when he could have been silent and safe. "We have here an honest man, a patriotic man, a truthful man, and we are to expel him, lest we shall be contaminated with honesty, truth and patriotism." Ames in fact "had no more idea of bribery than he has of lying. They are vices that do not belong to him." It was the press, "that damnable engine of libel and slander" that had made his name "a by-word." As for those who still hesitated to believe that Ames was as guileless as Nathaniel praised by Jesus in the Gospel, Butler had another line from Scripture. "Let him who is without sin cast the first stone." Almost his last words on behalf of Ames were the question, "Who shall go unwhipped if every man has every act of his life brought in judgment against him?"[82]

To Ames's critics in the House, he had done nothing but cash in on a sure thing, made certain by the government's largess. There had been no risk in the "Oakes Ames contract," written when his brother Oliver was president of the Union Pacific and the Ames crowd controlled the company. At the least sign that the contract was onerous, Ames and his brother by mutual agreement could have modified the contract or rescinded it altogether. In fact Oakes Ames did not intend to perform the contract; two months after it was made Ames assigned it to the seven trustees of the stockholders of the Credit Mobilier. The capital Ames put in the Credit Mobilier was quickly recouped, and the great profits rolled in. Meanwhile he headed off regulation and inquiry in Congress by his bounty to key members. It "is supposed that he knew enough of Scripture to know that 'where a man's treasure is, there will his heart be also.'" His acts "inveigling" members of Congress to invest were performed with "Satanic skill." It had been said that "Mr. Ames, in doing what he did, had no sense that he was doing an immoral act, or that he was even doing an indelicate act; that he regarded it as the same thing as going into a business community . . . by giving them shares. . . . [But] if a man's moral sense sees no wrong in that which our predecessors declared a penitentiary offense . . . is he fit to sit here . . . ?[83]

Ames's three letters to McComb were the center of the case against him and conclusive in the committee's view of his guilt:

> I am here on the spot and can better judge where they will go. . . .
>
> I don't fear any investigation here. . . .
>
> I have used this where it will produce most good to us, I think. . . .
>
> We want more friends in this Congress. . . .

These lines of Ames could not be forgotten or overlooked.

At a time when Credit Mobilier stock was worth at least 200, Ames had sold it at 100 to members of Congress, in the committee's judgment "to

enlist strength and friends in Congress who would resist any encroachment" on the Union Pacific's privileges and who would oppose regulation
of its rates or investigation into its relations with the Credit Mobilier.
Ames's purpose was "to influence their votes and decisions in matters to
come before Congress." His conduct was "bribery" and a violation of the
criminal statute against giving money or anything of value to a member of
Congress.[84]

Ames's attempt to explain away the damning letters as merely meant to
placate McComb was scouted. In effect, Ames was claiming now that the
letters informed McComb that "he was bribing members of Congress"
with the stock but that "in truth such was not the case," and his words to
McComb had been "a mere pretense on his part." Everyone of experience
knew that "old dodge of lobbyists" to pretend that they had expended
money with congressmen and to have great influence with them, when in
fact they had spent nothing and had no influence. "Mr. Ames, therefore,
in this explanation of his makes himself appear as playing the role of an
ordinary lobbyist, pretending to be exercising an influence on the
House. . . . Instead of that being any justification . . . it is but an aggrava-
tion of the offense." To explain away his bribery, he had had to paint himself in the darker color of a double crosser of his partners.[85]

The most ingenious argument for Ames was that bribery was a bilateral
act. It took two to commit it. If Ames was guilty of bribery, whom had he
bribed? Not Brooks, whose bribes had come from Durant and Dillon. Not
the two senators and twelve congressmen whom the committee accused of
nothing. The recipient of a bribe "must have some little inkling of the purpose." But the committee treated the recipients of Ames's bounty as innocent. Congressmen, it appeared, had taken presents. But "to give a
present to an individual is not a crime." Who, then, was bribed?[86]

The committee's position was that the innocence of the recipients it
named was irrelevant.

> The law does not require that the intent shall be known to the person to whom
> the present is made. It is the insidious attempt to undertake to bind over by ties
> of gratitude the man whose official action you wish to influence by it. It stands
> upon the same principle of law as that which relates to making presents to jurors
> or judges, or to treating a juror. You shall not use any of those influences that or-
> dinarily affect the human mind and the human judgment. Although the man
> you are practising upon may be entirely ignorant of your intent and your pur-
> pose, the law declares that you are guilty.

Such was the austere judicial view of the committee's chairman, Luke
Poland. In the racier language of Congressman Hawley of Connecticut:

> Mr. Ames says several times that he never made a promise to a Congressman,
> and never exacted a promise from one; that he would not dare to do so. Certainly
> not; that is not the way. Gentlemen certainly are remarkably ignorant of the style
> of the lobbyist if they suppose him to resort to anything so bald as that. The lob-

byists exact no promise, they make no promise. They offer an opportunity for an exceedingly favorable purchase, and the least said the better. . . . Innocent old man![87]

When Ames himself was asked by the committee about his motives in selling a piece of the C.M. at such favorable prices, he replied, "I am kind-hearted and want to help everybody." One recalls his sarcasm when Schuyler Colfax explained the motivation of Nesbitt, the government printer, in similar terms.[88]

When the investigation had begun, Ames had been "solicited and urged" to support the statements of "the panic-stricken men about him"; and he had done his best to shield the congressmen who had dealt with him, chiefly by a studied vagueness in his answers to the committee. At first, as one member put it, he was "mild, and coy, and gentle as a maiden with these gentlemen." His attitude and testimony changed "when he discovered that they intended to put the whole responsibility of this trans-action upon him alone." It was then that Ames retrieved from North Eas-ton the memorandum book with its record of what he had paid each con-gressional customer. In his first testimony to the committee on December 17, 1872, in the form of a prepared written statement, Ames had sworn as to Schuyler Colfax that he could not "remember having paid over to him any dividends." The memorandum book showed he had paid Colfax $1,200 in dividends. Ames was asked about his December 1872 testimony in February 1873, "Did you intend to speak the truth or speak a lie?" He did not reply to this question but a little later gave the answer: "I intended to make it as favorable as I could to Mr. Colfax, but when I heard it was said they intended to break me down I could not do otherwise than state everything."[89]

It was when he learned that "they" intended to break him that Ames adopted the strategy seen from Garfield's perspective as reflecting a deter-mination "to drag down as many men with him as possible." Ames wrote his family: "I think they will insist that all these men that are said to have rec'd stock from me will be put in the bill and be expelled with me. But I have not much fear of being expelled."[90] There was safety in the number involved. The strategy was dangerous because it redoubled the determi-nation of the others to sink him alone.

"Dear Wife," Ames wrote Evelina Gilmore Ames in mid-January 1873, "Don't feel uneasy on my account, as there will be no stain on my reputa-tion, whatever others may do. Am sorry that you feel so badly. Remember that the scriptures say that 'whom the Lord loveth he chasteneth.'" A stain on the family name—that was at stake for Ames. His wife's feelings—these were engaged in the outcome. He himself was suffering—that was why Hebrews 12:6 was appropriate.[91]

The issue finally before the House was not the expulsion recommended by the committee, but the milder remedy of censure. Twenty congressmen participated in the debate—twelve essentially supporting the committee, eight essentially for Ames. "Though a spirit of excitement and some panic prevailed," Garfield wrote dispassionately (i.e., he did not sense himself in grave danger), "the minds of the members of the House throughout the debate on the whole has [sic] been calm and fair, with the exception here and there of an ebullition of personal feeling."[92] Among the debaters, Butler and Poland stood out by contrast as antagonists. Butler was well-known, indeed notorious, nationally. A man from Massachusetts with a reputation as a brawler in its legislature; a Democrat who had voted to nominate Jefferson Davis for president and who became the personification of Yankee heavy-handedness as military ruler of New Orleans; a postwar Republican congressman; counsel for the Massachusetts men involved in the Union Pacific, Butler was generally regarded as a no-holds-barred politician. His speech on behalf of Ames made Ames weep, but Garfield thought it "more brilliant than solid," and Poland observed icily, "There is class of ingenious lawyers in the country who have an excellent faculty of getting their clients hung."[93] Poland himself was aloof, cool, unsentimental. He had, he told the House, never learned "how to play the buffoon or harlequin." Originally from Westford in northernmost Vermont, he had gone to school till he was seventeen, passed the bar at twenty-one, and been elected to the Supreme Court of Vermont in 1848; in that state, where judges had one-year terms, he was annually reelected for fifteen years, serving the last five as chief justice. He had been a United States senator from 1865 to 1867 and then did not refuse to serve in the Lower House. He was not only the antithesis of Butler, he was also far from the Ciceronian tradition. He admitted Ames's general reputation and focused on the single offense: "They say he is a self-made man, has acquired a vast estate by steady industry, has lived an honest life . . . but after all, the question is, Did he commit this crime?" The question cut through Butler's rhetoric.[94]

Apart from the strict merits of the case, the defenders of Ames continued to urge the danger of scapegoating in response to the clamor of the press. The "cry has gone forth, 'Crucify them! Crucify them!.'" Where there was doubt, especially as to jurisdiction, should the House brand Brooks and Ames as felons and bring on their families "lasting shame and sorrow?" Each man who "stands up in the image of the God who made him" would vote for acquittal.[95] The opponents of Ames dwelt on the general wickedness of the Credit Mobilier—"conceived in sin" and "brought forth in iniquity"; on the growing danger to honest government posed by great corporations, monopolies, railroads—the Credit Mobilier was "only the outcropping" of a system by which 200 million acres of public lands had been given to the railraods; and on the justified apprehension and anger of the voters. Bribery was "debasing." The "integrity" of the House, the "honor" of the government, the "purity" of our institutions were at stake. The American people were trying "Samson-like—an interesting image for the House—to burst their bonds. The public outrage was not the clamor of a mob, but an intelligent reaction to corruption. "We have no other protection so safe, certain and effectual." In Poland's sober words at the very end of his speech in reply,

> I quite agree that much that has been said by the press has been partisan and foolish, and there does not seem to have been displayed any very sincere wish to deal out exact justice to anybody. But I do not agree with those gentlemen [Butler and Bingham] that it is all clamor, or all fiction. The excitement and duty of the press over this matter is but the spray and the foam of a ground-swell beneath, that has foundation in the minds of the people. . . . [T]he country is filling rapidly with gigantic associations which command great influence and great money power. The people are fast learning . . . that, unless some check be found, their rights, if not their liberties, will soon be at the mercy of these great and fast-increasing monopolies.

Poland then submitted the case "to the judgment and conscience of the House." It voted 182 to 36, not voting 22, to "absolutely condemn the conduct of Oakes Ames."[96]

AMES DEAD; SONS DEFEND HIM, MASS. LEGISLATURE CLEARS

Ames himself sat in the House until the proceedings' end, even joining in the vote to table the resolution censuring others besides himself and Brooks. Outwardly, he maintained his bluff demeanor. Inwardly, according to a memoir authorized by his sons, and perhaps written by one of them, the hurt "lacerated his heart." He returned to a public reception in North Easton. Two month later, on May 5, 1873, he was stricken by pneumonia and paralysis. He died on May 8.[97] His sons and the Union Pacific worked to vindicate his memory. At Sherman, Wyoming, at the highest point on the line, the railroad built a cairn with portraits in granite on it of the Ames brothers. The sons built in North Easton a Victorian Gothic structure, the Oakes Ames Memorial Hall.[98] At its dedication in 1881 some 400 business and political figures came to commemorate Ames and listen to eulogies of his work. James Blaine wrote that Ames had been "distinguished among his associates, both in and out of Congress, for solidity and uprightness of character."[99] The sons' memoir—fifty pages long, forty-four devoted to defending Ames's role in the Credit Mobilier—was published to celebrate this occasion and an action in 1883 by the Massachusetts legislature. A vote of both houses adopted a resolution embracing General Butler's view of his punishment: "his unflinching truthfulness and honesty . . . made him the victim of an intense and misdirected public excitement." The memoir even repeated the staple argument used by Ames's friends in Congress—there could have been no bribe since the transactions were not bilateral. At the time the legislature acted, Butler was governor of the commonwealth, and three years later Ames's son Oliver was elected governor. The family name was safe in Massachusetts.[100]

The defense by the family has continued into the present generation. Charles Edgar Ames, a direct descendant of Oakes, has written *Pioneering the Union Pacific: A Reappraisal of the Builders of the Railroad,* which makes the ultimate economic argument. Although the Union Pacific eventually became insolvent under its load of debt to the government and underwent receivership, the receiver finally paid back the United States for its subsidy: "So the nation's taxpayers did not lose a penny. . . ."[101]

U.P. BOUGHT BLAINE'S BONDS

BOOKKEEPER SAYS. SPEAKER

NOT A DEADHEAD

The cartoon in *Frank Leslie's Illustrated Magazine* of March 1, 1873, which showed Oakes Ames as a rampaging elephant scattering the barnyard fowl, had shown "the Maine bird" perched out of reach. But was Blaine out of reach, people wondered. About the same time John Harrison, a government director of the Union Pacific, had begun telling friends that the railroad had engaged in a transaction that "would ruin Mr. Blaine and the Republican party." By the spring of 1876 this rumor and rumors linking Blaine to other railroads were appearing in the press. He was now the frontrunner for the Republican presidential nomination. Washington gossip attributed the circulation of the stories to his Republican enemies. In April Blaine rose in the House to make a sweeping denial of all the stories and to invite investigation. It was a bold maneuver, for the Democrats now controlled the House. In May they accepted his invitation. The House committed the investigation to a subcommittee of two Democrats and a Republican that was already looking into the Union Pacific.[102]

Blaine, it will be recalled, had set up the Credit Mobilier investigation after his meeting with Garfield and, as the committee's first witness, had sworn that he never received "a single cent derived in any manner or shape" from the Union Pacific. But the new committee now heard Harrison. In 1872 he had been warned not to inquire into certain bonds owned by the U.P. because they would involve Blaine. The warning had come from Edward H. Rollins, the U.P.'s treasurer. The bonds were seventy-five first mortgage bonds of the Little Rock and Fort Smith Railroad, purchased through a New York broker by the U.P. in December 1871 for $64,000. They were an odd investment, being the securities of another railroad, not readily marketable, and bought at a price that seemed absurdly high. Little Rock bonds with a par value of 100 were, if usable at all, worth 10 to 20 when pledged as collateral. Even the per share price was curious—not an even multiple but 85.6. Rollins did not deny that he had wondered about the transaction and warned Harrison not to ask about it. But he now told the committee he must have been mistaken to connect the bonds in any way to Blaine.[103]

Thomas Scott, president of the Union Pacific for a single year, 1871–1872, then testified that the bonds had been his, not Blaine's, and that he had bought them fifteen months earlier from the chief promoter of the Little Rock. Scott, the president of the Pennsylvania Railroad, had been trying to resuscitate the Union Pacific. He had served without pay, expecting to be well compensated if his efforts revived the road. By December 1871 the U.P. was reviving, and "the company owed me a very considerable compensation." At the same time Scott was short of cash, and he happened to owe the U.P. about $64,000. Accordingly, he proposed to the executive committee that they accept his Little Rock bonds and cancel his debt. The executive committee was composed of himself and such old associates of his as Andrew Carnegie and George Pullman. They agreed and bought the bonds, giving Scott an option to repurchase if the bonds went up.[104]

Scott's story was detailed, circumstantial, and unsupported. No documents to substantiate it existed—no recorded vote of the executive committee to cancel his debt or to buy the securities, no evidence that there had been a debt, no evidence of the option to repurchase. The executive committee had fixed neither the value of Scott's services nor the value of the bonds it was buying to compensate him for his services. Oddly, too, the Union Pacific had paid the New York broker by check for the bonds. If the bonds were in exchange for canceling Scott's debt, why was a check to a third party involved?

The committee next heard as witnesses Blaine's former broker in Boston, Warren Fisher, and Fisher's bookkeeper, James Mulligan. Fisher had gone bankrupt since his dealings with Blaine and might fairly have been described as disgruntled. He had made available to Mulligan letters which Blaine had written him, and it was inferable that he expected Mulligan to do what he started to do, bring the letters before the committee.[105] Before that happened, Blaine called on Mulligan and asked for the return of the letters as his property. Mulligan refused. Blaine then, according to Mulligan, "prayed, almost went on his knees—I would say on his knees—and implored me to think of his six children and his wife and that if the committee should get hold of this communication it would sink him immediately and ruin him forever." According to Blaine, he did not plead but he did argue. According to Mulligan, Blaine "asked me if I would not like a consulship." According to Blaine, "I jokingly remarked whether he would like to go abroad in some official capacity. . . . I would not say Mr. Mulligan falsifies; I do not want to say that at all. There might have been room for his putting a construction on what I said." The upshot was that Mulligan still refused to release the letters but twice gave them to Blaine to read. The second time Blaine kept them.[106]

Mulligan returned, empty-handed, to the committee to tell this astonishing tale. When the committee turned to Blaine, he declined to deliver "his property," supporting his refusal with a letter from two lawyers, one a prominent Republican, the other a prominent Democrat. Both were veterans of the affairs of the Union Pacific in Congress. One was Matt Carpenter, senator from Wisconsin and the author of the report of the Senate Judiciary Committee in 1871 recommending that the government could not withhold money to meet the interest on the bonds it had lent the U.P. The other was Garfield's old counselor, Jeremiah Black. Carpenter and Black advised that the letters were irrelevant to the committee's inquiry and that Blaine had no duty to surrender them.[107]

Blaine's tactics of publicly stealing back his letters of course riveted attention upon them. Garfield, an observer highly sympathetic to him, noted in his diary: "A new sensation in the Blaine investigation. A dramatic scene between himself and the Irish witness Mulligan." The word "Irish" contained a whiff of ethnic prejudice, detectable also in Blaine, partly of Irish descent himself, mocking Mulligan's pronunciation. The next day Garfield wrote, "The general impression tonight is that Blaine has suffered very serious [sic] from the Mulligan Letter business." Already the letters were "the Mulligan letters," although, accurately, they were "the Blaine letters." Two days later Garfield doubted that Blaine could "recover." He was "in this Dilemma. If he publishes the letters they will probably afford materials for campaign scandal. If he refuses, people will say there is something very criminal in them."[108]

Blaine boldly broke the impasse by reading the letters aloud to the House, scrambling their chronological order and not surrendering them for inspection. The result was at first a "triumph." Blaine appeared to have been candid. Nothing fatal had been revealed. But as the printed text of Blaine's oral reading became available, certain passages were "criticized," and Garfield worried about their effect on Blaine's presidential quest.[109] No letter was conclusive on the question of whether, through Scott, the U.P. had bought Blaine's bonds. But four references in the letters proved troublesome for Blaine. Writing to Fisher in 1869 while he was speaker of the House, he had sought an interest in the Little Rock, a railroad indirectly dependent on federal land grants. In one such letter he drew attention to the service he had gratuitously rendered the road as speaker by ruling out of order an amendment hostile to its grant. The unspoken implication was that he deserved thanks and could do more. The impression was strengthened by a second letter declaring in the jargon of a good railroad buff, "I do not feel that I shall prove a dead-head in the enterprise if I once embark in it. I see various channels in which I know I can be useful." As now explained by Blaine, the interest he sought was "what was called the bed-rock of the road, to let me be interested in the building of it." The explanation did not lessen the hint of service being offered for a price.[110]

Blaine had in fact become a bondholder of the Little Rock, not "at precisely the same rate as others paid," as he had assured the House on April 24, but as a salesman. Working with Fisher he had sold the Little Rock to a dozen friends in Maine and received a commission, indeed an extra large commission. It was paid in part in Little Rock bonds. This was the second troublesome matter. The letters showed beyond argument that Blaine had lied to the House in April.[111] These sales on commission apparently related to several later letters of a plaintive and harassed sort stressing Blaine's need for cash after the Little Rock investment turned sour. On April 18, 1872, he wrote Fisher, "You say that 'necessity knows no law.' That applies to me as well as you, and when I have reached the point I am now at I simply fall back upon that law." In the same letter occurred a third troublesome reference. Blaine mentioned "the sales of bonds which you spoke of my making" and declared, "I did not have the money in my possession forty-eight hours, but paid it over directly to the parties whom I tried by every means in my power to protect from loss."[112] The implication was that, embarrassed by his earlier bond sales in Maine, he had tried to bail out the friends who had bought the bonds, passing on to them "the money." But whose money had he had in his possession for forty-eight hours? Mulligan's memorandum on the letters indicated he believed Blaine here referred to the Union Pacific's purchase from Blaine of the Little Rock bonds.[113]

An explicit reference to the Union Pacific was a fourth embarrassment. A letter to Fisher disclosed that Blaine had $6,000 worth of land grant bonds of the U.P. which he had left with Fisher in January 1871 and now asked to be returned because "the bonds were only a part mine." Explaining this passage to the House, Blaine did not extricate himself. The bonds, he said, had been bought on "a very favorable basis" in 1869 on the advice of Congressman Samuel Hooper. They were bought by "a lady who is a member of my family" and then given to Blaine as security on a loan to her. The bonds were "literally all hers."[114]

Alternative inferences could be drawn. Either Blaine had had a deal for himself with the Union Pacific in 1869, or the U.P. bonds had been held by a close member of his family, a person whose property he treated as his own; and either he had, like an embezzler, put her bonds in Fisher's charge, treating them as his own without her consent, or she had formally pledged them to Blaine as security he could use as he liked and whose interest he would collect, so that in substance they were his. Blaine's claim of total disassociation from the affairs of the Union Pacific was destroyed.

As the Democrats pressed on with the committee hearings, and the time of the Republican presidential convention neared, Blaine collapsed at church on Sunday, June 11. He was brought home unconscious. After seeing him motionless on a bed in his front parlor, Garfield wrote, "If he dies of this, it will be the work of political assassination as really as though he had been stabbed to death." Blaine's paroxysm was no pretense. At nine in the evening Garfield found him still unconscious.[115] Near the climax of his political career his inner conflict over his old connection with the U.P. and his dread of exposure had taken outward and visible form.

The Republican Convention opened three days later, with Blaine very much alive and directing his forces by telegraph. For the Republican reformers, who had chafed for eight years at the charges of corruption in the Grant administration, the Blaine-Fisher correspondence constituted a fatal taint for Blaine. In the words of Congressman George Frisbie Hoar of Massachusetts, "I did not think it wise to put at the head of a movement for reform and for purity of administration, a man whose supporters must defend him against such charges. . . ." Blaine led on the first ballot with

285 votes, his next rival having only 124, but he could not get a majority. Hayes was nominated. So Blaine lost his best chance to be president and paid, not for the last time, for accepting the largess of the Union Pacific.[116]

BURN THIS LETTER!

In 1884 James Gillespie Blaine was at last the Republican candidate for president. He had been Garfield's Secretary of State and had been with the president in the Baltimore and Potomac railroad station when the disappointed spoilsman had assassinated him. He had seen Chet Arthur, "the Gentleman Boss," suddenly elevated to the presidency and become the backer of civil service reform, sanctified by the martyrdom of Garfield; but Arthur was still the embodiment of the most corrupt elements in the Republican party. The Stalwarts, the orthodox party members (mostly hacks, although Clover Adams reckoned John Hay among them), wanted Arthur in 1884; the Mugwumps, or virtuous independents, were ready to bolt; and the Half-Breeds, or those in favor of reform but not too much reform, were for Blaine. A certain *machismo*—the term was not then in use—characterized the attitude of the Stalwarts toward those too vigorously opposed to corruption. They were "Pharisees," "gentle hermits," "saints," or "dudes." In the words of the head of the Republican machine in New York State, the reformers were "the man milliners, the dilettantes and carpet knights of politics. . . . They forget that parties are not built up by deportment, or by ladies' magazines, or gush!"[117] Blaine could not have been accused of such refinement, and yet he was now acceptable to the Half-Breeds. In the view of that quintessential Half-Breed George Frisbie Hoar, now Senator Hoar, the cloud over Blaine in 1876 had lifted. The famous letters to Fisher had in fact proved nothing against him. The charges against him "would never have found credit for a moment except in minds deeply excited by the political passion which at that time raged to a degree wholly unknown in our political strife today."[118] Hoar, no whore, had not made accommodations but kept the angle of vision which permitted him to write that "the lesson" he had learned from the Credit Mobilier and other scandals was this: an "American statesman" should "never for any political advantage support or tolerate a corrupt man, or vote for a corrupt candidate," but he also should "never abandon his principles or quit political life because of its corruption." He could not afford an unblinking look at Blaine. Hoar had, in fact, been the key congressman on the Wilson Committee in 1873 when Harrison as a government director of the U.P. had tried to interest the committee in investigating the connection between Blaine's bonds and the U.P.[119] Appointed to the committee by Blaine, Hoar then and later looked straight ahead and at the surface. The Massachusetts delegation, headed by Hoar, led the movement at the Republican Convention that rejected Arthur and eventually accepted Blaine.

Carl Schurz, leader of the Mugwumps, on August 3, 1884, delivered a speech entitled, "Why James G. Blaine Should Not Be President." The tariff, the currency, the Mormons were all topics of national interest. "But this time, the Republican National Committee has, with brutal directness, so that we face it whether we will or not, . . . forced upon this country another issue, which is infinitely more important, because it touches the vitality of our institutions. It is the question of honesty in government." With this preamble, Schurz analyzed the letters of Blaine to Fisher and Blaine's reaction when Mulligan stood ready to disclose them. Speaking with the experience of a former senator, Schurz dwelt on Blaine's power at the time he wrote the letters. He was then "by far the most powerful man in the Government, next to the President." What did his power consist in, how could he affect the railroads with which he dealt? The heart of his power had been over "the composition of committees." It was to affect the exercise of this power that the railroads had been ready to deal with him. When Blaine, seeking an interest in the Little Rock's construction, declared that he would not prove to be a dead-head and referred to "channels" where he would be of use, here was *official power offering itself for prostitution to make money.* "And this is the man we are asked to elect President of the United States and to crown with the highest honors of the Republic. In the face of these facts?"[120]

Schurz spoke in Brooklyn, addressing in particular naturalized Americans from Germany, and his speech was translated into German and distributed in thousands of pamphlets. Blaine lost the election of 1884 to Cleveland by 219 electoral votes to 182. He would have won if he had had New York's thirty-six electoral votes. He lost New York by 575 votes out of over one million votes cast. Fraud on Long Island, General Butler as the Greenback Party's candidate getting 17,000 votes in New York, a famous expression of bigotry by a Blaine supporter—any of these factors, if different, would have meant that he carried New York and the election; so too if Schurz's speech to the German immigrants in Brooklyn had not been spoken, Blaine would have won; so too if the reform-minded of New York had not been moved by the facts; so too if one more incident had not capped the case against Blaine.[121]

In September, the Boston law firm of Sohier and Welch contacted Schurz and let him know that their client had letters "which would probably be of use to you in a political point of view."[122] Their client was James Mulligan. Remarkably, there were more letters from Blaine to Fisher, which Fisher had turned over to Mulligan and which Mulligan had not brought to Washington when he had testified in 1876.

The letters were of political use, and they were printed in the Boston *Journal* of September 15, 1884. One was decisive. It was dated April 16, 1876, eight days before Blaine had spoken in the House denying the rumors of his transactions with the Union Pacific and the Little Rock. The letter contained the draft of a letter for Fisher to sign, exculpating Blaine of any special deal on the Little Rock bonds. The draft, as prepared by Blaine for Fisher, ran, "I am sure that you never owned a bond of the road that you did not pay for at the market rate." The draft denied completely Fisher's knowledge of Blaine's role as a broker and Blaine's commission in bonds to which Fisher later testified as fact. Blaine's cover letter ended, "Burn this letter. Kind regards to Mrs. Fisher."[123]

Blaine's reputation was given the coup de grâce. Already the Democrats had the jingle,

> Blaine, Blaine, James G. Blaine
> Continental liar from the state of Maine.

Now they had,

> Burn this letter. Burn this letter.
> Kind regards to Mrs. Fisher.

Shortly before the election a great Democratic procession down Broadway contained a corps of men striking matches and burning letters and repeating this chant, recalling for all in New York who had eyes to see or ears to hear how Blaine had tried to fix the inquiry into the bribe he had received from the Union Pacific.[124]

17

The Citizen Censors

The concept of bribery lived in government. It affected the careers and lives of American officials. It was a political weapon, powerful if skillfully employed. The Credit Mobilier affair had illustrated each of these propositions. They were to be illustrated repeatedly in American politics, national and local. Case after case of corruption, federal or state or city, erupted into scandal and political battle. For the concept to have this power it was necessary for it to be alive in minds other than those of politicians. In the interest the idea held for novelists, journalists, concerned citizens, bribery sustained its grip on the American consciousness.

Industrial expansion, increasing accumulation of wealth, immigration by exploitable voters, postwar relaxation of moral standards are supposed to have produced an increase in bribery, and a consequent reaction. Certainly the gross amounts offered as bribes appear to be larger as national wealth increases. But no quantitative data exist to substantiate the belief that the number of corrupted officials increased. One has only a sense of a greater consciousness of the existence of corruption. Interaction occurs between political events and the bribery tradition inherited from Israel and

Rome, Pierre le Chantre and John Bromyard, Martin Luther and Edward Coke and Edmund Burke. Events are perceived through the spectacles the tradition furnished.

The Caricaturist of Congress.   Hot on the heels of the Credit Mobilier investigation, Mark Twain and Charles Dudley Warner published a novel, *The Gilded Age*—a potboiler, a forerunner in fictional form of the instant journalism that in our time has so often turned congressional scandals into money-making paperbacks; it bore the subtitle, "A Tale of Today." Here, for instance, is one of several characters apparently modeled on Oakes Ames: "In the party of which our travellers found themselves members was Duff Brown, the great railroad contractor, and subsequently a well-known member of Congress: a bluff, jovial Bost'n man, thick set, close shaven, with a heavy jaw and a low forehead—a very pleasant man if you were not in his way. He had government contracts also, custom houses and dry docks, from Portland to New Orleans, and managed to get out of Congress, in appropriations, about weight for weight of gold for the stone furnished." Or, more succinctly with unmistakable reference to the foundation of the Ames fortune, there is "that stuffy Congressman from Massachusetts—vulgar   ungrammatical   shovel-maker—greasy   knave   of spades."[1]

A railroad fraud is first described in terms of the Pennsylvania legislature by Mr. Bigler "of the great firm of Pennybacker, Bigler and Small, railroad contractors":

> "We'll buy the lands," explained he, "on long time backed by the notes of good men; and then mortgage them for money enough to get the road well on. Then get the towns on the line to issue their bonds for stock, and sell their bonds for enough to complete the road, and partly stock it, especially if we mortgage each section as we complete it. We can then sell the rest of the stock on the prospect of the business of the road through an improved country, and also sell the lands at a big advance, on the strength of the road. All we want," continued Mr. Bigler in his frank manner, "is a few thousand dollars to start the surveys and arrange things in the legislature. There is some parties will have to be seen, who might make us trouble."[2]

" 'It will take a good deal of money to start the enterprise,' remarked Mr. Bolton who knew very well what 'seeing' a Pennsylvania Legislature meant." Bolton's daughter Ruth, the heroine, intrudes:

> "Well, what would become of the poor people who had been led to put their little money into the speculation, when you got out of it and left it half way?" Bigler replies, 'Why, yes, Miss, of course, in a great enterprise for the benefit of the community, there will little things occur, which, which . . . and then there's so many poor in the legislature to be looked after. . . . Yes, an uncommon poor lot this year, uncommon. Consequently an expensive lot. The fact is, Mr. Bolton, that the price is raised so high on United States Senator now that it affects the whole market; you cannot get any public improvement through on reasonable terms. Simony is what is I call it, Simony. . . . "[3]

The president of a second railroad going west and dependent on Congress describes to a young stockholder his expenses in getting an appropriation:

> A Congressional appropriation costs money. Just reflect, for instance. A majority of the House Committee, say $10,000 apiece—$40,000; a majority of the Senate Committee, the same each—say $40,000; a little extra to one or two chairman of one or two such committees, say $10,000 each—$20,000; and there's $100,000 of the money gone, to begin with. Then seven male lobbyists at $3,000 each—$21,000; one female lobbyist, $10,000; a high moral Congressman or Senator here and there—the high moral ones cost more, because they give tone to a measure—say ten of these at $3,000 each, is $30,000; then a lot of small-fry country members who won't vote for anything whatever without pay—say twenty at $500 apiece is $10,000; a lot of dinners to members—say $10,000 altogether; lots of jimcracks for Congressmen's wives and children—those go a long way—you can't spend too much money in that line—well, those things cost in a lump, say $10,000. . . ."

In addition there is money in advertising "because you've *got* to keep the papers all right," and money to charities, and the result is finally that to get $200,000 in appropriations you have to spend $325,000. The expense still makes economic sense: the next time the railroad will go for a half million appropriation and the next time for one million. The president has secured the receipts of the congressmen he has already paid. "All these people are in the next Congress. We shan't have to pay them a cent. And what is more, they will work like beavers for us—perhaps it might be to their advantage."[4]

A newspaperman and old Colonel Sellers from Missouri discuss the morals of the current Congress: "To be sure you can buy now and then a Senator or a Representative; but they do not know it is wrong, and so they are not ashamed of it," says the newspaperman. Colonel Sellers replies that it is "sinful" and "shameful. . . . And yet when you come to look at it you cannot deny that we would have to go without the services of some of our ablest men, sir, if the country were opposed to—to—bribery. It is a harsh term. I do not like to use it."[5]

Several congressmen, including the derisively named Mr. Trollop, are described as buying stock in an enterprise known as the National Improvement "without paying a penny down"—"think of the happy idea of receiving dividends, and very large ones, too, from stock one hasn't paid for!" The speaker, Laura Hawkins, a country girl turned female lobbyist, tells Trollop: "Now you see, you had to know one of two things: namely, you either knew that the idea of all this preposterous generosity was to bribe you into future legislative friendship, or you *didn't* know it. That is to say, you had to be either a knave or a—well, a fool—there was no middle ground. *You* are not a fool, Mr. Trollop."[6] Colonel Sellers continues to maintain that "there is still a very respectable minority of honest men in Congress" and that they will investigate corruption. Of course no one will be expelled: "That would not be regular.... But all that inquiry is not lost. It has a good moral effect." Washington Hawkins, Laura's naive brother, asks, "Who does it have a good moral effect on?" Sellers answers, "Well—I don't know. On foreign countries, I think.... It shows that a man cannot be corrupt in this country without sweating for it. I can tell you that."[7]

Sellers goes on to say, "Look what Congress did to Mr. Fairoaks." "Well, what *did* Congress do?" asks the colonel's simple interlocutor. "You know what Congress did, Washington. Congress intimated plainly enough, that they considered him almost a stain upon their body; and without waiting ten days, hardly, to think the thing over, they rose up and hurled at him a resolution declaring that they disapproved of his conduct!... You can depend on it, Washington. Congress is vindictive, Congress is savage, sir, when it gets waked up once."[8]

Running through *The Gilded Age* is the attempt of Laura and Washington Hawkins to dispose of their ancestral acres in eastern Tennessee at a high price to the federal government. In this enterprise they have as a patron Senator Abner Dilworthy, a great friend of the Negro, who at length proposes an Industrial University in eastern Tennessee to educate blacks, to be situated on the Hawkins' property, and to be federally financed. The bill goes to the House where a key person is Mr. Buckstone, chairman of "the House Committee on Benevolent Appropriations." Laura flirts with him; badinage is as close to sex as the novel goes. Mr. Trollop, an avowed opponent of the bill, is finally won over not by bribery but by a move that, a century later, seems curiously innocuous. Laura, unknown to him, is the ghost writer of one of his important speeches. She keeps evidence of her collaboration and says she will reveal her part in his speech if Trollop fails to work for her bill. Trollop collapses before the threat.[9]

The bill passes the House with three million dollars authorized to buy the worthless Tennessee land. It is denounced by the metropolitan press as "iniquitous." Senator Dilworthy rejoices as the invective mounts—the public will react in his favor.[10] However, he himself encounters an unexpected disaster. Up for reelection by his state's legislature, he offers a persistent opponent, Mr. Noble, $7,000 in cash. Noble takes his money and then denounces him on the floor of the legislature, adding that there are fifty other members present with money in their pockets from Dilworthy. The legislature rejects Dilworthy, and the Senate rejects the Industrial University bill.[11]

The Hawkinses are left in the lurch. But Dilworthy, now a lame duck, demands an investigation by the Senate. Noble becomes its object. Dilworthy assures the committee that the $7,000 was borrowed by him from a nameless friend to help another young friend hoping to start a bank in a distant corner of the state; he gave it to Noble at midnight to take to his young friend. The committee threatens Noble for a while—"by his own confession he accepted a bribe"—but in the end it concludes that no bribe has been proved. When a senator "of the worn-out and obsolete pattern" moves to expel Dilworthy, he is met by the argument given by "the

Massachusetts General in the House," that Dilworthy's presence for the few remaining days of the Senate would not "contaminate the Senate to a dreadful degree." The Senate recognizes "that it could not be contaminated by sitting a few days longer with Senator Dilworthy, and so it accepted the committee's report and dropped the unimportant matter."[12]

In the winter session of 1868–1869, Mark Twain had been the secretary of Senator William Stewart of Nevada, and the Credit Mobilier must then have come to his attention, although he had left before Stewart opened his attack upon it. In his notebook he jotted down points about congressmen he had seen: Oakes Ames—"Car'd Pac RR as much or more than any"; General Garfield—"young, able, & scholarly—was chief of Rosecranz staff—preacher"; General Butler—"one reliable eye. Is short & pursy."[13] These impressions, digested for four years, were mixed in The Gilded Age with his immediate reactions to the session of Congress that rebuked Brooks and Ames. As early as March 4, 1873, he was seeking, unsuccessfully, to get Thomas Nast to illustrate his novel and describing it as an "essentially American book." He had the manuscript in hand by June.[14] He had used what the session provided, with small alterations. Dilworthy was modeled on Samuel Pomeroy, elected to the Senate in 1861 as a radical Republican, accused in 1873 of offering $8,000 in the Kansas legislature to obtain a vote for his re-election, cleared by the Senate and defeated for re-election. The Industrial University in eastern Tennessee was transparently Fisk Institute in Knoxville, the recent beneficiary of federal legislation. The retroactive doubling of congressional pay in 1873 had become "the Indigent Congressman's Retroactive Appropriation." The DeGoyler pavement contract, another of Garfield's "woes," was recalled by "Dobson's Patent Pavement," marketed by Bigler. There was a swing to New York City where Laura was tried for murder and acquitted before an Irish judge, unmistakably a creature of the Tweed ring, who had earlier made his fortune selling spittoons for the New York courthouse at $1,000 per spittoon.[15]

The main fare was provided by the Credit Mobilier investigation and debate. Dilworthy's story of his borrowing from an unidentified friend to lend the cash at midnight to Noble for another unidentified friend was not far from the kind of tale told the Poland and Wilson Committees by James Brooks, Cornelius Bushnell, and Schuyler Colfax. The $3,000 price per head of committee members was not far from the $2,500 figure used in Spence's memo on the disposition of the Union Pacific's $126,000. The argument against expulsion of a corrupt member was General Butler's. Undigested, chunks of the Credit Mobilier matter padded out the plot. At its best The Gilded Age was like a Mark Russell show lampooning at the Shoreham or on television the politicians of the present. It was funny because true. The truth, clean of pompous pretense, seemed absurd if measured by a standard higher than that used by Congress.

The religious imagery interwoven into the story linked it to the inherited learning on bribery. When Bigler calls the high market price of the Pennsylvania legislature "simony," it is of course a joke—an ironic joke that a lobbyist ready to buy legislators should denounce their high price by the ecclesiastical category. The joke cannot be appreciated without reference to the old religious meaning; and the novel as a whole cannot be understood without reference to the old religious tradition. The basic norm measuring what goes on is that of Colonel Sellers. He does not like to use the plain English Christian term for it, bribery, but he does; and when he does, he denounces bribery as "a sin" and "a shame." A minority of Congress is not corrupted—the notion of an elect, a possibly saving remnant, is preserved even as the effectiveness of the elect is being satirized because Congress is going to do little to check the corruption. In the end, evil is defeated and good rewarded. Dilworthy loses his election and his university bill. Laura the lobbyist dies ignominiously. In a plot that forms a counterpoint to the career of the corruptionists, Ruth, a hard-working doctor, is united to her truelove Harry who has labored to discover a coal field. The dénouement and the critique of the congressmen's action and inaction are intelligible only if a moral standard exists by which good and evil are judged. That moral standard is biblical. Even the punishment implied to be condign is from Genesis: Congress is weak and worthless, Sellers's jibes suggest, because it merely censures. What it should have done to corrupted members like Mr. Fairoaks is what God did to Adam.

During the Christmas holidays of 1874, General Garfield attended Mark Twain's adaptation of the novel as a play, *Colonel Sellers*. Garfield found the show, which had run three months in New York, to be "a piece whose stupidity is only equaled by the brilliant acting of Colonel Sellers." He added, "The play is full of malignant insinuations and would lead the hearer to believe that there is no virtue in the world, in public or in private life." The virtue to which Garfield referred, that traditional and transcendent virtue which required probity in office, was tacitly acknowledged as much by this participant in Credit Mobilier as by the author of the lampoon.[16]

The Alienated Observers of Power.   "Poor Blaine squeals louder than all the other pigs." The comment was that of Henry Adams to another young reformer, Henry Cabot Lodge, as he read Blaine's explanation of the Blaine-Fisher letters and thought of other squeals like those from Schuyler Colfax.[17] Sometime between 1876 and the summer of 1879 Adams composed a novel one of whose characters, Senator Ratcliffe, is often asserted to be Blaine, but if he is Blaine, he is so only in a moral sense. Ratcliffe is an ex-governor, a Midwesterner, a secretary of the Treasury, a power in the administration succeeding Grant's, none of which Blaine was. A "prairie giant," he has an underlying coarseness reminiscent of Adams's horrified Bostonian comments on Stephen Douglas—"gross, vulgar, demagogic." He has a family background in New England and "a kind of classical education at one of the country colleges there," two features which recall Garfield. His durability also suggests Adams's view of Garfield, of whom he wrote prophetically to his brother in 1869, with a nice sense of the uses of reciprocity: "So get ready to help him, for he may help you some day. We may never come up, but he probably will swim pretty strong."[18] Composed of parts of other men, Ratcliffe is still Blaine if we may assume, as it appears reasonable to do, that Henry Adams agreed with his wife Clover that Blaine "represents the corruption element as thoroughly as any man can."[19]

From Clover's letters to her father it is evident that she loathed Blaine, and the intensity of her dislike reflected her moral judgment on "the corruption element." Her feelings no doubt were those of a member of an established class toward a parvenu. Nowhere does she record that her uncle Samuel Hooper had been on the ground floor of the Credit Mobilier, acquiring 750 shares in 1865 from Oakes Ames: family was not to be put on the same level as the greedy newcomer. But the strength of her feelings against Blaine exemplify a new force in America—the hatred of educated women for the corruptionists. Women had been made the special embodiments of purity in nineteenth-century America. *Democracy* used a cliché in treating Madeleine Lee as the guardian of integrity. Women had also internalized the common image. Clover was among them. If Clover did not actually have a part in the composition of *Democracy*—there is some evidence she did—her feelings pervade the novel, and its heroine embodies her spirit, her values, her clear-eyed perceptions, and her unsparing judgments. Clover scorned "the ward politician"—her phrase for President Chester Arthur—and "the machine politicians." She laughed when her pert friend Emily Beale told Secretary of the Navy George Robeson to his face that he was bound for the penitentiary; and she blithely referred to Mayor Fernando Wood of New York as "an ex-forger." When Blaine with "his stained record" became secretary of State under Garfield, it was "a gross insult to the moral sense of the community." She and Henry resolved to attend no parties where he was a guest—a resolution that struck many contemporaries as quixotic. Writing her father, she referred to Blaine when he was nearly caught as "the rat-Blaine" and as "the Blaine-rat." Only a syllable separates these names from "Ratcliffe."[20]

Democracy, the Adams novel, appeared anonymously in 1880: Madeleine Lee, a widow of thirty, has come to Washington to try to understand "the heart of the great American mystery of democracy and government."[21] She is intelligent, spirited, and rich. She establishes a salon to which are attracted John Carrington, a forty-year-old Virginian and ex-rebel, now a Washington lawyer and lobbyist; Baron Jacobi, an old and cynical Bulgarian diplomat; C. C. French, a reforming young congressman from Connecticut; Nathan Gore, a historian from Massachusetts; and Silas P. Ratcliffe, senator from Illinois, a major power in the Republican Party and recently defeated candidate for nomination to the presidency. The time is shortly before a new Republican president takes office.

As the gentlemen swirl about Madeleine, with varying degrees of romantic interest, French speaks out for Civil Service reform. Ratcliffe replies "that the most famous products of Connecticut are Yankee notions, nutmegs made of wood and clocks that won't go. Now, your Civil Service Reform is just such another Yankee notion; it's a wooden nutmeg; it's a clock with a show case and sham works." Madeleine asks, "Surely something can be done to check corruption? . . . Is a respectable government impossible in a democracy?" Ratcliffe responds, "Purify society and you purify the government. But try to purify the government artificially and you only aggravate failure." Baron Jacobi comments:

> You Americans believe yourselves to be excepted from the operation of general laws. You care not for experience. I have lived seventy-five years, and all that time in the midst of corruption. I am corrupt myself. . . . Well, I declare to you that in all my experience I have found no society which has had elements of corruption like the United States. The children in the street are corrupt, and know how to cheat me. The cities are all corrupt, and also the towns and counties and the States' legislatures and the judges. . . . I do much regret that I have not yet one hundred years to live. If I could then come back to this city, I should find myself very content—much more than now. I am always content where there is much corruption, and *ma parole d'honneur* the United States will then be more corrupt than Rome under Caligula; more corrupt than the Church under Leo X; more corrupt than France under the Regent![22]

Madeleine is not convinced. "Mr. Ratcliffe seems honest and wise. Is he a corruptionist? . . . I must know whether America is right or wrong. Just now this question is a very practical one, for I really want to know whether to believe in Mr. Ratcliffe. If I throw him overboard, everything must go, for he is only a specimen." Carrington, who is becoming attached to Madeleine and sees Ratcliffe as a rival, is "very well aware that the weak side of the Senator lay in his blind ignorance of morals."[23]

A false February spring produces a June-like temperature shortly before the new administration comes in in March. The author observes:

> In such a world there should be no guile—but there is a great deal of it notwithstanding. Indeed, at no other season is there so much. This is the moment when the two whited sepulchres at either end of the Avenue reek with the thick atmosphere of bargain and sale. The old is going; the new is coming. Wealth, office, power are at auction. Who bids highest? who hates with most venom? who intrigues with most skill? who has done the dirtiest, the meanest, the darkest, and the most, political work? He shall have his reward.

Ratcliffe's friends fear that the new president will take away "their honestly-earned harvest of foreign missions and consulates, department-bureaus, custom-house and revenue offices, postmasterships, Indian agencies, and army and navy contracts. . . ." They plot with their leader to capture him.[24]

Ratcliffe outwits the president, becomes his secretary of the Treasury, and controls the key patronage. He is also riding high with Madeleine, until Mrs. Sam Baker, the widow of "a noted lobbyist" enters the scene. Her husband has died, leaving Carrington as his executor. Carrington has had access to his papers and has obtained information compromising to Ratcliffe. Mrs. Baker boasts to Madeleine about the success she and her husband had "in the lobby." Madeleine asks, "But how did you do it? did they take bribes?" She answers, "Some of them did. Some of them liked suppers and cards and theatres and all sorts of things. Some of them could be led, and some had to be driven like Paddy's pig who thought he was going the other way. Some of them had wives who could talk to them, and some—hadn't." The last words are choked on "with a queer intonation in her abrupt ending." Madeleine persists: "Now, how would you have gone to work to get a respectable senator's vote—a man like Mr. Ratcliffe, for instance?" Mrs. Baker does not answer directly, saying, "But you see, what we generally wanted was right enough."[25]

As these events occur, Nathan Gore has come to disappointment in his search for a diplomatic post. The president has dismissed him as a "man-milliner." Madeleine consoles him: "But after all, why should politicians be expected to love you literary gentlemen who write history? Other criminal classes are not expected to love their judges." For Ratcliffe, Madeleine is the judge: "You judge with the judgment of abstract principles," he tells her, "and you wield the bolts of divine justice."[26]

Obscurely aware of her suspicions, he decides to present himself to Madeleine as one who, from necessity, has not been entirely pure. Earlier in their acquaintance he had told her openly a story known to everyone in Illinois, how, when he was governor of the state during the war, he was afraid that the presidential vote of 1864 was going against the Republicans. "Had Illinois been lost then, we should certainly have lost the Presidential election, and with it probably the Union." Accordingly, he ordered the election officials in the northern counties to withhold their returns until all the southern counties were in and we "learned the precise number of votes we needed to give us a majority." He then directed what the northern returns would be. Madeleine had been unable to condemn this wartime action. Now, proposing to her, he tells her, "In politics we cannot keep our hands clean. I have done many things in my political career that are not defensible. To act with entire honesty and self-respect, we should always live in a pure atmosphere, and the atmosphere of politics is impure. Domestic life is the salvation of many public men. . . ."[27]

Madeleine is about to accept his proposal, but Carrington breaches his professional obligation of confidentiality, "because," he tells her, "I owe you a duty which seems to me to override all others." Drawing on the papers of the deceased Baker, he informs her of the circumstances in which, eight years earlier, the Inter-Oceanic Mail Steamship Company obtained "a heavy subsidy" from Congress to "extend its service round the world." The bill had passed the House and was stalled in a Senate committee, of which Ratcliffe was chairman. Ratcliffe had shown himself "decidedly hostile." "All ordinary kinds of argument and influence had been employed upon him, and were exhausted." At this point Baker asked authority from the company "to see what money would do." He received the authority, spent $100,000, and in forty-eight hours the bill was out of committee and passed by the Senate. According to Mrs. Baker, her husband delivered the $100,000 in bearer bonds of the United States to Senator Ratcliffe.[28]

All papers showing the transaction have been destroyed. The company books were "undoubtedly kept as to show no trace of it." Ratcliffe will deny it. How can Madeleine be sure it happened? Carrington suggests that she confront him with his letter setting out the story. She is already thinking of Ratcliffe as "a man who if law were the same thing as justice, ought to be in a felon's cell, a man who could take money to betray his trust." She is "impatient for the moment when she would see him again, and tear off his mask."[29]

When she does confront him, he says the story is "true in its leading facts; untrue in some of its details and the impression it creates." The occasion occurred when it was essential to prevent the government from falling into "the blood-stained hands of rebels." The National Committee had spent money freely, and it had borrowed a very large sum on pledged securities. The head of the National Committee and two senators came to Ratcliffe and told him that he must drop his opposition to the Inter-Oceanic's bill. Ratcliffe asked nothing more when they said that this action on his part "was essential to the interests of the party." If the money was paid at all, of which Ratcliffe himself has no personal knowledge, it was paid to a representative of the National Committee.[30]

As Madeleine listens to this story, she doubts that he knows "the difference between good and evil, between a lie and the truth." He talks of virtue and vice as the colorblind do of red and green. He suffers from an "atrophy of the moral senses." Yet he persists in his position. She did not condemn him when he told of his action as governor in which he "had even violated the sanctity of a great popular election and reversed its result." In comparison with that act, the money taken from the steamship company was "a trifle. . . . Perhaps its stockholders receive one dollar a share in dividends less than they otherwise would." And he insists that "there are conflicting duties in all the transactions of life, except the simplest." Was he in this case to abandon his obligations to the party and the Union?[31]

She hesitates. Earlier her sister had predicted that Ratcliffe "expects one of these days to find a bribe that will answer" in winning over Madeleine; and as she hesitates, he offers to abandon politics, at least for a period, to accept the American embassy in London, and to take her there where her "social position would be the best in the world." To this offer she responds: "Mr. Ratcliffe, I am not to be bought."[32]

He leaves in anger, is struck by Baron Jacobi with his cane as the result of jostling him at the door, and is left with "an impassable gulf" between his life and Madeleine's. As she heard his story, she "felt as though she had got to the heart of politics, so that she could, like a physician with his stethoscope, measure the organic disease." She now leaves Washington for Egypt to "look out for ever at the polar star."[33]

The Gilded Age was true but one-sided in its parody of the Credit Mobilier. *Democracy* is true, balanced, and fair—balanced because it does not present Ratcliffe as simply betraying his trust for purely selfish reasons, fair because it allows him to present a universal argument of bribetakers and bribegivers: necessity. The necessity of the country at war, the necessity of the country after the war, the necessity of the Republican Party, these are arguments Ratcliffe uses not implausibly. The story of the ratification of the Thirteenth Amendment, never mentioned, is in the background. Even if, as Adams indicates, the true story is that Ratcliffe had dragged the Party "into an enormous expenditure to carry his own State, and with it his own re-election to the Senate," and that "he himself had privately suggested recourse to Baker," the necessity of campaign funds is at the heart of American democracy.[34] The necessities he is allowed to plead are those of concrete situations. Madeleine is taxed with judging by "abstract principles." His argument is capped by the claim that there are always conflicts of duties where a choice must be made. Naïvely, Madeleine wants to keep morality uncomplicated, straight, and simple. Ratcliffe's position is not only fairly argued but fairly exemplified. Madeleine herself has just been saved only because, in a conflict of duties, Carrington chose love of her over his professional obligation to keep a secret.

The novel, however, sides with Madeleine. Carrington's early judgment on Ratcliffe's "blind ignorance of morals" is confirmed. Carrington's own breach did not involve selling a trust. Madeleine herself cannot be "bought," and she will not associate with a man who has been bought. The denial of Madeleine to Ratcliffe—the fixing of the "impassable gulf" between them—is the punishment Ratcliffe suffers for his sin.

Sin is what Ratcliffe is seen as committing, a sin judged directly by Madeleine who wields "the bolts of divine justice." Although God is not mentioned, the language of religious tradition is used. Writing Lodge, Adams had spoken of Blaine and Colfax as squealing pigs—shades of Cicero's Hog! But *Democracy*'s vocabulary is Christian. Ratcliffe in his incomplete confession acknowledges that his hands are not "clean," that he has engaged in an "impure" activity. In the novelist's direct intrusion into the novel, inserted just before his protagonists' journey to the shrine of George Washington at Mount Vernon (a shrine with a tomb with an unresurrected body) the language echoes the Gospels: In a true renewal of life there should be no "guile"; in the false spring of Washington there is a great deal. At either end of Pennsylvania Avenue stand the Capitol and the White House, and they are, like those hypocrites Jesus denounced, "whited sepulchers." The promise held out to him who has done "the dirtiest" work is a reverse application of Jesus' promise, that "he shall have his reward." At *Democracy*'s end, the "impassable gulf" is "the great chasm" which, in Luke 16:26, Father Abraham tells the rich man in hell that none may cross.

Only Jacobi, the European, admits that he is corrupt. All the Americans appear to act on the assumption that they have the innocence of the first

Adam. Ratcliffe, even when trapped, will not confess guilt. The corrupt European, acknowledging his sin, even if less repentantly than the sinner in the Gospel, goes away more justified than the American with the illusion of his innocence.

What of Madeleine herself? She does not acknowledge that she is saved only by Carrington's breach of trust. (When a year after the novel came out Jere Black broke a similar professional trust to reveal Garfield's corruption, he was to the Adams' close friend, John Hay "an old blackguard"). Madeleine's uncompromisingly harsh judgment on Ratcliffe reflects her own self-righteousness. The religious language is all borrowed and metaphorical. The judgment is now.[35]

The moral standard by which corruption is condemned is used without reference to redemption. "If I throw him overboard," Madeleine had said to herself about Ratcliffe, "everything must go, for he is only a specimen." When he is thrown overboard, she rejects American politics in toto as corrupt. Nothing opposes Baron Jacobi's statement that all are corrupt and his apocalyptic prediction of a climax of corruption in America about the year 1976. Ratcliffe is not permitted to find "salvation" in domestic life. Madeleine herself, one of the elect, saves herself only by withdrawal to the desert, only by a flight to Egypt. The last line of the book—Madeleine's— contrasts the *massa damnata* and the elect: "The bitterest part of all this horrid story is that nine out of ten of our countrymen would say I had made a mistake."

The bitterest part of all, however, was that *Democracy* used religious criteria and imagery without faith. Unlike Dante, the author did not turn from condemnation of corrupt rulers and a corrupt Church to God. Only the hope—better said, the possibility—of supernatural assistance exists. Actual judgment is on earth—Madeleine's in the first instance, the historian's in the longer run; and *Democracy* offers judgment in a form where Ratcliffe is forever damned.

Over twenty years later, after Clover had killed herself, Henry Adams was to refer to "my master Job," and later still he was to express in a prayer to the Virgin at Chartres a faith in a redeeming power that his niece believed sustained him at the end. But what he thought at the time *Democracy* was written was different:

> The newspapers discussed little else than the alleged moral laxity of Grant, Garfield, and Blaine. . . . In spite of all such criticism the public nominated Grant, Garfield, and Blaine for the Presidency and voted for them afterwards, not seeming to care for the question; until young men were forced to see that either some new standard must be created, or none could be upheld. The moral law had expired—like the Constitution.[36]

This retrospective passage, written much later in *The Education of Henry Adams*, appears to equate vindication of the moral law with results at the polls. No other sanction had seemed satisfactory. Small wonder that the younger Adams thought that the moral law had expired! His conclusion had the bitter pessimism of a man with a great political heritage who held aloof and was not counted. Voteless Clover and officeless Henry stood outside the power struggle, unable to influence outcomes but capable of invoking against the winners the bolts of judgment prepared in an earlier age by believers in divine judgment and divine retribution.

The Diary of a Concerned Citizen.   Novelists reflected the public consciousness of bribery and contributed to that consciousness a sense of its prevalence, effectiveness, and gravity. Other American citizens revealed their thinking only in private conversation, correspondence, and memoirs. They were the constituents Ames and Blaine and Garfield had to keep in mind. They were the readers of Mark Twain and Henry Adams. Such a citizen was George Templeton Strong, a lawyer in New York City, the son of a lawyer in New York City, the grandson of a judge in Massachusetts. Graduate of Columbia, forty-nine years old in 1867, a devout Episcopalian, Strong kept a diary, published only in 1952. Quotations from it follow:[37]

The Citizen lobbies in Albany, N.Y. and makes an incidental observation:
March 16, 1867. This is a most corrupt and profligate legislature. A legislator who is asked to oppose a lawless and mischievous measure, and who responds by putting his open palm behind him—wide open—inviting a little honorarium of greenbacks, is a bad fruit of our prevalent political theories. . . .

The Citizen regrets his (relative) poverty:
March 19, 1867. . . . What a dreary time this is! Ellie shews me some little gimcrack I gave her ten or fifteen years ago, and casually remarks, "How rich we were *then*"—! Very true. We are very poor now. But she takes whatever comes, like an honest, true-hearted Christian woman. If she bewailed herself, and deplored prices and the currency, as many women would, I think I should blow out my brains.

Corruption comes home to the Citizen:
March 21, 1867. . . . N.B. This house has changed its number. It has been No. 74 East Twenty-first Street ever since it has been inhabited—that is, since October, 1849. It is now No. 113 East 21st Street, re-numbered by order of the Common Council. Some tinman, influential among the blackguards and loafers of his ward, coveted the job of furnishing these new tin tickets. Our civic government, and I fear our state government, too, is utterly profligate and corrupt.

The Citizen observes an expensive municipal construction:
April 2, 1867. . . . Looked in at the New Court House this morning while waiting to keep an appointment at surrogate's office. One of its rooms fitted up and Court of Appeals sitting therein. Sorry to see that this building is not fireproof, though it is so costly a swindle.

The Citizen views the judicial system of his state:
April 9, 1868. . . . Bench and bar settle deeper in the mud every year and every month. They must be near the bottom now. Witness the indecencies done and suffered by Dudley Field, Barnard, Brady, Haskin, etc., in General Term of Supreme Court, as reported in the newspapers. Their reports are emasculated, and many bits of specially pungent Billingsgate are suppressed as too filthy for print. This combat of night scavengers was an affair of outposts in the great Erie Railroad war, the controversy of Drew and Vanderbilt. The Supreme Court is our *Cloaca Maxima*, with lawyers for its rats. But my simile does that rodent injus-

tice, for the rat is a remarkably clean animal. Johnny's pet is always cleaning himself. . . .

The Citizen makes an atrocious pun:

November 3, 1868. . . . Extras are strangely infrequent for the evening of an election day in this very Democratic city, controlled by the purest of the Cork-asian race, and their paucity is a good sign.

The judiciary's contribution to the naturalization of recent immigrants is noted by the Citizen, and he employs a Wagnerian metaphor. He regrets the escape of the enemy's fortress:

November 4, 1868. Fine day. Grant is certainly elected, but this state is lost, thanks to the enormous crop of fraudulent voters in the culture of which I believe Hoffman himself is none too good to have worked with Barnard and McCunn and other ornaments of the Bench. There is talk of contesting the returns, but it will come to naught, and the next session at Albany will be a long Walpurgis night of all political filthiness and corruption. . . . The new Tammany Hall, 14th Street, was on fire this afternoon, I hear, but unfortunately not burned up. . . .

The Citizen forecasts revolution:

May 20, 1869. . . . Last night, Law School Commencement, . . . four speeches, prepared without concert, should each have been mainly an expression of the same thought, viz., that corruption in our legislative bodies, our great corporations, and now even in the state judiciary, and in the sheriff's office, has at least reached a stage that must produce revolutionary action if no legal remedy can be found. Such things are "in the air." The strongest expressions to this effect received the loudest applause, and every condemnation of our accursed elective judiciary system brought down the house. I verily believe we are nearly ripe for a Vigilance Committee. No help from Albany can be hoped for. Railroad kings (Fisks, Vanderbilts, and the like) and scoundrelly "Rings" control our state legislation. The dishonesty of every man in public office is a violent presumption, and universally recognized as such. No decent man can take public office without imminent danger of losing caste, unless he compel the respect of a defrauded but corrupt community by the accumulation of at least one or two millions of fraudulent profit. This state of things cannot last much longer without an explosion.

Mention of two judges leads the Citizen to reflection on judicial office:

December 18, 1869. . . . N.B. Barnard and Cardozo (*arcades ambo*) seem to have fallen out a little. The stink of our state judiciary is growing too strongly ammoniac and hippuric for endurance. Like Trinculo, we "do smell all h——p——" whenever we read or hear of the sayings or doings of the average New York judge. He is as bad as the New York alderman, if not worse, because his office is more sacred. People begin to tire of holding their noses, and are looking about in a helpless way for some remedy. The nuisance must be abated somehow and that soon, but I see no hope of its abatement, except by a most perilous process, justified only by the extremest necessity, and after all constitutional remedies are exhausted. Some change is certainly needed most urgently. Law protects life no longer. Any scoundrel who is backed by a little political influence in the corner groceries of his ward can commit murder with almost absolute impunity. The sheriff's office is a den of Celtic thieves, roughs, and *Sicarii*. Law does not protect property. The abused machinery of Law is a terror to property owners. No banker or merchant is sure that some person, calling himself a "receiver," appointed *ex parte* as the first step in some frivolous suit he never heard of, may not march into his counting room at any moment, demand possession of all his assets and the ruinous suspension of his whole business, and when the order for a receiver is vacated a week afterwards, claim $100,000 or so as "an allowance" for his services, by virtue of another order, to be enforced by attachment. No city can long continue rich and prosperous that tolerates abuses like these. Capital will flee to safer quarters.

The Citizen, engaged professionally in litigation, reacts to the presiding judge, the father of a future justice of the Supreme Court:

December 21, 1869. Another dull December day, with an ash-colored sky, and with gaseous extract of damp streets by way of atmosphere. More Cardozo, and no progress. I think Nature meant Cardozo to sweep the court room, not to preside in it, and that he would look more natural in the dock of the Sessions than on the Bench of the Supreme Court.

The decent men (one or two anomalies excepted) organize. The Citizen identifies a type of judicial bribery and reinforces a prejudice:

February 2, 1870. . . . Last night's meeting (Twenty-sixth Street and Fifth Avenue, at George C. Anthon's school building) was successful. It sought to create a "bar association" and appointed committees for that purpose. The decent part of the profession was well represented. Nearly two hundred were present, and among them was the virtuous D. D. Field. Van Winkle was in the chair. Speeches by Judge Emott, Henry Nicoll, Evarts, John McKeon (!), D. B. Eaton, S. J. Tilden, and others were generally rather good, though too subdued in tone to suit my taste. But Choate and others told me that they thought moderation is best at first. I have not much hope of good from this movement, but it may possibly accomplish something.

Here is a specimen—a very mild specimen—of the way in which the Supreme Court of the state of New York does business. In these Schermerhorn partition suits, the parties—all *sui juris* and all represented—agreed on three commissioners, all well known as experts in real estate and as beyond exception. When the interlocutory decree appointing them is moved for, Mr. Justice Cardozo says that Mr. Gratz Nathan, another little Jew and a nephew of the judge's, must be a commissioner and that we may choose which of the three we will strike out to make room for him! Nathan would do no service and would charge $10,000 for doing it. Cardozo would confirm the charge and probably pocket half the money. . . .

The Citizen holds judicial office to be a disqualification for a position of social respectability and fiduciary responsibility:

April 17, 1870, EASTER SUNDAY. . . . Braem seems much gratified by his election—or rather, by his nomination—to Trinity Church vestry. Vinton was anxious that one Spencer, a justice of the Superior Court and a regular attendant at Trinity, should be put on the ticket. What we hear of his personal character seems in his favor. But when his name was brought up at our little conference on Thursday week, his position on the bench was held a fatal objection to him. He must have been put there with the approval of the Ring and is, therefore, open to violent suspicion of being everything a vestryman of Trinity Church should not be. The objection is unanswerable, but what an illustration it is of the degradation of this city! A seat on the bench of the Superior Court, where Duer and Oakley sat twenty years ago, is now *prima facie* evidence of dishonesty and has become a disqualification for any office connected with the administration of an important religious trust.

Two judges and Alderman William M. Tweed turn the Citizen's mind to thoughts of revenge:

October 18, 1870. . . . If misrule could ever justify assassination of the ruler, ours would justify it; for in such *canaille* as Bill Tweed and Barnard and Cardozo we have only tyrants, but tyrants beneath contempt—vulgar swindlers who ought to be in the penitentiary. . . .

The Citizen, jubilant, recalls another diarist:

November 9, 1870. . . . Hoffman and Tammany triumphed yesterday, of course, but by a reduced majority. Some twenty-six thousand votes seem to have been kept from the polls by the terror of U.S. marshals, federal bayonets, and courts that "Tammany does not own," and which are, therefore, prepared to punish fraudulent voters. Oakey Hall runs far behind his ticket, "which do please me mightily"—to quote Pepys.

The Citizen meditates on sovereigns:

April 21, 1871. . . . Congress has adjourned, after passing the Ku-Klux Bill, from which little good is to be expected, and after a disgraceful interchange of Billingsgate between the Hon. B. F. Butler and certain other "honorable" blackguards. The state legislature is about to become inodorous and adjourn. The Ring has carried all its measures with the help of a Republican member, O. Winans of Chautauqua, who ratted opportunely (I hope he had self-respect enough to insist on a good price), and the city of New York is now at its mercy—autonomy, self-government, rights of suffrage, and "democratic principles" being ignored. "Boss" Tweed and his tail are sovereigns of this city and county. Perhaps the title "Boss of New York" will grow into permanence and figure in history like that of the doge of Venice. All titles have their beginnings, and we may be ruled henceforth by a series of bosses, hereditary or nominally elective. This may prove a degree better than the direct rule of 30,000 beastly Celtic bogtrotters.

The Citizen adjusts the means to the end, and puns:

July 22, 1871. . . . The *Times* is creating a deep sensation by detailed statements of vast sums embezzled by the Ring, with names, dates, and amounts. Some clerk in the Comptroller's office has been bought, no doubt. An unclean job, but one must fight the Devil with fire. As yet there appears no answer. But even Bill Tweed the Boss (that is *Der Böse*), Oakey Hall, Sweeny & Co., cannot let three distinct (verifiable) charges of fraud go by default.

The Citizen finds the *Times's* case established:

July 26, 1871. . . . The New York *Times* continues its revelations, which are making an impression that I hope will last. Mayor Hall replies at last, feebly and irresponsibly, severely criticizing the motives of the editor. These disclosures of Tammany's iniquity may now be considered as taken *pro confesso.*

The corruptibility of the press; the short memory of the electorate, according to the Citizen:

July 27, 1871. . . . The New York *Times* revelations seem to be discussed in nearly every newspaper in the country, except the *Herald* and others of this city. They are mostly bought by the Ring. Even the *Post* and the *Tribune*, generally reputed honest, speak out less boldly than they should, because they value the advertising patronage of Tweed and Company. The feeble babbling of the *World* in defense of Oakey Hall is contemptible. "He might have been compelled to sign these (flagitious) warrants by a mandamus"; possibly. But why did he interpose no objection, make no resistence, or public protest, and at least warn the community of these enormous frauds to which he now pretends that "the law" compelled him to be an accessory?

Significant fact that $40,000 of city bonds put up at auction yesterday found no bidders. But it's a great misfortune that these disclosures are made at this time; for everybody is out of town, and vigorous action is impossible. By next October everyone will have begun to think of something else, and there will be no vigorous campaign against these thieves and ruffians.

The citizenry organizes. The Citizen's father-in-law and the current John Jacob Astor hang back:

September 4, 1871.... Grand meeting on Tammany frauds at Cooper Institute at eight. Walked down with Murray Hoffman, Jr. Had a card for the platform, but the crowd and heat were beyond endurance; so I adjourned to the committee room awhile with Dr. Lieber, [Oswald] Ottendorfer of the *Staats-Zeitung*, Peter Cooper, and others, and then looked at the auxiliary open-air meeting. Both seemed earnest and uproarious. Havemeyer was speaking when I left the hall, constantly interrupted by earnest plaudits. But the minds of a New York assemblage are as running water. The impressions of today are effaced tomorrow.

The disease of this community lies too deep to be cured by meetings, resolutions, and committees. We the people are a low set, without moral virility. Our rulers, Tweed and Company, are about good enough for us. The Alcibiades of New York is Mr. James Fisk. Mr. J. G. Bennett, Jr. who makes money by printing the advertisements of abortionists ... is elected "commodore"—or some such thing—by the aristocratic Yacht Club of New York, and is a leader of fashion in the Belmont clique. John Astor, Willy Duncan, William T. Blodgett, and others sit in the same railroad direction with vermin like Bill Tweed.

In discourse with Astor and Mr. Ruggles in Wall Street about this meeting, I found neither inclined to be "prominent" in it. Mr. Ruggles fears these villains might take vengeance on him by stopping certain improvements now in progress to the damage of sundry uptown lots of his. But his conscience is a little uncomfortable.

The Citizen's father-in-law joins the fray. The Citizen weighs the mixed motives of a judge:

September 5, 1871.... Mr. Ruggles is on the Executive Committee of Seventy appointed by last night's meeting. The Seventy make their first move against the Powers of Darkness tomorrow (papers prepared in advance). Mr. Justice Barnard (!!!) is to be asked for an injunction against what Shakespeare calls the "ring the country wears," forbidding further issue of city and county bonds, and so on. This does not look promising, but its result depends on the degree of importance the politic Barnard attaches to this reform movement. He will, of course, rat whenever his interests require it. This movement is formidable; its success may lead to his impeachment. These "caterpillars of the commonwealth" have done all they can for his advancement. By appearing in the new rôle of an honest and fearless judge he may escape mischief and gain much kudos with unthinking people. These considerations may lead him sorrowfully to decline the huge bribe that is doubtless within his reach and try to act with the semblance of uprightness. I have sundry intimations that he will do so. But he is an evil beast and will most probably aim at amusing the reformers, without doing substantial harm to his old allies in corruption.

The Citizen observes the tergiversations of his rulers:

September 7, 1871. This morning Justice Barnard, on motion of Barrett, granted order to show cause against perpetual injunction in the suit of John Foley against the mayor, aldermen, William M. Tweed, and others. The announcement was received with indecent but pardonable applause from a crowded courtroom. But it is mere order *nisi*. It was very possibly agreed upon as judicious by Tweed, Oakey Hall, and Company after free consultation with the judge. It may be a mere tub prudently thrown to the anti-Tammany whale. Tammany needs some "stern and incorruptible" Democratic judge to play off against a "possibly somewhat extravagant Democratic mayor and comptroller," at least until the November election is over.

The Citizen doubts the permanency of reform:

September 22, 1871.... The *World* sees at last that the wounds of the Ring are probably mortal; so it declares that they were inflicted by the Democratic party! "Lord, Lord, how this *World* is given to lying!!!" For weeks it has been denouncing all charges against Tweed and Company as a mere party clamor, cunningly devised by hungry radical office-seekers. But I fear our labor for reform will be in vain. We may succeed in breaking this Ring, but another will soon be riveted round our necks. A sordid and depraved community cannot govern itself without corruption. Cutting out a cancer or a gangrenous spot does not *cure* a patient whose blood is thoroughly poisoned. . . . When we the people learn (among other things) to consider wealth basely acquired and ignobly enjoyed a reproach and not a glory, we shall have a right to hope for honest rulers.

The Citizen sees the Party side of corruption:

October 5, 1871. . . . That synagogue of Satan, the Rochester "Democratic" Convention, talks bravely against corruption and fraud. But it allows the Tammany delegation from New York to be magnanimous and withdraw "so as not to embarrass the convention." It has not the courage to kick Tweed and Company into the street. It declines to admit a "reform delegation" claiming to represent the city "Democracy." Some think this is a stunner for Tweed. . . . But I do not so see it. Tammany is still the vital centre of the state Democracy, and Tweed is entitled by strict Democratic rule to the votes of all true Democrats. He and his pals are not read out of the party. Perhaps it's as well. The prospect of the Republicans is brightened by Democratic tenderness for these notorious scoundrels and thieves. The convention may have slightly chilled the ardor of city rascaldom without having secured cordial support from comparatively honest rural Democrats. The party could not afford to lose the services of Oakey Hall's noble army of repeaters, or the control of city funds wherewith to buy up invertebrate Assemblymen. It could not spare the great fraudulent majorities that are rolled up at every city election; so it dared not make thorough work against corruption and goes into the fall campaign with the filthiness of Tweed and Company in its skirts just a little wiped off. . . .

The Citizen reports that the Boss' crimes are established:

October 26, 1871. . . . Morning papers published full, detailed, tangible proof of Boss Tweed's iniquities—footing up between three and four millions—and announced that this swindler would be held to bail today in a suit instituted by O'Conor. Bail is set at $1,000,000. The order of arrest was granted by an Albany judge.

The Citizen compares the Boss to a figure of mythology, with a glancing shot at the press:

October 28, 1871. . . . Tweed magnanimously submitted to arrest yesterday and was held on bail for one million dollars. Respect for the illustrious defendant compelled the sheriff to make the arrest in person and not by one of his deputies. Tweed is a grand moral spectacle—statuesque as a demigod in Greek tragedy. Although "interviewed" and badgered at least nine times a day by "one of our reporters" (as the vultures interviewed Prometheus), he is always calm and great, if not perfectly grammatical—and that defect may be chargeable on the reporters. With wise forecast, he is preparing (so far as may be) for the struggle and for the possibility of adverse fortune by divesting himself of his impedimenta and by transferring the spoils of many happy years of swindling (real estate and securities) to his wife and children and confidential pals. I wish I could hope to see the scoundrel hanged, but he will be elected to the State Senate on November 7. . . .

The Citizen notes repercussions of the Boss' rout:

November 20, 1871. . . . The "Guardian" Bank for Savings (Bowery), William M. Tweed, President, and the "Bowling Green" Bank for Savings (Broadway), both being rotten fungi got up by members of the Ring to facilitate their swindling operations, have severally faintly exploded and have gone into the custody of receivers. Sundry other savings banks, officered by members of the same conspiracy, are reported in danger.

Comparative anatomy by the Citizen:

November 22, 1871.... Connolly has resigned in form, at last. Oakey Hall (with many a wry face, no doubt) appoints the detested Andrew H. Green in his place. He is also putting decent men upon the Park Commission—most reluctantly. He is an invertebrate rascal. But His Scoundrelism William M. Tweed holds on to his place, grim and undismayed. The basalt columns of the Giants' Causeway are not more rigid than Boss Tweed's backbone....

The Citizen distinguishes the Mayor from his dependents:

December 2, 1871.... Oakey Hall, once so jaunty and cocky, is said to be sadly wilted down, like a broken lily, in fact. His wife and daughter in Europe are driven from one hotel to another by people who point at them as the family of one of the Great American Swindlers. One can't help pity the poor things. Hall himself, who had a kind of social position once, is now very generally cut, as he deserves to be. He is less callous and far less heroic than some others of his gang, and he is understood to feel this acutely. He suffers also a good deal from Nast's stinging caricatures in *Harper's Weekly.* I hope these will be republished in some permanent form.

Heartening signs for the Citizen; a medieval anecdote furnishes him with an analogy for modern lawyers:

December 16, 1871.... Indictment for felony against Tweed, and he was lodged in the Tombs but was bailed out by Mr. Justice Barnard. He has a great array of counsel. Connolly is indicted for a misdemeanor. Judge Learned of Albany reduces Connolly's bail to half a million, but leaves Tweed's at the original amount (this in the civil suit). General Frank Barlow, who has recently had occasion to call on Tweed, says he finds that chieftain in a broken and demoralized condition, confessing that he has lost heart and quails under the concentric fire now playing on him....

The Bar Association is pusillanimous; its members are afraid to get up a case against Barnard, Cardozo, and Company, though abundant proof of corruption is within their reach. If they should fail, Barnard and the others would be hostile to them, and they would lose clients....I feel inclined to resign from this Bar Association. Sorry to see John Burrill among Tweed's counsel. As to the Fields (père et fils), Stoughton, Fullerton, and that blatant beast John Graham, they would take retainers from Satan himself. As between Michael and Satan disputing for the body (or the assets) of Moses, they would prefer to be concerned for the latter....

Social sanctions, approved by the Citizen:

December 21, 1871.... A general meeting of the Union Club is called for Friday night to consider a resolution that Oakey Hall's membership is prejudicial to the character of the club. There are sixty-five signatures. Oakey Hall feels this very keenly and has been begging and praying O'Conor to help him—talking about his young daughter whose prospects would be blighted by the infliction of a social stigma on her papa, and so on. O'Conor has been rather melted, I regret to say. Belmont's enthusiasm for Oakey Hall seems to have cooled down a little. Hall wrote yesterday to Denning Duer, acting president of the club, that he feels he is "unwilling the serenity of the club should be imperiled" by differences of opinion on a merely personal question; and that in case the proposed meeting should happen not to take place, he would like this to be considered as his resignation.

The Citizen invokes Isaiah 1, 6 as Albert Cardozo and George Barnard are investigated:

February 3, 1872. . . . The Assembly at Albany is "going for" Cardozo and Barnard at last, and its Judiciary Committee is instructed to take up the charges of the bar association against those learned judges. Only one legislator voted against the reference and that was the notorious Tom Fields, who has a natural antipathy to investigations. So far, well. We are living in a day of ruffianism and of almost universal corruption. Life and property are as insecure here in New York as in Mexico. It is a thoroughly rotten community. "The whole head is sick and the whole heart faint. From the sole of the foot even unto the head, there is no soundness in it but wounds and bruises and putrifying sores. Run ye to and fro through the streets of Jerusalem and seek in the broad places thereof, if ye can find a man, if there be any that executeth judgment, that seeketh truth." Unless some peaceful and lawful remedy be found, a dangerous convulsion cannot be far off. To degrade venal judges and restore confidence in the courts is manifestly the first step toward reform. . . .

Legal ethics, according to the Citizen:

February 26, 1872. . . . The legislative committee is diligently investigating the judicial career of Judges Barnard and Cardozo. Results, if any, are kept very close. E. H. Owen (!!!) and Fullerton attend on Cardozo's behalf, and Bidwell (!!!!) is retained "for consultation." This is for the sake of his white cravat and his high character, for there can be nothing to consult about, and there has been no consultation. Cardozo wants to be able to talk about "my eminently respectable counsel, Mr. Bidwell and Mr. Owen." As to Fullerton, he and his client are well suited to each other. Bidwell took this retainer reluctantly, feeling bound by the strict rule that forbids a refusal, unless there be an actual prior retainer on the other side. But I think he was wrong, and that that rule applies to none but judicial proceedings. On investigations by legislative or congressional committees, and the like, counsel do not appear professionally and as sworn officers of a court, but merely as experts in badgering witnesses; and they have a perfect right to accept or decline that function. This committee is no tribunal. I regret that Bidwell should have befouled his fingers by touching—even formally—such filth as Cardozo. The immaculate Barnard is weak enough to publish a "protest" against Mr. S. J. Tilden's acting as a member of this committee, because Tilden has publicly denounced him and is not impartial. Impartiality is the first qualification of a judge, but it is not essential to a prosecutor, or to him who collects evidence for a prosecution.

The Citizen ponders the evidence and acknowledges the fitness of imprisonment without trial:

March 27, 1872. . . . The New York *Times* publishes transcripts of the bank accounts of Cardozo and Gratz Nathan, and they present coincidences that are curious and instructive. Connolly having evaporated and disappeared and his evidence being essential to the conviction of Brady and Haggerty, the voucher-stealers, their trial cannot be brought on, and Cardozo (perhaps not improperly) admits them to bail. So they will go unpunished. But it is comfortable to think that the scoundrels have been locked up for several months.

The Citizen records a victory, but is uncompromising:

May 1, 1872. The virtuous Cardozo has resigned, but I trust his impeachment will not be thereby abated. . . .

The Citizen cites an earlier authority on bribery:

August 20, 1872. . . . Exit Judge Barnard—convicted by a nearly unanimous vote on nearly all the articles of impeachment, unanimously removed, and disqualified from all future office 33–2. Very good, as far as it goes. But downright Bishop Latimer would have gone a step further. "There lacks a fourth thing to make up the mess, which, so God help me, should be *hangum tuum,* a Tyburn tippet to take with him. . . . Yea, an were it my Lord Chancellor himself, to Tyburn with him!" Latimer is right. Barnard's skeleton neatly hung on wires in a glass case should "point a moral and adorn" the new court house. . . .

A lawyer for the defendants invades the Citizen's home:

February 1, 1873. . . . Our campaign against scoundrelism in high places makes no progress. Boss Tweed's jury disagreed, some of them being beyond all question bribed, and the report of the Bar Association in the matter of D. D. Field was a mere wordy apology for doing nothing in the premises. That impudent scoundrel came here last night to Ellie's reception uninvited. Perhaps he thought that as the Cyrus Fields were invited and also his daughter-in-law, Mrs. Laura (née Belden)—his next-door neighbors on either side—he was invited by implication. I could not very well order him out, for I did not know but that Ellie might have thoughtlessly sent him a card. But I received him with sad civility, and people generally did not seem disposed to cultivate him. . . .

More social sanctions, applauded by the Citizen:

April 5, 1873. This evening in Century Club. The case of Frederick A. Lane came up. He sent in his resignation, which was laid on the table. Then came the motion to expel, which William P. Lee opposed in a forcible-feeble way. There was no reply, and the motion was carried 85 to 3. The three were William P. Lee, Hitchcock, who is an editor of the *Sun* and therefore presumably without moral sense, and one Goodridge, said to be a personal friend of Lane's. For the charges against Lane, *vide* the proceedings and evidence on the trial of Judge Barnard.

At the hour of triumph, the Citizen is pessimistic:

November 19, 1873. Everyone expected Boss Tweed's jury to disagree—they were out so long—but they brought that scoundrel in guilty this morning; thank Heaven. Sentence is postponed till Friday. Pity he can't be hanged. But he'll get a new trial, I suppose, and probably get off altogether, the rank, old felonious dog-fox!

The Citizen registers approval:

November 22, 1873. Boss Tweed the *Meister-Dieb* sentenced to twelve years and a moderate fine. Good as far as it goes.

The Citizen uses the Book of Common Prayer to celebrate:

November 29, 1873. . . . Mr. Attorney-General Barlow writes to ask Mr. Sheriff Brennan why Boss Tweed still lingers in the Tombs and is not consigned to the penitentiary. Mr. Brennan replies that he is waiting for an "intimation" from Judge Davis or the district attorney. Mr. Barlow rejoins that the sentence might be considered a sufficient intimation to the sheriff of his official duty in the premises, and that if he, the sheriff don't do it rather promptly, the Governor will know the reason why. So Mr. Tweed was this afternoon translated from the Tombs to Blackwell's Island—the "Isle of Sinners"—cropped, shaved, washed, and arrayed in his penitential garment of many stripes. "For this and for all other mercies," and so on!

What's biting the Citizen? Personally, he's suffered very little from corrupt officialdom, as far is recorded here only the indignity of having the number of his fine house altered. There is no indication—rather the contrary—that he greased the palm outstreched to him on March 16, 1867; and he still got the bill defeated. He and his co-counsel rebuffed the attempt by Cardozo noted on February 2, 1870; the judge's nephew was not named to appraise the real estate; the partition suits were not lost.[38] City taxes? In his day they were infinitesimal; he never mentions them. Yet the Citizen is an angry man—the judiciary is a sewer; Judge Cardozo should be sweeping the courtroom, if not on trial himself. "Beasts" and "dog-foxes," "caterpillars" and "vermin," the objects of the Citizen's scorn are subhuman. Lawyers, the Citizen has observed, are less clean than rats; the community as a whole is "thoroughly rotten" or "sordid and depraved." Even when the tide is turning on September 4, 1871, the people are "without moral virility" and the disease is "too deep to be cured" by what they do; and the whole is ruled by "his Scoundrelism," Boss Tweed. Images and invective recall John Bromyard; but the Citizen is not preaching. Bursts of anger not intended to stir others to action, his words exist as memorials to the Citizen's state of mind.

What's biting the Citizen? New York, in the past twenty-five years, had trebled in size, growing from 371,000 in 1845 to one million inhabitants in 1870.[39] It is, as the Citizen's entry of December 18, 1869, implies, "rich and prosperous." The Citizen himself has a profession and practice as a lawyer; a house; several servants. Yet his interests have been more philanthropic than profit-seeking—the great work, during the late war, of the Sanitary Commission; the New York Philharmonic, of which he becomes president; Columbia College, of which he is a trustee; Trinity Church, of which he is a vestryman. He has not been sought as counsel by stock speculators, railroad magnates, large industrialists. He knows of fortunes being made, and comparatively, and in his own estimation, he is "very poor." It is a fair inference that he feels envy toward those making the fortunes and is censurious of the means they employ. When those means are bribes, he can satisfy his envy in justified reproaches.

Public outcry against the corruption of New York City is not a postwar phenomenon. On June 4, 1852, the *Times* had editorialized on "Our City Government—Its Corruption and Imbecility" and regularly criticized the aldermen. Denunciation of "rings" had become a commonplace in New York politics of the 1860s. "Ring" had the remarkable advantage of sounding specific while identifying no one, or conveying a knowing sense of conspiracy while not indicating names, number, or purpose of the conspirators. In the 1864 municipal elections the winning candidate, John "Toots" Hoffman was charged with being in "the Tammany Ring," although he was not yet Tammany Hall's Grand Sachem. At the same time a Tammanyite attacked his critics as members of "the Corporation Ring," while the *Times* denounced "the Ring of the Board," that is, the ruling aldermen. Hearings in 1865 on garbage dumping led the *Herald* to speak of "the rings" that ran New York. In 1867 the *Herald* referred to Mayor Hoffman and "the Lunch Club Ring," also described by opponents as "the City Hall Ring." In 1868 the *Herald* gave the history of "the famous Tammany Ring." It is in terms of this established newspaper term that on May 20, 1869 the Citizen refers to "scoundrelly Rings" in the plural and that on April 21, 1871 he finally refers to "the Ring" ruling New York City. Tweed, Grand Sachem of Tammany since 1869, is first mentioned by the Citizen on October 18, 1870, and is identified as "Boss" only on April 28, 1871. The Citizen takes his views from the papers.[40]

It is all the better from the Citizen's perspective that the bribery is connected with Democrats. The Citizen, by the end of the war, had become a loyal Republican. The Democratic Party had been associated with secession, with near-treason during the war, and with cultivation of the votes of the foreign-born. It is easy for the Citizen, with scarcely a smile, to describe the Democratic State Convention as "that synagogue of Satan." There are individual Republicans he castigates—he cannot stomach Benjamin Butler—and there is the sellout, Winans of Chautauqua. These are exceptional cases. The Republican Party is never indicted by him. Yet he could not have been unaware of the cries that corruption permeated the Grant Administration.

During the period of the diary entries just reported, the charges involving the Credit Mobilier were being made by the *Sun*—whose editors were "presumably without moral sense"—and were then investigated and reported on in Congress. In the *North American Review* in early 1869 Charles Francis Adams, Jr., had asked, "Who, then, constitute the Credit Mobilier? It is but another name for the Pacific Railroad ring. The members of it are in Congress. . . ."[41] The Citizen never mentions the Credit Mobilier, much less the involvement in it of the Republican leadership in the House. He is aware of corrupt railroad speculators (Drew, Fisk, Gould, Vanderbilt), to whom he refers disapprovingly. The makers of the Union Pacific, so closely connected with his party, are unnoticed. Corruption for the Citizen is a city and state phenomenon, associated with Tammany, "the vital centre of the state Democracy."

Tammany is not only Democratic. Its strength is derived from the Irish immigrants it has naturalized, registered as voters, cultivated by favors and office. The Citizen is a man of strong feelings, apt to denounce as a class any group—Southerners, for example—who endanger his peace of mind. In New York it is the Irish who are the block most visibly associated with his enemies. The Citizen is suspicious of Jews, too—his reaction to Cardozo, to Cardozo's face and to Cardozo's nephew, and his pun on "Cork-asian" dominance, show it ("Cork" refers to the Irish, "asian" to the East, whence the Jews are imagined to come). But Jews were not so numerous as petty officials or voters as those the Citizen describes as "Celtic bogtrotters." The Citizen does not conclude immediately from the race or religion of a man that he is bad. He acknowledges, without special comment, the presence of Jewish businessmen supporting the reformers and notes, without alarm, that the prosecutor of the Ring is to be Charles O'Conor. He cannot but be aware that the worst of the judges, George Barnard, is a Yale man of "American" antecedents; that the Ring's mayor, Oakey Hall, is an "American" with "social pretensions"; that Tweed's predecessor as Grand Sachem of Tammany, Governor Hoffman, is an "American" of Dutch ancestry; that the lawyers he so cuttingly denounced come from his own class and ethnic stock; that Bidwell, who defends Cardozo, is his own partner; and that the Boss himself is apparently of Scottish descent and certainly an "American" of at least two generations' standing.[42] The Citizen's anger is not confined to the foreigner. But what gives righteous fire to the Citizen is the thought that he, a descendant of old New Englanders and old New Yorkers, should be governed by a Boss whose strength rests on the immigrants. The stereotypes formed in the Citizen's mind are of a Jewish judge, created by the Ring, and of an Irish sheriff, created by the Ring, running the New York that had been governed by the Citizen's virtuous ancestors. To believe that these foreigners are bribetakers is to raise his sense of loss to a moral level.

The Citizen's sense of falling behind in the struggle for wealth and power, his dislike of Democrats, his resentment of the alien would not have found easy expression if the Citizen had not been able to associate his enemies with corruption. The Citizen does not care to probe his unconscious—the connection, for example, between his unrecorded sex life and his overt conduct; nor does he desire to relate even his conscious prejudices to the judgments he pronounces, on objective grounds he would assure you, on the governance of New York. "What's biting me?" the Citizen could have asked, and answered, "The crimes committed by public officials."

The evidence which the Citizen bothers to record to demonstrate criminality is not great: the extended hand, the overture from Cardozo, the unnecessary change in his street number. His impressions of the judiciary as the *Cloaca Maxima* depend on his own experience, reinforced by that of lawyers he knew. With little doubt he was familiar with an essay in 1869 by Henry Adams's brother, Charles Francis, Jr., in the *North American Review* which pointed to "judicial venality" in Commodore Vanderbilt's struggle for control of the Erie Railroad.[43] His view of the court house building as a swindle and of the Ring in general must be based largely on gossip, on what public opinion among the elite of New York take for public knowledge; the denounced building where the Court of Appeals sits is the same court house Mark Twain had furnished with thousand-dollar spittoons. When the *New York Times*, on July 22, 1871, provided dollar detail on "the Ring's" takings, it was the first time the Citizen had information—albeit unverified evidence—of the magnitude of its operations. When the principals of the Ring defended themselves weakly or not at all, the Citizen could hold that its depredations were confessed. Well before any criminal trial took place, the Citizen had decided who was guilty.

That foul deeds had been committed; that city contractors regularly paid off Tweed and his cronies; that the payoffs were thoughtfully regulated and meticulously divided—15%, for example, on the courthouse construction, producing 2.5% apiece for the six Democratic Alderman—was to be established by the contractors' testimony in court and by Tweed's extrajudicial confession to the alderman. In substance, although not in all details, the press had been right, the Citizen had been right in smelling rottenness. The Citizen is within his rights in saying that the crimes done by Tweed and his fellow officials were enough to rouse the wrath of any member of the community.[44]

Those crimes are variously described by the Citizen as "embezzlement," "thievery," and "swindling." The crime of which the Boss was actually convicted, and for which he was sent to jail, was neglect and dishonesty in examining the accounts of the city, a breach of a statutory duty incumbent on him as a member of an audit committee. Neither this crime nor the others mentioned by the Citizen was the crime of bribery. But bribery was the *modus operandi* of the Boss. Where the voters, the legislature, or the newspapers of New York needed to be won, Tweed was a bribegiver. Where the city had a say, Tweed took. When the Citizen denounces "corruption" generically, it is this system of payoffs he has in mind. Bribery is central.[45]

Whom or what does the concerned Citizen bite? The answer must be, No one, nothing, except with very soft teeth. We do find him applying social sanctions within his power—he helps turn down Judge Spencer for the Trinity vestry; he is for the expulsion of Mayor Hall from the Union League Club; he would not, if he could help it, invite David Dudley Field to his home. Mild as these measures are, they are not negligible against those with social aspirations. We do not find him taking stronger action. He does attend reform meetings, but he is not a speaker or a leader. He regrets to his diary that his father-in-law, Samuel B. Ruggles, is thinking of wriggling out of "the Committee of 70," but he is not on it himself. He no doubt gives his vote to the cause of reform. It is not evident that he gives his money. It is abundantly evident that he never thinks of running for public office. As he intimates on May 20, 1869, he will not risk "losing caste" by becoming a politician.

Bribery for the Citizen is a subject he can get worked up about. He is very definitely concerned. One can imagine that his conversation with Ellie, his wife, or Johnny, his son, or with an old friend would be as sharp as the diary in condemning the crooks in office. He is not moved to go further. The Citizen is familiar with some of the great public preachers against corruption—Isaiah and the other prophets; Bishop Latimer. The Citizen reserves his rage for his bedroom. The Citizen is a private character.

The Citizen, his editors observe, "seeks only his own approval." Seeking only that, he can be content with puns or irony about the "learned judges" and "the virtuous Cardozo" or indulging his cultural superiority in applying Virgil to Barnard and Cardozo (the *arcades ambo* of December 18, 1869).[46] But what ferocious thoughts he harbors in his privacy! On May 20, 1869, he thinks it must come to "revolutionary action" if a legal remedy for the corruption is not found. On December 18, 1869 he dreams of vigilante process. On December 21, 1869, he imagines Cardozo as a janitor or criminal defendant. On October 18, 1870 he suggests that assassination may be justified. On October 28, 1871, and November 19, 1873, he meditates on hanging Tweed. He is ready, rhetorically, on August 20, 1872, to hang Judge Barnard, and he indulges the fantasy of the judge's skeleton on display in the court house. More realistically, he is ready to send Tweed,

Barnard, and Cardozo to the penitentiary on December 18, 1869; he approves fighting "the Devil with fire"; he is delighted when Tweed is actually sentenced to twelve years (a sentence later found by the Court of Appeals to be illegal); and on November 29, 1873, he dwells with pleasure on the image of the imprisoned and humiliated Boss. His victories, like his anger and his jokes, are in his mind. His concern with bribery is real. The manifestation of his concern is emotional, mental, verbal.

The Confession of a Crusader.   In contrast to the concerned citizens who provided their votes and their hurrahs and their mental approval to reform, and in contrast to novelists like Mark Twain and Adams, who satirized corruption in fictional form, were the journalists who instigated or orchestrated campaigns against actual corruptionists. Charles Dana of the *Sun* had opened the attack on the Credit Mobilier; George Jones of the *Times* had started the downfall of the Tweed Ring.[47] The pattern was to be repeated by other crusading editors. One, Fremont Older, has left an account marked by unusual regret for what he had accomplished.

In March 1907 the eighteen members of the board of supervisors of the City of San Francisco publicly confessed to having been bribed by fight promoters to eliminate competition in boxing exhibitions; by the Pacific Gas and Electric Company to set the gas rate at eighty-five cents instead of at seventy-five cents per thousand cubic feet; by the Parkside Realty Company to give a franchise for a trolley on 19th Avenue leading to the company's new development in the Sunset district; by the Bay Cities Water Company to have the city buy for $10 million its water rights in the Sierra; by the Pacific State Telephone and Telegraph Company to deny a franchise to a rival telephone company; and by United Railroads of San Francisco to permit the conversion of its lines to overhead trolleys. For the telephone company matter, eleven supervisors admitted to receiving $51,000 each from the company's agent directly. All of the other bribes had been funneled through Abraham Ruef, the acknowledged power behind the administration of the mayor, Eugene E. Schmitz. Ruef, in turn, had used one supervisor, Joseph Gallagher, as his conduit to the others. For the trolley matter, Gallagher confessed to receiving, out of $200,000 paid to Ruef, $85,000 to be divided among the supervisors. The divisions were usually made with an exactness recalling the judgment of Iunius or the aldermen of New York. For the gas rate decision Ruef was believed to have received $20,000 from a major stockholder in PG&E, of which he had given $13,350 to Gallagher. Gallagher had kept $1,350 and paid $750 apiece to sixteen of the other board members, giving nothing to one member known as unfriendly to all public utility corporations. From the boxing promoters Ruef had gotten $18,000, of which Gallagher, given $9,000, had deducted 5 percent as a commission and distributed $475 apiece to himself and the seventeen others. For the Parkside franchise, Ruef had $15,000 down, $10,000 to come, but nothing had gone to the supervisors, who had not yet voted. The water deal was also incomplete; Ruef had been promised one million dollars if it went through. From the supervisors' confessions, published in the San Francisco newspapers, it was inferable that anyone wanting a license or a contract from the city, or the denial of a privilege to a rival, could get his way by paying Ruef.[48]

By December 1908, Louis Glass, vice-president and general manager of Pacific Telephone, had been convicted of bribery and sentenced to five years in San Quentin state prison; Eugene Schmitz, mayor, had been convicted of extorting $5,350 from the Poodle Dog, Delmonico, and Marchand's French restaurants as a condition of renewing their licenses, and sentenced to five years in San Quentin; and Abe Ruef, the boss, had been convicted of his part in arranging the United Railroads' permit and given fourteen years in San Quentin. The supervisors, enjoying immunity as long as they danced to the prosecutors' tune, replaced the imprisoned mayor with the designee of the prosecution.[49]

These results were accomplished in the face of determined resistance by the ruling ring. A newsboys' boycott and a truck drivers' strike had blocked distribution of the *Bulletin*, the paper that had promoted the prosecution. Fremont Older, its editor, had been kidnapped. R. A. Crothers, its publisher, had been felled by blows to the head. Before the prosecution had started, the supervisors had removed the district attorney and appointed Boss Ruef himself in his place, a maneuver only eventually undone by a judicial order. The first jury to try Ruef, having heard abundant testimony of his guilt, still had several jurors who voted for his acquittal so that no verdict was possible. A new jury was empaneled, and a man was caught trying to bribe a juror. The home of Supervisor Gallagher, turned state's evidence, was dynamited. After the second trial was finally under way, Frank Heney, the prosecutor, was shot in the courtroom at point-blank range, and the suspect, arrested, conveniently committed suicide while in public custody. As his death was probed, the police chief himself—equally conveniently—died by drowning.[50] The merit of overcoming all the obstacles and all the violence belonged to Heney, who survived; to Hiram Johnson, his assistant, who took over the trial when Heney fell; to William Burns, the famous detective, who was hired by private funds to work for the prosecution; to Rudolf Spreckels, a rich San Franciscan, who provided the larger part of the funds; and to Older, whose paper had been pursuing the ring in editorials, cartoons, and news stories since Schmitz first took office in 1901. Supported by an indomitable wife, Older had gone beyond the role of a journalist to put together the combination of Heney, Burns, and Spreckels which made the prosecution a success. At the height of the battle, Ruef, addressing a public meeting, identified Older as his principal opponent. He was right. If any newspaperman could believe that by his verbal assaults calling the citizenry to action, by his own shrewd strategy, and by his personal moral virtues such as courage, patience, and unflinching honesty, he had smashed a rotten city government, it was Older.[51]

Triumph turned to bitterness the day Ruef entered San Quentin, had his head shaved, and was clothed in the stripes of a convict. That day Older wrote in an editorial, "One should be very sure of his own rectitude before he feels a pharisaical gladness over the humiliation of Abe Ruef."[52] Older's self-doubts reflected disillusionment. The Supreme Court of California—on technical grounds of remarkable formalism—had reversed the conviction of Schmitz; Glass had been given a new trial which led to his acquittal.[53] The trials of Patrick Calhoun, the head of United Railroads, and Tirey L. Ford, its counsel—the men responsible for the $200,000 bribe—had ended in defeats for the prosecutors.[54] The unions had always resented the prosecution, because Schmitz had been the candidate of the Union Labor Party, whose strength lay in organized workingmen. Businessmen came to resent it, because the prosecutors had gone beyond the politicians to try the entrepreneurs whom the businessmen believed were the innocent victims of extortion. The Hearst paper, the *Examiner*, had sharply ridiculed the prosecution; other papers of the area eventually joined in rejecting it. Public opinion, high and low, was turned in its disfavor. The city seemed sick of having virtue vindicated. The electorate as a whole washed its hands of goodness by electing an anti-prosecution district attorney in 1909.[55] Ruef alone went to jail. As Older came to see it, Ruef was made the scapegoat for a system.[56]

In reparation, as it were, for what he had done, Older went to San Quentin and offered Ruef his friendship. He then began to work as hard for his parole as he had for his conviction and succeeded in freeing Ruef after he had served over four years of his term. Ruef, a Berkeley alumnus, reciprocated by giving the *Bulletin* "An Autobiographic Account of My Career from University to Prison, with an Intimate Account of the Corrupt Alliance between Big Business and Politics in San Francisco." Revealing no more than what had already been confessed by others and insisting that the money paid him by the big corporations had been "attorney's fees," Ruef struck the same note as the new Older—the system had made him what he was. Still, it was a confession of a sort; and Older, publishing other confessions by criminals in the *Bulletin*, came to think he should confess, too.[57]

When he finally did so, after leaving the *Bulletin*, he declared himself a believer in "the doctrines of Christ," whose "message was the most beautiful ever given the world." Yet he was attached to no church and, at least at the beginning of his editorship, he had "no ideals whatever about life, and no enthusiasm beyond newspaper success."[58] The paper he had served, he now admitted, had been mired in the same corruption he attacked in Ruef. The dominant force in state politics was the Southern Pacific Railroad and the political master of the state was not the governor but the SP's political manager, William Herrin. Among other ways of maintaining power the SP paid regular subsidies to newspapers throughout the state to assure their "friendliness." The *Bulletin* (circulation 20,000) was such a paper, getting $125 a month, raised to $375 when the SP needed its services in two local campaigns. The *Bulletin* also collaborated with the *Post*, a paper owned outright by the SP, in rigging the bidding on printing for the city; and the *Bulletin* took an extra $7,500 to oppose Schmitz, the labor candidate, when he first ran for mayor. Older's efforts at "house-cleaning" at the paper had proved "futile." Needless to say, the *Bulletin*, as it ardently attacked Boss Ruef, was silent about Boss Herrin.[59]

Its campaign against the Schmitz administration was a logical continuation of its purchased opposition to his candidacy. Once embarked upon it, the *Bulletin* published stories on civic graft that sometimes mixed facts and guessing and presented them as the known truth. For instance, it ran pictures of Schmitz, Ruef, and three police officials with the caption, "These Five Men, and Only These, Have the Power to Protect the Chinese Gamblers, Who Pay $9,035 a Month for Protection." Older had made up the dollar amount to convey a sense of having information which he did not in fact possess. As the campaign intensified, it became, in Older's own words, "most vicious." Although he had no specific knowledge of any crime they had committed, Older editorialized that both Schmitz and Ruef should be in the penitentiary; *Bulletin* cartoons frequently portrayed them in prisoner's stripes. When it looked as though a judge might uphold Ruef's appointment as district attorney and oust the chosen prosecutor, the *Bulletin* assembled a mob that overawed the court. When it came time to get hard evidence for the prosecution, Older printed a fake page of the *Bulletin* discrediting Golden Roy, an ex-convict trying to live down his past, and used the page to blackmail Roy into giving information on the ring. When it was necessary to get the supervisors to cooperate, Older worked with Roy to "trap" and then "terrorize" them into confessions implicating Schmitz and Ruef. With Roy he rehearsed a scenario that was used to make the supervisors think they were receiving a secret bribe from proprietors of a skating rink, while Burns's detectives stood by ready to catch them with the incriminating cash. Older acquiesced in an offer of immunity to Ruef to get him to talk and then did not doubt Burns when he claimed, with arguable accuracy, that Ruef had broken the agreement and so should be prosecuted. Older had heard William P. Lawlor, the judge who presided at Ruef's trial, say at the Family Club that "the dirty blankety-blank should be made to crawl on his hands and knees from the county jail and be tried on one of the big indictments." Yet Older remained silent when Judge Lawlor, challenged by Ruef to recuse himself as biased, swore in an affidavit that he was impartial. In summary, as Older put it, "I realized that we had to get down once or twice to Ruef's level in order to prove him guilty and get him into the penitentiary." Obsessed with "getting" Ruef, Older had been insensitive to the means employed; and gradually he discovered, "It was evil fighting evil." When he had a sense of loss at the moment of triumph, "it was the evil in me that brought defeat."[60]

Uneducated in any formal sense—a printer's devil who had become a reporter and then an editor—Fremont Older had found in the American version of the antibribery ethic the idiom by which he could sell his paper, be a big shot in San Francisco, even give focus and purpose to his life.

Now, as he regretted the result of what he had done, a sense of the ineffectiveness and vindictiveness of incarceration in a prison; a new belief that the system not the man was responsible; the observation that punishment had been selective and uneven and finally borne by one man alone; compassion for another human being's suffering; and the keen awareness of his own moral flaws and failures made Older judge himself with a sharpness which Cicero and Coke, Burke and Strong never showed. If Ruef was corrupt, Older confessed, so too was he. Confronting himself, Fremont Older had reached the stage of King Lear, mad on the heath—"None does offend, none—I say none."

The Conversion of a Muckraker.   The Puritan zeal of a rascal beadle could also congeal in another way, as the life story of another crusader was to illustrate.

In 1905 when Older was mounting his successful crusade against Ruef, the leading authority on graft in the nation was another Californian, Joseph Lincoln Steffens. Born in San Francisco in 1866, brought up in the upper middle class in Sacramento, educated at Berkeley, Steffens had been uncertain of the truth and eager to discover it, and like Henry Adams he had sought it in education on the European Continent. A cheat at cards and ready to cheat in his college geometry classes, he wanted to discover for himself whether "there was any moral reason for or against cheating in cards, in politics, or in conic sections."[61] He did not find his answer in Heidelberg, Berlin, or Paris, but returning to America with a wife to support he became a journalist in New York. Eventually, his work led him to cover the police and the Reverend Charles Parkhurst, who, in his sermons against prostitution and police corruption, "sounded like a prophet of old."[62] Curious, open-minded, pragmatic, an explorer, Steffens had little of Adams's burden of the past and none of George Strong's religious convictions and ethnic prejudices. Except that he was a believer in "democracy," he had still not set any foundations for a moral life. But in New York in the 1890s he, like most people, was certain that bribery was bad, and that bribery was the central cause of bad government in the cities: "Bribery was the answer to all our questions, bribery was wrong. Wasn't it?" Even Richard Croker, the boss of Tammany, "felt it was bad" and "never did and never could have defended bribery." An anti-Tammany journalist, Steffens accepted what he perceived as Parkhurst's plan for reform—"to elect good men," because "only bad men would take bribes."[63]

Lincoln Steffens, as he preferred to call himself, achieved his national reputation as *the* authority on bribery with a series of articles in *McClure's Magazine* beginning in October 1902. Under the title "Tweed Days in St. Louis" he reported on the corruption which prosecutions had exposed as existing under Mayor Henry Ziegenhein and Boss Ed Butler, and concluded his recital with the judgment, "The problem of municipal government in America has not been solved." His next article, "The Shame of Minneapolis," focused on Albert Alonzo Ames, the city's mayor and boss, and the payoffs he and his brother Fred, the police chief, received from criminals. In "The Shamelessness of St. Louis," Steffens enlarged on his first article, noting the boss's preference for describing his takings as "fees" or "presents" and the Missouri belief that "there was always boodling in St. Louis." Pittsburgh was his next target. He described how the ruling ring, allied with the Republican state boss, Senator Matthew S. Quay, had controlled Allegheny County as well as the city, and how a fight between Quay and the local ring had freed the city, only to have it fall back under a new ruler, Thomas Steele Bigelow, "the everlasting American Boss." From Pittsburgh, Steffens moved to Philadelphia, memorably characterized as "corrupt and contented." Here "the rake-off" was regulated, ranging from 5 to 25 percent. All the major interests—the large corporations, the universities, the clergy—were satisfied with what the ring, an offshoot of the Republican state machine, provided. A city charter won by reformers in 1885 was used to perfection to perpetuate the ring's control. Strangely, as it now seems, Steffens found that Chicago had almost licked corruption. It was "half free and fighting on." Its press was the nation's best, its aldermen "an honor to their country!" Finally, Steffens turned to New York on the eve of the November 1903 election and warned the unheeding majority, "Tammany is Tammany, the embodiment of corruption."[64]

These articles did not represent detective work. In St. Louis and Minneapolis, Steffens relied on indictments and trials; in Chicago and Pittsburgh on the word of reformers; in Philadelphia and New York on common gossip. His achievement was to put in the perspective of a national pattern a major problem of municipal government. Himself of English, German, and Irish origin, Steffens delighted in demolishing the common view of corruption, that some alien infusion into America was responsible. "The 'foreign element' excuse," he wrote, "is one of the hypocritical lies that save us from clear sight of ourselves." In New York corruption was attributed to the Irish; how did this explain St. Louis, a German town? Neither Irish nor Germans were strong in Minneapolis, a city of Scandinavians ruled by New Englanders. Pittsburgh was dominated by the Scotch and Scotch-Irish. Philadelphia was "the most American of our greater cities." Steffens could conclude, "We all do it, all breeds alike."[65]

What indeed were the constant factors? "The corruption of St. Louis came from the top," that is, from leading citizens of the city. In Pittsburgh the railroads began it. In Minneapolis corruption was caused by the prohibition of vices (drinking, gambling, prostitution) that were "inevitable," and the consequent resort to payoffs to permit them. In Philadelphia the big corporations were behind the state ring. In New York corruption came from prohibited vice, from the docks, from contractors compelled to comply with a myriad of building regulations, and, as everywhere, from the owners of street railways. Business, large or small, was the source of corruption when business depended on a privilege within the power of the city to give.[66]

Published in book form as *The Shame of the Cities*, the articles were, as

Steffens noted retrospectively, filled with "astonishment, shame, and patriotic indignation," reflecting "the taught ignorance," that is, the shared values, of Americans.[67] In an era when progressivensss in politics was associated with reform, they struck a responsive chord. If the business community could plead, "Don't knock, boost," it could not provide a respectable defense for outright bribery.[68] The prosecutor in St. Louis had said to Steffens, "Bribery is treason," that is, it destroyed democratic government. When Israel L. Durham, the boss of Philadelphia, asked him, "Just what is it I do that's so rotten wrong?," Steffens could answer that his crime was "disloyalty"—Durham had sold his neighbor's trust.[69]

The picture Steffens drew was not all dark. There were heroes nearly everywhere: Joseph Folk, the district attorney in St. Louis; Oliver McClintock and David Bruce, reformers in Pittsburgh; Hovey Clark, the grand jury foreman in Minneapolis. But in what had already happened in Philadelphia and Pittsburgh and was about to happen in New York it was evident that reform did not last, that corruptors were always ready to spring again upon a city. "Is democracy possible?," Steffens began his second article on St Louis.[70] As he looked around the nation and found bribery at all levels of government, he began to wonder. On all sides he was told, "That *is* the way it's done."[71]

Steffens was a valued consultant to Older and Spreckels and Heney in the San Francisco prosecution of Ruef and company and they entered into his pantheon of reformers. Yet the pattern set by the public utilities and the brothels and the real estate dealers of San Francisco was all too familiar. States turned out to be as bad as cities. Rhode Island, for example, was bossed by Charles R. Brayton and represented in the United States Senate by the creature of the sugar trust, Nelson Aldrich. New Jersey, whose corruption had been begun by the Camden and Amboy Railroad, was now owned by the big corporations.[72] Villages were no better than states. Like Baron Jacobi in *Democracy*, Steffens found corruption everywhere. Even the placid town where he now lived, Greenwich, Connecticut, was corrupt—Yankee voters were paid $2.50 for their votes, Italian voters $2.75.[73]

The president himself, Theodore Roosevelt, and old friend from New York, was not exempt from the general evil. When Roosevelt had fallen heir to the office through McKinley's assassination, the reformers had exulted. To the discouraged prosecutors of graft in San Francisco Roosevelt had written in 1908,

Indeed, if there can be any degrees in the contemptuous abhorrence with which right thinking citizens should regard corruption, it must be felt in its most extreme form for the so-called "best citizens," the men high in business and social life, who by backing up or by preventing the punishment of wealthy criminals set the seal of their approval on crime and give honor to rich felons. . . . Do not become disheartened. Keep up the fight.

Surely this president would never engage in corruption himself. But as he went into his second term, Steffens began to see him as "a shallow careerist." In a dialogue recalled by Steffens in an idealized form reminiscent of John of Salisbury's report on his conversation with Adrian IV, Roosevelt admitted to Steffens that he traded appointments for votes he needed in the Congress. Steffens asked him to name the worst appointment he had made. Roosevelt mentioned the brother of the mistress of a senator whom he had made a United States district attorney. Steffens got him to name his "next worst" and so on till a list of appointments made to win senators was in front of them. Steffens asked if this were not "the lowest form" of bribery, to buy votes with public office, offering not one's own money but public trusts as payment. Roosevelt would not agree. In a syndicated column, without naming names, Steffens then declared that the president did in fact engage in bribery. Members of the Cabinet buzzed like angry cardinals at the insult. The president's mild comment was, "This is a difference of opinion between two writers about the use of words."[74] Literally and in terms of the law on the books, Steffens was right. Politically and in terms of the law as applied, Roosevelt was right; and who was right morally depended on whose morals were taken as the measure. In 1907 Steffens was sure that his should be.

A shift began to occur in his thinking, partly due to external causes, partly to introspection. The president publicly denounced "the muckrakers," privately assuring Steffens he did not mean him. "Muckraker," in its original use in John Bunyan's *Pilgrim's Progress*, described an avaricious man who looked at the ground, exactly like Dante's avaricious men punished in the *Purgatorio* by looking downward. In Roosevelt's odd inversion it became a derogatory name for the critics of privilege, and the president's speech was a repudiation of corruption as a national political theme.[75] Steffens himself had gone to study Boston and found it "dying of hypocrisy." He began to wonder if "our ideals and our morality" were not the cause of civic evils. He noted that the Puritans had managed to seek both sanctity and wordly success by forming "as we all do, watertight compartments of the mind."[76] Was there not a real contradiction between morality and success in America? And had he not been thinking like a Puritan? He hated the imputation of being righteous, and as he examined himself, he found he too could be bribed—bribed by the desire to keep his job and to have his articles published. The righteous, he was to write in a passage reminiscent of Augustine's analysis of the temptations of the judge, are "bribed by their own money."[77] Being so, he concluded, they are no better or worse than those they condemn. Turning to the New Testament itself, he read it as the story of a man who attacked hypocritical privilege and was betrayed for a bribe.[78]

Steffens's evolution was to go further. He had found it easy to develop rapport with the real bosses and to admire their lack of the reformers' hypocrisy. Martin Lomasny, the Boss of Ward Nine, he had seen as the only man who could reform Boston.[79] At the same time by his standards democracy had been subverted almost everywhere in America through system-

atic bribery. "You cannot build or operate a railroad," Steffens told an audience of Los Angeles businessmen, "or a street railway, gas, water or
power company, develop and operate a mine, or get forests and cut timber
on a large scale, or run any privileged business, without corrupting or
joining in the corruption of the government." The fault, he suggested,
was not Adam's or Eve's or the serpent's, but the apple's—that is, the
prize which was held out made bribery necessary.[80]

Always admiring the strong men, and now giving up on the salvation of
democracy, Steffens was ready to applaud revolution when it came, first in
Mexico, then in Russia. He went to the Soviet Union, met Lenin, defended
Lenin's defense of terror, and announced on his return, "I have been over
into the future, and it works."[81] He went to Italy, met Mussolini, and
described him as "the divine Dictator." When Stalin liquidated the
kulaks, Steffens applauded the Soviet state as a regime that was "continuously radical and loyal to its purposes."[82]

A split in his consciousness remained. In 1931 he published his autobiography, tracing his conversion from muckraker of corruption to defender
of dictatorship. Lenin he celebrated because he had founded a new society "without possibilities of riches and poverty, graft, war, injustice, and
tyranny." The elimination of graft was still for Steffens a central desideratum. Yet for his new consciousness, Greek-Christian morality was mean-
ingless. First tentatively—"maybe bribery and corruption are acts of God"
and "muckrakers in general the agents of the Devil"; then decisively—"political business corruption [is] a natural, well-nigh universal process of change"—he concluded that his reforming passion had been misdirected. Each business, he thought now, bribed only because it had to
bribe. The new railroads had had to "tunnel" the old state politics as they
had had to tunnel the mountains in their way; and so with successive
business bribers. Hence, "all the various forms of corruption should be
regarded, not as felonies, but as evidence of friction in the process of pouring new wine into the narrow necks of old bottles." Mixing the modern
imagery of social engineering with the metaphor taken from the Gospels,
Steffens firmly and finally repudiated the tradition whose invocation and
application had made him famous. If Steffens were now right, bribery was
a dead issue, concern with it a deforming distraction.[83]

The Reticent Academicians

Journalists led campaigns against corruption, concerned citizens
grieved over it, novelists depicted and deplored it, but what of the old academic classes, the lawyers and theologians, and new academicians, the
psychiatric theorists and the political scientists and sociologists? Were
they among the censors?

The Law Schools. Oliver Wendell Holmes, Jr., then a justice of the
Supreme Judicial Court of Massachusetts, delivered a dedication address
in 1897 at Boston University Law School. Published in the *Harvard Law*

Review under the prophetic title "The Path of the Law," it set out in succinct form themes that were to be central to American legal education in the twentieth century; it pointed to the path that American law schools would follow. A central proposition of Holmes was this: "If you want to know the law and nothing else, you must look at it as a bad man, who cares only for the material consequences which such knowledge enables him to predict, not as a good one, who finds his reasons for conduct, whether inside the law or outside of it, in the vaguer sanctions of conscience." The bad man would "want to keep out of jail if he can." From his perspective, one could estimate what was truly law, that is, the occasions when public force would be applied by the courts.[84]

The bad man was a central image. What opportunities did the bad man have to refine the accuracy of his predictions by using bribes? That Holmes knew that certain opportunities existed can be inferred from the treatment of bribery in *The American Commonwealth* (1889), the work of an English observer and Holmes's intimate friend, James Bryce. According to Bryce, about one-quarter of Congress took cash, stocks, land, or other property for their votes or committee actions. Many state legislatures— New York, Pennsylvania, Virginia, Maryland, California, Illinois, Missouri, and Louisiana were mentioned by name—were as bad. Bribery in elections to office was "a sporadic disease, but often intense," as, for example, in New Hampshire. "Jobbery"—the award of government business to political supporters—was common. Patronage appointments were "usual." The "ugliest feature" of all was the domination of cities by "Rings and Bosses," who venally disposed of city contracts and franchises. Against this "dark picture," the honesty of the judiciary stood out. True, a shadow had been cast over it in Europe by the tales of the corrupt judges of the Tweed Ring. But these stories—Bryce recounted them even more luridly than Strong—concerned only three men; the stories loomed large in European eyes because they had happened in New York. The Tweed three apart, the state judiciary was incorrupt; and the federal bench was "above suspicion." In this vision of American corruption as depicted in the press and culled from conversations with legal *bien pensants* such as Holmes and Judge Thomas Cooley, Bryce presented the judges as the one element in the American legal system substantially unaffected by bribery.[85]

Imputing Bryce's understanding to Holmes, we may infer that the Holmesian bad man would not have tried to bribe a judge. But would he have refrained from other useful bribes? Bribes could change the laws and prevent the execution of the laws. With bribes one could stay out of jail and make a good deal of money besides. Holmes's bad man is, in fact, not pictured as using bribes in this effective way. He is not a truly bad man at all, but a hardshell Yankee intent on having his rights in the law courts. Reducing "law" to what *courts* do, and believing the courts to be incorrupt, Holmes paid no attention to the role that bribes would have had in a realistic account of the American legal system.

From the same New England class as Henry Adams, Holmes's response to post–Civil War America was not to assail corruption but to create a corner in which corruption did not operate:

> Who sweeps a room as for Thy cause
> Makes that, and the action, fine.

Holmes paraphrased George Herbert and applied the sentiment in a secular sense, sweeping the law clean of dirt. He wrote as though bribery did not exist.[86]

The strength of Holmes's convention was pervasively evident in three ways in the law schools: Classes were not taught in Bribery—it would have seemed ludicrous to put Bribery in the curriculum between Agency and Constitutional Law. Casebooks were not constructed on Bribery—if courses were not taught in it, casebooks were otiose. Law reviews scarcely ever touched the subject—if it was beneath consideration in the classroom, what place did it have in the professional journals?

In 1895, a student Note in the *Harvard Law Review* discussed a proposal of the attorney general of Massachusetts to make it a crime to give money to a voter but not for the voter to receive it; the Note was dry, jejune, and brief—scarcely more than a page. In 1919 a student Case Note reported a Canadian case in which a contract to sell land to the government, made through a legislator, was held unenforceable. These two short notices constituted the total treatment of bribery by the *Harvard Law Review* in the first fifty years of its existence from 1887 to 1937. The *Yale Law Journal*, from its beginning in 1891 to 1940, ran three student write-ups of cases in Idaho, Missouri, and New York; each was a minor instance of corruption; each was reported without comment. The *Columbia Law Review* from its start in 1900 to 1940 reported three slightly more significant cases, two from Missouri, one from New York; no commentary enlarged the student work. Students at Yale, the seat of the self-described Legal Realists, were not more curious than those at Harvard about the actual impact of bribery on the legal system. None of the Big Three as of 1940 had run comments on the Manton case (discussed below in chapter 18), the most famous bribery conviction of a judge in modern times. Nor had any of the less prestigious journals, with the solitary exception of a one-page treatment of a ruling on the Manton evidence in the *Rocky Mountain Law Review*. Among the less famous journals there was also a bare scattering of references to bribery cases of any sort. "Does Wealth Influence the Administration of Justice in Massachusetts?," asked a lawyer in the *Maine Law Review* and went on to say that improper inducements to judges were "wholly unknown" but that juries were "tampered with" by politicians and wealthy defendants connected "with the machine." No evidence supported either conclusion; no concrete proposals for reform followed. In the age of the city and state bosses, municipal and legislative corruption was a subject virtually taboo in legal academe. No one would believe that Justice Holmes, or the law school professors, or the law school students knew Lincoln Steffens's America where bribery *"is* the way it's done."[87]

Influential writers on jurisprudence ignored the effect of bribery on law. Two of the most influential were Europeans—an Austrian and an Englishman. Their very acceptability in America showed how, well into the 1970s, American law schools wanted to be insulated from touching the impurity of corruption. The Austrian, Hans Kelsen, in a work significantly entitled *The Pure Theory of Law,* propounded an account of law purportedly purified of political and moral factors. Law, for him, consisted in a set of norms "dynamically" established by judges and legislators and officials authorized to make norms by the Basic Norm setting up the legal order. Looking at rules and not at the persons setting the rules, Kelsen did not consider how the authorized norm-establisher could be dynamically affected by a bribe. The purity of law excluded such extraneous considerations.[88] The Englishman, Herbert L. A. Hart, adapting Kelsen, proposed a two-tiered layer of laws—secondary rules delegating power to make primary rules affecting conduct. Primary legal rules were attended by physical sanctions that were "prominent or usual"; in the normal system, sanctions were imposed "for a high proportion of offenses." Hart paid no attention to the impact of bribes on the formation of the rules or on their enforcement, or to the status of bribery law itself, so infrequently enforced by any physical sanction. If his theory were correct, bribery statutes were not laws or the American system of law was aberrant. As he left the subject unmentioned, no one drew either conclusion.[89]

Only in the 1970s were there signs of a change—signs which followed the surge in criminal law enforcement which will be taken up in Chapter 18. In 1979, for example, W. Michael Reisman, professor of law at Yale, published *Folded Lies,* in which he contrasted "the myth system," affirming values of personal and social importance and condemning bribery, and "the operational code" of the society, according to which bribery was acceptable. Utopians such as John Rawls, he wrote, reinforced the myth system and obscured the operational code. Law professors were classed with the Utopians; Kelsen and Hart were excellent exhibits.[90]

Posed half-way between scholarship and action, law professors typically repressed interest in the impact of corruption on what they taught. Speculative and practical impulses alike were frustrated if bribery was a significant element in lawmaking. Cases could be analyzed for doctrine. Standard legal scholarship consisted in doctrine-building. Corruption corroded the building blocks. Rules could be set out and reshaped on rational grounds. Corruption was an irrational force. The accomplishments of law professors were in the mind, in argument, on paper. Bribery destroyed confidence in the cases and made the rules the product of sordid bargaining. No obvious way existed for the law professor to detect the existence of bribery or to tame its power. George Templeton Strong had written of a respectable man losing caste by going into politics, stained as politics was by corruption. The law schools had no interest in their subject being reduced to the low-caste level of politics. Unable to analyze or to control corruption, unwilling to let their field appear to be contaminated, academic lawyers concentrated on more malleable matter.

The theologians.   Augustine had analyzed the sin of bribery as he had analyzed the sin of adultery. Theologians from Ysidro of Seville to Caterina of Siena had perpetuated and propagated the antibribery standard of Christendom. Simony had engaged the minds and challenged the exertions of reformers from Gregory I to Martin Luther. In nineteenth- and twentieth-century America, academic theologians had little to say on the subject.

Academic theological treatment of the topic had already withered in Europe. Detailed analyses of sins were, in general, a prominent feature of Catholic moral theology, directed as it was to the guidance of confessors and penitents. Usury had been explored extensively by this theology in the sixteenth and seventeenth centuries and a consensus reached permitting ordinary banking. A reader of academic theology would be familiar with all the ways a usurer might cloak his acts and all the ways a banker could justify his activity.[91] Sexual conduct had been analyzed elaborately, and the rules confining it to approved forms of marital intercourse stated in detail. A confessor drawing on academic moralists would find a mass of sexual material to guide him.[92] Bribery was different. In the golden age of Catholic casuistry, from 1550 to 1650, it was a minor subject. Thereafter it remained a topic in moral theology under the general heading of "Justice" or under the particular heading of "Duties Proper to One's State in Life."

Four factors can be hypothesized to have been at work. After the Catholic-Protestant split was definitive, Catholic theologians were defensively discreet about the Church: the spirit of Bernardino of Siena not that of John Bromyard prevailed. The monarchs of the age of absolute monarchy did not encourage criticism of their administration. The moralists had such a rich vein to explore in sexual morals that they had little incentive to foster another kind of purity. Academic theology had concentrated mainly on simony: as that subdivision of bribery declined in interest, its relevance to secular affairs was not perceived.

In mid-eighteenth century, Alfonso de'Liguori, summing up two centuries of casuistry in his *Theologia moralis*, still lacked a Latin action noun meaning bribery; he had to use a compound formula of noun and verb (*munera accipere*); and he still lacked a standard, nontechnical, unambiguous word for bribes. The best he could do was to condemn "big *munera* which are called *sportulae*," while still permitting unsought "little *munera*, which are called *xenia*, that is, food and drink." Treated perfunctorily and as it were by rote, bribery received little fresh analysis and sank in a repetition of bromides. Gaps and weaknesses abounded.[93]

Gaps—the omission of explicit treatment of legislators; the omission of explicit treatment of administrators; the omission of explicit treatment of voters; the omission of explicit treatment of bribes by lawyers—went back to medieval theology. Even in medieval days the failure to treat expressly of bribery of the prince qua legislator or to consider licit and illicit reciprocities in city-state government left large holes. Liguori, the most representative Catholic moralist of the eighteenth century, still explicitly connected bribery only with judges. Despite the spread of republican government in the nineteenth century, many of his modern successors continued in this tradition—for example, Augustinus Lehmkuhl, S.J. (German, 1888); Adam Tanqueray, S.S. (French, 1906); Benedict Merkelbach, O.P. (Belgian, the leading Dominican moralist in Rome, 1935); Arthur Vermeersch, S.J. (Belgian, the leading Jesuit moralist in Rome, 1937). Against this background of comparative neglect of the topic in Europe, Catholic theologians in America had little to say.[94]

Francis Patrick Kenrick, an Irish immigrant to America, educated at the College of the Propaganda in Rome, was an exception of a sort to the rule. Co-adjutor bishop of Philadelphia in 1841, he wrote a pioneering work for America, a Latin treatise on moral theology. Kenrick taught that lawmakers are sinners if they "waste the Treasury's money in matters of no importance and neglect to complete those things which would bring many advantages to the commonwealth; spend time in useless debates with waste to the Treasury; vote with the hope of reward or with a definite contract already made; take care to make or revise laws for the benefit of their own property with loss to others'." The idea that legislative faults were appropriate topics for moral theologians to analyze was faintly visible. The particular vice in being bribed to vote was not identified; the sin was treated on the same level as irresponsible palaver; and the Latin term for bribes was not employed. Largely dependent on European sources and models, and only faintly apprised of any problem by Kenrick, other American Catholic moral theologians did not face bribery as a major moral problem of nineteenth-century America.[95]

Weaknesses in the moral theologians' analysis of judicial bribery, inherited from the scholastic tradition, continued. Despite positive law to the contrary, Liguori and his successors saw it as morally lawful to give *munera* to a judge or his servants "to buy back (*redimere*) unjust harassment." This, wrote Liguori, "is not corruption, but insurance that one's own may be given one." The positive laws did not apply, for the laws "intend to prevent those giving *munera* corrupting the judges, but not their obtaining just judgment." Although the judge was put under moral obligation to restore the *munera*, Liguori left litigants wide scope for rationalizing: most litigants believe, know, are certain that their cause is just.[96]

Another weakness—the theologians' treatment of the obligation of restitution. If the judge received *munera* to give an unjust judgment, wrote Lehmkuhl in the late nineteenth century, he had no moral duty to return what he had received. He had received "the price accepted as the valuation of a dangerous and wicked action." At work here was the traditional analogy of a corrupt judge and a prostitute. As a whore could keep her hire, so could a judge. The judge did not get off scotfree: he still had the obligation to make up losses he had caused; but if he was paid to give an acquittal, what specific loss was he responsible for? Lehmkuhl neither asked nor answered this question. The state's right to the profit made by its agent was ignored. The same analysis reappeared in Vermeersch as late as 1937, Vermeersch enlarging the opening for payments by being uncertain whether it was a sin for a judge to take money for deciding one case before another. As far back as 1656 Blaise Pascal had poured scorn on the moralists denying the unjust judge's duty of restitution and permitting the receipt of presents to expedite a case—positions he found "at once horrifying, unjust, and extravagant," a morality calculated only to favor the corrupt judge. Writing polemically and ascribing only to Jesuit moralists these positions that could be found also among other casuists, Pascal showed a shrewd sense of what would shock his bourgeois audience. But what Pascal found disgusting in the seventeenth century was still being defended in the twentieth. Repetition of old discredited analyses reflected the stagnant condition of the field.[97]

Reflecting the silence of the European academic theologians, in America the *Homilectic and Pastoral Review* ignored bribery from the review's inception in 1900 until 1938. In that year John A. McHugh, O.P., analyzed the sin of "graft," noting that it was "so widespread that it can be met in practically every condition of life" and yet was not defined in any treatise of moral theology. Treating it as a synonym for bribery in any context, McHugh went on to state that graft was against commutative justice and against distributive justice; that it was a means of discrimination; that it despoiled the people; that it led to dishonesty and lies; that it contributed to "the modern pagan idea which views life as a racket"; and that, subordinating public good to a public servant's private good, it was against reason and natural law. None of McHugh's basic doctrine was new, but for generations of moral theologians it had not been said, repeated, expounded, or elaborated. Implicit in standard theological expositions of the preeminent place of the common good, the moral teaching on bribery had not been spelled out. Nor had the moralists faced a standard excuse, that custom excused. Custom could not excuse, McHugh sweepingly declared, because graft was "intrinsically sinful." The challenge McHugh offered, the argumentation he marshaled, the problems he pointed to did not lead to any substantial investigation of the area by the academic moralists.[98]

Addressing the problem of graft in a clerical journal, the *American Ecclesiastical Review*, in the early 1940s, Francis J. Connell, a Redemptorist and professor of moral theology at the Catholic University of America, acknowledged that its treatment in European works was "very meager." The reason was, he thought, that it was Americans who had raised graft to "a fine art" (the most modest, charitable, and naïve of explanations, overlooking entirely the kind of withdrawal from public morals which the Catholic Church in Europe had practised). Because of lack of theological grounding, the average priest was unsure what to say. It was evident that the Catholic clergy as a body were not "sufficiently definite and outspoken." There should be frequent sermons on the subject and detailed instructions to officeholders. The confessor of a public official should interrogate him about his public conduct if there was "some reason to believe that he was "addicted to dishonest practices." Connell noted that question 261 of the new edition of the Baltimore Catechism put as a sin against the Seventh Commandment the taking of a bribe by a public official. Although nothing was said of sin on the part of the briber, the sweeping reference to all public officials was unusual in catechetical instruction.[99]

Connell himself showed the error in the prevailing view on restitution of a bribe which treated it like a whore's *turpis contractus*. In the case of the prostitute's shameful contract, the right of no third party was injured. In the case of a bribe, either a specific person was damaged and was owed restitution, or the bribe belonged to the state whose agent unlawfully had sold what was not his to sell.[100]

This challenge to the dominant analysis was still made with hesitancy in the face of his European authorities to the contrary. Here and in his more general analysis of graft as violating commutative justice, Connell was aware that "some readers" would think him "over-strict." He did not press the obligation of restitution. He acknowledged the existence of Catholics who "in perfect good faith" believed they did not sin when they took "honest graft" by bribery. On general principles of moral theology, since their ignorance harmed the common good, their good faith should be disturbed; they should be told the truth. But the very existence of such ignorance was a commentary on the dearth of instruction. Again and again Connell felt impelled to observe that custom was not a defense. "Everybody is doing it," is the excuse he had repeatedly heard. It was no excuse with him, but his brief exhortations to the contrary scarcely met a problem he saw as widespread. He himself offered no analysis of the specific duties of lawyers or legislators where bribery was concerned, although writing about the duties of both; he developed no casuistry for the treatment of campaign contributions; he dealt only with the grossest instances of bribery.[101]

Irony of ironies, the churches born in the Reformation, owing so much to the cry against corruption at the time of their birth, did little to analyze the sins of corruption, their particular causes or their specific shapes. If the Catholic theologians did not reflect the full richness of the Christian heritage, they did at times treat the subject. Theologians of other Christian denominations were far less inclined to examine at all the issues it involved. The use of patronage, logrolling by legislators, the place of campaign funds—these and other difficult topics requiring discrimination between allowable and impermissible reciprocities were not usual matters of analysis for Protestant writers on love and justice. Opposition to corrupt civic government was at times a badge of honor for Protestant ministers—the preaching of Charles Parkhurst that so stirred Steffens in New York is an example. The spirit of reform breathed in many laymen's hearts. Academic theological treatment was largely wanting.

"Good works" as a way to earn salvation were discounted in some denominations. A "static"natural law morality was criticized. "Legalism"
was often seen as the enemy of Christian freedom. For these reasons,
casuistry did not flourish in Protestant churches. Lacking consensus on a
method, they did not develop a literature with a strong sense of a shared
set of themes and texts. Nonetheless, Protestant ethics was a distinct and
active field. Reviewing its characteristics in America, James Gustafson in
1971 emphasized its "fundamental interest" in "practical morality" and
instanced a variety of topics from civil rights to medical care which had
been specifically addressed by Protestant moralists. Bribery and simony
were not among them.[102]

Disinterest in these specific topics could be found in Lutheran moral
treatises ranging from such nineteenth-century works as Charles Ernst
Luthardt's *Apologetic Lectures on the Moral Truths of Christianity* (1889) and
Bishop Martensen's *Christian Ethics* (1897) to modern Lutheran treatments
such as Dietrich Bonhoeffer's *Ethik* (1949); in Calvinist writing such as Karl
Barth's *Ethik I* and *Ethik II* (1928) and Emil Brunner's *The Divine Imperative*
(1947); in a seminal, neo-orthodox work such as Reinhold Neibuhr's *Moral
Man in Immoral Society* (1932) and in Neibuhr's comprehensive *The Nature
and Destiny of Man* (1941, 1943); in Methodist Paul Ramsey's *Basic Christian
Ethics* (1953) and in Presbyterian William F. May's *A Catalogue of Sins*
(1967); in the work of Anglican bishops such as Kenneth E. Kirk's *Conscience and Its Problems* (1927) and Herbert Hensley Henson's *Christian Morality*, the Gifford Lectures of 1935; in Baptist evangelical theology like
Billy Graham's *The 7 Deadly Sins* (1955) and in graduate school theology
like *Ethics from a Theological Perspective* (1981) by Gustafson, an ordained
minister of the United Church of Christ and a university professor at
Chicago. A reader of these dozen authors would learn a great deal about
sin and self-centeredness, about generous love for God and help for one's
fellow, about greed and lying and infidelity. Without question a reader
reflecting the ethos of these writers would find certain kinds of reciprocity
beneath contempt—the same could be said of any reader responding to
the basic thrust of the Gospel. Like the early penitentials or the later sermons of Bernardino of Siena, these books struck at vices on which bribery
battened. Like the penitentials and Bernardino, they did not speak of the
specific contexts in which bribery could occur or about the distinctions
made, the rationalizations offered, the arguments involved in its definition and condemnation. The reader would not be told of the scriptural, patristic, and medieval heritage or the images and stories sustaining the
tradition. He would not learn anything of the prevalence of the sin or its
seriousness. Despite the writers' "fundamental interest" in "practical morality," the actual problems of judges, legislators, administrators, lawyers,
policemen, procurement officers, and lobbyists were not addressed. It
was as though at a certain level of theological sophistication or at a certain
level of class consciousness it was agreed that everyone knew what constituted bribery, that everyone knew that bribery was wrong, and that no
problems existed worthy of debate or discussion.

Three recent indexes are symptomatic of the neglect accorded the problems. *Baker's Dictionary of Christian Ethics* (1973) an Evangelicals' publication, has entries on Abortion, Cannibalism, and Kisses, but none on Bribes, Corruption, or Simony. An ecumenical work, *Concise Dictionary of Christian Ethics* (1979) has Birth Control, Euthanasia, and Masturbation among its topics, but not Bribery, Corruption, or Simony. The *Index Volume with Aids for the Preacher* to Karl Barth's great *Church Dogmatics* (9,000 pages of theological reflection published by Barth between 1932 and 1967) has among its subjects Abortion, Birth Control, Divorce, and War, but the preacher who looked for Bribery or Simony would get no aid. Sex and violence were amply treated by Christian moralists like Barth. The special reciprocities involved in bribery were not the object of the same kind of close attention.[103]

Psychoanalysts. The old academic disciplines of law and theology showed little taste for the study of bribery. Among the new fields of study, that which dealt with human aggression, obsession, and guilt, might have taken an interest in those reciprocities which were exploited aggressively against the social good, engaged in obsessively by those in power, and singled out as asocial and criminal by concerned critics. "Bribery" and "Corruption," however, do not appear in the index to the *Complete Psychological Works* of Sigmund Freud.[104]

In the 1920s, Franz Alexander, a Freudian psychoanalyst, collaborated with Hugo Staub, a Berlin lawyer to produce, *The Criminal, the Judge, and the Public*, the first psychoanalytic study of crime and punishment to be translated from the German and published in English. Bribery was adopted as a metaphor: neurotics and criminals were said to "'bribe' or disarm their conscience by means of a voluntary acceptance of some suffering." "All forms of psychoneuroses," Alexander and Staub went on, "are based on this 'bribery' mechanism; they represent a compromise made by the Ego in order to obtain simultaneous gratification of both the prohibited Id drives and the demands of the Super-Ego."[105]

Transmuted into a central explanatory figure of speech, the bribe was removed from politics. A single generalization was offered about bribery in government. Before every revolution, Alexander and Staub wrote, there are accumulated acts of injustice: "the corruption of those in power breaks down the power of their inner representative, the inhibiting forces of morality, and man is thus transformed into a plaything in the hands of his unchained instincts." The authors made no attempt to show that this sweeping, imaginative, half-metaphorical statement had any support in historical data.[106]

Psychoanalysis did influence the speculation of other social scientists about corruption. Harold D. Lasswell, political scientist at Yale University, writing about bribery for the 1930 *Encyclopedia of the Social Sciences*, observed its ubiquity and added, "The fact that it is often resorted to where cheaper means would seem appropriate . . . suggests that it gratifies drives which are organized very early in the life history of individuals." It was, he continued, a way of putting down "representatives of authority."

Lasswell offered nothing on the psychology of the bribetaker nor anything on the cheaper, more appropriate means available to the bribegiver. His speculation about early childhood was undeveloped.[107]

In a more extensive study, *Power, Corruption, and Rectitude* (1963), Lasswell and Arnold A. Rogow turned to the bribetaker, dividing politicians into "game politicians" and "gain politicians." The former saw politics as a game in which they obtained power, respect, self-righteousness, and affection in order to compensate for parental deprivations of these goods; the latter, lacking "rectitude standards" in their "early political training," saw politics as a variety of commercial enterprise. The age of "early political training" was left ambiguous, but the authors repeated Lasswell's 1930 thesis that corruption could ensue when "early" environment promoted "severe deprivation." No evidence was offered to demonstrate the relation between corrupt acts and the experiences of infancy and childhood.[108]

A later writer, Viennese by birth and Freudian by belief, Albert A. Ehrenzweig, professor of law at Berkeley, author of *Psychoanalytic Jurisprudence*, distinguished oedipal and nonoedipal crimes, the latter being crimes whose repression was weaker than that of oedipal crimes. Since the repression was "wholly or partly conscious," punishment could often fortify it effectively. Bribery, not mentioned, presumably fell within this category along with other offenses Ehrenzweig vaguely described as "political." The implication—not documented by any history—is that bribery would be more readily deterred by punishment than an oedipal crime such as murder. The only approximation to bribery, however, that Ehrenzweig actually dealt with was plea-bargaining. The mental mechanism causing neurosis and crime in Alexander and Staub's account closely resembled this transaction. Perhaps for this reason Ehrenzweig characterized plea-bargaining itself as "always morally reprehensible," "disgraceful," and "sordid." His psychoanalytic explanation was that it was a way of showing gratitude to an offender. Ehrenzweig—himself once a judge in Austria—did not comment on the usefulness of plea bargaining in tempering the law's rigidity, its place in reducing judicial congestion, or its status in America as a lawful reciprocity. Against it he directed the moral indignation and the rhetorical images of purity formerly reserved for bribery of a judge.[109]

Social Scientists.   Law professors tended to be silent, moral theologians exculpatory, psychoanalytic writers speculative. What of those whose academic specialties—modern ones—were the study of man, government, and society?

Anthropologists preferred not to use the term "bribe" at all. Concentrating on primitive groups in which offerings to the gods were customary and practices of reciprocity common, they appeared not to encounter the concept of the bribe in the societies they studied, and they refrained from applying the modern Western concept judgmentally. In addition, focus on certain functions of the offerings led them to practice a kind of reductionism, ignoring or eliminating differences they considered not germane to the functions emphasized. James Frazier, for example, in 1890 wrote his famous account of the religions of antiquity, describing the rich variety of sacrifices made to ancestors, gods, and totems. He said nothing of bribes. From his perspective, the functions of sacrifice were the same whether the sacrifice was a gift of oneself or a bribe to manipulate the deity addressed. Marcel Mauss in 1925 wrote his classic essay *Le Don* (The Gift) on exchanges in Polynesia and among certain North American Indians. He called all the exchanges "gifts"; there was no occasion, from his viewpoint, to introduce the term "bribe." The omission was the more striking as Mauss ended the essay on a note of moral exhortation, urging modern emulation of the exchanges he described. Indices of anthropological texts and subject catalogues of anthropological libraries (for example, the Kroeber Library at Berkeley) eschewed "bribe" as a topic. Anthropologists registered reciprocities; they did not classify bribes.[110]

Ruth Benedict's well-known anthropological account in 1946 of modern Japan was a spectacular instance of anthropological reticence. A primary concept in her work was *on*, the sense of obligation and indebtedness and mandatory reciprocity to ancestors, parents, emperor, teacher, and all others who benefit a person in the course of life. *On* was seen as central to Japanese ethics. A species of *on* was *giri*, a type of obligation for which there "is no possible English equivalent," because of the variety of obligations it encompasses. Among the examples of *giri* were "duties to nonrelated persons due to *on* received," for example, by a gift of money or a favor. *Giri*, the Japanese saying went, "is hardest to bear." It had to be repaid. Reciprocation was obligatory; and the reciprocation must be exact—too much was as bad as too little. Equivalence was essential. A person could be "cornered with *giri*."[111]

Clearly if a bribe was given, it would be natural to suppose that *giri* was expected in return. In contemporary Japan, where laws exist against bribery, one would expect an official to experience acute conflict between the *on* owed the emperor (which included obedience to law) and the *giri* he owed a favor-giver. The conflict was not mentioned by Benedict. The possibility of such conflict was not even envisaged. The term "bribe" was not used. One received only "gifts or favors."

Like the theologians, Benedict used the moral categories of Christian tradition for sexual conduct. She spoke of homosexuality, masturbation, pornography, and prostitution. In each case she noted how the prevailing Japanese norm differed from "English and American" norms and how sensitive the Japanese had been to "Western criticism." Contrast of this kind she did not attempt with bribery.[112]

"Bribery" indeed might have appeared absent from her vocabulary except that it entered her retelling of "the true national epic of Japan," the *Tale of the Forty-Seven Ronin*. The tale begins with two masters of ceremony receiving instruction in court etiquette from Lord Kira, the great daimyo of the court. One of them showers Kira with gifts, the other,

Asano, does not. Kira instructs the nongiver with bad grace and purposely tells him the wrong costume to wear. Asano accordingly appears before the Shogun ridiculously dressed and is so disgraced that the only honorable course left is to kill himself. A long cycle of revenge by Asano's retainers, the *ronin* of the story, is begun. They are to kill Kira for disgracing their lord. The revenge is for Kira's insult, not for his gifttaking. Nonetheless, commenting on the story, Benedict spoke of "the bribery theme at the outset." She offered no explanation of why she used this "Western" word to characterize giftgiving that seemed a normal way of acquiring *giri*. No line existed in her account between the obligation created by a gift and by a bribe.[113]

Unlike anthropology, early sociology knew the concept. A pioneering work, mixing philosophy, psychology, and sociology, *The Philosophy of Money* by Georg Simmel, devoted a short section to bribery, defined as "the purchase of a person." Simmel stated that a bribee tried to preserve his dignity and hide what he was doing to protect himself against" self-negation and self-devaluation which would result from his sacrificing his personality for a certain amount of money." In his dogmatic style he declared that money facilitated bribery not only by its usefulness in being passed in secret, but by its lack of the mark of prior ownership that land or cattle would have and in not making the psychological impact that a sexual bribe would. In support of his general remarks Simmel offered a random set of examples from classical Athens, medieval Florence, eighteenth-century England. Although his work could only have been written at the end of the nineteenth century and in Berlin, he wrote as though "bribe" and "bribery" were universal concepts, timelessly applicable in every culture.[114]

More modern sociologists who focused on function did not find the concept useful. In 1957 Robert K. Merton's magisterial work, *Social Theory and Social Structure*, saw the "key structural function of the Boss" as organizing, centralizing, and maintaining the scattered fragments of power, thereby satisfying needs "not adequately satisfied by legally devised and culturally approved social structure." For deprived members of society, the machine headed by the Boss humanized assistance and let them keep their self-respect. For businessmen, legitimate and criminal, it provided political privilege leading to profit. For the ambitious and uneducated, it provided social mobility. In short, "the functional deficiencies of the official structure generate an alternate (unofficial) structure." To recognize the functions performed by the "unofficial structure" was, Merton wrote, "to provide not an apologia for the political machine" but a basis for reform. True reform required either eliminating the needs or offering a structure to satisfy them. Otherwise one engaged "in social ritual rather than social engineering."[115]

Suppose the needs being human could not be eliminated and the structure could not be changed without revolution, or perhaps could never be changed, did not Merton's account function as an apologia? Studiously abstracting from morality, employing inoffensive words such as "unofficial," eschewing the terms "bribe" and "corrupt," Merton showed why the system worked as it worked. Explaining the system as it existed, he condemned no part of it. He did put in a category disfavored by its apparent inefficiency those acts, such as the prosecution of bribetakers, that changed neither needs nor structure. These acts were not engineering, that is, acts accomplishing change, but ritual, that is, acts without substantive effect.

A significant number of political scientists went further in abandonment of the bribe as a significant concept. Colin Leys, a specialist on modern Africa, wrote in 1965, "What Is the Problem about Corruption?" and stigmatized as "writers of the moralist school" those who saw corruption as always "a bad thing." Those involved in bribery, he observed, regarded it as "a good thing." For him, he implied, its badness or goodness was a question for investigation. Sometimes corruption led to results "not particularly nice" but unimportant to society. On occasion, bribes promoted efficiency and socially useful administration. Frequently, they served "persistent integrative needs of society." Examples from Africa, the Soviet Union, and the United States were cited in support of his argument against the uniformly negative evaluation of the bribe.[116]

James Q. Wilson, professor of government at Harvard, writing in the *New York Times Magazine* in 1968, authored an article entitled "Corruption Is Not Always Scandalous," which began, "Moral issues usually obscure practical issues, even when the moral question is a relatively small one and the practical matter is very great." Americans, he suggested, were inordinately "puritanical" if they subordinated the practical to the moral. He wondered aloud why cash or anything readily convertible into cash "converts a compromise or an exchange of favors into a corrupt act" while logrolling and patronage appointments were mysteriously exempt from public condemnation. He advocated discriminating between "those forms of corruption that impede the attainment of social objectives and those that may facilitate it." He did not, he wrote, mean to say that corruption was ever right: "Corruption by definition is wrong." But he went on to say what was "honest graft"—a concept attributed to George Washington Plunkitt of Tammany in 1900. Honest graft brought a profit to the officeholder and no harm to the public. In Plunkitt's example an insider's use of city planning information to buy up private property was honest graft. In Wilson's updating of Plunkitt, honest graft was the placing of insurance or bank deposits by a city to favor the insurance company or bank "willing to pay." When done to attract "necessary campaign funds," this was honest graft. In Wilson's opinion, unsupported by statistics but representing the shrewd guess of a keen observer of American politics, there had been "a rather sharp decline in the amount of dishonest graft over the last 30 or 40 years, but probably much less decline in the amount of honest graft."[117]

Wilson went on to distinguish the graft involved in capital formation to construct a major facility and that involved in the operation of the facility once built. The first kind of graft he suggested might have purchased "something of value," such as "an early decision to undertake a risky project." Hardly a port, city hall, or subway in a large American city, he intimated, was built without graft of this sort. The implication left was that this necessary graft was not bad. Operational graft, on the other hand, was explicitly said to be "judged by quite different standards": it could "play havoc with such facilities."[118]

Wilson also distinguished "integrative and disintegrative corruption." Disintegrative corruption was free-lancing by officials for their own benefit. Integrative corruption was seen in Mertonian terms. It coordinated independent governmental bodies so that the government as a whole could accomplish an objective; it was a way of overcoming fragmented authority. By implication it was close to being good. In spite of Wilson's disclaimer that he was not saying corruption was right, he treated honest graft, capital formation graft, and integrative corruption in such a way that they appeared to be of little practical consequence measured against the benefits they bought. Only after these distinctions were made did he observe that some kinds of corruption had "high symbolic costs," qualifying this apparent concession to the old purity ethic by his agnosticism about the price paid: "we know the least about such symbolic values."[119]

In *Comparative Political Corruption* James C. Scott in 1973 took a comprehensive view of corruption in a variety of Third World countries, drawing on unreformed England and machine politics in the United States for analogies. Thailand he found to resemble the England of James I with officials using monopoly concessions and licensing for their own economic and political advantage. In Indonesia under the Guided Democracy of Sukarno, "the 'corruption market' was so disorganized that 'prices' were highly unstable and delivery by 'sellers' was highly uncertain." As the rules of the game and security in office were uncertain, officials tried to squeeze as much as possible while in office. A far higher degree of corruption existed than in Thailand; indeed corruption in Indonesia "attained truly epidemic proportions." Haiti under François ("Papa Doc") Duvalier was even more corrupt. The government was the only source of wealth; the regime set no limits to its coercive authority. Neither traditional norms nor an independent authority nor a commercial class nor any other institution limited the dictator's power to extract money. "If any regime may be said to be *fundamentally* corrupt, it would be the Duvalier regime."[120]

Scott granted that "aggregate data are virtually impossible to find or to assemble." Hence, his grading of degrees of corruption had to be based on anecdotes and intuition. Implicitly, the grading was judgmental—the fundamentally corrupt Haitian regime was worse than the more gently exploitative Thai government. He noted a number of factors favoring corruption in the Third World: the continuation of traditional giftgiving; the force of ties and kinship; the demand for valuable governmental concessions exceeding the supply; the expansion of governmental functions; the great power of the bureaucracy relative to other sectors of the society; the relatively high status of civil servants, approached by peasants as superiors. Resistance to corruption, he concluded, depended on political authority and "the strength of certain political institutions and values."[121]

Invoking "values," Scott implicitly acknowledged the moral element affecting the growth or check of corruption; "corruption" itself was a value-laden word. Normative in his choice of basic concept and in his grading, he simultaneously maintained, "Far from being pathological, patterns of corruption and violence may actually represent channels of political demand without which formal societal arrangements could scarcely survive." He quoted the view of Myron Weiner, an authority on India, that American political machines should be emulated in the present state of Indian society; effective politics in the short run depended on "patronage, favor and bribery." Scott did not disagree. He himself observed, "Much of the corruption for which big-city machines in the United States were noted represented an informal integration of demands which the formal system all but excluded from cooperation." Corruption was "the alternative means of interest articulation." Characterizing corruption in this Mertonian way, quoting Weiner favorably, refusing to treat corruption as pathological, Scott declined to be a censor.[122]

Not all social scientists thought it desirable to drop the moral category. *Corruption: A Study in Political Economy* (1978) by Susan Rose-Ackerman, an economist at Yale University, analyzed the risks and benefits of bribery for a hypothetical legislator and showed that, operating on a purely economic basis, the legislator would be corrupt. Restraint, Rose-Ackerman reasoned, came from "personal honesty and a devotion to democratic ideals." She concluded, "If one wishes to understand the functioning of a democracy, it will not be possible to follow the conventional economist's inclination to ignore moral constraints upon self-seeking behavior." Conventional economics, like the substantial current of political science reflected in Leys, Wilson, and Scott, sought to analyze bribery without moral criteria. Rose-Ackerman's work was a protest against the prevailing mode.[123]

At work in the writing of Scott, Wilson, and Leys could be seen the ideal of a value-free social science, of an impartiality that understood everything and condemned nothing. The writers about Third World nations knew a second intellectual pressure—not to practice cultural imperialism, not to judge Africans or Asians as benighted by Western standards. A government had to be bad indeed—Papa Doc's reached that point—to be damned as "fundamentally corrupt." These academic inhibitions were reinforced by a silent secular injunction—not to use moral standards related to God. Judgment as to the social good is inescapably moral. Leys's emphasis on efficiency, Wilson's appreciation of the pragmatic accomplishments of crooked politicians, Scott's valuation of informal integration all acknowledged values. What they did not acknowledge were the values dominant in classic theocentric morality. As in much social science writing about sex, there was a perceptible inclination to make common behavior into the norm, a genuine uncertainty as to what other norm existed.

Even the historians of tradition, were not immune from revisionist inclinations. For Lucien Febvre the petty corruptions of the Church were not a sufficient cause for the Reformation; grander reasons had to be found. Leo Hershkowitz gave an account of Boss Tweed in which he emerged as harshly judged by his contemporaries, almost the victim of persecution. Abraham S. Eisenstadt wrote,

> America is a Christian commonwealth. The founding of its polity was an incident in the drama of the European reformation. To say that Americans are a Christian people is at once to define their perception of corruption and the role it has played in their history. Christianity informs their public life with a type of moral code; the degree to which their officials fulfill the code determines the American's sense of the officials' probity or corruption.

American politics were "a morality play" because of the Christian infusions. For Eisenstadt, like the later Lincoln Steffens, this mixture of piety and politics obscured the social phenomena. In the Gilded Age, Eisenstadt wrote, new national problems had arisen which could not be handled by the old structures, so "a new system of national politics had to be devised." The gentility, judging by the old standards and regretting their own lost power, had morally indicted "the new capitalists and the new politicians." No doubt critics like Henry Adams, Clover Adams, and George Templeton Strong fitted his description of an envious, judgmental gentility. Writing in the the 1970s, Eisenstadt held that "the Gilded Age—America's great age of political corruption—was the figment of the gentility's moral imagination." The Christian notions, inextricably intermixed with American democracy in this analysis, formed an ideological screen, distorting the dynamic social shift. "Moral" qualified "imagination," but bribery, like witchcraft, appeared to depend on the preoccupations and perceptions of the beholder; moral censure became an exercise in self-expression.[124]

The Darwinian Novelist.   The academic interest in bribery was tepid. But the true *trahison des clercs* from the perspective of the bribery tradition was its moral abandonment by a major American novelist. In Theodore Dreiser's trilogy, *The Financier, The Titan,* and *The Stoic,* bribery is the essential operation by which the protagonist, Frank Algernon Cowperwood, acquires his great fortune. Coming to maturity in Philadelphia just after the Civil War, Cowperwood launches his rise to wealth by becoming a member of the Philadelphia Stock Exchange and working out an arrangement with the city treasurer by which city funds are put at his disposal for his private speculation in return for the treasurer personally sharing in his profits. The scheme collapses under the pressures of a panic, and Cowperwood is convicted of embezzlement for one transaction in which he too casually treated the city's money as his own. Nothing is made of the bribery he has engaged in: it is how Philadelphia is run and how the state of

Pennsylvania in Harrisburg is run. Imprisoned by the state, Cowperwood makes life bearable by bribing the sheriff and the guards.[125]

On his release, Cowperwood speculates in stocks, makes some money, and leaves Philadelphia to seek a bigger fortune and social acceptability in Chicago. His first major enterprise there is to invade the gas business by bribing suburban town councils to grant franchises to his new company. Eventually he has enough of a position to challenge the old companies whose franchises cover the city. Bribing the boss of the Chicago councilmen, John J. McKenty, with the prospect of $300,000 to $400,000, Cowperwood aligns the city government with him against the old companies, who ultimately have to buy him out. Flush with the large profits of this transaction, Cowperwood enters the street railway business. Again a judicious amount of pressure from the bribed boss and the complaisant city councilmen force an established company to deal with Cowperwood. This time he takes over and expands the company, always with the city at his beck and call. A reform movement, stirred up by his enemies in the financial world, temporarily overturns Boss McKenty's rule of the council; but Cowperwood traps the reform mayor into a sexual adventure and successfully blackmails him into doing nothing to hurt his company.[126]

To keep his street railway franchises for another fifty years, Cowperwood turns to the Illinois legislature and bribes it ($50,000 for the Republican whip, $2,000 apiece to "the boys") to grant the extensions. Legislation to this end is cleverly attached to a bill setting up a Public Service Commission. Honest Governor Swanson vetoes the bill. Cowperwood has to settle for a law letting the Chicago City Council grant the fifty-year renewals. The press, a tool of Cowperwood's foes, stirs tremendous indignation against the extension, and ward meeting after ward meeting denounces the councilmen as boodlers, bribed to do Cowperwood's bidding. The council caves in to the pressure and refuses the extension. Cowperwood solaces himself with a mistress. He ultimately sets off to amalgamate the underground lines of London. He finds that cash bribery is not practiced in England, but subtler forms of reciprocity govern the grant of franchises. He dies before his final financial ambition is achieved.[127]

In external details the story is modeled on the life of Charles Tyson Yerkes, a Quaker financier from Philadelphia who came to control the street railways of Chicago. Edward Butler, a boss in Philadelphia in *The Financier*, is modeled on Edward Butler, the boss of St. Louis celebrated by Steffens. McKenty, the boss of Chicago in *The Titan*, is modeled on John Powers, a real boss of Chicago. City councilmen Tiernan and Kerrigan are based on Chicago councilmen Bathhouse John Coughlin and Hinky Dinky Kenna. Flatly naturalistic in tone, the narrative purports to be no more than the story of the life of one powerful, power-hungry man. No conclusions are drawn, no morals pointed. Cowperwood is portrayed as a man without spiritual or religious feeling, without a conscience. "He had none, truly." The absence of conscience is not held against him by his creator. He is insatiably promiscuous, and his lubricity, like his lust for power, is accepted by the author as a propensity beyond rational control. Cowperwood is a man without friends, a husband who betrays two wives and many mistresses, a father who is indifferent to his children once he has paid for their upbringing. His motto is, "I satisfy myself." In the hands of a Cicero or a Burke, he would be a Hog; and indeed his cool insouciance is startlingly reminiscent of Warren Hastings, whose self-explanation, "The Care of Self-preservation will naturally suggest the Necessity of seizing the Opportunity of present Power," could be his. But in Dreiser's hands, he suffers no moral judgment, and his final rebuff in Chicago is "a cataclysm"—a natural disaster—not condign retribution.[128]

In the course of the trilogy—begun in 1912 with *The Financier*, finished posthumously with *The Stoic* in 1945—the author steps in to speak in his own voice and denounce as unnatural "the Christian idea" of lifelong fidelity in marriage. He does not so directly attack the bribery ethic. But he does identify it with Christian belief. When the reformers want their councilmen to give up "all the perquisites of graft and rake-off," Councilman Kerrigan declares, "None o' that Christian con game goes around where I am." When two grafting members of the Illinois legislature are mocking clerical reformers, they parody the Christian line, noting "that the Lord has called us also to this work." Governor Swanson, who is shown refusing a bribe of $300,000 in cash from Cowperwood, is seen as motivated by "the selflessness of a Christian ideal and of a democratic theory of government." For Dreiser the connection with Christianity is not a recommendation. In his retrospective postscript to *The Titan* he asserts that words like "right, justice, truth, morality, an honest mind, a pure heart" are words meaning merely that a balance must be struck between the strong and the weak; the strong must not be too strong nor the weak too weak. The play of forces in society will inevitably produce the balance. Dreiser does not say what the criteria are by which "too strong" and "too weak" are determined. He accepts whatever balance exists. He is a chronicler of events, not a critic of morals. The guardians of the bribery ethic—the press and the clergy—are portrayed, in Philadelphia, as weak and hypocritical: in Cowperwood's observation, they "did not dare to utter a feeble squeak until some giant had accidentally fallen." In Chicago, the newspapers are more formidable and actually defeat Cowperwood; but they are ready to sell out for a bribe, or manipulated by men no better than Cowperwood, or, seeking to boost circulation, not disinterested. The bribery ethic is their convenient weapon.[129]

The distance between the bribery ethic in Dante and Shakespeare and in Dreiser is enormous. The language of the tradition can no longer be used to flay the corrupt. It has become "mouthings of pharisaical moralities—platitudes!" Brought up a Catholic with huge emphasis by his father on hell as God's punishment for sin, Dreiser has designed a trilogy that reads as a repudiation of retribution and the criteria on which retribution would be based. The study of the life of a man who by Christian criteria is a sinner, the work demonstrates by empirical observation, as it were, that no retribution exists. No Last Judgment awaits anyone. No judgment on earth is arranged by Providence or by the novelist imitating Providence. No redemption occurs, either. There is no saving Christ or Christ-figure. The titan rises by crookedness, fails when he gets too big, becomes a semistoic and dies like the animals whose struggle to live he believes is the secret of life. A vulgar Darwinism predominates. Dreiser's view of bribery is close to that of the disillusioned Steffens—a natural necessity in the America they know.[130]

Neutered, the tradition survives. Briberies are not moral events, but they are points of narrative interest. Unlike the details of the operation of Cowperwood's gas or street railway companies, the arranging of the key bribes is attentively told. Like Cowperwood's repeated adulteries the briberies are not morally disapproved but significant enough in the narrator's eyes to warrant talking about. What Christians call sin retains a powerful, even prurient, fascination. Where, for a naturalism unspoiled by moral curiosity, adulteries and briberies would be of no greater interest than a character's eating habits or physical regimen, Dreiser depends upon the tradition which invests these acts with importance. Denying that moral standards have any special standing, the Cowperwood trilogy focuses on incidents of sexual and civic infidelity given meaning by morality.

The Tradition Reasserted

Among the academicians a spectrum of attitudes toward bribery was discernible. For a minority, of whom McHugh, Reisman, Rose-Ackerman were representative, it was a serious social evil. For the majority, attitudes ranged from formal and uninterested disapproval to acceptance and rationalization of at least some forms of the phenomenon. Theologians downplayed the topic, often provided an excuse for the bribegiver, relieved the bribetaker of the obligation to account to his principal; nonetheless, they considered bribetaking a sin, offensive to God, repugnant to justice. Legal scholars who did not care to investigate bribery still knew that it was a crime and to be shunned. Psychiatric writers, explaining bribery by childhood deprivations, understood involvement in it as a personality disorder. For anthropologists the concept was a zero, a blank. The dominant social scientists found a positive value in some forms of bribery which were necessary to the functioning of the society—paradoxically for them corruption could, in some instances, be integrative. Journalists like the repentant Older and the later Steffens, historians like Eisenstadt, novelists like Dreiser were with the social scientists. The accusatorial aspect of the bribery tradition, so prominent in authors from Isaiah to Henry Adams, had no strong attraction for any of these observers of human relationships. They did not see their purposes served in arraigning a group or an institution as corrupt. They found no gratification in judging particular individuals as faithless officials or destructive corruptors. Distancing themselves from their own society in order to analyze it, they showed none of the passionate outrage at corruption that had marked rebukers of bribery like Ezekiel and George Templeton Strong, Gregory I and Edmund Burke, Cicero and the young Steffens. Their dispassionate disinterest was very different from the legal developments to be narrated in the next three chapters—developments that could have occurred only if the antibribery ethic was vigorously alive. The antibribery ethic was in fact robustly represented in the twentieth century among many Americans not affected by academic analysts or Dreiserian naturalists. In the novel, the journalistic exposé, and the biographer's verdict, the old tradition reflected and formed minds as censorious of corruption as the Citizen's.

Analogy.   The concept of the bribe, used metaphorically in a variety of forms, is central to Henry James's *The Ambassadors* (1901). Lewis Lambert Strether, a man of New England integrity, has been dispatched by his patron, Mrs. Newsome, to bring her son Chad back from Paris to America. Influenced by the delights spread before him by Chad and Chad's mistress, Madame Marie de Vionnet, Strether abandons his mission and stays on in Paris himself. New ambassadors led by Chad's sister Sarah arrive to bring Chad home. Will they succeed? Strether thinks, "and it all came to the question of Sarah's being really bribeable. The precedent of his own case helped Strether perhaps but little to consider she might prove so; it being distinct that her character would rather make for every possible difference. This idea of his own bribeability set him apart for himself; with the further mark in fact that his case was absolutely proved." In the legal language of precedent and judgment, Strether judges himself to have been corrupted in being deflected from his ambassadorial role.[131]

Modest self-deprecation when Strether applies the concept to himself, the term becomes sharper when he uses it in connection with his now-deserted patron, Mrs. Newsome. Part of her inducement to Chad to return is a share of the family business. "Oh damn the money in it!" Strether exclaims to Chad, who replies, "It's pleasant to a fellow's feelings to 'size-up' the bribe he applies his foot to." Strether answers, "Oh then if all you want's a kickable surface the bribe's enormous." From the parental perspective of Mrs. Newsome, the family business is a gift offered Chad to do his duty to his mother and to give up a meretricious relation with a married woman. As parents tend to see incentives they tender their children, it is reward, not bribe. Strether's perspective prevails: Chad, he has come to think, is under superior obligation to Marie de Vionnet; a material inducement to leave her is a bribe.[132]

Then there is Strether's own relation to Marie de Vionnet. She has given him a new vision of life. Is she his friend? In their final climactic encounter, she says to him, "The only safe thing is to give." He replies, "You've been making, as I've so fully let you know I've felt, the most precious present I've ever seen made." Giving him her trust, she gives something of herself.[133]

Reversal of conventional expectations and of Strether's initial judgment on his own bribeability: the offer to Chad he brought from home was a bribe; what he receives from Marie de Vionnet is a gift. The distinction between a material incentive and the present of a person's self is insisted upon. The difference between a bribe and a gift makes Strether's final position intelligible.

Even more remarkable: the moral focus of the novel is not on Marie de Vionnet's adultery. Strether is surprised, upset, shocked when he discovers that Chad's relationship with her is physically sexual. But this discovery is not decisive. Chad gives up the adulterous affair and is morally inferior: he has succumbed to the bribe or bribes from America. Marie de Vionnet makes a gift of herself and is morally superior: she has known what a gift is. The bribery ethic, drawn by James with a fine, firm line between bribe and gift, is more important than the sexual ethic. Written in 1901, the novel is an anticipation of an America of the future.

The tradition appears to weaken with the transposition of the bribe to domestic psychology. The social interest in governmental corruption has been lost. From the same intellectual milieu as Henry Adams and Wendell Holmes, Henry James, it seems, has been, like them, alienated from politics. Withdrawn to England from America, he has abandoned the political meaning of bribery. But where does his analogy get its force? The tradition gains strength from the dependence of the analogy on the vitality of the prime analogate.

In casual domestic contexts "bribe" was to be applied to any inducement given a child to persuade him to do what his parents wanted. The idea of a manipulative maneuver by the briber was retained from the classic concept, but the essential element of a breach of trust by the bribee was abandoned. In James both elements of the classic concept are kept. "Bribe," "bribeable," "bribeability" are words of reproach to Chad and Strether because their class has so firmly condemned bribery in the political arena.

The Political Novel. The prime analogate, the corruption of government officials, continued to receive the attention of American novelists. The master work of American novels treating of bribery was published in 1946: Robert Penn Warren's *All the King's Men*. In a setting evocative of Louisiana in the 1930s the classic themes of the tradition are woven together in the rise and fall of Willie Stark, who begins his political career by running for county treasurer in an upstate rural community, protesting the graft in a school bond issue. Lucy, his schoolteacher wife, is not in favor of "stealing." A city journalist asks, "Doesn't she know how they run things up in Mason County?" "They run 'em up there just like they run 'em down here," Jack Burden, the narrator replies. Willie is easily beaten, Lucy is fired. The bricks for the school construction come from a kiln in which the county chairman has an interest. A fire escape at the school collapses, killing three children. It is Willie's break. He becomes "the spokesman for the tongue-tied population of honest men." The state machine has been operating so long without serious opposition that "ease had corrupted them." But the machine sets Willie up to run for governor to split the rural vote and let its own candidate be elected. Angered when he finds out how he has been used, Willie runs the next time and wins. He is now a disillusioned and masterful politician, who himself rules by blackmail and bribery.[134]

Three arguments or pleas are made for Willie—first, that all judgments of bribery are relative and in fact colored by class. As Jack Burden says of an aristocratic critic of Willie: "Graft is what he calls it when the fellows do it who don't know which fork to use." The second is that bribery is a necessity. Willie's attorney general, Hugh Miller, resigns when Willie covers for a dishonest member of his administration. The Boss says Miller wanted to keep his "Harvard hands clean." Miller "wanted the bricks but he just didn't know somebody had to puddle in the mud to make 'em. He was like somebody that just loves beefsteak but just can't bear to go to a slaughter pen because there are some bad, rough men down there who aren't animal lovers and who ought to be reported to the S.P.C.A."[135]

The third argument is that corruption and corruptibility are universal—in the county and in the city, in the school board and in the governor's mansion, in Willie the quondam reformer as in the machine he beats. Judge Montagu Irwin is, for Burden, the symbol of integrity, but Willie tells Burden, "There is always something." He answers, "Maybe not on the Judge." And Willie says, "Man is conceived in sin and born in corruption. . . . There is always something." Burden discovers that Irwin as attorney general acquiesced in the interpretation of a contract urged by a utility; he subsequently received $44,000 in the stock of a related company and appointment as its counsel.[136]

Willie's defense is made, but counterarguments are heard. Even as he raises the plea of universality, Willie combines a biblical metaphor with a homely rural image to indicate the character of the grafter's activities. "Callahan's been playing around for a long time, and he who touches pitch will be defiled, and little boys just will walk barefoot in the cow pasture." Burden himself (a burden to himself) comes to understand the evil he collaborates in by working for Willie. Illumination is provided through a historical flashback where corruption is analogized to a practice of adultery and its cruel consequences.[137]

Judgment is pronounced on Willie—first by his wife, who leaves him. It is then pronounced again and again by Willie on others. Governor, he returns home to the farm and says, "I bet I slopped five hundred herd of hogs out of this trough. And by God, I'm still doing it. Pouring swill." Here the hogs are the state's legislators. In a variation on the sexual metaphor for corruption, Willie fantasizes that he runs a seraglio for Burden, and his bagman, Tiny Duffy, is "the Secretary of the Bedchamber." Duffy is endlessly abused by the Boss. He is "the Judas Iscariot, the lick-spittle, the nose-wiper." As Burden observes, Duffy becomes, "in a crazy kind of way, the other self of Willie Stark, and all the contempt and insult which

Willie Stark was to heap on Tiny Duffy was nothing but what one self of Willie did to the other self because of a blind, inward necessity."[138]

Lucy judges Willie, Willie judges himself, and Burden becomes a judge when he confronts Judge Irwin with his knowledge of his bribery. "It wouldn't stick in court," says Judge Irwin. Burden replies, "But you don't live in a court. You aren't dead and you live in the world and people think you are a certain kind of man. You aren't the kind of man who could bear for them to think different, Judge." Burden is literally correct: Irwin kills himself when he believes Burden will reveal the truth. For Burden there is then another discovery: the corruptible and corrupted Judge is his father.[139]

Bribery is a class category. What it describes pejoratively is done in all politics and has to be done. Yet it is evil as adultery is evil. It necessarily produces self-loathing. The shame of it can kill. Such are the paradoxes of *All the King's Men*, a compendium of themes and characters from the Western tradition on bribery. Hugh Miller is Brutus, the unreflective honorable man who benefits from the bribery of others. Meek Lucy Stark is Isabella or Madeleine Lee, the righteous woman who wields the thunderbolts of divine justice. Willie himself is as familiar as Dante with the pitch of Ecclesiasticus; his sense of sin is Christian; and Willie, assassinated, says with his last breath to Burden, "It might have been all different, Jack. You got to believe that." The epigraph of the book is from the *Purgatorio*: "Mentre che la speranza ha fior del verde"—"While hope wears a green flower." Hugh Miller is going back to politics, this time with knowledge, saying, "History is blind, but man is not." Last illusion or Christian option, what might have been all different in Willie's view is his rule by corruption.[140]

Targets, Alive and Dead.   In Britain the reputation of the judiciary had changed remarkably from Bacon's day. By 1853 Anthony Trollope, searching for a metaphor for the improbable, could write, "The bishop did not whistle; we believe that they lose the power of doing so on being consecrated; and that in these days one might as easily meet a corrupt judge as a whistling bishop. . . ." Whistling bishops were commoner in America. "There is always something," Willie Stark had said. "Maybe not on the Judge," Jack Burden had inaccurately replied. Most Americans would have replied like Burden if the question had been raised about judges of the Supreme Court of the United States. No whistling bishops there.[141]

On May 5, 1969, *Life* published a story with the caption, "Fortas of the Supreme Court—a question of ethics" and, beneath, a larger headline, "The Justice . . . and the Stock Manipulator." The article, by William Lambert, reported that Abe Fortas, a justice of the United States Supreme Court, had been paid $20,000 by the Wolfson Family Foundation; that Louis Wolfson, who with his brothers had set up the foundation, had been appealing a criminal conviction of securities fraud; that the Supreme Court had refused to hear the appeal and Fortas had recused himself so that he did not participate in this decision; that, while Wolfson was being investigated he had dropped Fortas's name "in strategic places"; and that almost a year after receiving the money, Fortas had paid $20,000 to the foundation.

According to Lambert, Wolfson met Fortas about the time Fortas was appointed to the Court in 1965. The $20,000 was paid him in January 1966. A Wolfson associate was told by Wolfson that a pending investigation by the Securities and Exchange Commission would be taken care of "at the top" and that Fortas was "joining the foundation"; Fortas flew to Florida and visited Wolfson for a day in June 1966, immediately prior to the SEC's disclosure of its investigation. Wolfson was indicted in September and October 1966; and Fortas "repaid" the foundation in December 1966. Paul Porter, Fortas's former partner and present "spokesman," was quoted as saying the money was paid to Fortas because Wolfson had asked Fortas to "outline future charitable and scholarship programs for the fund." In Porter's terms, it was "refunded" because "Abe had a whole sackful of petitions for writs; the business of the Court took so much of his time that he couldn't do the work for the foundation." Porter indicated that Fortas had expected to advise the foundation on education—the fund granted scholarships for theological studies. Carol Agger, Fortas's wife, was also cited as corroborating Porter and adding that her husband was also to advise the foundation on civil rights projects.[142]

Lambert asked rhetorically what counseling Fortas could have provided to justify his fee. The total income of the foundation was $115,000, its total grants $78,000. The $20,000 to an adviser seemed "generous in the extreme." The tax return of the foundation identified the payment as an "exchange," as though Fortas's services had been a capital asset.[143]

Invited by *Life* to explain his relations with Wolfson, Fortas wrote of "conversations" beginning in 1965 when Wolfson told him of the foundation's programs. He did not mention the $20,000 or any counsel he had given. Lambert pointed out Fortas's relation to Lyndon B. Johnson, president at the time of the Wolfson matter: "From Lyndon Johnson's days as a congressman through his term as President of the United States, Fortas was counsel and close confidant. . . . Fortas continued to advise and do favors for President Johnson after he took his seat on the Supreme Court in October 1965." Johnson indeed had unsuccessfully nominated Fortas to be chief justice of the Supreme Court in June 1968.[144]

Lambert accused Fortas of no crime. He went out of his way to say that Wolfson had used Fortas's name without Fortas's knowledge. As criteria for judgment of the affair, *Life* editorialized only with a box containing two of the Canons of Judicial Ethics: A judge's "official conduct" should be free "from the appearance of impropriety." A judge should not accept "inconsistent duties." These canons and the entire article did not mention bribery.[145]

Lambert had been assisted by leaks from the Internal Revenue Service, which told him of the foundation's tax return, and by the prosecutors of Wolfson, who told him of Wolfson's use of Fortas's name. The government had had all the basic information, and if the lower echelons of the government had taken the course prescribed by the criminal law, their information would have been transmitted to higher echelons for a decision as to prosecution rather than to the editors of a magazine. The government would have taken the initiative in enforcing the law. The law, however, was not formally enforced at all. Citizen censors, the editors of *Life* showed how deeply the bribery ethic could bite.[146]

As *Life*'s story came out, Fortas issued a press release beginning, "I have not accepted any fee or emolument from Mr. Wolfson or the Wolfson Family Foundation." He had, he then stated, been "tendered" a fee, which he "returned"; he had not communicated with any official about Wolfson or given Wolfson any legal advice. Immediately on publication of Lambert's article, the Justice Department subpoenaed the foundation's files and discovered in them a contract between Fortas and the foundation. In return for Fortas's service to the foundation, the foundation agreed to pay Fortas $20,000 a year for life and in the event of his death $20,000 to Carol Fortas during her life. The contract was at once shown to Attorney General John Mitchell, who the next day showed it to Chief Justice Earl Warren. Warren spoke to Fortas. The existence of the contract was leaked to the *Los Angeles Times*, which scheduled publication of its details for May 15. On May 14, 1969, Fortas resigned.[147]

The day he resigned Fortas filed with the Chief Justice a "memorandum with respect to my associations with the Wolfson Family Foundation." He stated that Wolfson had intended "to increase the Foundation's resources" and asked him "to participate in and help shape the Foundation's program and activities." The contract was drawn to compensate him for these "continuing services." He withdrew from it in June 1966 when he found he had not enough free time from judicial business and had learned that the SEC had asked for the criminal prosecution of Wolfson. He had canceled the agreement "subject to completing the projects for the year." In December he had "returned" the $20,000 "in its entirety," treating the services he had performed as "a contribution." While Fortas was on the Court, Wolfson "on occasion would send me material relating to his problems," but he had not "interceded or taken part in any legal, administrative, or judicial matter" affecting Wolfson. If Fortas were believed, no canon of judicial ethics had been violated. Nothing in his *official* conduct had the appearance of impropriety. To agree to advise the foundation was not to assume a duty inconsistent with his judicial role.[148]

Nonetheless, a single article in a national magazine and its consequences had been enough to remove from a position of great power an extraordinarily able and ambitious man. Fortas's official explanation of his resignation was that "the public controversy relating to my association with the Foundation is likely to continue and adversely affect the work and position of the Court." The "controversy" was over nothing, if he could be believed. At work in the calculations of the Justice Department, the chief justice, the press, and Fortas himself was the tradition on bribery. Discreetly but unmistakably, the bribery of a justice of the Supreme

Court had been made an issue. The citizen censors were active. Fortas had the choice of undergoing investigation or resigning.[149]

Resigning, he was not criminally prosecuted. His old firm did not take him back, but he was not disbarred. He was available for speeches and not unwelcome in law reviews. (No law review, indeed, chose to analyze the circumstances of his fall.) He was not eligible for high office or political recognition. He endured a limbo not dissimilar to Warren Hastings's after his impeachment had failed in the Lords or Francis Bacon's after his conviction. His own reaction after the event was, "It's just as if an automobile hit me as I stepped off the curb." Alive, he had become dead by the publication of what he had done.[150]

That Abe Fortas should have been on the Supreme Court at all was the decision of another man whose life was to evoke the censure of the censors, in his case most effectively after his death and, most unusually, from his biographer. Hog One was painted by a prosecutor, a great orator, in the heat of prosecution and in the aftermath of victory. Hog Two was depicted by another prosecutor and orator speaking over the heads of indifferent judges to posterity. Hog Three—for so Lyndon Baines Johnson appears in his biography by Robert Caro—was no longer alive to provoke anger by his arrogance; he was on trial in no judicial forum; but he was judged in a book that painstakingly detailed his life.

From his earliest days in politics at a small Texas teachers' college, Johnson in Robert Caro's biography wins elections by cheating, is characterized by a "passion for deception," and is obsessed with the pursuit of power. Fawning on those he needs, bullying those who need him, he is a rural creep, a Texan Uriah Heep, unctuous and humble before power; mean, mean-spirited, and vicious when in possession of it. Forty years later, reminiscing about his college enemies, Johnson is quoted, "They lost everything I could have them lose. It was my first real big dictat—Hitlerized—operation, and I broke their back good. And it stayed broke for a good long time."[151] As Caro puts it, "The desire to dominate, the *need* to dominate" are there from the beginning; also "the viciousness and cruelty, the joy in breaking backs and keeping them broken."[152]

Ambitious poor boy struggling to the top, Johnson is dependent on patrons and treacherous to those who befriend him. The most important public support for Johnson in his congressional district comes from the Austin *American-Statesman*. Its publisher is Charles E. Marsh. Cultivated by Johnson, Marsh is his close and admiring friend. Secretly, Johnson makes Marsh's mistress his own. The most important congressional patron for Johnson is the Texan who becomes speaker of the House, Sam Rayburn, who comes to regard Johnson as a son. Secretly, Johnson discredits Rayburn with President Roosevelt and "to help his own career" lyingly portrays Rayburn as the president's enemy; Rayburn suffers a kind of exile, Johnson becomes the president's prime man in Texas.[153]

Loyalty, obedience, subservience he expects and gets from his own subordinates. He shows them occasional cruelty and a "gift for finding a man's most sensitive point," supplemented "by a willingness—eagerness almost, to hammer at that point without mercy." Like Willie Stark with Tiny Duffy he tonguelashes his close associates. Johnson's wife, a shy, sheltered rich man's daughter of twenty-two, has been swept off her feet by him in 1934; after they are married, he orders her about in public, treats her as a servant at home, and by 1938 is engaged in his affair with the Marsh mistress.[154]

Disloyal, mendacious, vulgar, and vindictive, Johnson has only three assets: charm, ability to manage men, and determined energy. The charm is smarmy, the ability to manage reveals the will to dominate, the energy is exercised in ruthlessness. This monster is a master of bribery. Bribery runs through his rise to power. When he is first elected to Congress in 1937 at the age of twenty-eight, he buys votes—the votes of the rural boxes where the money goes to the sheriff or the county commissioners; the votes of the blacks who are sharecroppers in the county or slumdwellers in Austin, where the money goes to the blacks' leaders; the votes of the Czech immigrants in the countryside, whose price is higher. He also buys what he needs from the media, paying money for favorable stories in the small-town newspapers.[155]

Once in Congress Johnson devotes his great energy to securing statutory authorization for the Marshall Ford Dam, whose construction the contracting firm of Brown & Root has prematurely begun before the dam has been congressionally approved. He works with Brown & Root "as closely as if he were one of the firm's employees," not only getting the approval but successfully lobbying for larger appropriations, so that Brown & Root makes several million dollars. The relation between the Austin congressman and the contractors is strictly reciprocal. The contractors want their "money's worth." When they get it, they "balance the books" by providing Johnson with campaign contributions, "more funds, in fact, than he could possibly use."[156]

Johnson continues to get contracts for them. Without bidding and without experience in such work, Brown & Root in 1940 is awarded the contract for the $100,000,000 naval air base at Corpus Christi: it is a mark of Johnson's influence with the adminstration. When Johnson runs for the Senate in 1941, Brown & Root raises the necessary cash—partly by requiring subcontractors of the company to contribute, partly by giving "fees" to lawyers and "bonuses" to executives who are expected to pass the money to the Johnson campaign, partly by fictitious contracts with subcontractors who are asked to turn their "payments" over to the Johnson managers. Johnson uses the cash for advertising, for the purchase of favorable news, and for the purchase of votes. Mexican-American votes are bought wholesale from venal bosses in Duval and Starr counties: so the cycle of reciprocity turns, Johnson buying office through money he obtains by using his office to procure business for the contractors.[157]

In 1943 the Internal Revenue Service begins an investigation of Brown &

Root. Campaign contributions are not deductible as business expenses. The fictitious fees, bonuses, and subcontract expenses have been deducted. Brown & Root has broken at least three federal laws—against tax evasion, against a corporation contributing to a federal campaign, against a defense contractor contributing to a federal campaign.[158] The Internal Revenue agents note that Brown & Root had set up "a slush fund." Assistant Secretary of the Treasury Elmer L. Ivey says it appears "fraud" is present. Criminal prosecution threatens. Johnson asks to see President Roosevelt "as quick as he possibly could" on what is not "a Sunday School proposition." Johnson and Alvin Wirtz, a former Brown & Root lawyer, now undersecretary of the Interior, see Roosevelt. The same day a new agent is sent from Atlanta to Texas to make a separate report. The next day Ivey is summoned to the White House to report on the tax investigation. Within one week of Johnson's talk with the president, the criminal case is closed because of Brown & Root's "participation in the war effort"; the civil case is settled for one-fifth of what the investigating agent thought assessable. Brown & Root's reciprocal relationship with Johnson, and his with Roosevelt, have resulted in Brown & Root escaping criminal liability and civil fraud penalties.[159]

Narrating these events, Caro does not use the term bribe nor stop to characterize the conduct described in terms of its criminality under existing federal statutes. Johnson buys votes in violation of federal election law; Johnson influences the award of contracts in violation of federal bribery law; Johnson fixes a criminal case in violation of the statutes against obstruction of justice and conspiracy. Johnson's behavior does not impede his ascent. He is on his way to making a fortune in a television franchise dependent on government regulators whom he can influence; to becoming majority leader of the Senate; to being elected vice-president and to being elected president.

Observing his career, one could conclude that not only were the laws he ignored empty rhetoric but also that in America the antibribery ethic itself was dead. Both conclusions would be premature. The portrait of Johnson which Caro painted depends on the bribery tradition. Adulterer, hypocrite, ingrate, liar, and traitor in this account, Johnson rises by giving and taking bribes. Corruption is central to Caro's picture of Hog Three. By the law on the books and by the moral standards reflected in Caro's implicit condemnations, Johnson is guilty of bribery. By law as it was enforced and by the moral standards observed in practice by his political associates, Johnson is innocent. But the criminal laws which Johnson mocked were about to be brought to life. The tradition sustained in American writing from Adams to Caro was about to be given new political and legal vitality.

Like the censors of Republican Rome, the American censors did not pronounce their verdicts after a judicial hearing in which the defendent confronted the witnesses against him and had his say. Within the confines of their own creations the novelists, of course, could affix guilt definitively, but when the novels were read as reflections of reality—when they were taken to say that this was how the system worked—they acted as accusations rather than final judgments. Caro's biography, researched and documented though it is, must also count as accusation—the defendant has opportunity neither to answer or confess. The accusatorial character of the censors' verdict is more readily apparent in Strong's diary, Older's headlines, Steffens's muckracking, Lambert's innuendo. These accusations performed multiple functions. They sold books, magazines, newspapers; expressed anger, envy, frustration, prejudice; afforded explanation of financial or political success; championed purity at points where society was perceived as vulnerable to disintegration; asserted values derived from the Bible and the Western religious tradition; identified those guilty by the standard of unenforced criminal law. The most striking feature, on the whole, about the accusations was the intensity of interest they held for the accusers. Not for them the pallid pokings of the topic engaged in by formal academic analysis. For the censors, the accusations were page one news, magazine cover stories, subjects of burning personal indignation, central themes of their books. For them, whether or not a man took a bribe was of crucial concern.

Sometimes the accusations were actually substantiated in court, as Older's were. Sometimes the accusations were based on evidence already accumulated by others in a forum where the defendant had been heard, as were Mark Twain's. Sometimes the reaction of the accused appeared to be confirmatory of the allegations, as Fortas's flight under fire appeared to confirm Lambert. Sometimes the sources cited and the evidence presented seemed to make guilt probable as in Caro's account of Johnson. But the accusers themselves prosecuted no case, sent no one to jail. Like the preachers of medieval England or orators such as Cicero and Edmund Burke, they perpetuated a tradition in which a verdict was expected to be rendered by the state or by God more physical and definitive in its consequences than their merely verbal rebuke. Occasionally their cries led to such verdicts, as happened in the cases of Tweed and Ruef. Sometimes the expectations they sustained and shared were unsatisfied and resulted in alienation from political life as happened with Adams, exiled as effectively from American politics as Dante was from Florentine affairs; or desire for revolution, as was momentarily the case of Strong and ultimately the case of Steffens; or resigned acceptance of the reciprocities, criminal or not, that made the system work—Dreiser and the later Older were examples. The cumulative thrust of their work was otherwise. Their work, in the tradition that stretched back so far to prophets and popes, showed the need for reformation. Reform was what Lambert's articles achieved, what Caro's Catonian judgments called for, what *All The King's Men* still supposed possible. As long as hope wore a green flower, reformation would be tried. Educated in the tradition by the censors, twentieth-century Americans were to attempt reformation by the enforcement of the criminal law.

18

The Ideal Criminally Enforced

Abraham Lincoln transferred his corrupt secretary of War, Simon Cameron, to St. Petersburg to represent the United States as minister to Russia. James Fowler Simmons returned to Rhode Island from the Senate with his loot. No investigation by the executive branch followed the congressional exposures of the Credit Mobilier and the congressmen who had acquired its stock at bargain prices. No grand jury ever called James G. Blaine to account. Article II, section 4, of the Constitution had been stretched to permit the impeachment of judges, and in the course of time six federal district judges resigned under charges of corrupt conduct in office, and one district judge and one circuit court judge were impeached by the House for corruption and convicted by the Senate. In no instance did criminal prosecution follow. Federal criminal law against bribery was not, where leaders of the government were involved, enforced by criminal sanctions.[1]

Presidents, vice-presidents, members of the Cabinet, federal judges were immune. Legal realists, understanding by "the law" the statutes actually applied, would have to conclude that no *criminal* law against the bribery of these high officers was in force in the early years of the Republic, in the entire nineteenth century, or in the first quarter of the twentieth century. Over 140 years of American history elapsed before any one of this rank was criminally convicted as a bribetaker.

Breaks in the Pattern.   In the late 1920s the conviction of an ex-cabinet officer for bribery in office changed the prevailing rule or, rather, demonstrated that it was not of iron. In the late 1930s the conviction of a federal judge while still in office showed that even incumbency was not equivalent to immunity. Both cases depended on political incentives for their initiation, both were prosecuted with bipartisan cooperation. Read together, the cases were signs of a new seriousness about the criminal aspect of the bribe.

Teapot Dome was the tag for two transactions arranged in 1922 by Albert Bacon Fall, secretary of the Interior—leases to two oil companies of drilling rights in the Navy's oil reserves at Teapot Dome, Wyoming, and at Elk Hill, California. The leases were justified by Fall as necessary to prevent drainage from the government's land. The companies had the possibility of making very large profits. The conservationists—forerunners of today's environmentalists—attacked the contracts vigorously as a gross abandonment of the principle of preserving natural resources. Their complaints became effective when the Public Lands Committee of the Senate declared that the procurement of the leases had been "essentially corrupt."[2]

The committee's condemnation came in 1924, after Fall had left the Cabinet, and the president who had appointed him had died. The country had already heard many rumors of the corruption of the administration of the late Warren Harding of Ohio, dominated by politicians often denominated "the Ohio gang." The senator who had unearthed the basic facts was Thomas J. Walsh, a Democrat from Montana; and in a presidential election year the Democrats were certain to make a great deal out of the corruption of a Republican administration. There was on Democratic casualty: William McAdoo, Wilson's secretary of the Treasury, who turned up as counsel for one of the companies involved and saw his hope for the Democratic presidential nomination mortally wounded by this association. The main targets were Republicans: Harry Daugherty, attorney general of the United States and the chief of the Ohio gang, who had done nothing to investigate the culprits; and Edwin Denby, secretary of the Navy, who had passively assented to the leases. Both resigned. Public sentiment was that Washington needed to be "fumigated and sterilized," and "every faithless public servant" punished. Calvin Coolidge, the vice-president from Massachusetts who had become president by Harding's death, had every reason to distance himself from Harding. He appointed two special counsel—Atlee Pomerene, a Democratic ex-senator, and Owen Roberts, a Philadelphia Republican—to prosecute the wrongdoers. Choosing these independent and vigorous lawyers, Coolidge set in motion the process that led finally to Fall's imprisonment.[3]

Such a breach in the immunity of a former member of the Cabinet (also a former senator) was by no means a foregone conclusion. Roberts and Pomerene first secured judicial cancellation of the leases, described by Pierce Butler for a unanimous Supreme Court as "corruptly secured." The two oil companies were given no credit for what they had spent and were forced to pay back over $47 million.[4] The criminal suits were more difficult. Whether the explanation lay in sociology, in the reluctance of Washington juries in the 1920s to convict very rich men, or in effective lawyering, the two very rich men, Edward Doheny and Harry Sinclair, who had corrupted Fall, were acquitted in jury trials. Fall was tried with Doheny for conspiracy to defraud the United States and was acquitted with him. Sinclair was tried alone and acquitted. Doheny was tried alone and again acquitted. The cover stories—Doheny's that he had made Fall a $100,000 cash loan, delivered by Doheny's own admission in "a little black bag," a loan on which he had collected neither principal nor interest; Sinclair's that he was buying an interest in Fall's ranch—were apparently swallowed.[5]

After the failure of the conspiracy prosecution, Fall argued that his innocence of taking a bribe from Doheny was *res judicata*, for the bribe was one of the overt acts charged as part of the conspiracy. After Doheny's acquittal of bribery, Fall made the additional argument that if Doheny was innocent of giving a bribe, he could not be guilty of taking one. Nonetheless, on October 25, 1929, Fall, tried alone for accepting Doheny's $100,000, was convicted; and in 1931 the Court of Appeals for the District of Columbia upheld his conviction. His acquittal of conspiracy was treated as irrelevant. *Res judicata* did not apply for Fall was on trial for bribery, not conspiracy. Doheny's acquittal was equally no defense. Whatever Doheny's intent, in this case "the only mind that the jury was called upon to penetrate was the mind of Fall," and the jury by its verdict had found him to have taken Doheny's money with the intention of being influenced in his duties. Fall was sentenced to a fine equal to the bribe and one year in jail. President Herbert Hoover, once his colleague in the Cabinet, was as desirous as Coolidge to establish his distance from Harding and his cronies. Later (after his first choice was rejected) Hoover was to find Fall's prosecutor Roberts an eminently desirable nominee for the Supreme Court. Roberts's elevation as much as Fall's fall were the consequences of Teapot Dome. Hoover refused Fall's plea for clemency. In July 1931 Albert Bacon Fall entered a federal penitentiary.[6]

The causes of this result were various and convergent. Fall was careless—his display of sudden wealth at his ranch had awakened Walsh's suspicions in 1922; his untruthful explanations to the Senate bound him in such a tangle that he chose not to testify on his own behalf when he was tried. He was also vulnerable, no longer in the Cabinet or Senate, and Harding dead. He had been made into an archvillain for the conservationists. He had become a symbol of corruption to both parties. His exposure was accomplished by a singularly able senator, Walsh, and his two prosecutors were very accomplished lawyers. That he had received the cash from Doheny was undisputed—only his intent was at issue, and circumstances pointed strongly to the guiltiness of that intent. His case went to the jury after the great stock market crash, and his appeal was weighed during the Depression. For these multiple reasons, precedent was broken and a former member of the Cabinet imprisoned.[7]

Eight years after Fall's conviction, an even bigger bribery case was criminally prosecuted. In 1939 Martin T. Manton was the ranking judge in the most respected federal appeals court in the country. He had sat on the federal bench since 1916, when, at thirty-six, he had become the youngest federal judge in office. Within eighteen months of his appointment he had been promoted to the Court of Appeals for the Second Circuit. In 1922 he had been an active candidate for appointment to the Supreme Court of the United States. Yet even at this date his reputation was not good among leaders of the New York corporate bar. Chief Justice Taft, reporting what he had learned of their views to Pierce Butler, his candidate for the Court, noted that as a lawyer Manton had been an "ambulance chaser," and then had grown rich "through politics"; his partner had been Bourke Cockran, a Tammany congressman; he had gotten his judicial appointments from President Wilson through Tammany and the McCooey machine in Brooklyn; his reputed backer, Archbishop Patrick Hughes, "should be ashamed of himself" for supporting him; his political and "other" associations disqualified him; he was a man "utterly unfit" for the Court.[8]

The Judiciary Committee of the Association of the Bar of the City of New York (the big firms' bar association) was unanimously against Manton's promotion to the Supreme Court. Utterly unfit in the Chief Justice's estimation for the highest office, he had remained at what was the center of the corporate legal world when corporate business came into the federal courts. He was to vote in over 4,000 cases and to write over 1,000 opinions. For twenty-one years his fitness to sit on the court next to the Supreme Court in prestige and in power went unchallenged.[9]

Challenge finally came from a young lawyer originally from Michigan, unschooled by apprenticeship in a Wall Street firm, Thomas E. Dewey. Initiated by experience first in the United States Attorney's Office in Manhattan, then as a state-appointed special prosecutor, Dewey had achieved spectacular success in prosecuting members of Il Unione Siciliano (the quaint designation of the day for the Mafia) and other murderers and mobsters. He had seen Manton release two convicted gangsters, Lepke and Gurrah, on low bail. He had come across a garment manufacturer's books showing large cash transactions with the judge and wondered why the judge dealt in cash and where he kept it. No doubt he had heard other rumors.[10]

Dewey in 1939 was district attorney for Manhattan. Only thirty-six, he had already run once for governor, denouncing the corrupt Democratic machines in Albany, Buffalo, and New York City. Ambitious, courageous, outspoken on the tie between organized crime and governmental corruption, Dewey began to investigate Manton. On January 29, 1939, he wrote Hatton W. Summers, chairman of the House Judiciary Committee, setting out in succinct detail six cases in which Manton had received money from litigants. He made no accusation of crime. He said only that his investigation had been "with a view to possible criminal prosecution under the income tax laws of the State of New York."[11]

The next day Manton resigned his office—an almost open admission of guilt and if custom were followed a protection against impeachment or a criminal trial. The case Dewey had developed was too strong to be so easily disposed of. The federal government looked foolish for being so far behind. A Democratic administration could not now be seen as protecting its own. Manton was the product of an earlier era of Democratic politics, but he had been vocal in his criticism of the Supreme Court for blocking the New Deal, indicating none too subtly his availability for the Court if Pierce Butler should resign or die. Attorney General Frank Murphy must once have even seen him as a rival for this seat which was to become his. Murphy now authorized prosecution. John T. Cahill, an energetic young United States district attorney, obtained indictments by April 1939. By May, Manton was on trial. In two weeks he was convicted.[12]

Noncapital offenses, committed more than three years previously, were barred by a general statute of limitations. Overt acts in a conspiracy, however, could be introduced in evidence although older than three years, if the conspiracy had continued and if at least one act occurred within the three-year period. Cahill elected to prosecute under the conspiracy statute, even though the maximum penalty was two years' imprisonment instead of the fifteen years provided in the law against bribery of a federal judge. The statute prohibited conspiracy "to defraud the United States" "in any manner or for any purpose." Arrangement and acceptance of the bribes were shown as overt acts in the carrying out of the conspiracy.[13]

In the period 1932–1938, Manton had received large sums of money from litigants in at least a dozen cases—six patent suits, three receiverships, two criminal prosecutions, and one stockholders' suit. His payors included two poultry dealers; an insurance salesman; an engineer; a brewer; two lawyers; a fence for stolen bonds; a movie executive (Harry Warner of Warner Brothers); and several presidents of closely held companies. The payments had been made in cash or, if by check, to nominees of Manton. The sums were always substantial. In all, not less than $430,000 and perhaps as much as $600,000 had been paid. The amounts sometimes were in the form of loans, made without real prospect of repayment. The judge was assisted in these arrangements by two members of the bar, Bill Fallon, a defense lawyer known to professional criminals, and John Lotsch, the president of a small savings bank. The judge, Cahill told the jury, had made his office "a counting house." Testimony had shown "brokers and brewers and moneylenders lugging the cash into the judge's chambers." Witnesses had painted "an overwhelming picture of judicial corruption."[14]

On appeal, Manton argued that there was no defrauding of the United States and no obstruction of justice, because the cases in which he had been paid were correctly decided. In the appellate process he was only one of three members of any panel. Experienced judges—Harrie Chase, Augustus Hand, Learned Hand, and Thomas Swan—who had sat with him in the cases in question testified that his conduct in conference had in no way reflected bias. In several of the decisions the panel had been unanimous. In others, Manton had not written the opinion but only provided a concurring vote. In no appeals case could Manton by himself have produced victory for the litigant bribing him. Now he contended that bribery without harm done by the outcome could not establish the conspiracy of which he stood convicted.[15]

Writing for the court hearing his appeal, retired Supreme Court Justice George Sutherland rejected Manton's argument. Sutherland was willing to assume that all the cases were rightly decided. Correctness was not at issue. "Judicial action," Sutherland wrote, "whether just or unjust, right or wrong, is not for sale." The conspiracy was unlawful once Manton agreed to take money for the exercise of judicial power.[16]

Calvin Chestnut, imported from Baltimore to preside at Manton's trial, gave him the two-year maximum sentence possible under the conspiracy statute. A federal judge caught red-handed could scarcely have been given less. Manton entered a federal penitentiary in March 1940, a little over a year after Dewey's letter to Summers, and he was released eighteen months later. In November 1940 Dewey was elected governor of New York, his part in Manton's downfall making one of many strands in his reputation as a prosecutor. On the federal bench for twenty-three years, Manton was only fifty-nine when convicted; he died in obscurity in upstate New York, aged sixty-six.[17]

The Muzzled Criminal Law.   Fall and Manton remained exceptions. Prominent judges and lawyers, officeholders and businessmen could be suspect of bribery and not be investigated, or plainly guilty of giving or taking bribes and not be convicted of crime. Examples will illustrate.

Among the cases listed by Dewey in his letter to Summers was one in which Manton had received $250,000, the largest of the amounts enumerated in Dewey's allegations. The bribe was not cited in the criminal case against him, possibly because the complexity of the arrangement made it unappealing in a prosecution already provided with plenty of provable misdeeds. It was documented in a disbarment proceeding brought by the Justice Department itself against Louis S. Levy, the lawyer who had been the intermediary for the payment.

Levy was a founder of the *Columbia Law Review* in 1900 and Manton's mentor in law school. He had later supported his appointment to the bench. Friendship and business continued to bring them together. In 1932 Levy was the second-ranking partner in the medium-sized firm of Chadbourne, Stanchfield, and Levy. He was also counsel to the American Tobacco Company in a suit of great personal interest to its officers. A stockholder was seeking the return of $10,000,000 of bonuses paid to the company's executives. The case was in the Second Circuit before a panel over which Manton presided.[18]

A few days before the case was argued, Manton asked Levy for a loan of $250,000. With the apparent acquiescence of George Washington Hill, American Tobacco's president, and Albert Lasker, the controlling force in Lord and Thomas, American Tobacco's ad agency, the loan was made. A check was furnished by Lord and Thomas, made out to an individual nominated by Manton. In return, Lord and Thomas received the nominee's demand note carrying 5 percent interest and a pledge of stock of uncertain value. Lasker and the officials at Lord and Thomas made no effort to discover the purpose of the loan. It was never repaid. For practical purposes the money became Manton's. The true quid pro quo was the decision, delivered by Manton, upholding the bonuses. The disbarment proceeding, before Judge John C. Knox, focused on Levy as the arranger of the exchange. Knox found that Levy "in mind, heart, and action was venal and corrupt."[19]

No criminal prosecution followed. The statute of limitations forbade pursuit of what Levy had done in 1932. He had not been part of the continuing conspiracy of which Manton was guilty. He had, however, as Knox observed, been guilty of perjury in the disbarment proceeding. It was possible to prosecute him for his fresh crime by which he had tried to cover up his old bribery and retain his professional status. Exercising its discretion, the Justice Department chose not to take this course. Disbarment was considered penalty enough.

A second example from the debris around Manton: Edward Stark Thomas—Yale Law School graduate, former state representative, former treasurer of the Democratic party in Connecticut, former secretary of Governor Baldwin—had been a federal district judge since his appointment by President Wilson in 1913. He was the senior district judge of the Second Circuit as Manton was the senior circuit judge. In 1935 when Manton's henchman Lotsch had been indicted for taking a bribe as a special master in a patent case, Manton had made the unusual move of transferring Thomas from Hartford to Brooklyn for a month, so he could hear Lotsch's case. Manton knew his judge well. Thomas dismissed the indictment on the ground that Lotsch had never been sworn in as a master. Lotsch, according to his own testimony at Manton's trial, paid $10,000 to Manton to recompense Thomas for his help. Lotsch's testimony did not show that Manton had delivered the money, but as the federal prosecutors closed in on Manton, Thomas, on April 12, 1939, abruptly resigned from the bench. He sought temporary sanctuary in the Neuro-Psychiatric Institute and Hospital at Hartford, the modern equivalent of the Franciscan church in which Chief Justice Weyland had sought safety from his avenging master in medieval England. The mental institution was safer. Thomas lived until 1952, untroubled by further pursuit and remembered at his death only for the honors he had accumulated.[20]

Another resignation occurred in April 1939, as the shock waves of the

Manton affair reached the neighboring Third Circuit embracing Pennsylvania, New Jersey, and Delaware. The resigning judge was J. Warren Davis, native of North Carolina, a graduate of Crozier Theological Seminary, and ordained Baptist minister. Davis had graduated from the University of Pennsylvania Law School and been elected a state senator in New Jersey. President Wilson had named him to the district court in New Jersey and in 1920 promoted him to the appeals court. Twenty-five years on the federal bench, he came under investigation when Manton did, and a month after Manton was indicted, he resigned. The jig was up. Resignation, he reasonably supposed, would spare him harassment.[21]

Investigation, however, continued. In 1941 he was indicted for conspiracy to defraud the United States by accepting bribes. Payoffs to his bagman, Morgan S. Kaufman, were shown in two patent cases. In a third, a bankruptcy, the payment was confirmed by the payor, William Fox of Fox Films and Fox Theatres, a co-conspirator who pleaded guilty and became a government witness. The government, nonetheless, failed to convict. Hung juries in Philadelphia spared Davis and Kaufman. The government abandoned the prosecution. Fox, a bankrupt, alone went to jail.[22]

Civil litigation reopened the patent suits. To hear them the chief justice of the United States appointed three judges from outside the Third Circuit. The attorney general of the United States, in an extraordinary intervention, presented evidence on Davis's corruption. For the new court, Judge Morris Soper reviewed what had been established:

Universal Oil Products, jointly owned by Royal Dutch Shell and Standard Oil of California, was the holder of valuable patents for the cracking of oil. The parent corporations wanted to exploit the lucrative market for licenses of the patents, but they first wanted the validity of the patents judicially established. Universal brought a test case against Root Refining Company in Wilmington, Delaware. The usual appeal of the case would go to the Third Circuit, whose decision, given the complexity of patent cases, would probably not be reviewed by the Supreme Court.

Having chosen the forum and foreseen the path of appeal, Frank L. Belknap, Universal's general counsel in Chicago, selected the lawyers. Thomas G. Haight of Jersey City was to lead the trial team. Once counsel for Jersey City, then for Hudson County, he had been appointed by Wilson to the federal district court in New Jersey and promoted by him to the Third Circuit. After only six years as a judge, he had resigned and begun a successful patent practice in New Jersey. His relations with Manton and with Davis, who succeeded him on the bench, were very good.[23]

Haight opened the case before District Judge Hugh Morris, who made preliminary rulings. Morris then resigned as judge and, by prearrangement with Haight, appeared the next day in his old court as Universal's trial counsel. He was at once paid $2,500 as a retainer. Universal was now represented by two ex-judges. But appeal was inevitable. Haight was introduced by Judge Davis to Morgan Kaufman. Haight in turn brought Kaufman to Belknap's attention.[24]

In a complicated, technical case Kaufman—a lawyer whose highest employment had been as a referee in bankruptcy in the Middle District of Pennsylvania—had no skills. His base was Scranton, while the trial was in Wilmington. He had only one thing to offer—his intimacy with Judge Davis. Belknap hired him. In a single year Universal paid him $50,000.[25]

Half, at least, of his fees were approved by New York counsel for Shell and Standard of California—Richard E. Dwight, senior partner of Hughes, Schurman, and Dwight, and William D. Whitney, a younger partner of Cravath, de Gersdorff, Swaine, and Wood. The explanation for hiring Kaufman was that it was a "hold-off retainer," that is, he was retained lest the other side retain him. As Judge Soper, reviewing the facts, pointed out, the only reason why either side would have wanted Kaufman was his influence with Davis. The hold-off retainer operated as a preemptive bribe.[26]

The panel that heard Universal's case on appeal consisted of Davis, District Judge J. Whittaker Thompson, and Circuit Judge Joseph Buffington. Buffington was eighty years old, deaf, so near-sighted that he could not read a newspaper, and without a law clerk. He depended on Davis, who in the Fox bankruptcy wrote and sold to Fox the opinions signed with Buffington's name. Buffington was also an intimate of Kaufman. The panel, unsurprisingly, voted for Universal.[27]

Judge Soper, relating this history, drew its implications. Universal's conduct was "directed against the integrity of the court." The sale of justice had put the judicial process in doubt: the corruption of Davis had touched "the existence of the court itself." The records of the court "must be purged." The judgment in Universal's favor was vacated, and its suit dismissed.[28]

Kaufman and Haight had again collaborated in another patent case brought by American Safety Table Company against the Singer Sewing Machine Company. In the district court in Philadelphia, American Safety had been represented by the dean of the local patent bar, and lost. On appeal to the Third Circuit, American Safety employed Kaufman, who in turn brought in Haight, and won. The panel consisted of Davis and Buffington and a third judge, Albert Johnson, whose career will shortly be described. Black humor could not have designed more grotesque representatives of justice. Judge Soper refrained from this observation but finding that Kaufman had been paid by American Safety only for his influence with Davis, he vacated American Safety's judgment and dismissed its suit. Kaufman, he suggested, was "an apostate lawyer," American Safety "a corruptor of the Government itself."[29]

Belknap, Universal's "generalissimo," was dead. Morgan Kaufman, a small fish from Scranton, was disbarred. No criminal investigation, no disciplinary proceedings, no public words except Soper's laying out of the facts touched Richard Dwight, Thomas Haight, Hugh Morris, or William Whitney. The principals in American Safety, Standard Oil of California, Royal Dutch Shell, and Universal were not rebuked or even identified.[30]

Albert W. Johnson, Davis's colleague in the American Safety case, had his own career of unrequited crime. A Republican state legislator and a county judge in Scranton, he was appointed to the federal district court in 1925 by Calvin Coolidge; the senior senator from Pennsylvania—who presumably would have had a say in the appointment—was George Wharton Pepper, a leader of the Philadelphia bar. The selection was criticized by the local Scranton bar and press. In the next two decades Johnson's behavior far exceeded the prophecies of his most pessimistic critics. After six years of his regime the *Philadelphia Inquirer* observed that he confined bankruptcy trusteeships to a handful of lawyers, his son-in-law prominent among them. In 1933 Attorney General Homer Cummings announced a federal inquiry into "the receivership racket" in his district, but nothing came of it. Only after he had been on the federal bench for eighteen years did Johnson encounter a lawyer who became sufficiently aroused to bring him to book. Max Goldschein, a federal prosecutor, was told by a Scranton newspaperman that embezzlers whose conviction he had just obtained in Johnson's court had fixed the judge; their sentence would be nominal. The reporter's tip was true. Outraged, Goldschein helped launch a double-barreled investigation of Johnson by a federal grand jury and by a subcommittee of the House Judiciary Committee. The latter, chaired by Estes Kefauver, reported in 1945 that for over fifteen years—the bulk of his time in office—Johnson had been involved in "conspiracy against the administration of justice"; that he "notoriously engaged in the barter and sale of court offices, notably in the appointments of attorneys, trustees, receivers and similar offices"; and that "his decisions, decrees, orders and rulings were commonly sold for all 'the traffic would bear.'" Ten cases—all involving Johnson's judicial supervision of bankruptcies, receiverships, or reorganizations—were cited in support of these comprehensive condemnations.[31]

During the subcommittee's hearings—indeed after a single day on the witness stand—Johnson resigned, later renouncing even his pension rights to avoid any risk of impeachment. In 1947 he was tried in Pennsylvania with his bagmen, John Memolo (the borough lawyer) and Jake Greenes (a beer salesman) for conspiracy to defraud the United States. Greenes, memorably, had told the Kefauver subcommittee his view of collecting the bribes. "I felt like this might probably be a question of ethics involved, but I certainly had no idea there was anything too terrible about it." At the trial Greenes and Memolo were loyal to the judge, refused to testify against him, and were convicted. Johnson went free. He returned to the practice of law, was elected president of the local bar association, and had the chutzpah to sue for the restoration of his pension, contending that he had been mentally incompetent when he renounced it. The Court of Claims rejected this contention, observing that he "was perhaps more keenly conscious than ever before." Johnson's immunity from criminal punishment was nonetheless evident.[32]

In the most striking case investigated by Goldschein and Kefauver, Johnson had presided over the receivership of the Williamsport Wire Rope

Company, a small corporation coveted by its chief creditor, Bethlehem Steel. Johnson manipulated the receivership so that eventually in 1937 Bethlehem was able to acquire the company at a bargain price. For these services, he and several bagmen were paid "large bribes" by Bethlehem —in all $250,000, conveniently approved, in disguised form, in an order by Judge Johnson himself approving the sale of Williamsport. Fifteen years later, Bethlehem was found liable for this fraud and without admitting liability settled further litigation by paying the old Williamsport stockholders $6 million. The lawyer chiefly responsible for approving the bribes on Bethlehem's behalf was its outside New York counsel, Hoyt A. Moore, sixty-seven, a leading partner in the law firm of Cravath, de Gersdorff, Swaine, and Wood.[33]

When the Kefauver committee uncovered the facts in 1946 it characterized Moore's part in the arrangements as "corrupt connivance." In 1947 he went on trial with Johnson and successfully pleaded the three-year statute of limitations. He had had no part in Johnson's continuing conspiracy to sell justice; the events involving him were ten years old; he could not be touched. No disciplinary proceedings were brought against him by the Justice Department or by the respectable bar associations of New York City. His firm, which since 1944 had been known as Cravath, Swaine, and Moore, retained his name in its own. Writing the firm's biography a year after Moore's acquittal, his partner Robert Swaine did not refer to the Kefauver hearings, Moore's trial, or Moore's acquittal, significant though these events had been for the firm. Swaine did note, without indicating how it was accomplished, that Bethlehem's acquisition of Williamsport had been handled by Moore. In a section whimsically entitled, "What's in a Name?," Swaine discussed the alterations in the firm's name but not the significance of perpetuating Moore's. In a brief biographical section devoted to Moore himself, he observed that Bethlehem had been Moore's principal client and that Moore had devoted himself to Bethlehem's expansion. He concluded his account with this cryptic sentence: "No lawyer ever unreservedly gave more of himself to a client." To those familiar with the facts Swaine's "unreservedly" said a great deal. It was very much less than the canons of the profession would have said if they had been applied.[34]

Alive, at work, the bribery ethic had been enforced indirectly. Davis, Johnson, Thomas had resigned. Kaufman and Levy had been disbarred. Moore had been subtly rebuked by his partner. American Safety Table, American Tobacco, Bethlehem Steel, Universal Oil had been denied the fruits of the decisions in their favor. Impossible to explain these results if the bribery ethic was dead. But bribery as a crime remained dependent on status. Manton excepted, it was those on the fringe who went to jail—low-level lawyers like Fallon, Lotsch, Memolo; beer salesman Greenes; bankrupt Fox. Judges—Davis, Johnson—could not be convicted. Wall Street lawyers—Levy, Moore—were discovered too late to be convicted of bribery and were not pursued for perjury. Other successful lawyers—

Dwight, Haight, Morris, Whitney—were not even investigated criminally despite the circumstances suggesting that they had been accessories to bribery. Businessmen—George Washington Hill, Albert Lasker, the executives of American Safety, Bethlehem Steel, Shell, Standard of California, Universal Oil—were not called to account despite evidence indicating that they had controlled the cash employed and authorized its employment.

When the bribery ethic was enforced—exceptionally by criminal convictions, more often by lesser sanctions—patterns of corruption were unearthed that seemed long established. The cases did not involve sudden impulses to accept or to give money. As far as the eye could see, Johnson and Manton had been at it. When Manton needed a complaisant district judge, he knew Edward Thomas would serve his purpose: how else except by experience? Davis knew Johnson would be cooperative; both found old Buffington serviceable. Levy, when he was disbarred, was said by Judge Knox to have done the same thing twenty years before and escaped punishment then; Levy's understanding of Manton's needs went back thirty years. Moore, when he was approached by Johnson's bagman, knew exactly what was wanted; his skill in tucking the bribes into the plan approved by the judge himself did not reflect the inexperience of a novice in corruption. Haight had relations for nearly a decade with the bagman Kaufman. The corporate executives who authorized the bribes did not appear to regard the bribing of federal judges as other than a business decision, where advantages and risks were to be weighed, and the principal risk, as they correctly calculated, was giving up what was corruptly won. Business as usual encompassed bribery of courts.[35]

Long service on the federal bench by outstandingly corrupt judges—twenty-five years for Davis; twenty-one years for Johnson; twenty-three years for Manton—proclaimed the compatibility of public honor and judicial tenure with the secret practice of bribery. Close colleagues—men of the caliber and penetration of the two Hands—had seen nothing amiss. Local bar associations—provincial in Johnson's case; the prestigious Association of the Bar of the City of New York in Moore's—were so indifferent to the problem that they did not further investigate the lawyers who had secured acquittal of bribery well-documented in a nonjudicial forum. Weakness in the criminal law where the status of the bribetaker or bribegiver was high had the secondary consequence of weakening other sanctions against high-status bribers or bribees. The bar associations, ready to discipline lawyer-embezzlers, showed no desire to discipline a Johnson or a Moore.[36]

The Shrouded Beacon.   State enforcement of state criminal law against bribery was not substantially different from the federal practice. Governors, judges of courts of general jurisdiction, major state officers were, on the whole, exempt. Massachusetts may stand as an example. Steffens's reports on Connecticut, Minnesota, Missouri, New York, Pennsylvania, and Rhode Island and Robert Caro's later report on Texas suggest that it was not unusual.[37] The commonwealth was not dominated by a machine or run by a single party so that all protest against corruption would have been stifled. It was endowed with educated lawyers and generally able judges. It had a number of competing newspapers free to build circulation by uncovering graft. It was also a state, as Congressman Oakes Ames and his colleagues in the Massachusetts congressional delegation showed, not free from corrupt public servants. Real instances of bribery might have been expected to have been uncovered by partisan investigators, publicized by hostile papers, punished by vigilant courts. Political fights in the state were hard. Mollycoddling of criminals was not fashionable. Suspicion of corruption was often voiced.

The Massachusetts legislature, seated on Beacon Hill in Boston, was officially called the General Court. Neither its topographical association with light nor the nomenclature associating it with a judicial assembly put its reputation beyond doubt. For example, in 1891 a lobbyist familiar with its operations, in which he played a successful part, shared with Louis D. Brandeis, then a Boston lawyer (they both represented the same distiller), a list of legislators he knew could be bribed. Nonetheless, in the entire existence of the commonwealth from the Revolution to 1900, only one case came to the Supreme Judicial Court where officials were convicted of bribe-taking. Aldermen of Haverhill in 1895 were found guilty of conspiracy with liquor dealers to sell alcoholic beverage permits. Otherwise, so far as reported appellate cases indicate, Massachusetts public officials were blameless.[38]

Moral outrage about the state of the commonwealth was high in some circles. A Massachusetts Reform Club existed and attracted such speakers as that scourge of corruptionists, Carl Schurz. Brandeis, having heard him more than once, told his fiancée in 1890 that Schurz had affected him "as no other moral teacher ever has"—a strong tribute from an independent spirit. Holding Schurz's ideals, Brandeis was appalled at the liquor lobbyist's list of bribeable legislators. The lobbyist apparently intended to go on winning votes by payments. Brandeis gave him a lecture on the evils of bribery until—as Brandeis recalled the episode almost fifty years later—"tears ran down the liquor agent's face." His response did not change the nature of the legislature, and Brandeis did not always provoke such repentance. In a speech in 1903 Brandeis asked rhetorically if Bostonians meant to teach "that in Boston opportunity means the chance for graft?" In another publicly reported speech he added that the city's expenditures were enormously enlarged by "the high degree of corruption." Like his lecture to the lobbyist, these observations were directed to encouraging reform. He could not have supposed that they would lead to prosecutions.[39]

Enforcement of the bribery law against one level of officials did increase in the first half of the twentieth century. Councilmen of cities and selectmen of towns, municipal and state bureaucrats, clerks of court and an occasional mayor of a smaller city were convicted of bribery. Governors, major state officeholders, the mayor of Boston led charmed lives. James Michael Curley was shown, in a civil suit by the city of Boston, to have as mayor accepted $35,000 to fix a land damage suit against the city. He was ordered as a faithless trustee to turn his bribe over to the city. The statute of limitations did not bar prosecution for the bribery. He was not prosecuted for that crime, nor was he prosecuted for perjury for his lies defending himself in the civil case. His autobiography in 1957, vaguely but defiantly entitled *I'd Do It Again,* portrayed him as the champion of the poor, persecuted bipartisan patricians.[40]

In 1921 Daniel H. Coakley was disbarred for selling his influence to halt criminal prosecutions; in 1941 he was impeached and removed as a member of the Governor's Council for selling pardons to criminals; in neither 1921 nor 1941 was he tried as a criminal himself.[41] John Derham, a state district judge, was disbarred in 1954 for fixing a land damage case against the commonwealth; his payee, inferably the commonwealth's attorney general, was not identified beyond a reasonable doubt and escaped censure. The only one who went to jail as a consequence of the affair was the district attorney who exposed the bribe: the publicity he incurred led to his being investigated and convicted of federal tax evasion.[42] In 1960 a parole-revocation proceeding before Federal Judge Charles E. Wyzanski led to testimony by an engineer convicted of tax evasion that he had paid money to state legislators, a former Republican candidate for governor, a present member of Congress, and William F. Callahan, past commissioner of Public Works and present head of the Massachusetts Turnpike Authority—in all a "bounty" of $275,000 paid by the engineer in the course of obtaining contracts for his firm. The prosecuting authorities of the commonwealth did not stir to life.[43]

In the late 1960s a modest effort was made to apply the criminal law at higher levels. In 1967 Foster Furcolo, an ex-governor, was indicted for arranging to bribe six members of the Governor's Council to approve his nominee for commissioner of Public Works; significantly the money to secure this key public appointment—$15,000, or $2,500 per councillor—was furnished by a private contractor. Furcolo was acquitted; two councillors were convicted. In 1971 the deputy commissioner of banks was convicted of taking bribes from two big small loan companies (Beneficial Finance Company and Household Finance Corporation) to set the rates on small loans. Also in 1971, the state showed that Commissioner Callahan, now dead seven years, had arranged to have his son-in-law made a partner in an engineering firm doing business with the Turnpike; the son-in-law and the firm were convicted of bribery.[44]

These prosecutions showed that the criminal law was not obsolete and that it did not reach very high or very wide. A special commission on state and county buildings in 1980 investigated the expenditure of 17 billion dollars appropriated since 1968 for public buildings; it reported a 72 percent failure rate, that is, 72 percent of the construction had been unusable without repairs. It concluded that "at those crucial points where money and power come together, the system has been rotten." The pattern was "pervasive." In the award of construction contracts for public buildings, corruption was "a way of life in Massachusetts." The commission's functions were advisory and reportorial. No major elected officials were indicted. If the commission's conclusions were true—that the system was rotten, the pattern pervasive, corruption a way of life—the criminal law was scarcely enforced at all.[45]

Transition

A paradox: criminal law, federal and state, was infrequently applied to anyone, almost never to those of high status; yet there was continued expansion of the criminal law of bribery. The expansion was statutory and, to the extent that the statutes remained unapplied, purely theoretical. The stream of edicts of fourth-century Roman emperors on corruption is an appropriate parallel. Yet, as the sequel eventually showed, the tinkering with statutes could be seen as psychological preparation for hard enforcement. First, however, there were the legislative enactments.

Private Bribes. In the late nineteenth century state laws began to criminalize the bribery of private persons. New York was the pioneer, making it a misdemeanor in 1881 to give a "gift" to an agent, employee, or servant. Unlike governmental bribery, consent by the principal was a defense. The states were far from uniform and sometimes whimsical. Statutes were directed at the bribery of specific classes of employees—chauffeurs in Illinois, gardeners in Maryland! By 1932 there were only seventeen general statutes of the New York kind. But the trend continued. By 1980, the criminalizing states had doubled to thirty-four, and the tendency was now to include not only employees and agents but all fiduciaries. Seeking to reach payola in the record industry, eight states and the American Law Institute's *Model Penal Code* of 1962 added anyone professionally a disinterested expert. The basic crime as defined by the modern statutes consisted in conferring a benefit on an employee, agent, or fiduciary with intent to influence the recipient's conduct in his principal's affairs. Givers or receivers of such benefits committed bribery.[46]

Sometimes the statutes were employed defensively in civil litigation to void a contract. Rarely were they the basis of actual prosecutions. In New York, the country's commercial capital, no reported cases existed, eighty years after the pioneering law's enactment, where the statute had been criminally enforced and the conviction upheld. Those injured by a private bribe had more incentive to make the bribee turn over his bribe, or the briber turn over his profit, than to call in the police to vindicate the law.[47]

Literally read, the modern statutes applied to education and religion as much as to commerce: a teacher receiving a sexual favor from a student, a churchman practicing old-fashioned simony, could be held guilty of being influenced in the conduct of his principal's affairs. In these noncommercial areas the statutes were not brought into play at all. In commercial law they functioned as a symbolic backup to the ethics required by honest business.

Unlike any previous society, the United States now had statutes comprehensively extending the criminal law of bribery to almost every class and occupation. Who was not an agent, employee, or fiduciary? Amateur athletes, it might be answered. Between 1947 and 1960, thirty-two states made it a crime to influence sporting contests by bribes to officials or participants. Officials and professionals already fell within commercial bribery laws; now they and the amateurs were given special insulation from corrupting temptations. The statutes reflected the remarkable reverence in which sports were held in America, the self-interest of sports promoters, and a fear that gamblers had strong motivation to fix games. Almost never applied, they were occasionally enforced with great severity. A fixer of a basketball game in Iowa, for example, was sentenced to up to ten years' imprisonment, five times Manton's sentence for selling justice.[48] The connection of gamblers with the Mafia led to a federal criminal statute applicable to all sports affecting interstate commerce; the statute was expanded by judicial interpretation to include jockeys agreeing among themselves to rig their own race.[49]

It was not enough to protect the integrity of athletic contests. Television game shows, like athletics, provided vicarious pleasure for viewers identifying with a contestant. Their outcome could be affected by bribery or other collusion. The *Model Penal Code* and eight states made it a crime to rig any "publicly exhibited contest." The criminal net was now almost everywhere.[50]

Payments Affecting Public Power.   In 1600 only judges and witnesses could be *criminally* bribed, that is, found guilty of a crime for taking money to be influenced. By the eighteenth century the impeachment of Warren Hastings at least acknowledged that administrators fell within a class that could commit the crime. Legislators were a nineteenth-century statutory addition. By the mid-twentieth century, the usual statute included all officials and employees of government. The expansion did not stop here. Private persons were capable of influencing public decisions. The *Model Penal Code* of 1962, followed by fifteen states, added the officers and employees of political parties to the bribable class.[51] Logic cried out to continue further—party officials were not the only ones to have a say with officeholders. The *Model Penal Code*, followed by Idaho and, in a wondrously reforming spirit, New Jersey, put everyone among the bribables—the Code made any person selling political influence affecting a governmental appointment or transaction guilty of a crime. Political bosses, wives, mistresses, sons and daughters of officeholders, if they exercised their influence for a price, were within the law's scope.[52]

Loopholes and anomalies were attacked by modern legislation. The New York rule was that extortion was a defense for the bribegiver. In other words, if an official was asking money to do what he was legally bound to do, it was not the crime of bribery to pay him. The rule was the modern survival of the medieval moralists' position that it was not sinful to buy off official harassment (*redimere vexationem*). *The Model Penal Code* of 1962 rejected the rule. Its 1980 commentary characterized the citizen who payed an official in response to a threat as one willing "to subvert the legitimate processes of government." His duty was to resist the threat and report it. The penal law should "encourage resort to this option," not permit "a reprehensible invasion of government integrity."[53]

Some state laws restricted bribes to pecuniary benefits. The statutory trend was to define any favor, pecuniary or not, as a bribe. Such a definition on its face encompassed a broad variety of political activity. For example, city councilman A's promise to vote for B as mayor if B would support A's legislative proposals fell within the definition. Even state senator A's agreement to vote for state senator B's bill if B would vote for A's—logrolling characteristic of most legislatures—was not outside this definition. Read as they were written, the statutes extended the bribery rule deeply into political life.[54]

Intent "to influence" or "to be influenced" was sometimes hard to prove. Federal bribery law enacted in 1962 treated as bribery a lesser category of offense where intent of this kind did not have to be shown. Bribery was committed if a benefit was sought or offered "for" or "because of" an official act. Intent to affect performance of the act did not have to be proved to establish commission of the crime. Read strictly and not tempered by custom, the statute embraced the common American practice of giving the mailman five or ten dollars at Christmas; a federal crime was committed because the money was clearly given "for" the mailman's official service during the year.[55]

The law on the books was far more severe than the law enforced. As written, the statutes condemned customs as trivial as the postman's Christmas present and as pervasive as the politician's swap. At work appeared to be a dynamism, the reverse of the movement of the law "from status to contract."[56] Contract—the rule of reciprocity reached by private agreement—was replaced in government and out of government by law protecting duties defined by status. It was as if in a highly mobile society, uncertain of traditional loyalties, the criminal law of bribery could establish essential obligations.

Enlarged, refined, sealed-tight in theory against evasion, the criminal law had an educational significance, but no very great educational significance, if it were not more actively employed. Would the same forces that had led to its elaboration also lead to its application?

Two National Scandals.   On October 11, 1973, Spiro T. Agnew resigned as vice-president of the United States and pleaded *nolo contendere* to a single count of evading federal tax on income of $29,000 unreported by him when he was governor of Maryland. The prosecutors simultaneously filed in court and made part of the public record a summary of the evidence they had been prepared to offer if Agnew had not abandoned his defense. Their summary showed a man whose willingness to accept bribes had been uninhibited by fear of criminal prosecution.[57]

According to the prosecutors' statement, when Agnew first took office as governor, he had stated his belief that it was customary for engineers receiving nonbid contracts from the State of Maryland to make payments to the governor. For their part, the firms, except the large ones, shared this belief. Without explicit request or agreement, they paid. For example, in 1967, one engineer, Lester Matz, gave Agnew $20,000 in cash in a manila envelope, representing 1 percent on two years' worth of contracts. Through a real estate developer, I. H. Hammerman II, whom he used as a bagman, Agnew collected on other engineering contracts awarded by the State Roads Commission, splitting these sums, so that the bagman had 25 percent, the chairman of the commission 25 percent, and he himself 50 percent. Payments had been made to Agnew before he was governor when he was the executive of Baltimore County, and they continued when he was vice-president. Matz admitted giving him $2,500 for help in securing a federal contract, and when Matz was bothered by solicitors for the Nixon-Agnew presidential campaign of 1972, Agnew had reassured him with a quip: "Tell them you gave at the office."[58]

Agnew appeared to be a man who had accepted the morals of the system he had encountered. The son of Greek immigrants, he was a drop-out from college and the graduate of an unaccredited night law school. He had been an army officer in World War II, failed when he tried to start a law practice by himself, had been an insurance claims adjuster and the assistant manager of a supermarket. Appointed a member of the county zoning board, he had gone from there to his first elective position as county executive. A one-term governor of Maryland when Nixon selected him as his running mate, he had been elected vice-president at the age of fifty. Nothing, apparently, in his education or experience had led him to question the rightness of an official receiving payments from those doing business with the state. His joke about "giving at the office" showed a cheerfully cynical acceptance of the practice.[59]

Once facing federal indictment, he and his advisers showed great sensitivity to the charges of corruption. Negotiations for a plea were opened by him in September 1973 but were not concluded for a month, nearly breaking down over his reluctance to abandon his right to a trial unless the prosecution agreed not to make the charges of corruption public. Finally pleading to the single tax evasion count, he denied that he was guilty of any other wrong. Four days later he addressed the nation by radio and television. He said he had pleaded *nolo contendere* only "to still the raging storm"—a reference to the criticisms of the Watergate-beset administration. He declared that he had never enriched himself by the betrayal of a public trust. Like any poor public official, he had had to raise campaign funds to get elected. Contributions from contractors were one source of the funds. He spoke of corruption only to counterattack. The government's witnesses were "self-confessed bribe-brokers, extortionists, and conspirators." They had been given whole or partial immunity, and that immunity was "an open invitation to perjury." Immunity in the hands of an ambitious prosecutor could "amount to legalized extortion and bribery." As for what he was charged with in the government's summary, it boiled down to this: "that I permitted my fund-raising activities and my contract-dispensing activities to overlap in an unlawful and unethical manner. Perhaps judged by the new post-Watergate political morality, I did."[60]

Suggesting that what he had received from the contractors constituted campaign contributions, throwing the epithets of bribery back against his accusers, admitting only the technical charge of violating the Internal Revenue Code, Agnew demonstrated that socially and politically bribery was a far more damaging crime to be thought guilty of than tax evasion, felony though tax evasion was. As a tax-evader he could try to hold his head up. As a bribetaker he was lost. Obliquely, he acknowledged how moral notions color law. By what he called the new morality, his "fund-raising activities" could be considered "unlawful." The admission qualified and undermined the assertion of complete innocence. In making it, he appealed to public tolerance of campaign contributions and intimated that the law had been retroactively and unfairly altered by a new moral infusion. The morals he complained about, however, were at least as old in America as Adams's *Democracy*.

In the speech to the nation Agnew denounced the trade of testimony by a witness for immunity from prosecution as "legalized bribery"—a self-canceling phrase, marvelously useful as an unanalyzed rhetorical device. A comparable reciprocity, permitted by law, was at the center of the settlement of Agnew's own case. He had agreed to plead *nolo contendere* only in exchange for the prosecutor's promise to seek a light sentence for his crime. Attorney General Elliott Richardson explained to the court why the government had accepted this proposal: it had been "unthinkable" that the nation should have been required to endure "the anguish and uncertainty of a prolonged period" during which the guilt or innocence of the vice-president would have remained undetermined. In the background were the Watergate accusations against President Nixon, the real possibility that Nixon might be impeached, and the real danger that Agnew would then succeed him. To avoid "the unthinkable," Richardson had engaged in what had become a standard transaction in American courts, negotiation of a plea. As he told the judge, "No agreement would have been reached" if he had not agreed to "include an appeal for leniency." Formally, Agnew resigned and gave up his right to a trial in return for a recommendation for mercy. In the eyes of critics like Albert Ehrenzweig, plea bargaining was a corruption itself. It was undoubtedly a form of reciprocity recalling the fines by which English kings settled criminal cases or the pardons sold by medieval popes. But this exchange, according to the law and custom of the country, did not constitute bribery.[61]

As a result of this trade, Agnew was not sentenced to jail—unlike other tax-evaders who were lawyers and came before this court. He was given three years unsupervised probation and fined $10,000. He was also disbarred from practicing law by Maryland; and Maryland eventually (ten years later) recovered from him $268,482, the bribes received plus over

$100,000 interest. Mulcted seriously, disciplined professionally, punished mildly in terms of criminal sanctions, guilty legally of only one crime of tax evasion, Agnew suffered indirectly the historic punishment of bribetakers—extrusion from high office and disgrace. A laughing stock to his enemies (he had been bold in his defense of traditional virtues), an embarrassment to his friends, he entered the limbo of disgraced politicians, unelectable and unappointable to office. All these consequences, professional, social, and political, followed on the conviction of tax evasion which was the means of making public his "fundraising activities" with contractors doing business with him as governor. Agnew's case still showed that full application of the criminal law on bribery near the apex of power would be restrained by other considerations.[62]

On August 9, 1974, Richard M. Nixon resigned as president of the United States, his impeachment having been recommended by the House Judiciary Committee. Formally, he had not been charged with bribery. Article I of the articles of impeachment accused him of violating his oath of office by obstructing the administration of justice. The article then listed a variety of means by which he had obstructed justice, including making false statements, withholding evidence, and counseling witnesses to make false statements. Other means he was said to have used were "approving . . . the surreptitious payment of substantial sums of money for the purpose of obtaining the silence or influencing the testimony of witnesses . . . [and] rewarding individuals for their silence or false testimony."[63] In ordinary language, these were acts of bribery; and bribery, along with treason, was one of the two grounds the Constitution specified as a basis for impeachment. Debate at the Constitutional Convention, it will be recalled, had explicitly anticipated bribery by the president as a danger to democratic government. In the first article of impeachment the acts of bribery were deliberately subordinated, and the key constitutional term "bribery" was not itself used. An apparent design to make a more general indictment of Nixon's conduct in office predominated.[64]

A single act of bribery, proved, might not have been enough to topple the president; and in fact the investigation of his conduct and his ultimate departure were brought about by multiple convergent forces far exceeding the charge of bribery.[65] Bribery was nonetheless at the core of the hard evidence set out against him. By June 28, 1972, the evidence showed, the president's agents had begun to raise money to pay for "the legal expenses" of the defendants charged with the Watergate burglary of the Democratic National Committee; by September 1972, the amount provided them, $190,000, exceeded the probable cost of their lawyers; on March 21, 1974, the president conferred with his assistant, John Dean, on the raising of $120,000 more to pay a now-convicted defendant as the price of his silence. Arrangements to fix a case by money payments were violative of both the bribery and the conspiracy statutes.[66] When the president's men—presidential advisers John Ehrlichman and J. Robert Haldeman and Attorney General John Mitchell—were ultimately tried and convicted of conspiracy to obstruct justice, the arranging of "hush money" constituted an overt act in the proof of their conspiracy. Before their conviction, evidence of this criminality turned even partisan Republicans in Congress away from support of the president and made his impeachment or resignation inevitable.[67]

Widely regarded as a moral watershed, Watergate in its dénouement conformed to a traditional pattern—the antibribery ethic playing a decisive role, but not enforced criminally against the president himself. Watergate itself was not the critical step in the new criminal enforcement of federal bribery law. That step had already been taken under President Nixon himself.

The Larger Than Local Champion

Federal entry on the local scene can be understood as a facet of the larger tendency to federalize provincial preserves, a trend that ever since the Civil War had brought more and more power to Washington. The federal income tax, the securities regulation enacted under the New Deal, the civil rights legislation of the 1960s, were other signs and embodiments of the same dynamism. The push toward the center was stronger than party principles. In the late 1960s one local area yet unaffected by federal expansion was criminal corruption. Ideologically, President Nixon presented himself as a believer in decentralization. Yet under his administration, a combination of old laws, prosecutorial ingenuity, judicial imperialism, and new legislation approved by Nixon began an effective federalization of the law of bribery. Much as in the eleventh century, to the admiring applause of reformers, the central administration of the Church assumed responsibility for suppressing simony everywhere in theory, and in fact did so selectively far from Rome, so the federal leviathan emerged as the general foe of all graft and the selective chastener of civic corruption. From the perspective of reform, it was the age of Ildebrando; that an age of Leo X and Luther would follow did not figure in the federal calculations.

The Equation of Bribery with Extortion. Harbinger of what was to come was the prosecution of the Kenny machine in Jersey City, the work of two Nixon-appointed district attorneys, Frederick Lacey and his successor, Herbert J. Stern. New Jersey, according to Lincoln Steffens, had always been corrupt; Jersey City seemed the corruptest part of all. A reform led by an undertaker in 1905 had been quickly snuffed out. From 1918 to 1949 the city had been ruled by Boss Frank Hague. John Kenny, a Hague henchman, beat the machine in 1949 in the guise of a reformer; and in a spectacular gesture of repudiation the city actually sued Hague for $15,000,000 taken as bribes from municipal employees in the thirty-one years of his incumbency. The theory of the suit was upheld by the New Jersey Supreme Court; the money was not collected before Hague died. Kenny soon showed himself a boss in the mold of his mentor, and the law enforcement agencies of the state were unable to shake his hold. In 1970 the federal rescue was launched.[68]

Put into play was the Anti-Racketeering Act of 1934. The law had been enacted after a Senate investigation of big city gangsterism. The statute did not mention bribery. By the Hobbs Act of 1946, aimed at racketeering labor unions, the statute was amended to outlaw extortion—defined as the obtaining of the property of another with the other's consent under circumstances where that consent was "induced by wrongful use of actual or threatened force, violence or fear, or under color of official right." The sanction for violation was serious—a maximum of twenty years' imprisonment. On its face the statute had no application to bribery, and before 1970 it had never been applied to bribery. The leaders of the Kenny machine in Jersey City were charged with violation of the Hobbs Act.[69]

Kenny himself no longer held public office, but was, in the words of the court reviewing the evidence, "the absolute boss of the political party in power." He was seventy-seven, sure of his position, announcing that he would "spit in the eye" of the prosecutor who indicted him. Evidence developed at the trial showed that contractors with Jersey City or Hudson County were expected to pay 10 percent of the contract price to designated members of the machine. If they were known to be unwilling to pay, they were excluded from bidding. If they failed to pay after being hired, their final payments were delayed until the 10 percent was delivered. At the head of the recipients of the payments was Kenny. The liquid anonymity of large sums—$700,000 in bearer bonds in Kenny's possession; a secret bank account in Florida controlled by the mayor—were mute testimony to the success of the system and its criminal character. The defendants, with the exception of Kenny, were convicted. His trial was severed on the grounds of ill health. After his confederates were convicted, he pleaded guilty to tax evasion, was fined $30,000, and sentenced to prison for eighteen years. His sentence was then reduced to eighteen months; he spent most of his prison time in the prison hospital; and he was paroled within a year. His power was nonetheless broken. The main instrument of his machine's downfall had been the Hobbs Act.[70]

Bribery had been established on a massive scale, but how had the Hobbs Act been violated? Kenny's associates appealed. Stern, the successful prosecutor, published in Newark in the *Seton Hall Law Review* an article with the pointed title, "Prosecutions of Local Political Corruption under the Hobbs Act: The Unnecessary Distinction between Bribery and Extortion." The act, Stern wrote, was a major statute under which the federal government could "combat local political corruption where the state is either unable or unwilling to do so." At the core of his article was the contention that "extortion" under color of official right was equivalent to bribery. Blackstone's definition of extortion, he asserted, supported this position.[71] On this theory, it was apparent, he had prosecuted the Kenny crowd. On appeal, without discussion of the point, the Third Circuit Court of Appeals, speaking through Circuit Judge John Gibbons, upheld the convictions.[72]

For almost two centuries it had been black letter law that there was no federal common law of crimes—that is, federal judges lacked the power to turn evils into crimes the way English judges had done; every act which counted as a federal crime had to be an act proscribed by Congress. To a substantial degree, broad federal statutes and judicial self-confidence had made the black letter rule a myth. The Sherman Act, for example, made criminal "every contract . . . in restraint of trade." As any contract in some degree restrains trade, the courts had been forced to construct "a standard of reason" based on the judges' reading of English common law and past American practice—in short, to write a kind of common law gloss on the criminal statute. The judges' freedom to interpret the criminal law gave them in fact the power, if they chose to exercise it, of making new law—of creating in effect a new federal common law of crime. With *Kenny* this judicial freedom was exercised in regard to bribery.[73]

Stern's contention that Blackstone supported his interpretation was substantively inaccurate; and Congress had not treated extortion and bribery as the same. A statute banning extortion by federal officials had been on the books since 1909. It had never been interpreted to include bribery.[74] In statutes enacted as recently as 1961 and 1970, Congress had continued to use "extortion" and "bribery" as distinct terms.[75] As effectively as if there were federal common law crimes, the court in *Kenny* ignored Blackstone and congressional usage, for practical purposes amending the Hobbs Act and bringing into existence a new crime—local bribery affecting interstate commerce. Hereafter, for purposes of Hobbs Act prosecutions, such bribery was to be called extortion. The federal policing of state corruption had begun.

Equation of extortions and bribery was carried further. In *Mazzei*, a prosecution begun under the Nixon regime in 1972, a state senator had asked the owner of a building to pay 10 percent of the rent to an election committee if the senator arranged for the Commonwealth of Pennsylvania to rent the building. Convicted of extortion, the senator claimed on appeal that he had exercised no office in influencing the award. Everyone knew that legislators had no leasing authority. How could he have acted, or even have appeared to act, under "claim of official right"? Judge Gibbons, the author of *Kenny*, found this objection to be valid. Sitting *en banc*, the Third Circuit, in an opinion by Collins Seitz, disagreed. Mazzei's briber had believed that that was the way the system worked: he had to pay off the legislator. Coercion enough, said the court. When clout was perceived as needed to get the business of the state, payment for clout would count as Hobbs Act extortion. As no briber pays unless he thinks it is necessary to pay, the line between bribery and extortion disappeared.[76]

In the context of labor racketeering, courts continued to maintain that Hobbs Act extortion was distinct from bribery. The distinction offered was that the payor of extortion feared economic *loss*.[77] The distinction collapsed when applied to payments paid public officials. Bribers often paid officeholders to achieve economic *gain*. These acts were now regularly treated as Hobbs Act extortion. In *Hathaway*, for example, a consulting engineer from Philadelphia paid $25,000 or about 10 percent of his contract price, to the executive director of the New Bedford Redevelopment Authority to win the contract. At the trial of the director, the engineer testified that on other occasions he had bribed the majority leader of the Pennsylvania House, the treasurer of New Jersey, and the mayor of Lancaster, Pennsylvania. The engineer's *modus operandi*, in short, was bribery. If anyone was ready to pay, it was he. The First Circuit, per Levin Campbell, observed that he paid in New Bedford, Massachusetts, because he feared "preclusion from business with the Authority." The payee's conviction of Hobbs Act extortion was upheld. Similarly in *Salvitti*, the executive director of the Philadelphia Redevelopment Authority suggested that a certain lawyer be hired by a developer seeking a settlement of a disputed claim, and the developer hired the lawyer, agreeing to his fee with the understanding that he would not have to pay anyone else in City Hall. The developer observed, "When in Rome, do as the Romans do." The lawyer delivered $27,000 of his $75,000 fee in cash to the director, who was convicted of extortion: the "subtlety" of his communication to the payor was no defense when he clearly indicated that a payoff was expected.[78]

Prosecutions were brought under the Hobbs Act against a variety of bribetaking local officials—a Chicago alderman (*Staszcuk*); Chicago policemen (*Braasch* and *Crowley*); a Charleston, South Carolina, county councilman (*Price*); an Oyster Bay, Long Island, commissioner of public works (*Trotta*); a St. Louis building commissioner (*Brown*); the governor of Oklahoma (*Hall*).[79] The cases proclaimed the range and reach of federal power. The Hobbs Act was construed to apply to any act affecting interstate commerce in the smallest degree—to reach as far as the jurisdiction of Congress under the Commerce Clause had been construed to reach in the past forty years of judicial expansion of that jurisdiction. The impact on interstate commerce did not have to be actual; it needed to be only contemplated or potential or hypothetical.[80] In an economy as multistate as that of the United States, a bribe that did not have a potential effect on commerce between the states was hard to imagine. The one practical restriction on federal jurisdiction was the energy of local federal prosecutors. Lacking any national directive to pursue bribery under the Hobbs Act (indeed national directives would seem to have indicated the contrary), the United States district attorneys, spread thoughout the land, made individual decisions whether to bring local bribery within the Hobbs Act or not. Newark had led the way. New York, Baltimore, Chicago, Philadelphia, and Pittsburgh followed with particular vigor. In theory a crime anywhere in the nation, Hobbs Act bribery depended for its establishment on initiatives that varied with geography. By the mid-1970s, over 300 state officials were being prosecuted annually.[81]

The Federal Arsenal. The Hobbs Act, reinterpreted, turned out to be only one of a variety of federal laws under which local bribery could be punished. The Travel Act, the criminal laws on tax evasion, the mail fraud and wire fraud acts, conspiracy law, and, above all, the Racketeering Influenced and Corrupt Organization Act were found to speak to civic corruption.

Federal law piggy-backed on state law under the Travel Act, a 1961 product of the Kennedy administration's concern with the Mafia and union racketeers. Under the Travel Act, it was a federal crime, punishable by only five years' imprisonment, to travel or to cause others to travel in interstate commerce or to use interstate facilities to commit any of a list of enumerated crimes against state law, among them "extortion" and "bribery." Interpretation of the act was not restrictive. In *Perrin* "bribery" was held by the Supreme Court to include commercial bribery if state law made it a crime. In *Clark* a county purchasing agent was found to have "caused" a salesman to travel when the salesman came from out of state to pay the official a bribe. Causality in this sense consisted of the official being ready and willing to be bribed.

Bribery under the laws of the states was generally distinct from extortion. It did not bother federal appeals courts that in applying state law in a Travel Act prosecution they would need to distinguish two crimes no longer distinguishable for Hobbs Act purposes. Indeed, sometimes Hobbs Act indictments and Travel Act indictments were tried in the same case and "bribery" was treated as bribery under state law and extortion under federal law. In *Kenny* and *Hathaway*, for example, officials were convicted of taking bribes under the Travel Act, that is, bribes under state law; and for the same acts they were also found guilty of Hobbs Act extortion. In *Hall* a banker paid David Hall, governor of Oklahoma, a $50,000 "finder's fee"; the governor agreed to use his influence with the state employees' retirement board to get the board to buy $10 million worth of notes. The banker was held guilty of bribery under Oklahoma law, in breach of the Travel Act; the governor was convicted of Hobbs Act extortion.[82]

To fail to file a tax return, to fail to report income, to misstate the category of income, to deceive an internal revenue agent all constituted federal crimes. If a bribetaker in state office reported his bribes as ordinary income in the year of their receipt, the federal tax law was not broken. If he was too arrogant to believe he would be pursued, if he thought cash bribes could not be traced and so need not be reported, if he sought to treat bribes as capital gain in order to pay a lesser tax, he stood in federal jeopardy. Agnew had complained that "post-Watergate morality" had brought about his prosecution. But the tax laws which brought him to book were well established, and the investigation that led to his conviction was launched by an administration of which he was a part.[83]

Other federal statutes, like the Internal Revenue Code not mentioning bribery in express terms, reached both bribetakers and bribegivers. Two such laws dealt with communications. One made it criminal to use the mails, the other to use interstate "wire" (telephones or telegraph) "to defraud." Local bribery, carried out by letter or out-of-state telephone call, could be analyzed as mail fraud or as wire fraud, depending on the instrumentality employed. The mail fraud statute went back to 1872. The ease with which it encompassed any crooked scheme involving the mails made it a favorite of federal prosecutors pursuing a variety of white-collar crimes. Where money or property was obtained from the state by bribery, and the mail was used, the statute's application was straightforward. No need for the government to show that the bribe itself or the request for the bribe had gone through the mail—the statute came into play whenever the mails were used to propose a bribe, pay a bribe, distribute the proceeds of a bribe, or carry out the agreement obtained by a bribe.[84]

The case of Otto Kerner, Jr., governor of Illinois from 1961 to 1968, prosecuted under Nixon in 1973, illustrates how a basic crime of bribery could be made the subject of both tax evasion and mail fraud indictments. Governor Kerner and his bagman, Ted Isaacs, accepted stock in Chicago Thoroughbred Enterprises and in exchange favored the interests of the company's owner, Marjorie Lindheimer Everett, in setting racing dates, making appointments to the Harness Commission, and influencing legislation on horseracing. Kerner and Isaacs reported $159,000 apiece as long-term capital gain when they sold the stock in 1967. But they had received the stock in 1966. If it was a bribe, the stock was ordinary income to them in that year. To prove its tax case, the government proved the bribe. The failure to report in 1966 constituted evasion of the tax.[85]

As for mail fraud, it was indisputable that they had used the mail to transmit checks and correspondence relating to their transactions with Mrs. Everett. But what fraud had they committed? Fraud, their lawyers argued, must involve depriving someone of something of "definable value." Mrs. Everett had paid willingly and knowingly. "To defraud" in the mail fraud statute meant what it meant at common law—to get an economic benefit from the victim. Whose money or property had they taken by dealing with her? The Seventh Circuit dismissed the argument. Their fraud consisted in depriving the citizens of Illinois of the governor's "honest and faithful service." As "defraud" in the conspiracy statute had been interpreted to include Manton taking money for the exercise of judicial power even when the power was exercised to reach a just result, so "defraud" in the mail fraud statute was read to include the exercise of executive power for money. No financial harm to anyone had to be shown. Corruption of a public official was itself a species of fraud. When the mail was used in the course of the transaction, the crime of federal mail fraud was committed. For the first time at an appellate level, bribery of a public official where no money or property was obtained from the state was treated as fraud in the sense of the statute. So holding, the Seventh Circuit innovatively enlarged the statute's scope and in effect created a new crime.[86]

Back in the 1920s, Learned Hand had referred to the general conspiracy statute as "that darling of the modern prosecutor's nursery."[87] Its usefulness had been demonstrated in the prosecution of Manton. It remained a formidable supplement to the specific statutes. To conspire was a separate substantive crime apart from the offense that was the object of the conspiracy. The Jersey City defendants in *Kenny*, for example, were convicted of, and sentenced for, the substantive offense of conspiracy to violate the Travel Act. Fine lines were drawn between what counted under one statute and not under the other. Among other crimes, Governor Kerner and Isaacs were charged with violation of the Travel Act and also with conspiracy to violate the Travel Act in the collection of their bribes from Mrs. Everett. The basis for these charges was the defendants' use of interstate facilities: they had deposited the checks for their Chicago Thoroughbred stock in Illinois banks and the checks had cleared through the Federal Reserve Bank in Missouri. Conviction on the Travel Act count was reversed because, the Seventh Circuit said, the connection of their crime with the interstate facilities was fortuitous, peripheral, unintentional. Nonetheless, their conviction of *conspiracy* to violate the Travel Act was upheld. They had, the court said, conspired to distribute the proceeds of their bribes. Intention to conspire plus actual distribution was sufficient to establish their guilt. That their use of interstate facilities was unintentional was no defense to the conspiracy charge.[88]

The role of the federal judiciary—that mostly male, mostly white, mostly over forty, distinctly affluent elite—was critical in the expansion of federal supervision over local corruption. If the trial judges had not responded sympathetically to the new theories of the prosecutors and if the appellate courts had not sustained most convictions, the expansion would not have occurred. The federal judges felt little empathy for the bribetaking politician. No historical or technical distinction between bribery and extortion was to aid him to elude conviction in the way the ancient distinction between larceny and embezzlement had once aided white-collar thieves. The judges themselves were usually not innocent of political experience and connections; their first loyalty remained to the judicial system. Their corporate ethic spurned bribery. Manton, Davis, Johnson were not so much ghosts they wished to exorcise as failures extinguished from their memory.

A case in point was the treatment of Otto Kerner, Jr. His father had served thirteen years as a judge of the Seventh Circuit Court of Appeals. Before becoming governor he had himself been a judge of Cook County. From the governship he had gone by appointment of President Johnson to the Seventh Circuit. He had been sitting six years as a federal judge at the time of his indictment. Two of his colleagues on the bench testified at the trial to his good character. After his conviction he continued to sit as a judge while his appeal went before his fellows. The name the case bore on appeal was not his but that of his bagman, Isaacs. He presented to his colleagues a claim of privilege beneficial to them all—that the constitutional provision for impeachment of a federal judge, rightly understood, meant that a judge had first to be impeached and removed from office before he could be subjected to trial in, so to speak, his own court. Neither this cunning contention nor any other substantial part of his multifaceted appeal persuaded those who judged it. All his Seventh Circuit colleagues recused themselves. A panel was assembled from three other circuits. These representative judges upheld his conviction. They did so although to do so required them to make an unprecedented extension of the mail fraud statute and to squeeze out a difficult distinction between the Travel Act and conspiracy to violate the Travel Act. Issuing their opinion per curiam, they affirmed the corporate character of their judgment.[89]

Common accord existed in the federal judiciary, it appeared, that local corruption was an evil now to be stamped out, almost as vigorously as racial discrimination. That bribery was a great evil had been the contention of American censors since the days of Henry Adams. The federal judges reflected the consensus of concerned citizens, novelists, journalists. Little dissent was heard as the Hobbs Act received a gloss creating a new federal crime of extortion, as mail fraud came to include breach of fiduciary duty to the state, and as the federal courts created a federal common law of bribery.

RICO. The development was not, however, merely the result of judicial response to innovative prosecutions. It was also legislative. In 1970, in the second year of the Nixon administration, collaboration between the Democratic-controlled Congress and the Justice Department under John Mitchell produced the most comprehensive federal statute ever designed against bribery—the Racketeering Influenced and Corrupt Organization Act or RICO. Largely drafted by a single individual, G. Robert Blakey, a law professor on the staff of the McClellan Committee, the act could not have passed the Congress as it did by votes of 73 to 1 in the Senate and 341 to 26 in the House unless its dominant purpose had been supported by the executive branch.[90]

In fact, despite misgivings expressed by the American Civil Liberties Union, RICO was extremely popular legislation, seen as the legitimate outgrowth of repeated congressional investigations of the infiltration of organized, professional criminals—gangsters, mobsters, racketeers—into unions, businesses, and state and local government. The Copeland hearings in the 1930s, the Kefauver hearings in the 1950s, the McClellan hearings in the 1960s had publicized the power and plunder of these persons whose way of life was crime. The existence of the Mafia or La Cosa Nostra—an organization once the beneficiary of skepticism about its reality—had been demonstrated beyond cavil. No figment of the FBI, no politicians' imaginary scapegoat, this cruel conspiracy of 3,000 to 5,000 criminals had been shown to operate almost with impunity in certain American cities. The acronym of the new law recalled the name of the character played by Edward G. Robinson in *Little Caesar*, a movie about the Capone mob, and congressional enthusiasm for RICO was enthusiasm for ending the sway of "the mob." The statute was to deal with what its preamble described as "a highly sophisticated, diversified, and widespread activity"—organized crime—and to achieve "the eradication of organized crime in the United States." The managers of RICO, however, steadily rebuffed attempts during consideration of the bill to confine RICO to a specific set of gangsters, to limit its scope to the Mafia, or to create a "status crime" of being a member of the mob. The law reached anyone, professional criminal or not, who performed the acts proscribed by the statute.[91]

The original bill defined racketeering as "any act involving the danger of violence to life, limb or property" which was punishable by more than a year's imprisonment. The Justice Department argued that this definition was "too broad" and would tend to "a complete federalization of criminal justice."[92] It suggested specifying the crimes, and Congress agreed. Criminal justice as such was not completely federalized. The law of bribery was.

As passed, the bill treated as racketeering any act "involving murder, kidnapping, gambling, arson, robbery, bribery, extortion, or dealing in narcotics or other dangerous drugs" if the act was "chargeable" under state law and punishable by more than one year's imprisonment. RICO, like Dante, treated bribery as seriously as physical violence and indeed as worse than such physical violence as manslaughter and mayhem. Any act indictable under the federal bribery law, the mail and wire fraud laws, the Hobbs Act and the Travel Act, was also described as racketeering, so that RICO picked up and, as will be seen, enlarged federal power under all these statutes. Bribery was obviously only one of several crimes which RICO embraced. Nonetheless, the act's "Statement of Findings and Purpose" recognized that the money and power of organized crime were "increasingly used" to "subvert and corrupt our democratic processes." A close connection between organized crime and bribery was acknowledged.[93]

The structure of the statute followed that of the Travel Act. The listed offenses were not themselves made criminal—they were already crimes under state or federal law; but they were made predicates for the new crimes created by RICO. To commit two or more of the predicate offenses within a period of ten years was to engage in "a pattern of racketeering activity" which constituted a RICO crime if it affected an "enterprise." The new crimes created by RICO were defined in terms of such a pattern. The range of conduct thereby covered, together with the severity of the sanctions attached and the broad power given the attorney general in situations in which he suspected racketeering to launch civil investigations (where the burden of proof would be lower) put federal prosecutors in a position to sweep all graft before them.[94]

District attorneys at first had an inclination not to rely too much on this broad and untried statute. In the course of the 1970s its remarkable usefulness began to be appreciated. Key terms turned out to be "pattern" and "enterprise." Specifically, it was a RICO crime to invest income derived from "a pattern of racketeering activity" in any enterprise; to acquire any interest in an enterprise "through a pattern of racketeering activity"; to conduct an enterprise "through a pattern of racketeering activity"; or to conspire to do any of these acts. If the income derived from two separate bribes was invested in a company, a RICO crime was committed; if one acquired shares in a company by receiving two separate bribes of the company's stock, a RICO crime was committed; if one used one's official position to collect two bribes, a RICO crime was committed; if one paid two bribes to an officeholder, one violated RICO; if one conspired to do any of these things, one was guilty under RICO. Paying bribes, collecting bribes, investing bribes was racketeering.

It was unclear whether any two predicate offenses, committed within ten years of each other, constituted "a pattern" or whether the two acts had to be somehow connected. It was held in *Colacurcio* that separate bribes paid by different gamblers, each interested in weakening police enforcement of the gaming laws, were connected enough for the gamblers to be treated as an enterprise and for the individual acts of bribery to be treated as a pattern. It was held that several mailings all in furtherance of a single bribe—that of Salvitti, the Philadelphia redevelopment director—each constituted an offense under the mail fraud statute; taken together, they made up "a pattern," so that Salvitti was convicted not only of violating the Hobbs Act and of mail fraud but also of violating RICO.[95]

"Enterprise" was a deliberately chosen term, defined by the statue to include all individuals and all legal entities. Hesitation was experienced at first as to whether a unit of state government or the state itself could be an enterprise—had Congress really meant to say that American governments might be discovered which were conducted by a pattern of racketeering activity?

The overwhelming answer of authority was that it had. When a supervisor in the Department of Revenue of Pennsylvania accepted $500 a week to permit the smuggling of untaxed cigarettes, the Third Circuit held the department to be an enterprise conducted by racketeering, and the payment of several of the weekly installments to be a pattern constituting a RICO crime. The Fourth Circuit held the sheriff's department of Wilson County, North Carolina, to be an enterprise; when Sheriff Wilbur Pridgin accepted payoffs from local houses of prostitution he committed a RICO offense. A similar result was reached as to the sheriff's office in Hancock County, West Virginia. In a RICO prosecution against policemen taking money from moonshiners and lottery operators, the Fifth Circuit found the police department of Macon City, Georgia, to be an enterprise. The Seventh Circuit found the sheriff's department of Madison County, Illinois, to be a RICO enterprise when the sheriff was convicted of taking $50 per week per prostitute from houses of prostitution and $6 per car towed from towing companies. In Louisiana the state agricultural department was treated as an enterprise corruptible by RICO-banned acts. In Tennessee, charges that the governor's office in Governor Blanton's time sold pardons were found to be valid RICO counts: "the Office of the Governor" was an enterprise for RICO purposes. In South Carolina, state senator John D. Long was convicted of RICO racketeering when he sold his influence to procure state jobs. In cities as far apart as Philadelphia and El Paso, traffic courts were found to be enterprises, and bribetaking by the employees handling traffic fines was found to be punishable under RICO.[96]

The Supreme Court did not grant review in the many cases finding that governmental units could be "enterprises." Indirectly it approved these results in a case where a restrictive reading of "enterprise" had been boldly urged by counsel for a convicted criminal and was actually adopted by the First Circuit Court of Appeals. Novia Turkette, Jr., and eleven others were convicted under RICO of conspiracy to conduct an enterprise whose purposes were to steal and traffic illegally in drugs, to commit arson and insurance fraud, to influence the outcome of state trials, and to bribe police officers. The "enterprise," in short, was a blanket term covering the variety of crimes the gang had committed. Turkette's lawyers argued that a criminal enterprise could not be an "enterprise" within the meaning of the statute: otherwise the statutory language was somehow duplicative, making it a crime to commit certain crimes through an enterprise that would consist of the same crimes. First Circuit Judge Hugh H. Bownes accepted this argument, observing that "we think that the courts' natural antipathy to organized crime has clouded their perception of RICO, its purpose, and legislative history."[97] Fifth Circuit Judge Simpson in *Elliott* had taken a different view in upholding the Rico conviction of a gang whose enterprise consisted in "making money from repeated criminal activity" and whose predicate offenses included automobile theft, meat theft, arson, the sale of illegal drugs, jury-fixing, suborning a witness with a bribe, and murder. The enterprise in this case, Simpson wrote, could "best be analogized to a large business conglomerate" with a single chief executive officer and subsidiary departments to handle such matters as "murder and obstruction of justice." The corporate analogy was striking. As the chartering of lawful corporations had permitted government to regulate them, so organized crime was given recognition as an enterprise, that it might be better controlled.[98]

The Supreme Court in effect adopted *Elliott*, reversing *Turkette*, 8–1. Justice White wrote that interpretation of the statute must begin with the words of the statute. No limitation on "enterprise" was written into the statute; the courts should not read a limitation in. The reasoning of *Elliott* applied equally well where local governments were the enterprise.[99]

If the powers granted by RICO were employed, there was scarcely a corner of graft within the United States from governorships to traffic courts, from Anchorage to Macon City, that the federal government could not explore, and scarcely any bribetaking in local office that it could not enjoin. State statutes of limitations did not apply, and bribery offenses against state law, sometimes no longer prosecutable by the state, could—it was held in *Forsythe*—be reached by the federal authorities. Even acquittal of a state offense in a state trial was no defense to the federal charge: in *Frumento* the cigarette smugglers who had connived with members of the Democratic party in Philadelphia to fix the Bureau of Revenue were acquitted by a Philadelphia magistrate. For the same bribes they were then indicted and convicted in federal court under RICO. The predicate of the conviction was the offense against Pennsylvania law; in *Frumento* the federal court determined for itself that the predicate offenses had been committed.[100]

Federal encroachment on what had been state turf was manifested in other ways. A celebrated case was the combined RICO-mail fraud prosecution of Marvin Mandel, governor of Maryland. The owners of Marlboro Race Track were shown to have given the governer clothes, a bracelet for his wife, vacation trips, the payment of certain insurance premiums, and a share in two real estate ventures. In return the governor did not work to uphold his own veto of a bill giving Marlboro certain good racing dates, and he later helped promote a bill permitting Marlboro to merge with Bowie Race Track. Mandel was indicted under RICO. After deliberating 113 hours—believed to be a record in a federal criminal trial—the jury convicted Mandel, his bagman, the race track owners, and the lawyer who had arranged to conceal the identity of the owners. On appeal, the brief for Mandel vigorously attacked the federal government's intrusion into the state's affairs. In insisting that Mandel had breached his duty as governor to exercise independent judgment, uninfluenced by what he was given, the federal government was going beyond its proper limits and acting as though it was *parens patriae* of the state and its citizens, the brief contended. The Fourth Circuit shook off the argument that the government of Maryland was not the business of Congress. The court followed the precedent established in Governor Kerner's case, holding it was fraudulent for a public official to act in breach of his fiduciary duty, although no money or property was taken from the state. The mail fraud and bribery crimes of Mandel formed the predicate for his conviction under RICO. Congress, the court observed, had the right to keep the mail from being used to carry out fraudulent schemes.[101]

Immunity for actual legislative acts kept a corner of congressional activity free from supervision by the executive branch of the federal government. State legislators, the Supreme Court held, enjoyed no comparable immunity from federal prosecution for their committee actions, speeches in the legislature, introduction of legislation or votes: in a RICO prosecution of a state senator in Tennessee, the federal authorities were permitted to show that he introduced a bill and attended a committee hearing in furtherance of his obtaining of bribes. A state might grant such immunity to its own legislators, but comity did not require the federal government to honor it: "where important federal interests are at stake, as in the enforcement of federal criminal statutes," wrote Chief Justice Burger, "comity yields." State legislators were immune from suit under the federal Civil Rights Act. Where RICO was in play, comity—the courtesy of one sovereign to another—had very little place.[102]

The federal courts even began to assume a certain independence of the states in defining what the state offenses were which constituted RICO predicates. In *Forsythe,* a bail bond agency in Allegheny County, Pennsylvania, had been making systematic payments to aldermen, justices of the peace, and constables in return for these officials referring criminal defendents to the agency. The trial court dismissed a RICO indictment of the agency on the ground that the Pennsylvania bribery statute in effect at the time of these acts did not provide for more than a year's imprisonment for a briber, so the state offense did not fall within RICO. The Third Circuit, through Francis J. Van Dusen, noted that there was another Pennsylvania statute punishing "corrupt solicitation" by two years' imprisonment. Congress, Van Dusen said, had indicated that it wanted to define state offenses "generically." Was corrupt solicitation an activity "generally known or categorized" as bribery? Van Dusen concluded that it was and reinstated the indictment. The holding made potential defendents responsible for knowing what acts were "generally known" as bribery. Whatever the official description provided by a state statute, criminal defendants were held to a broader knowledge.[103]

A hypothetical variation of a real case will illustrate the extension of RICO accomplished by this ruling. What better criterion for determining what was "generally known" as bribery than the federal bribery statute itself? Under the heading "Bribery of public officials and witnesses," Congress treated gratuities to public officials as a variant of bribery; as the Third Circuit had put it, the statute covered bribery "and kindred offenses." New York also had a law against gratuities to public officials, sometimes politely called an antitipping statute. In the confirmation hearings of Nelson Rockefeller as nominee for vice-president of the United States, succeeding Gerald Ford in 1974, Rockefeller admitted that as governor of New York he had given or loaned thousands of dollars of his own money to New York officials—$510,000 in forgiveness of loans to the chairman of the Transit Authority, over $1,250,000 in all to public officers. His counsel, with chutzpah, maintained that the law did not apply to the governor; certainly no one had prosecuted him. The Senate Committee questioned Rockefeller about the gifts but did not treat them as fatal to his nomination. But the argument could have been made that Rockefeller was guilty of a RICO offense. What the New York law condemned was generic bribery: on this point the federal bribery statute was conclusive. Rockefeller had repeatedly violated the New York law. His claim of exemption from the New York statute was implausible; his motivation—to get better service—was that of anyone tipping a state employee; benign intentions could not make such acts legal. Hypothetically, a federal prosecutor could have brought the new vice-president down, and a federal court could have construed the state crime generically to sustain his conviction for racketeering. The federal ability to define state bribery by genus had opened the way for another broad addition to the federal common law of bribery.[104]

Not only was the federal reach longer, more tenacious, less circumscribed than the states'. Indictment under RICO associated the defendant with mobsters. Corporations, county magistrates, state bureaucrats, county police, governors were put in the same category as mafiosi.

Defense counsel complained in vain to the courts and to the press that Congress could not have had their respectable clients in mind when it condemned organized crime in RICO. All conduct similar to that of organized criminals was caught in the same mesh. The offense of bribery underwent not only a new scrutiny but also a verbal escalation. From being bribery it became, for the purposes of federal law enforcement, racketeering.[105]

Attached to violation of RICO were financial penalties of the most severe kind. The statute itself provided the remedy of triple damages for anyone harmed by a RICO crime. Judicially it was held that conviction under RICO (for racketeering designed to control the tavern business in Pierce County, Washington, by intimidation of tavern owners and the bribery of officials) operated as an estoppel in a civil suit for triple damages. The defendants could litigate the question of harm caused the plaintiff, they could not dispute their RICO guilt.[106]

Even more drastic were the provisions for forfeiture of a convicted defendant's interest acquired in violation of RICO or any interest "affording a source of influence" over an enterprise the defendant had operated in violation of RICO. Under these provisions the owners of the racetrack who had used this enterprise to bribe Governor Mandel forfeited their stock, estimated to be worth $2 million. When one of those subjected to the forfeit contended that he was not the mere nominee of a convicted defendant but the true owner, innocent of the RICO violation, he was told by the court that he must first seek relief from the attorney general. A motel which a RICO racketeer had used as a place of prostitution, bribing the local sheriff by paying his expenses when he resorted to the prostitutes, was forfeited under these provisions: the motel, being used as a means of bribery, had been operated in violation of RICO.[107]

Forfeiture of property used in the commission of a crime was familiar to American law. The claim that it was cruel and unusual punishment or that it violated Article III's constitutional ban on forfeiture of an "estate" was not sustainable. What was distinctive about RICO—what arguably made its forfeiture provisions less drastic—was that forfeiture was not decreed in a proceeding against the property where the constitutional protections of the criminal law did not apply, but as a punishment after a person had been tried criminally and found guilty. What was novel was that the forfeiture extended to property like the racetrack or motel, employed to pay a bribe.[108]

Did an "interest acquired in violation of RICO" include the profits of the racketeering? On this point the circuits divided and the Supreme Court was asked to decide. How far forfeiture could extend if the profits were included was shown in the case of Jack O. McNary, mayor of Lansing, a village in Cook County, Illinois, a case that illustrated also the application of forfeiture to a bribetaking official. McNary accepted various real estate partnerships netting him $85,000 in return for facilitating zoning changes favorable to his benefactors. He put $65,000 into his own lawful window and door business, B and M Manufacturing Company, and later transferred $103,000 from B and M to a second lawful business, Ports of Call. The federal government convicted him of RICO racketeering for accepting the zoning change bribes. The prosecution contended that McNary had commingled the $65,000 received from "a pattern of racketeering activity" with lawful income, tainting the latter. It claimed McNary's interests in B and M and Ports of Call as forfeit. The Seventh Circuit agreed. Interests forfeitable under RICO went beyond the enterprise operated in violation of RICO.[109]

Fact and Speculation.   RICO like the Hobbs Act purported to be national. In fact its impact depended heavily on local discretion. Nonetheless what was done one place would be imitated in another, there were national guidelines promulgated and unevenly enforced, and eventually a Public Integrity Section, established in the Justice Department, was given joint responsibility with the local district attorney for at least the final decision to pursue corrupt officials. Local federal initiatives were also affected by the signs of political approval they received: with the blessing of Senator Clifford Case, Lacey and Stern, the *Kenny* prosecutors, were made federal judges; with the blessing of the *Chicago Tribune*, James Thompson, the Hobbs Act prosecutor in Chicago, was in 1976 elected governor of Illinois. Under four different presidents—Nixon, Ford, Carter, Reagan—the application and expansion of federal bribery law went on.[110]

The dynamic movement to prosecute corrupt officials antedated Watergate. The movement, already perceptible under Nixon, was not markedly partisan: Agnew was among its first victims. RICO was created by a Democratic Congress collaborating with the Nixon administration. Presidential personalities, party ideology differed in the 1970s. No change in the presidency, no asserted distinction between the parties made any difference to the course of the law. So steady a development owed its power not as much to individual initiative as to the values dominant in the society.

Why at this particular time, it may be pressed, were such values dominant? Hypotheses can be advanced: The student movement of the 1960s directed mainly at the draft and the war in Vietnam, generated a skepticism of authority and a doubt in the value of law sufficient to cause academic lawyers to feel the need to come to the law's defense.[111] The judges, it may be supposed, acted in the same spirit to vindicate the law's authority and impartiality. What stronger course to take than to enforce it against corrupt officials even when the law was ambiguous enough so that the judges could have gone the other way?

This hypothesis can be reinforced with what was observable internationally: Communist ideology stressed the incorruptibility of revolutionary cadres while associating American capitalism with corruption and the support of corrupt regimes. As in the seventeenth-century conflict of Catholics and Protestants neither side wanted to be more relaxed than the other in championing sexual purity, so in the twentieth century the United

States could not be less publicly pure than its Communist rivals. It was a serious objection to its foreign policy, for example, that the government of the Republic of Vietnam was said to be "corrupt." In this area of morals affected by ideological rivalry an absolute standard of what constituted corruption was applied. The international standard encouraged enforcement at home.

A second, apparently contradictory hypothesis arises from the account given jointly by an anthropologist, Mary Douglas, and a political scientist, Aaron Wildavsky, as to the reasons why environmental causes became so powerful in America in the 1960s. In their analysis, there is a "center," composed of hierarchical forces for order, and a "border" consisting of sectarian forces critical of the center. Sectarians distrust the holders of public office. For them no one in high office is sacrosanct. They are egalitarians. They flourish among persons who have received a college education, and their strength in the United States is correlated to the remarkable rise, post-World War II, in the proportion of college-educated Americans. Dominating the media, and supported by the media, the sectarians maintain a continuous hostile surveillance of officialdom. Hierarchical notions that look on one class as "the criminal class" are offensive to them. Society is not divided into "us" and "them," at least it is not so divided along the old status lines, although a tincture of vulgar Marxism leads the sectarians to speak of a ruling class and to distrust the rich. White-collar crime in general becomes an inviting target for them, and in particular the application of the criminal law of bribery to high officers of the government is an attractive step. Those who make the application are rewarded by the appreciation of the press and their peers. The unhorsing of Fall by the environmentalists was a forerunner. Sectarians within the government go on to make the center less credible by exposing and prosecuting representatives of the central hierarchy.[112]

An anthropological analogy affords a third hypothesis: America, Tocqueville wrote in the 1830s, was far stricter than Europe in the purity of its morals—meaning thereby the public sexual morals of the Americans. The rules for sexual purity in a society may be read as a way of guarding the society at points at which it is vulnerable, a way of securing important entrances and exits, a way of avoiding ambiguities. One overall function of such rules, it has been argued anthropologically, is to impose order on the chaotic flux of existence. In the United States in the 1960s the rules on sexual purity underwent a marked decline in public acknowledgment and public acceptability, a decline marked by the repeal of many statutes on sexual behavior and eventually reflected in the late 1960s and early 1970s at the highest public level by the United States Supreme Court obliterating many of the traditional legal distinctions between the married and the unmarried. Americans, once so proud of their chaste superiority to most European nations, were no longer distinguished by public insistence on sexual virtue. If rules on purity—rules against social pollution—have an essential order-maintaining function entirely apart from their specific content, it may be supposed that as one type of purity regulation declined, a compensating increase took place in insistence on the purity of governmental conduct. The ancient parallel between sexual corruption and civic corruption, and the use of sexual metaphors to describe bribery, can be seen as confirmatory evidence that the bribery ethic has always had an antipollutant effect with one function analogous to the purifying function of the rules on sexual conduct. In the 1960s this function became dominant.[113]

Speculation could add that a special attractiveness could be found in the final release, apparently achieved by substitution, from the public Puritan sexual ethic as it had existed in laws forbidding abortion, adultery, contraception, fornication, and homosexual conduct and in laws discouraging divorce and strengthening marriage. Officials were now to bear the burden of purity. Relieved of responsibility, the electorate could indulge itself. To avoid disorder, to ward off national disaster, it was only necessary that the government itself be clean. George Orwell had forecast for 1984 a society in which electronic devices enforced a Puritan sexual regimen. He had not envisaged modern America in which wiretapping, photography, and television, not to mention elaborate traps created by governmental deceit, would be employed to enforce governmental integrity. In principle, it could be argued, technology performed the same function in Orwell's world and in the real America—purity was preserved.

No one of these hypotheses can be said to be demonstrated by what is presented here. It is the nature of social phenomena to appear over-determined, that is, multiple causes can retrospectively be postulated as bringing the phenomena about. Contradictory as they would be if only one cause were operating, the first and second hypotheses could both be true if different causes were at work. In this case there would be convergence, much as in the fourth-century Roman empire the apparently contradictory motivations of a static hierarchal landowning class and an upwardly mobile bureacratic class converged to produce intense concern with corruption. It is the nature of such hypotheses to be incapable of demonstration—there are no controlled experiments; it is hard to distinguish coincidence from causality. Confronted with multiple interacting social causes, each hypothesis isolates certain factors, treats them as critical, and adds its own assumptions about human motivation. Each hypothesis has a certain plausibility on its own terms. Each addresses what is amply demonstrated in this chapter on the criminal law and in the two succeeding chapters on campaign contributions and overseas bribery, namely, the marked shift in the treatment of corruption by the American legal system. In whatever way hypotheses account for it, that large central fact remains: in the late 1960s anticorruption law began to be criminally enforced more often than ever before.

At the level of political rather than anthropological explanation, the increase in prosecutions at a local level can be simply accounted for: federal supervision of local corruption removed the inhibitions on bribery prosecutions that often operated when bribery had to be prosecuted by local authorities. Not only outright corruption and not only the dictates of a political machine but also restraints imposed by friendship, political indebtedness, and political fear worked to discourage local prosecutors from pursuing local grafters. The agents of a superior system looking at those involved in an inferior system did not suffer the same inhibitions; and those in the inferior system were, often enough, insufficiently plugged into the higher system through congressmen or national party to influence it. Descending from above, supported by a judiciary sometimes called "imperial," the federal forces had an independence, an impartiality, and a sense of integrity that made the federal policing of bribery far more effective than the typical efforts of a state or city. The vigor of the supervision was testified to by the governors—Agnew of Maryland, Blanton of Tennessee, Hall of Oklahoma, Kerner of Illinois, Mandel of Maryland— who now fell within the federal net; and except in the exceptional circumstances of Vice-President Agnew, the sanction actively applied was harsher than had been usual for high bribetakers. Imprisonment was prescribed for Blanton, Hall, Kerner, and Mandel. Although parole substantially reduced the time the governors served, their incarcerations were not nominal.[114]

In the period 1970–1977, 43 mayors, 44 state judges, 60 state legislators, and 260 sheriffs or local police officers were federally indicted for corruption; most were convicted. In all, 369 state officials and 1,290 local officials were found guilty of corruption.[115] There was no way of knowing whether more corruption existed in the 1970s than at earlier times in the United States. A fraction of the cases would have documented Baron Jacobi's gloomy assessment of America in *Democracy* or provided a book for Lincoln Steffens. Both Jacobi and Steffens believed that corruption was universal in the America they knew. They would not have been surprised at the statistics of the 1970s. What was clear was that corruption was being investigated and punished on a scale unknown before. That phenomenon was tied to the emergence of a champion bigger than the locality.

Harsh criminal sanctions stopped at the vice-presidency, criminal law enforcement at the presidency. Would the country have wanted to convict vice-president or president as RICO racketeers? The legislature was different. What the federal government as a higher government could do to police the states, could not the Justice Department do to Congress?

Lawmakers before the Criminal Law

No statute with regard to bribery applicable to Congress existed before 1852. No convictions were obtained before the twentieth century. At the height of the Progressive Era, when muckrakers were denouncing the corruption of the Senate as "treason," the Roosevelt administration dusted off the Civil War statute against a member of Congress accepting "compensation" in any matter before a government department when the United States was a party. In Oregon where, before his successful prosecution of Ruef, Frank Heney was United States district attorney, wholesale land frauds were investigated, and Heney obtained the conviction of a senior Republican, John H. Mitchell, seventy years old, four times a senator from Oregon. Mitchell was sentenced to two years' imprisonment and died while his appeal was pending. The exemplary jailing of a veteran senator did not occur; moreover, Oregon was a long way from the capital for the lesson to have been conveyed; his obituary in the *New York Times* mentioned his conviction but did not use the ugly word bribe.[116]

Theodore Roosevelt's administration did convict and jail two naïves in national politics. Joseph R. Burton, a first-term Republican senator from Kansas, was found to have agreed to receive $2,500 from the Rialto Grain and Securities Company to stop a mail fraud investigation. Edmund H. Driggs, a Democratic ex-congressman from Brooklyn, was found to have been paid $12,500 by the Edward J. Brandt-Dent Company to use his influence while in Congress to secure a contract for the purchase by the United States of 250 cash registers.[117]

In the 1920s, John Wesley Langley, a veteran Republican representative from Kentucky, was prosecuted by the Coolidge administration and convicted of accepting $11,700 for his influence in obtaining permits for whiskey shipments into Kentucky. His formal conviction was for conspiracy to violate the Prohibition Act. In the 1930s two congressmen were convicted of violating a statute enacted in 1926 against accepting money to procure a federal appointment: Harry E. Rowbottom, a recently defeated Republican from Indiana, for selling post office appointments in Indiana; and John H. Hoeppel, a second-term Democrat from California, for selling for $1,000 a nomination to West Point. George E. Foulkes, a recently defeated Democrat from Michigan, was convicted of conspiracy to assess postmasters for political contributions.[118]

After a Senate investigating committee headed by Harry Truman in 1946 produced evidence of fraud in military procurement, Andrew Jackson May, a recently defeated Democrat of Kentucky, ex-chairman of the Military Affairs Committee, was prosecuted for accepting $58,000 to use his influence to secure contracts from the War Department for the companies of Henry M. Garsson and Murray Garsson. That May's actions occurred during World War II made them particularly scandalous. The offenses of which he was formally convicted were conspiracy to defraud the United States and accepting compensation to represent a party before a department.[119]

In 1949 J. Parnell Thomas, a Republican congressman from New Jersey, was convicted of a practice not unknown before—of taking what were euphemistically called "kickbacks" from the salaries of staff members, in effect continuous bribes for their appointments. The offense of which he was formally found guilty was receiving compensation for services in a matter where the United States was a party. In 1962 under the Kennedy administration, Congressmen Frank W. Boykin of Alabama and Thomas F. Johnson of Maryland were prosecuted for attempting to fix a mail fraud case; the formal crime of which they were convicted was receiving compensation to represent a party before a federal department.[120]

As of 1970, then, ten members of Congress had been convicted of crimes generically bribery. The standard dodges—"loans" in Langley's case; "legal fees" and "political contributions" in Boykin's and Johnson's—had been penetrated. A wide range of politicians had been brought to book. Before entering Congress, Burton had been a legislator in Kansas, Johnson in Maryland, Langley in Kentucky, Mitchell in Oregon; May had been a county judge. Over half were lawyers: Burton, Foulkes, Johnson, Langley, May, and Mitchell. Hoeppel, the seller of West Point, had been a master sergeant. Driggs was an insurance salesman, Boykin a businessman, Rowbottom an accountant and former salesman of "lubricating oils." Democrats had prosecuted Democrats Boykin, Foulkes, Hoeppel, and May and Republican Thomas; Republicans had prosecuted Republicans Burton, Langley, Mitchell, and Rowbottom and Democrat Driggs.

Of the ten convicted, only May had been a power in the House, and he had been defeated for reelection before his indictment. Langley, Boykin, and Thomas were veteran congressmen, the others were novices in national politics. The sentences the guilty received were not severe—the longest were Mitchell's, May's, and Langley's (two years). May served nine months and eventually received a complete Christmas Day pardon from Harry Truman, now president. May was readmitted to the bar in Kentucky, the Kentucky court finding a "second chance" required by "Christian principles." Langley also returned from prison to Kentucky law practice. Burton, Johnson, and Rowbottom served no more than six months. Boykin was merely put on probation; he was ultimately pardoned by President Lyndon Johnson. Driggs was given one day. In summary, the laws relating to the bribery of Congress were enforced in a nonpartisan way, sporadically and symbolically and very mildly. The major sanction was political oblivion.[121]

The pace of prosecution quickened in the 1970s. Two congressmen were convicted of technical violation of the statute on campaign contributions—not a bribery statute but a law drawing an essential line between bribery and donations; their cases will be discussed in Chapter 19. John V. Dowdy, a veteran Texas Democrat, was prosecuted for accepting money to stop a Justice Department investigation of a Maryland home improvement firm; his conviction was reversed, except on three counts of perjury—in effect, but not in form, he had been tried for bribery. Three congressmen—Charles C. Diggs, Jr., Democrat of Michigan; James F. Hastings of Pennsylvania, and J. Irving Whalley, Republicans of Pennsylvania—were convicted of taking kickbacks from employees; the mail fraud statute was used to secure the convictions. Bertram L. Podell, Democrat of Brooklyn, was convicted of receiving compensation—$41,000—to influence the Civil Aeronautics Board in the choice of an air route. Joshua Eilberg, Democrat of Pennsylvania, pleaded guilty to accepting compensation for helping a Philadelphia hospital receive a federal grant.[122]

Three members of Congress were actually charged with bribery. Under the Nixon administration, Frank J. Brasco, Democrat of New York, was indicted for conspiracy to receive bribes to influence truck-leasing contracts from the Post Office; he was convicted in 1974. Also under Nixon, Senator Daniel B. Brewster, Democrat of Maryland, was charged with soliciting bribes; ultimately in 1975 he pleaded no contest to a charge of receiving payments for his official act, a crime under the illegal gratuities section of the bribery statute. During the Carter administration, Daniel J. Flood, Democrat of Pennsylvania, chairman of the Labor-HEW Appropriations Subcommittee, was indicted for conspiracy in receiving bribes to influence his actions as chairman of the subcommittee; after one trial resulted in a hung jury, Flood pleaded guilty to defrauding the government.[123]

Compared to the past 180 years, the amount of attention to congressional bribery in the 1970s was remarkable. Like the Justice Department's supervision of the states, it antedated Watergate: *Brasco*, *Brewster*, and *Podell* were cases begun under Nixon. Culprits ranged from powerful incumbents like Flood to lame ducks like Brewster. Democrats predominated, impartially prosecuted under Democratic and Republican administrations alike. Sentences continued to be light—Brasco received three months, Eilberg and Flood were put on probation, Brewster was merely fined. Political death was the true sanction.[124]

Article I of the Constitution provided as to senators and representatives that "for any Speech or Debate in either House, they shall not be questioned in any other Place." Seeking to convict Congressman Johnson, the government introduced evidence of a speech he had given praising savings and loan associations. The Supreme Court held this evidence to infringe the congressman's immunity from questioning. Seeking to convict Senator Brewster, the government introduced evidence of legislation he had agreed to back in committee and on the floor. The Supreme Court held that this evidence did not infringe the constitutional immunity. In modern practice, only a fraction of a congressman's time was spent in speech, debate, or actual voting. In all the rest of his activities, the Court's decision in *Brewster* left a member of Congress vulnerable to prosecution.[125]

The culmination of all the efforts to curtail and punish bribery among legislators occurred near the end of the 1970s in the police operation known by its governmental code name of Abscam. It could not have taken place except in a society drenched in the antibribery ethic. No comparable antibribery effort had ever been mounted by any nation against criminal bribetakers among its own lawmakers.

The Honey and the Sting.   Enacting the Foreign Corrupt Practices Act in 1977, Congress revealed its deep distrust of overseas corruption. In Abscam congressmen were to encounter the corrupt alien in America and, expecting corruption, were to be themselves corrupted. At the same time reality and fiction were to be so mingled that crimes impossible of commission were to become occasions of punishment. Imagination was made to serve reason by scenarios in which liars' tales were used to test the presence or absence of virtue and criminal predisposition.

Abscam began in 1978 with the creation of Abdul Enterprises by the Federal Bureau of Investigation. Abdul Enterprises, a fictitious company, represented Kambir Abdul Rahman and Yassir Habib, two imaginary, fabulously wealthy Arabs interested in investing in the United States and unconcerned about the technical restraints of American criminal law. The plausibility of such a company depended on the common knowledge that there were oil-rich Arabs looking for investments and the common belief that Arabs would be more indifferent to American law than Americans. The company's purpose was to serve as a decoy.[126]

As its code name, a fusion of Abdul and scam, proclaimed, Abscam was a deceit perpetrated by the government, in colloquial terms a "sting" or operation in which would-be swindlers would be made dupes themselves. "Sting" in the argot of the streets had been made familiar to everyone by George Roy Hill's movie *The Sting*. Beyond the streets' usage was the most famous use of the word in the English language—St. Paul's, "O Death, where is thy victory, O Death, where is thy sting?" (1 Cor 15:55). As ancient folklore had it, gifts are ambivalent, lifegiving or poisonous. Not by chance *Gift* in German means poison. Stings depended on poisonous gifts associated with death. Stings were also associated with bees. They provoked another apiarian image. The money pot provided by the FBI was envisaged as honey. The sting was successful when would-be criminals sought to touch the honey and were captured in their crimes.

Abscam was successful because of money, modern technology, and the skills and sophistication of its personnel. One million dollars were deposited by the government at the Chase Manhattan Bank in the name of Abdul Enterprises to give the company credibility and a credit reference. Bribes of up to $100,000 were paid by Abdul with funds advanced by the FBI. Electronic recording equipment was provided the principal actors who interacted with the potential criminals. Telephone calls were frequently recorded. Video cameras caught on film the conversations, the agreements to accept payments, and the actual delivery of cash.[127]

Never before in history had movies been made of government officials being paid off. Not only were the officials surreptitiously filmed; the movies were played to courts, committees of Congress, the audiences of public television. A nation, at least the interested part of a nation, was instructed in corruption by videotapes of the bribing. Such cinematographic evidence proved to be overwhelming. Juries—usually interested in two things: did the defendant commit the act? is the defendant a bad person?—saw the defendants commit the acts, and the circumstances surrounding the acts made the defendants look terrible. Eight different juries—ninety-six different men and women in Brooklyn, Philadelphia, and Washington—found the Abscam defendants guilty.[128]

Personnel was an extraordinary combination of the lawbreaker and the law enforcer, of the unscrupulous and the scrupulous, of the knavish and the conscientious and the astute. Out front was a first-rate scalawag, Melvin Weinberg. According to his memoirs, recorded in the third person by a journalist, he was a liar and a thief as a schoolboy, dropping out completely in the eighth grade. Later he was hired by a glass workers' union to break the windows of employers of nonunion glaziers. He cheated a cousin who befriended him with a position in his business. He swindled an insurance company. He took $10,000 from a doctor for a promise, unfulfilled, to kill his wife. He ran a series of "front-end scams," that is, he took substantial down payments of cash on the false representation that he would produce loans or other returns for those paying him. Although for five years he netted $250,000 a year, he never paid any income tax. At almost all opportunities he indulged his voracious sexual appetite. In 1977 he was convicted of wire fraud in violation of federal law. On probation and desirous of keeping a girlfriend out of the federal clutches, he agreed to become a confidence man for the FBI.[129]

Weinberg was chosen by the government to be the chairman of Abdul Enterprises. With assured knowledge of human greed, with a lively sense of the prospects that entice greedy men, with abundant energy for imposing himself on his marks, he worked for almost two years at catching other criminals. Outside of Chaucer's Somonour or Pardoner one has difficulty thinking of a rascal so devoted to deceit. Amply compensated—he received at least $150,000 from the FBI[130]—he was not motivated merely by money. He rejoiced in the swindling itself. His delight was in making men into monkeys. His joy was the greater the more sophisticated, the more astute, the more prestigious, the more powerful were his dupes. Uneducated except by the streets, he dominated those educated by colleges and honored by universities. A swindler formerly outside the law, he now swindled swindlers who had prospered in American society. A criminal, he turned lawmakers into lawbreakers like himself.

Teamed with Weinberg were the law-abiding, the dutiful, the conscientious, including a man congruously named Good. Supervisor of the FBI office at Hauppage, Long Island, John Good picked Weinberg for his talents and oversaw his efforts. Son of an FBI agent himself, embued with the ethic of the Bureau, streetwise but disciplined, Good matched Weinberg's flamboyant gusto with his own intense and sober zeal. Other trained FBI men played with professional sang-froid the parts of Arabs or their representatives. At the top, William Webster, director of the FBI, a lawyer and former judge of the United States Court of Appeals for the Eighth Circuit, took responsibility and infrequently monitored his agents' actions.[131]

Outside the FBI, other lawyers from the Department of Justice participated in the planning and execution—among them Thomas Puccio ("the Pooch"), head of the Organized Crime Strike Force in Brooklyn, who was to be the chief prosecutor of the criminals caught; Irving Nathan, deputy assistant attorney general, the Washington overseer of the operation; Philip Heymann, a professor from Harvard Law School, who as the assistant attorney general in charge of the Criminal Division approved the plan; and, at the apex of responsibility, Attorney General Griffin Bell and his successor, Benjamin Civiletti. Those at the top who permitted, encouraged, and directed Abscam as it brought to book seven members of Congress were neither politicians nor vigilantes. Their choice of targets was not motivated by partisan considerations, nor were they driven by ordinary bureaucratic motives. Lawyers, serving the government for a limited time, they sought to make the Justice Department effective against crime, and they did not discriminate in favor of the powerful when the powerful fell into their hands.[132]

Abdul Enterprises when it began in March 1978 was not focused on the corrupt officeholder. Those at first attracted to the wealthy Arabs were sellers of stolen art, thieves of securities, forgers of certificates of deposit. As word of the Arabs' prodigious fortune spread in criminal circles on the Eastern seaboard, a forger doing business with them proposed that they build a casino in New Jersey; a friend could assure them of a license from the state. The friend was Angelo Joseph Errichetti, a member of the state senate, mayor of Camden, and the most influential Democratic politician in southern New Jersey. Energetic, pragmatic, and corrupt—without apparent conscience as to taking money as an official—Errichetti had a character entirely comprehensible to Weinberg. The common word for engaging in sexual intercourse was always in Errichetti's mouth. With it he violently reduced complexities to banalities he could dominate. "I'll give you Atlantic City," he assured Weinberg, adding inappropriately to an apparent representative of Arabs, "I'll be your rabbi." Not honest even with his own confederates in crime, Errichetti connived with two Philadelphia lawyers, Howard Criden and Ellis Cook, in an attempt to hoodwink Weinberg and his Arab friends. Promising to produce Mario Noto, deputy director of the Immigration Service, Errichetti and Criden presented Cook in his place. In a moment of high comedy, recorded on film and later shown on public television, Tony Amoroso, FBI agent posing as a representative of the Arabs, met Ellis Cook, Philadelphia lawyer, posing as Noto. Cook gave himself away inadvertently by saying his name was "Nopo." Disconcerted, the FBI agent awkwardly backed off from the encounter. But this abortive scam came late. Most of the time it was to Errichetti's self-interest to come up with real officials.[133]

Through Errichetti, Abdul Enterprises was able to bribe a bribetaking member of the New Jersey Casino Commission, its vice-chairman, Kenneth MacDonald. Then the circle of corruption was enlarged. Errichetti brought in George Katz who had once lent him money: the loan had led to Katz's garbage collection contract with the city of Camden, a transaction in the pattern of John Jacob Astor's with James Monroe and only one of Katz's many successes with corrupt officials in New Jersey. Abscam scooped in Katz. Insatiable and unwitting, Errichetti led the government agents further—to those who gave contracts for sewers in parts of Connecticut and New York as well as New Jersey; to members of the Philadelphia City Council open to bribes for building permits, zoning waivers, and the other licenses without which any construction in a modern city is stalled; and climactically to corruptible members of Congress. For Errichetti the motivation was elemental, a share of the payoff Abdul would make to each official. In Weinberg's view, Errichetti was "the Judas goat" whom other officeholders followed into the snare of Abscam.[134]

The congressmen first produced were Michael "Ozzie" Myers and Raymond Lederer, two Democratic hacks representing respectively southern New Jersey and a part of Philadelphia. Myers, a man armed with braggadocio, was happy to be paid to stand ready to introduce a private bill letting Abdul Rahman and Yassir Habib remain in the United States. Lederer, a former head of the Philadelphia Probation Department and a member of the Philadelphia Police Athletes' Hall of Fame, took the Arabs' money for the same purpose. "I'm no Boy Scout," he affirmed. Reporting his outside income to Congress pursuant to the Ethics in Government Act of 1978, he described his share of the bribe as a "consulting fee."[135]

Word of the rich Arabs went higher. Errichetti brought in Frank Thompson, Jr., sixty-one, a veteran of the New Jersey legislature, congressman from Trenton since 1954, chairman of the House Committee on Administration and the Subcommittee on Labor–Management Relations, his status as a pillar of the liberal Democratic establishment recognized in his being a trustee of the Kennedy Center, a regent of the Smithsonian, the holder of an honorary doctorate of laws from Princeton. Thompson, too, accepted payment for being ready to help the Arabs with a private immigration bill. Further, he offered to produce an equally open colleague, John Michael Murphy of Staten Island. A West Pointer and hero in Korea, now fifty-three, Murphy was chairman of the Committee on the Merchant Marine and Fisheries. A more conservative Democrat than Thompson, he was known particularly for his partiality to his old West Point classmate Anastasio Somoza, dictator of Nicaragua. Thompson was as right about Murphy's willingness to help the Arabs for money as Errichetti had been about Thompson.[136]

One more member of Congress was recruited by the mayor of Camden: Harrison Arlington Williams, Jr. "Pete" Williams was the senior United States senator from New Jersey, the chairman of the Committee on Labor and Human Resources and of the Subcommittee on Securities, Housing, and Urban Affairs, the fifth-ranking Democrat in the Senate. Sixty, a graduate of Oberlin College and Columbia Law School, Williams had been in Congress for twenty-three years, his status, like Thompson's, acknowledged by Princeton's honorary degree of laws. A liberal, known as a friend of labor, he had not committed himself in the contest between Senator Edward Kennedy and President Carter for the 1980 presidential nomination. His prominence and his fence-sitting position in this battle meant that the Justice Department had to proceed with great caution in his regard; a mistake as to his venality would have been politically expensive. Errichetti was not mistaken about him, but something other than cash was needed as bait. What he was offered and found attractive was 18 percent in a titanium venture the Arabs would finance by a loan of $100 million; the business of the enterprise would be largely with the government of the United States. Senator Williams's quid pro quo for his stock was to be the use of his influence with the government to get contracts for the enterprise.[137]

Other middlemen brought in John Wilson Jenrette, Jr., of Ocean Drive Beach, South Carolina, a former city judge and South Carolina legislator, now serving his third term in the House of Representatives; and Richard Kelly, the sole Republican, a former federal assistant district attorney and state circuit judge, now in his third term as a congressman from Florida. The two ex-judges joined Williams as lawyer officials entangled by Abscam. Other lawyers receiving money from the apparent Arabs were George X. Schwartz, president of the Philadelphia City Council, a former partner in a substantial Philadelphia firm, and Louis Johanson, a member of the Philadelphia city council. Lawyers also played a role as intermediaries. Howard Criden, a former Pennsylvania prosecutor, helped Errichetti in recruiting congressmen. He divided the spoils with his partners, Johanson and Ellis Cook. When Congressman Meyer, for example, got $50,000, Errichetti kept $15,000 of it, Criden $9,000, Johanson $6,500, and Cook $4,500. Ultimately, Criden was convicted of a RICO crime for conducting the affairs of the law firm itself through "a pattern of racketeering activity." Williams's seventy-year-old bagman, Alexander Feinberg, was a member of a three-man Camden law firm, a former solicitor for the New Jersey Turnpike in the acquisition of land, and currently counsel to the Delaware Port Authority. He was described by his neighbors as "cultured" and "very distinguished" and by a public official who had worked with him as "an all-around nice guy." He took an equal share with Williams, 18 percent of the titanium enterprise, for his services.[138]

Middlemen were extremely expensive, but when money came so easily, with scarcely any economic cost to the officeholder, the corrupted officials were disinclined to resist the middlemen's demands. In effect, the officials paid the middlemen part of their bribes as finders' fees and obtained protection, so they thought, from detection. Use of intermediaries was part of their prudence in negotiating and accepting a bribe. At a lunch on October 7, 1979, at the Plaza Hotel in New York, for example, a million dollars to be paid to Williams was discussed by him with Feinberg and representatives of Abdul Enterprises. How was it to be handled? "Use Alex," Williams said. As to the proposed sale of the titanium enterprise, the senator remarked, "Everybody is—er—protected, everybody is—er—protected—in other words not out front." "Yes, sub rosa, sub rosa," murmured Feinberg, giving the liturgical antiphon of the go-between. The operators of Abscam, seeking to catch the principals, strove to penetrate the protection. The problem was to "strip the insulation" from them, Weinberg declared. If Williams was to get his bribe, he would have to "stand bare-assed naked in Macy's window and do his own dirty work." The image of what was desired, with its sexual undercurrent, reflected not only Weinberg's res-

sentiment but also his frustration at Williams's initially effective use of Feinberg to shield himself.[139]

Cash was the medium normally used for bribes. Crassness in its handling was deprecated. When a representative of Abdul openly produced bills to give to the bribeable vice-chairman of the Casino Commission, the recipient characterized the display of money as "crude and insulting." When Williams opened a hotel desk drawer and found greenbacks stashed in it, he felt queasy and intuited something was wrong. Normally cash was delivered decently clothed by an envelope. Even a briefcase full of bills was unclean in the eyes of Thompson and of Murphy, each requesting Criden to "take care" of it rather than touch it with their own hands.[140]

The same impulses, a mixture of prudence and pride, could be discerned at work in oral discourse. No officeholder dealing with Abdul Enterprises said, "I want a bribe, payoff, kickback." An acceptable euphemism for paying a bribe was "doing the right thing," a phrase that simultaneously asserted the obligation of reciprocity and converted the criminal act into virtuous conduct. "I'm not looking for any money," Thompson stated in the morning, returning in the evening to have a briefcase stuffed with $50,000 handed over on his behalf to Criden. When the supposed sheik told Williams he wanted to give him "some money" for being ready to help him with an immigration bill, Williams said sharply, "No, no, no, no." Willing to accept shares of stock made out to Feinberg and endorsed to him in blank, Williams was offended by the blatant mention of cash.[141]

Williams was also cautious, although not equally so, in committing himself to get government contracts for the enterprise in which, without any investment on his part, the Arabs were offering him an 18 percent share. At no point did he promise specific orders or declare the amount of federal business he could obtain. At the most what he indicated was that he would use his best efforts as an experienced, prestigious, and well-connected senator to get "the government"—a vague entity—to patronize the titanium enterprise. "And if this can be put together," he told the sheik, "in my position with, within our government here, which goes back decades, and knowing as I do the people that make the decisions, with, when we've got it together, we move. We move with our government. . . ." He was, he stated, "in a position to go to, ah well, you know, right to the top on this one." He could get the president "enthusiastic and excited" about the titanium venture. Later an expert for the defense, a professor of linguistics, could plausibly testify that Williams in response to requests for more specific assurances used only "lax tokens," that is, noncommittal words of a positive import, providing feedback to his companions without committing himself to them. Williams was unwilling to put himself in a position where Yassir Habib could assert that the senator had undertaken an obligation to deliver a particular contract or a specific dollar result. By his vagueness he believed he protected himself against any charge of dereliction of senatorial duty.[142]

Abstractly taken, his words were compatible with innocence. Only in context with other words and deeds—specifically his direction to the Arabs to use Alex Feinberg and his acceptance of the free stock—was his intention to be paid for his influence evident. Never touching a penny in cash, never bargaining for what he got, never offering or giving more than vague cooperation in return, Williams maintained his innocence of bribery before a jury and before his fellow senators. The idea that for such actions he should forfeit membership in the Senate by a vote of his colleagues struck him as "preposterous." Federal appeals judge Jon Newman stigmatized his denial of wrongdoing as "brazen," but such is the power of verbal disguises that it is credible that he believed in his own innocence even after the jury had found him guilty and the Senate Ethics Committee had determined on his expulsion from the ranks of living senators.[143]

Bribing the Dead.   Caught *in flagrante delicto* on camera, with the ambiguity of their language resolved against them by their eventual acceptance of either cash or stock, the congressmen must have wished that they could have plea-bargained. But on the prosecution's side, with such evidence in its possession there was little to move it to bargain; and on the defendants' part, with their political lives at stake, there was a strong motive to go to trial and either explain what they had done or convict the government of abuses entitling them to an acquittal. A trial was had by each.

Three principal lines of defense were employed by different defendants —entrapment; lack of due process; and play-acting. Entrapment, sometimes called a "statutory defense," was more accurately a defense created by a gloss most American courts had added to the criminal statutes. It was a defense not recognized in England, countries of the Commonwealth, France, or Germany. The gloss ran that the legislators had not intended the statutes to apply to those the government entrapped into commission of a crime. Decoys to catch criminals were a familiar feature of American law enforcement. In the nineteenth century marked envelopes containing money were sent through the mails with the intention of trapping a thief in the post office. In recent times policemen disguised as helpless vagrants were used to trick and catch urban muggers. Narcotics agents gave dope peddlers the opportunity to sell to them. Government agents disguised as fences bought stolen goods and captured the thieves who had delivered them. Each of these operations, objectively viewed, was a trap by which an unwary criminal was caught. None was entrapment in the sense of the gloss. To establish entrapment as a defense it was necessary for a defendant to show that the government had done more than provide bait or an opportunity to commit a crime: the government had to have induced the defendant to commit it. In the federal courts, once inducement was shown, the prosecution had the burden of proof: it could negate the defense by showing that the defendant was predisposed to commit the crime. Standard instructions to a jury stated that a person "ready and willing" to commit a crime was not entrapped by being presented with an opportunity. Even if a defendant had had no "previous intent and purpose," his ready and willing predisposition could be inferred—the jury was told—from the way he responded to the opportunity as it arose before him. The government could, for example, show that the defendant engaged in "morally indistinguishable" behavior when not induced by the government; or that the defendant had formed a design to commit the offense prior to the inducement; or that the defendant gave "a prompt and unhesitating agreement to the corrupt proposal." The government had to demonstrate that the defendant was of a frame of mind such "that once his attention is called to the opportunity to commit the crime, the crime is the product of his own preference and not the product of government persuasion."[144]

Entrapment, it has been observed, is a defense easy to claim and hard to prove as a matter of law—that is, hard to establish so convincingly that a trial judge can take the issue from the jury and dismiss the prosecution or that an appellate court can reverse a conviction because the defendant was entrapped. If an adult of ordinary mental competence engaged in sexual intercourse, how easy would it be to show that he or she was seduced if predisposition to the act negated the claim of seduction and willingness to do the act suggested predisposition? If extreme cases can be imagined, extraordinary insight would generally be required to distinguish seduction from willing surrender; no judge could do so regularly as a matter of law. For similar reasons of judicial incapacity, the distinction between entrapment and willing response was normally left to the impenetrable discretion of jurors who did not have to explain or articulate their reasons. Left to the jury, entrapment became a dangerous defense—to demonstrate that he was entrapped, the defendant had to concede at least tacitly that he had committed the crime; he admitted he was a bad, if gullible, person. Guided by standard instructions, no jury found the congressmen trapped by Abscam to have been entrapped.[145]

After conviction, certain Abscam defendants argued that the court should reverse their convictions as a matter of law. They had, they claimed, been "overpowered" by the amounts of money offered. District Judge George C. Pratt rejected the contention. Even if a congressman had thought he was to get a full $50,000, this sum "in these inflationary times" was not overpowering. Moreover, as a matter of policy this contention was unacceptable. Every man might have a price, but "when that price is money only, the public official should be required to pay the penalty when he gets caught." The argument was equally rejected when Senator Williams pointed to the millions of profit dangled before him for his cooperation and argued that such bait, offered by the government, had denied him due process of law. Judge Jon Newman doubted if the size of the bribe could ever be unconstitutionally large "when offered to a person with the experience and sophistication of a United States Senator."[146]

The defense of lack of due process went deeper than the defense of entrapment. It elevated criticism of the government's conduct to a constitutional level, claiming that Abscam violated principles of governmental decency essential to civilized society and further that, as the citizens whose rights were thereby injured were legislators, the executive branch of government had endangered the independence of the legislature. The due process argument was pressed with great earnestness on behalf of Senator Williams by Erwin N. Griswold, former solicitor general of the United States. Abscam, he declared, was "typical of the sort of governmental abuses which the due process clause was designed to prevent. It is, indeed, the sort of thing which King John abjured at Runnymede in 1215." In addition, he contended, the pictures presented by the video tapes were distorted. Made by prosecuting officers, they were "set up so as to emphasize the facts the prosecution wants to stress." Their use *en masse* had had the prejudicial impact of isolating with apparent but misleading objectivity the target of the cameras. The taperecordings at the heart of Abscam's success were in this view themselves an element of unfairness in the government's prosecution of Williams.[147]

Griswold's contentions did not persuade Judge Pratt, who scoffed that they came down to saying "while a little 'truth' is permissible, large quantities of 'truth' are unconstitutional." But similar arguments proved acceptable in other cases. Judge John Fulham, who had presided at the trial of the Philadelphia councilmen, held that the government's conduct had been "outrageous" to such a degree as to be unconstitutional. The defendants had been tempted not only by cash but also by the prospect of the Arabs investing in a big development project in Philadelphia; the government agents who had duped them had insinuated that, such was "the Arab mind," unless they took the cash, the Arabs would take their legitimate investment elsewhere. Judge Fullam set aside the jury's verdict of guilty. On appeal of his decision, Federal Circuit Judge Ruggero Aldisert agreed. Recalling from his boyhood the stories of refugees from Eastern Europe about the use of *agents provocateurs* by the secret police, he wrote, "To the Department of Justice, its operation was a taste of honey; to me, it emanates a fetid odor whose putrescence threatens to spoil basic concepts of fairness and justice that I hold dear." Sitting en banc, the Third Circuit Court of Appeals outvoted Judge Aldisert, 7 to 2, and in an opinion by Judge Dolores Sloviter reversed Judge Fullam.[148]

William Bryant, seventy, a black born in Alabama, who presided at the trial of Congressman Kelly, reacted to Abscam like Aldisert and Fulham. During a bench conference he told the lawyers that the case had "an odor to it that is absolutely repulsive. . . . It stinks." The government claimed that the congressmen brought to the honey pot had been self-selected bribees. But Kelly had been brought to the Arabs' representatives to discuss lawful investments in his district, and the middleman who brought him doubted that he would take cash. Judge Bryant could see no reason for the government to have dangled money before the congressman, except to test his virtue. He doubted that testing virtue was a permissible governmental purpose, but, putting that doubt aside, he offered an objective test of "outrageous conduct"—it occurred when the government did not model its temptation on reality. Kelly had rejected a bribe when first offered—"I got no part in that"—but the undercover agent had persisted in offering money. Anyone other than an agent, Judge Bryant held, would have given up at the first refusal by the congressman for fear of being reported and prosecuted. Only the knowledge that he was safe from any charge let the agent press his offer. Without realistic restraint, the government's conduct was fundamentally unfair. Judge Bryant set aside the jury verdict against Kelly. On appeal, he was reversed, and the verdict was reinstated. Due process, the Court of Appeals for the District of Columbia held, had not been violated. Circuit Judge Ruth Bader Ginsburg thought Judge Bryant's test speculative and held that Abscam had not reached a level of outrageousness of constitutional proportions. In both the Philadelphia case and *Kelly*, male appellate judges joined female appellate judges in rejecting the due process claims; in both cases the women on the appellate bench were less sympathetic to the defendants' claim than the male district judges.[149]

The third defense, play-acting, took two forms. Congressman Kelly had the chutzpah to tell the press that he took the cash to trap criminals who were trying to bribe him; he had even spent part of the cash to make the bribers believe that they had hooked him; ultimately he had planned to turn them over to the FBI. This defense, seriously pursued in court, struck even sympathetic Judge Bryant as "bizarre" and "nearly farcical," without a scintilla of evidence offered in its support. Senator Williams told the Senate that he had never agreed to use his interest to secure contracts; he had, in effect, been stringing the Arabs along: "Yes, there was puffing. Yes, there was exaggeration," he said. [But] "I never did anything but brag foolishly about my importance." A defense of this kind—boldly risking the obloquy attached to double-dealers—could be risked only because those doing the bribing were themselves play-acting. It failed to convince any jury.[150]

A variant of the play-acting defense was Congressman Myers's that, as he had not intended to deliver what the bribers sought, he had not been "influenced" within the meaning of the federal bribery statute. Argued to the Circuit Court on appeal, this defense was held by Judge Newman to be inadequate as a matter of law. "Being influenced" in the bribery statute did not refer to an official's true state of mind but to the state of mind he showed the briber. If a congressman manifested an intention to be bribed, he was guilty even though in his heart he meant to swindle his payors.[151]

Play-acting by an Abscam bribee had greater strength as a defense if it was considered in conjunction with the play-acting of the Abscam bribers. Knowing that they were in fact American citizens not Arab sheiks, the bribers could not have intended that the bribees introduce immigration bills on their behalf and could not have believed that they could do so. If Myers had the intention of deceiving them by a false promise to use his office, they were in a position where they could not have been deceived. In other decoy cases the false appearance created by the government does not affect the essentials of the crime—the post office employee steals the marked envelope, the thug attacks the apparent derelict, the dealer sells the nark the dope, the thief delivers the property to the undercover fence. But how could a fictitious Arab be induced to believe that a congressman would help him when the Arab, actually an agent of the government, knew he needed no help? True, it might be observed that the congressman took real money: there was an actual payoff. But if the payoff was for nothing—the congressman was acting; the payor could not be aided—was the crime bribery? The question was even harder in Williams's case. He had not taken real money but shares in an imaginary titanium business. What was the crime in taking Monopoly money for a pretended use of office that the payor knew could not be an actual use of office? One answer was that Williams did not know the stock he received was valueless, so he must have thought he was being paid. Yet if he was not in fact paid and in fact did not intend to deliver contracts to the sheik, and his payors knew that they had given him nothing and that he could do nothing for them, was there a bribe? Case law said that if you were charged with hunting deer and you shot a decoy made to look like a deer and put out by game wardens, you were innocent: there had been no deer within the meaning of the wildlife code. Was a sham bribe different from a stuffed deer?[152]

Questions of this kind, in this form, were not addressed by the district or circuit courts. In effect, the appellate decisions upholding the Abscam convictions disbelieved the play-acting claim of the defendants or, rather, refused to disturb the jury verdicts which rejected the claim. The appeals courts also accepted the conclusion that as a matter of law A could bribe B with something without value if B thought it was valuable, and B was bribed if he intended A to believe he would use his office on his behalf, although A knew B could not deliver. Pretending to be bribed would be treated like being bribed.

The fate of the bribees was also real. All had been convicted by juries, sentenced by judges, and their convictions upheld by appellate courts. Jenrette, Kelly, Lederer, Myers, Thompson and Williams had been convicted of bribery. Murphy had been convicted of the lesser offense of taking money "for" an official action. Kelly, Lederer, Myers, and Williams had also been convicted under the Travel Act. Thompson and Williams had been convicted of criminal conflict of interest. The government —mercifully or prudently—had not charged any of the Abscam congressmen with violating the more severe laws, the Hobbs Act and RICO. Jenrette, Lederer, Murphy, Myers, Thompson and Williams were sentenced to fines ranging from $20,000 (Murphy) to $50,000 (Williams). All were sentenced to jail—Kelly to a maximum of only 18 months, Jenrette to two years, the rest to three years. The first batch of Abscam defendants to enter prison were photographed by the *New York Times* as if to provide ocular evidence that a congressman would actually be imprisoned. The political careers of all seven ended. Jenrette, Kelly, Murphy, and Thompson were defeated for reelection; Lederer resigned. Myers, with little debate, suffered the fate which Blaine's influence had spared Ames and Brooks. He became the first congressman in history to be expelled for bribetaking. The greatest political brouhaha was in the Senate where Pete Williams, not up for reelection until 1982, continued to proclaim his innocence.[153]

When the Ethics Committee began its investigation in 1980, the Senate was controlled by the Democrats, and the committee chairman was Howard Heflin, former chief justice of the Alabama Supreme Court. The committee understandably put off its hearings so as not to prejudice Williams's trial. When the committee resumed its work in the summer of 1981, the Republicans had organized the Senate, and Malcolm Wallop of Wyoming was chairman. Wallop and Heflin worked harmoniously in presenting to the full Senate the Ethics Committee's case against Williams. Although the Republicans had control by only three votes and Williams's ouster would mean his replacement by a Republican, there was no suggestion of party politics in the proceedings. Since two-thirds were necessary for expulsion, no narrow partisan case would have prevailed. The membership of the Ethics Committee was not merely bipartisan; it ranged from Jesse Helms, conservative Republican of North Carolina, to Thomas Eagleton of Missouri, self-described as "the showcase liberal" on the committee. In its unanimous recommendation for his expulsion, Williams could read his doom.[154]

In the Senate debate that followed, he had one outright defender, Daniel Inouye, Democrat of Hawaii, who began by emphasizing that expulsion was an extreme measure. In the entire history of the Senate only traitors had ever been expelled. Did Williams, "a good man," deserve this drastic fate? Admitting that "I felt uncomfortable. I felt embarrassed . . . by conversations which we would associate with a gang of thugs," Inouye argued that the videotapes of Williams created an exaggerated picture of his culpability. He had been a fool to talk as he did with the people he had met. These "vile and putrid scenes" had contaminated him with their "dirt," so that he appeared to be a criminal as well.[155]

Inouye's main focus was on the conduct of the FBI, attempting to show not so much that it had engaged in technical entrapment as that the executive branch had encroached on the independence of the legislature. This theme was picked up by other senators less interested in defending Williams than in criticizing those who had set up or approved Abscam. Who had chosen the particular congressmen who became its targets? Corrupt middlemen. In one case at least they had been mistaken. Senator Larry Pressler of South Dakota was persuaded to meet Abdul's representative who indicated it would be "no problem" to contribute to his dark-horse presidential campaign and pushed him to promise he would help the Arabs with a private bill. Pressler had been taped as replying, "In any event, it would not be proper for me to promise to do anything in return for a campaign contribution. . . . So maybe . . . that makes it impossible for you to, you know, help out. . . ." Here was an instance of an innocent senator being tempted by the most disguisable kind of donation, a campaign contribution. In the words of Senator Alan Cranston of California, Pressler had been "targeted on the spur of the moment." The temptation which he had survived so well had been "a shocking example of misbehavior by the FBI." Williams, Cranston argued, had also been put to a "cruel, unreasonable test."[156]

Senator John Stennis, eighty, a conservative Democrat from Mississippi, indicating that he condemned Williams, still gave it as his opinion that "this activity of the FBI is a national disgrace." Senator Sam Hayakawa, a conservative Republican, amended the Lord's prayer: "Lead us not into temptation, especially let us not be led into temptation by the slimy crooks, the con men, and hustlers hired by the Justice Department." Senator Inouye observed that the FBI had proved "that perhaps all of us are ultimately corruptible," but it was not the business of the executive branch "to discover at what point the uncorrupted can be corrupted." Speaking for himself, Williams declared that he had been trapped by "grand masters of deceit." He insisted on Abscam's effect on the independence of the legislative branch. He pointed to the limbo in which he had lived between the government's disclosure of the sting operation and his actual indictment: "Can you imagine the oppressive feeling I had whenever the President called me about a vote that was critical to his administration?"[157]

For all that senators had to say about the threat to Congress as a coordinate branch of government, for all the scorn that was heaped on Abscam and Abscam's authors, for all the frissons felt by senators who thought, "It could have been me," very few were willing to spare Williams some form of senatorial condemnation. As a substitute for the ultimate casting out, Cranston proposed that he be censured, arguing spiritedly that censure was more than a slap on the wrist: "Anyone of us would feel disgraced if we were censured." Even Inouye, embarrassed by the tapes, did not claim that Williams's behavior had been beyond reproach.[158]

The tendency from Cicero to Burke had been to paint official bribetakers as thorough villains. This temptation was avoided by those who criticized Pete Williams. To Stennis, ready to expel him, Williams had been "an almost ideal member of this body." For David Pryor of Arkansas, a member of the unanimous Ethics Committee, he had been "a respected colleague and dear friend." According to Heflin, who marshaled the arguments for expulsion, "In the fields of education, labor, the arts, banking, securities, and housing, Senator Williams has been an accomplished legislator." Recognition of all his good acts could not alter judgment on what he had done—there were no scales in which the good might outweigh the bad. Resolutely the Ethics Committee insisted that Williams's explanation of his conversations with the sheik as mere bragging was itself condemnatory: if he had intended to do nothing for the sheik but take his money he was as much a confidence man as Weinberg. By this, his own admission, he was a swindler. Disbelieving him, the committee found him in fact a bribee. Like stained Senator Staienus in Cicero's classic presentation, whichever alternative was adopted, he was corrupt. "There can be no compromise," affirmed Chairman Wallop, "with bribery, influence peddling, conflict of interest, and ethically repugnant conduct."[159]

As, near the end of a week of debate, sentiment for his expulsion grew, Jeannette Williams went on television to plead her husband's cause. A wife's belief in the integrity of her husband was advanced as evidence. A wife's loyalty was displayed to evoke the empathy of anyone capable of identifying with a spouse standing by her beset mate. The association of domestic and political virtue was ancient, a part of the legend that corrupt men were perfectly corrupt. But the association here was ineffective, and Senator Inouye acknowledged to the Senate that Jeannette Williams's television apperance had been a mistake.[160]

Williams tried one other appeal, an appeal that implicitly recognized the religious roots of the bribery prohibition. Agents of the FBI had earlier shown themselves no slouches in Scripture. The government's cunning in dividing its personality had not been entirely without biblical warrant, and the yacht in Florida on which they had brought Weinberg, Errichetti, and Criden together with Williams in July 1979 had been named "The Left Hand." None of their guests had been sufficiently familiar with Matthew 6:3 to ask of what activity of the right hand the left was being kept in ignorance. Now Williams presented to the Senate an advertisement published in the *New York Times* by ministers, largely Presbyterians and Methodists of conservative orthodoxy, with a banner headline, "Don't Expel Senator Williams." Studded with quotations from both Old and New Testaments, the statement denounced Abscam as a criminal conspiracy by the government. The ministers quoted Proverbs 17:23, "A wicked man taketh a gift out of the bosom to pervert the ways of justice" and applied the text to condemn the government. As Senator Williams saw the matter, "the preachers" had raised their voice to denounce "an abomination." For himself, he did not hesitate to quote St. Paul, "I have fought a good fight" (2 Titus 4:7) as applying to his own case. He did not allude to Paul's famous challenge to the sting of death.[161]

Running through much of the hostile reaction to Abscam was the thought of the ancient Christian prayer which Senator Hayakawa had echoed: "Lead us not into temptation." If we do not want God to arrange our temptation, neither do we want the government. The thought entered into the doctrine on entrapment, the opinion of Judge Bryant, the Protestants' protesting ad. Maybe Senator Inouye was right: all were ultimately corruptible. If the FBI had used the same investigative technique against any sector of the government, an equal number of bribable officials would have been captured. One person with great responsibility for Abscam said as much to the author of this book: so "the old hands" of the Department of Justice had informed him. On the other hand, what kind of virtue was it that could not survive temptation?

Levity, often a characteristic of senatorial exchanges, was rare in the debate over Williams's fate. Expulsion was symbolic execution, too serious for jokes. Senator Moynihan reported having an FBI tape on which William Rosenberg, a felon employed in the course of Abscam, declared that he could deliver Senator Jacob Javits to the Abscam operators for $25,000 and Senator Moynihan for $50,000. Moynihan had called FBI Director Webster about this lying boast, and Webster had said, "Weren't you complimented?" Moynihan had rebuked the jest of the FBI director as unseemly. Speaking now to the Senate on the abuses of Abscam, Moynihan added that Rosenberg had also said he could deliver Senator Robert Kerr. Moynihan remarked that Kerr at the time had been dead almost seventeen years. Russell Long of Louisiana asked, "Might we assume that that might be some great feat, if the FBI actually succeeded in bribing someone in his grave?"[162]

The question was in the realm of imagination, but Abscam itself was a creation of imagination in which acts impossible of accomplishment on behalf of fictional creations had been the measure of criminality. "Death takes no bribes," Benjamin Franklin had said. But the dead? Senator Long's grotesque supposition seemed appropriate. It evoked memories of gifts given the dead in other times and cultures, and here the image of the dead was central—Senator Kerr was physically dead, Senator Williams would be collegially dead if expelled, there had been his moral death much earlier, and the sting had brought death to all it touched. On March 11, 1982, seeing expulsion as inevitable, Williams resigned.[163]

Purity codes of two different kinds had been in conflict. Louis Brandeis, such a strong champion of governmental purity from corruption, had expressed the other code in a classic dissent delivered in 1928. In his view the courts should refuse to permit "a detective-made criminal" to be punished, not out of deference to the rights of the criminal but "in order to protect the Government. To protect it from illegal conduct of its officers. To preserve the purity of its courts." The case to which he addressed himself involved drugs not bribes, so he did not have to choose between purity of means and purity from corruption. His broad declaration that "a desirable social end" could not justify "foul means" would range him with those rejecting Abscam as foul. The same choice of procedural purity was evident in the vocabulary of Judge Bryant ("It stinks") and Judge Aldisert ("a fetid odor"). In the 1980s the desire for purity in office had proved stronger.[164]

Antibribery ideals triumphed. No legislator, however high his status, was exempt. With only a corner of constitutional immunity remaining, Congress was in as nearly subordinate a position before the Justice Department as were county sheriffs and city councilmen. Congress of course could change the law governing the FBI, but when in the wake of Senator Williams's resignation Congress set out to do so, its efforts ended in a compromise unlikely to disturb the 462 undercover stings then being conducted by federal agencies. Aggressive techniques for trapping the criminal, including criminal bribees in Congress, were essentially undisturbed.[165]

Reciprocity remained central to politics. Federal prosecutors would decide which reciprocities were criminal. Federal judges would decide if the prosecutors' distinctions should be upheld. Definers of what exchanges constituted bribery, these prosecutors and judges were unlikely to forego their new power. Employing means that would have been criminal if employed by private persons, the executive branch was in a position to supervise every government official in the country from traffic court clerks to senators. The judicial branch was in a position to approve or disapprove this supervision. Enforcers of the antibribery ethic by the criminal law, these prosecutors and judges had become the guardians of honest government, local, state, and national, in America. At the center of this supervisory system created by the Hobbs Act, the Travel Act, the Internal Revenue Code, the mail and wire fraud statutes, the conspiracy statute, and RICO, and "the federal common law" based on these acts, was the crime of bribery. A new stage in the use of the concept of the bribe had been reached. This epoch, which began about 1968, caused unprecedented pressure for the creation of a clear line between what could lead to disgrace and prison and the voluntary contributions that were the fuel of politics in a democracy.

19

The Donations of Democracy

Democracy does not work without campaigns for office. Campaigns require money. Unless only the rich are to run, the money must be raised. If the government supplied it, the danger of manipulation by incumbents would be great. If the money comes from citizens, they give it to candidates they expect to vote, on at least some issues, in accordance with the donors' desires. Normally, at any rate, money is given to an officeseeker whose views on important issues coincide with the giver's. The money is given with the hope, expectation, purpose that particular views will be translated into particular votes. A tacit reciprocity exists. How is money given a candidate different from a bribe?

Nineteenth-century usage made the verb "to contribute" and the noun "contribution" central to the answer to this question. As early as 1829 New York passed a statute entitled "An Act to Preserve the Purity of Elections" forbidding anyone "to contribute money" for an election except for printing. The law was interpreted in 1842. An entrepreneur who had performed a contract to build a log cabin on Broadway to promote the presidential campaign of William Henry Harrison was denied payment of the contract price of $1,000. The case struck a theme that would recur and become stronger. Preservation of purity could lead to total prohibition. The statute—not heard of again in New York politics—was a linguistic benchmark. "Purity" was its aim. "Contribute" was the normal way of designating a political payment. "Contribution" in the New York court's opinion was the normal noun for the action of contributing and the normal noun for what was contributed. The verb "to contribute" was employed in the same sense in a federal statute of 1867: government officials were not "to require or request" the employees of naval yards "to contribute or pay any money for political purposes." "To contribute" here was in effect to offer a quid pro quo for keeping one's job with the Navy; Pepys would have understood. But a request to a working man to contribute was condemned not as extortion or as a request for a bribe; it was condemned as a distinct practice deserving special statutory attention.[1]

Unless stigmatized by a specific law, a contribution was marked off from a bribe, which was criminal, and at the same time subtly distinguished from a gift, which was gratuitous. The word was the American equivalent of *contributio*, the Latin term the fifteenth century had used to distinguish a lawful payment for a pardon from a sinful bribe or a free gift. A contribution was what one made, in other contexts, to a partnership or a charity. It was, if not precisely an investment, something shared with another whose purposes agreed with one's own, who was in the process of furthering those purposes, who responded to the contribution by using it for those purposes. A contribution in politics, wrote Theodore Roosevelt, that most practical of progressive Republicans, was received by him "without any kind of promise, expressed or implied." In the same sentence he added that he accepted it on the principle that the one making it had "no end to serve except to assist the cause he is championing." Roosevelt did not acknowledge the tension between his absence of a promise and the donor's desire to assist a cause. The donor gave, relying on the candidate to furnish the assistance. Did not reliance depend upon, or create, reciprocation? And if one gives to get reciprocation in office, is one not giving in order to influence official conduct?[2]

If the contribution was small, it might not even come to the candidate's notice or, if it did, be too insignificant for anyone to expect it to influence his conduct. No reciprocation would be created. But if the contribution was large enough to be known to the candidate, it appeared to be payment whose expected effect would be to lead to a response by the candidate after he was elected. That the money went to pay for campaign expenses or to a campaign committee not the candidate himself did not appear to alter matters materially: the candidate wanted to be elected and so benefited personally from whatever help he got in his campaign. Small contributions, insignificant individually, could have the same effect of expected influence if they were aggregated and handled through a single conduit. How and why, then, were large or aggregated campaign contributions linguistically and legally distinguished from bribes?

Seven hypotheticals will illustrate the range of this question:

1. A gives to X, a candidate, out of dislike or distrust of Y, X's opponent.

2. A gives to X out of admiration for his character and a belief that the country will be better with him in office.

3. A gives to X because of X's general sympathy to a particular industry, section of the country, or economic class.

4. A gives to X because X has a principled stand on a specific issue.

5. A gives to X because he needs "an insurance policy" guaranteeing he can present his position to X—that is, although A has such status that legislators listen to him, he wants to be sure that he will always have access to X.

6. A gives to X because he has no other way of getting access to him.

7. A gives to X because he expects X to vote for a specific bill.

In Case 1, nothing is expected of X, and he is being rewarded for nothing. No reciprocity exists, no bribery can be suspected. In case 7, the donation is made with the expectation of X's response in official conduct. Full reciprocation is anticipated. The distinction between bribe and contribution is close to collapsing. In Case 2, X is getting a kind of reward but for something—his character—that could scarcely have been shaped to win this sort of reward. No reciprocation, no bribery. In Case 6, A is making a payment of the kind frequently used in the past to win the attention of a judge. In the judicial instance the emperor Constantine saw it as a way of corrupting the courts. Not only did the money get the judge's time: it prejudiced him in favor of the payor. An analogous observation holds true of the legislator. The evil may be less specific because unlike a judge the legislator is not judging between two parties but looking at a range of alternatives. Nonetheless, the access buyer is paying not only for attention but for favorable attention. The payment is close to what would be called a bribe if made to a judge; but access to, and favorable attention by, a legislator has not generally been regarded in the same way as an approach to a judge. Case 5 is only a slight step from Case 6 and still more benevolently viewed: the president of a large union or corporation does not have to pay to get access to a legislator—"insurance" of the access is seen as benign. In Cases 3 and 4 the contribution does not cause the candidate to take a position; he already has taken the position; but the contribution does reward him for his stand. If a litigant gave a judge a present for a principled opinion in his favor, modern law would treat it as a species of bribery. Usage did not and does not, however, treat as a bribe a campaign contribution to a legislator whose stand one admires.[3]

The hypotheticals show that a legislator is not in the position of a judge. The judge's office is modeled on the paradigm of the transcendent Judge of the Bible and a sharp line distinguishes him from the litigants before him. The legislator, on the contrary, is his constituent's *representative*—at least such is the non-Burkean view of legislators that predominates in practice. A certain identity of interest is expected to exist between constituent and legislator; and it is easy for every contributor to see himself in the role of a constituent. Given the acceptance of this mutuality of purpose between contributor and legislator, the prevailing assumption in America has been that campaign contributions normally fall in the range of cases where specific votes are not being bought. The campaign committee, distinct from the candidate, has become the regular vehicle for such payments, and the fact that a public cause as well as the candidate's own welfare is served by the campaign has softened the perception of benefit to the candidate in the gift. The existence of a substantial number of acceptable purposes in campaign-giving has made it difficult to mark off the cases where law and language would say "bribe." At times "campaign contribution" has been a code word used as a flimsy cover for a payment intended to enrich an official personally in exchange for an official act specifically benefiting the payor. These cases have not disturbed the normal assumption that a campaign contribution is different from a bribe.[4]

Isolating the Corporate Donor. American experience, however, caused the normal assumption of legitimacy to be doubted and to lead to the drawing of legal lines stamping certain campaign contributions not precisely as "bribes"—the harshest word was avoided—but as "corrupt." Ever since the Credit Mobilier affair had dramatized the possibilities on a national stage, corporations as corruptors had been a recurrent theme of national, state, and municipal politics. Already when Adams wrote *Democracy* the obvious rejoinder of a senator accused of receiving $100,000 from a corporation for his vote was that the money had been given to meet campaign expenses of his party. For a Madeleine Lee the answer was an admission of guilt: the senator still had sold his vote. But there was a time lag between the perceptions of the Madeleine Lees and public action. In 1894 her view was given nuanced recognition by Elihu Root, a lawyer highly familiar with corruption in New York, whose clients included the corporate corruptors, although he did not serve them corruptly. When a corporation gave $100,000 or even $50,000 to a campaign, Root pointed out to the New York State Constitutional Convention, it was "upon the understanding that a debt is created from a political party to it; a debt to be recognized and repaid with the votes of representatives in the legislature and in Congress or by the action of administrative or executive officers who have been elected in a measure through the use of money so contributed." Root did not say this creation of reciprocity was bribery but he asked the constitutional convention to cut through ambiguity and evasion by isolating corporations as contributors. Their donations were to be prohibited "precisely because laws aimed directly at the crime of bribery so far have been ineffective."[5]

Root's idea was not accepted then, but his solution was put forward nationally a decade later by President Theodore Roosevelt, who came to support it not only from his great admiration for Root but from his own experience. Running as the incumbent in 1904 he was proud of his part in creating, within the Department of Commerce, a Bureau of Corporations to gather information on the big corporations. He selected George Cortelyou, his secretary of Commerce, as his national campaign manager. The *New York Times* explored the implications of the appointment. "Buying the President" was the title of a *Times* editorial on October 1, 1904, denouncing it as "a national disgrace" and noting Cortelyou's collection of campaign contributions from companies within his department's jurisdiction. Alton B. Parker, the Democratic candidate, lacking other good issues, took up the cry. The Republican party, he implied, was blackmailing the non-contributing corporations.

"Cortelyouism" briefly became a noun describing the Republicans' game. A gift of $100,000 to the party by Standard Oil, a particular object of Roosevelt's hostility in the past, was singled out by critics in the press. Roosevelt, saying he knew of no such contribution, ordered Cortelyou to return it if it had been made. He denounced Parker's charges of extortion as falsehoods. His own innocence of what his campaign committee had been doing was proclaimed and plausible. When later John Archibold, president of Standard Oil, revealed that he had given the Republican committee $125,000 in cash and that it had never been returned, Roosevelt was ready to believe him to be a liar. Corporations in fact contributed over $1,000,000 to the Republican campaign—far more than they gave the Democrats. After it was all over, Roosevelt followed Root's advice and asked Congress to prohibit all corporate contributions.[6]

Directors should not be able to use stockholders' money for political purposes; flat prohibition "would be, as far as it went, an effective method of stopping the evils aimed at in corrupt practice acts"—these were Roosevelt's two reasons. The Senate Report that brought in the bill in 1906 observed laconically, "The evils of the use of money in connection with political elections are so generally recognized that the committee deem it unnecessary to make any argument in favor of the general purpose of this measure. It is in the interest of good government and calculated to promote purity in the selection of public officials." It was irrelevant to the law's intent, though not to its mildness, that the author of the report, Senator Joseph Foraker of Ohio, could be described by Roosevelt as "one of the most unblushing servers and beneficiaries of corporate wealth within or without office that I have ever met." The law evoked the familiar terms of the Western tradition against bribery. "Corrupt practices" were to be diminished, "purity" was to be promoted by the absolute restriction on corporations. Recommended by Roosevelt; its purpose applauded by Parker; welcomed by Samuel Gompers, the head of the American Federation of Labor; and accepted by the servers of corporate wealth, the prohibition became law as the Tillman Act in 1907.[7]

The act as passed broadly forbade "any corporation whatever" to "make a money contribution in connection with any election" for president, senator, or congressman. The original bill's attempt to prohibit all contributions in any election, national or state, by corporations engaged in interstate commerce had been dropped. The phrase "money contribution" was narrow. The phrase "in connection with" was dangerously vague, given that the First Amendment guaranteed freedom of speech. The penalties were mild—a maximum of $5,000 fine for the corporations and $1,000 for an officer or director consenting to a contribution. The only bite in the law was a provision of up to one year's imprisonment for a consenting officer or director. The Tillman Act's description of the offense—"make a money contribution"—was studiously neutral.[8]

Roosevelt, however, had mentioned "corrupt practice acts." "Corrupt practices" was a standard phrase in America by the 1840s; the English had enacted a Corrupt-Practices Act in 1883. In 1910 Congress added its own "Federal Corrupt Practices Act," a statute requiring the reporting of all contributions to national elections. A corporation that made a contribution and concealed it was now guilty of two crimes, and national party committees receiving corporation contributions were under a criminal obligation to report them. The next year, 1911, the law against corporate giving was extended to include primaries. But in 1913 a gap was allowed to develop. The Seventeenth Amendment providing for the popular election of senators was adopted. The provisions of the law against corporate gifts were such that they applied only to the election of senators by state legislatures. For a dozen years nothing was done to fill the hole. In 1921 another hole was opened. The Supreme Court held that Congress had no constitutional power to regulate spending in any primary. In 1925, in the wake of the Fall affair and other scandals of the Harding administration, an amended Federal Corrupt Practices Act patched up the statute, including within its scope the direct elections of senators, eliminating primaries, and expanding "money contribution" to "contributions."[9]

In 1940 an amendment of the Hatch Act against "pernicious political activites" made it a federal felony, punishable by five years' imprisonment, for a contractor with the government to contribute to a federal campaign. In 1943 the War Labor Disputes Act extended the ban on contributions to labor unions, and the Taft-Hartley Act continued this legislation into peacetime. The impulses behind these pieces of legislation pointed to different assumptions about the basic law's effectiveness. The contractors were presumably specified in 1940 because it was believed that they had been undeterred by the general law against corporate contributions. The unions were included in 1943 because it was believed that they should be under the same restraints as the corporations; the law was taken to have at least some deterrent strength.[10]

Enforcement of the statutes was in fact slight. Neither major party was anxious to offend its donors, discipline its campaign chairman, or prosecute its own winning candidates. The Roman law against *ambitio* is the legislation's appropriate analogue. The laws were symbolic reminders not to spend too much. In 1916 the federal district attorney in Pittsburgh had the Brewers' Association indicted for violation of the Tillman Act. The brewers replied with the obvious challenges to the law's constitutionality: it was too vague and it infringed their association's freedom of speech. The district judge ruled against them and the association did not find the ruling worth appealing. Thirty-two years later, another district attorney evoked the law to indict eighteen auto dealerships in Michigan; two defendants were tried and acquitted, the rest pleaded nolo contendere and acquiesced in small fines. Between 1950 and 1961 over 100 complaints of violation were processed by the Justice Department; only three resulted in indictments; and in no case was the sanction so serious as to lead the defendants to appeal to higher courts. A single case in the 1960s resulted in a nolo contendere plea and a $100 fine. Desultory enforcement of this kind left the law's constitutional and statutory significance undeveloped by corporate advocates. Only labor unions were sufficiently hampered by it to bring constitutional challenges to the Supreme Court.[11]

The lack of legal development meant that practices that could have been stamped as evasions of law grew up without check. Corporations gave bonuses to their employees, permitted padded expense accounts, or paid consultants' fees on the understanding that the money would be turned over to a campaign. Corporations contributed to trade associations that took political stands. Corporations paid for partisan propaganda disguised as "institutional advertising." Experts spoke of such evasions as inviting "public cynicism" and of the laws as "moribund." They even pointed to reports of occasional—although only occasional—"outright violations." A famous incident occurred in 1956 when during a legislative contest affecting the oil industry $2,500 in cash was contributed to the campaign fund of Senator Francis Case of South Dakota and Case on the floor of the Senate denounced the payment. Less dramatically, the purchase by corporations of lapel pins and advertising space in campaign books was noticed as a widespread illicit practice. Most significantly, the experts estimated that $200 million was spent in the presidential campaign of 1964. Without corporate contributions on a large scale it was unlikely that such a total could have been reached. No prosecutor, no major politician claimed that the figures showed that corporations were spending millions of dollars in bribes. The distinction between bribe and contribution held. But massive evasion of the law indicated that "corrupt practices" were flourishing.[12]

The same tide that brought about the new criminal enforcement of the bribery law described in Chapter 18 brought about reform in the campaign laws and did so at about the same rate of momentum. In 1946, just after World War II, the Governmental Regulation of Lobbying Act was passed—a comprehensive effort to require reporting by those whose work urging legislative action also offered a conduit for improper payments to members of Congress. In 1962 a bipartisan committee appointed by President Kennedy to report on campaign expenses stressed their rapid rise and, urging legislative reform, remarked candidly that the recipient of a large contribution was "in moral hock" to the donor. Under Lyndon Johnson a series of proposals were advanced to change the unrealistic statutes. "More loophole than law, they invite evasion and circumvention," President Johnson told Congress of the Federal Corrupt Practices Act and the Hatch Act. According to Robert Caro's biography, Johnson spoke with peculiar authority. Under President Nixon the first comprehensive changes since 1925 were enacted. The new statute, enacted at the beginning of the 1972 presidential year, permitted taxpayers to contribute one tax-deductible dollar to a fund for presidential campaigns: the dilemma of raising campaign funds and aggregating them in a way that did not have the influence of a bribe was solved in principle at the cost of making the government the collector. At the same time numerous loopholes in the old laws on reporting were closed.[13]

From 1907 to 1972 Congress and succeeding Republican and Democratic administrations reflected ambivalence about campaign contributions. Contributions from ineligible donors and unreported donations were not stamped as bribes. Violation of the law merely produced something described as "illegal." The new legislation in 1972 continued in this direction. The Federal Corrupt Practices Act was repealed, and the terminology of corruption was not employed.[14] Campaign contributions were treated as a subject for technical regulation very different from shameful bribery. Yet the ban on certain classes of contributors was continued, reflecting the belief that their contributions were corrupting, while the provisions on reporting reflected the belief that only pure contributions could be reported so that by insisting on reporting, impure contributions would be eliminated. A zone of illegality was created where the full force of the antibribery ethic did not operate yet where the antibribery ethic was at work. The same societal tendencies that made the Nixon administration the first enforcer of federal bribery law against local corruption and made a Democratic Congress collaborate with the Nixon administration in creating RICO led the Democratic Congress to pass, and the Nixon administration to accept, the reform legislation whose application was to contribute to the undoing of the Nixon administration's donors at the moment of electoral triumph.

Watergate.   The same factors that produced acceptance of the new legislation enhanced the likelihood of its enforcement. The precise way in which enforcement was accomplished depended on the accidents of politics: the Watergate burglary in 1972 of the headquarters of the Democratic National Committee became in 1973 the subject of investigation by a select committee of the Democratic-controlled Senate. Realigning his forces to meet the threat, Nixon named a new attorney general, Elliott Richardson, a member of his own cabinet but from the Eastern Seaboard wing which was in fact hostile to him. Richardson could take office only if confirmed by the Senate. In his confirmation hearings the Senate Judiciary Committee obtained a promise from him that he would appoint an independent special prosecutor. Richardson's eventual choice was Archibald Cox, professor of law at Harvard Law School and solicitor general under President Kennedy—another Eastern Seaboard liberal. Whether Richardson and Cox are viewed as members of the new "border" acting against the new center, or representatives of the old "center" driving out interlopers, they were in a camp ideologically and socially distinct from those Cox was to bring to account. The terms of Cox's responsibilities were worked out by him and Richardson with the approval of the Democratic-controlled Judiciary Committee. The special prosecutor was given jurisdiction of very great flexibility. It included not only offenses "arising out of" the burglary but "all offenses arising out of the 1972 presidential election for which the Special Prosecutor deems it necessary and appropriate to assume responsibility." Without stretching, the jurisdiction included campaign finances if the special prosecutor thought their investigation appropriate. Whether he should think so or not was left to his discretion.[15]

Richardson was confirmed and Cox appointed by the end of May 1973. Cox proceeded to appoint a staff of thirty-seven lawyers. The news media gave him high visibility and strong support as the antagonist of the president. In July the chairman of American Airlines informed him that the corporation had contributed $55,000 to the Committee to Re-Elect the President. Cox revealed the crime to the press and invited other corporate officers to confess, announcing that "their voluntary acknowledgment will be considered a mitigating circumstance in deciding what charges to bring." For the first time in the life of the Tillman Act, now sixty-three years old, major attention was focused on its enforcement.[16]

An offshoot of the Watergate Committee's probe led to the criminal indictment of Secretary of Commerce Maurice Stans, the chief Republican fundraiser. Common Cause, a liberal, non-party, political action organization, sued the Committee to Re-elect the President and obtained an order that it disclose contributions made to it over an eighteen-month period. The combination of the Watergate prosecutor's activity, the Stans indictment, and the Common Cause suit discomfited corporations that had contributed to Nixon's reelection. Instead of reaping the rewards of victory, they saw themselves as the likely objects of criminal investigation. Fifteen prominent corporations—among them Braniff Airways, Goodyear Tire and Rubber, Greyhound, Minnesota Mining and Manufacturing, and Phillips Petroleum—pleaded guilty to making illegal campaign contributions and were fined. The Northrop Corporation and its chief executive Thomas V. Jones pleaded guilty to violation of the statute prohibiting contributions by government contractors; the company and Jones were fined. The Associated Milk Producers pleaded guilty to making a corporate contribution and two of its officers were sentenced to prison. Maurice Stans pleaded guilty to accepting an illegal campaign contribution and was fined. But no corporation provided such a complete account of its illegal political activities as was now furnished to the government and the world by the Gulf Oil Corporation. The report by Gulf showed that, beyond the estimates of any expert on the American political process, the law against corporate contributions had been systematically flouted.[17]

Off the Books in the Bahamas.   Gulf Oil Corporation in 1973 had assets of about twelve billion dollars, gross revenues of about eighteen billion, and a net income of about one billion. Claude C. Wild, Jr., vice-president and head of its "Government Relations Office," conducted its legislative program in Washington. In July 1973 Wild informed Gulf's chairman and chief executive officer, Bob R. Dorsey, that he had given $100,000 of Gulf funds in cash to the Committee to Re-Elect the President. Gulf at once retained outside counsel, who advised confession to the Watergate prosecutor. This was done. Return of the money was demanded by the company. The money was obtained from the committee. Gulf's board of directors, up till now unadvised of the gift, was summoned to a special meeting, and told.[18]

Gulf had been founded by the Mellon family of Pittsburgh and the family still controlled 20 percent of the stock. Whatever the sins of the ancestors, the descendants were grandly devoted to philanthropy, often large individual contributors to the Republicans in lawful ways, and hugely respectable. The National Gallery of Art, the Mellon Collection at Yale, the Mellon Foundation were embodiments of their munificence. The modern Mellons appeared to know nothing of Wild's activities. They became indignant that Wild should besmirch their name. Responding to their views, the board's reaction was swift. It asked that outside counsel investigate thoroughly and report in a month; that procedures be set up to prevent such apparently unauthorized gifts being made in the future; and that the audit committee of the board be informed of all matters of fiscal substance. The posture of the directors was clear: Wild had acted on his own. Contributions of the kind he made were not company policy. The directors disavowed him and would not let this sort of misconduct happen again.

Four months later, Wild and the company were charged with a single violation of the federal law against corporate contributions. On the same day, by prearrangement with the Watergate prosecutor, they pleaded guilty. Wild was fined $1,000, Gulf $5,000. The corporation appeared to have contained the affair with virtually no damage and at almost no cost.[19]

The damage and the cost were to come. The affair had provoked the attention of the Securities and Exchange Commission. Charged by federal law with receiving accurate financial reports from corporations registered under the law, the SEC's concern with bribery had hitherto seemed remote. The head of the Enforcement Division, Stanley Sporkin, was a lawyer with strong ethical convictions. He saw the relevance to his domain of Gulf's transgression. The chairman of the commission, Ray Garrett, a Republican appointee, was a conscientious lawyer open to persuasion by the staff. With his assistants David Doherty and Robert Ryan, Sporkin pressed further. Six months of inquiry and negotiations followed. They culminated in a consent decree being entered against Gulf: the SEC accused Gulf of civil violations of the Securities Exchange Act, and, without admitting the accusations, Gulf agreed not to violate the Act in the future. It submitted to an injunction requiring it, under pain of contempt of court, to abide by its agreement.[20]

As part of the settlement and judicial decree, Gulf consented to appoint a Special Review Committee—whose chairman would not be connected with the company—to look into Gulf's political contributions. John J. McCloy, former chairman of the Chase Manhattan Bank and former president of the World Bank, headed the committee. Its other members were Nathan Pearson, a financial adviser, and Beverley Matthews, a Toronto lawyer, both men being directors backed by the Mellons. Its lead counsel was William E. Jackson of the Wall Street law firm of Milbank, Tweed, Hadley and McCloy, the son of Robert Jackson, the Supreme Court Justice. Reviewing the investigation already made and examining afresh employees of Gulf, with the cooperation of the company but without power to compel testimony or to take oaths, the McCloy committee produced the most comprehensive account ever made of political payments by a corporation.

In part, the McCloy committee's report must be understood as an indictment—it was produced by persons critical of what had gone on. In part, it must be understood as confession—Gulf agreed to the report being made and did not dispute its findings. Of all the documents reviewed in this history of bribery—a term the committee avoided—this report is most marked by a conscientious lawyer's desire to distinguish evidence from suspicion.

According to the report, William K. Whiteford, (the chairman of Gulf), Archie Gray and David Searls (Gulf's top legal officers), and Joseph E. Bounds (administrative vice-president) decided in 1959 to set up a fund from which cash could be paid for political purposes at home and abroad. Whiteford believed that other oil companies already had such funds in place. The timing of his move coincided with the opening of a publicly announced political program by Gulf in Washington.

Bahamas Exploration Company (Bahamas Ex.), an almost inactive Gulf subsidiary, was selected as the vehicle for the operation. A bank account of $250,000 was opened for it in Nassau with Gulf corporate funds; further transfers of money followed. William Viglia, a lawyer at headquarters in Pittsburgh, was sent to Nassau to handle the account. Gulf's books reflected transfers to Bahamas Ex. but not their purpose. Accounting for the money after it reached Bahamas Ex. was fictitious. The Bahamas Ex. books regularly showed not the receipt of funds but merely "deferred charges." These charges were always written off by year's end. What was actually done with the funds was not recorded.[21]

In fact, Gulf's man in Nassau spent his time turning Bahamas Ex.'s bank account into dollars—a slow process since large amounts of United States dollars were not instantly available and the local casino was the chief source of them for the local bank—and putting the dollars in a safe deposit

box. Then either Viglia or another courier designated by headquarters delivered the dollars in the United States. In a typical year there would be
over a dozen deliveries, usually in amounts of $25,000 per delivery. Be-
tween January 1960 and July 1972 a total of $5,186,000 of Gulf funds was
transferred to Bahamas Ex. and at least $4,530,000 was returned to the
United States in dollars. A slightly different arrangement brought in
another $400,000 between July 1972 and July 1973, when the Watergate in-
vestigation ended the business. The dollars were delivered to Claude
Wild, Gulf's vice-president for governmental relations.[22]

The cash received was distributed by Wild personally or by his staff,
which included an assistant for "legislative liaison" and regional vice-
presidents of Gulf's Government Relations Department. The money was
usually distributed in plain envelopes. The recipients were officials,
usually legislators or members of their staffs.[23]

Those getting the cash were both Democrats and Republicans. Next to
the $100,000 given the Committee to Re-Elect the President, the largest
amount was $50,000, delivered over several months to Lyndon B. Johnson,
then a senator and majority leader of the Senate, through his assistant,
Walter Jenkins.[24] The next highest recipient of cash—$25,000 delivered to
"a personal confidant"—was Hubert Humphrey, then a senator cam-
paigning for vice-president.[25] Deliveries of envelopes were also made to
persons connected with the campaigns of Senators Howard Baker, J. Glenn
Beall, Wallace Bennett, and Marlow Cook, and Congressman James Burke.
Envelopes were delivered directly to Senator Howard Baker, Congressman
Hale Boggs, Senator William E. Brock, Senator Howard Cannon, Congress-
man Joe Evins, Congressman Craig Hosmer, Congressman Chet Holifield,
Senator Edward Mechem, Congressman Melvin Price, and Congressman
Richard Roudebush. Cash was delivered in some form to the campaigns of
Senator Henry Jackson and Congressman Wilbur Mills.[26] Other cash con-
tributions were made by Wild's subordinates situated in different parts of
the country. His Pennsylvania agent, for example, contributed cash to the
campaigns of Congressmen Frank M. Clark, John H. Heinz, and William S.
Moorhead. There was a special arrangement with Hugh Scott, senator
from Pennsylvania, Gulf's home state. Each spring and each fall Wild
presented him with $5,000 in cash.[27]

Cash was also dispensed to state officials. William H. Avery, governor of
Kansas, received an envelope at his office. Another envelope was delivered to Preston Smith, governor of Texas. George Bloom, a Pennsylvania
utility commissioner, received an envelope. Various Pennsylvania state
legislators got from $100 to $1,000 apiece, with one Republican leader getting $7,000 to be split among other politicians. A staff member of the New
Jersey Turnpike Authority, who had provided helpful information on
plans for the turnpike's location, had bargained for nothing but stood in
need of a "thank-you"; Wild provided $10,000 which, funneled through a
Wilkes-Barre intermediary, expressed Gulf's thanks. In Texas, Wild
regularly supplied cash to Ira Butler, a Fort Worth lawyer, who represented

Gulf before the state agency regulating oil and gas, the Texas Railroad Commission. Every year Butler gave cash—usually about $1,000—to any commissioner opposed for reelection. He also contributed cash from Wild to a campaign for attorney general of Texas and to several candidates for election to the Supreme Court of Texas.[28]

Even after the committee had identified about two dozen congressional recipients and a dozen or so state recipients, it had trouble finding out how much anyone got. Often the bearers of the envelopes did not know what they contained—the contents could have been mere messages, but then why did Wild use Gulf officials as the messengers? Not more than $330,000 was accounted for by positive testimony. $4,400,000 was distributed to recipients who remained anonymous. No doubt some of the named donees shared in this bounty. The others have never been identified.

The outside law firm that had looked at Bahamas Ex. at the directors' request in 1973 had suggested that, once begun, the cash-generating mechanism "could and did self-perpetuate."[29] Those who got it started —Whiteford, Bounds, and Wild—were knowledgeable, as were the then general counsel David T. Searls and his successor, Archie Gray. But no one else knew about the fund. Even Gulf's man in Nassau, the courier who brought the cash, did not know its purpose; and Wild himself professed to be ignorant of the kitty the cash came from.[30] Extraordinarily, a pump that produced $400,000 a year for over a decade functioned with no one touching it. Only the strong hand at the nozzle—Wild's—gave direction to the spray of currency.

Of those responsible, Whiteford, Gray, and Searls were dead, Bounds was retired, and Wild confessed to making the $100,000 gift and resigned. The pleasing conclusion was that no current officers were implicated. The review committee found this carefully constructed analysis implausible. To begin with, the key man in arranging the transfer of funds, the comptroller William T. Grummer, had himself been a courier carrying cash back to Pittsburgh. His successor, to the committee's expressed skepticism, could not remember who authorized him to continue the transfers, and the successor's successor, Frank C. Anderson, acknowledged being worried that Bahamas Ex. cash went to Wild. Anderson's successor admitted to making transfers to Bahamas Ex. on the basis of handwritten notes or simply oral requests from Wild, whose responsibilities in Washington had not the remotest connection with operations in the Bahamas. He understood what was meant when he received this undated memo on Wild's Washington letterhead: "Fred—Would you please make a deposit of 200 to the proper account. Claude." "200" meant $200,000. The note indicated that the comptroller must have known that Wild exercised authority over Bahamas Ex.'s cash; it also showed conclusively that Wild knew where the cash came from—"the proper account" which the comptroller needed to be reminded to keep supplied with funds. The pump could not have continued to produce cash without the comptroller's conscious collaboration in the off-books set-up. Advice on the fictitious bookkeeping entries to be made to cover the operation came continuously from the comptroller's office. Its staff joked about the man "with the little black bag."[31]

How independent was Wild in his disbursements? He came to Gulf's staff in 1959, thirty-six years old, a graduate of the University of Texas and its law school, the son of a Lyndon Johnson operative in Texas. He was told by Searls and Gray that Gulf wanted to build an organization that would give Gulf "muscle" in politics. He regarded himself as responsible to Searls, Gray, and chairman Whiteford. His first task was to deliver the cash Searls had promised Jenkins for Lyndon Johnson. Increasingly he was allowed to exercise his own discretion, within limits. In 1963, for example, when his Louisiana agent suggested a $40,000 gift to Senator Russell Long, he sought authorization from Whiteford. (The authorization was given; the committee heard no evidence as to the gift's delivery.)[32]

Beginning in 1963 Wild looked on Royce Savage, then Gulf's general counsel, as his boss. In company terms, Wild "reported directly" to Savage; it is not clear what he reported or how often. According to Wild, he once gave Savage "an accounting"—a single handwritten piece of yellow paper without copies. Also, according to Wild, his accounting was disturbing to Savage: "In all sincerity he didn't like it and he told me he didn't like it. He was trapped like—not trapped, but we were involved in this merry-go-round, and how do you get off?"[33]

Savage, Wild's boss, had been for twenty-one years a federal district judge in Tulsa. In 1960, when chief judge of the northern district of Oklahoma, he had presided over a nonjury trial of the country's twenty-nine leading oil companies, criminally charged with conspiring to fix prices after the Suez crisis. Gulf was among the defendants. Unexpectedly, at the conclusion of the government's case, Judge Savage had stated from the bench, "I have an absolute conviction, personally, that the defendants are not guilty" and entered a nonappealable judgment on their behalf. When nineteen months later he resigned to become Gulf's general counsel, President Kennedy accepted his resignation without the usual expression of good wishes, and the *New York Times* editorially expressed the two contradictory views that there was not "the slightest ground" for thinking that Savage had been moved by improper considerations in dismissing the government's case, and that in going to work for Gulf he had shown "poor judgment," because "his action tends to lessen public confidence in the independence and integrity of the Federal judiciary." Moving to Pittsburgh, Savage had entered the world of big business, eventually becoming a Gulf director and a member of the top management team. Wild customarily referred to him as "Judge Savage," and no doubt he brought an aura of the bench with him.[34]

Savage was acutely conscious that Chairman Whiteford resented lawyers getting into "policy decisions." He did not challenge Whiteford on the arrangements made with Wild. A year or so after his first accounting on the yellow pad, Wild gave him a second accounting of the same general and simple character as the first. Whiteford had now retired, and Savage proposed the establishment of a "Good Government Fund," to which individual Gulf employees would voluntarily contribute. The proposal was designed to avoid illegal contributions by the corporation. Savage once described it as "therapy," then denied that he had used the word. To the review committee he admitted that he knew that Wild made substantial political contributions but contended he had never received any accounting.[35] Wild had said that the annual $10,000 in cash to Senator Hugh Scott had come about because Savage "had not liked" an earlier arrangement by which Scott's law firm was on retainer from Gulf for $20,000 a year. The retainer had been terminated, and the cash replaced it. Savage denied that he knew of the new arrangement. His own position was that "never in service with Gulf did I handle any cash contribution to any political figure."[36]

After Savage retired in 1969, Wild reported to Gulf's chief executive, E. D. Brockett. Back in 1963 the two Texans, Brockett and Dorsey, had been kept out of earshot of the discussion of the proposed $40,000 Louisiana contribution because Whiteford considered them "Boy Scouts." Brockett told the review committee that in fact he knew nothing of the Bahamas Ex. cash or Wild's "extracurricular activities" until the Watergate revelations. Equal ignorance was asserted by Dorsey, Brockett's successor as chief executive officer and the person to whom Wild "reported" from 1972 to 1975.[37]

The committee cautiously observed that Wild was "one of the best known and most effective lobbyists in Washington" and that he was known by congressmen to be a "likely source of political contributions." The committee wondered if "alert" chief executives of Gulf would not have inquired into where his money came from. Specifically as to Dorsey the committee suggested that if he "did not know of the nature and extent of Wild's unlawful activities, he perhaps chose to shut his eyes to what was going on."[38] The committee's view chimed with Wild's on the consciousness of top management: "It was one of those things, I guess, that they—nobody wants to talk about but everybody realizes it may be going on."[39] The blindness of Brockett and Dorsey was a more telling commentary on the status of the disbursements than direct supervision of them would have been. If they chose not to know what "may" have been going on, it was because they knew they could not know and permit its continuance.

The innocence of the management of Gulf was matched by the innocence of the recipients. The review committee said it was "acutely conscious" that contributions had often been solicited from Gulf by candidates. This "merry-go-round" had involved a "pattern of joint involvement."[40] Joint involvement is the usual symbiotic relationship of contributor and candidate. But candidates were not anxious to admit that they had received criminal gifts or broken several federal criminal laws—on contributions from corporations, on contributions from contractors, on the reporting of contributions, and arguably even on unlawful gratuities and bribes. The candidates had received no bribe or unlawful gratuity, they thought, for they had promised nothing specific in return. Nor had they violated the law against contributions by corporations or by contractors when they were unaware of the source of the funds. Recipients had assumed that the money they received was Wild's own or the gift of individual Gulf employees. The idea that Gulf Oil Corporation was subsidizing them in cash had apparently not occurred to them. Wild's title and job, his ready access to funds, his lobbying activity—none of these factors informed them about the corporation behind his gifts. Their innocence had persisted although, on occasion, recipients had received one sum by check—the lawful contribution of the Good Government Fund—and another amount in cash, whose anonymous form might have raised a question.[41] That envelopes and cash were, in themselves, badges of criminality they did not admit. That there was nothing criminal, wrong, or even unusual in receiving $2,000 or $25,000 or $50,000 in bills was their tacit and unanimous position.

Reform of Congress was not the business of the Gulf review committee; the reform of Gulf was. The committee's aim was that "so far as humanly possible" steps be taken to eliminate illegal political payments by the company.[42] Its recommendations illustrated a paradox. Multinational corporations had a greater capacity to concentrate cash and hide their tracks than any briber in history. At the same time they were peculiarly subject to bounds and restraints. They depended for their existence upon a multitude of professionals. If the professionals could be made responsible, the corporation could be chained.

Specifically, the committee's first recommendation was that off-the-books accounts be prohibited. They had "no place in any publicly-held company." They provided an opportunity for abuse by the company's own employees. Moreover, the practice of keeping everything on the books was "in itself a built-in deterrent to improper importunities from outsiders." The directors had already set up new controls on the issuance of checks and disbursements of cash and had expressly forbidden illegal contributions. The committee's first recommendation, coupled with the increased powers given the company's auditors, assumed that the recordkeeping of accountants would act to inhibit illegal payments. Its second recommendation responded to "the unfortunate role played by a succession of Gulf's General Counsel," that is, Grey, Searls, and Savage. The committee proposed that the general counsel be "the keeper of the company's legal conscience." Incumbent on him would be the duty to protest if the company broke the law—to report first to the chief executive, then to the directors. The review committee stopped short of the view of some modern authorities on legal ethics that if all else failed, the general counsel had a duty to inform the government.[43]

By the very size which allowed them to exert influence, the large corporations were vulnerable to public disapproval. The committee believed that Gulf had been so buffeted—so subjected in its view to "publicity and commotion"—that the corporation would probably never again violate the law against political contributions. The crucial decisions would remain with top management. Prevented from closing their eyes by the company's accountants and lawyers, the chiefs of the corporation would undoubtedly decide to obey the law and avoid the payments functionally indistinguishable from bribes.[44]

The Interest of the SEC. Interaction of the ancient concept of corruption and the modern law of securities regulation produced the Gulf report. The Securities and Exchange Commission had no general policing function and no special charge to prevent corruption. Its mission was to prevent fraud on investors in a company with stock registered under the Securities Exchange Act. Because corrupt practices were a crime, because they had, therefore, to be hidden on a corporation's books, a corporation committing them had to engage in fictitious accounting and fraud under the securities laws. The interest of the SEC in accurate accounting created for it an interest in discouraging corruption and illegal political payments. It was the SEC's suit that had finally flushed out Gulf's system of illegal disbursements.

Suppose an intelligent and cynical investor said, "It is to my interest and the company's interest that bribes be paid on occasion. I don't care if the amounts are buried on the corporation's books if, comparatively speaking, they are not too large. Four hundred thousand dollars a year spent for political purposes is less than one-tenth of one per cent of Gulf's income. It is an infinitesimal amount, certainly an amount of no material significance to me as an investor. It was being spent in the wise discretion of experienced corporate officers for corporate purposes. It did not help my appraisal of Gulf to have the payment of these sums disclosed. When the SEC decided to force disclosure, it acted as a policeman or the holder of a roving commission. It departed from its statutory purpose."

To that complaint the SEC had an answer: It is never within the purposes of a corporation to commit a crime. Therefore the money was never spent for corporate purposes. Every investor is entitled to know if part of his investment is being used contrary to corporate purposes, criminally, so that he may disassociate himself from such an unlawful enterprise. It is always fraudulent to take money, however small the amount, on the pretext of lawful business and then use the money to break the law.

That answer might satisfy a conscientiously law-abiding investor puzzled by the SEC's concern about payments in violation of domestic law. But suppose bribes were paid overseas? Are investors and corporations citizens of the world, called on to be obedient to the law of every country? And suppose a bribe abroad is no crime but the custom of the country? The Gulf report implicitly raised these questions.

Omaggi. Gulf in 1966 had $200 million invested in plastic and fertilizer plants, shipping, and a large refinery in South Korea. With the encouragement of the American government, Korea was preparing for a democratic election. The incumbent party thought its expenses in a democratic election would be high. The incumbent party turned to foreign investors, especially American ones, to finance its campaign. A high offical in the secretariat of President Park asked Gulf for $1 million dollars. The request was "accompanied by pressure which left little to the imagination." Gulf President Bob Dorsey in Pittsburgh approved the payment. It was recorded at headquarters as a transfer to Bahamas Ex.[45]

Four years later, in 1970, there was a much heavier election challenge to the incumbents. S. K. Kim, a leader of the incumbents, summoned Korean Gulf Oil's "vice-president for governmental relations" to his office and told him that Gulf must contribute $10 million. Gulf's answer was postponed until Dorsey, on his way to Korea on other business, arrived. He at once informed Kim that the request "was almost preposterous." Kim said, in effect, although "substantially more roughly," "I'm not here to debate matters. You are either going to put up the goddamned money or suffer the consequences." Dorsey left in anger but eventually agreed that Gulf would contribute $3 million. He was, he said later, not afraid of nationalization. The payment was made because, in his judgment, "the opportunity to continue a profitable business, without unwarranted and inhibiting government interference, required it." The payment was recorded as a transfer to Bahamas Ex. and the funds were then routed through a Swiss bank account. From it, nine checks for $200,000 apiece, and $1,199,790 in cash went to make up the sum in Korea.[46]

Payments of this sort seemed to their makers to be no crime under American law, and it was at least arguable that they were not criminal in Korea: they could have been characterized not as bribes but as money extorted by the threat of official reprisals. If the money had been required in order to prevent official violence to Gulf's property, extortion would have been established. When the dominant party demanded the money as a condition for continuing business, the threat was less extreme but nonetheless coercive. A fine line separated money paid to prevent unjust intereference by officials from money paid to secure government business. No doubt an even finer line could be drawn between what was paid to fend off disaster and what was added voluntarily to increase good will—one part being extorted, the other part a willing bribe. It was Dorsey's position that the millions paid were to prevent harassment. On this basis a medieval moralist would have said that Gulf was justifiably buying off harassment, paying a kind of ransom. If a Korean court followed "the New York rule," extortion was a good defense to a charge of bribegiving. Dorsey was not a medieval moralist or knowledgeable in New York law. He did not inform the directors of what he had done. The payments were "rather delicate." Any revelation would have been "embarrassing."[47]

The large payments supplemented a second kind of off-the-books arrangement in Korea, the "Gray Fund," amounting to about $10,000 a year. The purpose of the Gray Fund was not to pay for "specific administrative or legislative favors" but "to ease access" to government agencies and "to obtain expeditious but routine action." The explanation for its existence was the low salaries of the bureaucrats who needed "gratuities" to supplement their income. Payments here were remarkably like those St. Augustine had discussed in the context of the Roman Empire in Africa and had treated as distinct from unjust bribes yet the sort of thing a devout man would avoid taking.[48]

Italy was a country which Gulf entered after World War II. Of particular interest, given the common belief of Americans in Italian corruption, there was here a large gap between most rumors about Gulf's activities in Italy and credible evidence. The Gulf review committee examined two suspicious sums, $868,000 spent in connection with the expansion of Gulf's Milan refinery and $1,200,000 spent for rights to a pipeline. The committee concluded that both expenditures were made in legitimate commercial transactions.[49]

But an off-the-books fund was run by Gulf in Italy, formally known as the "Special Account" and informally called the *Fondo Nero* or "Black Fund." In Korea, the review committee had noted the excuse of Gulf that cash tips had been used to expedite the flow of business "through the bureaucracies of a relatively inexperienced government," as though lack of experience was a relevant factor. No one could have said that Italian bureaucracies were inexperienced. Payments were, nonetheless required. For example, in the 1960s Gulf was expanding its marketing in Italy, acquiring gas stations from other companies and opening new ones. It needed permits to operate the stations. For this purpose cashier's checks paid for by the Black Fund were sent to Gulf district managers, who then disbursed the cash among the bureaucrats. The amount spent was comparatively trivial—$23,000 over a decade or no more that $2,300 a year.[50] On occasion Gulf also distributed gas coupons to officials.[51] The giving of such *omaggi,* or gifts, the committee concluded, "to lubricate the sluggish machinery of petty bureaucracy, was and is an accepted way of life which did not involve significant sums, considering the nature and volume of the government contacts." Regular corporate accounts as well as the *Fondo Nero* were drawn on to provide the cash. The practice, the committee reported, "was characterized as tipping rather than bribery and was not considered unlawful."[52]

By the passive mood "was characterized" the committee dodged the question of who did the characterizing. Tipping in its usual sense indicates open remuneration for private service with the employer's consent. Its meaning was extended when it was used to cover surreptitious payments to government functionaries. In Italy as in Korea the payments were a venial form of the practice familiar to Augustine in Roman Carthage.

"Tipping" in Italy, "paying ransom" in Korea, Gulf had conformed its practice to local conditions. The committee did not fault management for doing so but for falsifying the accounts; and the false accounts were a perverse reflection of the antibribery ethic. Management was afraid of being called bribers; it shrank from explaining Korean or Italian conditions to the directors; it took the route of avoiding explanations by concealing what needed to be explained.

Gulf's political contributions in the United States, one might urge, represented a similar conformity to local mores. Federal law made the contributions criminal, but federal lawmakers, often of great respectability, accepted them. The payments were morally no worse than political contributions to President Park's party in Korea or *omaggi* to Italian bureaucrats. They were the custom of the country. If management hid the practice from the directors it was from fear of the need for explanations. There was nothing wrong in the contributions in themselves. The antibribery ethic distorted their treatment by requiring that they be hidden.

Against this conclusion, the explicit provisions of American criminal law spoke. The custom was a "corrupt practice." In the United States the plain envelopes with cash were Gulf's way of access to the holders of political power. Those who authorized the envelopes had overstepped the line drawn by statute. The antibribery ethic not only led to the concealment of the payments, it also gave purpose to the law by which they were crimes. That $400,000 a year to American politicians could not be shrugged off as the custom of the country was soon manifest in the reactions to the Gulf review committee's report, which, packaged commercially as a paperback in half a million copies, was soon available to everyone.

Responses.   Before the disclosures forced by the Watergate prosecutor, no commentator on the loopholes in the Corrupt Practices Act and its easy evasion had suggested that any major corporation regularly broke the law and systematically distributed corporate cash to officeholders and candidates. The gap between the Gulf Report and academic speculation was extraordinarily instructive in how difficult it was to measure the amount of corruption even in a society that prided itself on its openness and on its press. Corrupt practices flourished under the noses of respectable directors, under the eye of a reasonably vigilant Washington press corps, under the scrutiny of academic analysts. The critics knew only what insiders made available.

Once the news was out, the leading newspapers—the *New York Times*, the *Washington Post*, and the *Wall Street Journal*—gave generous coverage to the report. The *Wall Street Journal*, while the Gulf investigation was under way, pondered "the rationalizations" offered by businessmen, including the extortion defense now offered by the Gulf management for what it had paid in Korea. The *Journal* did not reject the rationalizations out of hand but observed that payoffs bought "only short-term surcease" and that there was "a great deal of bargaining strength from taking a position that is morally and ethically sound." The conclusion of an editorial entitled "Business and Baksheesh" was that "the SEC may have stretched its mandate a bit, but the results have been well worthwhile." When the review committee report became public, the *Journal* told its readers that the Gulf board of directors must decide the fate of the executives involved in "the slush fund."[53]

"Slush fund" was a term that had been in common use in America for at least thirty years to describe money set aside to pay for corruption. It was a contemptuous phrase. Slush, in the experience of Northeastern city dwellers, was liquid, loose, messy, and dirty. The connotations of urban slush carried over to the political usage. Slush fund was a term designating money to be dishonorably employed.

A story leaked to the *Journal* on January 13, 1976, revealed that the Mellons intended to "clean up" the Gulf slush at a directors' meeting scheduled for that day.[54] An extended two-day board meeting in fact occurred and was reported on the basis of "inside sources" in the *Journal's* lead story of January 15, under the headlines,

> Morality Play
> Gulf Officers' Ouster
> Was Boldly Engineered
> By Mellon Interests

Brockett and Dorsey had been excluded from acting with the other directors, who then numbered twelve. Five were solidly in the Mellon camp. A Sister of Mercy, Jane Scully, recently made a director, had been neutral at first but swung to the Mellon side, and in the end the directors acted unanimously. In an atmosphere "sort of like a jury room," they demanded the resignations of Dorsey and three other high officers. Dorsey was less than two years from retirement, two of the others were only fifty years old. All were accompanied by lawyers who presented their pleas to the Mellons' lawyers, but the latter and the board remained adamant. Without release from liability or other protection, the four were made to resign. A new president, unconnected with the slush, was brought in from Gulf Canada. The headline "Morality Play" punningly summed up the action: A "play" had been made by the Mellons. A symbolic drama had been enacted.[55]

Repercussions continued. A stockholders' suit was brought against Gulf, the four retired officers, and thirteen others, seeking to recover for the corporation the money illegally spent. The company acquired leverage over Dorsey and the other retired executives by suspending their stock options. They were given the alternatives of joining in a settlement or litigating the suspension, too. On September 30, 1976, a settlement of the stockholders' suit was reached. Dorsey lost half his stock options or about $400,000 and incentive pay of $250,000. The other resignees suffered proportionally in financial penalties. Two retired officers also were forced to give up pay for 1975—Judge Savage, $100,000, and former Chairman Brockett, $150,000; while former vice-president Bounds was required to forfeit a pension. The insurer of the liability of Gulf officers and directors kicked in $2,000,000. The company agreed to pay the defendants' legal expenses (say $400,000) and up to $600,000 of the plaintiffs' fees. The McCloy investigation itself had cost the company $3,000,000. For roughly $4,000,000, the company got back something over $3,000,000. The measure of success was not monetary.[56]

Other miscellaneous penalties were exacted. The Treasury invoked the

Bank Secrecy Act of 1972 and sued Gulf for all the cash brought into the country from the Bahamas after the Act's enactment. Under the law, all the unreported dollars were forfeit. Gulf settled for $229,000 or 90 percent, a percentage accurately reflecting the small chance it had of succeeding in a trial and the largest penalty ever collected under the Act.[57]

In Bolivia, Bob Dorsey was convicted of bribery for a gift of a helicopter to the Bolivian president. As he was not in the country for his trial, the effect of the verdict was only to increase the unlikelihood that in retirement he would travel in Bolivia. The Bolivians, incredulous about the informality of Texas-style executives, insisted on condemning him as "Robert Dorsey."[58]

Announcing its settlement with its executives, the company revealed that it had been reimbursed $57,261.55 by the recipients of illegal contributions, but the reimbursers were not identified. It later became known that Senator William Brock had returned $5,000 and Congressman John Heinz $8,000. Heinz issued a statement drawing attention to his net worth of $1,300,000 and to his being the beneficiary of a trust fund of $11,000,000; for one as rich as he, he implied, the acceptance of Gulf's $8,000 was an unintentional oversight. In an article entitled "Getting Off Scott-free," *The Wall Street Journal* scolded the Senate's Ethics Committee for ignoring the case of Senator Hugh Scott and pointedly observed that he was the Republican leader in the Senate and had appointed the Republican members of the Ethics Committee. When Scott was defeated in the 1976 primaries by Heinz, interest in his case lapsed. Only one congressman was in fact prosecuted for partaking in the Gulf bounty—James R. Jones of Oklahoma, Lyndon Johnson's former appointments secretary. He was indicted by the Watergate special prosecutor, pleaded guilty to a failure to report a contribution, and was fined $200. He said the Gulf money—$1,000–$2,000—had been given him to pay a campaign debt, and that it had been delivered in cash by Judge Savage. Jones, not charged with bribery but a technical misstep, was reelected and subsequently became chairman of the House Budget Committee.[59]

Only one Gulf executive went to jail, a lawyer who was an unlikely candidate for imprisonment. He was William Viglia, the keeper of the funds and courier from the Bahamas. He had been given immunity from prosecution to tell a Watergate grand jury about Bahamas Ex. and was charged with perjury in his testimony. He was now seventy-one years old and pleaded guilty. He was sentenced in Tulsa to a year in jail for his mistaken loyalty to Gulf.[60]

In this vengeance visited on a miserable underling the criminal law exhausted itself. The true and comprehensive sanction for the corporation's conduct was the association of its name, linked alliteratively by its advertising with goodness, with the corrupt practices it had paid for in Washington, the states, and the world. Life imitating language, Gulf had greased, lubricated, oiled government officials around the globe. By its well-publicized confession, Gulf cooperated with its critics and mitigated, although it did not escape, punishment. Secret cash payments to political figures for political purposes were not called bribes but once the safe zone created by statute was deserted the payor appeared as a corruptor.

The Increasingly Difficult Distinction. While the Gulf investigation was going on, an entirely distinct case presented to the courts issues highly relevant to the recipients on Capitol Hill of Gulf's cash-filled envelopes—the case of Senator Daniel Brewster, already noted in Chapter 18 as an instance of enforcement of the criminal law. Brewster, Democrat of Maryland, was on the Post Office Committee of the United States Senate. Cyrus Anderson was a registered lobbyist for Spiegel, Inc., a mail order catalogue company. In 1967 Anderson called on Brewster, told him of Spiegel's opposition to higher postal rates, and handed him an envelope containing $5,000 in cash. Brewster said he "would do all he possibly could to be of assistance to Spiegel." Four months later a bill raising postal rates was introduced in the Senate. Anderson discussed with Brewster how to defeat the bill and had his companion hand the senator an envelope containing $4,500 in cash. In July 1967, Brewster's administrative assistant, at Brewster's order, called Anderson and asked if more money was forthcoming. After several calls, Anderson offered a Spiegel check for $5,000 with the payee blank; the administrative assistant filled in the name of a campaign committee. Within seven months Spiegel had contributed $14,500 to Brewster directly or to his campaign committee. In 1970 Anderson, Brewster, and Spiegel Inc. were indicted for bribery.[61]

The indictment was dismissed for violating a senator's constitutional immunity. On the government's appeal, the Supreme Court divided on uncharacteristic lines, an indication of the way the antibribery ethic pushed against other loyalties and principles. Two social liberals, Brennan and Douglas, and a centrist, White, accepted Brewster's contention that a bribery prosecution would be an inquiry into the motivation of a legislative act. Members of Congress, Brennan wrote, were never entirely free from political pressures to vote one way or another. The line between legitimate influence and an outright bribe could be "more a matter of emphasis than objective fact." No distinction, White observed, had been offered by the government between a bribe and a campaign contribution. It would confer on the Executive "enormous leverage" over the legislative branch to permit prosecution for taking a political contribution.[62]

Justices Marshall, Blackmun, Stewart, Burger, Powell, and Rehnquist, a spectrum whose usual positions ranged from highly liberal to highly conservative, accepted Solicitor General Erwin Griswold's argument that "taking a bribe" was not a legislative act. At the trial there would be no need for inquiry as to how Brewster had actually voted. There was a possibility of abuse by the Executive, but Congress was not "without weapons of its own." If the Court now underestimated the potential for harassment, Congress could always exempt its members. Bribes, "perhaps even more than Executive power, would gravely undermine legislative integrity and defeat the right of the public to honest representation."[63]

At the trial that followed, two provisions of modern federal bribery law, enacted in 1962 at the initiative of the Kennedy administration, came into play. Under the heading, "Bribery of public officials and witnesses," one subsection, *b*, punished by fifteen years' imprisonment anyone "corruptly" giving anything of value to an offical "to influence any official act," and subsection *c* equally punished any official "corruptly" getting anything of value "in return for being influenced in his performance of any official act." Two other subsections, *f* and *g*, punished by two years' imprisonment anyone giving anything of value to a public official "for or because of any official act performed or to be performed" and any official receiving such. Subsections *b* and *c* with their use of "corruptly" and "influence" and heavy penalty evidently sought to deal with a more serious offense than subsections *f* and *g*, which omitted "corruptly" and "influence" and set a lesser penalty. "Corruptly" characterizing the *b* and *c* offenses apparently added something to the description of the crime, but what? Often used in older bribery statutes, the word could be considered mere rhetoric specifying nothing as to the elements of criminality to be proved. The drafters of the Model Penal Code had dropped the term entirely, and their 1980 commentary declared that it had no content: it merely left the courts to decide case by case, without statutory guidance, what acts should be characterized as done "corruptly." The trials of Anderson, Brewster, and Spiegel exemplified this point.[64]

The statute, and the courts interpreting it, drew a line between a payment made "corruptly" with "intent to influence" an official act and a payment "for" an official act. The distinction was murky. The statute classified both kinds of payments as bribery. The courts taking account of the lower penalty set for the second kind called it a "gratuity." But in social function was there any difference between paying "for" the performance of an official act and paying "to influence" an official act? Was not the difference at most in the degree of proof of intent? In calling one form of bribery a gratuity were not the courts falling into the linguistic ambiguity of earlier ages where no clear word for bribe existed and the ambiguity required that, context by context, the meaning of the term be established? And what was the difference between paying "for the performance of an official act and contributing to the campaign of a legislator whose voting record one wanted to reward?[65]

Two of the payments made by Anderson were made not to a campaign committee but to Brewster directly; it may appear easy to say these payments were not campaign contributions. To do so, however, would be to ignore the custom of which the Gulf Report was such convincing evidence, that cash was often delivered on Capitol Hill classed by both payor and recipient as a campaign contribution. That custom was relied on by Anderson: he had only done what many other lobbyists did. Essentially his position was that what was generally done could not be criminal.

Spiegel, Inc., pleaded guilty to giving Brewster two bribes of the *f* kind and was fined $20,000. Anderson, after a trial, was convicted of bribery.

All three of the payments he had made for Spiegel were found by the jury to be of the *b* type. He was fined $30,000 and sentenced to $1^1/_2$ to $4^1/_2$ years imprisonment. This result seemed incongruous—the company guilty of only *f* type bribery, its own agent guilty of the more serious, "corrupt" *b* offense. But the incongruity might be explained by the mildness usually used with a defendant willing to plea bargain and give up the right to a trial. The different treatment of Anderson and the corporation paled beside the different treatment accorded Anderson and Brewster.

In the very trial in which Anderson was found guilty of corruptly giving money to Brewster, the senator was found guilty of only the lesser offense of receiving money "for an official act to be performed." Anderson appealed. How could he have "corruptly" influenced Brewster, while Brewster was not corruptly influenced? It was the old complaint of Oakes Ames. The appellate court replied as Luke Poland had to Ames, the briber could be corrupt in intent, while the bribee was "insensitive to any influence."[66]

The same judges who upheld Anderson's conviction gave Brewster a new trial. The grounds were error by the trial court's instructions to the jury on the differences between corrupt *c* bribes, unlawful *g* payments, and entirely innocent campaign contributions. The instructions given were found to have been "indigestible," indeed, incomprehensible. The statute gave "great difficulty." The trial judge "strove manfully." Still, the necessary "fine distinctions" had not been made. But the statute, Circuit Judge Malcolm Wilkey wrote, was not unconstitutional because the trial judge had "faltered." Judge Wilkey himself hesitated to say what proper instructions would be. From what the court had said, he wrote, "we trust a trial judge can distill the elements on which the jury should be instructed to focus." To reach this conclusion was for the appeals court itself to falter. The differences between *c*, *g*, and innocent campaign contributions appeared too tenuous to bear explanation.[67]

Brewster did not take great advantage from the confusion—he eventually pleaded guilty to the crime of which the first jury had convicted him, that is, of receiving money for the performance of an official act. But the inability of both trial and appellate courts to articulate the difference between innocence and guilt pointed to a grave problem in the statute and the graver and more general problem of satisfactorily distinguishing a campaign contribution from a bribe.[68]

Anderson and *Brewster* seemed to make the existence of bribery turn on the specificity of what was sought—Brewster's vote on postal rates. But the general rule was that nothing very specific needed to be proved in order to establish bribery. "No particular act need be contemplated by the offeror or offeree," the court said in Governor Kerner's case. "There is bribery if the offer is made with intent that the offeree act favorably to the offeror when necessary." Senator Williams was convicted of bribery when he had promised the Abscam Arabs nothing but his general willingness to help get contracts. How did a legislator letting a contributor know he agreed with him on "the issues" differ from an offeree ready to help an offeror when necessary? If *Anderson* and *Brewster* were correct, how could the envelopes containing cash delivered by Gulf on Capitol Hill be distinguished from the envelopes found in these cases to constitute bribes?

The Push for Purity. Campaign contributions could be criminally punished as bribes. Yet Congress had never classified illegal contributions as bribes. When in 1972 Congress had reformed the election laws and abandoned even the terminology of corrupt practices, it could have been argued that a firm separation had been made between corruption and bribery on the one hand and election law violation on the other. No doubt it would have been in the self-interest of many members of a legislature to create this kind of disassociation.

In 1974—two months after Watergate had climaxed in the president's resignation and two months after the Court of Appeals for the District of Columbia had decided *Brewster*—Congress reformed the election laws again. The continuing tendency to segregate election law violations from criminal bribery was visible. A Federal Election Committee was created. A bureaucratic regulatory body, not the Justice Department, was to be the normal overseer of compliance. The problem of campaign contributions was approached as a problem of funding. The federal subsidizing of presidential elections was strengthened and expanded to include presidential primaries. Less reliance on any identified donor was encouraged and more dependence cultivated on the anonymous taxpayers whose checkoff on income tax returns could generate the Presidential Campaign Fund. The new provisions on contributions were first inserted in the United States Code as part of Title 18, "Crimes and Criminal Procedures." They were then transferred to Title 2, "The Congress." The push for purity led the codifiers in this symbolic fashion to separate campaign funds from association with criminality.[69]

Tacitly, the provisions for new sources of funding acknowledged the corrupting effect of the oldfashioned system. Restrictions in the new law embodied other tacit admissions. To contribute more than $100 in cash to a federal campaign was made a crime—that the use of cash was a badge of bribery was implicitly acknowledged. For a member of Congress to receive more than $1,000 as an honorarium for a speech was made a crime—the use of an honorarium as an easy vehicle for a payoff was implicitly recognized. Individuals were limited to contributions by check of no more than $1,000—no one could be supposed to buy much influence or access with this kind of contribution.[70] If large cash campaign contributions did not operate as bribes, limitations of this kind made little sense. When the new legislation, under attack by Senator James Buckley as unconstitutional, came before the Supreme Court, the Court treated the reforms as supplementary to the repression of bribery.

In *Buckley v. Valeo*—an opinion of 144 pages, curiously issued per curiam—the Court upheld the restrictions on contributions. It said, "To the extent that large contributions are given to secure a political *quid pro quo* from current and potential office holders, the integrity of our system of representative democracy is undermined." The Court conceded that quantified data did not exist. "Although the scope of such pernicious practices can never be reliably ascertained, the deeply disturbing examples surfacing after the 1972 election demonstrate that the problem is not an illusory one." In this sentence "pernicious" functioned as a synonym for "corrupt." The most telling phrase were the words "deeply disturbing." The Court habitually dealt with a variety of crimes which it usually did not bother to describe as disturbing, let alone deeply disturbing. In using this phrase here the Court reflected less the individual psychology of the opinion writer than a common response to the perception of large sums of money being used to obtain official action.[71]

Bribery statutes were not in themselves sufficient to reach the evil: "laws making criminal the giving and taking of bribes deal with only the most blatant and specific attempts of those with money to influence governmental action." Less blatant, less specific attempts to exchange money for response by an officeholder could be prohibited by the laws limiting campaign contributions. "The reality or appearance of corruption," the Court held, could be the legitimate object of preventive legislation.[72]

Reality or *appearance* could be the object of prevention. Purity in the sense of the New York legislature of 1829 was what the Court was upholding. Purity in this sense was now a major purpose of the national government at the same time that purity in the sense of laws designed to uphold the family was being discarded. It is instructive to compare *Buckley v. Valeo* with the cases on pornography finding an absence of quantifiable harm in pornographic material; or with the Court's incomprehension at the purpose of sexual purity statutes—Justice Brennan, for example, finding "wholly without rational purpose" Congress's restriction of certain federal benefits to persons related by blood or marriage; Justice Stevens, for example, finding New York's law against the public dissemination of contraceptives "irrational and perverse." The Court's opaqueness on the sexual issues was not due to the individual willfulness of the Justices: it at once reflected and proclaimed the public abandonment of the old rules on sexual purity. Unself-consciously compensating, as it were, the Court upheld with vigor the rules on political purity.[73]

The Era of the PACs. The rules were not as strict as they looked. Individuals could give $1,000 to a candidate in a primary, a second $1,000 in the run-off, a third $1,000 in the general election. Spouses' and children's contributions were counted separately. $20,000 could be given a national political party as distinct from a campaign committee. Contributions to state parties were not limited, and by an amendment adopted in 1979 state parties could spend money to get out voters in a presidential election. Still, appearances were protected. The PACs threatened even appearances.

In the 1930s the unions had pioneered in forming political committees for fundraising, and by the 1940s "PAC" referred to the Political Action Committee of the CIO, a fundraising and fund-dispensing organization of legendary power. Its financial organization was changed but its capabilities were not crimped when Congress put unions under the same ban as corporations by prohibiting them from contributing to campaigns for federal office. The PAC itself was not a union. It became "the paradigm union political fund" and began to be copied by trade associations and general probusiness groups.[74]

Under the Nixon administration, a federal prosecution challenged a committee that had collected over one million dollars from members of the Pipefitters Union and contributed to federal campaigns. Union officials ran the committee. Union members paid the committee regularly. Often they were under the impression that they had to pay if they were to remain in the union. The union was convicted of violating the Corrupt Practices Act (unrepealed at the time of the prosecution). The Supreme Court, 6–2, reversed, accepting the dodge: the committee was not the union. While the case was pending on appeal, lobbyists for the AFL-CIO obtained legislative insurance against losing the case and gave the Court a nudge as to the result Congress expected—as part of the comprehensive election reform that became law in 1972, Congress specifically authorized unions to set up and administer "separate segregated funds," which could contribute up to $5,000 to any one candidate. Corporations were given the same privilege. *Pipefitters* wrote a gloss on this new provision. A prophetic dissent by Lewis Powell predicted that the Court was creating an opportunity "heretofore unrecognized" for every union and corporation. The corporations, he observed, were more numerous than the unions.[75]

The Federal Election Commission that had been created by the 1974 reform law enlarged on *Pipefitters* by explicitly advising that a union or corporation could use its own money to administer a political action committee or PAC, leaving all donations the PAC collected to be used as contributions. The era of the PACs had arrived. Few experts at this date foresaw how the PACs would increase, and how $5,000 given to several candidates multiplied by the rapidly increasing number of PACs would reach an enormous total. In 1974 there were 100 PACs, by 1976 there were 450, by 1982 there were over 3,000. By the 1980s they had become a far more important source of funds for congressional candidates than were the national parties. The influence they acquired was a major factor in the decline of the strength of the parties as organizations affecting Congress; their influence was correlated to their cash contributions.[76]

Through the 1980 elections unions gave more to PACs than corporations, and PACs gave more to Democrats than to Republicans. It was predictable, however, that corporate PACs would continue to increase and that corporate contributions would outmatch labor's. By an amendment sponsored by the unions in 1974, government contractors could have PACs. Defense contractors quickly set them up. In general, the larger the corporation, the more likely it was to have a PAC. All the big oil companies, for example, had them, although it was only in January 1983 that chastened Gulf joined the others. PACs abounded among corporations sensitive to legislation and government regulation.[77]

Corporate PACs customarily solicited their top management or all their management personnel for contributions and sometimes their stockholders as well. PACs were authorized by a corporation's chief executive officer, and their strategy was responsive to the corporation's leadership. Not the alter egos of the corporations, the corporate PACs were "at the very least their surrogates" and were "so considered by their employee/shareholder members, and more importantly, by the recipients of PAC funds and the public." The source of the PACs' money was individuals—contributing in 1980, on an annual average, $81 to corporate PACs. Did the multiple sources and small amounts make the practice innocuous if the effect of the aggregated contributions redounded to the corporation's credit?[78]

The question could not be confined to the corporate PACs if the impact of the contributions was the criterion. All PACs were open to question, including those formed by trade groups, unions, and by nonbusiness groups pursuing ideological goals. How was the PACs' acquisition of influence to be described? *Inc.*, a business magazine, described the process in 1982 in terms of what politicians wanted "to sell" and the public "to buy"; the magazine instructed businessmen in calculating the cost–vote ratio in purchasing an "equity share" in a congressman. A small share in the chairman of the House Budget Committee was better than a big share in a freshman congressman. The language was as frank and as insensitive as that of an old-time hawker of indulgences. Congressmen were scarcely less candid: "Organized special interests don't contribute to congressional candidates for the fun of it; they do so to get things done." Representatives of PACs spoke only slightly more discreetly, using the ancient terms of evasion: "With a little money, they hear you better," declared a major contributor. "PACs are not buying anyone. They're rewarding," said another. Access was all that was purchased, said a third. *Congressional Quarterly*, a journal devoted to the doings of Congress, observed that the rewards depended on "loyalty." Willingness to reciprocate was the message the PACs themselves conveyed to their donees.[79]

Reward not bribe, access not vote—the claimed distinctions had circulated since the days of Rome. The PAC representatives did not suppose that they could be confessing to federal crimes. They assumed—no doubt reasonably—that what was otherwise criminal was licensed by the license given by the election law to organize PACs in the first place.

An analogy with an old moral issue appeared relevant. In the analysis of usury advanced by theologians of the thirteenth century it was a sin for the lender to lend expecting or hoping for specific gain by a gift from the borrower; but it was no sin if the lender merely believed that his borrower might be generous. A very fine line separated sinful usurious intent and blameless awareness of the likelihood of reciprocity. It was a line too fine to be maintained except in the interior judgment of a soul. A similar mental line seemed to distinguish the lawful gift to a candidate from a bribe. "Almost a hair's line difference," said Russell Long, a senator superbly equipped by experience to know, separated a campaign contribution from a bribe. Had the statutes been able to supply the hair?[80]

Critics saw the PACs as "the new road to corruption," the legislative process "inherently distorted, even corrupted," with access purchased and, "at worst," votes being actually traded for money. In the view of Daniel H. Lowenstein, former chairman of the California Fair Political Practices Commission, a "special interest group"—that is, any group organized to lobby and raise money for candidates voting "right" on the group's issues—was open to the charge of actual bribery. Writing in 1984, he declared that "most special interest contributions are bribes." Under our system of campaign finances, he contended, "politicians and interest groups engage routinely, not in 'legalized' bribery, as is commonly supposed, but in felonious bribery that goes unpunished primarily because the crime is so pervasive."[81]

Lowenstein spoke explicitly in terms of law as it was written, not as it was enforced. He pointed out that his analysis showed that "bribe" was "a contested concept," that is, a concept whose normative meaning depended on political values. His analysis of the gap between written law, interpreted in terms of his values, and law, as enforced, meant that prosecutors had great discretion, if they came to share such values, to treat as bribes much of the ordinary financing of American campaigns.

In the 1980s a case decided under state law showed how much prosecutorial discretion existed; the case could be read as indicative of what could be done under federal law. Wanda Brandstetter, a volunteer working for ratification of the Equal Rights Amendment, handed a member of the Illinois House of Representatives a note that read, "Mr. Swanstrom the offer to help in your election and $1,000 for your campaign for Pro ERA vote." Wanda Brandstetter, like many citizens, assumed that the offer of a campaign contribution could not constitute a crime. She was charged under the Illinois bribery statute with offering "personal advantage and property" to Representative Swanstrom, convicted of bribery, and sentenced to a fine of $500 and 150 days of public service. The appellate judges thought her conduct "differed only subtly" from conduct protected by statutes or the Constitution. They nonetheless upheld her conviction.[82]

Wanda Brandstetter was no doubt not the first woman to be guilty of bribegiving but her conviction in a case where prosecutorial discretion was so doubtfully exercised had a double significance. Women were no longer on the pedestal of purity where nineteenth-century thought had placed them; they were in the political arena. The chastity that had once been enforced by law in the sexual area would now be enforced in terms of purity from corruption.

At the federal level, the discretion of federal prosecutors, controlled as it was by custom, had so far been exercised not to treat the PACs as bribers.

Public, reported payments made by PACs by means of checks were not counted as bribes. But Congress was in a position little different from the papacy in, say, 1500. No one then had shown why payments for indulgences were not simony, sinful like other simoniacal gifts, except that the papal curia authorized them. The pope depended on their sale for a good share of his income. Was the curia, short of a cataclysm, to cut off the sale? Congressmen were like members of the curia who had to run their congregations and needed gifts from their petitioners to do it. The sin of simony hovered over a required gift; bankruptcy and failure threatened the congregation without an income. However arbitrary, a line had to be drawn. Congressmen whose campaigns had to be funded drew a not dissimilar line and used not dissimilar licenses. The distinction between what was lawful and unlawful was subtle to the *Brandstetter* court, fine to the *Brewster* court, almost a hair to Senator Long—in fact the distinction was made on no principled basis. Depending on the decision of the prosecutor and the will of the judges, many contributions could be classed as bribes.

Meanwhile, federal law enacted by Congress began to reach further and further to criminalize the bribery committed by Americans everywhere. Federal bribery law had been applied to the most local American activities. Where the PAC licenses did not apply, it was being enforced against the congressmen themselves. Finally the federal standard was to be stretched to cover the world.

20

The Ambassadors of America

"In Intelligence operations, money is an essential ingredient; even where other motives arise—as patriotism or ideological affiliation—money, however little, or its equivalent, must be dropped in, like a touch of bitter in a mint julep, to validate the deal. Only when money has passed is the mystical union fully established." In these words Malcolm Muggeridge recalls his work for the English secret service in World War II. "I found," he writes, "that bribery, which inevitably played a large part in my Lourenço Marques activities, had as many subtleties and diversities as seduction. Thus, in certain circumstances, the passing of money had to be engineered in such a way that it seemed to happen of itself, which, in seduction terms, was the equivalent of lolling or reaching out an arm as though by accident." There is an implicit moral criticism in his comparing his bribing activity to seduction. The critique is muted. It is taken for granted that intelligence activities will go on; that governments will bribe the officials of neutral foreign governments; that the techniques are standard and the practice universal. When the Americans arrive in Lourenço

Marques, they are not different; they merely raise "the accepted tariff of bribes to astronomical proportions."[1]

"If our Minister in Chile had been worth his salt he would have bought up all the telegraph people"—so Lord Fisher, First Sea Lord, to Winston Churchill, First Lord of the Admiralty, on January 25, 1915, as the British Navy hunted the *Dresden* off the coast of Chile. There is no reserve, no shame in the thought of buying up the Chilean telegraphers. To the contrary, the failure to bribe is a criticism. The British Minister, Francis W. Strange, is "effete" and "seems a bloody fool" for doing nothing.[2]

Muggeridge was a distant agent of Churchill's government in World War II, Fisher was his immediate subordinate in World War I. In neither case can one suppose that Churchill disapproved of a technique so taken for granted in dealing with foreigners. Contrast his reaction when his son Randolph suggested that he had made a small gift to Leslie Hore-Belisha with an ulterior motivation (the time was 1938; Churchill was still out of office, Hore-Belisha was in). Churchill was deeply offended at Randolph's light-hearted comment. He wrote:

It was a base thing for you to suggest the small gift I gave was given to curry favor presumably in the hopes of gaining political or personal advantage. It was given out of kindness of heart, & of some pity wh I felt for a man I do not much like, but who had appealed to me for advice and spoken much of his loneliness, etc. I wonder that you are not even now ashamed tht such a thought shd have sprung so readily to yr mind and yr lips. I hve not deserved it of you.[3]

Insinuation that even a small present to a cabinet officer will function like a bribe is "base." The same Churchill is not in disagreement with Fisher about Chile and presides over a government that routinely employs bribery like Muggeridge's abroad. What is the distinction? In war against an enemy much is permitted by ordinary morals that is ordinarily prohibited; but Chile and Portugal were not enemies, and, as Muggeridge intimates, intelligence operations also go on in peace. A war-born sense of urgency underlays Fisher's frustration but does not account for his assurance that bribery is an unobjectionable option. At bottom is the conviction that bribing foreigners is not like bribing your own. The bribery ethic stops with your countrymen. Fisher, Muggeridge, Churchill, representative Englishmen, are representative of the tradition. Foreigners, it is easy to believe, are corrupt anyway. "Isn't everybody corrupt there?" is the question James Bryce reported that Englishmen usually asked a traveler who had come back in the 1880s from the United States. In paying off a foreigner one merely conforms to local custom.[4]

The bribery ethic had been fashioned in part in response to bribes paid by subject peoples—by the Sicilians in Cicero's time, by the Indians in Hastings's. It had indeed been easier to see the wrongs of bribery at a distance than at home. But those bribed had been high officials of the home government; it was the purity of the imperial nation which the bribery ethic protected, objection had not been made to bribes paid the Sicilians or the Indians. Although the meaning of bribery was colored by a strong ethical content, its definition for many government officials, even those as morally sensitive as Churchill, was by law; and law stopped at national boundaries.

Bribery abroad was not boasted of at any time. Muggeridge's disclosure, although not unique, is uncharacteristic of secret service agents—there are secrets that are kept. The British government did not publicly announce the buying of friendly officials. The ethical connotations of bribery operated as a restraint, as did, even more, an awareness that all civilized countries had some laws on bribery—the bought officials could not be publicly identified. Discretion, but not moral objection, accompanied the payment of overseas bribes.

Necessity, the rationale for bribery during war or for intelligence, was equally present for any nation dependent on foreign commerce when commerce was protected or obtained by bribery. At the turn of the century Joseph Conrad put the argument in terms of Charles Gould, the fictional English manager of an American mine in the hypothetical Latin American state of Costaguana: "Charles Gould was competent because he had no illusions. The Gould Concession had to fight for life with such weapons as could be found at once in the mire of corruption that was so universal as almost to lose its significance. He was prepared to stoop for his weapons." Gould has the belief and justification that once "the material interests get a firm footing," there will be order and security, and "a better justice will come afterwards." A better justice later, but Gould does not think himself unjust as he sends his agent each month to pay off the junta in the capital.[5]

Suppose the belief in a better justice came to be seen as a colonialist's illusion. Suppose the confident separation of breeds without the law from the law-abiding became doubtful. Suppose the bringing together of the world by communications meant that national boundaries were easily disregarded. Suppose a greater sense of the dignity of each people became more general. Such suppositions became realities a generation after World War II. Under the immediate impact of American political events, and under American auspices, they affected the bribery tradition, hitherto so nationalistic in its application, and made its ambit global.

The development is best exemplified by what happened in the 1970s to Lockheed Aircraft Corporation of Burbank, California, a company that bore a relation to the government of the United States in significant ways similar to that which the East India Company had held to the government of England. Lockheed was in the 1960s the nation's largest defense contractor, dependent for its existence on procurement orders from the Defense Department; by the same token, the Defense Department was dependent on it for planes and missile systems. Like the East India Company, Lockheed did a large part of its business with foreigners. A substantial part of its revenue came from the sale of military and commercial aircraft abroad. In 1971, as Lockheed's credit faltered, the United States did what England had done for the East India Company: it made its own credit available—in this instance by a guarantee of Lockheed's borrowings up to $250,000,000. The creation of a government agency, the Emergency Loan Guarantee Board, or ELGB, made the relation closer by giving the ELGB vague supervisory authority over a corporation that still remained entirely owned by its stockholders. The hybrid character of this public-private entity made it peculiarly exposed to the political currents and the requirements of law in the 1970s.

As Lockheed's payments abroad to the officials of foreign governments became public before a global audience, the main questions present in any historical presentation of bribery were implicitly raised: If these payments were to be called bribes was it by application of American law or by application of American ethics or by application of foreign law or foreign ethics? If the law of any country was chosen, was it law as announced or as enforced? If an ethical standard was used, what group's standard was to be chosen? Without formally addressing these questions, the accountants, lawyers, and directors of Lockheed, the Emergency Loan Guarantee Board and the Securities and Exchange Commission, two committees of the United States Senate, and governments from Japan to the Netherlands struggled with answers to them. To a striking degree, once the payments were public—once, so to speak, the money was out on the table—there was agreement about their ethical status. Ethically the concept of the bribe was now universal or almost universal. The upshot of the Lockheed affair and similar disclosures by other American corporations was to be an effort by the United States to give the concept universal legal significance.

Lockheed's case divides into three stages—revelations at home, within the company and the country; foreign repercussions; and confessions.

Domestic Disclosures

Ever since 1933, Lockheed's income and expenditures had been inspected, tabulated, reconciled, and summarily stated to its stockholders and the world by its public auditors, Arthur Young and Company. Two hundred persons were employed, 25,000 hours of time were spent in the annual outside audit. Up to 1971, so far as the record was to show, Arthur Young and Company had known nothing of the off-the-books accounts, the frauds and the deceptions covering the payments with which eventually every newspaper reader was to be made familiar.[6]

From 1972 to 1974 the auditors showed uneasiness but required the corporation to make no changes. The usual veils were in place. The usual assumptions were made. Inside and outside accountants and lawyers were quiescent. The knowledgeable directors were content. Lockheed, with remarkable foresight, had not violated the bribery or election laws of the United States even to get the $250,000,000 guarantee from the Nixon administration and a closely divided Congress. Lockheed had been unscathed by the Watergate prosecutor. Its way of doing business overseas was untouched.[7]

What changed this comfortable contentment? The Watergate prosecutor's program for disclosure of illegal corporate campaign contributions, coupled with such admissions as those made by Gulf, had shown that the money a corporation sent out of the country might return —laundered, as the phrase went—to be used illegally in the United States. A second factor entered the situation in 1975.

On February 3, 1975, Eli Black, chairman of United Brands Corporation, threw himself from the twenty-second story of the Pan-American Building in New York. The dramatic death of the chief executive of a major corporation excited the attention of the SEC. The Commission investigated the company, the biggest American producer of bananas and since its start in 1900 under the name of the United Fruit Company, a power in Central America. The SEC found among other matters that had preyed on the mind of Black, a former rabbi, was an agreement he had made to pay $2,500,000 to high officials of Honduras to relax a tax on bananas. Payment of half of this amount had precipitated a power struggle at United Brands before his death.[8]

In April 1975 the SEC sued United Brands, charging the company with securities fraud in not reporting to the SEC the $1,250,000 installment paid. News of the suit could not be confined to the United States. The Honduran parliament began an inquiry, and when President Oswaldo Lopez Arellano refused to open his bank records to the investigators, a military coup removed him.[9]

That the suicide of a company's president and the fall of a country's president should be linked to a large sum paid high government officials by an American corporation became arguments for Stanley Sporkin and the enforcement staff of the SEC: secret overseas payments by a corporation were of material interest to investors. Such transactions should now be disclosed—not with the aim of leading their makers to suicide but to inform the investing public. The SEC asked all companies subject to its sway to reveal to the Commission "questionable" payments made by them abroad. Like the Watergate prosecutor, the Commission implied there would be leniency for the guilty who confessed, harshness for the guilty who kept silence. A questionnaire requesting this information reached Lockheed at the end of April 1975.[10]

Converging on Lockheed's situation was an investigation being conducted by the Senate headed by Senator Frank Church, Democrat of Idaho. Hostility aroused by the increase in the price of Arab oil, sentiments fanned by the Israeli lobby, and anticapitalist ideology symbolically represented by the Institute of Policy Studies all fed into Church's Subcommittee on Multinational Corporations. The committee looked into OPEC, then into the Arab League's boycott of Israel. On June 9, 1975, it took up Northrop Corporation, a major supplier of aircraft to Saudi Arabia.

Northrop had already pleaded guilty to a felony: a federal contractor, it had contributed to a federal campaign. Its executives may have had the sense that its competitor had escaped too lightly. Admitting having paid

$450,000 to a Saudi agent, Adnan Khashoggi, and $750,000 to a Swiss agent, Hubert Weisbrod, its executives now testified to channeling commissions on sales to European governments to a Swiss corporation. They described this device as "based on the Lockheed model," an analogy widely interpreted as suggesting that their conduit for improper payments had been copied from Lockheed. The spotlight of public attention was turned in Lockheed's direction.[11]

The incident led Arthur Young and Company to a new and stringent stand. No doubt, the Watergate and SEC probes had already made the auditors apprehensive. Now they announced that they would not certify Lockheed's accounts unless the officers signed statements that all payments to consultants were in accordance with contracts and duly recorded on company books. This request was no more than the description of the arrangements already furnished to outside counsel, and it was the description that had satisfied the auditors before. In the climate of 1975 the officers would not sign.

With uncertified accounts, the company could not send out proxy material for a stockholders' meeting already scheduled for July 18, 1975. The sudden delay caused questions. First the board of directors, then the ELGB, then the SEC and the staff of two committees of the Senate came to know part of the truth: Lockheed had been making payoffs abroad. On August 24, 1975, the treasurer of Lockheed, a fifty-four-year-old bachelor, shot himself to death.[12]

The first outside agency to react to the information about the payments was the Senate Banking Committee, headed by Senator William Proxmire of Wisconsin, a critic of the government's guarantee of Lockheed's debts. Without attempting to say whose definition of bribery he was using—presumably it was the ethical definition that he believed to be accepted by American morals—Proxmire denounced the payments as bribes. Opening hearings on "Lockheed Bribery" on August 25, 1975, Proxmire called attention to the connection between the guarantee and what he called the bribes. The Banking Committee had been assured in 1971 that Lockheed had enough orders to repay the loans guaranteed, but "none of us ever suspected at the time that the ability of the company to achieve its projected sales figure was in any way dependent on bribes to foreign officials." Lockheed, Proxmire suggested, had either misrepresented its condition or withheld material information. He wanted to know what the ELGB, chaired by Secretary of the Treasury William Simon, would now do.[13]

To say that bribery overseas was company policy in which the United States acquiesced was to make an unprecedented admission. No American official in 1975 would have made himself the defender of bribery anywhere. The ELGB, Secretary Simon told Proxmire, "does not and will not condone illegal and unethical activities by American business here or abroad." On the other hand, he said, the Board did not want to put Lockheed at a competitive disadvantage or force it out of business.[14]

In public hearings with the secretary of the Treasury before him, Prox-mire assumed that Secretary Simon agreed that the payments were bribes; on the basis of this assumption Proxmire observed that there was a contra-diction in Simon's position. The secretary of the Treasury said he "abhorred bribery." He also said he would take no action to stop it. The ELGB, if it chose, could refuse to extend the guarantee and Lockheed would go bankrupt; the government's leverage was decisive if it wished to use it. "Do you have any question at all that these are not bribes?" asked Proxmire. Simon had not. He had been misunderstood. The ELGB would require that the bribery stop. A resolution had been prepared for a Sep-tember 8 meeting of the Lockheed directors. "This will stop and stop now?" asked Proxmire. "Yes, sir. That is correct," answered Simon.[15]

Daniel Haughton, Lockheed's chairman, followed Secretary Simon as a witness in the open hearings. He doubted that Lockheed's treasurer had killed himself because of the furor over the payments; he had just "been working very hard." Haughton refused to disclose the recipients of the money. He denied that loans guaranteed by the United States had financed the payments. Total advances on foreign sales had always ex-ceeded commissions. Proxmire asked, "You are requiring the country to whom you sell to in effect pay the bribe or make the payment?" "Well, we try to," answered Haughton. "You say these bribes paid off to the best of your knowledge? It was money well spent?" pressed Proxmire. "I don't necessarily call these bribes," Haughton replied. "Maybe the customer does not feel that way about it." Proxmire asked, "How do you feel about it?" "Well," said Haughton, "I feel under the circumstances that it is a cost of winning the competition."[16]

Proxmire paid no attention to Haughton's refusal to acknowledge that the payments were bribes. He denounced "the imperial corporation" which flouted the laws of other countries and now stood "a self-confessed briber," compounding its fault by refusing "to give the government and the public details of the bribes." His tone implied that this position would not last long. His severity reflected the popular American feeling put more lightly by the satirist Russell Baker in a column in the *New York Times* called "My Money Lies over the Ocean." Baker wrote, "I believe everyone should have an equal opportunity to get rich on the Lockheed Corpora-tion's money. After all, Lockheed's money is really my money, since I pay the taxes that keep it from collapsing." Unlike any ordinary American cor-poration operating overseas, Lockheed had to account to the government, the taxpayer, the censorious citizen.[17]

The Lockheed directors met on September 8, 1975, and adopted as com-pany policy a resolution whose effect, Haughton said, was to ban "payments" to foreign officials "directly or indirectly." The term "bribes" was avoided. Negotiations with the SEC for a consent decree were approved. The ELGB was assured that Lockheed would implement the new policy fully.[18] Four days later the Church committee, armed with Lockheed documents obtained from the auditors, continued the exposures with Haughton again its witness.

"Lockheed does not defend or condone the practice of payments to foreign officials," Haughton began. "We only say the practice exists, and that in many countries it appeared, as a matter of business judgment, necessary in order to compete against both U.S. and foreign competitors." Necessity, it appeared, was Houghton's justification. The boldness of this position was almost at once belied. Haughton no longer had the company behind him.[19]

Lockheed payments in Iran, the Philippines, and elsewhere were publicly exposed. Lockheed's relations with Dasaad Musin, its intermediary in Indonesia under Sukarno, were, for example, explored at length. Dasaad, rated by Lockheed as being in "a unique position" with Sukarno, customarily took a 3 percent commission. When, three years after Sukarno's fall, Dasaad finally lost his influence, he was eliminated as an agent. The commission rose to 5 percent and Lockheed found itself dealing directly with Indonesian military officers, paying part of the 5 percent into an account called with rich irony "The Widows and Orphans Fund."[20]

Dasaad's operations paled besides those of Lockheed's representative in Saudi Arabia, whose name might have been extravagantly invented by Dickens. Adnan Khashoggi was a Stanford-educated Saudi who first came to prominence in arranging the Saudi purchase of tanks from France. Also employed by Northrop, he had been Lockheed's agent since 1964. In the five years looked at by the committee, 1970 to 1975, commissions paid by Lockheed on Saudi sales amounted to $106 million. Khashoggi had received most of the money, dividing it with anonymous officials whose names Lockheed correspondence, except for a reference here or there to a Saudi prince, did not reflect. The commissions typically went to Lockheed's "consultant," Triad Financial Establishment, a Liechtenstein corporation, controlled by Khashoggi. Typically, too, one sale required several contracts, each setting out a different commission, because Khashoggi, as a Lockheed letter delicately put it, had "a personal need for several documents in lieu of one." For example, a sale of C-130 military planes in 1967 was effected with one consultant's contract to Triad showing a 2 percent fee; a second contract of the same date showing a 5 percent fee; and a third showing a 5 percent fee plus $41,000 per plane. Inferably, different officials were shown different contracts. Khashoggi's commissions became higher in 1973 as, according to Haughton, "more players" became involved.[21]

Haughton was pressed hard to be specific as to why payments anywhere had been necessary. Did he actually know of similar payments made by Lockheed's competitors? He had come armed with a recent article in the London *Sunday Telegraph* describing the French Defense Ministry as "Le Ministère des Pots-de-Vin," or "The Ministry of Bribes," and Khashoggi as the usual middleman. Haughton said smart American newspapermen would tell you "that this is in fact a way of life overseas." But he himself provided nothing of his own knowledge. The most he would say was, "Well, a lot of times we don't win, we lose," leaving the implication that when Lockheed lost there had been a payment by someone else.[22]

Senator Clifford Case, Republican of New Jersey, referred to the payments as "bribes." Haughton challenged him : "We call them kick-backs." Senator Church asked what the difference was. Haughton replied that a kickback was "where you have something in the price . . . that you return to the buyer." He continued, "A bribe to me is where you go to somebody and say I would like for you to do something for me, and I will pay you *x*. Now that is the way it comes through to me. I am not an author-ity on these matters." Senator Church did not resist the opening: "If you are not one, I don't know who is." No senator picked up Haughton's evi-dent equivocation: a kickback, as he described it, went back to the buyer; but the payments of which he spoke went not to the buyer but personally to the agents of the buyer.[23]

Lockheed correspondence referring to the payments was often encoded. The code for "consultant" was "locust." The senators inquired how the word had been chosen. The answer was that a computer had selected it. Senator Charles Percy, Republican of Illinois, commented, "Maybe a com-puter can think." Senator Church said, "Even the computer had a con-science." Senator Case told the story of a man convicted of cheating his clients; the judge asked if he was not ashamed of cheating those who trusted him; the criminal asked, "Whom else can you cheat?" This subver-sion of "people who necessarily have to put their trust in you," Case went on, was why Lockheed's operations were regarded with disgust.[24]

Senator Joseph Biden, Democrat of Delaware, asked Haughton whether he would condone Biden stuffing ballot boxes if his opponent did it; Haughton replied no.

BIDEN: Then I would be curious to know why not.

HAUGHTON: In the first place, it is against the laws of the United
    States.

BIDEN: That hasn't stopped you.

HAUGHTON: I haven't stuffed any ballot boxes.

For Haughton, the line was clear—dishonesty depended on American law. The senators were bewilderingly bent on being universalists.[25]

Senator Church observed, "When you pass fat wads of money to these foreign officials, you greatly influence whether they are going to buy an airplane or whether they are going to import some wheat. . . . Look at the result of the latest Italian election where the Communists made startling gains because of the common perception that the Communist Party was the only one that wasn't involved in gigantic ripoffs." To these remarks, Haughtons's response was to reread his statement repudiating the making of payments in the future.[26]

The hearings were hard for Haughton, laughed at and lectured by the senators; but the area of disclosure had been limited. Negotiations with the SEC continued. Lockheed retained the Washington law firm of Rogers and Wells, whose senior partner, William Rogers, had been secretary of

State from 1968 to 1972. On November 28, 1975, the firm obtained from Rogers's successor, Secretary of State Henry Kissinger, a letter to the Justice Department. Kissinger asked Justice to give consideration to requesting a federal court to issue "a protective order" prohibiting "premature disclosure" of the names and nationalities of certain foreign officials alleged to have received "covert payments from Lockheed." Kissinger's reason was that "the making of any such payments and their disclosure can have grave consequences for significant foreign relations interests of the United States abroad." Kissinger did not characterize what was done as bribery but he "reiterated our strong condemnation of any such payments." He did not wish, he wrote, to block law enforcement by the United States. In effect, he stuck to the old rules. Bribery overseas was foreign policy not domestic crime.[27]

This diplomatic intervention was successful. In the federal district court where the SEC complaint was pending, the SEC was forbidden to release names and nationalities. But the order had no impact on the Church Committee, which continued to examine documents subpoenaed from Arthur Young and Company. In the view of Lockheed's president, "Somebody, for some reason, wanted to further expose Lockheed activities."[28]

On February 4, 1976, the Church Committee made public a new selection of documents culled from the Lockheed files. Among bank entries by Crédit Suisse, transfers of foreign exchange by Deak & Co., and receipts for yen in cash signed by Lockheed's "confidential agent" Yoshi Kodama, with even the proper revenue stamp attached, one receipt stood out:

> August 9, 1973
>
> I received One Hundred Peanuts
>   (s) Hiroshi Itoh

Itoh, soon to be identified as a contact with the office of the prime minister of Japan, must eventually have been struck by the incongruity of this code. In later receipts, "Peanuts" became "pieces." But the harm was done when the document was captured by the Senate's investigators. Nothing could have been more dangerous than to have been made ludicrous.[29]

Another document certain to whet public interest was a letter handwritten by Roger Smith, Lockheed's former general counsel, at the time the letter was written a company consultant in Europe. It was addressed to Charlie Valentine, director of contracts at Lockheed-Georgia, a Lockheed subsidiary, and dated from the Grand Hotel, Rome, March 28, 1969. Its subject was a "Legal Retainer Agreement" with the Lefevres, Italian lawyers. Under the heading "Compensation to Third Persons" Smith wrote: "Please hold on to your seat, as what follows may be a shocker to you (I am somewhat inured due to the P-3 exercise). To get you in the proper state of

mind, you should know that Ovidio Lefevre (this is strictly his department) states that Gelac [Georgia Lockheed], if it wishes the maximum run
of success, must be prepared to go as high *as* $120,000 *per airplane* for the
cumshaw pot." The money would go to "the party" and to "the Antelope
Cobbler." "The party"—presumably the Christian Democratic party in
control of the government—was put derisively in quotation marks, indicating Smith's belief that this was a fib. The Antelope Cobbler was
unexplained code. "Get out your little black book" was all Smith wrote by
way of explanation. With such delectable phrases spread before the
public—the cumshaw pot, the Antelope Cobbler, and the little black book
joining the One Hundred Peanuts—Lockheed's fat was in the fire.[30]

Senator Percy announced, "Previous hearings of this Subcommittee
have dealt with payoffs, bribes and corruption in the less developed
world. Many people, including diplomats at the OCED, have scoffed at
these practices as being unimportant because they constitute standard
business practices in the third world. Today we shall see that those 'standard business practices' come quite close to home. . . . We will deal with in-
dustrialized nations . . . allies of the United States." William Findley, the
Arthur Young partner in charge of the Lockheed account, testified about
cash payments made by Lockheed in Europe and Japan and an off-the-
books account in Geneva.[31]

Two days later Lockheed's president, A. Carl Kotchian, was put on
public display. He testified about the off-the-books account in Switzerland, then about a million dollars paid to "a high government official in
the Netherlands." Senator Church asked if Kotchian wouldn't call the
million dollars a bribe. Lockheed's management still resisted the characterization. Kotchian answered, "I think, sir, that as my understanding of a
bribe is a quid pro quo for a specific item in return . . . I would characterize
this more as a gift. But I don't want to quibble with you, sir."[32]

Senators touched on Lockheed payments in Germany, Italy, and
Sweden. Japan was the main area of concentration. "All I really remember," Kotchian wrote of the hearing later, were "the crew of reporters
from Japan and other European countries" and "the tremendous television lights." He also remembered "being very severely questioned and interrogated by the senators." He felt "particularly uncomfortable" when
asked to divulge the names of the Japanese who had recommended the
payments to high government officials: "all in all, it was a very painful two
and a half hours."[33]

Among the most pained people of all were those at the United States
Department of State. James D. Hodgson, secretary of Labor under Nixon,
had been for eighteen years Lockheed's expert on industrial relations. In
1973–1974, he had been a senior Lockheed vice-president at Burbank.
When in 1974 he was selected for a diplomatic post by the Ford administration, the appointment must have been intended as an American seal of
approval for Lockheed, unless the administration was more naïve than it
is usually credited with being. In an open, honorific way his selection con-

firmed Lockheed's special status. At the time the Church committee produced its disclosures and Lockheed became a word of ill omen in Japan, Lockheed's veteran officer was the American ambassador to Japan.[34]

Unprecedentedly, governments around the world had been told by American senators in the most public of forums, a Senate hearing, that they had been bribed. Disclosure of the payments and their denunciation as bribery put each affected government on the spot: would it look further? Implicitly the Church committee asked other governments to cooperate in enforcing a universal ethic. Would they respond? Reactions in the Netherlands, Italy, and Japan were representative.

Foreign Repercussions

Colonel Pantchoulidzew and the Legacy of the World Wildlife Foundation. No names were mentioned when Kotchian told the Church Committee about $1,000,000 paid to a high official of the Netherlands and declined to quibble as to whether the million was a bribe or not. Almost immediately a leak from the committee revealed the name of the recipient. It was His Royal Highness, Bernhard, Prince of the Netherlands, consort of Queen Juliana. In Holland, Bernhard formally informed the prime minister that Kotchian's testimony was untrue. The prime minister, four days after Kotchian's statement was made, created a "Commission of Three" to determine the truth.[35]

The swift appointment of the commission, its membership (an eminent judge, an accountant, and a banker representative of the three major parties, Christian Democrat, Labor, and Liberal), and its actual inquiries were evidence of the gravity of an open charge of bribery. The monarchy, a largely symbolic institution, was touched when the prince consort stood accused of such activity. The final report of the Commission of Three was completed six months later. In its remarkable mixture of boldness and timidity, bluntness and circumspection, reservations and self-contradictions, it was eloquent evidence of the difficulty experienced by members of the Dutch establishment in acknowledging that the prince of the Netherlands had brought shame upon himself and his adopted country.

According to what the commission learned from the Lockheed files and officers and set out in its report, the idea of paying H.R.H. Bernhard had originated in late 1959 under the regime of Robert Gross, then the chairman of Lockheed. Gross was "a personal friend" of the prince. It was their "long friendship" which "inspired the idea of a gift." That Lockheed had just won a Dutch military contract for its F-104 Starfighter had "no connection whatever." The gift was to be a Lockheed Jet Star, a present which would "create a favorable atmosphere for the sale of Lockheed products in the Netherlands." But Lockheed "could not find any suitable way of transferring the ownership of the aircraft to the prince free of charge." The company consequently decided to give him cash. The amount was arrived at by calculating "what commission would be payable on the machines to be supplied to the Netherlands in the coming three years." This amount was rounded off to $1 million.[36]

The Commission of Three recited this story without comment—a "gift" that had no connection with the sale of the Starfighter yet had a cash equivalent fixed in terms of a commission on the Starfighter; a gift that was supposed to create favorable publicity yet could not be made publicly; a gift from a "personal friend" (as though there were impersonal friends) yet was to be made by the corporation. The method of payment, set out in a letter from Roger Smith, Lockheed's general counsel, to Gross, was arranged in this way: Smith visited the prince at his palace at Soestdijk on September 30, 1960, and was told that the million should be paid through Hubert Weisbrod, a Zurich lawyer (also Northrop's agent). Smith would be contacted three days later at the Hotel Dolder in Zurich with instructions as to the bank account into which Weisbrod should deposit the money. The contact would be made by a member of the staff of the prince's family with an unforgettable name, Colonel Pantchoulidzew. In due course Pantchoulidzew made the arrangements, and Lockheed paid $1 million into the account.[37]

The commission did not say that H.R.H. Bernhard had accepted the money as a bribe. In part, at least, this conclusion was not reached because the commission could not find out what he had done for the money. In part, it was because the commission found that the procurement of the Starfighter had not been influenced by him. As far as Bernhard had left any visible trail, he had been promoting not the Starfighter but a rival product produced by Northrop. "If the gift offered had indeed influenced his judgment, this opinion would have had to be worded more harshly. But the Commission has found no evidence of this." Unlike Congress dealing with James Brooks in 1873, the Commission of Three would not find a man bribed unless they could find that he had delivered.[38]

The commission did, however, discover two later incidents, inexplicable if H.R.H. had been merely a passive bystander when Colonel Pantchoulidzew helped start the million dollar bank account. In 1968 Lockheed's P-3 Orion was losing out to the Bréguet Atlantique as the Royal Dutch Navy's choice for an antisubmarine plane. Kotchian sent Smith to visit the prince at Annecy, France, to offer him $500,000 if he could get the decision reversed. The commission, in the strongest passage in its report, said the offer had "all the features of an attempt at bribery" but "was evidently not felt by the prince to be dishonorable or improper." Bernhard declined it because the decision had already been made. Kotchian, however "wished to show his appreciation of the prince's honesty by offering $100,000 just the same." The $100,000 was paid from Lockheed's off-the-books account. The prince said he never got the money. The payee, Victor Baarn, was believed by the commission to be fictitious. The commission engaged in its own mild irony when it reported that "it was said" that the $100,000 was in appreciation of the prince's honesty.[39]

The second incident occurred in 1974. The Royal Dutch Navy was again looking at the P-3 Orion. H.R.H. in his own hand wrote Smith (at the time counsel to Coudert Frères, the New York–Paris law firm) suggesting that Lockheed might now succeed and that a 4 percent commission for the life of the program, payable to Weisbrod, would be appropriate. Lockheed headquarters calculated that the commission being requested would amount to between $4 million and $6 million, and turned it down. Smith reported to the prince that it was too much. When the Lockheed calculations were mentioned to him, H.R.H. "was astonished and said that he had only a sum of about $1 million in mind." He accordingly wrote Lockheed again, stating that since 1968 he had spent a great deal of time and effort to get the right decisions made and to prevent wrong decisions based on political considerations. A rejection of his proposal would never have happened in the days of Robert Gross or Courlandt Gross. He would do no more about the procurement program, a statement the commission found to be a "concealed threat." The letter made an impression in Burbank. Smith was instructed to proceed to the palace at Soestdijk and open discussions leading to a flat $1 million if four aircraft were ordered. The prince agreed and said the money should be paid into a Geneva bank account. Removal of the antisubmarine planes from the navy budget led to the whole deal falling through.[40]

Confronted with his own handwriting, Bernhard said he would have "considered it impossible that he could have written such things." But the texts he had penned came, he said, from Fred Meuser (another Lockheed agent) and Smith, and in his mind "the whole thing" was only a way of being able "to make a big contribution to the World Wildlife Fund," an environmentalist charity of which he was president.[41]

Like a many-faceted tutelary deity, the prince was a patron of tourism, alpine sport, and hunting. The prince's thought in the context of the investigation that an environmentalist motive would cover him was an instructive index of what rated high among good causes. Nothing in fact in the correspondence with Lockheed suggested that the six or four or one million dollars for which he negotiated would be contributed to the World Wildlife Fund. As an unpersuasive footnote to this unpersuasive explanation of his motive the prince declared to the commission that Meuser, now as he believed the beneficiary of Lockheed's $1 million, had recently promised him to leave a large portion of his estate to the WWF.[42]

Taking Bernhard's story at face value, the Commission of Three primly observed that a good end could not justify bad means. It characterized Lockheed's requests of the prince in 1968, and the prince's requests of Lockheed in 1974, as "improper" and even as "extremely questionable." The commission said generally that Bernhard's relations with Lockheed had gone "awry." It spoke of the proposed gift of the Jet Star as a conceivably proper gesture but went on, "When a gift of money was made in its place the relations became sullied." In this sentence the language usually used to describe the dirty effect of bribes was employed. The prince's later initiatives were "completely unacceptable."[43]

The commission submitted its draft "to the prince and his advisors." Its final report bore the marks of negotiation and compromise. Overriding its harsh language was a milder voice saying only that the prince's conduct had been "extremely unwise and imprudent." Faced with the prince's own handwritten assertion to Lockheed that for years he had worked for "the right decisions," the Commission of Three was unable to find that his judgment had been bought.

Bernhard was forty-nine years old when he met Roger Smith in Soestdijk in 1960, and he was sixty-three when he dealt with him in 1974. He was of royal descent, a nephew of the last prince of Lippe, no ill-educated royal scion but a hardworking German, with an earned law degree from the University of Berlin as well as an honorary law degree from the University of Utrecht. He was not innocent of big business; in his youth he had been an employee of I.G. Farben and in his later years he founded the Bilderberg Conferences "to further human relations between leading personalities in Europe and the United States." He was not penniless or dependent on a small allowance. His salary from the government was about $300,000 a year, his wife's $1,700,000. In his appearances before the commission he complained of a bad memory, spoke of using the drafts others provided, and seemed unaware of the implications of his actions. The Commission of Three made nothing of his sophistication and experience. The commission's most general conclusion was that the prince had put himself "in a dubious light."[44]

Surprise or astonishment appeared to be the prince's standard reactions to any new information showing him in a greedy posture. The shaming effect of his transactions, however, was noted by the commission in a comment on the reaction of the Dutch defense officials and the senior technical and administrative staff of Lockheed: "The latter regarded it as a slur on years of devotion and dedication that the products of the company should owe their success partly to underhand methods, and in the same way the Netherlands defense officials who were interviewed felt the assumption that the policy they had followed and the decisions they had taken might not rest on a purely business basis to be an unexpected and gravely disturbing censure."[45]

The technical people felt the sting of shame. Was Prince Bernhard truly impervious? His evasions before the commission may be explained, no doubt, by his desire to keep his royal job and his view of what would really hurt him. It was better to tell an implausible story than to admit publicly that he had been bribed. His words when he saw his own letter to Lockheed asking for $1 million, that he "would have believed" these things impossible for him to write, were true. It was impossible for him to maintain his image of himself and see himself as the person addressing Lockheed as its willing agent.

When the reports from the Church committee had first reached the Netherlands, the Dutch were described journalistically as "shaken." Labor, the party in power, had less sympathy for the monarchy than had the Christian Democrats or Liberals, but only the Communists had wanted to condemn Bernhard without investigation. The prime minister, Joop M. den Uyl, had urged suspension of judgment but said that bribery would not go unpunished.[46] When in August 1976 the Commission of Three presented its report, den Uyl was presented with a problem, reflected in two public actions, one by the prince, one by the government.

Speaking to Parliament and releasing the report, den Uyl announced that the prince had "damaged the national interest." The prime minister believed in "equality before the law," for Bernhard as much as for anyone else. For that reason the government was not going to initiate a criminal investigation. If there had been offenses, some were barred from prosecution by the passage of time, others, more recent, were uncertain to be established. Also a prolonged investigation "would have serious consequences for the head of state"—here the special status of Bernhard as the queen's consort was acknowledged as a factor. Finally, equality before the law was again invoked: the prince had "already suffered drastic consequences as a result of his behaviour." In short, he was punished enough by what the government now required. As in any plea bargain, the government had laid down conditions for not seeking the maximum penalty. That a bargain had been made was indicated by den Uyl saying that the government's decision had been discussed with the prince.[47]

The conditions were two. The prince was required to resign all the functions that had caused him to confuse his interests with the nation's. He was required to resign every military position and every business directorship, and did so. The second condition was that the prince apologize to his countrymen. A public statement set out his confession:

> I have not been critical enough in my judgment of initiatives presented to me.
> I have written letters that I should not have sent.
> I have not observed the caution in this matter which is required in my vulnerable position as consort of the Queen and Prince of the Netherlands.
> I admit and sincerely regret this.[48]

The sequel was foreseeable. Bernhard would sit by Juliana as she opened parliament in the fall, no longer resplendent in air force uniform. His daughter Beatrix would substitute for him in awarding the Erasmus Prize. He and the queen would cancel their trip to the United States to celebrate the American bicentenary. He would even resign as president of the World Wildlife Fund. Stripped of his functions but not of his royal rank, disgraced but not jailed, freed from making any restitution unless

Meuser's promised legacy to the WWF was taken seriously, the prince learned the Dutch estimation of his offenses.[49]

The Italian Style.   The Italians, wrote the *New York Times* Rome correspondent, were "not all that surprised" by the revelations about Lockheed bribery because "envelopes of varying thicknesses are such an everyday part of Italian life." This analysis was perhaps more reflective of American assumptions about Italy than about what had actually happened. In fact, as the article itself noted, the ruling Christian Democrats had been politically damaged by the case.[50]

The Italian police moved quickly to arrest suspects. By March 1976, General Diulio Fanali, former chief of staff of the air force, was in custody. Indictments were slower, because two principals, both ex-ministers of Defense, were members of Parliament. Eventually, Parliament lifted their immunity, and Luigi Gui, a Christian Democrat, Mario Tanassi, a Social Democrat, and nine others went on trial for "aggravated corruption" in connection with the purchase of fourteen Lockheed Hercules planes in 1970–1971. In thirty years of Christian Democratic rule no cabinet minister had been convicted of a crime in office. A panel of judges was specially set up by Parliament. While the trial was in progress, Giovanni Leone, the president of Italy, was rumored to be "il principale personaggio corrotto" or chief person corrupted. He had ties from university days in Naples with the principal intermediary "di corruzione." Leone (Lion) was caricatured in the press as an antelope. On July 15, 1978, he resigned.[51]

In May 1979, General Fanali, ex-Minister Tanassi, Tanassi's secretary, and two others were convicted and the others acquitted. The conviction could not be appealed. Fanali was sentenced to one year, nine months in prison, Tanassi to two years, four months. The prison sentences were comparable to those given congressmen convicted of bribes in the United States. A separate government agency, the Audit Office, ordered the principals to turn over to the state the $1,600,000 they were found to have received. The court that convicted Fanali and Tanassi added on its own motion a finding that $500,000 had gone to an Italian politician not yet identified. Bribery, in short, was punished, and punished criminally, and about as quickly and incompletely as was usual in America where high government officials were concerned.[52]

Japanese Politicians and Prosecutors.   It took no longer for the news from Washington to be transmitted to Japan than for suspicion there to be pointed at ex-Prime Minister Kakuki Tanaka and for the connections of Lockheed's agent Kodama with ex-Prime Minister Kishi to be noted. The current prime minister, Takeo Miki, who came from Kishi and Tanaka's party, the Liberal Democrats, announced, "I will make it a point of honor for Japan to investigate the Lockheed contribution and to clarify the issue for our people." His statement used the preferred term of American politics "contribution" and combined a bold promise to investigate with a nicely ambiguous phrase about "clarifying the issue." Meanwhile the Liberal Democrats decided to postpone as long as possible the next general election so that the scandal might die down. The opposition threatened to bring parliamentary debate to a halt unless a full-scale investigation was assured by the government. The Public Safety Commission, charged with responsibility for the Japanese police, made a rare political statement, urging the prime minister "to make clear the truth of the Lockheed contribution issue." Otherwise the PSC saw the possibility of "social disorder." The political principals kept silence, and the Japanese intermediaries stonewalled.[53]

Arrests, resignations, indictments, and trials followed. A prime Lockheed agent, Yoshi Kodama—known in Japanese terms as a *kuromaku* or black curtain, that is, one exercising control behind the scenes—had a stroke, which dispensed him from testifying before Parliament, but he was indicted in March 1976, and his assets were seized by the tax authorities. In June 1977 he went on trial for tax evasion and breaking the foreign currency laws in connection with the Lockheed payments. In his opening statement to the court, he said he had received $178,571 per year from 1969 to 1976 as a Lockheed consultant and received nothing else from Lockheed in these years. Also in March 1976, a month after Kotchian's testimony before the Church committee, Hiro Hiyama, chairman of Marubeni, Lockheed's sales agency, resigned, and Marubeni announced it would not handle any more business for Lockheed. Marubeni's executive director, Toshiharu Okubo, testified before Parliament that he had signed receipts acknowledging receiving "units" from Lockheed, but that he did not know what the "units" referred to. For this testimony he was indicted for perjury, and he resigned from Marubeni.[54]

On July 26, 1976, Itoh—the recipient of the "Peanuts" and Marubeni's contact with Prime Minister Tanaka—was indicted. The net was cast wider with the indictments of Tanaka's secretary, Toshio Enomoto, and Kodama's secretary, Tsuneo Tachikawa. On July 27, 1976, Japan was, in the language of journalism, "stunned" by the arrest of Tanaka himself. On August 16, Hiyama, Okubo, Itoh, and Tanaka were jointly indicted under Articles 197 and 198 of the Penal Code. Kotchian was named as a co-conspirator but was not indicted. The Marubeni men were charged with paying Tanaka 500,000,000 yen in four installments; Tanaka was charged with having received this bribe "in connection with his duties" as prime minister. He was also charged with violation of the Foreign Exchange and Foreign Trade Control Law. If the case against the former prime minister were proved, he would be liable to three years' imprisonment for the foreign exchange offense, to five years' imprisonment for bribery, and a fine of triple the bribe and confiscation of the bribe by the tax authorities, a potential liability of two billion yen.[55]

Public excitement was such that when Kichiro One, president of Japan Broadcasting Company, visited Tanaka after he was released on bail, One was compelled to resign his post. Yasuhiro Nakasone, the secretary-general of the Democrat-Liberal Party (later the prime minister), was so besieged by telephone calls that he taperecorded a message denying his involvement with Lockheed. The Liberal Democrats' loss in December 1976 of an absolute majority in the lower house of Parliament was attributed, in part, to public reaction to the scandal. In January 1977 Kenji Osano—an intimate of Tanaka's and a large stockholder in All Nippon Airways, whom Kotchian had also used—was indicted for perjury, and Tanaka's trial began.[56]

Four years later, in November 1981, Tokyo district court gave its first verdicts. Tachikawa, Kodama's secretary, was found guilty of currency violations in setting up a dummy company in Hong Kong with $350,000 received from Lockheed. He was sentenced to four months' imprisonment. Osano was found guilty of perjury in telling Parliament that he had not acted as Lockheed's agent; he was sentenced to one year in prison. Crucial to his conviction was the deposition of Kotchian, given in the United States. Osano had argued that the deposition was inadmissible under Japanese law, and he appealed on this point. On January 26, 1982, Tokuji Wakasa, chairman of All Nippon Airways, and five other officials of ANA were convicted of foreign exchange violations and of perjury before Parliament. Wakasa was sentenced to three years in jail but was given a five-year stay of execution. Meanwhile in Tanaka's trial a surprise witness was the divorced wife of his former secretary Enomoto, who testified that her husband had helped transfer money received from Marubeni. A wife testifying against a husband was itself a notable event in Japan. "A bee stings once before it dies," she said in a declaration given headline attention. Her sting and others were effective. In conformity with Japanese practice, the prosecution asked for the punishment that should be imposed on the former prime minister before the verdict was given. It was five years in jail. On October 12, 1983, Tanaka was found guilty of accepting $2.1 million in bribes from Lockheed. He was sentenced to a fine equal to the bribes and to imprisonment of four years. Appeal postponed execution of the verdict.[57]

Swift in arresting suspects, deliberate in trying them, the Japanese ground down the recipients of the bribes. Strikingly, the bribetakers were either politicians or corporate officials. Ordinary bureaucrats were not involved. No go-between was able to argue that bribes were only a special form of *giri*. No recipient was heard to say that *on* to his benefactors justified his course. The simple prescriptions of Western-style criminal law prevailed. Those who had disgraced Japan by bribery that was openly demonstrated were not to be protected.

Confessions

The Autobiography of an Airplane Salesman.   American ambivalence about bribery was nowhere better reflected than in a remarkable document published in Japan by A. Carl Kotchian himself—his own account, entitled *Lockheed Sales Mission*, of how he sold the Tri-Star to All Nippon Airways. Written in English and translated into Japanese, the book appeared in summary form as "Reflections of Mr. Kotchian" in the *Asahi Shrimbun* of August 21, 22, and 23, 1976.

Kotchian calculated the total paid to sell the Tri-Star as follows, converting yen into dollars at rates varying with the time of payment:

To Marubeni as regular commission	
$160,000 per plane, reduced by a credit	= $2,900,000
To Kodama, one billion, 895 million	
yen in several installments	= $6,274,000
To Okubo for the office of Prime Minister	
Tanaka 500 million yen	= $1,831,000
To six officials/politicians	= $100,000
To the president of ANA	
$50,000 per plane plus $179,000	
cash in 1974 for "rent" of the Tri-Star	= $879,000
TOTAL:	$11,984,000[58]

Containing such precise information on prices paid and exact descriptions of his intermediaries, and coming at the height of public excitement in Japan, Kotchian's book could not have been welcome to his Japanese associates. What moved him to make this most complete admission ever made by a private payor of government officials?

Kotchian entered on his sales mission to Tokyo with what would conventionally be described as "an all-American background." He was born in 1914 in a small pioneer town, (Kermit, North Dakota), his parents being Adolphus C. and Mamie Bonzer Kotchian. As an undergraduate he had studied economics and management at Stanford; he had gone on to graduate from the Stanford Business School. Beginning as an accountant at Price, Waterhouse in 1936, he had soon moved into aircraft accounting. He had been with Lockheed since 1944, rising from budget manager to chief cost accountant to president in 1967. At six feet, he was so tall that he could not conceal himself on his covert visits to his agents in Japan. The American character of his antecedents and attitude was similarly undisguisable.[59]

Reflecting on his experience and recapitulating his thoughts in *Lockheed Sales Mission*, Kotchian noted that the sale of airplanes was "inevitably related to the government of the country concerned. There comes the question then of why it is necessary to make payments." His answer, in part, was, "I was convinced that our competitors were doing the same thing. That is to say, I thought that the pledge of money was like admission to a ball game. And if you didn't pay the admission, you were not even qualified to participate in the game. . . ."

As for the request of payments to the 6 politicians, I did not ask why the money was necessary, because I was fully aware of the decisive influence that government high officials would have on the importation of the aircraft. Under such circumstances, was it really possible, from the standpoint of reality, to say, "No, I refuse to pay." I thought of all the effort expended by thousands of Lockheed men and women since the conception in designing and developing the L-1011 Tri-Star; our superhuman effort to avoid bankruptcy because of our own financial difficulties as well as similar difficulties of the engine maker; the successive defeats in both the KSSU and Atlas competitions in the European theater; I thought of the painful final efforts of the last 70 days; and I thought of being told that "If you make this payment, you can surely get the order (of as many as 21 airplanes)." I must admit that my moral and ethical considerations gave way to the commercial gain that we had been seeking for so many hard days and weeks and years.

The total of almost $12 million was less than 3 percent of what Lockheed expected to receive on the sale of twenty-one Tri-Stars. For this reason, the payments were "worthwhile."[60]

Moreover,

such disbursements did not violate American laws. I should also like to stress that my decision to make such payments stemmed from my judgment that the Tri-Star payments to ANA (All Nippon Airlines) would provide Lockheed workers with jobs and thus redound to the benefit of their dependents, the local communities, and stockholders of the corporation. . . . I should like to emphasize that the payments to the so-called "high Japanese government officials" were all requested by Mr. Okubo and were not brought up from my side. When I was approached by saying "500 million yen is necessary for such sales" from a purely ethical and moral standpoint, I should have declined such a request. However, in that case, I should most certainly have sacrificed commercial success. . . . Finally, I want to make it clear that I never discussed money matters with Japanese politicians, government officials, or airline officials.

He discussed "money matters" only with the black curtain, Kodama, or with Marubeni's man, Okubo.[61]

Kotchian's memoir never uses the term bribe. He does speak of a payoff to the office of the Prime Minister. "Squeeze," a term used in Asia for a request for a bribe, he employs to describe ANA's open request for a discount, with the implication that the payments to ANA's president were similar in character. He does not use Haughton's preferred term, "kickback." Sometimes he speaks of "disbursements" or simply "money," "cash," or gives the amount in dollars or yen. His usual word is "payments." He refers generally to the payments as not violating United States law. He never mentions the criminal law of Japan. When he speaks of the "ethical and moral," he appears to use the two adjectives together for emphasis. He gives no definition of what they mean, nor does he convey a sense of their specific reality for him. He makes no reference to God or Providence, and he uses none of Oakes Ames's biblical language. He has a modern product to sell and is a modern man, at points in his sales campaign half-jokingly, half-seriously invoking superstitions such as the bad luck of Friday the 13th and the good luck of a papier-mâché Daruma. "Reality," as he poignantly evokes it in his closing explanation, consists in the constraints imposed by his devotion to Lockheed's service.

Kotchian does not profess shame, admit guilt, or ask forgiveness. Of the approximately $12,000,000 in payments that he authorized he is most sensitive about the last-minute $100,000 to the six politicians, but even as to this payment the assurance that it would be "decisive" was "extremely persuasive and attractive at that time." Illness which he incurred at the climactic moment of clinching the sale would bear interpretation as psychosomatic; it is connected by him with the preceding frustrating delay not with the payments. He and his wife Lucy, he says, have suffered. The suffering appears as inflicted from without, imposed on him by the investigations conducted by the governments of the United States and Japan. The one sign he gives that all does not look right to him is his anxiety to make clear at the start of his book that Lucy, who accompanied him, knew nothing of the payments.[62]

If he has none of the overt motives of a penitent, why does he write? His own explanation is ingenuous: "We [Lucy and I] made many friends in Japan. We respect its culture, admire its art, enjoy its society. It is for these reasons that I write this book. It is an accounting to the Japanese people from the best of my recollection."[63] Strikingly, he did not publish his book in the United States: he did not, it may be inferred, wish to confess at home what was open to characterization as bribery; he presumed that his Asiatic audience would take a less puritanical view.

An accounting, then by an accountant, an accounting even in the literal sense of totaling the money spent to bribe the leaders of Japan, not an apology. Yet it is an extraordinary act in the history of bribery—the one who made the payments publicly and without necessity identifying amounts, occasions, methods, and recipients. The criminal law of Japan was plain. It was a crime to give or to receive a bribe. Bribetakers in Japan were in fact sometimes prosecuted and even occasionally imprisoned.[64] Can the purpose of Kotchian's act—which overtly accomplished only the destruction of the reputation of his Japanese allies and even endangered their liberty—be other than apologetic? Is not Kotchian accounting to the Japanese by saying, "I only did what your representatives expected?" Is that not his own defense, admitting the facts, pleading Japanese mores, ignoring the law of Japan? And his selection and isolation of certain facts carrying the tale of the payments—do not these acts acknowledge the moral significance of what he has done even as he declines to accept blame or acknowledge guilt? Like Oakes Ames's notebook, his memoir constitutes a series of confessions revealing more of the author than he had in mind.

Report to the SEC. Kotchian confessed to the Japanese people, Kotchian and Haughton to the Senators, Bernhard to the Dutch. Tanassi and Tanaka were tried. The SEC still awaited an accounting. Like the penitent going to confession in the Catholic Church, the confessing corporation was asked and motivated to confess fully—if it did so, absolution would be given; if it concealed a sin or two, these hidden faults could damn it.

Given the choice of making a clean breast of it and going away washed white, or hiding some impurities and being found out later, many companies that confessed, confessed all. If anything impaired the accuracy of their confessions, it was that they were too full. Cautious counsel were inclined to put everything in, to let the doubtful be confessed with the certainly illegal, so that all would be forgiven at once. Some companies probably chose not to tell their lawyers everything, and some lawyers were not cautious. Whether overinclusive, underinclusive, or absolutely accurate, the confessions of the corporations constituted the most complete, the best-documented, the most convincing admissions ever made in the long history of bribery.

Approximately 500 corporations came forward to confess to the canonical offense of making unreported, questionable payments overseas. Characterized as "questionable" rather than as bribes—the father confessors here being indulgent to the qualms and scruples of the penitents—the payments very often were sums paid to government officials to influence their official acts. As a percentage of American corporations doing business abroad, the number of penitents was not large—less than 1.5 percent. As a percentage of corporations registered under the securities laws, the number was still small—less than 4 percent. But in quality of products, resources, and prestige the corporations were magnificent; and their confessions could not go unnoticed. Of these confessions, none was to paying a larger amount of money than Lockheed's, which came as part of its 8-K report filed with the SEC in May 1977.[65]

Lockheed confessed to using a number of devices to conceal the payments: backdated contracts; multiple contracts for a single transaction; false invoices; shell corporations; straw payees; the regular use of bearer checks or cash. It confessed to departures from standard accounting practice to accumulate the money used: an off-the-books account in Switzerland opened in the name of two lawyers; a deposit box in Geneva containing at times over $300,000 in cash; transfers through Swiss subsidiaries not recorded on the subsidiaries' books. It confessed to transporting large amounts of cash in unorthodox ways—huge amounts of yen for Japan, for example, were picked up physically by couriers in Hong Kong and delivered to Lockheed's man in Japan bundled in newspapers. It confessed to having no protection against its own employees taking a share of a payment made to a foreign official by a side arrangement that part of the cash they paid be returned to them. It confessed that the normal beneficiaries of its bounty were the employees of national airlines, foreign political parties, and the officials of governments around the world. It did not treat every commission to a middleman as questionable; if it had, it would have had to include in its tally the whole $106 million paid on Saudi sales. Adopting a more liberal rule, by which a substantial part of Khashoggi's pay was legitimate, it still reached a remarkable sum for the five years, 1970–1975, covered by the report. Lockheed confessed to paying in those years over $30 million which it called questionable.[66]

The review committee, consisting of outsiders new to the company, laid the blame for everything squarely on Kotchian and Haughton. Kotchian had been "the architect" of the strategy; Haughton had "fully supported the program." The two leaders were formally accused of having "encouraged a distortion of ethical values in the Company's marketing efforts overseas." If they had thought their actions were "wholly justified," it was "inconceivable" that they would not have informed the board of directors.[67]

These strong conclusions could be made to appear a "Gang of Two" approach in which all the evil of the corporation was ascribed to two men, now happily dispensed with. But to characterize the report in this way would be to caricature it. The committee provided enough historical data for any reader to discover that the practice of payments antedated the Haughton-Kotchian regime; and the recommendations of the committee for improving the status of the inside auditors and for instructing company counsel that they were expected always to live up to "the highest standards of their profession" reflected a sense that both sets of professionals had failed. The blame placed on Kotchian and Haughton was a recognition that they had made the big decisions in the years surveyed.[68]

The committee recognized that payments of the kind made had been "endemic" in a "number of foreign countries." Yet it refused to equate endemic practice with necessity. It described the "entire situation" as "an unnecessary tragedy for both the individuals involved and for the Company."[69]

To describe Haughton and Kotchian's overthrow and the pillorying of Lockheed as a tragedy was a concession to sentiment—a concession the committee was able to afford as it put a distance between itself and the chief actors. Using this distant voice, the committee spoke as though it did not speak for Lockheed. From the inside point of view, a sinner is not the victim of a tragedy but is himself responsible for his sin. The adjective "unnecessary" revealed this other viewpoint—an unnecessary tragedy, a kind of contradiction in terms, is one that the victim could have prevented. Speaking from this inside viewpoint, the review committee entered the formal confession of Lockheed.

"Moral" was not employed even as little as Kotchian used it in his autobiography. "Moral" for the chairman of the committee meant the petty regulations against dancing that prevailed in the South of his youth.[70] But the report reflected a moral view. In this respect the formal report of the review committee had one dimension missing from the curiously flat, utterly secular tone of Kotchian's admissions. Unlike a religious confession, the report did not ask pardon of anyone, but it did contain one essential element of a religious confession, a firm purpose of amendment. Lockheed's "basic need" was "a change of attitude and approach that must permeate the whole organization." The committee repeated once more the cliché that the payments were part of a "way of life." The committee declared that this way of life "should be dead" for Lockheed. The ancient religious imagery of Paul exhorting the Christians of Corinth to be dead to the old man echoed in this recommendation for the conduct of the newly washed defense contractor.

The Criminal Standard Made Universal

Unethical perhaps but not criminal under American law was the self-characterization of the confessants to the SEC disclosing their payments. Yet they needed to confess only because the SEC took the position that to have hidden the payments was a species of securities fraud. Confession was the alternative to prosecution.

Once the payments were analyzed in the light of existing criminal statutes it was seen that as many as nine American laws could be criminally violated by a bribe paid abroad. Three of the laws expressed an American antipathy to foreign bribes. Since 1958 bribes to foreign officials could not be counted as "ordinary and necessary expenses" deductible from income for federal tax purposes; the willful treating a bribe as a deduction violated criminal provisions of the Internal Revenue Code.[71] Under the Export-Import Act a seller whose sales were financed under the act had to certify that he had not paid bribes to make them. A similar provision applied to sales under the Foreign Assistance Act. A great deal of American commerce abroad was done under the auspices of one or the other act. When false certificates showing no bribes paid were filed, a general federal criminal statute against false statements to a federal agency was broken.[72]

Two statutes caught the means often used in making foreign bribes. The Bank Secrecy Act, in force since 1970, required the reporting of transfers of more than $5,000 cash in or out of the country. The penalties imposable became serious—five years' imprisonment and a $500,000 fine—if the law was broken to further the commission of any other federal crime, a condition arguably met by many transfers for bribery overseas. The general conspiracy statute made any agreement to defraud the United States a felony. It could be applied to a plan to deduct bribes willfully in violation of the Internal Revenue Code.[73]

The mail and wire fraud statutes were also germane, and with them RICO. The wire statute expressly applied to "foreign commerce," and telephone conversations and cables were a regular part of overseas bribery. The mail was necessarily used to effect the sales achieved through bribery. Whether depriving a foreign people of honest government was within the fraud condemned by the statutes was an open question. To hold that it was was only to expand the meaning of fraud a little more than the Governor Kerner case had done in 1969. The federal "common law crime" of bribery was capable of such expansion. If mail and wire fraud was committed twice, RICO was violated, and overseas bribery became federal racketeering.[74]

Sleeping, the laws had let corporate counsel sleep. Enforced, they surprised counsel and clients with their bite. Confessions continued to be made to the SEC. Ultimately, United Brands, whose payment to Honduras had kicked off the whole sequence of investigations and exposures, pleaded guilty to wire fraud. Lockheed too pleaded guilty and was fined $647,000 for false statements on the financing of its overseas sales and for wire fraud on payments channeled through a front in the Cayman Islands. Its chief American competitors, Boeing and McDonnell-Douglas, were eventually convicted of crimes in the sale of planes abroad: McDonnell-Douglas pleaded guilty to wire fraud and false statements, and paid $55,000 in fines and $1,200,000 in civil damages; Boeing pleaded guilty to false statements and was fined $400,000. Tactfully, in none of the cases did the prosecutors invoke RICO.[75]

Old law was good enough to catch the bribers. Innovative legislation appeared unnecessary. Such was not the conclusion of Senator Proxmire who with Senator Pete Williams (it was three years before Abscam) introduced what was to become the Foreign Corrupt Practices Act of 1977. No law specifically criminalizing bribery abroad existed. All the statutes violated had been peripheral, related to the means or to the reporting of bribes. Nothing explicitly prohibited an American from paying for a favor overseas. No such law had ever been framed in this country or anywhere else. It was now proposed.

Succinctly, Senator Proxmire's report for the Banking Committee stated the need: The "revelations" to the SEC had had "severe adverse effects." The effects were four: Foreign governments friendly to the United States in Japan, Italy, and the Netherlands had come "under intense pressure from their own people." The "image of American democracy" had been "tarnished." Confidence in the financial integrity of American corporations had been impaired. The efficient functioning of capital markets had been hampered.[76]

Proxmire's report did not remark the irony that without the actions of the Senate committees and the SEC itself there would have been no revelations affecting the image of American democracy, friendly governments, or corporate reputations. The committee did not note that Lockheed alone was the cause of the problems in the three countries it named, nor did it note that in each case the country affected had coped with the revelation without a change in government. The committee did not demonstrate that the disclosure of slush funds had actually affected the price of any stock. The committee's bill passed the Senate 87 to 0 and the House 349 to 0. If the reasons given did not persuade, the title and purport of the bill did. Like a vote against obscenity in the nineteenth century, a vote against bribery in 1977 was certain of public approval in America. No member of Congress cared to stand as the champion of corruption at home or abroad.[77]

In some ways the Foreign Corrupt Practices Act (FCPA) was like any law on domestic bribery. Its structure was modeled on the mail and wire fraud laws. The essential crime was the use of the mails or other means of interstate commerce for the condemned purpose. The condemned purpose was to further any payment to a foreign official, party, or candidate for office in order to influence an official act. The statute went further than most antibribery laws in spelling out that the crime was committed if the payment was made to an intermediary—to any person the payor had "reason to know" would transmit what he got to an official. This provision, designed to strike at the use of the ubiquitous middleman, was to make American companies nervous: when did they have reason to know? The FCPA went a good deal further than domestic antibribery law in its financial sanction—a possible one million dollar fine for the company. The five years' maximum imprisonment provided for company directors, officers, or employees was severe but not unusual.[78]

"Payments"—also "gifts" and "offers"—were what the act condemned. "Bribe" was not used. In this way the FCPA avoided an obvious difficulty: was the meaning of "bribe" determined by the law of the foreign country or by federal law? But the question could not be wholly avoided. The adverb "corruptly" was introduced before the phrase defining the crime —the offense was "corruptly to use the mails." Awkwardly placed, the qualifying adverb required interpretation. The Proxmire committee report said, not enlighteningly, "The word 'corruptly' connotes an evil motive or purpose, an intent to wrongfully influence the recipient." Old-fashioned and eliminated as obsolete in many modern bribery statutes, "corruptly" meant "by bribes." Inescapably an American court applying the law would have to decide whose standard measured "evil motive," "wrongfully," or "bribes."[79]

In some ways the Foreign Corrupt Practices Act was less stringent than laws already applicable to American bribers overseas. To violate the FCPA, the bribe had to be for the purpose of getting or keeping business. The United Brands bribe to get a tax break in Honduras—the transaction that had started the SEC on its inquiries and had led to the company's wire fraud conviction—would not have fallen under the new law. The FCPA also exempted from its scope payments to employees whose duties were "essentially ministerial or clerical." Proxmire's report said the exception covered payments for such matters as "expediting shipments through customs"; "placing a transatlantic telephone call"; "securing required permits"; or "obtaining adequate police protection." In this discrimination the FCPA drew a line unknown in typical laws applicable to bribes at home. The FCPA was less formidable too in that its violation was not a predicate of RICO. No corporation could become a federal racketeer by two violations of the FCPA as it could by two acts of mail or wire fraud. If the tacit message of Congress was that the FCPA was to be used to the exclusion of other federal criminal statutes, offenders were benefited by the new law.[80]

Enforcement was assured by requirements as to accounting, requirements intended, so the committee said, "to operate in tandem with the criminalization provisions of the bill to deter corporate bribery." Corporations were required to keep books reflecting their transactions "accurately and fairly" and "in reasonable detail." They also had to maintain internal accounting controls good enough to provide "reasonable assurances" that transactions were executed in accordance with management's instructions; management was not to have the excuse that it did not know what its bribegiving employees were doing.[81]

The accounting requirements were set out as an amendment to the Securities Exchange Act. Every company registered under the act, not merely those doing business abroad, had to keep accurate, fair, and detailed books and had to maintain effective internal controls. To violate any of these provisions was to be guilty of securities fraud. Far more than foreign corrupt practices fell under the new rules. If a company was bribing at home, it was under the same obligation to record the transaction accurately as if it were doing it abroad. At the same time, only corporations whose stock was registered under the act were bound by it. A multitude of closely held corporations, such as contractors and construction companies, liquor stores and gambling enterprises—potential domestic bribers— were put under no obligation by the FCPA. The act's deterrent effect on bribery at home was confined to the publicly held corporations whose stock was required to be registered.[82]

Even the latter were exempted from fair and accurate accounting if the transactions concealed met one description—they were entered into in cooperation with a federal agency for national security purposes. This small exception chimed with a larger one: Congress bound the executive branch in no way by the new law. The most likely American paymaster of foreign officials did not suffer the slightest restraint. The necessities of intelligence were treated as decisive. "Citizens" were bound by the prohibition on payments, but the United States itself was as free as ever to bribe abroad.

Omission of the government itself was notable and paradoxical in a law treating foreign officials like one's own. After all, the intelligence agencies had no immunity in paying bribes at home. After all, Lockheed itself—the classic illustration of the evils the law aimed to prevent—was in many ways an extension of governmental activity. Lockheed's preservation as a defense contractor by foreign sales could have been described as a national security project more important than many acts of espionage. After all, was it more scandalous, more harmful to the good name of America for an American corporation to corrupt a government than for the United States itself to do so? The law's limitation revealed a limit to the universalism the United States embraced.

Another exception to the law was almost unavoidable if the feelings of foreign governments were not to be wholly disregarded. In theory, no doubt, if it became criminal for an American to corrupt a foreigner, it became criminal for the foreigner to conspire with the American to arrange for his corruption. The FCPA did not incorporate this theory into statute. Unusually although not uniquely—for there had been election laws that applied only to the candidates who paid, not to voters who took—the FCPA focused its sanctions on the payor. The notion that paid foreign officials could, if captured, be tried as accessories to an American's crime was not entertained.[83]

One aspect of the FCPA was absolutely unique. Its prohibitions applied only to payments intended to influence a country other than the United States. For the first time in the history of the world, a measure for bribery was introduced into law that was universal as far as those subjected to the law were concerned. For the first time, a country made it criminal to corrupt the officials of another country. America's ambassadors—that is, its businessmen—were to show American purity throughout the globe. Secular requirements had never so comprehensively embraced and extended the bribery ethic.[84]

V

Conclusions

21

The Future
of the Bribe

Moral concepts are ideas bearing on the pursuit of the Good, that which satisfies basic human needs. As these needs are both personal and social, earthly and transcending earth, so moral concepts have personal and social dimensions, worldly and transcendental aspects. What constitute basic human needs and what contribute to their fulfillment have been matters of discovery, debate, and development. Moral concepts found enshrined in traditions do not stay the same. They undergo transformation. They are subject to investigation and criticism. They expand, shrink, or disappear. They depend on what reason can determine and what is perceived as the demand and example of God. The bribe has had the life of a moral concept.

The idea preceded the word. It was discovered in the Ancient Near East and entered into the commandments of Israel. It was developed in Greece and Rome and became a shibboleth of orator-politicians. It entered the religious and political life of the Roman Empire. It was imparted to tribes and peoples unused to the restrictions it generated. It was put on the banner of religious reform in the eleventh century and stayed there for over

500 years. It found full articulation in the poetry of Dante, in the plays of Shakespeare, and in the invention of a vocabulary tailored to the thought. It became part of the common law of England. It expanded its sway from judges to high administrators to legislators. It entered the American Constitution and became the stuff of American political conflict. It was adapted to social and familial and psychological contexts. It began to be a serious element in the criminal law as actually enforced. It formed a standard known to every country in the world and was honored by hypocrisy where unobserved in conduct.

The idea was not universal. It was applied analogously, and the line of development was not linear. Weakly in the Ancient Near East and in early medieval Europe, fitfully in Jacobean, Stuart, and Hanoverian England and in the United States throughout its history, the connection between the idea and the pursuit of the Good has been perceived. Faintly or vigorously realized, the moral character of the idea has persisted. Will it continue to persist?

Consider the life of two other moral concepts, slavery and usury. Slavery at one time was not a moral issue: its modalities might be adjusted, its existence was taken for granted. Its relation to the basic personal and social needs of human beings was first raised in a serious sustained way in the eighteenth century. At first the economic aspect of the matter dominated. Antislavery criticism interfered with property. The lost labor could not be replaced. The moral question whether human beings could pursue the Good treating other human beings as slaves was obscured. Ultimately the moral question was decisive. Fogel and Engerman's recent attempt to rationalize Southern slavery in economic terms is anachronistic; it has been settled that slavery is not to be judged economically but in terms of basic human needs, that is, morally.[1]

In contrast to slavery, the kind of banking system a community should have is usually seen as an economic question. Yet from the twelfth to the seventeenth century in Western Europe the regulation of banking and credit was regarded as so related to basic human needs that moral judgment dominated the economic. Lending at a profit fell under moral scrutiny and a large portion of credit transactions came within the condemned category of usury. Except in Islam, the ordinary operations of banking are not now judged by criteria of a moral character. Usury as a moral concept has withered.

Is bribery more like slavery or more like usury? Is the idea likely to remain vigorous and even expand its dominance, so that more reciprocities will be challenged and rooted out as contrary to the satisfaction of true human needs? Or is bribery likely to shrink, to be applied only in cases of spectacular official greed as usury is invoked where rates of interest become bloated? The future of the bribe depends on whether bribery remains a matter of moral focus and judgment. Reasons, now to be examined, exist for seeing the matter in two conflicting ways.

The Nonmoral Nature of Exchanges with Officeholders

By bribery is meant improper reciprocation with an officeholder for an act intended by society to be gratuitous. To approach the matter neutrally, "exchange with an officeholder" will be substituted for "bribery." Five arguments exist why such exchanges should not now be subject to predominantly moral judgments. These arguments are directed at the moral nature of bribery today. When reference is made to history it is to be understood that the argument is by analogy, to analogous not identical concepts of bribery.

1. *Everybody does it.* Wherever one looks, whatever time or place or country, exchanges with officeholders are found. From the mayors of Nippur and Nuzi in 1500 B.C. to the mayor of Lansing, Illinois, in 1976, payoffs have been made. From the Roman Curia under Innocent III to the Supreme Court of the United States under Earl Warren such exchanges have been arranged. In religious representations as ancient as *The Book of the Dead* and in secular reporting as recent as the *Wall Street Journal* such exchanges are commemorated. No religion has banned exchanges with the divine officeholder. No government has ever ruled without exchanges by and with the rulers.

"All sects, all ages smack of this vice." This observation, made apropos fornication in *Measure for Measure,* is equally apt here.[2] Women, it is true, appear to smack of it less than men, for in the case of bribery special opportunities must be conjoined to appetite. Only officeholders can be the objects of bribes, and women have been officeholders less frequently than men. The sex differential apart, there is no common denominator isolating those who do participate in bribery and those who do not. Romans and Visigoths, Englishmen and Africans, Catholics and Jews, pagans and Protestants, capitalists and Communists, imperialists and patriots have engaged in these exchanges. It was done by officeholders in the England of Edward I and in the England of James I and in the England of George III. It was done in the America of Abraham Lincoln and the America of Teddy Roosevelt. It has been a way of life in Iran and Indonesia, Italy and Japan, our state houses and our national capital.

What has been done everywhere at every time cannot be contrary to human nature or destructive of the human pursuit of the Good. Universal, vast, ineradicable, bribery is a practice that accompanies the human condition.

2. *It is necessary to do it.* Such a practice cannot be counter to basic human needs; rather, it must itself meet human needs. The second argument builds on the observation underlying the first argument: what is commonly done must be done if one is to live and act in the world.

To take one example, from the life of an illustrious philosopher, when Germany annexed Austria, Ludwig Wittgenstein was in England; his two sisters lived in Vienna; they became subject to the Nazi laws on race.

Wittgenstein went to Germany, negotiated with the Nazi authorities, and made an arrangement whereby for a certain sum put at the disposal of the Reichsbank from the family fortune in Switzerland, the two sisters would remain undisturbed.[3] In short, the Germans were bribed not to apply the racial code. But does it make moral sense to put this foresighted and courageous action of Wittgenstein in a morally reprehensible category? Generally speaking, is it not true that all payments made to prevent the application of unjust laws are justified? Wittgenstein's case is, indeed, an example of the class covered generally by the scholastics' phrase *redimere vexationem*—to buy back harassment. When you have a right to a civil good—property, fair treatment, peace—you have a right to prevent its unjust denial.[4] To use effective and necessary means of securing the right is not unjust. These means include an exchange with the powerholder who is unjustly denying you your due.

The same reasoning holds true of the removal of unjust laws. The classic case is the passage of the Thirteenth Amendment. Let us take it as proved that Abraham Lincoln through his agents did use presidential patronage to obtain the necessary Democratic votes or abstentions. Did not his pure purpose justify his trading? Would it really have been morally preferable for him to have acquiesced in the continued enslavement of the blacks until he could get the amendment enacted without the use of any quid pro quo? A great human need for liberty had to be met. Lincoln took the means necessary to meet the need.

What holds as to political necessity holds as to commercial necessity. There is no reason to rank lower the exigencies of economics. "Was it really possible, from the standpoint of reality, to say, 'I refuse to pay'?" Carl Kotchian asks and knows the answer is No if he is to sell his company's planes. As Daniel Haughton puts it, payments were "necessary in order to compete against U.S. and foreign competitors."[5] Kotchian and Haughton are representative reciprocators with officeholders. They reciprocated not out of desire to violate the law or malice toward anyone, but because they had to be reciprocators if they were to stay in business. Business necessity was their motivation. Business necessity was their justification.

The necessity that binds the donor, it may be objected, is not a necessity that binds the recipient. True, the recipient is bound by different necessities—the necessity of obtaining campaign contributions, the necessity of finding funds for his party, the necessity of maintaining a standard of living congruent with his office. The officeholder is a needy man, nearly everywhere not officially compensated in a way commensurate with his responsibilities and power. His acceptance of reciprocities is itself token and evidence of his needs.

Anthropologists who have found exchanges the rule in the societies they have investigated do not describe one group of recipients as more grasping than another: the exchanges represent an equilibrium of needs. American political scientists who have studied Third World countries have found reciprocation with official officeholders playing a part in the transition of the countries from colonies to democratic nations. They have discovered an important truth. Such exchanges help to build nascent political parties. Such exchanges lessen the impersonality of government. Such exchanges overcome the inertia of bureaucracy. Such exchanges, in short, make the country run. They are a functional necessity in the new nations. Is not as much now admitted of the city and state machines once so scorned for their reliance on reciprocities? In the period of the vigorous expansion of the United States, in the building of the strongest nation in the world, did not the reciprocal exchanges in every American city from New York to San Francisco function to provide the necessary capital construction? Did they not function in Washington to provide the necessary railroad connections? We should not condemn with moral judgment what has been needed to make other systems, and our own, work.[6]

3. *Reciprocities are formally indistinguishable.* The usury prohibition known to medieval Europe broke down because it became impossible in practice to distinguish unlawful usury ("profit on a loan") from lawful interest, lawful profit on foreign exchange, and lawful partnership income.[7] A similar phenomenon can be observed here and is indeed implicit in the two preceding arguments that reciprocity with an officeholder is normal and necessary. A multitude of reciprocal exchanges are generally accepted as legitimate. No satisfactory criteria exist by which these exchanges can be distinguished from what bribery prohibitions classify as bribes.

To begin with, there are gifts. The difficulty of distinguishing bribes from gifts was signaled in antiquity by the language. *Shoḥadh, dōron, munus*—are they to be translated gift or bribe? Wise ambiguity. We hesitate because the Hebrews, Greeks, and Romans hesitated. Who could be certain that the gift was a corrupt gift? The Greeks had a word for it, runs the proverb. The Greeks did not have a word for bribes because all gifts are bribes. All gifts are given by way of reciprocation for favors past or to come.

The difference between a bribe and a gift lies, for some, in the nonspecific and tacit character of the request for reciprocity that accompanies a gift. Consider Kotchian's response to Senator Church's question as to what Lockheed got for its $1 million to Prince Bernhard. Kotchian replied, "It was from a great good will and helpfulness in various programs that were going on in that area. . . . My understanding of a bribe is quid pro quo for a specific item in return, and I would categorize this more as a gift. But I don't want to quibble with you, sir."[8] Quibbling indeed is the right term to describe the attempt to segregate bribes from gifts; or (a *reductio ad absurdum* of the moral argument) shall we distinguish by size—one million dollars is a bribe, one hundred is a gift? As in the prince's case, a gift is not made out of the air but with an appreciation of who the donee is and what he has done or will do. Dealing with intelligent donees, the donor may reasonably expect a better return if he is not specific. The essence of the transaction remains reciprocal.

Gifts overlap with another subdivision of reciprocities, tips, which are equally hard to tell from bribes. The paradigm of a tip, it will be said, is a payment whose minimum amount is set by custom, given a waiter after he has provided service; the waiter has no legal right to even the minimum; the waiter's employer is aware of the practice and takes it into account in setting the waiter's salary. Nothing distinguishes the paradigm from the practice of Christmas gifts to mailmen. Yet such gifts to mailmen and any other tips to federal employees are by law classified as bribes.[9] The law is not peculiarly arbitrary in this instance. Any attempt to isolate one set of reciprocities and stigmatize them as illegal or immoral must be arbitrary.

Throughout much of the world, low-level government officials depend on tips to supplement their salaries. They are exactly like waiters, poorly paid because their governmental employers know they will be compensated by those who use their services. The Foreign Corrupt Practices Act distinguishes the grease that goes to them from the bribes it condemns. The distinction discloses the arbitrariness in classifying reciprocities.

The tip to the official is excused because the official is said to be underpaid. Will this distinction hold? The cabinet minister in many countries is underpaid, considering his responsibilities and comparing his government salary with that paid by the private sector. If the low-level official is entitled to a kind of "occult compensation," designed to give him an income commensurate with his work, the same logic holds for the cabinet minister: he is entitled to a gift to bring his income up to a proper standard. The rationale for the tip destroys any effort to stigmatize the larger payment to the minister.[10]

The tip, it might be said, is only for the execution of a nondiscretionary task; and it is only for the proper performance of a task not its perversion. But surely many of the acts tipped are precisely for the exercise of discretion—for putting one application ahead of another, for not examining every article of luggage, for overlooking minor failures to meet the regulations. As for being tipped only for doing the job the right way, the high-level donee may make the same claim: "I selected the airplane our country needed most. I am being rewarded for an act which was beneficial to the country and fair to all competitors."

The only difference between what is jocularly called "lubrication" and a bribe appears to be the amount. Even a difference in magnitude is not always suggested. "Machinery stuck for lack of grease," wired a Lockheed representative in Saudi Arabia where Lockheed payments were by the thousand and the million.[11] What would be one man's bribe in terms of amount would be a more affluent man's tip. Such a varying yardstick is insufficient to show that bribes and tips to officials are different.

Gifts, tips, and campaign contributions! A chapter has been devoted to these "donations of democracy," these gifts without which the whole electoral system would disappear or become dependent on the dole of a central government agency. Nothing in that chapter established a functional difference between campaign contributions and bribes. All that was shown were governmental efforts, usually clumsy, half-baked, and ineffective, to channel contributions, publicize them, and limit their amounts and origins. Lines were drawn between contributions and bribes. Each line was arbitrary—corporations could not give; corporations could give only by arranging for a committee; contributors could give only so much to one committee, etc. No line reflected a substantial moral distinction. The system presently in force—lawful contributions through PACs—is simply one of licensed bribery.

Look again at a federal court of appeals trying to distinguish bribes and subvarieties of bribes such as illegal gratuities and campaign contributions in the cases of Anderson and Brewster. The court entangles itself in verbiage. The distinctions are not intelligible. Reason does not know how to distinguish. The only discernible lines are those arbitrarily drawn by election statutes.[12]

Did any functional difference exist between bribes and the campaign contributions made so widely by the Gulf Oil Corporation? When Gulf's lobbyist disbursed cash to Lyndon Johnson and other leaders of the Congress, did he have to say, "Vote for Gulf on such and such an issue"? The recipients knew who the donor was and for what company he worked. Whether the amounts delivered were called gifts, bribes, or contributions, they accomplished the same objective. They induced and rewarded gratitude and reciprocal response in the recipients.

Campaign contributions may be considered a subspecies of a larger class—access payments. "I'm not paying for my congressman's vote," the large contributor will say. "I simply want to be sure he will listen to my side of the case." In *The Book of the Dead* Ani's gift to the gods is for access. Bailiffs of imperial judges and clerks of Roman cardinals took money on their masters' behalf, that they should give time to the case. If everyone gave the same amount, as is done when court fees are paid, no particular reciprocity would be set up between the receiver of an access payment and its maker. But in every age the maker has had the opportunity of making his case appear particularly attractive by what he gives. Ani's platter for the gods was put together to be pleasing. The access money received by Roman bailiffs was perceived as a common way of influencing the court. The access money taken by curial clerks was seen to be symptomatic of a Roman Curia where everything was for sale. Access payments in the form of campaign contributions are not uniform. The access bought by the large donor is the same as influence. In most contested matters the ear of an official is needed to obtain the result desired. The access payment in fact and function, if not in hairsplitting theory, is a payment to establish reciprocity with the officeholder.

Access payments, campaign contributions, tips, gifts—the ways in which exchanges with an officeholder may be made are so many that no exhaustive list can be made. Need one catalogue the forbearances, the appointments, the promotions, the kindnesses to siblings and in-laws, the sexual favors paid for or voluntarily given, or the business opportunities afforded, which constitute the common coin of reciprocity as much as cash and which, escaping legal condemnation, are morally indistinguishable as returns to officeholders? The perfect impossibility of making any but arbitrary definitions of what is morally acceptable and what is "bribery" is evident.

4. *It is immorally enforced.* A moral idea that lives by immoralities is a contradiction in terms. Such is the notion of the bribe. When certain exchanges are categorized as bribes, enforcement of their condemnation is inconsistent; intemperate; hypocritical; an expression of envy. The idea is made effective by technicalities, lies, and bribes.

When the antibribery ideal is invoked it is inconsistently applied. At the level of law, the great unevenness has been demonstrated. The crime of bribery needs two for completion; in its inception in Israel the Law (like the Prophets and Wisdom) only condemned the bribetaker—the first fatal inconsistency. A second inconsistency—the crime is the more dangerous the higher the official: from ancient Israel to America, the general rule has been, the higher the official, the greater his immunity from prosecution for bribery. If the bribetaker has been high enough—the lawmakers of Israel, the Senate of Rome—he has been completely immune.[13]

When a law has existed and been applied, it has been applied fitfully. Warren Hastings suffered shame; his predecessors, surely little different in their rule of Bengal, received honor. Oakes Ames and James Brooks were disciplined and died in disgrace; James Garfield and James Blaine, their partners, became, respectively, President and Secretary of State. Richard Nixon was forced out of office for planning certain condemned exchanges; Lyndon Johnson rose to the presidency on the back of such exchanges. Such a hit-or-miss notion as bribery can be the convenient weapon of journalists and politicians as simony once was of preachers and religious reformers. Neither bribery nor its subspecies simony have today the consistency, the stability, the exigency of a true moral concept.

From Cicero to Caro the haters of bribery have been driven to create "Hogs," caricatures of human beings, devoid of redeeming characteristics, so that in pillorying the caricature they can express their devotion to the antibribery ethic. Their devotion has led them to reduce human beings to objects. Their devotion, as in Burke's case, has put them in the unChristian posture of unforgiving hatred of the bribetaker.[14]

Hypocrisy in the enforcement of the antibribery ethic is common. Cicero, the great foe of bribery, will not subject his clients, the knights, to the bribery law. Richard Nixon, whose administration creates federal "common law" bribery to bring down the Kenny machine, plots to give bribes. The Watergate Committee, nearly all of whose members took money from Gulf, judges Nixon.

Often enough, popular dislike of a bribetaker reflects a sense that he is getting something the critics would like to have themselves. How much the monastic complaints about the Roman Curia incorporate ill-natured envy! How much the impotence of the Adamses inspires ill-will in the portraits of the powerful in *Democracy!* How often is the journalist a man of action *manqué* revenging his frustrations! Just as a large ingredient of sexual puritanism is the malice of the sexually deprived toward the sexually content, so the desire to repress bribery conceals the desire to share the fruits of office. Small wonder that accusations of bribery can be fruitfully analogized to accusations of witchcraft. Accusations of either practice satisfy the deep resentments of the accusers.

Their dispositions are uncharitable and hypocritical; their motivation jealous, and their means are typically foul. They catch a briber on a technicality—William Tweed is skewered on an accounting statute, Spiro Agnew trips on a tax law. They do not blush to manipulate statutes to punish crimes that the statutes were not meant to prevent. They exploit illegal leaks of government information as William Lambert did to topple Abe Fortas. They encourage treachery by a man's associates or employees, as Coke must have done to catch Bacon. They set up hoaxes such as Abscam which depend on sustained deception and lying by agents of the government. They capture bribeable congressmen by having the government furnish the bribe money.

The antibribery ethic is supposed to encourage trust. Enforcement of the antibribery ethic is destructive of trust. Dante's insight in the *Inferno* was profound: those who pursue bribees are themselves diabolical in their pursuit. They pretend to defend a moral ideal. They express hatred and envy, they practice immoral duplicity.[15]

5. *The material effect of the exchanges commonly condemned is either trivial or undemonstrated.* At best, the bribery rules, which have been so extravagantly expanded, are like the taboos on sexual intercourse, which were so extravagantly expanded by elaborate biblical provisions about certain classes of kin, virgins, and the menstruous, all of whom were shielded from sexual encounters. Purity rules of this kind, designed to impose order on chaos and prevent national catastrophe, rest on no rational basis and prevent no substantive harm. Taboos, they should be discarded when no actual injury which they avert can be identified.

The work of the world is concerned with the distribution of goods and services. What matters first is how much there is to distribute and next that the distribution be fair. But fairness is notoriously difficult to determine *a priori*, and in practice circumstances that appear accidental such as inherited wealth have as much to do with distribution as factors that might appear more fundamental (to philosophers anyway) such as inherited brains. The effect of reciprocal exchanges with officeholders upon fair distribution is miniscule compared with the effect of the inheritance of property. The effect of such exchanges upon the production of goods and services is undemonstrable.

In the typical case of such an exchange in connection with the purchase or sale of a government asset, the payment to the official is calculated as a percentage like the 3% of Dasaad Musim. It is true that middlemen enjoying great influence and a quasi-monopoly position such as Khashoggi have asked more; but it is reasonable to regard a Khashoggi as extraordinary. If one puts the average at between 5% and 10% of the price, it is not unrealistic. An increase of this sort in the cost of goods, inflationary though it may be, cannot be called substantial. If 90 to 95 percent of what a government spends is being paid for actual goods and services, the cost of a payment built into the purchase price is *de minimis*.

Lex non curat de minimis, "The law pays no attention to trifles," runs the old adage. What is true of law is *a fortiori* true of morality. Morals are concerned with what aids or impedes the fulfillment of basic human needs. A small increase in the cost of government, an increase probably less than what is due to sheer waste and inefficiency, is not the sort of thing with which morality concerns itself.

It will be said that the receipt of a favor encourages an official to accept shoddy work or to order a product the government does not need. Let the official be condemned then for the cheating which is the gravemen of the offense. But if, like Samuel Pepys, he buys the best quality work and contracts for only what is necessary, what substantial injury is done the government if he is enriched at the same time? By the same token the commissioner who votes for what he believes to be a reasonable rate of return deprives no one of anything if he is rewarded by the regulated utility for his reasonableness. The commissioner who selects the best qualified applicant for a television license or a redevelopment project or a liquor permit and pockets remuneration from the company selected has inflicted no material harm. The governor who helps a racetrack get dates for racing determines a schedule indifferent in itself. The judge who takes money voluntarily offered by the litigant he thinks is right has taken nothing from the loser and nothing unwillingly from the winner.

The modern American cases, it is true, say that bribery defrauds the people of honest government.[16] Honest government, however, has no cash value. Intangible ideals such as justice, trust, honor have no place in the calculation of material harm. To bring in the ideals is to smuggle in the moral idea, much as though such ideals as chastity, virginity, and fidelity were brought into a frank discussion of the material harm in sexual promiscuity. If we stick to what can be measured by any material standard no one has ever demonstrated that a country with all kinds of reciprocal exchanges with officeholders, such as the United States, has had less goods and service distributed than a country such as ——. But who can say which country has fewer reciprocal exchanges? A comprehensive comparative study of all the forms of reciprocities with officeholders, which is the necessary predicate to any judgment of harm done, has never been made. In the absence of such a study, the harm is undemonstrated. Given the probability that no study could isolate the effect of reciprocity from other factors such as the political maturity of the country, the state of its economy, the degree of personal freedom of its citizens, their intelligence and character, the existing distribution of wealth, and a dozen other interacting sociopolitical conditions, the harm is undemonstrable.

The foregoing arguments show that reciprocal exchanges with officeholders are engaged in everywhere; that as far as is known no time or country is free of them; that they have been a way of life as much in the United States as in Saudi Arabia; that they are necessary to the conduct of business; that no intelligible moral line distinguishes one type of reciprocity from another; and that in themselves, apart from separable effects such as cheating and deception, the material harm done by them cannot be known and falls, for want of demonstration, into the category of trifles ruled by etiquette, convention, and purity taboo, not morality.

The Arguments Evaluated

1. The first argument has shown illustratively, but not exhaustively, that bribery has been practiced by some persons of every country, race, or creed. It is essentially a quantitative argument, and its failure to produce quantitative data is its first deficiency. As the final argument on the same side contends, bribery has never been quantified. We have no statistics showing how many do take bribes or have taken them. The argument is unproved.

The argument suffers from a second deficiency, the assumption on which it rests—that what should be done is what is done. This assumption, particularly prominent in recent arguments on sexual morals, has no validity. Many common practices—torture, religious persecution, the denial of rights to those born out of wedlock—are known to be wrong. Slavery was once "a way of life" in almost every country in the world. Its ubiquity did not change its moral character. The very question being examined is whether bribery is in the same category once occupied by slavery as a general but detestable custom.

2. The second argument does not show that bribery is necessary but that it has been thought necessary, just as the maintenance of slavery was thought necessary even by such critics of the system as Jefferson.[17] What is perceived to be necessary is often a function of what risks one is willing to run. No absolute constraint compels a business to bribe, just as no force made anyone a slaveholder. Many persons doing business in American and abroad assert that they have prospered without bribery. Only a fraction of American companies—less than 4 percent of those registered with the Securities and Exchange Commission—have confessed to paying bribes abroad; so that even in circumstances where confession was solicited without penalties and even as to business in countries where bribery statutes were weakly enforced, it was seen that only a small number of corporations actually found it necessary to bribe. Companies such as Gulf and Lockheed, which have repented of their corrupt ways, are as prosperous as when they were the paymasters of politicians throughout the world. If, as has been asserted, business has been lost in certain countries because it is now an American crime to bribe abroad, the loss has not been shown to be as much as 5 percent of the American total for the country. It was argued earlier that even 5 percent was *de minimis*. Surely, a drop of less than 5 percent is an index that bribes are not necessary for most businesses. Necessity, it seems, is not only the tyrant's plea but also the plea of those too used to taking the easy course. When required to reform, businesses discover that what looks like inexorable reality is a mirage generated by their fears.[18]

The plea of necessity is restated by those who insist that bribery has a social function. Functional observations prove too much if they are translated into moral argument. Tweed's New York, Ruef's San Francisco functioned by bribery. Railroads were constructed, traction lines laid, airplanes manufactured because bribes worked to diminish the capital risks of the corporations involved. Thailand and Haiti run because officials are paid off. Bribes have a function. Every persistent practice has a function, else why would it persist?

Cannibalism had a social function. Child sacrifice had a social function. Child marriage had a social function. Racial segregation had a social function. To convert observation into argument, an assumption is added: that human beings always know their own needs and the right way to meet them. On this assumption, it follows that every functional practice, since it fulfills a human need, is moral. Few believe the assumption. When Haiti is pronounced "more corrupt" than Thailand, the implicit judgment is made that, however functional, bribes interfere with the fulfillment of basic human needs, otherwise why speak of corruption?

The great maxim, "Whatever is, is right," makes moral judgment vacuous by depriving it of any criterion. Moral judgment must always be comparing what is done to satisfy human needs with what could be done, and it must always be scrutinizing the needs themselves. Functionally useful, bribes sometimes satisfy the wrong needs—for example, the need to make several million dollars without risk—and they do so by a method always destructive of trust. The social purpose a bribe serves does not make the breach of trust disappear.

One kind of necessity remains, the necessity to bribe to prevent oppression. It is a necessity alleged only on behalf of the bribepayer. It is no defense at all for the bribetaker. He must bear the full moral weight of being a bribee. As to bribers, relief of oppression is urged in mitigation or excuse. Not merely the victim of extortion because he is the initiator actively seeking to pay, a Wittgenstein or a Lincoln urges superior moral obligations that outweigh the obligation not to bribe.

Where the right of war exists, so does the right of usury, ran a scholastic maxim.[19] A similar rule holds of bribery. In actual warfare, bribery is a weapon, less lethal than a bomb, which may justly be employed. Social orders may exist where the bonds of civic friendship have been so far dissolved that the state of society approaches warfare, at least as to the oppressed. The Germany in which Wittgenstein acted was in such a state. In such conditions it is necessary to "buy back harassment."

The existence of exceptions does not disprove a moral rule. Exceptions subvert a moral rule only if they are easily admitted and widely extended.

General social trust must have disintegrated if war, or a state approximating war, has come into being. The excuse of buying off harassment cannot be evoked in a merely individual situation; the damage to the common good is too great. The case as to Lincoln's supposed bribery is unproved. Judged as a hypothetical case, it must be condemned: it did occur in the course of an unfinished war, but it did not involve a measure taken against the enemy; it did, as hypothetically admitted, subvert the democratic process. It is not like Wittgenstein's action. The exception is admissible only when the social order and attendant trust are seriously impaired.

3. The third argument pretends that no distinction can be drawn between bribes and other reciprocities. All are reciprocities; they must be either all good or all bad. In structure the argument is like those of ultra-Puritans or ultra-libertarians who say there is no difference between marital and other sex. For the ultra-Puritan, all sex is condemned; for the ultra-libertarian, all sex is permissible. The distinctions on which civilized conduct depends disappear in a raw reductionism.

Defensible definitions, not dependent on the lines drawn by legal statutes, can be drawn. To draw them it is necessary to go beyond the words "gift," "tip," "contribution," and "bribe" and not to accept the use of the first three words to conceal bribery. It is necessary to sketch the salient characteristics of the transactions these words denote as types.

A gift—I speak of our developed sense of the term—is meant as an expression of personal affection, of some degree of love. It is given in a context created by personal relations to convey a personal feeling. The more it reflects the donee's interests and the donor's tastes the better. The more completely it is a gift the more completely it declares an identification of the giver with the recipient. In modesty or shyness gifts may sometimes be made in secret; but secrecy is not their necessary concomitant. The donee is glad to acknowledge the donor. The size of what is given is irrelevant. What counts is how much the donor expresses identification with the recipient. The gift once given is wholly the donee's and no one else's—it is with this donee and not someone else that the donor identifies. Sacrifice is a supreme gift: the donor identifies wholly with the donee.

It would be idle to pretend that donors are usually not responding to favors given or hoping for favors to come. The donor, however, does not give by way of compensation or by way of purchase. No equivalence exists between what the donee has done and what is given. No obligation is imposed which the donee must fulfill. The donee's thanks are but the ghost of a reciprocal bond. That the gift should operate coercively is indeed repugnant and painful to the donor, destructive of the liberality that is intended. Freely given, the gift leaves the donee free. When the love the gift conveys is total, donor and donee are one, so the donor has no one to whom to respond. Every gift tries to approximate this ideal case. A present of any amount is a gift when it conveys love.[20]

At the center of the Western tradition, endlessly instructive on the difference between gift and bribe, is the transaction known as the redemption—a term which as late as Shakespeare could be used ambiguously. But,

> Lawful mercy is nothing kin to foul redemption.

By a bold capture of language, Christian thought changed the meaning of the word redemption from payoff to liberation, achieved by a gift. The gift is of Christ, made by Christ, to us:

> The giver gives Himself.

God identifies with us to the point of being able to divinize us:

> He who became a participant in our nature
> [makes] us co-sharers in His divinity.

A chasm separates this uncoerced and uncoercive, loving, exemplary action from the manipulatively motivated, exploitative, secret exchange we call a bribe.[21]

Between the polar opposites of bribe and gift lie a variety of transactions like tips and contributions. The tip is remuneration for the work of an employee, given according to a custom known and consented to by the employer. Given for service, it is intended to create no identification between tipper and tippee. The service has been given in expectation of the tip. Proportionality exists between the two. Size is significant. A very large tip is either a gift or a bribe.

The tip is meant to reward past acts and influence future ones. It affects the employee's exercise of discretion. The employee is faster, more attentive, more imaginative in expectation of the tip. As the employer knows and consents to the custom and its impact on the employee's discretion, no conflict exists between the employee's loyalty to the employer and the employee's response to the remuneration. Only low-level employees, however, receive tips. High-level employees make too many discretionary decisions where single-minded loyalty to the employer is important for the employer to consent that his agents be distracted by the tip's influence.

Campaign contributions are imperfect gifts because they are usually not set in a context of personal relations; they are intended to express a limited love—an identification with a cause. They are not wholly the recipient's —their purpose is restricted. They are given in response to work done or expected to be done. They are not tips because they are not given to low-level employees but to those who if elected must exercise discretion in public affairs. They do not express or create overriding obligations, that is, there is no absolute obligation on the part of the contributor to recognize past work by the candidate; and there is no absolute obligation on the part of the candidate to do the work the contributor expects. Absence of absolute obligation creates one difference between contributions and bribes. Size is thus a relevant characteristic. A large contribution can create an overriding obligation; its proper name becomes bribe.

Contributions normally differ from bribes in a second way. They are not secret. They are given openly. They are recorded and reported. Above a very small amount, they are given in a traceable form, not in cash. They are not disguised or laundered. The difference between secrecy and non-secrecy bears on accountability. The contributor acknowledges that he stands with this candidate. The candidate acknowledges that he takes this contributor's money. Voters know with whom the candidate identifies. Political accountability is preserved.

A bribe is not an expression of love. The briber seeks to move the bribee to serve the briber's interest. The more impersonal the medium, as Simmel observed, the better; if sex is used, it is as a commodity.[22] The bribe never belongs to the bribee but in equity and morals to the principal for whom the bribee had a duty to act. The bribe is necessarily secret. If it becomes known, the bribee is damaged, disgraced, incapacitated from delivering on the bribe. Deceit and lies are the bribe's normal accompaniment, necessary to protect its secrecy. The accountability of the briber and the bribee are not to the public but to each other. Equivalence and hence size are important. The larger the amount relative to the recipient, the greater the pressure created.

The bribe is intended to reflect or to create an overriding obligation. The briber pays because he feels he must reciprocate or must have reciprocation. The bribee delivers because he must. Angelo is double-damned because he takes a bribe and does not act upon it; so is Hog in Cicero's classic indictment. In the obligation created by the bribe, moral paradox abounds. Reciprocity is basic to human society. To violate the trust put in reciprocity is, generally speaking, immoral. The briber relies on the general trust put in reciprocity to impose an obligation contrary to the special trust placed in the officeholder. The bribe creates a conflict of duties nonexistent in the case of the tip; a secret, absolute obligation different from the contribution; a loveless compulsion unknown to the gift.

"Bribe" is used today not only in its primary sense of an exchange with an officeholder but in the sense of any inducement given to alter conduct that would naturally be otherwise. In this derivative usage some of the differences between a bribe and a gift disappear. In their primary senses, a bribe expresses self-interest; a gift conveys love. A bribe subordinates the recipient to the donor, a gift identifies the donor with the recipient. A gift brings no shame, a bribe must be secret. A gift may be disclosed, a bribe must be concealed. The size of a gift is irrelevant; the size of a bribe, decisive. A gift does not oblige; a bribe coerces. A gift belongs to the donee; a bribe belongs to those to whom the bribee is accountable.[23] When a parent gives something to a child to get him to do something, is it a gift or a bribe? Normally what is given belongs to the child; it is disclosed; no shame attaches; sometimes love is expressed. At the same time the child is subordinated to the donor; size is not irrelevant; coercive obligation is imposed. If we make no objection to what is given, we say gift. If we disapprove morally, we say bribe.

Difficulties in discerning differences in the derivative usage do not change the main question, the moral distinguishability of gifts, tips, contributions, and bribes to officeholders. These can be masked as one another; but the masks are removable. The one million dollars paid by Lockheed to Prince Bernhard was no gift. It was paid in secret. Its size was decisive. It was meant to bind. We cannot be misled by Kotchian's quibble. The half-million dollars loaned by Nelson Rockefeller to a New York public official was too big for a tip, and its recipient was not low-level. It was too big for a gift. Its size created an obligation to the lender going beyond repayment of the loan. Uncondemned by New York law, its moral status is evident.[24] The ten dollars given at Christmas to the mailman—literally a bribe by federal law—is a classic tip and its inclusion within the law an error. Campaign contributions can be bribes, as successful prosecutions have established. Cash and secrecy are today the normal badges of criminality. But contributions can also be distinct from bribes, meant not to manipulate an officeholder but to identify with him and the cause he supports. No doubt in close cases the motivations of contributor and candidate are morally significant; it is not surprising that moral lines should depend on motivation. The entire set of laws on campaign contributions can be read as an effort, clumsy surely but persistent also, to reinforce the moral line already in existence between bribes and contributions.

The access payment, too, may be readily classified. If the payment is small, open, and uniform for all, it will of course be no more than an entrance fee, as morally legitimate as any fee charged for the use of a court. Large, secret, variable, it bears the marks of what is given in expectation of official action. The pretense is then made that only attention is purchased. The pretense is transparent. In its ancient form of a price paid to a judge's servants, or in its modern form of a substantial campaign contribution, it is accompanied by the tacit understanding that the attention bought will be favorable. Access payments of this sort are bribes.

Intermediate cases, borderline cases exist. What moral concept is free of them? Gray depends on black and white. The most difficult area is that of employment. Is a person given a job as a payoff or on the merits? Motives may be mixed when the President makes an appointment or when a private corporation hires a former government employee. Double effect can often be found—choice of a responsible appointee, reciprocation of an official favor. As in countless other situations of double effect, a moral judgment is required to determine the predominant motive and consequences. The difficulty of the judgment does not destroy the moral nature of the concept being employed. If sexual favors are used, are they predominantly expressions of simple lust or affection, or are they intended chiefly to influence official action? If banking favors are extended, do they reflect business judgment or are they benefits conferred to obtain official responses? The existence of a second effect other than the obtaining of governmental action cannot obscure or disguise a real purpose of bribery. At the same time there will be cases where bribery is neither intended nor effected. Close cases, the necessary weighing of complex elements, accentuate the moral character of the judgments needed.[25]

Convention plays a large part in the development of any area of morals. Convention will mark off areas where reciprocities are tolerable, acceptable, desirable from those areas, extending beyond the hard-core central case of cash for official actions, where immoral payoffs are present. The necessary appeal of moral judgment to conventional guidelines does not mean that the basic principles are merely conventionally related to the moral good; the conventions are always subject to criticism and revision in the light of basic principles.

4. The fourth argument is a species of familiar gamemanship. It involves an objection applicable to all moral ideas, and uses it to attack a particular moral idea as if no other moral idea were open to it. If the objections were sound, no moral idea would survive. Yet the argument itself, to succeed at all, appeals to morality. It is self-destructive.

What moral idea has not been exploited by the envious and the hypocritical? What moral idea has not been treated to rhetorical overkill? Patriotism, piety, purity—all positive moral concepts—and negative moral concepts such as avarice, pride, and usury all have been used extravagantly. Bribery is not special in the abuse made of the basic idea.

What moral idea has ever been consistently enforced by law? From anger to xenophobia, many sins have never been punished by law. As to such moral notions as fraud which the law does undertake to incorporate, the law acts spottily and with indifferent success. The moral character of bribery does not depend on its thorough application by statutes or by prosecutors. The objection, however, is particularly ill taken today when the moral idea animates an immense expansion of the criminal law of bribery, so that the law includes commerce and sports as well as politics; is applied to congressmen and governors as well as to sheriffs and mayors; and is made a measure for American conduct in every country.

Unlike some vicious actions, bribetaking is the peculiar vice of a distinct class. To be a bribee one must hold a position of trust. To expose bribery is ordinarily to go against those who have, or recently had, power. Special efforts not necessary for the correction of humbler vices are required. Add that reciprocal exchange is the natural form of relationship with strangers, and enforcement of the antibribery ethic goes against the grain. It is not surprising, and it is not disastrous to the moral concept, if extraordinary measures need to be taken to assert the duty not to receive a bribe.

A moral government will not resort to foul means to enforce the ethic. Abscam went too far: the government that touches pitch is also stained. But no injury is done a bribetaker when his co-conspirator is led to confess their common crime. No injury is done a bribee photographed in the act. No injustice is done when bribers or bribees are punished for other crimes they have committed although their participation in unpunished bribery is the reason for their prosecution. Next to tyranny, corruption is the great disease of government. Skillful surgeons need more than a single way of curing the disease.

5. The fifth argument invites morality to overlook bribery as too trivial for its high concerns. Joined to the first three arguments it is hypocritical, pretending on the one hand that bribery is universal and necessary and, on the other hand, that it is too small to notice. Isolated and taken on its merits, the argument is morally obtuse. Using a quantitative measure, it doubts the effect of bribery on material goods. But the common good of any society consists not only in its material possessions but in its shared ideals. When these ideals are betrayed, as they are betrayed when bribery is practiced, the common good, intangible though it be, suffers injury.[26]

The quantitative argument further overlooks the effect upon individual persons of engaging in behavior everywhere felt as shameful and contrary to social ideals. To take a bribe is commonly understood as a prostitution of one's office. To pay a bribe is to play the part of a professional seducer. Secrecy and deceit are the common badges of the bribe and must be practiced by the parties to it. To accept a bribe is to take on the necessity of lying. Human beings do not engage in such acts without affecting their characters, their view of themselves, their integrity.[27]

Finally, the quantitative argument innocently ignores the massive popular discontent that can be ignited by corruption. No doubt, there is an element of envy in this discontent. No doubt, the discontent is often politically fanned and exploited. But the envy stirred and the political passions manipulated get their strength from the shared perception that a real evil is being perpetrated by the corrupt officials. In relatively stable countries such as Japan and Italy, revelations of corruption have affected the electoral strength of the ruling parties. In less stable African nations, corruption has been an invitation to coups and revolution. In the nonCommunist world, capitalist corruption has been effectively used to attract disillusioned youth to Communism. In the Soviet Union and Eastern Europe, corruption has prevented the realization of the announced ideological objectives. West or East, bribery has a political impact corresponding to the moral magnitude of the issue.[28]

The question was asked if bribery as a moral concept was more like usury or slavery. The answer is that today it is like neither. Usury has little vigor as a moral concept; bribery has much. Slavery is indisputably immoral; the morality of bribery is debated.

The closest parallel is furnished by sexual morality. That genital intercourse is primarily for procreation and permitted only in marriage; that intercourse with another's spouse is wicked and with a person of the same sex worse; that faithful, free, marital intercourse is significantly set apart from random sexual acts—these propositions constituted the proclaimed

Western sexual ethic from A.D. 500 to the mid-twentieth century. Buttressed by auxiliary rules of lesser importance such as the ban on contraception, the main lines went unchallenged. They were incorporated into the law of every Western nation. Adultery and homosexual acts were crimes. Marriage was a state with multiple legal privileges.

This ethic had its foundation in religious belief, and with the erosion of belief, it crumbled within Western society in general; within a religious tradition the ethic may still hold. Against it in the twentieth century was urged the universality of practice. Abroad, in many parts of the world, it was not honored. At home, as the Kinsey studies were cited to show, it was not observed. What was generally done, it was then argued, must be necessarily done; and what was generally and necessarily done could not be wrong.

Intrinsically, the sexual act was the same whatever its context. Harm in the act was undemonstrated, undemonstrable, at most trivial. The distinction between the conjugal intercourse of sterile spouses and the intercourse of homosexuals became blurred. The auxiliary rules were discarded. Then the laws protecting marriage were either left unenforced or actually repealed. The legal privileges of the married shrank to almost none. The distinction between living together and marriage became almost invisible. Rape and the exploitation of children remained condemned. Between consenting adults any sexual act appeared acceptable.[29]

Could the bribery ethic undergo the same decline so that only extortion and the exploitation of great disparities in bargaining power would remain condemned? The question, put now at the height or near the height of the embodiment of the bribery ethic in law, seems preposterous. Does not the bribery ethic assure an essential condition of government, while sexual sins are merely private acts? But sexual morals once were thought to speak to issues more central to society than government. Privatization is only a symptom of their fall. If the bribery ethic were to be regarded as obsolete, it too would be privatized.[30]

Historically, the tie between the ethics of bribery and sexual ethics are close. It is not simply that they were formed in the same religious milieu and taught by the same religious tradition and depended on the command of the same God. They have shared the same language. "Corruption" is a state of civic graft or sexual depravity. Bribed judges are "whores," who have "prostituted" their office. Francis Bacon, as he said in self-defense, was at least a virgin in the king's affairs. "Fig-leaves" covered his shameful acts of bribetaking. Even cynical rejections of the two ethics are alike in implying that true "virility" cannot be confined by the feminine virtues the ethical standards incorporate.[31]

The parallelism of language and metaphor points to an analogy deeper than the linguistic. At the core of each ethic are two moral concepts—fidelity and gratuitousness. Genital acts and official acts, must be faithful, and they must be unpaid. Neither kind of act is in the realm of commerce. Both require loyalty. The Western ethic as to each draws lines that distinguish purchased action from free action, lines that depend on the special status of a gift. The Western ethic as to each teaches that human fidelity is possible and in one case is the foundation of the human family, in the other of the social enterprise. The usual sanction as to each is internal, the judgment of conscience, sometimes reinforced by public shame.[32]

Intention, context, ceremony set off one sexual act from another. Reductionists look at the physiological process and find adultery, prostitution, and conjugal intercourse indistinguishable. Ceremony marks off the marital setting, and marriage provides the context in which the intention to express faithful love governs intercourse. In the same way intent and context distinguish campaign contributions, gifts, and tips from bribes. In each case the physical act of payment is the same. Nothing in the physical action itself, everything in the relational aspects makes the moral difference.

Alike by the analogical values at their center, relying on the same metaphors and the same sanctions, rooted in the same religions, the sexual ethic and the bribery ethic carve out of common reciprocities a special realm of sacred gratuitousness and insist on creating distinctiveness by context. If the sexual ethic has been abandoned, the bribery ethic is likely to have a similar fate. It is already presaged by the kind of arguments just summarized, now available in the literature of social science.

Against this future is not only the obvious fact that the two ethics deal with different sets of acts alike only metaphorically. There is the observable phenomenon that as public recognition of the sexual ethic has declined in America, public recognition and enforcement of the bribery ethic have increased. Whether or not the movement is compensatory, it is evident that the bribery ethic is not narrowly tied to the sexual ethic, and that a society for substantial periods can promote one and not the other. Considerations other than analogy will decide the future of the bribe.

Conclusions

There are four reasons why bribery is likely to continue to be morally condemned:

1. *Bribery is universally shameful.* Not a country in the world which does not treat bribery as criminal on its lawbooks. There are some laws such as those on gambling that are constantly broken without any particular sense of shame attaching to the offense. Bribery law is not among them. In no country do bribetakers speak publicly of their bribes, or bribegivers announce the bribes they pay. No newspaper lists them. No one advertises that he can arrange a bribe. No one is honored precisely because he is a big briber or a big bribee. No one writes an autobiography in which he recalls the bribes he has taken or the bribes he has paid. Pepys's diary is for himself; Kotchian's accounting to a foreign nation an anomaly. Not merely the criminal law—for the transaction could have happened long ago and prosecution be barred by time—but an innate fear of being consid-

ered disgusting restrains briber and bribee from parading their exchange. Significantly, it is often the Westerner with ethnocentric prejudice who supposes that a modern Asian or African society does not regard the act of bribery as shameful in the way Westerners regard it.

The shame affects even those caught with little more than fig leaves to protect their modesty. For Francis Bacon what he received as chancellor from litigants were "gifts" not bribes. For Chairman Haughton of Lockheed what Lockheed paid constituted not bribes but "kickbacks." In the files of the great corporations engaged in bribery on a world scale the term "bribe" itself is not the usual description for a payment; euphemism is essential.

Shame and hypocrisy in the use of language are vice's tribute to virtue. Shame may be culturally conditioned. Shame so strong and so general is acknowledgment that there is something objectionable in the conduct that goes beyond the impolite and the merely illegal. Shame does not conclusively establish but it points to the moral nature of the matter.

2. *Bribery is a sellout to the rich.* In any situation ruled only by money or its equivalent, the deeper pocket will prevail. If judicial judgments could be bought and paid for, there would be a market in judgments as there is in soybeans and potatoes. The same holds true of the decisions of regulatory agencies, of public authorities, of government procurement officers, of legislators. If bribes were not morally objectionable, we would live in a world of pure plutocracy where wealth would be the measure of all things.

Only in caricature or jeremiad is there such a predominance of wealth over all other values. Our culture, and the culture of every nation, cultivates values other than wealth. Part of the cultivation is resistance to the encroachment of money into every sphere, and part of the resistance depends on the moral condemnation of bribery.

In judicial proceedings, efforts not totally useless are made to make factors other than money determine the outcome: the skill of the lawyers and the prudence of the judge as well as more general ideals such as fairness and truth are given a weight that would be reduced to zero if bribery were acceptable and money alone counted. In legislative proceedings, the security of the country, the welfare of particular groups, the success of an administration are all values that work against the dominance of money and make its employment through bribery a repugnant intrusion. Regulatory agencies and public authorities have the well-being of rich and middle class and poor before them; if money buys their decisions the interests of all but a few are injured. In each of these forums where public policy is made, if bribery were regarded as an inconsequential matter, wealth would swallow up the other values. To claim, "The rich usually have it their way anyway" is not responsive to this observation, in part because it fails to acknowledge the accommodations the rich must usually make to "have it their way," in part because it blurs the difference between a society in which money talks and a society in which money would rule. It is not, I should suppose, the experience of anyone familiar with any of the governmental processes of the United States that success in them is a direct correlative of money. But if bribery were to be cynically put beyond moral censure, there would be no bounds to the triumph of wealth. Such a triumph would be contrary to the pursuit of basic human needs, and what is necessary to prevent it is a moral matter.

The advocate of the acceptance of bribery as a nonmoral matter may say he does not go so far. His position is that bribery, like pornography, may be restrained if it thrusts itself too boldly on the citizenry, if it flaunts itself in public areas where decent conventions prevent its acknowledgment, if it fails to pay rhetorical tribute to other values a society honors. To accept bribery is to accept the way things are, not to proclaim a regime where mammon is publicly enthroned as sole monarch.

This rejoinder is unconvincing. Once it is accepted that decisions may be paid for, a market is introduced. The bribery ethic gradually extended its sway from courts to high-level administration to legislatures. The process could be reversed. Old markets in legislatures, government procurement, and public employment could by degrees be restored. Once the restraint of conscience accepting the moral ideal is removed, there is no obvious or convenient point where it would be wrong to bribe. The democratic commitment to equality before the law, however haltingly realized, is too great to permit such a regression.

3. *Bribery is a betrayal of trust.* Trust, that is, the expectation that one will do what one is relied on to do, is a precious necessity of every social enterprise. The notion of fidelity in office, as old as Cicero, is inextricably bound to the concept of public interest distinct from private advantage. It is beyond debate that officials of the government are relied upon to act for the public interest not their own enrichment. When they take bribes they divide their loyalty. Whether or not they consciously act against the public interest, they have adopted a second criterion of action, the proper reciprocation of the bribe. Their resultant conflict of interest is always a dilution of loyalty, always a betrayal of trust.

A trust cannot be betrayed if a trust is not imposed, cynics may say. Everyone knows that leaders act for their political advantage. No one trusts them to act always selflessly for the public good. The cynical objection fails to note that action motivated by political expediency carries with it political accountability. The trust, although tempered, is that officeholders will act accountably. It is supposed, not unreasonably, that perceptions of political advantage by the accountable officeholder will often coincide with what is the public good. For a bribe there is no accountability but to the briber.

The social injury inflicted by breaches of trust goes beyond any material measurement. When government officials act to enrich themselves they act against the fabric on which they depend, for what else does government rest upon except the expectation that those chosen to act for the public welfare will serve that welfare? The trust comes with the office. A person is no mere powerholder but an officer of government because he is invested with this trust. The trust cannot be repudiated without denying the responsibility inherent in the role and thereby denying the role itself. As the trust reposed in a mother is central to the family, so the trust reposed in the officeholder is central to government. To preserve this trust, to keep it from betrayal, is to protect what reason requires in the pursuit of the Good. The condemnation of bribery functions to this end and in so doing functions as the command of morality.

4. *Bribery violates a divine paradigm.* The imitation of God lies at the root of the bribery prohibition. God "does not take *shoḥadh*," the Book of Deuteronomy proclaims. The God of Israel is not turned from the widow and the orphan by the wealth of their opponent. The God of Israel judges impartially. No human gift can blind God's eye or bind His judgment. Nothing, as the Book of Job teaches, can compel the Creator to reciprocate. Fixed in the biblical basis of Western culture is the model of the Ruler-Judge who is above all attempts to bribe Him. We are to be like Him. Fixed in the Christian tradition which has been recurrently invoked to reform our civilization are the image of what cannot be bought, the paradigm of the Donor who identifies with the donees, and the teaching that what is freely received must be freely given. Generous gift and base bribe are demarcated forever by religious example and instruction.

The argument, it will be urged, is too nationalistic and too religious. It is too nationalistic because it appeals to a tradition nurtured in the West and fully accepted only in the American commitment to recurrent reformation. It will not work in a world in which Western or American values cannot dictate morality. It is too religious because it depends on a belief in God and belief in a nonbribeable, giftgiving God. It will not work with those who believe God is bribeable or bribegiving. It will not work in a secularist society where belief in God is either not admitted or not acknowledged to have consequences.

Nonetheless for those who believe in God and who believing in Him believe that He is the source of morality, the argument works. "Be holy because I the Lord your God am holy" is the law of Israel (Lv 19:2). "Be you therefore perfect even as your Father in heaven is perfect" is the law given by Jesus (Mt 5:48). Jews and Christians are called to this imitation of God. It is a moral call, based on religious command; for one of the great human needs is for divine example; for, as Plato says, God is the measure of all things. As the God of Job and Jesus does not take or give bribes, so cannot those who imitate Him.

One's origins, one's experiences, one's existing balance of values go into the perception of one's ends; at the same time the ends chosen affect the person one becomes. The dynamism of movement to ends determines what one regards as human needs and affects one's choice of the means necessary to satisfy them.

From the perspective taken here, the shame of the briber and the bribee are true indicia of violation of the human good; the acceptance in practice of plutocratic rule is abhorrent; the trust reposed in government is inherent in public office, which becomes raw power without it; and the divine paradigm is real. Personal and social needs are frustrated by the act of bribery, which violates the basic need to honor by action not mere words values other than wealth, the basic need to trust one's government, the basic need to be like one's heavenly Father. The nature of bribery is contrary to the nature of the human person in its full development.

Going beyond the data, I venture a prediction: as slavery was once a way of life and now, whatever analogues in economic duress remain, has become obsolete and incomprehensible, so the practice of bribery in the central form of the exchange of payment for official action will become obsolete. The movement to restrict by law many forms of reciprocal exchange with officeholders incorporates the thrust of a dominant moral idea. The conventions that give concreteness to the idea of the bribe will be refined and made responsive to the needs satisfied by human trust and human conformity to God's example.

Appendix

Prices

DATE	OFFICIAL	AMOUNT	DISCUSSION: CHAPTER
74 B.C.	Senator (Rome)	40,000 sesterces	2 at note 12
73 B.C.	Governor (Sicily)	80,000+ sesterces	2 at 58
A.D. 431	Grand Chamberlain (Byzantium)	200 gold pounds	4 at 80
1204	Pope	100 silver pounds	7 at 53
1618	Chancellor (U.K.)	50–1,000 pounds	12 at 95–104
1664	Clerk, Naval Board (U.K.)	300 pounds per year	13 (7/16/64)
1694	Speaker of House (U.K.)	1,000 guineas	13 at 35
1780	Governor (Bengal)	40,000 pounds	14 at 36
1795	Legislator (Georgia)	$600–$1000	15 at 31
1813	Secretary of State (U.S.)	$5,000 (loan)	15 at 51
1862	Senator (U.S.)	$50,000	15 at 84
1867	Committee Chairman (U.S. Congress)	$80,000	16 at 70
1868	President (U.S.)	$25,000	16 at 71
1871	Congressman (U.S.)	$2,500	16 at 80
1871	Speaker of House (U.S.)	$64,000	16 at 103
1871	Alderman (New York)	$2\frac{1}{2}\%$	17 at 44
1905	Supervisor (San Francisco)	$475–750	17 at 48
1905	Boss (San Francisco)	$115,000+	17 at 48
1905	Senator (U.S.)	$2,500	18 at 117
1908	Voter (Connecticut)	$2.50–2.75	17 at 73

Prices

DATE	OFFICIAL	AMOUNT	DISCUSSION: CHAPTER
1922	Cabinet Officer (U.S.)	$100,000	18 at 5
1932	Mayor (Boston)	$35,000	18 at 40
1932	Circuit Judge (U.S.)	$250,000 ($2^{1}/_{2}\%$)	18 at 19
1937	District Judge (U.S.)	$250,000	18 at 33
1959	Councillor (Massachusetts)	$2,500	18 at 44
1965	Prince (Netherlands)	$1,000,000	20 at 36
1966	Supreme Court Justice (U.S.)	$20,000/year for life	17 at 147
1966	Governor (Illinois)	$159,000	18 at 85
1967	Governor (Maryland)	$20,000 (1%)	18 at 58
1970	Sheriff (Illinois)	$6 per car towed	18 at 96
1970	Mayor (Illinois)	$85,000	18 at 109
1970	President (Korea)	$3,000,000	19 at 46
1970	Redevelopment Authority Director (Massachusetts)	$25,000 (10%)	18 at 78
1972	Presidential Candidate (U.S.)	$100,000	19 at 24
1972	Vice-Presidential Candidate (U.S.)	$25,000	19 at 25
1973	Prime Minister and associates (Japan)	$12,000,000	20 at 58
1974	President (Honduras)	$2,500,000	20 at 8
1978	Governor (Oklahoma)	$50,000	18 at 82
1979	Congressman (U.S.)	$50,000	18 at 141

Caveat

It is impossible in tabular form to discuss whether, beyond a reasonable doubt, the price was paid and whether, by some standard of the culture involved, it was regarded as a bribe. Consult the chapters listed for discussion.

List of Abbreviations

[References to Latin and Greek texts, unless otherwise noted, are to the numbered sections in the Loeb Classical Library, various editors, Cambridge, Mass.: Harvard University Press, 1927– .]

ANET   James B. Pritchard, *Ancient Near Eastern Texts relating to the Old Testament* (Princeton: Princeton University Press, 3rd. ed. 1969)

CC   *Corpus Christianorum. Series Latina* (Turnhout: Brepols, 1953– .)

CSEL   *Corpus scriptorum ecclesiasticorum latinorum* (Vienna: C. Geroldi, 1866– .)

DAB   *Dictionary of American Biography* (New York: Charles Scribner's Sons, 1953– .)

DNB   *Dictionary of National Biography* (Oxford: Oxford University Press, 1921 [reprint of the 1885–1890 ed.]– .)

Eubel   Conrad Eubel, *Hierarchia catholica medii et recentioris aevi* (Regensburg, 1913–1923)

Mansi   J. D. Mansi, *Sacrorum conciliorum nova et amplissima collectio* (Paris, 1899–1927)

MB   *Materials for the History of Thomas Becket* ed. J. C. Robertson and J. B. Sheppard (London, 1875–1885)

MGH   *Monumenta Germaniae Historica* (Berlin, 1826– .)

NCE   *New Catholic Encyclopedia* (New York: McGraw-Hill, 1967)

PG   J. P. Migne, *Patrologiae cursus completus. Series graeca* (Paris: Migne, 1857–1866)

PL   J. P. Migne, *Patrologiae cursus completus. Series latina* (Paris: Migne, 1844–1880)

RS   *Rolls Series* or *Rerum britanicarum medii aevi scriptores* (London: Longmans, 1858–1846)

X   *Decretales Gregorii IX, Corpus iuris canonici,* Vol. II, ed. E. Richter and E. Friedberg (Leipzig, 1879–1881)

Notes

CHAPTER 1: BENDING THE BOND OF RECIPROCITY (PP. 3–30)

1. Marcel Mauss, *The Gift*, trans. Ian Cunnison (New York: W. W. Norton, 1967) 31–45; originally "Essai sur le don," *L'année sociologique* (1925) 13–14, 30.

2. Anonymous, "The Poor Man of Nippur," trans. O. R. Gurney, *Anatolian Studies* 6 (1956) 145, with corrections 7 (1957) 135, and further emendations in Jerrold S. Cooper, "Structure, Humor and Satire in the Poor Man of Nippur," *Journal of Cuneiform Studies* 27 (1975) 168. For a discussion of the date, see Edmund I. Gordon, "A New Look at the Wisdom of Sumer and Akkad," *Biblioteca orientalis* 17 (1960) 140. See also O. R. Gurney, "The Poor Man of Nippur and Its Folktale Parallels," *Anatolian Studies* 22 (1972) 149–158.

3. An instructive instance of Western cultural preconceptions is afforded by the translations of the line, "What is your problem that you bring me a gift?" Gurney, the first modern translator of the tale, rendered it "What mean you by this outrage that you bring me a bribe?" This version portrayed the mayor as a high civil servant indignant at an open attempt to corrupt him. It was a translation that could not be sustained. Only a year later Gurney amended the line to read, "What is your crime that you bring me a bribe?" This was much better but too specific in suggesting that a donor to an official could only be a criminal and still too ethnocentric in translating the Akkadian *šulmānum* as "bribe." By this translation Gurney attached all the opprobrium of Western culture to a term that in its Mesopotamian context was either ambiguous or innocent. Gordon, op. cit. 140, n. 139, also treats the gift as a bribe and sees "some relationship" with the Sumerian proverb, "Let a goat be carried in your right hand, let a present (*kadra*) be carried in your left." Only in the 1970s did Cooper correct these errors with "What is your problem that you bring me a gift?"—a translation that catches exactly the expectation of the official that he is to reciprocate for a present which is itself entirely expectable. In conformity with my view of similar ancient terms, I have changed Cooper's "gift" to "offering." Hans Martin Kümmel, "Bestechung im Alten Orient," in Wolfgang Schuller, ed. *Korruption im Altertum* (Munich: R. Oldenbourg, 1982) 62, cites Gurney, translates Gurney's "bribe" into German as *Bestechungsgabe* (bribe).

4. J. J. Finkelstein, "The Middle Assyrian Šulmānu Texts," *Journal of the American Oriental Society* 72 (1952) 78–79.

5. Ibid. 77–78.

6. Urukagina is quoted in F. Charles Fensham, "Widows, Orphans and the Poor in Ancient Near Eastern Legal and Wisdom Literature," *Journal of Near Eastern Studies* 21 (1962) 130.

7. "The Laws of Ur-Nammu," trans. J. J. Finkelstein, *ANET* 524; on Ur-Nammu's own gifts, see Samuel Noah Kramer, *The Sumerians* (Chicago: University of Chicago Press, 1963) 130–131.

8. "The Protests of the Eloquent Peasant," trans. John A. Wilson, *ANET* 407–410.

9. "The Code of Hammurabi," trans. Theophile J. Meek, *ANET* 178.

10. Cf. Mauss, *The Gift*, 15–16.

11. The "balance of Re" and the offerings of the deceased are noted by Henri Frankfort, *The Intellectual Adventure of Ancient Man* (Chicago: University of Chicago Press, 1946) 108. For the spell, see R. O. Faulkner, *The Ancient Egyptian Coffin Texts* (Warminster, England: Aris & Phillips, 1973) 1, 35. The date of the invention of scales is given by Bruno Kisch, *Scales and Weights* (New Haven, Conn.: Yale University Press, 1966) 22. There seems to be hard evidence of Egyptian belief in judgment after death only circa 2100 B.C., although it is possible to argue that the belief arose as early as 2500 B.C., Siegfried Morenz, *Egyptian Religion*, trans. Ann E. Keep (Ithaca, N.Y.: Cornell University Press, 1973) 129. As Frankfort observes, earlier Egyptians thought that the righteous man was in harmony with the divine order; no judgment was needed, Henri Frankfort, *Ancient Egyptian Religion* (New York: Harper & Row, 1948 ed.) 118.

12. "The Protests of the Eloquent Peasant" 409–410.

13. "The Installation of the Vizier," trans. John A. Wilson, *ANET* 213.

14. "From the Autobiography of Rekh-Mi-Re," trans. John A. Wilson, *ANET* 213.

15. *The Book of the Dead—The Papyrus of Ani*, ed. E. A. Wallis Budge (London: The Medici Society, 1913) Plates 1–4.

16.   Frankfort, *Ancient Egyptian Religion* 118 (on the magic used by the deceased). For the ritual in selected cities, see Pierre Montet, *Everyday Life in Egypt in the Day of Rameses the Great,* trans. A. R. Maxwell-Hyslop and M. S. Drower (London: Edward Arnold, 1958) 307—308.

17.   See the translated texts of these laws, *ANET* 159—163, 522—525.

18.   Compare "The Code of Hammurabi," 5, *ANET* 166 with *The Babylonian Laws,* ed. G. R. Driver and John C. Miles (Oxford: Clarendon Press, 1955) 1, 69. The text is analyzed without reference to bribery by Julius G. Lautner, *Die richterliche Entscheidung und die Streitbeendigung im altbabylonischen Prozessrechte* (Leipzig, 1922) 45—49, 66—67.

19.   "Ur-Nammu," trans. S. N. Kramer, *ANET* 584; W. G. Lambert, *Babylonian Wisdom Literature* (Oxford: Clarendon Press, 1960) 129 (Shamash); John A. Wilson, *The Burden of Ancient Egypt* (Chicago: University of Chicago Press, 1951) 48 (*Ma-at*).

20.   Driver and Miles, eds. *The Babylonian Laws* 1, 69, n. 2; Lambert interprets the hymn to Shamash as providing only for the punishment of reneging judges, in the same way as I argue Hammurabi can be read, Lambert, *Babylonian Wisdom Literature,* 320.

21.   Leonard W. King, *The Letters and Inscriptions of Hammurabi* (London: Lugac & Co., 1900) 3, 20. King's interpretation follows on p. 22. *Tātu* is translated into the German for bribe in M. San Nicolo, "Bestechung," *Reallexikon der Assyriologie,* ed. Erich Abeling and Bruno Meissner (Berlin and Leipzig: Walter de Gruyter & Co., 1938) 2, 19. Kümmel, "Bestechung im Alten Orient," in Schuller, *Korruption* 56, notes that general usage does not support such a translation, but he seems to think it supportable in the context of Hammurabi's letter.

22.   *ANET* 213.

23.   Compare "Edict of Harmhab," in James H. Breasted, *Ancient Records of Egypt* 3, 31—32 (Harmhab = Horemheb), with Kurt Pflüger, "The Edict of King Haremheb," *Journal of Near Eastern Studies* 5 (1946) 265. Breasted has "reward from another," Pflüger "bribe of another." Wolfgang Helck, "'Korruption' im alten Ägypten" in Schuller, *Korruption* 67, has *Geschenke* (gifts). See also Alexandre Moret, "Un procès de famille sous la XIXe dynastie," *Zeitschrift für Ägyptische Sprache und Alterthumskunde* 39 (1901) 39.

24.   Ostraka-Cairo 25207, trans. Adolf Erman, "Gebete eines ungerecht Verfolgten und andere Ostraka aus der Königsgräbern," *Zeitschrift für Ägyptische Sprachen* (1900) 38, 23—27 (prayer to the Sun-god); "Praise of Amon-Re," *Papyrus Bologna* 1094, trans. Ricardo A. Caminos, *Late Egyptian Miscellanies* (London: Oxford University Press 1954) 9.

25.   A. Leo Oppenheim, *Ancient Mesopotamia* (Chicago: University of Chicago Press, 1964) 158 (Hammurabi's Code "in many essentials represents a traditional literary expression of the king's social responsibilities"); J. J. Finkelstein, "Ammisduqa's Edict and the Babylonian 'Law Codes,'" *Journal of Cuneiform Studies* 15 (1961) 103 (Mesopotamian codes are "royal apologia and testaments").

26.   "A Prayer for Help in a Law Court," trans. John A. Wilson, *ANET* 380; Ptahhotep is quoted in David Lorton, *The Judicial Terminology of International Relations in Egyptian Texts Through Dyn. XVIII* (Baltimore: Johns Hopkins University Press, 1974) 43.

27.   "The Instruction of Amen-Em-Opet," trans. John A. Wilson, *ANET* 424. I have altered "bribe" in Wilson's translation to "reward" on the ground that Egypt like Mesopotamia had not developed a term with the specific sense "bribe."

28.   "Advice to a Prince," Lambert, *Babylonian Wisdom Literature* 112; discussion of the genre at 110—111; see also M. Weinfeld, "Ancient Near Eastern Patterns in Prophetic Literature," *Vetus Testamentum* 27 (1977) 195, who translates *kat-ra* as "bribe" and sees "the violation of morality" as the cause.

29.   Riekele Borger, *Die Inschriften Asarhaddons Königs von Assyrien,* Supp. to vol. 9, *Archiv für Orientforschung* (1956) 12 (Eshaddon prophet). Borger translates a form based on *kat-ra* (here translated as "offerings") as *Bestechung* (bribery). "Advice to a Prince" also says, "If the adviser or chief officer of the king's presence denounces them [the citizens] and so obtains *tātu* from them, at the command of Ea, king of Apsu, the adviser and chief officer will die by the sword. . . ." Lambert, 115. Lambert here translates *tātu* as *bribes* where "offerings" would appear more apt; as he himself writes, "Akkadian does not distinguish between 'present' and 'bribe,'" *Babylonian Wisdom Literature* 320.

30.   "Hymn to the Sun-God," trans. Ferris J. Stephens, *ANET* 388. Emendations in the translation have been made by me on the basis of discussion with Professor Anne Kilmer and consultation of Lambert, *Babylonian Wisdom Literature,* 133. I follow Lambert translating "*tātu*" as "present," not "bribe." Lambert goes too far in saying that only the judge who takes *tātu* and reneges is condemned by these verses. Lambert translates the lines following those on the judges as referring to investors in "unscrupulous trading missions" abroad,

while Stephens translates the lines as condemning usurers, making the hymn closer to Psalm 15.

31.   On the etymological connection of *šulmānum* with *šulman* (health), see Kümmel, "Bestechung" 61. An Assyrian of the later empire pointedly regrets that he knows no one at the royal court "to whom I might give an offering (*šulmānum*) to receive me and take up my cause," Finkelstein, "The Middle Assyrian Šulmānu Texts" 78−79. *Feqa* is used to designate tribute paid to a conquering invader by a rebel vassal of the pharaoh, "The Piankhi Stele," in James H. Breasted, *Records of Ancient Egypt* 4, sec. 802. Akkadian *kudrum* is Sumerian *kadra* or *kat-ra*, Kümmel, "Bestechung," 61.

32.   P. Dhorme, "L'emploi métamorphique des noms des parties du corps en hébreu et en akkadien," *Revue biblique* 30 (1921) 524; cf. A. Leo Oppenheim, "Idiomatic Accadian, *Journal of the American Oriental Society* (1941) 61, 260. Cf. the later rabbinic pun explaining *shohadh* as *she-hu-had*, "he is one"—that is, the judge is one with the donor. See Chapter 3, n. 24.

33.   Isaiah 40:12 implies that the Lord has weighed the hills and mountains. Proverbs 11:1 and 20:23 teach that the Lord abhors false scales. Proverbs 16:11 teaches, "Scales and balances are the Lord's concern. All the weights in the bag are His business." But in none of these passages is God weighing man. Perhaps He is by implication the weigher in Psalm 62:9, when the psalmist says, "All men are faithless. Put them in the balance and they can only rise." But the passage is ambiguous. In Daniel 5:27 when Daniel explains the dream of Belshazzar, he says "*tekel:* you have been weighed in the balance and found wanting." Again, by implication only, God may be the weigher, and He is weighing a man on earth, not after death.

34.   Plato, *The Laws* (Loeb Classical Library ed. 1926) 10, 905 D and 10, 908E.

35.   When the Massoretic text was made in the seventh century A.D., the symbolism of the shoe had become obscured and the text was amended to conform with Deuteronomic law. The reference in Amos 2:6 to a shoe was replaced with "life-price to turn a blind eye." But Jesus ben Sirach in his life of Samson has retained the shoes (Ecclus 46:19), and the Septuagint and Old Latin have the text as translated above. It has been persuasively argued that they are correct in E. A. Speiser, "Of Shoes and Shekels," *Bulletin of the American Society for Oriental Research* 77 (1940) 15.

36.   In an ancient chapter of the *Book of the Dead* the deceased prays, "May naught stand up to oppose at my judgment . . . nor that which is false be uttered against me before the great god." Egyptian criminal procedure as old as the third millennium focused on the witness, requiring him to take the "Oath of the Lord" to speak truthfully and often preparing him for the oath by administering a beating. In one especially well-documented criminal prosecution, the Tomb Robbery Cases, for example, the witnesses were regularly prepared for testimony by the administration of the oath and the bastinado. The laws of Hammurabi set out clear and strong sanctions against false accusers. See *The Book of the Dead—The Papyrus of Ani* 237−238; John A. Wilson, "The Oath in Ancient Egypt," *Journal of Near Eastern Studies* 7 (1948) 135; T. Eric Peet, *The Great Tomb Robberies of the Twentieth Egyptian Dynasty* (Oxford: Clarendon Press, 1930) 20−24; "The Code of Hammurabi" 1−4, *ANET* 166.

37.   It has been forcefully argued that Deuteronomy as originally written was teaching rather than law, see Calum Carmichael, *The Laws of Deuteronomy* (Ithaca, N.Y.: Cornell University Press, 1974) 258. For recent discussion of Deuteronomy as the book of the law discovered under Josias, see W. Dietrich, "Josia und das Gesetzbuch," *Vetus Testamentum* 27 (1977) 13.

38.   Compare Job 36:20 in the *Jerusalem Bible* (a version that warns generally against knowing relatives) with Job 36:19 in the *New English Bible* (the better text, where any reference to nepotism is absent).

39.   Isaiah 10:1−2—especially in the Septuagint and Vulgate translations with their emphasis on "writing"—could be argued to refer to legislative drafting. However, the passage concludes with a reference to "judgment," and the usual commentary restricting it to judges seems more probable.

40.   The Hebrew *šalōnīm*, used in Isaiah 1:23 in parallel with *shohadh*, is derived from the Assyrian *šulmānum*, Finkelstein, "The Middle Assyrian Šulmānu Texts," 79. In his denunciation of the evil leaders of Jerusalem, Micah says,

Her rulers sell justice,
Her priests give direction in return for mehir,
Her prophets take shohadh for their divination.

                                                              (Mi 3:11)

Mehir is used in Deuteronomy 23:18 to refer to the pay of a male prostitute. Here it functions in parallel with *shohadh*. It is used again of the contemptible king in Daniel, who will "distribute land for *m'hir*" (Dn 11:39). But the term is not used in other contexts where it would be appropriate if payment to an official were regularly recognized as base and contemptible.

41. Popular poetry, quoted by Plato, *The Republic* 3, 390E.

42. Roland de Vaux, *Les Institutions de l'Ancien Testament* (Paris: Editions du Cerf, 1960) 2, 304–315. De Vaux categorically denies that the prophets categorically rejected gifts, ibid. 344–347. The biblical view, he holds at 2, 341, is, "Dieu se lie en acceptant le don."

CHAPTER 2: THE PREFERENCE OF THE PROFESSIONALS (PP. 31–54)

1. Cicero, *Pro Murena* 24.

2. *Dōron* meant gift or offering in Greek. It could be argued to be ambiguous but in the classic orations of Athens, so familiar to educated Romans as a model, a charge of taking *dōron* was a charge against one's opponent regularly made in fifth- and fourth-century Athens and as stereotyped in use as "Your father was a slave," or "Your mother was a prostitute." See Hermann Wankel, "Die Korruption in der rednerischen Topik und in der Realität des classischen Athen," in Schuller, ed. *Korruption im Altertum* 30–35, 50. *Dōron* in such political context clearly meant "bribe" as in such phrases as "to be charged with *dōron*," (Aeschines, *Against Ctesiphon* 232); "to be judged for *dōron*" (Lysias, *Against Epicrates and His Fellow-Envoys* 3), "to convict of *dōron*" (Aristophanes, *The Clouds* 591). The meaning is also found in such compounds as *dōrodeketes* (a taker of *dōron*) (Job 15:34) and *dōrodekeo* (take as *dōron*) (Herodotus, *History* 6, 72). The fourth-century Greek politician Timarchus was accused by Aeschines of consuming "the wages of his prostitution and the fruits of his *dōrodokia*" or bribe-taking (Aeschines, *Against Timarchus* 154). Demosthenes charged Aeschines himself with *dōrodokia* and was told that one "who wants to arouse the anger of his hearers over *dōrodokia* must himself refrain from such conduct." (Aeschines, *On the Embassy*, 3). In other words, a substantive noun denoting habitual acts of bribery existed in Greek. There was also *to dekazein*, "the paying of ten," used, for example, by Aristotle, who says "the paying of ten" began with Anytus who successfully "paid ten" in the jury when, in 409 B.C., he was tried for having lost Pylos to Sparta (Aristotle, *Athenian Constitution* 27, 5). There was also the adjective *dōrodokos*, clearly meaning bribetaking: in Plato's *Republic* 3, 390, Adeimantus declares, "We cannot let our men be bribetaking (*dōrodokous*) or money-loving." Again, in Plato, *Laws* 12, 955, where a law is mentioned which says "Do not serve for *dōroisi*," and is backed by the death penalty, the Greek word definitely means "bribe."

Nonetheless there are classic Greek texts in which specific words for bribery are not used. Thus, according to a famous story of antiquity, Cambyses, king of Persia, had a judge, Sisamnes, who "received money to give an unjust judgment." Cambyses discovered what he had done, had him killed and flayed and covered the seat of justice with his skin, appointing in his place Sisamnes' son, Otanes, with the reminder never to forget in what way his chair was cushioned (Herodotus, *History* 5, 25). The word used for "being given money" is *chremasi*, a generic verb for being paid. Another, later example: Aristotle, approving the change in the government of Athens which permitted lawsuits to be decided by large bodies of citizens, observed that "the few are more easily spoiled (*eudiaphthorōteroi*) by gain and favor than the many," Aristotle, *Athenian Constitution* 41, 2. In a similar vein in the *Politics*, he defended citizen assemblies judging cases on the ground that "in many cases a crowd judges better than a single individual." He argued, "The many are more incorruptible (*adiaphthorōteron*)—just like the larger stream of water, so the multitude is more incorruptible than the few," and went on to say that an individual was more easily roused to anger or a similar emotion than was a crowd, Aristotle, *Politics* 3, 1286a. Aristotle, pointedly perhaps, does not mention corruption by bribery in either work.

The Romans, familiar as they were with Greek examples, did not create Latin equivalents of *dōrodokia*, *dōrodokos*, or *to dekazein*.

3. The background of the case, Cicero, *Pro Cluentio* 43–45; Cicero's engagement for Fabricius, ibid. 49–50.

4. Ibid. 43–47.

5. Cicero, *Brutus*, 205.

6. From the root *mei/moi*—the root also incorporated in *mutuum* and our own "mutual"—*munus* had the suffix *nus*, the form used to designate a social or judicial act. In a primary sense, *munus* means "a reciprocal gift imposed by custom." Jacques Michel, *Gratuité en droit romain* (Brussels: Université libre de Bruxelles, 1962) 480–482.

7. *Pro Cluentio* 53–54, 65–67.

8. *Pro Cluentio* 59 (Fabricius' conviction); ibid. 25 (Oppianicus' political background); Erich S. Gruen, *The Last Generation of the Roman Republic* (Berkeley: University of California Press, 1974) 174, 517 (Quinctius' career).

9. See *Pro Cluentio* 30 for the background of senatorial judges. The Loeb edition regularly translates *iudices* as jury. A good counterexample is the use of *juges* in a standard French translation of *Pro Cluentio* by Pierre Boyancé, Cicéron, *Discours* (Paris: Société d'édition "Les Belles Lettres," 1953) vol. 8.

10. "Judges I want," Cicero to Atticus, 65 B.C., *Letters to Atticus* 1, 2, ed. D. R. Shackleton Bailey (Cambridge: At the University Press, 1965—1967); Cicero to Atticus, June 61 B.C., *Letters* 1, 16 ("everything was in that"); Cicero, *In Verrem* 2, 1, 158 (skirmishing on selection of Hog's judges); *Pro Cluentio* 55 (Iunius' ties).

11. *In Verrem* 2, 1, 157 (Hog and Iunius); Cicero, *Pro Caecina* 28—29 (Falcula's blind vote).

12. *Pro Cluentio* 87. Compare the use of *sequestra* to mean bawd, Apuleius, *The Golden Ass* 9, 15. *Sequester* is sometimes the same as *interpres*, the fixer or go-between who sets up a deal (cf. *In Verrem* 1, 36).

13. *Pro Cluentio* 69—72.

14. Ibid 74—75.

15. Ibid. 71.

16. *In Verrem* 2, 2, 78 (Bulbus and Staienus); ibid. 1, 29 (the judgment of the court); ibid. 1, 39 (the senator-judge who took from both).

17. *Pro Cluentio* 78.

18. Ibid. 77 (Quinctius); *In Verrem* 1, 29 (Caesonius).

19. *Pro Cluentio* 91, 103, 113.

20. On the court's original purpose, Cicero, *Divinatio* 65; on its extension, *Pro Cluentio* 104.

21. Ibid.

22. Ibid. 97 (Bulbus); *ibid.* 99—100 (Staienus).

23. Ibid. 98 (Gutta and P. Popilius); ibid. 127 (Gutta and Aquilius); *In Verrem* 1, 39 (G. Popilius); ibid. 1, 39 (Septimius); *Pro Cluentio* 135 (Egnatius). Were Gutta and P. Popilius also expelled from the Senate for their corrupt decision? Gruen, *Last Generation* 527, 529, so concludes, citing *Pro Cluentio* 127, 131—132. I would infer from Cicero's fuzzy presentation that it was not the sole ground of censure.

24. *Pro Cluentio* 148, 151, 154. A common but unproved assumption is that the *lex Cornelia* not only incorporated the old law but also obliterated it. See, e.g., H. Grose Hodge, "Introduction," *Pro Cluentio*, ed. cited, 211—212. The contention of C. Joachim Classen that Cluentius is *not* now being tried for attempted judicial murder by money seems totally mistaken in the light of *Pro Cluentio* 9, cf. Classen, "Cicero, the Law and the Law Courts," *Latomus* (1978) 37, 605—606. Two other poisonings also form part of the case against Cluentius, *Pro Cluentio*, 165 and 166.

25. *Pro Cluentio* 124 ("Teach us"); ibid. 82 (clean accounts).

26. Ibid. 38—39.

27. Ibid. 33—35.

28. Ibid. 21—24.

29. Ibid. 64.

30. Compare *ibid.* 9: "Corrupuisse dicitur A. Cluentius iudicium pecunia" and "sed vereor ne mulier me absente hic corrupta sit" (Clinia of the virtuous Antiphilia in Terence, *The Self-Tormentor* 232). For senatorial usage, see a proposed decree of 74 B.C., which ran, "Si qui sunt, quorum opera factum sit ut iudicium publicum corrumperetur. . . ." (*Pro Cluentio* 136).

31. *Pro Cluentio* 148—149, 157. The relevant text apparently ran: "Qui eorum coit, coierit, convenit, convenerit, consenserit, falsumve testimonium dixerit, quo quis iudicio publico condemnaretur. . . ." Cicero does not give the text as a whole.

32. Ibid. 146.

33. On the composition of the courts, Gruen, *Last Generation* 29—30.

34. *Pro Cluentio* 150—152.

35. Ibid. 153.

36. *In Verrem* 2, 2, 181: "vehementerque illum ordinem observo." Cf. Thomas N. Mitchell, *Cicero: The Ascending Years* (New Haven, Conn.: Yale University Press, 1979) 100.

37. Cluentius, *Pro Murena* 67; Cicero, *Pro Sestio* 133—135.

38. *Pro Murena* 70, 71.

39. Ibid. 74.

40. Lily Ross Taylor, *The Voting Districts of the Roman Republic* (Rome: American Academy in Rome, 1960) 3—16 (the early history of tribal elections); Gruen, *Last Generation* 214 (legislation 67 B.C.); Cicero to Atticus, June 61 B.C., *Letters* 1, 16 (later legislation); *In Verrem* 2, 3, 162

(thief and distributor). Between 90 and 60 B.C., there were at least seven successful prosecutions for *ambitus*, Gruen, *Last Generation* 207, 272, 304, 527, 529, 531; Gruen, *Roman Politics and the Criminal Courts, 149–78 B.C.* (Cambridge, Mass.: Harvard University Press, 1968) 306–310. The law, not totally a dead letter, was a loser's last resort. As Cicero observed, it was hard to run well for office while simultaneously compiling information against your opponent to use in a prosecution of him for *ambitus*, *Pro Murena* 46.

41.   Cicero to Atticus, June 61 B.C., *Letters* 1, 16. The term translated as "hire" is *merces*. On the translation of *aerarii* as "cash-takers," see Bailey, ed., *Letters to Atticus* 1, 315 where the term is translated "bribe-takers."

42.   Idem: "rem manifestam illam redemptam esse a iudicibus." Other examples: *In Verrem* 2, 5, 117 (a Sicilian captain): "Metum vigarum nauarchus, homo nobilissimus suae civitatis, pretio redimit"; ibid. 2, 2, 186 (on endangered Syracusans): "pretio sese redemerunt"; ibid. 2, 1, 142 (award): "Si pupillo opus redimitur, mihi praeda de manibus eripitur"; ibid. 2, 2, 69 (a prisoner's friends): "fuissent auctores redimendae salutis"; Hog himself: "Ut primum e provincia rediit, redemptio est huius iudicii facta grandi pecunia," ibid. 1, 16. For discussion of the action noun, see David Daube, *Roman Law: Linguistic, Social, and Philosophical Aspects* (Edinburgh: At the University Press, 1969) 29–63.

43.   *Pro Caecina* 71–72. The passage is effectively used by John Kelly, *Roman Litigation* (Oxford: Clarendon Press, 1966) 32–33, to show the force of corrupting factors in the Roman courts.

44.   Cicero to Atticus, June 60 B.C., *Letters* 2, 1, 8.

45.   Cicero to Atticus, December 5, 61 B.C., *Letters* 1, 17: "dicit enim tamquam in Platonis *politeia*, non tamquam in Romuli faece sententiam."

As for Athens itself in Plato's day, Aeschines, declaiming against Timarchus, gives an instance where an attempt to bribe members of the popular assembly was charged. According to him, death was provided by law "for him who bribed as for him who was bribed." No direct testimony as to the bribes was introduced but, because the accused were unable to defend themselves against old age and poverty, they were put to death (Aeschines, *Against Timarchus* 87–89). This apparently political decision is ambiguous evidence on the enforcement of the law on domestic bribery. According to Lysias, it was easily supposed that one made money out of one's office (Lysias, *On the Property of Aristophanes* 49). Wankel, "Die Korruption in der rednerischen Topik" 36, gives an instance of the death penalty being threatened for Ergocles for his bribetaking while on a military expedition (Lysias, *Against Ergocles* 3); but Ergocles' death sentence is explained elsewhere as due to his embezzlement of public funds (Lysias, *Against Philocrates* 3). Wankel also cites the case of the death penalty imposed on Timagoras in 367 B.C. for taking lavish gifts from Artaxerxes when serving as ambassador to him from Athens (Plutarch, *Pelopidas* 30, 6); but Plutarch shows himself a little skeptical about the alleged reason, noting that the Athenians only laughed when Timagoras' shield-bearer boasted of what he had received from the Persian king. In any event, what was done about bribes from foreigners is no evidence of what was done about bribery at home. As to that, Isocrates, *On the Peace*, sec. 50, in 355 B.C. provides a partisan but not unrealistic comment: "Although prescribing the penalty of death for bribing, we elect as generals those conspicuous for it." Wankel, 38, citing this text, does not dissent.

46.   Compare Cicero, *De officiis* 3, 43, with Cicero, *Epistolae ad Familiares*, Letters 53, 55, 57, 58, 59, 61. One apologist for Cicero's *humanitas* in the letters is W. Glynn Williams, "Introduction," in the Loeb edition at 5.

47.   *In Verrem* 1, 28.

48.   *Divinatio* 41.

49.   Cicero, *Pro Murena* 24 ("greatest gratitude"); on clients' gratitude: E. Badian, *Foreign Clientelae* (Oxford: Clarendon Press, 1958) 165–167; on Cicero's client, Publius Sulla, and the financing of his house, Cicero to Atticus, January 61, *Letters*; cf. D. R. Shackleton Bailey, *Cicero* (New York: Charles Scribner's Sons, 1971) 46, n. 1; on the ungrateful freedman, Dionysius Pomponius, see Cicero to Atticus, February 22, 49, *Letters* 8, 4; on the relation of power and goodness in the *boni*, T. R. Wiseman, *New Men in the Roman Senate* (London: Oxford University Press, 1971) 174.

50.   *In Verrem* 2, 5, 136, a purported quotation from Hog.

51.   Cicero to Atticus, June 61, *Letters* 1, 16, 6: "nummulis acceptis ius ac fas omne delere, et quod non modo homines, verum etiam pecudes factum esse sciant, id Talnam et Plautum et Spongiam et ceteras huius modi quisquibis statuere numquam esse factum." Bailey argues that all three names were those of real persons, with Plautus ("Flatfoot") and Spongia ("Sponge") selected for comic purposes. Bailey, ed., *Cicero's Letters to Atticus* 1, 318.

52.   Cicero to Atticus, July 17, 65, *Letters* 1, 1.

53. *Pro Cluentio* 202 ("that assemblies...").

54. Cicero, *De re publica*, in Ammianus, *Res gestae* 30, 4, 10.

55. *Pro Cluentio* 139: "Omnes enim illae causarum ac temporum sunt, non hominum ipsum ac patronum."

56. *In Verrem* 2, 1, 104–114 (the will of Annius); ibid. 2, 1, 115–118 (Hog's edict); ibid. 2, 1, 123–124 (the will of Trebonius); ibid. 2, 1, 125–126 (the approach to Ligus); ibid. 2, 1, 137 (Chelidon's house); ibid. 2, 1, 130–149 (the temple caper).

57. The examples, all from *In Verrem*, are as follows: to release a criminal, 2, 5, 65 (pirate captain); to let a master ransom his slave, 2, 5, 24 (Apollonius' case); to let prisoners be visited, 2, 5, 118 (Hog's lector Sextius); to let a man be executed with minimal suffering, 2, 5, 118 (Sextius' deal); to let executed men receive burial, 2, 5, 120 (burial of Heraclius); to release sailors from duty, 2, 5, 62 (Sicilian sailors); to let a captain escape punishment, 2, 5, 117 (Phalacrus); to relax treaty obligations, 2, 5, 50 (payments by Messana); to appoint a provincial senator, 2, 2, 122 (senator of Halaesus); to appoint tax assessors, 2, 2, 133 (Sicily); to rig an election to the priesthood, 2, 2, 128 (high-priest of Cephaloedium).

58. Ibid. 2, 2, 68–75.

59. Ibid. 2, 5, 33 (youth); 2, 1, 78 (Lampsacus); 2, 5, 34 (Chelidon); 2, 5, 28 (Sicily).

60. Ibid. 2, 5, 160–162.

61. Ibid. 2, 4, 93–95 (Aesculapius); 2, 4, 103–104 (Juno); 2, 4, 106–114 (Ceres).

62. Ibid. 1, 19 ("You're acquitted"); ibid. 1, 25 (Hortensius and the Sicilians); ibid. 1, 26–28 (Metellus and the Sicilians); ibid. 2, 1, 17 (*magna pecunia* to Cicero); 1, 16 (*grande pecunia* to buy the court); 1, 40 (the fat third year).

63. Ibid. 1, 22–23.

64. Ibid. 1, 24–32.

65. Ibid. 2, 5, 188: "iste nefario quodam furore et audacia instinctus bellum sacrilegum semper impiumque habuit indictum." Ibid. 2, 2, 9: Hunc [Verrem] denique ipsum pertullisent si humano modo, si usitato modo, si denique uno aliquo in genere peccasset." Wankel, "Die Korruption in der rednerischen Topik" 45, also hesitates to suppose that the rhetorical and the real coincide.

66. Ibid. 2, 5, 189.

67. *Divinatio* 57 (Circean potion); Plautus, *Miles Gloriosus* 4, 2, 67; *In Verrem* 2, 1, 121: "negabant mirandum esse tam nequam esse verrinum"; ... "Sacerdotem exsecrabantur qui verrem tam nequam reliquisset"; ibid. 2, 4, 53: "Nam nos quidem facimus in Verrem, quem in luto volutatum totius corporis vestigiis invenimus."

68. Aeschines, *Against Timarchus* 154.

69. *In Verrem* 2, 2, 27.

70. Ibid. 2, 2, 70.

71. *Turpe* applied to appearance: e.g., Plautus, *Poenulus* 1, 2, 131; Cicero to Atticus, October 54, *Letters* 4, 18 (judges' filth).

72. *In Verrem* 1, 28.

73. *In Verrem* 2, 1, 131: "pupillos et pupillas certissimam praedam esse praetoribus" (put in Hog's mouth); ibid. 2, 1, 113: "cur hanc dolorem cineri eius atque ossibus inussisti...?" (addressed to Hog); ibid. 2, 1, 114: "Eripias tu voluntatem mortuis...?" The Reclaimables Inquiry took jurisdiction although civil redress was also open to Roman citizens, *Divinatio* 18 ("Nam civibus cum sunt ereptae pecuniae, civili fere actione et privato iure repetuntur").

74. Ibid. 2, 2, 78: "Etiam si illud est flagitiosum, quod omnium rerum turpissimum maximeque nefarium videtur, ob rem iudicandum pecuniam accipere, pretio habere addictam fidem et religionem, quanto illud flagitiosius, improbius, indignius, eum a quo pecuniam ob absolvendum acceperis condemnare...."

75. Ibid. 2, 2, 76.

76. *Pro Cluentio* 159: "habere in consilio legem, religionem, aequitatem, fidem; libidinem autem, odium, invidiam, metum, cupiditatesque omnes amovere..."; *In Verrem* 2, 5, 188: "fides in agenda, eadem vestra sit in iudicanda." "Fides" means both the quality of character that produces constancy in a relation and the foundation of the faithful relation, the pledge or commitment that has been made, see *Thesaurus Linguae Latinae* (Leipzig: B. G. Tuebner, 1912–1926) 6¹, 663.

77. *Pro Cluentio* 164: "Quod ad vestrum ius iurandum pertinet." Ibid. 195: "Vos iudices, quos huic A. Cluentio quasi aliquos deos ad omne vitae tempus fortuna esse voluit." *Pro Murena* 2: "cum omnis deorum immortalium potestas aut translata sit ad vos aut certe communicata vobiscum...." *Pro Cluentio* 159: "non se reputare solum esse neque sibi quodcumque concupierit licere." Ibid. 159: "maximeque aestimare conscientiam mentis suae, quam ab dis immortalibus accepimus, quae a nobis divelli non potest."

78. To Atticus he wrote, apparently without reason for hypocrisy or modesty, that he saved the state from Catiline by "divine guidance," Cicero to Atticus, June 61, *Letters* 1, 16. In the next line he referred, more lightly, to the need for help from "some god." His last formal view expressed at the end of *The Nature of the Gods* is that Balbus, the spokesman in the dialogue for belief, was, it seemed, "closer to the image of the truth," *De natura deorum* 3, 95.

79. *In Verrem* 2, 5, 184–189.

CHAPTER 3: THE MORALS OF THE CHRISTIANS (PP. 55–82)

1. See W. D. Davies, "The Moral Teaching of the Early Church," *The Use of the Old Testament in the New and Other Essays: Studies in Honor of William Franklin Stinespring*, ed. James M. Efird (Durham, N.C.: Duke University Press, 1972) 316–317.

2. Cf. J. Duncan M. Derrett, "The Footwashing in John XIII and the Alienation of Judas," *Revue internationale des droits de l'Antiquité* (1977) 3rd Series 24, 14–15.

3. Joachim Jeremias, *The Parables of Jesus*, rev. ed. S. H. Hooke (New York: Charles Scribner's Sons, 1963) 154, translates Luke 18:5, "so that she may not finally deafen me," thereby losing completely the idea that the widow is shaming the judge. Literally it means "so that she may not hit me under the eye," and the English idiom "give a black eye" is an accurate equivalent. Jeremias at 156 also characterizes the judge as "brutal"; he is far from the mark.

The Roman tribune Claudius Lysias, when he hears that Paul is a Roman citizen, exclaims, "With a great sum I obtained this citizenship" (Acts 22:28). The implication is that he purchased Roman citizenship, perhaps from a favorite at the imperial court, see F. F. Bruce, *Commentary on the Book of Acts* (Grand Rapids, Mich.: W. B. Eerdmans, 1954) 446; Dio Cassius, *History* 60, 17, 5. The author of Acts makes no moral judgment of this transaction.

The parable of "the unjust steward," Luke 16:1–8, is often understood in a way that makes it analogous to a case of bribery—the steward "bribing" the debtors of his master by discounts. David Daube has convinced me that this analysis is wrong. The "steward of unrighteousness," as he is called, is like "the unrighteous judge" of Luke 18:3–6, wicked in the work he has done prior to the good act which is the subject of the parable. In that good action he is exercising his lawful powers as an administrator to discount the debts of needy debtors. There is nothing unlawful in his winning friends this way, and his master thinks he has acted wisely. See David Daube, "Encomium Prudentiae," *Aufstieg und Niedergang der römischen Welt*, ed. Hildegard Temporini and Wolfgang Haase (Berlin and New York: Walter de Gruyter & Co., 1984), vol. 25³.

In contrast, Jeremias at 181 says that the steward is trying "to cover up his embezzlements by falsifying the accounts." One does not cover up embezzlements by reducing the resources at one's disposal! Jeremias at 46 states that the master may, in one telling, have been the Lord, and that the steward is "criminal." As Daube shows, the master is a bad type, an avaricious rich man; and if the steward were criminal in his action, it would have compounded his difficulties not eased them.

4. On the image of the good shepherd as king, see G. W. Ahlström, *Royal Administration and National Religion in Ancient Palestine* (Leiden: E. J. Brill, 1982) 2.

5. Josephus, *The Jewish War* 2, 273; for the example of *exagorazein* and examples of *lutron*, see Stanislas Lyonnet and Léopold Sabourin, *Sin, Redemption and Sacrifice: A Biblical and Patristic Study* (Rome: Biblical Institute Press, 1970) 80–82 (*lutron*); 107 (Plato's case).

6. Ibid. 86 (Philo's usage); 90–93 (Old Testament usage as to *lutron*, etc.); 110–112 (Old Testament sense of "acquisition"). On God's position as new owner in the Old Testament, see in particular David Daube, *The Exodus Pattern in the Bible* (London: Faber & Faber, 1963) 42–46.

7. Lyonnet and Sabourin, *Sin, Redemption and Sacrifice* 79 (the question raised); 103 and 119 (the authors' answer).

8. For an excellent exegesis of the teaching on the imitation of Christ, see W. D. Davies, *The Setting of the Sermon on the Mount* (Cambridge: At the University Press, 1966) 94–99.

9. Volusianus as reported in Marcellinus to Augustine, Letter 136, sec. 2, *S. Aureli Augustini Epistulae*, ed. A. Goldbacher, CSEL 44, 94–95 (1904).

10. Paul Veyne, *Le pain et le cirque* (Paris: Editions du Seuil, 1976) 47.

11. Cf. Ceslas Spicq, O.P., *Les épîtres de Saint Pierre* (Paris: J. Gabalda, 1966) 67–68.

12. Augustine to Marcellinus, Letter 137, secs. 9–15, CSEL 44, 133–142. The reference to Luke 3:14 at 141 is to the message of John the Baptist when soldiers asked him, "What ought we to do?" and he answered, "Do not extort, do not blackmail. Be content with your wages."

13. Marcellinus, tribune and imperial secretary and "vir clarissimus" in official records, is

addressed by Augustine as "carissimo ac desiderantissimo filio" in Letter 138, *CSEL* 44, 126. On the relation between the Church and her sons in office, John Matthews, *Western Aristocracies and Imperial Court* (Oxford: Clarendon Press, 1975) 127–145. As to Paul's point, it does not matter whether "the household of Caesar" is Nero's own establishment, as used to be held, or an imperial outpost in Asia, as today is more commonly believed. See Joseph A. Fitzmyer, "The Letter to the Philippians," *The Jerome Biblical Commentary*, ed. Raymond E. Brown, Joseph A. Fitzmyer, and Roland E. Murphy (Englewood Cliffs, N.J.: Prentice-Hall, 1968) 2, 253. For the Old Latin version of Job 36:5, see Pierre Sabatier, *Bibliorum sacrorum latinae versiones antiquae seu Vetus italica* (Reims, 1743) 1, 895.

14. Augustine, *Contra duos epistulas Pelagianorum* 2, 7, *PL* 44, 580.

15. *Didascalia Apostolorum*, ed. R. Hugh Connolly (Oxford: Clarendon Press, 1929) 38–41. (I paraphrase Connolly's translation); cf. also the fourth-century Arian adaptation of the *Didascalia*, *Constitutiones apostolorum* 2, 6, and 2, 42, ed. Francis X. Funk (Paderborn, 1905) 38–39, 132–133.

16. Jerome on Amos 6:12, quoting Isaiah 5:20, *PL* 25, 1067.

17. Julian, *Ad Florum*, quoted by Augustine, *Contra Iulianum* (*Opus imperfectum*) 1, 38, ed. Michaela Zelzer, *CSEL* (1974) 85¹, 28 (italics supplied); Quodvultdeus, *Sermo de symbolo contra iudaeus, paganos et arianos* c. 4, ed. R. Braun, *Opera*, *CC*, vol. 60 (1976) 231: "Exspectatur enim dies iudicii; aderit ille aequissimus iudex qui nullius potentis personam accipiet, cuius palatium auro argentove nemo corrumpet." Augustine, *Enarrationes in Psalmos* 45, 6, ed. Cyril Lambot, *CC* 38, 523.

18. Pelagius, *In Epistolam B. Pauli ad Romanos* 2, 1, in *PL Supp.*, ed. A. Hamann 1, 1120; Augustine, *Enarrationes in Psalmos* 32, 1, *CC* 38, 256.

19. Augustine, *In Joannis Evangelium Tractatus CXXIV*, Tract 30 at 10, 7, 24, ed. R. Willems, *CC* 36, 292–293. Augustine's text was apparently unusual among Latin versions, although some other versions read, "Do not judge according to the person," see Sabatier, *Bibliorum sacrorum latinae versiones antiquae seu Vetus italica* 3, 422.

20. Augustine to Macedonius, Letter 153, sec. 23, *CSEL* 44, 423: "Sed non ideo debet iudex vendere iustum iudicium aut testis verum testimonium, quia vendit advocatus iustum patrocinium et iuris peritus verum consilium; illi enim inter utramque partem ad examen adhibentur, isti ex una parte consistunt."

21. Slaves *redimantur*: *Codex Theodosianus* 3, 1, 5 (A.D. 384); *redemptos*: ibid. 5, 7, 2 (A.D. 409); *redemptio ex servitute*, ibid. 4, 8, 7 (A.D. 331).

Guardians paid off (*redempti*): ibid. 3, 5, 12 (A.D. 422); chaperons paid off (*redempti*): ibid. 9, 24, 1 (A.D. 320); buy up (*redimant*) enforcers: ibid. 2, 13, 1 (A.D. 422).

"Non sit venale iudicis velum, non ingressus redempti.... Aeque aures iudicantis pauperrimis ac divitibus reserentur." Ibid. 1, 16, 7 (A.D. 331). Cyprian, *Ad Donatum*, Letter 1, 10, *PL* 4, 214: "Quis inter haec vero subveniat? Patronus? Praevaricatur et decipit. Iudex? Sed sententiam vendit.... Nullus de legibus metus est. De quaesitore, de iudice, pavor nullus. Quod potest redimi non timetur." Jerome, *In Amos*, *PL* 25, 1046.

22. Augustine, *Contra Iulianum* 3, 3, 9. *PL* 44, 706: "Ubi redemptio sonat, intelligitur et pretium"; *PL* 44, 707: "Redemptor ipse respondeat, dicat ipse mercator: 'Hic est,' inquit, 'sanguis meus'"; Augustine, *Enarrationes in Psalmos*, Ps 136, 7, *CC* 40, 1968: "Si redimimur, captivi eramus. Qui nos redimit? Christus. A quo nos redimit? A diabolo"; Augustine, *De nuptiis et concupiscentia* 1, 22, *CSEL* 42, 235 (from the power of the devil); Augustine, *De Trinitate* 3, 15, *PL* 42, 1029 (devil not enriched but obliged).

23. Ambrose to Constantius, Ambrose, *Epistolae*, Letter 72, *PL* 16, 1299); Jerome, *In epistolam ad Ephesios; PL* 26, 480–481; John Chrysostom, *Fragmenta* on 1 Peter 1, 18, *PG* 69, 1053; Origen, *In Evangelium Matthaei* 20, 28, *PG* 13, 1397.

24. Augustine on Psalm 25:13, *CC* 38, 149. For the anticipation of Augustine in Cicero, see Chapter 2, n. 54. As to the parallel development, not direct precedent, in *The Babylonia Talmud*, Rabbi Ashi said that if a man guards an orchard from outside, "all of it is protected. But if he guards it from inside, only that section in front of him is protected and that which is behind him is not protected," *Yebamoth* 21a, *The Babylonian Talmud*, ed. I. Epstein (London: Soncino Press, 1936), Pt 3¹, 123–124. With this general principle in mind of the need for a guard about the law, the rabbis said "even an offering of words is forbidden." Samuel, one of two judges of the rabbinic court at Neharden in the Persian Empire, circa A.D. 240, is said to have been offered a helping hand on board a ferry. He disqualified himself from judging the case of the man who had offered the hand. The Palestinian rabbi, Ishmael bar Rabbi Jose, circa A.D. 200, was offered a basket of fruit by his tenant on Thursday, instead of the tenant's usual offering of fish on Friday. He disqualified himself from hearing the tenant's case. A man removed a bird from the head of Rabbi Amenar, who then disqualified himself from

judging his case. All these exempla are offered in the Talmud, *Kethuboth* 105b, (Vol. 14, 677—678) which also gives the punning reason of Raba the Master (d. 247) for the Deuteronomic prohibition of *shoḥadh*: a judge who takes it becomes so well-disposed to the giver that with him "he is one" (*she-hu-had*). Mari, son of R. Ashi, used to disqualify himself as a judge where a scholar was concerned because a scholar was "dear to him as himself, and a man cannot see anything to his own disadvantage," *Shabbath* 119a, 4, 585.

The rabbinic ideal should be compared, however, with the casuistry of *Sanhedrin* 29a (23, 175) where the Misnah teaches, "A friend of one of the litigants is not permitted to act as a judge," but says, "friend" means "groomsman," and Raba limits this disqualification to the day of the wedding.

25.   Augustine, on Ps 25:13, CC 38, 149: "Munera non solum pecunia est, non solum aurum et argentum, non solum exenia sunt; neque omnes qui accipiunt ea [money, gold, silver and *exenia*] accipiunt munera. Aliquando enim accipiuntur ab ecclesia. Quid dico? Petrus accepit, Dominus accepit, loculos habuit, ea quae mittebantur Iudas auferebat." Augustine on Psalm 49:28, CC 38, 596 (corrupt judge).

26.   J. N. L. Myres, "Pelagius and the End of Roman Rule in Britain," *Journal of Roman Studies* 50 (1960) 21. Myres's article is marred in three respects. First, he thinks that the bad meaning of *gratia* meant that Pelagius' critique of theological *gratia* had social implications. This suggestion is without foundation. Second, he ignores the range of meanings of *gratia* and its good sense in the Theodosian Code and in writers like Ambrose. At 30 he tries to find significance in the absence of references to *gratia* in a bad sense in legislation after 419, as though the Pelagian controversy which reached its climax in 419 taught the imperial draftsmen not to use *gratia* in its unfavorable meaning. But the Theodosian Code itself was put together by the imperial draftsmen in the 430's. If *gratia* in a bad sense was now *verboten*, why did they preserve so many decrees using it this way? It is clear, I suggest, that they had no trouble distinguishing good and bad meanings. In the same way Innocent I attacks the bishops who show *gratia* (favoritism), Innocent to Agapitus and others, Epistle 39, PL 20, 606, and also attacks the heretics who write against God's *gratia* (favor), Innocent to Augustine and others, Epistle 31, 5, PL 20, 596. Third, Myres supposes that Pelagius' theory reflects a more passionate hatred of human injustice in the courts than does Augustine's. Myres was corrected on his claim that Pelagius had a social program by J. H. W. G. Liebeschuetz, "Did the Pelagian Movement Have Social Aims?" *Historia* 12, 227 (1963), but Liebeschuetz did not clear up the impression that Pelagius somehow had firmer convictions than Augustine about human justice. A useful contrast to Myres's views is provided by Ignacio Pérez de Heredia y Valle, "Die Sorge um die Unparteilichkeit des Richters im Allgemeinen in der Lehre der Synoden und der Väter vom IV. Jahrhundert bis zum Ende der Väterzeit," *Archiv für katholisches Kirchenrecht* (1979) 148, 380—408.

27.   *Codex Theodosianus* 1, 16, 3 (A.D. 319); ibid. 6, 4, 22 (A.D. 373); ibid. 2, 1, 6 (A.D. 385); ibid. 9, 40, 16 (A.D. 398). Ambrose, *De officiis ministrorum* 2, 24, PL 15, 144; Council of Hippo, c.14, Mansi 3, 849; Myres at 50.

28.   *Codex Theodosianus* 13, 1, 9 (372). Note that *beneficium*, while used more often than *gratia* in a positive sense in the Code, is here used in a negative sense; ibid. 1, 1, 4 (393): "Generale praeceptum beneficio speciale anteferendum est." Implicitly, of course, this decree recognizes that favors have legal status and will be lawfully accorded. Exemptions—with which the *Internal Revenue Code* sec. 503(c) would afford one of numerous comparisons in our legal system—are for professors, physicians, and in some instances for their children, *Codex Theodosianus* 13, 3, 1–19 (A.D. 321–428); for all manner of artisans, ibid. 13, 4, 2 (A.D. 337); for teachers of painting, ibid. 13, 4, 4 (A.D. 374); for bishops, ibid. 16, 2, 1–47 (A.D. 313–425); for officials of the palace, ibid. 6, 35, 1–14 (A.D. 314–425); for the secret service, ibid. 6, 27, 1 (A.D. 354); 6, 27, 8 (A.D. 435).

29.   Ibid. 13, 10, 8 (A.D. 383): "abolita specialium immunitatium gratia"; ibid. 11, 1, 26 (A.D. 399): "Nullum gratia relevet"; ibid. 9, 38, 5 (A.D. 371): "Indulgentia . . . poenae gratiam facit." For other examples of the positive use of *gratia*, see ibid. 1, 6, 4, (A.D. 365): certain requests for privilege in Rome, asked as a favor (*gratia*), are to be referred to the emperor for final decision; ibid. 6, 24, 3 (A.D. 365): members of the imperial guard who obtain their positions by patronage or the favor (*gratia*) of the powerful are taxed at a higher rate than those enrolled after service—here the use of *gratia* is not disapproved, it is treated as a legitimate avenue of entry into the guard, but veterans are not to be taxed to death. Similarly in ibid. 6, 18, 1 (A.D. 412) retired counts who have earned the title outrank counts who have purchased the title or acquired it by favor (*gratia*)—the emperor is not treating this high title as illegal when it is bestowed by grace.

30.   Ambrose, *De obitu Valentiniani* sec. 9, CSEL 73, 334 (1953): "Videns haec Valentinianus

integrae plenae gratiae respondet . . ."; Ambrose, *De obitu Theodosii* sec. 12, *CSEL* 73, 377: "Quantum igitur est deponere terrorem potentiae, praeferre suavitatem gratiae!" ibid. sec. 33, *CSEL* 73, 388: "Et ego . . . dilexi virum misericordem"; ibid. sec. 16, *CSEL* 73, 379: "[Christus] maluit in hunc mundum redemptor venire quam iudex."

31.   Macedonius to Augustine, Letter 152, sec. 2, *CSEL* 44, 394; Augustine to Macedonius, Letter 153, sec. 3, *CSEL* 44, 398; ibid. sec. 4 at 398–399; ibid. sec. 9 at 405. See *Codex Theodosianus* 9, 40, 16 (A.D. 398) (decree permitting some intervention).

From the perspective of the prefect of Rome in 384—the perspective of a proud pagan prefect—clemency in a judgment given by anyone less than the emperor was corruption. See Symmachus, *Relationes*, in *Prefect and Emperor: The "Relationes" of Symmachus A.D. 384*, ed. and trans. R. H. Barrow (Oxford: Clarendon Press, 1973) 234–236: "Alia est enim condicio magistratuum, quorum corruptae videntur esse sententiae, si sint legibus mitiores, alia est divinorum principum potestas, quos decet acrimoniam severi iuris inflectere."

The tradition of the bishop as intercessor has not lapsed. One reads in the life of John XXIII: "It is not known what Roncalli may have said to the German commander. From that moment, each time death sentences were issued against Greek partisans who had fallen into German hands, Monsignor Roncalli sent a petition of clemency to the Field Marshall and each time the death sentence was commuted to life imprisonment." Giancarlo Zizola, *The Utopia of Pope John XXIII*, trans. Helen Barolini (Maryknoll, N.Y.: Orbis Books, 1978) 39.

32.   The Council of Milevis to Innocent I, *CSEL* 44, 664; Augustine to Sixtus, Letter 194, sec. 7, *CSEL* 57, 181.

33.   When Western bishops led by the grand old man, Ossius of Cordova (aged 87), met in 343 to rebuff the Arians, they enacted canons against bishops moving to bigger sees, a practice believed to be helpful to the Arians. See Council of Sardica, Canons 1 and 2, *Ecclesiae monumenta iuris antiquissima*, ed. C. H. Turner (Oxford: Clarendon Press, 1939) 1, 452–455, 490–492; Hamilton Hess, *The Canons of the Council of Sardica* (Oxford: Clarendon Press, 1958) 76–79. The practice is denounced in canon 1 as motivated by avarice and the love of domination and in canon 2 as carried out by those who did not scruple "to corrupt a handful" with rewards and "hire." The Latin *praemium*, "reward," had its Greek parallel, *misthos*, "hire" or "reward." Absence of any specific accusation of buying *gratia* suggests that the legal and political potency of accusations of this kind had not yet been fully grasped.

34.   Basil to the Choirbishops, Letter 53, *Lettres*, ed. Yves Courtonne (Paris: Société d'Edition "Les Belles Lettres," 1957) I, 137–138 [= *PG* 32, 397]; Basil, *Ethikon*, *PG* 31, 788–789; *Canones Apostolorum* in *Didascalia et Constitutiones Apostolicae* 8, 42, 29, ed. F. X. Funk (Paderborn, 1905) 1, 572–573; cf. *Constitutiones apostolorum* 6, 7, 3, ibid. 1, 316–317.

35.   John Chrysostom, *Peri Parthenias*, *PG* 48, 550.

36.   Palladius, *Dialogos*, *PG* 47, 47–51. For a discussion of the identity of Palladius, see Chrysostomus Baur, O.S.B., *John Chrysostom and His Time*, trans. M. Gonzaga (Westminster, Md: Newman Press, 1959) 1, xxii–xxvi.

37.   Ambrose, *Expositio evangelii secundum Lucam* at Luke 4:54, *CC* 114, 125 and Lk 9:18–21, *CC* 114, 338; Jerome, *In Matthaeum*, *PL* 26, 62–63 and 158; Augustine, *Enarrationes in Psalmos*, Ps 130, sec. 5, *CC* 40, 1901.

Many modern translations translate *peristeran* in the Temple scene as "pigeon," while translating the same Greek word in the baptismal scene as "dove," thereby breaking the relation between the two stories. I assume it would be ludicrous to say that the Holy Spirit descended on Jesus "like a pigeon" or to translate Matthew 10:16, "Be harmless as pigeons." If "dove" is retained in these places, there is good reason to keep "dove" in the Temple story, and there is authority for such translation; see John L. McKenzie, *Dictionary of the Bible* (Milwaukee, Wisc.: Bruce Publishing Company, 1965) 203.

38.   Pelagius to Demetrias, *PL* 30, 22; Julian, *Expositio libri Job* 41, 2, *PL Supp.* 1, 1677; on the attributions to Pelagius and Julian, see Gerald Bonner, *Augustine and Modern Research on Pelagianism* (Philadelphia: Villanova University Press, 1972) 7.

39.   Augustine to Sixtus, Letter 194, sec. 4, *CSEL* 57, 178: "Quod autem personarum acceptorem deum se credere existimant, si credant, quod se ullis praecedentibus meritis, cuius vult, miseretur. . . ." Ibid. sec. 5 at 179: " 'Sed iniustum est,' inquiunt, 'in una eademque causa hunc liberari, illum puniri.' " Ibid. sec. 31 at 200: ". . . isti, qui personarum acceptorem fieri existimant deum, si in una eademque causa super alios veniat misericordia eius, super alios manet ira eius. . . ."

40.   Ibid. sec. 4 at 178–179: "atque ibi potius acceptionem nullam fieri personarum, ubi una eademque massa damnationis ac offensionis involuit, ut liberatus de non liberato discat, quod etiam sibi supplicium conveniret, nisi gratia subveniret: si autem gratia, utique nullis meritis reddita sed gratuita bonitate donata."

41.   Julian, *Ad Florum*, quoted by Augustine, *Opus imperfectum* 1, 38, *PL* 45, 1059 *CSEL* 85¹, 28: "sine fraude, sine gratia."

42.   Augustine, *Epistolae ad Romanos inchoata expositio* 8, *PL* 35, 2093: "Non omnis gratia est a Deo. Nam et iudices mali praebent gratiam in accipiendis personis aliqua cupiditate illecti aut timore perterriti."

43.   Augustine, *Opus imperfectum* 1, 39, *PL* 45, 1064 *CSEL* 85¹, 29: "qui negas gratiam ubi nulla est acceptio personarum."

44.   Ibid. 1, 38 at col. 1064, *CSEL* 85¹, 28.

CHAPTER 4: "LEST MONEY SHOULD PREVAIL AT THE DEPARTMENT. . . ." (PP. 83–113)

1.   Augustine, Sermon 107, 7, *PL* 38, 631.

2.   Augustine, *Enarrationes in Psalmos* 25, 13, *CC* 38, 150: "Accusat quasi accepta sint munera"; "caecos oculos dirigit in iudicem."

3.   *Codex Theodosianus* 1, 27, 1 (A.D. 318?): irremovability of case before bishop; 1, 27, 2 (A.D. 408): bishop's judgment valid and enforceable by office staff; 16, 11, 1, (A.D. 399): bishop's compulsory jurisdiction over cases involving religion; 16, 2, 41 (A.D. 411): clerics must not be accused except before bishops. Even before the last two decrees, a case from Antioch in 381 where monks brought those complaining about them into the bishop's court shows that the jurisdiction of the bishop was not easy to avoid where a religious issue was introduced; see Libanius, *Orationes* 30, 11, discussed by John Matthews, *Western Aristocracies and Imperial Court* (Oxford: Clarendon Press, 1975) 141.

4.   Julian, *Ad Florum*, quoted in Augustine, *Opus imperfectum* 1, 42, *PL* 45, 1065–1066, *CSEL* 85,¹ 30.

5.   Julian, *Ad Florum*, quoted in Augustine, *Opus imperfectum* 3, 35, *PL* 45, 1262, *CSEL* 85,¹ 375.

6.   These questions are, respectively, from J. Patout Burns, "Augustine's Role in the Imperial Action Against Pelagius," *Journal of Theological Studies*, New Series 30 (1979) at 81; Otto Wermelinger, *Rom und Pelagius* (Stuttgart: Anton Hiersemann, 1975) 199; Peter Brown, *Augustine of Hippo* (Berkeley and Los Angeles: University of California Press, 1969) 362; and Peter Brown, "The Patrons of Pelagius: The Roman Aristocracy Between East and West," *Journal of Theological Studies*, New Series 21, 62 (1970). For the charges against Theophilus, see Palladius, *Dialogos*, *PG* 47, 26.

7.   Augustine to Marcellinus, Letter 139, sec. 3, *CSEL* 44, 152; Augustine, *De peccatorum meritis et remissione et de baptismo parvulorum ad Marcellinum libri tres*, Preface, *PL* 44, 108; Augustine, *De spiritu et littera*, *PL* 44, 201.

8.   Wermelinger, *Rom und Pelagius* 94–164. On the normative role of the see of Peter, *Codex Theodosianus* 16, 1, 2 (A.D. 380).

9.   Julian, *Ad Florum*, quoted in Augustine, *Opus imperfectum* 1, 10, *PL* 45, 1054, *CSEL* 85,¹ 10.

A number of modern historians—Brown, *Augustine of Hippo* 362; Burns, "Augustine's Role in the Imperial Action Against Pelagius" 67; Wermelinger, *Rom und Pelagius* 196—have indicated that the Africans took the initiative in the appeal to Ravenna. They have been misled by the ultimate outcome being what the Africans wanted, and they have ignored the only evidence available—Julian's explicit statement that "we clamored for judges," followed by his statement that Augustine in *Marriage and Concupiscence* had praised Valerius for blocking this request. If the Pelagians were clamoring for imperial judges, they must have taken the initiative at Ravenna.

10.   Honorius and Theodosius to the Praetorian Prefect Palladius, April 30, 418, *PL* 56,¹ 490–493. On Zosimus' condemnation of Pelagius, see Wermelinger, *Rom und Pelagius*, 204.

11.   On Constantius and Marcellinus, see Orosius, *Historiarum adversus paganos libri* 7, 42, 16, *CSEL* 5, 558–559; Galla Placidia to Aurelius, March 20, 419, Galla Placidia to Augustine and others, March 20, 419, Letters 27 and 28, *Collectio avellana*, ed. Otto Guenther (Vienna, 1895), *CSEL* 35, 73–74. The letters are misentitled as letters from the emperor. The evidence on the African channels at Ravenna is reviewed by Wermelinger at 197–199.

12.   Augustine to Valerius, Letter 200, sec. 1, *CSEL* 57, 293.

13.   Augustine, *De nuptiis et concupiscentia* 1, 2, *CSEL* 42, 213.

14.   On Firmus's mission to the Roman clergy in 418, Augustine to Sixtus, Letter 194, sec. 1, *CSEL* 57, 176. Firmus is described to Valerius as "vir sanctus nobisque, ut ab illo scire potuisti, familiarissima caritate coniunctus," Letter 290, sec. 1, at p. 293. He does not sound like a bagman.

15.   Julian, *Ad Florum*, quoted in Augustine, *Opus imperfectum* 1, 10, PL 45, 1054, CSEL 85,[1] 10–11.

16.   Ibid., CSEL, 85,[1] 10.

17.   Honorius and Theodosius to Aurelius, bishop of Cathage, PL 56, 493, 494.

18.   Julian, *Ad Florum*, quoted in Augustine, *Opus imperfectum* 6, 18, PL 45, 1541: "Quid enim tam prodigale quam quod Poenas eloquitur?"; Julian in ibid. 4, 56, PL 45, 1372: "patronus asinorum."

19.   Augustine, *Confessiones* 9, 4, 7, CSEL 33, 202; ibid 6, 10 (Alypius' "amazing" probity).

20.   Augustine, *Opus imperfectum* 1, 42, PL 45, 1066, CSEL 85,[1] 30–31.

21.   Ibid. 3, 35, PL 45, 1262, CSEL 85,[1] 374–375.

22.   Augustine to Fortunatus, Letter 115, CSEL 34, 661–662; Augustine to Generosus, Letter 116, CSEL 34, 663. According to Symmachus writing Ambrose in A.D. 396–397 on behalf of his friend Caecilianus, it was unusual for Ambrose to intervene in a purely "financial" lawsuit, Symmachus, *Epistolae* 3, 36, ed. Otto Seeck, *Q. Aurelii Symmachi quae supersunt* (Berlin: Weidmann, 1883) 82.

23.   The scope of the *Lex Julia repetundarum: Digesta Justiniani* 48, 11, 1, 3, 4, 6, 7; ibid. 48, 11, 9 (Papinian); on 100 goldpiece limit, ibid. 48, 11, 6; on penalties, ibid. 48, 11, 7. On shakedowns, ibid. 47, 13, 1 and 2; on punishment of petty judges, ibid. 48, 19, 38; on making the case one's own, ibid. 5, 1, 15, 1, and Kelly, *Roman Litigation*, 104–116. On the murders of Papinian and Ulpian, A. Arthur Schiller, *Roman Law* (The Hague: Mouton Publishers, 1978) 353, 361.

24.   See Richard B. Stewart, "History and Policy Analysis," *Stanford Law Review* 31 (1979) 1159 at 1161, reviewing James E. Krier and Edmund Ursin, *Pollution and Policy* (Berkeley: University of California Press, 1977). On the sale of office in the Empire, Wolfgang Schuller, "Prinzipien des spätantiken Beamtentums," in Schuller, ed., *Korruption im Altertum* (Munich: R. Oldenbourg, 1922) 203, and Wolfgang Schuller, "Amterkauf im römischen Reich," *Der Staat* 19 (1980) 54–71.

25.   *Codex Theodosianus* 1, 16, 7 (A.D. 331) (Constantine's access legislation); ibid. 8, 1, 4 (A.D. 344): accountants for the judges ordinary are subject to torture; ibid. 8, 1, 6 (A.D. 362): accountants falsifying accounts of municipalities are subject to torture; ibid. 8, 1, 7 (A.D. 362): public record keepers are subject to torture; ibid. 8, 1, 8 (A.D. 363): accountants subject to torture; ibid. 8, 1, 9 (A.D. 365): accountants torturable if they fail to notify judge of tax due and delinquent; they also become liable for the tax; ibid. 8, 1, 12 (A.D. 382): an accountant who transfers money from one account to another "to correct the wrongdoing of the judge" is subject to the severest punishment; ibid. 8, 1, 14 (A.D. 398): civil accountants are not to mix with military accountants "to the ruin of all." These legal provisions on accountants are among the prime proofs often given of corruption; they indeed reflect a strenuous effort to curb it.

26.   Chronologically considered, the principal decrees against judicial corruption in the fourth and early fifth centuries preserved in the Theodosian Code are the following: *Codex Theodosianus* 11, 30, 5 (A.D. 316), Constantine at Arles to the proconsul of Africa: favoritism (*gratia*) shall not delay an appeal to the emperor. Ibid. 1, 16, 3 (A.D. 319), Constantine at Sirmium to the governor of Corsica: provincials have the right to appear before the governor to prefer charges of "negligence or avarice" against members of his office staff. Suit may be brought against anyone who has judged unjustly, corrupted by a reward (*praemium*) or influence (*gratia*). Ibid 1, 16, 6 (A.D. 331): Constantine at Constantinople to the provincials: access to be free. Ibid. 6, 4, 22 (A.D. 373), Valentinian to the Senate: those senators who with the aid of the judges become "vendors" and "sell Roman law at auction" shall be punished. The influence (*gratia*) of the powerful in trials shall cease. Ibid. 1, 16, 13 (A.D. 377), Valentinian at Mainz to the praetorian prefect: no provincial shall visit a judge secretly. Ibid. 9, 27, 4 (A.D. 382), Gratian to the praetorian prefect: penalties against misbehaving judges may be exacted from them or their heirs. Ibid. 9, 27, 5 (A.D. 383), Theodosius at Milan: all trial judges and judges ordinary of a province "shall keep their hands off money and patrimonies. They shall not consider another man's lawsuit their prey. A judge of a private lawsuit who is a trafficker (*mercator*) shall be [subject to the death penalty]." Ibid. 2, 1, 6 (A.D. 385), Theodosius at Milan to the praetorian prefect: if any person proves that his case has not been heard, or that it has been delayed, by the arrogance or by the favoritism (*gratia*) of the judge, the judge shall pay the fisc the value of the case, and his principal office staff shall be deported. Ibid. 9, 27, 6 (A.D. 386), Arcadius at Constantinople to the provincials: If a person "of any class whatever" has been shaken down "in any manner" by a judge, he shall report the crime and be vindicated. So too any person who knows that "a sentence as to law" has been sold and any person who knows "that a punishment has been remitted for a price or inflicted through corrupt cupidity." Ibid. 11, 30, 48 (A.D. 387), Theodosius at Milan to the praetorian prefect: a judge shall be

fined fifty silver pounds if he permits an appeal through favoritism (*gratia*); and his office staff shall be fined a like amount. Ibid. 9, 40, 15 (A.D. 392), Valentinian at Constantinople to the praetorian prefect: stigma and fines are provided for governors of provinces and judges if they sell their connivance in schemes of criminals to escape punishment after conviction by feigning either appeal or the intervention of clerics. Ibid. 9, 40, 16 (A.D. 398), Arcadius at Mnyzus to the praetorian prefect: clerics and monks may intervene in a criminal case and appeal if the safety of a person is threatened by the error or favoritism (*gratia*) of a judge.

27. Principal instances: Ammianus Marcellinus, *Rerum gestarum libri qui supersunt* 14, 9, 1–3: the treason trials at Antioch under Constantine's young nephew Gallus Caesar in 354; Ammianus was on the staff of Ursicinus, a general who unwillingly participated in the trials; 15, 2, 9: the treason trials in Milan under Constantius in 355; Ursicinus, accompanied by Ammianus, was on the scene but himself was under suspicion; Ammianus says that some rich men "bought acquittals at monstrous prices" ("absolutionem pretiis mercarentur immensis"); 15, 13, 2: the trials connected with the murder of the governor of Syria when Musonianus was praetorian prefect in the East, 354–355, where the poor were convicted, and the rich authors of the crime, having paid huge bribes, are freed; 19, 12, 1: the treason trials at Scythopolis conducted in 359 by state secretary Paulus who "sought profit from the rack"; 26, 10, 9–14: the lawsuits launched by Emperor Valens and his gang after Valens's accession to power in the East in 365, by whom the rich and powerful were robbed before judges falsely imitating Cato; 30, 4, 2: the deals made between 365 and 375 by Valens's judges, who "sold the cases of lesser folk to army officers or the palace powers"; and 28, 1, 34 the traffic conducted in judgments by Maximinus, acting prefect in Rome in 369, aided by one Victorinus who is said "to have sold Maximinus' decisions." Indirect punishment: ibid, 14, 11, 24: the end of cruel Gallus Caesar; 22, 3, 11: the end of Paulus, a Spaniard (14, 5, 6) known as Hellman (19, 12, 1) or the Chain (22, 3, 11).

28. John Kelly, *Roman Litigation* (Oxford: Clarendon Press, 1966) 116.

29. Augustine to Macedonius, Letter 153, sec. 23, *CSEL* 44, 423.

30. *Codex Theodosianus* 11, 11, 1 (368–373?): ". . . sive xenia aut munuscula, quae canonica ex more fecerunt, extorserit vel sponte haec quae improbata sunt oblata non refutaverit, ablatis omnibus facultatibus ultimo subiugetur exitio. . . ."

31. Augustine to Macedonius, Letter 153, sec. 24, *CSEL* 44, 423–424.

32. Martial, *Epigrams* 2, 13: "iudex petit, et petit patronus;" Petronius, *Satyricon* 14: "Quid faciunt ubi leges ubi sola pecunia regnat. . . ? Ergo iudicium nihil est nisi publica merces et eques in causa qui sedet, empta probat." Apuleius, *Metamorphoses* 10, 33: "Quid ergo miramini, vilissima capita, immo forensia pecora, immo vero togati vulturii, si toti nunc iudices sententias suas pretio nundinantur, cum rerum exordio inter deos et homines agitatum iudicium corruperit gratia. . . ." The reference is to Paris selling his judgment to Venus. The Loeb editors insert "*si*" before *vilissima* on the ground that the lawyers should not be called "to marvel at their own degradation." But I do not know why not, and the editors note than no manuscript supports the *si*.

All of the above examples are cited by Kelly, *Roman Litigation* 37–40, to show that corruption was a feature of Roman litigation. He also includes Ovid, *Amores* 1, 10, 38 and 40, which simply says that a judge whose "bag is open" has not been well selected, and a court which makes big money is "dirty."

33. The quotations are, respectively, from (1) Ferdinand Lot, *La Fin du monde antique et le début du moyen âge* (Paris: Editions A. Michel, 1951): "Tout le monde vole. Les employés (*officiales*) trafiquent des audiences judicieuses." (As evidence of this statement Lot goes on to cite Constantine's law *against* such payments, cited at n. 34 below). (2) Andreas Alföldi, *A Conflict of Ideas in the Late Roman Empire*, trans. Harold Mattingly (Oxford: Clarendon Press, 1952) 30: "The whole of the Roman Empire . . . [in which] nothing could be done without baksheesh." (3) Stewart I. Oost, *Galla Placidia Augusta* (Chicago: University of Chicago Press, 1968) 218: "The age . . . venal and corrupt judges . . . ubiquitous corruption and injustice of the times." (4) A. H. M. Jones, *The Later Roman Empire 284–602* (Oxford: Basil Blackwell, 1964) 1, 399 ("judicial corruption was normal and systematic"); 1, 409 (provincial governors "almost invariably venal"); 1, 470 (judges "as a rule venal"); 1, 502 (judicial corruption "an endemic evil").

For earlier statements on the same theme, see Otto Seeck, *Geschicte des Untergangs der antiken Welt* (Berlin: Siemenroth & Troschel, 1901) 2, Appendix, 101, 513, 531; Samuel Dill, *Roman Society in the Last Century of the Western Empire* (London: Macmillan, 1899) 199.

34. *Codex Theodosianus* 1, 16, 7 (A.D. 331).

35. E.g., Jones, *The Later Roman Empire* 3, 90 at n. 68 and 69, documents his claims of endemic corruption by citations of the Theodosian Code (9, 27, 5, and 9, 27, 6 cited at n. 26

above); Marcian, Novel 1, pr., cited below at n. 91; and Justinian, Novel 8, pr. cited below at n. 98–100; and Pope Gregory I to the Empress Constantina, June 1, 595, cited in Chapter 5, n. 19. Other documentation consists in a cross-reference to his own 1, 399 which in turn depends on Justinian, Novel 8. Jones's "evidence" thus is entirely composed of instances of accusations.

36.   Dill, *Roman Society* 230.

37.   See Peter Brown, "Sorcery, Demons, and the Rise of Christianity from Late Antiquity into the Middle Ages," in Mary Douglas, ed., *Witchcraft Confessions & Accusations* (London: Tavistock Publications, 1970) 21–34.

38.   Ammianus, *Res gestae* 30, 4, 3: (oratory hateful to good men); ibid. 30, 4, 21 ("shake booty"); ibid. 30, 4, 22 (losers blame their lawyers).

39.   Augustine to Macedonius, Letter 153, sec. 10, *CSEL* 44, 406; ibid. sec. 25 at 424–425.

40.   Augustine, *De Sermone Domini* 1, 16, 50, ed. Almut Mutzenbecher, *CC* 35, 55–56.

41.   Schuller, "Prinzipien des spätantiken Beamtentums" 203–207. On recruitment to the bureaucracy, compare Matthews, *Western Aristocracies and Imperial Court* 41.

42.   Ammianus, *Res gestae* 15, 7, 1 on Leontius "in disceptando iustissimus"; 26, 3, 1 on Apronianus, "iudex integer et severus"; 27, 3, 3 on Symmachus; 27, 3, 11 on Viventius, "integer et prudens Pannonius"; 27, 9, 8–10 on Praetextatus, noted for "integretatis multiplices actus et probitatis," who in judging "nihil ad gratiam faceret"; 28, 4, 1 on Olybrius, "iustorum iniustorumque distinctor et arbitror plenus"; 15, 7, 6–10 on Bishop Liberius; 16, 8, 5–6 on Mavortius and Ursulus; 16, 7, 6 on Eutherius; 27, 7, 1–9 on Valentinian; 14, 9, 1 on Ursicinus at Antioch; 15, 6, 1–3 on him at Cologne. On Romanus and his accusers, 28, 6, 7–29.

43.   Ibid. 14, 11, 25 (Nemesis); ibid. 28, 6, 25 (eye of Justice).

44.   Ibid. 14, 11, 25.

45.   Sylvanus Senex, Valentinus, Aurelius, Innocentius, Maximinus, Optatus, Augustinus, Donatus, and Other Bishops from the Council of Cirta to the Donatists, Letter 141, sec. 1, *CSEL* 44, 235: "vestros episcopos dicere cognitorem praemio fuisse corruptum." For classical use of *praemium* in a negative sense, see Juvenal, *Satura* 3, 56, where an informer is told not to take a reward but to stay in with his friend, Hog.

46.   See S. Lancel, *Gesta Conlationis Carthaginiensis*, *CC* 149A (Turnhout, 1974) x–xiii.

47.   W. H. C. Frend, *The Donatist Church* (Oxford: Clarendon Press, 1952) 159.

48.   Ibid. 168–226.

49.   *Codex Theodosianus* 16, 6, 4 (Feb. 12, 405): "... ut haeresis ex schismate nasceretur"; ibid. 16, 5, 38 (Feb. 12, 405) (madness of Donatists); ibid. 16, 11, 2 (March 5, 405): the foregoing edict is to be posted in Africa; ibid. 16, 5, 39 (Dec. 8, 405): without delay due punishment is to be given "Donatistae superstitionis haereticos"; ibid. 16, 5, 44 (Nov. 24, 408) (pestilence); ibid. 16, 11, 3 (Oct. 14, 410, to Marcellinus).

50.   Augustine to Marcellinus, Letter 133, sec. 3, *CSEL* 44, 83; Marcellinus at the conference, *Gesta* 1, 8, 58.

51.   Honorius and Theodosius to Marcellinus, *Gesta*, 4, 54–55.

52.   *Ibid.* 55–56.

53.   Augustine to Caecilian, Letter 151, sec. 8, *CSEL* 44, 388.

54.   Marcellinus, Edict, Jan. 19, 411, *Gesta* 1, 5, 56–58.

55.   Ibid. 57 and again at 58.

56.   42 *United States Code Annotated* (1959 ed.) sec. 1455(d).

57.   *Gesta apud Zenophilum*, *CSEL* 26, 185, 194. The testimony against Silvanus comes from his own deacon Nundinarius. They had quarreled and Silvanus had had Nundinarius stoned. His testimony is that of an insider, who is very biased. On the affair, see Frend, *The Donatist Church* 18–21, 161.

58.   Augustine to Glorius and others (all Donatists), Letter 43, sec. 17, *CSEL* 34, 99.

59.   Augustine to Marcellinus, Letter 133, sec. 1, *CSEL* 44, 80–81 (crimes of the defendants).

60.   Ibid. sec. 2, 82: "Imple, Christiane iudex, pii patris officium"; ibid. sec. 3, 83.

61.   Augustine to Apringius, Letter 134, sec. 1, *CSEL* 44, 84 (divine judgment); ibid. sec. 4, 88 ("on account of Christ").

62.   Augustine to Marcellinus, Letter 139, sec. 2, *CSEL* 44, 151.

63.   An excellent exposition of their friendship is made by Madeleine Moreau, *Le Dossier Marcellinus dans la correspondance de Saint Augustin*, *Recherches augustiniennes* (Supplement of *Revue des études augustiniennes*) IX (1973), 146–173.

64.   Augustine, *De civitate Dei contra paganos* 1, Preface, *CSEL* 40¹, 3.

65.   Augustine to Caecilian, Letter 151, sec. 8, *CSEL* 44, 388: "Quantum decus honestatis, qui splendor gratiae...."

66. Ibid. sec. 6, *CSEL* 44, 387: Marinus a Catholic; sec. 4, 385: Caecilian his close adviser; sec. 5, 386: assurances given African bishops; sec. 4, 385: Apringius' injury to Caecilian. On the suppression of Heraclian's revolt, Frend, *The Donatist Church* 292–293. On Caecilian as praetorian prefect in 409, Matthews, *Western Aristocracies and Imperial Court* 292. Caecilian had been a protégé of Symmachus, see n. 22 above.

67. Ibid. secs. 5–6, 385–386 on Caecilian's promises and the brothers' execution.

68. Augustine, *Confessiones* 6, 2, *CSEL* 33, 114–115.

69. Augustine to Caecilian, letter 151, sec. 4, 385: "non erat grande negotium procurari aliquem qui diceret, quod salute promissa dicendum ille [Marinus] mandasset. Omnia in ista tempore suffrangabuntur...."

70. Orosius, *Historiarum adversus paganos libri* 7, 4, 17, *CSEL* 5, 558–559.

71. Augustine to Caecilian, Letter 151, sec. 3, 384, ("impious cruelty"), sec. 6, 387 ("wicked cruelty"); sec. 10, 390 ("blind cruelty"); sec. 11, 391 ("gratuitous cruelty"); sec. 11, 390 (displeased emperor). In contrast, Marcellinus' own "deeds against the Donatists" were posthumously confirmed by Honorius, and he himself was given posthumous rehabilitation as "spectabilis memoriae vir," *Codex Theodosianus* 16, 5, 55 (A.D. 414).

72. Augustine to Caecilian, Letter 151, sec. 8, *CSEL* 44, 388.

73. Jerome to Marcellinus and Anapsychia in Augustine, Letter 165, *CSEL* 44, 541. Jerome addresses them as "vestra unanimitas" and salutes them at the end (sec. 3, 545) as "domini vere sancti."

74. Augustine to Caecilian, Letter 151, sec. 9, *CSEL* 44, 389.

75. Jerome, *Contra Pelagianos* 3, 19, *PL* 23, 588–589.

76. Roman Martyrology, *Acta sanctorum*, ed. Bollandists (Paris and Rome, 1865) April, vol. I, 540.

77. F. van der Meer, *Augustine the Bishop*, trans. Brian Battershaw and G. R. Lamb (New York: Sheed & Ward, 1961) 192.

78. Augustine to Caecilian, Letter 151, sec. 12, 391. As Moreau, *Le Dossier Marcellinus* 101, remarks, "Tout se passe comme si, au fond de lui-même Augustin avait le sentiment que Caecilianus avait, plus ou moins activement, trempé dans l'exécution de Marcellinus...."

79. Augustine to Caecilian, Letter 151, sec. 14, *CSEL* 44, 392: "... adhuc vis esse catechumenus, quasi fideles non possunt, quanto sint fideliores atque meliores, tanto fidelius et melius administrare rem publicam."

80. Text in Edward Schwartz, *Concilium Universale Ephesenum* (Berlin: Walter de Gruyter & Co., 1922) 1, 4, 222–225.

81. Batiffol, "Les Présents de Saint Cyrile à la court de Constantinople," *Etudes de liturgie et d'archéologie chrétiennes* (Paris: Grimaldi, 1919) 154–155. For Nestorius' view, see *The Treatise of Heracleides*, trans. from a Syriac translation by G. R. Driver and Leonard Hodgson as *The Bazaar of Heracleides* (Oxford: Clarendon Press, 1925) 132.

82. Schwartz, *Concilium Universale Ephesenum* ix–x.

83. See ibid. x–xii for Irenaeus' career; 60–61 for Irenaeus' impressions of the court on his arrival from Ephesus; and xiii for Irenaeus' intention to vindicate himself and Nestorius. Nestorius on Irenaeus, *The Bazaar of Heracleides* 117.

84. Batiffol, "Les Presents de Saint Cyrile" 176. The same position is argued, with more embarrassment, by Charles J. Hefele, *A History of the Councils of the Church* sec. 150, Eng. trans. (Edinburgh, 1883) vol. 3, 112–114.

85. Cyril, *Homilae diversae* 4, *PG* 77, 993.

86. *Codex Theodosianus* 16, 5, 66.

87. Acacius to Alexander, Schwartz, *Concilium Universale Ephesenum* 85. Hefele, *A History of the Councils* sec. 150 (vol. 3, 112), notes Acacius' reputed age.

88. Nestorius, *The Bazaar of Heracleides* 279–282 (money paid the commissioner; Cyril's escape); 350 (the presents and the written documents).

89. Ibid. 97. Without analyzing the documents, Driver and Hodgson accept the accusations of Acacius and the letter of Epiphanius as "evidence" of "Cyril's bribery," ibid. 282 n. 1.

90. Historians since at least the time of Louis de Tillemont have accepted the genuineness of the Irenaeus documents, see F. Nau, trans. *Le Livre d'Héraclide de Damas* (Paris: Letouzey & Ané, 1910) 367. It is typical that Nestorius' accusation, made in a sermon, that Cyril was using "arrows of gold" against him is cited as confirmatory evidence! (Nau 369). By this standard, the more an accusation is repeated, the more credible it is. Hefele, *A History of the Councils* sec. 150 (vol. 3, 113) finds Acacius' letter unconvincing but at sec. 156 does not subject the Irenaeus documents to the same scrutiny. In the course of writing this book I have not en-

countered anywhere—not even in the copious confessions made by American corporations to the Securities and Exchange Commission or in the corporate files made public by committees of the United States Senate—anything close to the kind of detailed laying out of a plan of bribery that is contained in the letter from Epiphanius or anything as specific as the list of presents and particular recipients attached as a schedule. The uniqueness of the documents is not reassuring as to their authenticity as papers authorized by Cyril.

91.   *Codex Iustiniani* 9, 27, 6. In 450 the Emperor Marcian refers to "the venal self-seeking of the [provincial] judge," which the emperor has "cut off"; now "no offered wealth will make a strict mind effeminate." But the emperor notes that the crowd of appeals from the provinces betrays a want of confidence in the provincial judges, Marcian, Novel, 1, pr. and 1, Paul M. Meyer, ed., *Leges Novellae ad Theodosianum pertinentes* (Berlin: Weidmann, 1954) 181–182.

92.   Council of Chalcedon, canon 2, *Conciliorum oecumenicorum decreta*, ed. J. Giuseppe Alberigo et al. (Bologna, 1973) 88. On the Council's christological compromise, Pierre-Thomas Camelot, O.P., *Ephèse et Chalcedoine* (Paris: Editions de l'Orante, 1961) 149; Jaroslav Pelikan, *The Christian Tradition: A History of the Development of Doctrine* (Chicago: University of Chicago Press, 1971) 1, 265–266.

93.   Gennadius, *Epistola Encyclica*, PG 85, 1613–1617.

94.   *Codex Justiniani* 1, 3, 30.

95.   Ibid. 1, 1, 8, 19.

96.   *Digesta Iustiniani* 48, 11, *De lege Iulia repetundarum*, and 47, 13, *De concussione*.

97.   *Codex Iustiniani* 9, 27, *Ad legem Iuliam repetundarum*.

98.   *Novella Iustiniani* 8, Preamble.

99.   Ibid. c. 1.

100.   Ibid. c. 7 ("pure hands); c. 9 (fifty days); Edict to the archbishops and bishops, post Novel 8; ("dedicated to God"); Oath (for Illyricum), post Novel 8 ("share with Judas").

1.   Patrick, *Confessio*, in *Libri Epistolarum Sancti Patricii Episcopi*, ed. Ludwig Bieler (Dublin: Stationery Office, 1952) 86. For the background, Ludwig Bieler, *St. Patrick and the Coming of Christianity* (Dublin: Gill & Son, 1967) 41–49; R. P. C. Hanson, *St. Patrick* (Oxford: Clarendon Press, 1966) 175–187.

2.   Patrick, *Confessio* 87. On the brehons, see Bieler, *St. Patrick and the Coming of Christianity* 69, and Kathleen Hughes, *Early Christian Ireland* (Ithaca, N.Y.: Cornell University Press, 1972) 57.

3.   Patrick, *Confessio* 77 (*munera*); 85 (*munuscula*); 85–86 (took no price). Patrick was referring to Samuel as described in Ecclesiasticus 46:23 of the Latin Vulgate (Ecclus 46:19 in the New English Bible). The Vulgate's translation of 1 Samuel 12:3 may also have been in the back of his mind: Samuel says he will make restitution "if I have received an offering (*munus*) from the hand of anyone."

4.   Ibid. 1, 86–87; Hanson, *St. Patrick* 157 (Patrick's seniors); 154 (his use of Psalms).

5.   Caesarius, Sermon 229, 6, *Sermones*, ed. G. Morin (Turnhout, 1953), CC 104, 910.

6.   Caesarius, Sermon 1, 12, CC 103, 9.

7.   Caesarius, Sermon 13, 2, CC 103, 65.

8.   Caesarius, Sermon 32, 1, CC 103, 139.

9.   Caesarius, Sermon 26, 2, CC 103, 115.

10.   Caesarius, Sermon 1, 12, CC 103, 9.

11.   Second Council of Braga, c. 3, Martin, *Opera omnia*, ed. Claude W. Barlow (New Haven, Conn: Yale University Press, 1950) 119–120.

12.   Ibid. canons 4–7, 120.

13.   Gregory, *Moralia in Job* 9, 53, ed. Marc Adrien, CC (1979) 143, 494.

14.   Gregory, *Moralia* 26, 26, PL 76, 374–375.

15.   Gregory to Theoctista, Oct. 590, Gregory, *Registrum epistolarum*, ed. Paul Ewald and Ludwig M. Hartmann, 2nd ed. (Berlin: Weidmann, 1958) 1, 5–7.

16.   Gregory, *Regula pastoralis* 2, 2, PL 77, 27 (cleanness of rulers); ibid. 77, 102 (conjugal intercourse). Gregory to Augustine, July 601, *Registrum* 1, 340–341.

17.   Gregory, *XL Homiliarum in Evangelia libri duo* 1, 17, 13, PL 76, 1145.

18.   Gregory, *Moralia* 19, 56, CC 143A, 1001. The emphasis of Gregory on practice reflecting the interior life is finely developed by Claude Dagens, *Saint Grégoire le grand* (Paris: Etudes Augustiennes, 1977) 75–81.

19.   Gregory to the Empress Constantina, June 1, 595, Gregory, *Registrum* 1, 324–325.

20. Gregory to Peter, Subdeacon, July 592, *Registrum* 1, 135, 137.
21. Gregory to Honoratus, Deacon, July 592, ibid. 1, 132.
22. Gregory to Queen Brunichildis, Sept. 597, ibid. 2, 5 (pallium); Gregory to Queen Brunichildis, Sept. 595, ibid. 1, 383 (her goodness); Jeffrey Richards, *Consul of God* (London: Routledge & Kegan Paul, 1980) 214 (Disraeli). On Brunichildis's incest, F. Holmes Dudden, *Gregory the Great* (New York: Longmans, Green, 1905) 2, 73.
23. Gregory, *XL Homiliarum in Euangelia libri duo* 1, 17, 13, *PL* 76, 1145.
24. Synod of Rome, July 5, 595, canon 5, Mansi 10, 435.
25. Gregory to Virgil, Aug. 12, 595, *Registrum* 1, 369. Gregory to all the bishops of Gaul under Childebert, Aug. 12, 595, 1, 373; to Childebert, Aug. 15, 595, 1, 374. *Simoniacum* as an adjective meaning simoniacal is found in an account of the deeds of Pelagius I. Appointed bishop of Rome by grace of Justinian, he in 556 is said to have declared that to obtain any office in the Church, from doorkeeper to bishop, "by gold or promises" was, as all knew, "simoniacal," *Liber pontificalis*, ed. Louis Duchesne (Paris: E. de Brocard, 1955) 1, 303. Duchesne dates this account to 579–590, ibid. 1, ccxxxii, but more recent authority interprets Gregory I to Secundinus, May 599 (*Registrum* 2, 147), to show that the lives of the popes at that time did not go beyond 555, E. Griffe, "Le *Liber pontificalis* au temps du pape Saint Grégoire," *Bulletin de littérature ecclésiastique* 57 (1956) 65–70.
26. Gregory to John of Corinth, Aug. 15, 595, *Registrum* 1, 377; to all the bishops of Hellas, Aug. 15, 595, 1, 379.
27. Gregory to Clement of Byzacena, Oct. 593, ibid. 1, 247; to John of Prima Justiniana, Nov. 594, 1, 297; to Januarius, May 594, 1, 259; to Maxim, Sept. 595, 1, 382; to the bishops of Epirus, Sept. 595, 1, 386; to Brunichildis, Sept. 597, 2, 6; to Anastasius, April 599, 2, 134; to Syagrius, Etherius, Virgil, and Desiderius, July 599, 2, 206–207; to Aregius, July 599, 2, 211; to Theodoric and Theudebert, July 599, 2, 201; to Isacius, Feb. 601, 2, 298; to Aregius, June 601, 2, 315; to Theudebert, June 601, 2, 323; to Theodoric, June 22, 601, 2, 319; to Clothar, June 22, 601, 2, 324; to Columbus, March 602, 2, 355; to Victor, March 602, 2, 356; to Eulogius, July 603, 2, 406–407.
28. Gregory to Eulogius, July 603, ibid. 2, 406.
29. Gregory to Syagrius, July 599, ibid. 2, 213–214. For the later nonaction, see Council of Paris, Canons, *Concilia Galliae*, ed. Carlo De Clerq, CC 148A (1963), 275–286; Richards, *Consul of God* 214 (on Brunichildis).
30. Synod of Rome, July 5, 595, canon 5, Mansi 10, 435. Gregory to Clement, October 593, *Registrum* 1, 247.
31. Gregory to Maxim, Sept. 595, ibid. 1, 382; Gregory to Marinianus, bishop of Ravenna, July 599, 2, 172; Richards, *Consul of God* 207.
32. God's Consul: Epitaph, Appendix V, *Registrum* 2, 470.
33. On the diffusion of Gregory's works, Dagens, *Saint Grégoire le Grand* 441.
34. Ysidro, *Sententiarum libri III* 3, chap. 52 "De iudicibus," *PL* 83, 724–725. The reference to "wolves in the evening" comes from the Old Testament prophet Zephaniah 3:3 where the Latin Vulgate spoke of judges in these terms.
35. Ibid. 3, c. 53, c. 54, *PL* 83, 726.
36. Ysidro, *De differentiis verborum*, at "Emere" *PL* 83, 29 (definition of *redimere*); Ysidro, *Sententiarum* 3, 54, *PL* 83, 726, and 3, 60, *PL* 83, 733 (on buying back sins).
37. Ysidro, *De differentiis verborum* at "Donum" and at "Munus," *PL* 83, 28 and 47; Ysidro, *Etymologiarum libri XX*, Book 6, c. 19, *PL* 82, 254; Ysidro, *Sententiarum* 3, 54, *PL* 83, 725 (bad judges look at *dona*).
38. Ysidro, *Etymologiarum* 8, 5, "De haeresibus Christianorum," *PL* 82, 298.
39. Note, for example, how he is repeated and paraphrased (without acknowledgment) by Rabanus (776?–856), the abbot of Fulda, the Benedictine center of eighth- and ninth-century German scholarship. See, e.g., Rabanus, *Homilia* 58, "De iuste iudicando et falsis testibus non recipiendis," *PL* 110, 108–109.
40. *Adamnan's Life of St. Columba*, ed. and trans. Alan Orr Anderson and Marjorie Ogilvie Anderson (London: Thomas Nelson & Son, 1961) 1, 51, 318–322. On Adomnán as the preferred spelling, John Ryan, S.J., *The Monastic Institute* (Dublin: Gill & Macmillan, 1971) 3.
41. *Adamnan's Life* 180 (Preface, sec. 2).
42. Bertram Colgrave, "Introduction," *The Life of Bishop Wilfrid by Eddius Stephanus* (Latin text and English translation) (Cambridge: At the University Press, 1927) x.
43. Aedde, *Vita Sancti Wilfirthi*, in ibid. c. 21, p. 44.
44. Ibid. c. 24, 48.
45. Ibid. c. 25, 50.
46. Ibid. c. 28, 54.

47. Ibid. c. 29, 58; c. 32, 66; c. 33, 66; Roman sources on Agatho: *Liber pontificialis*, 1, 350.
48. Aedde, *Vita Sancti Wilfirthi*, c. 34, 70.
49. Ibid. c. 36, 74 (the king's offer); c. 43, 86 (Theodorus' tribute).
50. Ibid. c. 63, 136.
51. Bede, *Historia ecclesiastica*, ed. Bertram Colgrave and R. A. B. Mynors (Oxford: Clarendon Press, 1969) 3, 5, p. 226, p. 228.
52. Ibid. 4, 1, 331 (on Theodorus); 5, 19, 522, 524, 528 (Wilfrid's troubles and death).
53. Ibid. 5, 21, 548, 540.
54. Teodulfo, *Versus contra iudices*, ed. Ernst Dümmler, *Theodulfi Carmina, MGH-Poetae latini* (Berlin: Weidmann, 1881) vol. 1, lines 165–167. Teodulfo's poem is the basis for G. Monod, "Les moeurs judiciaires au VIIIᵉ siècle," *Revue historique* 35 (1887) 2–17.
55. Ibid. lines 125–152.
56. Charlemagne, *Admonitio generalis, MGH-Leges*, sec. 2, *Capitularia regum francorum* 1, 53, 55, 58.
57. Teodulfo, *Versus contra iudices* lines 799–809 (witnesses).
58. Ibid. lines 212–220, 243–252.
59. Ibid. lines 172–176, 179–204, 253, 285–288.
60. Ibid. lines 675–679 (assessors); lines 433–434 (doorkeepers); lines 715–732 (servants).
61. Teodulfo, *De libris quos legere solebam, MGH-Poetae latini* 1, 543.
62. *Versus contra iudices*, lines 693–702.
63. Ibid. line 33 (Samuel); line 67 (Hezekiah); line 77 (Josiah); lines 301–302, 313, 319–320, 326, 333–334 (effect of *munera*); line 450 ("high-throned"); lines 514, 554 (last judgment); lines 629–632 (responsibility to poor); line 835 (Thunderer).
64. Ibid. lines 269–270 (a strong city); 283–287 (the little things).
65. Three years after Teodulfo's visitation, the same sort of guidance as that of 789 was given in a general capitulary from Charlemagne addressed to royal deputies. Flattery, fear, and reward were again listed as the subverters of justice, together with "the defense of kinship"—a specification of the kind of love that could corrupt. No acknowledgment was made of the gap between Charlemagne's standard and prevailing practice. No sanction was provided for *munera*-givers. Reliance was placed on motivating the deputies to help the helpless and to look for heavenly reward. See Charlemagne, *Capitulare missorum generale, MGH-Leges*, sec. 2; *Capitularia regum francorum* 1, 92. Teodulfo had meant to move Charlemagne, J. M. Wallace-Hadrill, *The Frankish Church* (Oxford: Clarendon, 1983) 218.
66. Teodulfo, *Capitula ad presbyteros parochiae suae* c. 16, PL 105, 196.
67. Teodulfo, [Second Diocesan Statute] *La législation religieuse franque de Clovis à Charlemagne*, ed. Carlo De Clerq (Louvain: University of Louvain, 1936) 1, 334, 341.
68. See John T. Noonan, Jr., *Contraception: A History of Its Treatment by the Catholic Theologians and Canonists* (Cambridge, Mass: Harvard University Press, 1965) 152–167.
69. Finnian, *Penitential*, in *The Irish Penitentials*, ed. Ludwig Bieler (Dublin: Dublin Institute for Advanced Studies, 1963) 82–84; Cummaine [Cummean], *Penitential*, in ibid. 116–118. For the authors, Bieler, *The Irish Penitentials* 4–7.
70. Columbanus to Gregory I, PL 77, 1064–1066; Columbanus, *Poenitentiale*, in Bieler, *The Irish Penitentials* 96–107. Bieler at 5 accepts it as in substance the work of Columbanus.
71. Bede, *Marci Evangelii Expositio* 14, 11, CC 120, 608. For the penitential of Theodorus of Tarsus, the *Canons* of Gregory, the penitentials of St. Bede and Egbert archbishop of York, and the penitentials of Pseudo-Bede and Pseudo-Egbert, see F. W. H. Wasserschleben, *Die Bussordnungen der abendländischen Kirche* (Halle, 1851).
72. *The Old-Irish Penitential* c. 3, trans. D. A. Binchey, in Bieler, *The Irish Penitentials* 267. On its place in Old Irish prose, ibid. 47. For the Roman law, see Chapter 2 above at n. 31.
73. Finnian, *Penitential* c. 18 (magic), c. 22 (false oath), c. 47 (unbaptized child).
74. "Sinodus Hibernensis Decrevit," in ibid. 171.
75. D. A. Binchey, "Penitential Texts in Old Irish" in ibid. 50.
76. *Canones Hibernenses*, in ibid., "De arreis," c. 7, 165.
77. "The Old-Irish Table of Commutations," ed. and trans. D. A. Binchey, in ibid. 278–279.
78. Pseudo-Cummean, *Excarpsus*, H. J. Schmitz, ed., *Die Bussbücher und das kanonische Bussverfahren* (Düsseldorf, 1898) 603.
79. Pseudo-Bede-Egbert, *Excarpsus*, in ibid. 698.

1. *Missale romanum* (Tours, 1955) at "Offertorium." For the general meaning of reform, Gerhart B. Ladner, *The Idea of Reform* (Cambridge: Harvard University Press, 1959, 26 and 35.

Ladner's magisterial work, focused on reform in the patristic age, has only a single generic reference to reform and none to bribery and simony as objects of reform.

2. Humbert, *Libri III adversus simoniacos*, F. Thaner, *MGH—Libelli de lite imperatorum et pontificum*, vol. 1 (Hannover, 1891), Bk. 2, chapter 36 (Hungarians, etc.); 3, 20 (Catiline; blind ambition); 3, 22 (culpable silence); 3, 34 (robbers).

3. Emile Amann and Auguste Dumas, *L'Eglise au pouvoir des laïques* (Paris: Bloud & Gay, 1942) 98–100. On the lack of enforcement in the tenth and eleventh centuries, ibid. 472–473. On Humbert, see Rudolf Hüls, *Kardinäle, Klerus und Kirchen Roms* (Tübingen: Max Niemeyer, 1977) 131–132; on Hugues, ibid. 158–159. See also H. E. J. Cowdrey, *The Age of Abbot Desiderius* (Oxford: Clarendon, 1983) 84.

4. Synod of Rome (A.D. 1059), *Acta*, Mansi 19, 907–908.

5. See Humbert, Bk. 1, c. 4–13, c. 16, c. 18. For the use of Giovanni's life of Gregory I, J. Joseph Ryan, *Saint Peter Damiani and His Canonical Sources* (Toronto: Pontifical Institute of Mediaeval Studies, 1956) 162.

6. Humbert, Bk. 3, c. 32.

7. Ibid., Bk. 1, cc. 14–15.

8. Bonizo, *Liber ad amicum*, ed. Ernst Dümmler (*MGH—Libelli de lite* vol. 1), Bk. 6, p. 592.

9. Synod of Rome (A.D. 1063), *Acta*, Mansi 19, 1024. John Gilchrist has argued that the view underlying this decree—the dominant view as he sees it—was that power was conferred by simoniacal ordination, although grace was not, John Gilchrist, "Simoniaca haeresis and the Problem of Orders from Leo IX to Gratian," *Proceedings of the Second International Congress of Medieval Canon Law*, ed. Stephan Kuttner and J. Joseph Ryan (Vatican City, 1965) 224–230. Gilchrist's interesting argument seems to me to rest on the belief that theory and practice coincided—a belief too often generally refuted to rely on here.

10. Humbert, Bk. 1, c. 14; Bk. 2, cc. 11, 17, 19, 34–36, 42–43.

11. Bonizo, *Liber ad amicum*, Bk. 6, 600.

12. Council of Reims (A.D. 1049), *Acta*, Mansi 19, 739–741.

13. Bonizo, *Liber ad amicum*, Bk. 6, 592.

14. William of Malmesbury, *De gestis regum anglorum*, ed. William Stubbs (London, 1889) *RS*, 90², 324.

15. Bonizo, *Liber ad amicum*, Bk. 6, 600 (accusation against Hugues); Bk. 7, 603 (swindlers at Saint Peter's).

16. Gregory VII to Beatrice and Matilda, June 24, 1073 [JL 4782] *Epistolae* 1, 11.

17. Garsius, *Tractatus*, ed. Ernst Sackur (*MGH—Libelli de lite*, vol. 2) 427–428. The satire is analyzed in John Yunck, *The Lineage of Lady Mead* (Notre Dame, Ind.: University of Notre Dame Press, 1963) 71–76.

18. Alfons Becker, *Papst Urban II* (Stuttgart: Anton Hiersemann, 1964) 32 (Bruno); 55 (*pedissequus* of Gregory); 96 (choice of name); 97 (letter to Hugues). Augustin Fliche, *La Réforme grégorienne* (Paris: Bloud & Gay, 1940) 199–202 (reputation).

19. Urban II to the Clergy and People of Amiens, Dec. 20, 1091, *PL* 151, 335 (JL 5455); Urban II to the Clergy and People of Amiens, July 18, 1093, *PL* 151, 362 (JL 5486).

20. Urban II to Foulque, Feb. 24, 1094, *PL* 151, 378 (JL 5509); Urban II to the Archbishop of Reims, May 13, 1094, *PL* 151, 388 (JL 5522).

21. Urban II to the Clergy and People of Limoges, Oct. 10, 1094 (JL 5528), *PL* 151, 551.

22. "Judicium Urbani Papae" (JL 5382), Gratian, *Concordantia discordantium canonum* C. 31, q. 2, c. 1. The details are discussed in John T. Noonan, Jr. "Power to Choose," *Viator* 4 (1975) 419–420. "Dearest friend" reference in Urban II to the abbot of San Juan de la Peña, *PL* 151, 374 (JL 5501).

23. Urban II to Sancho Ramirez, July 1089, Gratian, *Concordantia* C. 31, q. 2, c. 3.

24. Ryan, *Saint Peter Damiani and His Canonical Sources* 161.

25. Burchard, *Decretorum libri viginti*, Bk. 19, "De Poenitentia," *PL* 140, 949–977. Burchard does remark at 977 that "unjust judgments" are one of the fruits of avarice.

26. Burchard, ibid. Bk. 1, "De primatu Ecclesiae," chap. 21 and 22, *PL* 140, 555.

27. Burchard, ibid. Bk. 16, "De accusatoribus et testibus," chaps. 2, 25 and 27, *PL* 140, 909, 913, 914.

28. On Yves and Urban II, Noonan, "Power to Choose."

29. Yves, *Decretum* 6, 341, *PL* 161, 341 (judges); ibid. 1, 293; 2, 84; 5, 75–97, *PL* 128, 179, 351–356 (simonian heresy).

30. John T. Noonan, Jr., "Gratian Slept Here: The Changing Identity of the Father of the Systematic Study of Canon Law," *Traditio* 35 (1979) 159–161.

31. Gratian, *Concordantia*, C. 1, q. 1.

32. *Regula Sancti Benedicti* 58, 25 (no power over own body); 59, 4 (own reward), *The Rule of*

St. Benedict, ed. Timothy Fry. O.S.B. (Collegeville, Minn.: Liturgical Press, 1980) 268, 272. For the history of the controversy, see Joseph H. Lynch, *Simoniacal Entry into Religous Life from 1000 to 1260* (Columbus: Ohio State University Press, 1976) 3–9 (economic functions of the gift); 9–18 (negotiations over it); 71–75 (early criticism); 83–90 (the affair of St. Pantaleon); 90–93 (Gerhoch's critique, based on his *Liber de simoniacis*, ed. Ernst Sackur [*MGH—Libelli de lite* vol. 3] 268–269).

33.   Gratian, *Concordantia* C. 1, q. 1, c. 1 (Humbert on favor); c. 7, citing [pseudo-]Ambrose on Simon Magician; c. 8 (Chalcedon); c. 11, citing [pseudo-]Gregory Nazianzen on Simon Magician and on Gehazi; c. 16 citing [pseudo-]Ambrose on Gehazi; c. 19 citing St. Ambrose on Simon Magician; c. 21 citing Thrasius, bishop of Constantinople in 787, on Simon Magician and on Judas's sale of Jesus; c. 23 citing Jerome on Michah, on Simon Magician, and on the temple dove-sellers; c. 117 citing Gregory I on the temple dove-sellers. Gratian's final answer is given in dictum post c. 10, C. 1, q.2.

34.   Ibid. C. 1, q. 1, dictum post c. 106 (on orders); dictum post C. 24 (the analogy with the sale of Christ). Gilchrist, "Simoniaca haeresis" 227, argues that Gratian treated the question as one "of canonical authority," not validity. I do not read the dictum post c. 106 in this sense, although it must be admitted that, as more than one hand added dicta, contradictory dicta may be found. Gilchrist appears to rely on a dictum (ante c. 24, C. 1, q. 7) dealing with orders conferred by heretics generally, not with those conferred by Simonians.

35.   Ibid. C.1, q. 1, cc. 126–130 (*Codex*); C. 2, q. 6, c. 41 (Novel 46 as given in the *Authenticum*). On the revisor's additions of Roman law, see Noonan, "Gratian Slept Here" 164.

36.   Gratian, *Concordantia* C. 23, q. 1, c. 5.

37.   Ibid. C. 11, q. 3, c. 78 (Ysidro); c. 79 (Jerome); c. 83, citing Bede on Mark 14, 11.

38.   Ibid. C. 11, q. 3, c. 66.

39.   Ibid. C. 11, q. 3, c. 72 (Ysidro); c. 71 (Augustine).

40.   Ibid. C. 14, q. 5, c. 15.

41.   Helmut Gleber, *Papst Eugene III* (Jena: Gustav Fischer, 1936) 13–15.

42.   Bernard of Clairvaux to Eugene III, Letter 238, *PL* 182, 429.

43.   Ibid. *PL* 182, 430.

44.   John of Salisbury, *Historia Pontificalis* c. 6, ed. Reginald L. Poole (Oxford: Clarendon Press, 1927) 13–15. Poole supplies the name of Petronilla and data on the first excommunication, ibid. XXIII–XXXIV. Raoul sought a *divortium*, i.e., annulment. *Pecunia interveniente*, John's phrase, parallels *pretio interveniente* in the rubric to Gratian C. 1, q. 1, c. 124. Cf. Richard Helmholz, "Canonists and Standards of Impartiality for Papal Judges Delegate," *Traditio* 25 (1969) 386 at 396.

45.   Ibid. c. 6, p. 14. See ibid. c. 42, for John's use of someone else (the upright Ulger) to criticize Innocent II taking *munera* from King Stephen of England.

46.   Ibid. c. 6, 14–15.

47.   Bernard to Cardinal Hugues, Letter 290, *PL* 182, 496.

48.   William de Newburgh, quoted in Poole, *Historia pontificalis* 117.

49.   Bernard, *De consideratione ad Eugenium Papam*, Bernard, *Opera*, ed. J. Leclerq O.S.B. and H. M. Rochais, O.S.B. (Rome: Editiones Cistercienses, 1963) 3, 3, 13.

50.   Ibid. 2, 14, 23.

51.   Ibid. 2, 14, 23. Book 2 was begun July 1148, Book 3 was written later, in 1152, "Introduction" 381.

52.   John, *Historia pontificalis* c. 29, 62.

53.   Régine Pernoud, *Aliénor d'Aquitaine* (Paris: Editions Allin Michel, 1965) 86.

54.   John, *Historia pontificalis* c. 41, 80–81. In one other episode John's view of Eugene is ambiguous. When the Abbot Suger died in 1151, the French king ceased to protect his relatives. Suger's nephew Simon lost the royal chancellorship "from the suspicion of an odious name" and took refuge with Eugene. The pope gave him the unprecedented privilege of being answerable to any accusation only before the pope in person. With such patronage Simon and the king were reconciled; the privilege caused wonder, and bishops noted that this kind of privilege seemed to favor bold sinners (*Historia pontificalis* c. 44). The "odious name" means that Simon was suspect of simony. John does not pronounce on his guilt but seems to share the surprise at Eugene's solicitude for him.

55.   The case illustrates one resolution of a dilemma often debated by medieval canonists and theologians: should a judge act on the record or on the basis of his conscience as formed by information not on the record? For the history of the debate, see Knut W. Nörr, *Zur Stellung des Richters im gelehrten Prozess der Frühzeit: Iudex secundum allegata non secundum*

conscientiam iudicat (Munich: Münchner Universitätsschriften, Reihe der Juristischen Fakultät 2, 1967).

56. Bernard, *De consideratione* 3, 3, 13.
57. Ibid. 3, 3, 13.
58. Ibid. 4, 5, 13.
59. Ibid. 4, 5, 14.
60. Ibid. 4, 5, 15; cf. Chapter 3, n. 24, above, on the rabbis.
61. Ibid. 3, 2, 7 ("How long do you sleep?"); 3, 3, 13 (Paul quoted); 4, 4, 12 (qualities needed for curia).
62. The Clerks of Thomas Becket to Guillaume, archbishop of Sens, early 1172, Letter 307, *The Letters of John of Salisbury*, ed. W. J. Millor, S.J., and C. N. L. Brooke (Oxford: Clarendon Press, 1979) 2, 746–748.
63. See Poole, ed., *Historia pontificalis* 117, and David Knowles, *The Episcopal Colleagues of Thomas Becket* (Cambridge: At the University Press, 1951) 13. Knowles takes the position that the letter is not in John's manner. But it is the curial information, not the style, that would come from John; John, as the *Historia pontificalis* shows, could be very sharp when he chose to be.
64. Poole, *Historia pontificalis*, XV–XVI.
65. John of Salisbury, *Policraticus*, ed. Clement C. I. Webb (Oxford: Clarendon Press, 1909) 6, 24, sec. 624.
66. Ibid. 6, 24, 623.
67. Ibid. 5, 10, 663. Note that by this time, if not earlier, *gratia*, used to refer to divine favor, is more naturally translated into English as "grace."
68. Ibid. 5, 10, 563.
69. Ovid, *De arte amatoria* 2, 279–280, cited in John, *Policraticus* 5, 10, 565. For Cossus and Veiento, as it reads in Juvenal, see Juvenal, *Satura* 3, 184–185.
70. John, *Policraticus* 8, 23, 813. For "Saint Clairvaux," ibid. 5, 16, 578.
71. Ibid. 5, 10, 565.
72. Ibid. 5, 15, 576.
73. Ibid. 5, 10, 564–565.
74. Ibid. 5, 10, 565.
75. Ibid. 5, 10, 563.
76. Ibid. 6, 23, 622.
77. Ibid. 5, 10, 566.
78. Gilbert Foliot to Thomas Becket, 1166, Letter 225, *Materials for the History of Thomas Becket*, ed. J. C. Robertson and J. B. Sheppard, Rolls Series 67 (London 1875–1885) [henceforth MB] 5, 522. The quoted words are those of Thomas's enemy, Gilbert Foliot. Uttered in a letter to Thomas, they have the ring of truth.
79. John of Salisbury, *Metalogicon*, ed. Clement C. I. Webb (Oxford: Clarendon Press, 1929) 4, 41.
80. John to Cardinal Gualtero, late 1167, letter 235, *Letters of John of Salisbury* 2, 434.
81. John, *Metalogicon* 4, 41.
82. Adrian IV to the King of England, *Pontificia Hibernica*, ed. Maurice P. Sheehy (Dublin: M. H. Gill & Son, 1962) 1, 15–16.
83. John, *Metalogicon* 4, 41.
84. John, *Policraticus* 6, 24, 624.
85. Ibid. 6, 24, 623. For a similar modern account of a reformer's conversation with a friendly ruler, see Chapter 17, n. 74, below.
86. Ibid. 6, 24, 624–625. John does not say to Adrian—is his silence tactful?—what he says elsewhere in his book, 5, 15, 577, that Eugene III "received no offering from any man in litigation or from anyone he believed about to litigate."
87. Ibid. 6, 24, 625—626.
88. David Daube, *Civil Disobedience in Antiquity* (Edinburgh: At the University Press, 1972) 30. The original is Livy, *Ab urbe condita*, ed. W. Weissenborn and H. J. Müller (Berlin: Weidemann, 1962) 2, 32.
89. David Knowles, *Thomas Becket* (London: Adam and Charles Black, 1970) 87, 93.
90. *Decretales Gregorii IX* 5, 3, 18. For comparison with the PACs, see Chapter 19, n. 75, below.
91. John of Salisbury to Thomas, 1164, Letter 136, *The Letters of John of Salisbury* 2, pp. 6, 8.
92. Ibid. 2, 8–10. John's references were to Terence, *Adelphi* 219, and Virgil, *Ecloga* 2, 57.

The preceding line of Virgil reads: "You are a country fellow, Corydon. Alexis does not care for *munera*"—an implied compliment to Alexander III, a good-natured joshing of Thomas? For a similar, modern use of the *Eclogues* to affect superiority to *munera*-takers, see Chapter 17, n. 46, below.

93. Ibid. 2, 14.
94. Gilbert Foliot to Thomas, *Multiplicem*, 1166, Letter 225, *MB*, 5, 523–524. The authenticity of *Multiplicem* is demonstrated by Knowles, *Becket* 171–180.
95. Ibid. 28.
96. "[M]agnificus . . . nugator," John to Bartholomew of Exeter, 1166, Letter 187, *Letters* 2, 244.
97. David Knowles, *Archbishop Thomas Becket: A Character Study* (London: Geoffrey Cumberlege, 1949), printed from *The Proceedings of the British Academy*, vol. 35 (hereafter Knowles, *Character*) 13.
98. Foliot to Thomas, *Multiplicem*, *MB* 5, 543.
99. Knowles, *Becket* 97–98, 104
100. Knowles, *Colleagues*, 92–95.
101. Alexander III to Thomas, *Quod minor* [undated] Letter 94, *MB* 5, 178; Alexander III to Thomas, *Quoniam dies*, June 1165, Letter 95, *MB* 5, 179–180.
102. John to Thomas, July 1166, Letter 175, *Letters* 2, 158; Knowles, *Becket*, 109.
103. Ibid. 113–114.
104. John to Thomas, July 1166, Letter 175, *Letters* 2, 162–164.
105. John to Bartholomew of Exeter, July 1166, Letter 174, *Letters* 2, 148–150.
106. Ibid. 2, 144.
107. Knowles, *Becket* 118.
108. John to Alexander III, January 1167, Letter 213, *Letters* 346, 348.
109. John to Alexander III, c. Sept.-Oct. 1167, Letter 219, *Letters* 2, 370–372.
110. Ibid. 2, 376.
111. John to Magister Raymonde, chancellor of Poitiers, Oct. 1167, Letter 224, *Letters* 2, 388.
112. Foliot to Thomas, *Multiplicem*, 1166, Letter 225, *MB* 5, 524, 538.
113. John to Thomas, July 1166, Letter 175, *Letters* 2, 154.
114. John to Bartholomew of Exeter, c. Feb. 1169, Letter 288, *Letters* 2, 642.
115. John to Guglielmo of Pavia, c. Oct. 1167, Letter 229, *Letters* 2, 402.
116. John to Thomas, Sept-Oct. 1167, Letter 228, *Letters* 2, 400.
117. Cardinals Guglielmo and Otto to Alexander III, 1167, Letter 342, *MB* 6, 282.
118. John to John of Canterbury, bishop of Poitiers, Nov.-Dec. 1167, Letter 233, *Letters* 2, 424.
119. John to Cardinal Alberto, late 1167, Letter 234, *Letters* 2, 428–432.
120. John to Cardinal Gualtero, late 1167, Letter 235, *Letters* 434–436. The reference to Thrasymachus was from Plato, *The Republic*, Bk. I, 338a.
121. John to John of Poitiers, late Nov. 1167, Letter 230, *Letters* 2, 412.
122. John to John of Poitiers, c. May 1168, Letter 275, *Letters* 2, 580–582.
123. John to Thomas, Spring-Summer 1168, Letter 278, *Letters* 2, 598–600.
124. John to Magister Lombardo, July 1168, Letter 279, *Letters*, 2, 606.
125. Knowles, *Becket* 120.
126. Ibid. 121; Graziano was identified as Gratian the canonist by Hermann Reuter, the nineteenth-century historian of Alexander III, Reuter, *Geschichte Alexanders des Dritten* (Leipzig, 1864) 3, 443 and 791, but this interesting identification has not stood up. See John T. Noonan, Jr., "Was Gratian Approved at Ferentino?," *Bulletin of Medieval Canon Law* 6 (1976) 15 at 22.
127. John to Baldwin of Exeter, late Aug. 1169, Letter 289, *Letters* 2, 652–654; on the letter, see Noonan, "Was Gratian Approved" 21–22.
128. John to Baldwin, late Aug. 1169, Letter 289, ibid. 650. For the date of John meeting Graziano, Knowles, *Becket* 123.
129. Thomas to Graziano, 1170, Letter 663, *MB* 7, 281.
130. The Co-Exiles of Thomas to Graziano, 1170, Letter 665, *MB* 7, 289–290.
131. Thomas to Graziano, 1170, Letter 695, *MB* 7, 352.
132. Knowles, *Becket* 124–125, 128; Thomas to Cardinal Alberto, 1170, Letter 662, *MB* 7, 279–280; Thomas to Graziano, 1170, Letter 663, *MB* 7, 282.
133. Thomas to Cardinal Alberto, Letter 662, *MB* 7, 280; Thomas to Graziano, 1170, Letter 663, *MB* 7, 280.

134. Knowles, *Character* 20, 131. For Thomas's view of the essential conditions, see, e.g., Thomas to his clerks, Alexander and John, 1169, Letter 610, *MB* 7, 173–179.

135. Knowles, *Becket* 137–148.

136. William Fitzstephen, *Vita Sancti Thomae*, *MB* 3, 121.

137. His messenger to Thomas, 1164, Letter 61, *MB* 5, 119.

138. Magister David to Gilbert Foliot, 1171, Letter 752, *MB* 7, 480.

139. The King's Messenger to the Archdeacon of Poitiers, 1171, Letter 751, *MB* 7, 477–478.

140. Roger of York to Hugh of Durham and other prelates, Dec. 13, 1171, Letter 766, *MB* 7, 505–506.

141. See John, *Letters*, vol. 2, 374, 404, 664.

142. See n. 35 above and Chapter 4 at n. 96.

143. X 5, 3, 13.

144. Thomas to Graziano, 1170, Letter 663, *MB* 7, 282.

145. Knowles, *Becket* 37.

146. John to Pierre, abbot of Saint-Rémi, Dec. 1170, Letter 304, *Letters* 2, 722.

147. John to John of Poitiers, early 1171, Letter 305, *Letters* 2, 728.

CHAPTER 7: THE QUARTER AND THE ROAD (PP. 173–205)

1. Gui de Bazoches to a Friend (1175?–1190?), printed in *Chartularium Universitatis Parisiensis* I, 55–56; discussed in Astrik L. Gabriel, *Garlandia: Studies in the History of the Medieval University* (Frankfurt: Josef Knecht, 1969) 50.

2. Pierre le Chantre, *Verbum abbreviatum*, c. 23, *Contra acceptores munerum*, etc, PL 205, 82 (catalogue of types of *munera*-taking); 83 (shearers, etc.); 83–89 (Old Testament authorities); 85 (the Fathers; *munuscula*); 86 (Romans; "God alone in mind"). On his background as a judge, see John W. Baldwin, *Masters, Princes and Merchants: The Social Views of Peter the Cantor and His Circle* (Princeton, NJ: Princeton University Press, 1970) 1, 8.

3. Pierre le Chantre, "Liber casuum conscientiae," *Summa de sacramentis et animae consiliis*, ed. Jean-Albert Duguaquier (Louvain, 1954–1967) III, 2b, 579 (restitution by judge); Pierre le Chantre, *Verbum abbreviatum*, c. 51, "Contra advocatos," PL 205, 160 (sale of judgment simonian); ibid. c. 25, "Contra simoniam existentem," etc., 95 (Simonian sells God).

4. Pierre le Chantre, *Summa de sacramentis* 3, 2a, 93 (*acceptio personarum* as simony).

5. Uguccio, *Summa* (Admont MS. 7) at C. 11, q. 3, c. 66, "Qui recte iudicat." *Nemo presbyterorum* became X 5, 3, 14.

6. Pierre le Chantre, *Verbum abbreviatum*, PL 205, c. 24, *Contra clericos* etc., 90–91.

7. Ibid. col. 92 (sale of absolution; "pre-oiled"); 93 (nets; marriages).

8. LeChantre, *Summa* III, 2a, 38–39 (practice in Roman curia; judges-delegate); III, 2a, 153 (penny of justice); III, 2a, 35 (St. Thomas).

9. Ibid. III, 2a, 3, 35–36. On Lukás, see Astrik Gabriel, *Les Relations dynastiques franco-hongrois au moyen âge* (Budapest: University of Budapest, 1944) 21.

10. Alain de Lille, *Liber poenitentialis*, ed. Jean Longère (Louvain: Editions Nauwelaerts, 1965) 2, 54 (restitution of simoniacal gains); 2, 53 (judge's obligation of restitution); 2, 155 (need for judge to be free from sin); 2, 49 (offerings as penance for avarice); 2, 34 (less sin if the girl pretty).

11. On Courson and le Chantre, Baldwin, *Masters, Princes and Merchants* 1, 17–18; on Courson's origin, Gabriel, *Garlandia* 25.

12. Robert Courson, *Summa*, c. 14, ed. in part V. L. Kennedy, C.S.B., "Robert Courson on Penance," *Mediaeval Studies* (1945) 7, 330–331.

13. Courson, *Summa*, c. 15, 332–333 (confessor as Simon Magician); 334 (restitution); c. 9, 315–316 (left-handed appointments).

14. Ibid c. 8, 313–314.

15. J. J. Francis Firth, C.S.B., "Introduction," Robert of Flamborough, *Liber poenitentialis* (Toronto: Pontifical Institute of Mediaeval Studies, 1971) 2, 8–9.

16. Ibid. 133.

17. Ibid. 123 (types of *munera*); 183–185 (restitution).

18. F. Broomfield, "Introduction," Thomas de Chobham, *Summa confessorum* (Louvain: Editions Nauwelaerts, 1968) XXVI–XXXVI.

19. Ibid. 518–520 (judge not Simonian but sinful; a litigant can buy back his right); 502–503 (apparitors and shakedowns).

20.   Jacques de Vitry, "Exemplum," *The Exempla of Jacques de Vitry*, ed. Thomas Frederick Crane (London: Folk-Lore Society, 1890) 14. Nero in legend was the backer of Simon Magician, Cowdrey, *Age of Abbot Desiderius* 84.

21.   Jacques de Vitry, 14.

22.   Ibid. 15.

23.   Baldwin, *Masters, Princes and Merchants* 1, 18.

24.   Helene Tillmann, *Pope Innocent III*, trans. Walter Sax (Amsterdam: North-Holland Publishing Co., 1980) 2–3 (on Lotario's title, his time in Paris, and on the promotions of Corbeil, Courson, and Langton); Baldwin, *Masters, Princes and Merchants* 1, 317 (on le Chantre's reforms realized by Innocent III); Gabriel, *Garlandia* 58 (on the *pierres* or rocks from the quarry).

25.   But see also Kenneth Pennington, "The Legal Education of Pope Innocent III," *Bulletin of Medieval Canon Law* 4 (1970) 70–77.

26.   Tillmann, *Pope Innocent III* 4.

27.   Michele Maccarrone, "Innocenzo III Prima Del Pontificato," *Archivio della R. Deputazione Romana di Storia Patria* 66 (1943), 85–88.

28.   The edited text: Lotharius, *De miseria humane conditionis*, ed. Michele Maccarrone (Lucca: Thesaurus Mundi, 1955); Maccarrone, Preface, XXXVII, gives the date and at XI refers to Petrarch and Bernardino. The "A" version of Chaucer's *Legend of Good Women*, lines 414–415, refers to the poet's translating the "Wrecched Engendryng of mankinde." No copy of this translation exists and it may be only that Chaucer meant he used the work in *The Canterbury Tales*, see Eleanor Prescott Hammond, *Chaucer: A Bibliographical Manual* (New York: Peter Smith, 1933) 92. On Pietro Galloccia, "un influente patrono," Michele Maccarrone, *Studi su Innocenzo III* (Padua: Editrice Antenore, 1972) 346.

29.   Lotario, *De miseria*, Bk. 2, chap. 1 ("three big things); 2, 4 ("woe to you"); 2, 5 ("profit in the coffer"); 2, 6 ("insatiable").

30.   Ibid. 2, 11 (lawful wealth); Anonymous, *Gesta Innocentii PP III*, PL 214, c. 4, col. xviii (wonder at his resources); Lotario, *De miseria* 2, 5 (expenses exceed fruit won).

31.   Ibid. 3, 20 (the Last Judgment); 3, 18, 19 (the incorruptible Judge). Earlier curial usage of "the royal road," John, *Historia pontificalis* c. 38.

32.   Ibid. 1, 4 (embryo's food); 1, 28 (food for mother); Walter J. Ong, *Fighting for Life: Contest Sexuality and Consciousness* (Ithaca, N.Y.: Cornell University Press, 1980) 54 (archetype).

33.   Lotario, *De miseria* 1, 24 (dreams); *Gesta* c. 6, col. xx (the dream); ibid. c. 1, col. xvii (Claricia). On the biographer, Maccarrone, *Studi* 88: "acuto conoscitore dell'animo del pontefice," and on the biography, 189: "fonte preziosa per conoscere la mente e l'azione di Innocenzo III."

34.   Innocent III to the Archbishops and Bishops of France, Jan. 9, 1198, *Die Register Innocenz III*, ed. Othmar Hageneder and Anton Haidacher (Graz-Cologne: Hermann Böhlaus, 1964) (hereafter *Register*) 1, 4. For the objection raised as to his age, *Gesta* c. 5, col. xix.

35.   Ibid. c. 1, col. xvii (counts of Segni).

36.   Maccarrone, *Studi* 14.

37.   Innocent III, *Sermo II in consecrationem Pontificis Maximi*, PL 217, 657–658. I follow Tillmann, *Pope Innocent III* 40, in accepting this sermon as given at the time of his consecration.

38.   Innocent's view of the matter is summarized, *Gesta* cc. 48–49, cols. xciv–xcvi.

39.   Innocent III to Philip II of France, May 17, 1198, *Licet dextera Domini*, *Register* I, 243–245.

40.   *Gesta*, c. 24, col. xlvi.

41.   Ibid. c. 55, col. cii; on Philip's resumption of life with Ingeborg, Tillman 341.

42.   Innocent to Richard, Aug. 15–Sept. 15, 1198, *Register* 1, 536–538. Christopher R. Cheney, *Pope Innocent III and England* (Stuttgart: Anton Hiersemann, 1976) 275, n. 7, remarks on the "acid" tone of Innocent's reference to Richard's now lost letter.

The case for Lotario's having been the monks' advocate is based on hearsay and inference. It consists in three pieces of evidence: (1) the explicit assertion of Ralph of Coggeshall that he was (Ralph, *Chronicon Anglicanum*, ed. Joseph Stevenson [London: Rolls Series, 1875, vol. 66]89); (2) a letter from the monks of Canterbury to their prior in June or July 1187, suggesting that he arrange for "Lord Lotario, Pilio's partner," to come to England from the curia on their business (*Epistulae cantuarienses*, ed. William Stubbs [London: Rolls Series, 1865, vol. 38²] 68); (3) the inference to be drawn from King Richard's almost immediate assumption that Innocent as pope will favor the monks. Against these bits of information it can be pointed out that Ralph does not give his source; that "Lord Lotario" could be another curialist of the same name, as Tillmann, *Pope Innocent III* 17, shows existed; and that none of the monks' later correspondence refers to Lotario as their agent. On the other hand, the king's pointed suspicion is hard to account for, and the monks' letter of 1187 shows them thinking in terms of very influential curialists—Cardinal Hyacinto, for example, the future Celestine III; our Lotario, on the way to being a cardinal, fits this mold.

43. Prior Godfrey and the Convent of Canterbury, circa Nov. 6, 1190, *Epistulae cantuarienses* 457. On the pope's view of the friendless monks, *Gesta* c. 42, col. lxxxiii.

44. Innocent to Archbishop Hubert Walter, Nov. 23, 1198. *Register* 1, 652; Innocent to Richard, Nov. 20, 1198, *Register* 1, 658; Innocent to Richard, Dec. 22, 1198, *Register* 1, 713.

45. Innocent III to Archbishop Filippo, Sept. 23, 1198, *Ut nostrum, Register* I, 555 [=X, 13, 12, 1].

46. Innocent III to the Prelates and Priests of Lombardy, Oct. 2, 1198, *Cum ab omni, Register* 1, 569–570. The decretal in edited form, with the reference to *turpia lucra* omitted while the general sense is preserved, appears in X, 3, 1, 10, *Quum ab omni*. On *turpe lucrum*, see John T. Noonan, Jr., *The Scholastic Analysis of Usury* (Cambridge, Mass.: Harvard University Press, 1957) 30. The biblical paraphrase is from Jeremiah 1:10. In the twelfth century a sermon of Pierre Abélard denouncing the worldliness and litigiousness of monks says that "we [we monks] hire [*conducimus*] judges or orators, at no small price, to cover our unjust actions." Giles Constable, *Religious Life and Thought (11th–12th Centuries)* (London: Variorum Reprints, 1979) translates *conducimus* as "bribe." I do not believe Abélard speaks so strongly: he is referring to the practice of paying for judges as well as lawyers.

47. *Gesta* c. 41, col. lxxx (the three reforms in Rome).

48. Ibid. c. 41, col. lxxxi.

49. Gerald of Wales, *De iure et statu menevensis ecclesiae*, ed. J. S. Brewer (London: Rolls Series, 1863, 21³) 101–102 (prologue addressed to Stephen Langton); 178–182 (the first phase); 254 (told by pope not to worry; 257 (200 pounds to salute the pope); 263 (the offers intensify); 265 (part of cardinals corrupted; Ugolino and papal clerks press him); 266 (pope acts for opponent); 267–268 (decision). Cheney, *Pope Innocent III and England* 138, n. 57, on Gerald's details carrying conviction, and 139 on the upshot after Innocent's decision.

50. *Gesta*, c. 44, cols. lxxxvii–lxxxviii. On the old associations, Innocent III to Konrad, circa Feb. 17, 1199, *Register* I, 826.

51. *Gesta*, c. 44, col. lxxxviii.

52. Thomas of Marlborough, *Chronicon Abbatiae de Evesham*, ed. William Dunn Macray (London: Rolls Series, 1863, 29) 142. On Thomas and Langton, ibid. XX. For the case, see also Cheney, *Innocent III and England* 196–199.

53. Thomas, *Chronicon* 146. For the pound–mark ratio, William E. Lunt, *Financial Relations Between the Papacy with England to 1327* (Cambridge, Mass.: Medieval Academy of America, 1939) 1, 640.

54. Thomas, *Chronicon* 153. On Pietro da Benevento, see Maccarrone, "Innocenzo III Prima del Pontificato" 81.

55. Thomas, *Chronicon* 200. Innocent's judgment entered the Decretals as *Ex ore sedentis*, X 5, 33, 17.

56. All details in Innocent III to "our cousin Giovanni Oddone," July 1204, *PL* 215, 387. Tillmann, *Pope Innocent III* 128, says the Abaiamonti "had refused to accept the pope as judge despite the many securities they were offered." She fails to note that the security offered was merely as to their freedom not as to the justice they might expect. For Innocent's stern view of the corrupting effect of "the kindness of kin" (*presidium propinquorum*, literally, "the protection of propinquity"), Lotario, *De miseria* 2, 27.

57. Innocent III to Riccardo, Oct. 9, 1204, *PL* 215, 422–424, sets out almost all the details. It is followed in *Gesta* c. 137, cols. clxxxvi–clxxxviii, which also tells of the pope's flight. For cousin Ottaviano, *Gesta* c. 23, col. xlii.

58. Innocent to Riccardo, Oct. 9, 1204, *PL* 215, 424; *Gesta* c. 139–140, cols. cxc–cxciv (interlocutory judgment; Riccardo's financial effort; brother-in-law Pietro Annibale). On the tower, Tillmann, *Pope Innocent III* 294. On the retention of the property, Ferdinand Gregorovius, *Storia della città di Roma nel medio evo*, trans. Luigi Trompeo (Rome: Editione Frezza, 1941) 8, 49 n. 64.

59. Innocent III to Stefano, July 11, 1208, *PL* 215, 1443–1445 (judgment and details in Stefano's case). For the initial commission in the Bayeux election, Innocent to the Bishop of Dole, etc., April 22, 1205, *PL* 215, 594 [=X 1, 6, 29]. For Robert's consecration, Eubel, *Hierarchia catholica* 1, 14. On the benefice to Stefano in Bayeux, Maccarrone, *Studi* 125. For references to "the cardinal nephew," ibid. 124–125.

60. Innocent to the Clergy and People of Fermo, Jan. 13, 1205, *PL* 215, 767; see Maccarrone, *Studi* 13.

61. *Gesta* c. 23–24, cols. xxxviii–xlvi; Maccarrone, *Studi* 183–187.
62. *Gesta* c. 39, cols. lxx–lxxiii, for Innocent's view of the taking of Sora and the price of the neighboring land; Maccarrone, *Studi* 189–194, for a history taking into account the different perspective of Monte Cassino.
63. *Gesta* c. 39, col. lxxiii, Maccarrone, *Studi* 193–198.
64. Innocent III to Riccardo, "Our Brother, Count of Sora," Feb. 24, 1209, *PL* 216, 13–14, for details; Maccarrone, *Studi* 196, n. 1, for the palace and Paolo's inheritance.
65. Innocent III to Riccardo, Feb. 24, 1209, incorporating the notarial testimony to the homage at Ferentino, *PL* 216, 14–15.
66. Innocent to the Count of Celano, Dec. 6, 1206, *PL* 215, 1034.
67. Innocent III to the Bishop of Fiesole, March 13, 1204, *PL* 215, 304.
68. Innocent III to the Bishop of Vercelli and the Abbot of Tileto and the Priest Albert, Jan. 29, 1206, *Qualiter et quando*, X 5, 1, 17; cf. *PL* 215, 848.
69. *Gesta* c. 4, cols. xviii–xix (young cardinal's integrity); c. 41, col. lxx (plans).
70. *Gesta* c. 42, col. lxxxii ("supereminent intelligence"); c. 42, cols. lxxxv–lxxxvi (constant impartiality of Innocent); c. 17, col. xxx (pitch).
71. Innocent III to the Abbot of S. Stefano di Bologna and *Magister* Gregorio, Oct. 14, 1211, *PL* 216, 472–473.
72. *Magna Carta*, c. 40, James C. Holt, *Magna Carta* (Cambridge: At the University Press, 1965) 326.
73. On Langton's role, Cheney, *Pope Innocent III and England* 375–376.
74. *Gesta* c. 131, col. clxxv.
75. Ibid. c. 131, col. clxxvi.
76. Ibid.; see also Cheney, *Pope Innocent III and England* 150–154.
77. *Rotuli litterarum patentium*, ed. T. Duffus Hardy (London: Record Commission, 1835) 1, 69a.
78. *Gesta* c. 131, col. clxxvi.
79. Cheney, *Innocent III and England* 298–302.
80. John to All Christ's Faithful, May 15, 1213, *PL* 216, 878–880.
81. Lunt, *Financial Relations* 1, 59 (yield from Peter's pence); 172 (the income to 1327); Cheney, *Innocent III and England* 332–337 (on the whole affair).
82. Matthew Paris, *Chronica majora*, ed. H. R. Luard (London: Rolls Series, 1872–1883, 57²) 565.
83. Innocent III to John, July 6, 1213, *PL* 216, 881.
84. *Rotuli litterarum clausarum*, ed. T. Duffus Hardy (London: Record Commission, 1833) 1, 140b and 180a.
85. Anonymous draft, "The Unknown Charter of Liberties," attributed to Langton's influence, W. L. Warren, *King John* (Berkeley: University of California Press, 1978) 215, 217. Langton's canon: *Statutes of Canterbury*, c. 52, in F. M. Powicke and C. R. Cheney, eds., *Councils and Synods with Other Documents Relating to the English Church* (Oxford: Clarendon Press, 1964) 2¹, 34.
86. Innocent to the Magnates and Barons of England, March 19, 1215, C. R. Cheney and W. H. Semple, eds., *Selected Letters of Pope Innocent III concerning England, 1198–1216* (London: Nelson, 1953) 194; Innocent to Stephen, archbishop of Canterbury, and his suffragans, March 19, 1215, ibid. 196; on the whole affair, Cheney, *Innocent III and England* 368–376.
87. Roger Wendover in Matthew Paris, *Chronica*, RS 57², 615–616; Cheney, *Innocent III and England* 382.
88. Innocent III to All Christ's Faithful, Aug. 24, 1215, *Etsi karissimus*, Cheney and Semple, *Selected Letters* 216.
89. Ibid. 215 ("steadiest man") 216 (Jeremiah quoted).
90. Lotario, *De miseria* 3, 19. Alexander III's *Causam quae* became X 1, 29, 17.
91. Innocent III, *Sermo I*, at the Lateran Council, Mansi 22, 968, 969, 972. The constitutions of Lateran IV were the personal work of the pope, Antonio García y García, *Constitutiones Concilii quarti Lateranensis una cum Commentariis glossatorum* (Vatican City: Vatican Library, 1981) 6–8.
92. Fourth Lateran Council, Canons, c. 7, *Irrefragibili*, Mansi 22, 991–994 [= X 1, 31, 13.]
93. Anonymous, *Dialogus inter euntem ad curiam et venientem a Roma de malis moribus curie*, Appendix to Peter Herde, *Beiträge zum päpstlichen Kanzlei- und Urkundenwesen im dreizehnten Jahrhundert* (Munich: Michael Lassleben, 1967) lines 28–52. Tillman, *Pope Innocent III*, notes that under Clement III the curia was "a laughing-stock" for its venality; she then struggles, against the evidence, to show that Innocent's regime was different.

94.   Buoncompagno, *Ars rhetorica*, printed in Geoffrey Barraclough, "The Making of a Bishop in the Middle Ages," *Catholic Historical Review* 19 (1933) 314–316.

95.   Ibid. 281, 297–302; Cheney, *Innocent III and England* 110.

96.   Barraclough, "The Making of a Bishop" 308.

97.   *Gesta*, c. 41, col. lxxxi (admiration for Innocent); Barraclough, "The Making of a Bishop" 302 (crowning with laurel).

98.   Hans Martin Schaller, "Studien zur Briefsammlung des Kardinals Thomas von Capua," *Deutsches Archiv für Erforschung des Mittelalters* 21 (1965) 372, 388–391.

99.   An excerpt of the *Summa dictaminis* has been edited by Emmy Heller, "Der kuriale Geschäftsgang in den Briefen des Thomas v. Capua," *Archiv für Urkundenforschung* 13 (1935). The dates of the letters are given at 198.

100.   A horse, Letter 120 in Heller, "Der kuriale Geschäftsgang"; a mule, Letter 115; food, Letter 109; bedspread, Letter 104; cloth, Letters 15, 117, 125; vases, Letter 110; wine, Letter 121; skins, Letter 122; gold, Letter 113; *xenia*, Letter 51; *beneficium*, Letter 17; *munuscula*, Letters 17, 117 *dona*, Letters 4, 103, 105, 111, 112; *munera*, Letters 103, 107, 112, 121, 122, 123, 125. Monastic donor, Letter 108; Hungarian prelate, Letter 104; agent for Norwich, Letter 105.

101.   Ibid., Letter 112 (don't rush it); Letter 113 ("pure liberality"); Letter 118 (prohibition); Letter 119 (own intention); letter 18 (pope difficult).

102.   Ibid., Letter 103 (*munus*—no *munera*); Letter 111 (*donum*—no *dona*); Letter 105 (no obligation); Letter 116 (thanks when you stop).

103.   Ibid., Letter 4 ("ready hands"); Letter 17 ("fatter recompense"); Letters 123 and 124 ("educated hands").

104.   Ibid. 200.

105.   Stephen Langton, *Veni, Sancte Spiritus*, in *Graduale Sacrosanctae Romanae Ecclesiae* (St. Pierre de Solesmes Abbey, 1974) 254.

106.   Langton, *Veni*, *Graduale* 254.

107.   Innocent's insensitivity to a man being a judge in his own case was not confined to cases involving his relatives. When complaint was made to him of fraud on the part of Pietro d'Ivrea, patriarch of Antioch, he wrote the patriarch committing the complaint to him with the words, "Carefully judge your own self." Innocent III to the patriarch of Antioch, Oct. 12, 1215, PL 216, 697.

108.   *Gesta*, c. 4, cols. xviii–xix (Innocent's standard); Innocent to the Abbot of S. Stefano and *Magister* Gregorio, PL 216, 472 ("sometimes after an affair is judged").

109.   Honorius III to the bishops of France, Jan. 28, 1225, *Recueil des historiens des Gaules et de la France*, ed. Léopold Delisle (Paris, 1880) 19, 763–764. Gerald of Wales also refers to the scheme, attributing it to Innocent and saying it was a plan for the pope to appropriate "unbreakably for himself" one-tenth of cathedral revenues. He makes no mention of the quid pro quo for the tax being accepted, Gerald of Wales, *Speculum ecclesiae* (London: Rolls Series, 21⁴) 304–305.

110.   For his giftgiving, see *Gesta*, c. 149, cols. ccxxvi–ccxxviii.

111.   Tommaso di Celano, *Vita Secunda S. Francesci Assisiensis*, ed. Fathers of the College of S. Bonaventura (Quarrachi, 1927) 21–24.

112.   Maccarrone, *Studi* 301.

CHAPTER 8: BUY BACKS (PP. 206–238)

1.   Gregory IX to His Beloved Sons, the Doctors and Scholars dwelling at the University of Bologna, *Rex pacificus*, Sept. 5, 1234, *Decretales Gregorii IX*, ed. Friedberg, pp. 2–3.

2.   Raimundo da Peñafort, *Summa de poenitentia et de matrimonio* (Rome, 1608) 2.35 and 2.36. For the general obligation of confession, Fourth Lateran Council, c. 21, *Omnis utriusque sexus*, Mansi 22, 1007–1010 [=X 5, 38, 12].

3.   On Alexander: The Franciscans of the College of S. Bonaventura, Preface to Alexander, *Glossa in quatuor libros sententiarum* (Quaracchi: College of S. Bonaventura, 1951) 7*–24* and 68*; on Thomas, James A. Weisheipl, *Friar Thomas D'Aquino* (Garden City, N.Y.: Doubleday, 1974) 10, 27–33.

4.   Alexander, *Glossa* n. 4, 25, vol. 4, 442.

5.   Alexander, *Summa theologica*, ed. Fathers of the College of S. Bonaventura (Quarrachi: College of S. Bonaventura, 1930) vol. 3, p. 807 (preaching); 3, 796 (honest service). For Pascal's treatment of comparable casuistry, see Chapter 17, n. 97 below.

6.   Ibid. 3, 379 (relative to secular post); 3, 805 (relative to spiritual benefice); 3, 380 (good

man chosen over better man). Thomas Aquinas, *Summa theologica* (Rome: Leonine ed., 1903) 2–2, 63, 2, obj. 1 (custom) and *ad* 1 (relative's appointment); 2–2, 100, 5 (price).

7.   Alexander, *Glossa* 4, 493 (excommunicate); Alexander, *Summa theologica* 3, 809 (*redimere vexationem*).

8.   Ibid. 3, 382 (prelate and rich man); Thomas, *Summa theologica* 2–2, 63, 3.

9.   Cf. the implication of Celestine III to the Bishop of London and the Prior of Brokenbridge, X 5, 3, 28, *Dilectus filius R* (ecclesiastical payor entitled to restitution if ecclesiastical payee does not keep promise to refrain from harassment).

10.   Alexander, *Summa theologica* 3, 377.

11.   Thomas, *Summa theologica* 2–2, 63, 1.

12.   Aristotle, *Nichomachean Ethics* Bk. 5, 1131b–1132a.

13.   Thomas, *Summa theologica* 2–2, 61, 1 (distributive justice); 2–2, 63, 4 (judge).

14.   A consumptible is "a thing whose use is its consumption"—e.g., wine. Thomas considers money to be a consumptible and holds it to be unjust to put a value on its use different from the value of the principal, Thomas, *Summa theologica* 2–2, 78, 1.

15.   Alexander, *Summa theologica* 3, 381.

16.   Ibid. 4, 618.

17.   Thomas, *Summa theologica* 2–2, 67, 1–4. In the previous generation it had been debated whether *acceptio personarum* included taking *munera*, see Guillaume d'Auxerre, *Summa aurea*, ed. Jean Ribaillier (Grottaferrata: Collegio di S. Bonaventura, 1982) 2, 691 (Bk. 2, tract 23, c. 4). Guillaume concludes that taking up a person is a different sin from taking *munera*.

18.   Albert the Great, *In primam partem psalmorum commentaria*, Ps. 25, *Opera omnia*, ed. A. Borgnet (Paris: Vives, 1895) 15, 73.

19.   *Ad Christum judicem* [=*Dies Irae*], *Analecta hymnica medii aevi*, ed. Clemens Blume, S. J., and H. M. Bannister (Leipzig: O. R. Reisland, 1915) 54, 269. On the twelfth-century line, ibid. 273–274. On the hymn's disputed date and authorship, J. Szöverffy, "Dies Irae," *NCE* 4, 863–864.

20.   Honorius, *Elucidarium* 3, 12, *PL* 172, 1165: Peter Lombard, *Sententiae in IV libris distinctae* (Grottaferrata: Collegio di S. Bonaventura, 1981) 4, 45, 1. On Honorius' dates and origin, Edward A. Synan, "Honorius of Autun," *NCE* 7, 129.

21.   Thomas, *Scriptum super quatuor libros sententiarum Magistri Petri Lombardi*, (Parma: Pietro Fiaccadori, 1852–1873) 4, 48, q. 1, art. 4, sol. 4.

22.   *Ibid.* 4, 47, art. 1, sol. 2, (vol. 7, 1153), following Augustine, *De civitate Dei* 20, 14, *CSEL* 40², 461–462.

23.   Lotario, *De miseria* 3, 19.

24.   Alexander, *Glossa* 4, 443.

25.   Thomas, *Summa theologica* 3, 48, 5.

26.   "Redemptio enim emptionem significat iteratum." Thomas, *Scripta super quatuor libros*, Bk. 3, D. 19, q. 1, art. 4, obj. 1. This is stated as an objection, but the Reply to the Objection does not deny the basic idea that a purchase is involved. Similarly, Thomas's second treatment of the question, a Parisian quodlibet, declares, "Respondeo dicendum quod ad emptionem duo requiruntur," Thomas "Utrum alia passio Christi sine morte suffecisset ad redemptionem humani generis," *Quodlibet* 2, art. 2, *Opera omnia* (Parma, 1852–1873) 9, 473. In the third developed treatment in the *Summa theologica*, Thomas writes, "dicendum quod ad hoc aliquis redimat, duo requiruntur: scilicet actus solutionis et pretium solutum," Thomas, *Summa theologica* 3, 48, 5.

27.   Thomas, *Summa theologica* 3, 48, 5, and 48, 4 ad 3; acting by mandate of the Father, ibid. 3, 48, 5 ad 2.

28.   Thomas, *Scriptum super quatuor libros* 3, 19, 1 ad 4, art. 4, sol. 1.

29.   Ibid. 3, 19, 1, art. 4, sol. 1. On earlier medieval developments, see D. E. De Clerck, "Questions de sotériologie médiévale," *Recherches de théologie ancienne et médiévale* 13 (1946) 150; D. E. De Clerck, "Droits du démon et nécessite de la rédemption; Les écoles d'Abélard et de Pierre Lombard," ibid. 14 (1947) 32; J. Patout Burns, "The Concept of Satisfaction in Medieval Redemption Theory," *Theological Studies* 36 (1975) 285.

30.   Thomas, *Summa theologica* 3, 48, 4 ad 2 and ad 3.

31.   Thomas, *Scriptum super quatour libros* 3, 19, 1, 4 at *Sed contra*.

32.   Thomas, *Compendium theologiae ad fratrem Reginaldum* c. 227, *Opera omnia* 16, 67–68 (death for death, tree for tree); Thomas, *Quodlibet* 2, 2, ibid. 9, 473–474 (any suffering of Christ sufficient).

33.   Thomas, *Scriptum super quatuor libros*, 3, 20, q. 1, art. 3, "Solutio"; *Compendium theologiae* c. 227, *Opera omnia* 16, 67–68 (death maximum evil).

34. Urban IV, *Transiturus*, Aug. 11, 1264, *Les Régistres d'Urbain IV*, ed. Jean Guiraud (Paris, 1901) 2, 424.

35. Thomas, *Pange lingua, Officium de Festo Corporis Christi, Opera Omnia* 15, 234. For a discussion of Thomas's authorship, see John T. Noonan, Jr., "Bribery, Agency and Redemption in Thomas Aquinas," *Recherches de théologie ancienne et médiévale* (1982) 49, 161–162.

36. Thomas, *Lectio I, Officium de Festo Corporis Christi, Opera omnia* 15, 254. Cf. "Ordo Missae," *Missale Romanum* (Tours, 1955) 218: "Deus qui humanae . . . da nobis per huius aquae et vini mysterium eius divinitatis esse consortes, qui humanitatis nostrae fieri dignatus est particeps. . . ."

37. Thomas, *Summa theologica* 3, 59, 2.

38. Ibid. 3, 59, 2, citing John 5:27; ibid. 3, 59, 1, citing Acts 10:42.

39. Ibid. 3, 59, 2.

40. Ibid. 3, 59, 1.

41. Ibid. 3, 49, 5.

42. Anonymous, *Dies irae.*

43. Peter Abélard, *Ethica seu Scito te ipsum, PL* 178, 673.

44. Council of Clermont, canon 2, Mansi 20, 816.

45. Urban II to All the Faithful in Flanders, Dec. 1095, *Epistolae et chartae ad historiam primi belli sacri spectantes*, ed. Heinrich Hagenmeyer (Innsbruck: Wagner, 1901) 136; Robert the Monk, *Historia Iherosolimitana* 1, 2, in *Recueil des historiens des croisades: Historiens occidentaux* (Paris, 1841–1910) 3, 729; Foucher de Chartres, *Historia Hierosolymitana*, ed. Heinrich Hagenmeyer (Heidelberg, 1913) 1, 3 (p. 324): "eternal rewards." The popular understanding of Urban II's position is reviewed in James A. Brundage, *Medieval Canon Law and the Crusader* (Madison: University of Wisconsin Press, 1969) 146–149.

46. Bernard to the Clergy and People of Eastern France and Bavaria, *Epistulae* 363, *PL* 182, 566–567 (the letter was also sent to the English People, Bruno Scott James, *The Letters of St. Bernard of Clairvaux* [1953] 460).

47. Brundage, *Medieval Canon Law* 154.

48. Innocent III, "Expeditio pro recuperanda Terra Sancta," in Charles Joseph Hefele, *Histoire des Conciles*, trans. H. Leclerq (Paris: Letouzey & Ané, 1913) 5,[2] 1395.

49. Brundage, *Medieval Canon Law* 133–136. Specimen receipts in William E. Lunt, *Papal Revenues in the Middle Ages* (New York: Columbia University Press, 1934) 2, 517–518.

50. Ibid. 1, 121.

51. Thomas, *Summa theologica* 2–2, 88, 12 ad 3.

52. Thomas, *Scriptum super quatuor libros* 4, 20, q. 3, art. 3, sol. 1 ad 1.

53. Ibid. 4, 20, q. 1, art. 3, sol. 1 ad 2.

54. Thomas, *Quodlibet* 2, 8, 16, *Opera omnia* 9, 484. On Hughes of St. Cher and "treasure," Erwin Iserloh et al., *Reformation and Counter Reformation*, trans. Anselm Biggs and Peter W. Becker (New York: Seabury Press, 1980) 43.

55. Thomas, *Scriptum super quatuor libros* 4, 45, q. 2, art. 2 (*suffragia* for the dead); 4, 20, q. 1 art. 3, sol. 1 (indulgences good after death); sol. 2 (they are worth as much as preached); q. 1, art. 4, sol. 4 (obtainable for another by a man not in state of grace and can eliminate all purgatorial punishment); *Quodlibet* 2, 8, 16, *Opera omnia* 9, 484.

56. Thomas, *Scriptum super quatuor libros* 4, 20, q. 1, art. 3, sol. 2 ad 3.

57. See, for example, Lunt, *Papal Revenues* 2, 458 (20 *grossi* for plenary indulgence under John XXII).

58. Thomas, *Scriptum super quatuor libros* 4, 20, q. 1, art. 3, Quaestincula 3, and sol. 3.

59. Bonaventura, *Commentaria in quatuor libros sententiarum Magistri Petri Lombardi* (*Opera omnia*, ed. College of S. Bonaventura, Quarrachi, 1889, vol. 4, p. 537) 4, 20, Part 2, art. 1, q. 4 ad 1. On the date, Ignatius Brady, "Bonaventura, St.," *NCE* 2, 658–659.

60. Kurt Weitzmann, ed., *Age of Spirituality: Late Antique and Early Christian Art, Third to Seventh Century* (New York: Metropolitan Museum of Art, 1979) 556, 558.

61. Charles Rufus Morey, *Early Christian Art* (Princeton, N.J.: Princeton University Press, 1942) 169.

62. Emile Mâle, *Religious Art in France: The Twelfth Century*, trans. Marthiel Mathews (Princeton, N.J.: Princeton University Press, 1978) 407 and 511 n. 87.

63. Ibid. 408–409; Emile Mâle, *Notre Dame de Chartres* (Paris: Flammarion, 1963) 104–105.

64. Louis Réau, *Iconographie de l'art chrétien* (Paris: Presses universitaires de France, 1957) 2, 739–740.

65. See Honorius, *Elucidarium* 3, 13, *PL* 172, 1166.

66. Thomas, *Scriptum super quatuor libros* 4, 48, q. 1, art. 2 ad 2. Mâle, *Religious Art* 408, con-

tends that Honorius is followed in the various representations of the crucified Judge, but he ignores the implication that those who see the Crucified must be among the damned.

67. Réau, *Iconographie* 2, 733; Mâle, *Religious Art* 414.

68. "Offertorium," *Missa defunctorum, Missale Romanum* (Turin, 1955) 100*: "sed signifer sanctus Michael repraesentet eas in lucem sanctum." On the development of the prayer, Josef Beran, "L'Offertorio 'Domine Iesu Christe' Della Messa Per I Defunti," *Ephemeirides liturgicae* 50 (1936) 140−147. On the passage of certain souls through "purifying fire," Augustine, *De civitate Dei* 21, 26, CSEL 40², 571.

69. Mâle, *Religious Art* 413, 417.

70. Peter Lombard, *Sententiae* 4, 45 on the *diversa receptacula* of souls after death, following Augustine, *Enchiridion* c. 109; Thomas, *Scriptum super sententias* 4, 45, 1, sol. 2.

71. Emile Mâle, *The Gothic Image: Religious Art in France of the Thirteenth Century*, trans. Dora Nussey (New York: Harper & Brothers, 1958) 377 (on Bourges). Mâle, however, thinks it more probable that the object is not a chalice but the lamp of the Wise Virgin, so that the Redeemer is not in the scales; Dominique Manson, "Amiens," in Stefano Bottari, *Tesori d'arte cristiana* (Bologna: Officina grafiche Poligrafici il Resto del Carbino, 1968) 3, 287 (on Amiens).

72. Peter Lombard, *Sententiae* 4, 47, 2.

73. Thomas, *Scriptum super quatuor libros* 4, 47, q. 1, art. 2, sol. 2.

74. Honorius, *Elucidiarium* 3, 11 and 14, *PL* 172, 1164 and 1167.

75. Lotario, *De miseria* 3, 20 (no patronage); 3, 19 (only advocate the Lord).

76. Bernard of Clairvaux, *Sermo II de adventu Domini, PL* 183, 43.

77. Bernard of Clairvaux, *Sermo infra Octavum Assumptionis B.V. Mariae, PL* 183, 429.

78. Bernard of Clairvaux, *In navitate B.V. Mariae sermo de Aqueductu, PL* 183, 441.

79. Bernard of Cluny, *Mariale, Analecta hymnica medii aevi*, ed. Guido Maria Dreves (Leipzig, 1907) 50, 436 (Rhythm 7, "To whom shall I stretch"); 50, 451 (Rhythm 14: "Go-between"); 50, 426 (Rhythm 1: "If you fear"); 50, 426 (Rhythm 3: "Give the gifts"); 50, 452 (Rhythm 14: "Good mother"); 50, 434 (Rhythm 5: "Give them and me"); 50, 448 (Rhythm 12: "Star of the sea"); 50, 436 (Rhythm 7: "Make the formidable"); 50, 447 (Rhythm 11: "Just Judge"). On Bernard of Cluny, Frederic J. E. Raby, *A History of Christian-Latin Poetry* (Oxford: Clarendon Press, 1953) 315.

80. Guatier de Coinci, "Dou moigne que Nostre Dame resuscita," *Les Miracles de Nostre Dame*, ed. V. F. Koenig (Geneva: Droz, 1961) 2, 227−236; 230 lines 82−83.

81. Charles Diehl, *Manuel d'art byzantin* (Paris: Picard, 1926) 2, 545.

82. Mâle, *Religious Art* 417.

83. Mâle, *Notre Dame de Chartres* 105.

84. Manson, "Amiens"; Anne Prache, "Notre Dame," in Bottari, *Tesori* 3, 7.

85. For Torcello, Diehl, *Manuel* 2, 545. For Amiens and Notre Dame, Mâle, *The Gothic Image*; Manson, "Amiens."

86. Réau, *Iconographie* 2, 742.

87. Henry Adams, *Mont-Saint-Michel and Chartres* (Boston: Houghton Mifflin Co., 1904) 195.

88. Ibid. 145.

89. For negative evidence, see Gertrud Schiller, *Iconography of Christian Art*, trans. Janet Seligman (Greenwich, Conn.: New York Graphic Society, 1972).

90. Bottari, *Tesori* 3, 125. Other examples of Judas being offered money are a capital in the Autun cathedral and an eleventh-century Gospel illumination, Schiller, *Iconography* 2, 24.

91. On the authors, Samuel E. Thorne, "Introduction" to Bracton, *De legibus et consuetudinibus Angliae*, ed. George E. Woodbine (Cambridge, Mass.: Belknap Press of Harvard University Press, 1977) 3, xxxvi. On the proper spelling of the author's name, see Ralegh-Bratton, *De legibus* 3, 79, and Frederick W. Maitland, *Bracton's Note Book* (London: C. J. Clay & Sons, 1887) 1, 14. On the place of the book in English law, ibid. 1, 8.

92. Ralegh-Bratton, *De legibus* 2, 19.

93. Ibid. 2, 302.

94. Ibid. 2, 20 (judgments are God's); 2, 302−303 (God to be imitated).

95. Ibid. 2, 303.

96. Ibid. 2, 337.

97. G. O. Sayles, "Introduction", *Select Cases in the Court of King's Bench under Edward I* (London: Bernard Quaritch, 1936) LXVI and LXXVII (the retainers to the judges).

98. Ibid. CX−CXI.

99. *Warin de Monchesney v. Robert de Hecham*, Case 743, *Bracton's Note Book* 2, 565.

100.   Ralegh-Bratton, *De legibus*, 2, 254.

101.   Limits on the king: ibid. 2, 1; 2, 33; 2, 110; 2, 304–305; 3, 42–43. On the reinstatement of *Magna Carta*, William Sharp McKechnie, *Magna Carta* (Glasgow: Glasgow University Press, 1905) 164.

102.   Ralegh-Bratton, *De legibus* 2, 21–22.

103.   Anonymous, *Narratio de passione iusticiariorum*, printed as Appendix I in *State Trials of the Reign of Edward the First*, ed. T. F. Tout and Hilda Johnstone (London: Royal Historical Society, 1906, Camden Society, 3rd Series, vol. 9) 95.

104.   Ibid. 95–98.

105.   Respectively, *Annals of Dunstable*, ed. Henry R. Luard (London: Rolls Series, 1861, 36³) 355, 357; *Flores historiarum*, ed. Henry R. Luard (London: Rolls Series, 1890, 95³) 70; Thomas Wykes, *Chronicon*, ed. Henry R. Luard (London: Rolls Series, 1869, 36⁴) 319–321.

106.   Exchequer, *Rotuli Hundredorum* (London, 1812) 1 (14); also with an English translation, Helen M. Cam, *The Hundred and the Hundred Rolls* (London: Methuen, 1930) 251–257.

107.   *Rotuli* 3, (Flitte); 46 (Dustebery); 298 (Haywardeshow); 314 (Lincoln); 540 (Geldecross).

108.   Helen M. Cam, *Studies in the Hundred Rolls* (Oxford: Clarendon Press, 1921) 191.

109.   Ibid. 192.

110.   Ibid. 191.

111.   *Statutes of the Realm* 1, 26–39; 71–95; see also Cam, *Studies* 86, 121, 226–228.

112.   Tout and Johnstone, "Introduction," *State Trials* XI–XIII, XXXIX–XLIII; Sayles, "Introduction," *Select Cases* L–LIII.

113.   *Annals of Dunstable* (London: Rolls Series, 1861, 36³) 355–356; Tout and Johnstone, *State Trails* XXIX–XXX.

114.   *William de Bardwel v. Ralph de Hengham and others*, Tout and Johnstone, *State Trials* 49–51.

115.   Ibid. XXX (fine paid, subsequent career); 218 (conviction); 232–234 (acquittals or no judgment); Sayles, *Select Cases* LXVII (conviction analyzed).

116.   Tout and Johnstone, *State Trials* XXXI (fine paid) and 210–219; in *Agatha de Newcastle v. Brompton* (216–217) *munera*-taking was charged.

117.   Ibid. XXXII (Saham's fine); XXXI (Solomon's fine); 40, 218–219, 244–247 (Saham's cases); 242–245 (Solomon's cases).

118.   Sayles, *Select Cases* LXXII.

119.   Ibid. LXXIV.

120.   Ibid. LXXV.

121.   L. F. Salzman, *Edward I* (London: Constable & Co., 1968) 85.

122.   *Thomas de Goldington v. Nicholas de Stapleton*, Tout and Johnstone, *State Trials* 82.

123.   Ibid. 81–83.

124.   Ibid. 84.

125.   On the appropriateness of this appellation, see F. W. Maitland, *The Constitutional History of England* (1913) 18. Medieval Moscow affords another comparison. The Sudebnik or law code of 1497 denounces bribetaking by judges, but sets no sanctions. No sanctions are documented in practice, Daniel H. Kaiser, *The Growth of the Law in Medieval Russia* (Princeton University Press, 1980) 119–120.

CHAPTER 9: THE POUCHES AND THE PITCH (PP. 239–263)

1.   Dante Alighieri, *La Divina Commedia, Inferno*, Cantos 21, 22, and 23, lines 1–56. I have made the translation consulting many predecessors. If it must be accepted that any translation is a betrayal, I am convinced that it is preferable to betray Dante's sound rather than his sense; that all rhymed translations into English do frequently harm his sense; and that generally the best translation is the prose of Charles Singleton in *The Divine Comedy*, trans. with a commentary by Charles S. Singleton (Princeton, N.J.: Princeton University Press, 1970–1975).

2.   *Inferno*, Canto 1, 49–50 (the wolf); *Purgatorio*, Canto 20, 10–13 (the wolf cursed); Dante, *De monarchia*, ed. E. Moore (Oxford: Clarendon Press, 1916) 1, 11, 69 ("worst enemy of justice"); *Inferno*, Canto 11, 22–24:

> D'ogne malizia, ch'odio in cielo acquisita,
> ingiuria è il fine, ed ogne fin cotale
> o con forza o con frode altrui contrista.

3.   Dante, *Il Convivio*, ed. Maria Simonelli (Bologna: Casa Editrice Prof. Riccardo Pàtron, 1966) 1, 12, 9 (justice most human virtue).

4. *Inferno*, Canto 11, 25–27:

> Ma perché frode è de l'uom proprio male,
> piú spiace a Dio; e però stan di sotto
> li frodolenti, e piú dolor li assale.

5. Dante, *De monarchia* 1, 11, 93: "Karitas seu recta dilectio illam [iustitiam] acuit atque dilucidat"; *Inferno*, Canto 3, 5–6 (Divine Power made me); ibid. Canto 11, 55–56:

> Questo modo di retro par ch'incida
> pur lo vinco d'amor che fa natura;

Ibid. line 52:

> La frode, ond' ogne coscienza è morsa.

6. *Inferno*, Canto 21, lines 41–42:

> ogn' uom v'è barattier, fuor che Bonturo;
> del *no*, per li denar, vi sa fa *ita*.

Canto 22, line 53:

> quivi mi misi a far baratteria.

Ibid. lines 86–87:

> . . . e ne li altri offici anche
> barattier fu non picciol, ma sovrano.

7. Compare Cantos 21 and 22 in John Ciardi, trans., *The Inferno* (Bloomington: Indiana University Press, 1971), with Henry Boyd, trans., *The Divina Commedia* (London, 1802) 1, 267, 269, 277; Henry Francis Cary, trans., *The Vision of Hell, Purgatory and Paradise of Dante Alighieri* (first published 1806, here cited in 1901 ed., London: George Bell & Sons); Charles Eliot Norton, trans., *The Divine Comedy* (Boston: Houghton, Mifflin Co., 1902); Dorothy Sayers, trans., *The Divine Comedy* (London: Penguin, 1949); Geoffrey L. Bickersteth, trans., *The Divine Comedy* (Oxford: Shakespeare Head Press, 1965), and Singleton.

8. Singleton, *Inferno: Commentary* 368.

9. Pietro Alighieri, *Commentarium*, ed. Vincentio Nannucci (Florence, 1845) 210.

10. *Purgatorio*, Canto 8, line 53 (Judge Nino); Singleton, *Inferno: Commentary* 367–371 (Lucchese); 383 (Gomita).

11. *Ibid.* 385 (Zanche); 369 (Bonturo). The story of being "half of Lucca" is also told by commentators apropos Martino Bottaio, said to be the alderman delivered by the demon; ibid. 368–369: "Shake me," Bonturo or Martino said to Boniface VIII, and when the Holy Father did, the Lucchese responded, "You have just shaken half of Lucca." On the constituency of a leader of "the party of the people," see Lauro Martines, *Power and Imagination: City-States in Renaissance Italy* (New York: Alfred A. Knopf, 1979) 67.

12. Pietro Alighieri, *Commentarium* 210.

13. Singleton, *Inferno: Commentary* 392, follows a version of the tale in which the mouse escapes and accepts the interpretation of the fable offered by Neil M. Larkin, "Another Look at Dante's Frog and Mouse," *Modern Language Notes* 77 (1962) 94–99. The majority of the commentators have interpreted one of the two fighting devils to be the frog, the other "the mouse," and the pitch to be the hawk. The majority interpretation starts from the more common version of the tale that has both mouse and frog destroyed but does not do justice to the innocence of the mouse or Dante's stress on the need for a steady look at beginning and end. For the Florentine decree of November 6, 1315, see "Documents Concerning Dante's Public Life," compiled by George R. Carpenter, Dante Society, *Eleventh Annual Report* (1892) 51–53.

14. Pietro Alighieri, *Commentarium*, 212. The offensive lines are totally replaced in Henry Boyd's translation, *The Divina Commedia* 274.

15. Pietro Alighieri, *Commentarium* 210, 214.

16. John D. Sinclair, *The Divine Comedy: Inferno* (New York: Oxford University Press, 1948) Canto 21.

17.   Boniface VIII to the Bishop of Florence, *Pridem ad vestram perducto*, April 24, 1300, printed in G. Levi, "Bonifazio VIII e sue relazioni col Commune di Firenze," *Archivio della Società Romana di storia patria* 5 (1882) 450–452; Boniface VIII to the Bishop and the Inquisitor of Florence, *Perlato pridem ad audientiam vestram*, May 15, 1300, in ibid. 455–458. For the events, Thomas S. R. Boase, *Boniface VIII* (London: Constable & Co., 1933) 248–250, 276–277.

18.   Judgment of the Podestà, Jan. 27, 1302, in "Documents Concerning Dante's Public Life," ed. George Rice Carpenter, Dante Society, *Tenth Annual Report* (1891) 48–54.

19.   Judgment of the Podestà, Jan. 27, 1302, in ibid. 48.

20.   *Inferno*, Canto 11, line 52.

21.   Dante to Anonymous (a Florentine Friend) post 1315, in Dante, *Epistolae*, ed. Paget Toynbee (London: Oxford University Press, 1966) 156.

22.   Judgment of the Podestà, March 10, 1302, in ibid. 52–54.

23.   *Paradiso*, Canto 17, lines 54–55:

> Tu lascerai ogni cosi diletta
> più caramente. . . .

24.   Robert Davidsohn, *Geschichte von Florenz* (Berlin: Ernst Siegfried Mittler & Sohn, 1908) 2^2, 152–175.

25.   The names have incited much inconclusive speculation, Singleton, *Inferno: Commentary* 376. A number appear to be compounds, as follows:

Ali (wing) + *chinar* (to bend) = Bentwing (or, alternatively, *Hellequin*, a devil's name related to our Harlequin)
Calcar (trample) + *brina* (white hairs) = Trampleage
Cagna (bitch) + *nazzo* (nose) = Curnose
Barba (beard) + *riccio* (curl) = Curlbeard
Drago (dragon) + *nazzo* (nose) = Dragonnose
Graffiare (to claw) + *cane* (dog) = Clawdog
Scarmigliare (to rumple) = Rumpler
Mala (bad) + *coda* (tail) = Badtail
Lib (for *libero* or free) + *ic* (letters added for sound) + *occo* (for *occhio* or eye) = Free Eye or Walleye (This combination is the most debatable. No one has produced a completely convincing account of what Dante intended).

In addition, *Rubicante* appears derived from *rubeor*, to turn red; and *Farfarello* means Little Devil. As for *Ciriatto*, Francesco da Buti, circa 1395, suggests that "*Ciri, ciri*" is a hog call (see his *Commento supra La Divina Commedia*, ed. Crescentino Giannini (Pisa, 1858) 1, 558. *Ciro* is Tuscan for pig, Leo Spitzer, "Two Dante Notes," *Romanic Review* 34 (1943) 260. See also Ernesto Giacomo Parodi, *Lingua e Litteratura* (Venice: Neri Pozza, 1957) 2, 354–356.

26.   *Blake's Dante: The Complete Illustrations to the Divine Comedy*, ed. Milton Klonsky (New York: Harmony Books, 1980) Plates 38–45, especially Plate 41.

27.   *Paradiso*, Canto 17, lines 49–51:

> Questo se vuole e questo già si cerca,
> e tosta verrà fatto a chi cio pensa
> là dove Cristo tutto di si merca.

Boase, *Boniface VIII* 248–249, observes that it is unlikely that Dante had much importance to Boniface, but notes that by the spring of 1300 men in the curia believed that "Pope Boniface wants to give himself all of Tuscany."

28.   *Inferno*, Canto 19.

29.   Robert Brentano in his review of thirteenth-century popes puts Nicholas III high among the nepotists, Brentano, *Rome Before Avignon* (New York: Basic Books, 1974) 182. For the views of Pietro Alighieri, see *Commentarium*, 195–197. Singleton, *Inferno: Commentary* 368, treats simony, "the buying and selling of church office," as the ecclesiastical equivalent of his "barratry," the buying and selling of public office. But in each case his definition is too narrow; simony is, of course, the sale of *spiritualia*, including such things as absolution and ordination.

30.   Singleton, *Inferno: Commentary* 342.

31.   *Paradiso*, Canto 17, line 51.

32.   E.g., Singleton, *Inferno: Commentary* 338, 340, quoting the Florentine chronicler Giovanni Villani.

33. Pierre de Peredo, Charges against Boniface VIII, Oct. 6, 1303, in *Histoire du Differend d'entre Pape Boniface VIII et Philippe le Bel Roy du France*, ed. Pierre DuPuy (Paris, 1665) 212 (go-betweens in election cases; uncustomary charges), 213 (*exploratores*), 214 (no accountant could count); Guillaume Nogaret, Charges, September 7, 1304, before the *Officialis* of Paris, in ibid. 240 (manifest usurer, "sodomite," heretic); the Bishops and Clergy of France, Articles Against Boniface VIII, in ibid. 333–334 (accusation against Simone de Spini and question attributed to Boniface, "Nonne Papa Romanus dominus est omnium, specialiter bonorum ecclesiarum?"). As Boase, *Boniface VIII* 106, suggests, this remark, if made, was probably an ad hoc argument, not a serious claim. The cynical view that the man who owns everything cannot be corrupt is a kind of commentary on Dante's utopian view in *De monarchia* 1, 11, 80–90, that the ideal ruler is to have everything he wants, because "greed is the sole corruptor of judgment and hindrance to Justice."

34. *Purgatorio*, Canto 19, lines 117–126.

35. *Inferno*, Canto 19, line 98:

e guarda ben la mal tolta moneta;

and line 72:

che sù l'avere e qui me misi in borsa.

36. *L'Ottimo Commento della Divina Commedia*, ed. Alessandro Torri (Pisa, 1827) 1, 348–349.

37. Pietro Alighieri, *Commentarium* 198.

38. Writing the six Italian cardinals at Avignon in 1314 Dante tells them that they despise "the fire sent from heaven" and "strange fire burns on the altars—you sell doves in the temple where those things which cannot be measured . . . are made sellable." "Each has married a wife—covetousness," Dante to the Italian cardinals (circa May–June 1314), *Epistolae*, Letter 9, 131, 133.

39. *Paradiso*, Canto 18, lines 91–93:

DILIGITE IUSTITIAM primai
fur verbo e nome di tutto il dipinto;
QUI IUDICATIS TERRAM fur sezzai.

Ibid. line 96:

pareva argento li d'oro distinto.

40. Ibid. lines 115–123.

CHAPTER 10: THE MONKEYS AND THE BEARS (PP. 264–310)

1. Anonymous, *Book of Vices and Virtues*, ed. W. Nelson Francis (London: English Early Text Society, 1942) 34–36; cf. Dan Michel, *Ayenbite of Inwit*, ed. Richard Morris (London: Early English Text Society, 1866) 43–44.

2. *Book of Vices* 37–38; cf. *Ayenbite* 41–42.

3. Anonymous, *Memoriale presbiterorum*, excerpted in William A. Pantin, *The English Church in the Fourteenth Century* (Cambridge: At the University Press, 1955) 205.

4. John Mirk, *Manuale sacerdotis*, excerpted in ibid. 216 (Master Symon); G. R. Owst, *Literature and Pulpit in Medieval England*, 2nd ed. (Oxford: Basil Blackwell, 1961) 276 ("benefice with sin").

5. John Mirk, *Instructions for Parish Priests*, ed. Edward Peacock (London: Early English Text Society, 1902) 31.

6. John Thoresby, *Instructio*, printed as *The Lay Folks' Catechism*, ed. T. F. Simmons and H. E. Nolboth (London: Early English Text Society, 1921) 92.

7. Henry of Lancaster, *Livre de Seyntz Medicinés*, ed. E. J. Arnould (Oxford: Anglo-Norman Text Society, 1940) 17 (killing), 22 (lechery).

8. Ibid. 74 (beau present).

9. Ibid. 37 (Jesus on Judgment Day), 236–238 (intercessors and scales).

10. Pantin, *The English Church* 147. On the development of preaching and aids to preaching in the preceding century, see Richard H. Rouse and Mary A. Rouse, *Preachers, Florilegia and Sermons* (Toronto: Pontifical Institute of Mediaeval Studies, 1979) 43–64.

11. John Bromyard, *Summa praedicantium* (Venice, 1586) 2, 96v at *Munus*, ante art. 1 (Ps 25

in the Vulgate = Ps. 26); 97r–v, art. 1 (sin); art. 2 (exceptions and examples); 2, 99r, art. 3 (Job invoked); 2,100r (restitution); at *Iustitia*, art. 7, 2,428r (treason to God). On the dates and on the book's predecessor, see Leonard E. Boyle, O.P., "The Date of the *Summa Praedicantium* of John Bromyard," *Speculum* XLVIII (1973) 533–537, reprinted in Boyle, *Pastoral Care, Clerical Education and Canon Law, 1200–1400* (London: Variorum Reprints, 1981). Boyle dates the work as begun by 1330 and finished about 1348. It was based on an earlier work of Bromyard's, *Opus trivium*, a treatment of the three laws—divine, canon, and civil.

12.   Bromyard, *Summa praedicantium* at *Munus*, 97 r–v, art. 1 (comparisons); art. 2 (God blind); 98v, art. 3 (deny God and self); 99v, art. 3 (whore's hire); at *Simonia*, 364v, art. 2 (worse than the married Judas).

13.   Ibid. 2, 99r at *Munus*, art. 3 (bailiffs, jurors); 99v (prelates; judges selling commutations to robbers); 1, 403r at *Iudices*, art. 6 (custom contrary to charity); 1, 428r at *Iustitia*, art. 7 (sale for 6 pence).

14.   Ibid. 1, 427v at *Iustitia*, art. 7 (pillars); 1, 157r at *Correctio*, art. 4 (shield of friendship).

15.   Ibid. 1, 34v at *Advocatus*, art. 3 (*munera* paid by lawyers); 35v at art. 4 (effect of client's fee); 44r at *Adulterium*, art. 1 (*divortia*, i.e., annulments; implication that some annulments will not be granted).

16.   Ibid. 2, 98r–v, at *Munus*, art. 3 (return of *munus*).

17.   Ibid. 1, 45r at *Adulterium*, art. 2 (payments to summoners and judges); 1, 159r–160r at *Correctio*, art. 8 (analysis of commutation); at 161v (devils' partners); 2, 92v–93r at *Mundus*, art. 4 (punish a purse; proctors of devils). It has been observed that the penance could "not expose a person holding a responsible position to such humiliation that it would henceforward be impossible for him to exercise his authority." Rosalind Hill, "Public Penance: Some Problems of a Thirteenth-Century Bishop," *History* 36 (Second Series) (1951) 216. Bromyard ignored this kind of justification for money commutations.

18.   *Summa praedicantium* 2, 138r–139r at *Ordo clericalis*, art. 2 (scarcely 1 in 100; abundant life); 2, 363v–364r at *Simonia*, art. 1 (loans; licenses to pardoners; sale of patronage; *munus* of service and tongue); 365v, art. 4 (Sarah's husbands).

19.   Ibid. 1, 222v at *Electio*, art. 6 (piggish clerics; mercenary vicars; final accounting; spiritual eunuchs); 1, 158v, art. 5 (damned pig).

20.   Ibid. 1, 359v–360v, at *Honor*, art. 2. (the Venice edition has substituted "prelates" for "cardinals," which is the word used in the 1518 Nuremberg edition); ibid. 1, 99r, at *Munus*, art. 3 (servants).

21.   E.g., ibid. 2, 97v at *Munus*, art. 2 (Seneca); 2, 365v at *Simonia*, art. 4 (Ildebrando); 1, 399r at *Iudices*, art. 2 (Innocent III); 1, 399v, art. 4 (St. Bernard); 1, 401r, art. 5 (judge's hand oiled); 1, 404r, art. 7 (Cicero).

22.   Ibid. 2, 98v at *Munus*, art. 3.

23.   Ibid. 2, 141v at *Ordo clericalis*, art. 2 (state of modern Church); 154r–154v, art. 7 (infidels, lords, incurable wound).

24.   Brunton, excerpted in Owst, *Literature and Pulpit* 246 (dumb dogs); Brunton, excerpted in Owst, *Preaching in Medieval England* (Cambridge: At the University Press, 1926) 19–20 (Simon Magician).

25.   "Forbiggynge," Anonymous, Sermon, excerpted in Owst, *Literature and Pulpit* 282; Waldely, excerpted in ibid. 266; Philip, excerpted 269; Wimbledon, excerpted 280. Wimbledon's status, Pantin, *The English Church* 236.

26.   Brunton, quoted in Owst, *Preaching in Medieval England* 40.

27.   John Wyclif, a severe judge, said in 1379 that "the majority or all" of the friars in England were silent on simony, Wyclif, *De simonia*, ed. Herzberg-Fränkel and Michael H. Dziewicki (London: Trübner, 1898) c. 8, 98.

28.   Richard FitzRalph, Sermon, Feb. 7, 1352, printed in Aubrey Gwynn, S.J., "Two Sermons of Primate Richard FitzRalph, *Archivum Hibernium* 14 (1949) 58–62.

29.   *Ibid.*, 53 (Joseph and his brothers); 62 (promotions for *munera*).

30.   Aubrey Gwynn, "Richard FitzRalph, Archbishop of Armagh," *Studies* 22 (1933) 389 (ancestry), 402 (Oxford); Gwynn, "Richard FitzRalph at Avignon," *Studies* 22 (1933) 591, 595 (Grandisson and Lichfield), 597 (litigation at Avignon); Gwynn, "Richard FitzRalph, Archbishop of Armagh," *Studies* 23 (1934) 398 (nephews); 399 (selection for Armagh); Gwynn, "Richard FitzRalph," *Studies* 26 (1937) (cult).

31.   Aubrey Gwynn, "The Sermon-Diary of Richard FitzRalph, Archbishop of Armagh," *Proceedings of the Royal Irish Academy* (1937) 44, sec. C., no. 1, 39–41 (1340 and 1341 sermons); L. L. Hammerich, "The Beginning of the Strife Between Richard FitzRalph and the Mendicants," *Det Kgl. Danske Videnskrabernes Selskab*, Hist.-fil. Med. (1938) 26, sec. 3, 31 (Dominican sermon).

32.   FitzRalph, "Sermon-Diary" in Gwynn, "The Sermon-Diary of Richard FitzRalph" 36.

33. Bromyard, *Summa praedicantium* 1, f. IV at *Prologus*.

34. Owst, *Literature and Pulpit* 236, 285.

35. Gwynn, "Two Sermons," *Archivum Hibernium* 14 (1949) 50, gives the bishops of the province and their tenure of office.

36. Gwynn, "Richard FitzRalph," *Studies* 23 (1934) 397.

37. *Summa praedicantium* 1, f.lr at *Prologus*.

38. William Langland, *Piers Plowman*, ed. W. W. Skeat (London: Oxford University Press) 2, 8–20. References are to the B text.

39. Modern English writers have rendered Mede as "Lady Fee" (J. F. Goodridge, *Piers the Ploughman*, Penguin Books, 1959); or said Mede stands for "the desire for reward" (Morton W. Bloomfield, *Piers Plowman as a Fourteenth-Century Apocalypse* (New Brunswick, N. J.: Rutgers University Press, 1961) 111, cf. p. 6); or identified Lady Mede with graft (Donald and Rachel Attwater, *Piers Plowman* [London: J. M. Dent, 1957] ix, 202). None of these approximations preserves the ambiguity of *munus* or mede. The ambiguity is pointed out by Elizabeth Salter, *Piers Plowman* (Cambridge, Mass.: Harvard University Press, 1962) 97, when she says that Mede "is both bribery and reward."

40. Cf. Bloomfield, *Piers Plowman* 38.

41. *The Simonie* 11, 9–16, in Thomas Wright, ed., *The Political Songs of England* (London: Camden Society, 1839); Elizabeth Salter, "Piers Plowman and 'The Simonie,'" *Archiv. für das Studium der neueren Sprachen und Literaturen* 203 (1967) 248–250.

42. On Langland's clerical status and on the value of the autobiography, E. Talbot Donaldson, *Piers Plowman* (New Haven, Conn.: Yale University Press, 1949) 218–219, 226.

43. On the date, Skeat, *Piers Plowman* 2, 274, n. 447.

44. Wyclif, *De simonia*, c. 1, p. 9 (Avigonian nest), c. 3, pp. 27–31 (pope's simony by aspiration and appointments), c. 4 ("worst merchants"; "Luciferian domination"; "pseudo-pope"), c. 5 (annates; antipopes and Antichrist).

45. Ibid. c. 1, p. 4 (few prelates not heretics) c. 6, pp. 70–83 (Simonians by motives, lifestyle, charges).

46. Ibid. c. 1 (simonian promotions, collegiate churches and universities; silent friars; c. 2 (simonian business with cardinals; simonian judges and patrons; c. 7 (simonian monks); c. 8 (cooperators in simony).

47. Wyclif, *De civili dominio*, ed. R. L. Poole (London: Trübner and Co., 1885), 1, 1–14 (basic theory); 1, 37 and 2, 12 (forfeiture); 2, 39 (treason); 4, 482 (Statute of Mortmain); 4, 484 (eminent domain). The legal arguments are emphasized in William Farr, *John Wyclif as Legal Reformer* (Leiden: E. J. Brill, 1974) 129, 136, 152.

48. Joseph H. Dahmus, *The Prosecution of John Wyclyf* (New Haven, Conn.: Yale University Press, 1952) 79 (shift in government support); Herbert B. Workman, *John Wyclif* (Oxford: Clarendon Press, 1926) 1, 286, 293 (bulls to England); Pantin, *The English Church* 177–178 (English critics, notably Adam Easton, O.S.B., at the curia).

49. Wyclif, *De simonia*, c. 1, 4.

50. Ibid. c. 1, 2.

51. John T. Noonan, Jr., *The Scholastic Analysis of Usury* (Cambridge, Mass.: Harvard University Press, 1957) 32–33.

52. Wyclif, *De simonia* c. 1, 8 (sodomy), 10 (Judas); cf. Peraldus, *Summa de virtutibus et vitiis* (Venice, 1497) at *De avaritia*. On Wyclif's use of Pérault, see Johann Loserth, *Johann von Wiclif und Guilelmus Peraldus* (Vienna: Wien Akademie der Wissenschaften, Ph.-hist. Kl. Report 180, 1916) 14.

53. J. A. Robson, *Wyclif and the Oxford Schools* (Cambridge: At the University Press, 1961) 14 (Wyclif as pluralist); Workman, *John Wyclif* 1, 209–210 (Lutterworth); 1, 240–253 (Bruges); 1, 275–281 (relation to John of Gaunt); Wyclif, *De simonia* c. 2, 21 on restitution owed by Simonians.

54. Ibid. c. 7, 93 (Urban VI; secular lords); c. 8, 99–100 (simonian judges).

55. Ibid. c. 7, 94 (stop offerings); c. 8, 101 (old men drunk with avarice).

56. Clement VI, *Unigenitus, Extravagantes communes* 5, 9, 2, in Friedberg, ed., *Corpus iuris canonici*.

57. Wyclif, *De ecclesia*, ed. Johann Loserth (London: Trübner & Co., 1886).

58. Ibid. c. 29, 551 (fantastic imagination); 560 (no release from debt to God); 561 (*regalia* of deity); 564 (past merits not distributable); 568 (God distributes merits); 586 (connection of punishment to sin); see Introduction, xvi, xxiv, on the date of c. 23 devoted to indulgences.

59. Wyclif, *De dissensione paparum*, in *Political Works in Latin*, ed. Rudolf Buddensey (London, 1883) 2, 574 ("our Urban"); Wyclif, *Cruciata*, in ibid. 2, 592 ("manifest lie"); 594 (future

treasure); 595 (each an Antichrist); 609 (Bernard and Eugene); 612 (frivolous injury).

60.   Dahmus, *The Prosecution* 84 (charges against Wyclif); Workman, *Wyclif* 2, 236–241 (the mix of factors).

61.   Dahmus, *The Prosecution* 93–98.

62.   Workman, *Wyclif* 1, 328, suggests that Lollard was also confused with Middle English *loller*, loafer, and punningly related to Latin *lolia* or tares.

63.   Geoffrey Chaucer, *The Canterbury Tales*, ed. F. N. Robinson (Boston: Houghton Mifflin, 1957) F 1517–1520. These abbreviations are adopted: C = Clerks's Tale; F = Freres Tale; MLT =Man of Lawes Tale; P = Prologue; Pers = Persouns Tale; PT = Pardoners Tale; ST = Somonours Tale. Chaucer's use of "brybe" as a verb appears to be a metaphorical adaptation of the French *briber*, to eat greedily, to beg bread; see Randall Cotgrave, *A Dictionary of the French and English Tongues* (London: Adam Islip, 1632) at *briber*. In making a transformation of the verb, Chaucer's usage begins a new career for the word; in French, the noun *une bribe* meant only a piece of bread given to a beggar. The French for one giving a bribe was *un corrompeur par dons*, and the French verb for bribe or corrupt was *corrompre*; see Cotgrave at these words. On the apparitors and their blank citations, see Robert E. Rodes, Jr., *Ecclesiastical Adminstration in Medieval England* (Notre Dame, Ind.: University of Notre Dame Press, 1977) 138.

64.   P 223–225 (Frere Huber an easy man). The number 20,000 for the friars in England is put forward hypothetically in Wycliff, *Sermones*, ed. Johann Loserth (London: Trübner & Co., 1888) 2, 435.

65.   ST 2150–2151, 2248–2286.

66.   PT 671, 687.

67.   Chanouns Yemans Tale 1313.

68.   Petrarch, *Epistulae seniles*, in *Sources and Analogues of Chaucer's Canterbury Tales*, ed. W. F. Bryan and Germaine Dempster (New York: Humanities Press, 1958) 318.

69.   Geoffrey Sheperd in *Geoffrey Chaucer*, ed. Derek Brewer (Columbus: Ohio Unversity Press, 1975) 270: Chaucer "never discloses his commitment in religion"; 272: "There are still chinks in his narration through which can be glimpsed a black pessimism."

70.   E. Talbot Donaldson, *Speaking of Chaucer* (New York: W. W. Norton, 1970) 173.

71.   Thomas Aquinas, *Summa theologica* 1, 29, 3.

72.   Caterina to Gregory XI, probably Jan. 1376, *Epistolario di Santa Caterina da Siena*, ed. Eugenio Dupré Theseider (Rome, 1940), Letter 54, 214–215.

73.   Caterina to Abbot Berengarius, after May 17, 1375, ibid. Letter 51, 199 (re-sellers); Caterina to Raimundo da Capua, about April 1, 1376, ibid. Letter 65, 274–275.

74.   Caterina to Gregory XI, June–July 1376, ibid. Letter 71, 294–295.

75.   Petrarch, *Rime sparse*, in *Petrarch's Lyric Poems*, ed. Robert M. Durling (Cambridge, Mass: Harvard University Press, 1976) Poem 114, 223 (impious Babylon); Poem 136, p. 281 ("nest"); Poem 137, p. 281 (avaricious); Poem 138, p. 283 (disgraced whore).

76.   Caterina to Gregory XI, June–Sept. 1376, *Epistolario*, Letter 74, 304–305 (wolves, lamb); Caterina to Gregory XI, June–Sept. 1376, ibid. Letter 77, 314 (reformation).

77.   Matthew Spinka, *John Hus* (Princeton, N.J.: Princeton University Press, 1968) 59 (Wyclif's writings to Prague, the Goose); Jan Hus, *Super IV sententiarum*, ed. Wenzel Flajšhans and Marie Komínková (Osnabrück, 1966 reprint of 1905 ed.) 4, 25; Jan Hus, *Contra Cruciatam*, ed. Jaroslav Ersil, *Opera Omnia*, vol. 22, (Prague: Academia Scientiarum Bohemoslovaca, 1966); Jan Hus, *Simony*, trans. Matthew Spinka, in Spinka et al., *Advocates of Reform* (Philadelphia: Westminster Press, 1953) 193.

78.   Hus, *Simony*, Spinka trans., 213 (*gulden* for Prague archbishopric); 217 (annates); 219 (Hodek and Hůda); 224–225 (bishop's charges and attempted defense); 234 (monks); 242–246 (priests); 253 (shearers).

79.   Ibid., 255–257 (laymen); 260–266 (cooperators).

80.   Hus, *Contra cruciatam* 131, 134 (nothing conveyed); John Hus, *Quaestio Magistri Johannis Hus disputata . . . de indulgentiis sive de Cruciata Papae Johannis XXIII fulminata contra Ladislaum Apuliae Regem* in *Historia et monumenta Johannis Hus atque Hieronymi Pragensis, Confessorum Christi* (Nuremberg, 1715)1, 222 ("Look, a blind man . . ." and quoting *Bulla Commisariis* 1, 214); 223 (do not priests buy?); 226–227 ("With what face. . . With what face. . . ?"); 228 (Christ's tribunal); 232 (buy back ancestors); Matthew Spinka, *John Hus' Concept of the Church* (Princeton, N.J.: Princeton University Press, 1966) 113, on open palms of pardoners.

81.   Spinka, *John Hus* 114, 161 (case in Prague and Rome).

82.   Jan Hus, *Knizky Proti Kuchmistrovi*, excerpted and translated in Spinka, *John Hus' Concept of the Church* 107–108.

83.   Hus, *Simony*, 221.

84.   Jan Hus, *Contra Stephanum Palecz*, ed. Jaroslav Ersil, in Hus, *Polemica* (Prague, 1966) 237. The line is found in Hans Walther, *Initia carminum ac versuum medii aevi posterioris latinorum* (Göttingen: Vandenhoeck & Ruprecht, 1959) 199.

85.   Jan Hus, "Appeal from the Pope's Condemnation," Oct. 18, 1412, *The Letters of John Hus*, trans. Matthew Spinka (Manchester: Manchester University Press, 1972) 217.

86.   Spinka, *John Hus* 226 (vindication); 233 (Goose cooked). Spinka takes the position that Hus did not secure a safe conduct in advance, although he had been promised one by the emperor and after his arrival in Constance the emperor issued him one, ibid. 221, 228.

87.   Ibid. 265–290. On Hus's orthodoxy, see Paul De Vooght, O.S.B., *L'hérésie de Jean Hus*, 2nd ed. (Louvain: Publications universitaires, 1975) 1, 517, where the author hopes that the Church will annul "le verdict injuste et néfaste" pronounced by Constance on Hus.

88.   Mansi 27, 640 (John XXIII cited before Council); 641 (cardinals decline to be proctors); 654 (pope suspended); 662–673 (initial charges); 684–699 (report of prosecutors).

89.   On deposition for notorious heresy in canonist theory, Brian Tierney, *Foundations of the Conciliar Theory* (Ithaca, N.Y.: Cornell University Press, 1953) 61.

90.   Mansi 27, 684.

91.   Ibid. 685 (second charge); 685 (third); 687 (twelfth); 689 (twentieth).

92.   Jean Gerson, *Tractatus de simonia*, *Oeuvres complètes*, ed. P. Glorieux (Paris: Desclée, 1965) 169–173.

93.   Mansi 27, 704.

94.   Ibid. 27, 715–716.

95.   The operation of what could be called "compensatory orthodoxy" is frequently to be observed in theology and politics.

96.   Hus to His Friends in Bohemia, June 24, 1415, *Letters*, trans. Spinka, 190.

97.   Conrad Eubel, *Hierarchia catholica* 1, 32.

98.   Spinka, *John Hus* 290, 298.

99.   Bernardino, *Sermones "de diversis,"* Sermon 5, preamble, *Opera omnia*, ed. College of S. Bonaventura (Quarrachi, 1950) 7, 408.

100.   Bernardo Giustiniani, *Orationes* fol. L2, quoted by Patricia H. Labalme, *Bernardo Giustiniani* (Rome: Edizioni di storia e letteratura, 1969) 86 ("powerful in example as in word"); D. Pacetti, "Bernardine di Siena, St.," *New Catholic Encyclopedia* 2, 345–347 (biography).

101.   Bernardino, *Sermones "de diversis,"* Sermon 4, art. 1, c. 2, *Opera* 7, 455.

102.   Bernardino, *Sermones "de tempore,"* Sermon 18, art. 2, c. 7, *Opera* 7, 300–301.

103.   Bernardino, *Sermones "de diversis,"* Sermon 4, art. 1, c. 2, *Opera* 7, 455.

104.   Bernardino, *Quadragesimale de evangelio aeterno* 18, 3, 1, *Opera* 3, 326–327.

105.   Bernardino, *Sermones "de diversis,"* Sermon 8, art. 3, c. 3, *Opera* 7, 469.

106.   Bernardino, *De christiana religione*, Sermon 39, art. 2, c. 3, *Opera* 1, 508.

107.   Bernardino, *Le Prediche volgari*, ed. Ciro Cannarozzi, OFM (Florence: Libreria Editrice Fiorentina, 1934) 5, 297, 300.

108.   Ibid. 5, 104–105.

109.   Ibid. 5, 15.

110.   Bernardino, *Sermones "de diversis,"* 4, 3, 3, *Opera* 7, 491.

111.   Bernardino, *Le Prediche volgari* 5, 507–508; cf. Bernardino, *Quadragesimale de christiana religione*, Sermon 33, preamble, *Opera* 1, 401, on restitution in general.

112.   Cf. Bernardino, *Quadragesimale de evangelio aeterno*, Sermons 36–45, *Opera* 4, 203–416.

113.   Bernardino, *Le Prediche Volgari*, ed. Luciano Bianchi (Siena, 1884) 2, 288.

114.   Ibid. 2, 283; cf. Bernardino, *Prediche volgari di S. Bernardino* (Siena, 1853) 228.

115.   *Le Prediche Volgari*, ed. Cannarozzi, 5, 15.

116.   Bernardino, *Le Prediche volgari di S. Bernardino* (1853) 211. On the use of animal stories by the oppressed, see David Daube, *Civil Disobedience in Antiquity* (Edinburgh: At the University Press, 1972) 53–54, 71, 130–131. See also Francis Klingender, *Animals in Art and Thought to the End of the Middle Ages* (Cambridge, Mass.: M.I.T. Press, 1971) 379: Animal imagery is a common language for all of medieval society, and animal stories present "realistic appraisals of adult situations," "as seen from the point of view of those who are themselves neither lions nor foxes."

117.   [Thomas à Kempis], *De imitatione Christi* (London: Kegan Paul, Trench, Trübner & Co., 1892) Bk. 1, c. 24, sec. 1, p. 82.

118.   Egidio of Viterbo, Oration, May 2, 1512, Mansi 32, 670; see on Egidio's view of Rome, John W. O'Malley, S.J., *Giles of Viterbo on Christ and Reform* (Leiden: E. J. Brill, 1968) 132–134.

119.   Leo X, *In apostolici culminis*, Mansi 32, 845–846; Leo X, *Bulla Reformationis Curiae*, Mansi

32, 874–879.

120. Lucien Febvre, "Une question mal posée: Les origines de la réforme française et le problème des causes de la réforme," *Au Coeur religieux du XVIe siècle* (Paris: Sevpen, 1957) 68 [Article originally published in *Revue historique* (1929) vol. 161]. Cf. G. R. Elton, "Introduction: The Age of the Reformation," *The New Cambridge Modern History* (Cambridge: At the University Press, 1958) 2, 1–22; Steven E. Ozment, *The Reformation in the Cities* (New Haven, Conn.: Yale University Press, 1975) 116–120.

121. Martin Luther, *Sermo de duplici iustitia* (Weimar: Hermann Böhlau, 1884), *Werke* 2, 146 (1518 preaching); Luther, "Von der Freiheit eines Christen Menschen," *Werke* 7, 26, (1520); Luther, *Der Kleine Katechismus*, *Werke* 30, 249 (Article 2 of the Creed: the Redemption). For the old stereotype and criticism of it, Lucien Febvre, *Un destin: Martin Luther* (Paris: Editions Rieder, 1927) 21, 57–76. For the development of Luther's religious views, ibid. 58–65.

122. Martin Luther, *Wider Hans Worst*, *Werke* 51, 541. Hans Sausage (Hans Worst) was a derogatory name applied by Luther's opponent Duke Henry of Braunschweig to John Frederick, elector of Saxony, but taken over by Luther and applied by him to Duke Henry. Hans Sausage was a stock carnival character who carried a long leather sausage about his neck. He had earlier appeared in literature in Sebastian Brant's *Ship of Fools*, see Eric W. Gritsch, trans. *Against Hanswurst, Luther's Works* (Philadelphia: Fortress Press, 1966) 41, 181–182.

123. Erwin Iserloh, "Martin Luther and the Coming of the Reformation," in Iserloh et al., *Reformation and Counter Reformation* 45.

124. Albrecht of Brandenburg, *Instructio summaria* in Walther Köhler, ed.; *Dokumente zum Ablassstreit von 1517* (Tübingen: Mohr, 1902) 104 ("execution of the business"); 110 (purpose of fund-raising); 111 ("*pro contributione*," "*ad contribuendum*"); 112 (rates); 113 (wives); 114 (confessional letters); 116 ("buy back";"*contribuentes*," souls in Purgatory); 117 (compositions); 118 (religious); 122 (simony to take for confession).

125. Johann Tetzel, Specimen Sermon II in *Documents Illustrative of the Continental Reformation*, ed. B. J. Kidd (Oxford: Clarendon Press, 1911) 18.

126. Martin Luther, "95 Theses," Walther Köhler, *Dokumente zum Ablassstreit von 1517* 132, 136, 138, 140.

127. Iserloh, "Martin Luther and the Coming of the Reformation" 45.

128. Luther to Leo X, September 6, 1520, *Werke* 7, 6.

129. Nicholas Manuel, *Die Totenfresser*, quoted in Ozment, *The Reformation in the Cities* 111–114.

130. Luther, *Wider Hans Worst*, *Werke* 51, 498 (archdevil's whore, anti-Christlike and anti-God, devil's bride); 499 (stuck in whore's behind); 500 (Last Judgment paintings); 524 (partial judge no judge). For the illustration, see *Biblia* (Wittenberg, 1541). Giles Constable has pointed out the continuity of criticism and satire in the battle for reform while observing that the new religious sentiment of the Reformation time is often emphasized by historians who do not notice similar expressions in the twelfth century, Constable, *Religious Life and Thought (11th and 12th centuries)* (London: Variorum Reprints, 1979) chap. 15, 27–30, 40.

131. Leo X, *Cum postquam*, Nov. 9, 1518, in Kidd, ed., *Documents* 39–40.

132. Adrian VI to Francesco Chieregato, Nov. 1522, ibid. 109–110.

133. Lay estates of the Diet, "Centum Gravamina," ibid. 113–114.

134. Johann Eck [Memorandum I], "*In tribus cardinibus*," *Acta reformationis catholicae*, ed. Georg Pfeilschifter (Regensburg: Friedrich Pustet, 1959) 1, 109–111. Eck is "Dr. Sow" in Luther, *Wider Hans Worst*, *Werke* 51, 542.

135. Eck, "*In tribus cardinibus*" 112–115.

136. Ibid. 115–116.

137. Johann Eck [Memorandum X], "Ad sedandum Lutheri tumultum," *Acta reformationis catholicae* 146.

138. Johann Eck [Memorandum IX], "Etsi, Beatis
sime Pater," ibid. 145.

CHAPTER 11: TO RANSOM AND REDEEM BUT NOT CORRUPT (PP. 313–333)

1. Hugh Latimer, Fifth Sermon Before King Edward, April 5, 1549, in Latimer, *Sermons and Life*, ed. John Watkins (London: Aylott & Son, 1858) 171–172 (wife or servant); ibid. 176 (no king in England).

2. Latimer, "Third Sermon Preached Before King Edward," March 22, 1549, ibid. 124 ("They all love bribes"); ibid. 129 (Joshua); ibid. 132 (Cambyses).

3. Ibid. 168–169.

4. Ibid. 169–170.

5. Ibid. 173 (jurors); Latimer, "The Last Sermon Preached Before King Edward," 1550, ibid. 243 (silver basin), 244 (allowance of bills).

6. Third Sermon, March 22, 1549, ibid. 132.

7. Fifth Sermon, April 5, 1549, ibid. 163.

8. First Sermon, March 8, 1549, ibid. 94−95 (yeomen's sons); Seventh Sermon, April 19, 1549, ibid., 214 (unpreaching prelates).

9. *The Whole Bible*, trans. Myles Coverdale (London, 1535); (1 K 3 in Coverdale = 1 Sam 3 in the *NEB*; Dt 17:1 in Coverdale = Dt 16:19 in the NEB); *The Bible*, trans. by Thomas Matthew (London: John Rogers, 1549 print of the 1537 translation); *The Great Bible*, trans. Myles Coverdale (London, 1539).

10. Latimer, "Fifth Sermon Before King Edward," April 5, 1549, *Sermons* 175.

11. *The Bible and Holy Scriptures Conteyned in The Olde and Newe Testament* (Geneva, 1560); *The Bible Translated According to the Ebreu and Greeke* (London: Christopher Barker, 1578); *Biblia* (Wittenberg, 1541); *La Bible* (Geneva, 1588).

12. Latimer, "Third Sermon," March 22, 1549, *Sermons*, 124; Edmund Spenser, *The Fairie Queene*, ed. Ray Hefner (Baltimore: Johns Hopkins University Press, 1936) V, 9, 24, 9, and V, 9, 54, 9 ("brybes"); V, 2, 9 ("Lady Munera"); V, 2, 23, 3 ("meede"). The change from the fifteenth century is measurable. The *Promptorium parvulorum* of Galfredus Grammaticus, O.P., the first English-Latin dictionary, composed about 1440, translates "Brybery, or brybe" as "*Matigulum*," presumably derived from *manticulare*, to defraud or steal. A "brybour" is a *Manticulus*. "Brybn," a v rb, is translated by *maticulo* and by *latrocinor* ("I steal"), *Promptorium parvulorum*, ed. A. L. Mayhew (London: Early English Text Society, 1908) 48, 49, 65. In each instance the one taking the bribe is the active, initiating party, as in Chaucer. Strikingly, Galfredus does not find *munus* appropriate for *brybe* or *corrupere* for *brybn*.

13. George Whetstone, *Promos and Cassandra*, Geoffrey Bullough, ed., *Narrative and Dramatic Sources of Shakespeare* (New York: Columbia University Press, 1958) 2, 442−513: "Ne yet shall Coyne corupt . . . ," Part I, Act 1, scene 1; "raunsome" and "raunsome great," I, 3, 4; "apparelled thus monstrous," I, 3, 7; "raunsomed" and "If love or hate . . . ," Part II, 3, 3; "forced fault," II, 1, 7; "free of evil intent," II, 3, 3; "measure Grace," II, 5, 5.

14. "by wit or wyle," ibid., I, 2, 4; "som grace" and "a Lawier too long," I, 3, 6; "halfe his brybes," I, 5, 4.

15. "by the corruption of brybes," II, 2, 3; "common Barriter," II, 3, 3.

16. Giovanbattista Giraldi Cinthio, *Hecatommithi*, in Bullough, *Narrative and Dramatic Sources* 2, 420−430; "since without offense . . . It would have been more fitting . . . ," 428.

17. E.g., George Lyman Kittredge, ed., *The Complete Works of Shakespeare* (Boston: Ginn & Company, 1936) 97. Citations to Shakespeare are to this edition. For Augustine's story, see Chapter 4 above at note 40.

18. *Promos and Cassandra* II, 2, 4.

19. *The Oxford English Dictionary* (Oxford: Clarendon Press, 1934) 4, 384.

20. The questioning of the authenticity of *Henry VIII*, begun by James B. Spedding in the nineteenth century, is today rejected by many authoritative critics, see R. A. Frapes, "Introduction" to *Henry VIII* (Cambridge, Mass.: Harvard University Press, 1957) xv−xxvi.

21. Ser Giovanni, *Il Pecorone*, in Bullough, *Narrative and Dramatic Sources* 1, 472−475.

22. John E. Neale, *Essays in Elizabethan History* (London: Jonathan Cape, 1958) 64−65 (Cecil, Coke, and common practice). Joel Hurstfield in *Freedom, Corruption and Government in Elizabethan England* (London: Jonathan Cape, 1973) speaks of literary evidence of corruption in Elizabethan England as unacceptable (p. 138); rejects the application of "new, nineteenth-century standards" to the practices of the age (p. 159); and accurately observes that "corruption" has been a concept unanalyzed by most historians (p. 140). He does not acknowledge that by one standard—that of the moralists of the Elizabethan age speaking in the literature—the sale of offices was corrupt.

In Thomas More's *Utopia* Ralph Hythlody declares himself in favor of laws decreeing "that offices should not be obteined by inordinate suyte or by brybes and giftes . . . for so occasion is given to the officers by fraud and ravin to gather up their money again; and by reason of giftes and bribes the offices be given to rich men, which should rather have been executed by wise men . . . ," Thomas More, *Utopia*, Bk. I, n. 66, ed. J. H. Lupton (Oxford: Clarendon Press, 1895 [Latin and English translation of 1581 by Ralph Robynson]) 108. Robynson's "by inordinate suyte" translates More's *ambiantur*; his first "brybes and giftes" is a free paraphrase; his second "giftes and bribes" is a translation of *munera*.

Representative Catholic moral theologians of the seventeenth century taught that it was mortal sin to appoint an unfit person to secular office—the act violated the fidelity owed by the ruler, Juan de Lugo, *De iustitia et iure* (Venice, 1751) [first published in 1642] Disputatio 34, "Vices Opposed to Distributive Justice," n. 2. It was debated whether there was a moral obligation to appoint the more worthy among several fit candidates. In practice, Lugo concluded, "If the more worthy are not regularly sought and chosen, the unworthy will be chosen"—hence the more worthy should be regularly preferred, ibid. n. 21. But if offices should be given to the more worthy, could they lawfully be sold by the prince? On this question, the moral theologians split, some permitting sale "to the worthy," at moderate prices, to meet a necessity of the state, others holding it sinful.

23.   Purchase and sale also occur at a humbler level. Justice Shallow picks six men to serve Sir John Falstaff as soldiers. Only four need go. Two of the men pay Bardolph, Falstaff's lieutenant, to let them go; and Falstaff, advised by Bardolph that he has "three pounds to free Mouldy and Bullcaff," rejects them while Shallow, who is not privy to the payoff, protests that they were "your likeliest men." No comment is made on the transaction and the word "bribe" is not used. Shakespeare merely observes with realism and wry humor a scene of military recruitment, *King Henry the Fourth* 3, 2, 215–248.

24.   Cf. G. Wilson Knight, *The Imperial Theme* (London: Oxford University Press, 1931) 81–83.

25.   James I, *Basilikon Dōron. Or His Maiesties Instructions to His Dearest Son, Henry the Prince. The Political Works of James I*, reprinted from the edition of 1616 (Cambridge, Mass.: Harvard University Press, 1918), 39.

26.   Josephine Waters Bennett, *Measure for Measure as Royal Entertainment* (New York: Columbia University Press, 1966) 85.

27.   F. R. Leavis, "The Greatness of 'Measure for Measure,'" *Scrutiny* (1942) 10, 244.

28.   G. Wilson Knight, "Measure for Measure and the Gospels," in Knight, *The Wheel of Fire* (London: Oxford University Press, 1930) 84, 91.

29.   Geoffrey Chaucer, "The Persouns Tale" 775. Measure also meets measure in *King Henry the Fifth*, Act 2, scene 2, lines 39–180, where the three lords who urge the king not to be merciful but just to a man who railed against the king are treated with justice, not mercy, when their their own traitorous plot against the king is discovered. Part of the treachery of these men capitally punished involves the receipt of bribes from France—"foreign hire" (1. 100)—and "the golden earnest of our death" (1. 168).

30.   The fullest exposition of the Christian character of *Measure for Measure* is Roy W. Battenhouse, "'Measure for Measure' and Christian Doctrine of the Atonement," *Proceedings of the Modern Language Association* (Dec. 1946) 61, 1029. See also the essays by Knight and Leavis cited above, n. 27 and n. 28. Leavis observes at 340 "how close in this play Shakespeare is to the New Testament." See also G. Wilson Knight, *The Sovereign Flower* (London: Methuen & Co., 1958) 208: Shakespeare's Christianity in *Measure for Measure* "may be closer to the Gospels themselves than to any Christian system."

CHAPTER 12: ANGELO (PP. 334–365)

1.   Ben Jonson, "Lord Bacon's Birthday," *Works*, ed. C. H. Herford, Percy Simpson, and Evelyn Simpson (Oxford: Clarendon Press, 1954) 8, 225. Dates from January through March are given in the Gregorian style.

2.   Bacon to James I, James Spedding, *The Letters and Life of Francis Bacon* (London: Longmans, Green, Reader & Dyer, 1874) [Hereafter Spedding] 7, 168–169.

3.   Spedding 7, 168.

4.   John Donne, Sermon No. 15, Jan. 30, 1620 *Sermons*, ed. Evelyn M. Simpson and George R. Potter (Berkeley and Los Angeles: University of California Press, 1962) 2, 313.

5.   "Proceedings Against Mr. Wrenham," Star Chamber, 1618, in T. Cobham, ed. *State Trials* 1, 1059–1086. The statement of the case in the text draws on the accounts of both Wrenham at 1066–1071 and Yelverton at 1066–1069.

6.   James I, Speech in the Star Chamber, June 20, 1616, *The Political Works of James I*, reprinted from the edition of 1616 (Cambridge, Mass.: Harvard University Press, 1916) 1, 334, 337.

7.   Wrenham's speech in Star Chamber, *State Trials* 1, 1068; Yelverton, 1061; the petition's color, 1071.

8.   *Ibid.* 1060 (Yelverton: "as far as equity"); 1064 (Yelverton: "the razor of his tongue"); 1072 (Crewe); 1066 (Yelverton: "as justice is not to be recompensed").

9.   Ibid. 1066, 1069 (Wrenham's speech).

10.   Ibid. 1071.

11.   Ibid. 1072–1075 (Coke's judgment); 1065 (his role against Foorth).

12.   Ibid. 1076.

13.   Ibid. 1078.

14.   Launcelot Andrewes, *Pattern of Catechetical Doctrine* (Oxford: John Henry Parker, 1842) 271, 274.

15.   *State Trials* 1, 1081.

16.   Ibid. 1085.

17.   "Wrennum's Case," *Popham's Reports* 135, *English Reports* 79, 1237.

18.   *State Trials* 1, 1081 (Andrewes); 1083 (Wallingford).

19.   Andrewes, Sermon No. 10, At the Opening of Parliament, 1621, *Ninety-Six Sermons* (Oxford: John Henry Parker, 1843) 5, 205–206.

20.   Ibid. 213, 215, 216.

21.   On the purpose of Parliament, Robert Zaller, *The Parliament of 1621* (Berkeley and Los Angeles: University of California Press, 1971) 18; on Bacon's part in the preparations, Spedding 7, 140–156.

22.   Bacon's Speech, Jan. 30, 1621, as reported by Henry, Earl of Huntingdon's Diary, Lady De Villiers, ed., *The Hastings Journal of the Parliament of 1621, Camden Miscellany*, 3rd Series, vol. 83 (London: Royal Historical Society, 1953) 2.

23.   Speaker Richardson's Oration, in Villiers, *Hastings Journal* 3.

24.   Bacon's Speech to the Speaker's Oration, Spedding 7, 178–179.

25.   Zaller, *The Parliament of 1621* 57.

26.   Spedding 7, 187.

27.   Ibid. 7, 210. On bills of conformity to prevent collecting of a debt, Anonymous, "Diary," Wallace Notestein, Frances Helen Relf, and Hartley Simpson, eds., *Commons Debates 1621* (New Haven, Conn.: Yale University Press, 1933) [Hereafter *Commons Debates*, with the particular diary or set of notes indicated] 2, 222. On John Hall's case where both Cranfield's and Bacon's courts had taken jurisdiction, ibid. 4, 51 (Pym's Diary). It has been plausibly suggested that Sackville was more responsive to Bacon's enemy, Lionel Cranfield, than Bacon supposed, Menna Prestwich, *Cranfield* (Oxford: Clarendon Press, 1966) 292–293.

28.   Spedding 7, 209.

29.   Christopher Aubrey, Information in Star Chamber, *Commons Debates* 7, 387, 389; Aubrey, Petition to the Commons, summarized by the Committee on Courts, ibid. 4, 155 (Pym's Diary).

30.   Ibid. 2, 238 (Anon. Journal); on Hastings's parliamentary constituency, ibid. 6, 429.

31.   Ibid. 2, 239 (Anon. Journal) and 4, 160 (Pym's Diary).

32.   Bacon, "Of Great Place," *Essays, Works*, ed. James Spedding, Robert Leslie Ellis, and Douglas Denton Heath (London, 1878) 6, 400 [Hereinafter, *Works*].

33.   Bacon, *De Dignitate et Augmentis Scientiarum, Works* 1, 763–764.

34.   Bacon, Speech May 1617, Spedding 6, 190–192.

35.   Bacon, Speech, July 1617, Spedding 6, 211.

36.   Bacon to Buckingham, March 7, 1621, Spedding 7, 191–192.

37.   Huntingdon Diary, *Hastings Journal* 27–29.

38.   Ibid. 27.

39.   Ibid. 27–28. According to Coke, the king was "the supreme Judge over all other Judges" when sitting with the Lords, *Prohibitions del Roy* (1607), 12 Co. Rep. 64, 77 *English Reports* 1342.

40.   Ibid. 29.

41.   Ibid. 29–31.

42.   Catherine Drinker Bowen, *The Lion and the Throne* (Boston: Little, Brown, 1957) 76–82 (the competition for the appointment as attorney general); 118–123 (Coke's marriage); 155–156 (Bacon and Essex's trial); 168–169 (Bacon's letter to Coke); 338–341 (Coke's transfer from Common Pleas); 380–390 (Coke's humiliation and removal from King's Bench); 394–407 (Coke's daughter's marriage). *Bonham's Case*, 8 Co. Rep. 118a, 77 *English Reports*, 652; *Proclamations* 12 Co. Rep. 74, 77 *English Reports*, 1352; James's Speech in Star Chamber, *The Political Works* 1, 334, 337.

Despite the long history of intense rivalry between Bacon and Coke, historians from Thomas Macaulay to Catherine Drinker Bowen have underemphasized Coke's part in Bacon's downfall—partly due to not weighing heavily enough the impact of James's speech of March 10, partly due to not attaching importance to Coke's critical interventions on the procedure and evidence, see, e.g., Bowen, *The Lion and the Throne* 425–426, and Bowen, *Francis Bacon* (Boston: Little, Brown, 1963) 186. Above all, there is a failure to appreciate the fact that the host of witnesses against Bacon needed to be identified, recruited, organized. Prestwich, *Cranfield* 289, recognizes Cranfield's role.

43. *Commons Debates* 2, 221 (Anon. Journal).

44. *Commons Debates* 4, 155 (Pym): the petition; ibid. 5, 298: the letters; *Journal of the House of Lords* 3, 79: the letters dated; *Commons Debates* 5, 44 (Belasyse Diary): Hastings on Aubrey's purgatory; 5, 45: Finch's comment; 6, 64 (Thomas Holland's Notes): the box and Bacon's remark.

45. *Lords' Journal* 3, 56–57: Egerton's petition; *Commons Debates* 6, 64–65 (Holland's Notes): the ewer and the pounds delivered; ibid. 5, 298 (Smyth's Observations): the loan, the conversion to gold, the amount to Sharpeigh; 2, 225 (Anon. Journal): Young's confirmation of Egerton.

46. Ibid. 5, 296 (Smyth's Observations).

47. Bacon to Buckingham, Spedding 7, 213.

48. *Commons Debates* 4, 160 (Pym's Diary).

49. Ibid. 2, 235–237 (Anon. Journal).

50. Ibid. 2, 226.

51. Ibid. 2, 239.

52. Ibid. 2, 241.

53. Ibid. 2, 241–242: bribery unpunished if one witness not enough; ibid. 4, 168 (Pym's Diary): brothel as witness.

54. Ibid. 2, 240: Christopher Neville quoted in Anon. Journal on the Chancery as labyrinth; 4, 167. William Noy quoted in Pym's Diary on destruction of the land and breach of oath; 5 406: Noy quoted in Smyth's Observations on distribution of king's conscience; 5, 306: Thomas Crewe quoted on blinding bribes.

55. Spedding 7, 215. According to Coke writing in 1628 after Bacon's fall, William Thorpe, chief justice of the King's Bench, was found guilty of taking bribes of five felons under Edward III, suspended from office, and deprived of all his lands for having thus "maliciously, falsely, and rebelliously" broken his oath to the king. Thorpe was, however, pardoned and his lands were restored. Coke takes the position that the precedent is not a good one, for Thorpe's offense was wrongly treated as treason. In Coke's view, bribery is neither treason nor felony but "it is a great Misprision, for that it is ever accompanied with Perjury." Edward Coke, *The Third Part of the Institutes of the Laws of England* (London: M. Flesher, 1644) c. 68, 145–146. Coke also notes that none of the judges charged under Edward I were convicted of bribery. He is left with a single precedent: certain judges who took a "small" bribe of 4 pounds and were fined 4,000 marks under Edward III, ibid. 147. The clearest authority he cites is Deuteronomy 16:19.

56. Bacon to the Lords, March 19, 1621, Spedding 7, 215.

57. Lord Treasurer, Report on Conference with the Commons, *Lords' Journal* 3, 53.

58. *Commons Debates* 2, 244 (Anon. Journal).

59. Ibid. 5, 56 (Belasyse Diary).

60. Churchill's testimony as reported by Committee on the Courts, ibid. 2, 247–248 (Anon. Journal).

61. Ibid. 5, 56 (Belasyse Diary)

62. Ibid. 2, 248 (Anon. Journal).

63. Zaller, *The Parliament of 1621* 29.

64. *Commons Debates* 2, 248 (Anon. Journal).

65. Ibid. 2, 252 (Anon. Journal).

66. Ibid. 2, 251–252 (Anon. Journal); ibid. 4, 171 (Pym's Diary).

67. *Lords' Journal* 3, 55.

68. *Notes of the Debates in the House of Lords officially taken by Robert Bowyer and Henry Elsing, Clerks*, ed. Frances Helen Relf (London, 1924: Camden Society, 3rd Series, vol. 42) [hereafter Relf] 29, 37.

69. *Lords' Journal* 3, 58: committees; 3, 60: interrogatories and Meautys and Hunt's request for delay; see also Villiers, *Hastings Journal* 32, for interrogatories.

70. Relf 31; *Lords' Journal* 60.

71. *Lords' Journal* 3, 61–62; on Borough or Burrows, Spedding 7, 324, n. 1.

72. *Commons Debates* 7, 591 (Newsletter of Samuel Albyn to [John Rawson?]) March 28, 1621.

73. James I, *Basilikon Dōron, Political Works* 1, 39; James I, "Speech in the Star Chamber, June 20, 1616," *Political Works* 1, 331; Francis Bacon, *The Beginning of the History of Great Britain, Works,* 6, 278–279.

74. Bacon to James I, March 25, 1622, Spedding 7, 226.
75. *Lords' Journal* 3, 70.
76. Ibid. 69.
77. "Memorial of Access" (1622), Spedding 7, 352.
78. Spedding 7, 232–235.
79. Bacon, "Memoranda of What the Lord Chancellor Intended to Deliver to the King, April 16, 1621, upon His First Access to His Majesty After His Troubles," Spedding 7, 237–238.

Catholic moral theology of the seventeenth century held that the judge was morally bound to give a just decision and could not charge a litigant a price for his decision, see Juan De Lugo, *De iustitia et iure* (Venice, 1751; first published, Lyons, 1642). Disputation 37, "The Obligations Relating to Public Judgments, Especially the Obligations of a Judge," number 126. Suppose a litigant gave the judge *munera*. According to some authorities—Baldus; Gabriel; Antoninus as read by Lugo—it was always against natural law for a judge to receive them. Others—Navarrus was specified—felt it was not precisely against natural law but had such dangers and disadvantages that positive law most appropriately condemned the practice, Lugo, Disp. 37, no. 128. Lugo himself thought it was "naturally unlawful" when, given the amount, the circumstances, and the persons, the *munera* would usually induce perversion of judgment. It was "humanly impossible" for a judge during litigation to receive a large offering—a house or a vineyard—and not bend his judgment in favor of the offeror. A judge might be found "so upright or so boorish to condemn the offeror after taking his offering"; but moral rules must respond to what usually happens—so fornication is forbidden because usually a child conceived in fornication suffers parental deprivation and although this disadvantage might cease in a particular case, the sin is judged by what usually happens. A judge who trusted in his own integrity could easily be "insensibly affected" by an offering. On the other hand, the reception of small offerings, made out of politeness, was not condemned by natural law. Far more important, offerings made after the litigation was over were not naturally unlawful—then there was no danger of perversion of justice, Lugo, Disp. 37, nos. 129–130.

80. Bacon to James I, April 21, 1621, referring to their conversation of April 16, Spedding 7, 241.
81. *Lords' Journal* 3, 75.
82. Ibid. 3, 79–80.
83. Bacon to James I, April 20, 1621, Spedding 7, 240.
84. Bacon to James I, April 21, 1621, Spedding 7, 241–242.
85. *Lords' Journal* 3, 81.
86. Ibid. 3, 82 (Bennett's case); 3, 84 (Bacon's submission).
87. Bacon, "The humble submission and supplication of the Lord Chancellor," Spedding 7, 242–244.
88. *Notes of the Debates in the House of Lords,* ed. Samuel Rawson Gardiner (London: Camden Society, 1870) = *Camden Miscellany,* 1st Ser., 103, 13–17 [Hereinafter, Gardiner].
89. Ibid. 19. But see his position in the *Institutes,* above, n. 55.
90. *Lords' Journal* 3, 87; Gardiner, 23.
91. Bacon, "The Confession and humble Submission of me, the Lord Chancellor," Spedding 7, 252–262.
92. "Charges against the Lord Chancellor," summarized by Bacon in his Confession, Articles 24, 25, 26, Spedding 7, 259–260; cf. *Lords' Journal* 3, 79. [All the articles are cited as reported in the Confession.]
93. Bacon, "Confession," Spedding 7, 260.
94. "Charges," Article 27, Spedding 7, 260.
95. "Confession," Spedding 7, 260–261.
96. "Charges," Article 3 (Hoddy's Case); Article 5 (Monk's case); Article 8 (*Fisher v. Wrenham*); Article 13 (*Wroth v. Mainwaring*); Article 18 (Dunch's case); Article 22 (Ruswell's case), all as reported in Bacon, "Confession," Spedding 7, 253–259. On Sherburne or Sherborne, Spedding 6, 326 and 337; on Hatcher, ibid. 6, 336.
97. Ibid., Article 11 (Scott's case); Article 12 (Lentall's payment), Spedding 7, 255–256.
98. Ibid., Articles 1 and 2 (*Egerton v. Egerton*); Article 4 (Lady Dorothy); Article 16 (*Aubrey v. Brunker*), Spedding 7, 253–257.
99. Ibid., Article 6 (*Trevor v. Ascue*); Article 14 (Hansby's case); Article 17 (Mountague's case); Article 19 (Reynell); Article 20 (Peacock), Spedding 7, 254–259.
100. Ibid., Article 15, Spedding 7, 256–257.

101. Ibid., Article 7, Spedding 7, 254.

102. Ibid., Articles 9 and 10, Spedding 7, 255.

103. Ibid., Article 21, Spedding 7, 259.

104. Buckingham to Bacon, Nov. 18, 1618, Spedding 6, 377; and Buckingham to Bacon, June 12, 1618, ibid. 6, 312–313.

105. "Charges," Article 4, Spedding 7, 253.

106. Ibid., Article 17, Spedding 7, 258 (on Thelwall); Article 28, Spedding 7, 261 (on servants).

107. That the vice was "of the times" has been the commonest plea of Bacon's later apologists. Often they make no distinction between gifts to judges and to other officeholders and no distinction between small presents and large ones (e.g., Bowen, *The Lion and the Throne* (428–429). But judges were regarded differently from others. As Coke pointed out in the *Institutes*, bribery was a crime committed only by those "in Judicial Place," Coke, *The Third Part of the Institutes* 145–146.

In 1533, after Thomas More had resigned as lord chancellor and was in disfavor with Henry VIII, John Parnell, a London draper, complained to the king that More decided against him in a suit brought by Geoffrey and Richard Vaughan, London mercers, and that for making the decree (entered January 20, 1531) he had received from Vaughan's wife "a faire greate gilte Cuppe for a bribe." More was called before the King's Council to answer the charge. He admitted receiving the cup as a New Year's gift, much after the decree was issued, and added that he ordered it to be filled with wine, drank a toast to the lady, and returned it to her as a New Year's gift to her husband. His account was confirmed by other eyewitnesses according to his son-in-law, William Roper, who is the source of this story. William Roper, *The Lyfe of Sir Thomas Moore, Knighte*, ed. Elsie Vaughan Hitchcock (London: Humphrey Milford, 1935 = Early English Text Society, no. 197) 61–63. Roper recalled "another time" when More had given a decree against Lord Arundell in favor of a rich widow, Mistress Crocker. She had then presented him with a New Year's gift of a pair of gloves and, within them, forty pounds in gold. More took the gloves and returned the money, saying, "Mistress, since it were against good manner to forsake a gentlewoman's newe yeares gifte, I am content to take your gloves, but as for your money I utterley refuse," ibid. 63. In a third case, while his suit was pending, one Gresham gave him a New Year's gift of a fair gilt cup fashioned much to More's taste. More took it and gave the messenger a cup of his own, "not in his fantasie of so good a fashion, yeat better in valewe," to be delivered to Gresham, ibid. 63–64. Roper recites these stories to show More's "innocency and cleereness from all corruption or evil affection" (ibid. 64) and opines that, if he had not "from all corruption of wronge doinge or bribes taking kept him self so cleere that no man was able there with once to blemish him," the king would have readily heard such charges against him (ibid. 61).

Roper, a lawyer, prothonotary, and member of Parliament, wrote More's life about 1556 (ibid., Introduction, xlv). It is noteworthy that he is not surprised at the efforts made by litigants to make substantial payments to the chancellor, and he sees nothing amiss in More's courteous treatment of them, even when as in Gresham's case the gift was made before the case was decided. At the same time Roper is clear that these New Year's gifts could be characterized as "bribes." Note also how More's courteous return of a more valuable cup parallels Innocent III's treatment of the bishop of Würzburg (see Chapter 7 above at n. 51); how More's courteous refusal of Mistress Crocker's gift is paralleled by Bacon's courteous acceptance of Lady Dorothy's gift (see above, n. 62), and how the trick of hiding cash in gloves is still being practiced in Pepys's day (see Chapter 13 below, at the Pepys Diary entry of Feb. 2, 1664).

108. For a psychological study of Anthony and Ann which reflects interestingly on Francis Bacon, see Daphne Du Maurier, *Golden Lads* (Garden City, N.Y.: Doubleday, 1975). For the oracular character of Francis's talk, see William Raleigh [his chaplain as lord chancellor], *Life of the Right Honorable Francis Bacon*, the introduction to *Resuscitatio* (London, 1637). For Bacon on the cardinal importance of the law's certainty, Preface, *Maxims of the Law, Works* 7, 319. For Bacon's youthful poverty, Spedding 2, 106–108 (arrested for debt); ibid. 3, 79–81 (has to borrow from a cousin). For his reference to his soul as a stranger, "A Prayer, or Psalm," Spedding 7, 230–231.

109. Social tensions of the age could also be hypothesized to be an explanation of why the political forces of the day converged in the prosecution of Bacon's bribery. Witchcraft prosecutions afford an analogy. In the age of Queen Elizabeth, witchcraft became a matter of importance in English life. Parliament legislated three times against witches (1542, 1563, 1604). King James, while still in Scotland, wrote a book about them—*Daemonologue, in Form of a Dialogue*, Keith Thomas, "The Relevance of Social Anthropology to the Historical Study of En-

glish Witchcraft," in Mary Douglas, ed., *Witchcraft Confessions and Accusations* (London: Tavistock, 1970) 49. Witches appeared on the London stage—*Macbeth* is only the most famous example—and a 1587 treatise on their "Subtill Practices" reported people saying "there is scarce any towne or village in all this shire, but there is one or two witches at the least in it," Alan Macfarlane, "Witchcraft in Tudor and Stuart Essex" in ibid. 81, quoting George Gifford, *A Discourse of the Subtle Practices of Devilles by Witches and Sorcerers.*

Anthropologists have speculated that the rise of interest in witchcraft—and an accompanying outburst of accusations of witchcraft—reflect tension and conflict in English communities over gifts and loans, Thomas, "The Relevance of Social Anthropology" 63; Macfarlane "Witchcraft" 95. In a time of religious transition, the correct treatment of gifts and loans had become uncertain, producing anxiety and guilt. One response to the interior conflict was to project upon the would-be donee or borrower a malevolent power. Accusations of witchcraft "almost always arose from quarrels over gifts and loans, when the victim refused the witch some small article, heard her muttering under her breath or threatening him, and subsequently suffered some misfortune." Thomas "The Relevance of Social Anthropology" 62; cf. Macfarlane, "Witchcraft" 92.

Such an account of the underlying mechanism by which the person who was denied a favor was viewed as a witch is necessarily speculative and does not include all cases. (Gifts from an undesirable donor were also regarded as signs of witchcraft.) The main elements of the witchcraft phenomenon, however, offer a suggestive analogy to bribery—uncertainty over the treatment of gifts; changes in religion sharpening the articulation of the problem; a marked increase in discussion of the subject. In the case of witchcraft, moreover, there was not merely discussion but prosecution. In three villages of Essex county, for example, there were under Queen Elizabeth more trials for witchcraft than for murder; in this single county, Essex, with a population of approximately 100,000, there were over 700 formal cases of witchcraft in the period 1560—1680. Of those persons prosecuted, seventy-four were executed. The peak of the trials was in the ecclesiastical and Assize courts in the 1580s and 1590s. At that time, in Essex, witchcraft was second only to theft in frequency of prosecution (Macfarlane, "Witchcraft" 81—83). Nothing like this happened as to bribery. Elizabeth did not conduct any inquest into bribery in the fashion of Edward I. Her judges underwent no passion. While witchcraft trials flourished, and confessions of witchcraft substantiated the belief in its prevalence (ibid. 95; Thomas, "The Relevance of Social Anthropology" 53—54); bribery was little touched by the law.

It could be speculated that the prosecution of Bacon was a reflection at the highest level of society of an unease about gifts analogous to the village phenomenon. The religious tension of the court is disclosed in the punning references to Purgatory and Redemption. The moral tension about offerings is explicit in Shakespeare's plays. The spectacular affirmation in Bacon's case that certain offerings were wrong resolved an oppressive ambiguity.

110.   Robert Tittler, *Nicholas Bacon* (Athens: Ohio University Press, 1971) 80: Nicholas Bacon's lawful salary.
111.   Bacon to Buckingham, 1621, Spedding 7, 296.
112.   Bacon to Buckingham, Jan. 30, 1622, Spedding 7, 328; *Reports of Cases Decided by Francis Bacon,* ed. John Ritchie (London: Sweet & Maxwell, 1932) vi (number of cases). None of the cases in which bribes were confessed to is among these reported cases.
113.   "Receipts and Disbursements, Beginning the 24th of June, 1618, and ending the 29th of September, 1618," Spedding 6, 327 (expenditures), 336 (receipts).
114.   *Lords' Journal* 3, 98—101; Gardiner, 41.
115.   *Lords' Journal* 3, 12.
116.   *Commons Debates* 2, 268 (Anon. Journal).
117.   Spedding 7, 276.
118.   *Lords' Journal* 105.
119.   Bacon to Prince Charles, June 7, 1621, Spedding 7, 287—288.
120.   Gardiner, 63—64; *Lords' Journal* 3, 106.
121.   Bacon to Buckingham, May 31, 1621, Spedding 7, 280.
122.   Bacon, "Memorial" [in anticipation of conferring with Buckingham, 1621], Spedding 7, 313.
123.   Ibid.
124.   Bacon to Buckingham, May 31, 1621, Spedding 7, 280; Bacon to Buckingham, June 4, 1621, ibid. 281; Bacon to James, June 4, 1621, ibid. 281.
125.   "A Warrant to Mr. Attorney for An Assignment of Your Lordship's Fine," Sept. 20, 1621, Spedding 7, 301.

126. Williams to Buckingham, Oct. 27, 1621, Spedding 7, 310.

127. "A special pardon," Spedding 7, 307, (first draft), and Williams to Buckingham, Oct. 27, 1621, referring to what was before Williams, Spedding 7, 310.

128. Ibid.

129. Bacon to the duke of Lenox, Jan. 30, 1622, Spedding 7, 327.

130. Buckingham to Bacon, circa Oct. 10, 1621, Spedding 7, 305.

131. Selden to Bacon, Feb. 14, 1622, Spedding 7, 332–333.

132. Bacon, Petition to the House of Lords, circa Dec. 1621, Spedding 7, 321–322; Bacon to Gondomar, circa Dec. 1621, Spedding 7, 318–319.

133. Bacon to Lord John Digby, Dec. 31, 1621, Spedding 7, 322. Tobie Mathew, his bagman in certain of the transactions, was secretly a Catholic priest ordained by Cardinal Bellarmine in 1614, "Matthew Sir Tobie," *DNB* 13, 64. That he was also a Jesuit has not been established, ibid. 67.

134. Bacon to Buckingham, March 5, 1622, Spedding 7, 340–341.

135. Bacon to Mathew, Feb. 28, 1622, Spedding 7, 336; Bacon, Untitled memo, Spedding 7, 338.

136. Bacon to Cranfield, circa March 12, 1622, Spedding 7, 347.

137. Bacon to Buckingham, circa Nov. 1622, Spedding 7, 397.

138. Bacon to Cranfield, circa March 12, 1622, Spedding 7, 347.

139. Bacon to Tobie Mathew, March 27, 1622, Spedding 7, 364.

140. Ritchie, *Reports of Cases Decided by Francis Bacon* XXV.

141. Spedding 7, 347.

142. Quotations from, respectively, Meautys to Bacon, Nov. 25, 1622, Spedding 7, 397; Bacon to Buckingham, undated, Spedding 7, 397; Bacon to Buckingham, Feb. 5, 1623, Spedding 7, 403.

143. Bacon, Last Will and Testament, April 10, 1621, Spedding 7, 228.

144. Bacon, Last Will, Dec. 29, 1625, Spedding 7, 539–545.

145. Lord John Campbell, *Lives of the Lord Chancellors* (London: John Murray, 1857) 3, 146.

146. Spedding 7, 289–291; 393–394, 521.

147. Bacon, draft of letter from James I to the Attorney General, Spedding 7, 519–520.

148. Bacon to James I, Aug. 1624, Spedding 7, 518–519.

149. For the Commons' charges against Bennett, *State Trials* 1, 1145–1154. For the Star Chamber conviction and sentence, see *Bennet v. Easedale, Cro. Rep.* 55, 79 *English Reports* 651.

150. Bacon to James I, Spedding 7, 519.

151. Bacon, "The First Psalm," *The Psalms—translated when sick in 1624, Works,* 7, 277.

152. Bacon's treatment can be compared with the history of an auditor of the Sacred Roman Rota, Francesco Maria Ghislieri, at a slightly later date. In 1648 rumor reached Innocent X—a former auditor himself and sensitive to the court's reputation—that one member, "valuing profit more than Conscience, had put Justice on sale." According to the record of the affair made by Angelo Celso, another auditor, three auditors asked the pope to ascertain the delinquent and make an example of him. No one was louder in decrying the evil than Ghislieri, who was a Bolognese of great erudition, twenty years on the bench and next to the dean in seniority. Ghislieri indeed declared that the dean was showing too much coldness in such an important matter. The pope ordered that the tribunal proceed secretly and extrajudicially to find the culprit.

Under pretext of discussing the affairs of the Nazareth, a boys' home for which they were responsible, the auditors met at the dean's home and decided that each would withdraw in turn while the others discussed his "integrity." The dean went out first and was quickly exonerated. Ghislieri was next, and when he was gone, several auditors reported that he had received money "from cases." One auditor said he had seen a note from Ghislieri to Cardinal Montalto asking for 500 gold *scudi*, and that the cardinal had later told this auditor that he would not pay more, "but would prefer rather to lose the case." An auditor also said that the Princess Rossano told him that Ghislieri's vote was assured in a Sarsina case thanks to 1,500 gold scudi paid him by Prince Borghese; and a second auditor said that the prince had spoken in a guarded way indicating he had made such a payment. Two auditors said Ghislieri had received 400 *scudi* from Princess Verula, but later refused to give the intermediary a receipt and showed himself hostile to her interests without repaying the money. The story had been told then by the princess herself, who did not mind the loss of the money as much as Ghislieri's discourtesy.

In a case from Rome on a fiduciary account of the Maximi, Ghislieri wrote one party that he needed 80 doubloons. The party refused to pay and passed Ghislieri's note to another auditor, so that he could prevent Ghislieri prejudicing his cause. In another Roman case, the Robigni partnership litigation, Ghislieri got 2,000 *scudi* from the Robigni, according to report. One advocate, Roncone, had also told auditors about the rumors about Ghislieri. His reputation had spread to Perugia and other court circles. Ghislieri, the auditors also observed, was "habituated to gambling and heavily burdened by debt." It was decided to report him to the pope and to ask him "in favor of the Tribunal" to make Ghislieri a bishop.

Called back into the room to hear his colleagues' verdict, Ghislieri knew from the long time they had taken that he had been found out. Waxen, with a trembling voice, he asked them to have regard for his reputation and that of his relatives and of Bologna. No one answered, but all the other auditors went out in turn with no one else being found culpable. The next morning the dean informed Innocent X, who six months later made Ghislieri bishop of Terracina, a small seacoast diocese. Ghislieri still had the chutzpah to petition to keep his auditorship, "according to the custom of other auditors"; and three cardinals tried to persuade Innocent X not to remove him from the Rota. The pope, however, was firm; and Ghislieri was snubbed by his old colleagues, Emmanuele Cerchiari, *Capellani Papae et Apostolicae Sedis* (Rome: Vatican Polygot Press, 1920) 2, 146–150, where the report of Celso is excerpted and supplemented by references to the diary of another auditor, Pietro Ottoboni.

The place of bribery at the Roman court in 1648 is not very different from that at the English court in 1621. Selling justice, when it becomes a public affair, is recognized as wrong. Still, Cardinal Montalto is willing to pay 500 *scudi*: he only balks when the price goes up again; Princess Verula is annoyed at a doubledealer's ingratitude. Ghislieri is a gambler and a doublecrosser as well as a bribetaker, but when his crimes are established, it is the opinion of both his colleagues and the pope that he will be sufficiently punished if he is promoted to high priestly office with an income somewhat greater than his official salary as an auditor; and three cardinals think this punishment too heavy. In contrast, an under-datary under Innocent X, charged with forging the pope's signature on official documents and selling them for personal profit was tried, convicted on April 15, 1652, and executed, Ludwig Pastor, *History of the Popes*, vol. 30, 43–44. The under-datary had been depriving the pope of income; Ghislieri, like Bacon, had been a "virgin" as to cheating the boss.

Ghislieri's punishment had one element in common with Bacon's—disqualification for the future from high office. He could not return to the Rota, could not be its dean, could not be archbishop of Bologna or a cardinal or the pope himself—all offices to which an auditor of the Rota could legitimately aspire, see John T. Noonan, Jr., *Power to Dissolve: Lawyers and Marriages in the Courts of the Roman Curia* (Cambridge, Mass.: Harvard University Press, 1971) 52–54. But he was spared the public shame which public confession and formal judgment by the Lords visited on Bacon. The difference is between St. Bernardino's quiet style as to high ecclesiastical corruption and Bromyard's open denunciation.

CHAPTER 13: THE CONSCIENTIOUS CLERK (PP. 366–391)

1.   All diary references are to *The Diary of Samuel Pepys*, ed. Robert Latham and William Matthews (Berkeley and Los Angeles: University of California Press, 1970–1976).

2.   The relation with Warren continued to be strengthened—e.g. Feb. 6, 1665: "So to my office; and among other things, with Sir W. Warren four hours or more, till very late, talking of one thing or another, and have concluded a firm league with him in all just ways to serve him and myself all I can; and I think he will be a most useful and thankful man to me." Here the aim is not to serve the king and Warren, but Pepys and Warren; Pepys underlines, as it were, "in all just ways."

3.   E.g., entries for 1660 at March 18 (a piece of gold and 20 silver shillings for the commission of a captain); March 30 (two letters each containing a piece of gold "from some that I had done a favour to"); March 31 (20 shillings down and a note for 4 £ for the commission of a captain); April 1 (30 shillings for another); April 23 (40 shillings for another); May 1 (a French *pistole* for another); June 19 (5 £, "wrapped in paper," from Lady Pickering who desired to ingratiate herself with Pepys so Sandwich would help her husband, a prominent Cromwellian); June 21 (five gold pieces and a silver urn for a captain's commission); July 7 (100 £ asked by Pepys for "a clerk's place with me"; July 13 (two pieces from Lady Honywood for dispatching a ship to bring her ambassador husband home from Denmark). For his mounting net worth in the same year, see Jan. 4 (uses Navy's funds to pay his house rent because lacking money of his own); June 3 (100 £ clear); and December 10 (240 £ clear).

4.   Quotations from Pepys in Arthur Bryant, *Samuel Pepys* (New York: Macmillan, 1933–1939) 2, 24–25.

5. Ibid. 21–28.

6. Percival Hunt, *Samuel Pepys in the Diary* (Pittsburgh: University of Pittsburgh Press, 1958) 153–156.

7. Bryant, *Samuel Pepys* 1, 111–112. The subtitle of the third volume of Bryant's biography is "The Saviour of the Navy," referring particularly to Pepys's work with the Special Commission of 1686 (3, 282).

8. Ibid. 2, 34.

9. Latham and Matthews, "Introduction" cvi.

10. Ibid. cix.

11. Latham, "Introduction" cxxiii–iv. A different approach appears in the *Companion* to the Latham and Matthews edition of *Diary*, published as volume 10 of the edition in 1983. Writing on "Finances," Henry Roseveare speaks of Pepys's income as composed of "fees, perquisites, gratuities, and downright bribes" (131). He notes that Pepys's income rose dramatically during the Second Dutch War as he received "a golden shower of bribes and gratuities." He notes that after 1667, as Pepys became nervous about public criticism of the Navy, "we learn little more about bribes, gifts and profits" (133). He also notes that although the sale of office was barred by statute, Pepys openly discussed the sale of his (131).

12. *Diary*, Dec. 10, 1662, and note 1 thereto of Latham and Matthews.

13. *Diary*, Feb. 20, 1665. That the letter here referred to was ineffective is inferable from Pepys to Sir William Coventry, Dec. 23, 1665, *Further Correspondence of Samuel Pepys, 1662–1679*, ed. J. R. Tanner (London: G. Bell & Sons, 1929) 91–92; and that this second letter failed is inferable from Pepys to Coventry, Feb. 6, 1666, ibid. 157.

14. For this calculation, see the figures provided by Latham and Matthews for six months of Tangiers victualling, note 3 to *Diary*, Jan. 24, 1663.

15. Latham and Matthews, note 1 to *Diary*, Dec. 29, 1662.

16. Latham, "Introduction," cxxiii–iv (the salary); Roseveare, "Finances," in ibid. 10, 130 (data on incomes of time).

17. Diary, Jan. 28, 1660 ("discoursing on the happiness"); Latham, "Introduction" cxxiii (from 25 to 7,000 pounds); ibid. xxxix ("grown rich").

18. Martin Howard Stein, "Health—A Psychoanalyst's View," *Companion* to the Diary, vol. 10, 179–180. The play between Pepys's consciousness and what is suppressed is also suggested in the passage of July 20, 1667, recounting Cooling's cynical talk of bribes. A poor Oxford scholar made up of other people's pastiches is an analogy for Cooling made up of bribes. The most famous poor Oxford scholar of English literature was Chaucer's Clerk. Pepys thought Chaucer "a very fine poet" (June 14, 1663); cited him (Aug. 9, 1664); spoke of "my Chaucer" when he had his copy of Chaucer's *Works* bound (July 7, 1664); collated a number of Chaucer manuscripts and owned an engraved portrait of the poet (June 14, 1663, note 1). To a man familiar with Chaucer the contrast between the Clerk and Creed must have been not far from the front of his consciousness.

19. Ibid. May 18, 1661, and accompanying note 1 on Pepys and Bacon.

20. Richard Ollard, *Samuel Pepys* (New York: Holt, Rinehart & Winston, 1974) 284. Pepys, Ollard observes at 118, is "corrupt."

21. William Ames, *Conscience with the Power and Cases Thereof* (London, 1639) Bk. 5, 283–284.

22. Ibid. Bk. 5, 229–230.

23. Ibid. Bk. 5, 231.

24. Ibid. Bk. 5, 123.

25. Ibid. 124–126.

26. Richard Baxter, *A Christian Directory, or A Summa of Practical Theologie, and Cases of Conscience* (London, 1673) 4, 150–151.

27. Ibid. 4, 116.

28. Ibid. 4, 119.

29. Ibid. 4, 118.

30. Ibid. 4, 82 ("Directions Against Scandal"); ibid. 254–256 ("Directions Against Covetousness").

31. Richard Charles Browne, "Ashburnham, John," *DNB* 1, 634–635; Pepys, *Diary* 7, 417–418 (Sept. 2, 1667).

32. D. T. Witcombe, *Charles II and the Cavalier House of Commons* (Manchester: Manchester University Press, 1966) 62–65 (on the political situation and "the Canary patent"). Pepys indicates that Clarendon had not been unfaithful to the king, but Pepys's informant, Sir William Coventry, did tell him apropos the movement against Clarendon "many things not fit to be spoken," *Diary* 8, 415 (Sept. 2, 1667). Bribery could well be indicated.

33.   John Milward, *The Diary of John Milward*, ed. Caroline Robbins (Cambridge: At the University Press, 1938) 131–135.

34.   Ibid. 132 (defense); House of Commons, *Journal* 9, 24 (punishment); Witcombe, *Charles II* 64 (foreign money).

35.   Nearly thirty years later, again as a by-product of a political fracas as an administration fell, the Commons took a formal stand against the bribery of its members—this time against bribery of legislators qua legislators. Sir John Trevor had been speaker of the House under James II—an ideal selection at the time because he was identified with the militant Protestant interest yet was the first cousin of George Jeffreys, James's trusted legal adviser. He had also been master of the rolls while Jeffreys was lord chancellor. In that high judicial capacity he advised his cousin in a judgment by Jeffreys which enriched Jeffreys's son's fiancée by a large amount—Jeffreys behaving as abominably as Portia, and Trevor little better (James McMullen Rigg, "Trevor, Sir John," *DNB* 19, 1149–1150; H. Montgomery Hyde, *Judge Jeffreys* [London: George Harrap, 1940] 259 [the case of Jeffreys's future daughter-in-law; see also *Baden v. Pembroke*, 2 *Vernon's Reports* 52 and 213, 23 *English Reports* 644 and 739]).

With great dexterity Trevor had survived the Glorious Revolution, James's flight, and Jeffreys's imprisonment, and by the mid-1690s he was back in his old Jacobite positions, speaker of the House and master of the rolls. No doubt this ability to endure excited envy and distrust.

When the administration of his patron, the earl of Sunderland, began to crumble, Trevor was fair game. Two new parliamentary leaders, Charles Montagu and Thomas Wharton, began the parliamentary revolt by an accidental discovery that Henry Guy, secretary of the treasury, had accepted a sum from a regimental agent to expedite payment of the soldiers' wages. Guy was dismissed and committed to the Tower, Trevor helping the process on. Then Montagu and Wharton turned on Trevor and, doubtless inspired by a discreet hint, demanded that the accounts of the chamberlain of the City of London be inspected (J. P. Kenyon, *Robert Spencer, Earl of Sunderland* [London: Longmans, Green, 1958] 269–271]).

The inspection almost instantly revealed an order of the London Common Council of Feb. 12, 1694, directing the chamberlain to pay to "the hon. sir John Trevor, knight, speaker of the hon. house of commons, the sum of 1000 guineas, as soon as a Bill be passed into an act of parliament, for satisfying the Debts of the Orphans and other creditors of the said city." On the back of the order was an endorsement that the 1,000 guineas were delivered to Trevor on June 22, 1694, in the presence of two named councilmen. Testimony by members of the council filled in the background. The City had borrowed from the Orphans' Fund and needed help from Parliament to repay the money. The bill had failed in two or three earlier efforts. The City's solicitor opined that paying Trevor was the only course to take; otherwise, "the Bill would not go." Those acting for the orphans indicated that the bill would cost 2,000 guineas and that they would have to put up what the City didn't. One councilman had protested the City's paying. Everyone else seemed to think it routine enough for a record of the order to be made and kept, although Trevor's name was filled in only at a date later than the date of the order itself. Still, "the discourse at the community was, That the Speaker was the person to whom the sum was to be given." The chamberlain's books revealed that on June 22, 1694, there had also been a payment of 100 pounds to Paul Jodrell, clerk of the House, and 20 guineas to Mr. Hungerford, chairman of the committee to whom the Orphans' Bill was referred (*Corbett's Parliamentary History of England* [London: T.C. Hansard, 1809] 5, 901–906).

On March 13, 1695, Trevor informed the House he was sick. On March 14, Paul Foley, the chairman of the committee that had investigated the accounts, was elected speaker in his place (House of Commons, *Journal* 11, 272). On March 16, Trevor was expelled from the House "being guilty of a high Crime and Misdemeanour, by receiving a Gratuity of a Thousand Guineas." Ten days later Hungerford was expelled as well (ibid. 283).

In the same spirit of reform, the Commons also received the petition of the 400 licensed hackney-coachmen of London reciting that the licensing commission had, "by receiving Bribes, and by other undue means, acted corruptly." Three of the five commissioners were found guilty and were then removed by the king (Cobbett 5, 896). The Commons also investigated large-scale corruption—that effected by the East India Company which had been engaged in battle over the renewal of its charter. Production of the East India Company's records showed nearly 90,000 pounds spent by Sir Thomas Cook, a governor of the company, and accounted for vaguely as spent in connection with the charter. The inference was drawn that the money had been spent corruptly. When the Commons tried to track down specific sums, 5,500 guineas were shown to have been paid by Sir Thomas Cook to Sir Basil Firebrace, who in turn delivered them to Charles Bruce, who gave them to John Robart, the Swiss servant of the duke of Leeds, lord president of the King's Council and the second or third man of the kingdom. Robart fled to the Continent, the duke denied getting the money, the Commons impeached him, the Lords failed to try him. Leeds being already in political trouble, the impeachment marked the end of the duke's political ascendance (Andrew Browning, *Thomas Osborne, Earl of Danby and Duke of Leeds* [Glasgow: Jackson, Son & Co., 1951] 1, 517–521).

The penalties meted out for bribery were political and moderate. Leeds lost power but continued as lord president of the Council; Oxford gave him an honorary doctorate in civil law (ibid. 523–526). Jodrell, the clerk of the House, was not removed. As for Trevor, he did not return to Parliament, but, censured for committing "a high crime," he continued as master of the rolls, the second highest officer of Chancery, until his death twenty-two years later; he became a privy councillor in 1702 and died possessing personalty worth over 60,000 pounds (Rigg, "Trevor, Sir John," 1150). The penalty for bribetaking by a politician in these days of William III was, in a word, political, but political without substantial disgrace. Abstractly considered, to take a bribe was ground for expulsion from Parliament. Concretely, only a failing and disliked politician had to fear this sanction. Other instances of parliamentary discipline for bribery in the eighteenth century were not less political, see House of Commons, *Journal*, vol. 18 (1714–1718) 493, and vol. 19 (1718–1721) 542.

36.   John Dryden, "Absalom and Achitophel," lines 186–191, *The Poems of John Dryden*, ed. James Kinsley (Oxford: Clarendon Press, 1958) 1, 221–222. The lines were added in the second edition, ibid. 4, 1884. *Abbethdin* = "father of the court of justice," one of the two presiding judges in a Jewish civil tribunal, ibid. Achitophel is the adviser of Absalom in his rebellion against King David (2 Sam 15:12, 31, 34; 2 Sam 16:15–23; 2 Sam 17:1–23).

Shaftesbury's modern biographer, K. H. D. Haley, raises the question whether Yeabsly told Pepys the truth about his bribe. He could have been trying to convince Pepys "that he could continue his support of the contractors in safety," Haley, *The First Earl of Shaftesbury* (Oxford: Clarendon Press, 1968) 136. Haley does not take into account Pepys's entry of Sept. 23, 1667.

CHAPTER 14: HOG TWO (PP. 392–424)

1.   Edmund Burke, "Speech in Opening the Impeachment," Third Day, Feb. 18, 1788, Burke, *Works* (Boston: Little, Brown, 1867) 10, 7: "plans and systems"; Burke, "Speech in General Reply," Eighth Day, June 14, 1794, *Works* 12, 295: "muck and filth"; Burke, "Speech in General Reply," First Day, May 28, 1794, *Works* 11, 175: "captain general of the gang."

2.   Burke, "Speech in Opening," Fourth Day, Feb. 19, 1788, *Works* 10, 142.

3.   Ibid.

4.   Burke, "Speech in General Reply," Ninth Day, June 16, 1794, *Works* 12, 349. See also Burke to William Baker, June 22, 1784, in Burke, *Correspondence*, ed. Holden Furber (Chicago: University of Chicago Press, 1965) 5, 155; cf. H. V. Canter, "The Impeachments of Verres and Hastings: Cicero and Burke," *Classical Journal* 9 (1914) 199; Keith Feiling, *Warren Hastings* (London: Macmillan, 1954) 341 ("the vile and abhorred"); Charles Fox, Manager for the House of Commons, Speech, June 7, 1790, *Speeches of the Managers and Counsel in the Trial of Warren Hastings*, ed. E. A. Bond (London: Longman, Green, Longman & Roberts, 1860) 2, 271.

5.   Peter J. Marshall, *The Impeachment of Warren Hastings* (London: Oxford University Press, 1965) 85 (vote); *Report from the Committee of the House of Commons Appointed to Inspect the Lords' Journals*, April 30, 1794, in Burke, *Works* 11, 4 (length of sessions).

6.   Feiling, *Warren Hastings* 371–372, 383 (financial benefits); 386 (East Indiaman named); 393–394 (honored by Oxford, Parliament, Privy Council).

7.   Thomas Macaulay, "Warren Hastings," in Macaulay, *Miscellaneous Works*, ed. Lady Trevelyan, (London: The Jensen Society, 1907) 3, 291.

8.   Feiling, *Warren Hastings* 368.

9.   Marshall, *Impeachment* 189–190.

10.   Hastings, "Minute," 1781, quoted by Burke, "Speech in General Reply," Eighth Day, June 14, 1794, *Works* 12, 302;; Marshall, *Impeachment* p. x (value of *lakh*); P. J. Marshall, *East Indian Fortunes* (Oxford: Clarendon Press, 1976) 216–217 (expectations of Indian fortunes).

11.   George Dempster to Burke, Aug. 4, 1772, in Burke, *Correspondence* 2, 322 (choice of Hastings); Holden Furber, *John Company at Work* (Cambridge, Mass.: Harvard University Press, 1951) 27 (employees in Bengal).

12.   See Burke, *Correspondence* 5, 251, n.3: passage time to India.

13.   Furber, *John Company at Work* 11: company structure; ibid. 269: directors' patronage; Marshall, *Impeachment* 30 and 169: the Sulivans.

14.   "An Act for establishing certain Regulations for the better Management of the Affairs

of the East India Company, as well in India as in Europe," 13 Geo. 63 (1773), sec. 7 (governor-general created); sec. 10 (Hastings named); sec. 8 (obedience required); sec. 13 (court created); sec. 37 (information to be supplied government). On the state of Bengal in 1770 and its relation to maladministration by the Company, see *A Comprehensive History of India*, ed. A. C. Banerjee and D. K. Glose (New Delhi: People's Publishing House, 1978) 722–728.

15.   Furber, *John Company at Work* 237, 260–264.

16.   Burke to William Burke, post March 1782, *Correspondence* 4, 430 (4,000 pounds); ibid. 7, 425, n. 6 (French refugees); Burke, "Memoranda for Consideration" (For Rockingham, post March 1782), *Correspondence* 4, 424 (Baton de Marechal).

17.   Peter J. Marshall, "The Personal Fortune of Warren Hastings," *Economic History Review* 17 (2nd Series; 1964) 284–294; Furber, *John Company at Work* 79–80 (on remittances through Dutch).

18.   Burke to Philip Francis, Dec. 29, 1782, *Correspondence* 5, 60. Marshall, *Impeachment* 11–17, for Burke's developing attitude.

19.   Marshall, *Impeachment* 19–20.

20.   Ibid. 23 ("accidental and temporary"); William Blackstone, *Commentaries on the Laws of England* (Oxford, 1765) 4, 260 (impeachment).

21.   Burke to Francis, Dec. 10, 1785, *Correspondence* 5, 242–243.

22.   Marshall, *Impeachment* 40–50: on Pitt and Dundas; ibid. 58: impeachment voted; ibid. 62: "idealism and prejudices."

23.   House of Commons, Articles of Impeachment, in *House of Lords Sessional Papers, 1794–1795*, ed. F. William Torrington (Dobbs Ferry, N.Y.: Oceana Publishers, 1974) [hereafter Lords, *Evidence*] 7 (preamble); ibid. 34–36 (Sixth Article).

24.   Blackstone, *Commentaries* 4, 9, 2 (*peculatus*); ibid. (Chitty's edition 1825) 4, 17, 1 (on the technical requirements of embezzlement).

25.   *The Trial of Thomas Earl of Macclesfield* (House of Lords, 1725) in T. B. Howell, ed. *A Complete Collection of State Trials* (London: T. C. Hansard, 1812) 16, 1397 (opinion of judges), 1389–1399 (dissenting Lords); William Blackstone, *Commentaries* 4, 10, 17 (bribery defined); ibid. "Introduction," 1, 105 (extent of English law); *Rex v. Vaughan*, 4 Burrows 2494 (King's Bench, 1769) (Mansfield's views).

26.   Covenant of Hastings with the Company, Feb. 10, 1769, *Evidence* 960 (the covenant); 13 Geo. III, c. 63, sec. 23 (the statute); Robert Dallas, Counsel for Hastings, Speech, May 9, 1793, *Speeches ⌐f the Managers and Counsel* 3, 511 (Hastings's oath as Governor)

27.   *Macclesfield's Case, State Trials* 16, 786 (presents customary); 16, 1394 (conviction).

28.   Alexander Pope, *The Iliad* 1, 29–30 and 40–44, in *The Poems of Alexander Pope*, ed. Maynard Mack (New Haven: Yale University Press, 1967) 7, 67.

29.   Dallas, Speech, May 9, 1793, *Speeches of the Managers and Counsel* 3, 570, 579; Hastings, Address (in writing read by him), June 2, 1791, ibid. 2, 503.

30.   Munni Begam to the Governor General and Council, June 11, 1775, Lords, *Evidence* 1038; Robert Dallas, Counsel for Hastings, Speech, May 9, 1793, *Speeches of the Managers and Counsel* 3, 534.

31.   Charles James Fox, Manager for the House of Commons, Speech, June 7, 1790, ibid. 2, 288–295, Robert Dallas, Speech, May 9, 1793, ibid. 3, 568.

32.   Ibid. 3, 562–568; 3, 526 (English custom).

33.   Lords, *Evidence* 117–118.

34.   A detailed basis for inference as to the part of Hastings and his associates is provided by an aide-mémoire kept by George Vansittart, a Company employee on the Calcutta board of trade, Lucy S. Sutherland, "New Evidence on the Nandakumar Trial," *English Historical Review* 72 (1957) 438–465. The aide-mémoire, intended only for Vansittart's own use, is contemporary with the events, guarded, and self-justificatory. It appears to record only matters bearing on Nanda Kumar, so that, for example, a reference to seeing the governor is properly read as seeing the governor about Nanda Kumar (Sutherland at 463 n. 2). The aide-mémoire establishes the deep involvement with the prosecution of Vansittart, "Hastings' most trusted friend and subordinate at this time" (Sutherland, 444) and by implication Hastings's own involvement.

A little over a month after Nanda Kumar's formal charges against Hastings, on April 19, 1775 (the day of Paul Revere's ride!), Kamal-ud-din confessed that he had earlier made false charges against Hastings and his closest associates. Kamal-ud-din was a farmer of revenue, appointed to his post by Hastings and now in financial trouble. No reason was given for his sudden candor which conveniently implicated Nanda Kumar and one Fowke, a merchant on the Council Majority's side. Three indictments were immediately secured against them on the grounds of conspiracy against Hastings, Vansittart, and Barwell, Hastings's ally on the Council (Sutherland, 440, 458–459). The Council Majority responded two days later by publicly visiting Nanda Kumar. Vansittart noted, "a great noise is made about the town of Nundcomar's power and favour and inability of the Court of Justice to hurt him" (Vansittart in Sutherland, 451). Next day, Saturday, Vansittart conferred with Kamal-ud-din and saw Hastings on the business. Sunday he was visited by one Sudar-ud-din, an ex-servant of Nanda Kumar's (Sutherland, 446). Three days later this person brought to see him Mohan Prasad, an Indian high in Hastings's favor (Sutherland, 443). Mohan Prasad showed Vansittart a bond he said Nanda Kumar had forged and announced he was ready to prosecute him. Vansittart advised him on the choice of counsel (Sutherland 451–452). Vansittart then gathered information to support the case and got reports on Nanda Kumar's defensive strategy from false friends of the latter. On May 9, Kanta, Hastings's *banyan*, delivered one piece of information. On May 11, Vansittart consulted Hastings in person and later in the day delivered to Mohan Prasad's counsel a memorandum on the case (Sutherland 454–455).

In summary, unexpectedly but conveniently an Indian indebted to Hastings produced a confession which let the Hastings group launch three criminal cases against Nanda Kumar. (The same helpful Indian turned up as the star witness for the prosecution in the forgery trial, Sutherland, 462). When this ploy was met by the Council Majority, a more drastic move was made, in which the Indian actors were Nanda Kumar's ex-servant and an Indian much favored by Hastings. They moved only after checking with Vansittart and following his advice on the lawyer to use. Vansittart helped to develop the evidence and to provide the prosecution with guidance. On two occasions Vansittart specially consulted Hastings as to what to do with regard to Nanda Kumar; throughout the business he may be seen as acting for Hastings as his "most trusted friend and subordinate." It is fair to conclude that without the management of Vansittart and without the encouragement of Hastings indicated by Vansittart's participation, the prosection of Nanda Kumar on a capital charge would not have been begun.

For the doubt as to the forgery statute applying to the document and the probability that it did not apply in India at all, see J. Duncan M. Derrett, "Nanda Kumar's Forgery," *English Historical Review* 75 (1960) 232, 236, 237. For the jurisdiction, see North's Regulating Act, 13 Geo III, c. 63, sec. 14, which, enumerating cases of which the king's charter gives the Supreme Court jurisdiction, entirely omits the crime of one Indian acting against another Indian in a private transaction. The lack of jurisdiction was specifically charged by Gilbert Elliot (a later governor-general of India) in the draft "Articles of Charges of High Crimes and Misdemeanors against Sir Elijah Impey, presented to the Commons, December 12, 1787," House of Commons, *Sessional Papers of the Eighteenth Century* vol. 63, *East India Company. Sir E. Impey, 1787–1788*, ed. Sheila Lambert (Wilmington, Del.: Scholarly Resources, 1973) 4. For Nanda Kumar's Petition to the Council, August 1775, ibid. 27. A record of the original trial is published as "The Trial of Maha Rajah Nundocomar, Bahader, for Forgery," in Howell, *State Trials* 20, 923–1078. For the quotation from the Hastings supporter, Marshall, *Impeachment* 141. For Macaulay's observation, Macaulay, "Warren Hastings," *Miscellaneous Works* 15, 233; for the Indian view of the savagery of Nanda Kumar's execution, K. A. Ballhatchet, "European Relations with Asia and Africa," *New Cambridge Modern History* (Cambridge: At the University Press, 1965) 8, 226.

35.   Marshall, *Impeachment* 62 (Impey impeachment fails); for the common law view of a defendant's elimination of a witness, see, e.g., *People v. Spaulding*, 309 Ill. 292, 141 N. E. 196 (1923); see generally J. Wigmore, *A Treatise on the Anglo-American System of Evidence in Trials at Common Law* 2, §278 (3d ed. 1940) (suppression of evidence receivable against a defendant as an indication of his cause's lack of truth and merit). James F. Stephen, *The Story of Nuncomar and the Impeachment of Sir Elijah Impey*, (London: Macmillan, 1885) defends Impey but fails to deal with these points satisfactorily.

36.   Hastings to the Secret Committee of the Honourable Court of Directors, May 22, 1782, Lords, *Evidence* 1115.

37.   Ibid. 1114.

38.   The Directors to Hastings, March 19, 1784, ibid. 1149–1150.

39.   Covenant of Hastings with the Company, 1772, ibid. 961.

40.   Hastings to William Devaynes, Chairman of the Court of Directors, July 11, 1785, ibid. 1151–1152.

41.   Larkins to Devaynes, Aug. 5, 1786, enclosing Paper No. 1, ibid. 1153, 1157.

42.   Marshall, *Impeachment* 154.

43.   *Evidence* 1118.

44. Larkins, Cross-examination, ibid. 2733.

45. *Evidence* 1156.

46. Larkins, Cross-examination, ibid. 2733–2734, 2770.

47. Ibid. 2730 ("detached piece of paper"); 2742–2743 (not his account, does not know who kept); 2755 (does not read Bengal language).

48. Ibid. 2731–2732.

49. Marshall, *Impeachment* 91–92 (Hastings's view of *zamindari*), 153–154 (the Dinajpur case); Burke, "Speech in Opening the Impeachment," Third Day, Feb. 18, 1788, *Works* 10, 61–62 (Hastings corrupt as judge).

50. Ibid. 10, 62.

51. Charles Fox, Speech, June 7, 1790, *Speeches of the Managers and Counsel* 2, 367–368.

52. Hastings, Testimony, House of Commons, quoted by John Anstruther, Manager, Feb. 16, 1790, ibid. 2, 245 (Hastings's account of transaction); Charles Cornwallis, Testimony, Lords, *Evidence* 2724 (Nabakrishna's command of English); Vansittart's aide-mémoire in Sutherland, "New Evidence" 452 (Nabakrishna's help to prosecution).

53. Hastings to the Honourable Court of Directors, Feb. 21, 1784, *Evidence* 1120, 1146.

54. Larkins, Cross-examination, ibid. 2763.

55. Anstruther, Speech, Feb. 16, 1790, *Speeches of the Managers and Counsel* 2, 246; Burke, "Speech on the Sixth Article," Third Day, May 5, 1789, *Works* 10, 370–371.

56. Anstruther, Speech, Feb. 16, 1790, *Speeches of the Managers and Counsel* 2, 246; Fox, Speech, ibid. 2, 352; Burke, "Speech on the Sixth Article," *Works* 10, 372.

57. Ibid. 10, 373; Anstruther, "Speech," February 16, 1790, *Speeches of the Managers and Counsel* 2, 245; Marshall, *Impeachment* 151 (date of Nabakrishna's appointment as *zamindar*).

58. Ibid. 150–151.

59. *Evidence* (May 5, 1794) 2775. Marshall writes at 151, "At first sight, it seems difficult to avoid the conclusion that Nobkissen had bribed Hastings to send him to Burdwan. There were, however, strong grounds why Hastings should have accepted Nobkissen's petition without any personal inducement . . . the imputation of bribery remains unproven." Marshall's reasoning would clear of bribery any judge who had "strong grounds" for a decision apart from the present he received.

60. "Bengal book-keeping," Burke, "Speech on the Sixth Article," Fourth Day, May 7, 1789, *Works* 10, 404.

61. Burke to Dundas, Nov. 1, 1787, *Correspondence* 5, 356–357.

62. Edward Thurlow, Speech, March 24, 1795, *Debates in the House of Lords on the Evidence delivered in the Trial of Warren Hastings* (London: Debrett, 1797) 218 ("fairly and honorably possessed"); Burke to Henry Addington, March 5, 1795, *Correspondence* 8, 177–178 and accompanying notes (on Thurlow as advocate); ibid. 7, 372 n. 3 ("but with horror"); Burke to William Adam, Jan. 4, 1791, ibid. 6, 199 ("the Closetstool of Bribery"); ibid. 6, 199 n. 1 ("a very Nasty Business"); Marshall, *Impeachment* 27–28 (Hastings's early relations with Thurlow).

63. Burke to Thomas Burgh, July 1, 1787, *Correspondence* 5, 341 (on bishops); Burke to Henry Dundas, June 7, 1793, ibid. 7, 372 (on Thurlow).

64. Marshall, *Impeachment* 27 and 84.

65. Burke to Dundas, June 7, 1793, *Correspondence* 7, 373.

66. Burke to Francis, Dec. 10, 1785, ibid. 242–243 (emphasis in original).

67. Burke to Francis, circa Jan. 3, 1788, ibid. 5, 372 ("I must dilate upon it"); Burke, "Speech in Opening the Impeachment," *Works* 10, 7 (Hastings's systematic bribery); ibid. 10, 14 (Governor's hands like an idol's); Burke, Speech in General Reply, Seventh Day, June 12, 1794, ibid. 12, 163 ("a bribe here and a bribe there"); ibid. 12, 277 ("that most atrocious and wicked"). Burke, Speech in Reply, Third day, June 3, 1794, ibid. 11, 306 (close connection of vices).

68. Burke, "Speech in Opening the Impeachment," ibid. 10, 30 ("murdered not only the accuser"); Burke, Speech on the Sixth Article, First Day, April 21, 1789, ibid. 10, 218 ("murdered this man") (emphasis in original); Burke, Speech on the Sixth Article, May 5, 1789, ibid. 10, 317 ("murder" in popular sense).

69. Burke, "Speech in Opening the Impeachment," Third Day, Feb. 18, 1788, ibid. 10, 7 ("bribery, filthy hands"; "staining," "purity"); Burke, Speech on the Sixth Article, Second Day, April 25, 1789, ibid. 10, 251 ("sty of disgrace"); Burke, Speech in Reply, Eighth Day, June 14, 1794, ibid., 12, 269 (Swift quoted); ibid. 12, 275 (in love with Munni), ibid. 12, 277 ("we hate the crime"); ibid. 12, 317 ("great encyclopedeia"); ibid. 31 (comparison to Satan). James Erskine St. Clair, Manager, Speech, May 30, 1791, *Speeches of the Managers and Counsel* 2, 477 (unjust steward). The lines of Swift's are from Jonathan Swift, "Phillis, or The Progress of

Love," lines 99–100, Swift, *Poems*, ed. Harold Williams (Oxford: Clarendon Press, 1937) 1, 225. Burke to Charles O'Hara, April 24, 1766, *Correspondence* 1, 252 ("too virtuous to be honest").

70. Marshall, *Impeachment* 33 quoting Scott to Hastings, Jan. 18, 1786 ("ravings of a madman"); Feiling, *Warren Hastings* 358 (Burke's "hatred of others"); Burke, Speech in Reply, First Day, May 28, 1794, *Works* 11, 165–166 (Hastings' demeanor); Hastings to the Directors, Nov. 11, 1773, Lords, *Evidence* 2829 ("The Care of Self-preservation").

71. Feiling, *Warren Hastings* 348 (punishment before accusations); ibid. 370–371 ("bound to stake"); 382–383 (legal expenses over 70,000 pounds); Marshall, *Impeachment* 84 (6,000 pounds spent by Scott during trial); Marshall, "The Personal Fortune of Warren Hastings," *Economic History Review* 17, 298 (over 20,000 pounds spent by Scott, 1781–1786).

72. Feiling, *Warren Hastings* 383 ("total insignificance"); Marshall, *Impeachment* 33 (peerage postponed in 1784).

73. Furber, *John Company at Work* 235 (on Macpherson); Lord Charles Cornwallis to Lord Sydney, Jan. 7, 1788, *The Correspondence of Charles First Marquis Cornwallis*, ed. Charles Ross (London, 1859) 1, 310; Cornwallis, Testimony, Lords, *Evidence* 2719–2720 (Hastings's reputation); Cornwallis to Dundas, Dec. 31, 1790, *Correspondence of Cornwallis* 2, 68 ("Leadenhallstreet principles"); Cornwallis to the directors, Nov. 1, 1788, quoted in Franklin and Mary Wickwire, *Cornwallis: The Imperial Years* (Chapel Hill: University of North Carolina Press, 1980) 50 ("temptations, danger and discredit"); Cornwallis to John Moffeux, Dec. 16, 1787, *Correspondence of Cornwallis* 1, 318 ("shocking evils," "plunder"); Cornwallis to Dundas, Nov. 1, 1788, ibid. 2, 383 (Macpherson as impeachable as Hastings).

74. Holden Furber, *Henry Dundas* (London: Oxford University Press, 1931) 23 ("no broken fortune"); ibid. 133 (Lord Hobert in 1793 seeks governorship of Madras to restore fortune); Furman, *John Company at Work* 240, 256 (reduction of corruption); Percival Spear, ed., *The Oxford History of India*, 3rd rev. ed. (Oxford: Clarendon Press, 1958) 532 (Cornwallis's remark); for a summary of Cornwallis's accomplishments, Stanley Wolpert, *A New History of India* (New York: Oxford University Press, 1982) 195–200. In contrast, Hastings is compared favorably to Cornwallis because of his sympathy to Indian languages and culture by David Kopf, who does not advert to the corruption issue, Kopf, *British Orientalism and the Bengal Renaissance* (Berkeley: University of California Press, 1969) 13–26, 239.

75. Jonathan Swift, *Gulliver's Travels*, ed. Herbert Davis (Oxford: Basil Blackwell, 1959) Part III, chap. VIII (English yeomen); Part IV, chap. VI (chief ministers). Emphasis in original.

76. James Burgh, *Political Disquisitions or An Enquiry into Public Errors, Defects, and Abuses* (Philadelphia: Robert Bell & William Woodhouse, 1785) vol. 1, Book V "Of Parliamentary Corruption" 267 ("bribery, corruption . . ."); 269 ("filling their *pockets*"); 270–272 (offices); 277 (secret service); 278 (lottery tickets); vol. 2, 275 ("the modern plan of government").

These views of a critic of the system may be compared with Lewis Namier's classic analysis, *The Structure of British Politics at the Accession of George III* (London: Macmillan, 2d ed. 1951). Landlords delivered their tenants' votes in parliamentary elections; it was thought normal for the tenants to be responsive to their wishes (68–69). Nepotism determined the choice of parliamentary candidates and was "an acknowledged principle in administration" (359). Businessmen entered Parliament as a good way to get a government contract or were paid off by a government contract for running in an expensive constituency; even the parliamentary franking privilege was used for business profit (46–49). Patronage—expressed in appointments and promotions in all branches of government, civil, ecclesiastical, and military; in contracts; in the distribution of titles; in the award of totally discretionary pensions—was the way an administration nourished its parliamentary following. Discounting the need of any administration to use much secret service money for political bribes, Namier generalizes at 176:

> Bribery, to be really effective, has to be widespread and open; it has to be the custom of the land and cease to dishonor the recipients, so that it may attract the average self-respecting man. Such were the political emoluments in Great Britain about the middle of the eighteenth century, and the real mystery about the secret service fund of that time is why it should have existed at all, when, to say the very least, nine-tenths of the subsidizing of politicians was done in the full light of the day.

Namier's use of "bribery" in the passage is curious. If a reciprocity really does not "dishonor the recipients" and does attract "the average self-respecting man," in what sense is it a bribe? Not in the sense of the criminal law in force, not in the sense of the moral standard in use. Namier appears to be guilty of taking some modern moral notion of what "bribery" is and applying it to characterize common eighteenth-century practice. It is much as though a twenty-first century historian wrote about modern America observing the open campaign contributions of the PACs and finding the secret bribery of politicians mysterious, when "nine-tenths" of the subsidizing was done, through lawful PACs, "in the full light of day." But there is a sense in which Namier's term is justified. In the eyes of critics like Burgh the practices were dishonoring, not to be engaged in by any self-respecting man, immoral, and subject to political sanction. Precisely the same phenomenon exists today in the United States where the PACs are assailed by a few critics as corrupting although lawful: by the higher standard of the critics they are a form of licensed bribery (see Chapter 19 at note 81 below).

77.   Fuber, *Henry Dundas* 32 (the "Scottization" of India under Dundas); 59, 61 (his nepotism); 23−25 (his Scottish machine). Holding a sinecure as treasurer of the Navy, Dundas borrowed money from his subordinate, Alexander Trotter, the paymaster of the Navy; the latter was embezzling Navy funds on a grand scale to finance his private speculations. Dundas apparently knew of the embezzlements and accepted the loans as a quid pro quo for his toleration, ibid. 157−161. For his role in these transactions Dundas in 1805 was censured by the Commons and then impeached, but acquitted by the Lords, ibid. 155−164. His biographer writes in his defense that the embezzlements "occasioned no actual loss to the Government. Trotter was uniformly successful and paid all his Navy accounts," ibid. 149. This is what every embezzler hopes for—that he will be "uniformly successful."

78.   Burke, *Correspondence* 1, 63, headnote (the pension); Burke to Henry Flood, May 18, 1765, ibid. 1, 193 ("I had earned it"); Samuel Johnson, *A Dictionary of the English Language* (London, 1785) at "Pension" and "Pensioner."

79.   Burke to Flood, May 18, 1765, *Correspondence* 1, 192 ("extremely disgustful"); Burke to John Monck Mason, post May 29, 1765, ibid. 1, 196 ("ministerial fortune"); Burke to Charles O'Hara, Dec. 23, 1766, ibid. 1, 285 ("crooked politicks").

80.   Lord Fitzwilliam to Burke, June 26, 1794, ibid. 7, 555 ("credit and reputation"); Richard Burke Sr. to Juliana French, April 6, 1782, ibid. 4, 437 (Burke family's jobs); ibid. 5, 96 (Champion's job).

81.   Burke, "Memorandum" [to Rockingham, circa March 15, 1782], *Correspondence* 4, 424, ("You need stipulate"); Burke to Richard Burke Jr., post Nov. 25, 1782, ibid. 5, 52 ("reward for publick service"); ibid. 5, 82 n. 7 (7,000 pounds); Burke to an Unknown Lord, May 19, 1796, ibid. 9, 12 ("best and dearest part,"); ibid. 5, 324 n. 3 (brother as counsel); Burke to Edmund Malone, Feb. 12, 1788, ibid. 5, 378 (son is clerk).

82.   Burke to Thomas Lewis O'Beirne, Aug. 27, 1787, *Correspondence* 5, 32 (pension for sister); Burke, *Correspondence* 1, 351 n. 2 (William Burke's contribution to Beaconsfield); Burke to Francis, June 9, 1777, ibid. 3, 348−349 (recommendation of William); John Bourke to Francis, April 29, 1777, quoted in Burke, *Correspondence* 3, 348 n. 1 ("nearest and dearest"); Burke to Philip Francis, June 9, 1777, ibid. 3, 348 ("Indemnify me"); Burke to William Burke, March 27, 1782, ibid. 4, 430 ("new arrangements"); Cornwallis to Lord Rawdon, Dec. 2, 1789, *Correspondence of Cornwallis* 1, 450, 452 (scandalous exchange rate; most unnecessary job); ibid. 464 ("to pay his court").

83.   James Boswell, *Life of Samuel Johnson* (London: Oxford University Press, 1952), April 3, 1778 (Burke and Johnson); Oct. 12, 1779 ("must be bribed").

84.   Burke to James Boswell, April 23, 1782, *Correspondence* 4, 445; *Rex v. Vaughan* 4 Burrows 2494 (King's Bench, 1769) (Mansfield's opinion).

85.   Burke, "Speech in Opening of Impeachment," Third Day, Feb. 18, 1788, *Works* 10, 7 (less suspicion of pecuniary corruption); Burke, Speech on the Sixth Article, First Day, April 21, 1789, *Works* 10, 161 (no clear terms for bribes). William Blackstone's fears about dangers he would encounter in the legal profession may be read as contrary to Burke's complacency. Aged twenty-two, he wrote the following verses as he contemplated a legal career:

> Then welcome Bus'ness, welcome Strife,
> Welcome the Cares, the Thorns of Life,
> The Visage wan, the pore-blind Sight,
> The Toil by Day, the Lamp at Night,
> The tedious Forms, the solemn Prate,
> The pert Dispute, the dull Debate,
> The drowsy Bench, the babbling Hall,
> For thee, fair Justice, welcome all!

Thus, though my Noon of Life be passed,
Yet let my Setting Sun, at last,
Find out the still, the rural Cell
Where sage Retirement loves to dwell!
There let me taste the home-felt Bliss
of Innocence and inward Peace!
Untainted by the guilty Bribe,
Uncursed amid the Harpy-Tribe,
No Orphan's cry to wound my Ear,
My Honour and my Conscience clear,
Thus may I calmly meet my End,
Thus to the Grave with Joy in Peace descend.

William Blackstone, "The Lawyer to his Muse," Blackstone, "Select Poems and Translations" (MS, Boalt Hall, University of California, Berkeley) 76–77.
86.   Burke to Laurence, July 28, 1796, *Correspondence* 9, 62–63.
87.   Burke to Dundas, March 22, 1792, ibid. 7, 114 ("no more than a scuffle").
88.   Burke to Richard Shackleton [his lifelong friend], May 25, 1779, *Correspondence* 4, 79; Burke, Speech on Mr. Fox's East India Bill, Dec. 1, 1783, *Works* 2, 439 ("All political power"); Burke, "Speech in Opening of Impeachment," Third Day, Feb. 18, 1788, *Works* 10, 12 ("every office of trust . . . forbids bribes").
89.   Burke, "Speech on Moving His Resolutions for Conciliation with the Colonies," March 22, 1775, *Works* 2, 181.
90.   Burke, Speech in Reply, First Day, May 28, 1794, *Works* 11, 225 ("one law for all"); Burke to Mary Palmer, Jan. 19, 1786, *Correspondence* 5, 255 ("I have no party"); Burke, "Speech in Opening the Impeachment," Fourth Day, Feb. 19, 1788, *Works* 10, 144 ("When the God"). On the centrality of Christian belief for Burke and on the importance of this passage, see Gerald W. Chapman, *Edmund Burke: The Practical Imagination* (Cambridge: Harvard University Press, 1967) 271–273.
91.   Burke to Palmer, Jan. 19, 1786, *Correspondence* 5, 257.
92.   Burke to Dundas, March 22, 1792, ibid. 7, 114, 116.
93.   Burke to William Windham, Jan. 8, 1795, ibid. 8, 113 (Indian Vomit); Burke, Speech in General Reply, Ninth Day, June 16, 1794, *Works* 12, 398.
94.   Feiling, *Warren Hastings* 340.
95.   Burke, Speech in General Reply, Ninth Day, June 16, 1794, *Works* 12, 395.
96.   Burke to Dundas, June 5, 1795, *Correspondence* 8, 260.
97.   Burke to Lord Loughborough, March 7, 1796, ibid. 8, 406. Emphasis in original.
98.   Burke and Edward James Nagle to Laurence, Feb. 12, 1797, *Correspondence* 9, 238.
99.   John Brook, "Edmund Burke," in Lewis Namier and John Brook, *The House of Commons, 1754–1790* (New York: Oxford University Press, 1964) 2, 153.
100.   Burke, Speech in General Reply, May 28, 1794, *Works* 11, 180.
101.   For comparison and contrast, consider the view of corruption in imperial China under the Ch'ing dynasty as reported in modern works using largely eighteenth-century sources. Administration of justice was the responsibility of the district magistrate, who was also in charge of the collection of taxes and the preservation of order in the area. The magistrate was appointed by the central imperial government, rotated every five years, and chosen from outside the province so that he would not be influenced by family connections. In the eyes of the uneducated he was the representative of the local god or of the judge of the underworld; he also represented the emperor, the Son of Heaven, John R. Watt, *The District Magistrate in Late Imperial China* (New York: Columbia University Press, 1972) 17. Usually only acquainted with elementary legal principles, he came with a secretary trained in the law. His staff, provided from the province, consisted in clerks who did the preparation and transcribing of documents and runners who acted as police, bailiffs, process servers, torturers, and jailers. He brought with him personal servants including a gate porter through whom access to him was controlled. From the time of Yung-cheng (1723) the central government paid the magistrate *yang-lien yin* ("money to nourish honesty") but this salary was insufficient to meet his public expenses and private expectations. It was taken for granted that he also receive *lou-kuei* ("customary fees"). It was expected that he make money out of the tax collections. Magistrates regularly retired with substantial fortunes, T'ung-Tsu Ch'u, *Local Government in China under the Ch'ing* (Cambridge: Harvard University Press, 1962) 22–31.

The customary fees were not regarded as corrupt, but they were clearly of a kind that could influence the magistrate in performing the many acts that lay within his discretion. They extended to payments to his servants including the "gift for arriving at a post" (*tao-jen li*), the "festival gift," and the "New Year gift"; also the *men pao* or gift given the gatekeeper by one wanting to see the magistrate or deliver something to him, Ch'u, *Local Administration* 88.

Other payments are classified by modern authors, drawing on imperial edicts and manuals by magistrates for their characterizations, as corrupt. Runners and clerks are said to be habitually engaged in corrupt transactions. Runners are alleged to take payments from criminals not to apprehend them; to shake down the innocent with the threat of arrest; to threaten those they bring to court with chains unless paid "chain-release money" (*chieh-so ch'ien*); to keep persons in uncomfortable imprisonment unless paid; to lighten a sentence of flogging if compensated. Clerks are said to be adept at delaying cases and at altering documents for a price. Specific dodges are noted. A runner will collaborate with a clerk to get official papers in blank; the names of those singled out for extortion will then be filled in. A clerk will be paid by a defendant to improve a plaintiff's pleadings by clumsy alterations, so that the forgery is obvious and the magistrate believes that it was committed by the plaintiff to aid his cause; the practice is common enough to have its own name, "cutting out and pasting in." Personal servants are apt to be more controllable than the low-level personnel who constitute runners and clerks; but they too can often be paid for favors. A special provision of law provides for their punishment—the first time they are convicted, the characters *tsang-fan* ("bribery criminal") are to be tattooed on their arm; the second time, on their face. Officials are not to employ tattooed servants. The key servant is the gatekeeper, whose control of access makes his position highly profitable for him in corrupt ways. The secretary, the legal expert, is sometimes, though not often, corrupt. Corruption by the magistrate is considered possible but it is not emphasized as a problem, ibid. 49–50, 68–70, 88, 92, 256; Watt, *The District Magistrate* 211, 222.

The Chinese ruling class clearly carried very far the practice of blaming the staff for corruption; one thinks of Chancellor Bacon blaming his servants. The magistrate—an alien in the district in which he presides—is pictured by the sources as buffeted by pressure from the local gentry and as more or less helpless to prevent serious extortion and bribery among his subordinates. In theory the law does punish a magistrate for taking a bribe. There is a scale of punishments ranging from seventy strokes to strangulation depending on the amount of the bribe, Ch'u, *Local Government* 234–235. There is also a set of Disciplinary Regulations providing for a magistrate's removal for "avarice." A magistrate could be dismissed for conniving at a clerk's bribery and disciplined for offering a present "to please" another official, Watt, *The District Magistrate* 19, 171. The sources give no example of any magistrate being beaten or strangled for bribery. The co-existence of the Disciplinary Regulations, with their far milder penalties, suggest that the criminal sanctions against bribery by magistrates were not regularly employed. Even as to the Disciplinary Regulations, the sources do not supply specific instances where taking a bribe led to removal. Annual review by the central government of a magistrate's performance focused on two things: his ability to collect taxes and his ability to suppress robbers, ibid. 174–175. Money and public order were the chief concerns of the central government, not the magistrate's purity. There is no evidence offered that the central government made a serious effort to fix a line between customary fees and bribes or to enforce anti-bribery rules. On the books, for example, the law treated it as bribery for a magistrate to buy supplies at an "official price" well below the market price. In practice, even the most virtuous magistrates did not think they could survive without buying at the "official price," Ch'u, *Local Government* 30.

The imperial government's view appears to have been that there was a great deal of corruption, that low-level personnel was chiefly responsible for it, and that law existed on the books for its correction but could not be enforced. That, beyond the official government position, there was considerable suspicion of corruption on the part of the higher end of the judicial order is indicated by a variety of evidence. When the virtuous secretary Wang Hui-tsu (1731–1807) gave an innovative ruling in an inheritance case, he was believed to have been bribed, Watt, *The District Magistrate* 218. When two clans litigated against each other before a magistrate, bribery was expected, ibid. 219. In *The Dream of the Red Chamber*, a classic eighteenth-century novel, Chapter 86, an upper-class man kills a surly waiter. He is tried for murder, confesses, and is convicted by a magistrate. The magistrate sends his decision to the defendant's family with an oral message that he knows the family is well off. The family responds by sending several thousand taels to the magistrate, who orders a retrial. The defendant now claims it was an accident; the witnesses change their stories; the clerk alters the footnotes to eliminate evidence of a sustained assault. The magistrate orders the case continued. The defendant's family realizes he will be released if they make a "few more payments" to the magistrate's staff and compensate the deceased victim's family, Tsao Hsueh-Chin and Kao Ngo, *A Dream of Red Mansions* [*The Dream of the Red Chamber*] [Peking: Foreign Language Press, 1980] trans. by Yang Hsien-Yi and Gladys Yang, 2, 80. This translation from Maoist China is able to rationalize the novel as exposing "the corrupt and reactionary nature of the superstructure in the last period of Chinese feudal society," Publisher's Note, ibid. 1, VI.

The problem of the access payments to the gate porters recalls imperial Rome and papal Rome. The dodges of the runners recall Chaucer's summoner. "Cutting and pasting" brings to mind the charge against Nanda Kumar. What is conspicuous in China are (1) the absence of advocates, a class with a professional interest in preserving the courts from bribery; (2) a political system that encourages charges of corruption against magistrates; (3) a religious tradition that emphasizes the paradigm of an unbribeable deity.

CHAPTER 15: "THOROUGH AND MOST ADROIT POLITICIANS" (PP. 425–459)

1. Congress of the United States, Declaration of Independence. Text in Julian P. Boyd, *The Declaration of Independence: The Evolution of the Text* (Princeton: Princeton University Press, 1945). The reference to the "Supreme Judge" was added by Congress to Jefferson's draft, ibid. 34.

2. An Act for establishing a High Court of Chancery, Acts of October 1777, Chapter XV, *The Statutes at Large, being a Collection of all the Laws of Virginia*, ed. William Waller Hening (1824) 9, 389. A similar oath was set for other judges in 1779, ibid. 10, 90. For the royal judges' oath, see Acts of November, 1753, ibid. 6, 326. The oath of office for judges of the United States—invoked as a solemn climax by John Marshall in *Marbury v. Madison*, the fundamental case establishing judicial review of acts of Congress—also provided that judges should administer justice, "without respect to persons," see *Marbury v. Madison* 1 Cranch 137 at 180 (1803). For Sisamnes, see Chapter 2, above, n. 1.

3. *Page v. Pendleton and Lyons, Administrators, Virginia Reports Annotated* 2, 221–222.

4. John Randolph, quoted in B. B. Minor, "Memoir of the Author," *Virginia Reports Annotated* 2, 91.

5. A Declaration of the Rights of the Inhabitants of the Commonwealth of Massachusetts, *Acts and Laws of the Commonwealth of Massachusetts* (Boston, 1890), article 29, p. [8]. The judges' salaries, ibid. p. 17.

6. The Declaration of Rights, *Laws of Maryland*, ed. Virgil Maxey (Baltimore, 1811) 1, 14.

7. Acts of October 1776, *Statutes at Large* 9, 189; Acts of 1782, ibid. 11, 124.

8. Max Farrand, ed., *The Records of the Federal Convention of 1787* (New Haven, Conn.: Yale University Press, 1911) 1, 21 (Madison's Notes for May 29, 1787).

9. See Bernard Bailyn, *The Ideological Origins of the American Revolution* (Cambridge, Mass.: Harvard University Press, 1967) 43, 48, 86; Milton Klein, "Corruption in Colonial America," *South Atlantic Quarterly* 78 (1979) 57 at 70–71. Charles Carroll of Carrollton to Charles Carroll, Sr., January 29, 1760, and Charles Carroll, Sr., to William Graves, December 23, 1768, quoted in Bailyn *Ideological Origins* 91–92; "corrupt and prostituted minority," Philadelphia handbill, quoted in ibid. 126. For Dr. Johnson's view, see Chapter 14 above at n. 83. Colonial governors in America had often been perceived by Americans as avaricious men, out to make money from their office, see, for example, Stanley N. Katz, *Newcastle's New York* (Cambridge, Mass.: Harvard University Press, 1968) 33–35. Relief in England from their oppressions was generally viewed as expensive to obtain (ibid. 96). "'Connections,' 'interest,' and 'influence' were the ingredients of Anglo-American political in-fighting," ibid. 200. It was against the background of this experience, not on a tabula rasa, that the Americans framed their laws.

10. *Records of the Federal Convention* 2, 65–69 (Madison's Notes for July 20, 1787).

11. Ibid. 2, 186 (Madison's Notes for Aug. 6, 1787) (the elimination of "Corruption"); 2, 550 (Madison's notes for Sept. 8, 1787) (Mason's inquiry). On the meaning of "high crimes and misdemeanors" as "a category of political crimes against the state," Raoul Berger, *Impeachment: The Constitutional Problems* (Cambridge, Mass.: Harvard University Press, 1973) 61.

12. *Records of the Federal Convention* 2, 600 (Report of the Committee of Style).

13. Ibid. 2, 389 (Madison's notes for Aug. 23, 1787).

14. Ibid. 3, 327 (Debate in Virginia Convention, June 17, 1788, and accompanying note).

15. Ibid. 2, 254 (Madison's notes for Aug. 10, 1787).

16.   Ibid. 2, 66 (Madison's notes for July 20, 1787).

17.   Ibid. 1, 20 (Madison's notes for May 20, 1787).

18.   Ibid. 1, 388 (Madison's notes for June 23, 1787); and ibid. 1, 391–393 (Robert Yates's notes for June 23, 1787).

19.   Ibid. 2, 285–289 (Madison's notes for Aug. 14, 1787).

20.   Ibid. 2, 442 (Madison's notes for Sept. 3, 1787).

21.   Ibid. 1, 217 (Madison's notes for June 12, 1787).

22.   See Gerald T. Dunne, *Hugo Black and the Judicial Revolution* (New York: Simon & Schuster, 1977) 52–54. A legal challenge to Black's appointment was dismissed for lack of standing on the part of the petitioners, *Ex parte Leavitt* 302 U.S. 633 (1937).

23.   *The Federalist*, ed. Henry Cabot Lodge (New York: G. P. Putnam's Sons, 1888), No. 78, 490–491.

24.   Ibid. No. 83, 522–523.

25.   Ibid. No. 67, 425.

26.   Ibid. No. 10, 54.

27.   1 *Statutes of the United States* 46 (customs entries); ibid. 117 (judges).

28.   Charles Warren, "New Light on the History of the Federal Judiciary Act of 1789," *Harvard Law Review* 37 (1924) 73 (on the federal common law of crime).

29.   James Madison, Albert Gallatin, Levi Lincoln, Commissioners, "Georgia Land Claims," *Report to the House of Representatives* Feb. 16, 1803, U.S. Congress, *American State Papers: Class VIII–Public Lands* (Washington: Gales & Seaton, 1832) 1, 153–155.

30.   Ibid. 141; Charles Homer Haskins, "The Yazoo Land Companies," American Historical Association, *Papers* (New York: G. P. Putnam's Sons, 1891) 5, 83.

31.   List of shareholders and legislators in Madison et al., *Report* 141; vote 144; depositions of witnesses before Georgia Legislature, 1796, reprinted 144–149.

32.   Georgia Act of Feb. 13, 1796, quoting the convention of May 10, 1795, in ibid. 156–158; "chugging a sapling," ibid. 149.

33.   Ibid. 150 (refund of purchase price); U.S. Congress, *Annals* (8th Cong. 2nd Sess.), Feb. 1, 1805, 1131 (resumé of Georgia congressman's views by Samuel Dana, chairman of Committee on Claims).

34.   "An abstract of all of titles . . . recorded," in Madison et al. *Report* 220–228; Haskins, "The Yazoo Land Companies" 99 (Hamilton's opinion).

35.   *Annals* (5th Cong., 2nd Sess.), March 20, 1798, 1278 (suspicion; cosmetic change); *U.S. Statutes at Large* 1, 549–550 (act as passed); Madison et al., *Report* 134 ("cannot be supported"; compromise proposed). For the Massachusetts names before 1798, ibid. 141, and compare Allen Chamberlain, *Beacon Hill* (Boston: Houghton Mifflin, 1925) 59 (Bulfinch and Scollay). For the total Boston investment, Haskins, "The Yazoo Land Companies" 88.

36.   Gideon Granger to Nathaniel Macon, Speaker of the House of Representatives, Feb. 7, 1805, printed in *Annals* (8th Cong., 2nd Sess.), 1110–1112 (Granger's interest in Yazoo; his employment by Yazoo claimants); 1113 (the view of Attorney-General Lincoln).

37.   Henry Adams, *John Randolph* (Boston: Houghton-Mifflin, 1883) 9–10 (Randolph's education); 23 (Randolph in Augusta).

38.   John Randolph, Speech, *Annals* (8th Cong., 2nd Sess.), Jan. 29, 1805, 1024 ("subjects which pollution has sanctified"); 1026 ("gross and wilful prevarication"); 1028 ("swindlers of 1795"); 1031 ("sophisticated trash").

39.   Randolph, Speech, Jan. 31, 1805, ibid. 1104.

40.   Randolph, Speech, Jan. 29, 1805, ibid. 1031, 1033.

41.   Randolph, Speech, Jan. 31, 1805, ibid. 1106–1107.

42.   Granger to Macon, Feb. 7, 1805, ibid. 1113 ("virtue enough"); Matthew Lyon, Speech, Feb. 1, 1805, ibid. 1125; William Findley, Speech, Feb. 2, 1805, ibid. 1159–1162.

43.   See the pleadings in *Fletcher v. Peck*, 6 Cranch 87 (1810). On the Massachusetts case (1799), Haskins, "The Yazoo Land Companies" 99; George Blake holds a Yazoo title on Feb. 28, 1797, Madison et al. *Report*, 221.

44.   John Quincy Adams, *Memoirs*, ed. Charles Francis Adams (Philadelphia: J. B. Lippincott, 1874) 1, 546–547 (March 7 and March 11, 1809). Adams's report of what the Chief Justice said in open court does not appear in the reporter's account of *Fletcher v. Peck*, 6 Cranch 87.

45.   Albert J. Beveridge, *The Life of John Marshall* (Boston: Houghton, Mifflin, 1919) 3, 586 (Martin drunk); *Fletcher v. Peck*, 6 Cranch 87 at 130 ("indecent in the extreme"); 132 (act void against innocent purchaser). Gerald T. Dunne, *Justice Joseph Story and the Rise of the Supreme Court* (New York: Simon & Schuster, 1970) 70–74 (Story and Judge Wetmore).

46. Henry Adams, *History of the United States during the First Administration of Thomas Jefferson* (New York: Charles Scribner's Sons, 1909) 2, 214.

47. George M. Troup, Speech, Jan. 20, 1813, *Annals* (12th Cong., 2nd Sess.) 858.

48. *U.S. Statutes at Large* 3, 117 (March 31, 1814); Adams, *History of United States* 2, 45–46 (cost of Louisiana).

49. Adams, *John Randolph* 182 ("original sin"; Alpha and Omega); 193 (St. Thomas of Cantingbury); 258 ("a Yazoo man").

50. Robert V. Remini, *Andrew Jackson and the Course of American Freedom* (New York: Harper & Row, 1981) 15 ("Era of Corruption"); John Quincy Adams, *Memoirs* 4, 319 (March 29, 1819: Baltimore); 6, 87 (Oct. 26, 1822: Savannah); E. J. Hale to William R. Hale, July 3, 1824, quoted in Remini, *Andrew Jackson* 25 (high officers "not quite so good").

51. John Jacob Astor to James Monroe, Jan. 1821, excerpted in Kenneth Wiggins Porter, *John Jacob Astor* (Cambridge: Harvard University Press, 1931) 2, 726 (the interest on the loan; loan overdue); Monroe to James Madison, March 28, 1828, ibid. 2, 727 (time of loan and arrangement for release); 2, 893–894 (Astor's normal practice as to security for his loans). Monroe's letter to Madison is also printed in Monroe, *Writings*, ed. Stanislaus Murray Hamilton (New York: G. P. Putnam's Sons, 1903) 7, 164, but "J J Astor" is garbled as "J J Orton" and "release" is read as "return." For Monroe's salary as secretary of State, *U.S. Statutes at Large* 2, 250 and 713.

52. Astor to Monroe, Feb. 18, 1813, in Porter, *Astor* 1, 215 (first letter quoted); Monroe to Astor, May 1816, ibid. 2, 695 (request for blank licenses for Canadians); 2, 725 (critical years for American Fur); 2, 726 (Astor's habit of writing Monroe).

53. Ibid. 2, 725. Spelling as in original; see Chapter 4 above at notes 80–83 for Epiphanius' letter.

54. Astor to Monroe, post March 1825, quoted in George Morgan, *The Life of James Monroe* (Boston, 1921) 436; Monroe to Madison, March 28, 1828, in Porter, *Astor* 2, 727.

55. *The Papers of Henry Clay*, ed. James F. Hopkins (Lexington: University of Kentucky Press, 1961) 2, 686 (the mortgage document); 3, 533 (Astor's receipt for $5,000, showing loan was unpaid on Dec. 8, 1823); Porter, *Astor* 2, 713 (end of appropriation); Astor to Clay, March 26, 1823, *Papers of Henry Clay* 3, 402; Porter, *Astor* 2, 905 (1833 loan).

56. Biddle, Memorandum, printed in Reginald C. McGrane, *The Correspondence of Nicholas Biddle* (Boston: Houghton Mifflin, 1919) 357–358.

57. Remini, *Andrew Jackson* 375.

58. Porter, *Astor* 2, 713; *Papers of Henry Clay* 3, 110–111 (De Wolfe as client). On De Wolfe as a still active slave trader at the time, John T. Noonan, Jr., *The Antelope* (Berkeley: University of California Press, 1977) 28, 84.

59. Webster to Biddle, Dec. 21, 1833, in McGrane, *Correspondence* 218. Emphasis in original. For the context, Arthur Schlesinger, Jr., *The Age of Jackson* (Boston: Little, Brown, 1946) 84.

60. William Wirt to his wife, April 17, 1822, quoted in Noonan, *The Antelope* 81; John Quincy Adams, *Memoirs* 4, 82 (April 28, 1818).

61. Noonan, *The Antelope* 41 (Berrien as Cicero); 114 (the "Portuguese" fraud); 143–144 (the Spanish-Portuguese connection); 59–60 (Davies's decision and resignation).

62. Ibid. 112–116 (the decision); 138–142 (the cash settlement); 146–151 (congressional action); 152 (sale to White). Wilde is down on Biddle's list of borrowers for $6,000, McGrane, *Correspondence* 359. Could the Bank have financed part of the purchase of the Africans of the *Antelope?*

63. B. W. Leigh to Biddle, Aug. 21, 1837 ("so universal") , and Aug. 28, 1837 (Marshall's disposition of stock), McGrane, *Correspondence* 285–288.

64. Alexis de Toqueville, *Democracy in America*, trans. Henry Reeve, Francis Bowen, Phillips Bradley (New York: Alfred A. Knopf, 1956) 1, 278–279.

65. Adams, *Memoirs* 6, 448 (Dec. 19, 1824: Jennings); 6, 473–474 (Jan. 20, 1825: Scott); 6, 468, and 6, 473, 475 (Jan. 15 and Jan. 21, 1825: McKim). On McKim, see also Noonan, *The Antelope* 90–91.

66. Charles Francis Adams, Note, *Memoirs* 6, 465.

67. Adams, *Memoirs* 6, 453 (Dec. 23, 1824) ("walk upon fires"); 6, 457 (Jan. 1, 1825); 6, 464–465 (Jan. 9, 1825).

68. Samuel Flagg Bemis, *John Quincy Adams and the Union* (New York: Alfred A. Knopf, 1956) 58.

69. Clay to Brown, Jan. 23, 1825, ibid. 40; Remini, *Andrew Jackson* 128 (Clay supporters' information); Adams, *Memoirs* 6, 508 (Feb. 11, 1825) (Adams's statement).

70. Ibid. 6, 484 (Jan. 30 and 31, 1825); 6, 491 (Feb. 3, 1825); 6, 501 (Feb. 9, 1825: God's blessing invoked).
71. Andrew Jackson to John Calhoun, Aug. 1823, Remini, *Andrew Jackson* 15 ("corrupt to the core"); Jackson to John Coffee, Jan. 10, 1825, ibid. 87−91 (emphasis in original); Jackson to William Lewis, Jan. 29, 1825, ibid. 87 ("Intrigue," etc.).
72. Louis McClane to his wife, Feb. 6, 1825, ibid. 90.
73. Andrew Jackson to William B. Lewis, Feb. 7, 1825, *Correspondence of Andrew Jackson*, ed. John Spencer Bassett (Washington: Carnegie Institution, 1928) 3, 276 ("Barter of office"); Jackson to Lewis, Feb. 14, 1825, ibid. 3, 276 ("*Judas* of the West); Jackson to Squire Grant, Feb. 18, 1825, ibid. 3, 276 (*like Judas of old*); Jackson to John Coffee, Feb. 19, 1825, ibid. 3, 277 ("I weep"). Andrew Jackson Donelson to John Coffee, Feb. 19, 1825, quoted in Remini, *Andrew Jackson* 195; Andrew Jackson to John Overton, Feb. 10, 1825, ibid. 96 ("sheep").
74. Jackson to Lewis, Feb. 14, 1825, *Correspondence* 3, 276; *Niles Weekly Register*, July 5, 1828 (Jackson's views; emphasis in original); Remini, *Andrew Jackson* 141 ("Jackson and Reform").
75. Ibid. 376 ("Let the cry"); Jackson to Sarah Jackson, May 6, 1832, ibid. 364 ("redeeming spirit"). The secular use of "redeem" and "redemption" was well established by 1765: in Blackstone's *Commentaries* (1765) 2, 159, a mortgagor can "redeem" his estate by paying principal, interest, and expenses; if he is fraudulent, he loses "the equity of redemption." Savings banks were established by 57 George III, c. 105, schedule A (1817). "Save" in the secular sense of accumulating money was several centuries older.
76. Rachel Jackson to John Donelson, quoted in Remini, *Andrew Jackson* 7−8, 119−120.
77. Claude G. Bowers, *The Party Battles of the Jackson Period* (Boston: Houghton-Mifflin, 1912) 32 ("Clay's fight"); Remini, *Andrew Jackson* 143−150 (effect on Rachel).
78. Preston King, Speech, Dec. 7, 1852, *Congressional Globe*, 32nd Cong., 2nd Sess., 26, 23.
79. Millard Fillmore, "Third Annual Message to Congress," Dec. 6, 1852, *Zachary Taylor— Millard Fillmore: Chronology, Documents, Bibliographical Aids*, ed. John J. Farrell (Dobbs Ferry, N.Y.: Oceana Publications, 1971) 104.
80. Preston King, Speech, Jan. 6, 1853, *Congressional Globe* 26, 242−243 (bill reported); *New York Revised Statutes* (1846) 2, 761. On Haven's career, *Biographical Dictionary of the American Congress*, compiled by James L. Harrison (Washington: Government Printing Office, 1950) 1283; on Haven's partnership with Fillmore, *Zachary Taylor—Millard Fillmore* 50; *Congressional Globe* 26, 242 (amendment).
81. Ibid. 249 (Congressman Stanton of Ohio on congressional practice); 289−290 (Stephens of Georgia on well-known examples); 291 (Stevens); 295 (King); 301 (the vote).
82. Ibid. 365 (Jan. 21, 1853) (the bill); 392 (Jan. 29, 1853) (amended bill). On Badger's career, *Biographical Dictionary of the American Congress* 801;
83. *Congressional Globe* 26, 392 (Hale speech); 10 *U.S. Statutes at Large* 170−171 (1853).
84. *Congressional Globe*, 37th Cong., 2nd Sess., 2774 (bill introduced); 2958−2959 (Judiciary Committee amendments and discussion); 3061 (report on Simmons).
85. Ibid. 3260−3261, 3378.
86. Ibid. 3320 (report of Judiciary Committee); *Biographical Dictionary of the American Congress* 1813−1814 (Simmons's resignation); S. Rep. 169 37th Cong., 2nd Sess.; 1 *Statutes* 577 (statute).
87. Henry Adams, *The Great Secession Winter of 1860−1861*, ed. George Hochfield (New York: Sagamore Press, 1958) 19, 27.
88. Gideon Welles, "Diary," *Atlantic Monthly* (1909) 103, 369 (Lincoln's vow); J. G. Randall, *Lincoln the President* (New York: Dodd, Mead, 1953) 2, 154−155 (Lincoln's earlier broaching of subject); Abraham Lincoln, Fourth Annual Message to Congress, Dec. 6, 1864, *Collected Works*, ed. Roy P. Basler (New Brunswick, N.J.: Rutgers University Press 1953) 8, 149−150 (Lincoln's commitment).
89. *Congressional Globe* 38th Cong., 1st Sess., 2995; James F. Rhodes, *History of the United States* 5, 50 (composition of House).
90. Lincoln, *Collected Works* 8, 149.
91. John B. Alley in *Reminiscences of Abraham Lincoln*, collected and edited by Allen Thorndike Rice (New York: North American Review, 1888) 575 ("among the greatest"); 585−586 (activity for Amendment). Emphasis in original.
92. Albert Gallatin Riddle, *Recollections of War Times* (New York: G. P. Putnam's Sons, 1892) 324−325.
93. John G. Nicolay and John Hay, *Abraham Lincoln: A History* (New York: Century Company, 1890) 10, 84−85.
94. Rhodes, *History of the United States* 5, 50; Julian quoted in James Garfield Randall and

Richard N. Current, *Lincoln the President* 4, 310; Stevens quoted in James M. Scovel, "Thaddeus Stevens," *Lippincott's Monthly Magazine* 61, 550 (1898).

95. See Harry J. Carman and Reinhard H. Luthin, *Lincoln and the Patronage* (New York: Columbia University Press, 1943) 227, 331–333.

96. Abraham Lincoln, Second Inaugural Address, *Collected Works* 8, 333. On the theology, William J. Wolf, *The Religion of Abraham Lincoln* (New York: Seabury Press, 1963) 186.

97. Carl Sandburg, *Abraham Lincoln* (New York: Harcourt, Brace, 1939) 4, 361.

CHAPTER 16: CREDIT MOBILIER (PP. 460–500)

1. Ames to McComb letters, published in Select Committee to Investigate the Alleged Credit Mobilier Bribery, *Report No. 77*, House of Representatives, 42nd Cong., 3rd Sess., Feb. 18, 1873 [hereafter Poland Committee] 4–7.

2. On Ames, see Charles Edgar Ames, *Pioneering the Union Pacific: A Reappraisal of the Builders of the Railroad* (New York: Appleton-Century-Croft, 1969) 66–96; Allen Nevins, "Oakes Ames," *DAB* 7, 251.

3. Public Law, July 1, 1862, *Statutes at Large* 12, 489–498, as amended by Public Law, July 2, 1864, *Statutes at Large* 13, 356–365.

4. Robert W. Fogel, *Union Pacific: A Study in Premature Enterprise* (Baltimore: Johns Hopkins University Press, 1964) 57 (funds needed); 86 (effect of easy pass).

5. The easy pass was discovered before the Ames crowd took over, ibid. 117–119.

6. A French Crédit Mobilier had been founded in 1852 by Emile and Isaac Péreire to do a general banking business. As its name implied, it was authorized to deal in personal property. It built the Paris Gas Works and then engaged in railroad construction. Later destined to collapse in scandal, it was still highly successful in 1864. George Francis Train, a public relations man associated with Durant, suggested using its name for the American company. In the view of at least one New England family of C.M. stockholders this was "a woeful mistake," creating a sinister foreign impression of the company, Rowland Hazard, *The Credit Mobilier of America* (Providence, 1881) 15–17.

7. J. B. Crawford, *The Credit Mobilier of America* (Boston, 1880, reprinted Greenwood Press, 1969). Despite its author's avowed impartiality, this book is essentially a brief for Oakes Ames.

8. Peter Dey to Grenville M. Dodge, Dec. 8, 1864, quoted in Stanley P. Hirshon, *Grenville M. Dodge, Soldier—Politician—Railroad Pioneer* (Bloomington: Indiana University Press, 1967) 109; cf. Select Committee of the United States Senate, *Affairs of the Union Pacific Railroad Company*, *Sen. Report No. 78*, 42nd Cong., 3rd Sess., Feb. 20, 1873 [hereafter Wilson Committee], 668–669 (Dey testimony, 2/11/73).

9. Hirshon, *Grenville Dodge* 34 (Herbert M. "Hub" Hoxie); 109 (Hoxie's payoff).

10. Fogel, *Union Pacific* 65, 71.

11. Wilson Committee 26, 29 (Oakes Ames's testimony, 1/14/73); XV (23 million profit); Fogel, *Union Pacific* 69 (disgraceful bookkeeping); 70–71 (range of possible profit); 72 (yield of government bonds); 73 (average capital of C.M.). A member of the family of one important stockholder estimated the profit at $15,000,000, a figure almost in the center of Fogel's estimate. Hazard, *The Credit Mobilier of America* 28.

12. *Wardell v. Railroad Company* 103 U.S. 651 (1880), affirming *Wardell v. Union Pacific R. Co.*, *Federal Cases* 29, 17164 (Cir. Ct. Neb. 1877). Justice Field found that the contract authorized by the Ames-run executive committee of the U.P. was an "utterly indefensible" fraud on both the company and on the government, ibid. at 657, 659.

13. Poland Committee 12 (McComb testimony 12/13/72); 23 (Ames testimony 12/17/72).

14. The *Sun*'s text is republished in part in Ames. *Pioneering the Union Pacific* 436.

15. James A. Garfield, *Diary*, ed. Harry James Brown and Frederick D. Williams (Lansing: Michigan State University Press, 1967) 2, 88 (Sept. 9, 1872); 2, 93 (Sept. 19, 1872).

16. Black to Garfield, Sept. 29, 1872, in ibid. 2, 89.

17. Poland Committee 46 (Ames testimony 12/17/72 as to reliance on Black); Oakes Ames to H. S. McComb, Sept. 17, 1867, quoted in Ames, *Pioneering the Union Pacific* 186 (Black as "channel" to Johnson).

18. William Stewart, Speech, April 5, 1869, *Congressional Globe*, 41st Cong. 1st Sess., p. 503, citing Fisk's complaint in his suit against the Union Pacific; Senator James Nye, Speech, April 6, 1869, ibid. 549.

19. Stewart, Speech, April 6, 1869, ibid. 534 ("a little curiosity"); 16 *U.S. Statutes* 57 (1869) (attorney general to investigate U.P.).

20. Garfield, *Diary* 2, 120 (Nov. 30, 1872; Dec. 1, 1872); Black Papers, Nov. 7, 1872, quoted in

William Norwood Brigance, *Jeremiah Sullivan Black: A Defender of the Constitution and the Ten Commandments* (Philadelphia: University of Pennsylvania Press, 1934) 215.

21. Garfield, *Diary* 2, 121; Poland Committee 1 (resolution).
22. Ibid. 1 (Blaine testimony 12/12/72).
23. Ibid. 186–189 (Wilson testimony 1/16/73).
24. Ibid. 188.
25. George H. Haynes, "Henry Wilson," *DAB* 20, 323–324.
26. Poland Committee 461 (Ames testimony 2/11/73).
27. Ibid. 185 (Patterson testimony 2/16/73).
28. Ibid. 457–458 (Ames testimony 2/11/73); 337 (Patterson receipt); 352 (Ames testimony 1/29/73).
29. James W. Patterson, "Observations on the Report," March 26, 1873, printed as an attachment to *Senate Report No. 519*, 42nd Cong., 3rd Sess., Feb. 26, 1873, XXIII–XXIV, XXXI.
30. Ibid. VIII.
31. William A. Robinson, "James Willis Patterson," *DAB* 14, 303.
32. Poland Committee 81 (Colfax testimony 1/6/73).
33. Ibid. 451–453 (Ames testimony 2/11/73); 288 (Ames testimony 1/22/73); 309 (Sergeant-at-Arms N. G. Ordway testimony 1/22/73); 484 (Colfax testimony 2/11/73).
34. Ibid. 484–485 (Colfax testimony 2/11/73).
35. Ibid. 485 (Colfax testimony 2/11/73); 493 (George Matthews testimony 2/11/73); 496 (Caroline Hollister testimony 2/11/73).
36. Ibid. 488, 507, 507–508 (Colfax testimony 2/11/73 and 2/19/73).
37. Ibid. 513–514 (Ames's cross-examination of Colfax 2/19/73).
38. James Ford Rhodes, *The History of the United States from the Compromise of 1850 to the Final Restoration of Home Rule in the South in 1877* (New York: Macmillan, 1918) 7, 15; William MacDonald, "Schuyler Colfax," *DAB* 4, 297; *Frank Leslie's Illustrated Magazine*; Feb. 15, 1873, 362, "The Pious Vice-Presidents"; ibid. March 8, 1873, 420 (the Colfax cartoon).
39. Garfield, *Diary* 2, 138 (Jan. 14, 1873).
40. Poland Committee 129 (Garfield testimony 1/14/73).
41. Ibid. 296–297 (Ames testimony 1/22/73); 354–356 (Ames testimony 1/29/73).
42. Garfield, *Diary* 2, 142–143 (Jan. 22, 1873).
43. Poland Committee 358 (Ames testimony 1/29/73).
44. Calvin C. Chaffee to Henry L. Dawes, March 9, 1881, quoted in Margaret Leech and Harry J. Brown, *The Garfield Orbit* (New York: Harper & Row, 1978) 176.
45. Garfield, *Diary* 2, 150 (Feb. 9, 1873, on Black's reassurance); Jeremiah S. Black to James G. Blaine, Feb. 15, 1873, quoted in ibid. 2, 90, n. 249.
46. Black to the editor of the New York *Sun*, Sept. 28, 1880, quoted in Leech and Brown, *The Garfield Orbit* 177; Allan Peskin, *Garfield* (Kent, Ohio: Kent State University Press, 1978) 515 (Hay's comment).
47. Poland Committee VII, IX (on Garfield–Ames relations); *Congressional Globe* 1835, Feb. 27, 1873 (motion to condemn Hooper, Dawes, Kelley, Garfield, Scofield, and Bingham ruled out of order); ibid. 1842, Feb. 27, 1873 (Garfield opposes further inquiry); Garfield, *Diary* 2, 156, Feb. 27, 1873 (would not leave House).
48. Brown and Williams, Introduction to Garfield, *Diary* 1, XVII–LII (synopsis of life).
49. Garfield, *Diary* 1, 285 (Sept. 28, 1857: *Imitation of Christ*); ibid. 2, 156 (Feb. 27, 1873: "attempt to censure").
There were two episodes in Garfield's sexual life that foreshadowed or paralleled the political affair. In 1855, after a long and fitful courtship he became engaged to Lucretia Randolph. A little later he met Rebecca Selleck and began a romance. Was it sexually consummated? Rebecca implied that it was; Garfield gave no indication that he remembered it that way after he married Lucretia (Leech and Brown, *The Garfield Orbit* 71–72, quoting Rebecca). Sometime later, he met a New York newspaperwoman, Lucia Calhoun, who according to Lucretia felt for him "the fire" of "lawless passion" (Lucretia Garfield to James Garfield, quoted in ibid. 195). Was adultery committed? According to Garfield writing Lucretia, he had here "come closest" to wronging Lucretia (James Garfield to Lucretia Garfield, July 6, 1867, quoted in ibid. 194). He judged it wise to retrieve and destroy his correspondence. Rebecca and Lucia may be compared to Oakes Ames: they thought they had their man. Garfield was vaguer about the transactions.
50. Garfield, *Diary* 2, 138 (Jan. 14, 1873: "I confess"); ibid. 2, 169, April 23, 1873: a "woe"; ibid. 2, 270 (Dec. 31, 1873: "the stormiest year").
51. Ibid. 2, 169, April 12, 1873 (counsel of Black); ibid. 2, 180, May 15, 1873 (pamphlet defense); *Congressional Globe* 1833 (Feb. 27, 1873) (Garfield abstention).

52. Rhodes, *History of the United States* 7, 68.

53. Garfield, *Diary* 2, 351, Aug. 3, 1874. The other two issues raised against Garfield are also relevant to our investigation. One was a scandal rumored rather than fully known, the other showed that corruption as such could be a less effective popular charge than an accusation of sheer greed.

The rumored scandal related to Garfield's services in 1872 in "The Chicago Pavement Case." The District of Columbia was engaged in a program of paving the city, getting Washington, so to speak, out of the mud. Alexander R. Shepherd, otherwise known as "Boss," was the dominant figure on the District's Board of Public Works. The lion's share of the District's income depended on congressional appropriations. The De Goyler-McClelland Company of Chicago was the holder of a patent on an "ironized," though wooden, paving block. It sought to participate in Boss Shepherd's program, for that purpose using a Chicagoan, George Crittenden. Crittenden secured the services of an ex-Congressman from Cleveland, the current marshal of the Supreme Court, Richard Parsons. Parsons, hired with a contingent fee, in turn engaged Garfield. De Goyler won a contract for about $750,000 worth of paving blocks. Parsons was paid $15,000 and gave $5,000 of this amount to Garfield. (Leech and Brown, *The Garfield Orbit* 178–180; Peskin, *Garfield* 377–381).

Before the 1874 elections only the bare outline of the story was known—that Garfield, chairman of the House Appropriations Committee, had obtained a big contract with the District for a Chicago firm. The size of his fee was known. It looked enormous. Congressmen were paid $5,000 a year. General Sherman, commanding general of the Army, was paid $4,900. Regional commanders, the heroes of the late war, were paid under $2,500. General Garfield, a lawyer of remarkably little experience—none of it, so far as known, in municipal improvements—seemed to have doubled his salary almost at will.

In 1877 a Democratic-controlled House, looking into District of Columbia affairs, turned up Crittenden's memo to the company: "The influence of General Garfield has been secured. . . . He holds the purse strings of the United States, is chairman of the Committee on Appropriations, and the strongest man in Congress and with our friends. . . . It is a rare success and very gratifying, as all the appropriations for the District must come through him." On the basis of this evidence, the Washington *Post*, then a brandnew Democratic paper, could wonder editorially if the Republicans of Ohio knew the kind of man they were voting for. In the 1880 presidential election, the Pavement Case was an issue. Only with the publication of Garfield's diary, however, was the evidence against him complete. Crittenden's boastful memo was dated May 30, 1872. On June 2, a Sunday, Garfield recorded: "In the afternoon drove out to A. R. Shepherd's five and a half miles in the country." Congress adjourned on June 10. On June 13, Garfield noted that he had been "working up the DeGoyler Patent Pavement and laying its claims before the Board of Public Works," and he was still working on the matter on June 17 and 18. On the 19th he recorded: "At 6 o'clock called on A. R. Shepherd and substantially concluded arrangements for Chicago plans." At 7:45 he left for Ohio. Garfield was indignant that his services should have become a political issue: "It is time that we ascertain whether a member of Congress has any rights." The editors of his diary, surveying his three or four days' work and his $5,000 fee, conclude that his employment "resulted rather from his commanding position in Congress than from his legal ability." (George Crittenden, Memorandum, May 30, 1872, quoted in Peskin, *Garfield*, 380; Washington *Post*, March 15, 1878, quoted in Leech and Brown, *The Garfield Orbit* 181. Garfield, *Diary* 2, 60, June 2, 1872 (visit to Shepherd); ibid. 2, 62, June 10, 1873; ibid. 2, 67, June 19, 1873; ibid. 2, 312, April 15, 1874 (rights of a member of Congress); Brown and Williams, note to *Diary* 2, 63–64, n. 198.)

The other issue that bothered Garfield in the 1874 election was his vote for what was derisively called "the Salary Grab," a 50 percent increase in congressional salaries, retroactive to 1871. The increase, which could have been rationally defended as a prophylactic against corruption if it had not been retroactive, Garfield found to excite more immediate public disgust than either the Credit Mobilier or the paving contract (Garfield, *Diary* 2, 355, Aug. 11, 1874).

54. Ibid. 2, 378, Oct. 15, 1874 (on bolters); Rhodes, *History of the United States* 7, 17–18 (Garfield's "vindication").

55. *Puck*, Aug. 25, 1880, reproduced Leech and Brown, opposite 200; Peskin, *Garfield* 492.

56. Ibid. 600.

57. *Frank Leslie's Illustrated Magazine* Feb. 1, 1873, 336 (the cake); ibid. March 1, 1873, 400 (the rogue elephant).

58. Alley, Poland Report 77 (Alley testimony, 12/19/74); Allison, 304 (Allison testimony 1/22/73); Ames, 19 (Ames testimony 12/12/72); Bingham 191 (Bingham testimony 1/16/73); Boyer 207 (Boyer testimony 1/18/73); Colfax 452 (Ames testimony 2/11/73); Dawes 112 (Dawes

testimony 1/13/73); Garfield 295 (Ames testimony 1/22/73); Grimes 19 (Ames testimony 12/17/72); Hooper 19 (Ames testimony 12/17/72); Kelley 199 (Kelley testimony 1/16/73); Logan 346 (Logan testimony 1/28/73); Patterson 457–458 (Ames testimony 2/11/73); Scofield 204–205 (Scofield testimony 1/16/73); H. Wilson 461 (Ames testimony 2/11/73); J. Wilson 212 (Wilson testimony 1/18/73).

59. *Senate Report No. 519*, 43rd Cong., 3rd Sess. (1873) II and 61 (Harlan); Union Pacific R.R. Co., *The Union Pacific Railroad Company: Its Construction, Resources, Earnings and Profits* (New York, 1867) 1 (Morgan).

60. John D. Perry to Thaddeus Stevens, June 24, 1868, set out in Fawn Brodie, *Thaddeus Stevens* (New York: W. W. Norton, 1955) 183; Dodge to Anne Dodge, March 5, 1867, quoted in Hirshson, *Grenville Dodge* 149; ibid. 191 (her stock).

61. Robert Speer (Democrat of Pennsylvania), Speech 2/27/73, *Congressional Globe*, Appendix 142 (golden eggs); Charles Eldredge (Democrat of Vermont), Speech, 2/26/73, ibid., Appendix 191 (baby act); William Niblack (Democrat of Indiana), Speech, 2/26/73, ibid. 1823 (breaking down report); Job Stevenson (Republican lame duck from Ohio), Speech, 2/26/73, ibid. 1819 (leviathans in a little tub).

62. Poland Committee 245–258 (Brooks testimony 1/21/73); 415 (Neilson testimony 1/31/73); XII (committee disbelief of story).

63. Ibid. 231 (Dillon testimony 1/20/73); 343 (Benjamin Ham testimony 1/28/73); XII–XIII (committee conclusions).

64. Ibid. XIV; William M. Merrick (Democrat, lame duck, of Maryland), Speech, 2/25/73, *Congressional Globe* 1727.

65. James Blair (*Republican of Missouri*), Speech, 2/25/73, *Congressional Globe* 1735 (no jurisdiction); Seth Wakeman Speech, 2/25/73, ibid. 1734 (no intent to bribe); Daniel Vorhees (Democrat, lame duck, of Indiana), Speech, 2/26/73, ibid., Appendix 154–157.

66. *Congressional Globe* 1832, vote to substitute, 2/27/73; ibid. 1833, vote to condemn, 2/27/73.

67. Vorhees, Speech, 2/26/73, ibid., Appendix 156; George Templeton Strong, *Diary*, ed. Allan Nevins and Milton Halsey Thomas (New York: Macmillan, 1952) 4, 478 (May 2, 1873); Allan Nevins, "James Brooks," *DAB* 3, 77–78.

68. Wilson Committee 297–299 (Oliver Ames testimony 1/25/73).

69. Ibid. 175–176 (Stewart testimony 1/18/73).

70. Ibid. 301 (Oliver Ames testimony 1/25/73).

71. Ibid. 471 (Snyder testimony 2/1/73); 287 (Oliver Ames testimony 1/24/73).

72. Ibid. 296 (Oliver Ames testimony 1/25/73).

73. Ames, *Pioneering the Union Pacific* 326–327 (on the suit and the change in meeting place); Oliver Ames to Major General Grenville Mellen Dodge, May 2, 1869, in Dodge, *Autobiography* (MS, Iowa State Department of History and Archives, 1865–1871) 943 (New York as sink of corruption), quoted in Ames, *Pioneering the Union Pacific* 327.

74. Amos Akerman to George J. Boutwell, Dec. 15, 1870, in response to his letters of Oct. 7 and Nov. 23, 1870, *Official Opinions of the Attorneys General of the United States* (Washington: Government Printing Office, 1873) 13, 368.

75. Wilson Committee 529 (Bushnell testimony 2/3/73).

76. Ibid. 530.

77. *Congressional Globe* 1402, 2/17/71 (Army Appropriations Act passes House); *Senate Report No. 375*, 41st Cong., 3rd Sess, 2/24/71 (Boutwell wrong); *Congressional Globe* 1849, 3/1/71 (Act passes Senate with amendments); *Congressional Globe* 1916, 3/2/71 (Congressman James Beck reports on Senate insistence); the Army Appropriations Act of March 3, 1871, sec. 8, *Public Statutes* 16, 525 (completed legislation). The other House conferees besides Beck were O. J. Dickey of Pennsylvania and John A. Logan of Illinois; the Senate conferees were C. Cole of California, John M. Thayer of Nebraska, and Frank P. Blair of Missouri. It is interesting to note that Ben Butler had suggested to Oakes Ames that Senator Carpenter be employed as counsel for the Union Pacific at a fee of $10,000, Poland Committee 448 (Ames testimony 2/11/73).

78. Wilson Committee 530–533 (Bushnell testimony 2/3/73).

79. Select Committee, *Misc. Doc. No. 176*, 44th Cong., 1st Sess. 16 (Dodge testimony 5/13/76); Hirshson, *Grenville Dodge* 31–32 (Dodge as lobbyist); 192–193 (Dodge's evasion of process).

80. Wilson Committee 345–350, 526 (Spence testimony 1/28/73 and 2/3/73).

81. Ibid. 263 (Oliver Ames testimony 1/24/73).

82. Benjamin F. Butler, Speech, 2/26/73, *Congressional Globe*, Appendix 179–180.

83. Luke Poland, Speech, 2/25/73, *Congressional Globe* 1719 ("knew enough of Scripture";

"no sense he was doing an immoral act"); William Merrick, Speech, 2/25/73, ibid. 1728 ("in-veigling"; "Satanic skill").

84. Poland Committee IV, XVIII–XIX.

85. Washington Whitthorne (Democrat of Tennessee), Speech, 2/26/73, *Congressional Globe* 1822.

86. Seth Wakeman (Republican lame duck of Vermont), Speech, 2/25/73, *Congressional Globe* 1732 ("some little inkling"); Blair, Speech, 2/25/73, *Congressional Globe* 1735 (present to an individual not a crime).

87. Poland, Speech, 2/25/73, *Congressional Globe* 1719 ("It is the insidious attempt"); Joseph Hawley, Speech, 2/25/73, *Congressional Globe*, Appendix 174.

88. Poland Committee 273 (Ames statement as cross-examiner of Patterson 1/21/73).

89. Robert Speer of Pennsylvania, Speech 2/27/73, *Congressional Globe*, Appendix 142 ("mild and coy"); Poland Committee 20 (Ames testimony 11/17/72); ibid. 469–470 (Ames testimony 2/11/73); anonymous, *Oakes Ames: A Memoir with an Account of the Dedication of the Oakes Ames Memorial Hall at North Easton, Massachusetts* (Cambridge: Riverside Press, 1884) 16 ("solicited and urged").

90. Oakes Ames to Mrs. Oakes Angier Ames, Feb. 22, 1873, quoted in Ames, *Pioneering the Union Pacific* 476.

91. Oakes Ames to Evelina Gilmore Ames, Jan. 18, 1873, quoted in ibid. 475.

92. Garfield, *Diary* 2, 156 (Feb. 26, 1873).

93. Ibid. 2, 155 (Feb. 25, 1873: "more brilliant than solid"); Poland, Speech, 2/27/73, *Congressional Globe*, Appendix 197 ("a class of ingenious lawyers"); *Oakes Ames: A Memoir* 41 (Ames wept). On Butler, Carol R. Fisk, "Benjamin Franklin Butler," *DAB* 3, 357–359; George F. Hoar, *Autobiography of Seventy Years* (New York: Charles Scribner's Sons, 1903) 1, 312.

94. Poland, Speech, 2/27/73, *Congressional Globe*, Appendix 195 (never learned to play the buffoon); 198 ("Did he commit this crime?"); James Fairbanks Libby, "Luke Potter Poland," *DAB* 15, 33.

95. Seth Wakeman, Speech, 2/25/73, *Congressional Globe* 1732 (cry to crucify them); Abram Comingo, Speech, ibid. 1733 ("lasting shame"); Benjamin Butler, Speech, 2/26/73, ibid. Appendix 182 ("who stands in the image of God").

96. Job Stevenson, Speech, 2/26/73, *Congressional Globe* 1819 ("only the outcropping"); Washington Whitthorne, Speech, 2/26/73, ibid. 1821 ("purity"); John Bird (Democratic lame duck of New Jersey), Speech, 2/26/73, ibid. 1827 ("debasing"; "no other protection"); Poland, Speech, 2/27/73, ibid. Appendix 198 ("I quite agree"); ibid. 1833 (vote on Ames).

97. *Oakes Ames: A Memoir* 46 ("lacerated his heart"); 48 (death).

98. A photograph of the structure, designed by H. H. Richardson, appears in ibid. 55.

99. James G. Blaine to Oliver Ames, quoted in Ames, *Pioneering the Union Pacific* 543.

100. *Oakes Ames: A Memoir* 139 (resolution of Massachusetts legislature, April 13, 1883–May 7, 1883).

101. Ames, *Pioneering the Union Pacific* 516.

102. Garfield, *Diary* 3, 274–275 (April 18, 1876: Washington gossip); James G. Blaine, "Personal Explanation," *Congressional Record* 4³, 2724–2725 (April 24, 1876) (Blaine denials); Select Committee, "The Disposal of the Subsidies Granted Certain Railroad Companies," House of Representatives, *Miscellaneous Documents No. 176*, 44th Cong., 1st Sess., June 7, 1876 (as to 1873 rumors).

103. Ibid. 18–23 (Harrison testimony 5/15/76); 26–29 (Rollins testimony 5/16/76).

104. Ibid. 45–50 (Scott testimony 5/15/76).

105. Ibid. 93–97 (Mulligan testimony 5/31/76).

106. Ibid. 98–101 (Mulligan testimony 6/1/76); 105–109 (Blaine testimony 6/1/76).

107. Ibid. 109–110 (Blaine testimony 6/2/76).

108. Ibid. 106 (Blaine testimony 6/1/76); Garfield, *Diary* 3, 300 (June 1, 1876); 3, 301 (June 2, 1876); 3, 302 (June 4, 1876).

109. Blaine, "Personal Explanation," *Congressional Record* 4⁴, 3604–3607 (June 5, 1876); Garfield, *Diary* 3, 302 (June 5, 1876: Blaine's triumph); 3, 304 (June 8, 1876: passages being criticized).

110. Blaine to Warren Fisher, Jr., Oct. 4, 1869, *Congressional Record*, 4⁴, 3606 (June 5, 1876); Blaine to Fisher, June 29, 1869, ibid. 4⁴, 3606.

111. Cf. Blaine, "Personal Explanation," April 24, 1876, *Congressional Record* 4³, 2725, and Blaine, "Personal Explanation," June 5, 1876, ibid. 4⁴, 3608–3609, including a contract between Blaine and Fisher, September 5, 1869, for the bond sales commission. The unusually high commission is analyzed in Rhodes, *History of the United States* 7, 195–196.

112. Blaine to Fisher, April 18, 1872, *Congressional Record* 4⁴, 3605–3606.

113. Mulligan, Memorandum, undated, but made about May 1876, summarizing the Blaine–Fisher letters; taken from Mulligan by Blaine and submitted by Blaine to the House, June 5, 1876, ibid. 4⁴, 3607.

114. Blaine to Fisher, April 13, 1872, ibid. 4⁴, 3607, followed by Blaine's "Personal Explanation."

115. Garfield, *Diary* 3, 305–306 (June 11, 1876).

116. Hoar, *Autobiography* 1, 379; Rhodes, *History of the United States* 7, 207–210.

117. Roscoe Conkling, quoted in Matthew Josephson, *The Politicos* (New York: Harcourt, Brace, 1938) 246–247. On Hay as a Stalwart, Clover Adams to her father, *The Letters of Mrs. Henry Adams*, ed. Ward Thoron (Boston: Little, Brown, 1937) 339.

118. Hoar, *Autobiography* 1, 279, 313 (the lesson).

119. Ibid. 1, 278 (appointed by Blaine); 1, 32 (key role); Wilson Committee (Harrison testimony 5/15/76).

120. Carl Schurz, "Why James G. Blaine Should Not Be Elected President," Speech at Brooklyn, Aug. 3, 1884, Schurz, *Speeches, Correspondence and Political Papers*, ed. Frederick Bancroft (New York: G.P. Putnam's Sons, 1913) 3, 225 ("But this time . . ."); 3, 228 ("by far the most powerful"); 3, 236 ("It means . . ."); 3, 243 ("And this is the man"). Italics in original.

121. Svend Peterson, *A Statistical Study of the American Presidential Elections* (New York: Frederick Ungar, 1963) 51 (the vote analyzed); cf. Hoar, *Autobiography* 1, 408 (the causes).

122. Sohier and Welch to Schurz, Sept. 1889, quoted in David S. Muzzey, *James G. Blaine: A Political Idol of Other Days* (New York: Dodd, Mead & Co., 1934) 301–302.

123. Blaine to Fisher, April 16, 1876, reproduced in ibid. 303.

124. Ibid. 304.

CHAPTER 17: THE CITIZEN CENSORS (PP. 501–563)

1. Mark Twain [Samuel Clemens] and Charles Dudley Warner, *The Gilded Age: A Tale of Today* (Hartford, Conn.: American Publishing Company, 1877) 122 ("the great railroad contractor"); 292 ("greasy knave of spades").

2. Ibid. 140–141.

3. Ibid. 142–143.

4. Ibid. 254–261. Italics in original.

5. Ibid. 328.

6. Ibid. 379.

7. Ibid. 466–468.

8. Ibid. 469.

9. Ibid. 386–387.

10. Ibid. 393.

11. Ibid. 519.

12. Ibid. 535, 540–542.

13. Mark Twain, *Notebook and Journals*, ed. Frederick Anderson, Michael B. Frank, and Kenneth M. Sanderson (Berkeley: University of California Press, 1973) 1, 455–456 (Clemens's work for Stewart); 493–494 (notes on congressmen).

14. Ibid. 518; Samuel Clemens to Elisha Bliss, March 4, 1873, *Mark Twain's Letters to His Publishers 1867–1894*, ed. Hamlin Hill (Berkeley: University of California Press, 1967) 75.

15. Twain and Warner, *The Gilded Age* 487. On Pomeroy, see Justin Kaplan, *Mr. Clemens and Mark Twain* (New York: Simon & Schuster, 1966) 166.

16. James A. Garfield, *Diary*, ed. Harry James Brown and Frederick D. Williams (Lansing: Michigan State University Press, 1967) 2, 412 (Dec. 30, 1879).

17. Henry Adams to Henry Cabot Lodge, June 7, 1876, *Letters of Henry Adams*, ed. J. C. Levenson, Ernest Samuels, Charles Vandersee, and Viola Hopkins Winner (Cambridge, Mass.: Harvard University Press, 1982) 2, 273.

18. Adams to Charles Francis Adams, Jr., Feb. 13, 1861, ibid. 1, 231 (on Douglas); Adams to Charles Francis Adams, Jr., June 22, 1869, ibid. 2, 39 (on Garfield).

19. Marian (Clover) Hooper Adams to her father (Robert William Hooper), Jan. 9, 1881, *The Letters of Mrs. Henry Adams*, ed. Ward Thoron (Boston: Little, Brown, 1937) 252.

20. Clover Adams to her father, April 9, 1882, ibid. 372–373 ("ward politician" and "machine politicians"); Clover Adams to her father, Jan. 9, 1881, ibid. 252–253 (Fernando Wood; George Robeson, "a gross insult"); Clover Adams to her father, Jan. 31, 1882, ibid. 337–338 ("rat-Blaine" and "Blaine-rat": the hyphens appear both times in the original letter, now in the Massachusetts Historical Society, although not reproduced in "rat Blaine" in the

published version). Clover's father, a shrewd judge of his daughter, thought that she had written *Democracy;* she denied that "I" (thrice underlined) wrote it, Dec. 21, 1880, ibid. 247. It does not seem to me that her denial excludes co-authorship with Henry. When John Hay published *The Bread-Winner* anonymously in 1883, Henry's brother, Charles Francis, reviewed it in *The Nation* suggesting that it had been written by the same hand that wrote *Democracy:* "It has the same coarse, half-educated touch." E. L. Godkin, *The Nation's* editor, sent the review to Henry who commented to Hay, "Never, No, Never since Cain wrote his last newspaper letter about Abel was there anything so droll." He signed the letter "ever your poor, coarse, and half-educated friend Henry Adams" and added as a postscript, "My coarse and half-educated wife has had a fit over her brother-in-law's Nast-like touch," Adams to Hay, Feb. 2, 1884, Adams, *Letters* 2, 534. Is there not an implicit acknowledgment by Henry of Clover's part in the book in applying to her the same adjectives his brother had applied to the author?

As to the conventional image of women in America as the embodiment of purity, and the social forces contributing to this image, see Ronald T. Takaki, *Iron Cages* (New York: Alfred A. Knopf, 1979) 140–141, 171–172. On Samuel Hooper's stock, Charles Edgar Ames, *Pioneering the Union Pacific* (Indianapolis: Bobbs-Merrill, 1969) 203.

21.   Henry Adams, *Democracy* (Leipzig: Bernhard Tauchnitz, 1882) 12.

22.   Ibid. 52, 59–60.

23.   Ibid. 61–62 (Madeleine's question); 84 (Carrington's view).

24.   Ibid. 91 (the author on bargain and sale in February); 118 (the fears of Ratcliffe's friends).

25.   Ibid. 164–165.

26.   Ibid. 139 (Madeleine as judge); 156–158 (Gore and Madeleine).

27.   Ibid. 87 (Ratcliffe's wartime fraud); 241–242 ("In politics we cannot keep our hands clean.").

28.   Ibid. 255–258. This story is inspired by the report of the Ways and Means Committee published Feb. 27, 1875, on the actions of the Pacific Mail Company in 1872 in obtaining the passage of a bill giving it a federal subsidy for ten years of $500,000 a year. According to the committee report, the company, between February and May 1872, spent $890,000 in connection with the legislation. A portion of this sum was said to have been used to buy off competitors; a large amount was never traced beyond straws or agents in Washington, among them John G. Schumaker, a lawyer-lobbyist. He had received $275,000, of which $10,000 was his fee, and of the rest of which he gave "no satisfying account." Another recipient was William S. King, postmaster of the House, whose testimony the committee found contradicted by unbiased witnesses. The committee, stymied by silent or lying witnesses, found no evidence of "a reward" paid to any member of Congress, but referred the testimony to the district attorney for the District of Columbia, *House Report No. 268* "China Mail Service," 43rd. Cong., 2nd. Sess. (1875). Schumaker, a Democrat from Brooklyn, was an ex-congressman, who was elected again after the committee report, *Biographical Dictionary of the American Congress 1774–1961* (Washington: Government Printing Office, 1961) 1569. King, a Republican from Minnesota, was also elected to Congress after the committee report, ibid. 1168. Neither Schumaker nor King was prosecuted.

29.   Adams, *Democracy,* 258–259.

30.   Ibid. 271–276.

31.   Ibid. 276–277.

32.   Ibid. 177 (Madeleine's sister on Ratcliffe's search for a bribe); 281–282 (the bribe).

33.   Ibid. 272 ("the heart of politics"); 283 ("the impassable gulf"); 285 ("the polar star").

34.   Ibid. 274.

35.   It has been argued that Adams moves from *Democracy* to explore religion in his *Esther,* R. P. Blackmur, *Henry Adams* (New York: Harcourt, Brace, Jovanovich, 1980) 11–15. But *Esther* is not a very religious book and it seems to me that the church here functions as a metaphor for government.

36.   Henry Adams, *The Education of Henry Adams* (Boston: Houghton-Mifflin, 1927) 280. Compare Henry Adams to his niece (Mabel Hooper La Farge), Jan. 28, 1897 ("my master Job"), in Henry Adams, *Letters to a Niece and Prayer to the Virgin of Chartres,* ed. Mabel Hooper La Farge (Boston: Houghton-Mifflin, 1920) 96. The poem to the Virgin reflects, according to La Farge, her uncle's ultimate faith.

37.   References are to George Templeton Strong, *Diary,* ed. Allan Nevins and Milton Halsey Thomas (New York: Macmillan, 1952). For his biography and antecedents, "Introduction," ibid. 1, xii–xx.

38. Ibid. March 16, 1867 (the bill defeated); Feb. 8, 1870 (Cardozo rebuffed).

39. Leo Hershkowitz, *Tweed's New York: Another Look* (Garden City, N.Y.: Anchor Press—Doubleday, 1977) 47.

40. Ibid. 25 (the 1852 editorial); 104 (the rings running New York); 116 (Hoffman and the Tammany Ring; the Corporation Ring); 117 (the Ring of the Board); 119 (the famous Tammany Ring); 127—128 (the Lunch Club Ring; the City Hall Ring); 137 (Tweed elected Grand Sachem). According to Samuel J. Tilden, *The New York City "Ring," Its Origin, Maturity and Fall* (New York, 1873) 11, "a ring" also implies the notion of encircling men in both major parties.

41. Charles F. Adams, Jr. "Railroad Inflation," *North American Review* 222 (Jan., 1869) 147—148.

42. See Hershkowitz, *Tweed's New York* (Tweed's ancestry: in the heat of battle the New York *Times* accused him of being Irish; other critics called him a Jew); 107 (Hoffman's ancestry); 225 (Barnard's). Alexander B. Callow, Jr., *The Tweed Ring* (New York: Oxford University Press, 1966) 37 (Hall's ancestry); 136 (Barnard a Yale graduate).

43. Charles Francis Adams, Jr., "A Chapter of Erie," *North American Review*, July 1869, vol. 224, 30.

44. Callow, *Tweed Ring* 163—197. Hershkowitz argues that the contractors' testimony shows them guilty of fraud, but not Tweed (Hershkowitz, *Tweed's New York* 220—221, 240—241). He gives little weight to Tweed's own confession quoted or paraphrased at 321—329. In the end, his spirited effort to show Tweed's guilt to have been greatly exaggerated is not persuasive. There is no reason to discount the confession and such detail in it as, for example (at 323) the $2^1/_2$ percent per supervisor.

45. Ibid. 234 (Tweed's crime); Callow, *Tweed Ring* 176—179 (newspapers); 209 (voters); 214—221 (legislature). Tweed's sentence of 12 years, an aggregate of the sentences on each count of a multiple count indictment, was pronounced void, *People ex rel. Tweed v. Liscomb* 60 N.Y. 554 (1875). The court observed at 542 that "great wrongs had been perpetrated," so "the public mind was greatly excited."

46. Nevins and Thomas, Introduction, *Diary* 1, xxxvi (Strong's attitude). The reference is to Virgil, *Ecologae* 7, 4:

Arcades ambo
Et cantare pares et respondere parati
(Both Arcadians, equal and ready both to sing and to give answer)

47. Callow, *Tweed Ring* 254—261.

48. Walter Bean, *Boss Ruef's San Francisco* (Berkeley: University of California Press, 1967) 87, 90, and 197 (the fight promoters); 89—90 and 197 (P.G. & E.); 95, 139, and 197 (Parkside Realty); 141—142 and 197 (Bay Cities Water); 104 (Pacific Telephone); 117 and 137 (United Railroads).

49. Ibid. 239 (Glass); 226 (Schmitz); 286 (Ruef); 227—230 (choice of mayor by prosecutors). The "immunity contract" between the supervisors and the district attorney is printed in Franklin Hichborn, *"The System" as Uncovered by the San Francisco Graft Prosecution* (San Francisco: James Barry, 1915) xxi—xxii.

50. Bean, *Ruef's San Francisco* 44 (attack on Crothers); 56—57 (boycott and strike); 166—169 (Ruef's appointment as district attorney); 275 (the dynamiting); 283 (the attack on Heney and the suicide); 285 (death of police chief). Fremont Older, *My Own Story* (New York: Macmillan, 1926) 128—136 (his kidnapping).

51. Bean, *Ruef's San Francisco* 56 (Ruef's acknowledgment of Older as opponent); 71—76 (Older's recruitment of Burns, Heney, Spreckels); Older, *My Own Story* 109 (his wife's support). Between June 1906 and May 17, 1909, the prosecution spent at least $213,000, of which Spreckels supplied $138,000, Hichborn, *"The System"* xxxiv.

52. Quoted in Bean, *Ruef's San Francisco* 309.

53. *People v. Schmitz* 7 Cal. App. 330 (1908) at 369—375 (opinion of the California Supreme Court per curiam); see Hichborn, *"The System"* 327—334, quoting among others Dean John H. Wigmore on the "vicious habits of thought" the formal reasoning displayed. *People v. Glass* 158 Cal. 650 (1910) was decided 5—2, with Justice Frederick W. Henshaw writing the plurality opinion. Years later Henshaw was shown to have taken a bribe for his opinion in the famous Fair will case, and permitted quietly to resign, Bean, *Ruef's San Francisco* 308.

54. Ford was acquitted in two trials, and there was a hung jury in a third, ibid. 254—255; Calhoun's trial also ended in a hung jury and the indictment was ultimately dismissed, ibid. 288, 303.

55. Ibid. 293—298.

56. Older, *My Own Story* 177–178.
57. Bean, *Ruef's San Francisco* 312–314; Older, *My Own Story* vii (effect on him of Ruef's confession).
58. Ibid. 2 and 11.
59. Ibid. 10 (bid-rigging); 15 (Herrin the state boss); 26 (*Bulletin* circulation); 17, 27, 31 (subsidies); 34–35 (futile housecleaning at paper).
60. Bean, *Ruef's San Francisco* 49 (headline on the $9,035); Older, *My Own Story* 42 (his actual lack of knowledge); 69 (most vicious); 88 (overawing court); 97–99 (blackmailing of Ray and the scenario of the trap); 159–160 (the immunity agreement with Ruef); 169 (Lawlor statement); vi–vii ("I realized" and "evil fighting evil").
61. Lincoln Steffens, *The Autobiography of Lincoln Steffens* (New York: Harcourt, Brace, 1931) 133.
62. Ibid. 198.
63. Ibid. 248–249.
64. Lincoln Steffens, *The Shame of the Cities* (1904) 19–41 ("Tweed Days"); 42–68 (Minneapolis); 69–100 (St. Louis again); 101–133 (Pittsburgh); 134–161 ("corrupt and contented" Philadelphia); 190–192 (Chicago press and aldermen); 203 (Tammany).
65. Ibid. 2 ("The 'foreign element' excuse"); 103 ("We all do it"); 135 ("the most American").
66. Ibid. 20 ("The corruption of St. Louis"); 48 ("inevitable vices"); 103 (railroads corrupt Pittsburgh); 145–146 (big corporations in the state ring); 204–209 (New York).
67. Steffens, *Autobiography* 375.
68. Ibid. 521.
69. Ibid. 372 (Folk); 418–419 (Durham).
70. Steffens, *The Shame of the Cities* 69.
71. Steffens, *Autobiography* 372.
72. Ibid. 465 (Rhode Island); 495 (New Jersey). The *New York Times*, June 20, 1894, 1, denounced Aldrich as a "disgusting hypocrite," pretending to oppose the Sugar Trust but actually "owned" by it. It stated that in 1892 he had received through its chief lobbyist, John E. Searles, $1,500,000 to buy the stock of the Union Railway Company, the traction line in Providence, Rhode Island. Aldrich categorically denied the story, ibid. June 21, 1894. The *Times* did not have in its possession two contracts modern research has discovered, whereby, early in 1893, Searles and his associates agreed to finance Aldrich in buying the traction line that was to be the foundation of his fortune, see Jerome L. Sternstein, "The Problem of Corruption in the Gilded Age: The Case of Nelson W. Aldrich and the Sugar Trust," in Abraham S. Eisenstadt, Ari Hoogenboom, and Hans L. Trefousse, eds. *Before Watergate: Problems of Corruption in American Society* (Brooklyn: Brooklyn College Press, 1978) 156–157.
73. Steffens, *Autobiography* 595–596.
74. Ibid. 577–579; Roosevelt to Rudolph Spreckels, June 8, 1908, printed in Hichborn, "*The System*" xxvii.
75. Steffens, *Autobiography* 357. In John Bunyan, *The Pilgrim's Progress*, ed. Roger Sharrock (New York: Penguin Books, 1965) Part II, 247, Christiana encounters "a man that could look no way but downwards, with a muck-rake in his hand." He rakes "the straws, the small sticks and the dust of the floor," while ignoring a celestial crown which he cannot see for his concern with earthly things. "Then said Christiana, 'O! deliver me from this muck-rake.'"
The term "muck-raker" precedes Bunyan in Arthur Dent's *Plaine Mans Pathway to Heaven* (1622) 91, where "The gripple mucke-rakers had as leeve part with their bloud, as their goods," quoted in William York Tindall, *John Bunyan, Mechanick Preacher* (New York: Russell & Russell, 1964) 197.
76. Steffens, *Autobiography* 607.
77. Ibid. 524.
78. Ibid. 526.
79. Ibid. 619.
80. Ibid. 572–573.
81. Ibid. 799.
82. Ibid. 807 (Stalin and kulaks); 813 (Mussolini); 825 ("continuously radical").
83. Ibid. 829 ("maybe bribes and corruption"); 862 ("political business corruption").
84. Oliver Wendell Holmes, Jr., "The Path of the Law," *Harvard Law Review* 10 (1897) 457, 459.
85. See James Bryce, *The American Commonwealth* (London: Macmillan, 1889) 2, 110 ("sporadic disease"); 124–125, 132 (Congress); 128 (legislatures); 130–131 (elections); 457 ("ugliest

feature"); 500–501 (judges). Bryce distinguished four meanings in the term corruption: it designated (1) cash payments to officeholders; (2) payments in kind to officeholders; (3) jobbery in contracts; (4) patronage appointments. He himself saw no difference between (1) and (2) but acknowledged that they seemed different to some—5 percent of Congress would take cash, 20 percent more would take property, ibid. 122, 132. On Holmes's intimacy with Bryce, Holmes to Frederick Pollock, Jan 23, 1922, *Holmes–Pollock Letters*, ed. Mark De Wolfe Howe (Cambridge, Mass.: Harvard University Press, 1946) 2, 87.

86.   O. W. Holmes, Jr., "Law in Science and Science in Law," *Harvard Law Review* 12 (1899) 443 at 463, quoting George Herbert, "The Elixir," *The Works of George Herbert*, ed. F. E. Hutchinson (Oxford: Clarendon Press, 1941) 185. Holmes gave no citation, punctuated differently from Herbert, substituted "cause" for "laws" (a Freudian slip), and was obviously quoting from memory.

87.   Note, "Proposed Changes in the Bribery Laws," *Harvard Law Review* 8 (1895) 415; Case Note, "Illegal Contracts," ibid. 33 (1919) 611. "Recent Cases," *Yale Law Journal* 8 (1889) 248; 10 (1900) 223; 14 (1904) 236. "Recent Decisions," *Columbia Law Review* 3 (1903) 122; 4 (1904) 214; 13 (1913) 643. *Rocky Mountain Law Review* 13 (1940) 67; L. C. Southard, "Does Wealth Influence the Administration of Justice in Massachusetts?," *Maine Law Review* 3 (1909) 52.

88.   Hans Kelsen, *The Pure Theory of Law*, trans. Max Knight (Berkeley: University of California Press, 1967) 110–114.

89.   H. L. A. Hart, *The Concept of Law* (Oxford: Clarendon Press, 1961) 76–79.

90.   W. Michael Reisman, *Folded Lies: Bribery, Crusades and Reforms* (New York: Free Press, 1979) 22. Reisman found Hart "not particularly useful" (8) and Kelsen to have outlined a type of command system (130).

91.   John T. Noonan, Jr., *The Scholastic Analysis of Usury* 358–362.

92.   John T. Noonan, Jr., *Contraception: A History of Its Treatment by the Catholic Theologians and Canonists* (Cambridge, Mass.: Harvard University Press, 1965) 303–340.

93.   Alfonso de' Liguori, *Theologia moralis, Opera*, ed. Gaudé (Rome, 1905–1912), Bk. 4, "Particular Commandments Proper for Definite States of Men," n. 216.

94.   Augustinus Lehmkuhl, *Theologia moralis* (Freiburg im Breisgau, 1888) 1, n. 808–809; Adam Tanqueray, *Synopsis theologiae moralis et pastoralis ad mentem S. Thomae et S. Alphonsi hodiernis moribus accomodata*, 7th rev. ed. (Paris: Desclée, 1922) 3, n. 1005 (same teaching at n. 1005 in the 1906 edition); Benedict H. Merkelbach, *Summa theologiae moralis ad mentem D. Thomae et ad normam iuris novi* (Paris, 1935) 2, n. 636; Arthur Vermeersch, *Theologia moralis: Principia—responsa—consilia*, 3rd. rev. ed. (Rome: Gregorian University, 1937) 2, 480. In an earlier work, in 1901, directed to "current questions," Vermeersch condemned "corrupting" a doctor or magistrate to exempt one from the draft, but had nothing on judges, lawyers, or legislators, Vermeersch, *Quaestiones de iustitia ad usum hodiernum scholastice disputatae* (Rome: Beyaert, 1901).

95.   Francis P. Kenrick, *Theologiae moralis* (Philadelphia, 1841) 1, 399, "De legumlatoribus." In practice, three different attitudes toward corruption were taken by the Catholic clergy, well-illustrated in San Francisco at the time of the prosecutions of Ruef and Schmitz. Peter C. Yorke, a priest deeply committed to the labor movement, used the weekly paper he had founded, the *Leader*, to defend Ruef: for him the bribery charges were insignificant measured against the cause of the worker (see James P. Gaffey, *Citizen of No Mean City: Archbishop Patrick Riordan of San Francisco* [Consortium Book, 1976] 368–371). Thomas V. Moore, the Paulist chaplain at the Newman Club in Berkeley, held a very different view. When he saw that the pulpit of the Paulist church in San Francisco bore a name-plate of benefactors including the name of Eugene Schmitz, Moore removed the plate and threw it in San Francisco Bay, subsequently recounting his action to a reporter for the Sacramento *Bee* (ibid. 464). Patrick Riordan, archbishop of San Francisco, was embarrassed by both men. He issued a general directive to his clergy against mixing in "newspaper controversies of a political character," with Yorke as his specific target; and he demanded Moore's removal by the Paulist superior general, telling him that Moore's interference in local politics had become "a grave scandal" (ibid. 371, 464).

96.   Liguori, *Theologia moralis*, Bk. 4, n. 212.

97.   Lehmkuhl, *Theologia moralis* 2, n. 809; Vermeersch, *Theologiae moralis* 2, 378. For the comparison of the judge's duty of restitution to the prostitute's, Juan de Lugo, *De iustitia et iure* (Venice, 1737) Vol. 2, Dispute 37, n. 126. For a classic discussion of the prostitute's nonduty of restitution, Juan Medina, *De poenitentia, restitutione, et contractibus* (Ingolstadt, 1581) Vol. 2, "Codex de rebus restituendis," Q. 19 and 20, 125–237. Compare Blaise Pascal, *Les Provincials*, ed. Louis Cognet (Paris: Garnier Frères, 1965), "Eighth Letter," 134 (only favor

corrupt judges); 136 (presents for expediting case, defended by Luis Molina); 144–146 (no obligation to make restitution for unjust decision).

98.   John A. McHugh, "Graft and Its Morality," *Homilectic and Pastoral Review* 38 (1938) 241 ("so widespread"); 242 (untreated by moral treatises); McHugh, "Human Law and Opinion Against Graft," ibid. 38 (1938), 476–478 (intrinsically evil, unjustified by custom); McHugh, "Graft Against Commutative Justice and Sincerity," ibid. 38 (1938), 841 ("modern pagan ideas").

99.   Francis J. Connell, "Dishonesty and Graft," *American Ecclesiastical Review* 112 (1945) 1 at 2 ("sufficiently definite"); at 9–10 (confessor should interrogate; *Baltimore Catechism*); Connell, "Graft and Commutative Justice," ibid. 112 (1945) 161 at 162 ("a fine art"; "very meager"); at 170 (frequent sermons).

A review of a representative number of catechisms shows that one of the most influential, that compiled by the Dutch Jesuit Petrus Canisius in 1565, had no specific reference to bribery in treating of the Seventh Commandment, but did include a scriptural citation of Psalm 15 (Psalm 14 in the Vulgate) on taking *munera* against the innocent. Later, setting out the cardinal virtue of justice, Canisius quoted Augustine using John the Baptist's words to condemn as an extortioner any public official seeking something beyond his salary, Peter Canisius, *Summa doctrinae christinae* (Augsburg, 1833) 1, 368 (Seventh Commandment); 4, 393 (extortion). The *Roman Catechism*, issued in 1566 by a commission under the presidency of Carlo Borromeo, was both more limited and more emphatic. Under the Seventh Commandment it spoke of the sin of "venal judges," who, "bent by a price and *munera*, overthrow the best cases of the poor and needy," *Catechismus Romanus* (Rome: Propaganda Fide, 1907) 403. The rhetorical force of the denunciation of such judges left it open for the hardhearted to believe that only bribes taken to deliver unjust decisions were meant (the same implication could be read into Psalm 15). Nothing was said of other officials. The small catechism of Canisius and such English translations as *Certayne Necessaire Principles of Religion* (1578; Scolar Press reprint, 1971) or *A Summe of Christian Doctrine* (1592) had nothing specific on bribery; nor did Laurence Vaux, *A Catechisme or Christian Doctrine, Necessary for Children and Ignorant People* (1599; Scolar Press reprint, 1969). Roberto Bellarmino, S.J., *Catechism*, translated into English in 1619 as *A Shorte Catechisme* (Scolar Press reprint, 1973) and into Welsh in 1618 as *Eglurhad helaeath-lawn* had nothing on bribery under the Seventh Commandment.

A French catechism translated into English and printed in Boston in 1852 was fairly comprehensive, asking, "When are magistrates and public men guilty of what is equivalent to theft?" and answering, "When they sell justice or, contrary to law, receive gifts from those whose cases are before them." The catechism cited Exodus 23:8; Deuteronomy 16:18; and Isaiah 1:23, among other biblical authorities, and went on to ask, "What do you mean by extortion?," and answered, "He is guilty of extortion who exacts what is not his due, or more than his due." Luke 3:13 was cited, and the writer specified that "a magistrate, a secretary, an agent are guilty of it, when they neglect to relieve or to do justice, until the client or sufferer offers a bribe. . . ." Stephen Keenen, *Catechism of the Christian Religion being with small changes A Compendium of the Catechism of Montpellier* (Boston: Patrick Donahoe, 1852).

Several catechisms, prepared near the turn of the century—about the time Lincoln Steffens was making his sweeping charges—avoided mentioning bribery altogether, among them Thomas L. Kinkead, *An Explanation of the Baltimore Catechism for the Use of Sunday-School Teachers and Advanced Classes* (New York: Benziger Brothers, 1891); William Byrne (vicar-general of the archdiocese of Boston), *The Catholic Doctrine of Faith and of Morals* (Boston: Cushman, Keating, 1902); Abbé Luche, *The Catechism of Rodez, Explained in the Form of Sermons*, trans. John Thein (St. Louis: B. Herder, 1898); Thomas J. O'Brien, *An Advanced Catechism of Catholic Faith and Morals* (based on the Third Plenary Council Catechism) (Chicago: John Oink, 1902); Joseph de Harbe, S.J., *Catechism of Christian Doctrine* (New York: Fr. Pustet, 1902).

Abroad, catechisms were not specific either, for example, D. Chisholm, *The Catechism in Examples* (London and Glasgow: R. and T. Washbourne, 1908); the Maltese catechism, *Dutrina Jew Taghlim Nisrani* (Malta, 1911); and the catechism prepared by one of the most influential cardinals in the curia, Pietro Gasparri, *Catechismus Catholicus* (Vatican City: Vatican Press, 1930).

In the United States, the Dominicans Callan and McHugh (the latter being the author who was later to call for more attention to graft) said nothing beyond the Tridentine text on judges in their *Catechism of the Council of Trent for Parish Priests*, trans. with notes by John A. McHugh, O.P., and Charles J. Callan, O.P. (New York: Joseph F. Wagner, 1923) 446. The *Baltimore Catechism No. 2* (Buffalo, 1929), question 375, asked, "*What is forbidden by the seventh*

Commandment?," and answered merely, "The seventh Commandment forbids all unjust taking or keeping what belongs to another." The change was striking when in 1941 the *Baltimore Catechism* declared, "Besides stealing, the seventh commandment forbids cheating, unjust keeping of what belongs to others, unjust damage to the property of others, and the accepting of bribes by public officials," *Baltimore Catechism No. 2* (Paterson, N.J.: St. Anthony Guild Press, 1941), question 261, 51.

The American example was not generally followed, and catechisms reflecting Vatican II have nothing specific on bribery, for example, Australian Bishops' Education Committee, *Good News of the Kingdom: The Australian Catechism* (London: Geoffrey Chapman, 1966); Franco Pierini, S.S.P., *Catechism of Vatican II*, trans. from the Italian by Kevin Mullen et al. (Staten Island, N.Y.: Alba House, 1967); and the Bishops of the Netherlands, *New Catechism*, trans. from the Dutch by Kevin Smith (New York: Herder & Herder, 1967).

Simony as a subject did not fare much better. Thomas Kinkead's 1891 catechism explained that money given at mass was not to pay for the mass because "you could not buy any sacred thing without committing it.... To buy a holy thing for money is the sin of simony—so called after Simon, a magician, who tried to bribe the apostles to give him Confirmation when he was unworthy of it" (Kinkead, *An Explanation of the Baltimore Catechism* at q. 269). However peculiar a version of Acts 8, Kinkead's account did, remarkably, emphasize sin on the part of the payor. Most catechisms ignored simony. Peter Canisius and Vaux treated it in a very cursory way under the Seventh Commandment and Gasparri mentioned simoniacal contracts under the First Commandment.

The usual brevity of catechisms does not account for the omission of bribery. For example, references to "cheating" are common; the Byrne 1902 catechism details such offenses against the Seventh Commandment as employees not doing an honest day's work; the Dutch 1967 catechism deals with plagiarizing ideas; and the Montpellier-Boston 1852 catechism shows what could have been said by all. None of the catechisms specify bribetaking by a voter or a legislator, or bribegiving by anyone to a public official.

Representative Protestant and Anglican catechisms are similar to the Catholic, omitting the subject—for example, G. F. Maclean, *A Class Book of the Catechism of the Church of England* (London: Macmillan, 1868) 96, refers to the Eighth Commandment which "forbids, besides open robbery, all kinds of dishonesty ... in fact every species of fraud and extortion." Nothing more specific follows. For another example, G. H. Gerberding, *The Lutheran Catechist* (Philadelphia: Lutheran Publication Society, 1910) 225, under "Helpful Hints on the Five Parts of the Catechism," says, "Show how property, both real and personal, can be acquired, viz. by gift, by inheritance, and most generally by labor; that all other ways are wrong, e.g. cheating and taking advantage of another's ignorance or necessity...." Dealing in futures and stealing an employer's time are both specifically condemned but not bribery.

100.   Connell, "Graft and Commutative Justice" 169 (*contractus turpis*); Connell, "Catholics in the Police Force," *American Ecclesiastical Review* 111 (1944) 349 at 353.

101.   Connell, "Graft and Commutative Justice" 163 (good faith); 169 ("over-strict"; custom no defense); Connell, "Catholics in the Police Force" 355 (policeman's option to give bribe to charity); Connell, "Dishonesty and Graft" 9 (custom no defense); Connell, "The Catholic Lawyer," *American Ecclesiastical Review* 11 (1944) 274 (nothing on bribery); Connell, "Catholic Legislators," ibid. 10 (1944) 338 (nothing on bribery).

102.   James M. Gustafson, *Christian Ethics and the Community* (Philadelphia: United Church Press, 1971) 28 (fundamental interest in practical morality); 75–82 (examples); 76 (lack of consensus); James M. Gustafson, *Ethics from a Theological Perspective* (Chicago: University of Chicago Press, 1981) 1 (factors affecting Protestant moral theology).

103.   Charles Ernst Luthardt, *Apologetic Lectures on the Moral Truths of Christianity*, trans. Sophia Taylor (Edinburgh: T. and T. Clark, 1889); H. Martensen, *Christian Ethics*, trans. Sophia Taylor (Edinburgh: T. and T. Clark, 1897); Kenneth E. Kirk, *Conscience and Its Problems* (London: Longmans, Green, 1927); see also Kirk's *Some Principles of Moral Theology and Their Application* (London: Longmans, Green, 1920); Karl Barth, *Ethik I* and *Ethik II* (1928) trans. Geoffrey W. Bromiley as *Ethics* (New York: Seabury, 1981); Herbert Hensley Henson, *Christian Morality* (Oxford: Clarendon Press, 1936); Reinhold Niebuhr, *Moral Man in Immoral Society* (New York: Charles Scribner's Sons, 1932); Reinhold Niebuhr, *The Nature and Destiny of Man* (New York: Charles Scribner's Sons) vol. 1 (1941), vol. 2 (1943); Emil Brunner, *The Divine Imperative*, trans. Olive Wyon (Philadelphia: Westminster Press, 1947); Dietrich Bonhoeffer, *Ethics* (London: SCM Press, 1955); Paul Ramsey, *Basic Christian Ethics* (New York: Charles Scribner's Sons, 1953); Billy Graham, *The 7 Deadly Sins* (Grand Rapids, Mich.: Zondervan,

1955); William F. May, *A Catalogue of Sins: A Contemporary Examination of the Christian Conscience* (New York: Holt, Rinehart & Winston, 1967); Carl F. H. Henry, ed., *Baker's Dictionary of Christian Ethics* (Grand Rapids, Mich., 1973); Bernard Stoecke et al., eds., *Concise Dictionary of Christian Ethics* (New York: Seabury, 1979); Karl Barth, *Church Dogmatics: Index Volume with Aids for the Preacher* (Edinburgh: T. and T. Clark, 1977); Gustafson, *Ethics from a Theological Perspective* (1981).

104.   Sigmund Freud, *The Standard Edition of the Complete Psychological Works*, trans. James Strachey (London: The Hogarth Press, 1974), vol. 24, Index.

105.   Franz Alexander and Hugo Staub, *The Criminal, the Judge, and the Public*, trans. Gregory Zilboorg (New York: Macmillan, 1931) 49.

106.   Ibid. 12.

107.   Harold D. Lasswell, "Bribery," *Encyclopedia of Social Sciences* (New York: Macmillan, 1930) 2, 691–692.

108.   Arnold A. Rogow and Harold D. Lasswell, *Power, Corruption, and Rectitude* (Englewood Cliffs, N.J.: Prentice Hall, 1963) 45–54.

109.   Albert A. Ehrenzweig, *Psychoanalytic Jurisprudence* (Leiden: A. W. Sijthoff, 1971) 212 (oedipedal crimes); 219 (plea bargaining).

110.   James Frazier, *The Golden Bough: A Study in Magic and Religion*, 3rd ed. (New York: Macmillan, 1935) Vol. 12, General Index (no entries on "Bribes"); Marcel Mauss, "Essai sur le don," *L'année sociologique* (1925).

111.   Ruth Benedict, *The Chrysanthemum and the Sword: Patterns of Japanese Culture* (Boston: Houghton-Mifflin, 1946) 99, 116 (*on*); 116, 133, 143 (*giri*).

112.   Ibid. 183–188.

113.   Ibid. 199 ("true national epic"); 200 (story); 205 ("bribery").

114.   Georg Simmel, *The Philosophy of Money*, trans. Tom Bottomore and David Frisby (London: Routledge & Kegan Paul, 1978) 384 ("purchase of a person"); 385 ("self-negation," silence); 388 (examples); see also Karl Joël on Simmel, quoted in Introduction, 8 (the datedness of Simmel's work).

115.   Robert K. Merton, *Social Theory and Social Structure* (New York: Free Press, 1957) 72–82 (the Boss); ibid. 76, 81. For a variant on the functional approach, viewing corruption as "a product of modernization," see Samuel P. Huntington, *Political Order in Changing Societies* (New Haven, Conn.: Yale University Press, 1968) 70–72.

116.   Colin Leys, "What Is the Problem About Corruption?," *Journal of Modern African Studies* 3 (1965) 218–223.

117.   James Q. Wilson, "Corruption Is Not Always Scandalous," *New York Times Magazine*, April 28, 1968, as reprinted in John A. Gardiner and David J. Olson, eds., *Theft of the City: Readings on Corruption in Urban America* (Bloomington: Indiana University Press, 1974) 29–32. Cf. William L. Riordan, *Plunkitt of Tammany Hall*, containing an interview in 1902 with George Washington Plunkitt, reprinted in Gardiner and Olson, *Theft of the City* 8.

118.   Ibid. 32–33.

119.   Ibid. 33–34.

120.   James C. Scott, *Comparative Political Corruption* (Englewood Cliffs, N.J.: Prentice-Hall, 1972) 57–68 (Thailand); 75 (English analogy); 80–84 (Indonesia); 85–89 (Haiti); 108 (American analogy).

121.   Ibid. ix ("aggregate data" lacking); 10–14 (causes).

122.   Ibid. viii ("Far from being pathological"); 114 (quotation from Myron Weiner, *Party Building in a New Nation: The Indian National Congress*, 1967); 146 ("Much of the corruption").

123.   Susan Rose-Ackerman, *Corruption: A Study in Political Economy* (New York: Academic Press, 1978) 216 ("If one wishes"); 218 ("personal honesty"). For an economic approach, W. H. Leff, "Economic Development Through Bureaucratic Corruption," *American Behavioral Scientist* (Nov. 1964) 8, 13; J. S. Nye, "Corruption and Political Development: A Cost-Benefit Analysis," *American Political Science Review* (1967) 61, 417.

124.   For Lebvre, Chapter 10 above at n. 125; Hershkowitz, n. 39 above; Eisenstadt, "Political Corruption in American History: Some Further Thoughts," Eisenstadt et al., eds. *Before Watergate* 198 ("America is a Christian commonwealth"); 199 ("morality play"); 220 ,"a figment").

125.   References are to Theodore Dreiser, *The Financier* (Cleveland: World, 1946); Dreiser, *The Titan* (New York: Boni and Liveright, 1925); and Dreiser, *The Stoic* (Garden City, N.Y.: Doubleday, 1947). The arrangements with the city treasurer of Philadelphia are discussed in *The Financier* 149–153; the bribing of the sheriff and the guards, ibid. 368, 459.

126. The bribing of McKenty, Dreiser, *The Titan* 89, 173.

127. The bribing of Illinois legislature, ibid. 480–481; English ways of getting franchises, Dreiser, *The Stoic* 13.

128. *The Financier* 109 ("He had none, truly"). For the models of the characters, see Donald Pizer, *The Novels of Theodore Dreiser: A Critical Study* (Minneapolis: University of Minnesota Press, 1976) 155–156, 161–162 (Yerkes); 163 (Butler); 184 (Powers, Coughlin, Kennan). For the quotation from Hastings, see Chapter 14 above at n. 70.

129. *The Financier* 146 ("the Christian idea" of fidelity); *The Titan* 338 ("None o' that Christian con game"); 515 ("the Lord has also called us"); 485 ("selflessness of a Christian ideal"); 551 ("right, justice"); 197–198 (bribe-seeking by newspaper editor); *The Financier* 135 ("a feeble squeak").

130. Ibid. ("mouthings of pharisaical moralities").

131. Henry James, *The Ambassadors* (New York: Charles Scribner's Sons, 1922) 2, 69.

132. Ibid. 2, 317.

133. Ibid. 2, 283. For a further extension of the bribe concept, see Graham Greene, *The End of the Affair* (New York: Viking, 1961) 149. Richard, the atheist, says to Sarah, who believes in God, "I love you more than I hate all that. If I had children by you, I'd let you pervert them." She says, "You shouldn't say that." He replies, "I'm not a rich man. It's the only bribe I can offer, giving up my faith.." The offer is a bribe because it is an extraneous reason for Sarah to love him.

134. Robert Penn Warren, *All The King's Men* (New York: Harcourt, Brace, 1946) 56 (doesn't favor "stealing"); 68 ("became symbolically the spokesman").

135. Ibid. 134 ("Graft is what he calls it"); 146 ("Harvard hands"); 272 ("wanted the bricks").

136. Ibid. 54 ("always something"); 234–241 (Irwin's corruption).

137. Ibid. 59 ("Callahan's been playing around"); 171–202 (Burden's instruction by history).

138. Ibid. 34 ("Pouring swill"); 43 ("Secretary of the Bedchamber"); 105 ("the other self of Willie Stark").

139. Ibid. 368 ("It wouldn't stick"); 370 (Burden's discovery).

140. Ibid. 425 ("It might have been all different"); 462 ("history is blind"). In an introduction to a republication of the book, Warren says that Louisiana in the 1930s and Huey Long, assassinated in 1935, gave him "a line of feeling and thinking that did eventuate in the novel" (Introduction to *Time* republication, 1963, xi). He also says that the inspiration for Willie Stark goes back to Talus, "the 'iron groom,' who in murderous blankness, serves Justice in Spenser's *Faerie Queen*" (ibid. xvi). This recollection may be compared with Spenser's work where a cruel Saracen named Pollente keeps a bridge and anyone passing over it must pay "passage-penny." The spoils go to Pollente's daughter whose name is Lady Munera. Sir Artegall, who has been brought up in justice by Astrea, fights and destroys Pollente. Talus then enters Munera's castle and hacks off her hands of gold and feet of silver and drowns her in the river outside, Edmund Spenser, *The Faerie Queen*, Book 5, Canto II. Warren must intuit that the blind Talus will take Pollente's place.

141. Anthony Trollope, *The Warden* (Oxford: Shakespeare Head Press, 1929) c. 3, 33. Between *Macclesfield's Case* in 1725 and 1975, fourteen cases have been noted in which Parliament investigated a judge or at least entertained criticism of his conduct. None of them involved judicial bribery. In 1865 the House of Commons censured Lord Westbury, the chancellor, for appointing as bankruptcy registrar a person who had bribed the chancellor's son. Westbury resigned, Shimon Shetreet, *Judges on Trial: A Study of the Appointment and Accountability of the English Judiciary* (Amsterdam: North-Holland Publishing Co., 1976) 140–151.

142. William Lambert, "The Justice . . . and the Stock Manipulator," *Life*, May 9, 1969, 33–36 (the May 9 issue appeared May 5). Wolfson's conviction: *Wolfson v. United States* 405 F.2d 779 (2nd Cir. 1968); *cert. denied* 394 U.S. 946 U.S. (1969).

143. Ibid., 36. The foundation's tax return was filed for a fiscal year closing in September 1966, so it did not record payment from Fortas in December 1966. Auditing the foundation, the IRS checked Fortas's return for calendar year 1966 and found he had not recorded a payment from the Foundation, apparently on the theory that to receive unrestricted use of cash in January is not income if you pay a similar amount of cash to your payor in December of the same taxable year, see Robert Shogan, *A Question of Judgment: The Fortas Case and the Struggle for the Supreme Court* (Indianapolis: Bobbs-Merrill, 1972) 216.

144. Abe Fortas to the Editors of *Life*, circa April 1, 1969, quoted in Lambert "The Justice" 36 ("conversations"); ibid. 34 (Fortas's relation to Johnson); *New York Times* June 27, 1968, p. 1 (Fortas nominated to be chief justice); ibid. Oct. 3, 1968, p. 1 (Fortas asks name to be withdrawn).

145. *Life*, May 9, 1969, 34.
146. Shogan, *A Question of Judgment* 216–217 (leaks to Lambert).
147. Abe Fortas, Press Release, May 4, 1969, printed in ibid. 277–278 ("I have not accepted"); Fortas to Chief Justice Earl Warren, May 14, 1969, printed in ibid. 279–282 (terms of the contract with the foundation); *Life*, May 16, 1969 (Mitchell–Warren meeting); Shogan, *A Question of Judgment* 249 (Warren discussion with Fortas).
148. Fortas to Warren, May 14, 1969, ibid. 279–282. Cf. John P. Frank, "Conflict of Interest and U.S. Supreme Court Justices," *American Journal of Comparative Law* 18 (1970) 754 at 755: "As a matter of straight conflict of interest Fortas had violated no rule then existing."
149. Fortas to Warren, in Shogan, *A Question of Judgment* 282.
150. Ibid. 261. Law review comment was restricted to incidental references in the course of articles on "conflict of interest," see Frank, "Conflict of Interest"; Note, "Extrajudicial Activity of Supreme Court Justices," *Stanford Law Review* 22 (1970) 587. Merely reciting synopses of the facts from *Life* and taking Fortas's statements at face value, such commentary did not reach the bribery issue. A student note, "Crossing the Bar," *Yale Law Journal* 70 (1969) 484 at 490, n. 42, asked if Fortas could properly say that like Coriolanus he was "Whoopt out of Rome" (*Coriolanus* 4, 5, 83).
151. Robert A. Caro, *The Years of Lyndon Johnson: The Path to Power* (New York: Alfred A. Knopf, 1982) 190 ("They lost everything," quoting a tape-recording of Johnson, April 27, 1970).
152. Ibid. 200.
153. Ibid. 483 (Johnson and Marsh's mistress); 334 (Rayburn's view of Johnson); 754 ("to help his own career").
154. Ibid. 352–353 (cruelty); 302–303, 354–355 (relation to Lady Bird).
155. Ibid. 406–407.
156. Ibid. 380 (Brown & Root's gamble); 474 ("as closely"); 475 ("more funds than he could possibly use").
157. Ibid. 583–586 (Corpus Christi base); 717–718 (Brown & Root raise cash); 720–721 (vote buying).
158. See Chapter 18 below at note 83; Chapter 19 at notes 7–10.
159. Ibid. 748 ("slush fund"); 749 ("fraud"); 751 ("not a Sunday School proposition"); 752–753 (disposition of the cases).

CHAPTER 18: THE IDEAL CRIMINALLY ENFORCED (PP. 564–620)

1. Robert W. Archbald, judge of the Third Circuit Court of Appeals, was impeached and found guilty by the Senate in 1913, see Joseph Borkin, *The Corrupt Judge* (New York: Clarkson N. Potter, 1962) 221; Halstead Ritter, district judge for the Southern District of Florida was impeached and convicted in 1936, ibid. 243–244. The six district judges who resigned under fire were Richard Busteed (Alabama, 1875), Mark Delahay (Kansas, 1872), Edward Durell (Louisiana, 1875), George English (Illinois, 1925), Cornelius Hanford (Washington, 1912), and Francis A. Winslow (New York, 1929), see ibid. 226, 229, 230, 231, 233, 256.
2. For the basic transactions, see *Pan-American Petroleum and Transport Company v. United States* 273 U.S. 456 (1927); *Mammoth Oil Company v. United States* 275 U.S. 13 (1927); for the promoters' estimates of their probable profits, see M. R. Werner and John Starr, *Teapot Dome* (New York: Viking, 1959) 77, 86; Burl Noggle, *Teapot Dome: Oil and Politics in the 1920's* (Baton Rouge: Louisiana State University Press, 1962) 39–49 (initial protests); *Sen. Rep.* No. 749, 68th Cong., 1st Sess., printed in 65 Cong. Rec. 10938–10949, June 6, 1924; ibid. 10945 ("essentially corrupt"). Salient testimony and documents are conveniently excerpted in Arthur M. Schlesinger Jr., and Roger Burns, *Congress Investigates: A Documented History 1792–1974* (New York: Chelsea House, 1975) 5, 2403–2551.
3. Noggle, *Teapot Dome* 61 and 101 (damage to McAdoo); 68 (Walsh's role); 163 (Democratic exploitation); 108, 114–115, 124 (Coolidge response); "fumigated and sterilized," ex-Senator Albert J. Beveridge to Gifford Pinchot, March 7, 1924, quoted in Noggle, *Teapot Dome* 124.
4. *United States v. Pan-American Petroleum and Transport Co.* 6F.2d 43 (S.D. Cal. 1925), aff'd, 273 U.S. 456 (1927) at 500 ("corruptly secured"); *Mammoth Oil Company v. United States* 275 U.S. 13 (1927); Werner and Starr, *Teapot Dome* 296 (the government's ultimate recoveries).
5. Noggle, *Teapot Dome* 84–86 (Doheny and Sinclair payments; "little black bag"); 185 (Fall and Doheny acquitted); 190 (new evidence on Sinclair payments); 197 (Sinclair cover story); 200–201 (Sinclair acquittal); 211 (Doheny acquitted). Doheny's counsel used the heinousness of the crime of which he was accused to argue for his innocence. He pointed to

the involvement in the delivery of the $100,000 of Doheny's son, a navy veteran, now dead, and asked, "Can you believe his mind was so corrupt that he had conceived bribery and that he had fallen so low that he should select his own son, whom a few years before he had given to the Navy, as the instrument of his bribery?" Could the jury believe that young Doheny was "a briber"? Unlike Fall who had remained a prisoner of his earlier lies and so did not testify in his own behalf, Doheny was a witness for himself, even producing a note—which the government assailed as bogus—for the $100,000. Werner and Starr, *Teapot Dome* 282–288.

6.   *Fall v. United States* 49 F.2d 506 (D.C. Cir. 1931), *cert. denied* 283 U.S. 867 (1931) at 510–511; Noggle, *Teapot Dome* 211 (Fall imprisoned).

7.   Fall's imprisonment, a benchmark in the criminal enforcement of federal bribery law, was not itself harsh. He spent most of the time in the prison hospital and was released after nine months. His fine was forgiven. The ultimate sanctions were more like those suffered by Bacon. A Westerner with the scorn of a self-made man for the government, he was reduced to seeking mercies from the government. Released, he encountered much social ostracism and complete political ostracism. Once a lawyer, he had no practice. The great ranch in New Mexico—the root of his money needs—had been mortgaged to Doheny's company after his troubles began; it was now foreclosed on and sold. Unable to support himself, he lived on work done by his wife running a restaurant and canning vegetables at home, ibid. 213–214.

8.   William Howard Taft to Pierce Butler, Nov. 7, 1922, quoted in David J. Danelski, *A Supreme Court Justice Is Appointed* (New York: Random House, 1964) 58–61. Taft's principal source was undoubtedly his brother Harry, a New York lawyer, who also provided the information on the bar association committee vote, ibid. 74.

9.   See Borkin, *The Corrupt Judge* 25–26, where the number of cases and opinions of Manton is given for a ten-year period.

10.   Stanley Walker, *Dewey: An American of This Century* (New York: McGraw-Hill, 1944) 28–44 (early career); 45–80 (prosecutions). For the incidents involving Manton, Rupert Hughes, *Attorney for the People* (Boston: Houghton, Mifflin, 1939) 319. The two gangsters, Louis ("Lepke") Buchalter and Jacob ("Gurrah") Shapiro had been convicted of criminal violation of the antitrust law for using bombs, acid-throwing, and beatings to monopolize the trade in rabbit fur. Four months after they had been found guilty, Shapiro's conviction was upheld and Buchalter's was overturned by an appeals panel of which Manton was a member, but where the opinion was by Chase, *United States v. Buchalter* 88 F.2d 625 (2d Cir. 1937). Dewey's intervention to request high bail in a federal case could have seemed an intrusion; but the release on bail of two violent criminals and the extraordinarily quick reversal are recalled as memorable by the trial judge, John C. Knox, *A Judge Comes of Age* (New York: Charles Scribner's Sons, 1940) 290–291.

11.   Thomas E. Dewey to Hatton W. Summers, Jan. 29, 1939, reprinted in the *New York Times*, Jan. 30, 1939, 1. On Dewey's 1938 campaign for governor, Walker, *Dewey* 99–102.

12.   *New York Times*, Jan. 31, 1939, 1 (Manton resignation); ibid. March 9, 1936, 8; ibid. March 15, 1936, sec. IV, 8 (Manton's criticism of the Supreme Court); ibid. March 3, 1939, 1 and March 25, 1939, 3 (indictments); ibid. June 4, 1939, 1 (Manton's conviction); J. Woodford Howard, Jr., *Mr. Justice Murphy: A Political Biography* (Princeton, N.J.: Princeton University Press, 1968) 191 (Murphy's role).

13.   18 *U.S. Code* (1940 ed.) 238 (bribery of judge); 18 *U.S. Code* 371 (conspiracy); 18 *U.S. Code* 582 (statute of limitations) and its application in *Hyde and Scheider v. United States* 225 U.S. 347, 368–369 (1912).

14.   Dewey to Summers, Jan. 29, 1939, in *New York Times*, Jan. 30, 1939, 1; ibid. June 3, 1939, 1 and 9 (Cahill summation); Borkin, *The Corrupt Judge* 53–79 (evidence at the trial).

15.   *United States v. Manton* 107 F.2d 834 (2nd Cir. 1939) at 845–846. On the testimony of the four circuit judges, *New York Times*, June 3, 1939, 9. On the return of the cash where the panel was not delivered, Borkin, *The Corrupt Judge* 78.

16.   *United States v. Manton* 107 F.2d 834 at 846.

17.   *New York Times* June 3, 1939, 9 (on Chestnut); ibid. March 7, 1940, 46 (Manton's imprisonment); ibid. Oct. 14, 1941, 25 (his release); ibid. Nov. 18, 1946, 23 (his death).

18.   *In re Levy* 30 F. Supp. 317, 318–319, 328 (S.D.N.Y. 1939); Borkin, *The Corrupt Judge* 82.

19.   *In re Levy* at 327, 329. The Manton decision is *Rogers v. Hill* 60 F.2d 109 (2d Cir. 1932), *rev'd* 298 U.S. 582 (1933).

20.   *United States v. Manton* 107 F.2d 834 at 841–842; *New York Times*, April 13, 1939, 1, 5 (Thomas to mental hospital); ibid. Jan. 22, 1952, 29 (obituary); Judicial Conference of the United States, *Judges of the United States* (Washington: Government Printing Office, 1978) 387 (Thomas's background); 101 F.2d v (resignation). Thomas's actions in the reorganization of

the Fox New England Theatres—a reorganization set in motion by Manton—were being investigated at the time of his resignation, *New York Times* April 13, 1939, 5.

21. Judicial Conference, *Judges of the United States* 97, and Borkin, *The Corrupt Judge* 97–98 (Davis's career); *New York Times*, April 22, 1939, 4 (his resignation).

22. See *Root Refining Co. v. Universal Oil Products Co.* 169 F.2d 514 (3rd Cir. 1948) at 517; *United States v. Fox* 130 F.2d 56 (3rd Cir. 1942).

23. *Who's Who in America, 1936–1937,* 1069 (Haight's career); Borkin, *The Corrupt Judge* 63–64 (relations with Manton); *Root Refining* above, n. 22 at 526 (Belknap).

24. Ibid. 526; Judicial Conference, *Judges of the United States,* 286 (Morris's career).

25. *Root Refining* 526–527.

26. Ibid. 527–529; *Martindale-Hubbell Law Directory* (1935) 795 (Dwight); Robert A. Swaine, *The Cravath Firm and Its Predecessors 1819–1948* (New York: privately printed, 1948) 2, 475 (Whitney).

27. *Root Refining* 533 (Buffington opinions written by Davis); Borkin, *The Corrupt Judge* 101 (Buffington's physical condition).

28. *Root Refining* 524 ("existence of the court"); 534 ("must be purged"); 535 ("against the integrity of the court").

29. Ibid. (switch to Kaufman and Haight); 536 (the panel); 541 (apostate lawyer).

30. Ibid. 541 n. 9 (disbarment); Borkin, *The Corrupt Judge* 126–137. In 1959, aged 75, Kaufman was reinstated, ibid. 136.

31. Committee of the Judiciary, *Report on the Official Conduct of Albert W. Johnson and Albert L. Watson,* H. Rep. 1639, Feb. 25, 1946, 79th Cong., 1 ("conspiracy," etc.); Borkin, *The Corrupt Judge* 141–142 (Johnson's background); 143 (*Philadelphia Inquirer,* March 23, 1934, cited); 144–145 (Cummings's announcement); 147–152 (Goldschein involvement).

32. *Report on . . . Johnson* 28 (Johnson's resignation); Borkin, *The Corrupt Judge* 185 (Johnson's acquittal; Greenes and Memolo); 186 (president of bar association); *Johnson v. United States* 104 F. Supp. 106 at 109 (Ct. Claims 1952), *cert. denied* 345 U.S. 389 (1952) ("he was perhaps more keenly conscious. . .", Jacob Greenes, Testimony, July 11, 1945, in *Conduct of Albert W. Johnson and Albert L. Watson, Hearing before Subcommittee of the Committee on the Judiciary,* 79th Cong., 1st Sess. (1945), p. 770 ("a question of ethics").

33. Borkin, *The Corrupt Judge* 167–178 (the case); 179 ("large bribes," quoted from the report of the special master, Albert Aston, to the District Court, Jan. 23, 1952); 181 (Bethlehem's settlement).

34. *Report on . . . Johnson* 31 (Moore's "corrupt connivance"); Borkin, *The Corrupt Judge* 185 (Moore's acquittal); Swaine, *The Cravath Firm* 2, 144 ("No lawyer"); 2, 541 and 574 (Williamsport acquisition); 2, 717–718 ("What's in a Name?").

35. On Buffington's extraordinary aid to Johnson's son when in 1934 the son was on trial for embezzlement, see Borkin, *The Corrupt Judge* 145: it included designating himself, the senior circuit judge, to preside at the trial and then ruling key evidence inadmissible. On Levy's earlier misdeeds, *In re Levy* 30 F. Supp. 317 at 329 (S.D.N.Y. 1939). Martin Memolo, Moore's contact, was jailed for income tax evasion and died before the trial of his brother John, Johnson, and Moore, see Borkin, *The Corrupt Judge.* 183. Sutherland's pathbreaking sociological work studied the criminal convictions of the top 70 manufacturing, mining, and mercantile corporations. He found only 2 convictions for bribery from 1850 to 1949, Edward H. Sutherland, *White Collar Crime: The Uncut Version* (New Haven: Yale, 1983) 24.

36. Moore apparently did resign from the Association of the Bar of the City of New York, Swaine, *The Cravath Firm* 2, 140.

37. See Chapter 17 above at notes 64–66, 151, 153.

38. *Commonwealth v. Smith* 163 Mass. 411, 40 N.E. 189 (1895) (the case of the aldermen). Reported Massachusetts cases did include prosecution of the briber of a local district judge, *Commonwealth v. Murray* 135 Mass. 530 (1883); the briber of a milk inspector, *Commonwealth v. Lapham* 156 Mass. 480 (1892); the briber of a councilman, *Commonwealth v. Donovan* 170 Mass. 228 (1898); and of a citizen taking a bribe as a juror, *Commonwealth v. Milliken* 174 Mass. 79 (1899). The bribable legislators: Alpheus Thomas Mason, *Brandeis: A Free Man's Life* (New York: Viking, 1946) 89, based on Mason's interview with Brandeis, July 21, 1940.

39. Louis Brandeis to Alice Goldmark, Oct. 20, 1940, *Letters of Louis D. Brandeis,* ed. Melvin I. Urofsky and David W. Levy (Albany: State University of New York Press, 1971) 1, 93; Mason, *Brandeis* 89; Louis D. Brandeis, Speech before the Good Government Association, April 8, 1903 ("that in Boston") and Speech before the Boot and Shoe Club, March 19, 1903, both quoted in ibid. 120–121.

40. *Boston v. Santosuosso* 298 Mass 175, 10 N.E. 2d 271 (1937) (on demurrer, Curley's liabili-

ty as a trustee established); *New York Times,* Feb. 17, 1938, 1 (Curley, after trial, ordered to pay); for the applicable statute of limitations, Massachusetts *Rev. Laws* (1902) chap. 218, sec. 52. Autobiography: James Michael Curley, *I'd Do It Again* (Englewood Cliffs, N.J.: Prentice-Hall, 1957). As a young man Curley had impersonated another person and taken a federal civil service examination in his behalf; he was convicted of conspiracy to defraud the government, *United States v. Curley* 130 F. 1 (1st Cir. 1904), *cert. denied* 195 U.S. 628 (1904). A difference appears in Curley's autobiographical treatment of the two episodes: he admits the impersonation, *I'd Do It Again,* 69; he treats the main evidence in the civil bribery case as perjured, ibid. 309.

41. *New York Times,* Sept. 20, 1952 (Coakley's obituary).

42. Chief Justice Stanley Qua, "In the Matter of Information of the Massachusetts Bar Association Relative to the Committee on Rules of the House of Representatives, House No. 2696," Feb. 3, 1952, printed, *Boston Globe,* Feb. 4, 1952 (land damage case; disbarment); *Boston Globe,* Feb. 23, 1956 (tax evasion convictions).

43. *United States v. Worcester* 190 F. Supp. 548 (D. Mass 1960) at 572 ($275,000 in "bounty").

44. *Commonwealth v. Kelley* 359 Mass. 77, 268 N. E. 2d 132 (1971) (Callahan's son-in-law guilty of bribery); *Commonwealth v. Favulli* 352 Mass. 95, 422 N.E. 2d. 422 (1967) (ex-governor Furcolo acquitted; two governor's councillors convicted); *Commonwealth v. Beneficial Finance Company* 360 Mass. 188, 275 N.E. 2d 33 (1971), *cert. denied* 407 U.S. 914 (bribery of Deputy Commissioner of Banks).

45. Special Commission Concerning State and County Buildings, *Final Report,* Dec. 31, 1980 (Boston: Secretary of State for the Commonwealth of Massachusetts, 1981) 3 ("way of life"); 4 ("pervasive," "rotten"); 12 (72 percent failure rate).

46. Note, "Bribery in Commercial Relationships," *Harvard Law Review* 45 (1932) 1248–1252 (history of law to 1932); American Law Institute, *Model Penal Code and Commentaries* (Official Draft and Revised Comments) (Philadelphia: American Law Institute, 1980) sec. 224.8 (draft statute on "commercial bribery and breach of duty to act disinterestedly" with citations to state statutes on this topic); McKinney's *Consolidated Laws of New York* (1944 ed.), *Penal Code,* sec. 439 (New York history; lack of employer's consent as element of crime).

47. Note, "Control of Nongovernmental Corruption by Criminal Legislation," *U. Penn. Law Review* 108 (1960) 848 at 853 (New York cases). There are no recorded cases in Massachusetts, ibid. 861. For an example of the criminal law in civil litigation, see *Sirkin v. Fourteenth St. Store* 124 App. Div. 384, 108 N.Y.S. 830 (1908); but cf. *Donamar, Inc. v. Molloy* 252 N.Y. 360, 169 N.E. 610 (1930) (law will not nullify executed contract, but purchaser may recover amount of bribe from his agent or from the seller).

48. Note, "Control of Nongovernmental Corruption" at 858 (32 states); *Model Penal Code,* sec. 224.9 (motivation); *State v. Di Paglia* 247 Iowa 79, 71 N.W. 2d 601 (1955), *cert. denied* 325 U.S. 1017 (1956) (severe penalty).

49. 78 *U.S. Statutes* 203 (1964), 18 *U.S. Code,* sec. 224, applied in *United States v. Walsh* 544 F.2d 156, (4th Cir. 1976), *cert. denied* 429 U.S. 1093.

50. *Model Penal Code* sec. 224.9.

51. Ibid. secs. 240 and 240.1; ibid., p. 31 (the states following the Code).

52. Ibid. sec. 240.7.

53. Ibid. sec. 240.1, 38–43.

54. Ibid. sec. 240.1, 11–12. See, e.g., *Illinois Annotated Statutes,* "Criminal Law and Procedure," chap. 38, sec. 33–1 ("any property or personal advantage"); *Louisiana Revised Statutes* (1974 ed.) sec. 14, 118 ("anything of apparent present or prospective value"). A case where a bribery conviction was obtained on facts similar to the hypothetical about the councilmen and a bribe is *People v. Montgomery* 61 Cal. App. 3rd, 132 *Cal. Rptr.* 554 (1976). The *Model Penal Code* would lead to a contrary result because it defines a bribe as "a pecuniary benefit" in cases where the quid pro quo is a vote, *Model Penal Code* sec. 240.1.

55. *U.S. Code* 18, sec. 201.

56. Theodore W. Dwight, "Introduction" to Henry Maine, *Ancient Law* (New York: Henry Holt, 1885), XL.

57. *New York Times,* Oct. 11, 1973, 1, and Oct. 12, 1973, 1.

58. George Beall, United States District Attorney, "Exposition of the Evidence Against Spiro T. Agnew accumulated by the Investigation in the Office of the United States Attorney for the District of Maryland as of October 10, 1973," *New York Times,* Oct. 12, 1973, 36–38.

59. *New York Times,* Oct. 11, 1973, 33.

60. "Transcript of Former Vice President Agnew's TV and Radio Address, October 15, 1973," *New York Times,* Oct. 16, 1973, 34; ibid. Oct. 12, 26 (preliminary negotiations).

61. Elliott L. Richardson, Statement to the Court, *New York Times,* Oct. 11, 1973, 35, and

Richardson as reported in ibid. Oct. 12, 1973, 26. For a criticism of the process, see Albert W. Alschuler, "The Changing Plea Bargaining Debate," *California Law Review* 69 (1981) 652, 658.

62.   *New York Times*, Oct. 12, 1973, 1 (sentence); ibid. May 3, 1974, 1 (state disbars); ibid. Jan. 5, 1983, 10 (restitution). The suit for restitution had been begun by students at George Washington University Law School and was only later adopted by the state itself.

63.   Committee on the Judiciary of the House of Representatives, "Impeachment of Richard M. Nixon, President of the United States," *Report No. 93–1305*, 93rd Cong., 2nd Sess., Aug. 20, 1974, 1–3.

64.   See Theodore H. White, *Breach of Faith* (New York: Atheneum, 1975) 308–311.

65.   Ibid. 331–333.

66.   Committee on the Judiciary, "Impeachment" 56 ($190,000); 71–73 ($120,000).

67.   *New York Times*, Aug. 6, 1974, 1. For the conviction of the president's men, Attorney General John Mitchell and Presidential Assistants John Ehrlichman and J. Robert Haldeman, *United States v. Haldeman* 559 F.2d 31 (D.C. Cir. 1976), *cert. denied* 431 U.S. 933 (1977).

68.   *Jersey City v. Hague* 18 N.J. 584, 115 A.2d 8 (1955); *New York Times*, Jan. 2, 1956, 1 and Jan. 10, 1956, 37 (death and will of Hague). Infrequently invoked against public officers, the principle was well established in trust and agency law that a fiduciary had to account to his beneficiary or principal for any bribe (whether or not dressed up as a commission or compensation), see Austin Wakeman Scott, *The Law of Trusts*, 3rd ed. (Boston: Little, Brown, 1967) vol. 2, sec. 170 (2); American Law Institute, *Restatement of the Law of Restitution* (St. Paul, Minn.: American Law Institute Publishers, 1937) secs. 128 and 197, and for exemplary cases, *In re Smith* 1 Ch 71 (1895); *Kelley v. Allin* 212 Mass. 327, 99 N.E. 273 (1910).

69.   The Anti-Racketeering Act of 1934, *United States Statutes* 48, 979, construed by the Supreme Court and the legislative history given in *United States v. Local 807 of International Brotherhood of Teamsters* 315 U.S. 521 (1942), amended by the Hobbs Act, *United States Statutes* 60, 420 (1946), *U.S. Code* 18, sec. 1951. For the remarks of the supporters of Hobbs, 91 *Congressional Record* 97th Cong., 1st Sess., Dec. 12, 1945, 11900, 11906. For the New York prototype, *New York Penal Law*, ed. McKinney, 1944, secs. 850, 854.

70.   *United States v. Kenny* 462 F.2d 1205 (3rd Cir. 1972), *cert. denied* 409 U.S. 914 (1972); *New York Times*, June 3, 1975, 37 (Kenny's career).

71.   Herbert J. Stern, "Prosecutions of Local Political Corruption under the Hobbs Act: The Unnecessary Distinction between Bribery and Extortion," *Seton Hall Law Review* 3 (1971) 1, 14–15.

72.   *United States v. Kenny* above, n. 70.

73.   For black letter law, *United States v. Hudson* 7 Cranch 32 (1812); *Krulewitch v. United States* 336 U.S. 440 at 457 (1949); cf. Charles Warren, "New Light on the History of the Federal Judiciary Act of 1789," *Harvard Law Review* 37 (1923) 49 at 73. For an example of judicial freedom, *Standard Oil Company of New Jersey v. United States* 221 U.S. 1 (1911) at 60 ("standard of reason"), interpreting the Sherman Act, 26 *Stat.* 209 (1890), 15 *U.S.C.* 1.

74.   *United States Statutes* 35, 1104, (1909) as amended, 18 *U.S. Code* sec. 872, interpreted in *United States v. Sutter* 160 F.2d 754 (7th Cir. 1947). As to Blackstone, see his *Commentaries* 4, 141 (extortion) following 4, 139–140 (bribery).

75.   *United States Statutes* 75, 948 (1961), *U.S. Code* 18, sec. 1952 and 84, 941 (1970), *U.S. Code* 18, sec. 1961.

76.   See *United States v. Mazzei* 521 F.2d 639 (3rd Cir. 1975), at 643 (majority opinion) and at 647 (dissenting opinion), *cert. denied* 423 U.S. 1014 (1975). *Mazzei* treats influence peddling as extortion. Some state courts had found influence peddling by a legislator not criminal at all: *State v. Nadeau* 81 R.I. 505, 105 A2d 194 (1954), *State v. Bowling* 5 Ariz. App. 436, 427, P.2d 928 (1967).

77.   *United States v. Duhon* 565 F.2d 345, 350–351 (5th Cir. 1978).

78.   *United States v. Hathaway* 534 F.2d 386, 395 (1st Cir. 1976), *cert. denied* 97 S. Ct. 64 (1976); *United States v. Salvitti* 451 F. Supp. 195 (E.D. Penn. 1978).

79.   *United States v. Staszuck* 502 F.2d 875 (7th Cir. 1974), *cert. denied* 423 U.S. 837 (1975); *United States v. Crowley* 504 F.2d 992 (7th Cir. 1974); *United States v. Braasch* 505 F.2d 139 (7th Cir. 1974), *cert. denied* 421 U.S. 910 (1975); *United States v. Price* 507 F.2d 1349 (4th Cir. 1974); *United States v. Trotta* 525 F.2d 1096 (2nd Cir. 1975), *cert. denied* 425 U.S. 971 (1976); *United States v. Brown* 540 F.2d 364 (8th Cir. 1976); *United States v. Hall* 536 F.2d 313 (10th Cir. 1976), *cert. denied* 97 S. Ct. 313 (1976).

80.   E.g., *U.S. v. Hathaway* above, n. 78, at 316; *U.S. v. Staszcuk* 517 F.2d 53, 59–60 (7th Cir. *en banc*, per Stevens, J., reversing on this point and giving a broad reading to congressional jurisdiction 502 F.2d 825).

81.   Charles F. C. Ruff, "Federal Prosecution of Local Corruption: A Case Study in the Mak-

ing of Law Enforcement Policy," *Georgetown Law Journal* (1977) 65, 1171 at 1172 (300 state officials), 1205−1206 (relevant Justice Department directives), 1211 (active local offices).

82. *U.S. v. Kenny, U.S. v. Hathaway; U.S. v. Hall. Perrin v. United States* 444 U.S. 37 (1979), interpreting *United States Statutes* 75, 498 (1961), 18 *U.S. Code,* sec. 1952 (commercial bribery included); *United States v. Clark* 646 F.2d 1259 (8th Cir. 1981) ("caused").

83. *Internal Revenue Code,* 26 *U.S. Code* secs. 7201 (attempt to evade), 7203 (wilful failure to file), 7206 (perjurious statement), 7207 (false statements to revenue officer).

84. 13 *U.S. Code* 1341 (mail fraud—golf balls, hotel expenses, and cash make up mail fraud bribe); 18 *U.S. Code* 1343 (wire fraud). For the history and popularity of the statute, see Jed S. Rakoff, "The Federal Mail Fraud Statute," *Duquesne Law Review* 18 (1980) 771. For an example, see *United States v. Caldwell* 544 F.2d 691 (4th Cir. 1976).

85. *United States v. Isaacs* 493 F.2d 1124, 1161 (7th Cir. 1974), *cert. denied* 417 U.S. 976 (1974).

86. Ibid. 1149−1150. For criticism, see Comment, "The Intangible-Rights Doctrine and Political-Corruption Prosecutions under the Federal Mail Fraud Statute," *University of Chicago Law Review* 47 (1980) 562. The Comment at 571 argues that the mail fraud statute, as amended in 1909, meant to reach only fraud for the purpose of "obtaining money and property." The Comment at 584−586 points out that the Kerner court purported to rely on *Shushan v. United States* 117 F.2d 110 (5th Cir. 1941), *cert. denied* 313 U.S. 574 (1941), a state bribery case prosecuted under the federal mail fraud statute, where the court did use broad language as to fraud but where in fact the defendants had obtained money at the expense of the state. This argument as to the statutory history has force. Nonetheless, the federal courts more probably were right in interpreting "defraud" analogously to "defraud" in the conspiracy statute used to convict Manton. See Abraham S. Goldstein, "Conspiracy to Defraud the United States," *Yale Law Journal* 68 (1959) 404 at 423−426, 436, and compare *United States v. Manton* above, n. 15.

87. *Harrison v. United States* 7 F.2d 259 at 263 (2nd Cir. 1925).

88. *United States v. Kenny* above, n. 10 at 1210; *United States v. Isaacs* above, n. 85, 1152−1153, applying *United States Statute* 35, 1096 (1909), as amended, *U.S. Code* 18, sec. 371.

89. *United States v. Isaacs* above, n. 85, at 1144.

90. *Congressional Record* 116, 972 (Jan. 23, 1970); Senate vote; *Cong. Rec.* 116, 35363; House vote (Oct. 7, 1970).

91. See G. Robert Blakey, "The RICO Civil Fraud Action in Context: Reflections on *Bennett v. Berg*," *Notre Dame Lawyer* 58 (1982) 237 (acronym); 249 (congressional investigations); 272−273, 276 (rejection of status crime); 302 (estimate of mafiosi). Professor Blakey was the principal draftsman of the statute. For its "Statement of Findings and Purpose," 84 *U.S. Stat.* 922−923 (1970). This statement applies to RICO as well as to other portions of the act, Blakey, "The RICO Civil Fraud Action" 248, n. 28.

92. Attorney General Richard Kleindienst to Senator John McClellan, Aug. 11, 1969, printed in "Organized Crime Control Act of 1969," *Senate Report* No. 91−617, 91st Cong., 1st Sess., 121−122.

93. 84 *Stat.* 941 (1970), *U.S. Code* 18, sec. 1961.

94. Ibid. sec. 1962. Sec. 1963, "Criminal penalties," prescribes the penalties for those violating sec. 1962 by performing the acts sec. 1962 says are "unlawful." Professor Blakey contends that sec. 1962 is "not a criminal statute," Blakey, "The RICO Civil Fraud Action" 243, n. 20. He goes on to say, "Indeed, RICO is not a criminal statute at all in the traditional sense, since its violation depends on the commission of at least two acts that violate *independent* criminal statutes; it does not 'draw a line' between innocent and criminal conduct." This exposition brings out how, in the area of bribery, RICO incorporates state law. Nonetheless, as the cases below suggest, the federal courts are interpreting the state law, and the standards set by sec. 1962 are standards of conduct whose violation is a federal crime.

95. *United States v. Colacurcio* 659 F.2d 684 (5th Cir. 1981); *U.S. v. Salvitti* 200 above, n. 78.

96. *United States v. Frumento* 563 F.2d 1083, *cert. denied* 434 U.S. 1072 (3rd Cir. 1972) (Pennsylvania Revenue Department); *United States v. Brown* 555 F.2d 407 (5th Cir. 1977), *cert. denied* 48 S. Ct. 1448 (Macon City police department); *United States v. Baker* 617 F.2d 1060 (4th Cir. 1980) (North Carolina sheriff's department); *United States v. Bacheler* 611 F.2d 443 (3rd Cir. 1979) (Philadelphia traffic court); *United States v. Thompson* 685 F.2d 993 (6th Cir. 1982), *cert. denied* 103 S. Ct. 494 (1982) (governor's office); *United States v. Sutherland* 656 F.2d 1181 (5th Cir. 1981) (El Paso traffic court); *United States v. Long* 651 F.2d 239 (4th Cir. 1981) (office of state senator); *United States v. Karas* 624 F.2d 500 (4th Cir. 1980), *cert. denied* 449 U.S. 1078 (1981) (West Virginia sheriff); *United States v. Dozier* 493 F. Supp. 554 (N.D. La. 1980) (Louisiana agriculture department); *United States v. Lee Stoller Enterprises* 652 F.2d 1313 (7th Cir. 1981), *cert.*

denied 102 S. Ct. 636 (1982) (sheriff of Madison County). *United States v. Barrett* 505 F.2d 1091 (7th Cir. 1974), *cert. denied* 421 U.S. 964 (1975) (Clerk of Cook County convicted under RICO); *New York Times*, June 10, 1981, 19 (Roy Blanton, governor of Tennessee, convicted under RICO). *United States v. Fineman* 434 F. Supp. 189 (E.D. Penn. 1977) (Pennsylvania speaker of the House and bagman treated as enterprise when alleged RICO offense was selling speaker's influence in admission to state-supported veterinary school and medical schools.) At the trial, the defendant was acquitted of the RICO charges but convicted of obstruction of justice, 434 F. Supp. 197.

97.   *United States v. Turkette* 632 F.2d 896 at 905 (1st Cir. 1980).

98.   *United States v. Elliott* 571 F.2d 880 (5th Cir. 1978) 898 ("conglomerate"); 904 (purpose was to make money from criminal activity).

99.   *United States v. Turkette* 452 U.S. 576 (1981).

100.   *United States v. Forsythe* 560 F.2d 1127 at 1134 (3rd Cir. 1977); *United States v. Frumento* above, n. 96, at 1087.

101.   *United States v. Mandel* 602 F.2d 653 (4th Cir. 1979), *en banc*, affirming in part and reversing in part *United States v. Mandel* 591 F.2d 1347, 1357–1358 (4th Cir. 1979); *New York Times*, Aug. 24, 1977, 1. For another example of RICO combined with other statutes, see the case of the sheriff of Madison County who was convicted of conspiracy to violate RICO, four counts of mail fraud, three counts of wire fraud, and four counts of false statements to agents of the Internal Revenue Service, *United States v. Lee Stoller Enterprises* above, n. 96.

102.   *United States v. Gillock* 445 U.S. 360 (1980) 373.

103.   *United States v. Forsythe* above, n. 100, at 1137.

104.   *U.S. Code* 18, sec. 201; cf. *U.S. v. Anderson* 509 F.2d 312 at 333 (D.C. Cir. 1974); *New York Penal Law* (1965) sec. 200.30; Appendix to [Milbank, Tweed, Hadley and McCloy, Counsel for Nelson A. Rockefeller], "Legality of Loans and Gifts by Nelson A. Rockefeller to Members of his Staff and to Other State Employees," Committee on Rules and Administration, United States Senate, "Nomination of Nelson A. Rockefeller of New York To Be Vice President of the United States," *Hearings*, Nov. 14, 1974, 685–687.

105.   See Barry Tarlow, "RICO: The New Darling of the Prosecutor's Nursery," *Fordham Law Review* 49 (1980) 167 at 170, and the complaint of the American Bar Association on the prejudicial impact of describing the accused as a "racketeer," 251.

106.   18 *U.S. Code* sec. 1963, applied in *Anderson v. Janovich* 543 F. Supp. 1124 (W.D. Wash. 1982).

107.   See *United States v. Hess* 691 F.2d 188 (4th Cir. 1982), applying 18 *U.S. Code* sec. 1963 (a); *United States v. Tunnel* 667 F.2d 1182 (5th Cir. 1982) (motel forfeited); *United States v. Rubin* 559 F.2d 975, 990 (5th Cir. 1977) (union office forfeited).

108.   *United States v. Thevis* 474 F. Supp. 134 (N.D. Ga. 1979), following the general teaching that forfeiture is constitutional, *Calero-Toledo v. Pearson Yacht Leasing Co.* 416 U.S. 663 (1974). On the novelty of forfeiture based on personal guilt, see G. Robert Blakey and Brian Gettings, "Racketeer Influenced and Corrupt Organizations (RICO): Basic Concepts—Criminal and Civil Remedies," *Temple Law Quarterly* 53 (1980) 1009 at 1036.

109.   *United States v. McNary* 620 F.2d 621 (7th Cir. 1980); *Russello v. United States* 52 *United States Law Week* 4003 (1983) (profits of enterprise are forfeitable).

110.   Ruff, "Federal Prosecution" 1208. Lacey was nominated to the District Court in October, Kenny was indicted in November, Lacey resigned to take office as a judge in January, *New York Times* Oct. 8, 1970, 53; Nov. 17, 1970, 1; Dec. 22, 1970, 20. Stern was confirmed as a judge in 1973, *New York Times* Dec. 20, 1973, 83. The support of the state's Republican senator, Clifford Case, would have been essential for these appointments.

111.   See, e.g., Lon L. Fuller, "Human Interaction and the Law," *American Journal of Jurisprudence* 14 (1969) 1.

112.   See Mary Douglas and Aaron Wildavsky, *Risk and Culture* (Berkeley: University of California Press, 1982) 155 (sectarian distrust of officeholder); 159 (importance of higher education).

113.   For the anthropology, see Mary Douglas, *Purity and Danger: An Analysis of Pollution and Taboo* (London: Routledge & Kegan Paul, 1966) 3–6, 160–161 (imposition of order, resolution of ambiguity by antipollution rules; 96 (entrances and exits). For changes in American public law and American sexual morals, see, e.g., John T. Noonan, Jr., "The Family and the Supreme Court," *Catholic University Law Review* 23 (1973) 255–274; John T. Noonan Jr., "Genital Good," *Communio* (1982) 45.

114.   *New York Times*, May 24, 1975 (Kerner paroled for lung condition after serving seven months); ibid. Dec. 4, 1981 (Mandel sentence of three years commuted after he had served 19

months); ibid. May 23, 1978, sec. III, 4 (Hall paroled after serving half of three-year sentence); ibid. Aug. 15, 1981, 8 (Blanton sentenced to three years).

115.   Blakey, "The RICO Civil Fraud Action" 306.
116.   See *United States v. Mitchell* 163 F.1014 (D. Ore. 1908) (Mitchell estate does not have to pay fine assessed against Mitchell in 1905); *New York Times*, Dec. 9, 1905, 6.
117.   *Burton v. United States* 202 U.S. 344 (1906); *New York Times*, Oct. 22, 1906, 1 (his imprisonment); *United States v. Driggs* 125 F.520 (E.D.N.Y. 1903) (demurrer overruled); *New York Times*, Jan. 8, 1904, 1 (Driggs's conviction and sentence).
118.   *Langley v. United States* 8 F.2d 815 (6th Cir. 1925), *cert. denied* 269 U.S. 588 (1926); *New York Times*, April 16, 1931, 52 (Rowbottom); ibid. Nov. 24, 1935, 26 (Foulkes); *Hoeppel v. United States* 85 F.2d 372 (D.C. Cir. 1936), *cert. denied* 299 U.S. 577 (1936).
119.   *May v. United States* 175 F.2d 994 (D.C. App. 1949), *cert. denied* 338 U.S. 830 (1949).
120.   *New York Times*, Dec. 1, 1949, 1 (Thomas); ibid. June 14, 1963, 64 (Boykin); ibid. Jan. 27, 1968, 33 (Johnson).
121.   *New York Times*, Sept. 7, 1959, 15 (May's pardon and reinstatement at the bar); ibid. Jan. 12, 1926, 1 (Langley); ibid. Oct. 18, 1931, 25 (Rowbottom sentence); ibid. Dec. 9, 1905, 6 (Mitchell sentence); *Congressional Quarterly Weekly Report*, Feb. 9, 1980, 19 (Boykin pardon).
122.   Select Committee to Study Undercover Activities of Components of the Department of Justice, *Final Report, Senate Report No. 97–682*, 97th Cong., 2nd Sess., Dec. 15, 1982, Appendix F, 685 (Diggs); 686 (Eilberg); 688 (Hastings); 698 (Whalley); *United States v. Podell* 519 F.2d 144 (2nd Cir. 1975), *cert. denied* 423 U.S. 926 (1975); *United States v. Dowdy* 479 F.2d 213 (4th Cir. 1973), *cert. denied* 414 U.S. 1117 (1973).
123.   *United States v. Brasco* 358 F. Supp. 966 (S.D.N.Y. 1974), *aff'd* 516 F.2d 816 (2nd Cir. 1976), *cert. denied* 423 U.S. 860 (1975); *New York Times*, Feb. 27, 1980, 1 (Flood); ibid. June 26, 1975, 19 (Brewster).
124.   Select Committee, *Final Report* 683 (Brewster sentence); 686 (Eilberg and Flood sentences).
125.   *United States v. Brewster* 408 U.S. 509 (1972). The decision of the Court in 1979 that not only past legislative acts but letters referring to them were excluded by the Constitution only slightly enlarged the area of immunity, *United States v. Helstoski* 442 U.S. 477 (1979) 488.
126.   *United States v. Myers* 527 F. Supp. 1209 (E.D.N.Y. 1981).
127.   Robert W. Greene, *The Sting Man: Inside Abscam* (New York: E. P. Dutton, 1981) 96–97 (the million dollar deposit); illustrations of electronic equipment and of tapes made, ibid. following 136, 155 ($100,000 bribe).
128.   See *United States v. Myers* 527 F. Supp. 1206, 1211–1212 (E.D.N.Y. 1981) (summary of results in jury trials); the author's own experience in the fall of 1980 (the showing of scenes of Abscam bribery on public television).
129.   Greene, *The Sting Man* 20–21 (Weinberg's childhood); 23 (his work for glaziers' union); 24 (his sexual appetite); 33 (his insurance company swindles); 36 (his cheating of his cousin); 43–45 (his front-end scams); 46 (the $10,000 from the doctor); 49 (his income and income tax); 73 (conviction); 74, 77 (deal for girlfriend).
130.   *United States v. Myers* 527 F. Supp. 1206 at 1240 (E.D.N.Y. 1981).
131.   Greene, *The Sting Man* 11, 75–76 (Good); *Congressional Record*, March 10, 1982, vol. 128, p. S 1897.
132.   Greene, *The Sting Man* 5, 175–176, 233–236 (Puccio); 8 (Bell, Civiletti); *New York Times*, Feb. 17, 1980, Magazine, 1 (Heymann); Irving B. Nathan, "A Fair and Effective Method for Fighting Public Corruption" (typescript, 1981, in files of the author).
133.   Greene, *The Sting Man* 118–119 (early Abscam); 126–128 (Errichetti); 201–202 (the Noto impersonation).
134.   Ibid. 142 (Judas goat); 155 (MacDonald); 165 (Katz); *United States v. Myers* 527 F. Supp. 1206 at 1212, n. 5 (sewer scandals); *United States v. Jannotti* 673 F.2d 578 (3rd Cir. 1982), *cert. denied* 102 S. Ct. 2906 (1982) (Philadelphia City Council).
135.   See *United States v. Myers* 527 F.Supp. 1206 at 1212 (convictions of Myers and Lederer); Greene, *The Sting Man* 193–197 (details on their receipt of bribes); *United States v. Myers* 692 F.2d 823 (2nd Cir. 1982) at 849 (Lederer's report of money).
136.   See *United States v. Myers* 527 F. Supp. 1206 at 1214; Greene, *The Sting Man* 211, 235–239.
137.   *United States v. Williams* 705 F.2d 603 at 608–612 (2nd Cir. 1983), *cert. denied* 52 U.S. Law Week 3440 (1983) (evidence summarized); *In the Matter of Harrison A. Williams Jr.: Report of Special Counsel to the Select Committee on Ethics, United States Senate*, Aug. 13, 1981 (Congres-

sional Information Service microfiche 1981, S−352-8) 8−20; *Who's Who in America 1980-1981,* 3531 (Williams's background).

138. See *United States v. Myers* 527 F. Supp. 1206 at 1212 (convictions of Jenrette and Kelly); Greene, *The Sting Man* 237, 244 (details); *United States v. Jannotti* 673 F.2d 578 at 580 (3rd Cir. 1982), *cert. denied* 102 S.Ct. 1096 (1982) (Schmitz, Johanson); *United States v. Myers* 692 F.2d 823 (2nd Cir. 1982) at 829−830 (recruitment of congressman); 833 (split of bribe); 847−848 (Criden, Cook); *In the Matter of Harrison A. Williams, Jr.* 75 (Feinberg); *New York Times,* Feb. 20, 1980, 22 (descriptions of Feinberg). At Williams's trial, Feinberg objected to being called a bagman and Williams's counsel made this description of him by the government a ground for moving for a new trial. Judge Pratt found it a fair characterization, *United States v. Williams* 524 F. Supp. 1085 at 1106 (E.D.N.Y. 1981).

139. *In the Matter of Harrison A. Williams Jr.* 86 (Plaza lunch); Greene, *The Sting Man* 171 (Williams in Macy's window).

140. Ibid. 155 ("crude and insulting"); "Response of Senator Williams," Select Committee on Ethics (Congressional Information Service microfiche 1981, S−352-9) 27 (queasiness at cash); *United States v. Myers* 692 F.2d 823 at 833 (2nd Cir. 1982) *cert. denied* 103 S. Ct. 2437 (1983) (Thompson, Murphy, and briefcases).

141. *In the Matter of Harrison A. Williams, Jr.* 73 (shares endorsed in blank); 94 (rejection of cash); *United States v. Myers* 692 F.2d 823 at 832−833 (Thompson); Greene, *The Sting Man* 162 ("doing the right thing").

142. *In the Matter of Harrison A. Williams, Jr.* 66−67, 69 (offers of Williams); *Congressional Record* 128, p. S 1623 March 4, 1982 ("lax tokens").

143. Ibid., March 4, 1982, p. S 1599 ("preposterous"); *United States v. Williams, supra* n. 137 at 612 ("brazen").

144. Ibid. 619 (summary of current federal law). See also *United States v. Russell* 411 U.S. 423 (1973); *Hampton v. United States* 425 U.S. 484 (1975); Roger Park, "The Entrapment Controversy," *Minnesota Law Review* 60 (1976) 176 (standard instructions); 264 (federal rule on the burdens of proof and persuasion); Note, "Causation and Intention in the Entrapment Defense," *U.C.L.A. Law Review* 28 (1981) 859, n. 1 (status of rule in other countries); Note, "The Serpent Beguiled Me and I Did Eat—The Constitutional Status of the Entrapment Defense," *Yale Law Journal* 74 (1965) 942.

145. See *United States v. Myers* 527 F. Supp. 1206, 1211−1212. The difficulty of simultaneously showing that one is innocent *and* entrapped is pointed out by Judge Newman in *United States v. Williams* above, n. 137, at 616.

146. *United States v. Myers* 1227−1228; *United States v. Williams,* 620. District Judge Fullam found $30,000 offered to the president of the Philadelphia City Council "a substantial temptation to a first offense"; he was reversed on appeal, *United States v. Jannotti* 673 F.2d 578 (3rd Cir. 1982) at 599.

147. Erwin N. Griswold et al., "Post-Hearing Memorandum in Support of Defendant Harrison A. Williams' Motion to Dismiss the Indictment on Due Process and Related Grounds" in *U.S. v. Williams* (E.D.N.Y. 1981), reproduced in Select Committee on Ethics, *Response of Senator Williams* (Congressional Information Service Microfiche 1981 S 352-9) 117 (video distortion); 121 (King John). In a nonadversarial context, Griswold developed his critique of Abscam further, urging that there should be limits, moral and legal, to committing the government "to actions which in other hands would be grossly illegal and grievously immoral," Griswold, "Quis Custodiet Ipsos Custodes? Some Reflections on ABSCAM," *Proceedings of the American Philosophical Society* 126 (1982) 452 at 459.

148. *United States v. Williams* 529 F. Supp at 1094 (1981) (Judge Pratt's view of Griswold's argument); *United States v. Jannotti* 501 F. Supp. 1182 (E.D. Pa. 1980) at 1194, 1203 (Fullam's opinion), *rev'd* 673 F.2d 578 (3rd Cir. 1982); ibid. 612−613 (dissenting opinion of Aldisert).

149. *United States v. Kelly* 539 F. Supp. 363 (D. D.C. 1982) at 372−374, n. 45; *rev'd, United States v. Kelly* 707 F.2d. 1460 (D.C. Cir. 1983) *cert. denied* 104 S. Ct. 264 (1983).

150. Ibid. 377−378 (Kelly); *In the Matter of Harrison A. Williams, Jr.* at 129, ("brag foolishly"); 136 ("puffing"). Kelly was not the only Abscam defendant to claim he had been trying to catch his bribers. In a separate Abscam operation, Alexander Alexandro, Jr., a veteran criminal investigator with the Immigration and Naturalization Service, agreed for $15,000 to arrange a "green card," entitling an alien to resident status, for a bogus Arab. Alexandro's defense was that he was planning to turn in those paying him. His conviction was upheld in *U.S. v. Alexandro* 675 F.2d 34 (2nd Cir. 1982) *cert. denied* 103 S. Ct. 78.

151. *United States v. Myers* 692 F.2d 823 (2nd Cir. 1982) 841−842.

152. *State v. Guffey* 262 S.W. 2nd 152 (Mo. 1952).

153.   *United States v. Myers* 692 F.2d 827−828 (sentences of Lederer, Murphy, Myers, Thompson); *Congressional Record* 126, H 10309 (Oct. 2, 1980) (expulsion of Myers); *New York Times*, July 8, 1983, I (photo of Erichetti, Johanson, and Lederer); ibid. Dec. 10, 1983, I, 1 (Jenrette sentence); ibid. Jan 13, 1984, IV, 15 (Kelly sentence). Sentencing Thompson to three years, Judge Pratt recommended that for health reasons he be paroled after three months, ibid. Oct. 26, 1983, II, 2.
154.   *In the Matter of Harrison A. Williams, Jr.* 3−5 (history of Ethics Committee treatment); *Congressional Record* 128, S 1454, 1457 (March 3, 1982) (Wallop and Heflin on lack of partisan feeling); ibid. p. S 1802 (March 9, 1982) (Eagleton).
155.   Ibid. vol. 128, p. S 1472 (March 3, 1982) (traitors expelled); p. S 1475 ("gang of thugs"); p. S 1476 ("vile and putrid scenes"); p. S 1477 ("good man").
156.   Ibid. p. S 1795 (March 9, 1982) (Cranston on Williams); ibid. pp. S 1903−1906 (March 10, 1982) (transcript of Pressler conversation) p. S 1906 (Cranston on Pressler).
157.   Ibid. vol. 128, p. S 1472 (March 3, 1982) (Inouye); ibid. S 1721 (March 8, 1982) (Williams); ibid. S 1900 (March 10, 1982) (Hayakawa and Stennis).
158.   Ibid. vol. 128, p. S 1794 (March 9, 1982).
159.   Ibid. p. S 1736 (March 4, 1982) (Wallop); p. S 1437 (March 3, 1982) (Heflin); ibid. p. S 1454 (March 3, 1982) (Williams expellable on either alternative); ibid. p. S 1899 (March 10, 1982) (Pryor); ibid. p. S 1900 (March 10, 1982) (Stennis).
160.   Ibid. p. S 1882 (March 10, 1982).
161.   Ibid. p. S 1993−1994 (March 11, 1982) (ad); p. S 1998 (St. Paul). For the Left Hand, see Greene, *The Sting Man*, illustrations following 136.
162.   *Congressional Record* vol. 128, p. S 1642 (March 4, 1982).
163.   Ibid. vol. 128, p. S 1999 (March 11, 1982). Benjamin Franklin, *Poor Richard: The Almanack for the Years 1733−1758*, collated by Yvonne Noble (New York: Heritage Press, 1964) 20 (for July 1742). The proverb is at least as old as *Everyman*, see Morris P. Tilley, *A Dictionary of the Proverbs in England in the Sixteenth and Seventeenth Centuries* (Ann Arbor: University of Michigan Press, 1950) D 149.
164.   For Brandeis's view, see *Casey v. United States* 276 U.S. 413 (1928) 423−425. (Casey, a defense lawyer known to the jailers at King County Jail and suspected of bringing drugs to prisoners, was approached by a convict, George Cicero, who offered him $20 for morphine. Casey took his order for the money and delivered the drug to an intermediary, Mrs. Nelson. Cicero and Mrs. Nelson were acting at the instigation of the jailers, and Casey was arrested after he had made the delivery. Holmes, writing for the majority, rejected Brandeis's claim that setting up Casey had violated the purity of the process. "We are not persuaded," he wrote, "that the conduct of the officials was different or worse than ordering a drink of a suspected bootlegger." Ibid. 419.
165.   Immediately after Williams's departure, the Senate created a bipartisan select committee chaired by Charles Mathias of Maryland to investigate undercover operations of the Justice Department. The committee's report criticized the department for failure to supervise Weinberg; for placing too much credence in the uncorroborated claims of corrupt middlemen that particular officeholders were bribable; for not keeping better records of telephone calls and meetings of the undercover operatives; for giving too much control of Abscam to Puccio; for leaks to the press. The committee pointed to no injustice done to the Abscam defendants (Select Committee, *Final Report* 15−22).
    Senatorial scolding to this point, the report had recommendations for legislation—to create specific authority for the Federal Bureau of Investigation, the Drug Enforcement Administration, and the Internal Revenue Service to conduct undercover operations; to require the attorney general to draw up rules for their conduct; to authorize and regulate the use of money in undercover operations; and to require annual reports to Congress on such operations that were completed or had gone on more than two years. An Undercover Operations Review Committee of six was to be created in the Justice Department. No specific individual was to be given opportunity or inducement to commit a crime unless there was "a reasonable suspicion, based upon articulable facts, that the targeted individual has engaged, is engaging, or is likely to engage in criminal activity." Congress was also asked to create an affirmative defense of entrapment: the defendant would be found innocent of the crime he had committed if he could show that federal agents "manipulated the defendant's personal, economic, or vocational situation to increase the likelihood of his committing that crime" (ibid. 25−29).
    Recommendations of this nature accurately reflected the ambivalence of the committee. Undercover operations, it had found, had expanded enormously—53 run by the FBI alone in 1977, 463 in 1981. Risk and benefit attended them—the risk of injury to the property, privacy,

and civil liberties of citizens and the creation of crime where none would have existed; the benefit of detecting criminal activity, "especially organized crime and consensual crimes such as narcotics trafficking, fencing of stolen property, and political corruption." The proposed entrapment defense could be expanded to include any tempting offer or interpreted narrowly to mean only a change of the defendant's life situation. The standard for offering an individual an inducement to crime could mean that evidence of criminal conduct by the individual was in hand, or that hearsay indicated he would be "likely" to commit the crime. The administrative recommendations could be read to bureaucratize undercover operations to the point of hamstringing them; or they could be read to put a congressional seal of approval on a technique that had already bagged six congressmen and a senator.

CHAPTER 19: THE DONATIONS OF DEMOCRACY (PP. 621–651)

1. New York *Laws*, chap. 373 (1829); *Jackson v. Walker*, 5 Hill 31 (1843) ("contribution"); Naval Appropriations Act of 1867, 14 *U.S. Statutes* 492 (March 2, 1867) ("to contribute").

2. Theodore Roosevelt to Senator Moses Edwin Clapp, Aug. 28, 1912, *The Letters of Theodore Roosevelt*, ed. Elting E. Morison (Cambridge, Mass.: Harvard University Press, 1954) 7, 622.

3. For an intelligent discussion of the issues, see Note, "Campaign Contributions and Federal Bribery Law," 92 *Harvard Law Review* 451 (1978).

4. For example, (1) *In re Crum* 55 N.D. 876, 215 N.W. 682 (1927): a bank cashier, charged with embezzlement, informed Charles Crum, the assistant attorney general in charge of his case, that he would like to contribute to his campaign fund in a recall election; he then sent Crum $700 in cash. The payment was held to be a bribe; Crum was suspended for six months from law practice. (2) *State v. London* 194 Wash. 458, 78 P.2d 548 (1938): Mel London, a roads supervisor in King County, Washington, asked a supplier of pipe to contribute to John Stevenson's campaign for governor; the supplier gave London amounts totaling $591 in cash; London was convicted of taking a bribe and sentenced to ten years' imprisonment. (3) *State v. Smagula* 39 N.J. Super. 187, 120 A.2d 621 (1956): six members of the Board of Education of Wallington said to a candidate for school superintendent, "If you want the job it will cost you $3,000." He asked, "What for?" They said, "Campaign money." The six were convicted of soliciting a bribe.

5. Elihu Root, *Addresses on Government and Citizenship*, ed. Robert Bacon and James Brown Scott (Cambridge, Mass.: Harvard University Press, 1916) 144.

6. Roosevelt to George Cortelyou, Oct. 1, 1904, *Letters* 4, 963, and accompanying note; Roosevelt to Clapp, Aug. 28, 1912, *The Letters of T. R.* 7, 603–604, 618.

7. Roosevelt, *Presidential Message to Congress*, Dec. 5, 1905, *Congressional Record* 40, 96 (1905); Committee on Privileges and Elections, "Money Contributions of Corporations in Connection with Political Elections," *Senate Report No. 3056*, April 27, 1906, 59th Cong., 1st Sess., 2. For Roosevelt's reference to Foraker, Francis Russell, *The Shadow of Blooming Grove* (New York: McGraw-Hill, 1968) 186. The rationale of protecting the stockholder was ultimately undermined by *Cort v. Ash* 422 U.S. 66 (1975), denying a stockholder a federal right to sue a corporation for money spent in violation of the election law.

8. *U.S. Statutes* (1907) 34, 864 (the Tillman Act). In comparison, Massachusetts law, enacted the same year, had the same mild penalties and prohibited contributions only from insurance companies, Massachusetts, *Acts and Resolves* (1907) chap. 576, sec. 22. Gradually, this typical state statute was enlarged to embrace banks, utilities, and finally all "business corporations," *Annotated Laws of Massachusetts* (1958) c. 55, sec. 7.

9. *U.S. Statutes* (1908) 35, 1103 (codification); ibid. (1910) 36, 822 (primaries), held unconstitutional in *Newberry v. United States* 256 U.S. 232 (1921); Federal Corrupt Practices Act, 1925, *Statutes* 43, 1070. On the English precedent, see Earl R. Sikes, *State and Federal Corrupt-Practices Legislation* (Durham, N.C.: Duke University Press, 1928) 123. For American usage, see the argument in *Jackson v. Walker supra* n. 1 at 29.

10. *U.S. Statutes* (1940) 54, 772; for the statutes on union contributions, War Labor Disputes Act of 1943, 57 *Stat.* 167–168; Labor Management Relations Act of 1947, 61 *Stat.* 159.

11. As to corporations, see *United States v. United States Brewers' Association* 239 F.163 (W.D. Pa. 1916); *United States v. Lewis Food Co.* 236 F.Supp. 849 (S.D. Cal. 1964), applying loose standard set for unions to corporate spending. Edwin M. Epstein, *Corporations, Contributions and Political Campaigns: Federal Regulation in Perspective* (Berkeley, Calif.: Institute of Governmental Studies, 1968) 17; for the labor unions, *United States v. CIO* 335 U.S. 106 (1948); *United States v. United Auto Workers* 352 U.S. 567 (1957), wherein at 585–587 Justice Frankfurter suc-

cinctly reviews the history of the legislation; *Pipefitters Local Union 562 v. United States* 407 U.S. 385 (1972).

12.   Robert Engler, *The Politics of Oil* (New York: Macmillan, 1968) 404–407; Select Committee of the United States, "Contribution Investigation," *Senate Report No. 1724,* 1956, 84th Congress, 2nd Sess. For methods used to evade the statute, Engler, *Politics of Oil* 366; Jeremiah D. Lambert, "Corporate Political Spending and Campaign Finance," *New York University Law Review* 40 (1965) 1039.

13.   Federal Regulation of Lobbying Act, 60 *Stat.* 839 (1946), 2 *U.S. Code* secs. 261–270; President's Commission on Campaign Costs, *Financing Presidential Campaigns: Report* (Washington: Government Printing Office, 1962) 11 ("moral hock"); Lyndon B. Johnson, "Special Message to the Congress on Election Reform: The Political Process in America," May 25, 1967, Lyndon B. Johnson, *Public Papers: 1967* (Washington: Government Printing Office, 1968) 1, 565; Caro, Chapter 17 above, at notes 151–159; Federal Election Campaign Act of 1971, 86 *Stat.* 11–19 (1972), 2 *U.S. Code* sec. 431.

14.   86 *Stat.* 20 (1972).

15.   Watergate Special Prosecution Force, *Report* (Washington: Government Printing Office, 1975) 4–5.

16.   Ibid. 5 (appointment); 7 (staff); 72–73 (American Airlines).

17.   Ibid. 158–162.

18.   Special Review Committee of the Board of Directors of Gulf Oil Corporation, reprinted as *The Great Oil Spill* (New York: Chelsea House, 1976) [hereafter *Gulf Report*] 2 (Gulf assets and income); 7–9 (the $100,000 gift and its return).

19.   Ibid. v (Mellon ownership); 9–11 (board action and fines); 33 (concealment from the Mellons); Watergate Special Prosecution Force, *Report* 158–159 (guilty pleas).

20.   *Gulf Report* 11–15.

21.   Ibid. 32–33 (the top planners); 36–40 (Bahamas Ex.).

22.   Ibid. 39 (accumulation of dollars); Appendix D (record of dollar deliveries in the United States); 51–52 (totals).

23.   Ibid. 68–85.

24.   Ibid. 63–64, 70.

25.   Ibid. 74.

26.   Ibid. 71, 76–78.

27.   Ibid. 72–73, 79.

28.   Ibid. 77, 79–80, 82–84, 245–246.

29.   Ibid. 220.

30.   Ibid. 225.

31.   Ibid. 225 (Grummer); 227 (Anderson); 50–51 (Wild's handwritten notes); 46 (accounting advice); 222 (black bag).

32.   Ibid. 63 (Gulf's "muscle"); 234 (Senator Long).

33.   Ibid. 228.

34.   Ibid. 226, 229; *New York Times,* Feb. 14, 1960, 1, 35 (case dismissed); ibid. Oct. 25, 1961, 36 (editorial and information on Kennedy).

35.   *Gulf Report* 226 (Good Government Fund); 228 (Wild's view of Savage's reaction); 231 (Savage's testimony to review committee); 232 ("therapy"); 233 (Savage's knowledge of Whiteford's attitude).

36.   Ibid. 72 (Wild on Scott); 230–231 (Savage on Scott).

37.   Ibid. 33 ("Boy Scouts"); 234–236 (Brockett); 268–270 (Dorsey).

38.   Ibid. 238, 294 (Wild's reputation); 276 (Dorsey's shut eyes).

39.   Ibid. 270.

40.   Ibid. 294.

41.   E.g., ibid. 78.

42.   Ibid. 290.

43.   Ibid. 285–292.

44.   Ibid. 292.

45.   Ibid. 98–101.

46.   Ibid. 101–103.

47.   Ibid. 105.

48.   Ibid. 108–110.

49.   Ibid. 145–156.

50.   Ibid. 109 (Korea); 133–145 (Black Fund).

51.   Ibid. 125, n.1.

52. Ibid. 125.

53. *Wall Street Journal*, June 2, 1975, p. 8 (editorial); ibid. Jan. 2, 1976, p. 5 ("slush fund"); ibid. March 11, 1976, p. 1 (Chelsea House printing of the Gulf report).

54. Ibid. Jan. 13, 1976, p. 38.

55. Ibid. Jan. 15, 1976, p. 1, 17, qualified Jan. 16, 1976, p. 6.

56. Ibid. Sept. 30, 1976, 18 (settlement); ibid. March 15, 1976, p. 3 (cost of McCloy investigation).

57. Ibid. Nov. 14, 1977, 40.

58. Ibid. Dec. 23, 1977, 8.

59. Ibid. Jan. 23, 1976, 8 (Scott); ibid. Jan. 30, 1976, 20 (Jones's guilty plea); ibid. Mar. 17, 1976, 27 (his fine); ibid. Sept. 30, 1976, 18 (reimbursement).

60. Ibid. June 7, 1976, 12 (indictment); ibid. July 6, 1976, 4 (guilty plea); ibid. Aug. 5, 1976, 10.

61. *United States v. Brewster* 506 F.2d 62 (D.C. Cir. 1974); *United States v. Anderson* 509 F.2d 312 (D.C. Cir. 1974).

62. *United States v. Brewster* 408 U.S. 521 (1977) 543 ("more a matter of emphasis"); 558 ("enormous leverage").

63. Ibid. 523–525.

64. *U.S. Code* (1982) Title 18, sec. 201; American Law Institute, *Model Penal Code and Commentaries* (Philadelphia: American Law Institute, 1980) sec. 240.1, pp. 5–9. A majority of recent statutes followed the *Model Penal Code* in eliminating "corruptly" or "corrupt" intent. When Wisconsin did so, it was held that a jury still had to be instructed that a "corrupt" intent was required; the court refused to believe that the legislation had meant to effect such a "cataclysmic" change as its elimination would mean, *State v. Alfonsi* 33 Wis. 2nd 469, 147 N.W. 2d 555 (1967). But what the cataclysmic change would have been is hard to say.

The survival of what appears to be confusing surplusage—"corrupt"—has a parallel in the law on usury. The statute of Henry VIII against usury describes it in terms of a "corrupt bargain," 37 Henry VIII, c. 9 (1545). American courts still determine the existence of usury in terms of "a corrupt purpose," *I.R.E. Financial Corp. v. Cassel* 335 So. 2d 598, 599 (Florida 1976) or "a corrupt intent," *Western Auto Supply Co. v. Vick* 277 S.E. 2d 360, 366 (North Carolina, 1981). The survival of "corrupt" could be read as a sign of the religious origins of both the bribery and usury prohibitions.

The *Model Penal Code* itself created a problem analogous to that created by judicial interpretation of the federal statute. The *Model Penal Code*, sec. 240, a section distinct from that treating of bribery, was entitled, "Gifts to Public Servants by Persons Subject to Their Jurisdiction." The harsh word "bribe" was not used, and the offense was classed as a misdemeanor. An awkward exception was made for gifts conferred on account of "personal, professional or business relationship independent of the official status of the receiver." Implicitly the exception acknowledged that the gifts condemned were those made on account of the official status of the receiver. But what were gifts of this sort if not bribes?

65. In *Irwin*, the first major case to construe subsection *f*, the Second Circuit had said it was meant to prevent "additional compensation or a tip or gratuity" (in *Irwin* a payment by a tax accountant to an employee of the Internal Revenue Service). The court went on, "The awarding of gifts thus related to an employee's official acts is an evil in itself . . . because it tends, subtly or otherwise, to bring about preferential treatment. . . ." *United States v. Irwin* 354 F.2d 192 (2nd Cir. 1965), 196, *cert. denied* 383 U.S. 967 (1966).

66. *United States v. Anderson* 509 F.2d 312 at 332.

67. *United States v. Brewster* 506 F.2d 62 at 68–73 (appeals court's own analysis); 76 ("faltered"); 77 (First Amendment implications); 79 ("strove manfully"); 82 ("indigestible"). Edward Bennett Williams, Brewster's particularly able counsel, had pressed hard the argument that the statute was unconstitutional because it appeared to condemn the acceptance of contributions arguably characterized as political activity protected by the First Amendment—how hard can be inferred from the court's attempt to grapple with the argument. Brewster's guilty plea is reported in *New York Times*, June 26, 1975, p. 19.

68. For the cases where "contribution" was merely a code for bribe, see above at note 4; for the rule as stated in Kerner's case, *United States v. Isaacs* 493 F.2d 1124 (7th Cir. 1974) at 1145; for Williams, see Chapter 18 above at n. 137.

One possible difference of a visible kind separated certain campaign contributions from *f* bribes: to violate *f* the payment had to be to the officeholder *himself*; arguably a payment made to a campaign committee did not fall within the statute. The court in *Brewster* made this distinction fuzzy by indicating that *f* was violated if the campaign committee was "merely a conduit" to the officeholder or was his "alter ego." It then became a question of fact whether any particular campaign committee was the officeholder's conduit or alter ego. The difficulty in distinguishing "alter egos" and "surrogates" can be seen in the literature on the comparable problem of distinguishing a PAC from its corporate creator, see below at n. 78. Even the court's fuzzy distinction was not useful when *b* bribes were at issue: *b* bribes could be paid to persons other than the official.

69.   *U.S. Statutes* 88, 1280—1288. See generally Joel L. Fleishman, "The 1974 Federal Election Campaign Act Amendments: The Shortcomings of Good Intentions," *Duke Law Journal* (1975) 851.

70.   *U.S. Statutes* 88, 1263, *U.S. Code* 2, 441a (limits); *U.S. Statutes* 88, 1268, *U.S. Code* 2, 441g (cash); *U.S. Statutes* 88, 1268, *U.S. Code* 2, 441i (honoraria).

71.   *Buckley v. Valeo* 424 U.S. 1 (1976) at 26—27. The Court referred to *Buckley v. Valeo* 519 F.2d 821 at 838—839 (D.C. App. 1975) for the "deeply disturbing examples." The lower court had cited contributions by Gulf Oil, by American Milk Producers, Inc., by the American Dental Association, and by H. Ross Perot. The lower court also referred to polls conducted by the Center for Political Studies at the University of Michigan showing a marked increase from 1964 to 1974 of those who believed that "the government" was run "by a few big interests."

72.   *Buckley v. Valeo* 424 U.S. 1 at 27—28. *Buckley v. Valeo* held unconstitutional the new laws' limits on spending by individuals; and this teaching was extended by Judge Malcolm Wilkey to hold unconstitutional the limits on spending imposed on PACs, *Common Cause v. Schmitt* 512 F. Supp. 489 (DDC 1980), affirmed by an equally divided Supreme Court without opinion, 455 U.S. 129 (1982). The central distinction insisted upon was between contributing and spending. As Judge Wilkey put it at 495, "The opportunity for venal politician/contributor relationships" could be constitutionally impeded.

The Supreme Court drew other lines as to regulations aimed specifically at corporations. It held unconstitutional as violating the First Amendment right of free speech a Massachusetts statute restricting political advertising by a corporation designed to influence a referendum, *First National Bank of Boston v. Bellotti* 435 U.S. 765 (1978): the risk of corruption, it said at 790, was simply "not present." But the federal restrictions on soliciting funds by a corporation were upheld in *Federal Election Commission v. National Right to Work Committee* 51 LW 4037 (1982): the court would not "second guess a legislative determination as to the need for prophylactic measures where corruption is the evil feared." That, of course, as *Common Cause* and *First National Bank* showed, was not literally true. The Court would balance the great guarantees of the First Amendment against its concern with the evil of corruption. Where the Court thought there was sufficient risk of the evil, prophylactic measures to achieve purity would be permitted. See the critique of the Supreme Court by Circuit Judge J. Skelly Wright, "Money and the Pollution of Politics: Is the First Amendment an Obstacle to Political Equality?" *Columbia Law Review* 82 (1982) 609.

73.   See *U.S. Department of Agriculture v. Moreno* 413 U.S. 528 (1973) at 538 ("wholly without any rational basis"); *Carey v. Population Services* 431 U.S. 678 at 715 (1977) ("irrational and perverse"). There were limits to the Court's concern for purity, especially where freedom of speech could be invoked. In *Brown v. Hartlage*, 102 S. Ct. 1523 (1982), a candidate for commissioner in Jefferson County, Kentucky, announced that he would serve for $3,000 less than the $20,000 salary fixed by law. He was overwhelmingly elected. His opponent sought to invalidate the election on the ground that the winner had by his offer violated the Kentucky Corrupt Practices Act, *Kentucky Rev. Stat.*, sec. 122-055. The highest court to consider the issue in Kentucky agreed and invalidated the election. The Supreme Court reversed. Public commitments by a candidate were "very different from the corrupting agreements and solicitations historically recognized as unprotected by the First Amendment." The First Amendment was held to protect the candidate's public promise.

74.   For the history, see Edwin M. Epstein, "The Emergence of Political Action Committees," in Herbert E. Alexander, ed., *Political Finance* (Beverly Hills, Calif.: Sage Publications, 1979) 161—162; *Pipefitters Local Union No. 562 v. United States* 407 U.S. 385 (1972) at 420 ("the paradigm"); at 430 (shift in financing).

75.   *Pipefitters* above, n. 11, at 390 ($1,000,000); at 449 ("hitherto unrecognized"); 86 *Stat.* 10 (1972) ("separate segregated funds"). On the AFL-CIO's role in the legislation, Epstein, "Emergence" 164—165.

76.   Federal Election Committee, Advisory Opinion 1975-23 (the *Sun Oil* opinion), 40 *Federal Register* 56584 (1975). Printing, mailing, and soliciting costs, plus an allocation of salaries and equipment could be borne by the corporation or union, see Comment, "Corporate Political Action Committees: Effect of the Federal Election Campaign Act Amendments of 1976," *Catholic University Law Review* (1977) 26, 756 at 771. On the PACs' multiplication, "Running with the PACs," cover story, *Time*, Oct. 25, 1982, 20—26.

77.   Edwin M. Epstein, "PACs and the Modern Political Process," unpublished paper dated Oct. 1982, 25–27 (preference of PACs for incumbents and Democrats), 32 (prediction of corporate PACs' increase); Epstein, "Emergence" at 166 (on how Labor—some unions being contractors with the government by reason of manpower training agreements—moved to get the 1974 amendment).

78.   Epstein, "PACs and the Modern Political Process" 13 ("surrogates"); ibid. 62 (average contributor).

79.   Tom Richman, "Picking a PAC," *Inc.*, Aug. 1982, p. 30, quoting Justin Dart, chairman of Dart Industries ("With a little money") and Andy Ireland, Democratic congressman from Florida ("Organized special interests"). *Inc.*'s analysis was given an even broader audience by being quoted in *Time*, Oct. 25, 1982, p. 24. An article in the *Wall Street Journal* noted that individuals identified as lawyers led all others in contributions to candidates for Congress and that a number of law firms with a practice in such areas as antitrust law, tax law, and government regulation of business were active in organizing PACs, one such PAC contributing at least $500,000 in all to candidates for the Senate and the House. Fred Wertheimer, president of Common Cause, criticized the lawyers' giving as "straight access buying." Thomas H. Boggs, a prominent Washington lawyer, denied that lawyers' contributions had anything to do with access-buying. "Access in this town is who you represent and not how much money you've given." John J. Fialka, "Making Friends: Legal Profession Tops All Others in Financing Candidates for Congress," *Wall Street Journal*, Aug. 18, 1983, 1. The Staff of *Congressional Quarterly*, ed., *Dollar Politics* (3rd ed., Washington, 1982) 48 ("rewards" and "loyalty"); 52 (organizers of top PACs in 1980); Elizabeth Drew, *Politics and Money: The New Road to Corruption* (New York: Macmillan, 1983) 78 ("with a little money").

80.   Russell Long, "Statement," in *Financing Political Campaigns, Hearings on S. 3496, Amendment No. 732, S. 2006, S. 2965 and S. 3014 Before the Senate Committee on Finance*, 89th Cong., 2nd Sess. 78 (1966). On the old distinctions on usury, see John T. Noonan, Jr., *The Scholastic Analysis of Usury* 104–105.

81.   Drew, *Politics and Money* 4, 77, 146; Daniel H. Lowenstein, "Poltical Bribery and the Intermediate Theory of Politics" (unpublished typescript) p. 55 and p. 81. Lowenstein's term "contested concept" drew on William E. Connolly, *The Terms of Political Discourse*, 2nd ed. (Princeton, N.J.: Princeton University Press, 1983) 10–43. I am indebted to Lowenstein, now a professor of law at the University of California Law School at Los Angeles, for a copy of his paper and for references to the cases noted above in n. 4.

82.   *People v. Brandstetter* 430 N.E. 2nd 731 (Ill. App. 1982) *cert. denied* 51 LW 3362 (1982). Note that *Brandstetter* had none of the characteristics of the cases summarized above, n. 4. There was no personal benefit to the payor, the issue was one of general legislation, and there was no indication that the money would go to the personal enrichment of the officeholder.

CHAPTER 20: THE AMBASSADORS OF AMERICA (PP. 652–680)

1.   Malcolm Muggeridge, *The Infernal Grove* (New York: William Morrow, 1974) 154, 173.

2.   John Fisher to Winston S. Churchill, Jan. 25, 1915, Martin Gilbert, *Companion Volume I, Part I* to Gilbert, Vol. III of *Winston S. Churchill* (London: Heinemann, 1972) 449.

3.   Churchill to Randolph Churchill, Feb. 16, 1938, printed in Gilbert, *Winston S. Churchill* 5, 898–899.

4.   James Bryce, *The American Commonwealth* 2, 121.

5.   Joseph Conrad, *Nostromo* (New York: Doubleday, Page, 1924) 84–85. Gould's reasoning is repeated tolerantly in Neil H. Jacoby, Peter Nehemkis, Richard Eells, *Bribery and Extortion in World Business* (N.Y.: Macmillan, 1977) 193–94.

6.   William Simon, Chairman of the Emergency Loan Guarantee Board, Statement, Aug. 25, 1975, "Lockheed Bribery," *Hearings Before the Committee on Banking, Housing and Urban Affairs*, United States Senate, 94th Cong., 1st Sess. [Hereafter Proxmire Hearings] 9.

7.   In the audit conducted in 1972, William Findley, the Young partner in charge of Lockheed, questioned a sales commission not because of its nature but because the consultant to whom it was to be paid had assigned the payment. He was told that the assignment was a method of paying the head of a foreign air force. He insisted the matter be brought to the attention of the company's chief financial officer and dropped it at that point. In this minor and benign way, the accountants had taken up and put down money paid as a bribe, Special Review Committee of the Directors of Lockheed Aircraft Company, *Report*, Exhibit A to Lockheed, Form 8–K, filed with the SEC, May 1977 [Hereafter *Special Report*] 44–45.

In the audit in 1973, Arthur Young and Company found a record of $100,000 in cash at the

Hong Kong office of Lockheed Asia and observed that the cash "might have been paid under-the-counter." They then noted, "OK, Mr. C. R. Warman is aware of this item." Warman was the local manager. The auditors also found substantial cash and bearer check payments in Japan and noted the existence of a schedule of yen purchases kept by E. H. Schattenburg, the treasurer of Lockheed Asia. As the audit neared its close in February 1973, Findley and Mayhugh of Arthur Young "expressed concern" over the large number of payments Lockheed made in cash. They tabulated the amount at $4.6 million and suggested that the audit committee of the board of directors be informed. President Kotchian told them that only in England and the United States could a plane be sold without payments. He added that the yen went to "somebody's war chest." Chairman Haughton observed that if they told the audit committee the committee's counsel would instruct it to tell the board, "so why don't you just put it in the *Los Angeles Times*?" (ibid. 45–47 and Exhibit 9, pp. 11–14).

Intended as a *reductio ad absurdum*, this rejoinder did not prevent the auditors from telling the audit committee. The information went no further. The committee concluded that the payments were "proper sales costs" and were not necessary to report to the full board. The *Los Angeles Times* was not, even indirectly, to be informed. The committee did ask that big cash payments be in accordance with a contract with the consultant receiving them; and to achieve this conformity a contract with him was signed, dated "as of 1969" (ibid. 47).

In 1974 Arthur Young and Company furnished the audit committee with a worldwide tabulation showing "commissions" of $140 million on sales of $1.3 billion. The committee now asked for the opinion of outside counsel. For this purpose, John Martin, the company's inside counsel, drew up a general description of the commissions. Repeating no doubt what he was told, Martin stated that the commissions were paid to consultants in accordance with contracts; that they were generally commensurate with what was paid for similar services; and that they were properly recorded on the books of the company. Martin added that no officer of Lockheed knew how the consultants disposed of the money they received. On the basis of this description, Coudert Brothers in Paris and the firm of Miller and Chevalier in Washington gave their legal opinions that the payments were legal. Accountants and lawyers, familiar though they might be with the airplane business, were content with Martin's formal description (ibid. 50–52).

8.   *Wall Street Journal*, April 9, 1975, 1 (SEC investigation); ibid. May 7, 1975, 1 (power struggle over bribe); *New York Times*, Feb. 4, 1975, 1 (Black's death).

9.   *Wall Street Journal*, April 10, 1975, 2 (SEC suit); ibid. April 23, 1975, 1 (fall of Lopez).

10.   *Proxmire Hearings* 7.

11.   Subcommittee on Multinational Corporations, "Multinational Corporations and United States Foreign Policy," *Hearings before the Subcommittee on Multinational Corporations*, 94th Cong., 1st Sess. Jan. 29, Feb. 5, 19, 20, 26, March 11 and 18, 1975, Part II, on "Political and Financial Consequences of the OPEC Price Increases"; May 16, 19, June 9, 10, July 16, 17, Sept. 12, 1975, on "Political Contributions to Foreign Governments" [hereafter *Church Hearings*]. The Arab League Boycott was explored Feb. 26, 1975, *Church Hearings*, Part 11, 195–228. The Institute for Policy Studies was heard from May 19, 1975, *Church Hearings*, Part 12, 59–105. Northrop Corporation was the subject on June 9–10, 1975, ibid. Part 12, 107–238. The "Lockheed model" is referred to at 124 and 131. Payments to Khashoggi are described at 120–121 and to Weisbrod at 136–137.

12.   *Church Hearings*, Feb. 4, 1976, Part 14, "Lockheed Aircraft Corporation," 303–306 (statement of William Findley); *Wall Street Journal*, Aug. 25, 1975, 14 (death of treasurer).

13.   Proxmire, Statement, *Proxmire Hearings*, Part 12, 1–2.

14.   Simon, Statement, Ibid. 5 and 8.

15.   Proxmire–Simon colloquy, ibid. 14–16.

16.   Daniel Haughton, Statement, ibid. 25 (total advances); Haughton–Proxmire colloquies, ibid. 31, 36 and 45; ibid. 48 (cause of suicide).

17.   Ibid. 54–55 (Proxmire); *New York Times*, Feb. 7, 1976, 21 (Baker).

18.   Haughton, *Statement*, *Church Hearings*, Sept. 12, 1975, Part 12, 345–346.

19.   Ibid. 346.

20.   J. W. Clutter to W. G. Myers, Interdepartmental Memo, Aug. 11, 1965, *Church Hearings* 12, 937 ("unique position"). D. D. Stone to W. G. Myers, May 7, 1968, ibid. 961 (Dasaad without influence); N. C. Ridings to D. W. Cedarberg, Aug. 8, 1967, ibid. 955–959 (Dasaad's position); C. Fred C. Meuser to Earle N. Constable, July 19, 1968, ibid. 962 (Dasaad still influential); E. E. Rainwater to N. C. Ridings, Oct. 2, 1970, ibid. 976 (payments to military); Haughton–Church colloquy, ibid. 376. Dasaad operated on a commssion that was strikingly flexible. In 1965, the Sukarno government bought three Jet Stars, priced at $1,774,000;

Dasaad took a 3 percent commission, but on the third Je*-Star the price was increased $100,000 with the understanding that Lockheed channel the extra money to Dasaad. Negotiations opened on a fourth Jet Star with the Indonesians suggesting another $100,000 which Lockheed would route to Dasaad; otherwise Indonesia would buy a Caravelle. Haughton turned the request down. Senator Percy interpreted the rejection as a "moral position"; but Haughton told the senators, "When I refused to let the fellows put another $100,000 on the fourth Jet Star for Indonesia, that airplane already had some commissions in it, and I thought it was enough" (ibid. 371 and 938–939).

21.   Ibid. 349 ($106 million commissions); see Lockheed Aircraft Corporation and Triad Financial Establishment, "Consultant Agreement," Sept. 1, 1967, reproduced in *Church Hearings* 1012–1014; Clay E. Eaton, Lockheed Interdepartmental Memo, Oct. 24, 1967, and contracts, ibid. 1011–1021; Alan Kaplan, Lockheed Interdepartmental Memo, Aug. 15, 1968, ibid. 1024–1025 (on Saudi's complaint against Khashoggi; the name of the Saudi has been deleted from the reproduction); Haughton, Statement, ibid. 12, 351 ("more players"). A Lockheed cable from Saudi Arabia to the home office, for example, read, "Machinery stalled for lack of grease." In such cases, Triad usually agreed to an assignment of part of its commission, and Lockheed made payments to numbered bank accounts in Switzerland or Liechtenstein, listed in the name of another entity, Lauvier Établissement, see Church-Haughton Colloquy, ibid. 351 ("machinery stalled . . ."); Triad Financial Establishment to Lockheed Aircraft Service Company, Feb. 4, 1971, ibid. 1045 (assignment to Lauvier Établissement).

A decree of the Saudi Council of Ministers required a clause in procurement contracts specifying that no agent had been used to secure the sale. The Council further required the price to be reduced by any fees paid. An interdepartmental memo of Lockheed took note of this official action and recommended ignoring it: "our failure to include the clause may possibly go unchallenged, with proper ground work, and at worst can be made to appear simply an oversight on our part," J. A. Davidson to W. W. Cowden, Interdepartmental Memo, Nov. 26, 1969, ibid. 1033. The decree had no apparent effect on the arrangements with Khashoggi.

22.   Ibid. 367, 382.
23.   Ibid. 367.
24.   Ibid. 368–369 (Case); 377 (locust).
25.   Ibid. 378.
26.   Ibid. 375.
27.   Ibid. Kissinger to Attorney General Edward H. Levi, Nov. 28, 1975. Text in A. Carl Kotchian, *Lockheed Sales Mission: 70 Days in Tokyo* (typescript, 1976, on file in the Law Library, University of California, Berkeley) Appendix, 31.
28.   Ibid. 13.
29.   *Church Hearings,* Part 14, 8 ("One Hundred Peanuts"); ibid. 329 (code interpreted); ibid. 181 (later receipts by Itoh).
30.   Roger Smith to C. M. Valentine, March 28, 1969, ibid. 14, 28–34 (italics in original).
31.   Ibid. 315 (Percy); ibid., 300–308, 327–342 (Findley).
32.   Ibid. 343–349 (off-the-books account); 349 (Netherlands); 353 (gift or bribe).
33.   Kotchian, *Lockheed Sales Mission* 19–20.
34.   *Who's Who in America 1980–1981* 1575.
35.   Commission of Three, *Report* [English translation supplied to the author by the Embassy of the Netherlands, Washington, D.C.; hereafter, Commission of Three) 1-1. The Commission members were A. M. Donner, Judge of the Court of Justice of the European Communities; M. W. Holtrop, former president of the Netherlands Bank; and H. Peschar, president of the General Chamber of Auditors.
36.   Commission of Three, 2–2, 2–6.
37.   Ibid. 2–7, 2–12.
38.   Ibid. 7–7. To a considerable degree the Commission ignored its own characterization of Bernhard's role. Bernhard did not have any official purchasing authority. Supreme commander of the Dutch Armed Forces in 1944, he had subsequently become inspector-general of the Army and Air Force and inspector-admiral of the Navy and held a seat on the Defense Council and the Air Force Council. Besides having this eminence in the military, he had devoted much of his energy to the promotion of Dutch trade, and he was especially active in the aviation industry. He had learned to fly during World War II and usually flew his own plane. He was an honorary director of KLM, the national airlines, and a director of Fokker, Dutch manufacturers of aircraft. Military and civilian officials consulted him on aviation questions. The officials assumed that they were speaking to a sophisticated and detached observer, unpaid by any company. His "good personal contacts" in aviation made it possible

"to get doors opened and contacts made." Access was what H.R.H. provided. The Commission of Three, looking for some exertion of authority which he did not have, or expression of opinion which he did not commit to paper, found nothing, ibid. 3−14 and 15.

39. Ibid. 2−14 (Smith sent to prince); ibid. 7−4 ("all the features"); ibid. 2−14 (prince's honesty appreciated).

40. Ibid. 2−16 and 17 (prince astonished); ibid. 7−5 (concealed threat); ibid. 2−17 (later negotiations).

41. Ibid. 2−18.

42. Ibid. 7−6. The prince's role as patron is described in Who's Who in the Netherlands 1962/1963, ed. Stephen S. Taylor and Marinus Spruytenburg (International Book and Publishing Co., 1963).

43. Commission of Three, 7−6.

44. Who's Who in the Netherlands (biography); New York Times, Sept. 24, 1976, sec. II, 8 (royal allowance); Commission of Three, 7−7 to 8 (conclusions).

45. Ibid. 7−8.

46. New York Times, Feb. 8, 1975, 1 and 9; ibid. Feb. 9, 1975, 1−2.

47. Joop den Uyl, Statement to Parliament, Aug. 26, 1976, English translation, New York Times, Aug. 27, 1976, 8.

48. Prince Bernhard, Statement, Aug. 23, 1976, English translation, New York Times, Aug. 27, 1976, 8.

49. New York Times, Sept. 9, 1976, 50 (Erasmus prize); ibid. Sept. 17, 1976, sec. IV, 13 (U.S. trip canceled; WWF resignation).

50. Alvin Shuster, "Post-Lockheed Picture Not At All Clear," New York Times, March 20, 1977, sec. IV, 2.

51. Wall Street Journal, March 23, 1976, 29 (Fanali arrest); Guido Campopiano, Memoria di Accuse Contro L'Onorevole Giovanni Leone ed altri scritti sull' Affare Lockheed (Milan: Sugarco Edizione Siri, 3rd ed., 1978) 10 (Leone).

52. Wall Street Journal, March 20, 1979, 20; ibid. July 24, 1980, 20 (restitution of bribes); ibid. Aug. 6, 1979, 15 (unindentified recipient).

53. New York Times, Feb. 7, 1976, 1 and 32; ibid. Feb. 8, 1976, 1, 8; ibid. Feb. 12, 1976, 49; ibid., Feb. 13, 1976, 49 (Public Safety Commission).

54. Wall Street Journal, ibid. March 4, 1976, 4; March 15, 1976, 6; ibid. March 16 (Kodama); ibid. June 23, 1976, 2; ibid. Sept 9, 1976, 12 (Okubo); ibid. June 3, 1977, 7 (amount received).

55. Ibid. July 26, 1976, 6; ibid. July 27, 1976, 22; ibid. July 28, 1976, 17; ibid. Aug. 10, 1976, 10; ibid. Aug. 17, 1976, 2. The text of the indictment has been furnished to me in translation by the Japanese Embassy in Washington.

56. Ibid. March 18, 1976, 1 (taperecording); ibid. Sept. 9, 1976, 10 (resignation); New York Times, March 20, 1977, sec. IV, 2 (election loss); Wall Street Journal, Jan. 24, 1977, 13 (Osano); ibid. Jan. 27, 1977, 15 (Tanaka trial).

57. Wall Street Journal, Nov. 6, 1981, 29 (first verdicts against Osano and Tachikawa); ibid. Jan. 27, 1982 (Wakasa); New York Times, Jan. 27, 1983, 66 (punishment asked for Tanaka); ibid. Oct. 12, 1983, 1 (Tanaka's conviction and sentence). Enomoto was convicted of violating foreign exchange laws and sentenced to one year; Hayama was found guilty of conspiracy to offer bribes and given $2^1/_2$ years in prison; Itoh received two years for the same offense; Okubo, also found guilty of conspiracy, drew a sentence of two years, suspended because of his forthright testimony, ibid.

58. Kotchian, Lockheed Sales Mission 225−230.

59. Ibid. 111 (height); Who's Who in America 1970−1971 1273 (other data).

60. Kotchian, Lockheed Sales Mission 230, 236−237.

61. Ibid. 231.

62. Ibid. 106 (payoff); 200 ("extremely persuasive"); i, iii (Lucy).

63. Ibid. 1.

64. Ministry of Justice of Japan, Criminal Statutes c. 35, articles 197, 198. Research and Training Institute, Ministry of Japan, Summary of the White Paper on Crime (1980) 18.

65. Securities and Exchange Commission, "Questionable and Illegal Corporate Payments and Practices," submitted to the Committee on Banking, Housing, and Urban Affairs, U.S. Senate, May 1976 (over 300 corporations as of this date); Note, "Effective Enforcement of the Foreign Corrupt Practices Act," Stanford Law Review 32 (1980) 561, relying on a figure of 527 reported by Newsweek, Feb. 19, 1979, 63; the figure includes some domestic payments.

Haughton and Kotchian had lost their executive positions immediately after the Church Hearings of 1976, although they had continued as "consultants"—that category of employee which Lockheed found infinitely elastic—and, represented by counsel in settlements with the company, had not gone away penniless. The new board of directors, representing a substantial infusion of outside directors, agreed to the consent decree requested by the SEC. By its terms, under penalty of being in contempt of a federal court, Lockheed could not pay any corporate funds "to, or for the benefit of, any official or employee of any foreign government" or make any false entry on its books to conceal such payments. By the terms of the decree Lockheed also agreed that a Special Review Committee of four new directors would report to the SEC on the payments it had made. *SEC v. Lockheed Aircraft Corp.*, Civil Action No. 76-0611, U.S. District Court for the District of Columbia, Final Judgment of Permanent Injunction, April 13, 1976, CCH, *Federal Securities Reporter*, p. 95, 509.

Lockheed operated in seventy countries. Forty-one were thought in need of scrutiny. A questionnaire was addressed to 600 key employees. The committee's legal staff conducted 220 interviews, the committee itself thirty. It could not compel testimony like a court, but it had the persuasive powers of the company's management behind it and, like the Gulf review committee, it was generally satisfied by the cooperation it received. It had unfettered access to the books, the auditors, the lawyers. By the time the task was finished, just a year later, its staff had reviewed 135,000 pages of documents (*Special Report* 10−12). The New York law firm Shearman & Sterling and the accounting firm Arthur Anderson & Co. assisted the investigation, which was directed by the committee's special counsel, former U.S. District Judge Arnold Bauman, see *Gaines v. Haughton* 645 F.2d 761 (9th Cir. 1981) at 767.

66.   *Special Report* 33 (amount), 30−35 (methods); ibid. Exhibit 8, "Funds Outside Normal Channels." As the review committee reported, a "consultant" on sales to a foreign air force received a large cash payment from a Lockheed employee and in 1974 kicked back $100,000 to the employee which he deposited to his personal account in Switzerland. The kickback came to light because the recipient and his wife broke up, and his wife let Lockheed know; Lockheed, suiting the punishment to the crime, deducted $100,000 from the next payment to the consultant. Where husband and wife stayed united, the chance was small of detecting bribes with this sort of reverse spin. Ibid. Exhibit 5, "Additional Information Concerning United States Activities," 8−9, 11−17.

67.   Ibid 2 and 40. The Special Review Committee consisted of Houston I. Flournoy, former controller of California and unsuccessful Republican candidate for governor; Joseph P. Downer, executive vice-president of Atlantic Richfield, a veteran of the oil industry; and Ellison L. Hazard, retired chairman of the Continental Group, an insurance man. It was eventually headed (after one resignation) by J. Wilson Newman, retired chairman of Dun and Bradstreet. Newman, like Haughton, had grown up in a small southern town; he was a lawyer; and as head of a famous credit-rating firm, he had vast experience with American corporations. Dun and Bradstreet was also the owner of the *Wall Street Journal*, and Newman approached his job with the *Journal's* commitment to capitalism and to the exposure of its corruptions. The committee under his guidance proceeded with great vigor to investigate Lockheed's practices.

A shareholder brought a derivative action against Haughton and other directors, charging that Lockheed was entitled to damages from them for breach of their fiduciary duty to the corporation and the waste of corporate assets of the company in making the payments. A special litigation committee of Lockheed, composed of outside directors, concluded that "sound business judgment" dictated that the claims should not be pursued. The shareholder's suit was summarily dismissed, *Gaines v. Haughton* 645 F.2d 761 (9th Cir. 1981), *cert. denied* 454 U.S. 1145 (1981). The failure of the directors to disclose the foreign payments in proxy solicitations between 1961 and 1975 was also held not to give a shareholder a cause of action under sec. 14a of the Securities Exchange Act of 1934, ibid. at 779.

68.   *Special Report* 60−61 (on improvement in internal audit and company counsel).

69.   Ibid. 62.

70.   Conversation of the author with Mr. Newman, June 1980.

71.   *Internal Revenue Code*, sec. 7201 (willful evasion), sec. 7206 (perjurious statement). Prior to 1958 the Internal Revenue Service had taken the position that bribes to foreign officials were not deductible under the general rubric of "ordinary and necessary expenses" unless the foreign government "acquiesced" in the bribes: the proviso left a large loophole. In 1958, in the golden years of the Eisenhower administration, the law was amended and a curious hypothetical standard introduced. No "payment" "directly or indirectly" made to a foreign official was deductible if the payment would have been illegal under federal law if federal law had applied to the official. The amendment, although requiring imagination to apply, was not unintelligible. The regulations defined an indirect payment as one that inured to the of-

ficial's benefit [*Internal Revenue Code*, sec. 162c, as amended by the Technical Amendments Act of 1958, sec. 6 and regulations thereunder *T.D.* 6448, *Cumulative Bulletin* 1960−1 at 55; *Senate Report* No. 1983, 85th Cong., 2nd Sess., reprinted *U.S. Code Congressional and Administrative News* (1958) 3, 4805 (prior policy of IRS)]. With the 1962 Kennedy changes in federal bribery law the text of section 162 set a stringent standard for deductibility. Payments made "for" or "on account of" the act of an official became nondeductible. Another amendment in 1969 changed "payment" to "illegal bribe or kickback" without materially altering the standard of section 162c as amended by the Tax Reform Act of 1969. In any year after 1958 in which a company had taken a deduction for an overseas bribe it had understated its tax liability and, if it did so willfully, committed a federal crime. Aroused by knowledge of how widespread the foreign bribes had been, the Internal Revenue Service in the spring of 1976 required large corporations doing business overseas to answer "Eleven Questions" directed at discovering the lawfulness of their deductions on sales abroad. For the applicable federal bribery law after 1962, see Chapter 18 above, at n. 104. For the Eleven Questions, see *Manual Supplement* 42G-348, 2 CCH *Internal Revenue Manual* 7455-51 (1976).

72.   8 *U.S. Code* sec. 1001 (false statements); 22 *U.S. Code* sec. 6 (1976) (the Foreign Assistance Act). See Comment, "The Foreign Corrupt Practices Act of 1977," *University of Kansas Law Review* 27 (1978) 636.

73.   The Currency and Foreign Transactions Reporting Act (Bank Secrecy Act), 84 *Stat.* 1121−1122 (1970), 31 *U.S. Code* secs. 1051−1143. On conspiracy to violate the tax laws, *United States v. Klein* 247 F.2d 908 (2nd Cir. 1957).

74.   Chapter 18 above at n. 93.

75.   *United States v. United Brands Corp.*, No. 78 Cr. 538 (S.D. N.Y., July 19, 1978), summarized in Stanley S. Arkin et al., *Business Crime* (New York: Matthew Bender, 1983) vol. 4, sec. 18.04; *New York Times*, July 1, 1982, D1 and D13 (Boeing). *Wall Street Journal*, June 4, 1979, 8 (Lockheed plea), ibid. Sept. 9, 1981, 12 (McDonnell-Douglas). On the Eleven Questions, see Frederic W. Hickman, "Tax Aspects of 'Sensitive Payments,'" *Taxes* 54 (1976) 865−875.

76.   Banking, Housing, and Urban Affairs Committee, *Sen. Rep.* No. 95−114, May 2, 1977, 3, reprinted *U.S. Code: Congressional and Administrative News* (1977) 3, 4101.

77.   *Congressional Record*, Dec. 6, 1977, vol. 123, 38599 (final Senate vote), 38603 (agreement to conference report); ibid. Dec. 7, 1977, vol. 123, 38779 (House vote on conference report).

78.   Foreign Corrupt Practices Act of 1977, secs. 103−104, 91 *Stat.* 1495−1497: codified 15 *U.S. Code* 78dd-1 and 78dd-2.

79.   *Sen. Rep. 95−114* at 10.

80.   Ibid. (grease); Arkin, *Business Crime*, sec. 18.04 (arguable nonapplication to United Brands case).

81.   Foreign Corrupt Practices Act, sec. 102, 91 *Stat.* 1494, codified 15 *U.S. Code* 78m(b); *Sen. Rep.* 95−114 at 7 ("operate in tandem").

82.   Securities Exchange Act, sec. 32, 15 *U.S. Code* sec. 78ff ("penalties"). The SEC announced it would apply a negligence standard in seeking civil injunctions to enforce the act, SEC, Accounting Series Release No. 242, Feb. 16, 1978, 14 *SEC Docket* 180−182 (1978).

83.   For a criticism of the FCPA's potential impact on foreign subsidiaries of registered American corporations, see Hubert Lenczowski, "Questionable Payments by Foreign Subsidiaries: The Extraterritorial Jurisdictional Effect of the Foreign Corrupt Practices Act of 1977," *Hastings International and Comparative Law Review* 3 (1979) 151.

84.   Four examples of the impact of the FCPA: In 1982 a further investigation by ITT of its own payments abroad, supplementing a report to the SEC in 1978, reported $5,700,000 in payments since 1975, some of them since the passage of the FCPA. A European agent of the company, for example, retained on a $2^1/_2$ percent commission, asked and received 17 percent more for an unidentified third party. A company "compliance officer" with his own auditing staff and direct access to outside counsel and the board discovered and reported the payments. New controls were put on the European agent (*Wall Street Journal*, June 4, 1982).

In December 1980 Ashland Oil, Inc., a large independent oil refiner, was hurt by the cut-off of crude oil from Iran and in great need of a supply. It found it in Oman. The company paid $1,350,000 to a Liechtenstein company connected with an Omani; and for $26 million it bought from a group including an Omani a chromium mine in Zimbabwe; the mine turned out to be worthless. When these payments came to the board's attention, they were a factor in the abrupt resignation of the chief executive officer; no crime was confessed or charged (*Wall Street Journal*, May 16, 1983, p. 4).

In 1980 the Sam P. Wallace Co. paid a bribe of $1,400,000 to John J. O'Halloran, chairman of the Trinidad and Tobago Racing Commission, to get a contract of $31,000,000 to build a race track in Trinidad. O'Halloran was a close associate of Eric Williams, prime minister and leader of Trinidad since its independence. The company's internal auditors discovered the false entries covering the payments and informed the board; the board notified the SEC. A criminal prosecution followed in which the company and the head of the subsidiary responsible pleaded guilty to violating the FCPA. The company was fined $530,000, the executive was fined $10,000 and given two years' probation; the company's legal costs were $2,000,000 (*Wall Street Journal*, May 20, 1983, 52).

In 1982 Ruston Gus Turbines, Inc. of Houston and Solar Turbines International of San Diego pleaded guilty to violating the FCPA by payments made to sell their equipment to Pemex, the Mexican government oil company. Donald Crawford was indicted for arranging these and other deals with Pemex with bribes of 4.5 to 5 percent, amounting to at least $10,000,000. He pleaded innocent and as of summer 1983 awaited trial. Mexico indicted three middle-level Pemex executives for receiving the bribes (*Wall Street Journal*, Feb. 23, 1983), pp. 1, 22.

CHAPTER 21: THE FUTURE OF THE BRIBE (PP. 681–706)

1. Cf. Robert W. Fogel and Stanley L. Engerman, *Time on the Cross* (Boston: Little, Brown, 1974) with Herbert G. Gutman, *Slavery and the Numbers Games* (Urbana: University of Illinois Press, 1975).

2. Shakespeare, *Measure for Measure* 2, 2, line 5.

3. These facts were given to me in the spring of 1982 by Wittgenstein's pupil, G. E. M. Anscombe.

4. Chapter 7 above at n. 9; Chapter 8 at n. 7.

5. Chapter 20 above at n. 19 and 60.

6. Chapter 17 above at n. 115–122.

7. See John T. Noonan, Jr., *The Scholastic Analysis of Usury* 229, 267–268, 338–339, 358–362.

8. Chapter 20 above at n. 32.

9. Chapter 18 above at n. 55.

10. For the idea and invocation of "occult compensation," see *Scholastic Analysis of Usury* 402.

11. Chapter 20 above, n. 21.

12. Chapter 19 above, after n. 80.

13. Chapter 1 above at n. 39; Chapter 2 above after n. 79.

14. Chapter 14 above at n. 69.

15. See the criticism of Abscam by Sissela Bok, *Secrets* (New York: Pantheon Books, 1982) 273–278; and see Erwin N. Griswold et al., "Post-Hearing Memorandum in Support of Defendant Harrison A. Williams' Motion to Dismiss the Indictment on Due Process and Related Grounds" in *U.S. v. Williams* (E.D.N.Y.), Chapter 18 above, at n. 147.

16. Chapter 18 above at n. 86.

17. See Thomas Jefferson, "Query XVIII, Manners," *Notes on the State of Virginia*, ed. William Peden (1951) 162–163 for Jefferson's criticism of the institution of slavery, which, as a Virginia lawmaker, he accepted as necessary. See John T. Noonan, Jr., *Persons and Masks of the Law* (New York: Farrar, Straus & Giroux, 1976) 53–54.

18. Cf. Czeslaw Milocz, *Native Realm*, trans. Catherine S. Leach (Garden City, N.Y.: Doubleday, 1968)142: "Since we ourselves define what necessity is, we draw a line between the 'necessary' and the 'possible.'"

19. See Noonan, *Scholastic Analysis of Usury* 101: "ubi ius belli, ibi etiam ius usurae."

20. See Chapter 8 above at n. 35. This account of a gift runs counter to Mauss's account of the gift in primitive societies and his notion that every gift, including sacrifices, is meant to compel reciprocation, see Marcel Mauss, *The Gift* 14–15.

21. Chapter 8 above at n. 35 ("gave himself"); Chapter 8 at n. 36 ("participant of our humanity"); Chapter 11 after n. 29 ("Redemption fair and foul").

22. Chapter 17 above at n. 114.

23. Chapter 18 above at n. 68.

24. Chapter 18 above at n. 104.

25. See Peter Knauer, "The Hermeneutic Function of the Principle of Double Effect," trans. Noonan, *Natural Law Forum* 12 (1967) 132.

26. See Jacques Maritain, *The Person and the Common Good*, trans. John J. Fitzgerald (Notre Dame, Ind.: University of Notre Dame Press, 1966) 50–52.

27. For Lancelot Andrewes Lamar, the flawed protagonist of Walker Percy's novel, his fam-

ily's world falls to pieces when he discovers $10,000 in his father's sock drawer confirming the charge that his father as an insurance commissioner had taken kickbacks; he compares it to a later experience when he discovers his wife to be unfaithful. In each case the impact of the discovery extends the effect of the infidelity to the disillusioned discoverer. Walker Percy, *Lancelot* (New York: Farrar, Straus & Giroux, 1977) 41–42.

28.   See Gregory Grossman, ed., *Studies in the Second Economy of Communist Countries* (Berkeley: University of California Press, 1984).

29.   John T. Noonan, Jr., "The Genital Good," *Communio* 8 (1981) 198–228.

30.   Ibid. at 227–228.

31.   Chapter 12 above at n. 80.

32.   Chapter 2 above at n. 76.

Table of Scriptural Citations

Table of Cases

Index